SOUTH ASIAN FOLKLORE

AN ENCYCLOPEDIA

SOUTH ASIAN FOLKLORE

AN ENCYCLOPEDIA

AFGHANISTAN | BANGLADESH | INDIA | NEPAL | PAKISTAN | SRI LANKA

MARGARET A. MILLS, PETER J. CLAUS, AND SARAH DIAMOND, EDITORS

Routledge
New York London

Editorial Staff
Project Editor: Laura Smid
Production Editor: Jeanne Shu
Production Manager: Anthony Mancini, Jr.
Production Director: Dennis Teston
Director of Development Reference: Kate Aker
Publishing Director: Sylvia Miller

Published in 2003 by

Routledge
29 West 35 Street
New York, NY 10001-2299
www.routledge-ny.com

Published in Great Britain by
Routledge
11 New Fetter Lane
London EC4P 4EE
www.routledge.uk.co

Routledge is an imprint of Taylor & Francis Books, Inc.

10 9 8 7 6 5 4 3 2 1

Printed on acid-free, 250-year-life paper
Manufactured in the United States of America

Library of Congress Cataloging-in-Publication Data

South Asian folklore : an encyclopedia / Margaret A. Mills, Peter J. Claus, and Sarah Diamond, editors.
p. cm.
Includes bibliographical references and index.
ISBN 0-415-93919-4 (alk. paper)
I. Mills, Margaret Ann. II. Claus, Peter J. III. Diamond, Sarah, 1976-
GR302 .S68 2002
398′.0954′03—dc21

2002023695

TABLE OF CONTENTS

INTRODUCTION AND INVITATION

This book has come into existence with the generous help of many individuals and groups, on three continents, over a period of years. It has been our goal to bring together the work of distinguished and rising scholars from varied disciplines, who have documented and analyzed cultural production across South Asia, in order to facilitate the cross-fertilization of ideas and to present this work to a growing, interested general public. For the purposes of this book South Asia is defined as the nation states of Afghanistan, Bangladesh, India, Nepal, Pakistan, and Sri Lanka. However, it is important to recognize that political boundaries and affiliations in this region, as elsewhere, have changed over the course of history. Furthermore, cultural production is not bounded by polity; quite often creative inspiration is derived from the movement of ideas, people, art, and technology across political boundaries.

At the outset of this project we were faced with the daunting challenge of representing the vast array of local traditions from each major cultural subgroup in South Asia. However, we quickly realized this task was impossible given the size of the region, its cultural diversity, and the uneven state of research. Some types of oral tradition, performance forms, and material culture have been deeply studied, many others have barely been documented. We began this project by seeking out people engaged in field research and in developing new ideas for modeling the complex processes of cultural production in South Asia. (We did not specifically recruit scholars working on folk musical forms, however, as a separate encyclopedia of South Asian music was produced by Garland Publishing, a member of the Taylor and Francis Group, in the year 2000). We asked many of these scholars not only to present their own new work, but to reflect on the contributions of earlier scholars. We also set out to try to ensure that scholars based in South Asia would be represented in the work. Over the time of this project, we have gratefully watched the expansion of new scholarship and we seized opportunities to include this work in the book.

Research publication on South Asian folklore and culture for western audiences has at least a 200-year history, and a complex politics attendant on that history. Starting from the late eighteenth and early nineteenth centuries, European travelers and colonialist scholars set out to document the cultural practices and beliefs of a wide range of South Asian cultural and linguistic groups. Although many European scholars were motivated by the desire to pursue the Enlightenment ideals of humanism through objective knowledge in a scientific approach to the comparative study of human life and culture, much of the research and writing of this period was also conditioned by imperialist political and social goals. For instance, British colonial civil servants compiled a vast quantity of information regarding local customs and identifications of caste and tribe (published in compendious volumes referred to as the Gazetteers), the production of which was sponsored by the British colonial government for the purposes of more effective political control. Similarly, dictionaries of vernacular languages and folklore compiled by missionaries assisted in their goal of religious conversion. Both these groups argued, and probably believed, that their efforts were intended for the betterment of South Asians. Some Orientalist and gentleman scholars were driven by other philanthropic aims. They saw South Asia as a font of information for the understanding of human history in general, yet inevitably, given their training, they for the most part pursued research oriented around European-derived concepts of civilization, folklore, and culture. Their work was central to the establishment of a range of newly emerging disciplines in Europe, from comparative and historical linguistics, comparative religions, and comparative mythology to world history, folklore, and anthropology. Despite their expressed appreciation for South Asian civilizations and culture, imperialist and racist undertones still were evident in much of this work. Thus although these early writings provide a major source of information for later scholars, many of the findings are now viewed with a critical and even skeptical eye.

From the early to mid-nineteenth century, a new generation of South Asian scholars and cultural connoisseurs set about documenting and collecting South Asian expressive traditions in their respective regions and languages. In this they built upon a far longer tradition of South Asian treatises on the arts, including some cultural matters we would see as relating to folk arts and lore. The substantial contributions to folklore field research and publications by some highly erudite colonial-period scholars, such as Pandits Ram Gharib Chaube and S.M. Natēṣa Śāstri, are only now being rediscovered and reassessed. Most South Asian and some European writers of this period viewed their work as contributing to a growing nationalist movement. Although many celebrated the aesthetic and moral power of South Asian cultures, some cast a more critical light on certain cultural traditions and practices, especially those labeled as primitive or backward by colonial authorities, or those apparently at odds with the dictates of elite or canonical textual authorities. Cultural reform movements, influenced partly by colonial ideologies and modernizing agendas, played a large role in public debates regarding the artistic merit and social value of various expressive traditions during this period, and many artists and performers were influenced by these ideas as well. The integrity and value of expressive traditions regarded by some as vulgar or based upon superstition continues to be a subject of public and private debate within South Asia. Despite the public controversy, many of these traditions have yet to be systematically researched by either local or foreign scholars.

Contemporary scholars of South Asian expressive traditions are making great strides to fill in the many gaps in our knowledge. However, in gathering this knowledge together in a single publication intended for an English-language readership, we confronted other limitations. One significant constraint was the lack of resources needed to translate substantial relevant work currently available only in South Asian language publications. Second, there are scholars of regional folklore who have developed archival volumes containing finely-detailed information which is not well represented in the highly condensed essay form of an encyclopedia entry.

Third, South Asian terms are not always readily applicable or translatable into European-derived categories. For example, terms such as *ballad* and *epic* have been debated and quite specifically defined in European comparative literature circles. These formal definitions need to be significantly adjusted to describe more adequately the full variety of performance genres, in South Asia and elsewhere, now designated by those terms. Many authors in the volume chose to avoid this problem by using indigenous terms with their approximate gloss in English. However, this then makes it more difficult for those readers who are less familiar with South Asian languages to locate specific areas of interest and to identify connections between similar genres across different regions. The Table of Contents, index, SEE ALSO lists, and articles describing general categories of expressive tradition were designed with this issue in mind to better aid our general readers, as will be further explained at the end of this introduction.

Helpful as it is for technical precision in case studies, one problem with using indigenous terms in the many different South Asian languages is that it can make it difficult to formulate a common theoretical framework with which to compare traditions and perspectives. Venerable tools developed in the Western European context, such as the Aarne-Thompson type-indexing system for folk narratives, do not necessarily capture the varieties of South Asian traditions very well, or indeed at all in matters of social use and meaning, yet some tools are needed to enable cross-cultural analysis. By bringing together the work of Western and non-Western scholars we hope to encourage the advancement of comparative theoretical frameworks more applicable to the South Asian context. One theory or paradigm that has received major attention in the West in recent years, performance studies, does seem productive also in South Asian research. Performance studies as a paradigm accommodate research strategies that are attentive to the organization and conceptualization of South Asian cultural categories by their users, as Stuart Blackburn's essay on performance studies in this volume illustrates.

This is not to advocate for a more homogenized voice for South Asian folklore scholarship. The diversity of views in this volume bespeaks substantive differences in intellectual goals and priorities. Linguistic and conceptual divisions complicate the efforts of internationally scattered and disciplinarily diverse scholars to speak generally and to share information with a wider public across the region and the world, but such diversity is also vitality for the field.

As editors we were also concerned that some Western-European derived categories are fraught with political baggage in the South Asian context. For example, the term *tribe/tribal* is highly problematic for those individuals and groups in South Asia who associate this designation with a history of political marginalization and exploitation. Not least of all, the utility of the terms *folk* and *folklore* has been subject to debate, as a comparison of their treatment by different authors in this volume makes plain. In the hands of different commentators, the term *folklore* may evoke a critique of modernism (and globalism), a primordial national heritage as in the case of European Romantic Nationalism, a subversive/resistant stand vis-à-vis some hegemonic elite culture, a fragile and eroding knowledge base, irrationality and false consciousness, and more. The selection or coinage of indigenous terms to translate *folk* and *folklore* in local languages also comes freighted with similar concerns because the terms may still be linked with the meanings of their Western European counterparts.

Only very recently has knowledge accumulated in regard to some topics, so that scholars have begun to trace in more detail webs of connections, interactions and exchanges of ideas, and expressive forms in everyday cultural productions across the region. The exploration of commonalities is additionally complicated, however, by the major functional role expressive culture plays in community identity formation. Expressive forms or activities are often claimed by one group or another as a key, proprietary component of their own unique heritage. Thus, identity politics are never far from the surface in cultural production, as many scholars in this volume acknowledge.

Another, related critical issue that has vexed folklore and cultural studies for at least the last two decades is the idea of the invention of tradition, briefly, the idea that tradition does not exist and pass down through generations as a primordial, autonomous force, but is actively created and recreated, claimed and reclaimed by each generation and subgroup of cultural participants in specific expressive acts. Some such processes are visible historically, as in the ability to date, to two or three centuries ago, caste *purāṇa* literature that establishes origin myths for various non-Brahmin castes in the idiom of the much older Sanskrit Purāṇa genre. Although the invention of some caste *purāṇa* literature can be approximately dated, the evocation of these texts as authoritative or not and their interpretation within specific contexts is itself an ongoing process of negotiation.

Although documenting specific moments of invention and reformulation of cultural matter claimed as traditional is currently in vogue within academia, we must be aware that this, too, is a politically freighted act because it undermines the sense of primordialness that gives indigenous cultural practitioners and experts their claim to status, authority, and power. A proper awareness of the politics of scholarship invokes Arjun Appadurai's 1991 admonition that folklorists and allied scholars need to look closely at the wider regimes of power affecting local expressive life, including, we would add, the politics of scholarship. Local performers and artisans may be well aware and able to critique the regimes of power and politics affecting their activities, but their critiques may sometimes not be openly voiced to outsiders. Likewise, the critique of ethnographic research itself may be part of local discourse, although scholars may be less likely to encounter such critiques directly or may choose not to acknowledge them. Hence, we feel strongly that scholars too must attend to the identity politics and power relations at stake in their research and publications.

Globalization and the associated fear of the homogenization of cultural forms is an especially contentious issue facing scholars as well as indigenous performers, artists, and artisans today. In South Asia as elsewhere, vernacular culture does not operate in an isolated or pristine environment of face-to-face oral communication, but in a complex and fertile exchange with written traditions and with mass media, regionally and globally, which some of this book's authors have begun to explore. Scholars may be rightfully concerned when, for instance, the creation of printed collections of song lyrics creates a fixed, authoritative canon and thus undermines the creativity and generative power of a living performance tradition. However, the phenomena of cultural standardization and globalization are not altogether new, as folklore research teaches us. Nor should *global* be taken as a synonym for *western* or *modern*. The compilation and dissemination of literary classics such as the *Pañcatantra* or the *Jātaka Tales* illustrate these points, as does, in a different way, the ancient South Asian development of technologies such as crucible steel production. Ancient canonical literature drew from and fed back into oral narrative performance traditions, and the literary works in their turn entered an intercontinental flow of culture both written and oral which was in progress well before the modern era. Technology transfer is an even older story, traceable through archeology and to be kept in mind in studying contemporary material culture production and circulation.

In considering the effects of modernity and globalization on cultural production, scholars may not wish to focus on the issue of preserving tradition in any simple sense, but rather on how different people use discourses of tradition and authenticity, and varied cultural and aesthetic forms including mass media forms, to position themselves relative to others. The issue is thus not for scholars to determine "What is the authentic tradition and how to maintain it?" but rather to determine "How are cultural traditions and ideas about authenticity being established, transformed, and contested locally and transnationally?" Considering the global in the local and vice versa, it is suitable also to remember that the importance of such a distinction to the culture-producers cannot be assumed: people participating in a given expressive cultural activity may be quite unaware of, or unmoved by, any such dichotomy in their cultural repertoire.

In connection with the interactions of mass media and local cultural production, intellectual property rights have emerged as a central ethical concern for folklorists. Although prior scholarly assumptions about the anonymity of folk cultural production served the purposes of cultural appropriation of various kinds, including for instance the appropriation for mass media of folk songs collected from local performers who are not remunerated, local cultural actors may recognize various forms of individual and group rights of property and performance. Mass media marketing may also create new monetary value for expressive forms whose value in their prior contexts was either intangible or non-monetary, requiring new institutional arrangements to pass the material benefits of media exposure back to the producers. Scholars may be tempted to intervene in such situations, but sometimes also choose willful obliviousness, as when advising economically marginal people to resist commodification of their cultural productions in the name of authenticity. While some folklorists recognize and champion the rights of individual master artists to credit for their work (indeed in many cases the work is already their livelihood in whole or in part), those who seek to extend the impact and financial viability of local expressive forms may find themselves in complex negotiations with both individual master artists and group entities, such as performing castes, guild-like organizations, or village organizations that have some corporate claims to control over the repertoire and over performance or production. The identification or creation of stars by documentarians may be problematical to the community of artist/producers, just as was the alleged anonymity of general exploitation.

Local distributions of power and authority along class, caste, or gender lines may also inhibit access to benefits for those directly responsible for artistic production. Folklorists working in areas of media-marketable performance may profit by lessons learned in the area of crafts and development when they seek to devise ethical positions and strategies to address such problems responsibly in our work. Implicated in these concerns, as we pursue our research, is our awareness of the political economy of access to resources necessary for carrying out primary research, for repatriation of documented materials generated by it, and for archiving and access to such materials in or near the communities of origin. This issue was one we were well aware of when searching for authors to write on particular topics, for typically the individuals and groups with the most knowledge about a living tradition are often the ones with the least opportunity or desire to publish their perspectives. With advancements in audio and video recording and the internet also comes the opportunity for researchers and others to provide a wider international audience for local South Asian artists to demonstrate their skills and creativity and to voice their perspectives.

Thus, this book presents only a suggestive sample of the huge range of South Asian cultural practices and productions and ways of documenting and interpreting them. Although we anticipate that readers may not find their favorite folklore topic discussed here, nonetheless in close to 500 articles by more than 250 authors, we endeavor to sample a wide range of folkore topics, from material culture to customs and beliefs, rituals, festivals and performing arts, as well as the huge diversity of verbal art forms. If this volume functions as an invitation or provocation to further research and publications to bridge its many gaps, to extend and fortify collegial discussions and cooperation across the region and the disciplines, and to introduce the cultural richness of the area to a general audience, together with the problematics of its study, it will have served its editors' purpose.

Organization of the Book

There are several types of article in this book, designed to serve various informational needs. General concept articles have headings that recognize major topics applied across the whole region and many domains of expressive culture or large arrays of local forms, such as "Gender and Folklore", "Epic", "Folk Art," "Material Culture," "Life Cycle Rituals" or "Theater and Drama". These general articles outline a general approach to the topic and its history, and in turn are intended to orient and direct the reader to a variety of case study articles listed in the SEE ALSO list at the end of each article, which describe particular cases that further develop issues related to the general topic. The approach of the case study scholar may differ substantially from that of the general article. Although most of the entries are item-centered in that they describe particular expressive forms, classes of objects, events or occasions, the approaches of the different scholars also demonstrate differences in their research methodologies and theories. In a number of cases, we commissioned a case study article on a particular regional form, knowing that there are analogous forms distributed widely across the region, which have not yet been studied at the same depth. Case study articles thus are also our invitation for further case work, leading to better comparative overviews of both subjects and research strategies in the future.

Case study articles are often listed under the indigenous term for a performance genre, emphasizing that single western genre categories may not serve to describe the precise shape, content, or purpose of the performance form (for instance, there are case studies of individual named types of performance that relate equally and simultaneously to epic, dance, drama, music, song, festival, gods and goddesses, worship, and so forth.) Use of SEE ALSO and index listings should help the nonspecialist negotiate the book to find a variety of articles of related interest, many under unfamiliar headings.

Some short definitional articles introduce a major non-English term or concept which is invoked in various case studies and general discussions, such as *kathā* (a type of narrative) or *dṛṣṭi* (evil eye). Other relatively short, definitional articles, with a general title such as "Folk literature" or "Song," were created to provide a gathering point for references to articles of related interest that would not necessarily be listed together in an alphabetical index, or be clustered in any one SEE ALSO list attached to another article. They are intended to facilitate focused browsing and the identification of linked and related discussions among the articles.

To the best of our authors' ability, foreign terms have been transliterated according to the Library of Congress transliteration system for the language in question. Applications of that system had to make allowances in some articles for terms that are used in various languages but differently pronounced and differently spelled in each, and for features of colloquial or nonwritten languages which are not well represented in the LC system, itself designed to represent unambiguously the spellings of terms in standard literary languages.

A set of maps of the region has been provided in the front of the book, for general reference as needed. Some of the illustrations directly illustrate articles' subject matter, others provide a more general visual sense of a set of related topics.

We wish to thank our Editorial Board members for their sustained support over the life of this project: Stuart Blackburn, Joyce Burckhalter Flueckiger, Alf Hiltebeitel, Frank Korom, Kirin Narayan, Velcheru Narayana Rao, Ranjini Obeyesekere, and Susan Wadley. In addition, a number of people were instrumental in carrying the production process forward: Lauren Cross, Christine Kray, Janet Loftis, Lee Ellen Martin, Leela Prasad, and Valerie Stoker. We also thank Jim Gair, Wilma Heston, and Carol Salomon for graciously providing eleventh-hour assistance as well.

References

Anderson, Benedict. 1991. *Imagined Communities*, rev. ed. New York: Verso.

Appadurai, Arjun. 1991. Afterword. In Arjun Appadurai, Frank Korom and Margaret Mills, eds. *Gender, Genre, and Power in South Asian Expressive Traditions.* 467–476. Philadelphia: University of Pennsylvania Press.

Bendix, Regina. 1997. *In Search of Authenticity.* Madison: University of Wisconsin Press.

Ranger, Terence, ed. 1991. *The Invention of Tradition.* Cambridge: Cambridge University Press.

MARGARET A. MILLS, PETER J. CLAUS, AND SARAH DIAMOND

LIST OF CONTRIBUTORS

Syed Jami Ahmed
Bangla Academy

Jon W. Anderson
Chair, Anthropology Department,
The Catholic University of America

Ali S. Asani
Department of Religion, Harvard University

Wayne Ashley
Art Institute of Seattle

Martha B. Ashton-Sikora
Independent scholar, Alameda, California

G. Whitney Azoy
The Lawrenceville School, New Jersey

Sabir Badalkhan
Dipartimento de Studi Asiatici,
Istituto Universitario Orientale

N.A. Baloch
Sindh University

Sumanta Banerjee
English Department, Scottish Church College, Calcutta

Jayant Bhalchandra Bapat
Monash University, Australia

Thomas Barfield
Anthropology Deparment, Boston University

Jerome H. Bauer
Department of Religious Studies,
Washington University, St. Louis

Susan S. Bean
Peabody Essex Museum, Salem, Massachusetts

Brenda E. F. Beck
Department of Anthropology, University of Toronto

William R. Belcher
U.S. Army Central Identification
Laboratory—Hawaii

Kishore Bhattacharjee
Guwahati University

Harihar P. Bhattarai
Folklore Department, The University of North Carolina
at Chapel Hill

Lorilai Biernacki
Religious Studies, University of Colorado at
Boulder

Purushothama Bilimale
Archives and Research Centre for Ethnomusicology
American Institute for Indian Studies, Gurgaon,
Haryana

Stuart Blackburn
Department of Languages and Cultures of South Asia,
School of Oriental and African Studies,
University of London

Gregory D. Booth
Department of Anthropology, University of Auckland

Donald Brenneis
Anthropology Department, University of California,
Santa Cruz

Timothy C. Cahill
Department of Religious Studies, Loyola University, New Orleans

Sarah Caldwell
Department of Religoius Studies, California State University, Chico

Marcia S. Calkowski
Department of Anthropology, University of Regina

Amy Catlin
Department of Ethnomusicology, University of California—Los Angeles

Bernard Cesarone
University of Illinois

Pabitra Chakraborty

Tushar Chattopadhyay
Department of Folklore, University of Kalyani

A. Chellaperumal
Department of Folklore, St. Xavier's College

Shafiqur Rahman Chowdhury
Folklore Department, Bangla Academy, Dhaka, Bangladesh

Peter J. Claus
Professor Emeritus at California State University, Hayward

Fred W. Clothey
Department of Religious Studies, University of Pittsburgh

Richard J. Cohen
Indo-American Centre for International Studies, Osmania University Campus

Daniel J. Cohen

Birendranath Datta
Tezpur University, India

Dick Davis
Department of Near Eastern Languages and Cultures, Ohio State University

Frank de Caro
Department of English, Louisiana State University

Robert J. Del Bontà
Asian Art Museum of San Francisco

Corinne G. Dempsey
Department of Religious Studies, University of Wisconsin at Steven's Point

K.N.O. Dharmadasa
University of Peradeniya

Sarah Diamond
Research Associate, Institute for Community Research, Hartford, Connecticut

Wendy Doniger
Department of South Asian Languages & Civilization, Divinity School, Swift Hall, University of Chicago

Veronica Doubleday

Mary Frances Dunham
Independent Scholar

Nancy Hatch Dupree
ACBAR Resource and Information Centre

David B. Edwards
Anthropology Department, Williams College, Williamstown, Massachusetts

John Emigh
Department of Theatre, Speech and Dance, Brown University

Carl W. Ernst
Department of Religious Studies, University of North Carolina at Chapel Hill

Anne Feldhaus
Department of Religious Studies, Arizona State University

Jacqueline H. Fewkes
Anthropology Department, University of Pennsylvania

Joyce Burkhalter Flueckiger
Department of Religion, Emory University

Richard A. Frasca
Center for the Study of World Religions, Harvard Divinity School

Rich Freeman
Department of Anthropology, University of Michigan

Peter Gaeffke
Department of South Asia Regional Studies, University of Pennsylvania

Surendra K. Gambhir
South Asia Regional Studies, University of Pennsylvania

M.J. Gentes
Department of Philosophy and Religion, Claremont McKenna College

Pika Ghosh
Art Department, the University of North Carolina at Chapel Hill

Henry Glassie
Folklore Institute, Indiana University

Ann Grodzins Gold
Department of Religion, Syracuse University

M.H. Goonatilleka
Department of Fine Arts, University of Kelaniya

Arjun Guneratne
Anthropology Department, Macalester College

Pamila Gupta
Department of Anthropology, Temple University

Katherine F. Hacker
Department of Fine Arts, University of British Columbia

Kathleen Hall
Graduate School of Education, University of Pennsylvania

William L. Hanaway
Department of Asian and Middle Eastern Studies, University of Pennsylvania

Suzanne Hanchett
Planning Alternatives for Change

Ian Hancock
Center for Asian Studies, University of Texas

Kathryn Hansen
Center for Asian Studies, University of Texas

Lee Haring
Emeritus Professor, Department of English, Brooklyn College, CUNY

Lindsey Harlan
Department of Religious Studies, Connecticut College

Lauri Harvilahti
University of Helsinki

Mary Elaine Hegland
Anthropology Department, Santa Clara University

Carolyn Brown Heinz
Department of Anthropology, California State University, Chico

Edward O. Henry
Department of Anthropology, San Diego State University

H.M.D.R. Herath
Sociology Department, University of Peradeniya

Wilma L. Heston
University of Pennsylvania

Alf Hiltebeitel
Department of Religion, George Washington University

John Clifford Holt
Asian Studies Department, Bowdoin College

Lee Horne
University of Pennsylvania

Hameeda Hossain
Bangla Academy

Mohammad Nurul Huda
Bangla Academy

Wayne R. Husted
Religious Studies Program, Pennsylvania State University

Stephen P. Huyler
Ohio State University

Linda Iltis
Comparative Religion and South Asian Studies, University of Washington

Khalid Javaid

Edward J. Jay
Professor Emeritus at California State University, Hayward

Syal Kakar
Pakhto Department, University of Balochistan

Nathan Katz
Department of Religious Studies, Florida International University

M. Whitney Kelting
Department of Religious Studies, Florida International University

Jonathan Mark Kenoyer
Department of Anthropology, University of Wisconsin—Madison

Aisha Khan
Department of Africana Studies, SUNY Stony Brook

David M. Knipe
Middle East Studies, University of Wisconsin—Madison

Frank J. Korom
Department of Religion, Boston University

S.A. Krishnaiah
Regional Resources Center, M.G.M College

Nayani Krishnakumari
Telugu University, Andhra Pradesh, India

Richard Kurin
Office of Folk Life Programs and Cultural Studies, Smithsonian Institution

Todd Lewis

Mark Liechty
Department of Anthropology, University of Illinois at Chicago

Hilde K. Link
Institut für Völkerunde und Afrikanistik, Ludwig-Maximilians—Universität München

Deryck O. Lodrick
Department of Anthropology, University of California, Berkeley

David N. Lorenzen
El Colegio De Mexico

S.D. Lourdu
Department of Folklore, St. Xavier's College

Philip Lutgendorf
Asian Language and Literature Department, University of Iowa

Owen M. Lynch
New York University

Tryna Lyons
University of Washington

Wynne Maggi
University of Colorado—Boulder

H. M. Maheswaraiah
Department of Kannada, Karnatak University

Firoz Mahmud
Folklore Institute and India Studies Program, Indiana University

Aditya Malik
Department of Philosophy and Religious Studies, University of Canterbury, Christchurch.

Peter Manuel
John Jay College, New Jersey

Nancy M. Martin
Religion Department, Chapman University

Lee-Ellen Marvin
Department of Folklore and Folklife, University of Pennsylvania

Ulrich Marzolph
Arbeitsstelle der Akademie der Wissenschaften

Eveline Masilamani-Meyer
Universitat Basel

Gregory G. Maskarinec
Department of Anthropology, University of Hawaii at Manoa

Michelle Maskiell
Department of History, Montana State University

Walter Harding Maurer
Department of Asian Languages and Literature, University of Hawaii

Mary McGee
Columbia University

Dennis B. McGilvray
Department of Anthropology, University of Colorado—Boulder

Abigail McGowan
History Department, University of Pennsylvania

Udaya Meddegama
Department of Singhala, University of Peradeniya

Barbara D. Metcalf
Department of History, University of California—Davis

Margaret A. Mills
Department of Near Eastern Languages and Cultures, Ohio State University

Diane Mines
Department of Anthropology, Appalachian State University

Mattison Mines
Department of Anthropology, Washington University

Mahendra Kumar Mishra
State Coordinator, Tribal Education in the Orissa Primary Education Programme

Anne Murphy
Seattle Art Museum

Isabelle Nabokov
Department of Anthropology, Princeton University

Peter Nabokov
Department of World Arts & Cultures, University of California—Los Angeles

P. Nagaraja
Center for Folk Culture Studies, University of Hyderabad

Vijaya Rettakudi Nagarajan
Department of Theology and Religious Studies, University of San Francisco

C.M. Naim
Department of South Asian Languages and Civilizations, University of Chicago

Savita Nair
Department of History, Mount Holyoke College

Sadhana Naithani
Centre of German Studies, Jawaharlal Nehru University

Kirin Narayan
Department of Anthropology, University of Wisconsin—Madison

Vasudha Narayanan
Department of Religion, University of Florida

Mumtaz Nasir
Lok Virsa, Pakistan's National Institute of Folk and Traditional Heritage, Islamabad

Mekhala Natavar
Department of Asian & African Languages and Literature, Duke University

Deborah L. Neff

Mark Nichter
Anthropology Department, The University of Arizona

Ulrike Niklas
South Asian Studies Programme, National University of Singapore

†George W. O'Bannon
Writer, curator, and speaker on oriental rugs

Ranjini Obeyesekere
Department of Anthropology, Princeton University

†Goverdhan Panchal
Government of Gujarat, India

David Pinault
Religious Studies Department, Santa Clara University

Leela Prasad
Department of Religion, Duke University

Frances W. Pritchett
Department of Middle East Asian Languages & Cultures, Columbia University

Regula Burckhardt Qureshi
Department of Music, University of Alberta

Kristin Rao
University of Maryland, College Park

Sura Prasad Rath
Department of English, Louisiana State University—Shreveport

Susan A. Reed
Department of Sociology & Anthropology, Bucknell University

George W. Rich
Department of Anthropology,
California State University—Sacramento

Robin Rinehart
Department of Religion,
Lafayette College

Rosane Rocher
Department of South Asia Regional Studies,
University of Pennsylvania

Ratna Roy
Evergreen State College

David Rudner
Harvard University

Abdul Razzak Sabir
Department of Brahui, University of Balochistan

Lorraine Sakata
School of the Arts & Architecture, University of California—Los Angeles

Carol Salomon
Department of Asian Studies, Cornell University

Amita Vohra Sarin
Independent researcher

William S. Sax
Department of South and Southeast Asian Studies,
University of California

Elisabeth Schoembucher
Universität Heidelberg

Karine Schomer
California Institute of Integral Studies

Vernon James Schubel
Department of Religious Studies,
Kenyon College

Graham M. Schweig
Department of Philosophy and Religious Studies
at Christopher Newport University, Virginia

Enayatullah Shahrani

Audrey C. Shalinsky
Department of Anthropology, University of Wyoming

T.N. Shankaranarayana
Department of Kannada, Kuvempu University

H. Sidky
Department of Anthropology,
Miami University, Oxford

Lee Siegel
Department of Religion, University of Hawaii

Brian Q. Silver
Voice of America, Washington DC

Nikky-Guninder Kaur Singh
Department of Religious Studies,
Colby College

Debra Skinner
Frank Porter Graham Child Development Center,
University of North Carolina at Chapel Hill

Anna Sloan
South Asia Regional Studies,
University of Pennsylvania

John D. Smith
Department of Oriental Studies,
University of Cambridge

Tony K. Stewart
Department of Philosophy and Religion,
North Carolina State University

Roderick Stirrat
Department of Social Anthropology in AFRAS,
University of Sussex

Pulikonda Subbachary
University of Hyerabad

Kirtana Thangavelu
Department of Art History, University of California, Santa Cruz

Gordon R. Thompson
Department of Music, Skidmore College, New York

Hugh van Skyhawk
Südasien-Institut

Sylvia Vatuk
Department of Anthropology,
University of Illinois, Chicago

M.N. Venkatesha

Bittu Venkateswarlu
Department of Folk Arts, Telugu University

Susan S. Wadley
Department of Anthropology, Syracuse University

Maxine Weisgrau
Department of Anthropology, Columbia University

Mark P. Whitaker
University of South Carolina

James M. Wilce
*Anthropology Department,
Northern Arizona University*

Clare M. Wilkinson-Weber
*Department of Anthropology,
Washington State University—Vancouver*

Joanna Williams
*History of Art Department,
University of California–Berkeley*

Susan G. Williamson
Albuquerque Academy Library

Deborah Winslow
University of New Hampshire

Richard Kent Wolf
*Hunter College,
City University of New York*

Dominik Wujastyk
Wellcome Library for the History and Understanding of Medicine

Serinity Young
Anthropology Department of the American Museum of Natural History, New York

Niaz Zaman
Department of English, Dhaka University

Phillip B. Zarrilli
Department of Drama, University of Exeter

Adam Zeff
University of Pennsylvania

Eleanor Zelliot
Department of History, Carleton College

Claus Peter Zoller
Universität Heidelberg

LIST OF ARTICLES

MAPS

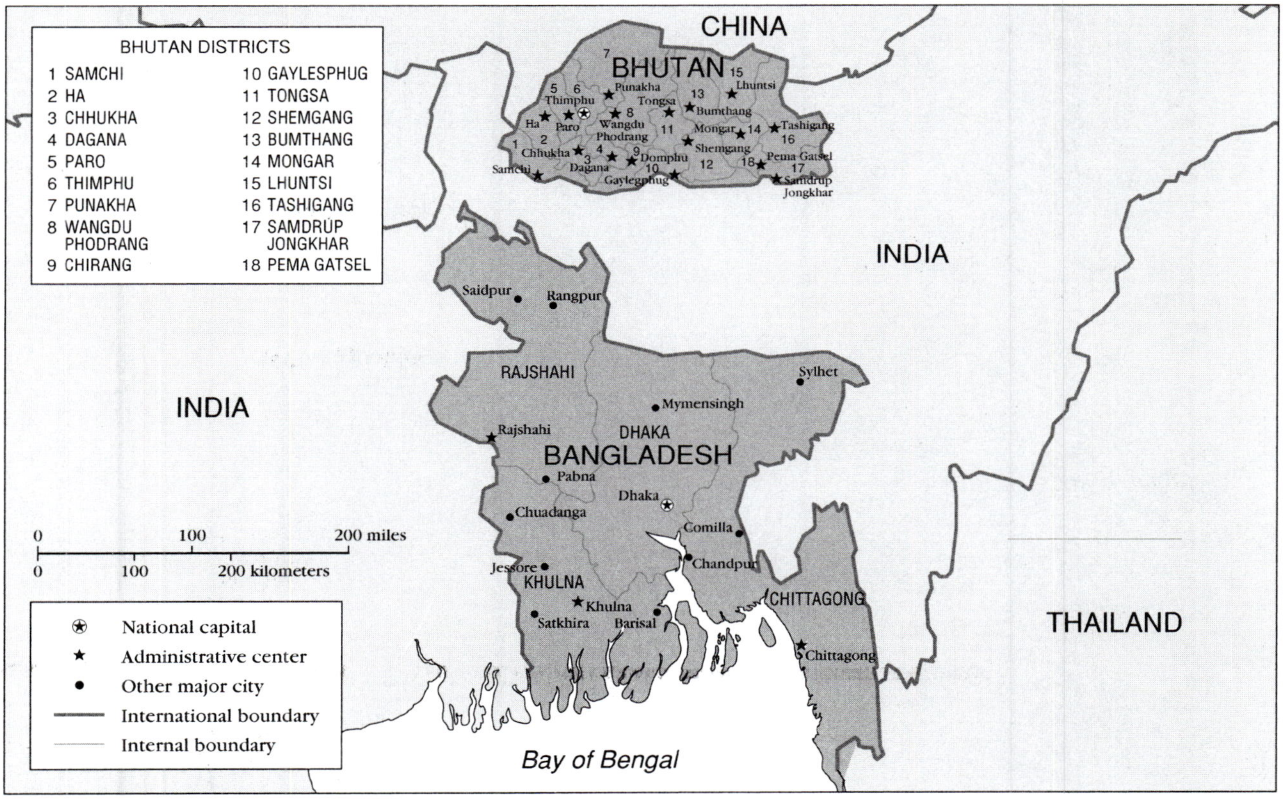

Bhutan and Bangladesh.

India, Nepal, Sri Lanka, and Maldives.

Pakistan and Afghanistan.

A

ACROBATICS

Acrobatics has been a distinct folk art form in South Asia since antiquity. Throughout much of the entire region today, performers belong to a seminomadic "tribal" community called Ḍombas, who are said to have originated in Andhra Pradesh. They move from place to place, settling in regions only long enough to learn about local conditions. In some places the same people also go by the name Candālas, an ancient Sanskritic term for untouchables. In Karnataka acrobats are called *kollāṭiga* ("rope walker") and their acrobatic performances are called *kollāṭiganāṭa* or *Ḍomba vidye* (Ḍomba knowledge).

Ḍombas perform a variety of gymnastic and acrobatic feats, including tumbling, tightrope walking, riding single-wheel cycles, pole and rope climbing, body contortions, feats of strength, and a wide variety of magic acts. Ḍombas are experts in manipulating an audience with their constant talk during performances. They are said to be able to mesmerize a crowd by their tricks. Ḍomba women also take part in many of the feats, doing tightrope walking and pole dancing. Often Ḍomba children are recruited into the tradition at a very young age, performing many of the same awesome feats as the adults, and inspiring special sympathy from the crowd.

Performances are held in the daytime, in the marketplace or in the street in front of a house. The performances appeal to audiences of all castes and creeds. Contemporary acrobats tend to imitate the music, dance, and gestures of television and film.

Because the Ḍombas exhibit great acrobatic skill, they are thought to possess remarkable willpower and control of body and mind. From this reputation, Ḍombas are called upon to perform a repertoire of additional services, such as making oracular predictions, performing exorcistic rites, and curing certain diseases.

Consistent with their seminomadic and tribal character, many Ḍomba families make and sell along the roadside a variety of handicrafts, notably horn and wooden combs, other miscellaneous utensils, and a variety of paper dolls. Traditionally, they raised donkeys and horses, both to carry their possessions and to sell along their way. They also buy and sell bullocks, oxen, sheep, and other domestic animals they acquire in their travels. Ḍombas are sometimes hired to do a variety of menial services such as decorating the marriage *pandal* (temporary canopy-like structure) or assisting at funerals.

Acrobats can be traced in Indian literature as far back as Kauṭilya's *Arthaśāṣtra* (ca. 396–312 B.C.E.), where *plavaka* (tightrope walkers) are mentioned among the names of artisans. They were said to be enemy agents who should not be allowed into the heart of the city. A fee (audience tax) was charged for their show. In Kalhaṇa's *Rājataraṅgiṇī* (The Saga of the Kings of Kashmir, 1148 C.E.) there is a description of an acrobatic performance, and it is said that King Cakravarman (923 C.E.) married an untouchable Ḍomba woman and made her his principal queen.

F. S. Mullay, a nineteenth-century British traveler, reported that at Chitvel in Cuddappa, Andhra Pradesh, there was once a king who invited all the gymnasts among his subjects to perform their feats. One of them, a member of Reḍḍi Ḍommara caste, exhibited such pleasing feats that he was awarded a ring, and a royal edict was issued that the wearer of the ring and his descendants should be the chief of the Ḍommara community. The ring contains a Telugu inscription stating that the wearer is the high priest (*mutliguru*) of all the Ḍommaras.

One incident relating to acrobatic performance has become a local legend in Karnataka. In a place called Ḍombana Koḍuge, a Ḍomba challenged the village headman and boasted he was such a master acrobat that

Village performer. Tamil Nadu, India. © Richard Rapfogel

he could fly like a bird. In turn, the headman offered him as much land as he could fly over. The Ḍomba made wings using winnowing trays and attached broomsticks to both arms. He jumped from the highest peak. Remarkably, he succeeded in covering a fair distance, and the people below cheered him on to fly further and further. But the equipment dislodged from his arms, and he crashed to the ground, dying on the spot. A small shrine was built in his honor, and it is said that every evening the people of the village light a lamp there in memory of the adventurous Ḍomba. As the headman had promised, the land up to the spot where the Ḍomba fell was reserved for the grazing of cows, and it was named after him. Until 1968 the land was left barren since the local people refrained from cultivation lest the cultivator should face misfortune. The Karnataka government has now developed the area into a small forest in their mini-forestry project.

Acrobat performers in Ladakh, Himachal Pradesh, according to J. S. Gally (personal communication), are known as *Bēḍa*. The priest of the *Bēḍa* plays an important ritual role at one particular temple when there is a famine. The priest first becomes possessed and then squats on a wooden board. The board is then placed on a tightrope, one end of which is tied to the temple and another end to a hill. The people drag him by a rope fixed to the board. Soon after his journey from hilltop to temple, devotees pluck his hair and clothes, believing that the relics will bring good luck. If he survives this tightrope journey, he will be treated as a god and highly respected. If he slips from the board and falls to his death during the tightrope journey, people regard his death as a sacrifice to the god.

Reference

Elliot, H. M., and John Dowson. 1964. *The history of India as told by its own historians*. Vol. 4. Allahabad: Kitab Mahal.

S. A. Krishnaiah

SEE ALSO

Andhra Pradesh; Professional Performers

AFGHANISTAN

The area now occupied by the state of Afghanistan is a patchwork of linguistic groups, reflecting three millennia of identifiable migrations and occupations. As a crossroads of trade routes (the "Silk Route") linking East and South Asia with northern Europe and the Mediterranean basin prior to the opening of European-dominated sea routes, Central Asia and Afghanistan experienced periods of artistic, scientific, and religious efflorescence (the latter as a center for Zoroastrianism, Buddhism, and mystical Islam), as well as devastating invasions. The modern state's boundaries are the product of pressures of nineteenth-century European imperialism, a classic "buffer state" created between Czarist Russia, which occupied the oasis city-states of Central Asia north of the Oxus River, and the British Raj expanding up to the foothills of the Hindu Kush mountains, north and west of the Indus River watershed. The boundary negotiated in the 1890s between the British and the Pashtun amir (king) of Kabul, the Durand Line, bisected territory still inhabited by ethnic Pashtuns and Balochis. The northern boundary likewise divided linguistic populations (Turkoman, Uzbek, Tajik). Afghanistan's population presently speaks around twenty different languages, the largest being Pashto, Persian in several dialects, various Turkic languages (Turkomān, called "Turkī," Uzbakī, Kirghiz), and Balochi. Pashto, Darī (as Persian is called), and Balochī are Indo-European, grammatically similar to European languages, while the Turkic languages are of a different family and closely related to the Turkish spoken in Turkey. A small population in the south, the Brahui, speak a Dravidian language related to the languages of South India and perhaps to that of the ancient, now-vanished Indus Valley civilization. People in Afghanistan now are often bi- or multilingual as needed in their daily affairs.

Prior to the nineteenth century, it is not clear that ethnicity or mother tongue was a key social or political identifier. Persian was the written lingua franca and

Twelfth-century Great Mosque. Herat, northwest Afghanistan, 1977. © Anthroarcheart.org

administrative language throughout Central Asia, Afghanistan, and large parts of India, while other languages, all with vigorous oral traditions, did or did not become literary languages to varying degrees. Some historians now argue that the important social categories in use up to the nineteenth century distinguished the majority who were settled, mostly agricultural people from the minority (perhaps 15 percent) of transhumant (seasonally migrant) nomadic animal herders, and from a small, socially marginalized assortment of craftspeople, entertainers, animal traders, and agricultural service workers, some itinerant, some settled, lumped together under various designations indicating low status (*jat, dom, loṛī, kherrāt*). Prior to 1980, it was estimated that 85 percent of the Afghan population made a living from agriculture and/or animal husbandry. With the closing of borders and land mine deployment in large areas of the country, and four years of drought along with continued hostilities from the late 1990s through 2001, the movements of nomads between seasonal pasture areas (sometimes between Afghanistan and Pakistan) have been largely curtailed. Animal populations have been destroyed as well as extensive traditional irrigation systems and agricultural lands.

Apart from settled versus nomadic lifestyles, the other long-standing source of social identity is religious, overwhelmingly Muslim in modern times, but including Sunni (an 80 percent majority), Ithna ʻAsharī ("Twelver") Shiʻa (in urban Herat and the central Hazārajāt mountain region), and Ismaʻīlī (in the eastern mountains of Badakhshān and the Wakhān Corridor). Small but ancient Jewish communities formerly residing in major cities have now virtually all relocated to Israel and elsewhere, and a small population of Hindu and Sikh tradespeople, also depleted by the late 1990s, were formerly found in cities and towns.

Twenty years of warfare following a Marxist coup (1978) and Soviet occupation (1979) have reshaped social relationships and cultural repertoires in ways that have yet to be assessed and are still very much in flux. One fourth of the estimated prewar population of just under twenty million was displaced to Pakistan, Iran, and more distant sites of refuge; an additional 15 percent or more were internally displaced by different phases of warfare before and after the Soviet withdrawal in 1989. A generation of interruptions of all phases of basic physical and social life (agriculture, village settlement patterns, marriage and mother-child survival, local circulation of goods and people for trade, services, and peacetime migration, education, life cycle and calendrical rituals, and festivals) has had potentially profound effects on dimensions of cultural knowledge such as verbal art traditions, music, and traditional technology (architecture, irrigation systems construction and maintenance, specialized production such as sericulture, distinctive local traditions in needle arts, pottery, metalwork, and jewelry making, and so forth). Wartime population shifts have also resulted in the acceleration of some cosmopolitan trends (for example, exposure to mass media, travel outside the home region) that were already under way in Afghanistan prior to 1978 due to extensive male labor migration and transfer payments, a slowly expanding national education system, and developments in mass media: radio plus a fledgling film industry and planning for national television.

The jihād (in the sense of a war in defense of religion) proceeded under a unifying ideology of righteous resistance to the secular Marxist regime and its Soviet supporters. The regime's early efforts (from 1978–1979) for enforced secularization and attempts at mass education, including compulsory adult female education, land, and credit reform, were flash points for a general uprising against the regime. Yet the resistance parties were more than a dozen and rivalrous, their leadership distinguished by different varieties of Islamist thought and by the regional and, to that extent, ethnic power bases of the different commanders. Major intervention by the United States and other regional and global political players resulted in large infusions of armaments and cash, turning participants in the national struggle into clients of various foreign entities. Accusations of foreign clientship (*vatanforūshī,* "homeland-selling" in Darī Persian) were and are a powerful traditional idiom of moral condemnation, going back at least to the Afghan-British interactions of the nineteenth century. What and who shall count as "real Afghan" is now a potent issue in an emerging defensive nationalism. A second destructive aspect of Afghan globalization is the development of the country as a primary producer of opium for processing into heroin, a major revenue source for warring factions that became the largest cash crop and source of hard currency in the war years.

Thus, any description of Afghan indigenous culture and cultural relations within the region becomes a mix of retrospection and speculation as to what will remain, what will revive, and what will emerge as salient cultural expressions in the coming years. Not only cultural but physical survival of Afghan individuals, families, and population groups depends on the future success of the extremely fragile process of national reconciliation and reconstruction under way since 2001. Return of diaspora populations, also now rapidly under way, potentially can restore both physical resources (including capital) and expertise (both traditional and cosmopolitan) needed for reconstruction, but tensions exist between the "stayed-on" and those who are perceived as having fled only to return as "carpetbaggers" corrupted by a life of exilic luxury and safety.

Since the late 1950s or early 1960s, the Afghan government sponsored journal publications designed to showcase Afghan traditional culture for a fledgling international tourist trade and for the satisfaction of nationalist intellectuals. The interest of the latter in documenting regional and local verbal arts, customs, and beliefs came to be framed and encouraged as a nationalist project, resembling the European nationalist language-and-folklore movements led by such scholars as the brothers Grimm in Germany and Elias Lönnrot in Finland. *Lamar,* the Ministry of Culture's journal published in the 1960s, made a point of framing certain local or regional performance forms, such as dance, as admirable components of a worldwide artistic heritage as well as a national one. Since dance, together with instrumental music, is religiously suspect to conservative Muslims, especially if it involves female performance before men, one can see the government's effort to celebrate Afghan regional dance forms (among other cultural expressions) as national heritage, as a potentially secularizing move. Likewise, *Lamar* and its successor journal starting in the 1970s, *Fūlklūr* (Folklore), generally avoided documenting local expressive forms that were pointedly religious and might inspire sectarian disapproval, such as religious praise poetry or religious healing practices. More "presentable" forms included proverbs, lyric and narrative poetry (including song texts but rarely documenting their tunes, perhaps due to a lack of ethnomusicologically trained indigenous scholars), folktales and other prose narrative, some local legends (including some local religious legends), and descriptions of local forms of life cycle rituals, especially wedding and birth customs (but not, for instance, funeral practices). *Fūlklūr* also downplayed specular features of *Lamar* which made it more like an Afghan *Life* magazine, with its abundant photos, drawings, and other graphics, and its mix of articles on contemporary national and international cultural topics as well as "folklore" in the sense of local ethnographic descriptions. *Fūlklūr* focused on print presentations of texts and verbal descriptions of "folk cultural" genres, materials, and activities, with very limited illustrations, a less technically demanding format, but also perhaps a less offensive one to Muslim observers.

Notable in the mid-1980s, during the Marxist period, was the appearance of several dozen local ethnographies and folklore monographs, published in Darī Persian or Pashto, under the sponsorship of the Ministry of Culture. These books for the most part presented field data collected by indigenous regional scholars prior to the 1978 coup. Some focus on a single genre or cluster of genres (for example, folk song genres); others attempt a more wide-ranging ethnographic profile of a locale or group; still others attempt to tie a locale to a major phase of regional history (such as a presentation of Sistān, a southwestern province, with reference to a historical interpretation of the Iranian national epic, *Shāhnāma*). Yet the combined effect of these publications was a substantial enhancement of cultural documentation of Afghanistan, beyond that of the 1960s and 1970s. Some new fieldwork was also being done, notably by the Tajikistani folklorist Ravshan Rakhmonov (Rahmoni), who conducted folk narrative research and made tape recordings of narrative performances in his free time while doing his "internationalist duty" as a translator for Russian advisors at some Kabul institutions of higher learning.

The Marxist regime's sponsorship of projects to document traditional culture, otherwise branded as backward in their ideology, was perhaps an effort to acknowledge and address local cultural constituencies, despite the intensification of hostilities all over the countryside, but if this was the goal, it seems quixotic, given the low literacy rate (30 percent or less overall, far less in rural areas), and the very limited circulation of such publications. The insecurity of the countryside caused a restriction of intellectuals, including some with ethnonationalist cultural interests prior to the war, to the safety of major cities, where they published their prior research.

The Sovietization of Central Asia was characterized by state sponsorship of distinctions defining the Soviet republics along ethnolinguistic lines. The division of the region into notionally ethnic "republics" served partly, if not mainly, to defuse pan-Islamist resistance in the early twentieth century. State-sponsored ethnic separatism could then be managed by the presence of Russian "seconds" at levels of bureaucracy from the top down. Both in Central Asia and in Afghanistan, one legacy of Western imperialism, most recently Soviet and global intervention, seems to be exacerbation of ethnic rivalries in local and regional politics, cultural constructions of essentialized difference being made into distinctions for which people fight and die.

One of the challenges for both scholars of Afghanistan's culture and cultural activists is to understand the interactions of transregional cultural commonalities and distinctions ethnic and otherwise, as a dynamic system or set of processes operating within and beyond national boundaries. The semiarid landlocked geography of Afghanistan presents some shared ecological challenges, from uncultivable deserts in the south to high mountains in the central and eastern regions. The staple grain, wheat, is grown at elevations up to about eight thousand feet, mostly dry-farmed and reliant on seasonal rains that fail periodically. For the poorest Afghans in hard times, wheat bread with tea and sugar (if affordable) sustain life. Outside of famine times, seasonal vegetables cooked with oil, dried legumes, and occasional helpings of dairy products are also basic to the diet. Meat may be seen only on festival occasions by poor families, even in better times.

Staple crops the world over, regarded as the staff of life by users, generally receive forms of ritual appreciation in traditional foodways. The foods prepared for *nazr* (women's votive offerings) in Afghanistan centrally involve wheat in the form of special breads, porridges, and *halvā* or cooked sweets. One noteworthy group of wheat-based ritual foods is prepared in various forms from Iran across central Afghanistan to the Karakorum Mountains of Pakistan. The basic ingredient is wheat sprouts that have been grown until they are about one inch high, then dried and ground into meal. The grain's own conversion of stored starch to sugar while sprouting ("malting") results in a sweet meal, which is then cooked for hours with water, oil, and additional wheat flour. The result is pudding-like *samanū* in Iran, or fudge-like in the case of *samanak* in the central Afghan Hazārajāt region and *ṣhoṣhp* in Pakistan's Chitral. This ritual food is particularly associated with *Naw Ṛūz*, the pre-Islamic, solar new year festival, celebrated at the vernal equinox. The sprouting of the wheat invokes the return of life in the spring, and the food is ceremoniously enjoyed by families and offered to friends during this season of visits and reconciliations.

Continuities in this and other folk cultural themes, forms, and practices across the country and the region would tend to support super- or transethnic views of Afghan and regional folklore. Yet at the same time, certain forms become marked as key items of ethnic or linguistic cultural heritage, linked to identity issues. All groups maintain and use stocks of proverbs, a resource for indirect yet trenchant social commentary in a regional cultural setting in which direct criticism of others' behavior is often to be avoided. The poetic phrasing of the proverb is special to each language and often draws on words and images particular and strongly salient to the language or dialect group. Yet the philosophical or psychological import is often shared across languages. Two traditions, Balochi and Brahui, assign special genre terms to narrative-based proverbs, those which sum up the point of a fable-like narrative and are comprehensible only to those somewhat familiar with the story. Yet all the traditions have such proverbs as well as freestanding ones.

Customs which are regional in scope may be locally or ethnically claimed. Throughout the region, there is a strong custom of female networks, such that women of an extended family and close friends visit one another for congratulations over good fortune, and for condolence and expressions of concern and support when a woman's family member is ill, in danger, or deceased. Among Pashtuns, this custom is regarded as part of *paṣhtūnwalī,* the unwritten ethnolegal code or standard of behavior that makes Pashtuns Pashtun in their own estimation. This reciprocal visiting custom is called *ghamṣādī* ("grief and joy") in Pashto. The expectation is that a woman being comforted will narrate the history of the trauma at some length and with dramatic detail, in response to her visitors' inquiry (*tapos*). The listeners then may respond empathetically (or competitively) by recounting some of their own misfortunes. Pashtun women judge each other's strength of character by their ability both to withstand these all-too-common trials and to articulate them movingly. One Pashtun woman discussing this custom explained, "[Visiting for condolence and support] is *sonnat* [Muslim proper behavior, modeled on that of the Prophet]; *how* we do it is our *riwāj* [custom]." Thus Pashtun proprietary custom is legitimated as Muslim duty. Yet among other ethnic groups as well visitation for condolence and hearing about others' personal experiences, not claimed as ethnically specific, are viewed as social obligation for members of extended families and other networks.

Some similar genres or performance forms, such as folk/oral quatrains (*chahārbaytī* in Darī Persian) are very popular across the region and among different ethnic groups but may go under different proprietary names. Quatrains are called *falak* in Badakhshān in the northeast and *sang gardī* in the Panjshir Valley just north of Kabul. *Falak,* "heaven," refers to the idea of fate, the "wheel of heaven," turning and doling out the sorrows of unrequited love and separation from home which are the staple themes of the quatrains. *Sang gardī,* "traveling among the stones," romantically refers to the practice of singing such short poems while walking the rocky hillsides of the Panjshir, their sound carrying across the landscape, and invokes a sense of freedom and pride in the home locale.

The chahārbaytī and related quatrain genres are most at home in Persian dialects, but other languages have equally famous and abundant short lyric forms, composed and memorized by ordinary people going about their lives, including the Pashto *lanḍay*. In contrast to the quatrain, the lanḍay couplet is asymmetrical; the first line must have nine syllables; the second, thirteen. Yet the content of lanḍay also favors themes of separation and unrequited love.

While verse epic is sparsely documented for Afghanistan (the most discussed epic being *Gūrughlī,* in Uzbek and Tajiki Persian forms, and current Afghan Baloch involvement with Balochi epic performance yet to be researched), there are rich traditions of prose romances and multi-episodic adventure tales in several languages. The effect of television and film on sustained narrative performance remains to be assessed. The prose romances performed in Herati Persian before the war were primarily romantic quest stories, a good number of them coexistent in oral and written (chapbook) form. The basic plot was "Boy learns of girl and falls in love sight unseen; boy meets girl; boy loses girl to a villain (resistant father or evil suitor selected by her parents); boy defeats villain (often with girl's help); return to boy's home and marriage." Some of these romances are especially prized for the *chahārbaytī* within them, which the hero and heroine use to speak their feelings and communicate. Such verses are sung by the narrator a capella, to a tune which is particular to the story and recognized as belonging to it. A new romance of this type, *Sīāh Mūī o Jalālī,* became popular in the 1950s as the true story of a poor young shepherd who fell in love with the daughter of his employer, a wealthy nomad, and began to sing inspired love poetry. This plot is unusual in that the traditional romance hero is a prince or noble who is temporarily incognito as a poor man, while Jalālī was a certifiable member of the underclass. The heroine's family first tried to banish or kill him, then reluctantly let him undertake to raise a large bride-price and marry her, which he did by dint of incredible labor as a shoemaker. His poems stud the narrative. He is said to have died young after the marriage, but the heroine was interviewed and photographed as an elderly woman by Maiel Harawi, an Afghan scholar who published a small chapbook on the romance in 1967.

Pashtun sung-verse romances, some of which have been made into commercial cassette recordings and marketed from Peshawar, are famous for a different type of modal plot or theme, that of the honor-death separating an idealized pair of lovers. A happily married couple, in one example, encounters difficulties because the wife has unwillingly let just her hand be seen by a strange man, when her husband is absent and she provides the stranger with some needed item from her husband's shop. In the tragedy that ensues, she insists that her husband, who loves her and does not doubt her, kill her to preserve family honor in the face of community gossip.

Fictional folktales (märchen, magic or wonder tales and animal tales told for entertainment or instruction) are abundant in Afghan languages, as are legends of local saints and other religious lore. Generally, concepts of truth and fiction are clearly implied in vernacular genre designations, but individual tellers and listeners may give varying degrees of credence to whole narratives or to elements within them, for example, non-sacred supernaturals or miraculous events. Indigenous scholarship has paid attention to particular tales and to bodies of tales in different communities, but comparatively little analytic attention has so far been given to performances in context and so-called "oral literary criticism," the concepts and opinions operating among participants in a particular tradition.

The richness of material culture in Afghanistan has only begun to be explored, with a few short articles in *Fūlklūr* on particular forms, and a few substantial monographs on, respectively, needle arts, small craft objects, vernacular architecture, and the social organization and activities of categories of craftspeople.

One area of emergent folklore is jihād or war lore, including martyrology, material culture in the form of illustrated "war carpets," and, more recently, rumors and reports about the objections the Islamist Ṭālibān had to certain local customs in different areas which came under their control. Critical reports are of course filtered through hostile sources (resistance elements and Western journalists) and thus are to be analyzed as resistance lore, rumors, and hearsay. In the realm of legend, in August of 2000 a version of the globally migratory "stolen organs" legend was leveled against the Ṭālibān by the United Front (later known as the Northern Alliance), alleging that they had harvested the vital organs of young male civilians for sale to brokers for "foreign" transplant recipients, leaving the victims to die while their organs were refrigerated and shipped out of Afghanistan.

Among the more problematic themes of recent oral history are the allegations that Ṭālibān and especially "outsiders," non-Afghan allies (Pakistanis, "Arabs") abducted attractive young girls and women from opposition families of different ethnic groups, and "married" them or held them as concubines. Abduction and rape being common in wartime, offenses against women are hardly unexpected, but the Afghan allegations present special problems in that some aggrieved families are said to prefer to declare their daughters dead rather than try to locate them, sexual shame being ineradicable. Thus a kind of "silenced history" is produced, no less potent because of the themes or processes of repression of individual witness narratives.

Western reporters during the Ṭālibān regime's hegemony abundantly reported the regime's objection to Western-style clothes and entertainments but more bemusedly noted the regime's rejection of some seemingly quaint or harmless local pastimes and practices. Kite-flying was forbidden; what was not reported in the West is that this sport of the windy spring season involves kite combats, in which the strings are coated with glue and ground glass and combatants try to rub their strings over that of a rival and cut it. Bets are made, and to this the Ṭālibān objected on religious grounds. Pigeon-flying was also a problem; pet pigeons are kept on urban roofs and in backyard aviaries for their appearance and the flying abilities of homing and "tumbling" breeds. Pigeon fanciers were already critically and somewhat humorously represented in Afghan folktales as a class of male ne'er-do-well just a cut above hashish-smoking fake mendicants. A third male pastime targeted by the Ṭālibān was egg fights. In spring, when eggs are boiled with onion skin to dye them light pink as part of spring celebrations, or indeed at any time among the boys who sell boiled eggs as snack foods in markets and bus stops, contests were held in which one contestant held his egg, large end up, firmly in his fist, while the second used the pointed end of his own egg to knock the other until one broke. The winner would take the broken egg (to sell if he were vending them) or some other small wager. The Ṭālibān news media reported one egg fight that ended in violence and the regime's decision to put a ban on the practice. Another custom that received Ṭālibān disapproval was fumigation with the smoke of wild rue (*isfand*) seeds, thought to ward off the evil eye and bad spirits. Mendicants and poor young boys could set up in business with a perforated tin can on a string, a glowing piece of charcoal, and some rue seeds, fumigating the doorways of shops and receiving small donations from the shopkeepers, but *isfandī* street kids in Kabul complained that "Arab" Ṭālibān condemned the practice as un–Islamic and sometimes beat them.

More significant customs, such as the various public and private celebrations connected with Naw Ṛūz, the solar new year at the spring equinox, were also suppressed as un–Islamic. In this they were on good religious-historical ground, but more significant, perhaps, was the sectarian dimension. The major public events of Naw Ṛūz, including the raising of a tall pole or mast (*janda*) wrapped in green fabric, which is auspicious to touch at the moment it is erected, take place at centers of Shi'a pilgrimage, the Shrine of 'Alī in Mazar-i Sharif and the Ziyārat-i Sakhī (Shrine of the "Benevolent," an epithet of 'Alī) in Kabul.

That the Ṭālibān were not entirely opposed to devotional activity at shrines, as were their Saudi Wahhābi ideological allies, is attested by the visit of Mulla Omar, the Ṭālibān leader, to the Shrine of the Cloak of the Prophet in Qandahar soon after the Ṭālibān gained control of that city. The cloak is only rarely to be viewed by anyone other than its custodians. The current shrine custodian's narratives of the visits of previous heads of the Afghan state suggest that only the righteous can dare to look at it, others being seized with fear when they try. Mulla Omar is reported to have removed the cloak from the shrine, against the better judgment of its custodians, and taken it to a central city mosque where he personally displayed it or, in some tellings, put it on, in a public display from the mosque roof met by shouts of "Amīr al-Mo'menīn!" ("Commander of the Faithful!") from the crowd. The title is that formerly held by the Caliphs, successors to the Prophet theoretically in authority over the daily lives of the entire Muslim community, before the thirteenth-century demise of that institution. The cloak's custodians, recently interviewed, are somewhat noncommittal on the significance of that event.

It is as impossible to offer an adequate summation of the range of Afghan folklore as it is to predict which aspects of vernacular culture will survive and flourish or develop anew under the conditions of radical social disruption which now prevail. It is clear, however, that long-standing values and principles of cultural style continue to figure fundamentally in the debates among Afghan citizens about the future shape of their culture and society.

References

Azoy, G. Whitney. 1982. *Buzkashi: Game and power in Afghanistan.* Philadelphia: University of Pennsylvania Press.

Badalkhan, Sabir. 2000. "Ropes Break at the Weakest Point": Some Examples of Balochi Proverbs with Background Stories. *Proverbium* 17, pp. 43–69.

Dor, Rémy. 1982. *Chants du toit du monde. Textes d'orature kirghize suivis d'un lexique kirghiz-français.* Paris: Maisonneuve et Larose.

Dor, Rémy, and Clas M. Naumann. 1978. *Die Kirghisen des Afghanischen Pamir.* Graz: Akademische Druck- und Verlagsanstalt.

Doubleday, Veronica. 1988. *Three women of Herat.* London: Jonathan Cape.

Dupree, Louis. 1973. *Afghanistan.* Princeton: Princeton University Press.

Edwards, David. 2002. *Before Taliban: Genealogies of the Afghan jihad.* Berkeley: University of California Press.

Frembgen, Jürgen W. 1989. *Naswar: Der Gebrauch von Mundtabak in Afghanistan und Pakistan.* Liestal: Stiftung Bibliotheca Afghanica.

———. 2000. *Lebensbaum und Kalaschnikov: Krieg und Frieden im Spiegel Afghanischer Bildteppiche.* Blieskastel: Gollenstein Verlag.

———. 2001. *Accessories: Islamische Kleinkunst aus Süd-, West- und Zentralasien.* (Mare Erythraeum IV). Munich: Staatliches Museum für Völkerkunde.

Gannon, Kathy. 2001. Taliban bans New Year's celebration. Associated Press release, 20 March 2001.

Grima, Benedicte. 1993. *The performance of emotion among Paxtun women: "The misfortunes that have befallen me."* Austin: University of Texas Press.

Heravi, Maiel. 1967. *Sīāhmūī.* Kabul: N.p. Chapbook.

Heston, Wilma. 1996. Rhyme and Repetition: Pashto Poetry and Song. In *Studies in the Popular Culture of Pakistan* (eds. William Hanaway and Wilma Heston) pp. 289–338. Lahore: Sang-e Meel for Lok Virsa.

Klimburg, Max. 1999. *Kafirs of the Hindu Kush: Art and Society of the Waigal and Ashkun Kafirs.* Stuttgart: Steiner.

Mills, Margaret A. 1990. *Oral narrative in Afghanistan: The individual in tradition.* New York: Garland Publishers.

———. 1991. *Rhetorics and politics in Afghan traditional storytelling.* Philadelphia: University of Pennsylvania Press.

———. 2001. The gender of the trick: Female tricksters and male narrators. *Asian Folklore Studies* 60(2): 237–258.

NNI News Service. 2002. Taliban accused of removing vital organs from Afghans. NNI News Service press release, Islamabad, 6 August 2000.

Olesen, Asta. 1994. *Afghan craftsmen: The cultures of three itinerant communities.* London: Thames and Hudson.

Onishi, Norimutsu. 2001. A tale of the mullah and Muhammad's amazing cloak. *New York Times* dispatch, 19 December 2001.

Paiva, Roland, and Bernard Dupaigne. 1993. *Afghan embroidery.* Karachi: Ferozsons Ltd.

Pedersen, Gorm. 1994. *Afghan nomads in transition. A century of Chang among the Zala Khān Khēl.* London: Thames and Hudson.

Poladi, Hassan. 1989. *The Hazāras.* Stockton, CA: Moghul Publishing Co.

Rahmoni, Ravshan. 1995/1374. *Afsānahā-yi Darī* [Tales from Persia]. Tehran: Soroush Press.

Reeve, William. 1999. Taliban resolve deadly "egg-knocking dispute." BBC dispatch, Rostaq, north Afghanistan, 6 February 1999.

Reut, Marguerite. 1983. *La Soie en Afghanistan: Lélevage du ver à soie en Afghanistan et l'artisanat de la soie à Herāt.* Wiesbaden: L. Reicher Verlag.

Reuters. 2001. Afghans brave Taliban whips to mark new year. Press release, 21 March 2001.

Sakata, Hiromi Lorraine. 2002. *Music in the mind: The concepts of music and musician in Afghanistan.* 2nd ed. Washington, DC: Smithsonian Institution.

Shahrani, Enayatullah. 1975. *Imsāl wa Hikam* [Proverbs and Wise Sayings]. Kabul: Government Printing Office.

Shahrani, M. Nazif. 1979. *The Kirghiz and Wakhi of Afghanistan.* Seattle: University of Washington Press.

Sullivan, Kevin. 2001. Kabul's lost women. Many abducted by Taliban still missing. *Washington Post* Foreign Service press release, 19 December, 2001.

Szabo, Albert, and Thomas J. Barfield. 1991. *Afghanistan: An atlas of indigenous domestic architecture.* Austin: University of Texas Press.

Thalhammer, Ingeborg. 1984. *Die Liedkategorien der Özbeken Nordwestafghanistans.* Vienna: Verlag des Verbandes der Wissenschaftlichen Gesellschaften Osterreichs.

Waldman, Amy. 2001. No TV, no chess, no kites: Taliban penal code from A to Z. *New York Times* dispatch, 21 November 2001.

MARGARET A. MILLS

SEE ALSO

Al; Aql and *Nafs;* Architecture, Afghanistan; *Atan; Badala; Buzkashī;* Carpets and Carpet Weaving; *Chaharbayti*; Circumcision; Courtship, Afghanistan; *Dom;* Folk Drama, Afghanistan; *Girau; Gurughli;* Islam; Jihad Poetry; *Malang;* Refugee Lore; Sacred Geography, Afghanistan

AGRICULTURAL DEVELOPMENT AND FOLKLORE, SRI LANKA

The majority of cultural festivals and ceremonies have multiple meanings that can be surfaced, examined, and used. These meaningful factors do not exist in isolation, or as superficial sociological phenomena. Their complexity is due to scientific, religious, social, and magical factors intertwined into a single event. Forms of ritual and festival which have a long history in Sri Lankan agricultural practice also have potentially positive roles in agricultural development. Their contribution ranges from practical impacts on crop management, to fostering and maintaining cooperative relationships among participants in present-day rural development programs. Three examples (*Vap Magula, kem,* and *attam kayya*) follow.

The Festival of the Plow, Vap Magula, is a collectively performed paddy land plowing ceremony several centuries old, in which virtually all paddy landowning families participate. It thus supplies a developed pattern of social integration, organizing water management in an atmosphere of mutual help, as well as its more general festival functions. In traditional Sinhalese society, rice production has for long been the primary and most important agricultural activity. Its success was determined by adequate and properly timed irrigation, supported by a highly developed inland water tank system connected with extensive canal networks. Successive kings centrally mandated the seasonal festivals, to be begun on auspicious days and organized by divisional level chieftains throughout the kingdom. In each village, with its associated tank and paddy fields, local leaders organized the festivals, with roles for astrologers, farmers, priests, local leaders, musicians, and singers. An auspicious moment for beginning plowing was determined by the local astrologer, in conformity with the more central initiatives. All trained buffaloes, plows, ropes, sticks, yokes, and other required tools were assembled. At least two days before the festival, water was diverted to the paddy fields and retained there. Food for the participants and animal feed for the festival period were assembled and prepared. Early on the festival morning, the buffaloes are brought to the field, harnessed and kept ready to start work at a precise time. All the farmers and their families assemble very close to the paddy fields. The village leader or most respected individual conducts the necessary religious ceremonies, then the plowmen are served with milk rice and oil cakes. The leader then enters the field at the astrologically determined auspicious moment and drives the first pair of buffaloes, to which the village's best plow is hitched. After he begins, all other plowmen join in, with up to twenty-five or more teams working in the field. The first team of plowmen may be replaced by others, while the first stops to enjoy refreshments. If a farmer is unable to participate due to illness or other problems, his fields will also be plowed by the group.

The festival food, called *muthețțuwa,* is collectively prepared by the village women and carried to the field before noon. At noon the animals are led to shade, watered, and fed. People enjoy their food, then return to plowing until evening, after which the draft animals are bathed and led to paddocks or sheds. The evening meal is also collective in some villages. If all fields have not been plowed, the collective work continues on the following days until all paddy land has been plowed. Vap Magula begins the farming for the year, brings people together, and provides opportunities for giving and receiving help, setting the tone of cooperation for the entire season's activities.

Apart from the manifest functions, latent functions of the festival include the pooling of resources—trained buffaloes, plows, energy, and goodwill. Social integration is served by inclusion of younger generations in the second tier of workers, and the sense of pride of performance and achievement attached to men's plowing well. Peasants discuss their labor exchange plans for the season while sharing food and drink. Most Sri Lankan villages include members of different castes. In rural areas, caste norms and values remain important, and people of different castes do not regularly exchange food or eat together. On Vap Magula day, lower caste villagers also participate, as audiences for the chanting of songs and poems by the superior Goigama caste members, and by receiving food and drink. The festival is seen as uniting the village, within and across caste lines.

The festival scenario also maximizes physical benefits to the land. The impact of the festival on water management practices is direct and critical. If individual farmers tried to begin plowing and its attendant irrigation on varied schedules, water wastage would be enormous. Collective irrigation and plowing keeps the water loss to 25 percent or less. Rice fields often must be kept wet for two weeks between first and second plowing, which provides for anaerobic decomposition of organic matter leading to formation of ammonium nitrogenous compounds that are relatively more stable in wet soil and more easily absorbed by the young plants. If the first plowing is completed in the shortest possible time, it integrates best with secondary land preparation activities.

Vap Magula models and enables collective action in farming. The strongly held belief in *nekata* (auspicious timing of beginnings) concentrates people's energies and controls procrastination. The village's farmers arrive at collective decisions, not only on when to plow, but usually on a single variety of rice to plant, so that those who have excess seed paddy can share with neighbors who may need it. This also ensures uniformity in growth, and thus water flow and maturation are synchronized to facilitate collective transplanting, manuring, irrigation, harvesting, threshing, and processing. A more uniform stand of the crop helps to obtain a better yield.

Kem designates a number of traditional ritual practices still used by farmers. The term probably derives from Sanskrit *kshema,* which denotes relief from difficulty, or immediate solution to a human problem. Kem rituals invoke religious and to some extent magical concepts, and may also embed observable practical effects which can be understood scientifically. During the last three or four decades, farmers have used pesticides on rice crops, yet still a few farmers use only kem practices as a natural and inexpensive means to control rice pests. Kem techniques minimize environmental pollution and collateral damage to other organisms, including desirable predators and parasites of rice pests. In the early 1990s, due to rising costs of pesticides and agrochemicals, interest in kem appeared to increase.

Hirima pidima (literally, "sun worship") is a form of kem to control rice stem borers, the larvae of moths that attack the transplanted rice seedlings, and can destroy the crop if unchecked. As soon as the stem borer moths are observed in any field, farmers get together to decide on a specific date for the ritual. The village leader collects unboiled paddy (unhulled rice) from each household. On a Sunday morning, before 5 A.M., the farmers gather, select the location for the ritual, and make a small *pahan păla,* a construction of sticks decorated with tender coconut fronds. The farmers pound the collected raw paddy and cook it with coconut milk. The *kapurala* (priest) chants over the milk rice and places it on a *mal bulat taṭuva* (a plate which also holds flowers and betel leaves) in the pahan păla. Finally all pray to the sun god to prevent pest damage to the crop. Each field owner then gets some milk rice, formed into small balls, and scatters them evenly around his field. Then all the farmers clap together and go away, to leave the fields without human visitors for three days. The milk rice attracts birds, and with no humans present, the birds linger and move freely around, feeding on stem borer moths.

Besides the psychosocial unifying effect of collective contribution to the ritual, a coordinated approach to pest control over contiguous fields has practical value. The birds' sustained presence to prey on the pests, a biological pest control method, can be seen as a latent value of the rite. Without the spiritual component, however, such a practice cannot be perpetuated adequately within a social system. Systematic application of the control method depends on its ritual requirements: 100 percent synchronized participation of village farmers, shared labor and materials.

Attam kayya (labor exchange) is a traditional labor form practiced by women, especially in the Anuradhapura District (North Central Province). Attam kayya is practiced for wedding ceremonies, agricultural festivals, farming operations such as transplanting, manuring, harvesting, and threshing, and also some domestic activities. It had already, by the early 1990s, served as the basis for the Regional Rural Development Bank (RRDB)'s organization of some credit unions for women. Labor exchange is a well-defined concept in traditional Sinhalese Buddhist social values. Attam kayya also includes the concept of *Pin Kayya* or spiritually meritorious labor. Work groups are composed of ten to one hundred close villagers or neighbors, usually of identical or similar status. The group members are notified of the date to assemble for work, usually around 8 A.M., working till 10 A.M. tea break, breaking again for a midday meal which the participants bring with them, then tea again at 3, finishing the session by 4:30 in order to return home by dark. Units of work are calculated as half days or whole days, and projects are organized to be completed within a maximum of two–three days. Group work includes songs or poems appropriate for the particular task. Male participants contribute, playing a local drum called *bummăḍiya.* Transplanting, weddings, and harvesting each have their own songs and poems, performed by the women workers collectively.

Pin kayya is labor donated to any disabled man or woman who needs assistance to get a farming operation completed. In this case, the cooperation, occasioned by reasons such as child delivery or serious illness, is solicited by the head of the household or his wife visiting each house in the village to tell about the disability and offer one betel leaf as a symbol of invitation. An individual accepts the betel leaf to promise participation. There is no obligation to reciprocate later. If no family member participates in the pin kayya, this is considered shameful for the family; thus each household tries to contribute at least one girl to work.

In the absence of capital or expensive equipment, poor peasant families in a subsistence economy thus command joint labor when needed. Such a collective institution can be adapted to facilitate collective capitalization (rural credit unions) and equipment purchase when resources permit. Adapting existing women's attam kayya groups to a rural credit scheme, the RRDB initially organized ten credit unions in which each union itself put up 10 percent of the lending capital, and the bank an additional 90 percent. Each group collectively cosigned on loans to individual members, as well as meeting monthly to organize labor exchange on a regular, every-Thursday cycle, and to decide on the order of loan applications from the group. Loans are made for such things as construction of crop storage facilities and purchases of fertilizer, water pumps, or housing. The collateral to the bank consists in the solidarity of the group rather than individual property or other assets. This extension of the traditional collective activities of women was designed to strengthen the women's decision-making skills as they extended into new types of collective projects, such as digging agricultural wells (fifty-nine new wells collectively constructed in one four-month period in the project region) and equipping them with pumps and other equipment through credit-union loans.

All three of these examples are derived from the present author (Herath)'s applied research experience as a sociologist attached to various government development schemes from 1978 onward. Thus traditional collective ritual and festival practices and indigenous labor arrangements in rural Sri Lankan communities can be and have been adapted to extend new benefits through rural agricultural development schemes designed to enhance and extend long-standing forms of local social cooperation and joint responsibility.

References

Herath, H. M. D. R. 1991a. Festival of plough (vap magula): A traditional ceremony associated with ploughing and its role in irrigation management and social integration. Delivered paper, Workshop on Cultural Factors in Rural Development, ICC/East-West Center, 26 May–1 June, 1991. Honolulu.

———. 1991b. Kem. Its cultural aspect and role as a strategy for pest control and participatory management. Delivered paper, Workshop on Cultural Factors in Rural Development, ICC/East-West Center, 26 May–1 June, 1991. Honolulu.

———. 1991c. Traditional labour exchange programme and women's development activities in the north central province Anuradhapura, Sri Lanka. Delivered paper, Workshop on Cultural Factors in Rural Development, ICC/East-West Center, 26 May–1 June, 1991. Honolulu.

H. M. D. R. HERATH AND MARGARET A. MILLS

SEE ALSO

Buddhism and Buddhist Folklore

AKHYAN

Akhyan (Gujarati/Hindi, "tale," "legend") in eastern Gujarat is the presentation of a (usually religious) story with music and exegesis. The best-known performance tradition of akhyan in Gujarat is that of the *man bhatt* (singer/performers). The title of the man bhatt derives from the large, globular bell-metal pot, or *man* (in the past, also known as a *gagar,* and thus *gagariya bhatt*), which serves as this *kirtankar*'s (singer/performer's) personal musical accompaniment. "Bhatt" is a family name common among some Gujarati Brahmans. The only practicing man bhatt—kirtankar Sri Dharmiklal Pandya of Vadodara—traces his tradition to Premanand (late seventeenth century) and credits Premanand with establishing the akhyan tradition through his translations of the *Mahābhārata,* the *Rāmāyaṇa,* and the *Purāṇas* into Gujarati. Man bhatt presentations focus on specific episodes (for example, the *Draupadī svayamvara* or "Betrothal of Draupadī" from the *Mahābhārata*) so that most akhyan are parts of larger stories. The repertoire also includes stories that are more specifically Gujarati, such as *Samalsah no Vivah,* regarding the wedding of the son of the regional poet-saint Narsinh Mehta. A characteristic of man bhatt akhyan (and a source of some past criticism) is the placement of epic figures in contemporary contexts and speaking in the vernacular.

The man bhatt presents an akhyan as a series of poems composed of smaller poems (in standard forms of Gujarati prosody) through song and recitation. Thus, each of these *kadavu* begins with a *chopai* (quatrain) followed by a number of *duhao* (couplets) and concludes with a special couplet (*valan*). Into the performance, the man bhatt inserts explanations of the actions of the characters and the moral significance for the audience. He (the performers are all male) also interjects appropriate music. For example, if, as in many of the most popular *akhyanao,* a marriage is part of the story, then the performer inserts a marriage song, the audience joining the man bhatt in the singing.

With metal rings commonly on two fingers of each hand, the man bhatt creates rhythms when he slaps his open palms on the shoulders of the pot, the rings clanging against the bell metal. Today, man bhatt Dharmiklal Pandya has the accompaniment of his sons on *tabla* and harmonium. In the previous generation, the accompanying instruments were the *jhanjh* (a pair of flat cymbals approximately six inches in diameter) or *cang* (small bell-metal cymbals) and the *pakhawaj* (a double-ended drum).

GORDON R. THOMPSON

SEE ALSO

Epic

ĀL

Āl is an evil female supernatural in Afghan Muslim folktale and legend who is regarded as a threat both to newborn babies and, in another manifestation, to young men, especially bridegrooms. *Mādar-i Āl* ("Mother of Āl") is an ugly old woman with long teeth and nails and glaring eyes who moves about at night and is thought to kill babies in their cribs. Her name is sometimes invoked to scare children into obedience. The burning of the seeds of wild rue (*isfand*) and fumigation of the vicinity of the baby with the smoke is believed to protect infants from her. In fictional folktales (*afsāna* in Persian) recorded by this author in Herat, Afghanistan, the *Āl-i Dil Kash* ("heart-pulling Āl") is a sinister female supernatural who may appear as a beautiful woman but who has elastic limbs and can stretch out her arms to seize the heart of a sleeping bridegroom and thus kill him. While Mādar-i Āl seems to have a stronger aura of belief around her, the Āl-i Pil Kash being more a fantasy monster, the two manifestations together prey specifically on those who should be dearest to women: new babies and new husbands.

References

Dupree, Louis. 1973. *Afghanistan*. Princeton: Princeton University Press.

Massé, Henri. 1954. *Persian beliefs and customs*. New Haven: Human Relations Area Files.

Poladi, Hassan. 1989. *The Hazāras*. Stockton, Calif.: Mughal Publishing Co.

MARGARET A. MILLS

ĀLHĀ (ĀLHĀ-ŪDAL)

The most popular heroic epic cycle of the North Indian heartland, *Ālhā* is known wherever Hindi and its dialects are spoken. Originating in the Bundelkhand region, it recounts the intertwined fates of the three principal Rajput kingdoms of North India on the eve of the Turkish conquest (late twelfth century C.E.): Delhi (ruled by Prithviraj Chauhan), Kanauj (ruled by Jaichand Rathor), and Mahoba (ruled by the Chandel king Parmal). The heroes of the epic are the brothers Ālhā and Ūdal, retainers of low social status but exceptional valor, whose cause is the protection of Mahoba and the defense of its honor. Called the "Mahābhārata of the Kali Yuga ('Dark Age,' the imperfect historical present)," *Ālhā* both parallels and inverts the themes and structures of the classical religious epic.

The cycle consists of fifty-two episodes in which the heroes confront enemies of Mahoba or the resistant fathers of prospective brides. It ends with the great historical battle between the kingdoms of Mahoba and Delhi, in which the Chandels were annihilated and the Chauhans so weakened they could not resist the subsequent attack of the Turks.

Ālhā is sung during the monsoon season. Performances occur at night, in the open, before multicaste all-male audiences, and consist of a single episode, referred to as a *laṛāī* (battle). A laṛāī can last less than an hour or a whole night, as the epic is not a fixed text but a tradition of composition in performance. Performance settings include informal sessions before a home, public events for a whole village or neighborhood, sessions at regional fairs associated with the epic, and, in urban environments, modern stage presentations, often competitions. More recently, *Ālhā* has been used by government, political parties, and sales promotion agencies. A laṛāī begins with an invocation to the central cult deity associated with the epic, Śāradā Devī of Maihar (in present-day Madhya Pradesh), followed by a background section situating the episode in the overall cycle. The unfolding of the laṛāī alternates between narrative that moves the plot forward and descriptive interludes that create emotional mood, and always ends with the climax of a great battle.

Ālhā singers include amateurs and semiprofess- ionals as well as professionals. Among the latter are *nāth*s (acrobats) and *jogī*s (wandering mendicants). Performance traditions are regionally differentiated by dialect, plot differences, melody, rhythmic pattern, and performance style, which ranges from solo recitation with drum accompaniment to group singing with full instrumental ensembles.

While *Ālhā* is an oral epic, the story is also found in a number of medieval manuscripts of the *Prithvīrāj Rāso* and the *Bhaviśya Purāṇa*. There is also a belief that the story was originally written by Jagnik, bard of Mahoba, but no manuscript has yet been found. Starting in the late nineteenth century, printed versions of *Ālhā* episodes and, eventually, the full cycle began to appear, and they continue to be published to this day in large quantities. Both older and recent *Ālhā* booklets are available in specialized library collections in India, England, and the United States. An English translation in verse was made by William Waterfield (1923). Field recordings are housed at the University of Washington's Archive for Ethnomusicology and the American Institute of Indian Studies' Archives and Research Centre for Ethnomusicology in New Delhi.

References

Schomer, Karine. 1989. Paradigms for the Kali Yuga: The heroes of the Ālhā epic and their fate. In *Oral epics of India*, ed. Stuart Blackburn et al., 140–154. Berkeley: University of California Press.

———. 1992. The audience as patron: Dramatization and texture of a Hindi oral epic performance. In *Arts patronage in India: Methods, motives, and markets*, ed. Joan L. Erdman, 47–88. New Delhi: Manohar Publications.

Waterfield, William, trans. 1923. *The lay of Ālhā: A saga of Rajput chivalry as sung by minstrels of northern India*. Oxford: Oxford University Press.

KARINE SCHOMER

SEE ALSO
Heroes and Heroines; Nāth

'ALĪ

'Alī ibn Abū Ṭālib (Caliph, lived ca. 600–661 C.E.), cousin and son-in-law of the Islamic Prophet Muḥammad, and fourth Caliph, was born in Mecca, circa 599 C.E. When Muḥammad began his mission, 'Alī was among the first to accept his message. 'Alī's life was thereafter dominated by an unwavering religious spirit and rigorous obedience to divine law. Soon after the *Hijra* (Muḥammad's departure to Medina, in 622 C.E., beginning the official era of Islam), 'Alī married Fāṭima, Muḥammad's daughter, and they later had two sons, Ḥasan and Ḥusayn.

An ardent supporter of the Prophet, 'Alī played a key role during the early Muslim campaigns. However, following Muḥammad's death (8 June 632), and throughout the reigns of the first three Caliphs, he did not serve in any official capacity. This changed in 656, when malcontents from Egypt came to Medina demanding reform and murdered Caliph Uthmān (17 June 656). 'Alī, the most eligible successor, was chosen Caliph. His ascension, however, was not universally acclaimed. Rivals used the circumstances of the election to impugn 'Alī's legitimacy, sparking a power struggle, called *Fitna* (time of trial), that split Islam along sectarian lines.

Opposition started with 'Āīsha, Muḥammad's widow, and two of the Prophet's former companions, Ṭalḥa and Zubayr, who ignited an uprising in Iraq. 'Alī rallied support in Kufa (henceforth to be his capital) and defeated the rebels outside Basra (4 December 656). With backing from Iraqi tribesmen, 'Alī next confronted Mu'āwīya, governor of Syria and Uthmān's nephew, who rebelled and demanded requital for Uthmān's death. 'Alī engaged Mu'āwiya's forces at Siffin (26 July 657), but the battle was indecisive. 'Alī returned to Kufa, only to be confronted by a new enemy, the Khārijites, fundamentalist sectarians who broke from his party and initiated a terrorist campaign. He dealt them a horrendous defeat at Nahrawān (17 July 658), but similar uprisings occurred elsewhere, forestalling further operations against Syria. Mu'āwīya, meanwhile, gained control of Egypt and commenced raids into Iraq.

On 24 January 661, the beleaguered 'Alī was assassinated by a Khārijite terrorist. He was buried in secret near Kufa. His son Ḥasan relinquished claims to the Caliphate, leaving Mu'āwīya master of the Muslim Empire. The political misfortunes of 'Alī—companion and kinsman of the Prophet, hero of the early wars, and last elected Caliph—subsequently led to a strong sentiment of veneration among his followers to his memory and to the Prophet's "house" as personified by 'Alī's descendants. This sectarian movement, which developed fully after Ḥusayn's martyrdom in Karbalā (10 October 680), was called *Shī'at 'Alī*. The Shī'a affirmed that 'Alī's was the true vision of Islam, as defined by Muḥammad, and that religious leadership (imāmate) legitimately belonged to him and his descendants. 'Alī is also the imam of the Isma'īlīs, who broke off from Shī'a during the eighth century.

During the subsequent centuries, pious legends transformed the historical 'Alī into warrior-saint, eminent champion of Islam, prophet, and culture hero. In Iran, Afghanistan, and Pakistan, *Ḥaẓrat-i* 'Alī, "His Excellency 'Alī," also designated by the epithets "*Amīr*" (prince, commander) and "*Sharīf*" (noble, honorable), figures in tales as a worker of miracles, protector of the weak, and slayer of dragons. The remains of the dragons slain by 'Alī are to be found near the cities of Bāmīyān and Kabul, in Afghanistan, where local people will point out geologic formations as the dragons' bones, with fissures said to be 'Alī's sword cuts. Ḥaẓrat-i 'Alī is also said to have created the enormous lake in Bāmīyān, appropriately named the *Band-ī Amīr* (Amīr's dam), by slicing the mountainside with his mighty sword, *Ẕūlfiqār,* the legendary weapon that, in the early wars, brought the enemies of Islam into submission.

Shrines have appeared in the numerous places associated with 'Alī's miracles. The most famous of these is at Mazār-ī-Sharīf (Tomb of the Noble One), in the Afghan city of the same name, which is said to be the true burial place of 'Alī. Local tradition has it that when 'Alī was murdered, his followers, in order to protect his holy corpse from desecration by enemies, assembled five coffins, loaded on the backs of five white camels. One of these contained 'Alī's body; the others were decoys. Each camel was then sent in a different direction, the one containing the blessed corpse of 'Alī being the one to reach Afghanistan. He was buried there in secret. The site remained hidden until the thirteenth century, when its location was revealed miraculously to religious elders in a dream. When the king was informed, he led an excavation party to the site. The party uncovered a stone tablet bearing an Arabic inscription stating that this was the resting place of Caliph 'Alī. The conviction on the part of the people of Afghanistan that 'Alī is buried in their country is a clear testament to his special place in the cosmology of South Asian peoples.

References

Caetani, Leone. 1905–1926. *Annali dell' Islam.* Vols. 9–10. Milan: U. Hoepli.

Fischer, K. 1978. From the Mongols to the Mughals. In *The archaeology of Afghanistan: From earliest times to the Timurid period,* ed. F. R. Allchin and Norman Hammond, 357–404. London: Academic Press.

Madelung, Wilferd. 1997. *The succession of Muhammad: A study of the early caliphate*. New York: Cambridge University Press.

Morony, Michael, trans. 1987. *The history of al-Tabar: An annotated translation, vol. 18, Between civil wars: The caliphate of Mu'awiyah*. Albany, NY: State University of New York Press.

Petersen, E. L. 1964. *'Alī and Mu'āwiya in early Arabic tradition*. Copenhagen: Munksgaard.

Wellhausen, Julius. 1975. *The religio-political factions in early Islam*, ed. R. C. Ostle. Trans. R. C. Ostle and S. M. Walzer. New York: American Elsevier.

H. SIDKY

SEE ALSO
Fāṭima; Muslim Folklore and Folklife; Sacred Geography, Afghanistan

ALI FESTIVAL

The so-called Ali festival celebrates the marriage of Kūttaṉṭavar, an important village god in northern Tamil Nadu and the Union Territory of Pondicherry. Kūttaṉṭavar is identified with the deity Aravāṉ (Sanskrit, Irāvat), the son of Arjuna and closely related to *Draupadī* and the *Mahābhārata* pantheon. The festival takes place in several villages, including Kūvākkam in South Arcot District and Piḷḷaiyārkuppam near Pondicherry, where transvestites, eunuchs, transsexuals, and hermaphrodites, all called *Ali* in Tamil, gather every year to celebrate.

The origin of this festival goes back to an episode known only in the southern tradition of the *Mahābhārata*: In the great war between the Pāṇḍavas and Kauravas, both parties stood equal in strength until finally the gods decided that the party in which a young hero would be ready to sacrifice his life in the next day's battle would attain the victory. Aravāṉ, the son of the Pāṇḍava hero Arjuna, was ready for the sacrifice, but, being a bachelor, his only condition was that he should first get married. Nobody came forth to give a daughter in marriage, knowing that she would be widowed the very next day. To solve the problem, Viṣṇu took the incarnation of a beautiful woman, Mohinī, and married Aravāṉ.

The female incarnation of Viṣṇu motivates the Ali to identify themselves with the god in this very special form and, hence, to participate actively in the annual temple festival. In fact, this festival forms the most important ritual event in the lives of the Ali. This is evident from the fact that, besides the very few local *Alikaḷ* (Alis), many people from Madras, and even from such faraway places as Bombay and Delhi, come yearly to attend the festival.

The village of Piḷḷaiyarkuppam possesses a small temple dedicated exclusively to Kūttaṉṭavar-Aravāṉ. The climax of this temple's yearly festival, which takes place over ten days altogether, is the two last days, vernacularly called Ali festival. On the festival day, from about noon onwards, groups of Alikaḷ start arriving. Every group has a traditional host in the village who provides food and housing.

In the later afternoon, joyful singing and dancing start in front of the Kūttaṉṭavar temple. In anticipation of the marriage ceremony, the Alis, all of them wearing saris and female jewelry, dance round dances (*kummi*), normally performed only by women, and sing improvised, often very erotic, songs. During the night, all of them, together with thousands of local villagers who participate in this ritual in fulfillment of vows, will become brides of the god.

In the early morning of the next day, the god—now a married man—will go around the village in a triumphant procession on a huge chariot in order to receive the offerings of the villagers, including betel, coconuts, bananas, flowers, camphor-flames, and here and there, a cock. At about noon, the god arrives back in front of his temple. At this moment, the whole atmosphere of the festival changes into its direct reverse. What was joyful becomes sad; instead of the erotic songs, lamentations are chanted (*oppāri*); and laughter is replaced by tears and weeping. A sort of general mourning hysteria spreads everywhere: The god has died on the battlefield, and all his brides are widows.

In a second procession, Kūttaṉṭavar is brought to the cremation ground—a harvested field at the outskirts of the village—where the funeral rites are carried out. The Alis now break their glass bangles and tear off their marriage badges (*tāli*). Then, they leave the ground and go back to the village to tie on white saris as a sign of their widowhood while the last remains of Kūttaṉṭavar are burnt, a ceremony to which women normally do not have access. The body (the procession effigy) of Kūttaṉṭavar is made of straw, but his head is made of wood and will be preserved. The Alis, all clad in their white saris, leave the village the same night. The festival is over.

References

Hiltebeitel, Alf. 1988. *The cult of Draupadī*. Vols. 1 and 2. Chicago: University of Chicago Press.

Niklas, Ulrike. 1998. "'The mystery of the threshold'—Ali of southern India." *KOLAM* 1 (January). http:www.fas.nus.edu.sg/journal/KOLAM/index.htm.

Shulman, David Dean. 1980. *Tamil temple myths*. Princeton: Princeton University Press.

ULRIKE NIKLAS

SEE ALSO
Aravāṉ; Draupadī; Hijrā (Transvestite) Performances

AMĪR ḤAMZA

The Prophet's paternal uncle Ḥamza ibn 'Abd ul-Muṭṭālib was one of the first converts to Islam, and remained one of its strongest defenders. When he was killed in the battle of Uhud (625 C.E.), his liver was cut out and gnawed by a vengeful woman whose relatives he had slain during an earlier fight. In Islamic story tradition, however, Amīr Ḥamza has taken on a much more complex and far-reaching life of his own. Between his Meccan birth and his grisly death, he spends much of his life in quests and adventures, in fighting *dev* (demons) and coping with beautiful but treacherous *parī* (fairies) in the magical realm of Mount Qāf. Although Ḥamza does occasionally convert unbelievers, the true territory of the story cycle is, as one Urdu version puts it, "battle, romance, magic, and trickery."

Although it originated as merely one of many medieval Persian oral romances (called *dāstān* and *qiṣṣa*), the Ḥamza story proved to have unique pan-Islamic popularity; it has inspired numerous versions in languages from Arabic to Malay. Versions exist in Hindi and Bengali, among other South Asian languages, but the cycle has developed with an extraordinary richness in Urdu. Besides many short versions, both old and new, the Urdu Ḥamza cycle includes as its great landmark the immense *Dāstān-e Amīr Ḥamza,* published by the Naval Kishor Press over roughly a twenty-five-year period starting in 1881. This version, written or dictated by several of the most successful oral narrators of the day, came to include forty-six volumes averaging over nine hundred pages apiece. Within such a span of prose, not only Ḥamza and his friends and enemies, but also their sons and even grandsons, had ample scope for adventure.

Within this fantastic cycle, narrative convenience was enhanced by reliance on the ubiquitous *ṭilism* named in the titles of many of the forty-six volumes. Ṭilism are magic worlds created by (non-Muslim) magicians. Within a ṭilism, nothing is what it seems: time and space expand or contract at the narrator's pleasure. Once trapped within such an escape-proof world, the predestined hero cannot break the ṭilism by simple prowess. Instead, he must follow the instructions on a special tablet, or must receive the guidance of a figure like Ḵhvāja Khiẓr (who wanders the wilderness, helping those who are lost or astray), or must manage to recite the unknown Great Name of God. Breaking a ṭilism normally kills the magician who made it and precipitates the hero back into "normal" narrative space and time at a point of the storyteller's choosing.

The Ḥamza cycle is a kind of ultimate efflorescence of sheer storytelling, dominated by a typically authoritarian romance narrator. Changing literary fashions have eclipsed the cycle for many years, but now bid fair to bring it back.

Reference

Pritchett, Frances W. 1991. *The romance tradition in Urdu: Adventures from the Dāstān of Amir Hamzah.* New York: Columbia University Press.

FRANCES W. PRITCHETT

SEE ALSO

Dāstān; Dēv; Muslim Folklore and Folklife

ANCESTOR WORSHIP

Ancestor worship or *śāddh* (Hindi) is practiced throughout South Asia. Many Hindus and Buddhists perform ancestor worship annually during *Pitṛ Paksh,* literally, "the fortnight of the ancestors." At this time, people worship their lineal ancestors (*pitṛ*s) with specialized śāddh rituals, often "feeding" them balls made of flour or grain (*piṇḍ*s) in a rite called *piṇḍān*. During Pitṛ Paksh, access to ancestors is considered most pronounced, although some people conduct śāddh rituals on other calendar occasions as well. In addition, many people perform śāddh rituals on auspicious occasions, such as marriage, birth of a child, prior to going on pilgrimage, and to win the approval and protection of ancestors for these events.

Śāddh practices are described in Vedic scriptures, and today's śāddh rituals remain similarly structured. Ancestor worship, however, displays much greater elaboration than these textually based practices.

Some believe ancestors bestow religious instruction or warn of impending dangers via dreams. Many people regard ancestors as sources of boons or curses. Some families incorporate particular ancestors into the household deity pantheon (*kul devatā*) to placate their anger, prevent their curse, or secure protection and favors, blurring the separation between ancestors and deities.

Buddhism displays internal tension about the utility of ancestor worship. Doctrinally, it is regarded as ineffective, but in popular ideology, ancestor worship is considered effective in transferring merit, especially to ancestors trapped as ghosts.

Jains do not engage in any śāddh practices. They believe in the instantaneous reincarnation of each soul after death, making most forms of ancestor worship, in their opinion, totally useless.

For Muslims, the *Śab-i-Barāt* festival is the most important time for ancestor worship. Adults and children stay awake the entire night, praying, and often fasting. People visit the graves of dead relatives to offer benedictions, and many prepare special foods for the ancestors. This yearly festival represents the most potent expression of Muslim ancestor worship directed toward those who died "normal deaths" caused by illness or old age. Souls who suffered violent or unusual deaths, however, may roam about, causing trouble for surviving relations. Like Hindu ghosts, such Muslim souls often require pacification and may demand shrines and regular worship.

Rituals associated with ancestor worship are extremely varied and resist generalization, but, frequently, domestic or public shrines (Hindi, *sthān*), ranging from simple stones to specially constructed buildings, are established to secure the blessings of ancestors considered dangerous, powerful, or spiritually advanced. If such shrines become widely renowned, they may develop into hero cults representing *śahid, pīr* (Urdu), *bīr*, or *brahm* (Hindi).

Tribal (*ādivāsī* or "aboriginal") groups in South Asia practice extensive ancestor worship. Ritualized food offerings and animal sacrifices to benefit ancestors are very common. In some parts of South Asia, tribal styles have profoundly affected Hindu, Buddhist, and Muslim practices of ancestor and hero worship. Elaborate shamanistic practices are found among many groups, such as the Santal, Sora, Naga, and Bhil, and have likely been most influential in their respective regions. Several tribal groups, including the Khasi, Munda, Ho, and Kol, erect and worship large upright stones in the form of dolmens or menhirs to commemorate ancestors.

References

Bhowmik, K. L. 1971. *Tribal India: A profile in Indian ethnology*. Calcutta: The World Press Private Ltd.

Blackburn, Stuart H. 1985. Death and deification: Folk cults in Hinduism. *History of Religions* 24(3): 255–274.

Gaborieau, Marc. 1984. Life cycle ceremonies of converted Muslims in Nepal and North India. In *Islam in India,* Vol. 1, *South Asia,* ed. Yohanan Friedman, 241–262. Jerusalem: The Hebrew University.

Gellner, David N. 1992. *Monk, householder, and tantric priest: Newer Buddhism and its hierarchy of ritual*. Cambridge: Cambridge University Press.

Jaina, Padmanabh S. 1980. Karma and the problem of rebirth in Jainism. In *Karma and rebirth in classical Indian tradition,* ed. Wendy O'Flaherty, 217–240. Berkeley: University of California Press.

Parry, J. 1994. *Death in Banaras*. Cambridge: Cambridge University Press.

Vitebsky, Piers. 1993. *Dialogues with the dead: The discussion of mortality among the Sora of eastern India*. Cambridge: Cambridge University Press.

DANIEL J. COHEN

SEE ALSO

Bhūta; Ghosts; Heroes and Heroines; Death Rituals; Exorcism; Hospitality; Melā; Paṇḍavlīlā; Religion

ANDHRA PRADESH

The state of Andhra Pradesh is situated on the central portion of the eastern seaboard of the Indian Peninsula, and spreads westward into the Deccan Plateau, extending up to 77 degrees east longitude. The northern boundary runs roughly across the 20 degrees north latitude line. The northern and western borders respectively correspond with the central latitudinal and longitudinal lines of India. Andhra Pradesh has a common inland boundary in the south with Tamil Nadu and Karnataka states, in the west with Karnataka and Maharastra, and in the north with Madhya Pradesh and Orissa. The Bay of Bengal lies to the east. The total area of Andhra Pradesh is 276,045 square kilometers.

The people now predominating in Andhra Pradesh are known as "Andhras" or "Telugus." Both terms can be used for the people, the country, or the language. We have ready reference to Andhras as a culture in the *Itereya Brahmana,* a text whose date is estimated as 800 B.C.E. Magastanese, the Greek ambassador, wrote in his memoirs that the Andhra territory in the eastern Deccan had a force of one hundred thousand infantry, two thousand cavalry, and one thousand elephants, besides thirty forts. Pliny's writings supported this statement. There are also references to Andhras as a people in the *Rāmāyaṇa* and *Mahābhārata.*

Andhra Pradesh comprises twenty-three revenue districts, spreading over three cultural subregions: Coastal Andhra, Rayalaseema, and Telangana. There are 264 towns and cities and 27,221 villages in this region. Geologically, the state may be divided into five parts:

1. Krishna Godavari Delta
2. the foothill zone
3. the Eastern Ghats
4. the Western Plateau and Basins
5. Hyderabad Plateau.

The first three are grouped into Coastal Andhra, while the fourth is in Rayalaseema and the last is in Telangana.

A riverine land, Andhra Pradesh has five major rivers and twenty-nine minor rivers. The mouths of the eastern coastal rivers served as ports up to the modern age, facilitating the development of Andhra as a maritime state.

The climate of Andhra Pradesh may be described as the tropical monsoon type, although annual fluctuations of rainfall in the state are sometimes drastic. Coastal Andhra is a rainy zone that often gets heavy storms and floods, while the western region called Rayalaseema is a relatively dry, endemically famine zone. The natural vegetation of the area varies from forest or mixed jungle, to thorny bush, to grassland. The forests have a rich variety of flora. The banyan, mango, tamarind, pipul, and neem trees are all very common in the state.

Population density is 242 people per square kilometer, which compares to the density of 267 in the rest of the country. The hilly areas that are tribal zones have less population, as tribal settlements are few and far between. The tribes of this region are the Koyas, Chenchus, and Savaras. They lead a semi-settled life, and many practice shifting cultivation along with some food gathering.

The main religion in the state is Hinduism, although a small amount of Buddhism is present. In addition to the Hindu gods Śiva and Viṣṇu, rural people worship village deities, but the rituals and ideas about the supernatural differ between these two modes of worship. Buddhism is not currently prevalent, although from 200 B.C.E. to 600 C.E. it was very influential. Buddhism facilitated the establishment of such educational centers as Sriparvata or Nagarjunakonda, Amaravati, and Ghantasala, and was also responsible for the construction of Buddhist *viharas* and stupas.

Other religious influences in Andhra Pradesh include Jainism, the Vīrasaiva cult, Islam, and Christianity. Jainism is one of the state's oldest religions. The Vīrasaiva cult appeared in the state in the eleventh century as a protest against Hindu ritualistic practices and the supremacy of Brahmans; it preached a casteless society, shunning untouchability. In the fourteenth century Muslim rule encouraged the spread of Islam, and Christianity was introduced about 1700 C.E. It spread mainly among the socially disadvantaged castes, whom it helped by trying to elevate their status in society.

Andhra Pradesh is rich in fine arts, and has contributed the world-renowned dance form *kuchipudi.* The musical compositions of Tyagaraja are famous among South Indian musicians, who cannot omit Tyagaraja's *kriti*s in their musical concerts.

Because the population is 80 percent rural, much of Andhra's folk culture emerges in rural contexts. The richness of its oral literature, folk performing arts, and folk religion make Andhra Pradesh an ideal subject for anthropological and folklore research. And although a considerable amount of research has been done in the past several decades by the state's folklorists, few of the results have been published in languages other than Telugu.

NAYANI KRISHNAKUMARI

SEE ALSO

Bull-Pulling Competitions; *Burra Katha;* Caste myths of Andhra Pradesh; *Oggu Katha; Perṇṭāalu; Vithi Nāṭaka; Watandari* System

ANGAY

Angay, or *cigyān,* is a form of women's oral improvisational poetry widespread among the Kakar and other Pashtuns of Balochistan Province, Pakistan. Pashtuns of various tribes populate northern and eastern districts of the province. The Loralai, Zhob, and Qilla Saifullah districts are the richest in Pashtun folk literature and poetry, including angay. This form was probably originated by the women of the Sandzarkhel subtribe of Kakars. It is now widely practiced by other Pashtun groups in Balochistan, but not found among the Pashtun tribes of Pakistan's Northwest Frontier Province (NWFP) or Afghanistan. It thus provides an example of the regional diversity of folk poetries within larger linguistic groups.

Angay are sung as part of the wedding ceremony, by the bride and her female companions, called *separyāne* (friends), young unmarried women of her own family and circle. The bride herself must sing, and if she does not, she loses credit in terms of her reputation for social competence. The poems are in monorhyme, with nine- or ten-syllable lines. Collected examples vary from three to fifty-three lines long, but most are from four to ten lines. Verses are improvised by the bride and her friends, but they are also remembered and repeated from place to place, perhaps with personal or place names changed. The bride sings in a special *āhang* (melody form) with a mournful, halting voice, with weeping sounds inserted regularly in the same place in the line. The bride, who must leave her home at marriage, is expected to be unhappy, and she remembers in poetry the deeds of her brothers, sisters, and parents. She may not only praise but also blame them for any perceived mistreatment of herself.

Though all have the same general poetic form, angay can be distinguished by types of content. Some of these include question-and-answer forms (*sawāl-jawāb*); songs including a curse or malediction against someone who has harmed the singer (*da sarawa angay*); poems by the bride's friends offering her encouragement; poems about rich and poor and the class system; satirical poems; songs of separation; laments for the dead; angay with philosophical content; angay with historical content such as the deeds of heroes who fought the British (Baloch Khan Kakar and his mother, Janata Ana, among them); and different topics of social protest and criticism.

The singing occurs on the last day of the marriage ceremonies at the bride's home, just before her departure for her husband's home. The bride, sitting on a *takht* (sitting platform), wearing a new dress and ornaments, and a special flower-embroidered veil (*gul ṭikray*), weeping and unhappy, begins the singing. Her friends, unmarried girls only, also weep and take turns singing. Every angay starts with a special, cryptic or nonsense verse, riddle-like and particular to that poem, which sets the rhyme for subsequent lines. A short example in translation is

There is a coin lying on the ground in the bazaar,
I'll be your sacrifice, oh my foolish brother,
You only come once to my new home,
Then you'll return to your white fort,
And leave me there in prison.
(from S. Kakar, *Angạy*, p. 385)

SYAL KAKAR

SEE ALSO
Wedding songs; Women's songs

ANIMAL PERFORMANCES

Dancing bears, snake charmers, trained bulls, fortune-telling parrots, and thieving monkeys are among the various animal acts one can see on the streets of India and other South Asian countries. The most common of these are snake charmers and trained bulls and bears. Other trained animals may be included as a part of performances such as fortune-telling and magic shows.

Snake Charmers

Snake charmers are identified by different descriptive terms in various parts of South Asia, such as *mādari lōg* in Rajasthan, Gujarat, and Maharastra; *bājigar* throughout the Punjab; *hāvādagaru* in Karnataka; and by many other names, depending on the specific caste or tribal communities. They are usually Muslim and wear Muslim dress: *payjam* (trousers), a black waistcoat, and a Muslim cap. Although they may devoutly attend the mosque on Friday for Nazam, many also accept and acknowledge Hindu deities.

They generally frequent weekly market fairs, annual temple fairs, Hindu pilgrimage places, and other periodic gatherings where people have idle time and look forward to entertainment. Many snake charmers have settled in cities where they make their rounds through suburban residential areas, local markets, and tourist centers, typically carrying one or more cane baskets or boxes containing their snakes. They also often carry pictures of gods, ancestors, or rich or famous patrons (such as film stars) whom they might have encountered. They display these on the street to attract the attention of passersby. The instruments they carry and play are various: a coconut shell fiddle, a wind instrument (*pungi*), a drum (*dhōlak*), or a flute (*pillangōvi*). Sometimes they bring and display a stuffed jackal, an animal also considered to be verminous.

They are usually associated with the cobra (several different species), but many also bring other snakes such as the python. Although it appears they have charmed the snake, making it dance to the sound of the pungi, the snake is probably only trying to keep the end of the instrument in its vision as it moves back and forth in front of it. Often the snake charmer will have a trained mongoose and will include a mock fight between these eternal enemies as a part of the performance. In addition to snake charming the performance repertoire often includes rope tricks, card tricks, and magic tricks done with iron rings and glass balls. Shows can last an hour or more and include jokes, film music, snake feeding, and information about the snakes.

In rural areas snake charmers are also employed to catch snakes and treat snakebites. They often sell twigs of an antisnakebite herb and amulets (*yantra*) to protect against snakebite. Many travel in family groups accompanied by their wife and children. The women usually do not take part in the performance, but male children often do, to the delight of the crowd. In some regions, snake charmers have places in the countryside where they meet annually with others of their extended family and community to discuss and allocate territorial rights, settle disputes, and arrange marriages among the dispersed families.

Bull Trainers

Bull trainers are usually men, but are occasionally accompanied by a woman who performs with them. The trainer leads a decorated bull or a pair of bulls that have been trained to perform various acts. They can be found widely in Andhra Pradesh, Karnataka, and parts of Maharastra. In Kannada they are called *kōlebasavaṇāṭa, gangettinavaru,* and *ettinavaru,* and have similarly descriptive identities in other languages. They are widely believed to be cowherds (Gollas) but it is often not clear to which, if any, of the many Golla castes they actually belong. There is said to be a particular place in Andhra Pradesh where bulls are specially trained, but in fact, not all are trained in that location.

The bull trainer's performance may include fortune-telling, but often, especially in urban areas, they merely go to the door of a house, call out or utter a few lines of song, and stand patiently waiting to see if anyone will come out to give them a coin or two. In rural areas their repertoire includes storytelling, particularly the story of the marriage of Rāma and Sīta. Although it is not exactly clear what the connection is between the bull trainers' other acts and this story, the trained bulls are almost invariably named after Hindu heroes, Rāma and his brother, Laksmaṇa. Bulls are regarded by Hindus as auspicious and as sacred representations of the god Śiva's mount, Basava or Nandi.

The bulls themselves perform simple tricks, nodding their head or pawing the ground in apparent answer to their trainer's questions. The trainer might, for example, give the bull simple arithmetic calculations to perform (adding two numbers), or ask the bull questions regarding a person's fortune; the bull responds with a single or a double nod of the head. Another common act is for the trainer to place himself (or his female assistant) under the feet of the bull and allow the bull to stand on his chest. Because the bull is regarded as auspicious and sacred, householders touch the feet of the bull and in return the bull gives its blessings. The trainer asks for small change, grain, or used clothing in return.

Trained Bears

In the southern states, bear trainers are most commonly Muslim men, but this is not necessarily the case in other parts of India. The bears are controlled by a stick connected to an iron ring through the bear's nose. Like the bull trainers, these men go from door to door. Bear trainers, though, need to do little to attract attention, for the very presence of the bear is enough to make people look twice. When they arrive at a house, they clank two iron bracelets together to cause customers to look out of the house. Although small children are apt to run at the sight of the bear, it is because of the children that the trainers come to the door. Mothers push the small children forward and coax them to touch the bear, give it food, and even sit on its back. Perhaps one reason for this is the belief that a child with many fears will not grow strong and healthy, and confronting the tamed bear helps to overcome fear and develop courage. If the child is too frightened to touch the bear, the trainer will take a few hairs of the bear and tie them to the child's neck as an amulet. The bear, too, is regarded as auspicious and few people will send the trainers away empty-handed. The bear walks upright on two legs and performs simple acts, which, with imagination and the suggestion of the trainer, can be interpreted as skits: "Boy going to school," "How the schoolmaster beats the schoolchildren," "How the herdsman tends his herd." The trainer communicates with the bear by means of signals struck with his bangles, and the bear also dances to the rhythm of the bangles. Occasionally, one encounters bear trainers at larger adult gatherings, where the men are challenged to wrestle the bear.

S. A. KRISHNAIAH

SEE ALSO
Acrobatics; Cow; Professional Performers

ANIMALS

See Animal Performances; Buffalo; Bull-Pulling Competitions; Cockfighting; Cow; Ibex and Goat; *Nāga*

AṄKEḶIYA

Aṅkeḷiya, or "horn game," is a set of rituals associated with the goddess Pattini. The rituals, traditionally held yearly in the month of Vesak (April/May) following the harvest, were formerly practiced by Buddhists and Hindus throughout Sri Lanka, with the exception of the North Central and Northern provinces and parts of the North Western Province. Taking place over a period of fifteen days, the sequence of rituals is performed exclusively by young and adult men.

The main aṅkeḷiya ritual involves the interlocking of two large horns, either sambur deer horns or wooden replicas. One of the horns is tied with jungle vines to a tree, known as the "horn tree"; the other is tied to a large pole, or "thunderbolt tree," which pivots in a hole in the ground. Two long tug ropes are attached to this pivoting pole. The village men divide into two teams—one representing Pattini and the other her consort, Pālaṅga—and at a designated time, they begin to pull on the tug ropes, causing the thunderbolt tree to move forward, thus putting pressure on the interlocked horns. The pulling continues until one of the horns breaks. The team whose horn snaps, loses; the winning team then celebrates its victory and humiliates the losing team through ritual acts, song, and verbal insult. The humiliation includes verbal sexual abuse pertaining to mother-son and sibling incest, obscene gestures of sexual intercourse, false and obscene invocations to deities, parodies of Buddhist prayers, and the construction of images of the opponents upon which degrading acts are performed.

In contemporary Sri Lanka the ritual of aṅkeḷiya is rarely performed; the decline of stable, agricultural-based villages has largely contributed to its demise. In the few areas where it is still practiced, the influence of urban middle-class values of propriety and emotional restraint have led to a considerable reduction in the performance of the obscene and humiliating aspects of the ritual.

Reference

Obeyesekere, Gananath. 1984. *The cult of the goddess Pattini.* Chicago: University of Chicago Press.

SUSAN A. REED

SEE ALSO
Buddhism and Buddhist Folklore; Games and Contests; Gods and Goddesses; Pattini (Goddess); Sri Lanka; Sinhala

AṆṆANMĀR KATAI

The *Aṇṇanmār Katai* (Elder Brothers Story) is a tale of epic proportions that is native to the Koṅgunāḍ region (parts of Coimbatore, Periyar, Tiruchirappalli, and Madurai districts) in Tamil Nadu. The *Aṇṇanmār Katai* is recognizable, despite variant story names

The sister crying, using traditional gestures, over the bodies of her dead brothers, and of their deceased assistant Cāmpukā, who lies in the foreground. © Eric Harris

and episodes, by the presence of three main characters: two elder brothers (known as Ponnar/Cankar or Periya/Cinna) and their younger sister Pārvati (alternatively, Tankāḷ or Arukkāni). The three were born together as triplets, but are always ranked by age in this story. The elder brother is generally quiet, even timid, while the younger is extroverted and aggressive. The youngest of all, the sister, has distinct magical qualities. Her are dependent on her goodwill and ritual blessings for their very survival in the war they fight against their male cousins for control of land earlier granted to their clan by a Cola king. On occasion, the Aṇṇanmār are also opposed to the king himself, to a group of forest dwellers called Vēṭṭuvas, and to the artisan (*Ācāri*) community of the region.

The two men eventually die heroically by impaling themselves deliberately on their own war swords in a kind of ritual suicide. Their sister performs the last rites and then follows them to heaven, where the three become minor divinities (*camikaḷ*). This triad is worshiped at local temples, usually at shrines belonging to agriculturally oriented families who identify strongly with the heroes' specific concerns. Other popular characters in the story include the brothers' strongman and first minister, a Paṟaiyā (an "untouchable" caste) named Cāmpukā, the heroes' huge dark horses named Nīlā (or Panca Kalyāṇi), their tiny pet dog Ponnācci, and the great wild boar who is allied with their enemies and whom they eventually defeat. Some versions of the story also describe the parents of the Aṇṇanmār at some length, and at least one begins with the life of the triplets' grandparents.

The Aṇṇanmār story is normally performed by singing bards who have learned their trade through a long apprenticeship to other, elder, singers (often relatives). Most often, the story is performed in front of a local temple dedicated to a goddess, although an open ground or large compound provides an adequate stage. It is commonly sung by a dynamic pair of bards whose storytelling skills are capable of attracting a large, appreciative audience. Sometimes one or more "actors" are added to the team, helping to partially dramatize selected story events. Minimal renditions last just a few hours and select only a few excerpts for retelling. More ambitious presentations require up to eighteen nights to complete. These much rarer, but very interesting, events best convey the true epic character of the story.

There is no fixed text or fixed constellation of characters and events. At least eight written variants of the story exist, of which at least four now circulate in printed form (see Beck, 1982). Scraps of archaeological and historical evidence combine to suggest that certain core events in the *Aṇṇanmār Katai* likely build upon folk memories of a fifteenth-century military campaign waged along the upper reaches of the Kāveri River (just north of the point where the districts of Ramanathapuram, Madurai, and Tiruchirappalli now meet). Though the sociological "bones" of the Aṇṇanmār story relate to this period, and very likely to real events, the tale has undergone much fanciful elaboration and poetic development over the centuries. By 1990, bards who knew and could sing the *Aṇṇanmār Katai* had practically died out. Due to competition from modern films and videos, younger persons are now not learning the tradition. A new era of interest in the story may emerge with the release of a full-length film variant, in progress.

References

Beck, Brenda E. F. 1982. *The three twins: The telling of a South Indian folk epic.* Bloomington: Indiana University Press.

———, trans. 1992–1993. *Elder brothers story:* Aṇṇanmār Katai. Madras: Institute of Asian Studies. (Complete text of one oral version in English and Tamil.)

BRENDA E. F. BECK

SEE ALSO

Epic; Heroes and Heroines; Tamil Nadu

'AQL AND *NAFS*

'Aql and *nafs* are paired concepts in Islam that identify and place fundamental aspects of human nature

within a cosmogenic frame. Developed in medieval juristics (*fiqh*) from Greek humoral theory and popularly believed to be Qur'anic in origin, the terms have passed into cultures from Morocco to Malaysia. As popular anthropology, they figure in conceptions and assessments of personality, gender, socialization, and social interaction. Formally, they identify microcosmic manifestations in a person of macrocosmic features of creation. 'Aql is reason or intellect, especially to know God's will; nafs is the unthinking drive of emotion, desire, or appetite that medieval philosophers identified with Aristotle's anima. In popular terms, 'aql is described as God's gift to His first creation, angels; nafs as His gift to jinn; and their combination as His gift to humans. Humans thus combine characteristics of self-absorbed jinn and God-minded angels, able both to recognize God's will and to act on their own.

'Aql and nafs typically are conceived as a balance that changes over the course of a life as the self develops from appetite-dominated infancy to elderly serenity through the socializing effects of religion, education, social experience, and maturation. They also figure in popular anthropologies of gender in which men are said to have more or more developed 'aql than women of the same age because they are more "socialized" to being public actors. In explanations that are more sociological than theological, 'aql figures as a sense that is developed in society for the situated, problematic character of social relations and experience. It is both cultivated in this context and, as cultivation, a manifestation of moral worth. Metaphysically, such notions affirm continuities between God and humans; practically, they place human action in relation to human nature as a fundamentally ambiguous construction.

"'Aql" and "nafs" figure in vocabularies of moral qualities and resources used by ordinary Muslims across the Middle East and South Asia in relating values of self-mastery to assessments of social order as similar kinds of control of passion by knowledge. This indigenous anthropology imagines a dialectic of complementary qualities whose balance, and realization, is always problematic. In this sense, nafs is identified with appetite, the momentary, and vitality. The problem it poses is mastery first of one's passions and then of social relations, including interactions with others, especially those who are presumed to be more or less "social"—leaders in comparison to followers, men in relation to women, the old in relation to the young. 'Aql is not intellect exercised in isolation, but in situated, immediate social relations. Discernment, particularly of the essential from the inessential, the apparent (*ẓāhir*) from the hidden (*bāṭin*), and judgment of what is right, fair, and doable are capacities of 'aql. Sufis, contemplating spiritual matters, concern themselves with a third term in this structure of personhood: *rūḥ*, the soul or spirit, which is eternal and is a matter of esoteric religious knowledge, in particular, the knowledge of God.

References

Anderson, Jon W. 1985. Sentimental ambivalence and the exegesis of "self" in Afghanistan. *Anthropological Quarterly* 58: 203–211.

Rosen, Lawrence. 1984. *Bargaining for reality: The construction of social relations in a Muslim community*. Chicago: University of Chicago Press.

JON W. ANDERSON

SEE ALSO

Jinn; Muslim Folklore and Folklife; Sufi folk poetry

ARAVĀN̲

Aravān̲ (Sanskrit, Irāvat), is a minor figure in the Sanskrit *Mahābhārata* with a much greater role in Tamil classical and folk *Mahābhārata* traditions, especially in the Draupadī and Kūttāṇṭavar cults. Worshiped as Aravān̲ in both cults, he is known as Kūttāṇṭavar only in his own. He is the son of Arjuna, third oldest of the Pāṇḍavas, and a snake princess named Ulūpī or Nākakan̲n̲i (Serpent Maiden).

In the Sanskrit epic, other than a brief account of Irāvat's birth in the first book, one hears no more about him until a single section in the sixth book, where he meets his death on the *Mahābhārata* war's eighth day. The ninth-century Tamil telling of the epic by the poet Peruntēvan̲ār in his *Pārata Ven̲pā* marks the first record of a dramatically different folk interpretation of the classical Sanskrit material, which itself then unfolds in both literary and oral folk forms.

Distinctive Tamil literary transformations start with Peruntēvan̲ār's portrayal of the war's beginning. Aravān̲ agrees to sacrifice himself on a new-moon night to Kāḷi, goddess of the battlefield, cutting his body in thirty-two places (a theme found in stories of the emperor Vikramāditya), so that, with Kāḷi's blessing, the Pāṇḍavas will win. To nullify Aravān̲'s prior agreement to sacrifice himself for the Kauravas, Kṛṣṇa makes it appear that the new moon occurs a night early. For his compliance, Aravān̲ obtains a succession of increasingly problematic boons that accumulate through further developments of his story. In Peruntēvan̲ār, he asks only to stay alive and die a hero on the war's eighth day, which allows him to retain his Sanskrit exit from the story. The fourteenth-century Tamil *Makāpāratam* of Villipūttūr Aḻvār adds Aravān̲'s wish to watch the war with his severed head for a few days—which oral folklore extends to the whole eighteen-day war. The boon of watching the eighteen-day war with a severed head offered on behalf of the Pāṇḍavas is given by Kṛṣṇa to heroes of other names—but most often variants of Barbarīka—in folklores found as far afield as Rajasthan, Himachal Pradesh, Garhwal, Kurukṣetra, Bundelkhand, Orissa, and Andhra Pradesh.

Tamil oral traditions then add a third boon: Aravāṉ's appeal for a prewar marriage to secure him ancestral rites denied to anyone who dies a bachelor. Kṛṣṇa arranges the one-day marriage, but the bride differs by region. Best known is the predominantly South Arcot version where Kṛṣṇa becomes Mohinī to marry the hero. In Kūttāṇṭavar festivals there, men and transsexuals dress as women to impersonate Kṛṣṇa-Mohinī in this role. Vowing to marry Aravāṉ for a day, they wear a *tāli* (marriage necklace), sever it when he dies, and lament his death as widows.

References

Hiltebeitel, Alf. 1988. *The cult of Draupadī*, Vol. 1, *Mythologies: From Gingee to Kurutsetra*. Chicago: University of Chicago Press.

———. 1991. *The cult of Draupadī,* Vol. 2, *On Hindu ritual and the goddess*. Chicago: University of Chicago Press.

———. 1995. Dying before the *Mahābhārata* war: Martial and transsexual body-building for Aravāṉ. *Journal of Asian Studies* 54(1): 447–473.

———. 1998. Hair like snakes and mustached brides: Crossed gender in an Indian folk cult. In *Hair: Its power and meaning in Asian cultures,* ed. with Barbara D. Miller, 143–176. Albany: State University of New York Press.

———. 1999. Barbarīka, Aravāṉ, Kūttāṇṭavar: Furthering the case of the severed head. Chap. 11 in *Rethinking India's oral and classical epics: Draupadī among Rajputs, Muslims, and Dalits*. Chicago: University of Chicago Press.

ALF HILTEBEITEL

SEE ALSO

'Alī; Draupadī; Kṛṣṇa; *Mahābhārata;* Marriage ceremonies; Tamil Nadu

ARCHITECTURE, AFGHANISTAN

Afghanistan provides an unusual context for understanding indigenous domestic architecture because, within a country the size of France, there exist an extraordinary number of distinct architectural traditions, nomadic and sedentary, associated with at least twenty different ethnic groups, most with their own language and distinct cultural heritage. The country's wide variety of mobile dwellings and permanent structures have all evolved in concert with a range of geographic conditions, climatic variations, and conservation of inherited traditions. There is also a surprising degree of competing cultural design traditions in houses, tents, and huts, often unrecognized by outsiders who are unaware of their social significance. For example, details in black tent design among nomads often declare at a distance the ethnic identity of the inhabitants.

Stock raising is the primary occupation of nomadic pastoralists in Afghanistan, who make up as much as 20 percent of the population. They take advantage of seasonally changing pastures, spending the winter in the lowlands and summer in the steppes or mountains. There are two major types of nomad dwellings: black tents and yurts. Most of the black-tent nomads are ethnic Pashtuns or Baloch, who make annual long-range migrations involving frequent moves. Most of the yurt-dwelling nomads are Turkic-speaking groups (Uzbek, Turkmen, or Kirghiz), who move only short distances.

Black tents are constructed of woven goat-hair cloth panels, which give the tent its distinctive color. The strips of tent cloth, each measuring about a meter in width and three to four meters in length, are pinned or tied together to create the top and sides of the tent. Stakes are driven into the ground to secure guy ropes that hold the tent cloth taut upon poles or a frame. In Afghanistan each tribal group has its own way of constructing and pitching a tent. The Durrani Pashtuns use a vaulted style, which employs ribs and sometimes T-bars to create the frame over which the cloth is stretched, while the Ghilzai Pashtuns employ sets of tent poles that create sharp peaks. Baloch, Brahui, and Taimani peoples each also have their own distinctive black tent.

Afghanistan forms the eastern end of a black-tent zone located within a broad band of desert and semi-desert environments extending from North Africa and Egypt through Arabia, Syria, Iraq, Iran, and Pakistan. It is the preferred variety in this arid zone because its goat-hair cloth absorbs the heat of the summer sun and provides considerable shade. When its sides are rolled up to allow a breeze, the interior is considerably cooler than the outside air. The black tent is also highly mobile and easy to erect quickly. However, the black tent is vulnerable to blowing over in high winds, provides little protection against cold, and is only moderately waterproof. For these reasons, its distribution is restricted primarily to the warmer and dryer parts of Afghanistan, particularly in the winter.

The yurt is an extremely sophisticated framed portable dwelling that employs round walls with a domed roof. It is found throughout Central Eurasia. Turkey, northern Iran, and northern Afghanistan constitute the southern margin of the yurt zone. The yurt is designed to withstand the most severe conditions encountered by any pastoral nomads. Its framework and form provide exceptional stability. It is easy to heat, and the use of heavy felt for insulation minimizes heat loss through radiation, even under very cold conditions. The yurt's stability and protection are unmatched in regions with severe winter cold, high winds, and rain or snow.

The yurt's basic structure consists of wooden lattice wall frames that expand and contract in a scissors-like motion. The lattice segments are tied together and linked to a door frame in order to form the circular wall. Long wooden struts are tied at equal intervals to the upper edge of the lattice frames and held secure at the top by inserting them into a compression ring. This stable structure supports the felt roof covering. Woven wool bands are wrapped around the outside of the lattice walls to create a compression ring that prevents the lateral thrust of the roof from pushing the walls out. The sidewalls may be enclosed by felt panels for insulation or covered only with a woven reed mat to allow air circulation.

In Afghanistan yurts are found only among Turkic-speaking nomads in northern Afghanistan and a few of their Persian-speaking neighbors such as the Central Asian Arabs and Firozkohi. However, yurt use has been in decline for some time, and many former yurt users have switched to permanent houses for winter use and rely on mobile huts for the summer. With the exception of the Kirghiz in the high Pamirs, the climate in areas of Afghanistan where nomads spend the winter is not severe enough to require a yurt, and in such situations the high cost of a yurt, its weight (250–450 kg in total), and its complex structure discourage its use. In addition, yurt use requires access to skilled artisans who produce the wooden parts. Thus, while the simpler and more mobile black tents have spread into northern Afghanistan over the last 150 years, yurt use has never spread south.

In addition to these two basic tent types, Afghanistan has a large variety of huts (*kappa*), used both by stock raisers and by villagers as summer housing. The most common is constructed by setting a couple of dozen poles into the ground in a circular or oval pattern four or five meters in diameter. The poles are bent towards the center, attached to one another, and covered with woven reed mats and, sometimes, felt. Variations in shape, number of poles, and coverings are common. There are also a variety of complex domed structures, created from reeds, found along the Amu River in northern Afghanistan, and vaulted huts of tamarisk in the southwestern region of Sistan that are relatively permanent.

In Afghanistan, domestic buildings rarely appear in isolation, but are normally part of a village complex in which individual units are integrated into a larger whole. Domestic architecture thus sets the physical parameters for community as well as family organization. Houses are typically square or rectangular in plan and employ sun-dried clay brick or pressed mud as their main building material. In cities, houses constructed of fired brick are more common. These are topped with domed roofs in the north and west of Afghanistan; in most other parts of the country, village houses use flat roofs. Other distinctive building types include stone houses found in the mountainous regions of the central Hindu Kush, heavy timber and stone houses in forested regions of Nuristan, and *qala* (enormous fortified farm compounds with clusters of individual residence units and courtyards surrounded by high walls and watchtowers), found predominantly in southern and southwestern Afghanistan.

Pressed mud or sun-dried brick walls supporting a flat roof constitute the most common variety of village building in Afghanistan. Standing alone, or more often as part of a multiple unit construction, such a building can be easily built with local materials. The main factor that has restricted the spread of flat-roofed buildings throughout the country is the need for poplar poles to support the roof; hence the use of domes where wood is scarce.

In Afghanistan, structures found in regions with cold winters, particularly in the mountains, are invariably flat roofed. This is because the multilayered flat roof provides better insulation than a curved roof (which consists of a single layer of bricks) and because the curved roof's high ceiling increases the cost of heating.

A key design problem of this and other buildings is the challenge of coping with the variation in the sun's radiation on a seasonal and daily basis. This problem is solved by orienting the building to maximize heat gain in winter and minimize it in summer, and to maximize light exposure in the morning and minimize it in the afternoon. Thus, doors, windows, and verandahs are located on southern or southeastern exposures, while western and northern exposures are avoided. Whole buildings are oriented (when physically possible) at 25 degrees east of south, the optimal orientation for passive heating or cooling for a unilateral rectangular structure at this latitude.

Domed and vaulted buildings of sun-dried brick are found throughout western and northern Afghanistan, where wood is scarce, because they do not require beams to support the roof. The walls of such buildings are more massive than those employing beams and flat roofs because they must compensate for the lateral thrust generated by the dome or vault. Vaults serve the same structural purpose as domes but are best built on rectangular plans. Domed and vaulted buildings offer a number of advantages in desert areas where temperatures fluctuate radically between hot days and cold nights. This is because curved roof forms dissipate more heat at night than flat roofs (particularly when the wind passes over them), while their higher ceilings allow warmer air to rise well above the residents below. The thick bearing walls necessary to support the roof also act as an efficient insulator. Ventilation in domed structures is often achieved by building an air vent at the apex of the dome that both catches breezes and funnels the hot air under the dome out of the structure.

Houses constructed with heavy stone walls that support multistoried compounds are found in high mountain valleys of the central Hindu Kush. Quoins—long pieces of wood—are used to interlock the stones at the corners, and the walls taper slightly in thickness as they rise to support two or three floors. The levels are stacked like stairs so that a building rarely has more than one story built directly atop another. Poplar beams spanning the space between the stone walls and resting on poles recessed in the top of the walls support the roof and floors. The roof must be carefully maintained by resurfacing on a regular basis and is vulnerable to melting snow, which is removed by the inhabitants with special wooden shovels. The houses employ common walls and roof space to form a cluster around a small courtyard, which is connected by a short enclosed corridor to the outside. The sheer stone walls with limited entries give a fortress-like appearance to the structure as a whole.

Timber and stone houses with elaborate post-and-beam construction are unique to Nuristan in the eastern Hindu Kush. The houses generally have at least two stories, with the family living quarters on top and rooms for storage or animal barns below. They are dug into steep mountainsides and stacked one atop the other because agricultural land available for terracing is extremely scarce. The roof of one house creates the only flat open space for building on the next level, and ladders provide access from one level to another. Unlike the rest of Afghanistan, where domestic architecture displays little or no ornamentation, Nuristan is renowned for its integration of artistic wood carvings into its village architectural tradition. These are produced by skilled artisans, who also ensure that all structures employ the same sets of dimensions.

The traditional qala, a type of fortified farm compound, has several obvious characteristics: it stands relatively alone on flat terrain; its compound enclosure is composed of a square or oblong plan with walls in the range of 40 to 80 meters per side, 6 to 8 meters in height, and 1 to 1.5 meters in thickness; it also has defense towers rising approximately one and one-third times the height of the walls at each corner and a gateway entrance bearing a guest house above it. The height, originally determined by defense requirements, is today calculated by the availability of the water needed to produce the huge quantity of mud required for the walls. With proper repair, qala last for generations and often house twenty or thirty families, usually the descendants of the original builder. While relatively uncommon today, the qala form has its roots in the Oxus civilization, dating to at least 3500 years ago, when this form dominated much of Central Asia.

References

Andrews, Peter A. 1997. *Nomad tent types in the Middle East*. Wiesbaden, Germany: L. Reichert.

Edelberg, Lennart. *Nuristani buildings*. 1979. Graz: Akademische Druck- und Verlagsanstalt.

Hiebert, Fredrik T. 1994. *Origins of the Bronze Age oasis civilization in Central Asia*. Cambridge, Mass.: Peabody Museum of Archaeology and Ethnology, Harvard University.

Olgyay, Victor, and Aladar Olgyay. 1963. *Design with climate: Bioclimatic approach to architectural regionalism*. Princeton: Princeton University Press.

Szabo, Albert, and Thomas Barfield. 1991. *Afghanistan: An atlas of indigenous domestic architecture*. Austin: University of Texas Press.

THOMAS BARFIELD

SEE ALSO

Sacred geography, Afghanistan; Mosques

ARCHITECTURE, BANGLADESH

In Bangladesh, hills rise to the north and east, but the vast delta of the center is lush and flat. Its topography is handmade, every elevation requiring an equal and opposite excavation. Earth, borne in headloads, has been heaped into platforms. Embanked by the rivers or meandering on the plain, long mounds lift habitable spaces above the damp fields. Bangladesh is a land of agriculture. Eighty percent of the population lives in its sixty-eight thousand villages.

The village has a common foundation built of earth, and it has a common roof shaped by the trees that rise to weave a canopy of leaves against the sun. Upon the shared foundation, beneath the shared roof, village buildings are lifted from the ground on constructed earthen platforms. Their walls are built of layers of clay, or blocks of clay, or impaled posts covered by woven strips of bamboo or sheets of corrugated iron. Their roofs are thatched or, increasingly, made of metal. Characteristically village architecture presents a mix of materials.

One feature of Bangladesh vernacular architecture that has attracted scholarly attention is the shape of the roof. Today the roof is usually a straight gable, but examples remain of the old form in which the eaves and ridge, framed of light members in tension, bend like rainbows. Especially in the fifteenth century, after the Muslim conquest and before the Mughals came, the curved roof of the village home was copied in masonry

The long, central path of the village of Rupshi. © Henry Glassie

on both mosques and temples, providing grand Muslim and Hindu monuments with a shared regional tone.

The households of the village are compounds—clusters of small buildings, diverse in material but similar in size and rectangular in plan. They are set separately but in close proximity around courtyards. The space of the village widens into zones for work, and it narrows into smooth paths, lined by nearly continuous walls, broken by entries that lead to the courtyards where food is cooked and people perform agricultural tasks. Behind the walls, village homes stream into a linked assembly, punctuated by the open courtyards, that manifests the commitment to both family and community unity.

Vernacular architecture has also developed in the city. In the capital, Dhaka, squatter settlements composed of village-like buildings of bamboo have been squeezed into the urban space, and, as in cities throughout the world, reinforced concrete has become a vernacular mode for constructing apartment buildings. In Old Dhaka, most notably in the neighborhood of Shankharibazar, stand examples of early urban housing. Narrow, deep buildings constructed of stuccoed brick have shops on the ground floor, two or three floors of living quarters above, and a breezy roof where a small temple stands.

The most splendid instances of vernacular architecture in Bangladesh are sacred buildings. The coarse structures of most mosques and temples are similar. Each is a rectangular building, ideally of masonry, with one or three doors on the front, shaded by a long a porch. On the Hindu temple, this porch often articulates with an arcade that runs around the courtyard. The mosque is elaborated in old examples by a high plinth and by three domes that rise above the prayer hall in the characteristic Mughal form. In the city, the mosque has been merged with the modern commercial building. Shops line the street, screening the prayer hall within, and more floors for prayer pile above into a high-rise house of worship.

The bamboo home of the village and the concrete home of the city are typically plain in style, lacking ornament, but the sacred building is usually richly decorated. In the Gupta and Pala periods, from the fourth to the tenth centuries C.E., temples were revetted with terra-cotta tiles. While terra-cotta fell out favor in the Sena period, around 1100 C.E., it was revived by the Muslim conquerors in the thirteenth century. Geometric and floral tiles covered the mosques. Figurative tiles depicting the deities and telling their stories, especially those of Kṛṣṇa and Rāma, coated the Hindu temples. Reaching its peak in Muslim architecture in the eighteenth century, terra-cotta ornament continues to be used, though now only on secular rather than sacred buildings. On mosques, notably the Koshaituli Mosque and the Star Mosque in Dhaka, the domes are sheathed with mosaics composed of broken bits of china and glass. This is the most common form of mosaic ornament in the twentieth century. In new mosques the mosaic is restricted to adorning a few key architectural elements: the domed minaret from which the faithful are called to prayer; the doorway that marks the transition from the noise of the street to the peace of the interior; and the mihrāb (the niche that orients prayer).

References

Ahmed, Khondkar Iftekhar. 1994. *Up to the waist in mud: Earth-based architecture in rural Bangladesh*. Dhaka: Dhaka University Press.

Glassie, Henry. 1997. *Art and life in Bangladesh*. Bloomington: Indiana University Press.

Hasan, Syed Mahmudul. 1987. Folk architecture of Bangladesh. In *Folklore of Bangladesh,* ed. Shamsuzzaman Khan, vol. 1, 424–445. Dhaka: Bangla Academy.

Khan, Muhammad Hafizullah. 1988. *Terracotta ornamentation in Muslim architecture of Bengal*. Dhaka: Asiatic Society of Bangladesh.

HENRY GLASSIE AND FIROZ MAHMUD

SEE ALSO
Mosques

ARCHITECTURE, BENGAL

An undulating, low-lying floodplain, Bengal is drained by a network of major rivers and drenched by torrential rains during the monsoon season. These geographical and climatic peculiarities of the land dominate patterns of existence and culture and shape its architecture. The dominant habitation pattern consists of small clusters of thatched huts sprinkled throughout the delta. The average Bengali village homestead is composed of a group of huts centered around an interior courtyard and often bounded by a low mud brick wall. In a more elaborate domestic compound, the hut closest to the entrance is typically reserved for receiving guests, while the inner ones are for sleeping and cooking. Other huts may function as cattle pens, storehouses, and home shrines.

Each hut in this complex is a single-roomed rectangular or square structure with walls constructed of a sheet of woven bamboo, reed matting, or, rarely, wood posts and beams, with layers of mud built up around this skeletal frame. The basic square unit of each hut may be aligned with one or more rectangular outer porches, so that a building may be wrapped completely by such shallow porches. These long outer porches are open, consisting merely of a sloping thatch roof with curved eave and edge, held up by vertical bamboo supports. Thatch, that is, dried rice straw or grasses of different kinds, depending on local vegetation, is piled upon a frame of crisscrossing bamboo strips to roof the structure. A hut can have a single roof slope down from the central spine to the periphery of the porch, or the porch can have its individual roof when there is significant difference in the height of the inner room and the verandah.

The downward curved eave of the thatch roofs (*cālā*) resulting from the bamboo frame is probably the most distinctive feature of Bengal's vernacular architecture. As bamboo is exceptionally strong and flexible, it provides a stable frame. A slight concave curve in the bamboo frame compensates for any potential sagging at the ends. The central bamboo or wooden post that supports the cālā roof is therefore made taller than the others. Consequently, while the slope of the thatch roof allows rainwater to drain off efficiently, the curved cornice at its end does not have any such utilitarian function. Instead, it derives from the adjustments made to accommodate the pliable nature of the bamboo.

These huts acquired value as regional markers during the period of Sultanate rule (thirteenth to late sixteenth centuries) in Bengal, particularly in the mosques constructed from the fourteenth century onward. (Palaces or any other forms of monumental architecture from this period do not survive.) The development of an identifiable regional architecture in preference to the importation of mosque styles from further west became part of the preoccupation of Afghan, Turk, and Persian rulers and elites, who were intent upon popularizing and legitimizing their regime and creating a regional culture distinct from Delhi and the neighboring Sultanate of Jaunpur, which provided periodic threats to their sovereignty. Sufis (charismatic saintly figures), who had also traveled east toward the Bengal delta, likewise perceived a local idiom as a successful way of presenting Islam, an alien faith to the common Bengal fisher and farmer. Thatch huts continue to provide congregational mosques for small local populations, and it is virtually impossible to recognize them as mosques when they are not occupied at prayer times.

More permanent mosque construction explores several aspects of the village hut complex. Sultanate mosque architecture showed a similar preference for numerous smaller structures rather than a single colossal structure. Small-scale constructions complement the settlement pattern, and taking into account the regular interruptions of transport and communication during flood season, probably allowed numerous, modest local mosques to serve local populations more effectively. Their spatial organization loosely corresponds to the clustering of huts in a domestic complex. Multiple spaces in addition to the main chamber for prayer accommodate the varied needs of the community for ablutions, burials, and communal meals during festivities. Bengal Sultanate mosques use the hut's basic form for their ground plans. The square or rectangular prayer chamber has an attached porch in the front (that is, east) and possibly two more along the side entrances to provide an intermediary zone. Larger mosques are created by multiplying the basic square unit to create multiple bays. Although a low dome caps this structure, this alien form is domesticated with the characteristic curved cornice of the hut. From its earliest tentative use in the Eklakhi Mausoleum at Hazrat Pandua, the curve became more pronounced over time, as also seen in the Qadam Rasul at Gaur.

When a new Hindu temple form emerged in the seventeenth century under the inspiration of Caitanya's *bhakti* devotional movement, these huts and their adaptation in mosque architecture provided satisfactory solutions for the new ritual and aesthetic needs of the young Vaiṣṇava community. The patrons of these monuments were landholders with restricted authority under Sultanate and Mughal rule (late sixteenth to mid-eighteenth centuries), rather than ruling dynasties. They probably found these smaller temple complexes easier to finance and control within their own territory than would have been the monumental single-towered temple type common to North India. Moreover, at the initial turbulent moment of Mughal rule, imperial authority was precarious and challenged by local leaders through guerrilla warfare and refusal to pay taxes. By allying themselves with an established regional form, they may well have been registering local resistance in their formal choices for architectural construction. The new formal connections between huts, mosques, and temples thus coincided with the new political alliances between Hindu landholders and the Muslim *pīr*s and overlords and with religious resonances between the mysticism of the Sufi spiritual leaders and that of the Gauḍiya Vaiṣṇavas. This climate fostered a cultural openness that stimulated experimentation in temple construction and provided a wide working vocabulary with multiple options for architects and masons.

The temple forms established in the seventeenth century draw heavily from vernacular huts and the immediately preceding mosques and mausoleums of the late Sultanate period that gave such a model monumental form. In fact, cālā, one of the names for these vernacular huts, is a term used commonly for the temple. Like the precedent domestic and sacred architecture, these temples are modest in scale and constructed in large numbers through the Bengal delta. These complexes are organized by function, with spaces for various activities clustered around an open courtyard within a walled enclosure. Most temples have a lower story consisting of a square or rectangular sanctum and one or more shallow rectangular covered porches flanking it. While the sanctum is the space of the resident deity, the porch provides shelter to visiting worshipers. Primary structures allocated for residence of the deity, for food preparation, for the entertainment of the deity, and for the sacred basil plant are oriented around the courtyard.

While an interior dome is used to cover the temple's sanctum, the exterior dome's function as a marker for mosques seems to have been recognized, since in temples the dome is never emphasized in the same way. In fact, domical roofing technology is often masked by a miniature square hut that constitutes the upper-level shrine. A long ridged vault covers the length of the rectangular porches, with bricks laid carefully to reproduce the sloping profile of a thatch hut. The resultant curved eaves and spine of these vaults give them the appearance of the interior of huts with a *do-cālā* or double-eaved thatched roof. In some cases, the interior ceilings even reproduce the crossing frame pattern of timber or bamboo that supports the thatch in a decorative terra-cotta veneer. The Keṣṭa Rāy Temple at Vishnupur (1655) explicitly reproduces the hut's entire roof features on the exterior. The lower story of this temple takes the *joṛ bāṃlā* form, that is, it consists of a juxtaposition of two rectangular huts aligned on their longer side. Each hut has two long sloping eaves with curved spine and ends.

The characteristic curved cornice of the lower story of the seventeenth-century temples reflects that of Sultanate mosques and tombs, derived ultimately from vernacular architecture. The elegant curve, now more pronounced in their transformation into brick, was imported from this peripheral province to the center of the Mughal empire at this time, where it was reproduced in pink Sikri sandstone and white marble for numerous palatial structures including Shah Jahan's throne in the Red Fort. There it signified the successful absorption of the rebellious province of Bengal and the exotic elements that were integrated into imperial style. This *baṅgālā* (architectural feature), as it was called, reflecting its regional distinctiveness, was then further disseminated to Rajasthan for Rajput palaces and ultimately brought back to Bengal in this particular reincarnation by Marwari merchants in the eighteenth-century mansions of north Calcutta.

The potential of the village hut as a marker of regional coherence experimented upon in mosque and tomb construction under Sultanate patronage was thus explored more fully in temples built by Hindu landholders during early Mughal rule. Its value as a Bengali form is also attested by its shared use for monumental construction between Hindu and Islamic modes of architecture. The further portability demonstrated by the curved eave is testimony to its successful deployment as a regional marker.

References

Eaton, Richard M. 1993. *The rise of Islam and the Bengal frontier, 1204–1760*. Berkeley and Los Angeles: University of California Press.

Hasan, Perween. 1989. "Sultanate mosques and continuity in Bengal architecture." *Muqarnas* 6: 58–74.

McCutchion, David J. 1972. *Late mediaeval temples of Bengal*. Calcutta: The Asiatic Society.

Michell, George, ed. 1983. *Brick temples of Bengal. From the archives of David McCutchion*. Princeton: Princeton University Press.

PIKA GHOSH

ARCHITECTURE, DOMESTIC: INDIA AND NEPAL

Until recently, the study of domestic homes and spaces built by India's village, tribal, or even elite urban dwellers has been neglected in favor of the subcontinent's classical temples, tombs, mosques, and palaces. Following construction of a "village complex" (*gram jhanki*) featuring fourteen examples of India's "folk" houses and their courtyards at New Delhi's Crafts Museum in 1972, however, appreciation of South Asia's owner-built, common dwellings that are unique to specific regions, ethnic groups, or castes has grown.

While the majority of India's vernacular dwellings remain walled with mud, beamed with recycled wood, roofed with vegetal thatch, and tied with human hands, their roofing profiles, room layouts, wall decorations, and ingenious adaptations of local building materials display wide variation. In isolated "tribal" areas some house types still express pre-Hindu traditions. These range from the "closed" style men's house, or *morung*, built by the Ao Nagas of northeastern Assam, which contrast steeply pitched roofs resembling the lofty sterns of old galleons with tiny, ground-level doorways for protecting occupants from surprise attack, to the barrel-roofed homes and dairies of the Todas of the Nilgiri Hills in western Tamil Nadu. Roofed with bundles of swamp grass bent over bowed rattan and bamboo frames and set within earthen depressions, Toda vaulted interiors are divided by gender, with men churning butter from their prized water buffalo in front, while women pound grain in rear rooms.

Starting from northern India, other regional dwelling styles include the two-storied, Kulu stone-block homes of Himachal Pradesh, resembling watchtowers with their distinctive wraparound verandahs and carved balustrades. Farther north, there are also the hip-roofed domiciles built by the Newars of Kathmandu, Nepal, whose vertical ordering of space, with kitchens on the third floor, maintains privacy for cooking—a common Hindu requirement—while removing smoke from living units. Other ethnic dwellings found in Nepal include the barn-sized Gurung structures, with their conical thatch roofs set upon elliptical, windowless, wattle-and-daub walls, and north towards Tibet, the Marpha communities whose compact, inward-facing houses shield their roof terraces, allowing occupants to work and store wood under the sky but away from bitter winds.

Further south, other distinctive house types associated with particular cultural areas include the sturdy, round *barmi* huts of the Kutch, in Gujarat, whose curved walls protect inhabitants from frequent sandstorms; the single-floored, rectangular *adi* dwellings of Arunachal Pradesh, whose interwoven green bamboo frames tied to teak uprights are elevated four feet above the ground on stilts, with a continuous porch on all four sides; and the *alponam* huts of the Nicobar Islands, their haystack-shaped roofs deflecting the ocean-borne rains, their wooden floors, raised safely beyond the reach of prowling animals, entered by ladders, which poke through trapdoors in the floor.

Ubiquitous building strategies for offsetting India's high temperatures involve the use of thick walls of puddled mud, wattle-and-daub, or sun-dried brick, keeping interior rooms darkened, providing deep roof eaves for maximum shade on exterior walls, and effective use of such "in-between" areas as verandahs, porticos, alcoves, or breezeways. Quality and durability of materials generally reflect income level. Where people can afford fired brick and fine plaster, they usually prefer them over hand-puddled adobe; where jackwood and teak are obtainable, they will generally replace bamboo for posts and beams; and where roofing tile is an option, it will be employed instead of palmyra leaf or grass thatch. For festive occasions, weddings, or birthdays, one often hires appropriate caste artisans to erect immense ornamental shades, known as *pandal* in Tamil Nadu.

Throughout India, kinship practices are commonly reflected in and reinforced by architectural designs and practices. Hence, the classic Indian patrilocal "joint family"—married brothers living together with their wives and children—produces, in its rudimentary form, a basic row house with adjoining family units sharing load-bearing walls. In northern Gujarat, however, where descendants of a common ancestor cluster around single courtyards, the added gateways in front of each extended-family compound, or *khadki*, turn a village into a group of kinship fortresses. Such is also the case in Chettinad, a region of interior Tamil Nadu where the financier Chettiar caste built their *nattukottai*, or family forts. In urban Gujarat, similar family houses, or *haveli*—renowned for their cantilevered upper balconies, intricately carved struts, and shaft-like *chowk* or small central courtyards—are grouped in microneighborhoods known as *pol*, with structures sharing a single street that can be sealed off for collective protection.

The complex relationships of social prestige, occupation specialties, and economics are also expressed in folk architecture. In Goa, for instance, the three types of houses—burnt mud and thatch, burnt mud and tile, and brick and mortar—are indexed to income and caste levels. For most Hindu Goans, poor and elite dwellings share symbolic features, such as cardinal orientation, placement of the fire, and gender-specific activity areas. In Goan Christian dwellings, however, these requirements, which spring from Hindu cosmological beliefs, are subordinated to more individualistic manipulations of space.

Across Tamil Nadu, a wide range of castes or occupation specialties also have their trademark temporary shelters: in sugarcane fields near Madurai, migrant field hands shroud their temporary A-frame shelters of back-woven palm flats with cane refuse; not far off, seminomadic Konar herdsmen hailing from Ramnad district set portable hemispherical roofs, woven and resembling overturned baskets, upon cylindrical walls within brush-fenced camps alongside their grazing goats; nearby, the roaming Narikuravar hunter bands pitch rows of their reed-mat pup tents directly on the asphalt road shoulders, while rumbling past them all are often *villu vandi*, or hay-roofed oxcarts, which provide mobile housing for celebrants traveling over many days to distant religious festivals.

For permanent homes, however, numerous symbolic practices help to create and maintain the "auspicious" Hindu habitation, as if protecting their occupants like a second skin. In South India an astrologer-advisor selects the day for chalking out room measurements, then digs a groundbreaking ritual pit in the northeast corner so as to bring the house-to-be into conformity with the "body" of primal man, the *vastupurusa* (the northeastern spot being his "head"). Reused wooden rafters and purloins must be ritually decontaminated, while, throughout the construction process, a demon-like *dristi* mask is often prominently displayed to discourage passersby from casting an evil eye upon the vulnerable structure. Before moving in, the owners host a house-blessing ceremony which climaxes with chanting of mantras and escorting a cow through all rooms before boiling her milk as the new kitchen's first function.

Once it is constructed, regular maintenance of the auspicious Hindu house entails proper rituals in its shrine or *puja* room, women's daily renewal of entryway "ground paintings" (known as *kolam* in Tamil Nadu, *jhetti* in Orissa, *mandana* in Madhya Pradesh, and *rangoli* in the Deccan), which welcome the sun god each morning, their offerings to *tulasi* plants in their rear courtyards, and periodic applications of purifying cow dung to interior and exterior walls. At annual harvest festivals, however, such as *Baisakhi* in Punjab, *Pongal* in South India, *Diwali* in Gujarat, or *Man Osha Chita* in Orissa, women hang special herb bouquets over the threshold and paint entire house walls with symbols of agricultural bounty.

Yet, India's folk buildings are also quick to reflect social and historical change. In the Gujarat *haveli*, for instance, one can note Maratha and Mughal influence in the slender, tapering columns on the uppermost balconies, while the iron balustrades are clearly a British innovation. As the British sought to segregate their own *dak bungalow* residences—quadrangular masonry buildings with high-pitched roofs projecting from porticos or verandahs—within European-only cantonments, well-to-do Indian merchant classes emulated their house designs, albeit often "Indianizing" them with Hindu social practices and traditional room dimensions. Indeed, a number of India's better-known vernacular traditions are actually the product of such a colonial era synthesis, from the Chettiar manor houses of Tamil Nadu, with their glowing plaster walls composed of finely crushed bivalve shells and coconut milk, to the Namboodiri *illam* of Kerala, with their shiny, pomegranate-stained black floors.

More recent architectural changes also illustrate the push and pull between tradition and modernity, as cement walls and tile or brick roofs become hallmarks of middle-class status. In "Westernized" neighborhoods of many Indian cities, the old gender division of domains within the house and associated oppositions between "pure and impure" have given way to the less rigid division between "public and private" spaces. Increasingly, personal idiosyncrasy in exterior facade design emphasizes the exterior display of individual achievement, replacing older, interior-oriented, room and hall plans, which, for many hundreds of years, followed Hindu building principles for protecting and perpetuating extended families behind their walls.

References

All India Handicrafts Board. 1974. *Village complex (Gram Jahnki)* New Delhi: Ministry of Industry, Government of India.

———. 1989. Chettinadu housing. In *Architecture, Design*, May-June, pp. 105–113.

Ifeka, Caroline. 1987. Domestic space as ideology in Goa, India. *Contributions to Indian Sociology* 21(4): 307–329.
Khambatta, Ismet. 1986. The meaning of residence in traditional Hindu society. In *Dwellings, settlements and tradition: Cross-cultural perspectives,* ed. Jean-Paul Bourdier and Nezar Alsayyad. New York: University Press of America.
King, Anthony D. 1984. *The bungalow: The production of a global culture.* London: Routledge and Kegan Paul.
Moore, Melinda A. 1990. The Kerala house as a Hindu cosmos. In *Indian culture through Hindu categories,* ed. McKim Marriott and Michael Moffat. New Delhi: Sage.
Noble, William A. 1987. Houses with centered courtyards in Kerala and elsewhere in India. In *Dimensions of social life: Essays in honor of David G. Mandelbaum,* ed. Paul Hockings. Berlin: Mouton de Gruyter.
Pramar, V. S. 1989. *Haveli: Wooden houses and mansions of Gujarat.* Ahmedabad: Mapin Publishing.
Roy, Onju. 1990. The merging of traditional and modern cultures in Nepal. *Architecture and Design*, May-June, pp. 73–83.
Steinman, Ralph M. 1989. Kolam: Form, technique and application of a changing ritual folk art of Tamil Nadu. In *Shastric traditions in Indian arts,* ed. Anna Libera Dallapiccola. Stuttgart: Steiner Verlag Wiesbaden.

PETER NABOKOV

ART

See Art, Tribal; Calendar Art; Folk Art

ART, TRIBAL

The term "tribal art" describes visual culture created both by and for tribal communities of South Asia, which in India alone constitute over sixty million people. The homogenizing rubric of "tribe" belies their very diversity: three hundred ethnic groups (so designated by the Indian government) that speak a variety of languages from the Indo-Aryan, Dravidian, and Tibeto-Burman families. The problematic term "tribe" was introduced into India in the mid-nineteenth century as an administrative and ideological category. The dual efforts of colonial administrators and ethnographers to know—and control—India's different peoples by imposing a classificatory system established artificially static, bounded categories, notably the hierarchical caste–egalitarian tribe dichotomy.

Extensive ethnographic collections, which were assembled during the colonial period and housed in newly founded museums, now constitute perhaps the largest single source of South Asian tribal arts. A major figure from this period is the British anthropologist Verrier Elwin, who supported Mahatma Gandhi's call for separate status for tribals or *ādivāsī* (original inhabitants), arguing for preservation of their unique lifestyles. Living among Gonds, Baigas, and Nagas for over three decades, Elwin documented in rich ethnographic detail the diversity of tribal cultures. His many publications remain a major resource for the study of indigenous cultures. However, the insistence on the cultural authenticity and purity of a tribe, as well as on the timeless, continuous quality of its art, are problematic conceptualizations that have persisted, to a certain extent, in scholarly and popular literature.

Despite its colonial legacy "tribal" still has a political utility in India today. India's constitution of 1950 granted "scheduled tribes" certain provisions and privileges, including a controversial policy of quotas or reserved seats in educational, occupational, and legislative arenas.

The vast majority of India's tribal population is concentrated in hilly, forested, and resource-rich regions: the southern Deccan; the extreme northeast; and a wide belt stretching across the middle of the country from Rajasthan, Gujarat, and the Vindhyan range in the west to the Eastern Ghats of Bihar, Bengal, and Orissa. This central zone is home to India's three largest groups: the Gonds, Santals, and Bhils. A selection of the art production of the Gonds and Bhils is discussed below.

Much of the visual culture of tribal communities reflects the once widely available resources of the forest, especially wood, bamboo, clay, and minerals. In addition to the ephemeral nature of many of these materials, production is often seasonal or cyclical, further emphasizing process rather than product. Highly abstract terra-cotta animals are presented by villagers at local shrines across central India as offerings to express gratitude for wishes granted. Left in piles in the compound, old terra-cottas decompose as new ones are added. The shrines themselves, dedicated to local protective deities, are built of wood and clay, which do not leave the historic imprint that stone architecture does. The historical depth of these tribal, highly regionalized traditions, then, must be discerned from other evidence. The rich mythologies of tribal communities and oral histories of artisans suggest visual traditions of some antiquity.

In Bastar district, in southeastern Madhya Pradesh, Gond shrines are the foci of periodic public religious activities rather than spaces for daily personal worship, prompting Elwin to speak of their "abandoned appearance." The temple precinct is clearly ordered and articulated as a communal space: the shrine itself, a modest structure—a single room with mud-plastered walls and wooden trusses to support a ceramic tile roof—is at the back of a large west-facing courtyard, demarcated by stone slabs. This rectangular space includes a wooden post in the center and a wooden swing to the north. When possessed by the goddess, individuals sit on this imposing seat, which is frequently studded with iron spikes. While the *pūjari* (village priest) is responsible

Memorials. Bastar District, Madhya Pradesh, India.

for conducting rites in honor of one among a constellation of regional goddesses, it is the person possessed (*siraha*) who, in the voice of the deity, answers queries from the assembled villagers concerning the welfare of individuals and the community. At these public events that combine aspects of religious devotion and community fair, animals are sacrificed at the wooden post, and villagers offer small clay bulls or elephants. More costly metal animals, as well as brass umbrellas and iconic images of the goddess—all produced by local brass casters and available at weekly markets (*hāṭ*)—are brought out from storage in the priest's home to be used on these ritual occasions.

Another prominent aspect of Bastar visual culture is the painted stone and carved wooden pillars erected by the Gond in commemoration of the deceased. Placed along the roadside, these memorials may carry a pictorial biography, or denote tribal ethnicity by the inclusion of scenes of dancing or hunting.

In Jhabua, Madhya Pradesh's most westerly district, stone slabs erected by the Bhils carry the image of a horse and rider—described by art historian Stella Kramrisch as an ancestral "Spirit Rider"—carved in low relief. Varying in height from two to as much as six feet, these *gātlā* are also made for the deceased, and are commissioned by his or her family because of the belief that the soul of the departed is restless, especially when the death is premature or accidental. Public rituals for installation and remembrance at festivals, such as *choṭi* (small) and *baṛā* (big) *navai,* bring together and help define a given community. Clay horses are offered at spaces designated for these east-facing gātlā as well as at small open-air shrines, or more typically, simple stone platforms dedicated to the goddesses Sāvan Mātā and Śītalā Mātā.

In Alirajpur, southern Jhabua district, the choṭi and baṛā navai offer opportunities to produce wall paintings known as *pithorā*. Prior to painting, the interior space is ritually cleansed by the artisan's wife, who, like the Bhil craftsman, must fast in preparation. The painter works in concert with the priest, who dictates the subject matter and placement of equestrian figures, domestic and wild animals, and village scenes. The ritualized production of pithorā is experienced by only a few; afterward the entire village celebrates the new harvest with a feast.

Contrary to the prevalent view of tribal art as unchanging or static, tribal arts reveal a vitality and a vigorous capacity to incorporate or borrow elements from other cultural systems, as well as to promote current values, attitudes, and aspirations. While one can speak of the continuity of a specific artistic tradition—an old gātlā with an inscription in Gujarati dated 1855 C.E., for example—the ability of people to change, revitalize, and reformulate indigenous arts must be emphasized. Brightly painted gātlā commissioned as recently as 1995 depict men on motorcycles or in planes, and are signed by the artisan; funerary structures in Bastar may now take the shape of miniature temples or cars.

Although in general craft production in South Asia is a hereditary occupation and a male-dominated domain, there are gender-specific tasks and technologies. Among the low-caste Kumhar, or potters, who have a large ādivāsī clientele in Jhabua, men exclusively work on the potter's wheel, whereas women craft hand-built forms such as the small horses. Rather than evincing the romantic position of the isolated and "authentic" tribal, patterns of craft production and consumption underscore a dynamic interaction between artisans and consumers. Indeed, this overview of tribal art would be incomplete without acknowledging the increasing commercialization and popularization of tribal arts for urban and international art markets.

Until quite recently tribal arts in South Asia received more attention from ethnographers and anthropologists than from art historians. In the formation of a canon of Indian art, the discipline has privileged sectarian and literate traditions, especially Hinduism and Buddhism with their monumental and datable art. At the risk of oversimplification, "tribal art" can be a useful category, because it makes an important intervention into a canon that has marginalized or excluded these other domains.

References

Elwin, Verrier. 1951. *The tribal art of middle India*. Bombay: Oxford University Press.

Hacker, Katherine F. 2000. Traveling objects: Brass images, artisans and audiences. *Res: Anthropology and Aesthetics* 37 (Spring): 147–165.

Jacobs, Julian. 1990. *The Nagas: Hill peoples of northeast India*. London: Thames and Hudson.

Jain, Jyotindra. 1984. *Painted myths of creation: Art and ritual of an Indian tribe*. New Delhi: Lalit Kala Akademi.

Kramrisch, Stella. 1968. *Unknown India: Ritual art of tribe and village*. Philadelphia: Philadelphia Museum of Art.

Shah, Haku. 1984. *Votive terracottas of Gujarat*. Ahmedabad: Mapin.

Swaminathan, J. 1987. *The perceiving fingers: Catalogue of Roopankar collection of folk and adivasi art from Madhya Pradesh, India*. Bhopal: Bharat Bhavan.

KATHERINE F. HACKER

SEE ALSO
Folk Art

ASSAM

Assam is the anglicized form of the local name of a state in the northeastern region of India, close to the country's borders with China, Burma, Bhutan, and Bangladesh. The basic term *asam* (pronounced *axam*) is popularly interpreted as a formation of Sanskrit derivation, meaning "peerless or unparalleled." However, the opinion generally accepted in academic circles is that the term has come from *Ahom,* the name of the ruling power of the neighboring Tai-Shan dynasty that was most dominant in the territory in the late medieval period.

In the ancient period, Assam was known by the names Prāgjyotisha and Kāmarūpa, which, along with the names of kings like Narakāsura and Bhagadatta, figure prominently in epic and Puraṇic literature. Recorded history speaks of several ruling dynasties, of whom the Varman line was the most illustrious. At various times during the medieval period, different parts of the land were under the control of the Chutiyas, the Barahis, the Kacharis, and the Bhuyans. In time there emerged two major ruling powers, the Ahoms in the east and the Koches in the west. The Ahoms came as invaders in the thirteenth century C.E. and soon became fully independent. Through their strong and uninterrupted rule, which lasted six hundred years, they effectively forged political, social, and cultural consolidation of different ethnic groups and sociopolitical forces. A more or less similar role was played in the western part by the Koches, whose descent can be traced to Bodo extraction. Several Muslim invasions, although successfully resisted by the Ahoms, left their own imprint. Serious internal conflicts and devastating Burmese invasions paved the way for British annexation in 1826. The British province with the present name included a large part of northeast India. After India's independence, the states of Nagaland, Meghalaya, and Mizoram were carved out of Assam.

Since early times, there had been migration of Aryans through and to Assam, settling in the region at different intervals. Segments of the original population had also been influenced in various degrees by Aryan religiocultural modes and mores. However, this part of India has always been a homeland of Indo-Mongoloid people. Scholars have also discerned some Austric and Dravidian elements. A large number of communities who stand at different levels of acculturation, integration, and assimilation vis-á-vis the Assamese-Hindu majority live in the hills and plains. Among the major tribal groups are the Bodos, the Rabhas, the Tiwas, the Misings, the Deuris, and the Sonowals in the plains, and the Karbis, the Dimasas, the Zemi Nagas, and the Kukis in the hills.

There is also a sizeable percentage of Assamese Muslims whose progenitors were early Muslim settlers taking local wives, early local converts, and Muslim artisans brought from the west. Their contribution to the overall sociocultural makeup is considerable. While there is a small Assamese Sikh community, Christianity has been embraced by certain segments of the tribal communities. Among the more recent large-scale settlers are Santals, Oraons, Gonds, and Mundas, whose ancestors were brought from the region around Orissa and Madhya Pradesh to work as indentured laborers in the tea gardens, and Bengali Hindus and Muslims from the former East Bengal (later East Pakistan and now Bangladesh). Also in recent times, there has been a sizeable influx of people from Nepal.

Cutting across sectarian barriers, the deepest and most abiding influence on Assam's society has been that of Śankara-deva (1449–1568), who spearheaded the neo-Vaiṣnava Bhakti movement in this region and was the harbinger of a renaissance with many-sided ramifications: spiritual, social, humanistic, literary, and artistic. A unique feature of Assam Vaishnavism is the institution of *satras* (monasteries), which have been centers for the cultivation and dissemination of all kinds of refinement. The *nām-ghar*s (prayer halls) constitute an adjunct of the satra institution at the grassroots level and serve as the focal points of the religious, social, and cultural life in villages. The satra-linked culture is marked by a constant folk-elite dialogue.

However, elements of Śaivism and Śāktism, which had powerful sway in the past, are prevalent even now at the folk level, and a substantial body of verbal folklore connected with the "lovable" god Śiva and the various forms of the mother goddess are widely current. Also extremely popular in western Assam is the worship of the snake goddess Manasā, locally called *Māre/Mārāi Pūjā,* around which revolves a whole range of folklore activities besides the rituals: narratives, singing, dancing, and playacting in the *ojā-pāli* style, shamanistic dancing called *deodhani nās,* and image making and painting done on *kūhilā* pith.

Assamese, a modern Indo-Aryan language, is the mother tongue of not only the nontribal majority but also of several tribal groups. It also serves as the lingua franca for others. While Assamese has a tradition of written literature going back to the thirteenth century, the various tribal languages belonging to the Sino-Tibetan family have lately made some progress in this direction.

With such a varied sociocultural background, Assam's overall stock of material in the various fields of folklore is predictably both voluminous and colorful.

The close rapport between the Aryan and the non-Aryan, and the pan-Indian and the parochial, is reflected in many forms of verbal folklore, particularly mythological narratives. Some of these link particular tribes or groups with popular Hindu gods or goddesses or with well-known characters of the epics, the object being to give a more respectable status to the tribes or groups concerned. Thus, the Kachari lineage is traced to Ghatotkaca, who was the son of the local non-Aryan heroine Hidimbā and the second Pāndava, Bhīma, of *Mahābhārata* fame; the Rajbansis claimed that their ancestors were Kshatriyas, the Aryan warrior class, who had come to the region to shelter themselves from the wrath of Paraśurāma, one of the incarnations of Viṣṇu; the Tiwas tell a story about the birth of their ancestor from the saliva of Mahādeva. There are other stories that represent attempts to ensure exalted lineages for ruling dynasties of non-Aryan origin. Well-known Purāṇic myths have also been modified in order to explain, for example, Assam's old name, Kāmarūpa, and the link of Kāmākhyā, originally a local deity, to the pan-Indian mother goddess. While the tribal groups have retained their own mythologies, mostly in verse and song forms, a portion of such material betrays signs of Hindu influence. Again, stories from the epics have percolated down to the popular tribal level. The *Rāmāyaṇa* story in particular has been a perennial favorite. For example, there is a Karbi version of the *Rāmāyaṇa,* known as *Sābin Ālum,* which is a veritable folk epic.

In the field of social folk customs, a notable feature is the absence of the dowry system that is prevalent in the rest of India. The Assamese custom has been for the bride's family to receive considerations in terms of cash (now practically discontinued) and other articles. The ceremonial presentation of ornaments and other things to the bride is an essential prenuptial ceremony.

Also interesting is the observance of the three *bihu*s which constitute a sort of festival complex basically connected with the traditional agricultural cycle. Coming at seedtime in mid-April, *Bohāg-Bihu* is also a spring festival and a new year festival. Ecstatic performance of bihu songs and dances with erotic overtones constitutes a striking feature of this festival. *Māgh-Bihu* is the harvest festival that comes in mid-January and is celebrated with feasting and the lighting of bonfires. Mid-October, in the lean season, is the time for *Kāti-Bihu,* observed without ostentation.

A distinguishing feature of the physical folk life is the dominant presence of bamboo, which provides materials not only for houses, fences, receptacles, mats, and many other things but also for certain food items. Another notable distinction is the universal practice of weaving by women of all communities, tribal and nontribal. In the nontribal Assamese society, weaving is not restricted to any particular caste, as it is in the rest of India, but is a skill cherished by women of even the highest castes. Spinning, weaving, and the execution of textile designs form the themes of a substantial body of verbal folklore of all the indigenous communities. All sections, including Brahmans and Vaiṣṇavas, are non-vegetarians. As in most other parts of India, areca nuts and betel leaves are highly valued items of cultural life.

Each of the communities, both tribal and nontribal, has its own stock of songs and dances, with themes ranging from the religious and ritualistic to the mundane and down to earth, from the sentimental and passionate to the carefree and the humorous. While the Assamese society can boast of a number of folk dramatic and semi-dramatic institutions like *ojā-pāli, dhuliyā, kuśān-gān, bhāri-gān,* and *putalā-nās* (puppet play), a very distinctive type of traditional performing art is represented by the *bhāonā* form of theater, which, owing its genesis to Śankara-deva, effectively combines elements of the classical Sanskrit drama with those of indigenous folk plays. Performance of various types of congregational hymn singing, known as *nām,* is widely popular.

References

Datta, Birendranath. 1978. *A handbook of folklore material of Assam and adjoining areas*. Guwahati: The Folklore Society of Assam.

Gait, Edward A. 1984 (1905). *A history of Assam*. Guwahati: L.B.S. Publications.

Goswami, Praphulladatta. 1967 (1948). *Folk literature of Assam*. Guwahati: Department of Historical and Antiquarian Studies, Assam.

Kakati, Banikanta. 1967 (1948). *The mother goddess Kāmākhyā*. Guwahati: Lawyer's Book Stall.

BIRENDRANATH DATTA

SEE ALSO
Bhāoyāiya Song; Marionettes; Tribal Communities, Northeast India

ATAṆ

Ataṇ is the generic name for various types of dance practiced by different Pashtun tribes of Afghanistan, and Pakistan's Northwest Frontier (NWFP) and Balochistan provinces. Men and women dance several varieties of ataṇ, some gender-specific and some not. The dancers are usually all male or all female, depending on the type of social gathering or occasion. In some areas, women from neighboring villages might gather in the spring in a pleasant outdoor spot to dance, as a sort of spring *mela* (celebration). The dancing in Pashtun regions of Balochistan is accompanied by sung poetry (*da ataṇ nāre,* "ataṇ songs"). In the Peshawar area of Pakistan ataṇ is also called *gada;* in the Kakar dialect of Balochistan provinces the dance is called *amạy;* in the Arnai dialect it is *laba*. There is a wide variety of named forms, including *da yawe waẓhe ataṇ* (one-shoulder dance), *da ghbargo waẓho* (double-shoulder), *sapatrey* (a Sendzarxel dialect name); *capa* (upside down); *shin atan* (green dance); *kamara amạy* (a Kakar form in which men and women formerly danced together, though they no longer do); *ṭalibi* (religious students' dance); *dreyaplay* (three steps); *nāṣiri* (named for a subtribe); local varieties such as the Arnai *khwara laba, hom, arvia,* and *xorkai laba;* the *sara'i atan* (illiterates' or wild people's dance); the *sala* and *globia* (exclusively women's forms); and others. The general form of the atan is a big circle or curving line, which may fragment at the end as the dance accelerates to a climax.

The Balochistan atan tradition includes songs in various meters, generally either in one-*bayt* (couplet) of $1\frac{1}{2}$-*bayt* (three half-line) stanzas. The syllable count is $6 + 11$, or $7 + 12$ in the couplet form, short half-lines alternating with long ones. Balochistan Pashtun dancers use *dhol* (large drum) and *sornā* (oboe) to accompany the song and dance. One interesting vocal form, the *sher zhaga* or "tiger voice," still performed by Sanatya Kakars around Muslim Bagh in Balochistan, begins with male dancers taking turns to sing *nāre* verses while dancing in a line or circle. Then, as excitement rises, the dancers begin a loud, rhythmic growling / wheezing meant to imitate tigers. The dance was performed either at weddings or on occasions to incite martial spirit for warlike activities. The use of nāre song with atan is found in a belt stretching from northeast Balochistan Province in Pakistan to Qandahar, Ghazni, and Wardak in Afghanistan. Not all Pashtun ataṇ have accompanying songs; Peshawar area ataṇ are generally accompanied only by drum and *sorna*.

SYAL KAKAR

SEE ALSO
Dance

B

BABY TALK

Individuals make different speech adjustments under varying contexts and according to various perceived aspects of their listeners. When speech adjustments occur only in response to particular listeners and they involve a set of modifications—phonological, syntactic, and lexical—these modifications are referred to as changes in speech register. The speech register called "baby talk" (also called language input or motherese) is commonly used by adults when speaking to young children.

Linguistic descriptions of baby talk exist for Bengali, Marathi, and Hindi, but no systematic comparison between adult speech and baby talk has been conducted with groups of caretakers in South Asia. A study of a diaspora community of Tamil speakers in Malaysia provides a beginning point for future research. This study examined fifteen female Tamil caretakers' adult speech and speech to their female children, aged one to three years, during spontaneous play. The sample of Hindu, non-Brahman families of South Indian origin was drawn from a lower-middle-class community in Kuala Lumpur (Williamson 1979).

In his cross-cultural description of baby talk, Charles Ferguson argues that baby talk is a simplified register. When compared to adult speech, it has several simplifying modifications; speech is reduced in syntactic complexity because it contains few multiclausal utterances. It is phonologically more intelligible, pitch is more varied, and morphological complexity is reduced. However, the Tamil study indicates a more complex picture: the presence of a variety of sentence types, the substantial frequency of word deletions, and inconsistent word order and case marking argue against Ferguson's hypothesis of a simplified register.

Comparing Tamil and English baby talk, we see variations in the proportion of sentence types (more imperatives in Tamil) and the amount of deletion (greater in Tamil), but similarities in the reduction of the length of utterances, reduction of clauses per utterance, phonological clarity, and high proportion of repetitions and imitations. Similar findings for greater phonological clarity, imitations and repetitions, and reduced length of utterances are indicated in studies of Bengali, Marathi, and Hindi baby talk (Dil 1971; Kelkar 1965; Das 1989). However, while case endings are reportedly not deleted in Bengali, they are dropped inconsistently in Tamil. In Marathi one may drop both verb and case endings. Modifications appear to be motivated first by conversational and situational needs and social status differences between caretaker and child, and then by the cognitive deficits of the child listener.

Specialized baby-talk names and lexicon reveal the high value attached to children and hope for their survival. For example, children may be addressed as "old man" or "old woman" or as "precious jewel." Girls may be addressed with male kin terms, but the opposite rarely occurs. A variety of reciprocal kinship terms and terms of affection are used for small children in Bengali. Caretakers sing nursery rhymes during bedtime rituals and use special terms to designate bogeymen, foods, games, and animals. Cultural beliefs may influence behavior toward infants. Newars in Nepal believe babies' memories of their past lives must be eliminated by childhood rituals to integrate them into this life. In addition, they believe babies are able to communicate with gods, goddesses, and other creatures in a divine language which they forget over time.

Cultural belief aside, we can ask to what extent baby talk is the first "language" learned by South Asian children. In the Tamil study, we find contrasts between input language and early child speech suggesting that simplifications in baby talk do not match those in child language, and vice versa. Baby talk serves as a register children learn in addition to mastering the adult language.

References

Das, Veena. 1989. Voices of children. *Daedalus* 118: 263–294.
Dil, Afia. 1971. Bengali baby talk. *Word* 27: 11–27.
Kelkar, Ashok. 1965. Marathi baby talk. *Word* 20: 40–54.
Snow, Catherine E., and Charles A. Ferguson, eds. 1977. *Talking to children*. Cambridge: Cambridge University Press.
Williamson, Susan Greenawalt. 1979. Tamil baby talk: A cross-cultural study. Ph.D. diss., South Asia Regional Studies, University of Pennsylvania.

SUSAN G. WILLIAMSON

BADALA

Badala is a Pashto word meaning "music, song, melody, verse." A particular song category may then be specified, for example, *da wāḍạ badala* (wedding song). The term badala is used particularly for a verse narrative that is sung either by an amateur at informal gatherings or by a professional on special occasions. In written form, a badala may also be called a *dāstān* or *qiṣṣa*. These narratives have been available in Peshawar, Pakistan, in chapbook printings since the late nineteenth century.

An amateur badala singer traditionally accompanies himself on a *rabāb* (stringed instrument) and may be accompanied by a friend with a *mangạy* (a clay pot to which a leather drumhead is sometimes added). Professional singers are usually accompanied by a drummer with paired drums (*tabla*), a rabāb player, and sometimes also a harmonium played either by the singer himself or by another musician.

The subject matter of a badala may be romantic or martial; the setting may be within or outside the Pashto-speaking area; the time may be present or past; and the characters may be entirely fictional or derived from historical persons. Written forms attest to more than a century of continued popularity for legendary romantic pairs such as the Pashtun Adam Khan and Dur-khanay, as well as Layla and Majnun, whose story is known throughout much of the Islamic world.

Several tune types are closely associated with the narrative singing. In contrast to the singing of lyric verse, where lines are often repeated, badala singing usually follows the narrative sequence with little or no repetition of couplets either in whole or in part. The length of a performance depends on a singer's skill, the audience's response, the number of interruptions for tea, meals, or other activities, and for professional singers, the depth of the patron's purse; performances in the past are said to have extended for several days. Short sequences of other forms of verse may be interspersed within a narrative, but are usually sung without interruption of the badala tune pattern.

References to badala singing (*badala wayạl*) in the traditional Pashtun guest house (*ḥujra*) occur in nineteenth-century folk texts. Since about 1980, audiocassettes of sung narratives labeled badala have circulated throughout Pakistan's Northwest Frontier Province. Professional singers have often memorized a number of badalas and are adept at improvising within the story's framework; the chapbook serves only as an occasional prompt. In other cases, a badala circulates as a cassette before its popularity leads to its printing as a chapbook. The form of badala common today is a series of couplets with either rhyming final hemistichs (AA, BA, CA, DA . . .) or a rhyme between hemistichs of each couplet (AA, BB, CC, DD . . .); in contrast to classical Pashto narrative verse, which uses a single rhyme pattern throughout, sequences of both these rhyme patterns may occur in the same badala. As with other Pashto verse, the badala meter is based on stress. The number of syllables per hemistich varies by a syllable or two, but twelve is most common. A major stress then falls on the third, seventh, and eleventh syllables, and a lighter, counter stress on the first, fifth, and ninth syllables.

Another form of badala, which is sung but does not generally circulate in cassette form, consists of a series of *chārbayta* (literally, four couplets). The Pashto chārbayta is a flexible stanzaic form with a refrain; it may have triplets as well as couplets and, despite its name, is not usually found in sets of four.

In the 1980s, as film songs in Pakistani languages came to be printed in chapbook form, the term badala was sometimes used for film songs in Pashto. One such chapbook, arranged by ʿĀlam Zeb and Imānat Khān "Ārif" Khaṭak, called itself "the first book of film songs" (*da filmī badalo ṛūmbe kitāb*) and was available in Peshawar in 1987. Like other chapbooks of film songs, this one includes the title of the movie and the name of the singer along with the words to the song itself. Although rhyming couplets predominate, many of its songs show shifts in rhyme patterns. Its sets of four hemistichs in the *rubāʿi* pattern (AABA) of classical Pashto and Persian at the beginning of some songs are a form not usually found in Pashto folk poetry.

References

Darmesteter, James. 1888–1890. *Chants populaires des Afghans*. Paris: Imprimerie Nationale.
Heston, Wilma. 1991. Footpath poets of Peshawar. In *Gender, genre, and power in South Asian expressive traditions*,

ed. Arjun Appadurai, Frank J. Korom, and Margaret A. Mills. Philadelphia: University of Pennsylvania Press.
Heston, Wilma, and Mumtaz Nasir. [1988]. *The bazaar of the storytellers*. Islamabad: Lok Virsa.
MacKenzie, D. N. 1958. Pashto verse. *BSOAS* 21(2): 319–333.
Zeb, ᶜĀlam, and Imānat Khān "Arif" Khaṭak, comps. n.d. *Filmī badale* [Film songs]. Peshawar: Zeb Ārt Publisharz.

WILMA L. HESTON

SEE ALSO
North-West Frontier Province

BAIT/BAYT

Bait compositions constitute the bulk of Sindhi folk poetry. As a form, the Sindhi bait developed early, probably under the influence of Arabic poetry during the Arab rule in Sindh (711–1050 C.E.). In the Arabic form *qaṣīda,* the bait is a verse composed of two equal parts, or *misras*. The opening bait of the qaṣīda, with its two rhyming misras, is thought to have been the model for the Sindhi bait, although it is possible that an indigenous form of Sindhi verse existed prior to 711 C.E. that so resembled the Arabic qaṣīda that it came to be called bait. A comparable poetic form in Hindi is called *dohira*.

Structural changes in the basic bait form were initiated beginning in the thirteenth or fourteenth century C.E. through the addition of "middle rhymes" (rhymes within lines) and of middle lines. These changes, which can be observed in the bait compositions of the first eminent Sufi poet, Qadi Qadan (1465–1551 C.E.), made the bait more flexible in structure, more varied in rhythm, and more amenable to changing forms of expression. The addition of intermediary lines extended the length of the bait, sometimes to more than a hundred lines, thus bringing into vogue the *drigha bait* (long bait), used for long narrations and usually recited or sung to the accompaniment of the *narr* (reed instrument).

The content of the bait has taken two diverse paths: On one hand, the bait has been used for didactic purposes, expressing spiritual, philosophical, and ethical ideas. On the other hand, it has become a vehicle for folk poetry and artistic narration. Thus, with the educated and the intelligentsia the bait has remained a poetic model par excellence for expressing higher ideas, while, with professional bards, it has become entertainment.

References

Baloch, N. A., ed. 1970. *Narr Ja Bait*. Sindhi Folklore Project, vol. 19. Hyderabad, Pakistan: Sindhi Adabi Board.
———. 1971. *Bait*. Sindhi Folklore Project, vol. 18. Hyderabad, Pakistan: Sindhi Adabi Board.

N. A. BALOCH

SEE ALSO
Sindh

BAIṬHAK

Baiṭhak literally means "sitting" or "a place to sit" in Hindko (a dialect of Punjabi spoken in the Peshawar area of Pakistan) and is the name of an exorcism ceremony for women in this region. The ceremony is initiated by families for healing an illness, sometimes physical but more often mental, of a family member (the "patient"). The occasion collects female friends and relatives together for a socially approved occasion in a society where the observation of *purdah* (seclusion) has been fairly strictly observed.

A room is thoroughly cleaned for the baithak, and new or freshly washed coverings are provided for the seating areas. Women who attend the ceremony bathe first and put on clean clothing. Food selection and preparation is done very carefully, both to please the guests and also to have available any particular food that a spirit, talking through the patient, may request. Choices of food vary according to the season. Groups of seven (for example, seven kinds of fruit) are especially auspicious.

Arrangements are made by the organizers to bring in a woman singer (*mīrāṣan*), sometimes with assistants, who specializes in the songs for this ceremony and who also knows the associated etiquette and rituals. The songs, which are in Hindko, are both Islamic and non-Islamic. The Islamic songs, which include songs in praise of God (Allah), his Prophet, Muhammad, and other holy persons, such as the Sufi saint ᶜAbd al-Qadr Gilani, are sung first. If these songs do not put the patient into a healing trance, songs invoking a hierarchy of non-Islamic supernatural beings are then sung. These songs are often to, or about, a particular fairy (*parī*), who may have been offended and therefore may have caused the patient's problem. During the singing, the patient goes into a trance and begins to sway back and forth and even move about as if dancing; it is with this movement that the healing takes place. Special care is taken so that the patient does not hurt herself due to the violence of her movements while in trance.

At the ceremony's conclusion, food is served and gifts, which may include money for the singer(s), are given to all those attending. The custom of holding this ceremony was still well remembered by older men and women living in Peshawar in the late 1980s, although they did not know of any having been held in recent decades.

Reference

Nasir, Mumtaz. 1987. *Baiṭhak*: Exorcism in Peshawar (Pakistan). *Asian Folklore Studies* (Nagoya) 46(2): 159–178.

MUMTAZ NASIR AND WILMA L. HESTON

SEE ALSO

Exorcism; Muslim Folklore and Folklife; Sufi Folk Poetry

BAKE, ARNOLD ADRIAAN

Arnold Adriaan Bake (1899–1963) was a Dutch ethnomusicologist, Sanskritist, collector, and scholar of Indian music. Bake's unique contribution to Indology was the extraordinary breadth of his scholarship, both diachronically and synchronically. He combined a vast historical knowledge, ranging from ancient India to the present, with a deep understanding of contemporary traditions gleaned from his fifteen or more years of survey research on the subcontinent. Bake's publications consist chiefly of some fifty journal and encyclopedia articles on a wide array of topics, from Vedic chants and classical music to hobbyhorse, circle, and stick dances in India, and the *cauṭṭanāṭaka* dance drama of Kerala.

Bake wrote his doctoral thesis for Ryks University in Utrecht on Indian classical music, translating an eighteenth-century Sanskrit musical treatise called *Sangītadarpanah*. It was probably during his first years in India from 1926 to 1929, while completing his doctoral research at the private arts school Shantiniketan in Bengal, that Bake was inspired to study India's folk and tribal musics by the school's founder, Rabindranath Tagore. He returned to India from 1931 to 1934 with a wax-cylinder recorder and silent 16 mm camera to document folk performances in Bengal, Nepal, Ladakh, and South India.

In 1937 he again returned to South Asia for an extended documentation tour beginning in Sri Lanka, continuing throughout South India, up the west coast as far as Gujarat, and ending in Sindh, using both silent 16 mm film and a Teficord for sound recordings. This unusual German machine could record up to one hour in duration and was used by Bake to document nearly a thousand items. Religious themes, gathered from Hindu, Muslim, Jain, Buddhist, Christian, and Jewish communities as well as tribals, predominate, but other types of folk and classical music are also represented, including work songs, music for folk dramas, and recreational music. Detained in India until 1946 due to World War II, he gave vocal recitals with his wife, pianist Cornelia Timmers Bake, that combined Western art song and renditions of Indian music, especially Bengali *kīrtan* and the songs of Tagore. On returning to Europe, he was appointed reader in Sanskrit with special reference to music at the University of London's School of Oriental and African Studies (SOAS), where he taught from 1948 until his death. His final field trip was in Nepal in 1955–1956, using tape recorder, still camera, and 16 mm silent film, as part of a team of scholars from SOAS.

Bake's film and audio collections are housed in SOAS, with copies at the Archives and Research Centre for Ethnomusicology, New Delhi, and the Ethnomusicology Archive of the University of California at Los Angeles. Most of his photographs and letters are archived in the Kern Institute, Leiden, with some letters at the India Office Library in London. The Nepalese materials have been studied by Carol Tingey, and the Indian materials by his student and colleague, Nazir Ali Jairazbhoy, with Amy Catlin-Jairazbhoy. Their continuing restudy of Bake's materials collected in Tamil Nadu, Karnataka, Kerala, and Gujarat has focused on comparing Bake's documentation of performances with contemporary renditions, and identifying the systems that sustain folk performance and those that contribute to change in traditional forms, such as classicization, modernization, institutionalization, and festivalization.

References

Bake, Arnold. 1930. *Bydrage tot de kennis der voor-indische muziek. Sangītadarpanah, The mirror of music and dance*. Utrecht: P. Geuthner Parys.

———. 1935. *Twenty-six songs of Rabindranath Tagore*. Paris: Bibliothēque Musicale du Musée Guimet.

———. 1963. Charlemagne in Malabar. *Folklore* 74 (Autumn): 450–459.

———. 1970. Stick dances. *International Folk Music Council Yearbook* 2: 56–62.

Jairazbhoy, Nazir Ali. 1991. Arnold Bake and the first restudy of his fieldwork. In *Comparative musicology and anthropology of music: Essays on the history of ethnomusicology,* ed. Bruno Nettl and Philip V. Bohlman, 210–227. Chicago: University of Chicago Press.

Jairazbhoy, Nazir Ali, and Amy Catlin. 1991. *The Bake restudy in India 1938–1984: The preservation and transformation of performance in Tamilnadu, Kerala and Karnataka*. A video-monograph. Van Nuys, Calif.: Apsara Media for Intercultural Education. Color, 1/2", 60 min.

Tingey, Carol: 1985. The Nepalese field work of Dr. Arnold A. Bake: A guide to the sound recordings. M.A. thesis, Department of Music, Goldsmith College, London.

AMY CATLIN

SEE ALSO

Dance; *Kīrtan*; Tagore, Rabindranath

BAKSHI

The *bakshī,* or *bakhxsī* (literally "singer of songs"), is the principal figure in the shamanistic traditions of the

Kazakhs, Kirghiz, and Uygur peoples of Central Asia, including the Turkmen of Afghanistan. Nineteenth- and early twentieth-century ethnographers described bakshī as men who possessed the ability to commune with supernatural beings on behalf of their communities or individual clients. These religious practitioners or ecstatics, who may correctly be called shamans, function as healers, mediums, diviners, and guardians of the psychic well-being of society.

Bakshī wear their hair long, and their accoutrements include a cap and sleeves of swan's down. Their ritual paraphernalia consists of a drum, fire, and magical objects, such as human bones, which they manipulate during their performances involving the singing of special songs. The bakshī's magical powers derive from his relationship with familiar spirits, called jinn, which he inherits from his father, and which, upon his death, will be transferred to his son. To commune with the jinn, the bakshī enters into a trance by beating his drum, singing songs, and reciting incantations in a specialized mystical language. He can then command his jinn to help him exorcise demons, prognosticate, and cure sickness.

The bakshī is also able to communicate with the spirits of the dead, which he accomplishes by reciting incantations while pouring the melted fat of a sacrificial animal on a fire. He is called upon by clients to provide this service during observances associated with ancestral cults. The shamanistic traditions of the bakshī, which derive from a wider Asiatic shamanistic complex, still persist in parts of Central Asia.

References

Baldwick, Julian. 2000. *Animal and shaman: Ancient religions of Central Asia*. New York: New York University Press.

Balzer, Marjorie M. 1990. *Shamanism: Soviet studies of traditional religion in Siberia and Central Asia*. Armork, N.Y.: M.E. Sharpe.

Castagné, Joseph. 1930. Etude sur la démonologie des Kazak-Kirghiz. *L'Ethnographie* 21–22: 1–23.

Centlivres, Micheline, Pierre Centlivres, and Mark Slobin. 1971. A Muslim shaman of Afghan Turkestan. *Ethnology* 10(2): 160–173.

Krader, Lawrence. 1963. *Peoples of Central Asia*, 130–133. The Hague: Mouton and Co.

Slobin, Mark. 1976. *Music in the culture of northern Afghanistan*, 98–99, 279. Tucson: University of Arizona Press.

H. SIDKY

SEE ALSO
Afghanistan; Jinn; Shamanism, Islam

BALANḌAY

Balanḍay is a form of folk poetry sung for weddings by Kakar Pashtun men from the Qilla Saifullah area of Balochistan, Pakistan. On the day of the wedding, men of the groom's party who have gone to the bride's home to claim her, after completing all the ceremonies there, return home with her in procession. People stand along the route to watch them. One man from the bride's side, usually someone adept in the poetic form who is from the bride's village but not from her immediate family, improvises poems demanding that the groom's people give him a *paga* (turban). First he praises them, but if they do not give the gift, he criticizes and abuses them in verse. If there is a poet in the groom's party, he may retaliate, starting a competition in abuse which the spectators enjoy. The basic form of the verse is two double lines, 7 + 12 syllables each, called *kāfiya*. One example runs as follows, possibly addressing both the poet's competitor and the British, who long tried to subdue the Pashtun tribes:

> The Amir lives in Kabul,
> And the British have settled in Quetta.
> I am a bubble on the stream,
> Oh, little man, I will put you under the mud.
> (translated from S. Kakar, *Pashtani Likwal*, vol. 2, p. 726)

SYAL KAKAR

SEE ALSO
Wedding Songs

BALĪ KHELĀ

Balī denotes a strong, stout man with some acrobatic skill, and *khelā* denotes a game or sport. *Balī khelā* is, hence, a sport played between two strong, stout, and skillful persons, a kind of folk wrestling or martial art, with ancient roots in the culturally distinctive greater Chittagong region bordering the Bay of Bengal (in the southeastern part of Bangladesh). It is distinctive to a group of people known as Chittāgongians or Cātgām̐iyās, who have managed to survive in this region, despite oft-recurring natural calamities in the form of cyclones and tidal waves. Balī khelā has become a symbol of the Chittāgongian people's strength and ingenuity, their unique cultural intrepidity, and their belief in the survival of the fittest.

According to oral history, balī khelā started among the Rohaingya tribe, who migrated from neighboring Myanmar (former Burma) and settled in the southern part of greater Chittāgong, now the Cox's Bazaar district. Another oral source claims that the ancient Arabian merchants introduced this game with a view to proving their physical superiority over their native counterparts. Still others believe that the Mojari tribe of the northern parts of Chittāgong—whose forefathers were thought to be professional soldiers in ancient Bengal—developed this game as a form of martial art.

In any case, balī khelā is entirely a men's sport, unique to this area, and is not practiced in any other part of Bangladesh. In the past, the participating bali were mainly Muslims, but now Hindus and Buddhists are also interested in the sport. In the northern Chittāgong region, balīs are also referred to by the term "malla." There are about one hundred bali or malla families; some of the most famous wrestlers include Rohaingya Bali, Lāilla Bali, Fāijjā Bali, Jābbār Bali, Maiggyā Bali, Akhtār Bali, Āmān Shah Malla, Chikon Malla, and Hari Malla.

The major balī khelā competitions begin in the dry season when crops are harvested and cultivable fields remain barren for a period. The games begin on the first day of the month of Baisākh in the Bengali calendar (mid-April), marking the festivity of the Bengali New Year's Day. The competition continues in various parts of the district, in all the major villages, until the end of May. The contest begins at noon and closes at sunset.

Balī khelā brings with it a colorful village fair. The sporting activities take place in an open field under the bright summer sun. The arena, generally rectangular, is marked with colorful flags on all four corners. The games begin with the younger balī participants and end with a contest between the two most famous balīs present. At the start, more than one pair of balī compete simultaneously, but in the final round only one pair competes. The promoters distribute medals and cash prizes among the participants. The winners in the senior competition receive gold medals. Winners in the junior competition are usually awarded a silver medal and the runners-up, a bronze medal. Each group also receives cash awards. The champion—he who wins the last bout of the day—is given the biggest gold medal and the largest cash award.

The acrobatic skills and tactics of the balī are known as *pāñc*. The most physically strong contestant does not necessarily win the game, since he may be tactically inferior to his opponent. The contestants are required to remove their shirts and other clothes from their upper bodies. They can wear lungi (a piece of cloth wrapped around the lower body from waist to ankle), but this has to be folded around the waist (*guc*-style) so that they can freely move their legs. Nowadays, the balī also wears brief trousers or shorts instead of lungi.

A balī engages his hands and feet to overpower his rival. He can touch his rival's body from head to waist with his hands, but he is not allowed to use his hands to pull on his opponent's legs, ears, or hair. He can use his legs to grip or hit his opponent's arms and legs. A referee moves about with a whistle to control the game. The player who succeeds in pinning his opponent's back to the ground is the winner. If two rivals compete for two or three bouts (each bout continuing for five to ten minutes) and no one is pinned, the game is a draw. In the case of championships, a win sometimes comes after the opponent simply falls to his knees (*ṭakkar*), but rules permitting such a decision must be declared prior to the game.

The winner makes a lap of honor around the ground, dancing like a butterfly, flapping his arms forward and backward like wings. The champion is carried on the shoulders of his group and *ḍhol* (drums) beat rapidly, announcing his victory. The celebrants continue to dance, making their way through the crowd of spectators, carrying pieces of colorful cloth to embellish their movements. During this time, spectators hand them small cash prizes. Ḍhol and *khañjani* (a pair of brass cymbals) accompany the dancing.

The town of Cox's Bazaar and the city of Chittagong have become major venues, holding the two most outstanding competitions in the region. The biggest contest of Cox's Bazaar district takes place in the town stadium in May. The most fascinating contest of the region, however, is Jabbar's balī khelā, held in the famous Laldighi maidan (square) in Chittagong, on 12 Baisākh (late April) every Bengali year. Jabbar, a famous balī who reigned as champion for a number of years, organized this contest. After his death, the local people have continued the event with active support from the government.

References

Āhmad, Oyākil. 1381 Bengali year 1974. *Bāṅglār Loksaṃskṛti* (Folklore of Bengal). Dhaka: Bangla Academy.

Musa, Monsur (ed.). 1944. *Muhammad Enāmul Hak Racanāvalī* (Works of Muhammad Enamul Huq). Pt. 3. Dhaka: Bangla Academy.

Caudhurī, Abdul Hak. 1988. *Caṭṭagrāmer Samāj O Saṃskṛtir Rūprekhā* (Outline of Society and Culture of Chittagong). Dhaka: Bangla Academy.

Isām, Samiul. 1992. *Bāṅglādeśer Grāmīn Khelādhūlā.* (Folk games of Bangladesh). Dhaka: Bangla Academy.

Mamun, Muntassir. 1996. The Festivals of Bangladesh. ICBS (International Center for Bengal Studies). Dhaka: Dhaka University.

MOHAMMAD NURUL HUDA

SEE ALSO

Games and Contests, Bangladesh; Martial Art Traditions

BALLAD, NEPAL

Lokgāthā is the word Nepali folklorists use to describe ballads, or folk songs that narrate a single incident. Nepali ballads are oral compositions put to melody, with simple narratives and short plots. Ballads have been sung since ancient times in Nepal. They are traditionally named after their raga (expressive mood of music), main character, function, or the time of their performance. For example, *cāñcari* is used to describe the ballads composed in cāñcari (raga resembling the melody of the *cāñcar* bird); *jeṭhe* are the ballads sung in the Nepali month of Jeṭha (May–June); and *goḍārī* are ballads sung during the weeding (*goḍāi*) season. Ballads are often performed along with dancing, which highlights their emotional power and accompanying melody. Other folk-song genres borrow stanzas and refrains with particular emotional appeal from well-known ballads, and ballads, too, are enriched through borrowing from other folk songs.

Ballads function especially as a bridge between epic traditions and popular folk songs, since many epics are now sung as ballads, and the stanzas of many ballads are sung in popular folk songs. For example, the following stanza from the ballad "Sītārānī Banaimā," which is thought to have been part of the lost Nepali oral epic *Rāmāyaṇa,* is today incorporated into a number of different popular folk songs:

Battīsai lacchinkī rī rānī bhāujū Sītālāī
Battīsai . . .
Rāmle die banibāsa
Rāmle . . .
Sītārānī banaimā laharī calyo manaimā.

To Queen Sītā, my sister-in-law, who has thirty-two noble qualities,
To Queen Sītā . . .
Rāma [the king] abandoned her and condemned her to exile in the jungle.
Rāma . . .
Queen Sītā is in the jungle; my heart is in turmoil.
(Collected and translated by the author.)

The stanza narrates the lament of Lakshmaṇa for his sister-in-law, upon his elder brother King Rāma's abandonment of his faithful wife Sītā. The incident and the melody of the ballad have such emotional appeal among Nepalis that the phrase "Sītārānī banaimā" (Queen Sītā is in the jungle) is a common folk expression incorporated into many folk songs.

Nepali ballads cover a variety of subjects and functions. In general, *bholāulo, puraṇagāthā,* and *maṅgalgāthā* are religious ballads sung mostly by males in the early morning. The main subjects of these ballads are the impermanence of human life, attitudes towards the materialistic world, the joy of devotion, and salvation through the grace of God. *Chaita, sabāī,* and cāñcarī deal with famous people and events of the past and are sung in commemoration or simply for entertainment. *Bhainī,* cāñcari, goḍārī, *asāre,* jeṭhe, *ohālī,* and *saṅginī* can have social or historical themes, and are sung in the fields during rice transplanting and weeding, for example, to reduce the monotony of work. *Rāmāyanī* ballads are composed in commemoration of deceased family members and are sung on the day of the *Gāījātrā* festival, celebrated on the first day of the dark moon in the month of Bhādra (August–September). In this festival, family members of people who died in the past year joke and console each other by singing and dancing to alleviate their grief. In the festival of *Tīj,* celebrated on the third day of the waxing moon in the month of Bhādra (August–September), Hindu women worship Śiva and Pārvatī through song and dance with the belief that their blessings will help their conjugal life to prosper. Tīj ballads cover a range of topics, from religious and historical events to contemporary social problems, such as discrimination against daughters, the depression of housewives, and so on. While grinding grain, some women sing *saṅginī* ballads, whose subjects are similar to the Tīj ballads.

Some ballads are recited rather than sung. *Pināsko kathā,* for example, is recited to relieve the sufferer of *pinās* (sinusitis). *Kavitta* is another recited form of ballad in which alliteration, rhyme, and rhythm substitute for melody. In one kavitta performance, *Khāṇḍo Jagāune* (initially a ceremonial vigil during the battles for unification of modern Nepal in the eighteenth century), a male performer narrates the martial exploits of his ancestors while invoking or worshiping the sword, finishing with the words "bairīkā ṭāukāmā ṭhwākka" (hit the sword on the enemy's head). Since Nepal is now in a time of peace, the performance has taken on a new meaning as a celebration of heroism and is performed as a part of matrimonial rites, especially among the Kshetrī (Kshatriya) caste.

Two musical castes, Huḍke and Gāine, earn their living in part by performing ballads. Huḍke, the tailor caste of western Nepal, are hired for festivals and ceremonies where, in costume, they dance and sing *bhārat* ballads to the accompaniment of the *huḍko* (hourglass drum) and other musical instruments. The bhārat portray the characters of kings and nobles of the past and, hence, they are performed as a symbol of proud cultural heritage and as a source of entertainment.

Gāine, who had previously gained the status of court musicians and messengers, but who are now mendicant performers, sing *karkhā* ballads commemorating the great deeds of a hero, mainly in raga such as *rāmkalī* and *dhansirī.* The two types of karkhā are *thāḍījas karkhā,* which describes the heroic deeds of a king, a nobleman, or a soldier, and *marhauṭe karkhā,* which describes the martyrdom of a hero or other meritorious person. All karkhā are accompanied by the *saraṅgī* (stringed instrument similar to fiddle). The Gāine have preserved the vast depository of karkhā through oral transmission for at least three centuries. In fact, karkhā of King Prithivi Narayan Shah (1723–1775), founder of modern Nepal, are heard even now during the reign of King Birendra Bir Bikram Shah (1945–present).

In addition to karkhā, the Gāine have recently started to compose broadside ballads whose common topics include *satī* (self-immolation of a widow on her husband's funeral pyre), suicide, murder, and love triangles. These hallads are commercially produced and sold on audiotape. Other balladeers of heterogeneous caste background perform broadside ballads on the streets of major cities and towns of Nepal. Chapbooks of these ballads contain one or two ballads along with three or four other songs, covering a wider variety of subjects, including murders, robberies, scandals, love triangles, and also editorials. These are popular among the common people, who do not hesitate to spend two or three rupees to buy a chapbook.

The contribution of the ballad to Nepali literature is immense. Nepali writers of various genres have borrowed from ballad plots, characters, melodies, figures of speech, and other expressions. For instance, *Munā-Madan,* the magnum opus of the poet Lakshmī Prasād Devkotā (1909–1959), and *Rājeswarī,* an outstanding work by distinguished poet Madhav Prasād Ghimire (1919–present), are based on the Newārī folk ballads "Jī Wayu Lā Lacchi Maduni" and "Mahārānī Bijyālakshmī," respectively. Future research will likely show how ballads continue to enrich Nepali culture.

References

Bhattarai, Harihar P. 1984. *Folk ballads of Seti zone: A research report*. Paris: UNESCO.

———. 1985. Folklore studies in Nepal. *Himalayan Culture* 3(1): 10–14.

Gaborieau, Marc. 1977. "Introduction." In *Himalayan folklore: Kumaon and West Nepal,* 2nd ed., H. K. Kuloy, ed., xi–xliv. Kathmandu: Ratna Pustak Bhandar.

Lienhard, Siegfried. [1974] 1992. *Songs of Nepal: An anthology of Nevar folksongs and hymns*. Delhi: Motilal Banarsidass.

Oakley, E. S., and Tara Dutt Gairola. [1935] 1977. *Himalayan folklore: Kumaon and West Nepal*. Kathmandu: Ratna Pustak Bhandar.

Pradhan, Kumar. 1984. *A history of Nepali literature*. New Delhi: Sahitya Akademi.

HARIHAR P. BHATTARAI

SEE ALSO
Dance, Nepal; *Rāmāyaṇa; Tīj* Songs

BALOCHISTAN: ORAL TRADITION

Until the second half of the twentieth century, the literature in the Balochi language was almost entirely oral, since writing was known only to a very few mosque-educated mullās and others with some reading knowledge of Qur'ān and sometimes also Persian. Even today the literacy rate is around 10 percent among male adults and 1 or 2 percent among women. Like other nonwritten languages, Balochi has a rich stock of oral literature comprising poems, prose, proverbs, riddles, legends, and folktales. The songs celebrate various life occasions in different forms. The most important named song types, distinguished by form, manner of performance, social position or gender of the performer, or the accompanying musical instruments, include

- *sipatē*—prayer-cum-praise songs, sung with no instrumental accompaniment by a group of women on the birth of a child
- *nāzenk*—women's praise songs for sons, brothers, and fathers, also sung without instruments
- *lōlī*—lullabies
- *hālō* and *lāṛō*—women's wedding and circumcision songs, sung with drums played by male *lūṛī,* professional musicians, together with hand clapping and slow circle dances
- *sōt*—short love songs, sung on festive occasions by men and women referred to as *sōtī,* with a variety of instruments
- *zahīrok*—songs of separation and travel, also sung while working, accompanied preferably by a *sūroz* (bowed fiddle)
- *līko*—very similar to zahīrok in content but distinct in singing style
- *ṛēhī* and *lēlaṛī*—similar to līko and zahīrok in content but different in melody
- *motk*—elegies, traditionally sung with no accompaniment up to the fourteenth or fortieth day after the death of a person, but because of the opposition of Muslim clergy, not practiced anymore
- *chōgān*—religious songs accompanied by ritual dances with no musical accompaniment, performed by the Ẕikri sect of Muslims
- *dāstānag*—short love songs sung in duet by a drone singer called *surrī* with a flute player (*nāṛi*).

Shēr, a highly refined, elaborated, and rich genre of Balochi oral poetry, is composed by Baloch of upper social status, and is memorized and performed by lower class lūṛī artisan-musicians, also called *domb* in eastern Balochistan and *pahlawān* (singers of heroic deeds) elsewhere. This is the only genre whose chronology can be partly traced through the characters mentioned. Based on content, the oldest datable samples belong to the fifteenth century, called the Classical period (Baluch 1977: 130ff.), and the heroic age of Balochi oral poetry, when the Baloch homeland was unified in a loose confederacy for the first time under Baloch rule with the city of Sibi as the capital. Famous shēr and *shērīdāstān* (prosimetrics) survive concerning the Rind and Lashar tribes' thirty years of tribal wars (fifteenth–sixteenth centuries), the hero Hammal's encounters with the Portuguese and other exploits (late sixteenth century), Shey Murīd and Hanī's romance (late fifteenth century), and many others. Among the later shēr cycles, the famous eighteenth-century epic celebrating the revenge of Bālāch Gorgej, who is famous as *Bālāch-i bergīr,* "Bālāch the Avenger," also gained universal popularity among the Baloch. Most of the characters of these heroic poems are believed to have been poets themselves, and the poetry of the epoch is regarded as a reliable record of important events.

The tradition of shēr composition continued into the first half of the twentieth century. Some late nineteenth- and early twentieth-century *shāir* (shēr-composing poets) achieved wide-scale popularity, even outside their areas of origin, thanks to the wandering lūṛī minstrels. As Hashomi discusses in his literary history, the most famous shāir of the Makran (coastal region) school are Mulla Fazul and his brother Mulla Qasum (nineteenth century), Mulla Bahadur (nineteenth century), Malik Dinnar Mirwadi (nineteenth century–twentieth century), Mulla Ismail (twentieth century), Mulla Ibrahim Raski (nineteenth century), Mulla Boher (nineteenth century), Izzat Lalla Panjguri, Mulla Nurmahmad Bampushti, Mawlwi Abdulla Pishshini (all twentieth century), and others. Eastern school poets include Jam Durrak, the poet laureate at the court of Mir Nasir Khan (ruler of Balochistan from 1749 to 1795), Taukali Mast (nineteenth century), the poet-lover-saint of the Mari tribe, Rahmali Mari 1 (nineteenth–twentieth century), the tribal poet (*rezwār shāir*) of the Mari tribe, Jawansal Bugti (twentieth century), the mystic poet of the Bugti tribe, Mulla Mazar (twentieth century), and others. The shēr-composing tradition ceased during the second half of the twentieth century when the Baloch, following the forcible inclusion of parts of their country into Iran by Reza Shah Pahlavi in 1928, and later into the new state of Pakistan in 1947 and 1948, were brought into formal contact with the Persian and Urdu languages. The traditional shāir was replaced by literary poets using Urdu and Persian prosody.

Unlike folk songs, which always have refrains, but not necessarily rhymes or fixed line lengths, shēr is always in verse with irregular rhymes, but with a number of lines of uniform meter. Shēr texts are memorized and, although different texts of a single shēr show some variations, no intentional changes are either admitted by the performer or tolerated by his listeners. Different types of shēr celebrate or record different events, but Baloch generally distinguish three main types based on content: *jangī shēr* (war epics/ballads), *'ishkī* (love epics/ballads), and *pēgumbarī* (religious poems, mostly dealing with the prophet and his companions, Islamic wars and the exploits of Muslim heroes against infidels, monsters, and superhuman beings of destructive nature).

When sung, a shēr is always accompanied by two instruments: a sūroz (fiddle) plus one or two *dambūrag* (lutes). The singer himself plays a two-stringed dambūrag and he may be joined by a *dambūragī* (dambūrag player) also called *panjagī* (helping hand), who plays the three-stringed dambūrag. Shēr can also be recited or chanted without musical accompaniment by men of any social background and status. While attitudes toward musical performance and musicianship are somewhat ambivalent (professional musicians generally being of the lowest status), recitation is highly regarded and rewarded as a *khānwādahī kār* (noble action) and a prestigious pastime. Almost every Baloch man, and many women as well, are proud to be able to recite some shēr or shēr fragments by heart.

While shēr as a literary genre has maintained uniformity across Balochistan in its performance, memorization, and transmission, other varieties of folk music and song are regionally distinct. Among travel and work songs, zahīrok is the most famous song genre in the south whereas līko dominates in the north and in the Sarhadd of Iranian Balochistan, in Afghan Balochistan, and among Balochi in Turkmenistan, and *ṛēhī* in the far eastern areas, into Punjab and Sind.

Dances are also regionally distributed: *chāp* (also called *dochāpī*) in the south, *suḥbat* in the north, and *drīs* in the east. The latter is included in all ceremonies of national importance, and hence could be regarded as the national dance of the Baloch. In performance, all these dances, including also *ambā* and *lēwā* (work and festive dances, respectively, of coastal fishermen), are very similar except that drīs performers hold two swords or sticks and cross them with the performers dancing on either side in turns. The movements of chāp, drīs, and suḥbat all include a halt step, step and turn, in a gradually accelerating circle. The first two forms are danced by men only. Women used to dance suḥbat in circles divided into male and female halves, but now women dance in all-female circles, in village contexts. Drīs music is provided by sūroz and one or more dambūrag, while other dances are performed to *ḍohol* (large cylinder drums) and *surnā* (oboe), the latter replaced by blown conch shell (*gurr*) for ambā and lēwā. Drīs is basically a war dance, which used to be performed before and after tribal battles to prepare for conflict or celebrate victory; however, it was also performed, like chāp and suḥbat, on other festive occasions. Performers of drīs are always males of upper social class; dochāpī and suḥbat are performed by persons of any social background, but predominantly by lower-status men; and ambā and lēwā are typically performed by fishermen, who are mostly of lower status.

Besides the festive dances, there are also healing and spiritual dances accompanied by religious chants such as *shekī, shēparjā,* and *mālid*. Particular to the Ẓikrī Muslim sect is *chogān* (a stepping circle dance), which is first performed at a slow tempo, gradually accelerating over the approximately hour-long performance. Chogān is danced by men only, to the accompaniment of a female devotional singer. The poetic lines in the beginning slow phase are about fifteen syllables long, shortening to three or four syllables in the fast, peak period of the dance.

Besides poetry and dance, Balochi also has a very rich stock of oral narrative traditions in the form of legends (*dāstān*) and stories (*kissa*), as well as verbal speech forms, such as riddles (*chāch*), proverbs (*batal*), and proverbs with background stories (*basīttuk*), sharing many themes with those found in other parts of the world. Numerous stories relate to supernatural beings (genies, monsters, fairies), hidden treasures (mostly guarded by serpents), magical objects, faithful animals, wars between kings, tests of wisdom in courts, and the like. Folktales relating to everyday social problems, such as the relationships of stepparents and stepchildren, faithfulness or unfaithfulness of siblings, sons, or wives, the fall of a proud and arrogant person, destruction of a tyrant, victories of wisdom over power, or a miser's loss of wealth, and the like are encountered everywhere in Balochistan. Although these folktales frequently have a moral lesson, their main aim is to entertain.

Like the singers of oral poems, the professional expert storytellers are usually lūṛī. Every village has one or more lūṛī families and, along with smithing, circumcising, drum beating, and leading dances on festive occasions, storytelling is one of their hereditary professions. The lūṛī's house has always served as a theater for the village folk. Until a few years back, before satellite television, people of all ages routinely gathered there during long winter nights and listened to the mythical and legendary stories. Unlike the singers and musicians, who are usually lower-class professionals, there are no restrictions of caste, class, gender, or even age for becoming a storyteller, and in domestic settings anyone with a taste for storytelling can become one. Thus, besides the lūṛī, in every village there are always several aged persons, both men and women, who recount stories to all the village folk, and especially to the children.

Tales are never to be told during the day. If unmarried persons tell tales in daytime, it is said that they will have an aged fiancé/e (*dishtār pīr bitt*), and if aged persons tell tales at the wrong times, it will cause the loss of prosperity in the house where the story is told. Formal occasions for telling stories include circumcision and wedding ceremonies of those families who cannot afford music and singing, times when a person is seriously ill and men and women spend a good part of the night in his or her company to give psychological support to the family, and during religious festivals, when men gather at the guest house of the village or tribal chief, or in front of a mosque, or at a village guesthouse to spend the night, or most of it. In villages, women may also be present, but in towns these are men's gathering places only.

Recordings of Balochi oral literature began during the nineteenth century when British administrators, travelers, and missionaries started collecting specimen texts to study the language. Some useful material was transcribed by literate Baloches at British request. The most systematic published colonial-period collection of any size is that of the British civil servant Longworth Dames in 1907, but his research, like most at the time, was limited to a small area inside or bordering on the Punjab. In 1900–1903, Mayer published some Balochi poems in India. Dames reprinted many of the poems collected by Leech, Mayer, and Hetu Ram. In 1855 A. Lewis had published his *Bilochi Stories* from Allahabad, and Dames included several stories in his *Textbook of the Balochi Language* (1891). During the early 1930s, I. I. Zarubin made an important folktale collection from the Baloch of Turkmenistan, then a republic of the Soviet Union.

The middle of the twentieth century marked the Baloch literary awakening. Several literary organizations were set up inside and outside Balochistan. Nowadays, more than a dozen Balochi magazines and periodicals, only a few of them regular, are published inside and outside Pakistan. The Balochi Academy in Quetta (founded in 1962) has published collections of Balochi poems from oral sources, as well as a series of nine collections of folktales. Most come from eastern Balochistan, where British administrators also did most of their collecting. Gul Khan Nasir, among his other publications on poetic traditions, has reconstructed two long epics, one about encounters between the coastal Baloch, under Mir Hammal Jiand, and the Portuguese during the sixteenth century, and another, the story of Dosten and Shīrīn. The hero, Dosten, is captured by the Moghul army while hunting, is reported dead, and then escapes to return to Shīrīn on the eve of her wedding to another man. Disguised as a minstrel (lūṛī or domb), he reveals himself by singing a song he had composed for her in prison and sent to her through a wandering minstrel. Nasir's compositions use almost all the recorded fragments of earlier versions of these tales, remaining mostly faithful to the original form and plot. M. S. K. Baluch, S. M. Mari, H. Mari, and Faqir Shad have also published important anthologies of oral poems. The present author is now beginning to publish his own taped collection of oral poems and folktales gathered over the last decade from this rich tradition.

References

Aksjonov, Sergej. 1990. Liko in the poetical folk art of the Baluch of Turkmenistan. *Newsletter of Baluchistan Studies* 7: 3–13.

Badalkhan, S. 1994. Poesia epica e tradizioni orali balochi: I menestrelli Pahlawan del Makrān. Ph.D. diss., Linguistics Department, University of Naples.

———. 1995. The changing contents of Baloch women's songs in eastern Makran. Paper presented at 3rd Conference of the SIE, Cambridge, England, September 11–15.

———. 2000. "'Ropes break at weakest points.' Some examples of Balochi proverbs with background stories." *Proverbium* vol. 17, pp. 43–69.

———. 2001. The role of audience in Balochi *sher* singing. In *Chanted Narratives: The Living 'Katha-Vachana' Tradition,* ed. Molly Kaushal. New Delhi: Indira Gandhi National Centre for the Arts, pp. 205–223.

Baluch, M. S. K. 1977 [1958]. *History of Baluch race and Baluchistan,* 2nd ed. Quetta: Gosha-e Adab.

Catalogue of the Balochi Academy [Quetta]'s Publications. N.d., n.p.

———. 1987. Insert in *Newsletter of Balochistan Studies.* Naples: Istituto Universario Orientale.

Dames, L. M. 1902. Balochi folklore. *Folk-Lore* 13(3): 252–274.

———. 1907. *Popular poetry of the Baloches,* vol. 2. London: Folklore Society.

Elfenbein, J. 1983. *A Baluchi miscellanea of erotica and poetry: Codex Oriental Additional 24048 of the British Library. AION* 43(2), suppl. 35 (Naples).

———. 1990. *An anthology of modern and classical Baluchi literature,* 2 vols. Wiesbaden: Harrassowitz.

Harrison, S. 1981. *In Afghanistan's shadow: Baluch nationalism and Soviet temptations.* Washington, D.C.: Carnegie Endowment for International Peace.

Hashomi, S. 1986. *Balochi Zabān o Adab kī Tārīkh* (The history of Balochi language and literature). Karachi: Said Hashomi Academy.

Lewis, Arthur. 1855. *Balochi stories as spoken by the nomad tribes of the Sulaiman Hills.* Allahabad: The Punjab Society.

Mari, Hayat. 1987. *Gāren Gohār* (Lost pearls). Quetta: Balochi Academy.

Mari, Sher Mahmad. 1970. *Balochī kahnen Shahirī* (Old Balochi poetry). Quetta: Balochi Academy.

Nasir, G. K. 1976. *Balochistān kī Kahānī Shāiron kī Zabānī* (The history of Balochistan from the tongues of poets). Quetta: Balochi Academy.

———. 1979a. *Balochī Razmīa Shāirī* (Balochi war poetry). Quetta: Balochi Academy.

———. 1979b. *Balochī 'Ishqīa Shāirī* (Balochi romantic poetry). Quetta: Balochi Academy.

SABIR BADALKHAN

SEE ALSO

Brahui Folk Literature; Dance; Epic; Folktale; *Mammā*

BAṆḌĀRA CULTS

Baṇḍāra cults are a folk tradition of religious worship, prevalent mainly among Sinhalese Buddhists, involving the ritual veneration of charismatic personalities posthumously elevated to the status of minor deities. Usually confined to the area of the former kingdom of Kandy in south-central Sri Lanka, the term "baṇḍāra" in ordinary usage signifies superior social status, and, in the context of a religious cult, it is an honorific appellation given to the person posthumously deified. Such deification is in harmony with the Buddhist belief in rebirth.

One illustration of a bandara is Kivulegedera Mohottala, a minor official who became a leader of the 1818 rebellion against the British. He was captured, tried, and executed, only to be deified soon after as Punchi Alut (younger, new) Bandara by the people of his area. His father (called Kivulgedera Alut Deviyo, wherein "deviyo" means "deity") and some others of his lineage had previously been deified. Another deified relative was Kivulgedera Bandara Deviyo, a farmer, who, hoping to win the hand of a pretty Moor (Sri Lankan Muslim) damsel, single-handedly harvested thirty acres of paddy in one day, subsequently succumbing to the exhaustion.

The bandara are often grouped into numerical sets, and so they may be propitiated in communal rituals. Thus, we hear of Baṇḍāra Pas Kaṭṭuva (a set of five) of the region of Uva, Baṇḍāra Hat Kaṭṭuva (a set of seven) of the northwest, and even a set of sixty-seven baṇḍāra (Hāṭa Hat Kaṭṭuva) propitiated in the *Kohoṁbā Kankāriya,* the most elaborate of all the ritual performances in the Kandyan area.

The conditions under which the deceased is elevated to the rank of a bandara deity generally include charismatic qualities such as extraordinary physical prowess, valor, or piety. But there are also instances when episodes of his or her life formed such a deep impression on people's minds that they led to deification. Kumara (prince) Bandara was the son of the Tamil usurper King Elāra (second century B.C.E.) who was executed for killing a calf while recklessly driving his chariot. Dahanaka (a personal name) Bandara was a village marauder who was trapped in a cave and buried alive by irate villagers. Gange Bandara (named after the river), the son of King Wimaladharmasuriya (1592–1604), was murdered by drowning on the orders of his uncle Senarath (1604–1635), who wished to secure the throne for his own progeny. Bhamana Bandara was an immigrant Brahman whose own brother killed him and cut up his body in a fit of rage.

Although usually associated with males, the title "bandara" is sometimes ascribed to female deities as well. The best-known female bandara is Henakanda Biso Bandara. Heṇakaňda Bisō means "Thunderbolt Queen," and she is so named because she was born from a large beli fruit which burst open thunderously, and she grew up to marry a king.

The regional provenance of baṇḍāra cults indicates that many of them have arisen in the peripheral areas of the former Kandyan kingdom. While the principal Buddhist deities—Nātha, Viṣṇu, Kataragama, and Pattini—have their main shrines in the center of the kingdom, the peripheral areas are left to be serviced by the baṇḍāra, albeit under the supervision of the principal deities, from whom the baṇḍāra have to obtain *varam* (warrant). Usually, a baṇḍāra deity's shrine (*dēvāle*) is a peripheral building in the compound of the devale of a principal deity. While the weapons (*āyuda*) of the principal deities are classical ones such as the trident and the sword, the baṇḍāra have rustic weapons such as the billhook (*kătta*) and the cane.

References

Dharmadasa, K. N. O., and H. M. S. Tundeniya. 1994. *Sinhala Dēva Purāṇaya*. Colombo, Sri Lanka: State Printing.

Obeyesekere, Gananath. 1979. Popular religions (of Sri Lanka). In *Modern Sri Lanka: A society in transition,* ed. Tissa Rernando and Robert A. Kearney. Syracuse, N.Y.: Syracuse University Press.

———. 1984. *The cult of the goddess Pattini*. Chicago: University of Chicago Press.

Parker, Henry. 1909. *Ancient Ceylon*. London: Luzac.

Seligman, C. G. 1909. Note on the bandar cult of the Kandyan Sinhalese. *Man* 9(77): 130–134.

K. N. O. DHARMADASA

SEE ALSO

Buddhism and Buddhist Folklore; Gods and Goddesses; Sri Lanka, Sinhalese

BAṆGĀṆĪ *MAHĀBHĀRATA*

The valley of the river Tons in the area called Baṇgāṇ in the westernmost hills of Uttar Pradesh is the home of an oral version of the *Mahābhārata*. The epic is called *Paṇḍuaṇ* after the five Pāṇḍava brothers, who, as in the Sanskrit *Mahābhārata*, fight against their cousins, the hundred wicked Kauravas.

The *Paṇḍuaṇ* is annually sung in February on the second day of the five-day festival "dance of the bards" (*Ḍaknatsaṇ*). The epic is performed by professional low-caste bards (*deuāḷ*) in front of temples belonging to the powerful deity Mahāsu. During the five days of the festival the bards re-create, through their performance of songs, ballads, epics, and sketches, the creation and history of the universe. On the first day creation myths and legends describing the advent of the god Mahāsu are sung. On the second day the *Paṇḍuaṇ* epic and some songs relating to the *Rāmāyaṇa* are performed. The second day thus is dedicated to divine and supernatural heroes. The main features of the remaining three days involve humorous and indecent sketches and songs that portray the mundane level. It is said that the world was ruled in the first age by giants, then in the second age by the heroes of the *Mahābhārata*. Now it is ruled by Mahāsu. The annual staging of the "dance of the bards" serves to reconfirm this concept.

Differing from other epic performances of northern India in which, typically, song passages (with end rhyme) alternate with explanatory comments in everyday language, the language of the *Paṇḍuaṇ* deviates almost persistently from everyday language. The bards employ four types of singing and dramatized speaking, and the poetic and skillful language of the epic frequently displays amazing deviations from the grammatical rules of ordinary Baṇgāṇi.

The *Paṇḍuaṇ* begins with an overture in heaven: in order to create an immaculate dynasty for governing the world, the gods undertake a pilgrimage to the lake Mānasarovar. Their ritual bath, however, is spoiled by the bath of a daughter of a low-caste cobbler. Consequently, the gods' plans are upset, and as a result not one, but two, families are created: the divine Pāṇḍavas and the demonic Kauravas. The god of the Himalayas has two daughters, Kuntī and Gāndhārī. The five Pāṇḍavas are born as the sons of Kuntī, who was made pregnant through the gaze of various gods, whereas the hundred Kauravas are the sons of Gāndhārī, who was made pregnant by different animals in the possession of various demonic beings. After some time the cousins start to quarrel, and the Pāṇḍavas are forced to leave the capital and live in the wilderness. There they kill a number of giants and thus end the giants' reign. From one of the giants they win a mysterious rod into which all knowledge is engraved. The Kauravas undertake a number of attempts on the lives of the Pāṇḍavas. However, all their efforts to poison or burn them fail. Before the final battle between the cousins begins, sixty-four fairies (*yoginī*) meet and decide its end. In the following battle all Kauravas are killed with the exception of their leader, Duryodhan. Duryodhan flees to Mānasarovar and enters the lake together with his family goddess. He intends to stay in the lake as a means to revive his brothers. However, he is roused by the Pāṇḍavas and finally killed.

The *Paṇḍuaṇ* uses a very archaic imagery and deviates in many details from the Sanskrit *Mahābhārata*. Oral *Mahābhārata* traditions in the Himalayas are not limited to the valley of the Tons, but also exist in Himachal Pradesh and other parts of the hills of Uttar Pradesh. Additionally, complex oral *Mahābhārata* traditions are found in at least three more regions of India: Rajasthan, Madhya Pradesh, and Tamil Nadu. A striking feature of these regional traditions is that they contain a number of similar elements—motifs and myths—which cannot be explained as common derivations from the Sanskrit *Mahābhārata*. Rather, they seem to suggest a very ancient and independent oral *Mahābhārata* tradition.

This is borne out by an Arabic translation of a *Mahābhārata* narrative from Sindh from the tenth or early eleventh century. The Arabic text was translated into Persian in 1026 and has come down in the form of a summary in a later Persian text with the title *Mujmil al-Tawārikh*. The language of this independent version of the *Mahābhārata* was not Sanskrit, but a northwestern variation of late Middle Indo-Aryan. This old Sindhi *Mahābhārata* contains several motifs unknown in the Sanskrit version, but found in present-day regional *Mahābhārata* traditions.

References

Chatterji, Suniti Kumar. 1949–1950. An early Arabic version of the Mahabharata story. *Indian Linguistics 11:* 156–163.

Singh, K. S., ed. 1993. *Mahābhārata in the tribal and folk traditions of India.* Simla: Indian Institute of Advanced Study; New Delhi: Anthropological Survey of India.

Zoller, Claus Peter. 1995. Oral epic poetry in the central Himalayas (Garhwal and Kumaon). *European Bulletin of Himalayan Research* 9: 1–7.

———. Forthcoming. *Die Panduaṇ. Ein mündliches Mahābhārata-Epos aus dem Garhwal-Himalaya* [The *Panduaṇ*. An oral Mahābhārata epic from the Garhwal Himalayas].

CLAUS PETER ZOLLER

SEE ALSO
Epic; *Mahābhārata*

BAṆGĀṆĪ BALL GAMES

Religiously determined ball games such as football, handball, and hockey are known from Himachal Pradesh and the hills of Uttar Pradesh. For example, in Baṇgāṇ, an area in the western Garhwal Himalayas, a football game is played annually in mid-January in villages where there is a temple of the powerful god Mahāsu. This agonistic game, called *iṇḍuaṛa,* is played by male Rajputs. Ideally, two teams are formed with players from two villages, the two sides of a valley, or two districts. The winner of the game—which usually lasts between one and two hours—is the team that manages to keep the ball longer on the side of the opponent than on its own side. The leather ball is usually filled with earth from a sacred field (*bastua*) belonging to the village where the game takes place.

The rules for determining the winner and the material used for stuffing the ball are related to the widespread belief in the central and western Himalayas that the land belonging to a village contains a specific power that permeates all living beings. In Baṇgāṇ this power is called *mīr*. Mīr is said to be especially concentrated in somewhat cube-shaped stone shrines called *jaga,* or in a specific center (*jiān*) in the necks of the ancient heroes (*mōṛ*). A jaga is not only an accumulator for mīr power, but also a female numinous being living in that shrine, who protects the village area. Every village aspires to increase or at least preserve the mīr power of its own jaga. Mīr powers could also be gained through sheep raids, wife-capture, headhunting, and agonistic ball games. Of these four practices, headhunting is not performed anymore and sheep raids and wife capture have become rare events.

In case of the ball games, the ball gets charged with mīr through contact with the players. By the end of the game, it predominantly contains the energy of the team—the losers—with which it has stayed the greater part of time. The winning team is allowed to keep the ball after the game for some time, or even bring it to its own village, in order for the other team's mīr, contained in the ball, to be absorbed.

In Baṇgāṇ the heads of slain hostile warriors were placed into the holy jaga shrines for the same reason. Similar practices connected with similar concepts are also known elsewhere. In some areas of eastern Himachal Pradesh the captured heads of hostile warriors were buried underneath the village temples, and meticulous accounts about the number of heads were kept. Similarly, in some areas of Garhwal, balls are buried near the village temples by the victorious teams of ball games.

The Baṇgāṇis regard the various mīr-containing trophies as "heads." The ball of the iṇḍuaṛa is sometimes called "head" (*mūṇḍ*) by the people; abducted women are occasionally termed *baḷi mūṇḍi* ("a woman who is a head"); and even an animal sacrifice for a jaga is called *jaga ri mūṇḍ* (a sacrifice, which is like a conquered head for the jaga). Conversely, real captured heads can be regarded as "balls" and can—according to local heroic songs and ballads—even be used for playing "hockey."

In eastern Himachal Pradesh and western Garhwal, the organization of the ball games and the practice of head-hunting are frequently connected with traditional divisions into geographical sections. Such sections are said to represent the ancient dominions of the Pāṇḍavas and Kauravas of the *Mahābhārata*. Consequently, it is sometimes stressed that both head-hunting and ball games are done according to the example of the heroes of the *Mahābhārata*, who, according to local songs and epics, not only fought against each other but also played the iṇḍuaṛa game.

References

Gairola, Tara Dutt, and D. A. Barker. 1917. Games and festivals of Garhwal. *Journal of the United Provinces Historical Society* 1(1): 160–167.

Lalit, C. R. B. 1993. Thodā: A martial game of the Khasha people of Himachal Pradesh. In *Mahābhārata in the tribal and folk traditions of India,* ed. K. S. Singh. Simla: Indian Institute of Advanced Study; New Delhi: Anthropological Survey of India.

Zoller, Claus Peter. 1993. On Himalayan ball games, head-hunting, and related matters. In *Flags of fame. Studies in South Asian folk culture,* ed. Heidrun Brückner, Lothar Lutze, and Aditya Malik. New Delhi: Manohar.

CLAUS PETER ZOLLER

SEE ALSO

Games and Contests; Godesses, Place, and Identity in Nepal

BANGLADESH

A modern nation-state created by the partition of India in 1947 and by a war of independence in 1971 which resulted in its separation from then West Pakistan (present-day Pakistan), Bangladesh is now among the ten most populous countries in the world, containing upwards of 130 million people, over 80 percent of whom are rural agriculturalists. The oldest cultivator population to arrive in the Ganges River delta and adjacent areas seems to have come from farther east (present-day Myanmar and Thailand). By 1000 B.C.E., Indo-Aryans were arriving from the Gangetic plains to the west. By 250 B.C.E., Buddhism had a strong presence, with an alternation of Buddhist and Hindu dynasties through the twelfth century C.E. Muslims began to arrive as migrants and missionaries as early as the eighth century C.E. In 1201 the Hindu Sena dynasty was defeated by the first Muslim ruler, Muhammad Bakhtiyar Khalji, followed by an intensification of Muslim immigration and Sufi missionary activity. Widespread conversion to Islam ensued, especially among the rural poor. Asim Roy argues that this conversion was of whole groups, a "caste mobility" phenomenon motivated less by theological interest than by opportunities for social advancement under Islam's egalitarian ethos. The social distinction between Urdu-speaking *ashraf* (in-migrating Muslim elites) and local, Bangla-speaking *atrap* (converts to Islam) remained potent in the Mughal, British colonial, and Pakistan periods of Bengali history.

Islam in Bengal was noticeably accommodating to prior local spiritual ideas and practices. It was and is also highly accommodating to charismatic experience as exemplified in the *Pir-murīd* (saint and disciple) relationship, veneration of saints (*pīr*), and verbal art genres derived from and sustained by Sufi practice and lore. Critiques of local religious practice appeared in reform movements from the sixteenth century onward, from within Sufism itself and also, beginning in the late eighteenth century, under the influence of the Arabian

Cycle rider. By Maran Chand Paul. Rayer Bazar, 1995. Slipped earthenware; 5 1/2 in. tall, © Indiana University Press

Wahhābī movement. The political message of Muslim reformism in the nineteenth century included appeals for unification through "purified" religious practice and opposition to oppressive Hindu *zamindar* landlords and British indigo planters, to both of whom the landless Muslim agricultural workers (*ryot*) were vulnerable.

At the level of practice, it is a matter of historical analysis and debate to what extent Bengali Muslim or Hindu reform movements of the colonial period and subsequently affected aspects of local religious practice and expressive culture, which include a rich tradition of visual representation of human forms (which orthodox Islam opposes), as well as personal recourse to saints, spirits, healers (*kabirāj,* who may specialize in both herbs and amulet-making), or exorcisers (*ojha*) for practical intervention in daily life problems. Hindu terms, concepts, and images, such as *dharma* (rules of life and behavior; justice), or aspects of *jātī* (caste) ideology regarding categories of persons, pollution, and so on coexist with Muslim ones in many contexts. Commentators including Sen Gupta and Glassie have noted the centrality of aspects of the Goddess (female divinity in general as expressed in particular deities) in Hindu popular devotional practice. Ideas and personages that have a widespread presence across Islamic lands may take on a particular character in Bangladesh, for instance, Khiẕr, the legendary peripatetic prophet/saint, who is known as Khijir Pir, Kwadja Khidr, or Kwaz, a spirit connected with water whose anger may be implicated in the all-too-frequent destructive flooding of the Ganges delta. The idea of jinn, spirits mentioned in the Qur'ān (Surah 72), is supplemented by *bhūta* and *petnī* (malevolent male and female ghosts).

The history of Bengali folklore studies, whether as colonial ethnology or as a cultural nationalist effort, can be traced well back into the British period. Sen Gupta traces the beginnings of indigenous folklore collecting to the advent of Bangla as the administrative language of the courts under the British, replacing Persian, in 1839. Lal Behari Day had published *Bengal Peasant Life* by 1874 and *Folk-Tales of Bengal* by 1883. By the 1920s Dinesh Chandra Sen published an overview of Bengali folk literature, and Nobel laureate poet Rabindranath Tagore and other prominent men of letters had taken as part of their project the recording and celebration of indigenous verbal genres, as well as the quotation of traditional themes and images in belles lettres. The idea of Bengali culture was and still is linked to Bangla language in particular, as demonstrated by the vigorous ongoing efforts of the Bangla Academy, Dhaka, to support cultural heritage performance and document oral genres in Bangla language. Such documentation included and still includes both Muslim and Hindu traditions, terms, and concepts, even today, in Muslim-majority Bangladesh, which was at least 85 percent Muslim by the 1990s. Bangla-speaking Hindus, the largest minority at perhaps 12 percent of the population in Bangladesh, constitute the majority in the adjacent Indian province of West Bengal. By the first census in 1872, Muslims already were relatively numerous in eastern British colonial Bengal; Hindus, in the western parts of the province. Bengal was divided into two separate, Muslim- and Hindu-dominated provinces by the British colonial administration in 1905, in a divide-and-rule strategy explicitly designed to combat the increasingly militant nationalist movement.

Also resident in Bangladesh are more than twenty named *ādivāsī* (Hindi, "original inhabitant," also called "tribal") groups, speaking various languages in the Tibeto-Burman and Dravidian language families, or dialects of Bangla. Ādivāsī groups, comprising as much as 12 percent of the population of India, represented not more than 1 percent of the population of Bangladesh according to the national census of 1981. A significant proportion of the Bangladeshi ādivāsī population is Christian, in the wake of colonial-period missionary efforts, while others are Hindu, Buddhist, or retain local spiritist belief systems.

Major migrations of settler-farmers and landless peasants accompanied colonialism and its aftermath. Numbers of Muslim settler/refugees occupied and cleared tracts in the plains of northwestern Bangladesh, west of the Brahmaputra, in the Chittagong Hills area, and elsewhere which had previously been controlled by ādivāsī groups who held and managed forested land jointly rather than owning it as individuals, practicing slash and burn agriculture, growing rice and cotton supplemented by hunting and foraging. Irresolvable differences in subsistence strategies on the land were part of a general pattern of cultural distinction. Local ādivāsī culture, called "primitive," was technologically simpler than that of preindustrial Bengalis, oral in use and transmission, while Bangla verbal culture and art had existed for several centuries in both oral and written forms. As in other nationalist movements which have tapped folklore as a cultural resource, the documentation of ethnic/linguistic minority lore and customs and their claiming (or not) as part of a national cultural heritage may become problematical in the face of accusations of physical and cultural repression and exploitation. Issues of cultural authenticity and rights of representation thus emerge in the discussion of ādivāsī-related matters in Bangladesh as they have in the history of "tribal" cultures facing territorial encroachment in the New World and elsewhere. While linguistic ethnonationalism has served as a unifying ground for Bangladeshi Muslims and Hindus, against the threat of communal violence, it gives non-Bangla-speaking minorities at best a less central role in the rhetorical construction of national culture and identity. Tribal folklife, which includes cotton weaving, bamboo and reed construction and weaving techniques for housing and a wide variety of utility items ranging from basketry to fish traps and snares, and personal adornment rules very different from either Muslim or Hindu conventions, remains very sparsely documented.

Oral histories and personal experience narratives, whether of local events in Bengali history and in contemporary Bangladesh, or of the Bengali diaspora experience in the United Kingdom and elsewhere, are also sparingly but intriguingly represented in recent literature. Studies such as Kotalová's analysis of rural gender-related social organization and custom, or Karlekar's study of nineteenth century elite Hindu women, are rich in subject matter for folklorists, but to some extent mute the voices of participants articulating and reflecting on these social standards in that they do not endeavor to preserve the coherency of verbatim narratives.

While the foundational efforts of Bengali folklorists prior to partition focused on Bangla verbal art genres and the heritage of Bangla language arts continue to loom large in Bangladeshi folklore scholarship, Firoz Mahmud in 1993 outlined the stake of Bangladesh in folklife studies, including material culture and a wide range of traditional activities shared by identifiable professional and residential groups. The rich material culture of Bangladesh provides distinctive items and media of artistic production taken as emblematic of national identity, whether it be *nakshī kāñthā* figurative needlework, the brocaded muslin *jāmdānī,* gauzy fabrics whose designs seem to float in space, or pottery horse sculptures. While jāmdānī has long been prized as a highly refined hand-weaving technique, superior to mechanized weaving and sought after by elites for fine saris and women's scarves (*dupāṭṭā*), kāñthā is a form of quilting which was originally a salvage art of the poor, making coverlets and other utility objects out of worn sāṛi and other recycled cloth, quilted in running stitch patterns with colored threads drawn from the sāṛi borders. Elaborately patterned kāñthā, mentioned in mystical poems, proverbs, and tales and celebrated in the populist romanticism of Jasimuddin's early twentieth-century narrative poem, "Nakshī Kāñthar Māṭh" (The Field of the Embroidered Quilt), fell out of fashion, if not of use, then was revived both as an icon of national identity and as an income-generating, marketable product, through direct intervention of folklorists and development specialists in the years after independence.

Pictorial representations of rural life in Bangladesh, village and river, serve to express a sense of national experience developed in dynamic popular art forms, especially vehicle painting and decorative terra-cotta. Representational forms in sculpture and bas-relief (icons, portraits, and representations of animals) are particularly richly developed relative to their development in other Muslim environments, with both Hindu and Muslim craftspeople contributing. Hindus are concentrated in crafts professions, as they are also in trade, but Muslim master craftspeople are also present. Close study of material culture production, including discussions with rural and urban artists and dealers, reveals the dynamic state of crafts in Bangladesh. Craftspeople strive to maintain aesthetic engagement in both process and design while responding to developing markets and fashions in such areas as cooking (clay *tandurī* ovens for the home) and décor (figural terra-cottas, statuary) in the urban middle class. As Glassie points out, traditional handicrafts for a wealthy audience (e.g., *jāmdānī sāṛī* cloth) stand a better chance of economic viability, in comparison to traditional utility handicrafts for everyday use, such as the pottery and brass now in competition with mass-produced utility items in plastic and stamped aluminum.

References

Abecassis, David. 1990. *Identity, Islam and human development in rural Bangladesh.* Dhaka: University Press.

Adams, Caroline, ed. 1987. *Across seven seas and thirteen rivers: Life stories of pioneer Sylhetti settlers in Britain.* London: THAP Books / The Tower Hamlets Arts Project.

Banerjee, Sumanta. 1989. *The parlor and the streets: Elite and popular culture in nineteenth century Calcutta.* Calcutta: Seagull Books.

Blanchet, Therese. 1984. *Meanings and rituals of birth in rural Bangladesh.* Dhaka: University Press.

Brauns, Claus Dieter, and Lorenz G. Löffler. 1990. *Mru: Hill people on the border of Bangladesh.* Basel: Birkhäuser Verlag.

Day, Lal Behari. 1883. *Folk-tales of Bengal.* London: Macmillan.

Glassie, Henry. 1997. *Art and life in Bangladesh.* Bloomington and Indianapolis: Indiana University Press.

Islam, Mahmuda. 1980. *Folk medicine and rural women in Bangladesh.* Dhaka: Women for Women Research and Study Group.

Islam, Mazharul. 1970. *A history of folktale collections in India and Pakistan.* Dhaka: Bengali Academy.

Karlekar, Malavika. 1991. *Voices from within: Early personal narratives of Bengali women.* Calcutta: Oxford University Press.

Khan, Shamsuzzaman, ed. 1987. *Folklore of Bangladesh.*, vol. 1. Dhaka: Bangla Academy.

———. 1992. *Folklore of Bangladesh*, vol. 2. Dhaka: Bangla Academy.

Khan, Shamsuzzaman, and Momen Chowdhury, eds. 1987. *Bibliography on folklore of Bangladesh.* Dhaka: Bangla Academy.

Kirkpatrick, Joanna. 1989. Reflections on popular art and culture in Bangladesh today: The persistence of graven images. In *Shaping Bengali worlds, public and private,* ed. Tony K. Stewart, 57–67. East Lansing: Michigan State University Asian Studies Center.

Kotalová, Jitka. 1993. *Belonging to others: Cultural construction of womanhood among Muslims in a village in Bangladesh.* Uppsala: Uppsala University.

Mahmud, Firoz. 1993. *Prospects of material folk culture studies and folklife museums in Bangladesh.* Dhaka: Bangla Academy.

Mey, Wolfgang, ed. 1984. *They are now burning village after village: Genocide in the Chittagong hill tracts, Bangladesh.* Copenhagen: International Work Group for Indigenous Affairs (IWGIA).

Roy, Asim. 1983. *The Islamic syncretist tradition in Bengal.* Dhaka: Academic Publishers.

Roy, Beth. 1994. *Some trouble with cows: Making sense of social conflict.* Berkeley: University of California Press.

Sen, Dinesh Chandra. 1920. *The folk-literature of Bengal.* Calcutta: University of Calcutta.

Sen Gupta, Sankar. 1967. *A survey of folklore study in Bengal: West Bengal and East Pakistan.* Calcutta: Indian Publications.

Timm, R. W. 1991. *The adivasis of Bangladesh.* Manchester, England: Minority Rights Group/Manchester Free Press.

Zaharul Haque, A. S. 1981. *Folklore and nationalism in Rabindranath Tagore.* Dhaka: Bangla Academy.

Zaman, Niaz. 1993. *The art of Kantha embroidery.* Dhaka: The University Press.

MARGARET A. MILLS

SEE ALSO

Architecture, Bangladesh; Architecture, Bengal; *Balī khelā;* Bāul Songs, *Bhāṭiyāli* Song; *Bhūta*; *Bicār Gān* Songs; Complaint; Foodways, Bangladesh; Games and Contests, Bangladesh; *Gāzīr Gajir Gān; Jāmdānī; Jārīgāni; Jhumar Jātrā* Drama; Jinn; *Kāñthā; Kerāmat;* Khvājah Khiẓr; Lālan Fakir; *Mārfatī* and *Murśīdī* Songs; *Mukhos Nācā;* Nationalism and Folklore; *Pathkabita;* Pottery, Bangladesh; *Sakta Song;*

Satya Pīr Sen, Dinesh Chandra; Song, Bengal; Syncretism; *Tabarrak; ᶜUrs*

BANGLES

The use of bangles or bracelets as a form of ornamentation is common throughout the world, but in South Asia bangles appear to have taken a specific role as a symbol of socioritual status and ethnic identity. The earliest bangles date to the Neolithic period (7000 B.C.E.) at the site of Mehrgarh, Pakistan. These were made from circlets of shell, or were composite bracelets made from beads of stone and shell. During the Indus Valley civilization (2600–1900 B.C.E.), we see a dramatic increase in the styles of bangles and the varieties of materials used to produce bangles. The range of materials includes shell, terra-cotta, stoneware, faience, alabaster, copper/bronze, and gold. Burials of adult women with shell bangles on the left arm are thought to represent the earliest use of bangles to define ethnic affiliation and possibly marital status. At present, among Hindu communities, women must remove or break their bangles at the death of their husbands, but women who die before their husbands are often cremated with the symbols of their married status, such as their red wedding sari, simple ornaments such as iron and lac bangles, an iron finger ring, or a necklace worn as a symbol of marriage, called the *mangal sutra* (auspicious thread). The mangal sutra is usually made of black glass beads alternating with gold or silver beads and is given to a woman during the wedding ceremony.

Green to blue-green glazed faience bangles were first made in the Indus cities and continued to be made in later periods until the development of glass technology during the Painted Grey Ware period (1100–800 B.C.E.). The early glass bangles were dark blue-green to black or yellowish brown. By the Early Historical period (600 B.C.E.) a wide variety of glass bangles were being produced, along with stone bangles made from agate and jasper.

During subsequent historical periods, bangles came to play an important role in ornamentation and for ritual purposes. In the Hindu traditions, women wear bangles to identify their marital status. Among contemporary Hindu communities, glass bangles are worn to mark important festivals or special social events. In some communities green glass bangles are worn as good luck for childbirth. Shell bangles are worn in many Bengali Hindu communities to represent the marital status of wives, to ensure the well-being of the family, and to ensure longevity of the husband. Ivory bangles are worn for the same general purpose in western India and Pakistan, and glass bangles are worn for these reasons throughout the subcontinent.

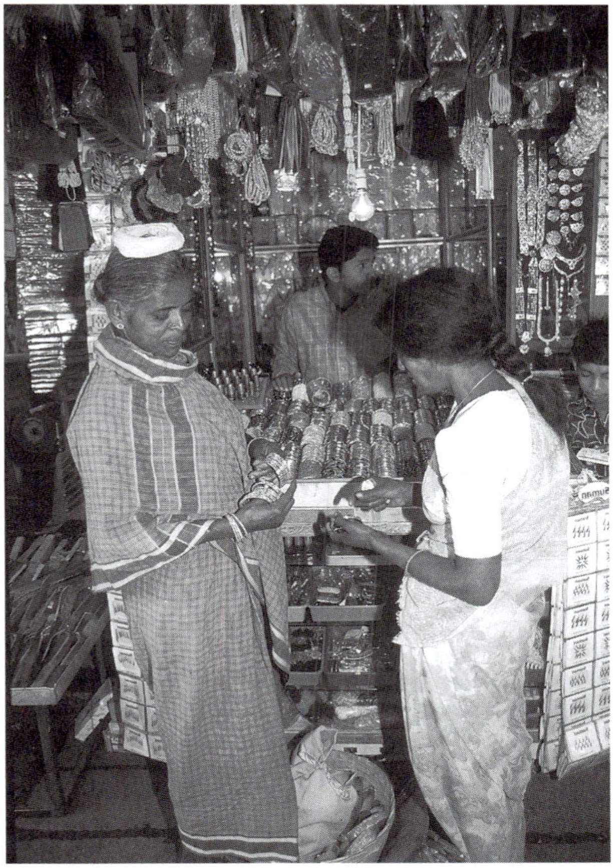

Women in a market look at the large bangle selection and decide which ones to buy. Karnataka, India. © Mimi Nichter

The styles of bangles not only signify ethnic affiliation, but also can be correlated to occupation and social status. In traditional communities, wide, heavy bangles made of ivory or shell that will not break easily are generally worn by women involved in heavy labor, while thin, delicate bangles made of the same materials are worn by elite women who do not engage in heavy manual labor.

In contrast to these more valuable materials, cheap and relatively fragile glass bangles are worn by women of all classes. Glass bangles are often broken intentionally to signify anger and sorrow, or simply to make room for a new set.

Bangles are also worn by men for functional as well as symbolic purposes. Among Sikh communities the man's iron bangle is worn as a religious symbol as well as a protection of the wrist in the course of battle. Holy men of both Hindu and Muslim sects wear specific types of bangles to identify their religious order or status and as protective amulets. Bangles made from gold or silver are worn by both sexes as a sign of wealth and status.

References

Kenoyer, J. Mark. 1992. Ornament styles of the Indus tradition: Evidence from recent excavations at Harappa, Pakistan. *Paléorient* 17(2): 79–98.

Parpola, Asko. 1990. Bangles, sacred trees and fertility: Interpretation of the Indus script relating to the cult of Skanda-Kumara. In *South Asian archaeology 1987*, ed. M. Taddei and P. Callieri, 263–284. Rome: Istituto Italiano per il Medio ed Estremo Oriente.

JONATHAN MARK KENOYER

SEE ALSO

Beads; Glass; Jewelry and Adornment; Material Culture

BĀRAHMĀSĀ

Literally "the twelve months," *bārahmāsā* refers to a poetic and song genre known across northern India (in languages such as Bengali, Hindi, Gujarati, Rajasthani, Bhojpuri, and Panjabi). The *bārahmasā* draws upon elements of both the climatic and cultural calendars of the area to tell a tale or to depict emotions. Each month and the relevant action/image associated with it are described in a line or perhaps in a stanza, depending upon the author. The primary focus is on the human year, as formed and mediated by the climatic year and its associated rituals and cultural events; the *bārahmāsā* explicate the progress of human beings through the psychological shoals of the annual cycle. *Bārahmāsā* focus especially on the imagery of extreme disjunctions, capturing the human moral and physical decline that occurs when the actions appropriate to a given month are left undone. A frequent image in *bārahmāsā* is the absence of one's lover during the rainy season months of *Aṣārh, Śrāvan, Bhādrapad,* and *Aṣvin* (Hindi) (July through October). This excerpt, from a song about one of the god Kṛṣṇa's loves, Lalita, captures this theme:

> In *Aṣārh*, the dark clouds gathered,
> In *Śāvan* [*Śrāvan*], the east wind blew.
> In *Bhādon* [*Bhādrapad*], I could not see the hidden path:
> The ponds and lakes are filled with water;
> In the month of *Kvar* [*Aṣvin*], Syam did not come to the house.

Bārahmāsā are an ancient poetic form, though no Sanskrit versions have been found. Most authors concur that it is a vernacular, non-Sanskritic poetic form related to, and perhaps derived from, the more popular *caumasā* (songs of the four months of the rainy season). In areas as separated as Bengal and Rajasthan, we find *bārahmāsā* inserted into longer poetic narratives, such as the Manasā *maṅgal* of Bipradās composed in 1495 C.E. in Bengali and an anonymous *dhola-maru* composed in western Rajasthan in the fifteenth century. Today, bārahmāsā are sung in rural communities throughout northern India, often as independent pieces, but sometimes as part of oral epics such as *Ḍholā* or *Pābūjī*. They are also available in chapbook form in urban markets. *Bārahmāsā* composed and published under colonial rule had titles such as "The Banning of Cow Slaughter." Thus, *bārahmāsā* is a genre easily adapted by local poets to a variety of topics and didactic themes. One of the most popular new *bārahmāsā* honors the recently deceased female ex-*dacoit* (robber/bandit) and political leader, Phoolan Devi. While retaining the format and core symbolism of the twelve months of the Hindu calendar, the popular folk bārahmāsā are extremely diverse in content and allow rural poet-singers opportunities to comment on a variety of issues.

References

Vaudville, Charlette. 1965. *Bārahmasā*. Publication de l'Institut Français d'Indologie, no. 28. Pondicherry: Institut Français d'Indologie.

Wadley, Susan S. 1983. The rains of estrangement: Understanding the Hindu yearly cycle. *Contributions to Indian Sociology* n.s. 17: 51–85.

Zbavitel, Dusan. 1961. The development of the baromasi in Bengali literature. *Archiv Orientali* 29: 582–619.

SUSAN WADLEY

SEE ALSO

Song

BĀUL SONG

The songs of the Bāuls are among the most popular Bengali folk songs. The Bāuls, who are found all over Bengal, belong to a syncretic devotional tradition that was influenced by all three major religions of the Indian subcontinent—Buddhism, Hinduism, and Islam—but also has distinctive features of its own. The term "Bāul" does not refer to a single homogeneous religious group. Rather, various Hindu and Muslim groups with similar beliefs and practices centering on the body and on bodily fluids go by the name Bāul, though not all such groups refer to themselves by that name. These groups are usually not divided along strictly sectarian lines. A Hindu guru may have Muslim disciples and vice versa.

The history of the Bāuls is obscure. Scholars place their origin anywhere from the fifteenth to the nineteenth century, but due to the oral and esoteric nature of the Bāul tradition, it is not possible to date its birth with any certainty. The earliest definite textual reference to the Bāuls as a religious tradition, however, is not until 1870. It is clear that the tradition reached its peak in the nineteenth and early twentieth centuries, when the majority of Bāul songs that comprise the present-day corpus were composed. Bāul songs continue to be composed to this day.

The majority of Hindu Bāuls reside in the state of West Bengal in northeastern India and the majority of Muslim Bāuls in Bangladesh. For the most part, the Bāuls come from the lower socioeconomic strata of society. Bāul singers earn their livelihood singing their often esoteric songs in villages at festivals or in the cities in the homes of patrons, and occasionally on radio and television. Although they may accompany their singing with a variety of instruments, those most closely associated with Bāul songs throughout Bengal are the *ektārā* (a one-stringed drone instrument held in the right hand and plucked with the fingers) and the *ḍugi* (a small clay drum hung from the left shoulder, or tied in front of the left hip, and played with the left hand). In addition to playing instruments, Bāuls in West Bengal generally dance as they sing.

The word "bāul," derived from Sanskrit *vātula* or *vyākula,* means "mad." To the public at large, the Bāuls do indeed seem "mad" in their unconventionality. They reject many established beliefs, customs, and practices. They strongly condemn the caste system and deny the authority of Hindu scriptures, such as the Vedas and Purāṇas, as well as the Qur'ān as interpreted by orthodox Muslims. They do not perform the rituals of either Hinduism or Islam; they worship neither in mosques nor temples, nor do they go on Hindu pilgrimages to Benares or the Muslim hajj (pilgrimage) to Mecca. Their appearance, too, sometimes sets them apart from other Bengalis. The dress of Hindu Bāul men in the area of Rāṛh, West Bengal, is particularly distinctive. They wear long, loose saffron-colored upper garments and patchwork coats made of rags, and their long hair is worn twisted in a topknot. It is this image that is associated with the Bāuls in popular imagination. To the Bāuls, the word "mad" does not have a pejorative connotation; in fact, they proudly affix to their names words meaning "mad," such as *pāgal* and *kṣepā.* The Bāuls associate madness with the rejection of everything that separates and divides people, such as caste and religion. They also associate it with love, with the direct experience of the divinity within the body gained from ritual sexual practices, or with the desire for that experience. Bāul lyrics frequently suggest that attempts to put their experiences into words sound to the uninitiated like the ramblings of a madman. For example, the Bāul poet Baidyanāth says in his song "Premer kathā balbo kāre sai?" (My Friend, Who Can I Tell About My Love?):

My friend, who can I tell about my love?
When I try to speak about it
people think I'm mad. (Bhāṭṭācārya 1971, 1026)

Bāul songs are generally short, consisting of three or four rhymed verses often ending in a signature line (*bhaṇitā*) in which the poet's name, and sometimes that of his guru, are mentioned. The songs are composed in simple colloquial Bengali and passed down orally from guru to disciple and from singer to singer. Literate Bāuls may record the songs in notebooks that they use to refresh their memories. The tunes of the songs tend to reflect the tunes of the singer's native region.

It is mainly through their songs that the Bāuls give literary expression to their beliefs and practices. Only rarely do they compose any treatises. The songs strongly condemn sectarianism since, as the song "Hindu yaban kṛṣṭānerā ki bhābe mane" ("What Do Hindus, Muslims, and Christians Think?") by Duddu Sāh states: "Heaven and the supreme guru are not the monopoly of any religion" (Bhāṭṭācārya 1971, 833).

Bāul songs express the belief that the body is a microcosm of the universe in which the creator resides and that it is the only means to liberation. For this reason, all rituals not centered on the body are considered a waste of time. In these *dehatattva* (truth in the body) songs, the body is often compared to an object, such as a house, a boat, or a city, as in this verse of Lālan Fakir's song "Āche ādi makkā ei mānab dehe" (The Original Mecca Is in This Human Body).

The original Mecca
is in this human body.
Mind, won't you take a look?
Why race all over the map,
huffing and puffing
till you're ready to drop? (Bhāṭṭācārya 1971, 572)

Bāul songs often describe the Bāuls' attempt to catch the elusive divine principle within. They express reverence for the guru or *murshid* who teaches the adept the secrets of their sexual rituals—which cannot be found in any text—and who is equated with the divine principle. In addition, they allude to the essential role of the woman who holds the key to the male adept's success in that *sādhanā* (method of realization). And finally, they hint enigmatically at those sexual rituals.

The Bāuls associate the male aspect of the divine principle with semen and its female aspect with menstrual blood. Through sexual intercourse during a woman's menstrual period, they seek to reunite the dual aspects of the divine principle which split apart when the world was created, and thereby to reverse the process of creation and regain the original state of nonduality. Since, according to Bāul belief, longevity is dependent on the preservation of semen, the male adept is taught by his guru to prevent ejaculation during intercourse.

Songs about sādhanā often use as sexual metaphors imagery from the activities of daily life—everything from fishing and farming to robbery and foreclosure.

The songs are also often composed in an ambiguous style in order to hide their ritual significance from the uninitiated. But no matter what the subject, the striking, evocative imagery of Bāul songs, their humor, and their catchy tunes give them wide appeal.

References

Bhāṭṭācārya, Upendranāth. 1971. *Bāṃlār Bāul o Bāul Gan* (The Bāuls of Bengal and Bāuls' Songs). 2nd ed. Calcutta: Orient Book.

Capwell, Charles. 1974. The esoteric beliefs of the Bāuls of Bengal. *Journal of Asian Studies* 33(2): 255–264.

———. 1986. *The music of the Bāuls of Bengal*. Kent, Ohio: Kent State University Press.

Das, Rahul Peter. 1992. Problematic aspects of the sexual rituals of the Bauls of Bengal. *Journal of the American Oriental Society* 112(3): 388–432.

Das Gupta, Shashi Bhusan. 1969. *Obscure religious cults*. 3rd ed. Calcutta: Firma K. L. Mukhopadhyay.

Dimock, Edward C., Jr. 1966. *The place of the hidden moon: Erotic mysticism in the Vaiṣṇava-sahajiyā cult of Bengal*. Chicago: University of Chicago Press.

———. 1987. The Bāuls and the Islamic tradition. In *The Sants: Studies in a doctrinal tradition of India,* ed. Karine Schomer and W. H. McLeod, 375–388. Delhi: Matilal Banarsidass.

Jhā, Śaktināth. 1999. *Bastubādī Bāul: Udbhab Samāj Saṃskṛtī o Darśan* (An analytical study of the materialistic outlook of Bauls of Bengal and their origin, society, culture and philosophy). Calcutta: Loksaṃskṛti Bibhāg, Pascimbaṅga Sarkār.

Openshaw, Jeanne. 2002. *Seeking Bauls of Bengal*. London: Cambridge University Press.

Salomon, Carol. 1979. The Bilvamaṅgal-Cintāmaṇi legend as sung by Sanātan Dās Bāul. In *Patterns of change in modern Bengal,* ed. Richard L. Park, 97–110. East Lansing: Asian Studies Center, Michigan State University.

———. 1991. The cosmogonic riddles of Lalan Fakir. In *Gender, genre, and power in South Asian expressive traditions,* ed. Arjun Appadurai, Frank J. Korom, and Margaret A. Mills, 267–304. Philadelphia: University of Pennsylvania Press.

———. 1995. Bāul songs. In *Religions of India in practice,* ed. Donald S. Lopez, Jr., 187–208. Princeton: Princeton University Press.

Urban, Hugh. 1999. The politics of madness: The construction and manipulation of the "Bāul" image in modern Bengal. *South Asia* 22(1): 13–46.

CAROL SALOMON

SEE ALSO
Bhāṭiyāli Song; Lālan Fakir; Song, Bengali; Syncretism

BEADS

Beads and pendants are important forms of ornament that have a very long history in the subcontinent. The earliest beads were made from natural marine shells, bone and antler, and possibly ostrich egg shell. These date from the Upper Paleolithic and Mesolithic periods, from eight thousand to more than eleven thousand years ago. Stone beads are documented extensively throughout the subcontinent beginning in the Neolithic period (around 7000 B.C.E.) and continuing through later periods up to the present.

The earliest stone beads are made from soft stone, such as limestone and soapstone, but by the early Chalcolithic period (4500 B.C.E.), we see the drilling and polishing of harder stones such as carnelian, banded agates, and jasper. During the Indus Valley civilization (2600–1900 B.C.E.), special lapidary techniques were developed to produce exquisite long carnelian beads that were exported to the surrounding regions of Central Asia, the Gulf region, and even as far as Mesopotamia. The Indus artisans produced many different styles of beads ranging in size from seventy millimeters in length to tiny beads of steatite (soapstone), measuring one millimeter in length and diameter. Special coloring techniques were developed to make permanent designs on beads, especially white designs on red carnelian. Beads of carnelian, lapis lazuli, turquoise, and copper were worn at the waist, the throat, and on the wrist. Tapered cylindrical amulets made of black stone or greenish colored stone have been found in association with female burials with shell bangles, and may have been a form of ornament worn by married women during the Indus period.

During the Early Historic period (beginning around 600 B.C.E.), the technique of coloring stone beads continued to be used, and a new technique of making white designs on beads that were blackened also appears. These beads, with white on red or white on black designs, became widespread during the early Hindu and Buddhist period (300 B.C.E. to 300 C.E.) and were traded as far as Southeast Asia and Tibet.

While many beads from prehistoric times may have been made from wood or seeds, these materials are preserved only at later dates. The sacred *tulsi* or basil wood is used to make beads worn by certain Hindu sects. A wide variety of sacred seeds, particularly the *rudraksha* (literally, "eye of Rudra," who is the god more commonly known as Śiva; *Elaeocarpur ganitrus*), are worn singly as amulets. Strands of beads made of sacred wood, seeds, or stone are used as prayer beads by all of the major religious sects of the subcontinent. Rock crystal and carnelian are the most popular stones, but amber, sandalwood, and a variety of other sacred materials are also used.

Beads of various materials are used as protective amulets, combined with gold or silver, or strung on cotton or silk thread. Married women among many Hindu communities wear a necklace (*mangal sutra*) that combines black glass beads with silver or gold beads. Men from many different communities wear agate, rock crystal, or garnet beads as protective amulets. Most communities of the subcontinent wear pendants made from stone or metal as protective amulets as well as for ornamentation. Many of these amulets are hollow and filled with sacred objects or written texts that protect the bearer.

Since antiquity, beads made in the subcontinent were traded to all parts of the known world and, even today, workshops in Khambhat (Gujarat) and Jaipur (Rajasthan) produce a wide variety of beads in semi-precious and precious stones for export to markets in Japan, Europe, Africa, and the Americas. Glass beads, many of which are imitations of popular beads made in other regions of the world, are produced near Delhi or in South India.

References

Francis, Peter, Jr. 1982. *Glass beads of India*. The World of Beads Monograph Series, 7. Lake Placid, N.Y.: Lapis Route Books.

Kenoyer, J. Mark. 1986. The Indus bead industry: Contributions to bead technology. *Ornament* 10(1): 18–23.

———. 1992. Ornament styles of the Indus tradition: Evidence from recent excavations at Harappa, Pakistan. *Paléorient* 17(2): 79–98.

Kenoyer, J. Mark, Massimo Vidale, and Bhan Kuldeep K. 1991. Contemporary stone bead making in Khambhat, India: Patterns of craft specialization and organization of production as reflected in the archaeological record. *World Archaeology* 23(1): 44–63.

JONATHAN MARK KENOYER

SEE ALSO

Glass; Jewelry and Adornment; Tibet; Tulsi (Basil)

BENFEY, THEODOR

Theodor Benfey (1809–1881) was a philologist and Sanskrit grammarian who taught at the University of Göttingen in Germany. His publications span dictionaries of Greek and Sanskrit, a Sanskrit grammar, and numerous translations of classical Indian texts. Benfey is known in folkloristic circles for his German translation of the *Pañcatantra,* possibly the most important Indic text for comparative studies of story literature.

In his introduction to the translation, Benfey expounded a diffusionistic theory of story-theme migration. Benfey, like many of his predecessors, chose India as a wellspring for narratological research. Drawing on the work of Silvestre de Sacy (1758–1838) and his students, he posited an Indic origin for the moral fable. His grand scheme included other genres such as märchen, which he also saw as originating in India. From there, he thought, the narrative genres diffused in many directions, ultimately reaching Europe via Africa and the Middle East. Because the *Pañcatantra* was such a popular source of entertainment and moral learning for Indians, Benfey supposed that this text—more than any other—could shed light on the mechanisms of diffusion.

Benfey saw a strong connection between the *Pañcatantra* and the Indo-Buddhist *Jātaka* tales, since both were educational, dealt with moral themes and parables, and made extensive use of animal characters. Possible Greek influence notwithstanding, Benfey was convinced that India must be the home of morality tales because the Indian populace was accustomed to the unique style of oral preaching put forth in the *Pañcatantra*. But he also admitted that writing played an important role in the dissemination of this corpus of stories. As India came into greater contact with Islamic and other cultures, Benfey argued, the oral mode of storytelling waned in importance. Thus, the Indian fables found new homes, carried in translated forms to numerous countries by traders, warriors, and monks.

Benfey's contribution to comparative studies cannot be underestimated, for scholars in many disciplines have commented extensively on his theory. Most important among these in the field of folkore studies was Emmanuel Cosquin (1841–1921), a collector of French folklore who went even further than Benfey by insisting that India was the indisputable home of all tales. Although he received much praise from his contemporaries, Benfey's ideas eventually came to be questioned by other European folklorists and philologists. In Russia, for example, proponents of the historical method utilized Benfey's insights, but a later revivalist, A. N. Veselovskiĭ (1838–1906), eventually refuted Benfey's thesis in asserting that the flow of influence can never be simply unidirectional. Joseph Bédier (1864–1937) was, perhaps, Benfey's most vocal opponent, arguing for a more plausible theory of polygenesis, or multiple origins.

Today, Benfey is taken more seriously as an Indologist than as a folklorist, yet his contribution to folklore theory has left an indelible effect. Tales do, after all, migrate, and even though his notion of a single point of origin should not be taken literally, his other points concerning the interrelationship between orality and literacy, as well as the role of human agency in the process of transmission, are still central to the growth and vitality of the discipline. It is no wonder, then, that he is often refered to as the "father of the historical-comparative method."

References

Bédier, Joseph. 1925. *Les Fableaux: Études de littérature populaire et d'histoire du Moyen Age.* Paris: E. Champion.

Benfey, Theodor. 1859. *Pantschatantra. Fünf Bücher indischen Fabeln, Märchen und Erzählungen,* 2 vols. Leipzig: F. A. Brockhaus.
Claus, Peter J., and Frank J. Korom. 1991. *Folkloristics and Indian folklore*. Udupi, India: Regional Resources Centre for the Folk Performing Arts.
Cocchiara, Giuseppe. 1981. *The history of folklore in Europe. Storia del folklore in Europa*. Turin, 1952. Trans. John N. McDaniel. Philadelphia: Institute for the Study of Human Issues.
Cosquin, Emmanuel Georges. 1922. *Les contes indiens et l'Occident.* Paris: E. Champion.

FRANK J. KOROM

SEE ALSO
Folktale, "Tale Type"; Story Literature, Sanskrit

BHAGAVATI RITUAL TRADITIONS OF KERALA

Bhagavati ("The Goddess") is the predominant Hindu deity of Kerala. Encompassing a wide range of divine personalities, Bhagavati in Kerala temples manifests as Kāḷi, Durgā, Lakṣmi, Pārvatī, and Sarasvatī, sometimes all in one day, and also encompasses local village goddesses associated with fever diseases. As Bhagavati, the goddess is conceived of as benevolent and powerful, simultaneously a chaste virgin and a caregiving mother. She is seldom portrayed in either mythology or iconography as being the consort of any male deity, but stands on her own. Her legends of origin differ from those of surrounding areas, and her cult combines indigenous local and later Sanskritic beliefs and practices. Almost every community in Kerala has its distinctive form of ritual worship, ranging from tribal costumed possession dances to elite Sanskrit operatic theater. The multiform ritual traditions associated with the worship of Bhagavati thus reflect Kerala's eclectic historical and social development. The best known ritual traditions are *Bhagavati pāṭṭu, guruti, kaḷam, muṭiyēṟṟu, paṭayaṇi, pāna, tīyāṭṭu, teyyam, tūkkam,* and *veḷiccappāṭu* performances.

The essential legend of Bhagavati central to all these ritual traditions is the *Dārikavadham,* an oral tale apparently indigenous to Kerala and well known there. While this legend shares a number of motifs found in other goddess traditions throughout South Asia, its essential features are unique to Kerala. Chief among these are Bhagavati's basic identity as Bhadrakāḷi, daughter of Śiva (born from his third eye), whose character is fierce and violent, and who kills the demon Dārika to restore order to the world. She is akin to Jaina nature spirits and snake deities known as *yakṣi*s, who are sexually voracious as well as deadly. The Sanskritic aspects of Bhagavati's mythology emphasize her dharmic, righteous anger, whereas folk legends and rituals of important Kerala temples clearly demonstrate her out-of-control sexuality and blood lust. The majority of ritual traditions devoted to Bhagavati enact some portion of the *Dārikavadham* story and are performed in order to appease and pacify the goddess. Many are accompanied by symbolic blood sacrifice (once actual, now done with a vegetable substitute known as *guruti,* a mixture of turmeric and calcified lime with water).

Thousands of temples to Bhagavati grace the landscape of Kerala, forming the core of daily worship for most Hindu Malayalis. Every Bhagavati temple holds, in addition to its regular devotions, an annual festival at which major ritual arts are commissioned. This plethora of performing arts, encompassing music, dance, theater, visual art, possession, curing, magic, comedy, and exorcism, has developed in response to the annual temple festival tradition and is the characteristic form of worship in Kerala. Major Bhagavati temples at which regular rituals are performed include Chengannur, Chottanikkara, Kanyakumari, Kodungallur, Mookambika, Pannayanarkavu, Paramekavu, Pazhayannur, and Tirumandankunnu. Two of these (Kanyakumari and Mookambika) are located outside of Kerala's present boundaries, in neighboring Tamil Nadu and Karnataka, but are connected by mythology and local tradition to Kerala goddess temples.

One of the unique features of Bhagavati worship in Kerala is the institution of the veḷiccappāṭu or oracle. Normally a male of the Nāyar caste, the oracle is attached as a ritual servant to the Bhagavati temple. He is not qualified to conduct the daily ritual offerings (*pūja*) in the inner sanctum; this duty is relegated to Brahmans. The veḷiccappāṭu's sole function is to become possessed by the spirit of Bhagavati and to pronounce oracles and give blessings to the faithful. Before the Temple Entry Act of 1936, all devotees but Brahmans were prohibited from entering into the inner area of the temple, so that the role of the veḷiccappāṭu was extremely important as in intermediary between the faithful and their deity. It also reflects the shamanic heritage of Dravidian religion, in which the enacted, felt, bodily presence of the deity is the essential form of *darśan* or contact with the divine. Veḷiccappāṭus serve other deities besides Bhagavati (although not the higher Sanskritic male deities such as Śiva and Viṣṇu), and lower-caste veḷiccappāṭus also are common in non-Brahmanac temples. Once a year, at the lowland Kodungallur Bhagavati temple festival, tribal female veḷiccappāṭus descend from the hills and participate in the ritual worship of the goddess.

The basic ritual of the veḷiccappāṭu is possession while holding the *vāḷ* or curved iron sword of the goddess. A belt of brass bells at his waist and brass anklets at his feet, the veḷiccappāṭu speaks for the goddess while in a trance, usually running wildly or bouncing in small vertical jumps. More elaborate versions of this kind of ritual are kaḷam and pāna. In kaḷam, a large portrait of Bhagavati is drawn on the temple floor out of colored powders—traditionally only white, black, red, and green, although other colors such as blue and yellow are now sometimes used as well. The two-dimensional powder drawing portrays Bhagavati in her fierce state, with weapons in her many arms and the severed head of the demon Dārika dripping blood from one of her lower left hands. Her eyes are wide and fangs protrude from her red lips. Her eyes, nose, and conical breasts are built up to protrude three-dimensionally from the floor. Once the kaḷam is completed, oil lamps, coconuts, areca flowers, rice, and bananas are placed at points around the circumference of the drawing, and offerings of light, mantras, ritual gestures, music, and food are made by a priest or the veḷiccappāṭu himself. Musicians sing Bhagavati pāṭṭu, songs of praise to the goddess, telling the story of *Dārikavadham.* The veḷiccappāṭu then unwinds the long hair of his head and runs his left hand through it while dancing in a trance and shaking the goddess's sword in his right hand. He dances in this manner over the kaḷam, eventually effacing it entirely. The mixed powders that remain are presented to the faithful as *prasādam* (blessed remains). In pāna a more elaborate sequence of offerings is presented along the same lines.

Concomitant to the kaḷam ritual is the offering of guruti (blood sacrifice or its substitute; see above). This is essential, but it normally is conducted outside the temple's inner sanctum, to the north or northeast. It is said to satiate demonic spirits and ghosts who accompany Bhagavati to war, but at other times it is the goddess herself who is believed to receive the offering of blood to sate her anger and heated state. Guruti is usually offered in the dead of the night, when ghosts and demons abound.

Perhaps the most important category of ritual worship dedicated to Bhagavati is that of dance-drama and theatrical possession performances. Although there are scores of such genres, the most important are muṭiyēṯṯu, paṭayaṇi, tīyāṭṭu, teyyam, and tūkkam. *Kathakaḷi,* the renowned operatic theater of Kerala, though once performed mostly in temples, has now moved largely to the commercial entertainment realm. Its stories, unlike the Bhagavati ritual arts, tend to focus on the Sanskrit epics and classical literature. All of these theatrical dance forms build on the principle of embodiment of deity central to the institution of the veḷiccappāṭu (oracle).

Teyyam is performed exclusively in the northern region of Kerala (formerly known as Malabar), and is closely related to the *bhūta kōla* ceremonies of Tulunad, southwestern Karnataka. Numerous fierce and blood-thirsty forms of Bhagavati appear amongst the teyyams. While possessed, actors may bite the heads off of live chickens and drink the blood in a display of the goddess's supernatural fury. The goddess gives oracles and blessings to her devotees through the actors during the teyyam performances.

Muṭiyēṯṯu, paṭayaṇi, tīyāṯṯu, and tūkkam are related art forms that enact different phases of the *Dārikavadham* story. Each is prevalent in a different region of central or southern Kerala. Muṭiyēṯṯu, often followed by *Dārikan* or *Garudan tūkkam* (hook-swinging), presents the story of the war between the demon Dārika and the goddess Bhagavati (as the fierce Bhadrakāḷi) in an all-night theatrical performance. Tūkkam is sometimes performed the day following muṭiyēṯṯu. This hook-swinging ritual is a symbolic form of human sacrifice. Once performed by inserting metal hooks into the skin of the back, today, tūkkam is done by suspension from a red belt at the waist. Its symbolic meaning is the offering of unlimited quantities of blood of the demon Dārika (or in some cases the mythical bird Garuḍan) to Bhagavati's ferocious assistant, Vētāḷam, following the war between Bhadrakāḷi and Dārika. The rite is believed to bring blessings to the performer and the community as a whole.

Paṭayaṇi, performed in the Pattanamtitta District of southern Kerala (formerly Travancore), and tīyāṭṭu, common to Ernakulam and northern Kottayam districts (formerly Cochin), both enact the return of Bhagavati from the war with Dārika, though in distinctive ways. In paṭayaṇi the goddess's ferocity upon her return to Kailāsam, the abode of her father Śiva, is mitigated by the comical sight of absurd and grotesque *kōlam*s, or caricatures, of herself and her attendants walking and singing in the night. The huge headdresses and costumes depict the goddess in highly abstract fashion, with scores of enormous eyelike circles in the headdress and breasts, distorted facial features, and wild gait. Obscene songs and the carrying of fire torches accompany the all-night paṭayaṇi performances. *Kāḷi tīyāṭṭu,* by contrast, is a solo performance within the temple sanctum, by a highly trained artist of the high temple-serving castes. After drawing an elaborate kaḷam and dressing himself, the artist seats himself on a stool in front of Bhagavati's shrine and proceeds to sing poetic verses describing the goddess's return to her father Śiva in Kailāsam. The verses are accompanied by graceful hand gestures and stylized facial expressions, highly reminiscent of kathakaḷi dance drama.

In addition to these temple rituals offered to the goddess Bhagavati, a plethora of lesser-known performative arts are cultivated by each community in Kerala. Tribal communities in the hilly regions perform embodied dances to various forms of the goddess such as Nīli,

Kūḷi, and Malavaḻi, all considered to be essentially nature spirits residing in the mountainous regions where they dwell.

Bhagavati is important to Malayalis not only as a legendary protectress, but as a deity of the land. For communities dwelling in the hills, she is the spirit of the mountains; for lowland agriculturalists, she is the paddy and the earth from which it grows; for toddy tappers, the graceful coconut palm is her form. The idea of human embodiment, then, is natural to the concept of Bhagavati as she permeates all living things through the energies of the soil. She is the essence of life itself, and as integral participants in the natural world, human beings can easily invoke, contain, and experience her presence through the myriad ritual arts. Bhagavati's worship intensifies during the hot summer months of the harvest, when the earth is dry and barren. The themes of heat and thirst have important symbolic value in understanding the goddess's cult. The complexity and wealth of Kerala's ritual arts dedicated to the goddess Bhagavati are a fertile field waiting to be tilled by enthusiastic scholars of the future.

References

Caldwell, Sarah. 1996. Bhagavati: Ball of fire. In *Devi: Goddesses of India,* ed. John S. Hawley and Donna Wulff. Berkeley: University of California Press.

———. 1999. *Oh terrifying mother: Sexuality, violence, and worship of the goddess Kāli.* Delhi: Oxford University Press.

Freeman, John R. 1991. Purity and violence: Sacred power in the teyyam worship of Malabar. Ph.D. diss., Anthropology Department, University of Pennsylvania.

Raghavan, M. D. 1947. *Folk plays and dances of Kerala.* Trichur, Kerala: Magalodayam Press.

Tarabout, Gilles. 1986. *Sacrifier et donner à voir en pays Malabar: Les Fètes de temple au Kerala (Inde du Sud). Ètude anthropologique.* Paris: École Française d'Extrême-Orient.

Thampuran, M. H. Kerala Varma. 1936. Kali cult in Kerala. *Bulletin of the Rama Varma Research Institute* 4: 77–97.

SARAH CALDWELL

SEE ALSO

Dārikavadham; Floor Designs; Gods and Goddesses; Hook-swinging; Kerala; *Kathakaḷi; Koḷam; Mutiyēṯṯu;* Pūja; Sacrifice; *Teyyam;* Theater and drama

BHAJAN

Bhajan is a devotional form of music found throughout all of India. The word "bhajan" is derived from Sanskrit, literally meaning "loving worship." It is appropriately named since this musical form emerged from and remains an integral part of the devotional (*bhakti*) movements that swept India beginning in the eleventh century. Bhajan usually consists of the responsory repetitions of a leader followed by a group, singing very appealing and melodious songs, but can also be the solo singing of a simple wandering mendicant. It is performed either in more intimate or larger congregational settings, in villages or cities, in the early morning hours of the day or, as is usual, in the evenings. These songs are filled with mystical fervor and devotion towards the divinity, and are comprised of poetic lyrics about God or saintly persons expressed in the vernacular. They are often performed in formal liturgical settings where sermons are presented and worship takes place or in informal gatherings of devotees called *bhajan mandal.*

A related musical form is *kīrtan* ("praising" or "chanting") which, like bhajan, was also an outgrowth of the bhakti movement, especially in Bengal. Although it has the same musical form as bhajan, kīrtan is usually accompanied by ecstatic dancing, often with arms in the air. This musical form was especially popularized by Caitanya (sixteenth century), an influential devotional mystic who toured all over India, while dancing to the chanting of the holy names of God. Kīrtan held on city streets is specifically called *nagar-kīrtan* ("praising God throughout the city"). Even today, one can observe the devotees of the Hare Krishna movement performing kīrtan on the streets of many major cities of the world. Another similar form of devotional song, influenced by the practice of bhajan, called *qawwālī,* was taken up by Sufis in Muslim India, who practiced love of God as their bhakti counterparts did.

The musical form of bhajan was originally motivated by saintly poets, whose bhakti poems then became lyrics for songs which were arranged according to Indian classical forms of ragas or *tālas.* The writings of saintly poets, such as Purandaradāsa (sixteenth century) from South India, Guru Nānak (sixteenth century), Sūrdās (sixteenth century), and Mīrābhai (fifteenth century) from the north, as well as Jayadeva Gosvāmin (twelth century) and Narottamadas (seventeenth century) from the east, became the lyrics of bhajans, through which devotion to God was expressed. These poets drew mostly from the *Bhāgavata Purāṇa,* the most popular of all *purāṇas,* specifically from the episodes of the tenth book describing Kṛṣṇa as the supreme being interacting with his most intimate devotees. Its classical roots make bhajan more sophisticated than folk music. Yet bhajan is more accessible than classical music, since anyone can sing and play bhajan without the technical precision that the classical demands.

The simple lyrical form of bhajan is a series of couplets that are each sung first by a leader and then repeated alternately by the group. Bhajan is found in a variety of vernacular languages or in the classical languages of Sanskrit or Tamil. Variety is also found in the degree of emotional intensity of the lyrics for the deity, depending upon whether bhajan expresses a more abstract theism or a personality-specific theism, the latter generally displaying much more intensity. The songs either praise God and his holy names or express longing for the Lord and the intense feelings of pain experienced in separation from the Lord. Lyrics can also be didactic in nature. The bhajan songs usually have a fairly simple musical accompaniment of some form of drum, small cymbals, and portable keyboard instruments.

GRAHAM M. SCHWEIG

SEE ALSO
Bhakti; Kīrtan; Purāna

BHAKTI

Bhakti, from the Sanskrit *bhaj*—"to share in, belong to, partake of, worship"—is the term for devotion to a particular deity widely practiced in the Hindu tradition. In its broadest sense, it can refer to those forms of worship associated with a temple, in which ritual is addressed to an icon (*deva-pūjā*) and viewing (*darṣan*) of the deity's representation is paramount. In this form, bhakti can include pilgrimage to sacred centers (*tirtha*), the taking of vows (*vrata*), devotional singing (bhajan), and the presentation of dramas, dances, musical recitals, and other forms of worship in collective settings. On the other hand, bhakti can also connote a devotee's intensely intimate experience with a personal deity (*iṣṭa devata, īśvara*). This experience is usually depicted as a relationship taking one of five forms—that of a servant to a master, a child to a parent, a friend to a friend, a parent to a child, or, most commonly, a beloved one to a lover. Bhakti is believed to enable the devotee to gain communion with the deity, to remain eternally in the deity's presence as an attendant, or even to gain complete union with the deity (*sājujyal*). Various metaphors are used in poetic tradition to describe this experience, from "wordless bliss" to "madness" or "intoxication."

Generally speaking, major bhakti movements can be discerned in those periods of Indian history when several religious and social currents converged. It particularly arises in the context of a pluralism of religious movements, such as Buddhist, Jain, Muslim, or Christian. Bhakti movements often selectively evoke earlier forms of "classical" (Sanskritized) religion, and appropriate popular or folk forms of religion. In later forms of bhakti, there is also the evocation of ethnic and regional themes that serve to localize the deity and make devotion a means through which identity can be affirmed and expressed.

The first major bhakti movement was that associated with the urban or epic age (third century B.C.E.–fifth century C.E.) in which theism, temple construction, and the use of iconography became a major part of the North Indian landscape, under the aegis of such dynasties as the Śakas, Kuṣanas, and Guptas. This devotionalism, as illustrated in the *Bhagavadgītā, Mahābhārata,* and *Rāmāyaṇa,* combined aspects of early brahmanism with forms of non-*vaidika* (popular) cultic theism, together with the selective appropriation of the ascetic (*śramana*) tradition found in Jainism and Buddhism. Bhakti was thus presented by the literati as the logical culmination of the earlier paths of wisdom (*jñana*) and action (karma).

The first major vernacular form of bhakti was expressed in Tamil country in the early centuries of the common era. Here poets, extolling the virtues of Śiva and Viṣṇu, especially their grace (*aruḷ*) and love (*aṉpu*), selectively borrowed from epic mythology, localized the deities' exploits in the Tamil countryside, and linked them to themes that were seen as part of a primeval Tamil consciousness. The movement provided a popular alternative to Jainism and Buddhism and helped make South India a major center of Hindu culture.

The late classical period, from the twelfth through the seventeenth centuries, found an explosion of the bhakti experience in many of the vernacular traditions. Major figures in this movement are to be found singing or writing in the regions of Bengal, Karnataka, and Rajasthan, and in languages such as Marathi, Hindi, Telugu, and Tamil. Poets could speak of the divine as one beyond form (*nirguṇa*), or as taking on very concrete manifestations (*saguṇa*) wherein the poet could appropriate the full range of the mythological exploits of a specific deity, not least of all its love for the devotee.

It is not a coincidence that this wave of bhakti was occasionally influenced by Sufism and became a popular alternative to an increasingly visible Islam.

The twentieth century witnessed still another resurgence of Hindu bhakti, characterized by the renovation of temples, renewed interest in pilgrimages, festivals, temple rituals, and participation in various forms of devotionalism previously accessible only to the higher classes. Once again, this neo-bhakti has come to embody a form of Hindu self-expression in the face of various alternative forces, including Christianity, globalization, and secularization.

References

Hardy, Franklin. 1981. *Viraha Bhakti: The early development of Kṛṣṇa devotion in South India.* New York: Oxford University Press.

Hawley, John S., and Mark Juergensmeyer. 1988. *Songs of the saints of India.* New York: Oxford University Press.

Ramanujan, A. K., trans. 1973. *Speaking of Siva.* Harmondsworth: Penguin Books.

———. 1981. *Hymns for the drowning.* Princeton: Princeton University Press.

Schomer, Karine, and W. H. McLeod, eds. 1987. *The Sants: Studies in a devotional tradition of India*. Berkeley: University of California Press.

FRED CLOTHEY

SEE ALSO
Bhajan; Darśan; Mahābhārata; Pilgrimage; *Rāmāyaṇa;* Sufi folk poetry; *Vrat Katha; Worship*

BHAKTI SAINTS

The saint poets of the *bhakti* (devotional) movements of Hindu India remain lively figures in the cultural and religious landscape, though their actual lifetimes range from the ninth to the eighteenth centuries. Their authority is based on religious experience, and they composed songs of love in their mother tongues for God, whether in manifest form (Viṣṇu, Kṛṣṇa, Rāma, Viṭṭhala, Śiva, or the Devī), or as the Lord beyond form. Among their number are women and members of very low castes (as well as Brahmans), and their life stories recount their suffering at the hands of the powerful—be they higher caste people, rulers, religious authorities, families, or husbands. They respond with defiance and absolute dedication, and their status as beloved of God is affirmed, often through divine intervention.

The works of some, like Sūrdās, the blind Kṛṣṇa devotee, have been incorporated into specific devotional sects, and others, like Kabīr, the iconoclastic weaver devotee of the formless Lord, and the leatherworker Raidās, have inspired low-caste religious movements. Still others primarily inhabit popular imagination, such as Mīrābāī, a high-caste woman whose public devotion to Kṛṣṇa and choice of a low-caste guru led to attempts on her life.

Devotional songs attributed to the saints are sung in temples but also in *jāgaraṇ*s, the all-night singing sessions held in homes that are so characteristic of rural religious life. Songs of numerous saints praising various manifestations of the divine are generally sung together, sometimes by professional caste musicians but more often by self-selected musicians and singers who provide this service out of dedication to God, or simply by gathered community members. Additionally, itinerant singers perform on trains or from house to house, and these songs are woven into daily life, sung to accompany repetitive work and played across the airwaves in commercial renditions.

Many songs bearing a saint's name reflect a particular style of religiosity and set of imagery associated with that saint rather than actual authorship. In some cases the saint's authority is lent to another's composition, or a well-loved saint is associated with a favorite song that is elsewhere and more consistently attributed to another. Further, as scholars have observed, songs attributed to the saints provide a language of resistance to oppression and religious hypocrisy for others who might not dare to speak out in their own names.

The saints' life stories provide the plot for epic songs, folk songs, and folk dramas performed by low-caste singers. The performances become an occasion for speaking about the performers' own lives, struggles, and religiosity as they, in some sense, make the saints over into their own image (as members of higher castes do in other genres, such as movies, dance ballets, comic books, and novels). The saints' names have become household words—blind singers are called "Sūrdās," and women perceived negatively as too independent or, alternatively, admired for living lives of similar devotion are called "Mīrā." Having entered the cultural vocabulary of India, these saints live on, inscribed in text and embodied in drama and life, their songs still sung, and new ones continually composed in their names.

References

Hawley, John Stratton. 1988. Author and authority in the bhakti poetry of North India. *The Journal of Asian Studies* 47(2): 269–290.
Hawley, John Stratton, and Mark Juergensmeyer. 1988. *songs of the saints of India*. New York: Oxford University Press.
Henry, Edward O. 1988. *Chant the names of God: Music and culture in Bhojpuri-speaking India*. San Diego: San Diego State University Press.
Lorenzen, David N., ed. 1995. *Bhakti religion in North India: Community identity and political action*. Albany: State University of New York Press.
———. 1996. *Praises to a formless God: Nirguṇī texts from North India*. Albany: State University of New York Press.
Martin, Nancy M. 2002. *Mirabai*. New York: Oxford University Press.
Mukta, Parita. 1994. *Upholding the common life: The community of Mirabai*. Delhi: Oxford University Press.

NANCY M. MARTIN

SEE ALSO
Gods and Godesses; Saints; Song

BHĀND PAṬHAR

Bhānd paṭhar is a robust, vital form of improvised secular theater, performed by semiprofessional troupes in the Kashmir Valley, most frequently at Kashmiri festivals honoring Islamic saints. As of 1980, before the recent fighting in Kashmir, there were over twenty-five troupes active. The performance season is traditionally inaugurated in June with a colorful gathering (*jashna*) of all the bhānd paṭhar troupes of a district. During the ensuing summer season, *shenai* and drums are used to summon the audience and accompany the action, and whirling *Sufiānā* dances are frequently interpolated into the stories. At the heart of the form, though, is the broad, farcical playing of the *maskharā*s, or clowns.

The bhānd paṭhar repertoire is culled from the entire history of Kashmir, and troupes have up to fourteen *paṭhar,* or story scenarios, in their standard repertoire; thus, clowns may emerge as servants of an eleventh-century Dārdic king and his wives (all played by male actors), as wily peasants trying to survive the whims of Persian overlords in the game parks of the thirteenth century, as haughty nineteenth-century English colonials and their less-than-loyal servants, as contemporary barbers from the town and country demonstrating their dubious tonsorial skills on laughing victims from the audience, or, in the repertoire of at least one troupe, as followers of Rāma and Hanumān. The appropriate lengths for the various paṭhar vary, as does the time of day for their playing: *dārda paṭhar,* for example, is appropriate to morning festivities, while *shikārga paṭhar* is always performed in the evening. Reflecting the historical range of the repertoire, the improvised dialogue features multilingual punning (Farsi, Punjabi, Kashmiri, Urdu), and even English gibberish.

Whatever the putative setting, though, the performances ultimately celebrate the endurance of the Kashmiri common man; the broad farcical acting style serves as a vehicle for satirical commentary as well as rambunctious play. *Bhānd*s seem to have originally come into Kashmir as court jesters, associated with the courts of Persia, and to have fanned out from the valley into much of northern India, attaching themselves to both Islamic and Hindu courts and often performing as strolling *bāhurūpiya.* While bhānd paṭhar itself is unique to Kashmir, the form has clear affinities with *rū hawzī* of Iran and even the Italian commedia dell'arte. Masks are used in portraying the animals featured in several of the paṭhar, and the tiger mask used is virtually identical to the lion mask of Iranian theater. In the 1970s and 1980s, the satirical capabilities of bhānd paṭhar and the comic skills of its actors were used in formal dramas commissioned for television and performed in Srinagar, Jammu, and New Delhi that focused on such contemporary topics as birth control and urbanization.

Reference

Mathur, J. C. 1964. *Drama in rural India.* New Delhi: Indian Council for International Relations.

JOHN EMIGH

SEE ALSO

Islam; Muslim Folklore and Folklife; Saints; Theater and Drama

BHĀOẎĀIẎĀ SONG

Bhāoẏāiẏā are regional folk songs of North Bengal and Assam, including the districts of Cooch Behar and Jalpaiguri in West Bengal, India; Dinajpur and Rangpur in Bangladesh; and Goalpara in Assam, India. They are composed in North Bengal dialect, and the riverine and forest landscape and toponyms of the region figure prominently in them. The singers and composers of the songs are typically employed as buffalo herders (*maiṣāl*), oxcart drivers (*gāṛiẏāl*), and elephant drivers (*māhut*), who sing the songs to pass the time as they travel from place to place, accompanying their song on the *dotārā,* a four-stringed instrument played with a plectum (pick). Bhāoẏāiẏā are slow songs, sung in a distinctive style characterized by the occasional insertion of the syllable *hā* after the vowels ā or e, as in the final word of the phrase "O ki pati dhahan" (for *dhan;* [O the treasure of a husband]).

The most common theme of bhāoẏāiẏā songs is love, particularly love in separation (*biraha*). Though sung and composed by men, they often take the persona of a woman whose lover's occupation requires him to lead a peripatetic existence. She addresses her absent lover by his profession and describes to him how she has suffered since he left, as in this verse of a well-known bhāoẏāiẏā song ("O ki gāṛiẏāl bhāi" [O oxcart driver, my friend]):

> O oxcart driver, my friend,
> how long must I go on
> watching the road for you?
> The day the oxcart driver left town
> this woman's heart was crushed.
> You drive your cart
> all the way to Cilmari port. (Pāl 1973, 5)

Besides the professions mentioned above, the woman's lover may be a merchant (*sādhu*), cowherd (*rākhāl*), or boatman (*mājhi*). She may also address him simply as "boyfriend" (*cyāṅṛā bandhu*) or "foreigner" (*pardeśiyā*), since she often makes his acquaintance as he passes through her village in the course of his travels. While the male character may be the woman's husband, more typically he is not. Like Rādhā in the Bengali Vaiṣṇava (the worship of Viṣṇu/Kṛṣṇa) tradition, she may even be married to somebody else (*parakīẏā*). In fact, the archetypal lover Kṛṣṇa (usually called by such names as "Kānāi" or "Kālā," which, like Kṛṣṇa, mean "dark" or "black") himself is the protagonist of some bhāoẏāiẏā songs.

References

Bhaṭṭācārya, Aśutoṣ. 1965. Añcalik saṅgīt (Regional songs). In *Bāṁlār Lok-sāhitya* (The folk literature of Bengal). Vol. 3, pp. 56–359. Calcutta: Calcutta Book House.

Pāl, Hariścandra, ed. 1973. *Uttar Bāṁlār Pallīgiti* (The folk songs of North Bengal), Vol. 1, *Bhāoẏāiẏa Khaṇḍa* (Bhāoẏāiẏa volume). Calcutta: Sanyal.

Ray, Sukumar. 1988. *Folk-music of eastern India with special reference to Bengal*. Calcutta: Naya Prokash.

CAROL SALOMON

SEE ALSO
Buffalo; Cow; Herders' Field Calls; Kṛṣṇa Song, Bengali

BHĀRAT LĪLĀ

Bhārat līlā is a form of improvised comic theater popular in the Ganjam Province of Orissa. While its characters are drawn from the *Mahābhārata,* a performance of bhārat līlā is very far from that magisterial epic work in its tone.

The central characters are Arjuna, Subhadrā, and the *dwārī,* a doorman or gatekeeper. The prominence of this last role, usually played by the leader of the troupe, has led to the form also being known as *dwārīnāṭa* ("the doorman's play"). The dwārī acts both as commentator and middleman in the duel of words that takes place as Subhadrā, urged on by her brother Kṛṣṇa and sister-in-law Satyabhāmā, tries to convince an uncharacteristically chaste Arjuna to take her as his new wife. Bawdy jokes, songs, and dances mix freely with an encyclopedic display of knowledge as Arjuna tests his would-be wife's comprehension of śāstric and purāṇic lore. The play thus functions both as ribald entertainment and an important conveyor of traditional knowledge.

While a single performance lasts about three or four hours, competitions (*bedi*) between two or more parties have been known to continue for several nights. In recent decades, Nabagana Parida has been the most prominent exponent of this form.

Reference

Dash, Dhiren. 1979. Jatra: People's theatre of Orissa. *Sangeet Natak: Journal of the Sangeet Natak Akademi* 52: 11–26.

JOHN EMIGH

SEE ALSO
Mahābhārata; Theater and Drama

BHĀṬIẎĀLI SONG

Bhāṭiẏāli are the folk songs sung and composed by the boatmen (*mājhi* and *māllā*) of East Bengal, particularly in the districts of Mymensingh, Comilla, Sylhet, Dhaka, Noakhali, and Chittagong, Bangladesh. Bhāṭiẏāli songs have slow tempos and free rhythm (*tāl*), and are traditionally sung solo by the boatman during leisure time, without instrumental accompaniment. This is in contrast to *sāri* songs, also sung by boatmen from East Bengal, which have measured rhythm and fast tempos, and are sung in a group, often in connection with boat races, to help keep the rowing synchronized. The term "bhāṭiẏāli" is derived from *bhāṭi,* most likely in its sense of "down-country," referring to their geographical origin in lower East Bengal, or possibly in its sense of "downstream journey," referring to the relatively easy trip down the slow-moving East Bengal rivers, during which the boatman has the time to relax and sing. The songs have also come to be associated with farmers and herders.

The main theme of bhāṭiẏāli songs is love. The songs are full of pathos and describe the loneliness of the boatman's daily existence spent apart from his beloved. They also complain of disappointment in love. Other themes include reflections on the ephemerality of life and on time wasted in idle pursuits. Often the songs are set on the broad rivers of East Bengal and tell of the difficulties and dangers involved in crossing these "shoreless rivers" (*akūl dariyā*), as in this verse of the song "Bandhu koi railā re" (O Friend, Where Are You?):

> O friend,
> the river has no bank, no shore,
> and the water's rough.
> In a crisis like this
> no one is with me.
> O friend, where are you? (Bhaṭṭācārya 1965, 330)

Many bhāṭiẏāli songs are symbolic: the river is the river of existence (*bhaba nadī*), the boat is the body, and the friend or helmsman is the Supreme, or the guru or *murshid* who is equated with the Supreme. The texts of such bhāṭiẏāli songs are indistinguishable from the songs of the Bāul religious tradition. It has been suggested that bhāṭiyāli were originally secular love songs but were later influenced by various types of religious folk songs such as Bāul, *mārphatī* (Islamic Sufi songs), and Hindu Vaiṣṇava (the worship of Viṣṇu/Kṛṣṇa) songs about the god Kṛṣṇa and his beloved Rādhā. Whatever may have been the origins, most bhāṭiyāli today reflect these influences.

References

Bhaṭṭacārya, Āśutos. 1965. *Ancalik saṅgīt* (Regional songs). In *Bāṃlār lok-sāhitya* (The folk literature of Bengal), vol. 3, pp. 56–359. Calcutta: Calcutta Book House.
Biśvās, Hemāṅgo. 1966. *Srīhaṭṭer lok-saṅgīter sur bicār* (A discussion of the tunes of the folk songs of Sylhet). In *Śrīhaṭṭer loksaṅgīt* (The folk songs of Sylhet), ed. Gurudaday Datta and Nirmalendu Bhoumik, 416–431. Calcutta: Calcutta University.
Datta, Gurudaday, and Nirmalendu Bhoumik, eds. 1966. *Śrīhaṭṭer loksaṅgīt* (The folk songs of Sylhet). Calcutta: Calcutta University.

Ray, Sukumar. 1988. Forms of Bengali folk-music: The eastern sector. In *Folk-music of eastern India: With special reference to Bengal,* 109–123. Calcutta: Naya Prokash.

CAROL SALOMON

SEE ALSO

Bāul Songs; *Mārphatī* and *Murśīdī* Songs; Song, Bengali

BHAVĀI

Bhavāi is a form of rural theater that is performed over a broad area in western India, including parts of Gujarat, Madhya Pradesh, and Rajasthan. Its origin is attributed to Asāita Ṭhākur, an outcaste Brahman who lived during the fourteenth century C.E. in what is now northern Gujarat. He claims to have formed the first so-called strolling (itinerant) troupe of *bhavāyas*—those who arouse sentiment—after having been excommunicated for dining with a Patel caste member's daughter while posing as her father in order to save her from a Muslim captor. (The grateful Patel gave Asāita Ṭhākur a small plot of land and financial support for a theater troupe, instituting a pattern of village patronage which is still in effect.)

Bhavāi is traditionally performed in conjunction with festivals honoring such aspects of *śakti* as *Ambāji* or *Bāhucharāji,* and *Nāvarātri* is regarded as a particularly auspicious time. Performances are frequently performed in temple courtyards or streets just outside of a temple in a space (*pauḍh*) sanctified by ritual. Invocations of Gaṇapati and of Kālī traditionally begin performances, and vignettes dealing with Hindu mythology and regional heroes are part of the repertoire. Most of the skit-like episodes are satiric, centering on the vices of various communities found in village societies: Brahmans, tailors, potters, barbers, sadhus, scavengers, and money lenders. Episodes, known as *veśas* (literally, "costumes") or *svāngs*, are performed in a mixture of Gujarati, Hindi-Urdu, and Marwadi that betokens the complex historical interconnections among communities in this region, and feature both songs and spoken dialogue in performance. The Nayak, or leader of the troupe, remains on stage as commentator, often joined by the clownish Rangalo.

Asāita is said to have composed 360 *veśas*, of which about 60 remain in the repertoire. Sample texts of these *veśas* were collected and printed in the nineteenth century, and these are still drawn upon by present-day actors. Both the music and the dance of bhavāi combine classical, folk, and popular elements: movements associated with *kathak,* a semiclassical dance, for example, may alternate with displays of *garba,* a regional folk dance, and with acrobatic skills. In recent years, as rural support has waned, there have been attempts in urban settings to honor and preserve bhavāi by teaching its skills in high schools and conservatories. And modern drama troupes in Ahmedabad, Bombay, and Delhi have been drawn to bhavāi's satiric comedy as a source of vitality.

References

Chandarvaker, Pushkar. 1973. *Bhavāi*: A type of folk drama of Gujarat. *Folklore* (Calcutta) 14(6): 217–223.

Richmond, Farley. 1969. *Bhavāi*: Village theatre of West India. *Papers in International World Affairs* (Michigan State University) 2: 13–28.

Varadpande, M. L. 1992. *History of Indian theatre,* vol. 2, *Loka Ranga, Panorama of Indian folk theatre*. New Delhi: Abhinav.

JOHN EMIGH

SEE ALSO

Kathak Dance; Nāvarātri; Sadhu; Theater and Drama

BHOPO

Bhopo is a generic term for bards and oracular priests belonging to the Nayak caste, an "unclean" scheduled caste, in Rajasthan. Bhopos travel in pairs from village to village to perform the epics of *Pābūjī* and *Devnārāyaṇ*. Typically, pairs are husband and wife—bhopo and *bhopī*—though all-male performances also occur.

Their performance incorporates an entire range of theatrical devices: dance, music, spoken and sung texts, and, most important, the use of an approximately eight-meter-long cloth scroll, called *paṛ,* on which scenes and characters from the deified heroes' epics are depicted.

References

Joshi, O. P. 1976. *Painted folklore and folklore painters of India: A study with reference to Rajasthan.* Delhi: Concept Publishing Company.

Smith, John D. 1991. *The epic of Pābūjī: A study, transcription and translation.* Cambridge: Cambridge University Press.

ADITYA MALIK

SEE ALSO

Devnārāyaṇ; Pābūjī; Paṛ

BHŪTA

The Sanskrit term *bhūta* is used in many regions of India to refer to a ghost, a wandering, dissatisfied soul, or a malicious spirit. In other regions, such as among the Tulu-speaking people of South Kanara district in Karnataka state, the term *bhūta* is used to refer to a variety of local spirits within the local cosmology with

Two bhūta in full costume at their annual bhūta kōla. Karnataka, India, © Mimi Nichter

the capacity to grant boons as well as cause harm, and to offer protection and blessings of bounty as well as inflict misfortune, illness, or crop failure. In this region, the bhūta pantheon is composed of anthropomorphic heroic bhūta—often heroes representing particular castes—and totemic bhūta that take on animal forms displaying male and female, as well as androgynous, characteristics.

Bhūta cults link the social domains of household, village, and kingdom, reproducing the ideology of the feudal relations that underlies the local social and moral order. At the household level *kuṭumbada bhūta* are regularly worshiped in shrine rooms through rituals meant to protect house space as well as matrilineal kin. *Jāgeda bhūta,* associated with particular neighborhoods, are housed in shrines and are routinely worshiped. At the village level, *ūrada bhūta* protect local boundaries. Malicious bhūta, often associated with the forests, crossroads, and unusual physical terrain, are controlled by talismans. In this way, the worship of particular bhūta is dependent on one's residence, caste affiliation, ties to a specific matrilineal household recognized to be central (*mūla sthāna*), and individual resonance, history, and alliance with other people and places.

During yearly rituals, caste interdependency is articulated. These rituals usually include possession, giving devotees an opportunity to interact with the spirits. Sometimes they provide devotees a sacred court for the hearing of disputes judged by possessed bhūta spirit mediums whose words and actions are interpreted throuqh intermediaries. At the kingdom level, aristocratic *rajendaiva bhūta* are worshiped during elaborate yearly rituals (*nema*), attended by the representatives of royal families and all prominent households. Rajendaiva bhūta, flanked by servant warrior *baṇṭa bhūta* who carry out their bidding, ensure the prosperity and justice within the kingdom in return for ritual tribute. Bhūta cults often contain congeries of spirits that reflect the dynamic history of each household or locale.

References

Ashton, Martha Bush. 1979. Spirit cult festivals in South Kanara. *The Drama Review* 23 (2): 91–98.

Claus, Peter J. 1989a. Behind the text: Performance and ideology in a Tulu oral tradition. In *Oral epics in India,* ed. Stuart Blackburn, Peter J. Claus, Joyce Flueckiger, and Susan Wadley, 55–74. Berkeley: University of California Press.

———. 1989b. "Kordabbu." In *Oral epics in India,* ed. Stuart Blackburn, Peter J. Claus, Joyce Flueckiger, and Susan Wadley, 231–235. Berkeley: University of California Press.

Prabhu, K. Sanjiva. 1977. *Census of India 1971. Miscellaneous (a): Special study report on bhuta cult in South Kanara District.* Series 14, Mysore (Karnataka). Delhi: Controller of Publications.

MARK NICHTER

SEE ALSO

Bhūta Kōla; Exorcism; Ghosts; Gods and Goddesses; Karnataka; Kordabbu; Spirit Possession and Mediumship; Supernatural Beings; *Teyyam*

BHŪTA KŌLA

For the Tulu-speaking people of coastal Karnataka, *bhūta* refers to a class of supernatural beings, and *kōla* means a ceremony for *bhūta*(s). A bhūta kōla is performed to appease and solicit assistance from the spirit(s).

Kōlas take place between December and July, from dusk to dawn, usually annually, at shrines located in rice fields, near trees, or in private homes. A shrine can be a stone, a pillar, a post topped with a small platform, an earthen platform, a swing, or a small building housing some of the above and the paraphernalia used in the ceremonies.

A space near the shrine is created for the ritual performance, and the ground is decorated with rice powder

Bhūta Ksētrapāla and Banta, © Martha Ashton-Sikora

patterns (*kolam/rangolli*). The shrine itself is sometimes decorated with palm-leaf-sculpted birds, animals, and geometric designs, as well as leaves, flowers, fruits, and vegetables. Prior to a kōla a palanquin containing the bhūta's paraphernalia—usually a mask, image, sword, shield, hand-held bell, and bow and arrow—is paraded to the shrine, accompanied by musicians and the village leaders, and then placed on the altar at the shrine.

During a ceremony both a dancer (*nalke*) and a priest (*pātri*) become possessed by the bhūta in a particular sequence. Typically, the kōla begins with the chanting of the bhūta's story (*pāḍdana*) by a member of the dancer's family while the dancer applies makeup. Once he is partially costumed, the dancer stands in front of the shrine, and, with the encouragement of intense music, he becomes possessed by the bhūta. He may hold fire torches to his chest or walk on glowing coals, demonstrating the veracity of his possession. He dances for several hours to mesmerizing music, pausing from time to time to add pieces to his costume.

In the next stage of the ceremony, the spirit enters and speaks through the pātri. The pātri is usually a member of the village community and, if the bhūta had been a human hero, then of the same caste as the bhūta. Otherwise, pātris are traditionally selected from the Billava (toddy tapper) caste. During this stage of the ceremony, the villagers make pledges and promises before the bhūta, ask for oracular predictions, and settle village disputes. When this work is finished, the bhūta then dispossesses the pātri and again enters the body of the dancer.

At this stage, the dancer is fully costumed. His adornment may include elaborate makeup, mask, and headdress, and a stiff apron extending horizontally at the dancer's waist (for receiving food offerings). Costume pieces are made of palm leaves, sculpted and painted palm flower sheaths, metal, cloth, or combinations of these. In the most elaborate celebrations (*nēma,* or *baṇḍi nēma*), the possessed dancer, along with the bhūta's paraphernalia and the bhūta's image, is taken in a special "cart" (*baṇḍi*), or on a carved wooden animal "vehicle," to nearby sacred places, receiving en route offerings of flowers, milk, and money from members of the village community.

Upon return to the shrine, a spokesman orates the bhūta's history and how the bhūta came to this particular place. He states that this kōla is performed according to tradition, asks the bhūta's forgiveness of any mistakes in the performance, and requests continued protection. The bhūta then blesses (or reprimands) village leaders, the sponsoring family, any special visitors, and local people. Afterwards, the bhūta receives animal or vegetarian offerings and then allows individual worshipers to ask advice for their problems. Finally, frenzied drumming and trilling wind instruments accompany rituals requesting the bhūta to leave the body of the dancer and thereby end the kōla.

Members of various castes participate in a kōla, providing certain services or items necessary for the ceremony. Although anyone can become possessed by the bhūta, the offices of spirit-medium (pātri) and ritual specialist (*pūjāri*) are frequently held by members of the Billava caste, and the caste itself is known as the Pūjāri caste. Only members of three castes can be dancers: Nalke (or Pāṇār), Parava, and Pambada.

References

Ashton, Martha Bush. 1979. Spirit cult festivals in South Kanara. *The Drama Review* 23(2): 91–98.

Ashton, Martha May Bush. 1979. beauty and the bhuta. *Illustrated Weekly of India,* 25 February.

Prabhu, K. Sanjiva. 1977. *Census of India 1971. Miscellaneous (a): Special study report on bhuta cult in South Kanara*

District. Series 14, Mysore (Karnataka). Delhi: Controller of Publications.

MARTHA B. ASHTON-SIKORA

SEE ALSO
Bhūta; Floor Designs; Ghosts; Karnataka; *Kordabbu; Pāḍdana;* Supernatural Beings; *Teyyam;* Tōṟṟam

BICĀR GĀN

Bicār gān, or argumentative folk song, is an important genre among the rich and varied folk songs of Bangladesh. This type of singing entertains and educates large numbers of people in both rural and urban areas of Bangladesh. The performers are usually touring professional singers. The Bangla word "bicār" means "to judge." In this sense, bicār gān means "songs of judgment." In practice, it is a duel between two folk singers. The themes of the bicār gān are debates on issues such as the differences between *shariyat* and *mārephat* (Islamic law and spiritual knowledge), the guru (spiritual teacher) and the disciple, man and woman, Hindu and Muslim.

The singing starts with songs praising Allah (God, in the Islamic tradition) and other prominent spiritual leaders including the Prophet Muḥammad, *pīr* (saints), and Hindu deities such as Rāma and Kṛṣṇa. Next, the actual singing contest begins, consisting of alternating questions and answers in song form. The bicār gān continues until the question-answer puzzle is settled. The arguments must be supported by the Qurān, *hadīth, Ramāyaṇa, Mahābhārata,* or other holy scriptures. The judges keenly observe the performance of each singer, evaluating them on their performance technique, musical talent, and the strength of their arguments. Debates may last an entire night, but more commonly today, they last only several hours.

In the earlier days, bicār gān were generally performed during the day. The stage was made of bamboo and wood (called *cauki,* meaning "platform"), with surrounding banana trees providing a canopy of leaves. The singers and their *dohārs* (assistant singers), sit on the cauki, while the audience sits in front of the stage on straw spread on the ground. Women traditionally would listen to the songs while sitting inside their homes, since they were not supposed to attend. Nowadays, the stages and decorations have undergone certain changes. Decorations are sometimes made of plastic, and the event may take place in a local theater instead of on a wooden platform. Women now sit side by side with men in the audience, and the performances usually take place at night. People from all walks of life, irrespective of caste, creed, and religion, participate. The audience gains mental peace and satisfaction as well as spritual knowledge from the performance.

SHAFIQUR RAHMAN CHOWDHURY AND LAURI HARVILAHTI

SEE ALSO
Games and Contests, Bangladesh

BIHAR: INDIA

Bihar, the second largest Indian state, has played a major role in the development of Indian civilization for two millennia. Beginning in the Vedic age and continuing until the Muslim conquests of the twelth century, Bihar's contributions read like a history of Indian religions. In more recent centuries, especially under the Mughals and the British, and into the present period of independent India, Bihar has perhaps lost its creative edge. Once the center of India's earliest empires, by 1765, Bihar was passed to the East India Company as part of the Diwani of Bengal; in 1911 Bihar and Orissa were broken off from Bengal into a separate province, and not until 1935 did the state take its present form. With a population of 95.5 million, Bihar has some of the lowest literacy rates in India (38 percent) and the highest levels of poverty.

Located in the middle and lower Gangetic region between the states of Uttar Pradesh and West Bengal, Bihar is bisected by the eastward flowing Ganga, creating a geographic division between the great alluvial plain of the north sweeping up to the Himalayas and the forested Chotanagpur Plateau in the south. This geographical division allowed for the isolation of numerous tribal groups on the southern plateaus despite the rise of many kingdoms and the full complexity of the caste system in the flat and fertile rice lands of the north. A further cultural distinction is frequently made between the North Ganga Plain and the South Ganga Plain. The latter is the region known as Magadha, which was the center of the Mauryan empire and always a crossroads between Bengal and centers of power to the west. In the centuries prior to the rise of the Mauryas, small kingdoms in this region attracted scholars and ascetics, among whom was the young Gautama, who achieved his enlightenment under the fig tree in Bodh Gaya, a hundred kilometers south of Patna. From the ancient capital, Pātaliputra (Patna), Emperor Chandragupta Maurya (321–297 B.C.E.) conquered west to the Indus and east to Assam, and his grandson Aṣoka adopted Buddhism, spreading the new dharma throughout his empire and beyond. Buddhist monastic universities at Nalanda, Vaishali, and Odantapuri furthered the development of Buddhist thought in later centuries. (The name of the state, Bihar, is derived from the numerous *vihāra,* or Buddhist stupas, that dot the landscape.) Vaishali was the birthplace of Mahavir, founder of Jainism, and Patna, the birthplace of Guru Gobind Singh, Sikhism's tenth guru. All the major Buddhist sites remain places of pilgrimage for Buddhists from around the world, especially Bodh Gaya, and Patna is sacred to Sikhs.

The North Ganga Plain was always somewhat remote from the political developments in the south, both in ancient times and today. From the terai region to the Ganga, rich rice lands and isolation have promoted a conservative culture dominated by Brahmans, especially in the center of this region known from earliest sources as Mithila or Videha. Here, except for Vaishali in the southernmost part, Hinduism resisted the heterodoxies of Buddhism and Jainism. According to the *Rāmāyaṇa,* this was the site of King Janaka's (Sīta's father) kingdom, and Sīta herself was a princess of Mithila. *Yajṇavalkyasmṛti,* the *Dharmaṣastra,* which is second only to Manu in codifying Hindu social practices, originated in Mithila, where Yajṇāvalkya was said to have lived and taught in ancient times, although the text is from a later period (perhaps the seventh century). And it was Brahman theorists in Mithila who, in response to Buddhist heterodoxy, first developed *Mīmāṃsā* philosophy, which sought a philosophical basis for a return to the authority of the Vedic texts.

The dominant landowning castes of Bihar are Brahman, Kayastha, Bhumihar, and Rajput, who together make up 13 percent of the population. Ahirs, Kurmis, Koiris, and Dhanuk are large and politically important middle-ranking castes, and among the twenty-three scheduled castes are Dusadh, Dhobi, Bhumij, Chamar, Musahar, and Pasi, the great majority of whom live in separate hamlets in Bihari villages. On the Chotanagpur Plateau are some of the largest tribal populations of India, second only to the northeastern region of India. The tribal population constitutes 8.29 percent of the total population of Bihar. Many of these are Hinduized and even consider themselves Hindu castes (e.g., Kharwar, Bhumij, Chero) or at least have adopted the cultural practices of their Hindu neighbors (e.g., Santhal, Oraon, Munda, and Ho). On the other hand, large numbers of Santhal, Oraon, Munda, Kharia, and Korwa have converted to Christianity. Because they also happen to inhabit Bihar's great industrial region on the Chotanagpur Plateau, where 20 percent of India's mineral resources are located, they are becoming a laboring underclass in cities like Dhanbad and Jamshedpur.

Folklore traditions follow linguistic divisions in Bihar. The languages of the Gangetic Plain region of Bihar are descended from one of the two *prakrits* (colloquial languages) spoken in ancient India, the Māgadhī language of the Mauryan empire. George Grierson, in his *Linguistic Survey of India,* classified these speech forms as "Bihari," a branch of Hindustani, with Bhojpuri (western), Maithili (north), and Magahi (central) as principal dialects. However, there really is no Bihari language, and most linguists today consider these distinct languages, rather than mere dialects.

It would be difficult to find a Bihar village, whether in caste or tribal regions of the state, without a rich selection of women's folk songs for auspicious occasions. Among the Bhojpuri-speaking peoples of the western districts of Bihar, women's songs are most often associated with rituals, particularly weddings, or with childbirth. Wedding songs are specific to sections of the rite itself but often consist of themes counter to the intention of ritual acts: the bride's sorrow at departing for her husband's house; insults to the groom, his family, and even the pandit. *Sohar*s are songs sung at or for the birth of a son. A separate class of songs is that of men's devotional songs, for instance, the *harikīrtan.* These are more heavily rhythmic and sung at specifically musical gatherings on occasions other than those devoted to women's songs.

The Maithili-speaking region of north Bihar, between the Gandak and Kosi rivers, is a distinct cultural region whose people have a high degree of self-consciousness as Maithils. Of the Bihar linguistic groups, only Maithili has a large written literature, perhaps because the medieval courts lavishly patronized the arts and the dominant Brahman caste was so oriented toward philosophy and scholarship. Of the numerous literary artists of Mithila, one name must be singled out, that of Vidyapati (b. 1350), a poet in the fourteenth-century court of Ṣiva Simha. He wrote in a wide range of lyrical styles, in Maithili rather than Sanskrit, and his songs are still sung in Mithila villages. It is difficult, and perhaps not useful, to distinguish between folk and literary forms, as they tend to form a spectrum rather than two separate classes. Of the many forms of song prevalent in Mithila, one must mention the *tirahūti* love songs for which Vidyapati is famous; *samdauni,* sung as a bride is leaving for her husband's house; *lagani,* sung by village women in the early morning while grinding grain; soha̩r, birth songs; and *nacārī,* songs of ecstatic devotion to Śiva.

Among Bihar's tribal groups, where the sexual life of young people is less controlled by *pardā* (rules of exclusion), another class of love songs celebrates the surreptitious encounters of young lovers. These are sung not at weddings but at public festivals, accompanied by flirtatious girls performing line dances, such as the *lagre* and *dahar* of the Santals.

In the visual arts, Bihar is famous for two somewhat recent traditions, the Patna style of painting, and Mithila folk art. The Patna style was a short-lived, Mughal-influenced form produced for the wealthy Hindu and Muslim elite in the eighteenth century. On sheets of glass, mica, and ivory, artisans painted miniature portraits and themes of Indian festivals and social life. Mithila art has become a thriving new tradition in recent decades as Maithil women adapt traditional wedding themes from their wall art to a paper medium. A great deal of attention has been paid to this art in Europe, North America, and Japan, and some of the best women painters have earned international reputations and awards from the Indian government. The art in its original form was, and still is, painted on the inner walls of courtyards and, especially, in the nuptial chamber, the *kohbarā ghar,* bringing the witness of the gods and certain magical themes to bless the union and ensure love and fertility.

Bihar has one classical dance form, that of *chau,* a masked dance performed annually during the festival of Chait Parva under the sponsorship of the Maharaja of Sareikella. Danced by males only, chau appears to have originated in a stylized dance of the hunt or warfare. In Mithila, folk dances invoke the gods and goddesses in such versions as *Rām-līla nāc, bhagat nāc, kirtaniya nāc, kunjvawi nāc, vidyapat nāc,* and *pūja ārati nāc*.

Folk traditions among tribal groups are quite distinct from those of caste-based villages, even where they have been influenced by Hinduism. In Hindu villages, performance events such as singing, rituals, and worship are almost always family or caste affairs, and the large public festival is rare. Among the tribal communities, however, there are large public festivals whose central rites are acts of devotion to the ancestors, spirits, or a major pan-Indian deity such as Śiva. Hook-swinging (*patta*) is practiced by Santals during *Baisakh* (April–May) or after finding a milk-giving stone incarnation of Śiva. Many other festivals involve tree worship, such as the widespread *Karam* festival, in which branches of the karam tree are brought from the jungle and set up in the village dance ground, where they are worshiped through dance, animal sacrifice, and the recitation of the myth of Karmu and Dharmu. These events are often ecstatic and orgiastic. Other popular tribal festivals are *Chata, Baha, Sarhul,* and *Sohrai*.

References

Archer, W. G. 1974. *The hill of flutes; Life, love, and poetry in tribal India, a portrait of the Santals*. Pittsburgh: University of Pittsburgh Press.

———. 1985. *Songs for the bride; Wedding rites of rural India*. New York: Columbia University Press.

Henry, Edward O. 1988. *Chant the names of God: Music and culture in Bhojpuri-speaking India*. San Diego: San Diego State University Press.

Mishra, Jayakanta. 1976. *History of Maithili literature*. New Delhi: Sahitya Akademi.

Roy Chaudhury, P. C. 1968. *Folk tales of Bihar*. Delhi: Sahitya Akademi.

Singh, Ajit K. 1982. *Tribal festivals of Bihar*. New Delhi: Concept Publishing Company.

Troisi, J. 1979. *Tribal religion: Religious beliefs and practices among the Santals*. New Delhi: Manohar.

Vidyarthi, L. P., and V. S. Upadhyay. 1980. *The Kharia: Then and now. A comparative study of hill, Dhelki, and Dudh Kharia of the central-eastern region of India*. New Delhi: Concept Publishing Company.

CAROLYN BROWN HEINZ

SEE ALSO

Birth Songs; *Cait Parab; Chau;* Mithila Painting; Myth; *Nāca; Rām Līla; Rāmāyaṇa*

BIHISHTĪ ZĒWAR

Bihishtī Zēwar is a work originally published in Urdu, circa 1906, and intended to be a complete guide for the education of Muslim girls from the perspective of the reformers associated with the North Indian seminary at Deoband (founded in 1867). The work has been translated into several Indian languages, including English, and has been continuously reprinted, often in brocade bindings suitable for presentation to a bride. The author of the work, Maulānā Ashraf ʻAlī Thānawī (1864–1943), was a graduate of Deoband, a scholar of *ḥadīth* (the narrations of Prophetic sayings and behavior), and an influential Sufi guide. Particularly in book Six, entitled "A Discussion of Custom by Category," he dissuaded girls from continuing the local customs (variously referred to as *rasm, riwāj, dastūr*) which were often the particular domain of women and which he deemed in conflict with the moral guidelines of the *sharīʻa* (norms and law).

Thānawī does not oppose these customs simply because they are shared with non-Muslims, but, rather, measures each one by carefully testing it against such principles as the illegitimacy of seeking public approval; the error of making what is optional obligatory (especially if what is obligatory, like prayer, is neglected); the failure to clearly state and pay promptly the wages of menials; the prohibition of incurring debt unnecessarily; or the error of causing hardship unnecessarily, as in the seclusion and lack of proper food and air prior to the wedding of the young bride, or the damage to health from inappropriate food and revelry. Book Six thus serves as a guide to the logic of moral reasoning engaged in by a scholar trained in the high Islamic tradition of ḥadīth and *fiqh* (jurisprudence), presented with verve as he catalogues, for example, some 103 points of error associated with weddings and deploys to ironic effect the rhetoric of speaking of custom as a law school of its own.

The book also, however, implicitly serves to document the very customs he condemns, customs current in the social milieu of well-born Muslims of North India at the turn of the century. While many seem arbitrary and trivial, together these customs marked distinctive styles of social relations and religious practice. Many customary practices sustained basic social institutions, among them *ne'ota,* the system of delayed reciprocity in which relationships are constituted by those who bring gifts for life-cycle rituals in the expectation that they will get such gifts in turn; *bhāt,* the practice of gifts to daughters and sisters that substitute, Thānawī insists, for the legitimate inheritance denied to women by local custom; and *jajmānī* (although the term is not used), the reciprocal obligations on such occasions as marriage enacted between patrons and menials (who receive gifts variously called *chattīs thāniya, purōtā, nēg, rīt,* and *bērgharī*). Other customs defined a mediational religious style associated with saintly intercession.

In condemning many customary practices, reformers like Thānawī were in accord with more Westernized reformers as well as with Hindu reformers who raised similar issues. Indian reformers, across the board, condemned extravagance and conspicuous consumption, and generally discouraged detailed rituals that tied people to auspicious times and places. The dissemination of normative standards fostered new self-consciousness not only between religious groups but also within those groups, as the more urban, educated, and well-born distinguished themselves from co-religionists deemed ignorant and given to error. Among other Urdu reformist texts of this period, Khwāja Altāf Ḥusain Ḥālī's *Majālis un-Nissa* (Convocations of Women) (1874) is also notable for two lists of "superstitious" folk customs associated with women.

References

Altāf Ḥusain Ḥālī Khwāja. 1986 [1874]. Majalis un-nissa. In *Voices of silence: English translation of Ḥālī's "Majalis un-Nissa" and "Chup ki Dad,"* ed. and trans. Gail Minault, 31–137. Delhi: Chanakya Publications.

Ashraf Alī Thānawī Maulānā. 1991 [1906]. *Perfecting women: Maulānā Ashraf 'Alī Thānawī's Bihishti Zewar,* ed. and trans. Barbara D. Metcalf. Berkeley: University of California Press.

BARBARA D. METCALF

SEE ALSO

Colonialism and Folklore; Gender and Folklore; Ḥadīth; *Jajmani;* Islam; Life Cycle Rituals; Muslim Folklore and Folklife

BIRBAL

Birbal (1528–1586) was a close companion of the Mughal emperor Akbar (r. 1556–1605), and has become well known in South Asian folklore as the hero of popular Akbar and Birbal tales. He was the son of Ganga Das, a Brahman of modest means from the district of Kalpi (near modern Kanpur). His real name was Mahesh Das, but he wrote his compositions under the pen name of "Brahm kavi" when he worked as court poet and bard at the Rajput court of Amber, prior to entering Akbar's service. Before this, he was employed by Raja Ram Chand at the kingdom of Rewa in central India.

Birbal joined the Mughal court in the early years of Akbar's reign (probably in 1562, when the king married the Amber princess). Akbar first gave him the title of *kab rai* (king of poets), and in 1572 bestowed on the minstrel the title *raja bir bar* (great brave or warrior). At that time, the mountain kingdom of Nagarkot (Kangra) was ordered to be seized and given to him as a fief. Contemporary Muslim historians referred to him as Birbar, a name today pronounced as Birbal.

Fourteen years older than Akbar, this charismatic Brahman bard was a powerful influence on the impressionable young king. He was hated by pious Muslims such as the historian Badaoni, who accused him of taking Akbar away from Islam by teaching him Hindu rituals such as sun worship. Along with liberal Muslim courtiers like Abul Faẓl, Birbal supported the syncretistic religious ideas of the visionary king. When Akbar formulated the *dīn illahī,* his so-called new religion, Birbal was the only Hindu courtier to officially join the emperor's circle of disciples.

Like many of Akbar's top nobles, Birbal was a man of versatile talents. He was a poet and a soldier who fought in several battles. He accompanied Akbar on his famous forced march to Gujarat in 1573, and also on the boat expedition to the eastern provinces in 1574. He held the military rank of a commander of two thousand when he was killed fighting Afghan tribes in Swat in February 1586, at the age of fifty-eight. Birbal's body was never recovered. His death is said to have grieved the emperor more than the loss of any other noble.

Birbal had served the king for half his reign, rising to take a place among the inner circle of nobles. He remained mostly at court by Akbar's side as an intimate confidant and friend, rather than as a minister with executive responsibilities. However, he was occasionally employed on diplomatic missions to Hindu kingdoms, including that of his former employer, Raja Ram Chand of Rewa. He was also sent on fact-finding assignments, such as investigating charges of government corruption in the Punjab in 1578. He was particularly concerned about the conditions of oppressed and needy people. When Akbar founded the Department of Administration in 1583, Birbal, along with other nobles, was put in charge of justice.

It is Birbal in the role of arbiter of justice that we see most often in the folk tales about him. In these stories, he uses his common sense and knowledge of human nature to solve cases brought before him. In other stories, he outwits the emperor or diplomatically puts him in his place. The close relationship of Akbar and Birbal is a historical fact, but the folk tales are part of a long-standing tradition of stories told about other courtier and king pairs in India. Jokes and anecdotes—some ranging toward the bawdy and obscene—are also told about Akbar and Birbal, most of them composed long after their time. Conversely, some of the motifs in Birbal stories are present in Persian, Arabic, and Sufi tales dating back several centuries.

References

Abdu-l-Qādir ibn-i-Mulūk S͟hāh, al-Badāonī. 1986. *Muntakhabut-t-Tawarikh* (The reign of Akbar: The choicest of histories), trans. W. H. Lowe and W. Haig. Vols. 2 and 3. Reprint edition. Delhi: Renaissance.

Abu'l Fazl Allāmī. 1989a. *Āīn-i-Akbarī* (Regulations of Akbar), trans. H. Blochmann. Vol. 1. Reprint edition. Delhi: Low Price Publications.

———. 1989b. *The Akbarnāmā* (Akbar's biography), trans. H. Beveridge. Vols. 2 and 3. Reprint edition. Delhi: Low Price Publications.

Aḥmad, K͟hwāja Niẓāmuddīn. 1936. *Ṭabaqāt-i-Akbarī* (History of Akbar's reign), trans. B. De. Vol. 2. Calcutta: Royal Asiatic Society of Bengal.

Marzolph, Ulrich, and Ingeborg Baldauf. 1990. Hodscha Nasreddin. In *Enzyklopädie des Märchens* (Encyclopedia of fairy tales), ed. Rolf Wilhelm Brednich, cols. 1127–1151. Berlin: Walter de Gruyter.

Naim, C. M. 1995. Popular jokes and political history: The case of Akbar, Birbal and Mulla Do-Piyaza. *Economic and Political Weekly* 17 June: 1456–1464.

Ramanujan, A. K., ed. 1991. *Folktales from India*. New York: Pantheon Books.

Sarin, Amita V. Akbar and Birbal (unpublished manuscript).

Sinha, Parmeshwar Prasad. 1980. *Raja Birbal life and times*. Patna: Janaki Prakashan.

AMITA VOHRA SARIN

SEE ALSO

Character Stereotypes; Heroes and Heroines; Mullā Nasruddīn

BIRTH SONGS

In rural areas of North and Central India, family and neighborhood groups of nonspecialist women celebrate the birth of a child by singing special songs at the home of the newborn. (One such performance is heard on Henry, 1981.) Because they are considered especially auspicious (*maṇgal*), these songs are also sung on other inaugural occasions and on appropriate festivals, such as *Kṛṣṇa Janamāśthamī*, as well. The songs are called by different names in different regions: *sohar* and *badhāī* in Uttar Pradesh and Bihar, for example, and *halre* in the Mewari-speaking area of Rajasthan. A closely related song category in eastern Uttar Pradesh and Bihar is the *khilaunā* or *khelaunā* (toy), considered to be in a more humorous and lighter vein.

Certain groups of professional musicians also perform birth songs. One such group is the male *pavaria*s (*pauria*s) of eastern Uttar Pradesh and Bihar (heard on Henry, 1981), but most notable are the *hijrā*s found across North India—surgically emasculated males who dress in women's clothing (see Nanda, 1999). (A sohar well performed by *hijrā*s is heard on the Tewari recording.) Groups of both types appear at the homes of the newborn and sing birth songs, and sometimes obscene insult songs as well, until they feel they have been appropriately compensated.

The texts of birth songs can be divided into three types. The first describes the events surrounding the birth of a child in Hindu mythology (Rāma, Kṛṣṇa, Gaṇeśa). The second deals with childbirth in the context of family relationships (such as the conflict between a woman and her mother- or sisters-in-law). These document the stereotypic tensions of joint family life. The third type is curious in that the texts have little or nothing to do with childbirth. They are mnemonic devices for ritual procedures, telling where and how certain deities are to be worshiped and what kinds of practices should be undertaken in pursuit of specific goals, such as fasts for getting a good husband. Tunes for birth songs vary regionally; for example, Bhojpuri sohar tunes differ from Maithili sohar tunes. Within a region, one tune may be used more than any other for birth song texts, but in neither Bhojpuri nor Maithili regions is *only* one tune used for sohar texts (Henry 1998, 2000a, 2000b).

Birth songs, in text and context, are related to the preference for male offspring. Tewari (1974) and Bryce (1961) both provide texts of birth songs indicating that female offspring are less desirable, and Henry (1988) asserts that in some families and communities, birth songs are sung only when males are born. This kind of sex discrimination, seen more at upper-caste levels, is apparently declining, and the songs are sung more often for both sexes among all castes.

The singing of birth songs has obvious consequences: it signals nearby residents of the blessed event; it transmits religious beliefs and practices; and "Listening to the conversation and the songs young girls at the songfest receive early training in what to expect when they reach childbearing age" (Jacobson, 1980).

References

Arya, U. 1968. *Ritual songs and folksongs of the Hindus of Surinam.* Leiden: E.J. Brill.

Bryce, L. Winifred. 1961. *Women's folk songs of Rajputana.* New Delhi: Ministry of Information and Broadcasting, Government of India.

Henry, Edward O. 1981. *Chant the names of God: Village music of the Bhojuri-speaking area of India.* Cambridge, Mass.: Rounder Records.

———. 1988. *Chant the names of God: Music and culture in Bhojpuri-speaking India.* San Diego: San Diego State University Press.

———. 1998. Maithil women's song: Distinctive and endangered species. *Ethnomusicology* 42(3): 415–440.

———. 2000a. Folk song genres and their melodies in India: Music use and genre process. *Asian Music* 31(2): 71–106.

———. 2000b. *Women's folk songs from India.* Recorded in India in 1995 and 1999. Cambridge, Mass.: Rounder Records. Compact disc.

Jacobson, Doranne. 1980. Golden handprints and red-painted feet: Hindu childbirth rituals in central India. In *Unspoken worlds: Women's religious lives in non-Western cultures,* ed. Nancy Falk and Rita Gross. New York: Harper & Row.

Nanda, Serena. 1999. *Neither man nor woman: The hijras of North India.* 2d ed. Belmont, Calif.: Wadsworth.

Tewari, Laxmi G. 1974. Folk music of India: Uttar Pradesh. Ph.D. diss., Wesleyan University.

———. n.d. *Folk music of India (Uttar Pradesh).* LP recording. Lyrichord LLST 7271.

EDWARD O. HENRY

SEE ALSO

Hijra (Transvestite) Performances; Life Cycle Rituals; Wedding Songs; Women's Songs

BOW SONG (*VIL PĀṬṬU*)

The bow song, which takes its name from a long hunting bow (*vil*) used for singing (*pāṭṭu*), is heard as ritual performance in local temple festivals throughout the southern districts of Tamil Nadu and sparsely in southern areas of Kerala and hill districts between Kerala and Tamil Nadu. This Tamil tradition belongs to a cluster of traditions along the western and southern coasts of India, such as (*teyyam* and *bhūta kōla,* in which singing the stories of deified local heroes and heroines causes spirit possession by the hero-god at whose shrine the performance occurs.

A bow song group consists of at least five musician-singers. A lead singer, male or female, plays the long bow (ten to fourteen feet) by striking its string with sticks and thus shaking the bells hanging from its wooden frame. A man plays a clay pot (*kuṭam*) by slapping a paddle on its mouth. Another plays a small, hourglass-shaped drum (*tuṭukai*). Either a man or a woman plays a pair of wooden blocks (*kaṭṭai*). And a man or woman plays a pair of small hand cymbals (*jālra*). Each group is led by an *aṇṇāvi,* or guru, who is often the lead singer. Although the bow, whose length and style of playing are unique among the musical bows of the world, is visually prominent, the drum is musically and ritually more important because its rhythms stimulate spirit possession.

Bow songs are performed in temple festivals, although in recent years troupes have begun to perform them in secular settings, such as school events and political campaigns. The music of the bow singers is also regularly heard on radio and occasionally on television. Each village in the region contains at least one, and usually many, small temples to local gods and goddesses. These temples (*kōvil*) range from stone temples to painted stones and trees; a distinctive kind of temple in the bow song region is a three-to-six-foot-tall obelisk (*pīṭam*) made of baked clay, covered in limestone paste, and mounted on a platform. Each temple contains a central deity and many associated deities, who are figures in the main deity's story or characters in their own stories. These stories are sung during the several days of the annual temple festival (*koṭai,* "offering") to honor the central and allied deities at the temple.

In local terms, the narrative world of the bow song is divided into "birth" (*piranta*) and "death" (*aḻinta* or *veṭṭupaṭṭa*) stories (*katai*). Almost without exception, birth stories are narratives about goddesses and gods of regional or even pan-Indian provenance—Śāsta, Kālī Ammaṉ, Muttār Ammaṉ—who are born in Kailāsa and descend to earth to inflict injury on the impious and to protect their worshipers. These regional deities are assimilated into the bow song world by the inclusion of local place names in their story, which describes a journey that ends when the deity takes up residence at the temple in whose festival the story is being performed. Death stories, on the other hand, are local histories, biographies of men and women who died a premature, cruel death, usually for challenging or transgressing caste boundaries, in disputes over land and love. Many death stories are elaborations of events in family, caste, and regional history, particularly conflicts between low castes (Paṟaiyaṉ, Cekkiliyār, Nāṭar) and high castes (Piḷḷai, Brahman). In the very popular story of Muttuppaṭṭaṉ, for instance, a Brahman man dies after marrying two women of an untouchable caste.

Although the bow song is the most common and important public performance event in the southern half of Tamil Nadu, its history is unclear. The earliest reference is a sixteenth-century poem, but the tradition is probably much older. Some extant manuscripts are dated to the late seventeenth century. Many bow song texts are written on palm leaf; several have been printed as chapbooks; and a few published with a scholarly

Bow song performance of Tampimar story, from palm-leaf manuscript. Tamil Nadu, India, 1978. © Stuart Blackborn

commentary. The language of the bow songs is a provincial learned Tamil, organized by conventional Tamil rhyme schemes: alliterative initial sounds of half-lines (*moṉai*) and of full lines (*etukai*). The pan-Indian scheme of repeating the last sound of one line in the first sound of the next line ("end-beginning," *antāti*) is also typical. As with most orally performed narratives, formulas are common, but the emphasis seems to be on memorization rather than improvisation. Memorization serves a ritual goal, too, for only an accurate narration of the story is thought to successfully invoke the presence of the deity. Historical veracity ensures ritual efficacy.

Reference

Blackburn, Stuart. 1988. *Singing of birth and death: Texts in performance*. Philadelphia: University of Pennsylvania Press.

STUART BLACKBURN

SEE ALSO

Bhūta Kōla; Epic; *Pāḍdana;* Tamil Nadu; *Teyyam; Tōṟṟam*

BRAHUI FOLK LITERATURE

The Brahui are the sole remaining Dravidian language-speaking population in what is now Balochistan in northwest Pakistan and southern Afghanistan, possibly descendants of the Indus civilization which preceded the arrival of Indo-European language-speakers in the Indus Valley. The Brahui, like the Balochi, are thought to have entered the Balochistan area as pastoral nomads, and subsequently for the most part settled into sedentary and semi-sedentary lifestyles. Most are now bilingual in Balochi and Brahui language.

History of the Brahui remains conjectural prior to the late sixteenth century when, following the end of the Rind Balochi sovereignty, an interregnum ensued during which the Arghun (Mongol-descended) Shah Beg raided from Kandahar into what is now Balochistan and Sind. In approximately 1604 C.E., Rais Ahmed, a nobleman of the Marwari tribe of Brahui, attained control over Kalāt in the highlands, which had remained free of Shah Beg's control and the center of Brahui population. In the mid-eighteenth century Brahui *khans* (chieftains) were still in control of Kalāt, south of Quetta, and sided with the Afghan Pashtun Ahmed Shah

Durrani in his rivalry with the Mughul emperors of Delhi. When a combined Hindu-Sikh force retook Lahore from Durrani control in 1758, Nāṣir, the Brahui khan of Kalāt, formed a Brahui-Balochi alliance to declare independence from Ahmed Shah Durrani as well. When Ahmed Shah was able to regain control of the area, however, Nāṣir Khan managed to restore an alliance with him while the Durrani forces continued incursions into the Punjab and Mughal territory to the south. In contemporary Pakistan, Brahui culture and politics are closely intertwined with Balochi. Brahui intellectuals have established a Brahui Academy located in Quetta, from which they have published literary works and collections of Brahui oral poetry and prose in chapbook form.

Brahui language is rich in oral literature, both prose and poetry. Prose genres include stories and tales, proverbs and riddles. Named song genres include *lailī mōr* (love songs), *bar nāzanā, laiko, hāllo* (marriage songs), *lōlī* (lullabies), *modā* (elegy), and others. Kamil Qadri wrote in 1972, "The antiquity of Brahui literature cannot be ascertained because it was not written but memorized and orally transmitted from generation to generation. In this process every poem or story has undergone change. A study of what is extant reveals that Brahuis have forgotten their past traditions."

Brahui folk stories are mostly created or re-created by nomads, shepherds, and farmers for the entertainment of their children and other family members. Mothers would tell stories to their children before going to bed. One can distinguish three kinds of folk stories popular in Brahui literature: those which are indigenous to Brahui language, those translated from other languages, and a third category of non-Brahui origin which have been "Brahui-ized." Some themes are pure Brahui, such as legends about the *mammā,* a large apelike creature known for its physical strength and resemblance to humans, and alleged to have been numerous in the past. Stories pertaining to kings, ministers, princes and princesses, merchants, deities, fairies, and so forth appear to have been translated from neighboring traditions, such as Persian. Another class of stories, distinguishable on a content basis, criticizes the cruel supremacy of the figures of *sardār* (tribal chief), *takarī* (notable persons), and landlords from the point of view of the oppressed classes. This criticism could be couched in symbolic terms, in portrayals in animal fables of cruel animals such as wolves, lions, snakes, and so on.

While the language of Brahui stories tends to be simple and understandable to both children and adults, portrayals of animals and birds have symbolic values and shades of meaning. In poetry, animals are also used symbolically, with reference to qualities such as color, speed, gait. Typical animal symbols are lion for bravery, crow for cleverness, dog for faithfulness, fox for greed, sheep for simplicity, ox for power, camel for tolerance.

Brahui folk song genres are mentioned above. In a poetry largely devoted to romantic themes, women in Brahui are depicted typically as *zebā* or *zebjān* (beautiful), *zebal* (pretty), *phuljān* or *ghuljān* (flower-like), *māhlanj* (lovely as moonlight), *bijlī* (electrical), *laadi* (delicately nurtured), *girdi* (with a beautiful gait), *mandar* (tiny, dwarf), *kelūṛā* (good player), *jānal* (part of the body), and *sauzō* (brownish). The beloved in Brahui folk song is thus portrayed with respect to her gait, color, attitude, and behavior.

Though no field studies exist to confirm it, Brahui folk songs are generally regarded as having been composed by shepherds and farmers during field work, and in major proportion by women. Besides romantic themes, Brahui folk songs also take up other human issues, such as shortage of water and rain, women's and men's labor, food shortages, hardships of the mountains and nomadic life, shepherding, travel difficulties, danger from wildlife, and difficulties of communication and information.

Shortage of water and rain is a common difficulty for Brahui nomads in their arid environment. A young shepherd boy sings a song to woo his beloved, which calls up a picturesque pastoral scene:

O! Zebo nanē dīr ete	O! Zebo (beautiful lady), give me water,
dīk nā hanēn ō nanē dīr ete	Your water is sweet, give me water,
gōdī gidān nā nanē dīr ete	O! Princess of the tent, give me water,
dīk nā hanēn ō nanē dīr ete	your water is sweet, give me water.

(Qadrī 1972:166)

While Brahui traditional norms do not favor love stories, it is interesting to note that the Brahui beloved is portrayed in poetry not as a young girl but as a married woman:

Gī kew nē naz gūlī pāt mana barī ā na
bala as tammānē śuminā are ā nā

My Beloved! I narrate you and your hard work,
Because your husband is a lazy and idle person.
(Mengal 1992:61)

Lailī mōr verses are composed of two-line stanzas. In one line, usually the first, a social or general problem is described, and the other line refers to the beauty, gait, or coquetry of a lady:

Cotolī cuka sē āsmān ṭi zigar kēk	A cotoli [sparrow] prays to his creator while flying,
lailī kanā tūsunē ustaṭi fikar a kēk	My beloved is sad due to life's hardships.
Bar kanā lailī mōr nokar nā jinda nā	Come, my Beloved, I am your servant,
sangati tamane mosum e sind a nā	There's a long journey before us up to Sind.

Bar nāzanā is the shortest form in Brahui poetry, comprising three verses in monorhyme and a fourth line refrain of *bar nāzana ji nāz a nā*. It was sung with *sironz*, a fiddle-like musical instrument:

Khwaja kanā nī us khudā	God! My master,
kapēs kanē dost ān jitā	Do not separate me from my Beloved,
katum kana ne kim fidā	I sacrifice my life for you,
Bar nāzanā ji nāz a nā	O! My Beloved, come with lovely gait.

Brahui folk songs differ from those of neighboring languages by their characteristic tunes. *Laiko* designates both the poetic form and a common tune of *zairok* poetry. It has three lines, in 5–7–5 syllables, like Japanese haiku. Also characteristic of Brahui folk songs are themes reflecting nomadic life, including allusions to difficulties of migration between the Kāchhī (the plains of Balochistan, now Sibi and Naseer districts) and Khurasān (the mountain region, presently Quetta and Kalat divisions) in search of pastures.

Brahui folk songs are most often sung without accompaniment. Instrumental music is made, however, by both Brahui men and women. The musical instruments most widely in amateur use include the *sironz* (a fiddle) and *dambura* (a plucked stringed instrument), both men's instruments, and the *daira* (frame drum like a tambourine), generally a women's instrument.

Epic poems are performed by specialist poets belonging to lower-status groups corresponding to scheduled castes in India, called *Lorī* in Brahui. Their traditional occupations in Brahui society are or were to serve people on the occasion of wedding ceremonies and funerary rituals, to play the *dhol* drums for marriage ceremonies or other festivals, to create and sing epic poetry during tribal warfare, and to make and repair agricultural tools and weapons, including guns, for the tribesmen.

Proverbs are plentiful in Brahui prose and occasionally found in Brahui poetry. In folk stories, proverbs are often densely employed and enjoyed for their cultural references, ease of understanding to those who know the culture, and wit. A folk story could contain from five to fifty proverbs, the most commonly used being those related to human feelings, natural beauty, and animal behavior. Conversational proverb use is also common in nomad camps and villages, especially by elders giving advice and directions to younger persons. Some Brahui proverbs retain very old morphological features of the language. Some frequently heard examples whose import will be easily comprehensible beyond Brahui contexts include

Duz nā řīš a kakasē	A guilty conscience needs no accuser.
Hušāřta xarwālhāk uff kēk panerte	A burnt child dreads the fire.
Tānke xāxar kappēs molh mafak	No smoke without a fire.
Amar dasōs hundun rūtos	As you sow, so shall you reap.

The paucity of Brahui proverbs in poetry is partly due to the length of proverbial phrases, many of which would be difficult to condense into the typically short lines of Brahui poetry. Yet proverbs do appear in folk and classical Brahui poems. Modern poets and short story writers also employ them. Proverbs themselves may take verse form. *Xan xan ān šarmṛngik* (equivalent to "out of sight, out of mind") has been rendered in couplet form as *ballah nā dosti ganda e, xan xan nā šarminda e*. Tājal, the poet larueate of Brahui, also uses proverbs, as in *ranga ṭi tūt ān zardalū zoor ganda nā wagē gut ā tour,* an allusion to the appearance of fruits, the gist of which is "first impresson is last impression."

In Brahui as in Balochi, a distinct genre of proverbs is recognized as such because they possess complete background stories, necessary for their comprehension. One well-known example is the saying *balwān nā barām*. The story goes that a foolish, simple man, Balwān (or Balo Khān), was engaged, but his father-in-law was greedy. He asked Balwān to bring the required bride-price to marry his daughter, so Balwān went to hie relatives and collected the stipulated amount. On his return, the father-in-law told him to bring more money, and this continued for many rounds, so that Balwān never succeeded in marrying and eventually died single. Now when work or plans are too prolonged, it is said, "This is like the marriage of Balwān."

References

Baluch, Muhammad Sardar Khan. 1984. *Literary history of the Baluchis,* 2 vols. Quetta, Pakistan: Balochi Academy.

Brahui, Abdul Rehman. 1979. *Wašetāk*. Quetta: Brahui Academy.

———. 1993. *Gwārikh*. 2nd ed. Quetta: Brahui Academy.

Dupree, Louis. 1973. *Afghanistan*. Princeton: Princeton University Press.

Mengal, Afzal. 1991. *Lalī Mōr*. Quetta: Brahui Academy.

———. 1992. *Shōshing*. Quetta: Brahui Academy.
———. 1994. *Chōtōlī*. Quetta: Brahui Academy.
Qadri, Kamil. 1972. All about Brahuis. *International Journal of Dravidian Linguistics* (Dept. of Linguistics, Kerala University), 1.
Sabir, Abdul Razzak. 1988. *Kalam-e Tājal*. Quetta: Brahui Adabi Society.
———. 1989. *Shāhī Kharwār*. Quetta: Shāll Publishers.
———. 1993. Descriptions of animals and birds in Brahui literature. In *Studies in symbolism and iconology*, vol. 7. Tokyo: Wako University.
Titus, Paul, ed. 1997. *Marginality and modernity: Ethnicity and change in post-colonial Balochistan*. Karachi: Oxford University Press.

ABDUL RAZZAK SABIR AND MARGARET A. MILLS

SEE ALSO

Balochistan: Oral Tradition; *Mammā;* Proverbs; Riddle, Balochi

BRASS BANDS

Private brass bands play a traditional role in wedding and other processions in India, Pakistan, and Nepal. South Asian processional musicians began the transition from indigenous instruments to European instruments in the mid-nineteenth century. To the extent that there is a standard ensemble, it is comprised of between eight and fifty bandsmen performing on clarinet, trumpet, and euphonium, together with snare and tenor drums. Saxophones, valve trombones, and E-flat clarinets are also found. Indigenous drums, the barrel-shaped *dholak* or *nāl,* are occasionally heard; the *tassa* (wide, shallow kettle drum) is frequently found in the central Deccan.

In the upper three-quarters of the subcontinent, the primary function of brass bands is to provide music for the *barāt,* the procession accompanying the bridegroom to his bride's home. Almost all Hindu and Sikh barāt, and most Muslim barāt as well, use brass bands. Bands may also be engaged to play for the *sanchaq* (a procession taking gifts to the bride) and the leave-taking *(bidāī)* when the bride leaves for her new home. Processions associated with circumcision (in Muslim communities), Sikh or Hindu religious events, or even (very rarely) funerals may also include brass bands.

A rich man celebrates a young daughter's vow to a goddess, © Diane Mines

Contemporary band repertoires are dominated by current Hindi film songs, but a small body of "standards" includes older, wedding-related film hits or other popular dance melodies. Some Western tunes, such as "Tequila," are also heard, although this song's introduction to South Asian culture was also mediated by the Hindi cinema. Some repertoire choices reflect the nature of the event, such as bidāī, when bands choose sad songs to accompany the conventionally sad mood of the bride's separation from her natal family. Slower, and often triple meter, songs (reflecting the six-beat *dādrā tāl* of Hindustani music) are common, as are tunes which approximate the Hindustani *rāg* (mode), *bhāīravī*. Pre-film melodies are rare, except in an obligatory march or fanfare with which many groups begin their performances. Most bands either know or are willing to learn regional folk or wedding songs to suit the ethnic identity of a particular patron family or group. For Sikh processions, such as on the birthday of the major Sikh gurus, many bands maintain a small repertoire of Punjabi and often religious songs.

Traditional elements of performance practice may be heard in some bands and in some regions; these include improvisation, heterophony, and vigorous syncopated solos by the drummers. These drum solos may sometimes require significant modification of the original melody, or may abandon the melody altogether, another traditional practice.

The historical antecedents of brass bands are earlier professional and semiprofessional processional ensembles. Except for isolated examples, most contemporary groups have no direct connection to earlier aristocratic or military bands. Many brass bands are owned and operated by families who previously had ensembles of *shahanāī* (a wooden, unkeyed conical double-reed instrument with a metal bell) and dholak drums. Musicians in this transitional period often combined indigenous and European instruments. These are still observable in some parts of the subcontinent. "Gunset" parties, made up of clarinets and indigenous drums, were one manifestation of this trend in southern and central India. Bagpipes were another intermediary instrument. As they gave up their shahanāī, many families spent a generation or more playing bagpipes, in response to popular taste, before proceeding to brass instruments. Bagpipe bands may still be found in parts of Bihar, Uttar Pradesh, and the Punjab.

The dominant social identity of most bandsmen in northern India is that of low-caste Muslim (often identified as Hāshimī, Khyām-kāne, or Rāīn) whose ancestors converted from Hinduism in the seventeenth and eighteenth centuries. In central India, Marāṭhā and scheduled caste families belonging to various branches of the large Dom caste are common. Especially in the Deccan, a large group of low-caste Māne-Yādhav (also referred to as Bajantrī) are both widespread and influential as brass bandsmen.

References

Booth, Gregory D. 1990. Brass bands: Tradition, change, and the mass media in Indian wedding music. *Ethnomusicology* 34(2): 245–262.

———. 1993. Traditional practice and mass mediated music in India. *International Review of the Aesthetics and Sociology of Music* 24(2): 159–174.

———. 1997. Socio-musical mobility among South Asian clarinet players. *Ethnomusicology* 41(3): 489–516.

GREGORY D. BOOTH

SEE ALSO
Circumcision; Colonialism and Folklore; Dom; Life Cycle Rituals; Marriage Ceremonies; Sikh Folklore

BRITISH FOLKLORE (IN SOUTH ASIA)

Britons who lived in South Asia during the historical period of colonization carried their folklore with them along with other aspects of their culture. These included both those who were educated, middle or upper-middle class, and those who can be called "common people," who might be most expected to perform folklore as conventionally conceived. However, there has been very little research on British folklore in South Asia.

Most Britons who went to South Asia did not settle there permanently, but rather undertook careers or spent military postings, returning periodically to Britain, where they finally retired. Thus, they were in contact with metropolitan British culture, but also formed a somewhat isolated subculture. Such genres as folk song flourished among the "other ranks" (nonofficer ranks) of the British Army stationed in South Asia and among those other working-class Britons who were sometimes employed in the lesser colonial services, such as railways and posts and telegraphs, and among those "Eurasians" with whom they sometimes merged. Drinking sessions in regimental canteens were a major occasion for singing. Regimental canteens might have particular musical reputations, with regiments that recruited from particular regions of the United Kingdom known for the local folksongs from that place.

The British "encounter" with South Asia also generated folklore. There were travelers' tales of sensational events from the earliest days of British commercial contact. East India Company records for Surat in 1698, for example, contain a story about a local monster without a head and with eyes in its breast. And several early sources recount the story of the Emperor Aurangzeb reproaching his daughter for appearing naked in public, when in fact she had been wearing seven layers of Dacca muslin (thus demonstrating the wonders of Indian fabric). As a British-Indian subculture of officials, army officers, and others evolved, its members developed a body of lore that included traditional customs, rituals, stories, and slang, whether borrowed from British or Indian sources, combined from the two, or created as something peculiar to the subculture itself. From the end of the nineteenth century, Britons going to postings in South Asia customarily donned their sun helmets at the Suez; on the voyage returning to Britain, they ceremonially cast them overboard at the same point, in a ritual that marked the boundary of their worlds. Some regimental officers' messes employed "lie books" in which tall tales were recorded. Traditional anecdotes reflected attitudes about lives lived as colonial expatriates. Legends about hauntings seem to have been a popular genre. In northern India these legends often involved the ghosts of Europeans killed during the "Mutiny" of 1857–1858.

It is difficult to say to what extent Britons assimilated South Asian folklore. European children in India certainly learned nursery rhymes in Indian vernaculars from family servants; however, because children customarily returned to Britain for schooling, these rhymes were often forgotten or became recollections of childhood rather than an ongoing British-Indian tradition. British residents in India also heard Asian folktales. Such occasions sometimes led to published collections, like *Old Deccan Days* (1869), which contains Gohanese Christian tales Mary Frere originally heard from her ayah (nurse-companion), Anna Liberata de Souza.

Folk ideas about South Asia, particularly India, played an important role in the British imagination. Although this is most easily seen in popular-culture sources, it is occasionally apparent in some folk genres, such as in the British broadside ballad "The Paisley Officer" (or "India's Burning Sands"), in which a woman, disguised as a soldier, follows her officer husband to India, only to perish there with him.

British folk traditions in South Asia certainly cannot be considered a major aspect of the folklore of the region, but are an interesting, if neglected, facet of the transplanting of European culture to South Asia during the colonial period.

References

Allen, Charles. 1976. *Plain tales from the Raj: Images of British India in the 20th century*. New York: St. Martin's Press.

Cox, Gordon. 1982. Songs and ballads of the wet canteen: Recollections of a British soldier in India. *Lore and Language* 3(7): 53–67.

de Caro, F. A., and Rosan A. Jordan. 1984. The wrong topi: Personal narratives, ritual, and the sun helmet as a symbol. *Western Folklore* 43: 233–248.

———. 1988–1991. Comentarios acerca del folklor de una élite colonial (Notes regarding the folklore of a colonial elite). *Cuadernos del Instituto de Antropología* (Notebooks of the Anthropology Institute) 13: 47–57.

Masters, John. 1956. *Bugles and a tiger*. New York: Viking Press.

FRANK DE CARO

SEE ALSO

Colonialism and Folklore; Frere, Mary Eliza Isabella; *Hobson-Jobson: The Anglo-Indian Dictionary;* Hospitality

BRITISH, FOLKLORE ABOUT

It was inevitable that during the many years of colonial rule in the subcontinent, local populations and British officials, missionaries, and their families interacted with each other in many ways. While there is abundant literature—both primary (as in British folklore collections and travelogues, for example) and secondary (subaltern scholarship, most notably)—on colonial imaginations of South Asian societies and cultures, there has not been as much study of South Asian perceptions and representations of the British. The evaluations were mutual, of course, and regional writing and everyday folklore richly display the wide variety of ways in which the social and political presence of the British was interpreted by local populations, who stereotyped, critiqued, caricatured, idolized—in short, counterimagined—colonial British culture and identity.

Perhaps the most frequent characterization of the British official in regional epics, songs, theater, and other narrative traditions is that of a politically repressive and imperialist figure. For instance, the well-known South Indian folk epic *Vīrapāṇḍya Kaṭṭapomman* dramatizes a historical encounter in the mid-eighteenth century between the British and the courageous Pāṇḍyan king. Kaṭṭapomman, who was hanged along with his brother for refusing to pay taxes. Versions of the epic depict the conflict as arising from the colonial system's incomprehension and intolerance of a rightful, ancient, kingly order that is usurped both to satisfy the personal ego of a particular British official, Major Jackson, and to enrich British coffers.

The forced collection of taxes by the British, commonly through aggressive means, is a recurrent theme in Indian folklore. A Gujarati legend recounts the exploits of a bandit, Babar Deva, who, after meeting a political activist, vows to fight British tax collectors rather than plunder indiscriminately. The self-declared authority of the East India Company and its officers is rarely accepted by protagonists in folk narratives, and more often than not, colonial power is proven to be subordinate to a higher moral or spiritual order to which the protagonist subscribes. Narayana Rao reports on two epics, the *Sanyāsamma Kathā* and the *Kāmamma Kathā,* both from West Godavari district of Andhra Pradesh, that depict the inversion of colonial authority by the supernatural powers of female protagonists.

Political events and policies of the colonial period provide a context for folklore about the British. In 1911, a British official, William Crooke, recorded women's songs in North India that registered their support for the Indian "Sepoy mutiny" of 1857. In theatrical and storytelling traditions like the *harīkathā* (story of Harī, or Viṣnu, narrated with music and singing), which provided a nationalist platform in the late nineteenth and early twentieth centuries, mythological battles between deities and demons symbolized confrontations between the Indians and the British. In Raja Rao's novel *Kanthapura* (1938), a folk singer enacts a harīkathā of the Gandhian struggle in which he depicts the British as demons. The 1875 Hindi play *The Blue Mirror (Nīldarpaṇa)* portrays a British planter as the rapist of an Indian peasant woman. This characterization, which exemplifies the depiction of British officials as power-wielding tyrants, predictably led to the hasty passing of a colonial censorship law, the 1876 Dramatic Performances Act.

In everyday speech in North India, the Indians referred to the British variously as *gōre-lōg* (white people), *safēd/lāl bandar* (white/red monkey), *Kompaniwāla* (East India Company people), *tōpiwāla* (hat wearer), or *firangī* (Frank derogatory for "Westerner"), with each of these carrying value judgments that ranged from oppressor and mischief-monger (monkey), to promiscuous individual (firangī in Urdu and Hindi also means "syphilis"). One Hindi folk song translated into English satirizes the British official as a tōpiwāla who assumes moral unaccountability beneath his topi:

> It [a topi] saves you from the heat;
> It saves [you] from the beatings;
> It creates fear among the natives.
> Having placed a hat upon your head,
> Commit all the atrocities you wish,
> It saves you from the eyes of God.
> (De Caro and Jordan 1984)

While the topi, the sun helmet made of pith, an avowed symbol of British identity in colonial India, distinguished the British community in India both from "natives" and from countrymen in England, it portended doom for the Indian *sipāhi* (anglicized "sepoy"). Forced by regulation to divest himself of all traditional accoutrements, the sipāhi was required to don instead the British Army uniform, which included the topi and leather belt. The scathing criticism that fellow Indians directed toward topi-donning sipāhis reflected a perception of the British as exploiters, proselytizers, and so on. Vivekananda in his Bengali essay, "The East and the West," observed that the British were stereotypically seen by Indians as power-driven, "... insane in their lust, drenched in alcohol from head to foot, without any norms of ritual conduct, materialistic, ... grabbing other people's territory and wealth by hook or crook ..." (Tapan Raychaudhuri 1988: 267).

Detailed scenes of colonial British life, both household and official, figure prominently in the genre known as "company art" or "company painting," which comprises paintings by Indian artists during the colonial period. These paintings, however, are complicated representations of Indian perspectives of the British, because the paintings were commissioned by British officials and consequently aimed to conform to the expectations set by the British. Nonetheless, Mildred Archer discovers that company paintings displayed uniquely "hybrid" views of the Indian artists who mediated between their impressions of the British and the specifications of the British patrons.

Perceptions of the British are also recorded in travelogues and memoirs like those by Behramji Malabari, who toured England in the late nineteenth century. Malabari's account praises the British, favors colonial rule, and recommends social reforms for Indian society that are endorsed by well-known British women. Such a perspective, however, is rare, and varies with the more complex image of the British delineated in Indian writing in English or in Indian films like Satyajit Ray's film depiction of Munshi Premchand's 1924 short story, *Satrañj ke Khilāḍi* (The Chess Players). Writers like R. K. Narayan, Mulk Raj Anand, Kamala Markandeya, and more recently, Shashi Tharur have created characters that represent the British as ubiquitously imperialist, semi-comical in their flawed comprehension of Indian language and culture, trapped between two worlds, and as occasionally sympathetic to the Indian nationalist cause. The *mēmsāhib* ("Ma'am + sahib," a term coined in British India by Indians to refer respectfully to the Englishwoman), a popular figure in Indian writing who emerges from middle-class Victorian England, is represented as being fascinated, appalled, and often confused by India, and as spending time socializing with other English families or "managing the natives" on the domestic front. Interestingly, a dessert presented in the 1850s by a Bengali confectioner to Lady Canning, the first vicereine, took the mēmsāhib's name, and was called "Lady Kenny" (or sometimes "Lēdikeni").

Characterizations of the British by people of the subcontinent constitute an emerging topic in South Asian research, which has begun to recognize the value of indigenous constructions of the British.

References

Archer, Mildred. 1992. *Company paintings: Indian paintings of the British period*. London: Victoria and Albert Museum.

Crooke, William. 1911. Songs of the mutiny. *The Indian Antiquary* 40: 123–24, 165–169.

Damle, Y. B. 1960. Harikatha: A study in communication. *Deccan College Research Institute Bulletin* 20: 63–107.

De Caro, Frank and Rosan A. Jordan. 1984. The wrong topi: Personal narratives, ritual, and the sun helmet as a symbol. *Western Folklore* 43(4): 233–248.

Dirks, Nicholas. 1987. *The hollow crown: Ethnohistory of an Indian kingdom*. Cambridge: Cambridge University Press.

Gautam, V. 1973. Some aspects of folklore as an agent of nationalism in the Bhojpuri-speaking area: 1917–1942—a case study. In *Essays in Indian folklore: Papers presented at the centenary festival of Raj Bahadur S. C. Roy*, ed. L. P. Vidyarthi, 180–190. Calcutta: Indian Publications.

Hankin, Nigel, 1994. *Hanklyn-Janklin*. New Delhi: Banyan Books.

Malabari, Behramji. 1893. *The Indian eye on English life; or, rambles of a pilgrim reformer*. London: A. Constable and Company.

Markandeya, Kamala. 1957 [rpt. 1971]. *Some inner fury*. Bombay: Jaico.

Masani, Zareer. 1987. *Indian tales of the Raj*. Berkeley: University of California Press.

Maya, D. 1997. *Narrating colonialism: Postcolonial images of the British in Indian English fiction*. New Delhi: Prestige Books.

Rao, Narayana Velcheru. 1986. Epics and ideologies: Six Telugu folk epics. In *Another harmony: New essays on the folklore of India*, ed. S. Blackburn and A. K. Ramanujan, 131–164. Berkeley: University of California Press.

Raychaudhuri, Tapan. 1988. *Europe reconsidered: Perceptions of the West in nineteenth century Bengal*. New Delhi: Oxford University Press.

Richmond. F. P. 1990. Characteristics of the modern theatre. In *Indian theatre: Traditions of performance*, ed. F. P. Richmond, D. L. Swann, and P. B. Zarrilli, 387–462. Honolulu: University of Hawaii Press.

Tharoor, Shashi. 1989. *The great Indian novel*. New Delhi: Penguin.

LEELA PRASAD

SEE ALSO

Character Stereotypes; Colonialism and Folklore; Legend

BROWN, WILLIAM NORMAN

W. Norman Brown (1892–1975) acquired his sympathy and interest for Indian civilization as a young boy spending five years with his missionary parents at Jabbalpur. He majored in Greek at Johns Hopkins University, receiving his B.A. in 1912. Like his father, George W. Brown, who received a Ph.D. in Sanskrit from Johns Hopkins, Norman Brown studied Sanskrit and Prakrit with Maurice Bloomfield, a comparative linguist and Vedic scholar. He also studied Pali and Arabic, and read Sanskrit with Franklin Edgerton, who remained an influential lifelong friend and colleague.

Brown's significant contribution to the field of South Asian studies is widely recognized. He was professor of Sanskrit at the University of Pennsylvania (1926–1966), chairman of the Oriental Studies Department (1937–1947), founder and chairman of the South Asia Regional Studies Department (1948–1966), founder and first president of the American Institute of Indian Studies, and editor of the *Journal of the American Oriental Society* (1926–1941).

Brown developed an interest in Indian folktales and story literature from his childhood experience in India and preparatory education by missionaries. He succeeded in generating a similar interest in his mentor and fellow graduate students. As Bloomfield was a scholar of Vedic and Jaina literature, he appreciated Brown's high estimation of India's story literature. Between 1910 and 1930, Bloomfield's students, among them Edgerton, Norton, Johnson, Burlingame, and Brown, published articles focusing on story motifs. Brown finished his dissertation in 1916 on "The Pancatantra in Modern Indian Folklore." Between 1919 and 1928, Brown published twenty-two articles and one monograph on story motifs in Indian literature. From 1922 to 1924, he was professor of English and vice principal of the Prince of Wales College (Jammu), where he edited the college journal, *The Tawi*. He encouraged his students to collect folktales in the villages and summarize them in *The Tawi,* while he also collected folktales. Later, at the University of Pennsylvania, he provided a student, Noriko Mayeda, this material for a dissertation. He co-published with Mayeda, *Tawi Tales: Folk Tales from Jammu*.

A research trip to India in 1928–1929 turned his interests in other directions, such as the study of Jaina literature, miniature painting, and the growing movement for Indian independence. He became progressively interested in Vedic literature for evidence of early Indian thought. Brown's ability to grasp the whole of Indian civilization is profound and rare.

References

Bloomfield, Maurice. 1916. On recurring psychic motifs in Hindu fiction, and the laugh and cry motif. *Journal of the American Oriental Society* 36: 54ff.

Brown, W. Norman. 1919. The Pancatantra in modern Indian Folklore. *Journal of the American Oriental Society* 39: 1–54.

Brown, W. Norman, and Noriko Mayeda. 1974. *Tawi tales: Folk tales from Jammu*. New Haven: American Oriental Society.

Rocher, Rosane. 1978. *India and Indology*. Delhi: Motilal Banarsidass. Contains Brown's complete bibliography.

RICHARD J. COHEN

SEE ALSO

Folklorist; *Pancatantra*; Story Literature, Sanskrit

BUDDHISM AND BUDDHIST FOLKLORE

Buddhism is a religious and civilization-wide movement that originated on the Gangetic plain in northern India about twenty-five centuries ago. The world's first missionary tradition, Buddhism—particularly its monastic elements—was visible in many of the court cultures of South Asian polities; its practices and institutions became embedded in the life of worldly power as that was known and practiced in the emerging regional states and cities of ancient India. For reasons that are still not fully known, Buddhism disappeared entirely from most areas of the Indian subcontinent just after the turn of the second millennium of the Common Era, although it continues to thrive as a vibrant cultural force in certain periphery regions of South Asia, notably Sri Lanka, Burma, Nepal, Ladakh, Sikkim, and Bhutan. Buddhism also has been reintroduced to India in the twentieth century, particularly among nominally Hindu and Muslim intellectuals, for whom it is conducive for thinking about "Indian identity" in a postcolonial context, and among Dalit communities, for whom it has been a powerful, inspirational counterculture for defending a social identity alternative to that given by upper-caste Hindu norms.

As a religious movement, Buddhism was translocal and universalist in its vision, and generally Buddhist ideas, practices, and institutions were supported and promoted in particular regions by rulers and merchants who had worldly aspirations that went beyond the merely local. Institutional Buddhism evolved as a tradition abetting the expansion of Indic civilization. This was so in ancient South Asia proper in the early centuries as tribal peoples were integrated into the first expanding states. This same phenomenon continued somewhat later over the Southeast Asia frontier where Buddhism coexisted with Brahmanical Hinduism, but was the dominant religion in most times and places there (and unlike its destiny of decline on the Indian subcontinent). Buddhism's alliance with state formation and expansion is one recurring trajectory in the faith's history (and it continues in the tribal areas of Thailand and Burma today). This was an interlocking sociocultural process that integrated expansive monastic institutions, the charisma of forest monk saints, the power of rituals performed by monks, the tradition's missionary ethos, the appeal of karma and compassion doctrines for rulers and ruled, alliances between monastery and merchants, and the legitimacy the tradition offered kings. It was vernacular folklore that communicated these basic teachings and legitimated the popular Buddhist practices that won the loyalty of the masses.

For many in South Asia's sociocultural elite, the grammar of cosmopolitan languages like Sanskrit and Pali was more important than knowledge of local lore about what was indicated, for example, by a gecko falling on one's head. Derived from a religious movement originating among ascetics, Buddhist philosophy was directed to a soteriology which Buddhists broadly understood as a transformation of the individual person through practices like meditation that ended in a freedom from suffering and ignorance for oneself and unbounded compassion for others. But elite-defined Buddhism, while it commanded patronage and prestige, and so shaped a polity's identity, was the actual concern of only very few. Only a small sample of men and women were ordained into the monastic order: since few among them could read the philosophical treatises, and even fewer still were thought to be in a position to pursue the strict practices that culminated in enlightenment, what we call canonical Buddhism was taken up directly by very few individuals. Thus, the splendors of Buddhist philosophy remained distant to even most monks and nuns, and further still from the pragmatic concerns of farmers concerned about crops, the health of loved ones, or flies in the kitchen. Civilizationally, then, the study of sacred stories and ritual among Buddhists was as important as meditation and philosophy.

As centrally visible as the great Buddhist monastics were in the elite cultures of South Asia, many also participated in South Asia's folk traditions. In fact, an early text identifies "the folklorist" (*tirascakathika*) as one of six monastic specializations (Lewis 2000:3). Indeed, their participation was key to the success of Buddhism as a distinctive religious movement. Buddhist folklorists, like Jains and others, adopted and adapted elements of the folk religion around them and connected them to their own system of religious reflection and meaning. This folk religion was only marginally different from the religious practices derived from later Vedic literature and its Brahman-mediated practices. These rituals focused on local deities known as *yaksa*s and *naga*s, and included notably an emphasis on a sense of the "divine" in a particular place and the approach to the "divine" through directly emotional and sensual forms of worship. Buddhist monastic discipline forbade direct involvement in such rituals, but householders were counseled in the Buddhist canons to respect all divinities in their midst, and make offerings to win their favors. What made individuals distinctly Buddhist was their revering the Buddha above all beings in the universe, and holding that his path was the only true means to final salvation. The popular narratives recounting the life of Shakyamuni the Buddha, perhaps the most widely spread Buddhist story, make these views plain through a wealth of incidents. Not only did Buddhists recognize the Indic deities, spirits, and ghosts and make offerings to them to seek local protection and aid from these resident supernaturals, they also incorporated these procedures to worship Buddha images and their distinctive memorial monuments, stupas.

Central to a consideration of Buddhist folklore is the tradition of *jātaka* and *avadāna* stories about the Buddha's previous lives. In the canon, appended to commentaries and ritual guides, and often redacted into further anthologies, they are the form of Buddhist literature for which we have the earliest datable evidence. These stories are represented visually at the earliest Buddhist memorial monuments, at stupas such as Bharhut and Sanchi from about the third century before the Common Era, and thus are linked to popular rituals. Jātakas and avadānas provide the most popular media in Buddhist culture, having been used over the centuries for didactic purposes, especially for the teaching of Buddhist doctrines and ethics to novice monastics and householders.

It is important to note that most of the stories preserved in the canonical languages were redacted for local audiences into a vernacular that was the local lingua franca. Most Buddhists until modern times were illiterate and so encountered jātakas and avadānas from the lips of monks or nuns, pondered them depicted as frescoes on monastery walls, or viewed them dramatically enacted by dancers or puppet performers. Students can miss the dynamism of this folklore by not having access to the vernacular context to note how artists can veer into modern political issues to recontextualize old disputes, elaborate on some themes while foreshortening others in a particular recitation, and even invert the classical norms. Though some of the vernacular translations from the various South Asian regions have been written down, few have been translated into English.

Modern scholars, noting that among the jātakas are various tales, riddles, and anecdotes that are known from elsewhere in South Asian cultures, have generally read this literature as a collection of folktales and thus have seen them more as sources about South Asian folklore than about Buddhism. T. W. Rhys Davids, one of the founding fathers of Buddhist studies, observed that the jātakas are "the most complete, the most authentic, and the most ancient collection of folklore in the world—a collection entirely unadulterated, as modern folklore stories so often are, by the inevitable process of passing through a Western mind" (Rhys Davids 1896: 78). But the size and scope of this narrative literature convey much about Buddhism, often conflicting with the views of the tradition conveyed by modernizers and Western exponents.

Creative engagement with and adaptation of South Asian folk traditions contributed strongly to the success of Buddhism as a religious movement that expanded outward to the ends of Asia. Monastic folklorists drew upon their rich story narratives to demonstrate how spirits can be integrated into a Buddhist worldview, how tribal norms need to be reshaped to be compatible with karma doctrine, and how a seemingly remote territory might indeed have been already sanctified for the faith by a long-ago visit by a future Buddha or a more recent visit by a renowned saint. It is indeed useful to look at the collection of popular narratives from early Buddhism as a vast resource suitable for redactors to adapt the tradition to new places and changing times. Such "domestications" were especially common in Buddhist history, where no central ecclesiastic authority ever controlled the religion.

The Buddha is remembered as saying that his teaching about suffering and the ending of suffering was key to understanding his career. Buddhists frequently turned to the material and practices of folk traditions to extend the Buddha's intent to understand suffering, perceive its causes, and ultimately end it in the world. Although Buddhism holds that natural causality shapes human life, it is karma—the causal mechanism that links intentional actions to this and future life consequences—that must be reckoned with to live a moral life that leads to fruitful spiritual development. Most Buddhist popular narratives in fact are case studies in karmic retribution, giving the listener the chance to understand this foundational teaching through an almost endless variety of circumstances, from the animal world to the royal palace, from the ascetic's primitive hut to the materialism of trade route.

Quite often the intention of the Buddhist narrative was to convey how to end suffering in an immediate sense, and what we see in canonical texts, such as those found in the sixth-century manuscript collection discovered at Gilgit in northwest Pakistan, is a sustained interest in how Buddhist rituals, particularly *bali* offerings to local gods and the copying of Buddhist texts themselves, can assist in warding off illness, natural disaster, poverty, untimely death, and human malevolence. In the same vein but at the opposite end of the South Asian Buddhist world in Sri Lanka is what is called *kem* in Sinhala; this includes such protective practices as the placing of written Buddhist verses in a kitchen to ward off flies. While one can say that there is nothing uniquely "Buddhist" about such practices, since they are generic versions of practices found in other folk traditions throughout South Asia, it is also crucial to note that passages from the canon find the Buddha asserting that his words can pacify and make auspicious any locality where they are chanted and ritually deployed. Indeed, it is in ritual manuals compiled by monks where additional stories are found: these narratives that describe the proper Buddhist origins of these practices are often recounted in the ritual itself. The stories associated with the *paritta* of the Pali canon, and the *raksha* literature from the Sanskrit canons connect the Buddha's teachings with the pragmatic needs of the great majority of Buddhists.

Generalizing from evidence found in contemporary communities in Sri Lanka and Nepal, we can also surmise specific local functions of folklore among Buddhists: to critique the pretensions of more elite men and women in the community, including monks; to promote the practice of certain favorite rituals; to criticize men or women for character faults; and to promote ethnic solidarity, as local redactions support group loyalty over the universal ethics found in the canon. In the cycle of stories about Andare in Sri Lanka is an example of the first: they mock the "wisdom" of this pundit by showing the disastrous effects of the impracticality that can be traced to his learning. Folklore in modern Nepal found in story collections and ritual texts provides a number of insights: that Buddhist merit-making "cheats death" by reuniting married couples after death and reuniting the rich with their wealth; that karma is *not* strictly individualistic, as actions by husbands and wives, patrons and shipmates, monks and kings may affect the destinies of others. Finally, heavenly rebirth was recognized in numerous passages as an exalted religious goal for good Buddhists to strive for.

By focusing on folklore and recognizing its centrality in Buddhist polities, we can understand that for householders, being Buddhist has meant being focused on the karma of merit-making (often collective in practice and effect) and seeking heaven; showing respect for elders, ascetics, and local deities; and with seeing one's own homeland as having been blessed by the Buddha's powers through ritual.

References

Brereton, Bonnie Pacala. 1995. *Thai retellings of Phra Malai: Texts and rituals concerning a popular Buddhist saint.* Tempe: Arizona State University Press.

Cowell, E. B. 1990. *The Jataka or stories of the Buddha's former births.* Oxford: Pali Text Society.

Dutt, Nalinaksha, ed. 1984. *Gilgit manuscripts Vol. I.* Delhi: Satguru Publications.

Hardy, Friedhelm. 1983. *Viraha-Bhakti: The early history of Krisna devotion in south India.* Delhi: Oxford University Press.

Lewis, Todd. 2000. *Popular Buddhist texts from Nepal: Narratives and rituals of Newar Buddhism.* Albany: State University of New York Press.

Rhys Davids, T. W. 1896. *Buddhism: Its history and literature.* New York: G. P. Putnam.

TODD LEWIS

SEE ALSO

Agricultural Development and Folklore, Sri Lanka; Goddesses, Place, and Identity in Nepal; *Jātaka* Tales; Vessantara

BUDDHISM, SRI LANKA

"Folk religion" is a term used by scholars to designate the domain of Sinhala religious practices having to do primarily with the propitiation of various deities and malevolent beings. Since the time of the first Western encounters with Sri Lanka, the coexistence of such practices with Buddhism has been problematic for European observers, including academics, largely due to the imposition of models of religious practice derived from Christianity. In many ways, folk religion has functioned as a residual category for anything not thought to be strictly Buddhist—the telling point here being that what constitutes folk religion largely turns on one's definition of Buddhism.

The earliest detailed account of Sinhala folk religion is that of Robert Knox (1681), who characterized the religion of the Kandyan peasants as the worship of "Gods and Devils," the Buddha being a "great God... unto whom the Salvation of Souls belongs." Later observers of Sri Lanka, then known as Ceylon, opposed the practices of folk religion, variously characterized as "animism," "demonism," or "kapooism," to Buddhism, which was conceived of as a rational, nonritualistic religion, charging the Sinhalas with being "corrupt" or "degenerate" Buddhists. The analysis of Sinhala religion in terms of a dualistic structure, and concerns about the alleged "authenticity" of Sinhala Buddhists, has largely continued to the present; in the second half of the twentieth century, the relationship between Buddhism and folk religion has been the subject of much scholarly interest, particularly among anthropologists.

The 1960s marked the beginning of an efflorescence of anthropological scholarship on the Theravada Buddhist societies of South and Southeast Asia. These studies were concerned with the relationship between Buddhism—as represented in the texts of the Pali literary canon—and society, as represented by the collectivity of religious practices. Intervening in the field of Buddhist studies, which had primarily addressed the textual and historical questions of classic Indology, anthropologists conducted field research on the range of existent religious practices. However, like their predecessors, they continued to analyze Sinhala religion in dualistic terms, making distinctions between text and context, precept and practice, village Buddhism and textual Buddhism, magical animism and Buddhism "proper." Terms such as these, opposing the so-called "little traditions" of the village to the "great tradition" of a translocal textual Buddhism, implied a hierarchical division between the two, valorizing the Buddhist texts as the standard against which local practices should be judged.

In a landmark essay, Gananath Obeyesekere (1963) challenged the divisions posited by scholars who had

Frescoes in Dambulla Buddhist cave retreats depict the Hindu deities Rāma, Viṣṇu, and Śiva as subservient to the Lord Buddha. Sri Lanka. © Anthroarcheart.org

suggested that religion in Buddhist societies could be analyzed in terms of vertical layers of non-Buddhist (e.g., animist, Hindu) and Buddhist elements. Advocating a holistic approach, Obeyesekere used the example of the Sinhala pantheon of deities and demons to argue that Sinhala Buddhism is a unified, internally consistent religious tradition, distinct from, but related to, the "great tradition" of Theravada Buddhism, defined as the tradition of Pali texts and Buddhist monks. Gombrich and Obeyesekere's (1988) study of religious change in contemporary Sri Lanka maintains the dualistic structure of Sinhala Buddhist religion, differentiating the spirit religion from Theravada Buddhism, but resists a hierarchical rendering of it. In their analysis, Theravada Buddhism derives its authority from the teachings of the Buddha as given in the Pali canon and interpreted by its commentators, while the term "spirit religion" is a "label of convenience" for those aspects of religious practice that concern the worship of gods and propitiation of demons. However, carrying forward Obeyesekere's earlier holistic framework, the spirit religion is viewed as closely linked with doctrinal Buddhism, which also recognizes the existence of gods and malevolent spirits, though it does not condone (or prohibit) their worship or propitiation.

Nineteenth- and twentieth-century reform and nationalist movements have resulted in vast changes in folk religion and Buddhism and in the relations between them. Initially, Buddhist modernists, bent on demonstrating the rationality of Sri Lankan religion, denounced the "superstitious" practices of deity propitiation and attempted to eliminate them altogether. However, as is evident today in the massive numbers of people who crowd pilgrimage sites and small urban temples, the gods are still very much alive. Indeed, it is among the urban and semi-urban Sinhala middle classes that there has been a rise in a wide variety of folk religious practices, some quite new. Perhaps the most significant recent change in the folk religion is the acceptance of spirit possession, particularly by women, as a positive phenomenon. Priestesses, a new religious role among Sinhala Buddhists, now practice in shrines that they themselves have founded.

The genealogy of categories scholars have used in their analyses of Sinhala religion has been the topic of considerable discussion in the 1990s. A critical issue examined by anthropologist David Scott is the extent to which scholarly inquiries focused on the "authenticity" of Sinhala Buddhists have been limited by their rootedness in Christian colonial conceptions. Drawing on the work of Philip Almond, Scott argues that the European preoccupation with doctrine and the location of religious authority in biblical texts has largely been responsible for the misguided concern with "authenticity" among colonial writers, anthropologists, and Buddhist scholars. In Scott's view, this essentialist concern should be abandoned in favor of questions about the ways in which the categories Buddhism and Buddhists are articulated in relation to sources of religious authority and power.

From a different angle, Jonathan Spencer and Charles Hallisey have also criticized the "scripturalist" approach of scholars who regard the Pali canon as the "original" and "pure" source of Theravada Buddhism. But, as Hallisey argues in a critique of Almond's work, it is also wrongheaded to suggest that representations of Buddhism by Westerners were shaped only by European values and expectations, "proceeding as if a genealogy of the West's account of Buddhism could be made without any reference to the people and places from which it is imagined to emanate" (32). Such a view, he argues, denies the possibility that non-Europeans played a significant role in the representations of Buddhism by Europeans, reifying "the West" and "the Orient" as clearly separate entities. Calling for more nuanced analyses of the encounters between Europeans and non-Europeans, stressing their heterogeneity, Hallisey suggests that "we should consider occasions where it seems that aspects of a culture of a subjectified people influenced the investigator to represent that culture in a certain manner" (33). In the context of Sinhala Buddhism, for example, Hallisey shows how T. W. Rhys Davids's view of Buddhism as rational and nonritualistic was shaped not only by his own European assumptions, but also by the views and examples of Sinhala monks he met while in Sri Lanka (47). Spencer similarly stresses the need for more subtle and heterogeneous accounts, calling for an expanded study of Buddhism, indeed of "the many possible Buddhisms" there have been in Buddhist history (210). Spencer suggests that such an expanded view would draw on evidence beyond the canon, to archaeology, vernacular Buddhist literatures, and ethnography.

The serious consideration of noncanonical sources in the study of Sinhala Buddhism will inevitably redefine the conceptual terrain of folk religion in more positive ways. Rather than viewing the practices of popular religious expression as deviations from an ultimate textual source, such a perspective will demonstrate how Sri Lankan Buddhist religiosity is embodied in myriad forms.

References

Almond, Philip. 1988. *The British discovery of Buddhism*. New York: Cambridge University Press.

Bechert, Heinz. 1978. On the popular religion of the Sinhalese. In *Buddhism in Ceylon and studies on religious syncretism in Buddhist countries,* ed. Heinz Bechert. Göttingen: Vandehoeck and Ruprecht.

Gombrich, Richard. 1971. *Precept and practice: Traditional Buddhism in the rural highlands of Ceylon*. Oxford: Clarendon Press.

Gombrich, Richard, and Gananath Obeyesekere. 1988. *Buddhism transformed: Religious change in Sri Lanka*. Princeton: Princeton University Press.

Hallisey, Charles. 1995. Roads taken and not taken in the study of Theravada Buddhism. In *Curators of the Buddha: The study of Buddhism under colonialism,* ed. Donald S. Lopez, Jr., 31–61. Chicago: University of Chicago Press.

Kapferer, Bruce. 1983. *A celebration of demons: Exorcism and the aesthetics of healing in Sri Lanka*. Bloomington: Indiana University Press.

Knox, Robert. 1681. *An historical relation of the Island Ceylon in the East Indies.* 1984 reprint of the original edition published in London. New Delhi: Navrang.

Obeyesekere, Gananath. 1963. The great tradition and the little in the perspective of Sinhalese Buddhism. *Journal of Asian Studies* 22(2): 139–153.

———. 1984. *The cult of the goddess Pattini*. Chicago: University of Chicago Press.

Scott, David. 1994. *Formations of ritual: Colonial and anthropological discourses on the Sinhala Yaktovil*. Minneapolis: University of Minnesota Press.

Spencer, Jonathan. 1995. The politics of tolerance: Buddhists and Christians, truth and error in Sri Lanka. In *The pursuit of certainty: Religious and cultural formulations,* ed. Wendy James, 195–214. London: Routledge.

SUSAN A. REED

SEE ALSO
Agricultural Development and Folklore, Sri Lanka; Buddhism and Buddhist Folklore; Spirit Possession and Mediumship; Sri Lanka, Sinhala; Syncretism

BUDDHIST SACRED GEOGRAPHY, SRI LANKA

Sri Lanka, just as any other country with an ancient civilization, has many sacred places, both classical and modern. Being a multireligious country, Sri Lanka has sacred places for every major religion of the world. Some popular sacred mountains and shrines, such as the Adam's Peak, Kataragama, Madu, and Munneswaram, are today frequented by many devotees, irrespective of their faith.

Pilgrimage to sacred places is an essential part of Buddhist culture. It is believed to be an excellent means of gaining merit. In the past, pilgrims would walk long distances to worship at their favorite sacred shrines. The greater the risks and dangers involved in the journey, the greater the merit one could earn.

Buddhist pilgrimage in Sri Lanka started with the arrival of Buddhism in the third century B.C.E. Upon conversion of the population by Arahant Mahinda, the first Buddhist missionary, the myth of (Sri) Lanka as the Dhammadīpa (the island of the truth) was created, along with other legends of the Buddha's three visits to the island and his purification and consecration of it. Thus, the island of Lanka was regarded by Buddhists as the chosen land of the Master for the protection of his *dhamma* (truth), which is perpetually protected and blessed by the *deva*. The myth of the Dhammadīpa has been further enhanced by records of donations by various kings of lands or of even the entire island to the order of Buddhist monks.

Throughout this history, the huge urban complex at Anuradhapura has been the most important religious center for Buddhists. It was there that Arahant Mahinda introduced Buddhism and established the Great Monastery, the Mahavihara. Under Mahinda's supervision the first *sīmā* (boundary of the monastery) was demarcated, symbolizing the firm establishment of the new religion in the island. Through the course of time, within and around the Great Monastery a number of temples, stūpas (Buddhist shrines), and other monastic buildings sprang up. Judging by the stone inscriptions and ruins of religious buildings, archaeologists surmise that Buddhism spread all over the island within a short period of time, probably within two centuries. Except for the Srī Mahā Bōdhi and other Bodhi trees (regarded as scions of the original tree under which the Buddha meditated) at sacred places, all the stupas were enshrined with *dhātu* (bodily relics of the Buddha). In addition to being relic chambers, some great stūpas such as Thuparama, Ratnamalie, Kelaniya, Mahiyangana, Mutiyangana, and Kirivehera are believed to have been constructed upon spots consecrated by the Buddha.

In the sacred geography of Sri Lanka, the traditions of *Atamasthāna* (the Eight Sacred Places) and *Solosmasthāna* (the Sixteen Sacred Places) are the most important landmarks. All these places are believed to have been visited by the Buddha, and are still frequented by devotees. Seven of the eight places of the Atamasthāna are located in Anuradhapura, while Chetiyagiri (or Mihintale) is located just nine miles from the sacred city. The temples and stupas in the sixteen places of the Solosmasthāna are scattered all over the island, including Nagadipa in the north and Kirivehera in the south.

The Temple of the Tooth Relic in Kandy attracts multitudes of pilgrims and visitors daily, more than any temple in the island. Since its arrival in Kandy in the fifth century C.E., the Tooth Relic has surpassed all other relics in the respect it has received. It has grown in importance as a symbol of sovereignty in the island.

Polonnaruva is the second most important ancient capital of Sri Lanka and still attracts thousands of visitors. However interesting and impressive are the ruins of Polonnaruva, as a sacred city it does not command as much respect as Anuradhapura. The reason for this is the absence of any myth or tradition identifying the city as a place visited by the Buddha. Further, none of its stupas or statues of the Buddha are said to contain relics of the master. Some other highly respected stupas, such as the Somawathie, Seruvila, and Tissamaharama, are believed to have enshrined some relic, either a corporeal one or an item used by the Buddha.

In recent times, pilgrims' itineraries have added new stūpas, temples, and images. For example, the Bōdhi trees at Getambe near Kandy and that at Kalutara, and the gigantic statues at Veherahena and Wevurukannala in the south are now included in most itineraries. Together with the myths of the Buddha's visits and the myth of the Dhammadīpa, other prevailing myths and legends enhance devotees' respect toward the island. The donation of the entire island to *sangha* (the Buddhist monastic system) by several past kings is one such legend. Another deeply rooted legend is that the king of the gods asked Buddha to protect the island. The chronicles further record that this island was blessed and consecrated not only by the most recent of the Buddhas, but by the three previous Buddhas as well.

In modern times, the genuine spirit of pilgrimage (that of suffering to earn merit) has been compromised by new transport facilities and entertainment. The number of visitors to sacred places has greatly increased as religious sentiment has been mixed with objectives of fun and tourism.

UDAYA MEDDEGAMA

SEE ALSO

Pilgrimage; Sacred Places; *Sri Pada;* Stūpa

BUFFALO

The buffalo is a symbol of evil, impurity, and death in Hinduism. A black buffalo is the *vāhana* (mount) of Yama, the Vedic god of departed spirits and judge of the dead. The buffalo is identified with various demons in Hindu mythology and is sacrificed by both Hindus and tribal peoples in South Asia.

The *Mahābhārata* and the *Purāṇa*s tell of the fierce *asura* (demon) Mahiṣa who waged war against the gods and became so powerful that he defeated them and displaced them from heaven. The gods wandered the world disconsolately until they were advised by Viṣṇu and Śiva to concentrate their powers, thus generating flames from which the great goddess Durgā emerged. Mounted on a lion, the goddess attacked the asura, who continually changed his form until he was finally slain in the guise of a buffalo. Durgā's victory over the buffalo-demon is celebrated in the *Daśaharā* festival (*Durgā Pūjā*) when Hindus sacrifice male buffaloes as offerings to the goddess, a ritual especially popular in Nepal, and in eastern India, where the *Śakti* (sacred female power) cult is strongly entrenched.

Dundubhi is described in the *Rāmāyaṇa* as a powerful buffalo-demon who challenges the gods to combat. Bhainsāsur is a malignant buffalo-demon of northern India who must be appeased to protect the crops. Mhaisāsur, an evil spirit of the Deccan, appears as a she-buffalo and is regarded as an incarnation of Sāvitrī, wife of Brahmā. The male buffalo is the symbol of the Jain *tīrthaṅkara* Vāsupūjya (literally "ford-finder," applied to the twenty-four great teachers of Jain tradition).

The buffalo's ritual role in South Asia appears to predate Hinduism and its Vedic antecedents (early Vedic texts indicate the buffalo may have been sacrificed to Indra and other deities, although no mention is made of the animal in later lists of acceptable sacrificial victims). The buffalo is depicted on seals from the Indus Valley, where both the wild Asiatic buffalo (L. *Bubalis arnee*) and the domesticated water buffalo (L. *Bubalis bubalis*) were known, and most likely had ritual significance in Harappan religion. The animal appears on seals by itself, in what seem to be hunting or sacrificial scenes, and, in the case of the so-called "proto-Śiva" seal, with the rhinoceros, elephant, and tiger surrounding a central figure seated in a yogic posture. This enigmatic, bovine-headed figure, long viewed as Śiva in his form of Pāsupati (Lord of Animals), wears a horned headdress and is clearly of cultic importance. The horns are buffalo horns, however, and it has been argued that this is not Śiva but a deity—perhaps a precursor of Mahiṣa—associated with the cult of the mother goddess and its related buffalo sacrifice that is so widely distributed in South India in later times. Another view sees the horned figure as female, perhaps the mother goddess herself.

In South India, where many traditions in popular Hinduism have their roots in Dravidian culture, buffalo sacrifice is closely related to the worship of village goddesses. Deities such as Polerammā and Yellammā, probably surviving forms of the once great mother goddess of the Indus Valley, are propitiated with blood sacrifices. Offerings include goats, pigs, and chickens, but the buffalo is the chief sacrificial victim. In many instances, the attendant of the goddesses is Potu Rāja, the "Buffalo King." The buffalo also fulfills the role of a "scapegoat" animal, being killed (or driven out of the village) to expiate sins, remove disease, or ward off ill fortune.

Buffalo sacrifice is common in the tribal cultures of the Indian subcontinent. Munda-speaking peoples of the Chota-Nagpur plateau sacrifice the buffalo as offerings to local agricultural deities, to propitiate village gods and goddesses, at times of epidemic and disease, and at funerary ceremonies. The sacrifice of the buffalo is also important for Dravidian tribes such as the Oraon and Khonds of central India. In the hills of northeastern India, where buffalo sacrifice is widespread, the *mithan* (L. *Bos frontalis*), a domesticated form of the wild buffalo or gaur, rather than the buffalo, has emerged as the focus of elaborate sacrificial rituals among groups such as the Naga and Chin.

Of all the peoples of South Asia, the Toda of the Nilgiri Hills in South India hold the buffalo as the most sacred. As a pastoral group, their entire economy revolves around the water buffalo, but certain female buffalo are selected as "temple" buffaloes and kept in sacred dairies, tended by a special class of priests. Elaborate rituals exist relating to the care of these sacred herds. The Toda sacrifice male buffaloes at funerals, but another custom of sacrificing calves has apparently been abandoned in recent years.

References

Hiltebeitel, Alf. 1978. The Indus Valley "Proto-Siva," reexamined through reflections on the goddess, the buffalo, and the symbolism of *vahanas*. *Anthropos* 73: 767–797.

Simoons, Frederick J., with the assistance of Elizabeth S. Simoons. 1968. *A ceremonial ox of India*. Madison: University of Wisconsin Press.

Walker, Anthony R. 1986. *The Toda of South India: A new look*. Delhi: Hindustan Publishing Corporation.

Whitehead, Henry. 1983. *The village gods of South India*. 2nd rev. ed. New Delhi: Asian Education Services.

DERYCK O. LODRICK

SEE ALSO
Bhāoyāiya Song; Dāsara; Goddesses, Hindu; *Nāvaratri*

BULL-PULLING COMPETITIONS

There are many different types of competitions involving bulls. Bull pulling is practiced in the Kadapa, Karnool, and Ananthapur districts of India's Andhra Pradesh state. A famous center of bull pulling, Thondapadu village in Ananthapur, has had many winning bulls. Regional, state, and national levels of competitions are usually held in February and March.

In this competition, called *bholam pandhya* (competition of stone slabs), heavy granite stones are tied to the neck of the bull with a chain. The stones measure $10.5 \times 2 \times 3$ feet (63 cubic feet). The bulls pull these stones a set distance; there are a 500-foot, a 1000-foot, and a 1500-foot relay. Betting on the race by spectators is permitted. Some owners will beat their bulls to induce them to move faster. The owners of the first bull to reach the target distance are rewarded with prizes in cash and gold. Inscriptions commemorating the competition are carved on the granite stones themselves.

Hybrid bulls are specially raised for the purpose of this competition. Champion bulls are used for breeding new, strong stock. Because maintaining these bulls is a matter of prestige, their owners treat them affectionately and provide lavishly for them. Kept in comfortable, spacious—even air-conditioned—housing, the bulls are provided with rich food and water. To prevent strain, they are trucked to distant competitions. Financial hardships such care causes are often ignored.

Bull-pulling enthusiasts believe theirs is a positive sport and more humane than Spanish bullfighting as there is no killing of the bulls. They also emphasize that the breeding programs help produce strong bulls and cows, which help the local population.

T. N. SHANKARANARAYANA

SEE ALSO

Animal performances; Buffalo; Cockfighting; Games and Contests

BURRA KATHA

The words *burra katha* come from the Telugu term for a one-headed finger drum—the *burra. Katha,* in this sense, means simply "story." Although enormously popular, *burra katha* is not a folk form of great antiquity. It was created in relatively recent times by the Communist Party of India. Its core formal elements, however, are primarily derived from the *jangama katha*. Jangamas are a caste of religious mendicants who formed itinerant performance groups to propagate the Shaivite religion. These groups may be seen today and are quite popular with the village audiences.

During World War II, the Communist Party began to adapt a number of folk forms to propagate an anti-Nazi message. The burra katha was one of these adaptations. The story content was composed by contemporary political writers, the performers were party members, and the performance itself was based on their observations of the traditional styles of Jangama artistes. Troupes are normally composed of three artistes: a main singer, who carries a *tambura* (stringed instrument) on his right shoulder and wears *andelu* (hollow brass ringlets with metal balls inside) on the thumb and forefinger of his left hand. A bright turban wrapped on his head and a red cloth held in his left hand complete his costume. As he sings, he moves forward and backward on the stage, occasionally dancing. His two accompanists (*vantalu*) wear similar dress and play the burra. The burra is used in performances like Jamgan katha and *sārda kadha* because its loud, sharp sound is associated with the emotional excitement of battle scenes.

In the 1950s, members of the troupes left the declining Communist Party, yet continued their dedication to the theatrical form. They began using folk narratives from a variety of traditional popular story traditions, such as the *Palnāḍu Katha, Bobbili Yuddham* (a historical battle in the twelfth century between Shaivite and Vaisnavite religions), *Katha* (the story of the battle of Bobbili in which local kings fought the French), *Abhimanyu Katha* (a story from the *Mahābhārata,* which is popular also in the regional forms of *Yakshagana*), and stories—especially those with strong social messages and powerful emotions—written by contemporary authors. Today, one finds troupes of Christian and Muslim as well as Hindu performers, all drawing upon the story repertoires of their religions both to entertain audiences and to propagate their religious messages. There are troupes of male performers, as well as female ones.

The burra katha owes much of its present distinctive style and form to a single artiste, Shaik Nazar, who trained many of the troupes. In the World War II era Shaik Nazar was used by the Communist Party to propagate anti-Nazism and party ideology through burra katha. After India gained independence in 1947 and the Communist Party was banned, Shaik Nazar, along with many other artistes, took up historical and mythological themes, preparing and performing scripts of *Palnati Yuddham* and *Bobbili Yuddham* and training burra katha troupes.

Today, burra katha is perhaps the most popular of all the theatrical forms of Andhra Pradesh, and is as popular in the cities as it is in the villages. Burra katha is financed by the neighborhood community. During a series of performances in a given locality, the community gives the performers room and board, and, at the end of the series, gives them a gift in kind and cash as a token of their appreciation.

Reference

Rama, Raju B. 1991. *Glimpses into Telugu folklore.* Hyderabad: Janapada Vijnana Prachuranalu.

BITTU VENKATESHWARLU

SEE ALSO

Tamāśā; Theater and Drama

BUZKASHĪ

Buzkashī (literally, "goat dragging") is an equestrian game played primarily by Turkic groups (Uzbek,

Turkomen, Kazakh, Kirghiz) in northern Afghanistan. In recent decades, other ethnicities, such as Tajiks, Hazaras, and even Pashtuns, have begun taking part. Central Asian in origin, buzkashī also occurs in the Muslim republics north of the Oxus River, in China's Xinjiang Province, and occasionally among Afghan refugees near Chitral and Peshawar in Pakistan. (Buzkashī bears no relationship to Pakistani polo.)

Played on horseback with the carcass of a goat or calf, games are traditionally sponsored by wealthy and politically powerful men (*khān,* pl. *khawānīn*), often in the context of a son's circumcision or marriage. Specialist riders (*chapandāz,* pl. *chapandāzān*) struggle against one another in a wild melee to lift the carcass off the ground and break free from the mass of other horsemen, who may number in the hundreds. Once clear of the mass, the rider drops the carcass and claims victory on behalf of his horse owner or patron (*sāhib-i-asp*). A town crier (*jorchī*), on horseback like everyone else, then launches into a stylized praise chant celebrating rider, horse, and horse owner. Prizes for the riders, donated by the game's sponsor, once included carpets or rifles but now consist mostly of cash. No sooner has one game cycle ended and its prize been awarded than a new group of riders forms where the carcass was last dropped. Forty or fifty such cycles may occur from mid morning to late afternoon. Some buzkashī festivals last three or four days. Except for behind-the-scenes preparation of food for male participants, women play no role in buzkashī and rarely even observe it as spectators.

Rules and Conflict

Lacking formal rules, teams, and officials, this traditional form of buzkashī—known as *tudabarai* ("emerging from a mass")—is replete with potential for dispute. Arguments arise most frequently over the interpretive issue of whether a rider claiming victory really broke free from other contenders. Such disputes may flare into open conflict in which the frame of already violent activity shifts from play to something more serious, especially when contending riders represent horse owners who are real-world rivals in local politics. From the sponsor's standpoint, a buzkashī succeeds, in part, to the extent that such overt conflict can be avoided or at least contained. Several days' worth of buzkashī prize money also tests the sponsor's financial resources. The host who can stage a dispute-free and prize-abundant buzkashī demonstrates his own political and economic power, earns considerable prestige, and enhances his position in real-world events that are typically dependent upon impression management.

Buzkashī in Kabul

Beginning in the mid-1950s, the Afghan government co-opted buzkashī, transformed it into a theoretically codified sport, and scheduled it in the capital city each October on the birthday of King Mohammed Zahir Shah. Subsequent nonroyalist regimes retained the October timing but shifted the occasion first to United Nations Day and then to the anniversary of the 1917 Bolshevik Revolution. Known as *qarajai,* the government form features uniformed teams, delineated rules, and military officers as referees. Always presented in the name of sheer play and fun, Kabul buzkashī tournaments also served as a symbol both of Afghan national unity and of governmental capacity for dispute-free control. The nationwide collapse of Afgan government control in the early 1980s was reflected in the year-by-year disintegration of Kabul buzkashī. By 1983 the Soviet puppet government abandoned all pretense at staging buzkashī. Local play continued with Afghan resistance commanders assuming the primary sponsorship role. In post-Soviet Afghanistan the primary locus of buzkashī has reverted to the provinces, where militia commanders, rather than traditional local leaders or Kabul-based government officials, assume the primary sponsorship role. A mid-1990s Taliban prohibition was frequently circumvented in the rural north. The Taliban collapse in late 2001 led to talk of a revived national tournament in Kabul.

Reference

Azoy, G. Whitney. 2002. *Buzkashi: Game and power in Afghanistan.* Prospect Heights, Ill.: Waveland Press.

G. Whitney Azoy

SEE ALSO

Afghanistan; Games and Contests

C

CAIT PARAB

Cait Parab, also known as *Caitra Jātrā,* is a holiday celebrated in the month of Cait (March–April). A number of fairs and festivals are celebrated by the people of eastern India during Cait: *Jhāmujātrā* of Goddess Mangalā; *Bāseli Pūjā,* celebrated by the fishermen in eastern Orissa; and the *Daṇḍa Jātrā* of Lord Śiva, celebrated in southwestern Orissa and West Bengal and associated with the Ṣākta and Śaiva cults. But the festivities associated with Cait Parab have a special significance for the tribal communities of the Mundāri language group in the Chotanagpur plateau of Bihar and Madhya Pradesh and the Dravidian language group in southern Orissa. For tribal communities like the Parajās, the Holvās, the Koyās, the Kondhs, the Bhatarās, the Bhumiās, the Goṇḍs, and others, Cait Parab is a spring festival. Although the celebration varies with each of the tribes, the Cait Parab of Korāput and Kalāhandi districts of Orissa adjoining the Bastar region of Madhya Pradesh has certain unique features, including ritual hunting, merrymaking with liquor, meat eating, and dancing.

The *mahul* flower, from which the local alcoholic beverage is made, is abundantly available in this season. Mangoes are also in season. The villagers offer the new mango to the goddess Dharnimātā (goddess of the Earth) on an auspicious day designated by the priest (*jāni*). This ritual, called *amba nuakhai,* celebrates eating the first mango (*amba*) of the season. Only after this, do the villagers start observing Cait Parab and begin its rituals and traditions.

In each village a sacred place of communal worship (*sadarguḍi*) is constructed. The men of the village go in a hunting party to the jungle with their bows, arrows, axes, and nets in search of deer, sambar, and bison. They are challenged by the women of the village to return with the prey, or else face ridicule. They never return to the village without a catch, since returning empty-handed represents impotency and a challenge to male pride. When they come with the quarry, women of the village receive them with dancing and singing. They offer the kill in front of the goddess and dance. The women cook rice and meat, serve liquor to all the community members, and a common feast is organized. The whole community, especially the young boys and girls, participates in singing and dancing irrespective of age and sex.

The rest of the festival season is spent in singing, dancing, and feasting. Young men and women assemble in the evening, to drink and celebrate. In addition to liquor made from the mahul flower, other alcoholic drinks include *salap, tāḍi,* and *landā.* Tribal youths play musical instruments called *ḍungḍungā* (a stringed instrument) and *ḍhāp* (drum). Hearing the music, the young women come forward to sing and dance. They take opposite sides and dance hand-in-hand with extempore verses, teasing, and challenging each other through song, thereby winning the heart of their beloved. Music, singing, and dancing continue for many nights. The pleasant romantic atmosphere of moonlit nights with the fragrance of wild flowers, soothing air, amid the calm and quiet jungle with its mysterious thick darkness, encourages the young people to choose their life partners.

MAHENDRA KUMAR MISHRA

SEE ALSO

Calendrical Ceremonies and Rites; Folk Art, Orissa; Tribal Folklore, Central India; Tribal Identity: The Bhils of Western Central India; Verbal Dueling

CALENDAR ART

Calendar art is ubiquitous in India. Prints of gods, mythical and historical heroes, and important contemporary figures are found everywhere and have been produced in India from the end of the nineteenth century until the present day. In many cases, these prints have been associated with calendars; hence the terms "calendar print" and "calendar art," although the prints are often found without a calendar attached.

The first prints produced for the Indian market were printed on foreign presses, primarily in Germany, where many patents for dyes and inks were held. Europe continued to produce some prints for the Indian market until at least the late 1920s, when Indian presses achieved the necessary technical level and the confidence of both the publishers and the buying market to ensure sales. Some of these Indian presses were run originally by German technicians.

Calendar prints do not illustrate traditional Indian taste as a rule, but rather display a fusion of Indian sensibilities with contemporary Western styles. The rise of the print took place at a time when much of India's own culture was ignored by the colonial elite. Many of the late nineteenth-century artists who painted the works that were transferred into prints were trained by Western artists who had come to India to teach European painting. The entire tradition of using Western styles has continued down to the present day. Most of the early artists, such as the pioneering Ravi Varma (1848–1906), who set up a press to reproduce his work in 1894, worked only in this style. Others, particularly from Nathadvara in Rajasthan, produced prints in this cosmopolitan Western style, while their traditional religious art was executed very differently. From the earliest times, only a Western style was deemed acceptable for prints. This is probably due to the printing technique itself, a chromolithographic process called "oleography," for which an oil painting was the only appropriate original. As time went on, the newer artists changed their printing techniques and the print style changed considerably as well, but it still retains its essential Western basis. Even when some of the original models for compositions are traditional Indian paintings, the modeling and perspective used in the prints owe much to Western styles.

Artists such as Ravi Varma, a portraitist of note, painted in a pure Western style with much modeling and shading, detailed textures of textiles, and a spatial setting, for his figure studies. The flat space and unshaded faces and bodies of much of traditional Indian painting are virtually unknown in calendar art. Compositions from traditional arts may appear, but the soft modeling of the figures in such prints as copies of the Tanjore style of the early nineteenth century makes them appear very different from the originals.

Many prints come into and go out of fashion quite quickly, but, others, for a variety of reasons, are not so short-lived and are constantly reissued, spawning a whole line of imitations. Some iconography has evolved within this medium. For instance, in the numerous versions of the goddess Lakṣmī, certain elements, such as money issuing from one of her hands, have become part of her iconography. In all likelihood, the modern Indian does not think of figures like Kṛṣṇa as seen in classical Indian sculpture or even in late Rajasthani painting; rather, he thinks of Kṛṣṇa as he appears in calendar art. As in the case of the early nineteenth-century woodcuts of Calcutta and the Punjab, the dissemination of many copies of these prints has spread the depicted themes and stories (primarily religious, but also secular in nature) over a wide area. This is why calendar art is surely one of the most important factors in keeping some of the old stories alive while developing new ones.

References

Del Bontà, Robert J. 1989. Calendar prints and Indian traditions. In *Shastric traditions in Indian arts,* ed. Anna Dallapiccola, Vol. 1, pp. 453–455, pls. 172–179. Stuttgart: Steiner Verlag Wiesbaden.

———. ed. 1984. *Calendar prints: Popular devotional art of India.* The ACSAA [American Committee for South Asian Art] Color Slide Project, Set 52. Ann Arbor: University of Michigan, Department of the History of Art.

Sharma, R. C., ed. 1993. *Raja Ravi Varma: New perspectives.* New Delhi: National Museum.

Vitsaxis, Vassilis G. 1977. *Hindu epics, myths and legends in popular illustration.* Delhi: Oxford University Press.

ROBERT J. DEL BONTÀ

SEE ALSO

Colonialism and Folklore; Folk Painting; Gods and Goddesses

CALENDRICAL CEREMONIES AND RITES

Much of the ritual life of South Asians is organized around the calendar. Generally speaking, the timing for, and the special intent of, rituals is tied to the seasons and to astronomical calculation, especially the cycles of moon, sun, and constellations. Often the seasonal and astronomical cycles are juxtaposed on one another and are further linked to the careers and exploits of particular deities and sacred figures.

Seasonal Rites

There is evidence that certain rites related to the agricultural process were practiced in prehistoric times. By the late Vedic period one finds both collective (*śrauta*) and domestic (*gṛhya*) rituals associated with the spring, the monsoon, the autumn, and the harvest seasons. In these rituals, plants and libations signifying the respective seasons are offered to deities by way of the fire sacrifice.

Today, rituals of planting, transplanting, and harvesting flourish. It is common, however, to juxtapose these agricultural rituals with those measured by astronomical cycles. For example, in parts of Karnataka, worship of the cobra and its presumed association with anthills (apparently, a metaphor of sexuality and the agricultural process) occurs shortly after the transplanting period in mid-August and again at the time of the completion of harvest in January. As Suzanne Hanchett has pointed out, each occasion occurs shortly after a solstice. Similarly, celebration of the birthday of the Kāveri (Cauvery) River, seen as the fecundator of Tamil Nadu's rice basin, occurs at the beginning of the first solar month after the fall equinox, and the Tamil harvest festival of *Poṇkal* occurs at the start of the first month following the winter solstice.

Astronomical Measures

Ritual chronometry is fundamentally determined by astronomic cycles, generally calculated by astrologers and published in vernacular booklets known as *paṇcāṇga*s (literally, five limbs). Of these astronomical measures, the most important are the lunar cycle, the solar cycle (both the day and the year), and the constellations (both those through which the sun "passes" during the year and those through which the moon "passes" each month). As a result, ritual time is generally marked throughout the Indian subcontinent by the conjoining of these cycles.

The Islamic Calendar

A notable exception to this principle of lunisolar conjunctions is the Islamic communities who follow an exclusively lunar liturgical calendar, comprising twelve months and a 354-day year as prescribed in the Qur'ān (10:6). Of these twelve months, four are considered especially sacred: Muḥarram, Rajab, Dhū al-Qada, and Dhū al-Hijja. The first of these is associated with the martyrdom of Ḥusayn, son of 'Alī, and the last is the month set aside for pilgrimage (hajj) to Mecca. In addition, the month of Ramaḍān is the occasion of the great fast. This was said to be the month in which the Qur'ān was first given to Muḥammad, the battle of Badr occurred, Ḥusayn was born, 'Alī died, and Mecca was reoccupied by the early Muslims. Each month, like the day, begins at sunset.

In contrast to the fasting (*ṣawm*) associated with Ramaḍān and Muḥarram, the Islamic calendar includes several days of feasting. The first day of Shawwāl, which succeeds Ramaḍān, is the occasion for *'Īd-al Fiṭr* (Feast of Fast-Breaking), when congregations meet (*ṣalāt*) for prayer, feasting, and giving thanks. Similarly, most Muslim communities observe the Feast of Sacrifices (*'Īd-al-Adha*) on the tenth day of the pilgrimage month, when Abraham's sacrifice of a ram is commemorated. The *Mawlid* (the Prophet's birthday), on the tenth day of Rabī ul-Awwal, has also been celebrated since the tenth century in many Muslim communities. In addition, Shiites are particularly apt to observe *Ashūra*, the commemoration of the death of Ḥusayn, on the tenth of Muḥarram, 672, with processions, mourning, self-flagellations, and the sharing of gifts. The birth or death of specific *pīr*s (saints) may also be celebrated in Muslim homes throughout the South Asian region. And although the Muslim liturgical calendar is lunar, some local Muslim communities celebrate New Year and certain agricultural ceremonies according to solar dates if it is the predominant regional custom to do so.

The Lunar Calendar

Inscriptions first mention lunar chronometry in the first century C.E. when reference is made to the fortnight (*pakṣa*) and the daily lunar stage (*tithi*). Of the lunar stages, the most important are the new moon (*amavasva*) and full moon (*pūrṇimā*), which were marked by rituals (*darśapūrṇamāseṣṭi*), even in the late Vedic period. The new moon serves as the beginning of the month in much of South India, Maharashtra, Gujarat, and Nepal. The full moon, on the other hand, marks the first of the month in much of North India and Telangana. The fortnight of the waxing moon (*śukla pakṣa*) is usually considered auspicious, while that of the waning moon is often inauspicious. Other stages (*tithi*s) of the moon may also be important in various parts of India, in some cases because they are equated with an event in the career of a deity. As a result, each such day may become the occasion for viewing (*darṣan*) or worship of the appropriate deity (*devapūjā*). The fourth *tithi* (*chaturthi*), for example, is generally associated with Gaṇeṣa, the sixth and eighth with goddesses, and the eleventh (*ekadaśi*) with Viṣṇu.

The Solar Cycle

The Indian solar year is divided into twelve solar months, each represented by the sun's entering into a constellation, known as a *sankranti*. These solar months are used in Bengal, Orissa, Tamil Nadu, and Kerala, whereas most other areas use a lunisolar measure of reckoning. In a lunisolar calendar, the month starts with the lunar cycle after the sun's sankranti. The solar year is further divided into two halves, each starting with the month (either solar or lunar) after the winter and summer solstices. These junctures are marked by special acts of vow taking (*vrata*), penitence, and ritual bathing (*snānam*). The period following the winter solstice is considered the light half of the year and is auspicious. It is a period often made congruent to the career of a deity. Christians, for example, follow such a rhythm when the birth of the Christ figure is celebrated just after the winter solstice at Christmas, his resurrection near the first lunar month after the vernal equinox, and his ascension forty days later, before the summer solstice.

In the solar calendar, further, the new year generally starts with the month (whether solar or lunar) after the vernal equinox (literally, the *meṣa sankranti*). An exception, however, is Gujarat, where the new year starts with the new moon of October-November (in effect, the ritual "midnight" of the year). This is an occasion otherwise celebrated by all Hindus as *Dīvālī* or *Dīpāvalī,* the festival of lights, when lamps are lit, new clothes are worn, work tools are honored, and ancestors are believed to visit.

The solar year is generally juxtaposed with the day, which is said to have twelve sacred or auspicious hours (*tirukkālam*). Six of those fall between dawn and noon and are homologized to the six "light" months of the year. The other six hours fall in the "dark" half of the day—three in the predawn, which are homologized to the months between the October-November new moon and the first month following the winter solstice. The other three are postdusk, and are homologous to the months following the autumn equinox. The period between the summer solstice and the fall equinox (and roughly between noon and dusk) is generally a slower ritual period (coinciding also with the southwest monsoon) when rituals associated with the agricultural cycle, penitence, and the repelling of evil tend to be more common, as they are in other "inauspicious" ritual seasons.

The Lunar Constellations (Nakṣatra)

The moon is believed to pass through twenty-seven constellations in its orbit around the earth each month, and each such "house" is ascribed mythical significance. At least some of these *nakṣatra*s were known to classical sages by the eighth century B.C.E. When the full moon occurs in or near the appropriate constellation in a given month, the festival marking the mythical event associated with that *nakṣatra* reaches its zenith. One example can illustrate this pattern. *Kārttikai* (sometimes known as the Pleiades) is the third constellation in the series. The moon is full (or nearly so) in the Pleiades in November-December, the time of the northeast monsoon in southeastern India. Mythologically, it is believed the *Kṛttika* maidens (Pleiades) suckled the young god Skanda on this day. Hence, the brief festival *Tirukkārttika,* observing the god's suckling by the Pleiades, is enacted at the confluence of the full moon and the *Kārttikai nakṣatra* in November-December. It is characterized by the lighting of lamps, as it is the dark time of the year, and the celebration of the decline of the monsoon.

Every juncture of the moon's orbiting of the earth and the earth's orbiting of the sun becomes a beginning or termination, a moment of breakthrough or commemoration. These rhythms are concentric, in that they are embedded in a series of smaller and larger cycles. The ritual life, not only of temples, but of families and individuals, takes its cue from these calendrical moments or "tempocosms." Each becomes the occasion for renewing vows, worshiping a deity, mastering the destructive forces of life, and, in other ways, becoming attuned to the rhythm of the cosmos.

References

Apte, V. M. 1958. Vedic rituals. In *The cultural heritage of India.* Calcutta: The Ramakrishna Mission Institute of Culture.

Babb, Lawrence A. 1975. *The divine hierarchy. Popular Hinduism in Central India.* New York: Columbia University Press.

Denny, Frederick M. 1994. *An introduction to Islam.* New York: Macmillan.

Hanchett, Suzanne. 1988. *Coloured rice: Symbolic structure in Hindu family festivals.* Delhi: Hindustan Publishing Corp.

Pandey, Rajbali. 1987. *Hindu* Samskaras: *Socio-religious study of the Hindu sacraments.* Delhi: Motilal Banarsidass.

Wilson, Guy R., and Glenn E. Yocum. 1982. *Religious festivals in South India and Sri Lanka.* Delhi: Manohar.

FRED W. CLOTHEY

SEE ALSO
Dīvālī/Dīpāvalī; Ponkal; Rituals

CANDAINĪ (LORIK-CANDĀ)

The epic tale of Lorik and Candā is performed from the Gangetic plains of North India to the central Indian region of Chattīsgarh. In this way it differs from many South Asian epic traditions that are regionally or linguistically bound or associated with specific caste histories, religious cults and festivals, or regional "historical" events. Nevertheless, Candainī performers and audiences understand the tradition to be rooted in specific performance and social contexts that shape the narrative emphases in very dramatic ways. Performance styles also vary. In both regions, the traditional style has been song-recitation; however, in Chattīsgarh, it has been adapted to the *nācā* dance-drama style. Also, in both regions, a few select sung episodes are now available on cassette tapes.

In the northern province of Uttar Pradesh, the epic is closely associated with the cowherding Ahīr caste, and emphasizes caste identity and boundaries. As a caste epic, martial elements of the narrative have been developed and elaborated. In Chattīsgarh, audiences and perfomers are multi-caste, and local communities identify it first with the region and only secondarily with the cowherding Rāuts. The Chattīsgarhi variant is primarily a love story that centers around the elopement of the hero and heroine; the battles are only those of a simple cowherd. The heroine Candainī is the character who initiates narrative action; she is bold, courageous, and resourceful. The female-centered nature of the Chhattisgarhi variant both reflects and contributes to a unique regional ideology.

At a young age, Candainī is married to Bāwan Bīr. Bāwan, however, has been cursed by the goddess Pārvatī to twelve years of impotence, and the young Candainī becomes impatient with her impotent husband. She returns alone to the village of her parents by way of a jungle, where she is accosted by the untouchable Baṭhuā Camār. She tricks him into climbing a tree, and escapes. His desire, however, is unthwarted, and he begins to harass her village to gain access to her. Candainī's mother appeals to the hero Lorik to save the village from the threats of the Camār. Uttar Pradesh variants elaborate at length the various episodes that dramatize this role of the protective hero, who is specifically called upon to protect the honor of the caste, usually through protection of its women.

Candainī meets and falls in love with Lorik in this period, and after numerous efforts, she finally persuades him to elope with her. Chattīsgarhi performances elaborate the many adventures of the hero and heroine as they pass through the forest and various kingdoms on their way to Hardī Gaṛh. After living some time in exile, Candainī gives birth to a son. Soon thereafter, Lorik receives a message from his wife that his family has lost all of its wealth and cattle, and that she has been reduced to selling milk and yogurt for a living. He returns home to reclaim his family wealth and honor—in Uttar Pradesh through battle, and in Chattīsgarh by simply wandering the countryside, collecting his cattle. In the northern variants, he ends up losing his military prowess and physical strength upon which his reputation was built, and finally commits suicide. In Chattīsgarh, he is dissatisfied as a householder and, one day, mysteriously meanders off into the countryside, never to be seen again.

References

Blackburn, Stuart H., Peter J. Claus, Joyce B. Flueckiger, and Susan S. Wadley. 1989. *Oral epics in India*. Berkeley: University of California Press.

Elwin, Verrier. 1946. *Folksongs of Chattīsgarh*. London: Oxford University Press.

Flueckiger, Joyce Burkhalter. 1996. *Gender and genre in the folklore of Middle India*. Ithaca, N. Y.: Cornell University Press.

Pandey, Shyam Manohar. 1979. *The Hindi oral epic Loriki*. Allahabad: Sahitya Bhawan.

———. 1982. *The Hindi oral epic Canaini*. Allahabad: Sahitya Bhawan.

JOYCE BURKHALTER FLUECKIGER

SEE ALSO

Epic; Madhya Pradesh and Chattīsgarh; *Nācā*; Uttar Pradesh

CARD GAMES

Scholars have not sorted out the world origin of playing cards, but card games were probably introduced into India around 1500 C.E. The immediate source of these games was Persian. Most, but not all, of the games are trick-taking ones derived from a game dubbed *Mughal ganjīfā*. The pack is made up of eight suits (sometimes ten), each headed by two court cards (king and minister), which are always the highest cards, followed by ten numbered cards.

The rules of these games are extremely complex, and memory is of the utmost importance. In half of the suits—the strong suits—the ten is the highest card after the court cards, followed by the smaller numbers; in the other half—the weak suits—the one is the highest card and the ten the lowest. Strong and weak suits are typical of some early European games, such as ombre. The relation between the two groups can sometimes reverse after dark or for some other arbitrary reason. All of the cards are divided among the players. The leading of certain cards is mandatory. Players do not have to follow suit, and there is no trump suit.

The original eight-suited Mughal ganjīfā was Hinduized by, for instance, changing the court cards into the Hindu guardian deities of the eight directions, or expanding them into ten suits to form the most common of all games: *Daśāvatarā ganjīfā,* named after the ten incarnations of Viṣṇu. In some parts of Orissa, two suits were added to the Daśāvatarā ganjīfā, bringing the total cards in the pack to 144. Larger sets add other suits of twelve cards each. Variations, including Rāmāyaṇa sets with half of the suits for Rāma and his followers and half for his foe, Rāvaṇa, and his confederates, exist. In either Hindu or Muslim contexts, the suits may consist of different flowers, animals, or some other fanciful conceit. King Kṛṣṇarāja III Woḍeyar of Mysore (1794–1868) devised a number of elaborate card games with packs of up to 360 cards.

In most cases, the indigenous Indian cards are round in shape with plain backs, varying from 20 to 120 millimeters in diameter. Rectangular cards are less common and are mostly from the earliest period. Corner indices, as in American cards, are absent, and the players must take in the full card at a glance, identifying the suits by their particular background colors and suit signs. Often the court cards are virtually identical from one suit to another, with the figure of the king or minister holding the suit sign.

A number of cards dating from the early Mughal period have survived, but most of the earliest cards date from the seventeenth and eighteenth centuries. A great number of styles have been identified, including both a courtly style and a less finished and refined bazaar style. Centers of large production are scattered over India, with many fine sets coming from Rajasthan and northern India, Kashmir and the Punjab Hills, Maharashtra, Orissa, Bengal, Andhra Pradesh, and Karnataka.

Reference

von Leyden, Rudolf. 1982. *Ganjifa: The playing cards of India.* London: Victoria and Albert Museum.

ROBERT J. DEL BONTÀ

SEE ALSO
Folk Art; Games and Contests

CARPETS AND CARPET WEAVING

Weaving is one of the earliest crafts developed by humankind. Carpet weaving worldwide has generally been considered women's work, because it contributes to hearth and home, and is still mostly done by women in traditional, noncommercial situations today. Carpet weaving evolved from the production of textiles. Exactly when is not known, but it must have existed by the second millennium B.C.E. Based on extant examples, it is assumed that carpet weaving developed in Inner Asia. This region was home to wild sheep, which were gradually domesticated for food and the fleece that was necessary for weaving. Native sheep types lived in a belt from North Africa across Anatolia and eastward in the mountain and desert regions of the Caucasus, Iranian Plateau, Central Asia, Afghanistan, the Himalayas, Tibet, and Mongolia. Carpet weaving spread throughout this region and became a well-established craft among many people of the region.

The oldest complete carpet in existence, the Pazyryk, is dated to the fourth century B.C.E. It was found at a Scythian burial site in the Altai Mountains. Where, why, and by whom it was woven remain in question. Its high standards of design, dyes, and technique prove that carpet weaving was a highly developed craft and art by this time. Only fragments of carpets exist from the Pazyryk carpet to the fourteenth century C.E., so knowledge of the history and development of carpets is spotty and speculative between those dates. Histories, records, and paintings show that carpet weaving was well established in the courts, cities, villages, and among nomadic tribes by the fourteenth century throughout the Near and Middle East and Central Asia. They were woven for both domestic and commercial purposes. There are carpet references in the Mongol era (thirteenth century), and they were woven in the Timurid courts (1370–1507 C.E.), although no extant carpet fragments are firmly attributed to them.

Carpet weaving refers to two general types of weavings, those with a pile surface and those without pile, called flat weaves. Many different techniques are used to weave both types. Pile weavings consist of threads called warps, wefts, and knots. Flat weaves have only warps and wefts. Some weavings are combinations of both flat and pile techniques. In general, two knot types are used, the asymmetric and symmetric. The former predominates east of a line northward through Iran and the Caspian Sea, and the latter to the west, although both types are found in all carpet-weaving areas. Although general statements may be made about the characteristics of discrete groups of weavings, categorical ones may not because of the idiosyncratic nature of the craft.

Carpets are woven for many different purposes and uses. In courts, cities, and villages, most are woven for floors and for commercial sale. Among nomads and villagers, weavings serve many domestic needs and the excess is sold. Types of domestic weavings are bags of various sizes for household and personal goods; tent bands to assemble yurts and tents; tack for horses and other animals; and special weavings for cooking, prayer, decoration, and festive occasions.

Among the principal traditional weaving people in Central Asia, Afghanistan, and Pakistan are the Turkmens, Kyrgyz, Uzbeks, Arabs, and Baluches. All of these are tribal people who use patterns, designs, dyes, and techniques common to nomadic and village weavers. The rugs of each group may generally be distinguished on the basis of patterns, colors, materials, knot type, weaving techniques, and general style. For example, Turkmen carpets are distinguished by the use of polygons, called *gul* (flowers), in all-over designs, primarily in different shades of red, with minor use of blues, brown, and white. A diagonal use of minor colors is typical. Other tribes emphasize such features as different colors or geometrical motifs, no diagonal color usage, or different density of weave.

Pile carpet weaving was introduced into the Indian subcontinent by the Moghuls (1526–1857 C.E.) in court workshops. It was expanded under the British in the late nineteenth century and is now established in many areas. Kashmir, Uttar Pradesh, Punjab, and Madras are major centers. Carpets are woven in city factories, villages, and in jails as a form of supervised or contracted labor for prisoners. Carpet weaving has always been a commercial rather than domestic industry in the subcontinent except among the Baluches of Pakistan. India, Pakistan, and Nepal are major producers of commercial carpets today.

The first Moghul carpets were based on Persian designs. Gradually, a Moghul style developed in which flowers became more realistic and animals native to the subcontinent replaced those found in Persian carpets. A distinctive red from lac dye, produced in India, predominated in these weavings. Special court-commissioned carpets with silk warps and wefts are among the most finely knotted carpets in the world. In the last half of the nineteenth century, this distinctive Moghul style disappeared in favor of Persian designs that continue today and are more popular in Western markets.

Today, the most finely woven carpets from India are produced in Kashmir. In other areas, commercial producers have established rug factories as a cottage industry in many towns where new designs are provided and, in some instances, vegetal dyes are being used. In Pakistan, the majority of rugs are made in patterns adapted from Turkmen rugs, but recently, finely woven rugs with Persian floral designs and patterns have been increasing. The output of carpets in India and Pakistan far exceeds their domestic production of wool, and now Australian and New Zealand wool is primarily used in their carpets. The use of child labor has been a continuing problem for Pakistan producers, although the use of child labor in the subcontinent is traditional to the culture and common in countries with large, illiterate populations. The Indian weavers are, in general, organized into village cooperatives, which appears to result in employment of an adult labor force.

In Nepal, rugs with Tibetan, Chinese, and contemporary patterns are woven in a technique adopted from Tibet. This technique employs a looping rod instead of individually tied knots, and results in a heavier pile and less finely woven rug. Both Tibetan and New Zealand wools may be found in these carpets.

Until recently, the study of Oriental carpets has been primarily conducted by historians of Islamic art, using designs and their transformation as the method of identification. In recent years, material analysis of structural elements and construction techniques—including thread materials, spin and ply of threads, type of knot, presence of warp depression, colors of warps and wefts, edge and end finishes—has been added as an analytical tool. With the creation of new laboratory techniques, such as chromatography and carbon dating, to study dyes and fibers, entirely new ways are opening to further refine the historical study of carpets.

References

Barber, E. J. W. 1991. *Prehistoric textiles.* Princeton: Princeton University Press.

Eiland, Murray L. 1981. *Oriental rugs, a new comprehensive guide.* Boston: Little, Brown.

Gans-Ruedin, Erwin. 1984. *Indian carpets.* New York: Rizzoli.

Hull, Alastair, and Jose Luczyc-Wyhowska. 1993. *Kilim, the complete guide.* London: Thames and Hudson.

Mackie, Louise W., and Jon Thompson. 1980. *Turkmen tribal carpets and traditions.* Washington, D.C.: The Textile Museum.

O'Bannon, George W. 1994. *Oriental rugs, a bibliography.* Metuchen, N.J.: Scarecrow Press.

Ryder, M. L. 1983. *Sheep and man.* London: Gerald Duckworth.

GEORGE W. O'BANNON

SEE ALSO

Handloom Weaving; Material Culture

CASSETTES

Cassette tapes are an audio mass medium that has had significant effects upon popular music and the music industry in South Asia. Prior to the advent of cassettes in the 1970s, the recording industry in South Asia had been thoroughly dominated by film music and by the virtual monopoly exercised by the Gramophone Company of India (GCI, absorbed by EMI [Electrical and Musical Industries] in 1931). Production of film music itself was concentrated in the hands of a small coterie of music directors and playback singers. A mainstream Hindi film song style had effectively marginalized other nonfilm popular music styles, while serving as the model for much regional-language film music.

The advent of cassette technology dramatically changed this situation. Cassettes and cassette players are cheaper, more portable, and more durable than records and phonographs, and have simpler power requirements. As such, they had begun to spread in South Asia in the early 1970s, and the subsequent liberalization of the Indian economy, in particular, precipitated their production and dissemination on a mass scale. Within a decade, cassettes effectively replaced vinyl records and caused a marked decentralization of the music industry.

In the mid-1970s, as cassette players proliferated among the urban middle classes of North India, music producers successfully marketed a simplified and stylized version of the Urdu *ghazal* (a poetic and light classical musical genre) as an alternative to the more populist film music. A cassette-based vogue of Hindu devotional music followed, including a mainstream, modernized version of the "stage *bhajan*" (a soloistic formal performance of a Hindu devotional song by a trained singer), and diverse lesser genres associated with particular cults, communities, and rituals.

By the early 1980s, cassettes and cassette players were becoming widespread among the lower classes and in rural areas previously enjoying little access to recordings; such communities thus came to constitute important new markets for the recording industry. At the same time, the lower production costs of cassette recordings enabled hundreds of small cottage cassette producers to emerge throughout the country, often orienting their output toward specialized local audiences previously ignored by GCI. These producers have marketed all manner of traditional folk, classical, and devotional genres, along with a variety of stylized versions of regional folk-pop music. While critics have deplored the commercialism and lewdness of much of the cassette-based regional music, cassette technology nevertheless can be seen to have invigorated regional and subaltern musical cultures which were previously on the defensive against mainstream film music. For their part, sales of film music have increased in the cassette era, especially among rural consumers; at the same time, sales of nonfilm genres like ghazal and regional music appear to have surpassed those of film music. Cassette technology has thus effectively democratized and demonopolized the South Asian music industry. Other entertainment forms such as narrative romances in Pashtu have also been successfully marketed on cassettes.

While cassettes have constituted a dynamic vehicle for the expression of local and subaltern values and aesthetics, the resistance of cassettes to censorship has posed some political problems for the South Asian polity. For example, aside from the use of tapes of songs and speeches by separatist movements and rival political parties in India, particularly divisive since 1989 has been the widespread dissemination of cassettes containing inflammatory Hindu militant speeches inciting violence against Muslims. Similarly, in Pakistan and wartime Afghanistan, cassettes of political songs, sermons, and speeches have also been extensively used as propaganda.

Reference

Manuel, Peter. 1993. *Cassette culture: Popular music and technology in North India*. Chicago: University of Chicago Press.

PETER MANUEL

SEE ALSO
Film Music; *Ghazal;* Song; Wedding Videos

CASTE AND STATE, INDIA AND NEPAL

Caste has been seen by Europeans as the key institution of Indian society ever since the Portuguese first arrived off the Malabar coast in the fifteenth century. The term derives from the Portuguese *casta,* connoting, among other things, the English concepts of race, hereditary social class, ethnicity, and profession. One problem with applications of this term is that it has no precise analogue in Indian languages; the single word *jat,* for example, can be glossed as ethnic group, race, tribe, or caste.

Caste is fundamentally a form of kinship. From the perspective of a peasant in an Indian village, a caste consists of a number of intermarrying lineages or extended kin groups. With few exceptions, these lineages are derived through the male line. Such a cluster of lineages, referred to in the anthropological literature by the native term *jāti,* may be concentrated in one area or be more widely dispersed. Structurally, as the anthropologist Bernard Cohn has observed, a jāti is a "system of actual or potential networks" of ties of blood and marriage. Members of a lineage marry people in other lineages of their jāti but not outside of it; the jāti is thus an in-marrying or endogamous group. A typical village in India will have a number of such jāti groups, ranked relative to each other. The term "caste" is best restricted to these jāti, which are structural units: groups of people who are formally linked to each other, most importantly through marriage.

The sociological reality of caste, as described above, is sometimes confused with the terms used to label jāti groups. All of the people who are described by a common name do not necessarily belong in the same jāti—that is, they do not have actual or potential links of any kind with one another. Such a caste name or category is simply a common label for a number of disparate and widely separated jāti groups lacking a common social structure. For example, a widespread caste name in North India is Baniya, a word meaning "trader." People who engaged in trade and formed jāti might have this term applied to them, even though jāti of Baniya in different parts of India do not necessarily interact or intermarry. Similarly, there are a great many jāti of Brahmans in India who share the same caste label and the same ritual occupation (that of priests), but who are not members of the same in-marrying group. Thus, for example, the term "Brahman" is a caste category, but "Kanya Kubja Brahman" refers to a particular jāti, a caste in the sociological sense.

The Indian sociologist G. S. Ghurye describes six essential features of the caste system. The first is that one acquires one's caste identity at birth. Second, castes in a given locality or region are hierarchically organized, based on ritual status defined by the relative purity or pollution of these groups. Third, there are restrictions on inter-dining and social intercourse between castes; the nature of these prohibitions varies from caste to caste and region to region. According to Marriott and

Inden, the underlying principle is that, through cooking, particles of the pure and impure substances that Hindus believe are inherent in individuals are transmitted from the cook to the food, and then to the body of the person consuming it. People of lower caste may eat food cooked by a Brahman because, being pure, he cannot pollute them, but Brahmans and people of higher caste generally may not eat food cooked by a person of a lower caste. Fourth, civil and religious privileges and disabilities are afforded to different caste groups linked to each other in a system. For example, caste groups may be segregated within the village, with untouchables (also called *Dalit* or scheduled castes) compelled to live in a separate hamlet and draw their water from a separate well. Fifth, a caste does not allow its members to take on an occupation that would be seen as degrading or polluting for that caste. Were a Brahman to work as a cobbler, for instance, he would be liable to outcasting by the rest of his community. In village life, most castes have been involved in agriculture, but they also have provided other services: blacksmithing, oil pressing, and ritual services such as shaving heads, beating drums, and so on. Sixth, there are restrictions on marriage. Endogamy (marriage within the group) is the dominant feature of caste society, with hypergamy (a woman marrying up) sometimes allowed. Women, however, may never legitimately marry down.

Both Indians and non-Indians often confuse *varna* with caste. While the sociological reality of caste varies from region to region in South Asia, varna is a common idiom used by many South Asians to talk about caste. Varna literally means "color," and may best be glossed as "estates," in much the same way as the word was used in European social theory of the medieval and early modern eras, particularly in France. The Orientalist A. L. Basham referred to varna as "classes." The varna system, which classifies people into four social and ritual categories, emerged in India during the Vedic period. The four categories (or estates) consist of the Brahman, whose duty (according to Mānu, the legendary author of the law code known as the *Mānu Smrtī*) was to study, teach, and perform sacrifices; the Kṣatriya, in whom was vested the power and duty to rule; the Vaiśya, whose task was to till the fields and pursue trades; and last, the Śudra, who was the servant to the three higher classes. The first three were distinguished from the last in being twice-born. Their second birth occurred through a ceremony investing them with the sacred thread, worn around the body for the rest of their lives, and initiating them into membership in their caste and lineage groups. In addition to these four varna, there were the outcastes or untouchables, considered too polluted or degraded to be admitted to the category of even the lowest varna.

While many previous scholars of South Asia (especially the French anthropologist Louis Dumont) have emphasized the ideology of purity and pollution as the structuring principle of caste, the central part played by the king or the state has become the focus of more recent scholarship. The Brahman-centered model of the caste system led to the idea that there was a contradiction between ritual status, as personified by the Brahman, and secular political power, as personified by the king or the Kśātriya. The British anthropologist Declan Quigley, drawing on earlier writings of the anthropologist A. M. Hocart, puts forward an alternative model of the caste system, decentering the notion of a ritual hierarchy based on attributes of purity and pollution, because, as he argues, "the orientation of castes is primarily to the dominant centre, not to each other" (1993: 166). The power of kingship—broadly defined as the rule of those groups that are able to exercise political power over others—is the center of his analysis. According to Quigley, the purity of the ruler is of central importance, not that of the Brahman. The purpose of the caste order, in which every caste must play its part, is to remove pollution from the ruler. This model of caste relations is reproduced at every level of society, being locally focused on the dominant caste. Typically, in much of India, local economic resources, especially land, are under the control of a particular kin group, forming the dominant caste. Thus, the Brahman himself may be a member of a service caste, who provides an essential service to the king or the locally dominant caste patron.

The centrality of secular power and Kṣatriya dominance in the caste system is also demonstrated by the nature of status mobility. Varṇā classifications are often used as a social idiom to legitimate claims to higher caste status; jāti may attempt to raise their social status by emulating higher castes and by claiming to belong to a varna of a higher status. Contentions often arise between jāti over whether a particular jāti group should be considered as Kśātriya, Vaiśya, or Śudra; its claims to belong to a particular varṇā will often depend on its current political and economic status, rather than its traditional caste occupation (often no longer practiced) or ritual status. According to the Indian anthropologist M. N. Srinivas, lower castes attempt to improve their relative status by emulating Brahmanical practices, a process for which he coined the term "Sanskritization." In fact, most lower castes model their behavior not on the local Brahmans, as Srinivas initially argued, but on the dominant caste. Only if the locally dominant caste (dominant in the secular, political or economic sense) were Brahman, would Brahman practices be imitated. Social-climbing lower-caste groups more frequently claim that they are of Kśātriya origin.

The institution of caste responds to and is molded by the power and priorities of the state. Before the British took control of India, caste ideology was upheld by the secular power of the ruler, who could promote or demote a caste and who was the final arbiter of its status within the hierarchy. States played an important role in organizing and maintaining the caste system, a factor unrecognized or unacknowledged by many scholars whose attention has been focused on the ideology of purity and pollution.

This role of the state is evident in the nineteenth-century Nepali state's attempts to deal with ethnic pluralism and the many different local caste systems of the newly unified country. Nepal emerged as a state during the latter half of the eighteenth century following the forcible unification of a number of formerly independent principalities and small kingdoms. (The country remained a near absolute monarchy until 1990, when a popular movement compelled the late King Birendra Bir Bikram Shah (1945–2001), a direct descendant of the eighteenth-century founder of the state, to concede sovereignty to the people and his executive authority to a democratically elected parliament, and to become a constitutional monarch.) In the nineteenth century, the ruling elite codified their perspective on the caste system in the Legal Code (*muluki ain*) of 1854, imposing a uniformity and rigidity on the many different local systems of caste. Its central principle was ascribed status, which persisted through all of the code's revisions until the code was finally replaced in 1964 by a new democratic constitution. However, the nineteenth-century reformulation into one "national" model served both to distinguish the social order in Nepal from that of British India and to symbolize the country's newly created unity.

The Legal Code of 1854 in Nepal recognized five hierarchically ranked categories: the Cord-wearing (or twice-born) castes, the Non-Enslaveable Alcohol Drinkers, the Enslaveable Alcohol Drinkers, the impure but touchable castes (including Muslims and Europeans), and the Untouchables. Each of these categories was internally stratified; the Cord-wearing or twice-born castes for example, were ranked into the Brahman, Thakuri, and Chetri castes. A key principle was the opposition between the clean castes and the untouchables. Within each of these two divisions, castes and ethnic groups were ranked relative to each other. In addition, confronted with the problem of how to deal with the so-called tribal groups, such as the Magar and the Gurung, to whom the consumption and offering of alcohol is an integral aspect of social and ritual life, the state developed another division between the Cord-wearing or twice-born castes and the alcohol-drinking castes. The twice-born castes dominated the state politically, while the rank and file of the army was substantially drawn from certain liquor-drinking ethnic groups. The alcohol-drinking castes were subdivided into two groups, with the lower ranking group enslaveable for debt and for other reasons. This second group included "tribal" groups, such as the Tharu and the Tamang, that unlike groups such as the Magar, Gurung, Rai, and Limbu, who played a more important role in the affairs of the kingdom, were politically and economically marginal to the state.

Despite the formal precedence given to Brahmans in this system, ritual status was clearly subordinated to secular power. The Legal Code allowed for the punishment of a Brahman: while it was considered sinful to put a Brahman to death (for treason, for example), he could be degraded out of his caste by being forced to eat pork and drink alcohol. Any children born to him after his degradation would assume his new status (a Non-Enslaveable Alcohol Drinker). Thus, the status of the Brahman or of any caste was controlled by the ruler.

The notion of the Brahman's ritual superiority to the king is also contradicted by the ideology of kingship, which emphasizes not only the king's role as the guarantor of the kingdom's prosperity but also his divine origin as an incarnation of Viṣṇu. Nepali peasants told Burghart (1996) that while "the embodied soul of the Brahman . . . is only an infinitely small fraction of the Supreme Soul," the king "is said to shine with one half of the fiery energy of the sun which is identified with the Supreme Soul." When the secular hierarchy of the polity intersects with the ritual hierarchy, the latter (for example, the status of the Brahman) is subsumed by the former.

As Burghart affirms, the ultimate guarantor of the caste system is secular power. Indeed, the king in traditional Hindu society "exercises the authority to order the relationships upon a territory between castes or between householders and ascetics." The ideology of caste ultimately depends on secular power for its dominance. Where that secular power no longer guarantees the ritual hierarchy, as in contemporary South Asian states, the ritual order is increasingly called into question by traditionally subordinated groups. In contemporary India, many so-called untouchable groups have rejected the caste system and their position within it, and have converted to other religions—Islam, Buddhism, and Christianity—in an attempt to escape its inequities.

References

Basham, A. L. 1971. *The wonder that was India: A survey of the history and culture of the Indian sub-continent before the coming of the Muslims*. London: Fontana.

Burghart, Richard. 1996. Hierarchical models of the Hindu social system. In *The conditions of listening: Essays on religion, history and politics in South Asia*. Delhi: Oxford University Press.

Cohn, Bernard S. 1971. *India: The social anthropology of a civilization*. Englewood Cliffs, N.J.: Prentice-Hall.

Dumont, Louis. 1980. *Homo hierarchicus: The caste system and its implications*. Chicago: University of Chicago Press.

Hocart, A. M. 1950. *Caste, A comparative study*. London: Methuen.

Höfer, Andras. 1979. The caste hierarchy and the state in Nepal. A study of the Muluki Ain of 1854. *Khumbu Himal* 13:2. Innsbruck: Universitätsverlag Wagner.

Marriott, McKim, and Ronald B. Inden. 1974. "Caste systems." *Encyclopedia Britannica, Macropaedia*. 3: 981–982.

Quigley, Declan. 1993. *The interpretation of caste*. New York: Oxford University Press.

Srinivas, M. N. 1966. *Social change in modern India*. Berkeley: University of California Press.

ARJUN GUNERATNE

SEE ALSO

Caste Mark (*Bindi, Boṭṭu*); Caste Myths of Andhra Pradesh; Person

CASTE MARK (*BINDI, BOṬṬU*)

A caste mark is an identity symbol of a community or group. An example is the red dot worn on the forehead by women in India. This ancient tradition has special significance for Hindus. The term *bindi* can be taken to represent the tradition in northern India and the term *boṭṭu* in southern India. Bindi means "round" in Sanskrit language; boṭṭu, derived from Dravidian sources, means "fingertip." The Sanskrit term *kunkuma* is synonymous with bindi, but kunkuma also has a meaning of *kēśara,* meaning "pollen of flowers." Historical references found in third- and fourth-century works (Vimala Jataka's drawings) indicate the antiquity of the tradition. Hinduism, as is well known, has a hierarchical system of varnas and castes. There is a view that the bindi, boṭṭu tradition was incorporated by the Aryans from non-Aryan peoples; the bindi, boṭṭu tradition is associated with the culture of women, whereas Aryanism is associated with the worship of male gods. All three important gods in Hinduism, namely Brahma, Visṇu, and Mahēśwara, are male gods.

The custom of preparing material for making bindi from soot is ancient. Soot is collected on a small plate held over the flame of castor seed oil lamp, and is worn on the forehead or on the cheeks to ward off the evil eye. The materials used for warding off the evil eye and for wearing on the forehead were traditionally prepared from native natural sources. The seeds of two evergreen trees, *Malotis philipensis* and *Crocus sativus,* are used in the preparation of kunkuma. These plants are found in large number in Orissa, West Bengal, Kashmir, Himachal Pradesh, and Assam. A red powder is produced when the seeds of these trees are broken up. This is pure kunkuma. Sometimes, raw fruits are soaked in water and a red liquid is obtained. When the liquid dries up, a red powder remains. This powder is used as kunkuma. Kunkuma can also be prepared from turmeric, jaggery, and asafoetida. Another way of obtaining kunkuma is by chemical action of sulphuric acid on turmeric roots. This kunkuma is made fragrant by adding perfumes. Black, deep red, blue, yellow, and rose kunkuma are now available. In addition kunkuma paste, rather than the traditional powder, is now available for wearing on the forehead.

The tradition of bindi, boṭṭu is based on religious and aesthetic considerations. The evolution of Hinduism is traced to the integration of peoples of Negritic, Austric, Dravidian, and Aryan origins. While Negritic racial features are today found among Hindu groups, Austric, Dravidian, and Aryan groups retain original racial and cultural aspects. A majority of Dravidian languages are found in southern India.

The tradition of applying a dot on the forehead is associated with sacrificial rites. Bindis are not only red, but white, yellow, brown, and black. The color red, however, seems to have special significance in ancient Indian culture. Having marked association with matriarchal families, the tradition of smearing female deities with red color has continued from early times to the present. There is the tradition of dotting with a finger the forehead of the female deity with blood of a sacrificed animal. Many tribes offer fowl, sheep, goats, and buffaloes to the deities, and their blood is smeared on the deity's forehead.

Dots of bindi and sandalwood paste are applied during worship of gods and auspicious rituals. There is a tradition of worshiping gods with the smearing of pastes of turmeric, vermilion, and sandalwood. Dots of turmeric are applied to the four corners of marriage invitation cards. Kunkuma is applied to the forehead and *mangaḷa-sūtra* (married woman's neck chain) on farewell by a woman whose husband is alive to one in similar circumstances.

Morning rituals include the application of kunkuma to the threshold. During a marriage ceremony, kunkuma is applied to the forehead of the groom after he puts on new clothing. Kunkuma is worn at the edges of a bride's new dress. This is considered auspicious and indicates good fortune for a wife. A woman wearing bindi or boṭṭu is considered to be auspicious and a woman without bindi is considered inauspicious.

Since bindi is a symbol of a married woman whose husband is alive, it is banned for a widow. The funeral of the dead husband's body is marked by throwing of kunkuma on the way. Kunkuma, which once graced the forehead of a wife, is wiped off on her becoming a widow. Unmarried girls and spinsters, however, can wear bindi.

Although it is common for Hindu women of all castes to wear bindi, there is variety in its application, indicative of caste differences. Brahman girls of Konkaṇ of western India wear small stickers or small dots of kunkuma or of black material. Smārtha Brahman women wear crescent-shaped kunkuma. Vaiṣṇava women wear a big round dot. Marathi Brahman women and Aryan women wear a dash-shaped kunkuma, and a few women put a small dark dot over the dash of kunkuma.

A few women get their foreheads tattooed in the shape of bindi. Saiva and Tamil women wear *vibhūti* (white burned cow dung) on their foreheads along with small black or red dots or dashes of kunkuma. A few women wear bindi of triangular shape, while others wear apple-shaped bindi. Some Saiva women wear four or five small dots of sandalwood paste.

Nowadays, a variety of bindi stickers are available. These stickers are in the shape of a flame, a star, an almond, and other symbols. Blue, green, and brown stickers are commonly available. In addition, bright and shiny stickers are also available. Many Muslim and Christian women have also begun wearing bindi, apparently under the influence of their Hindu neighbors. Now, widows also wear bindi as part of their makeup. Men who have applied kunkuma on their foreheads during strikes may be marking their determination to continue till victory.

References

Anantha, H. V., Krishna Ayyar, and L. V. Nanjundayya, eds. 1935. *The Mysore tribes and castes.* Mysore: Mysore University Press.

Kittel, Rev. F. 1968. *Kittel's Kannada-English dictionary.* Madras: Madras University Press.

H. M. MAHESWARAIAH

SEE ALSO
Dress; Metal and Metal-working

CASTE MYTHS OF ANDHRA PRADESH

A caste myth is a narrative of cultural identity of a particular caste. Often epic both in length and in the style of its performance presentation, it describes the origin and history of a particular caste and represents the worldview of the people who belong to it. Not merely a story or history of a caste, a caste myth is also a sacred narrative, as sacrosanct as a caste deity, whose story is usually contained in the myth.

Almost all of the castes of Andhra Pradesh have their own narratives. In Telugu, the language of Andhra Pradesh, the term for caste myth is *kula purāṇam* (literally, myth of a *kula,* or caste. The word *purāṇa* brings authenticity, sacredness, and antiquity to a caste history or story. Names of most of the caste myths are formed by placing the name of the caste in front of the word purāṇa. For example, narratives of this kind for the Gouḍa (toddy tapper) caste is *Gouḍapurāṇa,* for the Rajaka (washer men) caste, *Rajakapurāṇa,* and so on. Caste myths are narrated through various art forms by different castes. Distinctive musical instruments, staging techniques, and theatrical props are used in the various performance traditions. While the duration of the performances varies from three hours to three weeks, the usual length of a performance is one complete night, that is, seven hours. Caste myths of some economically and educationally developed castes are also available in written tradition in regional languages and even in Sanskrit.

A caste myth always tries to elevate the concerned caste into a high position in the social hierarchy. It frequently argues that the caste was born at the time of the creation of the universe itself, and that the originator of the caste is none other than the supreme god. Some caste myths depict the tools of the caste occupation as created by gods and the occupations as originating because the gods needed them. The caste myth of the Māḍigas, an untouchable caste, for example, depicts how their caste deity (*kula dēvata*), Jāmbavantuḍu, created the universe, their occupation, and the tools of their trade. The Māḍigas point to this myth as justification that they should not be treated as polluted or lowly.

In Andhra Pradesh there is a specific social system in which caste myths are propagated, the dependent caste system. For example, the caste myth of untouchable Māḍigas is the *Jāmbapurāṇam*. It is narrated by bards belonging to another untouchable caste, the Chindus, who are exclusively patronized by the Māḍigas, and who are thus dependent on them for their livelihood. The dependent caste system, though touched upon by some scholars, such as M. N. Srinivas and M. V. T. Raju, has not received the same importance in folklore and anthropological studies of India as some better-known systems of patronage such as *jajmāni* and *watandāri*. Most of the castes of Andhra Pradesh have some dependent caste to propagate their caste myths and recite their genealogies. Within some areas, each of the dependent castes has hereditary rights to recite genealogies and perform its art form, the narration of its patron's myth. The indigenous terminology for this jurisdiction is *mēra* and *mirāsi,* which also expresses the sum of yearly remuneration (in different forms) for their services. The dependent castes are called *arthi kulālu* (begging castes), *kulam biḍḍalu* (sons of the patron caste), *arthi biḍḍalu* (begging sons), or *gōtralavāru* (genealogists).

The patron castes are called *āsāmulu* or *yajamānulu,* both words meaning patrons or householders. There are several words to express the nature of yearly remuneration that dependent castes receive from their patrons for their obligatory yearly tours to their villages: *vaṇtana, kaṭnam, tyāgam.* These traditional relations between patron and dependent castes are alive even today.

Stories of the caste myths are usually adapted from the stories of the *aṣṭadaśa purāṇas* (the eighteen major Sanskrit purāṇas). They take characters and episodes from the Sanskrit purāṇas and add to them the story of their caste, creating an independent purāṇa. In the process, the caste myth tends to alter the values and social structure propagated by normally high-caste Sanskrit ideology, creating a "counternarrative." A caste myth also functions as oral codification of the norms, customs, and laws of the concerned caste, and, as such, governs the rituals and behavior of the caste. Each caste myth is regarded by the caste with pride and honor.

References

Raju, M. V. T. 1980. Persistence and change, a study of Watandari system in rural Telingana with special reference of Medak District. Ph.D. diss., Department of Anthropology, Andhra University, Visakhapatnam.

Srinivas, M. N. 1966. *Social change in modern India.* Berkeley: University of California Press.

Wiser, W. H. 1936. *The Hindu jajmani system.* Lucknow: Lucknow Publishing House.

PULIKONDA SUBBACHARY

SEE ALSO

Dependent Performing Castes; Epic; Gods and Goddesses; *Jajmāni;* Myth; *Purāṇa; Watandāri* System

CATHOLICISM, SRI LANKA

Sinhala Catholics form around 8 percent of the total Sinhala population of Sri Lanka. Most are concentrated along the western coast, although there is a series of small Roman Catholic enclaves in the interior of the island. The community was founded by the Portuguese in the sixteenth century. During Dutch rule in the seventeenth and eighteenth centuries, Catholics were subject to various degrees of persecution. The establishment of British rule at the end of the eighteenth century brought in a century and a half during which the Catholic Church and its followers formed a relatively privileged minority, but after independence in 1948 Catholics began to feel themselves increasingly marginalized in a Buddhist-dominated society. Not surprisingly, Sinhala Catholic folklore reflects the complex history of Catholics in Sri Lanka and the position of a minority religious community within the country as a whole.

There are a number of myths that center on the position of Catholic teaching in an Asian context. A frequent form of syncretism is the simple equation of Buddhist and Hindu supernatural beings with the saints of Catholicism. Thus, the god Skanda (otherwise known as Kataragama) is often equated with St. Anthony of Padua, while the goddess Pattini is equated with the Virgin Mary. Such identifications make no claim to a superior status for the teachings of the Church, but others are less egalitarian. One story, popular along the northwest coast of the island, claims that St. Sebastian is the elder brother of Mari (or Kāli) Ammā, a goddess of the Buddhists and Hindus. Another claims that the famous fifteenth-century Buddhist monk Sri Rāhula converted to Catholicism and became Francis Xavier, whose incorruptible body still lies in Goa. A third pits one of the most charismatic Catholic priests of the 1980s against a Buddhist priest rumored to be a sorcerer. A similar vein of thought can be seen in the acceptance of the existence of reincarnation for non-Catholics who will ultimately be reborn as Catholics before their final escape from rebirth.

The same sort of ambivalence can be seen in the forms of spirit possession and exorcism in Sinhala Catholic Sri Lanka. Traditionally, demonic possession was relatively rare and dealt with in the main by laymen who had access to certain powerful prayers collected in "Books of Protection." These originated during the Dutch period when there were few missionaries in Sri Lanka and functions otherwise associated with the clergy were delegated to laymen. Besides demonic possession, the prayers in such books cover a wide range of misfortunes from toothache to cattle disease. The prayers themselves, often said to be written by the famous Oratorian Father Joseph Vaz, are clearly modeled on Buddhist prototypes and are thought by their users to have power precisely because of the form of language used.

More recently, demonic possession has increased in importance, and other forms of exorcism have become popular. These center on particular people who are considered to have certain supernatural powers, rather than on particular prayers, as in older styles of exorcism. In effect, exorcism becomes a gift rather than a learned technique. This again is broadly in line with changes among Sinhala Buddhists, where new forms of religiosity and new forms of exorcism have become increasingly common. Yet while there is commonality, there is also difference: increasingly, the demons that afflict Catholics are the gods of the Buddhists and Hindus of Sri Lanka.

At different times the hierarchy of the Church has taken different attitudes toward the syncretic beliefs and practices of lay Catholics, and frequently, there have been disagreements among the clergy as to how to react to lay Catholic practice. The attitude of the Church as a whole has tended to vary as has its political position. During Dutch rule, priests had little choice but to adjust to local conditions, but with British rule, an increasing number of foreign priests entered Sri Lanka and attempted to regularize what they saw as decidedly heterodox beliefs and practices. In postcolonial Sri Lanka, the declining political power of the Church, coupled with the changes brought about by Vatican II, led to factions developing among the priesthood and, among some priests at least, an attempt to "indigenize" the Church. The result was that there was some decline in attempts to impose uniformity of belief and practice.

However, such tendencies developed in a rather convoluted way, in that those most interested in "indigenizing" Catholic belief and practice were also those who saw themselves as most "rational" and, thus, opposed to what they saw as superstition. This led to a number of attacks on long-standing traditions among Catholics. Thus, for instance, Easter celebrations along the coast had often involved the staging of Passion plays, with large puppets being used instead of actors. This appears to have had its origins in South India, and myths tell of how particular statues originated in particular Indian towns. In the 1930s, however, puppets were replaced by human actors in some Passion plays, supposedly as the result of visits by Sinhala Catholics to Oberammergau in Germany. Elsewhere, the use of puppets continued but was frequently attacked as superstitious and even as "non-Sri Lankan" by clerical critics. Such attacks also involved criticism of the supposedly magical powers of the statues used in the plays.

More generally, statues and images have an important role for many Sinhala Catholics. Some statues, notably those of St. Anthony at the famous Kochchikade church in Colombo and the Blessed Virgin Mary at Madhu, as well as the image of St. Anne at the pilgrimage church of Talawila, are said to have supernatural powers that derive from their origins. Traditionally, small images of saints such as St. Anthony of Padua and St. Benedict were buried in the foundations of houses during construction, and most Catholics wear small amulets bearing images of saints. Unlike the statues mentioned earlier, the power of these images is thought to reside in the prayers said over them, the same principle being used to explain the power of well-used rosaries.

Despite changes in the Church and in contemporary Sri Lanka, traditional forms of Catholic belief and practice continue to be important. Although particular forms of religiosity, for instance, the "Books of Protection," are falling out of use, others are developing in the fluid multicultural context that is contemporary Sri Lanka.

References

Boudens, Robrecht. 1979. *Catholic missionaries in a British colony: Successes and failures in Ceylon 1796–1893.* Immensee: Nouvelle Revue de Science Missionaire [New review of missionary science].

Peiris, Edmund, 1943. Sinhalese Christian literature of the XVIIth and XVIIIth centuries. *Journal of the Royal Asiatic Society* (Ceylon Branch) 35: 163–181.

Stirrat, R. L. 1982. Shrines, pilgrimages and miraculous powers in Roman Catholic Sri Lanka. In *The church and healing,* ed. W. J. Shiels. Oxford: Basil Blackwell.

———. 1992. *Power and religiosity in a post-colonial setting.* Cambridge: Cambridge University Press.

RODERICK STIRRAT

SEE ALSO

Christianity, Kerala; Exorcism; Festival of St. Francis; Kataragama; Religion; Saints; Syncretism; Theater and Drama, Sri Lanka; Worship

CAVITTU NĀṬAKAM

Cavittu nāṭakam literally means "kicking" (or "stamping") drama and refers to the Christian dance-drama of Kerala, dating from the latter half of the sixteenth century, in which all-male performers would take large, wide, hard, leaping/arcing steps/stamps as they danced dynamic choreography on a raised all-wooden stage and fought martial-arts-inspired stage battles with swords and shields. Similar in many ways to the uses of drama in New World proselytizing among Native Americans, the dramas of conquest indigenous to the Iberian Peninsula, and the development of Lenten dramas in the Philippines, *cavittu nāṭakam* was invented by Jesuits, working with Catholic converts, as a means of education and entertainment. Freely combining indigenous dance, martial arts, and music with European-inspired content and choral singing, in addition to biblical stories, a performance traditionally enacts the great epics and myths of Western Christendom. Stories of Charlemagne and of St. George and the Dragon are presented on Catholic feast days, at weddings, and at other major celebrations during the dry season in the central region of Kerala, where there is the highest concentration of Latin Christians.

During a performance, the troupe leader serves as on-stage stage manager, directing the action, encouraging the elaborately and regally costumed performers, prompting forgetful actors, and seeing that all-night performances keep moving in front of the painted backdrops. In a traditional performance, the comic character (*kattiyan*) serves as commentator and translator and often takes roles in the plays. Approximately thirty years ago, women began to appear on stage in women's roles. As late as the 1970s, a few new plays were written and companies gave occasional performances; however, in spite of attempts to revive interest and patronage, performances are seldom commissioned today.

References

Bake, Arnold Adrian. 1963. Charlemagne in Malabar, *Folk-lore* 74: 450–459.

Chummar, Chundal. 1978. Medieval religious drama of Europe and Chavittu-natakam of Kerala. *Malayalam Literary Survey* 2(3): 76–85.

———. 1984. *Christian theatre in India*. Trichur: Kerala Folklore Academy.

Raphy, Sabeena. 1964. *Cavittunatakam* (in Malayalam). Kottayam: National Book Stall.

———. 1969. Chavittu-Natakam, dramatic opera of Kerala. *Sangeet Natak* 12: 56–73.

Swiderski, Richard M. 1987. Representing representing: A *cavittunatakam* performance. *Asian Theatre Journal* 4(2): 177–190.

PHILLIP B. ZARRILLI

SEE ALSO

Christianity, Kerala; Comedians, Jesters, and Clowns; Dance; Kerala; Martial Arts Traditions; Theater and Drama

CENTRAL HIMALAYAN STATES

There is no universally accepted classification for grouping the peoples of the Uttar Pradesh Himalayas (Garhwal and Kumaon). Constant migrations and population shifts have led to complex patterns and the coexistence of varied categorizations. The ratio of the castes in Garhwal is roughly 60 percent Rajputs, 20 percent Brahmans, and 20 percent service groups.

One of the most striking differences between the caste systems of the plains and of the hills is the fact that in the plains there are multiple divisions of the castes, whereas in the hills one usually finds a twofold division between pure high-caste groups (Brahmans and Rajputs) and impure low-caste groups (Doms or Koḷṭas and artisan groups). Intermarriage between members of different castes within these two groups is quite common. In some parts of western Garhwal, where the percentage of Brahmans is below even 20 percent, the twofold division is interpreted by the Rajputs as built on an opposition between the "strong" martial Rajputs and the "weak" Koḷṭas. The Koḷṭas, on the other hand, quote myths according to which the first Rajput and the first Koḷṭa were brothers, and that, due to some mishap, the Koḷṭas lost their high status. According to another stratigraphic model prevalent among the Rajputs of western Garhwal, a distinction is made between original and secondary or derived castes: the Brahmans, Rajputs, and Koḷṭas are the original castes, and they are identified with the colors white, red, and black. The "secondary" or "derived" castes are the carpenters (Baṛi), musicians (Deuāḷ, Daki), and the gold- and blacksmiths (Sunār and Loār). They, too, are identified with the three colors. However, here, white and red are polluted by black. Carpenters and musicians are whitish, goldsmiths are dark red, and blacksmiths are black. Carpenters and musicians maintain close, multifarious relations with the regional deities, and the musicians—though low caste, they are fairly pure—frequently have their houses beside the village temples. Like the Koḷṭas, the members of the various "derived" castes have myths describing the high rank they originally held. The musicians, for instance, say that their first ancestor and the first Brahman were brothers.

Especially in the central and eastern areas the emigration of high castes from the plains to the hills has led to a twofold hierarchy of Brahmans and Rajputs. There is a difference between the so-called *asal* ("real") Brahmans and Rajputs, who are regarded higher in status, and the Khaṣ Brahmans and Rājputs. The Khaṣ (or Khaṣiya) castes form the largest "ethnic" group. They are mentioned as early as the *Purāṇa*s and the *Mahābhārata,* and they still dominate the western parts of Garhwal where a twofold hierarchy is not found. In contrast to the asal castes, who conform to the orthodox elite Hindu manners, the Khaṣiyas follow their own customary laws like bride-price and widow remarrying.

Whereas the names of the various low castes frequently denote their traditional occupations, the caste names of the upper division are frequently based on the name of their native village. In those areas where the social structures were dominated by Hindu kingdoms, however, many Rajput caste names correspond to hereditary administrative offices.

In connection with caste names referring to the place of origin, Jean-Claude Galey (181) remarks, "The importance still given today to titles, brotherhoods, and local origins may be the sign of an original system where territorial and clanic dimensions—two features ordinarily left aside from the characterization of castes and kept for the description of tribal populations—had here direct incidence over the definition of legitimate power." Exponents of this power were not only the kings and their representatives, or, especially in western Garhwal and eastern Himachal Pradesh, royal deities theocratically ruling over sharply outlined territories, but also Rajput clan chiefs (called Khūnd in the western districts) who appear in the local traditions as martial, freedom-loving warriors.

Whereas there existed a number of structural similarities between the old Hindu kingdoms of the central Himalayas and the theocratic deities with regard to hierarchical organization and multiplicity of functionaries, the characteristic patterns of the clan chiefs looked very different. In those areas where they had not become mere vassals of kings or powerful deities, the Khūnd clans were typically organized in moieties, called *śaṭi* and *pāśi*. Formerly, such divisions used to be exteremely hostile to each other; sheep raids, wife capture, and headhunting were common practice. The captured heads of slain enemies were buried either beneath the village temple (*thāri*) or placed into village sanctuaries called *jaga* ("place"). Such bloody clashes, which continued over generations, were said to be conducted according to the example of the war between the Pāṇḍavas and Kauravas.

References

Berreman, Gerald D. 1972 (1963). *Hindus of the Himalayas. Ethnography and change.* Berkeley: University of California Press.

Edye, E. H. H. 1994 (1921). The depressed classes of Kumaon Hills. In *Himalaya: Past and present,* ed. Maheshwar P. Joshi, Allen C. Fanger, Charles W. Brown, vol. 3, *1992–1993.* Almora: ASH (Association of Studies on Himalayas) Publication Series No. 5, 115–120.

Galey, Jean-Claude. 1992. Hindu kingship in its ritual realm: The Garhwali configuration. In *Himalaya: Past and present,* ed. Maheshwar P. Joshi, Allen C. Fanger, Charles W. Brown, vol. 2, *1991–1992.* Almora: ASH (Association of Studies on Himalayas) Publication Series No. 3, 173–237.

Joshi, L. D. 1929. *The Khasa family law in the Himalayan districts of the United Provinces India.* Allahabad: The Superintendent, Government Press.

Joshi, M. C. 1990. The Khasas in the history of Uttārakhaṇḍ. In *Himalaya: Past and present,* ed. Maheshwar P. Joshi, Allen C. Fanger, Charles W. Brown. Almora: ASH (Association of Studies on Himalayas) Publication Series No. 1: Introductory Volume, 193–200.

Lalit, C. R. B. 1993. Thoḍa: A martial game of the Khasha people of Himachal Pradesh. In *Mahābhārata in the tribal and folk traditions of India,* ed. K. S. Singh. New Delhi: Indian Institute of Advanced Study; Simla, Anthropological Survey of India.

Saklani, Atul. 1987. *The history of a Himalayan princely state. Change, conflicts and awakening (an interpretative history of princely state of Tehri Garhwal, U. P.) (A.D. 1815 to 1949 A.D.).* Delhi: Durga Publications.

Vidal, Denis. 1988. *Le Culte des divinités locales dans une région de l'Himachal Pradesh.* Institut Français de Recherche Scientifique pour le Développement en Coopération. Paris: Edition de l'Orstom.

Zoller, Claus Peter. 1993. On Himalayan ball games, headhunting, and related matters. In *Flags of fame. Studies in South Asian folk culture,* ed. Heidrun Brückner, Lothar Lutze, and Aditya Malik. New Delhi: Manohar.

CLAUS PETER ZOLLER

SEE ALSO

Baṇgāṇī Ball Games; Baṇgāṇī *Mahābhārata;* Caste and State, India and Nepal; Dom; Himachal Pradesh

CHAHĀRBAYTĪ

Chahārbaytī is a term commonly applied to folk quatrains in Persian, which are the basis of an important singing tradition in Persian-speaking areas of Afghanistan, Iran, and Tajikistan. *Bayt* is a simplified term; in Badakhshan (northeast Afghanistan) *falak* is also used. Chahārbaytī spring from a popular, improvisatory, oral tradition for men and women. Assumed to be of oral origin, the form is ancient, probably dating from at least the first centuries of Islam. Examples attributed to Baba Tahir of Iran (d. 1015) were preserved orally and subsequently written down.

Thousands of chahārbaytī and their variants exist, transmitted through singing. Men and women have composed them, but authorship is generally unrecorded, apart from rare instances, such as Jalalī (see below). The quatrains use colloquial language and often contain dialect words and local grammatical forms. For such reasons chahārbaytī has resisted conventional analysis and received scant attention from literary historians.

Chahārbaytī is itself ambiguous. *Chahār* (Persian: "four") and *bayt* (Arabic: literally "house" or "tent" but also "poetic couplet") renders the meaning "four couplets," whereas there are only two. According to Blum, in the dialect of Khorasan *bayt* is generally used for a single poetic line—hence the term *chahārbayti:* "fourliner" (Blum, 90). A synonymous term *dūbaytī* ("two couplets") is current in Iran, but in Afghanistan familiar only to the educated.

Confusion has been compounded by the use of other terms as synonyms for chahārbaytī. In his treatise on poetics, the Herati poet Jāmī (1414–1492) states: "For *Rubā'i* [literary quatrain] we meet occasionally with the names *Chahārbaytī, Dūbaytī,* and *Tarāna* [song]." Similarly Saifi's treatise (1491) equates rubā'i with dubaytī and tarāna. The literary quatrain, rubā'i, is distinct in meter and other formal properties. Farhadi makes this clear, as does Iwanow, who collected over 400 chahārbaytī in the district of Sabzevar (Iranian Khorasan).

The quatrain consists of four hemistichs (*misra'*). Each misra' normally contains eleven syllables, but this is flexible. Scholars describe the meter as a variant of

Arabic *hazaj*:

V – – – /V – – – /V – –

The rhyme scheme is normally aaba. An example from Herat demonstrates two other common features of chahārbaytī: (1) the first half of lines 2 and 3 is identical; (2) in lines 1, 2, and 4, the ninth syllable is formed by an additional suffix: "*o*" (after *kār, bīmār,* and *yār*) to render the necessary eleven syllables. This is an accepted convention for singing.

Alā bāghwān be bāghat kāro dārom
Bechīn yak dasteh gol bimāro dārom
Bechīn yak dasteh gol bimār kharāb é
Mesāle dasteh gol yak yāro dārom

Oh gardener, I need something from your garden
Pick me a bunch of flowers, I am ill
Pick me a bunch of flowers, it's bad to be ill
I have a sweetheart who is like a bunch of flowers.

Chahārbaytī content is usually melancholy and spiritual in tone. Principal themes are the passion of love (*chahārbaytī 'ishqī*) and separation from home (*chahārbaytī gharībī*). Some quatrains invoke the help of local saints, or refer to their shrines. Local place names occur, and rural imagery is common, especially in remote areas.

'Ishqī quatrains are infused with the imagery of Sufi mystical love, for example, the nightingale serenading the flower or the moth burning itself on the candle. The prototypical male lover is Majnun, a legendary Arab bedouin who went mad and pined away for love of Layla, whose family refused his suit. A corpus of quatrains attributed to Jalālī, a twentieth-century shepherd from Ghor (west Afghanistan), follows this model of suffering, sleeplessness, pain, and poetic inspiration. Jalālī was smitten with love for Sīāh Mū, whose father would not agree to their marriage. This quatrain is well known (phrases in parentheses added in performance):

(Akh) Jalālī āsheq-e rū-ye Sīāh Mū (āh del ārām eh)
Asīr-e chashm-e jādū-ye Sīāh Mū (jān-e mahbub)
(Ākh) kunad sojda Jalāli az sar-e seqd
Be mihrāb-e dū ābrū-ye Siāh Mū (jān)

Alas, Jalālī is in love with Sīāh Mū, o quiet heart
Captivated by the bewitching eyes of Sīāh Mū,
beloved soul,
Jalālī prostrates himself for the sake of being true
Before the prayer-niche of Sīāh Mū's eyebrows, dear

'Ishqī verses predominate in Farhadi's collection of quatrains from the Kabul region. In Badakhshān separation from home and the trials of fate are important. There the word *falak* ("firmament," "destiny"), synonymous with chahārbaytī, refers to the wheel of fate causing people to wander from home. A quatrain sung by Baba Naim (reported by Slobin) recalls the flight of refugees from Soviet Tajikistan (Kulab) to Afghanistan (Balkh) during the Basmachi uprisings of the 1920s and 1930s:

Charkh-e falak mārā be charkh āwordī
Kulāb budīm, mārā dar Balkh āwordī
(Jānam dar) Kulāb budīm o mīkhordīm āb-i shīrīn
Åz āb-i shīrīn bar āb-i talkh āwordī

O wheel of fortune, you spun us around
I was in Kulab, you brought us to Balkh
Dear, we drank sweet water in Kulab
You brought us from the sweet water to the bitter.

Some quatrains are more down-to-earth. In examples Shahrani translates from Badakhshān women, they criticize the cowardice of men they love.

O boy, why did you put on a man's turban?
When I fell in love with you, you did not care for me.
I swear to God I am in love with you.
Why did you put on a coward's turban?

Chahārbaytī are single entities, not sung in any particular grouping or order. They may be sung by anyone, although children are not normally concerned with such adult themes. Performance is solo. Sometimes singers take turns, "following" one another's verses. The male voice may be accompanied by a string instrument, such as *dutār* or *qīchak*. The term chahārbaytī also refers to a purely instrumental rendition of this style.

Intimate social gatherings for men or women provide the normal context for performance. These may be performed for relaxation, to enliven communal work, or as part of marriage or birth ceremonies. Quatrains are often sung at home. In Badakhshān they are sung in *qoshqāna* (guest houses). Men (but not women) may sing out in the open, working in the fields or minding sheep.

Traditional chahārbaytī melodies exist in a variety of melodic modes. They are in free rhythm, narrow in tonal range, and slow in tempo, with extended ornamental phrases at the end of each line. Additional cadential phrases are sometimes used. Professional musicians recognize regional melodies, for example, *Shomālī* (northern), referring to Parwan, north of Kabul; *Sarhadī* (from the border), referring to the border between Afghanistan and Iran, and other more local variations. Some paired chahārbaytī melodies exist, where two closely related but distinct melodies are sung in alternation, the one with the higher melodic range preceding the lower, for example, in the Shomāli style.

Some also have a chorus which is in rhythm, for example, *Sīāh Mū o Jalālī*. These versions of chahārbaytī performance are more like composed songs, popularized on the radio and taken into the repertoire of urban professional singers.

References

Blochmann, Henry. 1970. *The prosody of the Persians according to Saifi, Jami and other writers.* Reprint of Calcutta edition, 1872. Amsterdam: Philo Press.

Blum, Stephen. 1974. Persian folksong in Meshed (Iran), 1969. *Yearbook of the International Folk Music Council* 4:86–114.

Farhadi, Abdul Ghafur. 1955. *Le Persan parlé en Afghanistan: Grammaire du Kaboli accompagnée d'un recueil de quatrains populaires de la région de Kabol.* Paris: C. Klincksieck.

Herawi, Mayel. 1347AH. *Siahmu, Litan, Mariam* (quatrains in Persian). Kabul: Daulati Matba'a.

Iwanow, W. 1925. Rustic poetry in the dialect of Khorasan. *Journal of the Asiatic Society of Bengal* 21(3): 233–313.

Sakata, Hiromi Lorraine. 2002. *Music in the mind: The concepts of music and musicians in Afghanistan,* 2nd ed. Washington, D. C.: Smithsonian Institution Press.

Shahrani, Enayatullah. 1973. The 'Falaks' of the mountains. *Afghanistan* 26(1): 68–75.

Slobin, Mark. 1970. Persian folksong texts from Afghan Badakhshan. *Iranian Studies* 3(2): 91–103.

Utas, Bo. 1994. Arabic and Iranian elements in new Persian prosody. In *Arabic prosody and its applications in Muslim poetry,* 129–143. Stockholm: Swedish Research Institute in Istanbul.

Recordings of Chahārbaytī Performance

Baily, John. 1988. *Music of Afghanistan: Professional musicians in the city of Herat.* Cambridge: Cambridge University Press, accompanying audiocassette.

Sakata, Hiromi Lorraine. 1983. *Music in the mind: The concepts of music and musician in Afghanistan.* Kent, Ohio: Kent State University Press, two accompanying audiocassettes.

Slobin, Mark. 1972. *An anthology of the world's music. Afghanistan III. Music of the Tajiks.* AST-4007. Anthology Record and Tape Corporation, 135 West 41st St, New York, NY 10036. Long-playing record.

VERONICA DOUBLEDAY

SEE ALSO
Afghanistan; Song

CHAPBOOKS

Chapbooks are small, cheap, mass-produced booklets in paper bindings, written in simple poetry or prose and dealing with traditional subjects. Their subject matter includes, but is not limited to, traditional and modern romances and adventure stories (*dāstān*); retellings of traditional tales from Sanskrit, Persian, or Arabic literary sources; religious and secular poetry; religious stories of a popular nature; books of spells and charms; advice on marriage (based on traditional approaches rather than modern Western psychology); familiar selections of "classical" poetry (generally Persian); film songs and stories; and humorous stories and jokes. Excluded from this category are children's books, schoolbooks, instructional manuals, deliberately didactic works such as guides to prayer, and small books bound in boards (which would make them more expensive than paper-bound chapbooks). Chapbooks may be illustrated with simple line drawings. Chapbooks in Hindi and Persian are generally typeset, while those in Urdu, Pashto, Punjabi, and other languages of Pakistan are lithographed from copy written out by professional scribes.

Chapbooks usually come in two sizes: 4″ × 6″ and 7″ × 9.5″. Before World War II, chapbooks either had no cover, or a cover that duplicated the title page. Today they are almost always bound in colorful paper covers, often with pictorial designs inspired by the content of the book.

The term "chapbook" is of English origin and is used to denote these small books produced in South Asia because, first, the size, format, and contents of the South Asian books are very similar to those of European chapbooks, and second, because there is no single term in the languages of South Asia to denote them. Examples of chapbooks can be found in most of the languages used in northern India, Pakistan, and Afghanistan, and further afield in Iran.

Chapbooks began to appear in South Asia shortly after the foundation of Fort William College in Calcutta in 1800. This college was founded as a language training center for British administrators, and part of its program was to produce a series of simple printed books, written in good Hindi and Urdu, for student use. By virtue of this, Fort William became an early and important source of texts, many of which were retellings of traditional tales and stories that were soon taken up by commercial printers and issued in the form of chapbooks. As printing for a mass market developed and spread in the subcontinent, chapbooks became a staple item.

The chapbook industry is still lively in Pakistan, less so in India. The main centers of chapbook production in India were Delhi, Lucknow, and Calcutta. In Pakistan, Lahore and Peshawar, and more recently, Karachi, have been the most important sources of these books, with smaller cities such as Multan and Mardan contributing a share. Chapbook publishers are located in the older, more traditional parts of these cities, such as the Urdu Bazaar near the Jāma' Masjid in Delhi, Qiṣṣa Khwānī Bazaar in Peshawar, or Nau Likhā Bazaar in Lahore.

Chapbooks are sold most often by the publishers themselves. Other outlets are booksellers in the older parts of cities, "footpath"(sidewalk) sellers, and itinerant chapmen who travel from village to village selling small items, including chapbooks.

Chapbooks exist at the interface of oral and print cultures. Produced for the lowest economic level of the mass market, they are frequently read out loud by literate people to their unlettered families and friends. Their content embodies many of the values and worldviews of the various language groups that produce them. Some favorites, with long publishing histories, are *Śīt Basant* and *Vikram* in Hindi; *Fasāna-yi 'Ajā'ib, Gul-i Bakāwalī,* and *Chabīlī Bhatiyārī* in Hindi and Urdu; *Gul wa Ṣanaubar* and *Amīr Ḥamza* in Urdu; *Hīr Rānjhā* and *Sassī Punnūn* in Punjabi; and *Rāmdād Khān* and *Ādam Khān Dur Khānai* in Pashto. A measure of the shared culture of the subcontinent is the existence of such love stories as *Lailá wa Majnūn* in chapbook form in Hindi, Urdu, Persian, Pashto, and Punjabi.

While the chapbook industry is still alive, it is increasingly difficult for it to compete with modern forms of popular entertainment. The spread of literacy and the wide availability of electronic media have threatened chapbook publishers with a loss of their audience. A major function of chapbooks has been to carry and transmit traditional cultural values, so it seems unlikely that they will disappear immediately. Their future is, however, cloudy. Collections of older chapbooks can be found in the British Library and the India Office Library in London, and in the Library of Lok Virsa in Islamabad, Pakistan.

References

Hanaway, William L. 1995. Chapbooks in Pakistan. In *The other print tradition: Chapbooks, broadsides, and related ephemera,* ed. C. L. Preston and M. J. Preston, 127–143. New York: Garland.

———. 1996. Chapbook publishing in Pakistan. In *Studies in Pakistani popular culture,* ed. W. L. Hanaway and Wilma L. Heston, 339–615. Lahore: Sang-e-Meel.

Islam, Mazharul. 1970. *A history of folktale collections in India and Pakistan.* Dacca: Bengali Academy.

Jatoi, Iqbal Ali. 1980. *Bibliography of folk literature.* Islamabad: National Institute of Folk Heritage.

Pritchett, Frances W. 1985. *Marvelous encounters: Folk romance in Urdu and Hindi.* New Delhi: Manohar.

———, ed. and trans. 1991. *The romance tradition in Urdu: Adventures from the Dāstān of Amir Hamzah.* New York: Columbia University Press.

WILLIAM L. HANAWAY

SEE ALSO

Amir Ḥamza; Comic Books, India; *Dāstān;* Folk Literature; Hir Ranjha; *Kolum;* Mullā Nasruddīn

CHARACTER STEREOTYPES

Character stereotypes, vividly depicted in South Asian folklore, parody caste or ethnicity, exaggerate or overturn familial and gender roles, and satirize certain professions. While some character stereotypes are stock depictions, as in folktales (notably in the *Pañcatantra* and the Buddhist *Jātaka* tales), they are many times created contemporaneously in response to social and political situations, and, from a broader perspective, suggest shifting demarcations between "insiders" and "outsiders." Of the scores of stereotypes, the best known ones are the "greedy/miserly Brahman," the "witty minister," the "clever wife," the "fake holy man," the "wily barber," "the jester," and the "stupid politician." Like their counterparts elsewhere, such stereotypes frequently invert social expectations or norms; thus, the Brahman priest, supposedly learned and spiritual, is caricatured as foolish and obsessed with this-worldly possessions, and his elevated position in the social hierarchy is satirized. The tale of the Brahman and the coconut illustrates this: A Brahman in search of a coconut for his daily worship goes from vendor to vendor, hoping to get it at a lower and still lower price. He is finally directed to a coconut palm where he can get it at no cost. The tale ends with the miserly Brahman having to pay far more to get himself extricated from the top of the palm where he is stuck trying to pluck a coconut. The stereotype of the Brahman as a nitwit who will not deviate from his bookish learning is exemplified by the cluster of stories called "Paramānanda Śiṣyulu Kathalu," or "Tales about Paramānanda's Disciples," in Telugu folklore. These center on seven disciples of the fictional sage, Paramānanda, who come to grief because of their literal-mindedness. Among the countless illustrations of the Brahman caste's alleged greed, common to many folktales across the subcontinent, are the Assamese tale of the Brahman who, when rescued from drowning, is concerned that the rupee bill in his pocket is wet (Beck et al. 1987), and the South Indian tale in which a set of gold-hungry Brahmans are rebuffed with branding irons by Tenāli Rāma, the famous court jester (Ramanujan 1991).

In fact, the court jester who outwits learned scholars and royal personages, risking his life through impertinence toward those in power, is himself a distinctive stock character in South Asian folklore. Bīrbal, a nobleman in the Delhi court of the Mughal emperor, Akbar, Tenāli Rāma (also called Tenāli Rāmalingam, Tenāli Rāmakṛṣṇa, or Tenāli Rāman) in the South Indian Vijayanagara court of Kṛṣṇadevarāya (1509–1529), and Gopāl Bhār in the court of Kṛṣṇacandra Rāy of Nadia district in Bengal are three highly popular court jesters, about whom many times the "same" stories are told. Although widely popular, the historicity of these characters is contested; for instance, while tales place Gopāl Bhār, a barber by caste, in Kṛṣṇacandra Rāy's eighteenth-century court, critics believe that he is a fictional character created by the popular "Baṭṭalā"

("Under the Banyan Tree") presses of Calcutta. The court jester, or clown, solves conundrums (e.g., "How many crows are there in Delhi?" "How many stars are in the sky?"), teaches practical lessons, resolves problems, and provides worldly advice, and is not afraid of speaking the unpalatable truth to his master when others are silent because of fear or propriety. Each of these characters is a subject of much discussion in regional literature and literary criticism.

The "holy man," whether sannyāsī, fakir, mullā', or singing mendicant, has been an enduring and complex stereotype in representations of South Asia. The itinerant fake ascetic is a familiar figure in many folktales, as in the Assamese tale in which a *mullā,* invited to a pious couple's home, pretends to drive away a dog he claims to have "sighted" entering the *Kaabā* at Mecca. The *mullā's* claim to spiritual powers is exposed when he is unable to see the curry buried under the rice on his plate, placed by the woman of the house, who suspects his credentials (Goswami 1981). The term *Arjunasannyāsī* in Kannada and Telugu builds on this negative stereotype, and refers to Arjuna (one of the five Pāṇḍava brothers of the *Mahābhārata*), who in the guise of a sannyāsī gains access to the woman he wishes to marry. Another example of the bogus renunciant is the "Buddhist monk" in India, and especially in Sri Lanka, who is depicted in many jokes as consumed by worldly hunger for meat, wine, and sex, contrary to his Buddhist calling. Interestingly, stories of the Middle Eastern Mullā' Naṣruddīn, commonly told in South Asia, portray the *mullā* less of a fake holy man than a clever, foolish *mullā* who escapes difficult situations, including those of his own making, through his wit.

From a historical perspective, the figure of the holy man was a staple of the larger mythology of the "mystic Orient," and it was exploited in arguments that justified colonial rule. In nineteenth-century colonial writing—and also in early Indological scholarship—we find the classic stereotype of the *sādhu* or the fakir as either the austere, mystic renunciant capable of severe self-denial, representing an exalted spirituality, or a dangerous, cunning masquerader representing an uncivilized and backward culture. In popular media—cartoons and advertisements, for example—the fakir-sādhu image continues to be deployed as the mumbo-jumbo feat-performing character from the East; Narayan reports an advertisement for sports shoes in the *New York Times* that featured an "Ash-smeared, scantily clothed, and grinning . . ." sādhu on a bed of nails (1989: 71).

Character stereotypes of women in folktales range from the "hard-to-get beloved" or the "unfaithful lover," to the "clever/cruel wife" or "wicked mother-in-law." The *qawwālī* and *ghazal* traditions are famous for their poetic characterization of the women as elusive—mystical in the case of qawwālī—and yet real enough for her unrivaled physical beauty to be described in detail. She is depicted as coquettish, heartless, and unrelenting in her aloofness. A lover sings in a ghazal suspecting his beloved, *kal rāt tum kahāñ the batāna sahi sahi / dil lēke mēra hāth mēṅ kehte hai mujhse vōh, kyā lōge dām iske batāna sahi sahi* [Where were you last night, tell me the truth / With my heart in your hand you bargain, "What is the price of this, tell me the truth"]. The stereotype of the woman as the unfaithful wife fantasizing about secret lovers is also graphically portrayed in the bawdy *gālī* and *keśyā* songs sung by North Indian women during marriages. One *keśyā* verse illustrates:

> *Keśyā,* I brought a skirt from Agra, Lover
> and a wrap from Sanganeer:
> Lover, through the wrap the whole body shows,
> through the veil the fair cheeks show.
> Bite, bite the whole body,
> Don't bite the cheeks or husband will beat you.
> (Raheja and Gold 1994: 39)

More within the confines of the family, the woman is depicted as caught in the familial tensions resulting from a contest for the attention of her son or her husband, and for authority in the household. Mother-in-law/daughter-in-law folktales typically characterize one women as the persecutor, while the other through her wit develops strategies to avoid the persecution, and teaches a lesson to the aggressor. "The Clay Mother-in-Law," "The Clever Daughter-in-Law" (Ramanujan 1991), and "The Flowering Tree" (Beck et al. 1987) are examples of stories about oppressive in-laws and submissive wives. More often than not, however, the stereotype of the submissive wife is overturned in South Asian folklore. The wife is resourceful, witty, dominating, and holds the key to her husband's worldly success. A particularly illustrative story is reported by Wadley from Karimpur, North India, in which a king and a woodcutter temporarily exchange wives. The king's resourceful wife strategically manages to bring prosperity to the woodcutter, while the slovenly wife of the woodcutter puts the king through many losses: success and failure are all in the wife, concludes the narrator.

Perhaps the most exploited medium for the creation and perpetuation of stereotypes is humor, with ethnic jokes and jokes about public figures as the best-known types. Like the Irish or the Pole, the *Sardarjī* (the turbaned Sikh) is stereotyped as dim-witted, and the "Sardarjī jokes" have now become universally known. The politician, a frequent target, is made out to be poorly educated, uninformed, and generally incompetent to deal with local, national, and international situations in which he/she is constantly cast. Scores of actual politicians are made to fit this bill, and joke cycles develop around these figures, enlarging the stereotype. An uneducated erstwhile chief minister of Andhra Pradesh in South India, a joke recounts, asked his chauffeur, while driving by a theater which showed only Hindi films, what film was being shown there. When the chauffeur replied, "Under renovation undi sir" (It's under renovation, sir), the minister exclaimed in Telugu, "Oh, I didn't know English films were also screened here!"

An ingenious form of character stereotyping which, drawing sometimes on existing stereotypes, brings together ethnicity, language (particularly fluency in English) and political orientation in postcolonial contexts, is that of the emerging genre of the urban bilingual joking-question shared orally and through the internet among South Asian audiences. Through their circulation among a fluent English-speaking, often convent-educated community, these joking questions highlight the processes of insider/outsider demarcation common to stereotyping in general. They characterize, for instance, the Tamilian or the Gujarati as having pronounced regional accents when speaking English (creating thus the figure of "the vernac"), the Marwaris as misers, and the Sikhs as obsessed with their political struggle for an independent state. To illustrate: What did the Gujju (Gujarati) say on seeing the tomato lag in the vegetable race? Answer: Tomato ketchup!" ("Catch up!" pronounced in Gujarati-accented English) or How was wire invented? Answer: Two Marwaris spotted the same coin on the street! (The miserly Marwaris supposedly grabbed the coin, and stretched it in the tug-of-war that ensued.)

In the diasporic context of America and the United Kingdom, South Asian immigrants are stereotyped as belonging to one of two distinct socioeconomic groups. In the media, shows like David Letterman's "The Late Show" with Sirajul and Mujibur, the Bangladeshi convenience store owners, or "The Simpsons" with Apu, the 7–11 store owner, and "Seinfeld" with Babu Bhatt, the Pakistani restaurant owner, project the South Asian as locked in the professions of the "convenience store owner," the "cab driver," or the "motel owner." These characterizations are accompanied by images of uneducated, money-grubbing, large families crowded into small living quarters. The other stereotype is that of the upwardly mobile South Asian immigrant "doctor," or "software programmer," who is intelligent, hardworking and willing to take a lower salary in comparison to Euro-American or British colleagues. Unlike stereotypes in joking questions, which also focus on ethnicity and a lack of English-speaking fluency, media stereotypes such as the "unacculturated" Bangladeshis in Letterman's show have been denounced by South Asian groups as racist as, given their diasporic location, such depictions tend to conflate cultures with their stereotypes.

References

Beck, B. P. Claus, P. Goswami, and J. Handoo. 1987. *Folktales of India.* Chicago: University of Chicago Press.

Goswami, Praphulladatta. 1981. Assamese tales of priests and priesthood. *Journal of Indian folkloristics* 4.

Narayan, Kirin. 1989. *Storytellers, saints, and scoundrels.* Philadelphia: University of Pennsylvania Press.

Oman, Joseph C. 1905. *The mystics, ascetics and saints of India.* London: T. Fisher Unwin.

Ramanujan, A. K. 1987. *Folktales from India.* New Delhi: Penguin.

Raheja, Gloria G., and Ann G. Gold. 1994. *Listen to the heron's words: Reimagining gender and kinship in North India.* Berkeley: University of California Press.

Shulman, David. 1985. *The king and the clown in South Indian myth and poetry.* Princeton: Princeton University Press.

Wadley, Susan. 1994. *Struggling with destiny in Karimpur, 1925-1984.* Berkeley: University of California Press.

LEELA PRASAD

SEE ALSO

Bhavāi; Birbal; British, Folklore About; Comedians, Jesters, and Clowns; Gender and Folklore; *Ghazal; Mahābhārata; Malang;* Mullā Nasruddīn; Nepal; *Qawwālī;* Sikh Folklore; Song; Tribal Communities, Southern India

CHAU

Chau is a dance style practiced in eastern India in the Singhbhum, Mayurbhanj, and Purulia districts of the contiguous states of Bihar, Orissa, and Bengal. Although related, the three forms of chau—Seraikella, Mayurbhanj, and Purulia—are stylistically distinct. Dance scholars variously classify them as traditional, folk, or classical. While the Mayurbhanj and the Purulia chau are danced mostly by people of the scheduled caste or by the economically disadvantaged, Seraikella chau has remained the prerogative of the royal family, the *Kashatriyas* (the warrior class). The themes are mostly from the epics and the *purāṇa*s as well as everyday life, although Seraikella chau also uses lyrical, symbolical themes. Until recently, the dancers have traditionally been male in all three styles.

The origin of the term "chau" is controversial. It has been suggested that the word is derived from *chāyā* (shadow). Some have connected it to the Sanskrit word *chadma* (disguise). Both these terms stem from Seraikella chau, due to the masks (shadow disguise) used in the dance style. Still others have affirmed that "chau" comes from *chāuni* (military camp) because of its rootedness in the martial arts. In colloquial Oriya usage it means "armor" or "hunting stealthily."

There are characteristics common to all three chau styles, the first being a foundation in martial arts. None of the styles has a rich literacy tradition or well-documented history, yet all three have a rich vocabulary of stylized movements that have commonalities in spite of their uniquenesses. They are ceremonially performed around April and have strong connections with the worship of the sun and fertility rites. And, finally, all three syncretize the tribal, village, and Brahmanical/classical traditions.

Seraikella Chau

Seraikella chau is said to have retained its cultural heritage because the princely state of Seraikella never came under foreign yoke. It is ceremonially performed during *Caitra Parva* (*Caitra* festival), culminating in mid-April, although the rituals and the dance do not seem to be interdependent. The movements are based on exercises that are known as the *parikhaṇḍā* (*pari:* shield; *khaṇḍā:* sword). As in Mayurbhanj chau, Seraikella chau has elaborate stylized movements known as *cālis* (movements in space), *ṭopkās* (gaits), *uflis* or *upalayas* (cadences of movement derived from household chores, martial arts, and gaits of animals), and *bhaṅgīs* (movement patterns). What principally distinguishes Seraikella chau from the other two is in its use of restraint, both in the movements and in the masks used.

The masks are made out of dark clay from the Kharkai River and are extremely understated, relying heavily on pastels and symbolism, such as the essence of a swan rather than the physical manifestation of a beak. The dances are generally five to ten minutes in duration and performed mostly as solos or duets. The choreography, stylistic changes, and virtuosic dancing have remained the prerogative of the royal family, although the dance style today is egalitarian in its inclusiveness of all people.

Mayurbhanj Chau

Mayurbhanj chau is staged ceremonially twice a year. The primary performance is performed during Caitra Parva, culminating in mid-April. This style retains some of the ritualistic elements connected to the worship during this festival. Although there is a lack of written history, the Kalinga chronicles reflect a dominant martial tradition. As in Seraikella chau, there are ṭopkās, uflis, and bhaṅgīs in Mayurbhanj chau. Unlike Seraikella chau, this style is vigorous and acrobatic and includes group dances as well as solos. It is also the only style of chau dance that does not use masks, although the characters appear on stage with masklike faces.

Purulia Chau

Purulia chau is ceremonially performed during the annual sun festival in Bengal, again around April. Purulia chau is even more vigorous and acrobatic than Mayurbhanj chau in its martial movements. Similar to Seraikella chau, it is a masked dance, although the masks are realistic rather than symbolic and include the complete masking of body. Extending this realism, actors portraying animals crawl on all fours. The masks of Purulia use earth, torn pieces of paper and rags, or papier-mâché. The pieces are mostly group dances, fifteen to thirty minutes long.

References

Bhattacharya, Asutosh. 1972. *Chhau dance of Purulia.* Calcutta: Rabindra Bharati University.
Emmert, Richard, et al., ed. 1983. *Dance and music in South Asian Drama.* Tokyo: The Japan Foundation.
Gargi, Balwant, 1991. Chhau. In *Folk theater of India,* 166–181. Calcutta: Rupa and Company.
Kothari, Sunil. 1968. Chhau dances of Seraikella. Bombay: Marg 22(1): 5–29.
———. 1982. Chaitra Parva rituals—chhau dances. In *The performing arts,* ed. Saryu Doshi, 74–87. Bombay: Marg.
Pani, Jivan. 1968. Chhau dances of Mayurbhanj. Bombay: Marg 22(1): 30–45.
Patnaik, D. N. 1997. The chhau dance of Mayurbhanj: I. *Sangeet Natak* 125–126 (July–December): 19–30.
———. 1998. The chhau dance of Mayurbhanj: II. *Sangeet Natak* 127–128: 59–74.
———. 1999. The chhau dance of Mayurbhanj: III. *Sangeet Natak* 131–132: 21–43.
Singh Deo, Juga Bhanu. 1973. *Chhau: Mask dance of Seraikela.* Calcutta: Radiant Process.
Tsubaki, Andrew, and Farley P. Richmond. 1990. Chau. In *Indian theatre: Traditions of performance,* ed. Farley P. Richmond, Darius L. Swann, Phillip B. Zarrilli, 359–383. Honolulu: University of Hawaii Press.
Vatsyayan, Kapila. 1980. *Traditional Indian theatre: Multiple streams.* New Delhi: National Book Trust.

RATNA ROY

SEE ALSO
Bihar; Dance; Martial Arts Traditions

CHAUBE, PAṆDIT RAM GHARIB

The Indian folklorist, ethnologist, and linguist Paṇdit Ram Gharib Chaube (date of birth unknown, died 1914), though associated to doyens of colonial ethnography, such as William Crooke and George Grierson, has remained largely unknown for his contribution. The anonymity of Ram Gharib Chaube is reflective and symbolic of many neglected aspects of colonial folklore scholarship. The sources for his biography are few: two references in Hindi (C. Shukla, 1952; P. Shukla, 1955) and a letter written by him to his British associate

William Crooke (RAI MSS 139). However, the thousands of pages of manuscripts of Indian folktales (RAI and FLS Archives) written in English by him reveal, on the one hand, a scholar of immense capability, and on the other, the hermeneutics of colonial folklore scholarship.

Chaube was born, presumably in the 1860s, in the village of Gopalpur, Gola, Gorakhpur District, in the present-day state of Uttar Pradesh in North India. It seems he received traditional learning at home and formal learning at a government school. It is more certain that he went to Calcutta for higher education and graduated from the prestigious Presidency College. Thereafter he probably worked for some time in the Governor's House, but returned to the province of his birth and reached Mirzapur, where he was known to scholars of Hindi and Persian for his linguistic and poetic talents. His fame reached the district revenue collector of Mirzapur, William Crooke, who invited Chaube to join in the study of the tribal population of Mirzapur and the popular religion and folklore of the province at a high salary of Rs. 60 per month. For the next four years (1892–1896) Chaube is known to have been a full-time scholar, who became increasingly workaholic. In these four years were produced Crooke's most important scholarly works, but Chaube was not even in the list of people acknowledged for outside help. Only in Crooke's edited journal *North Indian Notes and Queries* (1891–1896) is Ram Gharib Chaube credited for a large number of entries. In addition, Chaube and Crooke worked on a methodologically defined folktale collection—oral narratives collected through the village schoolteachers. These were submitted in vernacular, and Chaube selectively translated hundreds of them into English and explained the layers of their meaning to Crooke. In 1896, Crooke retired from the Indian Civil Service and returned to England, and with him went the manuscripts of folktales. Subsequently, Chaube worked for George Grierson's *Linguistic Survey of Bihar* for some time. Toward the end of the nineteenth century he returned destitute and workaholic to his village. The lack of adequate recognition had created a split in Chaube's identity. He was known as a scholar, but not as the (co)author of his works. This split drove him to insanity, and the old bachelor died in his village of Gopalpur in 1914. The handwritten manuscripts of the folktales are the only record of the mind of an Indian folklorist of colonial India.

Chaube's manuscripts have been in London for most of the time since Crooke's return in 1896. The unpublished collection of the 158 narratives was surveyed by this author in 1996, was subsequently researched, and is presently in the press with four chapters of introduction to *Chaube and Crooke,* an analysis of the manuscripts and the larger context of colonial folklore scholarship. More than a century later, Chaube may find his rightful place in the discipline. That would, however, challenge many other long-held notions regarding the intellectual contributions of the so-called native assistants in the making of colonial anthropology and ethnography.

References

Folklore Society (FLS) Archives, University College, London.

Royal Anthroplogical Institute (RAI) Archives, William Crooke Papers.

Amin, Shahid, ed. 1989. *William Crooke: A glossary of North Indian peasant life.* Delhi: Oxford University Press.

Crooke, William. 1891–1896. *North Indian Notes and Queries.* A monthly periodical devoted to the systematic collection of authentic notes and scraps of information regarding the country and the people. Allahabad: "Pioneer" Press.

———. 1894. *The popular religion and folklore of northern India,* 2 vols. Allahabad: Government Publication.

———. 1896. *The tribes and castes of the north western provinces,* 4 vols. Calcutta: Office of the Superintendent of Government Printing.

Morrison, Charles. 1984. Three systems of imperial ethnography. British official as anthropologist in India. In *Knowledge and society. Studies in sociology of culture past and present,* ed. Henrika Kuklick and Elizabeth Long. Greenwich, Conn.: JAI Press.

Naithani, Sadhana. 1997. The colonizer folklorist. *Journal of Folklore Research:* 1–14.

———. 2002. To tell a tale untold: Two folklorists in colonial India. *Journal of Folklore Research* 39: 2–3.

Raheja, Gloria Goodwin. 1996. Caste, colonialism, and the speech of the colonized. Entextualisation and disciplinary control in India. *American Ethnologist* 23(3): 494–513.

Rouse, W. H. D. 1899. *The talking thrush and other tales from India collected by William Crooke and retold by W. H. D. Rouse.* London: J.M. Dent & Co.

Shukl, Chandrashekhar. 1952. *Ramchandra Shukl Jeevan aur Krititva.* Varanasi Vanivitan Prakashan.

SADHANA NAITHANI

SEE ALSO

Colonialism and Folklore; Crooke, William C.; Folklorists; Grierson, George A.; Natēsa Sastrī, Pandit; *Sangēndi Mahālinga*

CHRISTIANITY, KERALA

Over one-quarter of Kerala's population are members of one of a variety of Christian denominations. While a minority are Protestants, most Kerala Christians belong either to an ancient Syrian tradition, including Orthodox, Catholic, and Anglicized denominations, or Roman Catholicism, introduced by sixteenth-century Portuguese missionaries. The Syrian, or St. Thomas, Christians form a significant majority of Kerala's Christian population, tracing their origins to the conversion of high-caste Hindus by the apostle Thomas

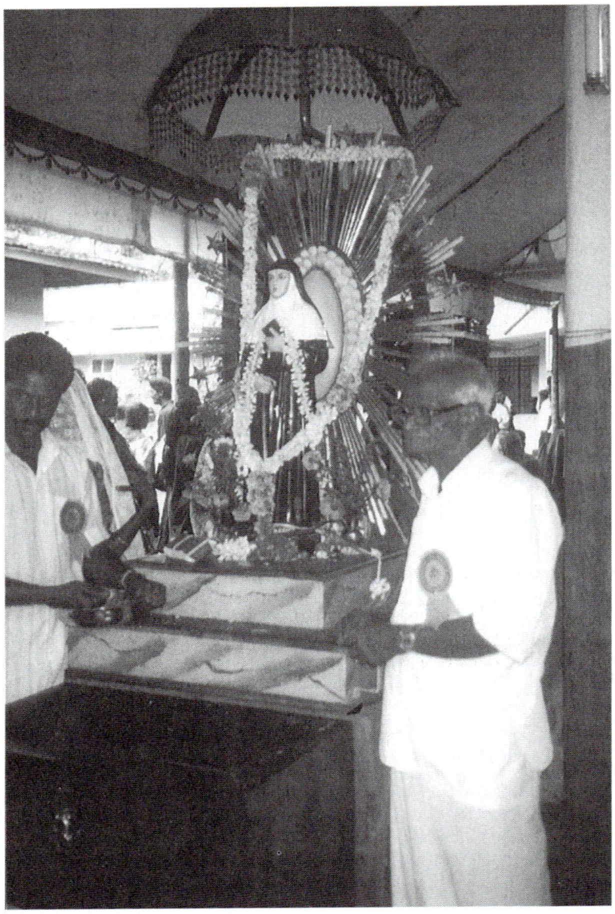

Volunteers at Sr. Alphonsa's birthday festival administer her blessings in the form of nērcha or prasādam. Kudamaloor, Kerala, India, © Corinne Dempsey

during his reported mission to South India. Large waves of Syrian merchants, arriving as early as the fourth century, and subsequent ties to West Asian ecclesial leadership contribute to a lasting Syrian influence upon much of Kerala Christianity.

Reflecting and supporting long-standing privileged status within the surrounding culture, many Syrian Christians (particularly Jacobite and Orthodox Syrian denominations centered respectively in Antioch and Kerala), as well as Roman Catholics belonging to the Eastern Malabar or Malankara rites, practice rituals similar to high-caste Hindus. Syrian Christian adherents of the Anglican-influenced Mar Thomites and Church of South India have abandoned many of these customs, however. Kerala Christian life-cycle rites—mirroring those practiced by South Indian Hindus—include the feeding of newborn babies a mixture of honey, powdered gold, and *vayambà* (an herb) to ensure their future prosperity. The highlight of Christian marriage ceremonies, similar to that of South Indian Hindus, is the groom's tying a necklace decorated with a gold leaf-shaped *tāli* around the bride's neck. Christians commonly decorate this jewelry piece, sometimes referred to as *minnà,* with a cross. A central feature of house-blessing rituals for Christians and Hindus alike is the *pāl kāchà,* or "milk boiling." To honor deceased family members, Christians annually perform Indian *śrāddham* (or, more colloquially, *cāttam*) feasts. While Keralite non-Protestant Christians typically celebrate these and other "Hindu-looking" rites with full support from church authorities, theological exegesis often differs from Hindu interpretation, rendering them, particularly on an official level, distinctly Christian.

In spite of current disregard, if not discouragement, from some clergy (particularly Roman Catholic and Protestant), many Christians heed astrological calculations and menstrual restrictions. Hindu astrologers commonly advise Christian clients and, until the first decades of this century, Jacobite and Orthodox Syrian priests regularly conducted their own astrological consultations. When planning events such as weddings or house blessings, most Christians observe *muhūrttam,* a system used throughout India for discerning auspicious and inauspicious time periods. During menstruation, women often abstain from entering church grounds or the church building itself, or from receiving the Eucharist, depending upon the individual and the efficacy of a particular church patron or festival.

The annual celebration of church saint festivals incorporates numerous Hindu traditions, such as the customary performance of traditional *ceṇdamēḷam* drumming played by temple musicians, which commonly leads Christian festival processions. Colored umbrellas associated with Hindu royalty (*muttukuṭa*) are a necessary adornment for the procession route and church festival grounds. *Alavaṭṭam* and *veṇcāmaram* (fanlike objects also associated with South Indian royalty) embellish the honored saint's garlanded statue as it brings up the rear of the procession. Until the mid-twentieth century, rooster sacrifices took place during a number of church festivals, with the festival committee serving the cooked meat as a blessing from the saint. Church festivals today more typically provide, as the saint's reciprocated offering, *nērcha* edibles, but in vegetarian form. A term used interchangeably with the Hindu *prasāda* by Kerala Christians, nērcha describes the offerings given to the saint that are left over and taken by devotees. Usually, but not always, referring to food, nērcha can be any blessed substance that is considered a "holy leftover." At festivals where devotees continue to bring live rooster offerings to saints, most commonly to St. George, churches auction them to festival participants. Fowl sacrifice, if performed at all, takes place outside the church grounds without clerical supervision.

While the atmosphere at today's prominent church festivals—complete with colorful processions, ear-splitting fireworks, animal auctions, vendors, carnival rides, and amusements—mirrors that of Kerala's temple festivals, many of these elements are a part of European festival traditions as well. Although it is nearly impossible to gauge the extent or flow of intercultural influences, the custom of offering *āḷrūpaṅgaḷ* figurines (ex-voto images, commonly corresponding to a part of the anatomy that has received or is in need of healing) to Kerala's saints as well as to Hindu deities appears to be a result of foreign influence. While the practice is not common in other parts of India, it has been widespread in Mediterranean Christian traditions for centuries. Keralite devotees most commonly offer silver or gold āḷrūpaṅgaḷ (also in the form of houses, babies, and snakes) during festivals and at major pilgrimage sites.

Also representative of interreligious dynamics in Kerala are local legends and rites. Most prevalent in the Kottayam District, a Syrian Christian stronghold, are tales linking village church saints with temple deities as siblings. Locally related by both Hindus and Christians, these stories describe sacred family members engaged in occasional spats, though ultimately reliant upon one another. Songs and stories about village church origins often convey similar themes of relational ambivalence. Depicting one segment of the Hindu community (commonly Brahman) as hindering Christians in their worship, these performances often describe a separate Hindu faction (usually members of the Nair caste) valiantly coming to the rescue. Also reflecting distinct yet interdependent religious identities is the local church and temple custom—practiced in a variety of locales—requiring a Hindu or Christian, reciprocally, to touch the *nilavilakkà* lamp oil (coconut oil for churches and sesame for temples) in order that it be purified.

As documented by Chummar Choondal (1983), Kerala Christian folk performances of song, dance, and drama provide further evidence of intercultural negotiations. For instance, the Portuguese-inspired *cavittu nāṭakam,* a dance drama performed by non-Syrian "Latin" Catholics, involving protagonists such as Charlemagne and St. George, incorporates Hindu *Kaḷaripayaṯṯà* martial arts and the Tamil language. Among the endogamous Knanaya Syrian Christians, however, who attempt to preserve an ethnicity separate from the rest of Kerala Christians, their *mārggamkaḷi* ballads describing the Indian mission of St. Thomas, while infused with Dravidian melodies, maintain Syrian liturgical chant sequences. While other Kerala Christian folk songs and ballads may suggest foreign influences as well, most currently use domestic language and melodies and, most recently, film song melodies.

References

Badone, Ellen, ed. 1990. *Religious orthodoxy and popular faith in European society*. Princeton: Princeton University Press.

Bayly, Susan. 1989. *Saints, goddesses and kings: Muslims and Christians in South Indian society 1700–1900*. Cambridge: Cambridge University Press.

Choondal, Chummar. 1983. *Christian folk songs*. Trichur: Kerala Folklore Academy.

———. 1988. *Christian folklore*. Trichur: Kerala Folklore Academy.

Dempsey, Corinne. 1998. St. George the indigenous foreigner in Kerala Christianity. *Religion* 28: 171–183.

———. 2001. *Kerala Christian sainthood: Collisions of culture and worldview in South India*. New York: Oxford University Press.

Neill, Stephen. 1984. *A history of Christianity in India: The beginnings to AD 1707,* Vol. 1. London: Cambridge University Press.

———. 1985. *A history of Christianity in India: 1707–1858,* Vol. 2. London: Cambridge University Press.

Raj, Selva, and Corinne, Dempsey, eds. 2002. *Popular Christianity in India: Riting between the lines*. Albany: State University of New York Press.

Visvanathan, Susan. 1993. *The Christians of Kerala: History, belief and ritual among the Yakoba*. New York: Oxford University Press.

CORINNE G. DEMPSEY

SEE ALSO

Catholicism, Sri Lanka; Cavittu Nāṭakam; Death Rituals; Film Music; Folk Music; Life Cycle Rituals; Marriage Ceremonies; Saints; Syncretism

CIRCUMCISION

Circumcision (Persian, *khatna*), the surgical removal of the foreskin of the penis, is required for all male Muslims, and the operation becomes the occasion for a celebration (*khatna sūrī*) of varying scale depending on local custom and the family's means. (Female circumcision [clitoridectomy] is not practiced in Muslim South Asia.) Muslim opinion varies as to the age at which the boy should be circumcised. Some groups circumcise infants a few days or weeks after birth, allowing a specified time to elapse after the birth to ensure the health of the child. Others hold that the child should be aged three to six, old enough to understand the significance of the event, since it is by it that the boy is "made a Muslim," as Persian-speakers say. While some families now choose to have the circumcision performed by a doctor at a clinic or hospital, the traditional circumciser is generally a specialist who is modestly paid for the service, performed in the boy's home.

The event can take place at any time of the year, except between the two great feasts (*'īd*), respectively for the end of Ramaẓān, the month of fasting, and that which takes place during the hajj, the pilgrimage to Mecca. In agricultural families, harvest time may be preferred because family resources are most abundant at that time. The operation is celebrated generally by the giving of a new suit of clothes to the circumcised boy, and by a sharing of special food, either in a meal to which guests are invited, or with portions of the special food sent as gifts to the family's nearby network of friends, relatives, and neighbors, or both. Very often the meal will include the meat of a slaughtered animal bought or selected for the occasion. For Muslims as for Jews, circumcision commemorates and reconfirms Abraham's willingness to sacrifice his son, and the sacrificial animal in the Muslim celebration, God's miraculous provision of an animal to take the child's place as victim. In less wealthy families, two or more brothers or cousins may be circumcised together so as to consolidate resources for a larger observance.

Besides food sharing, celebrations may include various kinds of entertainment. In western Afghanistan in the 1970s, this author attended a circumcision of two brothers, aged three and five, in an urban household of moderate means. The circumciser was a member of the local barber (*jat*) ethnic group, a low-status, largely endogamous group that also specializes in blacksmithing, professional music, and folk drama performance. The family paid for a performance by a traditional professional two-man *sāz duhul* (traditional double-reed woodwind and drum) ensemble, also from the *jat*. The performers played vigorous instrumental duets of traditional tunes, and also enacted a short stick-combat play (*cūb-bāzī*) in which one player used a long staff, the other a short striking stick. After the entertainment, held within the walls of the family's small house compound, the boys were circumcised with a knife briefly sterilized over a flame, their wounds dressed with sulfa powder and clean cloth bandages. A meal of stewed meat and rice, cooked by men connected to the family in large pots rented for the occasion, was then served to invited guests (mostly male and mostly extended family members, with males and females served separately) and distributed to nearby households.

At another, very modest circumcision event, in a village in the mountains of northern Pakistan in the 1990s, the circumciser was a local Sunnī mullā, who came to the household (an Isma'īlī Muslim one) around midday. The child was an infant and not the first son. The father, a shopkeeper, was at work, and the celebration included only the firing of a rifle into the air by the infant's sixteen-year-old cousin (his oldest "brother" by local calculations) and the distribution to the nearby households of relatives of portions of cooked meat and fresh wheat bread, cooked by the infant boy's aunt who resided in the same extended family household.

Among wealthier families, celebrations may be much more elaborate. In northern Afghanistan, circumcision celebrations, like weddings, are called *tuī*. Some wealthy landowners in the decades prior to the Afghan-Soviet war would, for such occasions, sponsor, besides a major feast with many guests, a *buzkashī* game in which as many as several dozen individual rider-players competed for prizes offered by the host, riding their own horses or those of wealthy sponsors.

MARGARET A. MILLS

SEE ALSO

Buzkashī; Dom; Islam; Jewish Folklore; Life Cycle Rituals; Muslim Folklore, Sri Lanka; Names and Naming Practices, Balochi

COCKFIGHTING

Called *kōḷikaṭṭa* in Kannada and *kōrikaṭṭa* in Tulu, cockfighting is a very popular sport in Tulunāḍu, on the west coast of Karnataka State. While cockfighting is generally organized as a form of entertainment or sport, it is a "fight to the finish" for the two specially trained cocks.

Customarily cockfighting is held on the days following festivals, public ceremonies, *jātra*s, and *bhūta kōla*s. The event starts in the late afternoon and goes on until late at night. A post-harvest paddy field or any level ground serves as the arena. The number of spectators who throng to the contests may vary between fifty and five thousand. Publicity is generally by word of mouth, but, these days, handbills or leaflets are printed and distributed to announce the event. The cock meant to take part in fighting receives special care and attention beginning at three months of age. As it grows up, it is allowed to take part in "amateur" contests with other cocks of the same age. After it acquires sufficient experience through such training, it is brought to the ring for its first deadly combat.

Fighting cocks are classified mainly according to their color: *boḷḷe* (white), *karboḷḷe* (black and white), *kempe* (red), *manjale* (yellow, turmeric), *kakke* (crow-colored, black), *nīle* (blue), *kuppule* (deep brown), *garuḍa būdi* (eagle and ash colored, gray), *karinīle* (dark blue), *kemmaire* (dark red), *giḍiye* (hawk-colored). Large cocks are called *paika;* small ones, *jīka*.

If the owner of the cock is rich and powerful, a large retinue of followers will accompany him as he takes it to the fighting arena. Some in the retinue are in charge of particular tasks related to the conduct of the sport: one is responsible for feeding the cock, another supplies water, and yet another fans it when it is wounded. There may also be a specialist in treating wounds. In the crowd, besides its owner, there may be many spectators who are admirers of a particular cock.

As the crowds gather, two cocks are matched with one another for the contest on the basis of their height, color patterns, and other factors. In Tulu this careful matching of appropriate fighting pairs is known as *pati malpuni*. Before the cocks are set against each other, the supporters of each make a bet. Sometimes as much as Rs. 500,000 ($10,000) is offered as a bet. When the betting is over, the two cocks are held a foot above the ground facing each other in a procedure called *derpuni* (driving forth, setting forth). There are specialists in both the fields of pati malpuni and derpuni.

The next procedure is to tie the blades on the legs of each cock. The blade is about two inches long and slightly curved, with a point at one end and sharp edges. There are many varieties of traditional blades, depending on their shape and place of origin: *ūra bāḷu* (native blade), *baḍekāyi bāḷu* (blade of the northern region), *nāgaragiri* (a place name), *ecimuḷḷu* (a kind of thorn), and *arekokke* (slightly curved). The thread used to fasten the blade to the cocks' legs is called *dōre*. After the blades are fastened, the two cocks face off in a procedure called *oḍḍāvunu* (displaying, showing off). Next, they are released and allowed to fight. If a cock is injured in the field, its people offer it support to revive it. The defeated cock goes to the owner of the winning cock. If both cocks die, each party retains its own. Curry made from the flesh of a fighting cock is said to be tastier than that of ordinary chicken and is also said to impart strength to those who eat it.

In cockfighting held as part of a jātrā or bhūta ceremony, a certain ritual, called *kōriguṇṭa,* is performed prior to the fight. Four or five days in advance of the contest, four thin poles of the *pālemara* (a tree that exudes a white sap that turns red over time; it has other ritual uses as well) are erected on the ground. Set apart for cockfighting, the poles are connected by lines drawn on the ground. The lines are also drawn on the inner area of the square, and the erected poles are also thus connected. One pole is fixed outside this betting ring. The chosen cocks are tied to two poles within the ring, freed after some time, and allowed to fight. These cocks have no blades fastened to their legs. After fighting for some time, the cocks are caught and brought to the bhūta shrine and later returned to their owner. This ritual, like others that take place during the bhūta ceremony, is performed in the presence of the leaders of the village.

People who take part in the sport of cockfighting closely follow a traditional *kukkuta pañcānga* (cock almanac), which gives details about the birth, growth, adulthood, old age, death, and other aspects of the lives of cocks. It also prescribes which colors of cocks should fight each other, mentioning the probable color of the winning cock on a particular day of the week or in a particular week of the month. Cockfighting enthusiasts have much faith in this almanac.

People of all classes and communities in the village take part in the sport, a very popular pastime for the rural folk of Tulunāḍu, and it is a matter of prestige to own a winning cock.

References

Blackburn, Stuart H., and A. K. Ramanujan, eds. 1986. *Another harmony*. New Delhi: Oxford University Press.

Bruckner, Heidrun, Lothar Lutz, and Aditya Malik, eds. 1993. *Flags of fame*. Delhi: Manohar.

Heesterman, J. C. 1993. *The broken world of sacrifice*. Chicago and London: University of Chicago Press.

Geertz, Clifford, 1993. *The interpretation of cultures*. London: Fontana Press.

Sturrock, J. 1894. *South Canara Manual*. Madras.

Upadhyaya, U. P., ed. 1996. *Coastal Karnataka*. Udupi: R. G. Pai Samshodhana Kendra.

PURUSHOTHAMA BILIMALE

SEE ALSO
Bhūta Kōla; Games and Contests; Jātrā/Yātrā

COLONIALISM AND FOLKLORE

Though the East India Company had been making political inroads in India since the eighteenth century, it was only in 1858 that British rule was formally inaugurated. A self-conscious imperial presence spurred the collection of folklore as a means to comprehend "the native mind" and thus to govern more efficiently. Field collections of performed folklore texts, beliefs, and customs were undertaken in various regional languages and among different religious and tribal groups. This trend displaced the Orientalist emphasis on studying ancient Hindu texts—in Sanskrit and accompanied by Brahmanical exegeses—as the key to Indian culture.

The study of folklore in India during the colonial period took place in dialogue with theoretical trends prevalent in England and in Europe generally: New field materials were evaluated in light of prevailing theories such as solar mythology, cultural evolution and survivals, and diffusion. Books and articles on Indian folklore were published both in India and in Britain. Many of the male folklorists working in India also took active part in the Folk-Lore Society in England. In India journal outlets for colonial folklorists included *North Indian Notes and Queries* (1891–1896), *Panjab Notes and Queries* (1883–1887), *Indian Antiquary* (1872–present), *Journal of the Anthropological Society of Bombay* (1886–present), *Journal of the Royal Asiatic Society of Bengal* (1905–1934), and *Man in India* (1921–present).

Folklorists of the colonial period fall into three groups: British administrators and female members of their families, missionaries (who were not always

British), and British-educated Indians. While women were prominent in the study of Indian folklore in the last half of the nineteenth century, by the early twentieth century, as the discipline became more established, they became marginalized, derided as too popular and not sufficiently scholarly.

Mary Frere's landmark *Old Deccan Days or Hindoo Fairy Legends Current in Southern India* appeared in 1868 and proceeded to go through several reprintings. This book brought together the folktales of Frere's nursemaid or ayah, a Lingayat convert to Christianity named Anna Liberata d'Souza. Frere was the daughter of the governor of Bombay. Her father, Sir Bartle Frere, supplemented the book with an introduction and notes. Indicating the attitude toward Indian folklore of the time, he wrote that it was important for "Government servants, . . . missionaries, and others residing in the country" to undertake such collections to understand "the popular, non-Brahmanical superstitions of the lower orders" (p. xiii). A similar book by the daughter of another civil servant was Maive Stokes's *Indian Fairy Tales.* First privately printed in 1879, it was reprinted in London the following year and received wide attention in both Britain and India. By the time *Wide Awake Tales,* collected by the wife of a magistrate, Flora Annie Steel, appeared in 1884, her coauthor, Richard Temple, had devised a comparative interpretive scheme for the study of Indian folktales, which he sets forth in the notes.

Richard Carnac Temple was a British civil servant in the Punjab, and a prolific folklorist. Among his many publications, the three-volume *Legends of the Panjab* (1884–1900) stands out for its groundbreaking emphasis on the performed text. Temple had trained scribes to record the poems of bards, and the book contains both transliterations and translations of the Punjabi language.

William Crooke, who served as district magistrate and collector of revenue in the United Provinces of Agra and Oudh, is another outstanding figure in the development of colonial Indian folklore. Like Temple, Crooke was a prolific writer. He is especially known for his painstakingly detailed book, *An Introduction to the Popular Religion and Folklore of Northern India,* first published in 1894 and subsequently revised and widely reprinted. As editor of *North Indian Notes and Queries* (1891–1896), Crooke created a forum for people to send in observations and initiate discussion on cultural practices and folklore texts of various genres. Along with British civil servants, educated Indians contributed extensively to this journal.

British interest in Indian folklore thus also spread to Indians: nationalist folklore can be seen as a direct reaction to and outgrowth of colonial folklore. The same pattern holds for Sri Lanka, where the folklorist Hugh Nevill is especially worthy of note.

An anamolous figure who deserves mention is Verrier Elwin, an Anglican priest turned Gandhian "philanthropologist" who began working among tribal groups in central and northeast India during the colonial era. He remained in India, becoming an Indian citizen after the British withdrew in 1947. A thorough scholar, careful ethnographer, gifted translator, and animated writer, Elwin remains a leading figure in the sphere of tribal folklore. In his introduction to *Folk-tales of Mahakoshal* (1944), Elwin also laid out the first comprehensive history of folklore study in India.

As Elwin pointed out, colonial administrators and missionaries were rarely faithful to folklore texts, tending to rewrite them in light of a Western audience, and to eliminate references considered off-color. "Native" folklorists, too, were guilty of doctoring materials so that they did not give a negative impression to Western readers. Collected materials also tended to be decontextualized, with little information provided on their role in actual people's lives. A notion of "authentic" tradition guided what was perceived as legitimate folklore, so references to changing social customs were screened out. Despite these shortcomings in the vast stores of folklore collected during the colonial era, scholars today continue to draw on these materials for historical documentation and for the persisting vitality of the recorded texts.

References

Crooke, William. 1894. *Introduction to the popular religion and folklore of northern India.* Allahabad: Government Printing Press.

Dorson, Richard. 1968. The overseas folklorists. In *The British folklorists: A history,* pp. 332–348. Chicago: University of Chicago Press.

Elwin, Verrier. 1944. Introduction. In *Folk-tales of Mahakoshal.* Bombay: Oxford University Press.

Frere, Mary. 1898 (1868). *Old Deccan days, or Hindoo fairy legends current in southern India.* London: John Murray.

Narayan, Kirin. 1993. Banana republics and V.I. degrees: Rethinking Indian folklore in a postcolonial world. *Asian Folklore Studies* 52: 177–204.

Ratnapala, Nandasena. 1991. Introduction: A brief survey of writers and writing. In *Folklore of Sri Lanka.* Colombo: State Printing Corporation.

Steel, Flora Annie, and Richard Carnac Temple. 1884. *Wide awake stories.* London: Trubner and Co.

Stokes, Maive. 1880 (1879). *Indian fairy tales.* London: Ellis and White.

Temple, Richard Carnac. 1884–1900. *The legends of the Panjab.* 3 vols. Bombay: Byculla Press.

Kirin Narayan

SEE ALSO
Brass Bands; British Folklore (in South Asia); British, Folklore about; Calendar Art; Chaube, Pandit Ram Oharib; Crooke, William C.; Diaspora [all regions]; Elwin, Verrier; Folklorists; Frere, Mary Eliza Isabella; *Kathak* Dancers; Nationalism and Folklore; Tribalism and Tribal Identity: The Bhils of West Central India

COMEDIANS, JESTERS, AND CLOWNS

Humor (*hāsya*) is an important part of theater in India. To fully appreciate this comedy, one must know the regional language(s), colloquialisms, and regional cultures—especially regional politics and religious beliefs. A visitor, however, can often comprehend the basic situation and be amused by the comedian's antics and body language, and facial and vocal expressions.

In most of the traditional theater forms, the comedian (*vidūsaka,* "jester" or "clown"), most often played by a male, is expected to have detailed knowledge of the epics and ancient stories of India, be well-versed in Sanskrit and the local language(s) and speech styles, and be up to date on contemporary politics, the local "who's who," and gossip. He must also be limber and acrobatic. Because of his knowledge and his abilities, the comedian traditionally commands a high position in the troupe.

Function in Theater

His purpose is to provide interludes of comic relief from the serious situations often being portrayed. Of all the performers in a play, the comedian is free to draw on the past and take from the present to connect the audience with the drama being performed. He reaches all segments of the audience through his ability to portray qualities from the sophisticated to the lowbrow. He mimics and makes fun of stereotypes, specific people, and situations from daily life. The comedian has the prerogative to act as he pleases and say whatever he likes, often including bawdy songs and obscene remarks and gestures.

An important or popular guest in the audience must accept that he or she might be vilified, ridiculed, or simply joked about by the comedian, and must not show offense. Even the gods are not spared the comedian's sharp tongue or ludicrous betrayal. God Śiva is sometimes played as a deaf and lame old man trying to seduce Goddess Pārvatī, who might be played as a prostitute. Hanumān, the monkey god, scratches humorously and uses his tail in creative ways. There are many comic scenes of the god Kṛṣṇa's sexual relationships with the milkmaids. At the end of such shenanigans the deities are asked not to hold a grudge, as the performance was all in fun.

Other clowning includes flirting, teasing females, being dim-witted, being the king's servant who puns on the king's words, and playing a Brahman as cunning or old and deaf. In contemporary theater, comic scenes include a Muslim husband nagged by his two Hindu wives and dialogues between the newlywed bride and the father-in-law, the thief and the police inspector, and the old miser and his young wife.

References

Ashton, Martha Bush, and Bruce Christie. 1977. *Yakshagana.* New Delhi: Abhinav Publications.
Ashton-Sikora, Martha Bush, and Robert P. Sikora. 1993. *Krishnattam.* New Delhi: Oxford and IBH Publishing Co., Pvt. Ltd.
Emigh, John, with Ulrike Emigh. 1986. Hajari Bhand of Rajasthan: A joker in the deck. *The Drama Review* 30 (1): 101–130.
Gargi, Balwant. 1966. *Folk theatre of India.* Seattle: University of Washington Press.
Hansen, Kathryn. 1992. *Grounds for play: The Nautanki theatre of North India.* Berkeley: University of California Press.
Richmond, Farley P., Darius L. Swann, and Phillip B. Zarrilli, eds. 1990. *Indian theatre: Traditions of performance.* Honolulu: University of Hawaii Press.
Shulman, David. 1985. *The king and the clown in south Indian myth and poetry.* Princeton: Princeton University Press.

MARTHA B. ASHTON-SIKORA

SEE ALSO
Character Stereotypes; Folk Drama, Afghanistan; Tamāśa; Theater and Drama

COMIC BOOKS, INDIA

India's first comic book series was launched in 1969 by G. L. Mirchandani's India Book House. This series, named *Amar Chitra Katha* (Immortal Picture Stories), also known as ACK, was the brainchild of Anant Pai (b. 1931) who wished to put Indian children in touch with their own cultural heritage. Prior to this, the only comic books available in India were imported ones featuring such superheroes as Superman, the Phantom, and Tarzan.

ACK comics highlight figures from Indian mythology and history. Each book measures approximately 7″ × 9 1/2″ and typically contains thirty-two pages, vividly illustrated in comic book format with dialogue in white balloons. The inside of the front cover contains a few paragraphs of information about the subject of the book, including, in some of the later issues, bibliographic references.

A total of 436 titles have been published in thirty-eight national and international languages, including

French, Japanese, and Swahili. As the primary audience for these books is English-speaking, middle- and upper-class families, each issue is first published in English. Hindi is the next most significant language of publication. Selected issues are also translated into the major Indian regional languages, such as Malayalam, Bengali, and Kannada, as well as little-known tribal languages like Halbi and Gondi.

At least a fourth of the comic books are devoted to Hindu myths, deities, and saints. *Krishna,* the first title in the series, has sold over a million copies. Almost sixty issues, including a forty-two-part miniseries, focused on the *Mahābhārata*. About 100 issues concentrate on folktales, including twenty-four books on Buddhist tales and eight on Akbar and Birbal stories. Often, several issues about a subject are combined into a "bumper issue." At least one-fourth of ACK comics cover historical subjects and biographies of historical figures, ranging from ancient kings to freedom fighters and other personalities in modern India. However, the series has been criticized for the underrepresentation of women and minorities as only twenty noteworthy women and merely a dozen or so Muslim figures have been featured.

In 1980 Anant Pai started *Tinkle,* a fortnightly subscription comic series published in English, Hindi, and Assamese, which contained nonfiction articles on history, geography, and science, as well as folktales. Children were asked to contribute stories, jokes, and anecdotes that were then scripted and illustrated by staff writers. Ten thousand letters poured in monthly from children around the country, some of which were published in the "Readers Write" column.

Because it combines visual images with simple verbal messages, the comic book format has proved to be a powerful and effective educational tool in India. The Amar Chitra Katha project has led to a phenomenal revival of interest in Indian mythology and folklore among urban English-educated Indians, and over 80 million copies of the comic books have sold (mainly in India, although about 3 percent have been exported to other countries). For a couple of decades, in the 1970s and 1980s, ACK books substituted for the traditional modes of transmission of oral culture (such as extended families and folk performances) which are fast disappearing from city life. However, due to competition from television and other media, sales of both Amar Chitra Katha and *Tinkle* comic books declined in the late 1980s. Although *Tinkle* remains in print, Amar Chitra Katha stopped publishing new titles in 1991, but continued to reprint eight to twelve older titles every month. The titles *Krishna* and *Hanuman* are now being marketed with accompanying audiocassette tapes in English, Hindi, Marathi, Gujarati, and Punjabi.

Several other publishers also entered the comic book market, but most did not survive for long. The Ramakrishna Math, a religious establishment, produces *Pictorial Stories for Children* featuring tales of saints and deities. Diamond Comics of Delhi is the only commercial publisher that has remained in the field, reprinting a few ACK titles in Hindi every month and also publishing its own series of Hindu mythology comics in English.

Diamond Comics are smaller than Amar Chitra Katha books. They are approximately 6″ × 7 1/2″ in size and usually consist of forty-six pages, although some are longer. In addition to mythological themes, Diamond Comics also present mysteries, adventure stories, and humorous tales. Newspaper comic strips by the cartoonist Pran have been compiled into numerous comic series. Typically, each comic book contains more than a dozen small stories, each two or three pages long, featuring the exploits of one of Pran's protagonists. Some popular Pran characters are a girl named Pinki, a public-spirited boy named Daabu, Shrimatiji, a middle-class housewife, and Chacha Chaudhary, a little old commonsense sleuth in a turban. Although the plots are thin and lighthearted, these little comic books give a visual window into contemporary urban India, as skyscrapers, banks, and stadiums form the settings for the stories. Unlike the mythology comics, these books aim to entertain rather than to educate.

References

Hawley, John Stratton. 1995. The saints subdued: Domestic virtue and national integration in *Amar Chitra Katha.* In *Media and the transformation of religion in South Asia,* ed. Lawrence A. Babb and Susan S. Wadley, 107–134. Philadelphia: University of Pennsylvania Press.

Pritchett, Frances W. 1995. The world of Amar Chitra Katha. In *Media and the transformation of religion in South Asia,* 76–106.

AMITA VOHRA SARIN

SEE ALSO
Birbal; Chapbooks; Folk Literature; Folktale; Kṛṣṇa; *Mahābhārata*

COMPLAINT

The category of complaint epitomizes a set of genres that leave their mark on conversations in South Asia without necessarily having a name. (Categories need not have names to be real.) Some performances of complaint are named, laments being chief among them and representing the marked end of the range of complaint forms. In Bengali, for instance, laments are known as *bilāp* or perhaps *jārī gān*. Their history reflects a dialectical relationship between oral and written forms, or

An old man sings a prayerful lament. © Jim Wilce

more fundamentally, between spontaneous, contextually grounded improvisation and structural features that enable audiences to recognize the genre(s). In Bengali there are centuries of text artifacts of even more forms of lament than can be denoted by either bilāp or jārī gān. These text artifacts may have arisen from spontaneous performances, often by women, and might at some stage have become models for other performances. Written examples of lament closely follow a prototypical content and occasion for lament, whereas spontaneous performances can surprise and even shock their audiences. In Bangladesh and the Punjab, for example, women are expected to lament spontaneously their departure from their natal homes at marriage and the deaths of certain kin, but they may also use recognizable lament forms to perform grief of other sorts. And whereas the former may be expected and welcomed, the latter may be punished.

Because lament can be loud and entail weeping and singing as well as language, it draws attention to itself and to the performer(s). That in itself is judged harshly in an ethos that is increasingly rationalized, demystified, self-controlled, and privatized. Other song genres in which women in rural Rajasthan and Uttar Pradesh voice complaints also draw dangerous attention to the performer. At the opposite extreme are nonverbal forms associated with—sometimes preceding, sometimes standing for—complaints. Bangladeshi Muslims may sigh loudly and wordlessly or exhale the name of Allah. This may precede or follow a complaint. It may serve to elicit a query that invites a fully verbalized complaint as a response. Some Bangladeshis treat complaints, even those elicited by questions, as inauspicious, *alakṣhmī,* the polar opposite of lakṣhmī. As auspiciousness herself, the goddess Lakṣhmī represents for Bangladeshis (even in some Muslims' discourse) the blessings of fertile soil and women. Thus, it is not only the self-indexing qualities of the named genres of complaint, but the very act of complaining and the effect that it is understood to have, that provokes criticism, called in Bengali both *abhiẏog* and *nāliś*. For both of those terms, "complaint" and "accusation" are accurate glosses.

These criticisms, or complaints about complaints, join with other forms of discourse in a category of metacomplaint, complaints about complainers or, conversely, complaints about something that is blocking one's complaint. Thus, there is the abhiẏog (accusation) of bystanders that one's (complaining) speech is inauspicious, alakṣhmī. Speaking openly about one's suffering and hardships (*duḥkha-kaṣṭer kathā balā)* is vulnerable to this critical metacomplaint. But secondary or metacomplaints may also be uttered by men or women who are in a position to make primary complaints, but complain instead about others' attempts to silence the lament or complaint. These sorts of statements may also be heard in conversations with druggists, doctors, and other healers. Examples recorded in Bangladesh include references to one's inability to get the complaint out, either because words fail one or because others interrupt. It is in all these forms of metacomplaint that the social significance of the primary genre(s) becomes clearest. Primary and secondary complaints reflect and highlight social tensions. Complaint is seldom dismissed as harmless, let alone portrayed as a cathartic or socially useful practice in South Asia.

The grammatical form typifying complaint varies across languages (in Japanese, use of the passive signals complaining). In many South Asian languages, complaint utterances need not include pronouns, either possessive (*my* head aches) or nominative (*I* feel). Instead of using grammatical forms that suggest that the self or a part of the self is a prototypical subject (an agent), the so-called dative or genitive (or "experiencer") subject construction is common in complaints, at least in Indo-Aryan languages. In Bengali, one says, "My much pain is," with both "my" and "is" as optional elements. Complaints uttered in English stand out for the salience of the *I*, whereas pronounless, impersonal, or "me-centered" constructions characterize complaints uttered in Indo-Aryan languages. (For example, "fever strikes," "my fever-fever strikes," and "fever strikes me" are common, whereas the grammatically possible "I perceive [feel] a fever" is not heard.) As a folk practice, complaint genres have a potential to shape language and its very structures. Some Bengali complaint forms are common enough that they seem to be undergoing grammaticalization, the reduction of free words to bound grammatical forms (for example, affixes). One example is *kaitāri nā,* a contraction of a phrase meaning "I cannot say [what's wrong with me] because someone keeps cutting off my story, because language escapes me, or because I am forming my complaint somewhat vaguely so as to invite my co-wives or other kin to construct it jointly with me." Thus we are confronted with the paradox that a genre that lacks an inclusive label might nonetheless contribute to the evolution of Bengali grammatical forms.

References

Gumperz, John, and Celia Roberts. 1991. Understanding in intercultural encounters. In *The pragmatics of international and intercultural communication,* ed. Jan Blommaert and Jef Verschueren, 51–90. Amsterdam and Philadelphia: John Benjamins Company.

Hopper, Paul J. 1996. Some recent trends in grammaticalization. *Annual Review of Anthropology* 25: 217–236.

Klaiman, Miriam H. 1980. Bengali dative subjects. *Lingua* 51: 275–295.

———. 1981. *Volitionality and subject in Bengali: A study of semantic parameters in grammatical processes.* Bloomington: Indiana University Linguistics Club.

Masica, Colin P. 1991. *The Indo-Aryan languages.* Cambridge: Cambridge University Press.

Raheja, Gloria Goodwin, and Ann Grodzins Gold. 1994. *Listen to the heron's words: Reimagining gender and kinship in North India.* Berkeley, Los Angeles, and London: University of California Press.

Wilce, James M. 1998. *Eloquence in trouble: The poetics and politics of complaint in rural Bangladesh.* New York: Oxford University Press.

JAMES M. WILCE

SEE ALSO

Folksongs, Nepal; Lament; *Silok;* Women's Songs

CONJURING

Conjuring has hardly changed over the centuries. The itinerant conjurer (*jādūgar*), entering the village with his son, calls an audience with his flute and the hourglass-shaped *damaru* drum. Once a crowd has formed the magic circle around him, the performance begins. A cloth ball revealed under half a coconut shell disappears only to reappear under another; a series of metal balls, each larger than the last, emerges from the magician's mouth; a mango seed, in a matter of moments, grows into a bush; a shawl, borrowed from an uneasy member of the crowd, is cut into shreds and then, after the wave of a magic wand, a puff of magic breath, and the muttering of magic words—"*gilli-gilli-gilli*" or "*yantru-mantru-jālajāla-tantru*"—it is whole again. To the horror of everyone present, the magician's son is decapitated, or dismembered, or perhaps his tongue is cut from his mouth. And when the child is healed, made whole, there is genuine awe. Wonder-struck by the powers of the magician, the villagers purchase his rings and amulets in hopes that they contain some portion of his strange magic. And they relish the pleasure of having been well deceived.

The villages are, these days, but the camping places between the cities and towns where the real money is to be made, where the rings and charms can be sold for many times what the magician himself has paid for them. On cluttered roadsides and street corners, in bazaars, markets, parks, almost anywhere, amidst any chaos, the itinerant conjurer, despite unrelenting police harassment, lays out his mat and squats down to begin beguiling the crowd. His son exhibits a dusty snake, performs the cups-and-balls routine, or makes a coin vanish. "*Jādū!*" (Magic!) someone calls out. The Hindi word for that entertainment is tinged with the dark meanings of the Sanskrit term from which it comes: *yātu,* indicating sorcery, witchcraft, black magic, and the powers and practices of evil spirits. The magician capitalizes on the associations—a touch of fear prods the astounded to reach into their pockets.

Many of the conjurers are born as blood members of a Muslim low caste, *Maslet*s, whose ancestors converted from Hinduism en masse several hundred years ago. Bound together by a secret language and secrecy itself, they are trained in a tradition of magic from infancy. The boys perform with their fathers until they are old enough to go out on their own. The girls perform—handle the snakes, are stuffed into baskets, have swords passed through their necks—until they are women. Then they are expected to bear new conjurers, to nourish them and teach them the ancient secrets of magic.

These entertainers are often called Madārī, a name that suggests an alliance with, or origin in, heterodox religious orders. They are confused with the fakir and the yogi. And the magician cultivates the religious associations: Performing near a mosque on Friday, the Islamic day of public worship, he'll whisper incantations that sound like the Arabic of the Qur'ān or invoke the name of the Prophet; in another part of town, near a temple later that day, he'll praise Śiva, Rāma, or Kṛṣṇa, and claim to have accrued his magic powers by meditating

Conjurer. Mamallapuram, Tamil Nadu, India. © Richard Rapfogel

in the cremation grounds. Aware that there is money to be made in religion, the street conjurer is now, as he always has been, a mock holy man. He probably evolved out of the magician-priest, the court figure who, in ancient India, was responsible for casting curses and binding spells, performing exorcisms and divinations, curing illnesses and warding off other evils, paralyzing enemy armies and entrancing women desired by the ruler. Apotropaic rituals were transformed into amusing skits; the magician-entertainer emerged, and magic shows became a fashionable courtly diversion in both classical and Moghul India. The magician, traveling from court to court, carrying a peacock-feather wand and a skull, earned his livelihood by performing both theatrical illusions and close-up sleights of hand.

The conjuring show is fundamentally a dramatic performance: each trick is a scene in an audience-observed play with a plot and characters, with a theme and an overall mood—the aesthetic sentiment of wonder as enhanced by alternating sentiments of humor and horror. The performance is a reminder that we cannot truly trust our senses, rely on reason, or know what is real and what is not. The persistence and universality of its appeal suggest a human need to be deceived, an innate and perverse propensity to take pleasure in deception.

References

Ayling, Will. 1981. *Oriental conjuring and magic*. Bideford, Devon: Supreme Magic.

Branson, Lionel H. n.d.[1922]. *Indian conjuring*. London: George Routledge and Sons.

Siegel, Lee. 1991. *Net of magic: Wonders and deceptions in India*. Chicago: University of Chicago Press.

Sorcar, P. C. 1960. *Sorcar on magic*. Calcutta: Indrajal.

LEE SIEGEL

SEE ALSO
Professional Performers

COSMOLOGY, HINDU

In canonical Hindu ideology, every soul (Sanskrit: *ātman*) is striving for release from the cycle of endless rebirths or reincarnations known as *saṃsāra* (Sanskrit). A soul achieves final liberation only by merging back into *brahman* (Sanskrit), the universal principle that comprises the totality of existence and nonexistence.

When this occurs, the ātman loses any trace of its prior identity. The attainment of ultimate liberation, known as *mokṣa* (Sanskrit) to Hindus, is directly comparable to the Buddhist idea of complete liberation called *nirvāṇa* (Sanskrit).

Mokṣa, or liberation, occurs only if all the accumulated residues of a soul's actions, called its *karma* (Sanskrit), adhering from all previous incarnations or existences, are consumed. This process of karma consumption, often described using metaphors of food, eating, and digestion, pertains to both good and bad karma that are attached to the ātman. If mokṣa is achieved, all traces of the soul cease to exist; mokṣa is a condition of ultimate nontransaction where nothing remains to perform any actions, and nothing remains to be transacted. Neither the ātman nor any of its karma will remain. The ātman now merges into the indescribable completeness of the universe (brahman). Mokṣa marks the cessation of reincarnation for the soul.

While mokṣa represents the ultimate aim of the Hindu religion, most people's goals, in belief and practice, are generally quite different, because mokṣa represents the exceptional occurrence in Hindu cosmological reference. Very few souls are considered far enough progressed to be anywhere near the achievement of final liberation. Generally, people assume that mokṣa is, for them, uncountable lifetimes away. Therefore, many people strive to achieve a better condition for the next, or perhaps a later, rebirth of their soul. This important aim is pursued in a variety of fashions.

Many undertake charitable acts to accumulate good karma in order to enhance their chances of attaining a better rebirth. Such endeavors often include giving food or money to beggars or to ascetics. Some make substantial donations of land, cows, or money, or give their daughters to Brahmans to increase their chances of attaining a better rebirth. Others give money for temple construction projects or sponsor religious festivals.

Large numbers of Hindus (and Buddhists) go on religious pilgrimages to accumulate substantial merit and thereby improve their chances of a better rebirth. Because places of pilgrimage represent points of sacred geography, they offer potent connections to divine realms. Pilgrimage centers are referred to in Sanskrit as *tīrtha*s, literally, "crossing places" or "fords"—locations where specific deities are considered to have come to the earth.

People also turn to specialists versed in complicated systems of astrology to find planetary influences that may be negatively influencing their lives and their potential for a better rebirth. Birth horoscopes are used to predict what the future portends and to assess what measures might be undertaken to counteract projected bad episodes anticipated in current or in later rebirths.

After a person dies, his or her soul experiences several forms of existence. Immediately after death, a person's soul exists in a ghostly state (Hindi: *pretyoni*), but, with proper ritual treatment, this condition is quickly resolved, and the soul becomes an official ancestor (Hindi: *pitṛ*). Once ancestor status is attained, the soul experiences the Hindu versions of heaven (Hindi: *svarg*) or of hell (Hindi: *nārak*), typically spending time in both regions. The duration of these experiences is said to depend on the karmic state of the soul. In this way, certain karma of the ātman are consumed, and, after these episodes are completed, the soul is often reincarnated into another earthly form of life, based upon its remaining karmic disposition.

Hindu cosmology teaches that, besides human beings, deities, as well as other classes of beings who exist in a variety of realms, are also subject to complex cycles of rebirth. In addition to the human realm, there are other planes of existence, often referred to in Sanskrit as *loka*. Conceptual representations of the loka vary considerably, and there are said to be anywhere from three to fourteen, but, most commonly, three loka are recognized: sky, atmosphere, and earth. Major Hindu deities, (e.g., *Śiva, Viṣṇu, Brahmā, Kālī, Pārvatī*), live in the realm of the sky, or the cosmos. In the atmosphere, all sorts of ghosts (*bhūt, pret*), demons (*piśāc, rākṣasa*), temptresses (*apsarā*), but also potentially friendly and helpful entities like ancestors (*pitṛ*), heroes and heroines (*vīr, satī*) and sages (*ṛṣi*) exist. In the earthly realm, humans, animals, and plants, as well as souls existing in inanimate forms as bodies of water, rocks, or mountains are found. The inhabitants of all the loka are subject to rebirth, albeit within enormously disparate scales of temporal existence. Importantly, the inhabitants of any loka may potentially interact with beings that exist in any of the realms of reincarnation.

In Hindu cosmology, the entire universe continually undergoes cycles of creation and destruction. This cyclic process is categorized into four periods, called in Sanskrit *yuga*. The basic characterization of each yuga is different, and each succeeding yuga is regarded as more degenerated than the prior one. Since human existence is only considered an aspect of the last and most corrupted of the four yuga, people often say that greed, corruption, poverty, shortness of life, and even death itself are to be expected in such times of decay and degradation. These conditions are inherent in the *Kali yuga,* the last of the four yuga.

Many lower-caste people blame their low social positions on human rebirth in the Kali yuga. For upper-caste groups, the numerical preponderance, as well as the purportedly nonreligious behavior of the lower-caste groups, is perceived as an obvious attribute of the present yuga. When the Kali yuga ends, the universe will be destroyed, but it will then be created anew and, once again, a glorious existence will prevail. But eventually, everything will degenerate, and the cycle will repeat itself again. It is in the very nature of existence. Mokṣa is the only way out of this cycle for any individual soul.

References

Eck, D. 1982. *Banaras: City of light.* New York: Alfred A. Knopf.

Fuller, C. J. 1992. *The camphor flame: Popular Hinduism and society in India.* Princeton: Princeton University Press.

Gold, Ann Grodzins. 1987. *Fruitful journeys: The ways of Rajastani pilgrims.* Berkeley: University of California Press.

DANIEL J. COHEN

SEE ALSO

Ghosts; Pilgrimage; Religion

COURTSHIP, AFGHANISTAN

In Afghanistan, traditional marriages begin with the groom's family identifying a possible bride for their son, and sending emissaries, usually senior female family members, to the girl's family to show interest in a match. The approach to a family not already related is circumspect. An emissary does not directly state her purpose, but a visit from relative strangers without stated purpose is read by the hosting women as *khostrūnī,* (Persian: "seeking" [a bride]). If the hostesses view the alliance as possible, the eligible daughter may eventually appear before the guests, for instance, serving their tea. If not, she will be kept out of view and this will be taken as discouragement. The match may still be pursued, if their reluctance is read as tactical or expressing the traditional, expected reluctance of families to give daughters in marriage. While Muslim values mandate marriage as natural and necessary for all those physically and mentally competent to form a family, the bride's family is expected to be cautious, and the bride herself extremely reluctant to consent to leave her mother and father's household.

Preliminaries between families who are already connected by blood or marriage may be more informal and direct, with individuals of similar status (brothers, fathers, mothers of the prospective pair) conversationally broaching the idea of a match. First cousins are generally preferred mates. In some groups (e.g., tribal Pashtuns) one or more male cousins may "claim" first right to marry a first cousin, and may object, even violently, if other suitors are considered. Families often prefer to give their daughters to relatives because the bride will not be entering a household of strangers, the couple may have played with each other as children (an index of compatibility), and the ongoing, diversified relations of the two families will bolster extended family leverage to manage any problems the marriage may develop.

While "daughter-seller" is a very bad insult among Afghans or all ethnic groups, negotiations of "bride-price," as it is pejoratively called in the West, the various kinds of payments made by the groom's family to the bride's, is central to pre-engagement negotiation. A family's joint investment in a marriage is seen to insure its stability both financially and socially. A girl's family wishing to discourage an unattractive match may simply demand a marriage payment well beyond the means of the suitor's family, another way of saying "no." Families of modest means with marriageable children of both sexes may decide to "exchange daughters," so that each family gives a bride to the other, and marriage payments are minimized. Exchange marriage also motivates each family to treat the new bride well, in protection of the daughter they have "given" to the other household. Negotiated resolution of, for instance, Pashtun tribal feuds may also include the marriage of a daughter into the enemy's household, the girl "given" as part payment of blood money for a feud killing. The girl serves as a kind of hostage, but as she matures and raises children, the rival families also become close kin.

Grooms' payments to the bride's family in marriages other than those for feud settlements are of several categories:

- the *pīshkash* or "milk money" which goes to the girl's family as compensation for the expense of raising her;
- the cost of outfitting the bride. The groom is expected to give his fiancée gifts of clothing or other personal adornment at each major holiday prior to marriage, and supply multiple suits of clothes, shoes, jewelry, and household equipment as part of her dowry. These things, together with more such donated by her family, are her personal property.
- the expense of the wedding feast (varying in size from a few dozen to hundreds of people) and any entertainment laid on for that, which could include professional musicians (a duo up to a small band), or in some areas, folk theater or a sponsored *buzkashi* match.
- The *mahr,* a stipulated amount in cash or kind (animals, land, etc.) promised but not transferred to the bride. It must be paid if she is divorced without cause, and may be computed as part of her share of her husband's estate, as a kind of insurance against divorce or widowhood. A wife can "forgive" her husband the mahr promised, and in some cases is pressed to do so, for instance, if she seeks a divorce which he refuses, on grounds of incompatibility or because of his marriage to a second wife.

Once the families have agreed on financial terms, the bride's family acknowledges this with a small ritual gift sent to the groom. In Herat, the traditional *nakh o sūzan* ("needle and thread") gift included a handkerchief, preferably of locally produced silk in bright emerald green, maroon, and purple striped patterns, and a stick-pin ("needle") of gold with a head in the shape of a cock.

After the bride's family's gift comes the *shīrīnī khorī,* "sweets-eating," when the bride's family serves guests from the groom's family and others invited with sweets, tea, and other snacks, and packets of sweets are sent back to members of the groom's family not attending. Those attending become traditional legal witnesses to the fact of the engagement. Either at this time or later, the *nikā* or marriage contract, stipulating all the payments and any other preconditions on the marriage, is read by representatives of both families and signed. The nikā in Afghan diaspora weddings may only be signed at the actual wedding feast, in a truncated sequence of ceremonies. It is also only during the nikā signing itself, sometimes just before the bride's transfer to the groom's home, that she is formally asked, by the *mullā* who is making the contract, whether she consents to the marriage.

Once the engagement is confirmed, the groom has both the right and the obligation to visit his bride's family with gifts for her, especially on the major Muslim feast days and secular holidays such as Naw Rūz (Spring New Year). Whether he is able to spend time with his bride, or even see her face, depends on local custom and the relations of the families. In the Herat area, local tradition favored the engaged couple with a practice called *nāmzād bāzī,* "fiancé(e) play," in which the couple, fully dressed, are put to bed together. The couple is expected to become familiar and affectionate, the groom overcoming the bride's fear of him, but sexual intercourse should not occur until after the wedding. One mother and mother-in-law from an outlying area laughingly described nāmzād bāzī in her youth: "They [bride's relatives] would *tie us up* in a *chādor* [floor-length modesty wrap] this way and that ([gesturing: around the waist, over the shoulder, and between the legs] and there was no *way* anything could happen! Now with these girls today . . . [with a significant glance at a daughter-in-law]—it's *different!*"

By the late 1970s, young people attending college were taking mate selection more into their own hands, choosing someone from among their own classmates, or proposing a match to the sibling of a close friend of the same sex. Such nominations might then be handed over to parents to negotiate the match in a more traditional process, if they would cooperate; elopements could risk dangerous levels of family estrangement. One of the early decrees of the Marxist government, in the autumn of 1978, attempted to put marriage choice in the hands of the young and make it easier for the poor to marry by limiting payments to the bride's family to the amount of silver coin stipulated in sayings of the Prophet, which by 1978 was only worth about U.S. $7. This decree was widely and violently opposed as a usurpation of family rights and responsibilities designed to ensure that marriage be an obligation taken on by whole families, not by light-minded or infatuated youth.

References

Doubleday, Veronica. 1988. *Three women of Herat.* London: Jonathan Cape.

Mills, Margaret A. 1983. "The lion and the leopard": The composition of a new fable in traditional style articulates a family dispute. *ARV: Scandinavian Yearbook of Folklore 1981:* 58–66.

———. 1993. "Of the dust and wind": Arranged marriage in Afghanistan. In *Everyday life in the Muslim Middle East,* ed. Evelyn Early and Donna Lee Bowen, pp. 47–56. Bloomington: Indiana University Press.

MARGARET A. MILLS

SEE ALSO

Gender and Folklore; Marriage Ceremonies

COW

The cow is widely revered as a symbol of fertility and motherhood in South Asia and occupies a central role in the rituals, beliefs, and practices of Hinduism. Although the cow is closely linked to worship of the mother goddess in ancient Middle Eastern civilization, its place in Harappan religion remains uncertain. The cow is noticeably absent from seals and other representations that attest to the prominence of the bull in Harappan culture. In the later Indian pantheon, however, the cow emerges as the emblem of Pārvatī, Durgā, Umā, and other manifestations of the mother goddess and continues to be associated with village goddesses in Hinduism today.

Vedic literature describes the economic importance of the cow in Aryan society and also affirms the animal's role in Vedic religious life. The cow was sacrificed to the gods and its milk and milk products used in ritual. The Vedas abound with figurative and mythological references to the cow. In the Vedic creation myth, Indra slays the dragon Vṛtra and releases the Cosmic Waters, which are said to be cows. The goddess Aditi, personification of the universe and nourisher of the earth, is referred to as a Cosmic Cow. Uṣas, the goddess of dawn—herself a cow—gives birth to the rosy Cows of Dawn (the rays of the sun).

There is little to indicate that cows were worshiped during the Vedic period. According to W. Norman

Brown (1957), the origins of the sacred cow concept lie in the Upanishadic era (c. 400–200 B.C.E.), with five factors contributing to its emergence: (1) the importance of the cow and its products in Vedic sacrificial ritual; (2) the literal interpretation of figurative uses of the word "cow" in the Vedas; (3) prohibitions against violations of the Brahman's cow; (4) the doctrine of *ahiṁsā* (noninjury); (5) and the association of the cow with the mother goddess cult. The cow's sanctity is firmly established in literary sources by the fourth century C.E. and henceforth remains a central fact of Hinduism. (Hindu attitudes toward the cow are restricted to humped zebu cattle [L. *Bos indicus*] and do not extend to other cattle species.)

The cow is of particular importance in the cult of Kṛṣṇa, and many Kṛṣṇa myths and rituals focus on the pastoral aspects of the deity. Kṛṣṇa's paradise is Goloka, the "Cow Heaven," where Kāmadhenu (also known as Surabhi), the wish-fulfilling cow created in the churning of the primeval ocean, resides. Festivals such as *Govadhana Pūjā* and *Gopāṣṭamī,* which celebrate specific events in the divine cowherd's life, involve *darśana* (viewing) of cows, feeding them special foods, the *go-pūjā* (cow-worship) ceremony, and *parikramā* (circumambulation) of cows. The five products of the cow (milk, clarified butter, curds, dung, and urine), known collectively as *pañcha-gavya,* are viewed as purifying and are widely used in ritual.

In Hindu thought, the cow is Go-mātā, the Cow Mother. She is a symbol of nonviolence, for her milk nourishes the calf without violating ahiṁsā. She is the bearer of *śakti* (power) and the bringer of good fortune and wealth. The cow is inviolate and should not be killed. The cow has thus become an icon of Hindu culture to be protected against the depredations of the non-Hindu. Cow protection is advocated in the Constitution of the Republic of India, and anti-cow-slaughter legislation has repeatedly emerged as an electoral plank of fundamentalist Hindu political parties.

The underlying source of the Hindu sacred-cow concept continues to be debated amongst scholars. Some scholars, Marvin Harris, for example, see the sacred cow concept as a mechanism for protecting an important economic resource within the specific ecological conditions and land-tenure systems of the Indian subcontinent, rather than as reflecting fundamental Hindu religious values. The resulting dialogue with opponents of this view has done much to focus interest on the religious, social, and economic position of the cow in India.

Although the cow achieves its highest status among the orthodox Hindu peoples of South Asia, the cow is also respected by Buddhists and Jains under the general tenets of ahiṁsā. In contrast, the cow traditionally has been sacrificed in many tribal cultures in the Indian subcontinent, a practice that has now, however, largely been abandoned. The cow has no special status in Islam, and diverging Hindu and Muslim attitudes towards the animal occasionally lead to communal unrest in India. Some Dardic-speaking groups in the Hindu Kush and Karakoram Mountains view cattle as impure animals, associated with female and demonic pollution, and treat the cow and its products with distaste.

References

Brown, W. Norman. 1957. The sanctity of the cow in Hinduism. *The Madras University Journal* 28(2): 29–49. [Reprinted 1964. *The Economic and Political Weekly* (Calcutta) 16: 245–255.]

Harris, Marvin. 1966. The cultural ecology of India's sacred cattle. *Current Anthropology* 7: 51–66.

Lodrick, Deryck O. 1981. *Sacred cows sacred places: Origins and survivals of animal homes in India.* Berkeley and Los Angeles: University of California Press.

Simoons, Frederick J., and Deryck O. Lodrick. 1981. Background to understanding the cattle situation in India: The sacred cow concept in Hindu religion and folk culture. *Zeitschrift für Ethnologie* 106(1, 2): 121–137.

Srinivasan, Doris. 1979. *Concept of cow in the Rigveda.* Delhi: Motilal Banarsidass.

DERYCK O. LODRICK

SEE ALSO

Gods and Goddesses; Herders' Field Calls; *Jungappa*

CRAFT

Craft, folk art, and decorative art are categories that evolved in early twentieth-century English usage to differentiate objects made by hand from those made by machine, and to distinguish from "fine art" objects of notable aesthetic or visual interest that were not considered art in the strictest sense. These new categories of material culture emerged from two separate but interrelated circumstances: the industrial revolution, which produced goods using machines and largely unskilled labor; and the arts and crafts movement together with modernism, which stretched the Western aesthetic canon to encompass works from the gamut of cultures and from all social strata.

As terms with a particular cultural and historical content, "craft," "folk art," and "decorative art" must be applied in South Asia with care. On the positive side, they encourage the consideration of the broad range of arts in this extraordinarily art-rich region. Localized specialties in particular media and techniques have gained much deserved attention, widening the scope of Indian art beyond the paintings, sculpture, and architecture made for rulers and religious elites. On the negative side, this classification forces a distinction between "craft," considered to be basically utilitarian, and "art," considered as the creative pursuit of aesthetic expression. In South Asia, just as the maker of a rice measure is constrained by requirements of size and shape, so the maker of a religious image is constrained by requirements of proportion and iconography. Both the rice measure and the religious image can be considered successful or unsuccessful, good or bad, according to technical, functional, and aesthetic criteria. The notion of craft also overdraws the distinction between handmade and machine-made: a twelve-spindle spinning wheel for making *khadi* (homespun) and a fly-shuttle loom, widely used by handloom weavers, could be considered either aids to handwork or machines. Finally, the term "folk art," with its connotations of naiveté and rusticity, often masks complex, cross-generational transmission of skills, honed techniques, and sensibilities in hereditary and caste-based professions so common in South Asia. The subcontinent's vast artistic output is of enormous range and depth.

Textiles are arguably South Asia's predominant art form. For millennia, finely woven and vibrantly dyed cottons have been exported globally, and textile production has been second only to agriculture in the South Asian economy. Today, there are about five times as many artisans working in textiles as in all the other arts combined. Numerous local textile arts have had international followings: the muslins of Dhaka were prized in ancient Rome, the block-printed cottons of western India were exported to medieval Egypt. Today, the embroideries of western India and Pakistan, the backstrap-loom brocades of Bhutan, the embroidered quilts (*kantha*) of West Bengal and Bangladesh are esteemed by collectors and museums in Europe, America, and Japan. *Ikat*s (in which yarns are tie-dyed before weaving) made in Orissa and Gujarat, tie-dyes of western India and Pakistan, and printed and painted cottons of western India, Tamil Nadu, and Pakistan have likewise gained recognition well beyond their regions. Other centers have become known for loom-embellished textiles, notably Banaras for gold and silver brocades, Dhaka for fine cotton brocades, and Kashmir for tapestry-woven woolens. Many other textiles could be mentioned; for example, there are the fine velvets and pile carpets made for the Mughal courts in the seventeenth and eighteenth centuries, or the tapestry-woven dhurri rugs currently made for export in designs ranging from long-established patterns to specially commissioned re-creations of American folk art motifs. Despite major changes in production in the last century, which have brought synthetic dyes, the jacquard loom, and competition with large-scale mechanized production, South Asian weavers, dyers, and embroiderers continue to create textiles of vigorous design and outstanding appeal.

Pottery is probably the most ubiquitous of South Asian arts, though in recent decades, the demand has been reduced by competition with metalwares and plastics. Most pottery produced in South Asia has been low-fired earthenware for roof tiles and food containers. Because Hindus consider pottery vessels to be easily contaminated and not suitable for reuse, and because low-fired pottery is so breakable, the demand for it was limitless. In thousands of villages, potters' wares have fulfilled local needs. In some places, such utilitarian pottery has achieved a striking elegance of form (for example, hand-formed vessels in Manipur) and vitality of decoration, such as that in Rajasthan. Clay has also been used for religious images throughout the subcontinent. Some images are very simply shaped and painted figures. Others exhibit great refinement; for example, the terra-cotta temples of Bengal (seventeenth–nineteenth centuries), faced with finely sculpted bas-relief tiles; the monumental horses dedicated to the god Ayyanar, which were built and fired in place in twentieth-century Tamil Nadu; and the unfired, painted and clothed images made today for Hindu festivals in eastern India.

Metalwares, like pottery, have been important as objects of everyday use at home and as objects for ceremony and ritual (and, in the past, as tools of war) with a long history in South Asia. The earliest known, a five-thousand-year-old bronze sculpture of a girl dancing, was excavated at Mohenjodaro in Pakistan. Perhaps the most famous metalwares from the subcontinent are the lost-wax cast images of Hindu deities made in the South Indian Chola empire (eleventh–twelfth centuries), widely admired as among the finest metal sculptures ever produced. Also highly regarded as a "folk" style are the votive images, vessels, and animals made in a distinct lost-wax technique (*dhokra*) in Bengal, Orissa, Bihar, and Madhya Pradesh. Vessels and utensils are created from sheet metal that is beaten into shape and sometimes elaborately engraved, like that in Moradabad and Jaipur. Metal engraving is the preliminary step in the inlay of gold and silver, which was highly esteemed for weaponry such as shields and sword hilts and for ceremonial objects like wine ewers and *pan* (betel) boxes. At Bidar in Karnataka a special method known as *bidri* was developed to inlay silver wire into an alloy of zinc that, when oxidized, turned matte black with shining silver designs. Repoussé work—patterning metal surfaces in relief from the reverse side—has been a specialty in copper, brass, and silver at many places, including Bhuj and Banaras. Enameled wares, though made in a number of centers, are best known from Jaipur.

Jewelry, principally in silver and gold, sometimes set with gems, is worn in great abundance in South Asia and serves as a repository of wealth across the region.

Ornaments, especially for women and for images of deities, but also for men, have been devised for the head, ears, nose, neck, upper arm, lower arm, fingers, waist, ankle, and toes. Jewelry has a central role in marriages, where relationships are established through gift exchange, and the occasion is elevated by gorgeous display, not only by the bride and groom, but by the guests as well. Silver, gold, and jewels are preferred where means allow, but glass, shell, lac-coated and painted wood, and beads of coral, turquoise, pearl, and other semiprecious stones are valued, too.

Works in stone and wood occur principally in architectural settings for which South Asia has been renowned for millennia. Well-known examples include Buddhist stūpa at Sanchi (second and first centuries B.C.E.); Hindu temples at Khajuraho (eleventh century C.E.) and Bhubaneswar (tenth century C.E.); fortress-palaces like those of the sixteenth-century *dzongs* in the valleys of Bhutan and the Mughal Red Forts at Agra and Delhi (sixteenth–seventeenth centuries C.E.); tombs such as the celebrated Taj Mahal (seventeenth century C.E.); and mansions, including the *havelis* of Gujarat, as well as farmhouses in Kerala and Bhutan. Modern architectural materials have replaced most of these uses of wood and stone, except perhaps in the construction of Hindu temples, where carved stone, especially images of the deities, remains important. Until the nineteenth century, household furnishings consisted mainly of cushions, carpets, and cloth floor coverings, and a modest quantity of wooden pieces, which at royal courts might be elaborately carved and ornamented with lac, ivory, or silver. Since the eighteenth century, beds, chairs, cabinets, and tables have become increasingly used; some centers became known for specialties, such as the elaborately carved furniture made in Mumbai (former Bombay), and the ivory veneering of Vizagapatam.

Painting, on walls, paper, and cloth, ranges from auspicious decorations for modest homes, for example in Rajasthan and Bhutan, to religious images that can be the focus of worship, such as the Kalighat paintings from nineteenth-century Calcutta, or present-day *pats* (paintings) from the Jaganath temple in Puri. In the past, Mughal, Rajput, and British rulers employed artists to paint portraits, record events, and even create visual representations of musical modes. Such works created for the ruling elites from the seventeenth to the nineteenth centuries have received the greatest recognition and esteem in the West. Recently some styles of wall painting (most notably Madhubani painting from Bihar, but also Warli in Maharashtra) have been successfully transferred to paper, making possible a broader market and greater appreciation. Elsewhere, in Rajasthan and Bengal, for example, paintings on paper and cloth have been created to represent narratives and serve as aids for the performance of both epics and local tales.

Many other media have been used by South Asian artists. Objects of precious materials such as ivory have been excavated at Mohenjodaro and are known to have been exported to ancient Rome. Mundane materials like *solapith* (the core of a reed) are carved into fanciful toys, garlands, and crowns for bridegrooms in Bengal. Baskets and mats made of cane, bamboo, grasses, and leaves are produced throughout the subcontinent.

Especially in India, the nationalist movement and later the government have supported artisanry as a source of employment for millions of people. The production of homespun (khadi) and handloomed cloth is subsidized; government cooperatives support small-scale industry; and a National Crafts Museum in New Delhi celebrates the achievements of India's artisans. Nongovernmental organizations have also entered the field, including the state Craft Councils of India, SEWA (Self-Employed Women's Association), and international agencies like the Ford Foundation. South Asia demonstrates that highly mechanized production and artisanry can and will coexist, and that art is not the preserve of elites.

References

Aryan, Subhashini, ed. 1993. *Crafts of Himachal Pradesh*. Ahmedabad: Mapin.

Birdwood, G. C. M. 1988 [1880]. *The arts of India*. Delhi: Rupa.

Dhamija, Jasleen, ed. 1985. *Crafts of Gujarat*. Ahmedabad: Mapin.

Huyler, S. 1996. *Gifts of Earth*. Ahmedabad: Mapin.

Jaitly, Jaya, ed. 1990. *Crafts of Jammu, Kashmir, and Ladakh*. Ahmedabad: Mapin.

Journal of Indian Art and Industry. 1884–1916. London.

Krishna, Nanditha, ed. 1992. *Arts and Crafts of Tamilnadu*. Ahmedabad: Mapin.

Nath, Aman, and Francis Wacziarg, eds. 1987. *Arts and Crafts of Rajasthan*. Ahmedabad: Mapin.

Saraf, D. N. 1982. *Indian crafts: Development and potential*. Delhi: Vikas.

Sen, Prabhas. 1994. *Crafts of West Bengal*. Ahmedabad: Mapin.

SUSAN S. BEAN

SEE ALSO
Folk Art; Handloom Weaving; Image-making, Metal; Material Culture; Quilting and Piecing

CRAFTS AND DEVELOPMENT, INDIA

India's crafts are known throughout the world by tourists and collectors alike as objects of beauty, excellent design, rich materials, and intricate workmanship. In the last ten years, however, they have also increasingly become known for the poverty of their producers. Recent government policy studies, articles in the popular press, and academic papers have all detailed the dire economic straits of artisans across India. In the face of declining markets, falling prices for products, and rising costs of raw materials, artisans are leaving their crafts for other trades or even manual labor; rather than continue the cycle of poverty into future generations, artisans encourage their children to leave crafts for more lucrative professions.

Not all the news about craftspeople is so bleak, however. One bright spot that emerges in many of the studies and articles is the number of organizations working to improve the economic status and stability of artisans. Such organizations, by training artisans to handle more of the production, distribution, and sale of their products themselves, are trying to return crafts to economic viability. At their best, they help artisans build their skills, adapt their products, and access the technological, financial, educational, and personal inputs necessary to compete in India's modern economy.

The current economic crisis facing India's artisans has several roots. One important one is decreasing consumer demand. Crafts face fierce competition from cheaper, often more durable, industrial products; in a rapidly changing economic landscape where machine-made goods are readily available even in the smallest villages, artisans making simple, utilitarian crafts can no longer earn enough to survive. Artisans making more decorative crafts have declining sales as well, in part because of the social stigma attached to crafts. Whereas machine-made goods are favored as symbols of modernity, urbanity, and affinity to the industrialized, sophisticated Western-oriented elite, crafts are seen by many as almost the opposite: namely, signs of provincialism and traditionalism.

On the supply side, a further factor contributing to the economic crisis is the skyrocketing costs of raw materials. Because of government policies favoring exports of raw materials and the industrial sector over handlooms and handicrafts, supplies of necessary materials like cotton thread, leather, and wood have shrunk to the point that artisans can no longer get good quality materials at affordable prices. When artisans are then forced to substitute with lower quality materials, product quality declines, prices fall, consumer dissatisfaction rises, and economic troubles increase.

What can be done to solve these problems? Historically, several approaches have been tried. Concerted government and institutional interventions in crafts date back at least to the 1850s, when the British colonial government started schools of arts and crafts in India to train craftsmen in design and production. With the interest of the independence movement in Indian-made goods, and Gandhi's particular focus on spinning and the production of cloth as nationalist activities, crafts projects took a more overtly political, nationalist flavor, and crafts products were worn and displayed as symbols of national pride. After independence in 1947, nationalist interest in, and image-making through, crafts was institutionalized through the creation of the All-India Handloom and Handicraft Board (AIHHB). Set up to promote and preserve Indian crafts and handlooms, the AIHHB has provided such services as the establishment of craft cooperatives, promotion of Indian crafts abroad, and sponsorship of National Craftsmen awards recognizing excellence in craftsmanship. On a regional level, most states have their own handicrafts boards, which market the craft products of their respective states on both a local and national level; the more aggressive of these state boards operate crafts emporia in major cities across the country.

Government efforts alone, however, have proven incapable of solving the problems facing artisans. Thus, in the last twenty years a whole crop of private, not-for-profit organizations have emerged that are attempting new approaches to improving the status of artisans. The specifics of the projects vary a great deal, on everything from which crafts are involved—from projects that aim at only high-end, museum-quality crafts and the master craftspeople who produce them, to projects that train slum women to do the most rudimentary embroidery on clothing for Western markets—to the goals to be achieved through the projects, with options including basic economic stabilization for artisans, empowerment of women, creation of a foundation for comprehensive rural development, and more. What all of the projects share, however, is a goal of improving the economic status, stability, and self-sufficiency of artisans. To reach these ends, many projects work to bring artisans more control over their products and production processes, by improving access to raw materials, increasing artisan contact with consumers (who may be geographically and socially far removed), and decreasing or even doing away with the middlemen who often control the most lucrative stages of the trade in crafts.

There have been some tremendous successes among these nongovernmental efforts. One widely cited example of such a success is the case of a group of weavers in the town of Phalodi, in the western, desert state of Rajasthan. Members of a low-caste community, the weavers had all but given up their traditional occupation because of shrinking markets and increasing competition, and ten years ago, mired in poverty, were turning to wage labor on road crews to survive. Today, after a decadelong association with a nonprofit organization. Urmul Trust, the weavers produce high-quality *khadi* (hand-spun, handwoven) cloth, traditional shawls, wall hangings and more, all of which are in high demand in upscale crafts boutiques in Delhi, Bombay, and other major cities across India. The social changes are equally marked. Literacy is up, men in this patriarchal area involve their wives in family leadership, both boy and girl children are being kept in school longer, and weavers are now confident in themselves as producers and leaders. Unlike many crafts projects, all of these changes have not come through the intervention of outside organizers alone. Indeed, although the Phalodi weavers as a group still remain affiliated with Urmul and call upon consultants for various projects, they have successfully assumed the leadership of all stages of their organization.

Another success story is that of the Self-Employed Women's Association (SEWA) in Lucknow, an organization of women producing a traditional white-on-white embroidery known as *chikan*. When SEWA was founded, women embroiderers in the northern Indian city of Lucknow faced numerous problems in earning money from their craft: they were poor, illiterate, unable to move around the city freely to buy materials or sell their products because of gender restrictions, and under the tight control of middlemen who paid the barest minimum for embroidery work while monopolizing profits. With only twelve women and Rs. 10,000 worth of stock when it was established in 1984, SEWA has grown to include four thousand members in and around the city, with 1992 sales of over Rs. 12 million, stores in Lucknow and Delhi, and annual weeklong exhibitions and sales in all the major cities of India. In the process of that growth SEWA has trained its members to take control of all levels of the organization, from accounting to materials distribution, production planning, sales, and management.

Beyond these two examples of very successful craft development projects, there are thousands of other nongovernmental, not-for-profit crafts organizations. Given the extraordinary success of groups like SEWA Lucknow and the Phalodi weavers, it is not surprising that there continues to be a great interest in crafts development. Indeed, new projects are starting all the time that use crafts as an entry point for comprehensive rural and urban economic and social development projects. Some of these new projects will be successful; many more will not. How one judges the projects singularly as either a success or failure is, of course, quite difficult, considering their diverse goals and methodologies. Some may earn high points for creating or expanding markets for crafts and increasing economic opportunities for artisans but do little to improve literacy, nutrition, or address other basic social issues. Other projects may have few marketing successes but have a strong track record in building leadership, self-reliance, and community organizing skills among artisans. Given this diversity, there is a need for a range of criteria suitable for assessing the merits and demerits of craft development projects. Such a range might include the ability of the project to improve artisan income; the quality of the crafts produced; the breadth of services or social programs offered (such as literacy training, violence prevention, education, and health care); the level of artisan leadership within the organization; or the financial self-sufficiency of the project. By looking at how an individual project measures across these topics, its full impact as a tool for social, economic, and artistic development can be measured.

The point of judging the success of a craft development project is, of course, to glean from one attempt lessons that can be applied in other places and organizations, and with other crafts. What makes the examples of the embroiderers of SEWA and the weavers in Phalodi so powerful is the hope that their successes can be replicated elsewhere. Yet, while there are lessons to be learned from every success, it is important to remember that each project is and will be different. In some ways, SEWA and Phalodi are impossible to reproduce. For one, both benefited from intensive, long-term involvements with gifted, committed designers: few organizations have such extensive access to that level of expertise. Additionally, SEWA owes part of its success to existing conditions in the market it entered: by beginning production when it did, the organization was able to take advantage of the poor quality of embroidery within the well-established, high-volume chikan market and create a niche for itself with a higher quality, distinct product. Few other organizations are able to create such clear product identity within existing markets, and many have to create their markets from scratch.

Whether or not individual successes are precisely replicable, craft organizations can and do still learn from each other. There is extensive communication between craft development projects, thanks in part to national exhibitions where producers from across the country come together to market their goods, meet customers, and swap stories with other craftspeople. With the expansion of these informational networks among producers, and given both the continued economic difficulties of artisans and the success of a few well-publicized projects, the growth in the numbers of craft development projects in India is likely to continue. This should be celebrated as evidence of attempts to improve conditions of craftspeople and critically evaluated to determine the direction and strengths of the field. As the field grows and matures, and as the inevitable changes in public taste shift crafts in and out of fashion, it will be important to evaluate the opportunities and constraints provided by different types of organizations and programs. Shifting markets and consumer demand will necessitate new products and new approaches to craft development; these new approaches can then be used as models for still further projects. Craft development projects have already proven their ability to effect change and empower producers; with continued support, interest, and attention, they should be able to continue to do so for years to come.

References

Cable, Vincent, Ann Weston, and L. C. Jain. 1986. *The commerce of culture: Experience of Indian handicrafts.* New Delhi: Lancer International.

Meister, Michael, ed. 1988. *Making things in South Asia: The role of the artist and craftsman.* Philadelphia: South Asian Regional Studies, University of Pennsylvania.

Rose, Kalima. 1992. *Where women are leaders: The SEWA movement in India.* New Delhi: Vistaar Publications.

Saraf, D. N. 1982. *Indian crafts: Development and potential.* New Delhi: Vikas Publishing House.

ABIGAIL MCGOWAN

SEE ALSO
Swadeshi; Toys

CREDIT SYSTEM (WOMEN'S PRIVATE BANKING IN RURAL INDIA)

The agricultural or artisan household in rural India typically operates as a joint productive and consumption unit, in which land and other assets are owned by males, and the senior male controls expenditure decisions. Yet, in most families, women are able to accumulate and maintain at least a small private store of goods and cash to use as they wish. They begin to do this when, at the time of marriage, their parents present them with a supply of clothing, metal utensils, jewelry, and cash. Thereafter, on ritual occasions, at certain calendrical festivals, when returning home for a visit, or when receiving a visit from natal relatives, they periodically receive similar gifts. They may do various odd jobs for neighbors to earn additional small sums for private use. Women of "service" castes receive small sums for performing assigned ritual duties at the life-cycle ceremonies of their families' higher-caste patrons. Furthermore, many women secretly divert funds from the household budget, selling small amounts of the family grain supply to local shopkeepers or overstating to their husbands the amounts paid out for food or other household necessities. In these ways, a frugal woman can amass a substantial nest egg; only in cases of dire family emergency would she be asked, or be expected to offer, to use any of it to defray ordinary household expenses.

Typically, a woman keeps her private money supply and valuable belongings in a locked trunk. But she may have reason to feel that, at home, her assets could be tampered with—for example, if she is at odds with other women of her joint family household, or if her husband is impecunious, perhaps even addicted to alcohol or gambling. Or she may experience the temptation to fritter away her money on small treats and trinkets instead of saving for a more important goal. She may then prefer to place her funds in someone else's safekeeping, in a practice called *paise dharna* (Hindi, literally, "to deposit money"). While the village shopkeeper is usually prepared to hold money and valuables for his customers, as well as lend them sums of money in times of need, rural women tend to prefer to rely on someone of their own sex for these services.

Informal female banking is an institution in many parts of India (for example, in Uttar Pradesh and Rajasthan). The banker is usually a mature woman who either lives in a nuclear family or occupies a senior position in a joint family household and has a husband who refrains from interfering in her autonomous pursuit of this kind of activity. In a 1965 ethnographic study one such woman was found to have served for over forty years as informal banker for eight of her female neighbors, who both deposited money and valuables for safekeeping and borrowed small amounts, usually against security in the form of jewelry or metal vessels. She kept no written records (she and her clients were all illiterate) and carried out all transactions in strict confidence. She kept her clients' goods in a locked storeroom in her house and never employed them for her own use. She neither paid interest on deposits nor charged it on loans, though in case of default, the items given as security were forfeited. It is not clear whether her interest-free policy is characteristic of all informal female banking in India, or whether it simply represented her personal mode of operating. She always spoke of her activities as a way of providing friendly assistance to longtime neighbors rather than as a moneymaking enterprise. Her activities provide an example of a mechanism by which, in a society characterized by patterns of sharp gender segregation and male dominance, female solidarity is both expressed and maintained.

References

Cottam, Christine M. 1993. Purdah magnates: Hidden traders in Rajasthan. In *Women, aid and development: Essays in honour of Professor T. Scarlett Epstein,* ed. C. M. Cottam and S. V. Rao, 1–21. Delhi: Hindustan Publishing Corporation.

Luschinsky, M. S. 1962. The life of women in a village of North India: A study of role and status. Ph.D. diss., Cornell University.

Vatuk, V. P., and S. Vatuk. 1971. On a system of private savings among North Indian village women. *Journal of Asian and African Studies 6:* 179–190.

SYLVIA VATUK

SEE ALSO
Girau; Jajmāni; Watandari System

CROOKE, WILLIAM

William Crooke (1848–1923) was born in Ireland and educated at Tipperary Grammar School. On a fellowship he received an undergraduate degree at the Trinity College of Dublin University. He passed the competitive entrance exam for the Indian Civil Service (ICS) in 1871, the same year W. A. Grierson started his service in the ICS. Crooke had an uneventful, mediocre career and in 1896 he took retirement as a district officer. The reason for this "official disapproval" was his inability "to bear fools or the pretentious gladly" (Temple). During twenty-five years as deputy collector and collector in the Etah, Saharanpur, Gorakhpur, and Mirzapur districts, spent largely in tents while assessing the tax basis of landholdings in hundreds of villages, he amassed a great factual knowledge about people and their lives in northern India. Temple says: "Here he could win the personal regard of the people, as besides being a great scholar, he was also a great sportsman and had shot many a tiger." He found some close friends among the scholar administrators of the ICS such as Grierson and Temple.

Since Crooke had no academic training in any discipline relating to India, his scholarship was that of a self-educated, inquisitive ICS official: he made huge lists of things, castes, terms, and stories, and tried to get information from insiders about the culture he had to deal with. He tried to explain and elucidate his lists with his ever increasing knowledge, and they provided him with materials for a rural and agricultural glossary of the North-Western Provinces and Oudh, which he circulated among his fellow officers before it appeared in 1879 as *A Glossary of North Indian Peasant Life.* His often serendipitous interests in the history of words and their meanings made him an ideal editor of the second edition of Henry Youle's *Hobson-Jobson: A Glossary of Colloquial Anglo-Indian Words* (1903), to which he added numerous tidbits. After his retirement he published a similar annotated glossary, *Tribes and Castes of Northern India* (1896).

The most original of his publications is *The Popular Religion and Folk Lore of Northern India* (2 vols., 1893; a second rewritten edition appeared in 1896), a remarkable achievement of his keen observations of village worship of godlings of nature, heroes, godlings of disease, and sainted and malevolent ghosts. He dealt also with the evil eye, tree and serpent worship, totemism and fetishism, animal worship, black art, and finally, rural festivals and ceremonies. He wrote this book as an attempt to balance the publications of his time on India, which were mostly based solely on the Sanskrit tradition.

His interest in customs and rites is also evident from his edition of Ja'far Sharif's *Qanun-i Islam* (which had been compiled at the request of and translated, enlarged, and published by G. A. Herklots M.D., of Dutch descent, in Madras in 1838) which appeared in 1922. The other book of this type was *Observations on the Mussalmans of India* by Mrs. Meer Hassan Ali, a European lady married to a Muslim in Lucknow (published in 1838 and edited by Crooke in 1917). In the introductions to both books Crooke meticulously brings together information about the authors. Moreover, he tries to rebut the "essentialistic view" of the authors and the translator from the point of view of his own knowledge of the wide diversity among the Indian Muslims.

After his retirement, he also wrote several summations of his many studies and the huge quantities of material at his disposal. One was the *North-Western Provinces of India, Their History, Ethnology, and Administration.* This book was first published in 1897. Further, he published *Natives of Northern India* (1907) and *Things Indian* (1906).

His wide knowledge of folklore and village life was invoked for a number of important new editions, such as James Tod's *Annals and Antiquities of Rajastan* (first 1829, with introduction and notes by W. Crooke, 3 vols., 1920), Herbert Risley's *The People of India* (2nd ed. by W. Crooke, 1915), and travelers' accounts of earlier centuries (Fryer, *A New Account of East India and Persia, 1672–1681* (1909); Tavernier, *Travels in India,* translated by V. Ball (1925).

His mine of knowledge was used for contributions to *Hastings Encyclopaedia of Religion and Ethics* and by the editors of several journals, such as *Indian Antiquary, Panjab Notes and Queries.*

At the end of his life, he received honors commensurate to his work and knowledge. He became the president of the Anthropological Section, British Association (1910) and of the Folklore Society (1911).

References

Osman, Mohammad Taib. 1971. William Crooke: An appraisal of his contribution to folklore. In *Folklore* 12: 200–217.

Shahid, Amin, ed. 1989. *A glossary of north Indian peasant life.* Delhi. With a long introduction on Crooke's method in the framework of the British administration of India.

Temple, Richard C. 1921–1923. William Crooke. In *Proceedings of the British Academy,* pp. 576ff.

PETER GAEFFKE

SEE ALSO

Chaube, Pandit Ram Gharib; Colonialism and Folklore; Folklorists; *Hobson-Jobson, the Anglo-Indian Dictionary*

D

DAHA-AṬA SANNIYA

In Sri Lanka, healing rituals, belonging to the broader category of *tovil* (demon dancing), combine astrology, *āyurveda* (an indigenous medical system), and demonology. These rituals are primarily practiced by Sinhala Buddhists; however, Tamil Hindus will also sometimes resort to such practices in worshiping the gods of the Hindu pantheon. Christians generally criticize these practices as witchcraft and demon worship, though some will privately seek the help of exorcists.

The *Daha-aṭa Sanniya*—popularly known as *Sanni Yakuma*—is the best example of a tovil ritual. *Sanniya* (pl. *sanni*) means "a disease" or "an ailment," and eighteen (*daha-aṭa*) such ailments are generally listed. The term *yakuma* means demon ritual. As expounded in the Indian treatises on ayurveda, the causative factors of the sanni are *vāyavya* or *vātika* (windy diseases), *āgneya* or *paittika* (rheumatic diseases), and *saumya* or *ślaiṣmika* (phlegmatic diseases). These are manifest somatically in morbid states of the three humors—aerial humor (*vāta*), bile (*pita*), and phlegm (*sema*).

In the sanni ceremony, however, a mythological dimension is added to the etiology; each ailment is presumed to be the work of a particular demon, who is symbolized by a dancer wearing the demon's mask. The entire ceremony is an exorcistic healing ritual, and the masks, healing devices. The sanni masks are small compared to the huge mask symbolizing the chief of the other sanni demons, called the *Mahā-kōla* or *Rājamulu Sanni Yakā*. The mask of the chief comprises a tall head mask symbolizing the demon. Attached are two flaps containing the eighteen smaller masks (used in the sanni rituals), in a form much like that of the skull-rack masks of Oceania. This is a mask of enormous proportion—tall, broad, and heavy. There is no evidence that it has been worn in the dance; it is kept on the side to symbolize the leader of the family of the sanni demons. The mask is in the form of a triptych with three slabs joined together by wooden props. It comprises a central, standing figure of a demon with two faces shaped like that of a *jarā yakā*. Masks of this genre, housed in local and a few foreign museums, are cylindrical in shape.

In carving the mask, the master carvers stick to specific and traditional iconographic specifications. For instance, the height of the entire mask should be six times the height of the bottom mask (normally forty-three inches), and the width of the mask should be six times the width of the bottom mask. The mask depicts the family of sanni characters with the demon in the process of crushing a human lying prostrate between his canine teeth. Mutilated limbs of other humans are carved on his head and on the hairy chest. The set of eighteen masks varies from village to village—atelier to atelier—and at least thirty-three such mask types have been documented.

The Sanni Yakuma ceremony is normally held after consulting the village astrologer in order to identify the demon seizure (*āveśa*), the type of disease inflicted, and the auspicious date and time at which the ritual should be enacted. The entire ceremony consists of three separate but interrelated phases: (1) chanting, offering of oblations, and the enactment of specific dance sequences intended to create a receptive mood in the patient; (2) the preparatory dances called the *dolaha-peḷapāḷi,* which clear the ground for the appearance of sanni demons on stage; and (3) the ritual dance of the sanni demons, which employs twelve *pāḷi* masks and eighteen sanni masks. (All eighteen sanni masks should be used in the ceremony.) The exorcists (*kaṭṭ-aṇḍiya/kaṭṭaṇḍi*) work as a group, each wearing a separate mask. The head exorcist conducts the ceremony and also wears a mask.

During the ritual operation, the exorcist administers local herbal medicines to the patient. The ritual is basically hypnotherapeutic in effect. The exorcist summons the demon and then puts him through his paces, in which the exorcist, through the incantation of mantras, cajoles him and instructs him to leave the patient. At the conclusion of the dance, the demon dancer removes his mask and appears before the patient as his normal self. The unmasking of this ambivalent character is intended to relieve the patient of any anxiety he may have had at the commencement of the ceremony.

References

Ames, Michael M. 1982. The magical arts of the Sinhalese Buddhists of Sri Lanka. *International Journal of Asian Studies* 2 (2).

Goonaratne, Dandiris de Silva. 1865–1866. On demonology and witchcraft in Ceylon. *The Journal of the Ceylon Branch of the Asiatic Society* 4(13): 1–117.

Goonatilleka, M. H. 1990. Sanni Yakuma: Its mythical dimensions and religious interaction. In *Ānanda: Papers on Buddhism and Indology. A Felicitation Volume Presented to Ānanda W. P. Guruge on His Sixtieth Birthday,* ed. Y. Yarunadasa, 130–140. Colombo, Sri Lanka: Felicitation Volume Editorial Committee.

Halverson, John. 1971. Dynamics of sanni exorcism: The Sinhalese Sanni Yakuma. *History of Religions* 10: 334–359.

Obeyesekere, G. 1966. The ritual drama of the sanni demons: Collective representations of disease in Ceylon. *Comparative Studies in Society and History* 2: 174–216.

M. H. GOONATILLEKA

SEE ALSO

Buddhism and Buddhist Folklore; Dance; Exorcism; Masks, Sri Lanka; Medicine, Ayurveda; Sri Lanka: Sinhala; Supernatural Beings

DAHE

Dahe, literally the plural form of *dahā* (a unit of ten), are poems in the Avadhi and Bhojpuri languages of Uttar Pradesh in India, on themes related to the martyrdom of Imām Ḥusayn, the grandson of the Islamic Prophet Muhammad. As a form of folk poetry, *dahe* (in Avadhi) and *daha* (in Bhojpuri) refer to short poems of two, four, or six lines—each two lines being both grammatically and semantically complete in themselves. These poems are publicly keened during certain nights—generally the seventh, eighth, and ninth—of Muḥarram, the first month of the Muslim calendar. As the name suggests, dahe were probably originally sung during the entire first ten days of Muḥarram, which are traditionally the most important days of ritual mourning for most Muslims, and in particular for Shīᶜa Muslims.

Dahe were probably first composed in the fifteenth century during the rule of the Sharqi dynasty of Jaunpur, since that is when many Muslim Sufi texts were also composed in Avadhi for the first time. Dahe singing gained further strength during the rule of the Nawabs of Avadh. Under the influence of these two Shī'a dynasties, the traditions of ritual mourning and setting up of *ta'ziya* (replicas of the imam's tomb) for veneration became well established in these regions and were adopted by their non-Shī'a and even non-Muslim subjects.

The public keeping or chanting of dahe is called *dahe ronā* or *dāhā kānā* (to cry out dahe). Groups of women—mostly non-Muslim, and exclusively from the lower professional groups or castes—visit the shrines of the ta'ziyah, singing dahe in a particular soulful melody, not very different from the keening sound made by the same women on other, more personal, mourning occasions. A prominent feature of their chant is the use of some refrain, often the last half of the second line itself. Men do not sing dahe, just as they do not take part in other public expressions of grief.

Curiously, though dahe are related to the commemoration of Imām Ḥusayn's martyrdom, his elder brother Imām Ḥasan, who also had a tragic end, gets mentioned more often. A notable feature is that the point of view adopted in the narration is often of the imām's mother, Fāṭima, daughter of the Prophet Muḥammad and wife of 'Alī. An emphatically feminine point of view is also indicated by the fact that the two most commonly used themes in dahe are the wedding of Imām Ḥasan's son Qāsim (martyred the next day) and the fate of his young widow (daughter of Imām Ḥusayn), and the death of 'Alī Asghar, the infant son of Imām Ḥusayn. In their fragmentary quality and their focus on the lamentatory, dahe are similar to the more literary genre called *nauḥa* and to the earliest examples of *marṣiya*.

Reference

Faruqi, Azhar Ali. 1981. *Uttar Pradesh Ke Lok Git* (Folk Songs of Uttar Pradesh), 275–284. New Delhi: Taraqqi-i Urdu Bureau.

C. M. NAIM

SEE ALSO

ᶜAlī; Heroes and Heroines; Islam; Lament; *Marṣiya; Muḥarram; Nauḥa; Ta'ziyah*

DANCE

Dance is an integral part of worship, life-cycle rituals, seasonal festivals, regional and national celebrations, and popular culture in South Asia. It would be impossible to enumerate all the different dances, yet issues of classification need to be addressed. National, religious, and ethnic divisions are foregrounded in the scholarship on South Asian dance. Most studies concentrate on the dances of a particular nation-state, providing a description of different dance forms, categorized as either "folk" or "classical," and organized by region and ethnic group. Although these categories are no doubt basic to understanding South Asian dance, it is important to consider how these categories are socially constructed and contested. The lived personal and collective histories of performers, audiences, and patrons also deserve more attention.

Large-scale festivals with displays of dances from different regions are used by the state to represent ethnic diversity in South Asia and to promote national unity. Yet shared histories, cross-cultural borrowings, and interethnic affiliations are not generally recognized in popular discourse or dance scholarship. Researching dance in South Asia presents the substantive challenge of identifying historical interrelationships among various genres of performance without glossing over sociocultural distinctions and conflicts. As Flueckiger (1996) has demonstrated in her research in the Chhattisgar region of middle India, neighboring groups are sometimes unaware of the commonalities between their folk traditions due to the emphasis on ethnic differences. Nor can South Asia be treated as an ontological reality outside of geopolitics. Long histories of trade, cross-migration, colonialism, globalization, and imperialism have shaped dance forms in South Asia and in the South Asian diaspora as well.

Deśī/Mārga

The Sanskrit terms *deśī* and *mārga* were used to classify dance in a medieval treatise on music and dance titled *Saṅgītaratnākara* (circa thirteenth century). The term *mārga* pertained to those dances (and *tāla,* rhythmical patterns) that adhered to the aesthetic rules outlined in the Brahmanical *śāstras,* and *deśī* referred to those dances that reflected regional tastes. This was not the first Sanskrit text to use these terms; however, it provided the most comprehensive discussion of deśī dance for its period. Although the deśī/mārga distinction is associated with "folk" versus "classical," these latter divisions are modern-day constructs. Today's dance forms do not encapsulate traditions of antiquity, despite the fact that they are often represented as such within nationalist discourse.

Use of the terms "folk" and "classical" may suggest a clear-cut division between rural and urban ways of life and between peasant and elite classes, but this ignores the powerful role of the state, religious institutions, and mass media throughout rural and urban South Asia. Whether or not a form of dance comes to be labeled as "folk" or "classical" often has more to do with the socioeconomic status of the performers, patrons, and audience members, as well as the degree of formalization and technique involved in the training. Typically, "classical" dance genres are associated with the elite classes and elaborate, formal training, whereas "folk" dance genres are associated with rural, marginalized communities and less elaborate, informal training.

Representations of folk and tribal dance in South Asia reflect the tendency within modern society to romanticize rural life and the preindustrial past. This is highly evident, for example, in "Bollywood" (Mumbai's movie industry) movies, which are enjoyed by South Asian audiences worldwide for their lively song-and-dance sequences. Many of these films contain bucolic scenes of villagers or tribespeople singing and dancing in colorful garb, conjuring up nostalgic images of rural peasant life. Folk dancers may take their inspiration from the everyday activities and experiences of rural peasants; however, they also incorporate urban, elite mass media and foreign influences. For example, Karagattam folk dancers of Tamil Nadu, South India, draw upon movements and gestures from "disco" dances featured in Indian cinema. While some people view such adaptations as corruptions of Indian tradition, for others these adaptations underscore the versatility of folk dancers to respond to contemporary conditions and concerns.

In examining the history of Indian classical dance forms of Odissi, Bhāratanāṭyam, and Kathak, one finds that they, too, have undergone significant change. In precolonial times, female dancers known as the *ṭawā'īf* of northern India and the *devadasi* of the South (referred to as nautch by the British) were not only dancers and singers but also courtesans and ritual specialists. They played important ritual roles in the *zamīndārī* (land-tenure system), temple, and court, and were supported by wealthy male patrons. With the shifts in power and cultural ideology that occurred under British colonial rule, these dance traditions underwent a period of declining patronage, only later to be "rediscovered" and reconstituted by urban elites during nationalist cultural revival movements of the late nineteenth and twentieth centuries. This new class of cosmopolitan performers altered the form, style, and meanings of the dances, performing them as national heritage on secular stages for middle- and upper-class audiences. As a result of these changes, many of the lower-class dancer-courtesans were disenfranchised from their tradition. Since today's dances contain modern influences, some dance scholars prefer to call them "neoclassical." Yet most audience members and performers continue to view these dances as representing their ancient heritage. Similarly, Kathak's Islamic roots in the Mughal courts of the sixteenth and seventeenth centuries have all but been erased from popular memory due to Hindu nationalism.

Dance and Religion

The close relationship between dancing and religion throughout South Asia raises another classificatory issue with the term "dance" itself. Western distinctions between dance, ritual, and drama do not readily apply. This is especially true in popular Hinduism, in which the duality of spirit and flesh found in Christianity and Islam does not exist. Hindu mythology and iconography are filled with images of dancing deities and devotees in both the Vaisnavite and Saivite sects: Śiva, or Nāṭarājā, performs the cosmic dance of life, Rādhā and Kṛṣṇa dance among the goatherds, and *apsaras* and *gandaravas* entertain the gods with celestial music and dance. Theatrical performance combined with dance is one of the many paths for attaining spiritual awakening and communication with the supernatural in Hindu religion. Like disciples of hatha yoga, dancer-actors (Sanskrit, *naṭa*) utilize meditation, prayer in the form of mantras, and somatic disciplines involving distinct movements and gestures to attain a state of bliss and to invoke divine blessings. Among Buddhist Newars of Nepal, Padmanarteśvara (a deity also referred to as Natsayadeo and Narteśvara) is considered the divine embodiment of dance and is ritually addressed by dancers and priests whenever they perform the dance of the Aṣṭamātṛkā (powerful goddesses of the Kathmandu Valley). A picture of Narteśvara is typically displayed in the beginning of the dance, while a song in his praise is sung (Khon 2001:14).

The earliest extant text concerning dance within the Sanskritic tradition is the *Nāṭyaśāstra,* a dramaturgical treatise, written by Bharata Muni sometime between the second century B.C.E and the second century C.E. The *Nāṭyaśāstra* contains thirty-six chapters on subjects ranging over the architecture of the playhouse, the emotional states of the performer and audience, body movements and gestures, makeup, music, percussive instruments, and so forth. Bharata expounded upon the importance of *bhava* and *rasa* in Sanskrit drama. Bhava is generally translated as mood, and rasa can be defined as a distilling of raw emotional experiences into aesthetic forms, which spectators can savor like the sweet taste of ripened fruits or honey. Bhava and rasa are important concepts in the performing arts in other parts of South and Southeast Asia as well. For example, Afghan women convey different expressive moods such as coquettishness (*nāz*) or showing off their charm (*shīwa*) in solo dances known as *ghamzagī* or *qandegī* (St. John 1993:61).

Music in the form of specific melodies (raga), drum rhythms (*tāla*), and songs is fundamental to dance. Many dancers wear brass bells around their ankles, and the rhythmic syllables made with their feet are synchronized with the drumbeats. This can lead to playful contests between the drummers and the dancers, as for example when a drummer uses offbeats and slurs to disguise the main rhythm or when either one picks up speed. In some cases, the drummers join in the dancing. There are many specific drum dances, most of them male, such as the *raban nätuma* dance of Sri Lanka, which is named after the *rabana* drum. The men sing verses from *Jātaka* tales while they dance and play the drums.

Dance is also found in most South Asian folk theatrical traditions as a means of livening up the plot and enabling the actors and audiences to enhance music and song kinesthetically. Historically, body gestures and gait were very consciously used in Sanskrit dramas to portray stock characters, such as the Rājā (king), the Vidusaka (clown), and the Brahman (priest). In Special Nāṭakam drama of Tamil Nadu—held on makeshift stages in streets during festival times—comic dance interludes, combined with music and song, keep audiences entertained throughout the night. In theatrical dance traditions, such as Kuttiyattam, Ottan Tullal, Taiyam, and Krishnattam of Kerala the performers act out *purāṇic* stories and may enter into a trance-like state as exhibited through distinct facial movements and body gestures.

The *Rāmāyaṇa* and *Mahābhārata* epics form the narrative structure for a host of theatrical performances involving elements of dance in South and Southeast Asia. The Rām Līlā and Rās Līlā held in Uttar Pradesh and other regions of North India are large-scale ritual reenactments of Rāma, Kṛṣhna, and Rādhā stories acted out by young boys who are specially selected for this role. In Bhāratanāṭyam, South Indian classical dance (most typically performed by a solo female dancer), the performer strikes distinct poses identified with particular gods and goddesses and uses gesture and movements to narrate and interpret stories from the epics and purāṇas. Dancers alternate between *nṛta,* pure dance; *nṛtya,* interpretive dance, and *nāṭya,* dance with dramatic elements. Stories drawn from the epics are also conveyed through Yaksagāna, a theatrical dance tradition of Karnataka in which actor/dancers dressed in elaborate makeup and costumes perform to the accompaniment of singers and musicians.

Numerous other texts, sculptures, and paintings provide information on dance in premodern South Asia. For example, Tamil *Caṅkam* literature, recorded on palm leaf manuscripts dating back to the second century, reveal myriad dance genres in the southern regions of India serving a host of functions ranging from the more serious tasks of communication with the gods and defending against evil spirits to the lighter activities of playful, celebratory expression and entertainment. Caṅkam poetry refers to male bards known as *pāṇar* and *iravalar* who accompanied the king to battle and female bards, known as *viṟali* and *pāṭin,* who sang and danced while playing a small lute. The goddess Koṟṟavai is described as dancing on the battlefield accompanied by ghosts, demons, and demon-women. Priests known as *vēlaṉ* ("he with the spear") performed a dance called *veriyatal* to drive out dangerous possessing spirits. Temple carvings and inscriptions also provide us with important information on dance, such as the Chidambaram temple built under the Chola kingdom of South India which is known for its striking dance sculptures and carvings.

Religious festivals remain the most important occasions for dance. Deities, spirits, and demons are invoked through dance to control forces of nature and human destiny. Dances are performed to cure people of illnesses, bring rain to ensure good harvests, promote well-being and fertility, and to provide for the overall prosperity of villages through appeasing and propitiating the spirits. Dance is linked with spirit possession in many parts of the world; in all world religions—even Islam, which discourages secular dancing—the dancing bodies of priests, shamans, and laypeople are vehicles through which trance occurs and spirits enter into the human realm. For example, followers of the Sunni Muslim Sufi order called Rifa'i in coastal areas of Balochistan practice a monthly meeting called Holy Eleventh Night's Charity in which men and women sit in separate circles, repeating their profession of faith (*kalima*) in a chorus. As they recite, members of the group begin swinging their bodies back and forth while circumambulating, thus bringing themselves to a state of religious ecstasy. Harmful spirits and demons, too, are controlled through dance, giving spiritual healers and exorcists power to ward off illness and other threats to their communities. Women of Makran, in coastal Balochistan, also practice a possession ritual to alleviate *gwāt* (wind spirit), which is thought to cause illness by attacking the person's heart and mind. An afflicted person seeks the help of a male or female spiritual healer (*gwāt-i-mat*), who performs a ceremony, known as *leb,* in which the gwāt-i-mat either asks the spirit to leave the possessed patient or uses other spirits to cast out the unwanted spirit.

The Chau dance of West Bengal is another such dance involving spirit possession. This dance is performed on the occasion of *Gājan* (the annual sun festival), which begins on the last day of the year and lasts up to several months. *Bhakta*s, or devotees drawn from various non-Brahman castes, perform daily religious rites in the vicinity of the Śiva temple, becoming kinsmen of the deity. For thirteen days prior to the festival they go to the temple and perform a ritualistic dance to a special tune and rhythm. Men and women of the community also participate in *cap*—a ritualistic, representational procession. The men wear masks and dress themselves as deities and also as women or animals such as tigers, bears, monkeys, and bulls. For example, a devotee of Kārttikeya (the god of war who rides a peacock) wears feathers attached to his back and a mask attached to his groin to give the appearance of riding a peacock. Rāvaṇa is represented by a mask of ten heads. Some devotees smear their bodies with mud, and wear dresses made of straw, rags, and skulls, as well as sticks and branches of trees. They travel through the village in procession, singing devotional songs, accompanied by the beat of a drum in a ritual called *telhalda,* which culminates in a dance in front of the temple.

Similar masked dances are found in Buddhist worship in Nepal and Sri Lanka, such as the *'bag 'cham* and the *kohoṁba kankāriya,* respectively. *'Bag 'cham* (masked dance) is held in Sherpa and Tibetan monasteries on the fifteenth day of the Mani Rimdu festival celebrated in the Everest Region. Wearing elaborate silk robes, masked dancers representing different deities perform a variety of different dances. *Dorje drolö* is the most important of the masked dances, performed as a solo dance representing the demon-slaying form of the divine saint Padmasambhava. Since this dance has great ritual significance, it is reserved for only the most talented dancers (Khon 2001: 197).

Life-cycle rituals and harvest festivals are other central occasions for dance in communities throughout South Asia. Marriage ceremonies typically call for celebration through dance. *Bhangra,* originally a Punjabi farmer's dance, is highly popular at Indian weddings. Bhangra music combines traditional Punjabi folk rhythms with pop culture musical elements of India and Great Britain. The *suā nāc* ("parrot dance") is an undulating circle dance, which is performed by *ādivāsi* (low caste, tribal) women of Chhattisgarh during the harvest month of *Kārtik* (October-November). Gond women perform this dance for audiences in their own villages and competitively with other villages. The dancers say that the primary reason for the dance is to raise money for the nine-day festival, called *Gaura,* which celebrates the wedding of the god Śiva and his consort Pārvatī.

The connection between dance and martial arts also deserves brief mention. Prior to the formation of modern armies, dances were used to display physical strength and readiness for combat. Various types of stick-fighting dances are common throughout South

Asia. The *kathi nāch,* a popular stick dance performed in Rajasthan during the annual *Durga Puja* festival, is characterized by participants moving in a circle while hitting the stick of the next person. This dance resembles the *dāndiā rāsa* danced with wooden sticks in Gujarat during festivals such as *Holi* and *Divali,* and *lī-keli,* a Sri Lankan stick dance. *Cillambāṭṭam* is another stick dance found in Tamil Nadu, which is performed with long wooden poles formerly used in combat.

Dances involving acrobatic feats are very popular in street fairs and religious festivals. Many folk dances involve the balancing of clay or metal pots and other objects on the dancers' heads (typically female dancers), such as the *charkhula* and *bhavai* dances of Rajasthan and *karagāṭṭam* or *kumbāṭṭam* of Tamil Nadu and Kerala, respectively. Such pot dances are associated with the worship of regional goddesses such as Sitālā in the North and Mariammaṉ in the South of India. Decorated pots are symbols of *śakti* (sacred female power) and thus figure prominently in ritualistic dance. The pots may be adorned with flowers and other objects, fire may be lit inside the pots, or multiple-tiered pots of graduated size may be used to form elaborate structures.

Dance and Resistance Politics

Folk dance provides a window onto the experiences, perspectives, and politics of subaltern communities. Folk dancers often use their performances to comment on their own lives and their society. Symbolism and verbal play are commonly used to convey veiled messages, or what James Scott refers to as "hidden transcripts." For example, karagāṭṭam—a folk dance genre of Tamil Nadu, South India, which is performed at Hindu temple festivals and life-cycle celebrations—is known locally for its bawdy humor, expressed in dialogues and songs, combined with erotic movements and gestures. Karagāṭṭam dancers use double meaning, mimesis, and parody to mock temple priests, depicting them as lustful and greedy, while also portraying politicians as corrupt.

Folk dance can serve as a form of cultural memory, collective identity formation, and resistance to hegemonic structures of power for subaltern communities. Even in the midst of tragic events such as natural catastrophes, social adversity, and political oppression, folk dances continue to enlighten and uplift the spirits of participants and audience members, providing testimony to human resiliency and the transformative power of creative expression. However, we must be wary of overromanticizing the resistant potential of folk dance. Folk dances can just as easily serve as hegemonic tools of dominant social groups, especially when they are viewed as archaic, naïve, or natural forms of expression.

Both folk and classical dance genres, and certainly the practitioners of these arts, have been profoundly affected by historical change. Nationalist movements at the turn of the twentieth century led to cultural revivalism in which various dances came to be viewed as national heritage and defined as "classical" or "folk." Yet simultaneously these traditions were being radically altered by new modes of cultural production. Scholars have recently come to recognize that most—if not all—South Asian dances have been invented and reinvented over time, such that attaching labels of "authentic" versus "inauthentic" and "traditional" versus "modern" is problematic. The use of such terms is implicated in cultural identity politics, which is why issues of identity, authority, and power are central to dance scholarship.

Dance serves to propagate social values and beliefs, to construct identity, and to convey veiled messages of resistance. However, in general, dance in South Asia has been less overtly politicized than urban street theater or cinema. Currently, some classically trained dancers are challenging the established canon, through rethinking the history, movement vocabulary, symbolism, contexts, and meanings of the dances in light of feminist thought and other contemporary sociopolitical concerns, while still maintaining elements of the formal technique and aesthetic of these distinctive classical styles. Yet only a relatively small cohort of activist-performers and scholars in South Asia emphasizes dance as a vehicle for social change.

References

Bose, Mandakranta. *Movement and mimesis: The idea of dance in the Sanskritic tradition.* Dordrecht: Kluwer Academic Publishers.

Diamond, Sarah. 1999. "Karagattam: Performance and the politics of desire in Tamil Nadu, India." Ph.D. diss. Anthropology Department. University of Pennsylvania.

Flueckiger, Joyce. 1996. *Gender and genre in the folklore of Middle India.* Ithaca, N.Y.: Cornell University Press.

Kersenboom-Story, Saskia C. 1987. *Nityasumangali: Devadasi tradition in South India.* Delhi: Motilal Banarsidass.

Kohn, Richard J. 2001. *Lord of the dance: The* mani rimdu *festival in Tibet and Nepal.* New York: State University of New York Press.

Scott, James. 1990. *Domination and the arts of resistance.* New Haven: Yale University Press.

Seneviratna, Anuradha. 1984. *Traditional dance of Sri Lanka.* Colombo: UNESCO.

Sultana, Farhat. 1997. "Gwat and gwat-i-leb: Spirit healing and social change in Makran" In *Marginality and modernity: Ethnicity and change in post-colonial Balochistan,* Paul Titus ed. Karachi: Oxford University Press.

St. John, Katherine. 1993. "A cultural and historical study of selected women's dance from Herat, Afghanistan, 1970–1980." Department of Dance, Brigham Young University.

Vatsayan, Kapila. 1976. *Traditions of Indian folk dance.* New Delhi: Clarion Books.

Waterhouse, David, ed. 1988. *Dance of India*. South Asian Studies Papers, No. 10. Mumbai: Popula Prakashan.

SARAH DIAMOND

SEE ALSO

Atan; Balochistan: Oral Tradition; *Bhavāi; Bhānd Pathar; Bhūta kōla; Burra kathā; Cait Parab;* Candaini (Lorik-Candā); *Cavittu nātukam; Chau;* Dance, Nepal; Epic, Nepal; *Gāmbhīra; Ghondala;* Govindji, Temple of; Jainism; *Jātrā/Yātrā; Jhumur Jātrā* Drama; *Kamsāle;* Karnataka; *Kātama Raju;* Kathak Dancers; *Kathakali*; Kerala; *Kohoṁba Kankāriya;* Life Cycle Rituals; Marriage Ceremonies; Masks; *Mukhos Nāc; Nācā;* Nationalism and Folklore; *Nautanki; Pāmpin Tullal;* Performance Studies; *Rām Līlā; Rāmāyana; Rāsa Līlā;* Spirit Possession and Mediumship; Sri Lanka, Sinhala; Tamil Nadu; *Terukkūttu; Teyyam;* Theater and Drama; *yaksagāna*

DANCE, NEPAL

Lokanṛtya and *lokanāca* are the traditional Nepali patterns of artistic movement, usually performed with song or musical accompaniment, that formalize and intensify kinesthetic experience and communication through culturally approved gestures and symbols. The terms "lokanṛtya" and "lokanāca" achieved currency only in the second half of the twentieth century; traditionally, folk dance, along with other ethnic, popular, traditional, and classical dances, and even dramas, were commonly called *nāca* (dance).

For centuries, Nepali dances have been used as vehicles of worship and as expressions of the people's most profound emotions and states of mind. Dances range from joyous celebration of the changing seasons, the harvest, or the birth of a child, to more ritualistic dances for the worship of deities or to appease evil spirits and ghosts. In most cases, even *nāca guru* (dance instructors) are unable to clarify the original meanings of specific sections of music or dance steps since they have become so conventionalized. Most people learn dances formally and informally from their gurus and their own family members. The costumes are customarily resplendent with extensive use of ornaments such as *śirphūla* (a flower made of gold) on the head to *paiñjarī* (golden or silver anklet) on the feet. Some of these dances are performed by men or women exclusively, but in most, they dance together. Among the folk instruments, *mādal* (a barrel-shaped drum) is the most popular.

Most ethnolinguistic groups have dances specific to them, such as the *jyāpu nāca* of Kathmandu Valley, and *magar nāca* and *durā nāca* of the hills of central Nepal. In addition to these ethnic dances, Nepali folk dances can be divided into three categories: religious, ceremonial, and social.

In the Hindu religious dances of the various regions of Nepal, the dancer seeks to express reverence for and interact directly with the divine. The religious dances of the Kathmandu valley, such as *navadurgā nāca, bhadrakālī nāca, svetakālī nāca,* and *hanumāna nāca,* are organized by the temples of the related deities—Navadurgā, Bhadrakālī, Svetakālī, and Hanuman, respectively. The dances are organized and performed on the temple premises during the religious festivals. For example, the navadurgā nāca is organized by the Navadurgā temple during the Daśaiṃ, a festival in celebration of the victory of the goddess Navadurga over the demon king Mahishāsura. The nāca are based on the deities' related *purāṇa,* such as Devīvagavat for Navadurgā, and glorify the deities' deeds. The nāca portray the characteristics of deities through the use of gestures, costumes, and masks, and it is believed that the deities will bestow their blessings upon the performers, sponsors, and audience. The masks are made of metal, wood, papier-mâché, or baked clay. Common musical instruments include drums, cymbals, and flutes. For all these dances, the invocation of Lord Ganeśa and Lord Śiva, the deities of success and dance respectively, is considered essential. The deities are invoked by the recitation of their hymns. Customarily, all the performers should be present in the invocation.

In the festival of *Tīj,* celebrated in the third day of the brighter moon in the month of Bhādra (August-September), the Hindu women worship Śiva and Pārvatī through song and dance in the belief that the goddesses' blessings will improve their conjugal life. The *khaiñjaḍi nāca* and *bālan nāca* are organized during religious fairs and festivals, in which men dance on the theme of *puraṇa, Rāmāyaṇa, Mahābhārata,* and *Bhāgavata* especially, to the beat of the khaiñjaḍī (tambourine).

Among Buddhists, *caryā* and *mani-rimdu* are distinguished dances. The Vajrāchāryas, members of the Buddhist priest class, perform the caryā dances with the ultimate aim of transcending duality by attaining a vivid conscious experience leading to the state of nirvana. For this purpose, the dancers put on masks of various types as required for different characteristics. Masks expressing compassion, love, and forgiveness are used for deities, and those evoking fear and terror are used for demons. The mask of the main character is made out of metal or wood, while those of subordinate characters are made of papier-mâche or baked clay. The *mani-rimdu* dance of Sherpas, who follow Mahayana Tantric Buddhism, has integrated the elements of Tibetan music and folk dances, especially the 'cham dance.

Jhāñnkrī nāca, a shamanic dance, crosses religious boundaries. The jhāñnkrī (shamans), dressed with exotic items such as porcupine quills and peacock feathers, perform their dance with leaps and jumps while beating *ḍhyāṅgro* (frame drums). They not only amuse the audience, but also, by communicating with the sacred and supernatural, attempt to protect people from evil spirits.

Ceremonial dances include dances at celebratory events, whether religious or secular, especially for rites of passage. *Ratyaulī,* performed at weddings by women of the bridegroom's party, is marked by joyous cajoling and teasing, especially of the bridegroom's mother and sisters. The members of ethnoprofessional musician castes such as Damāī, Bādī, and Bhāñnda are often hired to entertain, especially at weddings and other auspicious occasions. Damāī primarily play *pance bājā* (an ensemble of five kinds of instruments: trumpets, shawm, kettle drums, barrel drum, and cymbal); they also amuse the party with their *damāi nāca* dance, a comedic art, mocking or parodying the traditional songs and dances. Bhāñnda and Bādī charm the audience with dances from various sources, combining more traditional dances with those of contemporary Nepali and Hindi films.

Sakhiyā, bhailo, and *deusire* are festive dances. Sakhiyā is performed during the autumn festival Daśaiṃ (a celebration of the victory of the goddess Navadurgā over the demon king Mahishāsura). Bhailo and deusire are performed in the *Tihār* (festival of light and prosperity). Similarly, to celebrate the spring season, the *horī* dances are performed, especially in the Tarāi lowlands bordering North India. The *lākhe nāca,* the masked demon dances of Kathmandu Valley, are performed especially during the festival of *Indrajātrā,* celebrated in the honor of Lord Indra, the king of heaven and god of rain, on the fourteenth day of the brighter moon in the month of Bhādra (August–September). In these dances *jhyālinchā* (a teaser) teases *lākhe* (a demon) for the amusement of the spectators.

Social dances are performed for recreation, generally as part of events revolving around leisure activities and social interaction; they give expression to personal relationships, especially of love and courtship. In *deuḍā nāca,* boys and girls face off in separate lines and express their innermost desires in songs, while swaying back and forth. In the *dhāna nāca,* men and women of the Limbu ethnic group link arms and move in a circle counterclockwise with occasional steps backward and forward, all the while singing love songs. A wide range of leaps and jumps characterizes *tāmāṅ selo,* in which youths of the Tamang ethic group dance to the beat of the *ḍamphu* (frame drum). Among the Gurung and Magar ethnic groups, *cuḍkā, karuwā,* and *jhyāure* are the most popular dances; in these, boys and girls dance to the sound of pounding feet and the beat of the *mādal* (barrel-shaped drum) and *khaijaḍi* (tambourine). The *rodīghar,* a kind of nightclub of the Gurung ethnic group, provides youth with an institutional setting for singing, dancing, and entertainment.

Folk dance, though a widely performed Nepali folk genre, remains one of the least systematically studied fields. The folk dances described here are merely a sample of the vast repository of Nepali folk tradition. The growing cultural consciousness among various ethnic groups in recent years in Nepal and the increasing availability of new technologies to aid documentation have set an appropriate atmosphere for the preservation and promotion of Nepali folk dances. In this context, Nepali folk dance will continue to be an important site of knowledge, power, and cultural expression.

References

Bhattarai, Harihar P. 1985. Folklore studies in Nepal. *Himalayan Culture* 3(1): 10–14.

Jerstad, Luther G. 1969. *Mani-rimdu: Sherpa dance-drama.* Seattle: University of Washington Press.

Mandap, Kala. 1986. *Buddhist ritual dance.* Kathmandu: Kala Mandap.

Thapa, Bhairab Bahadur. 1968. Leading features of folk dances. In *Nepal monograph on Nepalese culture,* trans. Tirtha R. Tuladhar. Kathmandu: HMG Department of Information.

Varya, Tank Vilas. 1985. *Nepal: The seat of cultural heritage.* Kathmandu: Educational Enterprise.

HARIHAR P. BHATTARAI

SEE ALSO

Dances; Marriage Ceremonies; Nepal; *Tīj* Songs

DARGĀH

Dargāh ("court") is the term commonly used for the tombs of Muslim saints (*auliyā-i Allah*). A dargāh is an important place of *ziyārat* (pilgrimage). The model for this *ziyārat* is the pilgrimage to the tomb of the Prophet Muḥammad in Medina. According to popular belief, Muḥammad hears the devotions of Muslims at his tomb. Similarly, the auliyā (literally, "friends of God")—who are the designated representatives of the Prophet—hear the prayers of believers and may intercede with God in the name of Muḥammad. The auliyā are the invisible spiritual rulers of this world, and their graves are their palaces where devotees may seek their audience and *tufail* (intercession). The auliyā are spiritually present at the dargāh and, like earthly rulers, must be treated with respect and propriety (*adab*). A dargāh is a place of great spiritual power (*barakah*), where people come to fulfill vows (*mannat*), seek healing, or simply show devotion and respect. The dargāh of famous saints, like Mu'in ud-din Chishti in Ajmeer, is often an elaborate architectural monument built by Muslim rulers to demonstrate their devotion to the auliyā. Although tomb visitation is controversial, it is extremely popular, particularly during the annual *'urs,* celebrated on the death anniversary of the saint, and its accompanying festival (*melā*).

References

Currie, P. M. 1989. *The shrine and cult of Mu'in al-Din Chisti of Ajmer.* Delhi: Oxford University Press.

Troll, Christian W., ed. 1989. *Muslim shrines in India: Their character, history and significance.* Delhi: Oxford University Press.

VERNON JAMES SCHUBEL

SEE ALSO

Saints; Muslim Shrines; *ᶜUrs; Ziyarat*

DĀRIKAVADHAM

Dārikavadham (the death of Dārika) is a legend in oral transmission in Kerala and neighboring areas of Tamil Nadu, which forms the core of rituals and beliefs of the Bhagavati cult. The story tells of the birth, deeds, and death of the demon Dārika at the hands of the goddess Bhagavati (also Bhadrakāḷi).

The demon Dārika, after intense ascetic practice, secured boons of invincibility, a special weapon, and a secret mantra from the god Brahma. A drop of his blood would generate thousands of Dārikas and no man could kill him. Thus armed, Dārika began to commit numerous depredations. When Śiva came to know of Dārika's misdeeds, he opened his fiery third eye, and the enormous flaming form of Bhadrakāḷi emerged to destroy Dārika. Unsuccessful in battle, Bhadrakāḷi disguised herself as an old Brahman woman and went to Dārika's wife, Manodarī, who was repeating the secret mantra. After tricking her into telling the mantra, Bhadrakāḷi went through the forest and sought the help of the bloodthirsty Vētāḷam, leader of the forest ghosts and spirits. Manodarī, discovering the goddess's trickery, obtained a bucket of Pārvati's sweat and threw it on Kāḷi, covering her with smallpox. Hearing Kāḷi's cries for help, Śiva created Ghaṇṭākāṛṇan from his ear wax. Ghaṇṭākāṛṇan licked his sister's body to remove the smallpox but, out of modesty, could not touch her face, which remained scarred. Kāḷi returned to war. Vētāḷam spread her enormous tongue over the battlefield, drinking Dārika's blood as Bhadrakāḷi cut off his head. The furious Bhadrakāḷi returned to Kailāsam, holding Dārika's head in her left hand. On seeing the fearful goddess, Śiva attempted to calm her, saying, "Daughter, dance upon my naked body and release your temper." Doing this, she was satisfied, and, henceforth, began to receive offerings from devotees as a boon from Śiva.

Dārikavadham is sung in many ritual contexts of worship offered to the goddess Bhagavati in Kerala. Each caste has its own unique version of the songs. The agricultural Pulaya and Paraya castes, reputed to have ruled Kerala before the advent of the Brahmans in the early centuries C.E., perform *Dārikavadham* in Trichur and Palghat districts, wearing brass breasts and straw headdresses. In southern Kerala, *muṭiyeṭuppu, paraṇēṯṯu,* and countless other elaborations on the dance-dramas of *Dārikavadham* are performed with huge wooden headdresses and breastplates of silver or wood.

Published in Malayalam and Sanskrit as *Bhadrakāḷī Māhātmyam, Bhadrōlpatti,* and *Dārukavadham,* the story is also alive and well in oral tradition. Although texts such as *Devīmāhātmya, Devibhāgavatapurāṇa, Lingapurāṇa* (1.106), and the Tamil text *Tirukkūvam* contain closely related motifs, the full Kerala form of *Dārikavadham* does not appear in any of the Sanskrit *purāṇa*s (mythological texts) and appears to have its origin in oral tradition.

References

Mani, Vettam. 1975 [1964]. Ghaṇṭākaṛṇa. In *Puranic Encyclopedia,* 289. Delhi: Motilal Banarsidass.

Shulman, David Dean. 1980. *Tamil temple myths: Sacrifice and divine marriage in the South Indian Śaiva tradition.* Princeton: Princeton University Press.

SARAH CALDWELL

SEE ALSO

Bhagavati Ritual Traditions of Kerala; Gods and Goddesses; Kerala

DARŚAN

Sanskrit *darśana,* literally "seeing," pronounced without final "-a" in vernaculars, has come to have two distinct meanings. One refers to classical Indian philosophical systems or world "views"; six to a dozen such schools are well known. The other meaning indicates a religious "sight, vision, appearance" and is most frequently employed to state the experience of seeing, and being seen by, a divine being. For example, "This morning I went to the temple and took darśan of the Goddess. The Mother gave darśan to me."

Vedic, classical Hindu, and other traditions note the powerful consequences of being in the gaze of a deity, of being perceived by the deity. Puruṣa, Indra, Vāyu, Rudra, and Viṣṇu are all "thousand-eyed" gods; Brahma, with his four heads, sees all; Śiva and the Buddha perceive all worlds through the third eye of insight. The nine planetary deities constantly look upon all beings with a mixture of benevolent and malevolent effects. A god or goddess installed in a temple or shrine image (*mūrti*) is not consecrated until the moment of eye opening, a specific rite often involving a gold needle that activates sacred sight. To be seen by a divine being is always an awesome and transformative experience; the devotee hopes to go away from the encounter with an extension of divine protection, grace, auspiciousness.

Darśan is worship in its simplest and most direct form. Hindu households may have small images of gods and goddesses on an altar, numerous color lithographs of deities on the walls, perhaps a photo of a guru or renowned ancestor. Darśan applies to all, as it does to routine confrontations outside the house with innumerable shrines, temples, the processional image of a deity making its rounds of a village, sacred trees or rivers, holy men or women such as *sādhus* or ascetics. A devotee may clasp hands and nod in praise when passing a Hanuman temple even when it is closed, for the god sees through doors. Distant pilgrimages may be made to take darśan, for example, of the River Ganga, the city of Banaras, or Satya Sai Baba. Hindu pilgrims, walking fifteen days to take darśan of the god Viṭhobā on a special lunar day, may, because of the crowds, never reach his temple, but darśan of the temple spire from miles away can suffice. Jains may take darśan of images of *tīrthaṅkaras*; Sikhs of the Guru Granth Sāhib or the Golden Temple in Amritsar; Buddhists of an image of the Buddha, a stūpa, or the tooth relic at Kandy; Muslims of the *dargāh* of a saint. Traditions of meditation in Hinduism, Buddhism, and Jainism may also claim that intended visualizations of divine beings and gurus of the past are individual experiences of darśan.

References

Eck, Diana L. 1998. *Darshan. Seeing the divine image in India.* 3rd ed., New York: Columbia University Press.

Fuller, Christopher J. 1992. *The camphor flame. Popular Hinduism and society in India.* Princeton: Princeton University Press.

Gonda, Jan. 1969. *Eye and gaze in the Veda.* Amsterdam: North Holland Publishing Co.

DAVID M. KNIPE

SEE ALSO

Dṛṣṭi; Worship

DĀSARA

Dāsara ("ten days" or "destroying ten sins") is, technically, another name given for the *Nāvarātri* ("nine nights") festival, but is sometimes restricted to denoting the "Great Ninth" (*Mahānavami*) and the "Victorious Tenth" (Sanskrit: *Vijaya Daśamī;* Bengali: *Bijoya*) days of the Nāvarātri celebrations. The concluding ceremonies of the Dāsara festival commemorate either the victory of Durgā over the buffalo demon Mahiṣā or Rāma's conquest of Lanka. It is also believed that on the ninth day, the warrior Arjuna, in the epic *Mahābhārata,* recovered the weapons he had hidden in the *ṣamī* tree during his year of exile and then fought against the Kaurava army and won the battle. These victories are interpreted literally and symbolically in rituals.

On the ninth day, warriors worship their weapons (*āyudha pūjā*), and, by extension, craftsmen and other workers venerate their tools and implements; others understand the stories to mean the triumph of knowledge and learning over the darkness of ignorance. In parts of South India, educational materials (books, pens, pencils, and, today, computers and disks) and musical instruments are dedicated to Saraswatī, the goddess of learning and the performing arts. Finally, on the last day (the "Victorious Tenth" day dedicated to the goddess Lakṣmī in South India), there is a multidimensional celebration: new learning, especially of the performing arts, takes place, along with the honoring of music and dance teachers.

Historically, these two days were dedicated to martial celebrations by kings and warriors. Kings frequently led ceremonial forays to the borders of their kingdoms and ritually crossed boundaries to simulate attacks against enemies. Some of the best known and most majestic celebrations took place in Mysore, where the maharaja would worship the goddess Chamuṇḍī (a form of Durgā), ritually venerate the royal throne, weapons, and other symbols of royal power, and nine forms of the goddess Lakṣmī. On the tenth day he would ride on a gold seat on top of the royal elephant in a long and colorful procession to the northeast boundary of the city. After ritually hunting animals and worshiping the ṣamī tree, the torch-lit procession would come back to town for a royal durbar. In post-independence India, the grandeur and pageantry of the royal tournaments and processions have been replaced with more popular celebrations in which all weapons, tools, vehicles, and modes of transportation, including public buses and trains, cars, and bikes, are venerated. These are decorated with garlands and colored *kumkum* powder and dedicated to the goddesses through locally constructed neighborhood rituals, generally without the assistance of Brahman or other priestly personnel.

In Bengal, gigantic effigies of the goddess Durgā and other deities are consecrated and worshiped during the nine nights of the Nāvarātri festival; on the tenth day, the animating life believed to reside in them is said to depart, and the images, after being taken on a daylong procession, are submerged in a river or pond.

References

Biardeau, Madeleine. 1984. The sami tree and the sacrificial buffalo. *Contributions to Indian Sociology* n.s. 18(1): 1–23.

Kane, Pandurang Vaman. 1958. Vijayadaśamī. In *History of Dharmaśastra*, vol. 5, pt. 1, 188–194. Poona: Bhandarkar Oriental Research Institute.

Sivapriyananda, Swami. 1995. *Mysore royal dasara*. New Delhi: Abhinav Publications.

Stein, Burton. 1983. Mahanavami: Medieval and modern kingly ritual in south India. In *Essays on Gupta culture*, ed. Bardwell Smith, 67–90. Columbia: South Asia Books.

VASUDHA NARAYANAN

SEE ALSO
Nāvarātri; Ṣamī

DĀSTĀN

Dāstān is an extended, imaginative narrative, either oral or written. In premodern times, the terms "dāstān" and *qiṣṣa* were synonymous; they remain so in the chapbook industry in Pakistan, although in educated Urdu usage today, qiṣṣa has come to mean prose fiction. Dāstān are linear and episodic in form, may be contained within a frame tale, and usually contain a subplot parallel to the main plot.

Dāstān are generally romances of love, heroic stories of fighting, or Islamic religious narratives cast in a popular mold, and may have a didactic or vaguely Sufic content. The diverse major sources for dāstān in Afghanistan and South Asia are Arabic (mainly the *Alf Lailá wa Lailá*, or *The 1001 Nights*), Persian stories, Sanskrit (mainly the *Pancatantra* and the *Kathāsaritsāgara*, or *The Ocean of Story*), and the general stock of oral narrative current in that part of the world.

Narrated in Persian, Pashto, Urdu, Hindi, Punjabi, Sindhi, and other languages, dāstān were an important form of entertainment and, to some degree, instruction, among the Muslim populations of Afghanistan and India. They were recited or read aloud in private contexts such as peoples' homes or the royal court, and in public places such as village squares and tea houses. Dāstān reached their largest audiences and made their greatest impact when told by professional storytellers, known as *dāstān-gō* or *qiṣṣa-khwān*.

The dāstān of Amīr Ḥamza, the most widespread and influential dāstān in South Asia, probably reached the subcontinent from Persia in the twelfth century and was written down in the sixteenth century by order of Emperor Akbar. From the beginning until well into the twentieth century, the written and oral dāstān traditions flourished side by side and constantly interacted with one another. Translations, adaptations, and tales inspired by Persian models began to appear in writing in the seventeenth century in Deccani, and later in Urdu, Hindi, Punjabi, Pashto, Sindhi, and other languages. The two earliest Deccani dāstān—the indigenous story *Sub Ras,* and *Khāvar Nāma* from a Persian model—were written down in the seventeenth century. Others from the Persian tradition, such as *Chahār Darwīsh, Lailá and Majnūn*, *Ṭūṭī Nāma*, and *Bahrām wa Gul-andām,* were translated and adapted to local traditions. From the Sanskrit, via Persian, came *Qiṣṣa-yi Kāmrūp, Kalīla wa Dimna* (which also appeared in a later version called *Anwār-i Sohailī*), *'Īyār-i Dānish,* and *Khirad-afroz*. *Gul wa Ṣanaubar* and *Gul-i Bakāwalī* derive from other Indian sources. From *The 1001 Nights* came *Qiṣṣa-yi Saif al-Mulūk*, which was translated into Sindhi, Punjabi, Pashto, and Bengali.

Dāstān such as *Hīr Rānjhā* and *Sassī Punnūn̲* continue to be popular in Punjabi, and the tradition in Pashto is also thriving today with such tales as *Ādam Khān Dur Khānai, Yūsuf Khān Sher Bānu, Rāmdād Khān,* and *'Ajab Khān* representing both the amorous and heroic genres. Many Pashto, Punjabi, and Urdu dāstān are available today as chapbooks, and *Rāmdād Khān* is popular as an audio cassette.

References

Hanaway, William. 1994. Dāstān-sarā'ī. In *Encyclopaedia Iranica*, ed. Ehsan Yarshater, vol. 7, 102–103. Costa Mesa, Calif.: Mazda.

Heston, Wilma L., and Mumtaz Nasir. 1988. *The bazaar of the storytellers*. Islamabad: Lok Virsa.

Pellat, C., A. Bausani, Pertev Naili Boratav, Aziz Ahmad, and R. O. Winstedt. 1971. Ḥikāya. In *The encyclopaedia of Islam,* 2nd ed., ed. B. Lewis, V. L. Ménage, C. Pellat, and J. Schacht, vol. 3, 367–377. Leiden: E. J. Brill.

Pellat, C., H. Massé, I. Mélikoff, A. T. Hatto, and Aziz Ahmad. 1971. Ḥamāsa. In *The encyclopaedia of Islam,* 2nd ed. ed. B. Lewis, V. L. Ménage, C. Pellat, and J. Schacht, vol. 3, 110–119. Leiden: E. J. Brill.

Pellat, C., C. Vial, B. Flemming, Fahir Iz, L. P. Elwell-Sutton, J. A. Haywood, A. H. Johns, J. Knappert, and H. Zafrani. 1986. Ḳiṣṣa. In *The encyclopaedia of Islam,* 2nd ed., ed. C. E. Bosworth, E. van Donzel, B. Lewis, and C. Pellat, vol. 5, 185–207. Leiden: E. J. Brill.

Nakhshabi, Ziya' ud-din. 1978. *Tales of a parrot, the Cleveland Museum of Arts' Ṭūṭī-nāma,* ed. and trans. M. A. Simsar. Cleveland and Graz, Austria: Cleveland Museum of Art/Akademische Druck und Verlagsanstalt.

Pritchett, Frances W. 1985. *Marvelous encounters: Folk romance in Urdu and Hindi*. New Delhi: Manohar.

———. trans. 1991. *The romance tradition in Urdu: Adventures from the* dastan *of Amir Hamzah*. New York: Columbia University Press.

Schimmel, Annemarie. 1975. *Classical Urdu literature from the beginning to Iqbal*. Wiesbaden: Harrassowitz.

WILLIAM L. HANAWAY

SEE ALSO
Amīr Ḥamza; Cassettes; Chapbooks; Folk Literature; *Hir Rānjhā;* Story Literature

DEATH RITUALS

The stage of life of the deceased and the circumstances of death determine what kind of funeral will be performed for him or her. The older and more socially valued the person, the more elaborate the death rituals. In the Pakistan Punjab, Muslims reserve a death ceremony called *leda* for deceased elderly persons who have accomplished all their life tasks.

Full Hindu funerals require the designation of a chief mourner, preferably a son of the deceased. Similar to other life cycle rites, funerals involve specific gift-giving obligations on the part of certain kinds of relatives.

The outline of a Hindu funeral includes bathing the body and draping it with a shroud, carrying it to the cemetery or cremation ground with musical accompaniment, either interring or burning the body, and the bathing or otherwise washing of mourners on the return home. These acts are followed by a period of extreme restraint by the bereaved family, who cook as little as possible for ten to sixteen days, according to caste custom. After this the family is reintegrated with society through purification rituals and a feast of some sort. Most Hindus gather the charred bones (or perform a small offering at a grave) on the third day after cremation (or burial). Disposal of charred bones in a river is customary in many regions. Formal restrictions on the chief mourner are fully lifted after a year.

Simplicity and lack of ornamentation—bland foods, simple ritual items, and so on—set the tone for Hindu funerals. Music, performed by a specific service caste, may be unique in form.

Muslim funeral customs vary by region, but burial is universal. In the Telangana region of Andhra Pradesh, after a burial, Muslim funeral group members retreat forty paces away from the grave. For two days there is no fire in the family hearth; the family is fed by near relations. In Afghanistan close relatives of the same sex wash the body, and burial must never be done at night. Corpses are buried either lying on their right sides with faces toward Mecca or in an extended position with the feet toward Mecca. Nomads bury their dead along their routes, covering the faces with cairns.

In Pakistan close mourners avoid cosmetics and wear simple attire for at least a week. Friends and neighbors may help to dig a grave. A barber or a fakir (in the Punjab) will carry news of the death to others. A feast is given on the anniversary of the death according to the family's ability.

The Limbu of Nepal observe four days of mourning for a man and three for a woman. Sons of the deceased shave their heads. A funeral consists of a burial and a wake. At the conclusion of mourning the men of the house cook large pots of rice.

The Newar have a procedure that circumvents the risk of widowhood. A woman, usually a young woman without issue, places betel nuts on the chest of her dying husband and quickly divorces him.

References

Dube, S. C. 1955. *Indian village*. London: Routledge & Kegan Paul Ltd.

Dupree, Louis. 1973. *Afghanistan*. Princeton: Princeton University Press.

Nepali, Gopal Singh. 1965. *The Newars: An ethno-sociological study of a Himalayan community*. Bombay: United Asia Publications.

SUZANNE HANCHETT

SEE ALSO

Ancestor Worship; Lament; Life Cycle Rituals; *Mandecculu; Muḥarram; Oggu Katha*

DEPENDENT PERFORMING CASTES

Most of the castes of Andhra Pradesh, and of several other states of India, have one or more other castes or sections of their own caste that propagate their caste myths and recite their genealogies. The traditional relations between the patron castes and these performing castes varies, but it is almost always an intimate one and is often based on the metaphor of kinship, with the patron caste regarded as the elder brother or parent of the performing caste. Often, too, the relationship of the performing caste to their patrons is so exclusive that they are almost totally dependent on them for their livelihood. The relation between the patron and dependent castes does not necessarily remain exclusive; some patron castes have more than one dependent caste and vice versa. Different divisions of a single dependent caste will often have different castes as their patrons, preserving the one-to-one relation between patron and dependent families. In these and other ways the relationship differs from the *jajmāni* and *watanḍāri* systems with which it coexists in the villages of Andhra Pradesh.

In indigenous terminology the dependent castes are called *arthikulālu* (begging castes), *gōtrālavāru* (genealogists), *kulaṃbiddalu* (sons of the caste), *arthi biḍḍalu* (begging sons). The patron castes of the dependent castes are called *āsāmulu* or *yajamānulu*. The main occupational function of the dependent caste is to propagate the patron caste's myth (*kulapurāṇa*) through their traditional art form, but many of the dependent castes also entertain their patrons with magical and acrobatic performances, and perform various other duties, too.

Within the dependent caste, individual families hold the hereditary right to perform the *kulapurāṇa* and other duties for the patron families in a particular village, and no other family is allowed to perform the above activities and take remuneration from these particular families. This right (called *mirāsi, mēra, hakkubhktam,* or *vantana*) can be sold permanently to another dependent family in case the right-holder lacks heirs, or it can be leased out to others on a yearly basis.

Generally, male members of the dependent caste families perform the kulapurāṇa and genealogy recitation. Dependent performers visit their patrons once a year. They get remuneration in the form of grain, old and new clothes, cattle, and money. Some dependent castes also officiate at certain rituals for their patrons' families. On such occasions they get some special and extra remunerations. These remunerations are called *vantana, katnam, tyāgam, mēra,* or *saṃbhavana*. Even under current conditions of feeble patronage and the growing disinterest in village art forms performed by the dependent castes, the norms of inherited right are being followed with astonishing strictness.

Although the patron is paying for the dependent caste to perform services, the relationship between them is not considered commercial. One indication of this is that the performer gets his remuneration even when he does not perform; all he has to do is to appear at the patron's door. Yet the dependent performer does not see himself as a beggar. He would not perform his art form for any other caste but his patron's. In addition to the payments determined by rights, performers receive big gifts of various kinds when a wedding takes place in the patron's family. Furthermore, patrons are often willing to help their dependents meet the financial burdens of expensive occasions such as weddings. All these gifts, remunerations, and help are not for specific services. The dependents are treated as sons of the patron castes who, like relatives, have a right to their support. Even if the patron is known to be miserly on other occasions, he is not likely to deny help to his dependent performers' family. Humiliating the dependent performers is thought to incur *pāpam,* or sin, upon the patron's family, since the performers are propagating the sacred story of the patron's caste. There have been cases in which the caste headmen excommunicated families of a caste that insulted their performers.

Key to understanding the relationship between the patron and the dependent caste is the kulapurāṇa (caste myth), which depicts the origin and development of the given caste. The need to propagate the caste myth is to establish the caste's reputation and to establish the caste as an ancient and important one within the caste order. It is just such myths that have resulted in the caste system. Even in the context of a modern democratic society, the dependent caste relationship and the performance of kulapurāṇa, which preserves the identity of caste, are still alive.

References

Raju, M. V. T. 1980. Persistence and change, A study of Watandari system in rural Telingana with special reference of Medak District. Ph.D. diss., Department of Anthropology, Andhra University, Visakhapatnam, India.

Shah, A. M., and R. G. Shroff. 1959. The Vahīvancā Baroṭs of Gujarat: A caste of geneaologists and mythographers. In *Traditional India: Structure and change,* ed. Milton Singer. Philadelphia: American Folklore Society.

Singh, N. K., and Rajendra Joshi, eds. 1995. *Folk, faith and fedualism.* Jaipur, India: Rawat Press.

Srinivas, M. N. 1966. *Social change in modern India.* Berkeley: University of California Press.

Subbachary, Pulikonda. 1992. Janapada vijnanamlo asrita sahityam (A sociocultural study of the dependent caste system of Andhra Pradesh and a study of oral literature and art forms of the dependent castes). Ph.D diss., Department of Telugu, Osmania University, Hyderabad, India.

PULIKONDA SUBBACHARY

SEE ALSO

Caste and State, India and Nepal; Caste Myths of Andhra Pradesh; *Jajmāni;* Professional Performers; *Watanḍāri* System

DĒV

In the *Avesta,* the sacred writings of the Zoroastrian religion, the word *daēva, dēv* in Persian, is used as an appellation for a class of demonic beings in the service of Ahriman, the spirit of darkness, at war with the forces of Ahura Mazda, spirit of light, or God. Etymologically, dēv is cognate to the Sanskrit *dēva,* or god, but with the opposite meaning. Some linguists explain this in terms of a religious schism within the ancient Indo-Aryan population, whereby the deities of one branch became the demons of the other. Dēv are masculine spirits, incorporeal, but capable of assuming both human and animal forms. Often they appear as giants. They are nocturnal creatures who haunt unclean places, abandoned buildings, and rocky grounds, waiting to descend upon unwary humans. In the heroic Persian epic *Shāh Nāmah,* written by Firdawsī (eleventh century), the hero Rustam faces Akwān, a terrible shape-shifting dēv. The attributes of Firdawsī's dēv are identical to the Zoroastrian demons. Dēv exist alongside the lethal jinn, and *shaiṭān* (devils) in the demonology of Central and South Asian peoples. In popular folktales, however, dēv appear as amusing, simpleminded giants. In Afghanistan, a lazy person may be ridiculed by being referred to as *dēv zada,* "struck by a dēv," meaning that he or she has acquired the doltish capacities of the dēv. In children's fairy tales, dēv are sometimes cast as the protectors or servants of the *parī* (from the Zoroastrian *pairika,* or enchantress, but popularly conceived of as fairies).

References

Ananikian, Mardiros. 1925. The Dev. In *The mythology of all races,* ed. John Arnott MacCulloch, 86–88. Boston: Marshal Jones.

Bianchi, Ugo. 1977. L'inscription 'des daivas' et le zoroastrisme des Achéménides. *Revue de l'Histoire des Religions* 192: 3–30.

Shah, S. I. A. 1928. *Afghanistan of the Afghans.* London: Diamond Press.

H. SIDKY

SEE ALSO

Supernatural Beings, Nepal

DEVNĀRĀYAṆ

Devnārāyaṇ is the name of a folk deity worshiped primarily by the pastoral and farming community of the Gūjars in Rajasthan and northwestern Madhya Pradesh, India. The main feature of the cult is the performance of individual episodes from a two-part, forty-five-to-fifty-hour-long oral narrative that contains both sung and spoken sections (*gāv* and *arthāv*). The first part of this martial epic deals with the lives and deaths of Devnārāyàṇ's ancestors, the Bagaṛāvats, twenty-four sons of a "man-lion" and his twelve multicaste wives. Fervent devotees of Śiva, the brothers epitomize a heroic and warrior-like lifestyle that culminates in their self-sacrifice to the goddess Bhavānī in a momentous and gory war against a local Rājput chieftain. Whereas the first part of the epic is thus tragic and sorrow-ridden, the second, on the life and deeds of Lord Devnārāyaṇ, an incarnation of Bhagavān, or Viṣṇu, is marked by miracles and acts of healing that give testimony (*parcyo*) of the deity's divinity, while providing grounds for the establishment of the cult. Briefly, the episodes in the second part cover Devnārāyaṇ's birth, his childhood in a faraway maternal home, the return journey to his paternal home, the reunion with his four cousins, his three marriages, the defeat of the Rājput chieftain, and the creation of the first shrine, with his son as the first priest. Besides Devnārāyaṇ and his four cousins, the other main characters in the second part of the epic are his mother, Sāḍū Mātā, his wife Pīpalde, and Chochū Bhāṭ, the official bard and genealogist of the Bagaṛāvats.

Devnārāyaṇ's epic is performed during all-night vigils (*jāgraṇ*) by pairs of itinerant male singers called *bhopās,* a generic term for bards and oracular priests in Rajasthan. The performance incorporates an entire range of theatrical devices such as dance, music, spoken and sung texts, and, most important, the use of an approximately eight-meter-long cloth scroll, called *paṛ,* on which scenes and characters from the epic are depicted. The latter functions as a portable temple through which a sacred space is created invoking the presence of the deity, whose life-size iconic representation occupies the scroll's center.

The epic is closely related to the Gūjar community's self-perception as warrior pastoralists. As a deity, Devnārāyaṇheals and protects. Besides the householder singer-priests called bhopā, there are ochre-clad, renunciatory temple priests who carry the title of *dās* or *nāth.* The presence of the latter in the cult and in the epic suggests a connection to the influential medieval Śaivite ascetic order of the Nāth Sampradāya.

References

Malik, Aditya. 1999. *Stringing a necklace of heads: Sacrifice and death in the cult of Devnarayan.* In *Ways of dying: Death and its Meanings in South Asia,* ed. Elisabeth Schombucher and Claus Peter Zoller. Delhi: Manohar Publishers, p. 233–248.

Malik, Aditya. Powers of the timid: Aspects of humour in the Rajasthani oral epic of Devnarayan. In *Of clowns and gods, Brahmans and babus. Humour in South Asian Literatures,* ed., Christina Oesterheld and Claus Peter Zoller. Delhi: Manohar Publishers.

Singh, Bahadur. 1993. The episode of the golden Siva image in the Bagaravat. In *Flags of fame. Studies in South Asian folk culture,* ed. Heidrun Bruckner, Lothar Lutze, and Aditya Malik, 411–422. Delhi: Manohar Publishers.

ADITYA MALIK

SEE ALSO

Epic; Madhya Pradesh and Chattīsgaṛh; *Nāth; Paṛ;* Rajasthan; Śiva

DHĀMĪ

Dhāmī (oracular mediums) are found throughout the greater Karnāli drainage area of far western Nepal. Although dhāmī come from all castes, including those who wear a sacred thread as well as untouchables, the majority are Khas, descendants of the area's original inhabitants, a loosely grouped set of liquor-drinking clans who nevertheless wear sacred threads, giving them the designation "Matwālī Chetri." Each dhāmī is associated with one particular spirit and one particular shrine to that spirit, for a dhāmī is spontaneously selected by a single spirit, who alone possesses that individual. The possession is regarded as a consequence of the god's will, not the dhāmī's. If the dhāmī offends the spirit (such as by cutting his hair), it chooses to "ride" a different "horse." However, for important spirits, who often hold land grants and other property, the transition over generations tends to remain within a patrilineage, passing to son or nephew. Consequently, most dhāmī are male, though there is no rule demanding this, and exceptions (women called *dhāminī*) are fairly common. It is not unusual for a dhāmī's wife to succeed

Oracular Mediums (dhāmī). Nepal, © Gregory Maskarinec

him, especially when they have no son or until an infant son matures. There are also minor spirits always represented by women, such as the spirits of female vengeance suicides. The authentication process for a new dhāmī is complicated and often fiercely contested, with final selection resting with other dhāmī.

Most important of the oracular spirits are the "Twelve Brothers" Maṣṭā, whose festivals attract supplicants from all over western Nepal. Other dhāmī perform only for their own lineage, and some only for their own households. Maṣṭā (individual names of the "Twelve Brothers" are those of villages home to important shrines) has an autochthonous origin, while less important spirits are of human ancestors. Many require blood sacrifices, though some accept dairy products.

Oracular possessions take place on a regular basis, following the lunar calendar, commonly on new and full moons. These possessions take place in small shrines set outside villages or in throne rooms within the dhāmī's house. Dhāmī wear no special costume, although they observe restrictions of dress indicating subservience to a spirit. Most dress in homespun cloth and never wear footwear or caps. Many do wear turbans, to wrap up their long hair, which is never cut. A *dhaṅgrī* (the dhāmī's assistant) attends to technical details of the ceremony and interprets cryptic utterances. If drumming is involved, as at all major full moons, professional drummers of the tailor caste assemble to provide it, while village women often sing *māṅgal,* auspicious hymns to the spirit. On important occasions, dhāmī recite their spirit's *parelī* (personal history), but often they say nothing, simply distributing *ṭikā* (auspicious forehead dots) and "three grains" of *akṣetā* (ritually pure grains of raw husked rice) to supplicants, assurance that the spirit will attend to their problems. Dhāmī frequently consult one another. At yearly festivals at major shrines, groups of fifty or more dhāmī and dhāminī are simultaneously possessed. Rules regulating physical touch between castes are spectacularly suspended during these group possessions, when dhāmī from both ends of the caste spectrum, and from either sex, hoist one another onto their shoulders, physically reaffirming the hierarchical relations of the spirits they carry.

References

Gaborieau, Marc. 1969. "Note préliminaire sur le dieu Maṣṭa" (Preliminary remarks concerning the god Maṣṭa). *Objets et Mondes* 9(1): 19–50.

Sharma, Prayag Raj. 1972. Preliminary report on the art and architecture of the Karnāli basin, West Nepal. *Recherche Coopérative sur Programme 253 C.N.R.S.* (Cooperative Research of Program 253, National Center for Scientific Research). Paris: Centre National de la Recherche Scientifique.

Winkler, Walter. 1976. Spirit possession in far western Nepal. In *Spirit possession in the Nepal Himalayas,* ed. John T. Hitchcock and Rex L. Jones, 144–162. New Delhi: Vikas.

GREGORY G. MASKARINEC

SEE ALSO

Caste and State, India and Nepal; Gender and Folklore; Shamanism, Nepal; Shrines, Hindu; Spirit Possession and Mediumship

ḌHOLĀ

Ḍholā is an oral epic found primarily in eastern Rajasthan and western Uttar Pradesh. The first portion of the story has no known antecedents. The middle third is a variant of the Nala-Damayanti story from the *Mahābhārata.* The final portion is related to the ballad of Ḍholā-Mārū, known in western Rajasthan.

While the epic is named for Ḍholā, the real hero is Ḍholā's father, Rájà Nal. Nal is born to Rájà Pratham and Queen Manjhā after the king performs austerities to win an heir from the gods, Before Nal is born, Pratham, fearful for his life after being lied to by a devious astrologer, has Manjhā sent to the forest to be killed, but the sweeper sent to kill her refuses and brings the king a doe's eyes instead. Nal is raised by a trader and marries Motinī, the daughter of a demon. From Motinī, he receives magical weapons that aid him in further adventures.

Eventually Nal reunites with his parents, who decide to take a ritual bath in the Ganges River. In a battle over who should bathe first, Nal's parents are captured by Phul Singh Panjabi. Nal and Motinī must rescue his parents. Here the lead is taken by Motinī, who has access to the ritual knowledge of the Nāth yogis (tantric ritual practitioners) that allows her to defeat Phul Singh Panjabi's forces (which includes defeating the magic of his daughter). Motinī then departs for heaven so that Nal may marry a human bride and have offspring. Damayanti, in this epic, originally the daughter of Rájà Vasuki, king of the snakes, has taken birth as a human precisely to marry Nal. She chooses him at her *svayambār* (ritual where a woman chooses her husband), angering Indra, who desires her as his own bride. Indra inflicts twelve years of troubles on Nal and Damiyanti, who are forced to leave their kingdom of Navargaṛh. While in exile, Nal works as an oil presser. He eventually wins the daughter of the king for his yet unborn son, Ḍholā. Ḍholā and Mārū are married while still infants, after which Nal and his family return to Navargaṛh without Mārū.

Mārū eventually realizes that her groom is absent and seeks him out, with the help of a magical flying camel and talking parrot. Ḍholā, who was married a second time in a valuable military alliance, escapes from his second wife to reunite with Mārū. The epic ends with Ḍholā and Mārū dying together in a rising lake.

Nowadays, some local chapbooks containing the story have retitled it "Nal Purāṇa," recognizing the central importance of Rájà Nal. *Ḍholā* is performed by professional and semiprofessional singers from a variety of low- and middle-caste groups, and, less commonly, from the Brahman caste. In Harayana, *Ḍholā* singers are typically from the leatherworker caste in villages dominated by the Jat caste. Most derive a significant portion of their yearly income from singing *Ḍholā* and will travel from village to village to provide entertainment for religious functions or weddings. Singers are self-recruited and learn their trade by attaching themselves (as apprentices who also perform menial services) to known singers or troupes.

The core of the *Ḍholā* performance is a trained singer, accompanying himself on a *cikārā* (a two-string bowed instrument). In addition, a drummer, playing a *dholak,* and a *cimṭā* (steel tongs) player accompany the singer. Nowadays, a harmonium is often added for musical accompaniment. Generally, only one episode of the epic will be told in a single night's performance lasting five to eight hours. A second form of *Ḍholā* performance is the dance-drama, a form currently losing its popularity due to mass media. Commercial tape cassettes of *Ḍholā* are a new innovation very popular in rural areas. The audiences for *Ḍholā* are almost exclusively men, since women are often not permitted to attend public night performances. However, many women have heard at least portions of *Ḍholā* at a neighbor's house, where they sit on the roof, in a courtyard, or wedged into a corner of the verandah.

While not specifically a regional or caste epic, *Ḍholā* does contain significant social commentary as it plays upon the caste hierarchies of the multicaste farming communities of western Uttar Pradesh and eastern Rajasthan. Caste traits are caricatured, whether a Brahman priest or a low-caste oil presser, and caste interrelationships form much of the backbone of the story. The influx of rural migrants to urban areas, along with the spread of audiocassettes, have recently made *Ḍholā* a more popular urban phenomenon. Several printed versions of the epic exist in Hindi chapbooks. The most popular is that of Matol Sinh, a Gujar from Bharatpur District in Rajasthan.

References

Temple, Richard C. 1963. *The legends of the Punjab*, vol. 2. Patiala: Department of Languages.

Wadley, Susan S. 1989. Choosing a path: Performance strategies in a north Indian epic. In *Oral epics in India,* ed. S. Blackburn, P. Claus, J. Flueckiger, and S. Wadley. 75–101. Berkeley: University of California Press.

———. 1999. A Bhakti rendition of Nala-Damayanti: Todarmal's nectar of life. *International Journal of Hindu Studies* 3(1): 1–29.

———. 2001. Popular culture and the north Indian oral epic *Ḍholā. Indian Folklore Research Journal* 1(1): 13–24.

———. Forthcoming. *Rájà and the goddess: Inscribing caste and gender in the north Indian oral epic* Ḍholā.

Susan S. Wadley

SEE ALSO

Cassettes; Chapbooks; Dance; Gods and Goddesses; Heroes and Heroines; *Mahābhārata;* Nala and Damayanti; Professional Performers; Rajasthan

DIASPORA, AFRICA

Age-old civilizations; expansive land with varying climates and topographies; bouts with colonialism followed by brutal independence movements; greatly diverse ethnic, religious, and linguistic populations; growing but shaky economies; political instabilities; and cultural dynamism and resilience are among the features shared by the South Asian subcontinent and the African continent. An often unknown and understudied link between these two prominent world areas bracketing the Indian Ocean is the large and active South Asian migration to African countries. Reports from 1987 estimate almost 1.5 million South Asians in Africa, based predominantly in Mauritius, South Africa, and areas of East Africa, including Kenya, Tanzania, and Uganda. While areas of west, north, and central Africa have witnessed less sizable and historically more recent immigration, a South Asian presence there still deserves noting. Whether immigrants or descendants of immigrants in Africa, South Asians continue to stay connected to their places of origin. South Asians are part of African history as much as South Asians in Africa are part of South Asian history.

South Asian communities in Africa can claim roots back to early traders in the first centuries B.C.E. However, the more significant migrations and settlements occurred in the nineteenth century. South Asians have maintained and re-created many cultural practices in Africa while contributing to economic, political, and cultural life in the local societies. Today in parts of Africa, South Asians consider themselves as African as their neighbors, with varying degrees of identification with the parts of South Asia from which their ancestors emigrated.

South Asia and Africa have been connected for over two thousand years via a lively and lucrative trading system along the Indian Ocean coastlines. Spices, gold, slaves, and later textiles, household goods, and industrial materials were among the transported commodities. While South Asians have a long past as itinerant traders, only during the late nineteenth and early twentieth centuries did South Asians begin to settle on African soil. The first to settle were traders encouraged by the Sultan of Oman, who had recently relocated to Zanzibar Island. Several hundred traders resided in Zanzibar by the mid-1800s. Larger numbers of South Asians settled as merchants, entrepreneurs, and adventurers in south and east Africa through the latter half of that century. South Asian indentured laborers, who worked under contract following the abolition of slavery in the British empire in 1834, were recruited from bases in Calcutta and Madras, and were brought first to Mauritius and, after a few decades, to south African colonies. Once more, after the 1885 competition among European empires to claim uncolonized areas of eastern Africa, called the "Scramble for Africa," over 30,000 exported Indian indentured laborers arrived to work in British East Africa between 1895 and 1901. While only 20 percent of the laborers remained in Africa, others who accompanied and followed the trail from British India to British East Africa began to settle on the coasts and interiors of eastern Africa. Petty traders, artisans, shopkeepers, and farmers from western India, mainly Gujarat, Punjab, and Sindh, came to Africa with hopes of economic opportunity and served British, African, and South Asian populations.

While indentured laborers had little contact with their place of origin during the terms of their contracts, voluntary migrants, those who came independent of imperial contract and for commercial purposes, maintained social and economic links with areas of South Asia. Trade and familial networks often overlapped, since many merchants used extended, overseas kin networks as commercial networks. Religious pilgrimages, marriage alliances, and overseeing properties required strong contacts with South Asia, and were among the significant factors contributing to South Asian mobility and cultural maintenance, especially for those in eastern and southern Africa with close proximity to Asia.

Physical and emotional ties provided the resources and rationale for South Asians in Africa to reproduce a sense of community overseas. South Asians prospered economically by utilizing family business networks and fulfilling the needs of the local society. In part due to the inequalities of colonial societies and cultural plurality of newly independent ones, mistreatment, discrimination, exploitation, segregation, and exile have come to characterize the South Asian experience in Africa. A notable exception is Mauritius, the first in the indentured labor experiment, where South Asians represent well over half the population. While South Asians in many parts of Africa have been criticized over the last half century for social insularity, economic monopolization, and apolitical behavior, supporters argue that South Asian commercial organizations and political platforms address the needs of particular subgroups as well as the larger diverse pan-racial community. South Asians have organized their voluntary associations along religious and subethnic lines, such as Isma'īlī mosques, Swaminarayan temples of the Gujarati Samāj, and Goan Christian churches, and have simultaneously sought to maintain a unified community, some conflicts notwithstanding. South Asian philanthropy and participation in African economies have been noteworthy. As such, South Asians present a visible and well-established community of African citizens.

While contemporary South Asians may appear as a distinctive community in Africa, there exist so many overlapping practices with African societies that it becomes difficult to make claims of cultural proprietorship. Particularly in areas of food, language, and entertainment, interesting and debated cultural crossovers exist, of which there are certainly more than this short article can illustrate. These overlaps highlight a history of interaction. For example, a *samosa,* a spiced vegetable or meat-filled pastry, is considered as African to many Africans as it is Indian to many Indians. The same goes for *rotī/capāti* (a type of bread) and *biryani* (rice cooked with vegetables or meat), to name a few examples. Some innovations exist, however. Unlike

South Asians, east Africans eat samosas by biting off a bit of the pastry and squirting lime juice through the opening.

Linguistic exchanges over the centuries are present today. Elements of Kiswahili have been incorporated into Gujarati and Hindi (the main South Asian languages spoken in East Africa) and vice versa. The exact etymology of many words continues to be debated by scholars. For instance, *duka* (shop) and *dukawalla* (shopkeeper) appear to be products of centuries-old South Asian/East African commercial connections. Kiswahili and Gujarati–speaking South Asians living in East Africa would use the same word in both languages. Musically, video- and audiocassettes from India, along with America, China, and elsewhere, are extremely popular and are part of the entertainment offered by long distance bus services. Hindi films are distributed widely throughout Africa, and most always meet great commercial success. Finally, while international scholars, media sources, and governments have paid minimal attention to the over 1.5 million South Asians in Africa, communities of South Asian Africans maintain active networks of their own, both within Africa and abroad. News about political events, literature, economic opportunities, social gatherings, and much more spreads today mainly through websites and internet lists. "Namaskaar-Africana" is the primary and most active list by and about Asian Africans. List members from America, England, Africa, and India contribute regularly and help create a community of Asian Africans, most of whom no longer live in Asia or in Africa.

SAVITA NAIR

SEE ALSO
Food and Foodways

DIASPORA, CARIBBEAN

In response to the abolition of slavery in British West Indian territories, planters and colonial authorities undertook initial experiments with an alternative system of bound labor: indenture. Starting with an experiment in 1838 and becoming fully institutionalized in 1845, Britain's indenture project brought laborers from South Asia to the New World. By 1917, when indenture officially ended, over 400,000 predominantly Hindu and Muslim immigrants had left Uttar Pradesh, Oudh, Bihar, and Madras. Channeled in most cases through the emigration depots of Calcutta and Madras, they were sent to estates (plantations) primarily in Trinidad (143,939), Guyana (238,909), and Jamaica (36,412); they also went to Surinam (34,000), Martinique (25,509), Grenada (3,200), St. Lucia (4,354), St. Vincent (2,472), and St. Kitts (337).

While a number of laborers elected to return to India after their indenture contracts ended, the vast majority stayed on, forming small, dispersed village communities, and in some cases—for example, Trinidad and Guyana—eventually achieving demographic parity with Afro-Caribbean countrymen. In the 160 years of their settlement and assimilation into wider society, Indo-Caribbeans have moved from socially, economically, and politically marginalized status to being increasingly empowered claimants of state patronage and national recognition.

Bhojpuri, Hindi, Urdu, and Tamil are the languages the immigrants brought to the Caribbean; today Indo-Caribbean peoples speak the lingua franca of their home states. An exception are the elderly, or "older heads" as they are called in Trinidad, who, as first-generation Indo-Caribbeans, are still fairly well versed in the language of their immigrant parents. Yet numerous Hindi words and phrases (as well as some Urdu) are familiar to all generations of Indo-Caribbeans. In daily usage (both spoken and written) this lexicon tends to become Anglicized; for example, the English "s" is attached to a non-English ward to make it a plural.

The majority of Hindu immigrants and their progeny have remained adherents of Sanatan Dharm; other forms of Hinduism have been historically significant, notably Ārya Samāj. Most Muslims belong to the Ḥanafī school of Sunni Islam. Less common but quite important among Indo-Caribbean peoples is Presbyterianism. To a lesser extent they also follow other forms of Protestantism, for example, Anglican and evangelical or pentecostal movements, as well as Catholicism. Overall, however, the majority of Indo-Caribbean peoples identify as Hindu.

The cultural lifeways—arts, religions, foods, social organization—Indians brought with them to the New World shaped and were in turn influenced by cultures already present—African, European, Levantine, and East Asian (Chinese). In an ever-evolving relationship with local cultural forms, Indo-Caribbean expressive culture reflects two broad heritages: one from India and the other from the Caribbean.

Local Traditions

The expressive culture of the contemporary generation of Indo-Caribbeans is only a partial reflection of nineteenth-century traditions of the subcontinent. Demographic characteristics, different assimilation patterns, rates of religious conversion, and class mobility have helped to transform Indian music, art, and oral traditions in New World settings. With the early influence of Christianity, gradually rising socioeconomic status through increased formal education and skilled labor opportunities, and the increasing urbanization of agricultural communities through infrastructural improvements, Indo-Caribbean peoples invent and interpret "traditional" culture in diverse ways.

Indian identity in the Caribbean is, then, variously defined, depending upon perspective, context, and incentive. A common theme running through most versions and variations, however, is the perception among many Indo-Caribbeans that their roots lie in "folk" traditions, and that ideally Hindus should strive for a profile that also reflects Vedic or Brahmanic traditions, while Muslims should strive for an authentic, more pure form of Islam. Especially where the population numbers have been high, exogamy rates low, occupations concentrated, and identity politics strained (such as in Trinidad, Guyana, and Surinam, for example), two particularly significant emblems of Indo-Caribbean self-consciousness exist. One is the tension involving how to establish "authentic" and legitimate practices for "modern," Western life within the debated parameters of "traditional," eastern South Asian culture. The second emblem is the tension between defining and maintaining the distinctiveness of "Indian" identity within a hegemonic environment of Afro-Caribbean and Euro-American traditions and practices. The most commonly recognized forms of expressive culture among Indo-Caribbean peoples include ritual, music, and dance. In these arenas in particular, Indian food and dress, and also dimensions of expressive culture, may become particularly symbolically charged as signifiers of Indianness.

In all its forms, Indian tradition in the Caribbean must be seen within a context of cultural politics and its corollary, a gradual transformation in scale from village or neighborhood observance to nationally orchestrated event. The latter constitutes both those organized by associations—such as the interregional Sanatan Dharma Maha Sabha (SDMS) and Anjuman Sunnat-ul-Jamaat Association (ASJA), or Trinidad's National Council for Indian Culture (NCIC)—and those granted the status of national holidays by the state—such as *Dīwalī* and *E'īd-ul-Fitr* in Trinidad. Yet, again, moving toward higher profile as a political statement risks the gatekeeping on Indianness: determination of what gets performed and who can perform it becomes a more open frontier and hence contested terrain.

Ritual

Devotional "functions" or "prayers," as they are called, for example, in Trinidad, are regularly held throughout the year. Some, such as those in conjunction with E'id-ul-Fitr, *Bakra E'id,* and the *meeraj* (ascension) of the Prophet Muḥammad for Muslims, and Dīwālī, *Phagwa/Holī,* and *raksha bandhan* for Hindus, are calendrically based. Other "functions," such as Muslims' *maulid sharīf* (Qur'anic reading) and *haqika* (dedication of oneself or one's child to Allah with ritual sacrifice and prayers), and Hindus' *puja* (generic, devotional ritual to deities) and *bhandara* (ritual head-shaving of eldest son of newly deceased; closed to women), occur in accordance with particular occasions determined by participants. While observant Indo-Caribbean Muslims attend *jumma* (Friday prayers) at the *mosques,* for Hindus there is no requisite use of *mandirs* (temples) by devotees. If financial means permit, Hindus may build a "puja room" in the house for family use or, even grander and more conspicuous, a separate adjacent structure. Muslims may also, if space allows, designate a special room in the home for *du'ā* (prayer).

Of vital importance to ritual functions are clergy: historically paṇḍits and imāms have been key figures in keeping their respective religions alive. While their roles have undergone social transformations in more recent times, as religious and community leaders paṇḍits and imāms remain crucial in the pedagogical and propagative aspects of religious and cultural identity among Indo-Caribbeans. Others involved in rituals of various kinds and scale are religiocultural association leadership (for example, SDMS, ASJA, NCIC above) who, while lay, are very often active in promoting Indian / Indo-Caribbean identity.

Also a form of ritual, pilgrimage has not, by and large, been replicated among Indo-Caribbeans as it occurs in India. An important exception to this, however, is the hajj pilgrimage that Muslims embark on if they are financially and physically able.

Dress

Photographs and descriptions of early Indian immigrants to the Caribbean record the use of clothing and jewelry typical of mid-nineteenth century and early twentieth-century India. As they settled into Caribbean societies, immigrants and their descendants adopted the local Western wear. One notable exception is the *ornhi,* or veil, still worn by many elderly Hindu and Muslim women in public, a vestige of traditional head-covering that has become a key symbol among these Indo-Caribbean populations of the heritage of the subcontinent. In the last couple of decades other kinds of dress have become particularly emblematic of "Indian" identity, emphasized by the ritual, rather than routine, occasions of their use. Today the *shalwār kamiz* (known locally simply as shalwār) and sari are commonly worn by women on occasions, both religious and secular, where an Indian / Indo-Caribbean ambience is being emphasized. More recently, the *hijāb* or full head covering has become more common among Indo-Caribbean Muslim women.

Food

Cuisine may be the most pervasive dimension of Indo-Caribbean culture in the wider Caribbean. Many staples of the Indo-Caribbean diet are produced locally, including peppers, curries, and *masalas;* however, the indispensable garlic, lentils, some chutneys, and other spices are imported from abroad. Some foods are specifically designated as "Indian," such as *paratha* (a fried bread) or *bhaji* (like spinach); other foods such as *prasad* (offerings to deities) are made and eaten principally for religious rituals or other special occasions connected with Indo-Caribbean culture.

Indo-Caribbean dishes as well as cooking style, however, reflect long influence from Afro- and other Caribbean cuisines as well as North American forces. Thus, Indo-Caribbeans are as likely to serve *pilau* (meat, rice, and pigeon peas) or Caribbean-Chinese fried rice as any other population. At the same time, all manner of Indo-Caribbean cooking has become rooted in the region, such that curry goat *ṛotī,* for example, is as familiar to Afro-Jamaicans and Afro-Guyanese as it is among Indo-Trinidadians. The custom of "fast food" emanating from the United States has made fried chicken stands ubiquitous, including occasional *ḥalāl* (religiously permitted) options for Caribbean Muslims.

The centrality of food in symbolizing social relations is familiar in the popular art form of calypso (*soca*) music, where in carnival season food acts as a metaphor for such cultural dimensions as love, sex, race relations, and group identity. Also encoded in food are obeah (magical practices using supernatural powers) and *maljo* (the evil eye). When directed through food, obeah can affect a person physically or emotionally, causing illness or conquering one's will. If eating unusual or special foods, a person may "get" *maljo*—that is, become temporarily ill with minor symptoms—from the unintentionally transmitted envy conveyed by an onlooker.

When ritual functions are held, either in an individual home or in the public hall of the mosque or mandir, space is cleared and parts are partitioned for cooking the requisite food that will be "shared out" (significantly, never "served") and eaten after the event. Involving extensive reciprocity and communal labor, families and households contribute foods and utensils for cooking for several dozen to several hundred participants. The importance of commensality—the communal partaking of a meal—to these occasions is essential. To attend an event or visit someone's home and not eat inevitably communicates disdain or indifference to feelings which can, in turn, lead to social ruptures.

Music and Dance

As traditionally popular artistic expression and as a key component of religious practice in daily life, music has become an important symbol of Indo-Caribbean identity. Several forms exist. The first can be exemplified as music that is essentially religious in nature. Though there are many kinds of religious music among Indo-Trinidadians, the forms most frequently performed include *bhajan*s (Hindu hymns), *qasidah*s (Muslim devotional songs in praise of Allah or the Prophet Muḥammad), *chowtal*s (performed by Hindus annually during the spring festival of Phagwa/Holi), and the less extensive but important *marsiya* (songs associated with Muslim Hosay or Muḥarram observances). The most common medium for religious music is a group setting. Participants might be attending a devotional function in a mandir, masjid, or in someone's home; music and songs might be performed formally in a sponsored competition show or Indian television program. Whatever the setting, males and females of all ages can be involved. While qasidahs are usually sung without accompanying music and chowtals are generally only minimally accompanied by a few instruments (primarily percussion), bhajan singing characteristically includes several accompanying musicians, some of whom also sing.

A second example of music comprises Indian orchestras. For example, according to noted Indo-Trinidadian performer and musicologist Nasraloo Ramaya, from the early 1930s to the 1960s, informal groups of musicians began to develop into sophisticated performing ensembles, particularly through the influence of Indian films in Trinidad and the increasing availability of recorded music from India. Today orchestras commonly perform at weddings, parties, or festivals. Playing a variety of music, orchestras generally use electric organs and guitars, three or four kinds of drums, a harmonium, and occasionally a synthesizer, as well as male and/or female backup singers.

Another common musical form in the Indo-Caribbean is *tassa* drumming. Until relatively recently it was played solely on special occasions, particularly weddings (both Hindu and Muslim), festivals such as Trinidad's Hosay, and as accompaniment to the traditional singing style called *biraha,* now rare. Today villages or neighborhoods may have tassa drumming groups who play on diverse occasions, notably at weddings. During Carnival season, tassa drums sometimes accompany the steel bands.

Classical singing is also popular, and is distinguishable from film and folk music. Highly developed in Trinidad, it is known, for example, as *thumri, drupat, ghazal,* and *tilana*. A central singer plays his or her own harmonium and is accompanied by a drummer and a *dhantal* player, who do not sing. This musical form is commonly heard live, for example, at pūjās, but it is also readily accessible on Indian music radio stations—of which there are three in Trinidad alone—and via other media such as television programming.

Critically important to the continual evolution of Indo-Caribbean expressive culture is that Indian orchestras, tassa drumming, and classical singing, as well as chutney, a blend of Indian folk songs with the rhythms, beat, and lyrics of Caribbean music, are performed by guest artistes throughout the hemisphere as well as from further abroad. Hence it is not unusual for an Indo-Guyanese performer to be booked at Trinidadian venues, nor is it unusual for an Indo-Trinidadian performer to tour, for example, New York, Toronto, and London.

Most interpreters of dance styles try to emulate faithfully classical and contemporary forms in South Asia (primarily India). Formal instruction in a large number of schools and institutes for dance has become standard for those who wish it. Presentation of Indian dance often takes place as formal performance, either in local schools or on community (and sometimes national) stages. Easily available Indian films play an important role in providing styles patterned by Indo-Caribbean artistes, as they are locally known. These artistes are both male and female, and can range from primary school novices to adult professionals.

Contemporary Transformations

Expressive culture is always in flux. Among the most profound transformations in Indo-Caribbean aesthetic forms has been the advent of "crossover" music, a blending or amalgam of different kinds of rhythms, melodies, or styles. Although historically, "crossing over" has always been a part of Caribbean culture, certain forms among Indo-Caribbeans lend themselves more to permissible, even encouraged, "mixing" than others. Religious ritual, for example, is perceived as one domain that most significantly experiences the incursions of crossover as assault. Yet other expressive cultural forms, notably music, allow a porousness that suggests less concern with overlapping as problematic for authenticity. Beginning in the mid-1980s, Indian crossover music became increasingly popular, among the most prominent forms today being chutney.

There are several reasons for the recent rise in Indian crossover music. One is the recent discovery (since about the 1980s) of a very large potential market for crossover record sales intraregionally in the Caribbean, along with a global market of Caribbeans and other populations worldwide, including South Asians, interested in contemporary "world music" and experimental fusions of diasporic South Asian aesthetics. Another reason for the rise in Indian crossover music is the assertion of ethnic group consciousness, the use of cultural forms as emblematic of a distinctive identity that is in part expressed through such ethnic markers as music. A third factor is particularly evident in the current florescence of chutney music as public performance, the growth of this traditional folk art form into a nationally (and internationally) consumed media event.

Not limited to provincial efforts, expressive culture is mobile; this characteristic takes on particular significance in the Caribbean—a region both defined by diaspora and increasingly linked into the globalization of popular media. Whether clergy or classical singer, chutney artiste or dancer, Indo-Caribbean expressive culture is decidedly part of an international circuit, one that both shapes and is shaped by the history and experience of local peoples.

References

Guinee, William. 1992. Suffering and healing in Trinidadian Kali worship. Ph.D. diss., Indiana University.

Khan, Aisha. 1994. Juthaa in Trinidad: Food, pollution, and hierarchy in a Caribbean diaspora community. *American Ethnologist* 21(2): 245–269.

Look Lai, Walton. 1993. *Indentured labor, Caribbean sugar: Chinese and Indian migrants to the British West Indies, 1838–1918*. Baltimore: Johns Hopkins University Press.

Nunley, John W., and Judith Bettelheim, eds. 1988. *Caribbean festival arts*. Seattle: University of Washington Press.

Trotman, D. V. 1991. The image of Indians in calypso. In *Social and occupational stratification in contemporary Trinidad and Tobago,* ed. Selwyn Ryan, pp. 385–398. St. Augustine, Trinidad: Institute of Social and Economic Research.

AISHA KHAN

SEE ALSO

Bhajan; *Dīvālī/Dīpāvalī;* Food and Foodways; *Muḥarram; Marṣiya; Pūjā; Ta'ziya*

DIASPORA, FIJI AND THE SOUTH PACIFIC

South Asians constitute the single largest non-European ethnic group in the Pacific islands. Small communities are to be found in most Pacific island nations, and significant emigration to Australia and New Zealand, both directly from South Asia and from Fiji, has taken place since the relaxation of anti-Asian policies in the 1970s.

The largest South Asian diasporic community in the South Pacific lives in Fiji and consists primarily of the descendants of indentured immigrants who came between 1879 and 1919. About two-thirds of the immigrants left India through Calcutta, coming primarily from the Gangetic plain, while others, chiefly Tamil and Telugu speakers, departed from Madras. The community also includes the descendants of Gujarati merchants and a small Sikh community. Approximately 11 percent of the Fiji Indian population is Muslim, and there are some Christians, but the great majority are Hindus. Most Hindu Fiji Indians are members of the relatively traditional, devotionally focused Sanātan Dharam; some are followers of Sai Satya Baba; and a quite influential minority are members of the Ārya Samāj (originally founded in the late nineteenth century as a Hindu reformist and nationalist organization in Punjab). Fiji Hindi (FH), a cluster of linguistic varieties most closely related to the Bhojpurī dialect of eastern Uttar Pradesh, is by far the most widely spoken language.

The contours of expressive culture among Fiji Indians have been shaped by the various regional and caste origins of the immigrants, the leveling effects of indentured plantation work, decades of life in all-Indian rural communities separate from Fijian villages, and continued influences from India. The Indian influences come through traveling paṇḍits (Hindu priests and scholars) and *maulvīs* (Muslim religious leaders and teachers) who visit Fiji, through printed pamphlets and books, and through film, video, and recorded music. Contemporary Indian folk traditions in Fiji lie at the active intersection of memory, visions of India from media and other sources, and local experience. While the names of many performance genres remain the same as in South Asia, the characteristics and meanings of those genres have been dramatically transformed. The Urdu term *qawwālī,* for example, has come to denote a popular style of Hindu *bhajan*-singing; abusive texts sung by women at weddings in North India (*gāliya*) now figure most frequently in insulting songs exchanged between groups of men.

Several striking transformations in ritual practices have taken place. The once preeminent *Holī* festival has been displaced by *Dīvālī,* a festival honoring the goddess Lakṣmī, as the definitively Hindu holiday in Fiji. Special Dīvālī editions of the national newspapers are published, and colored lights are strung up in shop windows and throughout Indian residential areas. Visible to all Fiji citizens, Dīvālī (Dīpāvālī) is lively but decorous when compared with Holī (known for its rowdiness) and is locally regarded as the Hindu equivalent of Christmas. There also has been a dramatic rise of interest and participation by individuals throughout Fiji Indian society in ritual fire walking, originally a South Indian practice. Often undertaken to fulfill vows to particular deities, fire walking also serves increasingly as a public marker of Indian identity in Fiji, especially as some Fijian groups practice their own quite different styles of actually walking on quite hot stones. The most salient Fiji Indian dramatic genre is the *rām līlā,* usually staged by schools in conjunction with fund-raising fairs, and with children playing all of the roles. Very little traditional dance is evident.

Some traditional genres such as proverbs (*kahāvat*) occasionally figure in everyday conversation, but it is unclear whether such items have passed directly through oral transmission or have been learned through schoolbooks, which draw to some extent upon Indian sources, or from other published works. Similarly, stories (*kahāniya*) in fairly wide oral circulation have also been part of local school curricula. Apart from such texts as the *Mahābhārata* and, especially, the *Rāmāyaṇa,* published collections of religious exempla (*drshṭānt*) are perhaps the most important sources of "traditional" narratives. Personal experience stories, legends making Indian sense of Fijian landmarks (e.g., the overhanging rock formation thought to resemble a cobra's hood and now a shrine to Śiva), and historical (*itihāsik*) narratives about the early Indian days in Fiji are much more common than classic South Asian tales.

The Fiji Indian musical scene is very lively and complex. Solo voice accompanied by harmonium, *ḍhol* (mid-sized double-ended drum with goatskin heads), and *majīrā* (finger cymbals) or *bottil* (a pair of empty, upright, one-liter Fiji Bitter bottles struck rhythmically on the neck with a pair of heavy nails) is by far the most common form of village ensemble for both sacred and secular song. The most popular sacred genre is the bhajan qawwālī, a style of Hindu devotional singing; in distinction to its South Asian antecedents (bhajan, *harikīrtan*) this is a solo, rather than antiphonal, group style. Particular seasonal genres are also performed, such as *cautāl* during the Holī festival, and songs associated with religious services (such as the *kajlī bhajan,* often sung at *Rāmāyaṇa* readings) or with particular ritual events (such as the *telwan* songs associated with weddings) still occur. A few individuals know and perform major sung narratives such as *Ālhā*. Much more popular are songs from Indian films (*filmī gīt*), which constitute perhaps the most widely enjoyed genre. While many traditional genres, especially those associated with particular subcastes, have vanished or become exceptionally rare, music making is highly prized in Fiji, and performers and audiences continue to shape innovative and local styles of expression and enjoyment.

Much of the Fiji Indian diet is reminiscent of that of eastern Uttar Pradesh. It has also, however, been strongly influenced by the fact that most local farmers raise sugarcane and rely upon commercially available rice and sharps, a type of wheat flour grown and milled in Australia and considered especially good for chapati, which are usually eaten daily. Similarly, canned salmon and tuna are important staples, along with fresh fish and crab when available. Coconut oil is the most common locally produced cooking oil; commercial vegetable oil is also used. Relatively few Fiji Indians are vegetarians, especially in the countryside; chicken and goat are the most popular meats. One of the few remaining markers of attributed caste background has to do with raising pigs and eating pork, practices associated with people considered to be the descendants of *chamārs* (the subcaste name extended in Fiji as a general label for individuals of low-caste ancestry). Many cooks continue to grind and use particular mixtures of spices for different dishes, but commercially produced *garam masālā* is increasingly popular. Ritual and festival occasions are linked with particular foods. Jackfruit *tarkārī*, a dish in which meat, fish, or vegetables are cooked in a sauce with garam masālā and other spices, and puri, a deep-fried unleavened bread which puffs up when cooked, are featured at most Hindu weddings, and a goat is usually killed and cooked at Muslim feasts. Some traditional *miṭhāī* (sweets) are associated with specific festivals, for example, *lakri-miṭhāī*, sticks of deep-fried dough soaked in sugar syrup and dried, are associated with Dīvālī.

Several important foods have Fijian sources, principally *dālo* (taro), sweet potatoes, and breadfruit; these are generally served as tarkārīs, but breadfruit—parboiled, sliced thin, dusted with turmeric and chili, and fried—is a common snack. Perhaps the most salient borrowing from the Fijian diet is *yaqona* (kava), a drink made from the stalk and roots of the *Piper methysticum* plant. An important part of social and traditional ritual in Fijian villages, in Fiji Indian communities yaqona is often drunk by groups of male friends in the early evening, serving as a focus for informal sociability, gossip, and general conversation.

References

Brenneis, Donald. 1983. Passion and performance in Fiji Indian vernacular song. *Ethnomusicology* 29: 397–408.

———. 1987. Performing passions: Aesthetics and politics in an occasionally egalitarian community. *American Ethnologist* 14: 236–250.

———. 1991. Aesthetics, performance, and the enactment of tradition in a Fiji Indian community. In *Gender, genre, and power in South Asian expressive traditions*, ed. A. Appadurai, M. Mills, and F. Korom, 362–378. Philadelphia: University of Pennsylvania Press.

Kelly, John D. 1988. From *holī* to *dīvālī* in Fiji. *Man* n.s. 23: 40–55.

DONALD BRENNEIS

SEE ALSO

Ālha (Alha-Udal); Bhajan; Dīvālī/Dīpāvalī; Folk Music; Food and Foodways; *Hōlī; Qawwālī; Rām Līlā; Ramāyāṇa;* Song

DIASPORA, NORTH AMERICA

The majority of the South Asians settling in North America since the mid-1960s, now numbering over one million, are middle-class professionals and business owners. These families have long histories of migration, with previous generations having worked for the British colonial system, either in India or abroad in Britain and South Africa. Very little of their transplanted expressive cultures is "folkloric" in the sense of rural village traditions. Rather, the majority of expressive practices in the South Asian diaspora reflect elitist, mass cultural, and/or global concerns, being both closely tied to latest trends and styles from South Asian cities and responsive to the experience of living in North America. For example, while traditional embroidery and hand carvings are proudly displayed in homes, and skilled folk artists are brought to America from India for festivals and exhibits (via joint-governmental funding), few members of the diaspora community make traditional objects themselves. In part, this reflects historical social structures that associate crafts with particular subcastes. Such skills are rarely maintained by the families aiming for upward mobility over three or more generations. However, the middle-class and elite groups of all cultures have practices that are worthy of folkloristic investigation. In the diaspora, expressive forms, both folkloric and mass-mediated, are used to support cultural identity through extended family and community.

Festivals, foodways, and dancing are the most valued and supported folklore practices in the diaspora. South Asian communities in New York, New Jersey, Illinois, and Texas have emerged, supporting thriving business districts, places of religious worship, and cultural institutions. In recent years a greater number of the annual festivals of Hinduism are celebrated in more public gestures. The well-established Shri Maha Vallabha Ganapati Temple in Queens, New York, has observed a Ganesh "car festival" for several years. Traditional cooking has been maintained in most South Asian homes and is expected at extended family and community gatherings. Community publications and the Internet are important resources for the circulation of recipes. Cooking is primarily the responsibility of women, but many men boast that they learned to cook while living alone before their wives moved from India. Vegetarian diets are maintained by the majority of Hindu and Jain families. Dance is an extremely popular practice in the South Asian diaspora community. Navarātrī parties during late October and early November, in honor of the Goddess, are held in high school gyms and tent pavilions for thousands of participants. The primary activity at these gatherings is *garba* and *dandia-ras* folk dances and a few *bhangra* (another type of dance) numbers accompanied by local bands. Lessons in the classical dance form *bharatnātyam* are available in many communities, but young people prefer adapting dance routines from popular Hindi films. Young children, teenagers, and college students perform these dances at "cultural shows" sponsored by cultural societies, college groups, and multicultural programs in public schools. Among some of the examples of cross-cultural forms emerging in the North American diaspora are "rap performances" by young men during community cultural shows, expressing the joys and pains of being South-Asian American.

There may be a slight shift in the diaspora toward more egalitarian community leadership, where gender and age differences are less marked, and women appear to carry great leadership responsibilities in community events. At the same time, there are increased expectations for women to serve as the touchstone of South Asian cultural identity in the diaspora. Women are expected to demonstrate cultural identity visually for their families at cultural events by wearing clothing such as saris, *shalwār kamīz* outfits, or "half-saris" over skirt-blouse combinations for garba dances. Men are much less likely to wear South Asian clothing. Similarly, women demonstrate Sikh identity for the entire family by leaving their hair long, while men are often free to cut their hair.

Many of the cultural practices associated with middle-class homes in South Asia have been discontinued in North America. *Rangoli,* floor designs made with colored powders, cannot be used in most American homes where floors are covered in deep carpets. *Dīvālī* lights are more often strings of Christmas lights than oil lanterns. On the other hand, *mehndi*—designs made with henna on hands, feet, and face—has been continued by specialists available for hire. Many Hindu families keep a small *mandir* (god house) in the corner of the dining room closest to the kitchen. Daily *pūjā* (worship) is frequently performed by women before they go to work.

The narrative repertoire brought by South Asians to North America reflects over one hundred years of colonial influence. Education and exposure to literature are highly valued, Hindi films are adored. The traditional role ascribed to grandmothers as storytellers is not supported by nuclear households, except during visits with elder relatives. Children frequently learn sacred narratives via videotapes of the Doordarshan *Rāmayaṇa* series or Amar Chitra Katha comics. There is a growing repertoire of family stories and jokes relating bilingual and cross-cultural miscommunication, as well as jokes exploiting Indian regional stereotypes. For example, a college student told this anecdote about the misinterpretation of a traditional Gujarati greeting:

> When some Gujaratis answer the phone, they sometimes say, "Hari Om," which means "welcome." But someone misunderstood what that meant and told his mother that he didn't understand why he was asked to "hurry home!"

Compared to European immigrant groups of the late nineteenth and early twentieth centuries, South Asians in North America arrive with excellent financial resources and educational skills, which in turn provide access to better jobs, greater mobility, and leisure time. Many South Asian families can afford to travel to India bianually or annually. Resources are frequently invested in a diaspora culture more closely tied to the home culture than previous immigrant groups could manage. Furthermore, this emerging diaspora culture is not seen by the immigrants as a failure to assimilate to North American expectations, a shame thrust upon earlier immigrant groups. In addition to developing diasporic practices that promote group identity and cohesion, South Asians are adapting many of their cultural practices for inclusion in multicultural events, appropriately taking advantage of a rhetoric of public pluralism and civil rights developed by other cultural groups. Scholars of both immigration and South Asian culture will find much to research here.

LEE-ELLEN MARVIN

SEE ALSO

Comic Books; Character Stereotypes; Dance; *Dīvālī/Dīpāvalī;* Fairs and Festivals; Floor Designs; Food and Foodways; Gods and Goddesses; Gender and Folklore; Ratha Jātrā; Satya Nārāyaṇa Vrat Kathā; Worship

DIASPORA, SOUTHWEST INDIAN OCEAN

Beginning in the eighteenth century, immigration from the Indian subcontinent brought tradition bearers to Madagascar, Mauritius, Réunion, Seychelles, and the

Comoros. As early as 1636, Gujarati-speaking Indian merchants did business in Anjouan (Comoros). By 1770 in Mauritius, Tamil laborers from Pondicherry and Surat numbered about one-tenth of the population, while in Réunion, Indians were among the twenty-two thousand slaves. The abolition of slavery (in Mauritius in 1835, Réunion in 1848) led to the recruitment of thousands of Indian indentured laborers to work the sugar plantations. As immigrants, many claimed affiliation with higher castes than those they had been born into. Mauritian Indians, originating from Uttar Pradesh, Bihar, Madras Presidency, and Maharashtra, were allowed to purchase land and become smallholders, and they created an Indo-Mauritian culture, now increasingly secularized. Today they dominate Mauritius. In the Seychelles, five Indians arrived in 1778; a century later, Gujarati-speaking merchants and landowners arrived, subsequently maintaining extensive contact with the homeland. Today, elements of Indian culture are less visible in Seychelles, and convergence is the rule. Muslims (*zarab*) from Gujarat came to northwest Madagascar and Réunion in 1881–1900. Indian traditions are alive even in nationalistic Madagascar, where some six hundred Sunni Muslims live in Tamatave, the east coast port, speaking Mauritian Kreol. All these groups maintain traditions derived from the Indian subcontinent.

In Mauritius (or "Mirich Desh," as the first laborers knew it) the impact of immigration on folklore can best be detected. Indians and their descendants, while sharing the Mauritian Kreol language with everyone else, have ever defended their group's ethnicity. To them, "culture" means the heritage of the homeland. The indentured laborers in camps (only men at first) listened to recitations of the *Mahābhārata* and *Rāmāyaṇa* epics, sang sacred texts like the *Hanuman Chalisa,* and even built temples. Yet, knowledge of the customs and beliefs of other groups has made Mauritian folk religion a unique amalgam. Members of all groups know and participate in the traditions of others, while modifying certain traditions to set themselves apart. Tamils and Telugus, though speaking different languages from North India, share Hinduism with them. At home, Telugus observe *Shankantri, Shivratri, Dīvālī,* and other pan-Hindu festivals. They adhere to South Indian practices such as *ram bhajan,* an all-night ritual held at home by kinfolk and preceded by fasting. In the ritual, a mixture of vegetarian ingredients is offered to the god Rām by the priest, accompanied by song, dance, and prayers. Telugus also practice the annual *Ammoru Panduga* ritual, which propitiates seven Hindu goddesses and formerly involved sacrificing a cock; now, with the substitution of lemons, it has become a vegetarian ceremony. Telugus maintain their separateness in their rituals with observances that separate them from the Tamils; they worship the non-Sanskritic local deity Minissprince, also known in Réunion. Tamil temples house black stone images identified as the Roman Catholic Saint Theresa and the Virgin Mary. Creole Catholics of African extraction practice Indian rites; self-identified Hindus and Muslims go on pilgrimage to the grave of the blessed Père Laval. Religious symbols in the home, women's clothes, ornaments, ritual costume, and special foods remind people of their ethnic affiliations.

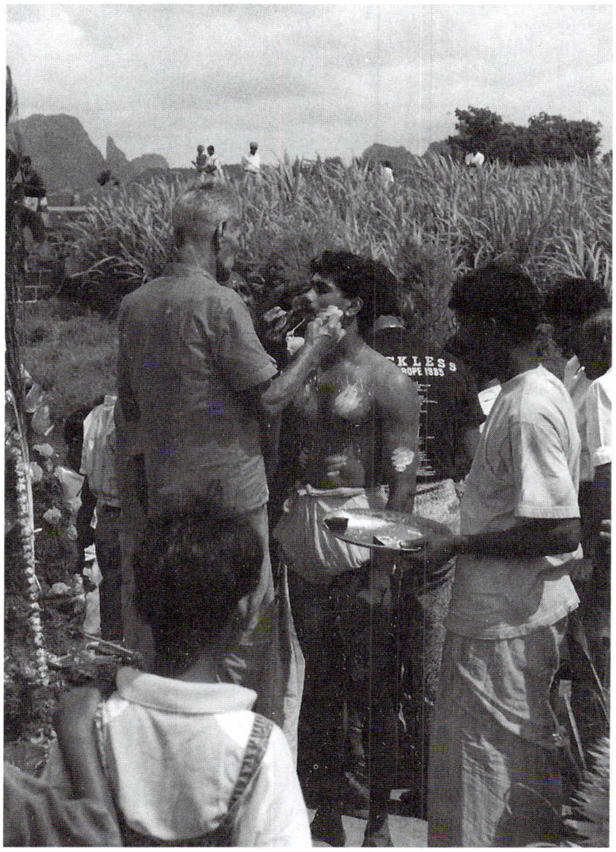

Tamil *Kavadi* ceremony. Mauritius, 1990. © Lee Haring

Mauritian villagers, both Hindu and Muslim, perform old-country folktales in the Bhojpuri language. An example is a tale known in Bengal and Afghanistan. In this version a daughter says "Sobur" (wait) to her father when he asks what to bring her from his journey. The father finds Prince Sobur, who falls in love with the young woman's picture. A magic fan transports him to her and they marry, but her jealous sisters work magic that causes him to disappear. (The latter episodes are strongly reminiscent of the internationally known tale,

"The Search for the Lost Husband," type 425 in the Aarne-Thompson Tale Type Index.)

As in the Caribbean, the cultures of the Southwest Indian Ocean turn both toward and away from their heritages to create new wholes. During religious festivals, Indo-Réunionnais recite traditional South Asian narratives in the island's Kreol language. In medicine, for example, "plants of Indian or Malagasy origin have a place in the therapeutic arsenal of a herbalist of European tradition without any modification of his conception of the relations between man and illness and between him and the active agents for a cure" (Benoist 1980, 36; translation, the author's). Illness impels people to cross the old barriers between Hindu medical practices, the herbal medicine of poor whites or Malagasy, Chinese consultation of divinities, and the separateness imposed by Islam.

Many issues call out for research. One is homogenization. Since Réunion became an overseas department of France, there has been strong pressure (resisted by Muslims) to conform to the schooling, televised commercialism, and linguistic standardization of France. Research in all the islands might identify expressions of resistance to the imposition of national culture. Another issue is whether Southwest Indian Ocean societies, in which castes, ethnic groups, and trilingual speakers cherish their differences, should be seen as pluralistic, syncretic, creolized, or a national amalgam. Finally and most important, in what ways and to what extent do the various islands resemble or differ from each other in performance styles? The varieties of South Asian diasporic folklore across the Southwest Indian Ocean are central to any understanding of the region's cultures.

References

Aarne, Antti, and Stith Thompson. 1961. *The types of the folktale*. Helsinki: Suomalainen Tiedeakatemia.

Baissac, Charles. [1888] 1967. *Le Folklore de l'ile Maurice* (The folklore of Mauritius). Paris: G. P. Maisonneuve et Larose.

Benoist, Jean. 1980. *Les Carnets d'un guérisseur réunionnais* (The notes of a healer from the island of Réunion). Saint-Denis, Réunion: Fondation pour la Recherche et le Développement dans l'Océan Indien.

Bissoondoyal, U., ed. 1984. *Indians overseas: The Mauritian experience*. Moka, Mauritius: Mahatma Gandhi Institute.

Haring, Lee. 1991. Prospects for folklore in Mauritius. *International Folklore Review*, pp. 83–95.

Nirsimloo-Anenden, Ananda Devi. 1990. *The primordial link: Telugu ethnic identity in Mauritius*. Moka, Mauritius: Mahatma Gandhi Institute.

LEE HARING

SEE ALSO

Dīvālī/Dīpāvalī; Epic; Fairs and Festivals; Folktale; Folktale, "Tale Type"; Gods and Goddesses; *Mahābhārata;* Muslim Folklore and Folklife; Narrative Classification; *Rāmāyaṇa;* Syncretism

DIASPORA, U.K.

The legacy of colonialism, since the seventeenth century, has forged ties between the British and South Asians in India as well as on British soil. South Asian dignitaries and students, servants and seamen, in small numbers, have long been part of British society. Following World War II, however, South Asian migration to the United Kingdom greatly increased as male laborers traveled from India, Pakistan, and later East Africa to meet the demand for factory workers. During the 1960s and 1970s their families joined them. The 1991 census estimated that nearly 1.5 million people of South Asian origin were residing in Britain. The greatest numbers are Indians, followed by Pakistanis and Bangladeshis. Some Indian families migrated directly from India (primarily Punjab and Gujarat), while the "twice migrants" (again largely Punjabis and Gujaratis) came from East Africa—Kenya, Uganda, Tanzania, Zambia, or Malawi—during the late 1960s and early 1970s. A 1994 survey estimated that 45 percent of British South Asians are Muslim, while 24 percent describe themselves as Sikh, 23 percent Hindu, 2 percent Christian, and 6 percent other.

The British "Asian" diaspora is extremely heterogeneous, including people divided by regional-linguistic, religious, sectarian, caste, class, migration, and generation-based distinctions. These cultural differences inform the ways British Asians give meaning to and participate in South Asian folkloric traditions. In the midst of this diversity, certain cultural traditions still shape the patterns of social life in Britain. Family, social, and religious structures have been reconstituted and adapted. The extended family system remains strong, and arranged or assisted marriages continue to join families of the same caste. Within families, respect for traditional authority relations and joint financial and social obligations still, in large part, reinforces strong family ties in Britain and across the globe. Cultural knowledge is communicated to children through the rhythms and routines of family life, the food that they eat, the folktales and stories they are told, the Indian films and wedding videos they collectively enjoy, and the domestic rituals they perform.

Participation in life cycle rituals and annual festivals varies considerably. The more observant Hindu families often set up a small *deri* (shrine) in a corner of their homes for worship. When space permits, Sikh families honor their holy book, the *Gūrū Granth Sāhib,* by placing it in its own room or shrine. Portraits of Gūrū Nanak and Gūrū Gobind Singh, as well as pictures of the Golden Temple, often hang in prominent positions in Sikh homes, while Hindus will display pictures of their deities. Life cycle rites related to marriage and the naming of a newborn child are commonly practiced by the observant and nonobservant alike. Hindu and many Sikh women and girls continue to celebrate *raksha bandhana,* tying amulets on their brothers' wrists to honor them. In times of need or thanksgiving, Sikh and Muslim families and friends will gather to participate in rituals (the Sikh *akhand path* or Muslim *khatme Qur'ān*) involving a continuous reading of their holy books, the *Guru Granth Sahib* or the *Qur'ān*.

Mandir (Hindu temples), *gurdwara* (Sikh temples), and *masjid* (mosques) can be found in most urban areas where substantial numbers of Hindus, Sikhs, and Muslims reside. Many now have space for wedding parties and other functions, and offer sports activities and language and religion classes for youth, as well as social activities for senior citizens. British work schedules require that services and festival events be held on weekends. Sikh families attend the gurdwara in greatest number for special celebrations, such as *gurpurb* festivals commemorating the births and deaths of the gurus and *Baisakhi,* the day when Guru Gobind Singh created the *Khalsa,* or Sikh brotherhood. Hindus in Britain also emphasize major annual festivals, such as *Dīvālī* (the festival of lights), *Navaratri* (the festival of nine nights in honor of the goddess), *Holī* (celebrating Prahlad's triumph over the demoness Holika), *Janamashtami* (Kṛṣṇa's birthday), and *Ramnavmi* (to remember Lord Rāma). Muslim families gather for the main feasts, *'E'Id-ul-Fitr* at the end of the fasting month of Ramaḍān, *'E'id-ul-Aḍha* (marking the sacrifice of Ismael by Abraham), and the birthday of the Prophet Muḥammad.

Folk customs and traditions have become forms of expressive culture, part of the symbolic ethnicity of South Asian groups in Britain. The urban landscape in many South Asian neighborhoods has been transformed into ethnic commercial centers, filled with shops selling saris and *salwar-kameez* (long tunic and trousers, for men and women), gold jewelry, and food items, as well as videos and music cassettes. Weddings, festivals, and other celebrations provide opportunities for wearing traditional dress and enjoying regional folk song and dance. Punjabi (*bhangra*) and Gujarati (*ras*) folk dances are particularly popular. Ethnic organizations sponsor music and dance performances as well as fashion shows and festivals. Language-based newspapers, radio, television, and, increasingly, the Internet are vehicles for cultural communication and entertainment. Support for traditional South Asian folk arts also comes from non-Asian sources under the umbrella of "multiculturalism." Multicultural curricula used in British schools frequently view "cultural difference" through a folklore lens, providing what has been referred to as a "sari, steel band, and samosa" view of Britain's racial "others."

Efforts to preserve or maintain South Asian traditions in Britain are being challenged by the inevitable forces of change influencing how Asians born and raised in Britain view and practice "their culture." Embracing "tradition" requires them to come to terms with a British racism that associates being "Indian" or "Paki" with being other, foreign, and inferior. More politicized British Asians have come to interpret aspects of South Asian custom from a feminist or neo-Marxist perspective, criticizing inequities seen to be inherent in the caste structure, arranged marriage practices, the dowry system, and the patriarchal family structure. Cultural tensions such as these inform the ways in which "tradition" is being reinvented in the production of "hybrid" cultural forms, in literature, music, dance, and fashion. As the third generation reaches adulthood, "folk tradition" continues to provide symbolic resources through which British Asian culture and identities are imagined and expressed, negotiated and contested as new ways of being British and Asian are fashioned.

References

Anwar, Muhammad. 1998. *Between cultures: Continuity and change in the lives of young Asians*. London: Routledge.

Bhachu, Parminder. 1985. *Twice migrants: East African Sikh settlers in Britain*. London: Tavistock.

Hall, Kathleen, 1995. "There's a time to act English and a time to act Indian": The politics of identity among Sikh adolescents in England. In *Children and the politics of culture,* ed. Sharon Stephen. Princeton: Princeton University Press.

James, Alan G. 1974. *Sikh children in Britain*. London: Oxford University Press.

Joly, Daniele. 1995. *Britannia's crescent: Making a place for Muslims in British society*. Aldershot: Avebury.

Knott, Kim. 1986. *Hinduism in Leeds*. University of Leeds Community Religions Project, Monograph Series.

Visram, R. C. 1986. *Ayahs, Lascars and princes*. London: Pluto Press.

Werbner, Pnina. 1990. *The migration process: Capital, gifts and offerings among British Pakistanis*. New York: Berg.

KATHLEEN HALL

SEE ALSO

Gūrū Nanak, Life Stories of; Life Cycle Rituals; Sikhism

DĪVĀLĪ/DĪPĀVALĪ

The *Dīvālī* festival takes its name, "Festival of Lights," from the practice of setting out rows (*āvalī*) of lighted oil lamps (*dīpa*) which invite the goddess Lakṣmī, the bringer of prosperity and auspicious fertility, to be present and bless the household or temple. Because Dīvālī is considered the means of renewing and securing abundance and wealth for the coming year, especially among merchant communities who settle accounts and open their new annual ledgers, it is one of the many "new year" celebrations of India. Though its customs and length differ regionally, common practices include:

- a predawn bath
- giving and wearing of new garments
- offering of water cupped in the hands to the ancestors (*tarpaṇa*)
- cleaning and decorating the house
- making and eating many kinds of sweets and other foods
- washing and decorating cows and bullocks
- special worship ceremonies (*pūjā*s) to Sri Lakṣmī
- taking of vows (*vrata*s),
- decorating with lit lamps.

The festival is celebrated by Hindus, Jains, and Sikhs.

As with most ritual celebrations in India, the scheduling of Dīvālī follows the annual lunar calendar of twelve months divided into two-week periods. The two weeks of the waxing moon is called the bright fortnight (*śuklapakṣa*) and that of the waning moon, the dark fortnight (*kṛṣṇapakṣa*). This bifurcation also applies to bright and dark halves of the year, based on the sun's apparent movement north and south on the horizon. Each of the lunar months begins on a new moon and each day of the bright and dark halves is numbered (first, second, third, fourth, etc.). The twelve lunar months are adjusted to fit the solar calendar and do not rotate through the seasons as in the Muslim calendar. The multipart Dīvālī celebration falls on days fourteen and fifteen of the dark half of the lunar month of Āśvina (September-October), though prayers for children and the taking of vows (*vrata*s) may begin on day twelve (*Vasubaras*) and the worship of coins on day thirteen (*Dhanatrayadaśī*). Each day is associated with particular customs and with events from the narrative tradition. The fourteenth (*Caturdaśī*) day is named for Naraka, a demon king killed by Kṛṣṇa, and his demise is celebrated as part of Dīvālī in some areas of India. The fifteenth day is the New Moon Day, the first day of the month of Kārttika (eighth lunar month), New Year's Day for merchants, and Dīvālī proper. The tradition of sacred narratives locates a number of important events on this day, including the dwarf Viṣṇu's (Vāmana) banishing of King Bali into the underworld (*paṭala*) after he took Bali's lands in three steps, Rāma's triumphant return to Ayodhya and coronation, the crowning of Vikramāditya in Ujjain, and Kṛṣṇa's saving of 12,000 abducted women whom he eventually marries because their families won't take them back.

As an agricultural festival, Dīvālī is part of a larger four-month ritual time cycle related to the alternation of dry and wet seasons, the southwest monsoon, and the grain harvest. The monsoon ends the dry season in May-June and initiates torrential rains, halting activity. This four-month period of celebrations around the monsoon season begins with Visṇu's falling asleep at the dissolution (or flooding) of the world. *Guru Pūrṇimā,* the honoring of teachers with gifts and worship on the full moon of the lunar month of Ashada (June-July), was originally the last day of instruction because of the monsoon. On the fifth day of the next lunar month of Śrāvaṇa, Nāgas, in the form of snakes, are worshiped during the *Nagapañcami* festival. *Navarātri* (nine nights) articulates the first nine days of the lunar month of Āśvina (September-October) and includes *pūjā*s to goddesses Saraswatī (on the seventh day), Lakṣmī (eighth day), and Durgā (nineth day). The tenth day of the bright half of Āśvina, called *Vijayā Daśamī* ("victory tenth") or *Dassera* (ten days), celebrates Durgā's killing of the demon Mahiṣāsura and also the god-king Rāma's defeat of Rāvaṇa. Dīvālī comes at the end of this four-month period, during the last few days of Āśvina and the first day of Kārttika. It completes Rāma's story with his return and coronation at Ayodhya and celebrates the harvest that is a product of the rains and the fecundity of Sri Lakṣmi.

Dīvālī's association with the harvest and the darkest part of the year, when ancestors return and must be propitiated to ensure further fertility, can be seen in the worship of Gaja-Lakṣmī. The securing of abundance is further amplified in Lakṣmī's union with the Yakṣa god of wealth, Kubera, who keeps his treasures buried underground. The plump, dwarflike figures of Kubera and Gaṇeśa (also worshiped during Dīvālī) have a close relationship with fecundity, the wealth of the "other" world, and Lakṣmī. Popular posters put up for Dīvālī depict Lakṣmī with gold coins flowing from her hands and Gaṇeśa with platters of his favorite sweets surrounding him. The entire ritual cycle, of which Dīvālī is a part, continues into the month of Kārttika with the reawakening of Viṣnu and the defeat of Tripurāsura by Śiva on the full moon day.

References

Fuller, C. J. 1992. *The Camphor Flame.* Princeton: Princeton University Press.

Kinsley, David. 1986. *Hindu Godesses.* Berkeley: University of California Press.

Lutgendorf, Philip. 1991. *The Life of a Text.* Berkeley: University of California Press.

M. J. GENTES

SEE ALSO
Calendrical Rites and Ceremonies; *Dasara;* Fairs and Festivals; Kṛṣṇa; *Navarātri; Pūja*

DIVINATION

Techniques of divination seek to discover the causes and outcomes of events beyond ordinary human knowledge. In South Asia, divination is typically employed during times of crisis, such as illness, sudden death, conflict, theft, or in connection with critical decision making—arranging a marriage, positioning a new house, timing a journey, or making a business deal. In fact, the Tamil word for divination, *kuṟi,* meaning "aim," implies the direction or course of action one should follow.

Except for astrology, which constitutes a special class of foretelling knowledge, most divining techniques in South Asia fall under four broad categories. Some rely on chance devices (random divination). Others interpret signs invested with ominous portent (semiotic divination). There are also techniques which require powers of second sight (intuitive divination). Still other methods depend upon direct communication with omniscient supernatural beings (intersubjective divination).

The process of random divination involves counting or statistical manipulations. In Tibet and adjacent countries (Nepal, Sikkim, Bhutan, and Ladakh), throwing dice (*sho-mo*) is widely used to cast a prophecy. Among tribal people of North India, the diviner throws rice into the air and counts the fallen grains by fours. The remainder—whether zero or an odd or even number—is interpreted with reference to memorized knowledge of the consequences. As described by the poets of the *Cankam* era, this method was also used two millennia ago in Tamil Nadu.

In semiotic divination, the spontaneous appearance of natural phenomena has portentous value. For Hindus and Buddhists, the flight path and cry of crows are assigned auspicious or inauspicious meaning. In South India, seeing a widow on the commencement of a journey or a special errand is a bad omen. In this category also fall dreams which augur success or sorrow.

For intuitive divination, a specialist scrutinizes parts of the human body (the palm of the hand) or substances such as fire, smoke, or rice, in order to formulate insights or revelations. A Munda shaman from Bihar stares at a packet of rice and reveals to his client what he sees. Throughout India, Hindu diviners study the flame from burning camphor until they discern patterns of the future. This form of divination requires innate or acquired powers of awareness, which are often attributed to low-caste priests or tribal women.

The revelations from intersubjective divination result from human beings communicating with a deity or the spirit of a dead person. In all religious systems of South Asia, this transaction takes place in two ways. A supernatural initiates the communication, instructing an individual—who is in a state of dream, trance, or meditation—what must be done. Or people deliberately induce themselves into such states in order to contact supernaturals. Hindu mediums, Tibetan reincarnate lamas, tribal shamans, and Muslim oracles (*dhāmī*) obtain their privileged rapport as a result of a spiritual election, extreme devotion, austere practices, membership in a priestly lineage, or apprenticeship with a master.

Each kind of divinatory method appears to express a distinct epistemology, cosmology, and sociology. But they may accommodate a single concept of fate. For instance, in South India the forces which guide human action are conceptualized as personal powers. Random divination is, therefore, also interpreted in terms of the workings of a spiritualized destiny, for its abstract patterns are said to result from divine intervention.

Thus, a Tamil deity might respond to a question from its devotee by influencing the throw of little packets that contain colored flowers. If the first bundle yields a white flower, the deity has declared the imminent end to an undesirable condition. A red flower signals a desired outcome. In Karnataka, divinatory stones located in or near temples fulfill a similar function. Devotees who can lift these big and heavy stones an odd number of times (usually five) obtain a positive response to their queries. In both examples, random divination becomes intersubjective. It may even be considered preferable to a seance with a trained or gifted oracle, since it allows communication with the deity that is not mediated by another human being.

The practices which seek to discover how best to act in the South Asian world are concerned not merely with the trajectory of past, present, and future events but with the human and personal significance of larger transcendental realities. Any investigation of divinatory methods requires not just an inventory of techniques but also an appreciation of the various theories that underlie South Asian cosmologies and systems of morality.

References

Beck, Brenda E. F. 1969. Colour and heat in a South Indian ritual. *Man* 4(4): 553–572.

Rinpoche, Lama Chime Radha. 1981. Tibet. In *Oracles and divination,* ed. Michael Loewe and Carmen Blacker, 3–37. Boulder, Colo.: Shambhala Publications.

Spencer, Dorothy M. 1970. The recruitment of shamans among the Mundas. *History of Religions* 10(1): 1–31.

Thurston, Edgar. 1906. Omens, evil eye, charms? Animal superstitions, sorcery, etc., votive offerings. In *Ethnographic notes in southern India,* 238–365. Madras: The Superintendent, Government Press.

Wayman, Alex. 1967. Significance of dreams in India and Tibet. *History of Religions* 7(1): 1–12.

ISABELLE NABOKOV

SEE ALSO

Dhāmī; Dreams; Exorcism; Fate, Hindu; Fortune Tellers; Geomancy; *Junjappa; Mailāra/Mallanna/Khandobā;* Numerology; Shamanism, Islam; Spirit Possession and Mediumship; Supernatural Beings, Nepal; Tibet

DIVINATION, BALOCHI

Pāl in Balochi, *fāl* in Arabic and Persian, describes procedures for the divination of future events or unknown facts by means of special knowledge and by reading and interpreting the appearance of particular objects and signs. While the term and some activities are shared among a variety of Muslim groups, this essay describes the commonest Balochi forms of the practice. The common belief among Balochis is that one is born with his/her destiny written of a guarded tablet (*lōh-i mahpūz*) and that the pious and/or those with special powers and techniques can read the hidden facts. Some of the commonest means of divination are discussed below.

Māsag

Māsag, one of the most widespread practices, is practiced by a *māsag-band,* "one who ties the māsag," usually a mature male but occasionally a female. Six equal-sized, long, slim splints of fresh dwarf palm wood are dedicated with spoken ("blown-on") spells, tied together end to end, and buried under a shallow covering of earth, with more spells, enjoining the māsag to tell the truth about the person or object. Then the diviner tries to separate the pieces without untying the knots binding them. The interpretation is made according to how they separate or remain connected. Accuracy is dependent on correct ritual, the expertise of the diviner, and other context factors. Acknowledged experts are sought out from some distance or called upon for a reading when they visit other places, to tell the outcome of a child's school exam, news of a traveling relative, recovery from illness, the fate of a lost animal, the coming of rain, and so on.

Many tales are told of successful divinations. In one example, a man met a prominent diviner while traveling and asked for a reading. He was told, "If you go home to your family, your wife will die, but if you stay away, you yourself will die." The client pressed the māsag-band for a more precise reading, and on the third try, the diviner was able to observe that a poisonous snake had hidden itself in the traveler's sack of flour. "If you had gone to your family, your wife would have opened the sack and been bitten and died. If you had remained away, you would have opened the sack to use the flour, and you would have died."

Āḍḍcārī

Āḍḍcārī (observing the bone) involves reading the scapula (flat shoulder bone) of a freshly killed mature ram or goat. Experts (*āḍḍcār*) predict the weather, natural calamities, wars, prosperity or famine, deaths of kings or other changes in government, and other matters of common interest. The scapula must be from a freshly killed, young adult animal, ritually prepared, carefully cleaned of flesh without scratching its surface so that the traces of vascularization on the bone are clear.

Other matters are divined by special means. The sex of an unborn child is discovered by throwing a freshly killed snake into the air three times and observing whether it falls upside down or otherwise. If it falls back uppermost, the child will be male. Shooting stars are believed to predict the death of important people. Some use the observed relations of the moon and clouds to predict rain or drought. The movement and color distribution in the flames and smoke of a household fire and any strange sounds the fire makes may predict calamities, epidemics, and such. If a fire makes a strange sound, calamity can be averted by reciting *Hōr o bārān, hōr o bārān* ("rains and showers, rains and showers") and sprinkling water on the fire. Drought being a great and frequent threat to arid Balochistan, much divination activity concerns rain.

Shirk o pāl

Shirk o pāl is the belief in certain actions or objects as auspicious or inauspicious. There are hundreds of taboos and omens attached to different objects and events. Among numbers, sixteen is unlucky (*shūmm*), worst of all if the sixteenth of the month falls on a Saturday. People do not initiate economic activity, begin a journey, or take any other important decision on the sixteenth of the month. Women do not wash their hair on the sixteenth, or on Saturdays, as it could be harmful or fatal to their fathers or brothers. A child born on the sixteenth of the (Islamic) lunar month is considered unlucky. A common curse is *shūmm o shānzdahī!,* "Unlucky [one], born on the sixteenth!"

Others

Other common divination signs include twitching eyelids (one or both, upper or lower, each predicts different things: the arrival of the north wind (grief and crying); ringing ears predict news (good in the right ear, bad in the left, with a protective formula to recite if the left ear rings); itching palms mean money (right is gaining, left is losing); gargling in the throat (a journey). Dogs howling toward heaven and the crowing of a cock are signs of misfortune or death (the dog is chased away, the fowl is killed and the meat given to dogs). A fox howling from the graveyard at night predicts a death, but if one throws chili on the fire and says, "Fox, your anus should burn!" the fox will feel the effects and the death will be averted.

SABIR BADALKHAN

SEE ALSO
Divination; Fate, Hindu; Muslim Folklore

DOHADA (PREGNANCY CRAVINGS)

Dohada (Sanskrit), *dohaḷa* (Pāli), *dohala* (Prakrit, Hindi), *doladuk* (Sinhalese), "two-heartedness," is the pregnancy whim, when the will of the fetus influences the moods and desires of the mother. The word is probably derived from Sanskrit (*dvi* + *hṛd*), literally "having two hearts"; from Sanskrit *daurhṛda,* "sickness of heart," "nausea," or "evil-hearted"; or perhaps from Sanskrit *doha* + *da,* "giving milk." Dohada is sometimes a euphemism for pregnancy.

The condition of having a second heart, causing vicarious cravings in the mother, is discussed in Sanskrit treatises on medicine and love, and in religious literature, where it is often interpreted as transfer of karmic substance (especially by Hindus) or as coordination of two people's karma (especially by Jains). In literature, the dohada motif is used as a stock embellishment. For example, many poetic descriptions of spring feature the pregnancy longings of blossoming trees. The *aśoka* tree longs for the touch of a maiden's foot in order to blossom, and the *kadamba* tree for the first thunder of the monsoon. Stories of pregnant humans and animals in dohada also abound, especially in the religious literature of the Hindus, Buddhists, and Jains, where they often have a formulaic character, serving, like dreams, to augur the birth of a hero. Dohada incidents often serve as a start motif, or are used ornamentally, having no obvious influence on the main events of a story.

Dohada stories usually involve some direct or indirect danger to the husband, who must perform heroic deeds to satisfy his wife's cravings, ensuring a safe and auspicious birth. Sometimes a dangerous dohada is satisfied by trickery, or dohada may be feigned to trick the husband. Dohada stories usually involve inauspicious, dangerous cravings, but, especially in a Jain context, may involve auspicious cravings for pious acts.

Examples of auspicious or good dohada are the craving of a Jain woman to hear continuously the Jain teachings, and to spend money for religious purposes, or the craving of a Buddhist woman to entertain the monks.

Cases of inauspicious or evil dohada are more numerous. For example, in the *Thūsa Jātaka,* Prince Ajātaśatru's mother has a dohada to drink blood from her husband King Bimbisāra's knee, which is satisfied; she gives birth, after an unsuccessful attempt at abortion, to a child who is destined to kill his father and seize his throne. The *Vipāka Sūtra* (a Śvetāmbara Jain canonical text) contains many especially sinister dohada stories.

Dohada is often satisfied by deceit. In the *Kathāsaritsāgara,* Queen Mṛgāvatī has a dohada to bathe in a lake of blood, which is satisfied by her husband, who makes for her a lake of red colored lac. In the *Pariśiṣṭaparvan,* the Machiavellian political theorist Cāṇakya (Kauṭilya), plotting to destroy the Nanda dynasty, searches for a suitable proxy to rule for him. A village chief's daughter has a dohada to drink the moon, and Cāṇakya promises to fulfill it if the infant is given to him to raise. The dohada is fulfilled when the mother drinks a reflection of the moon, and her son, the future Mauryan emperor, is named Candragupta, "Moon Protected."

Many stories involve feigned dohada. In the *Vidhurapaṇḍita Jātaka,* the queen, wishing to hear the sage Vidhura discourse on the *Dharma,* feigns dohada. In the *Nigrodha Jātaka,* a woman feigns pregnancy and dohada in order to improve her status in the household.

Similar tales are found in the world's folk and popular literature. (See Motif T571, "unreasonable demands of pregnant women"; Thompson 1957: 402–403).

References

Bauer, Jerome H. 1998. *Karma and control: The prodigious and the auspicious in Ívetāmbara Jaina canonical mythology,* ch. 5. Ph.D. diss., University of Pennsylvania.

Bloomfield, Maurice. 1920. The dohada or craving of pregnant women: A motif in Hindu fiction. *Journal of the American Oriental Society* 40 (1): 1–24.

Tawney, C. H., trans. *The ocean of story, being C. H. Tawney's translation of Somadeva's Kathā Sarit Sāgara (or Ocean of Streams of Story).* Delhi: Motilal Banarsidass.

Thompson, Stith. 1957. *Motif-index of Folk literature,* vol. 5. Bloomington: Indian University Press.

JEROME BAUER

SEE ALSO
Dom; Dowry and Bridewealth; Food and Foodways; Jain Folklore; *Jātakā* Tales; *Karma;* Life Cycle Rituals

DOM

The term *dom* is one of a series of negatively-tinged or even pejorative terms for endogamous, sometimes itinerant ethnic groups in Pakistan, Afghanistan, Iran and beyond, who are variously argued to be related to the European *Rom* (so-called "gypsies"), and to have dispersed into the Iranian plateau, the Near East and Europe from the Indus valley. While there is some overlap in the service occupations to which these groups are assigned (barbers, blacksmiths, sometimes leatherworkers and carpenters, sieve makers, rush mat weavers, musicians, folk actors and other entertainers, and allegedly, prostitutes), the names groups use for themselves, the ethnic identities they claim and their conjectural histories differ. Some of the professions (e.g. barbers, blacksmiths) live in settled city enclaves where they operate as private businessman, or in villages where they derive their income from standing client-relations with the surrounding population. Each family served contributes an annual fee made up of a share of the crop or equivalent, collectible by the serving families. Other, more itinerant groups have "circuits," ongoing relationships with communities where they stop to offer their services or wares. Musicians and acting troupes operate in a region, being paid on a negotiated fee basis for special events such as weddings or circumcisions, but making the rounds of the households they have served at harvest time to receive an annual donation as well.

Dom is a term used in various parts of Afghanistan, as well as in the Karakorum mountains and other parts of Pakistan, both for craftsmen and for professional musicians. In Hunza, the term described an underclass of craftsmen and musicians who lived as clients of the Mīr (Prince), Sunnis in an otherwise Isma'īlī area, in a small enclave adjacent to Baltit, the Mīr's capital seat. *Jat* or *jat o jūgī* is another pejorative catch-all term used widely in Afghanistan, as is *kherrāt*. Aparna Rao documents one group within this marginalized population, the *Gorbāt*. In Balochistan, the general term is *lūṛī* or dom, in either case denoting client populations of musicians and craftspeople living among the Baloch, attached as clients to individual families. The term lūṛī or *lūṭī*, transcribed as Persian *lūtī*, is also that used by Ferdowsi in the eleventh century C.E. Iranian national epic, the *Shāhnāma*, to describe a population of several thousand professional musicians said to have been sent to Persia from the Indus Valley at the request of the Sassanian king, Bahram Gur, in the fifth century.

Recent scholarly interest in the dom and related categories has generally either considered whether their marginalization in areas now predominantly Muslim is to be read as a remnant of caste ideology in those regions, or else has attempted to trace what are probably a series of migrations or displacements over several centuries of differently named low-status service-professional ethnic groups from the Indus Valley northward and westward. N. A. Baloch in discussing the development of Sindhi music illustrates the latter approach, with some richness of source material and detail.

References

Allana, Ghulam Ali, ed. 1982. *Folk music of Sind*. Jamshoro, Sind: Institute of Sindhology, University of Sindh.

Baghban, Hafizullah. 1978 (1976). *The context and concept of humor in Magadi theater*. Indiana University Dissertation. Ann Arbor: University Microfilms International.

Baloch, N. A. 1982. Prehistoric to early historic period: Developments under Islamic civilization. In *Folk Music of Sind*, ed. G. A. Allana, pp. 1–16.

Rao, Aparna. 1982. *Les Gorbat d'Afghanistan: Aspects Économiques d'un Groupe Itinerant "Jat."* Paris: A.D.P.F.

———. 1987. *The other nomads: Peripatetic minorities in cross-cultural perspective*. Köln: Böhlau Verlag.

Sakata, Hiromi Lorraine. 2002. *Music in the mind: The concepts of music and musician in Afghanistan*. 2nd ed. Washington, DC: Smithsonian Institution.

Westphall-Hellbusch, Sigrid, and Heinz Westphal. n.d. *The Jat of Pakistan*. Islamabad: Lok Virsa.

MARGARET A. MILLS

SEE ALSO

Balochi Oral Tradition; Folk Drama, Afghanistan

DOWRY AND BRIDEWEALTH

South Asia forms a contact area for the intersection of two seemingly contrary social customs, rooted in rather parallel human concerns. Generally speaking, Hindu and related marriage practice involves a substantial dowry to be transferred to the groom's family by the bride's family, in order to make the marriage. Without a dowry, girls cannot marry well or at all. In Muslim contexts, e.g. in Afghanistan and most of Pakistan, bridewealth, the transfer of substantial wealth to the bride and her family from the groom's family in order to make the marriage, is normal practice. Both customs have ethical rationales as well as possibilities for abuse attached to them.

In Hindu (and monogamous) India, the ethical injunction is to give the "gift of a virgin" in marriage willingly, not to expect payment in return. Furthermore, marriage should be exogamous, the girl joining a village where she is considered not to have blood relatives. This principle is referred back to the Brahmanical (classical Sanskrit) Laws of Manu, which lay out the basic social responsibilities of different categories of persons toward each other. The principle of free gift puts the responsibility for recruiting a suitable spouse on the girl's family. The elaboration of custom has led to enhancing the "free gift" substantially in cash and kind, presently including large appliances and motor scooters depending on family means. In recent decades, in upwardly mobile or aspiring lower middle class urban families in particular, the pressure on brides' families to provide additional donations, after the fact of the marriage and beyond the dowry then transferred, has resulted in some cases of notorious abuse, up to and including "dowry deaths" in which the alleged death of the young wife by suicide or accident (e.g. an exploding kitchen gas burner) was revealed to be a murder by one or more rapacious in-laws. At a wife's death, her dowry remains the property of her husband's family, and the husband is free to marry again.

In Muslim communities an apparently inverse institution, the "bridewealth" payments made by the groom's family, is thought to stem from a similar concern over the transfer of women from family to family, addressed by a tradition (*hadīth*) of the Prophet Muḥammad. In pre-Islamic times, it was said, men married as many women as they could afford, and there were abuses in the selling of women and their treatment afterward, as well as a sense of shame in families at being the ones to furnish a woman's sexual services to another family. The Muslim reforms by Qur'anic injunction limited the number of legal wives to four and enjoined the husband not to marry more than one if he could not treat them all equally. Additionally, sayings of the Prophet enjoined that daughters should be given joyfully and with celebration to other families as brides, that there should be no shame in wife-giving, and that in this reformed environment, the payment given their families to compensate their loss should be limited to the equivalent of a then-moderate amount in silver coin.

Muslim bridewealth payment in practice breaks down into various categories: payments to the girl's family, contributions to her personal property of jewelry, clothing and household equipment (which may be augmented or matched by contributions from her family), and the *mahr* or *mahrīya,* a stipulated payment in cash or kind to the bride which may be delayed and paid if she is divorced through no fault of her own, or widowed.

The Muslim institution also has its abuses: a girl's family may set the bridewealth very high to discourage an unwanted suitor (e.g. to oppose a love match, traditionally distrusted as a capricious, unstable basis for marriage). A husband wishing to rid himself of an unwanted wife without forfeiting the *mahr* may engage in psychological or physical abuse to the extent that she "forgives" him the *mahr* in order to be released from the marriage.

In both these systems, patriarchal values place superior power in the hands of the "wife-takers," the husband's family, who ultimately gain custody of a worker and producer of offspring for the patriline. Yet within the institution, subversive tactics and alternative interpretations reflected in such things as women's wedding songs and folk tales about marriage negotiation reveal a "folk" consciousness of strategies not only for abuse but for resistance or subversive correction of that abuse.

References

Mills, Margaret A. 1993. "Of the dust and wind": Arranged marriage in Afghanistan. In *Everyday Life in the Muslim Middle East*, ed. Evelyn Early and Donna Lee Bowen, pp. 47–56. Bloomington: Indiana University Press.

Raheja, Gloria, and Ann Grodzins Gold. 1994. *Listen to the heron's words: Reimagining gender and kinship in North India*. Berkeley: University of California Press.

Sharma, Rajendra Nath. 1980. *Ancient India according to Manu*. Delhi: Nag Publishers.

MARGARET A. MILLS

SEE ALSO
Courtship, Afghanistan; Gender and Folklore; Marriage Ceremonies

DRAUPADĪ

Draupadī is the heroine of the *Mahābhārata* in its classical Sanskrit versions, classical versions in other (mainly Dravidian) Indian languages, and folk versions of varied complexity all over India. The Sanskrit epic also calls her Kṛṣṇā ("Dark Lady"), Pāñcālī ("Lady from Pañcāla Country" or "Doll, Puppet"), and Yājñasenī ("Daughter of Yajñasena, i.e., Drupada," or "She Whose Army Is Sacrificial"). Her father sponsors a fire sacrifice for the birth of a son to avenge him against an enemy, and she is born gratuitously from the earthen altar (*vedi*) while a heavenly voice announces that she will bring doom to the warrior class. She marries five husbands, the Pāṇḍavas, the epic's chief heroes, and bears each a son who will die in the *Mahābhārata* war. It is unlikely that her polyandry is a historical or tribal memory.

When her eldest husband, Yudhiṣṭhira, wagers her as the last stake in the pivotal dice match, the winning Kauravas drag her, menstruating, into the hall, wearing a single bloodstained sari. Yet, she asks a subtle legal and philosophical question: Could Yudhiṣṭhira have bet her after he had bet and lost himself? Her question's insolubility saves the Pāṇḍavas from slavery, but not before provoking two scenes of violation: Draupadī's hair pulling and disrobing. The latter proves impossible. In the reconstructed Pune Critical

Edition, inexhaustible garments come forth to protect her as an unexplained wonder, but elsewhere in the same edition, she and Kṛṣṇa tell the universally known story that Kṛṣṇa supplied them in response to her prayers.

Draupadī then goes into exile with the Pāṇḍavas, where she continually calls for revenge. In rebuking Yudhiṣṭhira for his inaction, she says "We are all like puppets handled by the creator," which prods him to tell her that her argument is "heresy," and that, with his and her "patience," dharma will be victorious. Incognito for a year, she works as a hairdresser, and during the war, she does penance (*tapas*), sleeping on the ground to bring about the Kauravas' destruction. At his postwar coronation, Yudhiṣṭhira is congratulated: "By good luck, you have gone the way of Draupadī's mass of hair"—a likely allusion to a theme known in classical Sanskrit drama and classical vernacular and folk *Mahābhārata*s, but not explicit in the Sanskrit epic: that after her disrobing, Draupadī vowed she would not rebind her hair until she could dress it with Kaurava blood.

Draupadī's life is part of a divine plan in which gods assume human forms to rescue the goddess Earth from demons incarnate as kings, whose rule threatens to submerge Earth in the ocean. Draupadī incarnates the goddess Śrī, Earth's "Prosperity" and inconstant consort of kings (including Indra), but also the wife of Viṣṇu, who, in his descent as Kṛṣṇa, keeps things on course by favoring Draupadī and the Pāṇḍavas in all perilous situations.

Folk *Mahābhārata* traditions concerning Draupadī are especially rich in the Tamil Draupadī cult, in which the *Mahābhārata* is "offered" to her in narrative, dramatic, and ritual genres at her festivals (*viḻā, tiruviḻā*). Here she is a virgin goddess with enhanced destructive powers when she assumes the "form of Kāḷi," and, with a non-Sanskritic folklore about her birth from fire, gypsy (*Kuṟavañci*) disguise, firewalk, temple guardians (*Pōttu Rāja* ("Buffalo King," probably related to Mahiṣāsura), Muttāl Rāvuttaṉ (a Muslim), and Aravāṉ), and a second advent to save a local king and fort. She is also prominent in folk *Mahābhārata*s of Andhra Pradesh, Madhya Pradesh (Pandvani), Rajasthan, Garhwal (Pāṇḍav Līlā), and Nepal. In the Hindi *Ālhā* and Tamil *Elder Brothers Story,* she reincarnates as Belā and Taṅkāḷ, these folk epics' chief heroines.

References

Hiltebeitel, Alf. 1988. *The cult of Draupadī*. Vol. 1, *Mythologies from Gingee to Kurukṣetra*. Chicago: University of Chicago Press.

———. 1991. *The cult of Draupadī*. Vol. 2, *On Hindu ritual and the goddess*. Chicago: University of Chicago Press.

———. 1999. *Rethinking India's oral and classical epics: Draupadī among Rajputs, Muslims, and Dalits*. Chicago: University of Chicago Press.

ALF HILTEBEITEL

SEE ALSO

Akhyan; Ālhā (Ālhā-Ūdal); *Annanmār Katai;* Epic; Games and Contests; *Mahābhārata; Pāṇḍav Līlā;* Tamil Nadu; *Terukkūttu*

DREAMS

Dreams are pervasive in South Asian folk literature. Folk beliefs about dreams in South Asia are similar to those found in the classical traditions of South Asia as well as in other cultures from around the world. For example, most people distinguish meaningful from meaningless dreams, emphasizing the importance of dreams that occur around dawn and dreams sent by gods over those caused by bodily disorders, such as indigestion. Indeed, most of the dreams in Somadeva's *Kathāsaritsāgara* story collection take place at dawn and are sent by the gods. These basic ideas about dreams are also found in ancient texts such as the *Caraka* and *Suśruta Samhitā*s (medical texts) and in early Buddhist works such as the *Samantapāsādikā* (I.520–529), *Manorathapūraīī* (V.xx.6), and *Milindapañha* (IV.75), while the *Palijā taka*s are particularly rich in the dreams of women.

Overshadowing these theories in Hinduism, however, is the well-known idea that we are all participating in God's dream of creation. One version of this idea is contained in the *Kūrma Purāīa,* which describes the beginning of this *kalpa* (eon), when nothing existed but a vast ocean and Lord Nārāyaṇa (Brahmā; in other versions, Viṣṇu) sleeping on the coils of a great snake. As he sleeps, he dreams, and a wonderful lotus grows out of his navel from which arises all that exists; God's dream is the basis of our reality.

Shared Dreams

One type of dream preserved in various stories is the shared dream, a dream that appears on the same night to more than one person. While examples of such dreams can be found in other cultures, South Asia is an especially rich source for them. Examples from the *Kathāsaritsāgara* include:

- two Brahman cousins who perform austerities to Kārttikeya and then receive a shared prophetic dream telling them where to find a gūrū (I.12).

- three Brahman women, who remain virtuous wives even though they have been abandoned by their husbands, share a dream from Śiva (I.19–20).
- a king and queen worship Śiva in order to obtain a son, and he appears in both their dreams, predicting they will have a son. Later the queen dreams that Śiva gives her a fruit, and this is taken as confirmation of the first dream (II.136).

Shared dreams also occur in Buddhist stories such as the *Mahāvastu,* in which the Buddha's father, wife, and aunt all have dreams portending his departure from home (II.129–131). Another type of shared dream is one that transcends time, as when the Buddha has five dreams said to be the same dreams had by Buddhas of earlier eons recorded in *Lalitavistara* (I.296–297). A second example of this type is the conception dream of the Buddha's mother that is said to have been dreamt by the mother of the preceding Buddha, Dīpaṁkara, mentioned in *Mahāvastu* (I.205). Additional examples of such transtemporal shared dreams are contained in the Lotus Sūtra and the *Ārya svapna nirdeśa nāma mahāyāna sūtra* (*bKa' 'gyur,* vol. 25, text 48), which describe the dreams of Bodhisattvas. In these examples shared dreams are used to dramatize the essential sameness of all Buddhist heroes; their progress along the path leading to enlightenment is marked by dream signposts. Correspondingly, shared dreams also appear in stories about famous Buddhist religious figures in Tibet. One group of such dreams centers on Padmasambhava's departure from home when both his adopted father and his wife have frightening dreams.

An especially rich text in terms of dreams and folk beliefs is the popular biography of the Tibetan yogi and poet Milarepa (eleventh through twelfth century). This text is actually structured by the dreams that begin and end it, as well as anchor its pivotal center, when Milarepa passes from being a disciple to becoming a gūrū himself. It also contains the shared dreams that Milarepa's gūrū, Marpa, and Marpa's wife, Dakmema, have the night before Milarepa arrives to ask Marpa to be his gūrū. Marpa dreams of a *vajra* (a tantric ritual implement), while Dakmema dreams of a stūpa (Buddhist reliquary), religious symbols appropriate to announcing a Buddhist saint.

Conception Dreams

Some of the dreams presented thus far are also examples of the conception dream, a type of dream frequently encountered in the biographical literature of the Buddhists and Jains. Equally famous are the dreams of Queen Māyā, the Buddha's mother, and Queen Triśalā, the mother of Mahāvīra, founder of the Jains. In her dream, Queen Māyā sees a magnificent white elephant, which, by striking her right side with its trunk, is able to enter her womb. This dream is understood to be a prediction of the birth of a son who will be a world ruler either through kingship or renunciation. Many versions of Māyā's dream are among the earliest images preserved in Buddhist iconography and texts, and representations of this dream kept up an even pace with the spread of Buddhism. The Buddhist belief in conception dreams is also well documented in later Tibetan biographies, probably due in equal part to the popularity of Māyā's dream and earlier indigenous beliefs.

In the Jain case, on the night that Mahāvīra enters Queen Triśalā's womb she has fourteen sequential dreams of a white elephant, a white bull, a lion, the goddess Śri, a garland, the moon, the sun, a large flag, a vase, a lake, the milk ocean, a celestial abode, a heap of jewels, and a fire. When Queen Triśalā tells her dreams to her husband and asks him to interpret them, he says they mean that the couple will have a son who will be a great king. The next day, however, the king sends for the official dream interpreters who, citing dream interpretation books, say the dreams mean the child will be either a universal emperor or a *jina* (a Jain hero). Of particular interest is Triśalā's behavior after her husband interprets her dream. She says, "These, my excellent and preeminent dreams, shall not be counteracted by other bad dreams." The narration continues, "Accordingly she remained awake to save her dreams by means of [hearing] good, auspicious, pious, agreeable stories about gods and religious men" (Jacobi, 1968: I.240). Her words and actions are reminiscent of similar ritual activities from the Vedic period, though here they are in relation to auspicious dreams.

Propitiation and Diagnosis

Some of the earliest references to dreams are contained in the *Ṛg Veda,* in which several hymns appeal to various deities to dispel the effects of evil dreams (II.28.10, V.82.4–5, VIII.47.14–18, X.36.4, and X.16.4). In the *Arthava Veda* other appeals for protection from bad dreams are directed toward healing plants and salves (VI.9, IV.17, and X.3), in part due to a related belief that dreams can reveal the onset of illness. Ancient Indians also sometimes dreamt of the dead, but for them, as in many other cultures, contact with the dead is polluting and such pollution can occur in dreams as well as in the waking state. One of the ways to get rid of dream pollution is to transfer it to another object or to associate the dream with something ephemeral. Examples of this kind of thinking are found in the *Taittirīya-Āraīyaka,* which recommends a particular grass for removing the effects of bad dreams (X.1.7), and in the *Atharva Veda,* which states, "We transfer every evil dream upon our enemy" (VI.46).

The medical texts of ancient India, the *Caraka Samhitā* and *Suśruta Samhitā* (CS and SS), which are still in use today as part of the Āyurvedic system of healing, use dreams as a diagnostic tool. Sudhir Kakar's recent work has shown the persistence of these ancient ideas and the Āyurvedic approach to the whole person, in which dreams are considered a meaningful part of the person. This is not an idea unique to ancient India—dreams were used as a diagnostic tool by such well-known ancient Greek doctors as Galen and Hippocrates, as well as by ancient Mesopotamian doctors. Significantly, the CS contains many examples of premonitory dreams of disease and death that are similar to those seen in the epics and folktales.

In the SS, dreams seem to be caused by illness as well as being symptoms of it; certain dreams appearing to a healthy person indicate the onset of illness. In other words, a dream may be the first symptom. Fortunately, the text also has recommendations to avert the influence of dreams, such as reciting the *Gāyatrī,* meditating on a holy subject, or sleeping in a temple for three consecutive nights. It also recommends that "an evil dream should not be related to another," although this is challenged by the evidence of Indian folk and literary texts, in which the detailed telling of dreams, especially those thought to be inauspicious, is a stock device. This does not, however, preclude someone from keeping silent about his or her dreams, and the recommendation itself would seem to be connected to the idea that saying the dream out loud will contribute to or hasten its dreaded effect. The main point, though, is the notion that dreams have a lingering effect that can be avoided by appealing to divine power, an idea that persists from Vedic times to the present.

As we have seen, this lingering effect may also be a source of pollution (such as contact with the dead) or it may be viewed as part of the effluvia of the night that must be purified or washed away during morning ablutions. The philosophical texts treat dreams as effluvia when they assert a negative position, mainly referring to them as useless illusions or as useful only for signifying how real and powerful a force illusion (*māyā*) is in waking life.

In spite of the lively interest in dreams in the Vedas and related texts, few dreams actually occur in the epics, and then they play a very minor role. Two dreams that do occur in Valmiki's *Rāmāyaṇa* are of minor characters; however, both announce deaths, using the same images contained in the ancient Indian medical texts, for example, seeing a woman dressed in red, dragging someone toward the south. The few dreams in the *Mahābhārata* also belong to secondary or even liminal characters such as Karṇa and Bhīṣma. Dreams are, however, ubiquitous in the Tibetan epic of *Gesar* (*Kesar*), in which the hero continually receives dream visitations from Buddhist deities who offer him advice which he follows.

Divination

Because they link the internal and subjective emotional life of an individual with what appears to be objective outer events and symbols, dreams are believed to be a particularly potent form of divination. The dreamer is totally engaged in the dream activity and, upon awakening, feels compelled to describe the experience and to seek an interpretation that resolves it. The "objective" quality of dreams is perhaps most clearly expressed when dreamers say they "saw" (*dṛṣ*) the dream rather than "had" a dream. This use of language expresses the idea that dreams are experienced as given to individuals rather than created by them and emphasizes the external rather than the internal origin of the dream, thereby lending them a possibly divine authority. This thinking is expressed in hymn 4.9 of the *Atharva Veda* that appeals to an eye ointment, *añana,* for protection from troubled dreams, and in the Tibetan *Tangyur* (vol. 25, text 48) that recommends preparing and using a certain eye ointment when seeking an auspicious dream.

At the same time, dreams are a useful narrative device, acting as a deus ex machina to shift the action, define character, and express the inevitability of what follows. Not infrequently, they are the vehicles for divine appearances that reassure the audience not only of the immanence of divinity, but of the gods' enduring concern with the affairs of humanity. More research needs to be done on all these aspects of dream life, especially through interviewing living people about their dream beliefs and experiences.

References

Bays, Gwendolyn, trans. 1983. *The voice of the Buddha: The beauty of compassion.* (Original: *Lalitavistara*) Berkeley, Calif.: Dharma Publishing.

Bhishagratna, Kaviraj Kunjalal. 1963. *Sushruta Samhita.* 2nd ed. Varanasi, India: Chowkhamba Sanskrit Series.

bKa' 'gyur. 1980. Vol. 25, text 48. Oakland, Calif.: Dharma.

Bloomfield, Maurice, trans. [1897] 1979. *Atharva Veda.* Delhi: Motilal Banarsidass.

Bolling, G. M. 1913. Dreams and sleep (Vedic). In *The encyclopaedia of religion and ethics,* vol. 5, ed. James Hastings. New York: Charles Scribner.

Esnoul, Anne-Marie. 1959. *Les Songes et leur interprétation dans l'Inde.* In *Les Songes et leur interprétation* (Dreams and their interpretation) Paris: Editions du Seuil.

Griffith, Ralph T. H., trans. [1889] 1971. *The hymns of the Ṛg Veda.* Varanasi, India: Chowkhamba Sanskrit Series Office.

Jacobi, Hermann. [1884] 1968. *Jaina Sutras*. New York: Dover Publications.
Jones, J. J., trans. 1949–1956. *Mahāvastu*. London: Pali Text Society.
Kern, H., trans. [1884] 1963. *Lotus Sūtra, or Saddharmapuṇḍarīka* (The lotus of the true law), 278–279. New York: Dover Publications.
Lhalungpa, Lobsang P., trans. 1984. *The life of Milarepa*. Boulder, Colo., and London: Shambhala Publications.
O'Flaherty, Wendy Doniger. 1984. *Dreams, illusion and other realities*. Chicago: University of Chicago Press.
Sharma, Jadish, and Lee Siegel. 1980. *Dream-symbolism in the Śrāmaṇic tradition: Two psychoanalytical studies in Jainist and Buddhist dream legends*. Calcutta: Firma KLM.
Sharma, R. K., and Bhagwan Das, trans. 1977. *Caraka Samhita*, II.545–550. Varanasi, India: Chowkhamba Sanskrit Series.
Shastri, H. R., trans. 1953–1957. *The Ramayana of Valmiki*. London: Shantisadan.
Tagore, Ganesh Vasudeo, trans. n.d. *Kūrma Purāṇa*. Delhi: Motilal Banarsidass.
Tawney, C. H., trans. 1924. *Kathāsaritsāgara* (The ocean of story). London: Chas. J. Sawyer.
Tsogyal, Yeshe. 1978. *The life and liberation of Padmasambhava*, trans. Kenneth Douglas and Gwendolyn Bays from the French of Gustave-Charles Toussaint. Berkeley, Calif.: Dharma Publishing.
Van Buitenen, J. A. B., trans. 1975–1978. *The Mahābhārata*. Vols. 2 and 3. Chicago and London: University of Chicago Press.
Young, Serinity. 1999. *Dreaming in the lotus: Buddhist dream narrative, imagery, and practice*. Boston: Wisdom Publications.

SERINITY YOUNG

SEE ALSO

Chapbooks; Divination; Epic; Hinduism; Jainism; *Kalpasūtra;* Kathāsaritsāgara; Kesar; Legend; Life Cycle Rituals; Medicine, Ayurveda; Saints; Shamanism; Story Literature, Sanskrit; *Stūpa;* Tibet

DRESS

Uncut cloth, draped and tied, is the prevailing sartorial emblem of South Asia. From Pakistan to Bangladesh, from Bhutan to Sri Lanka, rectangles of cloth are worn sometimes as turbans, sometimes as upper cloths (variously known as *chādar, shāl, dūpatta, odhani*), and in many places as principal garments (sāṛī, *kira, lungī,* and *dhoti*). Everywhere, these garments coexist with cut and stitched clothing, as they have for millennia. But to the Western eye—unaccustomed as it is to anything other than an occasional scarf or neckerchief that is not tailored—the wrapped dress stands out.

South Asia is a region of daunting variety and complexity in dress. What people wear is the product of centuries of interconnected influences—social, cultural, political, and economic. Clothing is related to religion, region, caste, gender, stage of life, political belief, occupation, and occasion. For centuries South Asian sartorial styles have participated in transregional movements and been shaped by local preferences. For example, during the Mughal empire (sixteenth–eighteenth century), the court and the elite followed Persian models; in the nineteenth and twentieth centuries, Western dress has had a powerful impact and has been completely integrated into the sartorial scene. Today in urban areas among the middle class, jeans are popular with young men and suits with corporate businessmen. Women wear Western-style cardigan sweaters over their sāṛī and *shalwār kamīz* (baggy drawstring-waisted trousers and long tunics) and Western-style undergarments beneath. Across the region, shalwār kamīz, once worn principally in the northwest, have become popular with young women, especially in the cities, and are an intense fashion focus in which shape, length, and ornamentation change yearly. Among the dozens to be found in the region, one way of draping the sāṛī now predominates in the cities and towns and even in much of the countryside of India, Bangladesh, Nepal, and Sri Lanka. This style involves a length of cloth about one and one-half meters wide and five meters long, pleated in the front with its decorative border placed over the left shoulder and worn over a petticoat and with a blouse (*colī*). Fabrics, designs, and colors, as well as the cut of the sāṛī blouse—puffed sleeves, sleeveless, long or short torso—change rapidly, partly influenced by international fashion. No one, in town or country, is isolated from the impact of regional and international trends.

Everywhere, gender is a fundamental determinant of dress, and local preferences remain powerful factors in what people wear. Women in the northern and western areas tend to favor either a combination of full, gathered skirts (*ghaghra*) with fitted blouses (colī)—sometimes backless and sometimes hip-length—and a large shawl-like garment (odhani) tucked into the skirt and draped over the head; or loose trousers (shalwār) and tunics (kamīz) worn with head cloths (dūpatta). In the east and south sāṛī prevail, though they vary in length (four to nine meters) and are wrapped in many distinctive styles, usually with some of the cloth reserved for covering the upper body. This general pattern notwithstanding, there are many other quite distinctive styles to be found. In Bhutan, for example, women wear the wrapped kira, pinned at the shoulders and belted at the waist, in a manner visually similar to the unique Coorg style (Karnataka) of draping a sāṛī from the chest down and fastening it at the shoulder.

For men, as for women, tailored garments predominate in the north and west, and uncut wrapped garments in the east and south. Throughout South Asia, men's styles originating in the West—jackets with lapels, collared shirts, and trousers—have been widely adopted and are ubiquitous in town and country. Men's lower garments consist either of a style of pants (e.g., Western-style trousers, loose flowing *pāījāma,* or calf-hugging *cūrīdār*) or a wrapped and tied rectangle, usually about one and one-half meters wide and three meters long, draped sarong-like (*lungī*) or pleated and brought through the legs to create a divided garment (dhoti). Tunics (*kurtā*) and shirts, in a variety of styles, are the most common upper garments. Overcoats are worn in a wide range of styles, including sleeveless waistcoats, mid-calf length *sherwānī*s with stand-up collars and buttons down the front, and Western-style suit jackets. Shawls and shoulder cloths (cādar) may accompany almost any ensemble, except perhaps a Western-style suit. The enormous variety of turbans, caps, and other headgear worn reflects not only region, but also caste or ethnic group, religion, and politics.

Religious beliefs play an important role in dress. Hindus are enjoined to wear uncut, unstitched silk garments for the performance of many rituals. Partly as a result of this religious preference for untailored clothes, Hindus, especially men, often leave arms, torsos, and legs quite bare. By contrast, Islam encourages adherents, especially women, to keep their bodies well concealed, so the garments worn by both male and female Muslims usually cover heads, arms, torsos, and legs. Preferences for material also have a religious basis. While Hindus consider silk to be the purest fiber and prefer it, especially for rituals, Muslims are prohibited from the excessive luxury of pure silk garments and have devised mixed silk-and-cotton textiles (*mashrū'*) for formal wear.

Permutations and combinations of fabric, color, ornamentation, cut, and drape are countless, and the selection and deployment of these elements is critical to the way an ensemble is seen and understood. Clothing tends to be more colorful in the western and northern regions of South Asia; white is widely preferred in the east and south, although white predominates in men's wear in India, Pakistan, Bangladesh, and Sri Lanka. Colors are closely associated with the cycle of life, seasons, and festivals. Generally, younger women dress in brighter colors, and mature women (mothers and grandmothers) in darker, more sober hues. In many areas white is prescribed for widows, and red is preferred for brides, though, as with most such generalizations, there are counterexamples. On the southwest coast of India in Kerala, many brides wear white. In western India, women wear red to celebrate *Tīj* at the start of the monsoon season; for *Dīvālī,* the festival of lights, they prefer garments shimmering with silver and gold. In Bengal during *Durga Pūjā,* women wear sāṛī ornamented with red for the goddess. In different communities there are strong preferences for particular patterns and color schemes. In Pakistan and western India, the colors, motifs, and stitches of embroidered garments convey caste, ethnicity, and locality.

Fabrics of cotton, silk, and wool have been used in South Asian clothing for a millennium or more, and man-made fibers, developed in the twentieth century, have been eagerly adopted, especially rayon, often called "art silk" (i.e. artificial silk), nylon for wash-and-wear sāṛī, and polyester-cotton blends. In recent years, fashion for women of limited means has favored synthetic, easy-care fabrics with innovative (from a local perspective) patterns, while more wealthy women lavish their resources on more elaborate, labor-intensive, and costly fibers, weaves, and ornamentation techniques that are distinctive to their regions.

Individuals choosing what to wear or what to buy for themselves or their family members will be directed by gender and constrained by their means. They will be influenced by their educational background, their age and stage of life, and the choices available in the shops. They will take into account whether the outfit is for daily wear or for a special occasion or religious ritual. Choices of fabric, design, color, and cut will be made according to preferences for fashionable or conservative appearance, felt connections to local, urban, or international styles, as well as religious and political sentiments.

References

Chandra, Moti. 1973. *Costumes, textiles, cosmetics, and coiffures.* Delhi: Orient Longmans.

Goswamy, B. N. 1993. *Indian costumes in the collection of the Calico Museum of Textiles.* Ahmedabad: Calico Museum of Textiles.

Lynton, Linda. 1996. *The sari.* New York: Abrams.

Tarlo, Emma. 1996. *Clothing matters: Dress and identity in India.* Chicago: University of Chicago Press.

SUSAN S. BEAN

SEE ALSO

Bangles; Caste Mark (*Bindi, Boṭṭu*); *Dīvālī/Dīpāvalī;* Gender and Folklore; Gods and Goddesses; Jewelry and Adornment; Kalasha; *Swadeshi;* Tattooing

DRESS, PAKISTAN

Costume is one of the most vigorous and persistent dimensions of folk aesthetic in Pakistan, subject to highly specific regional and ethnic variations. Generally speaking, in Pakistan as elsewhere, women's dress tends to be more regional and more conservative of traditional elements than men's, men being more likely to adopt Western or generic urban elements for daily wear on at least some occasions. There is one main, basic garment type, the *shalwār-kamīz* ("trousers and shirt"), a long shirt over loose, drawstring-gathered trousers. Men's shalwār-kamīz tend to be in light or neutral monochrome colors, undecorated in most groups. Men's trouser drawstrings, like women's (neither of which should show in public), may be elaborately beaded or decorated with bright thread at the tie ends. The trousers of both men and women vary in width, tribal and nomadic people favoring more voluminous clothes for mobility and protection from weather.

The shalwār-kamīz was promoted as Pakistani national dress for women, over against the Indian sāṛī, but is in fact indigenous, in its male and female variations, across a wide band encompassing much of the northern half of the Indian subcontinent. Males top it off with a brimless cap, often decorated with regionally or locally distinctive needlework, with or without a *longī* or *pagrī* (turban cloth) wrapped around it, while in most areas, women wear various types of headscarves, shawls, or long draped cloths (*cādar*) covering head, shoulders, or at need, the whole body. This generic dress lends itself to subtle variation, not only in decoration but in use. The women's cādar, shāl, or *dūpatta* ("two-winged" or "two-sided"), a long scarf draped variously across the chest and over the shoulders, sometimes drawn up to cover the head as well, is a versatile garment that can provide modesty, shelter from the sun, wind, and rain, and in its sturdier varieties a bedsheet or a handy sling carrier for babies or other burdens. Many different colors, fabric types, and needlework decorations are used for these wraps. The ways of draping the dūpatta constitute a subtle repertoire for women to express varying degrees of modesty, religious observance, formality, informality, and fashion. Ways of wrapping the turban cloth for men who use it, its length (which can be three to six meters), its color, bulk, and material (cotton, silk, synthetic blends), on the other hand, serve as ethnic identity markers for men, while the turban cloth also can perform functions of bedsheet, weather protection, carryall, and possibly prayer mat.

Women's garments are the primary locus for the display of regional needlework, together with men's caps. The decoration of neckline or whole bodice, cuffs of sleeves or trousers, and sometimes seamlines and hems of the shirt on women's garments distinguishes ethnic group from group and even village from village in some regions. Women in Pakistan's northern areas wear very finely cross-stitched pillbox caps (called *koī* in Khowār language), a cap form generally reserved for men elsewhere in the country, along with the head and shoulder covering (shāl) worn by most other Muslim women.

Among Pashtuns in the North-West Frontier Province (NWFP) and quite widely in Afghanistan as well, the fine geometric counted-thread work called *qandahārī dūzī* ("Qandahar stitch") is executed by women in monochrome or bicolor to decorate men's shirt fronts extensively, but elsewhere, men's skullcaps alone receive such elaborate ornamentation. Women, on the other hand, often assemble as large and fine a wardrobe of local needlework-decorated garments as finances permit, as an important part of their trousseau. Several to several dozen outfits may go with the bride at marriage, prepared by her own efforts and by women of her family and her groom's, depending on local custom and the affluence and skills of the marrying families.

Some few groups depart from the general shalwār-kamīz style. In the Tharparker Desert of the southeast, adjacent to Rajastan, Hindu tribal women wear *kancera,* a fully embroidered, backless blouse held on by small cap sleeves and strings, and *ghagra,* a long, full skirt, covering their heads and backs with a long cādar or head veil, often colorfully tie-dyed, which can be drawn across the face and body if privacy is threatened. In some hot areas (Jhang, Khoshab), men wear colored *longī,* sarong-like fabric wraps, below the waist rather than shalwār.

In mountain areas of Sindh (Thana Bola Khan), Muslim women wear a snugly fitted pullover shirt (*gajj*) composed of small, square panels brilliantly embroidered on silk in a diversity of stitches, embellished with beads and sequins, with cloves, cinnamon and cardamom sewn into small bags and attached at the neck (cloves strung together with beads are included among married women's ornaments in many parts of the country). The neckline of the gajj is cut high and round on one side, with a slit opening extending the other. Unmarried girls wear the shirt opening slit toward the back; after marriage the slit side is placed toward the front, perhaps with symbolic significance, but also more conveniently for nursing a baby.

Several Balochi groups, also Muslim, decorate the women's wide, long-sleeved kamīz shirt not only with bodice and cuff embroidery but with a characteristic large, embroidered pocket (*jīp*), rectangular with a pointed top, attached to the middle front of the dress below the bodice.

Non-Muslim Kalasha women in the Northwest Frontier Province wear a distinctive long, loose, black homespun woolen gown woven from their own animals' wool, bloused around the hips with a wide scarlet fabric belt, together with multistranded necklaces of coral and coral-colored beads. The bright beads are a very important part of women's garb, indicating respectability and wealth: *ga acok* ("bare-necked") is an insult thrown at women who do not have many beads. Their distinctive *kupās* headgear, worn on special occasions, is a woolen strip, 8" or 9" wide, of black or brown wool homespun, sewn into a cap shape in front and draped flat for 16–18" down the back, covered with sewn-on cowry shells, beads, bells and buttons, with a red or maroon-colored woolen pompom or tassel at the crown of the head. The cap, which has structural affinities with some Tibetan headgear types, may be assembled by a man as a gift to his wife, either at marriage or after. A smaller type of headgear, *shushutr,* is also decorated with cowries and beads on a wool base and is worn during all waking hours by Kalasha girls and women, except (if they wish) when they are residing in the menstrual house while menstruating or recovering from a birth. Kalasha men traditionally wear mid-calf-length straight-legged, loose woolen trousers (supplemented by woolen leggings in winter) with a loose shirt and a woolen jacket or waistcoat. This same region has a distinctive male headgear, the tubular, rolled-brim "Chitrali" cap woven in homespun wool (*pattū*) in shades of cream, brown, or tan, which was adopted by some factions of Afghan *mujāhidīn* fighters during the Afghan- Soviet war. Kalasha men have traditionally worn this cap with a sprig of juniper, a pure and sacred plant in Kalasha religion, tucked into the brim.

References

Akbari, Nasreen, and Rosemary Crill. 1997. *Colours of the Indus: Costume and textiles of Pakistan.* London: Holberton.

Frembgen, Jürgen W. 1998. *Stickereien aus dem Karakorum.* Munich: Staatliches Museum für Völkerkunde.

Maggi, Wynne. 2001. *Our women are free: Gender and ethnicity in the Hindukush.* Ann Arbor: University of Michigan Press.

Mills, Margaret. 1994. The esthetics of exchange: Embroidery designs and women's work in the Karakorum. In *God is beautiful and he loves beauty: A festschrift for Annemarie Schimmel,* ed. A Giese and J. C. Bürgel, 331–345. Bern and New York: Peter Lang.

Yacopino, Felicia. 1977. *Threadlines.* Islamabad: Ministry of Industries, Govt. of Pakistan.

KHALID JAVAID AND MARGARET A. MILLS

SEE ALSO
Beads; Dress; Kalasha

DṚṢṬI

Sanskrit *dṛṣṭi* (in vernacular often pronounced *diṣṭi*) meaning, literally, "seeing, sight," has come to mean "evil eye" or "evil glance" in popular use, although the original Sanskrit carries no negative implications. *Dṛṣṭidoṣa,* in Sanskrit and vernaculars, is a deleterious effect on a person or object seen by an evil eye. In North India, Pakistan, and Bangladesh the Hindi and Urdu word *naẓar* carries both meanings, "sight" and "evil eye."

There is archeological evidence to suggest that the Indus Valley civilization had concerns for the evil eye. Ancient Vedic and classical Hindu traditions declare strong associations between the eye and the mind. Gods, goddesses, rulers, and powerful humans are all known to have effective, but not necessarily malevolent or damaging, gazes. Of the nine planetary deities (*navagraha*), all have powerful gazes and several are considered malevolent, foremost among them Śani (Saturn), whose dreadful glance decapitated Gaṇeśa. According to astrologers, Śani's effect (*doṣa*) on humans may last as long as seven and a half or nineteen years, and disease or ailments may be the result of Śani's gaze at a particular part of the body. Related notions of damaging eyes came into South Asia from Mediterranean and West Asian cultures, including medieval Islamic traditions.

According to folk belief throughout South Asia, nearly everyone's gaze is believed to mark another person, animal, crop, or inanimate object, although few are gazing with conscious malice and the viewer has no knowledge of what effect is taking place. Popular apprehensions are quite practical and concern, first, how to redirect a potentially damaging gaze; second, how to determine that an effect (doṣa) has taken root in the mind or body (usually the head); and third, how to remove an effect once it is diagnosed as dṛṣṭi-related.

Oral literary strategies to deflect an evil gaze are as old as the *Atharva Veda,* c. 1000 B.C.E. (e.g. 19.45.1). Throughout South Asia today, techniques are still everywhere in evidence. Life-size cloth-covered straw effigies hang from the top floors of buildings under construction; painted pots are upside down on poles near coconut palms; scarecrows with scarlet penises stand in crop fields; white gourds, coconuts painted yellow with demonic faces, or networks of cowrie shells and human hair hang over doorways; handprints on door jambs or walls are impressed with cowdung or blood from a sacrificed animal; elaborate threshold designs of powdered lime or rice are made by girls and women at dawn; cowrie shells, amulets, a woman's hair, or beribboned brass ornaments adorn the horns and necks of cattle. Obscene sculptures may decorate temple roofs and processional carts, and the image of a deity taken out in processions is not the real *mūrti,* which remains in the sanctuary. The Hand of Fāṭima serves the same protective purpose for many Muslims. All of these *dṛṣṭimūrtis* attract immediate attention and trick the gaze of a passerby into marking the lure and not a person, domestic animal, crop, house, or other valued object. One's own *dṛṣṭi* must also be guarded,

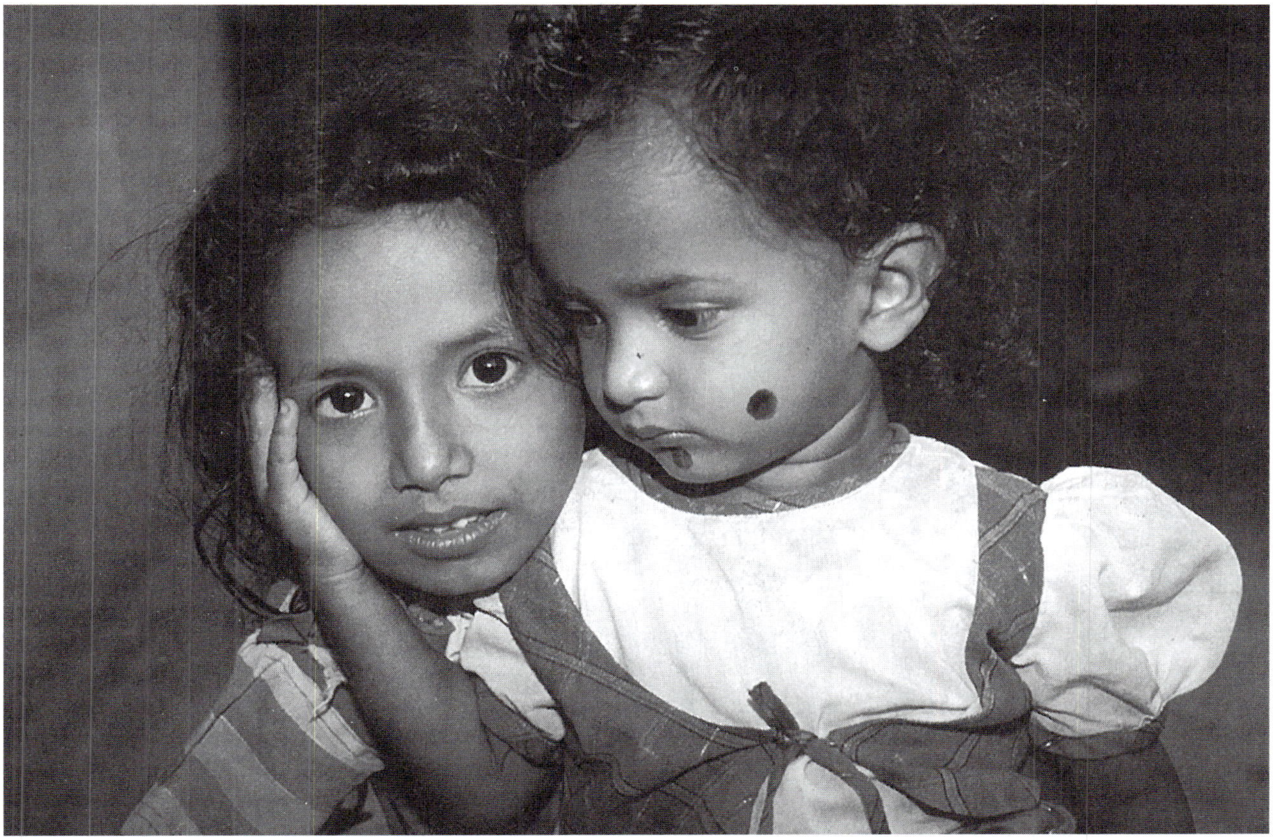

Dṛṣṭi (Evil Eye): Protective soot smear on child's cheek.

for example, in measuring harvested grain with averted gaze, lest it spoil, not from envy but from excessive pride.

Children are particularly vulnerable to an evil eye that may even prove fatal. No one should look at a sleeping baby; a father, who may not see the baby for several days after delivery, is then admonished not to gaze at his child with affection; a mother may frequently spit in the face of a child to degrade him with saliva pollution, thereby rendering him unfit for attention from an onlooker. Everywhere in South Asia a deliberately demeaning soot smear on a child's face makes her unworthy of notice, just as a degrading nickname (Stupid, Clown, Beggar, Manure Pile) or dressing a boy as a girl publicly mislabels the child. Black or red threads around a child's waist, wrist, or ankle are also widespread customs, as are amulets or metal tubes tied with black thread on children or adults, each containing mantras or sacred designs (*yantra*s) inscribed on copper or, for Muslims, phrases from the *Qur'ān* written on paper.

A pregnant woman or mother of sons may attract covetous glances from a childless woman and lose her offspring, a productive cow might dry up from a look while it is being milked, someone eating a meal may sicken if the dṛṣṭi of a passerby infects the food. It has been suggested that the origins of the forehead mark (*tilak, boṭṭu*) for women, who are partially or totally secluded from view in regions of South Asia, may have been as protective diverting marks on those women who did venture out in public.

Suspicion that the dṛṣṭi effect has occurred may call for ritualistic techniques at home or from specialists. In coastal Andhra, for example, one who has been in crowds, in the market, in a conspicuous position, such as giving a speech or accepting an award, may later feel "body weakness." Possibly, the effect of an evil eye is at work. A mother, wife, older sister, or senior woman in the neighborhood may take one or two hairs from the head of the person and, together with a pinch of rock salt and a red chili pepper, wave them around his head, first in one direction, then the other, three times. The affected one must then spit on the items and drop them into the kitchen fire. If the salt crackles in the fire, the extracted evil effect is being destroyed. If no sound is heard and symptoms persist, a local healer or exorcist may be consulted. He or she may wave a lime, an egg, or some chilis around the head of the afflicted one, and then drop these transferring items at a busy intersection where some unwitting person will step on them, catching, and further removing, the evil effect.

Most concerns about dṛṣṭi involve human-to-human sight, but gods, goddesses, ghosts, jinn, even animals (particularly snakes, crows, and cats) may deliver an effect. The curtain that sometimes separates devotee and a temple deity, like one that in certain regions divides bride from groom in marriage rites, protects both parties from the eye of the other until opportune ritualized times. Related to dṛṣṭi are other beliefs in certain regions about the evil mouth, evil foot, and evil shadow.

References

Abbott, John. 1932. The power of evil-eye. In *The keys of power. A study of Indian ritual and belief.* London: Methuen & Co.

Crooke, William. 1968 [1896]. The evil eye and the scaring of ghosts. In *The popular religion and folk-lore of northern India.* vol. 2. Delhi: Munshiram Manoharlal.

Dundes, Alan, ed. 1992 [1981]. *The evil eye. A casebook.* Madison: University of Wisconsin. [A. Stewart Woodburne, The evil eye in South Indian folklore, pp. 55–65; D. F. Pocock, The evil eye—envy and greed among the Patidar of Central Gujarat, pp. 201–210.]

Maloney, Clarence. 1976. Don't say 'pretty baby' lest you zap it with your eye—the evil eye in South Asia. In *The Evil Eye.* ed. Maloney, C., 102–148. New York: Columbia University Press.

Scott, David. 1991. The cultural poetics of eyesight in Sri Lanka: Composure, vulnerability, and the Sinhala concept of distiya. In *Dialectical Anthropology* 16: 85–102.

Thurston, Edgar. 1912. *Omens and superstitions in southern India.* London: T. Fisher Unwin.

Trawick, Margaret. 1990. *Love in a Tamil Family,* 93–97. Berkeley: University of California Press.

DAVID M. KNIPE

SEE ALSO

Caste Mark; *Darśan*; Fāṭima; Floor Designs; Ghosts; *Jinn*

E

ELLAMMA

Ellamma is one of the major village goddesses worshiped throughout Andhra Pradesh and Karnataka, southern Maharashtra, and northern Tamil Nadu. She is worshiped many forms:

- a stone or mud figure of the trunkless head of an auspicious woman (i.e., not a widow, the prominent insignia of the unwidowed status in this case being a glaringly big nose-ring stud and a big round mark of vermilion (*kumkum*) and turmeric powder)
- a termite mound
- a snake, usually a female cobra
- a stone figure of a human female infant lying on the ground face up.

In southern India, Ellamma is one of the Seven Sisters, or *śpta mātrikā.* She is an ambivalent mother goddess in the sense that the expression in her face is invariably smiling and appearing benevolent, but the features of her worship and the attributes of her powers, such as her power to cause epidemics and her appetite for buffaloes, goats, and hens, are all malevolent. Her worshipers are predominantly non-Brahmans. She is the caste deity for the tanner castes (the Mādigas and Baiṇḍlas of Andhra Pradesh, the Mahars of Maharashtra), who are part of the traditional, so-called untouchable communities who must live outside the village. For many non-Brahman households Ellamma is a household deity. Such households have an Ellamma *gadde,* or mud altar, on which an auspicious pot signifying Ellamma is placed. Budiga Jangama hamlets have Ellamma gadde in each household, and Budiga Jangamas worship several different kinds of Ellamma.

Unlike most of the folk goddesses whose identification with a specific classical goddess is usually vague and ambiguous, Ellamma is clearly identified with the classical (*purāṇic*) goddess Rēṇuka and is popularly referred to by the name Rēṇukāyellamma. Rēṇuka, wife of a Brahman sage, Jamadagni, and the mother of the militant Brahman sage Paraṣurāma, resembles Ellamma as well. The story content of the classical Rēṇuka myth and that of Ellamma are shared to a large extent.

The Ellamma myth, or *Ellamma Kathā,* exists in the oral tradition as an epic and is the main item in the repertoire of the Baiṇḍla (also Baiṇḍlōḷlu and Bavanīḍlu) caste, a performing caste patronized by the Māḍiga (tanner) caste. The Baiṇḍla also hold traditional ritual-officiating rights and duties for the Māḍigas. A fifteenth-century verse play called *Kriḍābhirāmamu,* whose major content is the description of the folk culture of Orugallu (the present town of Warangal in the Telangana region of Andhra Pradesh), describes a Bavanīḍu singing all the "stories of Paraṣurāma," obviously referring to the performance of the *Ellamma Kathā.*

This story provides an explanation of why Ellamma is worshiped in so many different forms. According to all versions of this story, Jamadagni, Rēṇukāyellamma's husband, came to suspect her chastity when he saw, through his supernatural power of vision, that she sympathized for a moment with the love play between a king and his queen when they came to the river where she was fetching water in a mud pot. He asked his sons to cut off her head as a punishment. Only the youngest son, Paraṣurāma, obeyed his father's orders and severed his mother's head with his axe. (*Paraṣu* means "axe" in Sanskrit.) When his father offered him a boon as a reward for his obedience, Paraṣurāma asked for the revival of his mother. The sage granted to Paraṣurāma his wish that the head of Rēṇukāyellamma would become a goddess and would be worshiped by the whole world. Since she died as a married woman, she became the goddess of auspicious (non-widow) status. Hence, her worship in the form of a trunkless head of an auspicious woman.

According to one of the most popular versions of the epic, she was found in the form of a snake by the king and queen. She then revealed herself as a child, and they raised and cared for her. Later in the story, out of anger, she again took the form of a snake and hid herself in a termite mound. The people, gods, and sages could entice her to come out of the termite mound only after ministering to her desires and offering her foods she was fond of. Hence, her worship in the form of a snake and a termite mound.

According to the version collected from northern Tamil Nadu, she was first found by a washerman in the form of an infant lying face up on the bank of the village washing tank. Hence, her worship in the form of a female child lying face up. Again, according to one of the Tamil Nadu versions, when Paraṣurāma set off to kill her, Rēṇukāyellamma ran screaming in fear into a forest where a Pāṇār (an untouchable community) woman embraced her in an attempt to rescue her. When Paraṣurāma caught up to her in the half-darkness of dusk, his axe cut off the heads of both Ellamma and the Pāṇār woman in a single stroke. When Paraṣurāma returned to the spot the next morning with the boon granted by his father to revive his mother, he found, to his astonishment, two heads and two bodies. When he reset the heads to the bodies, the head of Ellamma was put on the body of the Pāṇār woman and vice versa. The face of Ellamma with the body of a Pāṇār woman became the goddess Ellamma, and the other combination became Marimma. Probably this story relates to the exclusive association of Ellamma with the "untouchables" as their caste deity. According to the Telangana version, Ellamma took shelter in a tanner's house while being chased by Paraṣurāma. The tanner hid her in an underground tanning pit in a pool of blood. However, Paraṣurāma was able to induce Ellamma to come out in a frenzied trance-dance using the power of a percussion-and-string instrument called a *jamidiki*. Later, Paraṣurāma granted the tanner the boon that he and his lineage should become the Baiṇḍla performers who live on the narration of *Ellamma Kathā*. This explains how Baiṇḍlas derive from a subsect of Māḍigas (tanners).

The Rēṇuka temple of Mahur in southern Maharashtra, close to the borders of Andhra Pradesh, is such an important shrine of the Rēṇukāyellamma cult that, throughout the cult region, Ellamma is often referred to as Mahurayellamma. The village of Soundatti in Karnataka is where the biggest annual congregation of the Ellamma worshipers takes place. In addition to several such famous Ellamma shrines, Ellamma temples are found in almost all the villages of the region.

The word Ella[mma] has been found in personal names of both males (e.g., Ellayya, Ellanna, etc.) and females (Ellamma, Ellakka) from the earliest available Telugu inscriptions, indicating the antiquity of the popularity of the Ellamma cult. Indian folklorists often categorize Ellamma as a "frontier goddess," based on the contemporary meaning of the word *ella* as "frontier." However, the etymological origin and semantic history of the word "Ellamma" are yet to be scientifically traced. Telangana texts of the Ellamma epic derive the word from *yellu,* meaning "to emerge," linking it to the episode of the goddess being requested to emerge out of the termite mount. However, since this meaning of *yellu* is specific only to Telangana, the etymology is clearly case of a folk etymology.

In ancient Telugu literature there is a mention of the worship by kings and soldiers of a goddess called Ēkavīra. Ēkavīra temples are found even today in different parts of Andhra Pradesh. The attributes of Ēkavīra, such as her image as a disembodied head, match with those of Rēṇukāyellamma. The motif of termite mound worship is found in worship of other mother goddesses, such as Putt[a]lamma and Mariamma. And the worship of snakes in relation to mother goddesses is seen in Jāyamma of Karnataka, Mānasa Devi of Bengal, and Nāgarāju (also known as Subrahmanyam and Subbāryuḍu) of southern Andhra Pradesh. It is possible that the worship of Ellamma is related to and partially derived from one or another variant of these older images and the worship of these goddesses.

P. NAGARAJA

SEE ALSO

Dependent Performing Castes; Folk Etymologies; Goddesses, Hindu

ELWIN, VERRIER

Born in England, Verrier Elwin (1902–1964) was educated at Oxford, where he received a B.A. in literature and an M.A. in theology. Never a formal student of either anthropology or folklore, when Elwin first went to India in 1927, he did so to serve the poor. In part, he saw this as a way to repay India for his family's participation in the British rule of the subcontinent. In his words, "I thought . . . that I might go to India as an act of reparation, that from my family somebody should go to give instead of to get, to serve with the poorest people instead of ruling them, to become one with the country that we had helped to dominate and subdue" (Rustomji 1988, 13).

Upon arrival in India, he did devote himself to a life of service. His first few years were spent in a Christian *ashram* near Pune. It was during this time that he became active in the Indian nationalist movement and developed close relationships with prominent leaders, including Gandhi, Nehru, and Patel. At their suggestion he then shifted in 1931 to work and live with tribal groups in the Central Provinces, where he remained for twenty years, working for tribal uplift and researching tribal culture. While there he married, was divorced, and married again, both times to tribal women, the first of whom helped him significantly on his work on the Gonds. In 1954, at Nehru's request, he moved to the Northeast Frontier Agency, where he took up the position of anthropological consultant to the government, advising on tribal affairs and policies, a role he held until his death in 1964.

During his time in central India, Elwin became a keen observer of tribal culture and eventually published more than twenty monographs on tribal religious practices, marriage customs, folklore, and arts. Of these, perhaps the best known are *The Muria and Their Ghotul* (1947), *The Religion of an Indian Tribe* (1955), *Myths of Middle India* (1949), and *Myths of the North-East Frontier of India* (1958). He also wrote several books describing the problems facing tribal populations and suggesting new policy approaches. Elwin came to ethnographic writing through his development work among the tribals, and saw it as just another way to improve the lives and prospects of the people with whom he lived. One of the central goals of his publications and research was to demonstrate the rich cultural traditions and value of Indian tribal groups to the wider world. By doing so, he hoped to attract attention to the problems facing tribals and to build support for tribal development efforts. Even more important, however, Elwin hoped that his research on tribal beliefs, customs, and practices would help officials develop more sympathetic and informed policies toward tribal groups—policies that would work for change through existing tribal institutions, rather than impose a totally alien way of life.

Elwin's work has been criticized by anthropologists as being heavy on description and light on analysis. His primary interest, however, was never in academic anthropology. Instead, it was in the practical application of anthropology and ethnography to the development needs of tribal populations. In recognition of that interest, Elwin received many awards and honorary degrees, including the Padma Bhushan from the president of India in 1961.

References

Elwin, Verrier. 1947. *The Muria and their ghotul*. Bombay: Oxford University Press.

———. 1949. *Myths of middle India*. Bombay: Oxford University Press.

———. 1955. *The religion of an Indian tribe*. Bombay: Oxford University Press.

———. 1988. *Myths of the north-eastern borderlands*. Shillong: North-Eastern Hill University Publications.

ABIGAIL MCGOWAN

SEE ALSO

Folklorists; Tribal Communities, Northeast India; Tribal Folklore, Central India

EMBROIDERY

Embroidery is among the great artistic achievements of South Asia. Many distinct traditions have flourished throughout the subcontinent, reaching spectacular heights in northern and western India, Pakistan, and Bangladesh. Men and women of diverse castes, communities, and tribes use a variety of techniques and materials to fashion works ranging from the brilliant and vivid to the restrained and delicate.

The antiquity of embroidery in the subcontinent is hard to determine. Patterns carved on the garments of figures in Buddhist stūpa sculptures of the first and second century B.C.E. may represent embroidery, as may details on clothing depicted in the Ajanta frescoes of the fifth and sixth century C.E. We can be certain, however, that embroidery flourished at least four hundred years ago, for the oldest existing embroideries date to that time.

The uses of embroidery are many. Some, including appliqués of Puri and Tanjore, and selected embroideries of Rajasthan and Gujarat, have been made as temple hangings. Others have been produced for elite patrons, of which Mughal and Mughal-inspired court embroideries of the seventeenth century and eighteenth century C.E., and the nineteenth century C.E. *mocī bhārat* work of Bhuj, are outstanding examples. But a large proportion of traditional embroideries have been made for domestic use or for presentation. Women's embroidery—such as *kasuti* of Karnataka, the brightly hued garments, hangings, and animal decorations of Saurashtra and Kutch, the *sujanī*s (quilts) of Bihar—sheds light upon daily life, work, and the household, as well as on local interpretations of symbolic and mythic themes. Traditionally, *phūlkārī*s of Western Punjab, Punjab, and Haryana were made by women to mark transitions in their lives and events in the ritual cycle. On some, women stitched vivid representations of village life; on others, dense, brilliantly colored geometric designs (*phūlkārī bāghs*). Kantha quilts of West Bengal and Bangladesh bore stories from folk and epic literature, as well as stylized depictions of religious symbols and the natural world. *Chamba rūmāl*s of Himachal Pradesh are renowned for their subtly tinted miniaturesque narratives of unrequited love and Vaishnavite themes, including the life of Kṛṣṇa.

Commercial production is not new in South Asia. Kashmiri professional male embroiderers have stitched the intricate floral designs on woolen *amli* shawls for over two centuries. In the younger *namdā* (felt rug) and *gabba* (or flat-weave/blanket rug) industries of the area, embroiderers decorate floor coverings in chain stitch made with a hook. Lucknow *chikan,* whose delicate, white-threaded flowers and network embellish white cotton garments, also has a long commercial history, with possible antecedents in Bengal.

Embroiderers draw on a rich vocabulary of naturalistic and geometric designs, including visual symbols with rich folk and cosmological meanings. Deities; animals such as the elephant, parrot, and peacock; plants or plant motifs, like the lotus; and the famous *kalka,* or "paisley," recur in several traditions. Embroideries exploit a rich symbolic language of color, the textural possibilities of materials like silk, cotton, and leather, and a wide range of stitches. Embroiderers may also use beads (*moṭī bhārat* work of Gujarat), mirrors (numerous traditions of Baluchistan, Sind, Kutch, and Saurasthra), and cowrie shells (embroidery of the Banjara people of Maharashtra and Andhra Pradesh). *Zarī* embroidery uses gold and silver wires, sequins, and tubes. Applied on sari borders, furnishings, and bags, zarī embroidery is a thriving industry in several urban centers, including Surat (Gujarat), Madras, Lucknow, and Banaras.

Overseas trade in Indian embroidery dates back several centuries but became especially important in the colonial period. South Asian embroidery has influenced and enriched textile traditions elsewhere in the world, especially Europe. Some of its finest examples are housed in museums inside and outside South Asia. New materials and markets, as well as shifts in the contexts of use and production, have all transformed embroidery in the past century. Today, more embroidery is made for commercial purposes than for domestic use.

References

Chattopadhyay, Kamaladevi. 1977. *Indian embroidery.* New Delhi: Wiley Eastern Limited.

Dhamija, Jasleen. 1965. The survey of embroidery traditions. In *Textiles and embroideries of India.* Bombay: Marg Publications.

Irwin, John, and Margaret Hall. 1968. *Indian embroideries.* Ahmedabad: Calico Museum of Textiles.

Mirza, Shireen Nana Nee. 1990. *Sindhi embroideries and blocks.* Karachi: Department of Culture and Tourism, Government of Sindh.

Paiva, Roland, and Bernard Dupaigne. 1993. *Afghan embroidery.* Lahore: Ferozsons.

Zaman, Niaz. 1993. *The art of kantha embroidery.* Dhaka: University Press.

CLARE M. WILKINSON-WEBER

SEE ALSO

Crafts and Development, India; Dress; Dress, Pakistan; Gender and Folklore; Jain Folklore; Kāñthā; Material Culture, Pakistan; Quilting and Piecing

EPIC

The numerous and extensive epic traditions in South Asia are important both to the region's folklore and to the international study of this genre. While many folklorists around the world are familiar with the classical epics, the *Rāmāyaṇa* and the *Mahābhārata,* fieldwork and monographs since 1970 have expanded the known corpus of South Asian epics to several dozen epic-length stories of local and regional heroes and heroines, local gods and goddesses, oral tellings of the classical epics, and local caste myths, and more are reported each year.

Epics appear to be more common and widespread in South Asia, especially in India, than in any other region of the world. Although widespread, epic traditions are not evenly distributed, or at least evenly reported, across South Asia. Rajasthan, for instance, is a veritable epic factory (*Pābūjī, Devnārāyaṇ,* and many others), whereas Kerala has no known epic tradition (but *tōrram* and *dārikavadham,* however, are long narrative song traditions). Epics are performed in all South Indian regions: *Aṇṇanmār Katai* and bow song in Tamil Nadu; *Palnāḍu, Kanyakkā, Kāṭamarāja Katha,* and others told with painted scrolls in Andhra Pradesh; *Māle Mādēsvara* and others in Karnataka; *Kōṭi Chenayya, Siri,* and other *pāḍdana*s in the Tulu-speaking region of Karnataka. Comparatively few epics are reported from Maharashtra and Orissa, whereas several major epic traditions (*Ālhākhand, Ḍholā Mārū, Gūgā, Gopī Chand, Bhartharī*) are known across a wide geographical area in North India. Other epics are performed within specific regions, such as *Candainī* in the Chaṭṭisgarh region in Madhya Pradesh and the stories identified as "ballads" by D. C. Sen (1923–1932) in pre-independence Bengal. Among the so-called tribal cultures, stories of the goddess Persa Pen and of the god Lingal have been reported among the Gonds. All of the epics mentioned thus far are Hindu and are performed in India, although the genre is found also in other South Asian countries and religious contexts. The *Nabi-Baṇśa,* a sixteenth-century Bengali epic describing the life of the Prophet Muḥammad, for example, is known in both West Bengal and Bangladesh. In Sri Lanka, epic songs of the Kaṇṇaki cycle are performed in Sinhala and Tamil areas. The epic of Gesar [Kesar] is sung in Tibetan-speaking areas of the Himalayas and Central Asia, and in the Gilgit district of Pakistan. The Turkish-language epic of Gūrughī is known in Afghanistan, and in Nepal a cycle of songs about the Pāṇḍavas, heroes of the epic *Mahābhārata,* are sung.

Although no South Asian word accurately translates the English term "epic," the region is not unique in this regard. It is clear that long narrative songs about heroes and heroines, gods and goddesses, are an indigenous category in the locales where they are performed. The narrative itself may be performed in many styles and contexts, from folk song to folk theater, but the long, public, epic recitations typically belong to a wider genre identified by an indigenous term which translates as "story" (*kathā, kathe*) or "song" (*gīt, pāṭṭu*), and are sometimes marked by a special term derived from the performance style: *paṛ vācno* (reading the *paṛ* [scroll]) for the *Pābūjī* epic, or *vil pāṭṭu* (bow song) in Tamil. In fact, it is the occurrence of epics as living performance traditions that makes South Asia important as a place in which to appreciate the epic genre.

Thus, with some modifications, these traditions conform to the international consensus that epics are long narratives in verse about heroes. First, whatever their internal differences, South Asian epics have a strong story line, although most performance traditions include invocations to deities.

Second, South Asian epics contain verse material. But the distinction between prose and poetry—a distinction often used to distinguish legend from epic in the West—is misleading. Most South Asian epic performances also include non-sung portions of declamatory or explanatory prose (*vacanam, vārtā, arthāv,* for instance). It appears that song rhythms, rather than verse meters, structure oral performance, and that the distinction, and alternation in performance, between song and explanatory prose is fundamental to South Asian epics. Third, the heroic quality of South Asian epics is recognizable, although not identical to, that in epics from other parts of the world. Many epic heroes and heroines are, in fact, deified humans who died a cruel, untimely, and brave death, while others are romantic figures whose adventures are more amorous than martial; still others are religious mystics. Since heroes become gods, and no firm line separates humans from deities in Hinduism, epic and myth intermingle in South Asia; the *maṅgal kāvya* literature of Bengal, for instance, contains elements of both epic and myth. In these Bengali stories and many other kinds of oral literature, historical figures are quickly assimilated into a local, regional, and even pan-Indian pantheon, and power derives as much from spiritual discipline as from physical strength.

Finally, the contested criterion of sheer length is also met by nearly all narratives thus far identified as epic. In textual form these stories contain thousands—often tens of thousands—of lines, and they are sung for several nights, even weeks. In South Asia, length seems to distinguish epics from ballads (some of which are only a few hundred lines in length), although scholars are not of one opinion concerning the suitability of these labels. A related dimension of epic is narrative depth, typically three generations, which also separates most epics from ballads. Despite this lack of consensus as to what an epic is in South Asia, it certainly is not described by the narrow definition offered by Albert Lord: "Oral epic song is narrative poetry composed in a manner evolved over centuries by singers of tales who did not know how to write" (Lord 1960, 4). Further, South Asian epics are not, on the whole, composed in verse during performance by the oral formulaic method; some are memorized in large part, and many rely on sections of prose narration during performance.

An important characteristic of epics in South Asia, which separates them from legends, ballads, and other long oral narratives, is the ability to define a local worldview and to inscribe a group identity. This intimate relation between an epic and a community (caste, regional, religious) has been explored from several angles. Epics may provide a conceptual framework for an entire region, an authentic history for a specific caste, or legitimacy for a religious group. For these reasons, epic performances in South Asia are public presentations, with a particular profile. Performers are usually men (sometimes assisted by women), but women do play the lead part in some traditions. Performers belong to all groups in the caste hierarchy, although it is significant that Brahmans do not commonly perform epics, while low-status groups, including Untouchables, do. Also, many epic performances occur as part of a religious event, temple festival, wake, or family observance. This explains why spirit possession, when the spirit of the hero or god whose tale is sung enters one or more worshipers, is also common.

Epics are performed in an astounding variety of media in South Asia. A common assemblage would be a small group of male singers, accompanied by instrumentalists, although this core is often elaborated by the addition of costumes, dancers, and visual props. Visual storytelling is, for some reason, a preferred mode of telling epics: leather shadow puppets are used all over South India; long painted scrolls aid performers in Rajasthan and Andhra Pradesh; three-dimensional figurines, painted cards, and even portable boxes are used by epic storytellers in the Deccan area.

On the basis of narrative features, South Asian epics may be divided into three groups: martial, sacrificial, and romantic. Martial epics, such *Palnāḍu* and *Ālhā,* center on external struggles between men over land, women, and status (here the *Mahābhārata* and the *Iliad* provide parallels), usually leading to the death or disappearance of the heroes. By contrast, sacrificial epics (for example, the Telugu *Kanyakkā*), center on internal struggles or heroic acts, often suicide, by a woman. In both types, group unity is idealized, whereas in romantic epics (such as the Rāma story and the *Odyssey*), the plot turns on individual desire, especially the love quest in which the hero or heroine must rely on cleverness rather than physical power. The number of woman-centered epics, both sacrificial and romantic, in South Asia is noteworthy because it broadens the international definition of the genre.

The Hindu and Indian provenance of most South Asian epics may attest to the influence of the so-called classical epics—the *Rāmāyaṇa* and *Mahābhārata*. The story of Rāma and the story of the Pāṇḍavas are certainly very old and were written down in Sanskrit at an early date, perhaps at the beginning of the Christian era.

However, these epic stories are not now transmitted primarily in Sanskrit but in other languages, in oral performances, and in a multitude of different tellings and delivery styles. Epic performances of the Rāma story are especially numerous, including shadow puppetry in Kerala, women's group singing in Chattisgarh, and twenty-four-hour nonstop recitations in Hindi. The *Mahābhārata* is likewise the basis of several epic traditions, such as the Draupadī ritual drama, *terukkūttu*, in Tamil Nadu. Although literary texts of the Rāma story in regional languages have influenced the story line in many oral epic performances, the broad variation in what is called the Rāma story and the sheer number of its tellings caution against an overstatement of that textual influence.

References

Beck, B. E. F. 1982. *The three twins: The telling of a South Indian folk epic*. Bloomington: Indiana University Press.

Blackburn, Stuart, Peter J. Claus, Joyce B. Flueckiger, and Susan S. Wadley, eds. 1989. *Oral epics in India*. Berkeley: University of California Press.

Claus, Peter J. 1989. Behind the text: Performance and ideology in a Tulu oral tradition. In *Oral epics of India,* ed. Stuart Blackburn et al. 55–74.

Flueckiger, Joyce Burkhalter. 1989. Caste and regional variants in an oral epic tradition. In *Oral epics of India,* ed. Stuart Blackburn et al. 33–54.

Gold, Ann Grodzins. 1992. *A carnival of parting: The tales of King Bhartari and King Gopi Chand, as sung and told by Madhu Natisar Nath of Ghatiyali*. Berkeley: University of California Press.

Hiltebeitel, Alf. 1999. *Rethinking India's oral and classical epics: Draupadi among Rajputs, Muslims and Dalits*. Chicago: University of Chicago Press.

Honko, Lauri, in collaboration with Chinnappa Gowda, Anneli Honko, and Viveka Rai. 1998. *The Siri epic as performed by Gopala Naika*. FF Communications 265, 266. Helsinki: Academica Scientiarum Fennica.

Lord, Albert B. 1960. *The singer of Tales*. Cambridge, Mass.: Harvard University Press.

Lutgendorf, Philip. 1991. *The life of a text: Performing the Ramcaritmanas of Tulsidas*. Berkeley: University of California Press.

Narayana Rao, Velcheru. 1986. Epics and ideologies: Six Telugu folk epics. In *Another harmony: New essays on the folklore of India,* ed. Stuart Blackburn and A. K. Ramanujan, 131–164. Berkeley: University of California Press.

Roghair, Gene. 1982. *The epic of Palnāḍu: A study and translation of Palnāṭi Vīrula Katha, a Telugu oral tradition from Andhra Pradesh*. New York: Oxford University Press.

Sen, Dinesh Chandra. ed. 1923–1932. *Eastern Bengal ballads, Mymensing*. 4 vols. Calcutta: University of Calcutta.

Smith, John D. 1977. The singer or the song? A reassessment of Lord's "oral theory." *Man* 12(1): 141–153.

———. 1991. *Pābūjī: A study, transcription, and translation*. Cambridge: Cambridge University Press.

Stuart Blackburn

SEE ALSO

Akhyan; Ālhā (*Ālhā-Ūdal*); *Aṇṇānmār Katai;* Balochistan: Oral Traditions; Bow Song (*Vil Pāṭṭu*); *Candaini* (*Lorik-Candā*); Caste Myths; *Devnārāyan; Ḍholā;* Epic, Nepal; Epic, Sri Lanka; Epic, Tribal, Central India; Gods and Goddesses; *Gopī Cand; Gūgā;* Gujarat; *Gūrughlī;* Heroes and Heroines; *Hīr/Rānjhā; Junjappa; Kāṭama Rāju; Kesar; Mādēśvara* Epic; *Mahābhārata; Maṇgalkāvya; Pābūjī; Pāḍdana;* Palnādu; *Pāṇḍav Līlā; Paṛj; Rāmāyaṇa;* Shadow Puppetry; *Sirī*

EPIC, NEPAL

Epics, or long narrative poems composed in elevated style recording the valorous deeds of heroes and heroines, are called *mahākāvya* by Nepali academicians. Though Nepali folklore includes numerous folk epics, there is no term for "folk epic" in Nepali.

Other earlier epics may have been lost, or, though written, are no longer commonly performed; some have been reduced to shorter ballads and folk songs. Today, music, dance, and drama are often accompanied by the performance of folk epics. Due to their popularity in both secular and sacred contexts, some folk epics have even achieved the status of rituals that are performed during rites of passage.

The epic *Gesār,* performed by solo singers without instruments, is popular among the people of the remote Himalayan valleys who have been influenced by Tibetan culture. The title character Gesār, or as the people of northern Nepal call him, the "Little Man of Tibet," is a legendary king who brought both the tribal chiefs and supernatural beings under his rule in ancient times. The epic is performed by *sgrungpā* (minstrels) who sing the epic in verses of two long lines and occasionally recite prose in interludes between verses. The performance can last for several hours a day over a period of many weeks. Since the epic glorifies a mortal king, it is considered inappropriate for monks to perform it. However, both monks and common people can tell the heroic episodes of Gesār as folktales on any appropriate occasion or in any context.

The *Ḍāmphe ra Muralī* is a tragic epic sung only by the Gāine, a traditional minstrel caste from the hill region of Nepal, accompanied by the music of the *saraṅgī* (stringed instrument similar to the fiddle). Nominally a love story of two birds, *ḍāmphe* (*Lophophorus impejanus,* the national bird of Nepal) and *muralīcarī* (a bird that inhabits the bamboo groves of the plains), this epic symbolically narrates the love story of an adventurous mountain boy and a beautiful girl of the plain. The young ḍāmphe sees the muralīcarī in his dream and decides to marry her. Despite his parents' discouragement, he leaves the mountain in search of her. Finally, he reaches the plain and marries the muralīcarī and brings her back home. Unfortunately, the epic has a tragic end, as the ḍāmphe one day goes to a millet field in search of food and falls in a trap set by a mischievous old man. The Gāine enthrall their audience with their music, their picturesque descriptions of events and moods, and unparalleled similes and metaphors.

Another kind of folk epic, *bhārat* (also called *bhārau* or *bhārte,* as variations of the word *bhārat,* and *huḍkelī* after *huḍko,* or hourglass drum, the main musical instrument of the performance) is performed only by Huḍke, the musicians of the tailor caste of western Nepal. Huḍke may perform at festivals, where they are often hired by families for entertainment, or at religious fairs, where they usually perform on their own initiative as an act of cultural pride and entertainment. However, bhārat are not allowed to be performed on temple premises because these epics portray the characters of mortal kings and nobles, who are inferior to the deities.

While narrating the epic, the Huḍke performer plays the huḍko, dances, and mimes the episodes of the epic. He wears a special dress consisting of a white pleated skirt, a black waistcoat, and a white turban. Several bells hang on his shoulder, waist, and the straps of his huḍko, and to amuse the audience, he affixes yak or tiger tails as his own. As he dances to tell the story, the bells jingle, and his fur tail shakes. Between episodes he sings songs about the hero, especially on standard themes such as his physical appearance and dress. The performer is accompanied by two or four male assistants who accompany the song refrains with drums.

Among the epics accompaned by dance, *Soraṭhī* is the most popular and is performed with *mārunī* or *pāṅdure* dances in the eastern, central, and southern parts of Nepal. These dances amuse the audience through a variety of expressions. In mārunī dances, males dress like women and portray the attitude of youthful girls. In the simpler paṅdure dances, the male performers dance according to the narration of the epic. The *Soraṭhī* relates the legend of King Jaya Singh who could not have a child despite having fourteen wives. After begetting a daughter with his fifteenth wife, he is forced to abandon the child, only to meet her sixteen years later; not knowing her identity, he proposes marriage. Having all the while known who he was, at the wedding ceremony, the daughter asks how a man could dare to marry his own daughter. Shocked and dismayed, he arranges her marriage to his nephew Brijabhār.

The *Soraṭhī* is performed either in spring or autumn as a celebration of happy moments such as the welcoming of a family member returning home from a foreign country or marriage residence. The host family's courtyard is its stage, and the villagers and the relatives of the family are its audience. A gūrū directs the entire *Soraṭhī* performance, including the song and dance set to varieties of raga (expressive moods of music) and *tāla* (meter). A *pursuṅge* (male dancer) sings and dances with two or four mārunī, the male dancers dressed like women with bright colorful dresses. Generally, the roles of gūrū and pursuṅge are taken by the same person. Occasionally, a *ḍhantuwāre* (yogi) and a *lawarpānde* (clown) come on stage to amuse the audience with parodies and satires. The *garrābhāi* are the members of the chorus who accompany the artists with the *mādal* (barrel-shaped drum) and also serve to guard the stage from children and animals to ensure a smooth and undisturbed performance.

The *Ghāṭu* epic is named after the *ghāṭu rāga* (expressive mood of music), the principal rāga of the epic. The epic is performed among various ethnic groups of central Nepal, including the Bote, Darai, Dura, Gurung, Kumal, Magar, and Thakuri. Among the two types of *Ghāṭu, Baramāse* and *Satī, Baramāse Ghāṭu* can be sung any time of the year, whereas the *Satī Ghāṭu* should start on the *Śirpancamī,* the fifth day of the brighter moon in the month of Māgha (January–February) and should ideally conclude at the full moon of the month of Baiśākha (April–May).

The *Satī Ghāṭu* recounts the tragic saga of Queen Ambāvatī (ca. sixteenth century) who committed *satī* (self-immolation on the funeral pyre) after the martyrdom of her husband, Pasrāmu (Paraśurāma). For the performance, a platform stage is constructed and consecrated. The gūrū or *gūrūmā* (female guru) recites the epic, sprinkles water on the heads of two to eight well-dressed virgin girls (*ghāṭulī*), and invokes the gods and goddesses. The process is accompanied by the soft drumming of mādal, a barrel drum. All these actions put the girls in a semi-trance condition. Meanwhile, the gūrū or gūrūmā recites the stanzas of the epic while the ghāṭulī softly sway back and forth, repeating the stanzas. At the moment of the satī, the audience is typically overwhelmed by the tragedy and begins to cry. In addition to the tragic story, the *Ghāṭu* comprises a vast repository of knowledge regarding local history, geography, agricultural systems, food habits, and rituals and customs. People believe that the performance of the *Satī Ghāṭu* brings fecundity and prosperity not only to the ghāṭulī but also to their families and villages, and, hence, daughters are encouraged to participate in Ghāṭu before their menarche.

The heterogeneous nature of Nepali culture has engendered several epic traditions in Nepal. Other traditions not discussed here include, for example, the *Baḍkī Mār* of the Tharu and *Mani-Rimdu* of the Sherpa ethnic groups. The study of these traditions is just beginning, and future research will undoubtedly uncover new material and reshape existing classifications. This should lead to a richer, fuller understanding of the complexity of Nepali folk epics.

References

Bhattarai, Harihar P. 1984. *Folk ballads of Seti zone: A research report*. Paris: UNESCO.

———. 1985. Folklore studies in Nepal. *Himalayan Culture* 3(1): 10–14.

Gaborieau, Marc. 1977. Introduction. In *Himalayan folklore: Kumaon and west Nepal,* 2nd ed., ed. H. K. Kuloy, xi–xliv. Kathmandu: Ratna Pustak Bhandar.

Lienhard, Siegfried. 1992 [1974]. *Songs of Nepal: An anthology of Nevar folksongs and hymns*. Delhi: Motilal Banarsidass.

Oakley, E. S., and Tara Dutt Gairola. 1977 [1935]. *Himalayan folklore: Kumaon and West Nepal*. Kathmandu: Ratna Pustak Bhandar.

HARIHAR P. BHATTARAI

SEE ALSO
Dance; Gender and Folklore; Kesar

EPIC, SRI LANKA

Extended and imaginative narrative poems, which mythologize history and institutionalize aspects of culture by depicting heroic exploits from ages past, are ubiquitous in the literary and oral cultures of Sri Lanka. Sources of inspiration for poems of this genre may be Tamil Hindu, Sinhala Buddhist, or, as often, a combination of the two. They may be inspired by the experiences of a community's migration from India to Sri Lanka. In the epic village drama of *Sokari,* the heroine leads her family out of a troubled life in India and, after overcoming many obstacles, achieves a settled and peaceful existence in highland Lanka. Epics may also be inspired by idealizations of social roles (as in the Pali *Mahāvaṃsa*'s portrayal of Buddhist kingship, or the Tamil *Cilappatikāram*'s celebration of righteous and chaste motherhood), by eschatological hopes (as in the Sinhala *Anāgatavaṃsa*'s depiction of the ideal future age heralded by the arrival of the next Buddha *Maitrī,* or future Buddha), or by the need to create and identify sacred space (as in the many epic stories told about how various powerful gods came to inhabit local regions or pilgrimage shrines). They may be written elegantly as refined poems preserved in classical Tamil, Pali, or Sinhala; exist as popularized dramas enacted within village contexts; or simply be portions of petitionary prayers offered by priests praising the powers of deities on behalf of pilgrims. Two exemplary epics are discussed below.

Cilappatikāram

The South Indian Tamil epic *Cilappatikāram,* its sequel, the *Manimēkalai* (originally composed between 500 and 800 C.E.), and their more recent Sinhala recensions are central to the mythology of Pattini (literally "Wife"), a high goddess of great historical and cultural importance to both Sinhala Buddhist and Tamil Hindu communities for at least the past millennium. The epic story of Pattini is, without doubt, one of the best-known epics told throughout Sri Lanka. The goddess Pattini's incorporation into the Sinhala Buddhist pantheon of deities by the early fifteenth century C.E., and her eventual identity as one of the four national guardian deities of the late medieval Kandyan kingdom, signal not only inclusive religiosity or syncretism, but also the manner in which Tamil culture in general has been assimilated and transformed by the Sinhalese. In the Sinhala epic cycles, Pattini is first presented as offering alms to previous Buddhas in order to gain merit, and even aspires to attain Buddhahood herself. While Pattini is meditating on a mountaintop in quest of her enlightenment, Sakra, the Buddhist king of the gods, implores her to be reborn on earth to end a famine in the kingdom of Soḷī and to bring to justice the evil king of Pāṇḍi, who is attempting to become a virtual god on earth and who, like the great Hindu god Śiva, possesses the magical power of a third eye. Pattini agrees to Sakra's request to make things right in the world of suffering human beings and is soon miraculously conceived within a golden mango in the orchard of the evil Pāṇḍi king. Since no one can bring down the mango from the tree, Sakra, in his disguise as an old man, shoots an arrow, and the juice from the pierced mango sprays into the king's third eye, burns it, and renders him partially blind. Aghast and enraged, the evil king places the mango into a golden casket, which floats downriver only to be discovered by two merchants, one of whom takes it home.

In seven days beautiful Pattini emerges from the mango, grows up, and marries Pālanga, a son of the other merchant. But Pālanga is unfaithful to Pattini and squanders his extensive inheritance on a courtesan. Destitute, he returns to a forgiving Pattini, who gives him her gem-studded anklet for safekeeping before they both set off to Madurai, the capital of the evil Pāṇḍi king, to seek their fortunes.

Pālanga goes into the city alone and is betrayed by a goldsmith to whom he has attempted to sell the anklet. The goldsmith tells the king that Pālanga is a thief who has stolen his queen's anklet. Pālanga is tortured and executed. Pattini learns of this tragedy, and her sonorous lament forms one of the finest moments in all of Sinhala poetry. In her burning anger, she then approaches the evil Pāṇḍi king, dramatically tears off her left breast in a fit of rage, and fires it directly at the astonished king. Flames from her torn-off breast immediately consume the king, and eventually the entire city is ablaze and destroyed. Justice is rendered, a new order begins, and by her miraculous power, Pattini resurrects Pālanga and restores him to new life.

The *Manimēkalai,* the sequel to the *Cilappatikāram,* is certainly not as well known in Sri Lanka. However, it contains religious and folkloric elements of considerable relevance to the Buddhists of Sri Lanka. For instance, Pattini's daughter becomes a *bhikṣunī* (Buddhist nun), and it is clear that the author of the text views Pattini as being Buddhist even before her deification as a goddess. As a Buddhist deity, she aspires to be born in the dispensation of the future Buddha *Maitreya*. Thus, the *Manimēkalai* seems to indicate that Pattini was regarded as a goddess of importance for the heterodox (non-Hindu) religious traditions of South India.

The epic story of Pattini is told, and often dramatically enacted, in many rural villages at the time of the Sinhala and Tamil New Year in April. While the contemporary cult of Pattini remains quite complex, younger women, especially those who desire the birth of children, propitiate her at innumerable village shrines where she is celebrated as wife, virgin, and mother, and a symbol of purity, moral righteousness, forbearance, auspiciousness, renewal, and fertility. Pattini's epic story, in short, is a mythic and symbolic expression of traditional feminine power.

Mahāvaṃsa

A second epic of great paradigmatic importance in Sri Lanka, one associated with the valor of a long line of Sinhalese Buddhist kings responsible for maintaining the legacy of Lanka as the *dhammadīpa* ("island of dhamma" [Buddhist doctrine of truth]), is the monastic chronicle *Mahāvaṃsa,* first compiled in the fifth century C.E. monastic culture of Buddhist Anuradhapura but periodically updated into the eighteenth century. The *Mahāvaṃsa* begins with an account of three visits to Lanka made by the Buddha, in which he conquers and expels the *yakkha*s (demonized aboriginal inhabitants of the island who symbolize forces of chaos and malevolence) and thus renders Lanka fit for the establishment and preservation of his dhamma (doctrine). The epic then describes how the prototypical Sinhalese, led by their first king, Vijaya, a kinsman of the Buddha, arrive on the island just at the moment of the Buddha's earthly demise. Like the Buddha, they bring the island under control by defeating the yakkhas in preparation for the eventual coming of institutionalized Buddhism. This event finally occurs when the son (Mahinda) and daughter (Saṅghamitta) of the great Indian emperor Aśoka arrive from India and convert the populace, including King Devanāmpiya Tissa, to the Buddhist religion, thereby establishing the dhamma and *saṅgha* (monasticism) on the island.

The *Mahāvaṃsa* is chiefly concerned with describing the manner in which subsequent kings valorized and patronized the religion throughout the ages by maintaining civilized order, building monumental stūpa (reliquaries memorializing the Buddha), and supporting the saṅgha materially. The most celebrated of these kings, the great warrior Duṭṭhagāmaṇī (101–77 B.C.E.), is the subject of eleven of the original thirty-seven chapters comprising the *Mahāvaṃsa*. These chapters constitute one of the most important epics in Sinhala Buddhist culture, articulating a religiopolitical identity that continues to dominate much of Sinhala Buddhist political discourse even today. Duṭṭhagāmaṇī's epic begins at the point of his death in a previous life where, as a *bhikkhu* (monk) on the verge of attaining *arahant*ship (*nibbāṇa*/nirvana—transcendance of the cycle of earthly rebirth), he chooses to eschew this personal destiny in order to be reborn as the son of a previously barren queen who will reestablish Lanka as a domain fit for the preservation of the pure dhamma. His father, the king, asks Duṭṭhāgamaṇī never to fight the Tamils, who have by now invaded the island and taken over the capital city of Anuradhapura. Enraged (*duṭṭha*), the young prince assumes a fetal position, and analogizing himself to the island of Lanka, declares: "Over beyond the Ganga are the Damilas, here on this side is the Gotha-ocean, how can I lie with outstretched limbs?" (*Mahāvaṃsa* 22:86). Gāmaṇī places himself in exile in the remote southern reaches of the island until he is no longer able to contain his rage to displace the Tamil "usurpers" (analogues to the demonized yakkha, previously expelled or controlled by the Buddha and Vijaya).

Upon his father's demise, he defeats his brother in a battle for the Sinhala throne and commences a campaign in which he defeats some thirty-two Tamil rulers throughout the island. In an epic struggle he disposes of the great Anuradhapura Tamil king of forty-four years, Eḷāra, aided by warrior monks and by his own spear, upon which is mounted a relic of the Buddha. The *Mahāvaṃsa* thus celebrates Duṭṭhāgamaṇī for uniting Lanka "under one parasol of state" and praises his efforts made during the remainder of his long kingship to build massive stūpa reliquaries in honor of the Buddha and monastic complexes for the saṅgha. His story thus legitimates the practice of state warfare in defense of the religion. Indeed, his kingship illustrates the principle that the power of the Lankan state exists for the benefit of the Buddhist religion, a principle not lost upon contemporary Sinhala Buddhist politicians since independence.

References

Danielou, Alain. 1989, and T. V. Gopala Iyer, trans. 1989 *Manimekalai: The dancer with the magic bowl*. New York: New Directions.

Geiger, Wilhelm, trans. 1934. *Mahāvaṃsa or The great chronicle of Ceylon*. London: Pali Text Society.

Godakumbura, C. E. 1955. *Sinhalese literature*. Colombo, Sri Lanka: Colombo Apothecaries Co.

Obeyeskere, Gananath. 1984. *The cult of the goddess Pattini*. Chicago: University of Chicago Press.

Parthasarathy, R., trans. 1993. *The Cilappatikaram of Ilanko Atikal: An epic of South India*. New York: Columbia University Press.

Zvelebil, Kamil. 1975. *Tamil literature*. Leiden: E. J. Brill.

JOHN CLIFFORD HOLT

SEE ALSO

Buddhism and Buddhist Folklore; Epic; Fairs and Festivals; Gods and Goddesses; Heroes and Heroines; Hinduism; Lament; Life Cycle Rituals; Pattini; Shrines, Hindu; *Sokari;* Stūpa; Syncretism; Tamil Nadu

EPIC, TRIBAL, CENTRAL INDIA

Most central Indian tribes have their own epic narratives. The most commonly accepted terms for these are *purjā* (genealogical myth) and *gīt* (song). Singers go by different names in the various castes. Among the Goṇḍ tribes, the two major professional bardic groups are called *parghaniā*s and *padhān*s. The songs of Goṇḍ heroes are collectively distinguished as *Goṇḍvāni* epics, which include the stories of *Rājā Peimal Shāh, Rājā Hirde Shāh, Hirākhān Chatri, Rājā Lohāguṇḍi,* and *Cittalsingh Chatri*. The Goṇḍ also sing versions of the *Mahābhārata* and *Rāmāyaṇa,* locally called the *Pāṇḍavāni* and the *Rāmāyaṇi,* respectively. Among the Kondh tribes of southwestern Orissa, professional bards are called *marāl*s, *boguā*s, and *ghogiā*s. They sing both mythological epics, such as the *Govāutrā,* and secular, historical epics, such as the *Nāngmati Rājā Phulia* and the *Mārdava Rājā*. The Banjārā tribes also have a clan of bardic specialists, known as *bhāt*s, who sing narratives of the Banjārā heroes, *Lakhā Banjārā, Sirārām Nāik, Mithu Bhukhiā, Merrāmmā, Sobhānāik Banjārā,* and others.

Smaller tribes such as the Kamārs, the Bhunjiās, and the Agriās lack professional specialists, but there are experienced members of those tribes who sing their tribe's epics. The *Baḍdevtār,* for example, is a sacred narrative song concerning the ethnic origin of the Kamārs, and the *Gāndhu Pāradhiya,* the *Kokobhaini,* and the *Luhāgadiā Rājā* are secular historical epics. The Bhunjiās have similar historical epic songs on *Kholāgadiā Rājā* and *Kachrādhuruā*. Many tribes also have female epic singers, called *gurumāi,* who recite the myths of clan gods and goddesses. The gurumāi are unmarried elders, symbolically married to their village or clan god. In addition, within the tribal areas of central India, there are Hindu bardic castes who perform variants of such pan-regional epics as the *Candainī* (*Lorik-Candā*), the *Ḍholāmārū,* and the *Bānsgīt*.

Typically, bards form a subsection of the main tribe. It is their responsibility to maintain the tribal history and genealogy (*purjā*). The dominant section of the tribe, those who exercise land ownership and political power and who occupy the highest position in the religious hierarchy, may have a particular family of epic singers assigned to them. In more complexly structured tribes, each clan of a tribe may have its own clan bard. Bards attend all socioreligious ceremonies in their patrons' house, where they perform certain clan rituals as well as sing. The bard has certain customs and rules that must be observed so that the validation of the ritual can be maintained. The whole community meets the expenses of the singer, and all the members of the community, irrespective of age and gender, assemble at a common place in the first hours of the night and listen to their glorious history and the supernatural actions of their gods, goddesses, first progenitors, and cultural heroes.

Epic songs are sung in the tribe's own language and represent a distinct ethnic culture. The content of the epic songs concerns the origin of the earth, the birth of the group's supreme God, the birth of the first progenitor, the division of clans, and the procreation of succeeding generations. Most of the epic songs depict themes of love, war, victory, gaining or regaining of kingdom, or supremacy over other tribes. The stories tell of their struggle with other communities, their migration and settlement in certain regions, and the achievement of political and administrative power by their cultural heroes. The distinctive occupations and customs of the tribe are usually chartered in their epics.

Both purjā and gīt are thought of as cycles (*khenā*) and represent episodes within the tribe's larger epic tradition. Each episode is named according to the names of a hero and a heroine popular in the tribe's epic tradition. Generally there are two cycles, five cycles, or twelve cycles in the epic tradition of a particular tribal community. The songs within a tribe's epic tradition may be divided according to content and performance context as either sacred or secular. Both sacred and secular epic songs are believed to be true. Mythical songs form a part of the ritual, whereas secular songs are believed to be factual accounts of legendary heroes. Both secular and sacred epics have the social function of validating the tribe's beliefs and revitalizing its identity.

The singers use musical instruments while singing the narratives. Each tribe has its own musical instrument that represent a symbol (*bānā*) of its ethnic identity. The musical instrument is considered sacred, and it is believed that the clan god is represented in it. These instruments are each confined to a specific tribal group and the tribe uses only its own musical instrument to accompany epic recitation: the fiddle (*kikri*) for the Goṇḍs, a drum (*māndal*) for the Binjhāls, a single-stringed instrument (*ḍhunḍhuniā*) for the Kondhs, the sacred harp (*brahmavīṇa*) for the Devguniā, and *ḍambaru* for the Birthiā.

MAHENDRA KUMAR MISHRA

SEE ALSO

Candainī; Caste Myths of Andhra Pradesh; *Ḍholā;* Myth; Mythology, Hindu; Tribal Folklore, Central India; Tribal Music, Nilgiris; Tribalism and Tribal Identity: The Bhils of Western Central India

EXORCISM

Exorcism rituals, usually classified as indigenous healing rituals, are widespread all over South Asia. When a person gets ill, or a family is afflicted by severe problems, the causes for this crisis must first be identified. An acute individual crisis, such as sudden high fever, vomiting, fainting, or strange behavior, may indicate an illness that needs medical treatment. Problems such as childlessness, death of children, or loss of wealth may be attributed to an inauspicious planetary period. However, both kinds of problems may also be seen as the result of sorcery, or as the effect of an attacking malevolent ghost or demon. Further actions depend on the initial diagnosis.

If it is agreed upon that some supernatural being belonging to the category *bhūta* (malevolent spirits) or *prēta* (ghosts of the dead) is involved in the crisis, the affected persons still have several options, depending

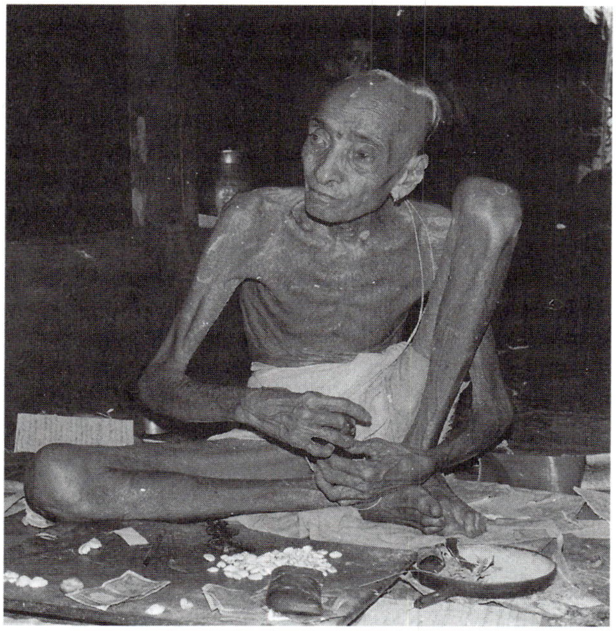

A famous exorcist reads cowrie shells to ascertain the problem and provide solutions. The exorcist appears thin because he severely limits his foods intake to enhance his spiritual powers. Karnataka, India. © Mimi Nichter

on exactly which being is producing the harmful effects. Exorcism and worship are two diametrically opposed methods for coping with ghosts or demons. If the possessing entity turns out to be the spirit of a deceased family member, it may have been demanding proper worship. Deceased family members, such as small children or young adults, have the ability to protect or harm their relatives. If they feel neglected, they may cause harm in order to draw their family's attention to their demands for the status of deified beings. As deified beings, they live in the realm of tutelary divine beings only if worshiped regularly. They are of ambivalent character and may harm their relatives if neglected.

If the entity is identified as a demon, or as a malevolent ghost who may have been manipulated by other people to do harm, efforts will be made to induce it to leave. The victim might be taken to a temple or shrine, where the presence of powerful deities or saints frightens the spirits so that they will leave their victim. Usually, however, an exorcist is called. With the power of his personal deity or with powerful mantras (verbal formulas) or *yantra*s (amulets), he might persuade them to leave. Less frequently, the possessing spirit might be forced out by measures such as inflicting pain or creating unpleasantness through burning shoes or pig's excreta. These are all minor forms of exorcism, performed as an immediate remedy in the acute stage of spirit possession. It is hoped that they will prove successful, but they frequently turn out to be insufficient or merely temporary.

If a minor exorcistic ritual turns out to be insufficient, other more elaborate and more expensive exorcism rituals have to be carried out. The most elaborate ones are the nightlong celebrations in Sri Lanka to demons such as Mahasōnā, the great demon of the cemetery. In this performance, a priest (*kapurāla*) and the victim get possessed by their respective divine and demonic entities, who continue to fight against each other until, eventually, the more powerful deity is able to defeat and drive away the demon. An exorcism of Mahasōnā is not only a healing ritual for a sick person, it is also a ritual for the benefit of all household members. The process of diagnosis and the arrangement of a major exorcism implies a great deal of preparation and involves many family members. It is an opportunity for the relatives of the victim to express and resolve social problems and various kinds of disputes among family members. Besides being a ritual of healing and of reordering social relationships, every exorcism ritual reestablishes the cosmic hierarchy. Ghosts and demons are able to interfere in a person's life only if there is an imbalance, be it social, psychic, or somatic. Once identified, spirits demand worship and attention to their status. In the subsequent ritual, deities and spirits confront each other, and the spirits are either put in their place and exorcised, or their demands are accepted and they are deified. In either case, they are exorcised.

Spirit possession and exorcism have often been explained in terms of sociological and psychological arguments. Both approaches result in an interpretation of exorcism as a forum for the oppressed to present their claims in public or to point publicly to unbearable psychic problems, and thus be able to control their environment more effectively. Society must react, since ghosts and demons are a danger not only for the individual but for the whole social group. As Kapferer (1983) rightly argues, spirit possession and subsequent exorcism rituals cannot be seen merely as a strategy on the part of the individual to get attention and emotional support, for they also bring into focus social, economic, and political problems affecting a victim and others. However, an exorcism also has to be seen as a ritual of transformation in which aesthetic forms, such as music, song, dance, and comedy, are capable of bringing patients and their relatives back into a normal conception of the world.

References

Blackburn, Stuart. 1985. Death and deification: Folk cults in Hinduism. *History of Religions* 24: 255–274.

Freed, S. A., and R. S. Freed. 1964. Spirit possession as illness in a North Indian village. *Ethnology* 3: 152–171.

Fuller, C. J. 1992. *The camphor flame: Popular Hinduism and society in India*. Princeton: Princeton University Press.

Kakar, Sudhir. 1983. *Shamans. Mystics and doctors: A psychological inquiry into India and its healing traditions*. Boston: Beacon Press.

Kapferer, Bruce. 1983. *A celebration of demons. exorcism and the aesthetics of healing in Sri Lanka*. Bloomington: Indiana University Press.

Obeyesekere, Gananath, 1977. Psychocultural exegesis of a case of spirit possession in Sri Lanka. In *Case studies in spirit possession*, ed. V. Crapanzano and V. Garrison, 235–295. New York: Wiley.

ELISABETH SCHOEMBUCHER

SEE ALSO

Ancestor Worship; *Baiṭhak; Bhūta;* Buddhism, Sri Lanka; Catholicism, Sri Lanka; Divination; Siri; Spirit Possession and Mediumship; Tibet

F

FAIENCE

Various glassy or vitreous siliceous pastes and glazed terra-cottas, commonly referred to by archaeologists as "faience," are the earliest form of glazed materials to be produced in prehistory and continue to be used in South Asia to produce containers, beads, bangles, and glazed tiles. Blue-green or deep blue glazed faience ornaments, primarily beads, pendants, and bangles, are well known from the Indus Valley civilization (2600–1900 B.C.E.), but they were first produced in the preceding Early Harappan period (3300–2600 B.C.E.) and continued to be produced during the Late Harappan (1900–1300 B.C.E.) and Painted Grey Ware periods (1200–800 B.C.E.).

In order to produce bangles, the artisans of the Indus cities developed a special high-strength compact faience (vitreous paste) by carefully grinding and refiring a colored frit (semi-vitrified quartz). The glazing was accomplished by including a flux in the paste so that after firing, the exterior was covered with a glassy surface and the interior was also strongly fused. The Indus faience bangles were colored with blue, blue-green, and white and decorated with multiple chevron designs. The white bangles were made to imitate shell bangles and had only a single chevron design. Faience beads, pendants, and gaming pieces were made with a larger range of colors, including blue, blue-green, azure, white, yellow, reddish-brown, brown, and black.

During the later periods, and even up to the present in Afghanistan, northern India, and Pakistan, a variation of faience technology has been used to produce beads, tiles, and vessels painted with blue and blue-green designs. In Herat and around Kabul in Afghanistan, glazed frit beads and pendants are still made using ancient techniques.

Glazed terra-cotta tiles and ceramic vessels are generally made with a terra-cotta body coated with a glaze made of crushed frit or glass and colored with various minerals to make a limited range of colors: blue, blue-green, azure, brown, yellow, and black. The tiles and ceramic vessels are first fired (bisqued) and then coated with glazes using two different techniques. In one process, a colored glaze is applied; in a second, mineral pigments are painted on the surface of the bisqued vessel or tile, and these are then coated with a clear glaze. Throughout the subcontinent, glazed tiles are used primarily in Muslim architecture, but they are also used in Hindu and Sikh architecture.

References

Kenoyer, J. Mark. 1994. Faience from the Indus Valley civilization. *Ornament* 17(3): 36–39, 95.

McCarthy, Blythe, and Pamela B. Vandiver. 1990. Ancient high-strength ceramics: Fritted faience bangle manufacture at Harappa (Pakistan), ca. 2300–1800 B.C. In *Materials issues in art and archaeology,* ed. P. B. Vandiver, J. Druzik, and G. S. Wheeler, vol. 2, 495–510. Pittsburgh: Materials Research Society.

Rye, Owen S., and Clifford Evans. 1976. *Traditional pottery techniques of Pakistan. Smithsonian contributions to anthropology,* No. 21. Washington, D.C.: Smithsonian Institution.

JONATHAN MARK KENOYER

SEE ALSO

Bangles; Beads; Glass; Pottery

FAIRS AND FESTIVALS

Fairs and festivals are enormously popular forms of celebration on the South Asian landscape. A festival (*utsava*) is usually a series of rituals and other activities commemorating a mythical event associated with a sacred figure or deity, and often occurring at significant seasonal or astronomical conjunctions. The festival is usually centered on a pilgrimage center, a temple, or a home. A fair (*mēla,* literally, "an assembly") is commonly a villagewide or intervillage (regional) celebration of important chronological or mythological moments, characterized by open bazaars, carnivals, cultural events, and other forms of entertainment. There are also a number of other terms in South Asian languages (Kannada, *jātra;* Telugu, *jātre;* Tamil, *viḻā*) used to designate types of religious celebrations which, while sometimes originally distinct or even unique in form, have gravitated to a more generalized cultural configuration. In contemporary practice it is difficult, therefore, to separate the two terms in the South Asian context. Both fairs and festivals often share common attributes: pilgrimage, various forms of play, milling crowds, and patronized performances of ritual, puppetry, oratory, music, pageantry, and dance.

Both fairs and festivals occur at specifically designated times, are centered around sacred spaces, and celebrate rhythms of divine and cosmic process and of seasonal and human activity. Both festivals and fairs—but especially festivals—have come to weave together classically derived priestly rituals with the need of common people for renewal and relief from the rigors of everyday life, and with the agendas of patrons who negotiate political and social alliances.

Festivals often serve as historical pageants and cultural performances insofar as they represent elements drawn selectively from participants' regional, local, or national heritage. While many festivals have been reinstated and made more grandiose in recent decades, the festival tradition has archaic roots in South Asia, dating perhaps to the elaborate platform sacrifices of the Indus Valley civilization and certain of the *śrauta* (corporate) rituals of the late Vedic age, especially such complex rites as the *aśvamedha* (horse sacrifice). During the age of kingship, chieftain-kings often sought to legitimate their status by patronizing festivals, and they made their courts, their capital cities, and their temples the venues for their enactment. In recent years, more and more people have come to participate in festivals, both in the public sphere and within their own homes. In villages and towns, residents from all walks of life celebrate festivals in varied ways, while patrons negotiate for the privilege of sponsorship in the temple or shrine whose presiding deity or saint is honored.

The Hindu festival calendar is determined by the conjunction of seasons, lunar cycles, the cycles of constellations, and the solar year. Generally speaking, the slowest season for festivals is the period falling between the summer solstice and the fall equinox. This is the time of the southwest monsoon and a season appropriate for rituals of protection and fasting. The former includes, in some rural settings of central India, the ritual protection of cattle at *harioli* (the new moon of July-August), and the propitiation of snakes (*nāga pacami,* in July-August). According to Lawrence Babb, for example, occasions for fasts may include those for the protection of children (e.g., *Bahuia Chauth* in August-September), and the feasting in honor of Pārvatī for the long life of one's husband (e.g., *Tija* in August-September).

Festival activity accelerates across the subcontinent as the fall equinox approaches and the southwest monsoon abates. *Gaṇeśa Chaturthi* (the "birthday" of Gaṇeśa) is celebrated for ten days in the latter part of August-September. This is observed most elaborately in Maharashtra, where Gaṇeśa is especially popular and where the festival was given a political character in the 1890s by B. G. Tilak (1856–1920). *Nāvarātra,* the "nine nights" of celebration in honor of the goddesses, is commemorated in September-October with special pomp in Gujarat, Bengal (where it is called *Durgapūjā*), and South India. Nāvarātra's last day dovetails with *Dāsara,* a celebration of Rāma's defeat of the demon Rāvaṇa, commonly reenacted in the pageant known as *Rām līla*. *Dīvālī* (*or Dīpāvālī*), the festival of lights, falls at the new moon of October-November. Dīvālī marks the "ritual midnight" of the year and serves as the beginning of the new year in some regions, especially Gujarat. It is accompanied by the worship of Lakṣmī, goddess of wealth, and merchants generally start a new fiscal year and venerate their account books at this time. Visiting ancestors are returned to their ancestral abode (*pitṛlōka*) with the accompaniment of lights and firecrackers.

The "light half" of the year begins with the month following the winter solstice. In Tamil Nadu, for example, *Ponkal* marks the official start of the "light half" of the year, falling on the day the sun enters the new zodiacal sign. It also celebrates the recent harvest. In the same region, *Tai Pūcam* falls on or near the full moon of January-February. The festival serves to commemorate the newly waxing solar year and coincides with a break in the agricultural cycle. It celebrates the power of such deities as Skanda to dispel the malevolent forces of the cosmos. Across the subcontinent, *Mahāśivarātri,* a fast day in honor of Śiva, is celebrated at the new moon of February-March. The major event of this month in North India, however, is *Holī*. Wood is collected for up to a month to build a bonfire in which the demoness Holika is symbolically burned. Holī is a pre-New Year form of catharsis when normal patterns of life are abrogated: colored water and mud are thrown on participants; lewdness is permitted; women can be aggressive toward men; social roles are reversed; meat can be eaten and *bhang* (hashish mixed with milk and yogurt) can be consumed. This time of relative "pollution," during which the plays (*līlās*) of Kṛṣṇa are reenacted, concludes with bathing, the purchase of new clothes, and preparation for New Year celebrations.

The New Year, for most of the subcontinent, starts with the month following the spring equinox. In rural areas of North India, this also starts the spring Nāvarātra, the worship of several goddesses for nine nights. The last day of this Nāvarātra is also the occasion of *Rāmnāvami* (Rām's ninth), celebrated as the "birthday" of Rāma, especially in Hindi-speaking areas. This also coincides, in central India, with the rural festival of *Javara,* in which the ritual planting of wheat occurs and seedlings are offered to the goddess. The goddess occasionally "possesses" dancers. Goats are sacrificed and ritual self-flagellation also sometimes occurs.

From March to May is a period deemed auspicious for marriage, especially in South India. Many Śaiva temples in South India hold a *Paṇkuṉi Uttiram* festival (a ritual reenactment of the marriage of god and goddess) at the full moon of April-May. In Madurai, Tamil Nadu, this festival, now known as the *Cittarai* festival, celebrates the marriage of Śiva and Mīnakṣi. In the seventeenth century, it was moved by the Nayakka kings to a date one month later (April-May). The festival in Madurai now culminates the New Year celebrations and coincides with the celebration of certain of Viṣṇu's exploits in a festival centered in the nearby temple of Āḻakār (the "handsome one").

During the month of April-May, as the weather becomes hotter, the beginnings of the agricultural year are celebrated in rural areas. In central India, for example, during the festival of *Akshaya Tritiya,* soil is symbolically broken and seed and manure are placed in fields. The new moon of May-June then marks *Savitrī Pūjā,* which is especially celebrated by women, who honor Savitrī as the ideal wife and mother and the epitome of self-sacrifice and benevolence. One of the major festival events of June-July, as the rainy season is beginning in Northeast India, is the *rathyātra* (chariot trip) of Kṛṣṇa in the form of Jagannāth. In his temple in Orissa, the festival represents Kṛṣṇa's journey to Mathura to kill the wicked demon Kamsa. The day following this festival (on the eleventh of June-July), Viṣṇu is said to go to sleep, thus representing the return of the southwest monsoon and the reduced festival season.

For Buddhists on the Indian subcontinent, the festival year is by no means as elaborate. The single most important festival occasion falls at the full moon of May-June, when the major events of Buddha's life—his birth, enlightenment, and death—are commemorated. In Tibetan Buddhist settlements, however, there are remnants of a Tibetan festival cycle in which a sense of a national politicoreligious order was symbolically enacted in monastic communities. In this cycle, the first month of the lunar new year (the one falling after the spring equinox) came to commemorate the fortnight when Buddha was believed to have performed triumphal miracles at Sravasti. Founded in 1409 by Tson-ka-pa, this festival historically included the crowning of the Buddha, Sakyamuni, by the king. The festival includes a national theater performance, masquerade dances in national dress, and butter-sculpting contests. Celebrations congruent with this historical pageantry are still to be found in Himalayan Buddhist communities of Ladakh and Nepal.

Islamic Festivals

There are two major festive days celebrated by most Muslims throughout South Asia. The first is the ᶜ*Īd al-Aẓḥa* (the feast of sacrifice). This occurs on the tenth day of Dhū al-Hijjah, the month of the hajj, or pilgrimage. After the event known as *jamrat* (stoning of pillars) that occurs on the pilgrimage, pilgrims and many Muslims in solidarity with them, commemorate Ibrahim's act of sacrificing a ram rather than his son Isma'īl. On this occasion, an unblemished sheep or goat is sacrificed *ḥalal* (i.e., with its face toward the *Kaaba* and with the incantation, "In the name of Allah"). This becomes an opportunity for remembering the goodness and mercy of Allah and human dominion over animals. The flesh of the sacrificed animal is distributed to the poor as well as to friends.

The other festive day is *'Īd al fiṭr,* the feast that ends the fasting month of Ramaḍān. During Ramaḍān, Muslims observe the fast (*ṣawm*) and abstinence (*imsāk*) from dawn to dusk each day. When the new month begins, families gather, sometimes in larger community settings, to celebrate in the sharing of foods that represent their ethnic and cultural heritage.

An important event for Shiite Muslims is ᶜĀshūrā, the tenth day of Muḥarram, the first month of the Islamic calendar. The day commemorates the martyrdom of Ḥusayn at Karbala in 680 C.E., as well as the deaths of other martyrs and saints. This fast day, which may have originally been grafted onto the Jewish Yom Kippur, is characterized by commemorative services at which the tragedies of Karbala are recounted. The day has grown in importance for Shīᶜas throughout history. By the tenth century C.E., under the Abbasids, commemorations were encouraged and led by professional mourners. In 962 C.E. a day of public mourning was declared in Baghdad and processions held. With the rise of the Safavid dynasty in Iran in the sixteenth century C.E., more impetus came for its celebration, including the development of the passion play (*ta'ziya*). Often today, ᶜAshūrā is marked by public displays of self-flagellation and mourning.

Finally, a number of Muslims continue to observe the birthdays of Muḥammad and of saints, known as *pīrs*. These occasions may be marked by a feast (*ᶜid*), by visits to the local *dargāh* (tomb-shrine), and/or by processions and services of prayer and remembrance.

References

Babb, Lawrence A. 1975. *The divine hierarchy. Popular Hinduism in central India*. New York: Columbia University Press.

Clothey, Fred W. 1982. *Rhythm and intent: Ritual studies from South India*. Madras: Blackie and Son.

Hanchett, Suzanne. 1988. *Coloured rice. Symbolic structure in Hindu family festivals*. Delhi: Hindustan Publishing Corp.

Harmon, William. 1989. *The sacred marriage of a Hindu goddess*. Bloomington: Indiana University Press.

Oster, Akos. 1980. *The play of the gods: Locality. ideology. structure and time in the festivals of a Bengali town*. Chicago: University of Chicago Press.

Thurman, Robert A. F. "Buddhist cultic life in Tibet." In *Encyclopedia of Religion,* ed. M. Eliade, vol. 15, 473–474. New York: Macmillan, 1987.

Welbon, Guy R., and Glenn Yocum. 1982. *Religious festivals in South India and Sri Lanka*. Delhi: Manohar.

FRED W. CLOTHEY

SEE ALSO

Bhūta Kōla; Dāsara; Dīvālī/Dīpāvalī; Festival of St. Francis; Holī; Jātrā/Yātrā; Kōla; Maharashtra; Maulid; Melā; Muḥarram; Nāvarātri; Ōṇam; Poṅkal; Rām Līlā; Ratha Jātrā; Sikh Folklore; Tījaji; Tij Songs; *Tiruvātira; Tūkka; ᶜUrs*

FATE, HINDU

Fate is an intensely ambiguous concept in Hindu mythology. Since the most common word for fate in Sanskrit, *daivam*, also means "pertaining to the gods" (*devas*), the statement "It happened because of *daiva*" can mean either "because of fate" or "because of the gods," two very different explanations for something that has no obvious material cause. Indeed, although the god Brahmā is often implicated in fate by the belief that he writes each child's fate on his forehead at birth, the *Purāṇas* often remark that even the gods have no power over fate (a point shared by Greek mythology). It is therefore hardly surprising that humans, too, often declare themselves powerless against fate. Yet both gods and humans often defy the decrees of fate, finding loophole clauses in the cosmic contract, often in the form of riddles.

Thus, the statement that a demon such as Namuci or Vṛtra or Hiraṇyakaśipu (the story is told of various demons) was fated never to be killed on land or sea, by day or by night, and so forth, is not so much contradicted as evaded by someone who kills the demon on the shore of the sea, at twilight, and so forth. So, too, human effort is often successfully employed against fate; thus, in the *Bhāgavata Purāṇa,* the wicked Kaṃsa defies the prophecy that he would be killed by a son of Devakī: "It is known that people like me can overcome fate, by the right combinations of spells and herbal medicines and constant effort." He is wrong, in this particular instance, but when Devakī's husband is about to hand over their son to Kaṃsa, Devakī harangues him and urges him to do something to counteract the fated prophecy. And she is right. A third invisible force overlaps with fate and the will of the gods: *karma,* the determining residue of one's good and evil deeds from a past life. But this, too, is often challenged by free will, the grace of a particular god, or even the casual and unjustified curse of a powerful sage or Brahman. Fate is therefore highly overdetermined, multivalent, and, in the end, unpredictable and incomprehensible.

References

Keyes, Charles, and Valentine Daniel, eds. 1983. *Karma: An anthropological inquiry*. Berkeley: University of California Press.

O'Flaherty, Wendy Doniger, ed. 1980. *Karma and rebirth in classical Indian traditions*. Berkeley: University of California Press.

WENDY DONIGER

SEE ALSO

Divination; Divination, Balochi; *Karma; Vrat Kathā*

FĀṬIMA

Fāṭima was the daughter of the Prophet Muḥammad and Khadijah, his first wife. Fāṭima was also the wife of the Prophet's cousin 'Alī ibn Abū Tālib, the first Shi'i Imām. Their two sons, Ḥasan and Ḥusayn, were the second and third Shi'i Imāms, and the only grandsons of the Prophet to reach adulthood. Thus, all *sayyids* (descendants of the Prophet) trace their descent from one of these two sons of Fāṭima. Known as Fāṭima Ẕahra (Fatimah the Shining), she is a focus of devotion among the South Asian Muslims, particularly the Shīᶜa, who refer to her as the sinless *sayyida* and consider her one of the fourteen *mas'umīn* (those protected from error)—a station she shares with Muḥammad and the twelve Imāms. She is an archetype of Muslim feminine piety—the perfect daughter of the Prophet, the perfect wife of 'Alī, and the perfect mother of Ḥasan and Ḥusayn. She is remembered for her generosity, which was so strong that she would occasionally give away all of the food in her household to the poor. She is also remembered for her courage in defending the rights of the family of the Prophet following the death of her father. Fāṭima, Muḥammad, ʻAlī, Ḥasan, and Ḥusayn are referred to in South Asia as the *Panjatan Pāk*—the Five Pure Ones. These five are represented by the *panja*—the five-fingered Fāṭimid hand on which each finger represents one member of the holy family. Fāṭima is the central element of this symbol—the person who links them all together. Because she is so deeply beloved by the Prophet and God, many Muslims believe that her intercession (*tufail*) is efficacious. Although especially important in Shīʻī piety, she is also venerated by Sunnis, particularly women. She is the focus of the most popular *muʻjizāt kahānī*s (miracle stories), which both Shiʻi and Sunni women read in the making of vows called *mannat*s.

References

Ayoub, Mahmoud. 1978. *Redemptive suffering in Islam*. The Hague: Mouton.
Hollister, John. 1953. *The Shiʿa of India*. London: Huzac.
Schubel, Vernon. 1993. *Religious performance in contemporary Islam: Shiʿi devotional rituals in South Asia*. Columbia: University of South Carolina Press.

VERNON JAMES SCHUBEL

SEE ALSO

ʻAlī; Gender and Folklore; Heroes and Heroines; Islam; Legend; Muslim Folklore and Folklife; *Panch Pīr;* Saints

FESTIVAL OF ST. FRANCIS

The festival of St. Francis Xavier is one of the few festivals in India that brings together Catholic and Hindu Goans in a celebration of their shared history and culture.

In the sixteenth century, Francisco de Jassu y de Xavier came to India from Spain to assist in establishing the Jesuit order in Goa, then under Portuguese colonial rule. His ten years of missionary efforts included conversions to Catholicism throughout India, China, and Japan. After his death in Malacca, on the western coast of Malaysia, on 3 December 1552, his body was shipped back to Goa and placed in St. Paul's Church, where a small, private viewing took place.

His body was first publicly exhibited in 1554 in Goa, where Dona Isabel de Carom began the popular practice of obtaining relics from the body: she bit off one of his small toes. Pope Gregory XV ordered the removal of St. Xavier's right arm after the saint's canonization in 1622.

To mark the significance of St. Francis's sainthood, the Goan Jesuits decided to hold a major festival, exposing his body for public veneration on the anniversary of his death. They placed the body in a silver casket and decorated the chapel holding it with a silver image of the saint and thirty-two pictures representing the "life and miracles of the Apostle." This continued until the end of the seventeenth century, when the Jesuits decided the risk of further damage to the fragile body was too great because of the steady increase in the number of visitors to his shrine. Private viewings of the saint's body were still allowed for important dignitaries visiting Goa, but only if special permission was granted by the Jesuit order.

The Archdiocese of Goa took control over the body of St. Francis Xavier after the Portuguese government suppressed the Jesuit Order in 1759. Consequently, the "Solemn Expositions of the Body of St. Francis Xavier" began with the body being exposed for a number of days, at irregular intervals, to mark such special occasions as the first arrival of pilgrims from the rest of India and Sri Lanka (1859); the anniversary of the canonization of St. Francis (1923); Goa's independence from Portugal (1961); and the International Eucharistic Congress held in Goa (1900) and Bombay (1965). Today, St. Francis Xavier's body lies in the Church of Bom Jesus in Panaji, the capital of Goa.

The festival of St. Francis Xavier continues to bring together annually not only Catholic and Hindu Goans but also returning Goans who live abroad and pilgrims from Europe, India, and other parts of Asia. For many Goans, the festival of St. Francis Xavier helps renew their cultural and historical ties, not only with one another but with a particular place. The larger expositions, held every ten years, bring in tourists from India and abroad who are eager to take part in the ritual display of St. Francis Xavier's body. During these festivities, Old Goa, in Panaji (Panjim), becomes a center for celebrating not only the life and miracles of the saint but also the unique culture of Goa.

References

da Fonseca, Jose. 1986 [1878]. *Sketch of the city of Goa*. New Delhi: Asian Educational Sevices.
Rayana, P., S.J. 1982. *St. Francis Xavier and his shrine*. Panjim: Imprimatur.

PAMILA GUPTA

SEE ALSO

Catholicism, Sri Lanka; Christianity, Kerala; Fairs and Festivals; Saints

FILM MUSIC

Film music, as a category, includes the music, song, and dance sequences accompanying commercial feature films. Because of its inherent and inextricable ties to the mass media, film music is better classified as commercial popular music than as folk music. At the same time, its influence upon and presence in folk culture is extensive and deep.

Film music started to emerge as a distinct musical genre with the advent of sound film in India in 1931. As in folk drama traditions and models like Parsi theater, actors alternated between speech and song, and soon almost all commercial films were musicals, in which five or six song and dance interludes would be inserted, whether structurally or gratuitously, into the plot. As the Indian film industry grew to be the largest in the world, film music became an increasingly pervasive feature of South Asian culture.

Until the mid-1940s, film songs were performed by singer-actors, like the renowned K. L. Saigal (1904–1946). Many songs consisted of *ghazal*s (simplified light-classical refrains) or stylized folk tunes. Film music acquired a more distinctive character after World War II, with the advent of "playback" singing, in which the actors would mouth songs separately recorded by professional singers. A syncretic mainstream film style soon emerged. On the one hand, this style retained traditional instruments like the *ḍholak* barrel drum, indigenous vocal ornamentation, and familiar rhythms and melodic modes. On the other hand, music directors combined these features with western instruments (especially violins), western concepts of orchestration, and chordal harmony. Rock and disco influence became increasingly strong from the 1980s. Meanwhile, by the late 1940s, film music had become thoroughly embedded in the glittery world of cinema culture, with its escapist fantasies, matinee idols, unabashedly commercial orientation, and its links to black money and corporate finance. Film songs are marketed separately as recordings, but many listeners prefer to hear them in their cinematic contexts.

Film music, like Indian cinema in general, has exhibited contradictory trends toward both homogeneity and diversity. Production has always been dominated by a handful of music directors and playback singers (such as Lata Mangeshkar and Asha Bhosle), and the industry has generally striven to create a common-denominator, relatively homogeneous style for an otherwise diverse mass audience. The growth of regional cinema has counterbalanced this trend to some extent, although regional film music styles, while drawing liberally from local folk genres, have also tended to imitate the mainstream Hindi style. For nearly half a century, film music marginalized all other kinds of commercial popular music, especially as marketed by GCI (Gramophone Company of India), which enjoyed a virtual monopoly of the recording industry in South Asia. The spread of cassettes from the mid-1970s decentralized the music industry and precipitated the flourishing of other forms of popular music, while also increasing sales of film music recordings.

Film music, a professional, studio-based art linked to cinema, is in many ways wholly distinct from folk music. Nevertheless, there is considerable mutual influence and interaction between the two genres. Many music directors have used folk song melodies as bases for film songs, whether in Hindi films or regional-language ones. Film influence on folk music is even more conspicuous. Folk musicians in innumerable genres resignify film tunes by setting new texts to them in local languages. Musicians also weave film songs, with their original texts, into various folk genres. Folklorists debate whether such practices represent creative atrophy or dynamic reappropriation. Equally controversial is the evidence that film music has contributed to the decline of numerous folk song genres throughout the subcontinent, at once broadening listeners' musical horizons while turning many into passive consumers, rather than creators, of music.

References

Manuel, Peter. 1988. South Asia. In *Popular musics of the non-western world: An introductory survey,* 171–197. New York: Oxford University Press.

Beats of the heart: There'll always be stars in the sky. The Indian film music phenomenon. 1992. Produced and directed by Jeremy Marre and Hannah Charleton. 60 min. Shanachie. Videotape.

PETER MANUEL

SEE ALSO

Brass Bands; Cassettes; *Mushā'ira; Qawwālī;* Song; Wedding Videos

FILM, VIDEO, AND TELEVISION VIEWING: NEPAL

Compared with India, whose electronic mass media industry dates to the early twentieth century and now is among the largest in the world, Nepal's experience with visual entertainment media is recent and limited. Although a few silent films may have been shown in public on occasion as early as 1901, and Nepal's Rana elites had their own private cinema halls from the 1930s, the country's first public hall opened only in 1950, just prior to the popular revolt that put an end to feudal rule. Following the political reorganization of 1951, a number of public cinema halls opened in the Kathmandu valley and in the Nepal Tarai (lowlands bordering north India). These halls screened mainly Hindi commercial films from India, with the occasional American or European film.

The 1950s saw the first Nepali language feature films. While often set in idyllic Nepali villages, these films followed many of the aesthetic and narrative conventions of the Bombay industry. In fact, many of the early Nepali films were made by Nepali speakers in India (for example, in Darjeeling). With a limited Nepali-speaking audience, and an even smaller number with access to cinema halls, Nepali-language film production remained very low, averaging one or two films per year from the 1960s through the 1980s.

In Nepal's capital, Kathmandu, people speak of the 1960s and 1970s as a "golden age" of filmgoing. During these decades, a visit to the cinema was a big event. Entire families would don their finest clothes. The cinema hall became a unique public setting in that the city's entire social spectrum—poor low-caste workers, students, merchants and civil servants, government officials, women and men, young and old—assembled in a shared ritual of mass consumption. While the audience on the main floor hooted and whistled at the action on screen, middle-class viewers seated above practiced a more sedate and restrained viewing aesthetic.

The "video boom," or the arrival of VCR technology, in Kathmandu soon put an end to this socially mixed cinema viewing. Following a brief but intense video boom in the late 1970s and early 1980s, when highly profitable "video parlors" sprouted like mushrooms, VCRs quickly became fairly common in middle-class homes around the city. Video parlors were soon replaced by video rental shops offering the latest Hindi releases as well as European, North American, and East Asian action films, martial arts pictures, and hard-core pornography (illegal but widely available). By the early 1990s, the city's middle-class viewers stayed at home to watch Hindi "social," "art," or "love-story" films, while the cinema halls offered low-cost, B-grade, Hindi *masalā* ("spice mixture," or formula) films to mostly poor, working-class young men. Even South Asian blockbusters had trouble filling local cinemas because, by the time these films reached Kathmandu, middle-class fans had already seen the films (often many times) on video at home. The few remaining video parlors are clandestine operations specializing in pornography for poor (often out-of-town) workers and schoolboys.

The one occasion when Kathmandu's cinematic audiences approximate their earlier social diversity is when screening Nepali-language films. Because Nepali filmmakers jealously guard their prints from video piracy, people have no choice but to pay for a cinema ticket, thereby allowing filmmakers to recoup their investments in a still very limited market. Even though most Nepali films are disparaged as poor copies of Indian commercial products, these vernacular films have an appeal that draws many middle-class viewers who would otherwise stay at home.

Nepali film production increased greatly following tax law changes in the late 1980s that made filmmaking more profitable. Indeed, Nepali films now often wait in long queues to be screened, competing with Hindi films that promise higher profit margins for hall owners. More films have meant higher demand for Nepali actors and actresses, but the market is still so limited that few film personnel are full-time professionals. In addition to low pay, actresses must contend with the social stigma associated with this highly public career. The growing film industry has also spawned a number of related enterprises, from Nepali film (fan) magazines to recording studios supporting professional musicians. A small number of Nepali film personnel have become successful in the Indian industry, either as dramatists, composers, or playback singers.

In Nepal, as in many other Third World nations, television broadcasting came only after VCR/TV technology was well established in urban areas. Televisions were first introduced simply as viewing appendages of VCRs, and people in Kathmandu still frequently refer to televisions as "screens." Nepal's King Birendra ordered a TV broadcasting feasibility study in 1980, but it was not until December of 1985 that Nepal Television (NTV) had its inaugural transmission. Partly in response to Indira Gandhi's push to expand Doordarshan's (Indian State Television) broadcast range prior to Indian national elections in 1983—which brought much of Nepal's Tarai within India's television reach—the Nepali government decided to go ahead with the project.

Although it was intended to promote a Nepali national consciousness, especially among Nepalis along the Indian border, NTV officials quickly discovered that producing a steady stream of nation-building, vernacular programming was both difficult and costly. With no private production houses and very little advertising revenue, with production hardware (donated by the Japanese government) in disrepair, with government funding cutbacks, and with the need to compete with Doordarshan for viewers, NTV was forced to turn to American and European media products which, hour for hour, cost a fraction of locally produced programming. Ironically, while vernacular programs are more popular with the mass of Nepali viewers, the few commercial enterprises able and willing to advertise on NTV typically prefer to sponsor Western programming, which attracts a smaller but more affluent audience of upper-middle-class consumers. NTV's experience is a classic example of how local and global market forces threaten to wrest control of the medium from its state masters by creating a context where, to remain economically viable, television—designed to foster the nation—ends up feeding its viewers an increasingly foreign diet.

Satellite television's arrival on the South Asian subcontinent in the early 1990s quickly began to transform media viewing patterns in Nepal. Whereas, even after the advent of Nepal TV, most urban Nepalis used their televisions mainly to watch videos, growing access to pan-Asian satellite broadcasts (from STAR TV) has meant a decline in demand for videocassettes. Between 1991 and 1996 the number of videocassette rental shops in central Kathmandu dropped by almost one half, while satellite dish antennas became common sights across the valley.

Media consumption patterns in Kathmandu often correspond to categories of class, gender, and age. While the cinema halls cater largely to young, urban, working-class males who favor Hindi mass-market releases, middle-class electronic media consumption is largely domestic and includes products from South Asia and beyond. For the most part, middle-class Hindi film viewers are women (both young and middle-aged) who watch video films at home. For women, Hindi videos in the afternoon are an important part of modern daily routines, often forming the focal point for small talk among women within an extended family or a neighborhood cluster.

Both men and women often use "realism" as the standard by which to judge a film's worth. Yet, ironically, while women use the term to separate good from bad Hindi films, middle-class men typically relegate all South Asian products to the "unrealistic" category and turn instead to East Asian, European, and American productions. Middle-class men and boys watch Hindi films at home, though they rarely express a preference for them. For many middle-class young men—be they part-time students, un- or under employed—watching videos and satellite TV is part of a daily routine. With time to kill, young men are avid consumers of "English" (generically non-South Asian) films and programs, from Taiwanese "kung-fu," to Japanese and European pornography, to American action/adventure films, "soaps," and MTV.

Frequently, males act as censors in the household, determining who can watch what. Women often complain that they would like to watch non-South Asian films but that they are forbidden to do so by a male (brother, husband, father). Because they are more likely to have sexually explicit content, women speak of feeling "uneasy" about viewing "English" films in mixed company. Yet for most women, this uneasy feeling comes less from embarrassment or shyness than from fear of being labeled loose or vulgar.

As Nepal moves into the twenty-first century, mass media consumption will likely continue to be an important domain in which class and gender identities are constructed and the boundaries between them policed and reproduced.

References

Baral, Dyuti. 1990. Television and children in Nepal: An assessment of viewing patterns. In *Occasional papers in sociology and anthropology,* ed. S. Mikesell, 67–76. Kathmandu: Tribhuvan University.

Khatri, Kem B. 1983. *Nepal's mass media.* Kathmandu: H. M. G. Ministry of Communication.

Liechty, Mark. 2002. *Class as cultural practice: Making middle-class culture in Kathmandu.* Princeton: Princeton University Press.

MARK LIECHTY

SEE ALSO

Gender and Folklore; Nationalism and Folklore; Wedding Videos

FIREWALKING, SRI LANKA

Firewalking is a ritual practice of Hindu and Buddhist devotees of deities, such as Pattini, Amman, Devol Deviyo, and Kataragama (Skanda), performed to fulfill vows and gain protection by walking over a bed of hot coals. While firewalking was earlier practiced almost exclusively by Tamil Hindus, since the mid-twentieth century the practice has been adopted by Sinhala Buddhists and incorporated into the annual festivals of many Sinhala shrines throughout the country.

In Tamil and Sinhala cosmologies, the element of fire is associated with anger and other unruly and powerful passions linked to the feminine. Among East Coast Sinhalas and Tamils, rituals are performed to cool down "hot" goddesses such as Pattini and Amman, whose anger causes fire, drought, and pestilence. During the annual festivals for these deities, humans avoid pollution, abstain from "heaty" foods, and partake of cooling foods, such as milk rice. At firewalking ceremonies, Tamil devotees smear their bodies with turmeric and carry margosa leaves, both cooling substances. Though most devotees emerge unscathed, some receive burns which are attributed to their lack of faith in the deity. On the East Coast, devotees say that the goddess lays down the end of her invisible sari to protect them from harm.

The prevalence of firewalking reflects social conditions. Among Tamils in the Batticaloa district, the number of those who walk the fire has increased dramatically since the occupation by Sri Lankan security forces in the mid-1980s. At one temple for the goddess

Pattirakāliyammaṇ in the early 1990s, more than 2000 devotees crossed the fire during the annual propitiation of the goddess, a dramatic increase over participation in the 1980s. Many of these firewalkers were young children, whose mothers promised the goddess they would walk the fire in exchange for protection; others were young males who made a vow while incarcerated in an army camp or prison.

It is believed that the first Sinhala Buddhist to walk the fire did so at the pilgrimage site of Kataragama in 1942. Early Sinhala firewalkers introduced Buddhist elements into the ritual, associating it with the Sinhala king, Duṭṭhāgamaṇī, and including the recitation of the three refuges and the chanting of protective verses (*pirit*). Contemporary Sinhalas walk the fire to prove their personal devotion to a god and to renew their powers to heal, prophesy, and banish evil influences. In recent years, firewalking and "fire-eating" have been put on display for tourists, performed as the climax of an evening of Sri Lankan drumming and dancing. Carrying lit torches, one or two firewalkers dance through the coals to powerful drum rhythms, throwing handfuls of resin to create large fireballs, which flash and disappear in the dimmed lights of a hall or the darkness of an outdoor courtyard.

References

Gombrich, Richard, and Gananath Obeyesekere. 1988. *Buddhism transformed: Religious change in Sri Lanka*, chs. 5 and 12. Princeton: Princeton University Press.

Lawrence, Patricia. 2000. Violence, suffering, Amman: The work of oracles in Sri Lanka's eastern zone. In *Violence and subjectivity*, ed. Veena Das, Arthur Kleinman, and Pamela Reynolds. Berkeley: University of California Press.

Obeyesekere, Gananath. 1978. The firewalkers of Kataragama: The rise of Bhakti religiosity in Buddhist Sri Lanka. *Journal of Asian studies* 37(3): 457–476.

———. 1981. *Medusa's hair: An essay on personal symbols and religious experience*. Chicago: University of Chicago Press.

———. 1984. *The cult of the goddess Pattini*. Chicago: University of Chicago Press.

SUSAN A. REED

SEE ALSO

Diaspora, Fiji and the South Pacific; Kataragama; Pattini; *Pirit; Pūjā;* Self-sacrifice; Skanda

FISH AND FISHING

Prehistoric remains show that fish have constituted an important food source for millennia in South Asia. Fish bones from the Neolithic site of Mehrgarh, located on the Kachhi Plain of Baluchistan in west-central Pakistan, reveal the use of carp and catfish as early as 6000 B.C.E. During the Harappan Phase of the Indus Valley Tradition (ca. 2600–1900 B.C.E.), fish were important food items for a portion of these prehistoric populations. Several species of catfish and carp were extremely abundant at the urban center of Harappa. The size of the bones suggests that many of these fish were in excess of two meters long and provided an important protein source. On several potsherds, ceramic motifs display fishermen using nets or fish designs. In addition to riverine fish, several marine fish bones (from jacks and marine catfish) have been recovered from Harappa. These fish remains probably represent a trade in dried or salted fish from the marine coastal zone some 850 kilometers distant. Nonperishable trade items, such as stone raw materials and copper from throughout the greater Indus Valley and beyond, are also known, but these fish remains help document the trade in perishable items as well.

Fish are common in ancient and modern religious symbolism throughout South Asia. In the prehistoric period this importance is revealed by the presence of fish-shaped faience and ivory tokens as well as a variety of fish-shaped signs present in the yet-undeciphered script of the Indus Valley civilization. Later, in the Sanskrit literature of the early historic period, fish, particularly *rohu* (*Labeo rohita* Hamilton), are mentioned as a sacrifice and an offering, both raw and cooked, to various gods, particularly Ganapati (Gaṇeśa). Fish also were offered to the *yakkha* (ogre-like spirits), the *nāga* (snake deities), and other divine beings. Offerings of rohu were commonly given in a *śrāddha*, a ceremony where food is offered to various animistic spirits (*mane*), but consumed by Brāhmaṇa, people of the Brahman caste. In later Hinduism (during and after the British occupation), one of the ten incarnations of Viṣṇu was in the form of Matsya, the fish. Sanskrit texts throughout the early historic period describe several fish species in terms of physical appearance as well as habitat preference and behavioral characteristics.

In the modern era fishing is still an important subsistence activity in the subcontinent, providing a major portion of the diet, particularly for people living in marine and estuarine zones. For interior populations, freshwater lacustrine and riverine fish are consumed in addition to marine species that have been traded inland. Although still traded in dried and salted form, it is more common to see fish shipped on ice by rail. Coastal and inland waters of South Asia possess a high diversity of important fish families. About 120 different families are found in marine and estuarine waters, including sharks, skates, rays, tunas, jacks, rock bass, trevallies, marine catfish, and grunters. Within freshwater lacustrine and riverine systems over 150 species and 68 genera exist, including important food fishes such as catfish, carps, snake-heads, and spiny eels.

Many types of fishing techniques are used in the subcontinent, including entrapment using nets and rigid fixed traps. In freshwater, casting nets and seine nets are preferred, while in marine environments, fixed nets that capture fish on the outgoing tide, as well as casting nets and hook-and-line, are the preferred inshore techniques. Near-shore techniques require the use of boats and make use of gill nets, bottom nets, and various purse seine nets in order to capture predatory fish, bottom-dwelling fish, crabs and lobsters, and octopi and cuttlefish. Along the coasts of southern India, beach seines are used with boats to harvest small inshore fish, such as herring and sardines.

In some areas of the western estuarine backwaters and the Gangetic delta region, rigid bamboo traps of various sizes and types are used and range from small basket traps to elaborate fixed weirs. In the western estuarine areas, a type of fixed platform lift net, known as a "Chinese fishing net," is used. Hook-and-line are used throughout the subcontinent, but only in the monsoon or in specific geographic areas such as in delta areas of Bangladesh. Fishing is also done by hand-spearing, draining ponds, spreading poison in the water, and using explosives to kill the fish by shock. Many local legends tell of the exploits of great fishermen who could dive below the surface and return with a fish in each hand and one between their teeth.

Within inland waters of northwestern India and Pakistan, the use of nets and hooks is linked with the seasonal flood cycles of the rivers. The main channels of the rivers are not the focus of fishing. Instead, the oxbow lakes and side channels that fill with water during the flood cycles are more easily harvested with nets. Hooks are used primarily within the main river channel during the nonflood autumn months.

Fishing grounds within the marine zone are often named for individuals or geographic locales as mnemonic devices in order to communicate locations. Along the Baluchistan coast of Pakistan, many of the areas are named for specific geographic markers used to triangulate specific loci in the ocean. A major geographic location like a mountain peak, a point of land, or a cove will have the same name as an offshore fishing ground. Some fishing grounds are named after the discoverer or record historical events, such as a boat capsizing on a subsurface rock.

Social aspects relevant to fishing include status, gender, and ethnicity. Fisherfolk, regardless of religious or cultural background, occupy a relatively low status in comparison to other occupational communities. Men are the chief harvesters and processors of fish, while women and girls perform traditional duties of family food preparation and upkeep within the domestic setting. However, throughout western and southern India and Bangladesh, many women perform duties as middle traders between incoming vessels and large-scale fishmongers. Some of these women have formed cooperatives and give loans to each other on a monthly basis. Children often assist the adults with tasks considered appropriate for their gender. For example, in Baluchistan, girls fetch water and herd goats during the day and help with cooking and food preparation during the evenings. Boys work in small-scale inshore fisheries and work with hook-and-line or casting nets until they are considered old enough to work on the boats. Boys often spend their afternoons repairing the various fishing gear, especially seine nets.

Fishing communities often comprise distinct ethnic groups, partially defined by their diet. For example, part of the ethnic definition of the coastal Makrani Baloch is that they "eat only fish." This helps to distinguish them from other Baloch peoples as well as from other ethnic and linguistic groups in Pakistan and Iran. Boat styles often indicate the ethnic affiliation of the owner, and this includes the painted motifs on the bow as well as minor structural differences in otherwise identical vessels. The Sindhi and Baloch fisherfolk of Pakistan can be distinguished by the cut of the bow of their vessels. Sindhi boats tend to have a curved vertical bow, while the Balochi vessels have an angled bow. Even modern fiberglass boats reflect these differing bow styles.

Throughout South Asia, fish are associated with curative powers for animals as well as humans. Water that has been used to cook or boil fish is used for healing water buffalo hooves in the Punjab regions of Pakistan, and the otoliths (ear stones) of marine catfish are traded for the treatment of kidney ailments by homeopathic healers. For many Makrani Baloch, illnesses such as fever or colds are cured by consuming fish, mollusks, and crustaceans.

In South Asian folk medicine, the world is classified according to a dichotomy of hot and cold. These divisions encompass animals, people, ethnic groups, and, especially, food. Fish are generally considered "hot," but inhabitants of the marine coast divide different fish species into finer gradations of hot as well as neutral categories. Eating fish during the hot summer months is often said to cause illness, heat rash, and an imbalance in the body. As heat is also a measure of virility and fertility, eating fish is often considered an aphrodisiac and a cure for infertility. In some modern Hindu marriage ceremonies, fish are offered as a blessing of fertility to the bride and the bridegroom. Regardless of religious affliation, it is common to see fish symbolism at wedding ceremonies throughout South Asia.

Although Pakistan and northwestern India have been emphasized in this essay, many of the symbolic and medicinal uses of fish are found throughout the entire subcontinent. The widespread nature of these beliefs suggests their ancient origins as well as the ongoing importance of fish to the people of this region.

References

Belcher, W. R. 1991. Fish resources in an early urban context at Harappa. In *Harappa excavations 1986–1990: A multidisciplinary approach to third millennium urbanism,* ed. R. H. Meadow, 107–120. Madison, Wisc.: Prehistory Press.

———. 1994a. Butchery practices and the ethnoarchaeology of South Asian fisherfolk. In *Fish exploitation in the past,* ed. W. Van Neer, 169–176. *Annales des Sciences Zoologiques,* vol. 274. Tervuren, Belgium: Musée Royal de l'Afrique Centrale.

———. 1994b. Multiple approaches towards reconstruction of fishing technology: Net-making and the Indus Valley tradition. In *From Sumer to Melluha: Contributions to the archaeology of southwest and south Asia in memory of George F. Dales,* ed. J. M. Kenoyer, 129–142. Wisconsin Archaeological Reports, No. 3. Madison: Department of Anthropology, University of Wisconsin.

Hora, S. L. 1935. Ancient Hindu conception of correlation between form and locomotion of fishes. *Journal of the Asiatic Society of Bengal (Science)* 1: 1–7.

———. 1948. Sanskrit names of fish and their significance. *Journal of the Royal Asiatic Society of Bengal (Science)* 14(1): 1–6.

Hora, S. L., and S. K. Saraswati. 1955. Fish in the Jakata tales. *Journal of the Asiatic Society (Letters)* 21(1): 15–30.

Parpola, A. 1994. *Deciphering the Indus script.* New York: Academic Press.

Pastner, S. 1977. Baluchi fishermen. *Old World Pastoralism* 6: 33–57.

Raychaudhuri, Bikash. 1980. *The moon and net: Study of a transient community of fisherman at Jambudwip.* Calcutta: Anthropological Survey of India, Government of India.

Suryanarayana, M. 1977. *Marine fisherfolk of north-east coastal Andhra Pradesh.* Calcutta: Anthropological Survey of India, Government of India.

Tietze, U., ed. 1985. *Artisanal marine fisherfolk of Orissa: Study of their technology, economic status, social organization, and cognitive patterns.* Cuttack: Vidyapuri.

WILLIAM R. BELCHER

SEE ALSO

Food and Foodways; *Gāmbhīra;* Gujarat; Life Cycle Rituals; Maldives

FLOOR DESIGNS

Floor design is a genre of nonverbal folklore, of folk art and material culture, usually embedded in ritual contexts of transformation of ordinary space into sacred space throughout South Asia. Rice powder paintings adorn doorways, household shrines, and open public Hindu ceremonial spaces. Although Hindu and tribal women are the primary exponents of this "ephemeral" painting tradition, men also perform this folk art form. Made with ground rice powders, bazaar-bought bright-colored powders, and wooden, aluminum, or plastic PVC piping stencils, floor designs are related to but distinct from wall paintings in function and symbolic presence; they can be performed ritually on a flat surface and can have layers of flowers, lentils, or unhusked rice overlaid to create a three-dimensional effect of breasts, lotuses, or *yantra*s. Whereas wall paintings last for months, these paintings on the ground are ephemeral and transitory. Sometimes, they are purposefully smudged by dancers, or other ritual specialists; at other times, they gradually disappear as people walk over them. These ground paintings are also called magic floor diagrams, and brief allusions to them are found in general works on ritual art, sacred art, ephemeral art, threshold art, and women's ritual art. They reproduce, in miniature form, large mappings and architectural templates of pilgrimage sites and temple architectural plans.

A Selection of the Terms Used for Floor Designs

Kolam	Tamil Nadu, Kerala
Kalam elluttu	Kerala
Pampin Tullal	
Sarpappattu	
Muggu	Andhra Pradesh
Alpana, Alpona	Bengal
Mandana, pglaya	Rajasthan
Aripan, Aripana	Bihar, Bengal
Rangavalli	Maharashtra
Rangoli	Maharashtra, Rajasthan, Uttar Pradesh
Sanjhi	Uttar Pradesh
Sathiya	Gujarat
Apna	Western Himalayas
Aipana, cauka purna sona rakhna	Uttar Pradesh

Women's Folk Drawings and Paintings

Throughout India, Hindu women create floor designs at the borders and thresholds of houses, shrines, communities, and temples. Floor designs have various names: *kolam* in Tamil Nadu, *muggu* in Andhra Pradesh, *kalam elluttu* in Kerala, *mandana* in Rajasthan, *alpana* in Bengal, among others (see table). In general, women in northern India create floor designs at special festivals or threshold ceremonies such as births, marriages, and deaths, whereas in southern India, floor designs are an integral part of daily life; for example, the *kolam* in Tamil Nadu is created daily before sunrise in front of the thresholds of most households. Throughout India, floor designs are one of the many folk arts that are visually based and centered or embedded within the lives of women.

Although this genre of various types of floor designs is relatively unexplored, ethnographically and theoretically, art historians, anthropologists, and religious studies scholars have begun to study them in recent years.

Men's Floor Designs

Men throughout South Asia create floor designs. Men frequently articulate a close connection between their ritual floor designs and the concept of the mandala; a mandala is a sacred drawing that represents the hosting of the divine in geometric, figurative, or pictorial terms usually found in tantric art. Women, on the other hand, rarely refer to any explicit connection between floor designs and tantric designs. Men's designs created on the ground also reflect a parallel ritual purpose to those of women. Men from tantric Buddhism, tantric Hinduism, folk Hinduism, and Jainism create a sacred enclosure for ritual to take place. There seems to be a structural similarity between these folk designs and the Nepalese and Tibetan Buddhist mandalas drawn for highly elaborate ritual occasions. In Kerala two performances rooted in the ritual designs drawn on the ground are the *pampin tullal* and the *kalam elluttu*. The pampin tullal, involving the creation of a huge and elaborate female goddess in colored powders, is well documented by Deborah Neff in her ethnographic study of the snake ritual. Clifford Jones has articulated, from an art historical perspective, the various detailed forms of the kalam elluttu.

Throughout Andhra Pradesh, men from varied communities roll out ritual designs with wooden stencils before a folk performance to mark off a sacred enclosure that is later erased by the feet of a dancing woman. Here it is embedded in a performance called *patam,* a ritual or folk theatrical performance, sometimes involving ritual possession.

Designs called *cauk* are drawn with rice and flowers during Islamic weddings throughout India. There is a paucity of ethnographic and religious literature on many of these forms because they fall between the disciplinary cracks of art history, anthropology, folklore, and religious studies.

References

Archana, Shastri. 1981. *The language of symbols: A project on South Indian ritual decorations of a semi-permanent nature.* Madras: Crafts Council of India.

Beck, Brenda. 1976. The symbolic merger of body, space and cosmos in Hindu Tamil Nadu. *Contributions to Indian Sociology* 10(2): 213–245.

Chatterji, T. M. 1948. *Alpona.* Calcutta: n.p.

Freeman, James. 1980. The ladies of Lord Krishna: Rituals of middle-aged women in eastern India. In *Unspoken worlds: Women's religious lives in non-western cultures,* ed. Nancy Falk and Rita Gross. San Francisco: Harper and Row.

Government of India. 1960. *Alpana.* New Delhi: Ministry of Information and Broadcasting.

Jayakar, Pupul. 1990. *The Earth Mother: Legends, ritual arts, and goddesses of India.* Revised edition of *The earthen drum: An introduction to the ritual arts of rural India* [1981]. San Francisco: Harper and Row.

Jones, Clifford. 1982. Kalam elluttu: Art and ritual in Kerala. In *Religious festivals in South India,* ed. Guy Welbon and Glenn Yocum. New Delhi: Manohar.

Kilambi, Jyotsna S. 1985. Toward an understanding of the muggu: Threshold drawings in Hyderbad. *Res* 10: 71–100.

Kramrisch, Stella. 1983. Unknown India: Ritual art in tribe and village. In *Exploring India's sacred art,* ed. Barbara S. Miller, 85–120. Reprint [1968]. Philadelphia: University of Pennsylvania Press.

Layard, J. 1937. Labyrinth ritual in South India: Threshold and tattoo designs. *Folklore* 48: 115–186.

Mode, Heinz, and Subodh Chandra. 1985. *Indian folk art.* New York and London: Alpine Fine Arts Collection, Ltd.

Mookerjee, Ajit. 1971. *Tantra asana.* Basel, Paris, and New Delhi: Ravi Kumar Books.

———. 1983. *Tantra art.* Basel, Paris and New Delhi: Ravi Kumar Books.

Nagarajan, Vijaya. 1993. Hosting the divine: The kolam in Tamil Nadu. In *Mud, mirror and thread: Folk traditions in rural India,* ed. Nora Fisher, 192–203. Santa Fe: Museum of International Folk Art.

Neff, Deborah. 1987. Aesthetics and power in pambin tullal: A possession ritual of rural Kerala. *Ethnology* 26: 63–71.

———. 1994. Special status performers: Fertility and power in a Kerala serpent ritual. Ph.D. diss., Dept. of Anthropology, University of Wisconsin, Madison.

Saroja, V. 1988. Tamil Panpattil Kolangal (Kolams in Tamil culture), Ph.D. diss., Madurai Kamaraj University, Madurai.

Saskena, J. 1985. *Mandana: A folk art of Rajasthan.* New Delhi: Crafts Museum.

Thangavelu, Kirtana. 1994. Letter to author. 12 December.

Woodruff, John. 1987. *Sakti and sakta.* Madras: Ganesh Publishers.

———. 1992. *The serpent power.* Madras: Ganesh Publishers.

VIJAYA RETTAKUDI NAGARAJAN

SEE ALSO

Folk Art; Folk Painting; *Kolam*

FOLK ART

We all know what folk art means. Or do we? Most people have a clear sense of typical examples, either from their own culture or from another, which are not easily generalized to diverse parts of the world. Some sense of what a definition in South Asia would want to include may emerge if we simply list the forms in one region—the state of Orissa, with which this author is most familiar. There are the products of the tribals—their distinctive, if simple, houses, jewelry, and wooden post-gods. The latter bring to mind the wooden triad enshrined in the monumental Jagannātha Temple of Puri. This immense shrine, built for a king in the twelfth century and today one of the four pan-Indian *dhāms* (abodes of Hindu sanctity), is surely not "folk" or vernacular architecture; yet the legendary connection between the wooden Jagannātha-Kṛṣṇa and tribal gods reminds us of the way rural forms constantly shape elite culture in South Asia. The paintings made for visitors to Puri include images that must be part of our definition. In the same villages where professional male painters produce their souvenirs, following canonical precepts, women annually decorate their walls as a ritual act taught orally to them by their mothers. Among the products of the potter, the term "craft" may seem appropriate to vessels in daily use, although some of these are of profound religious significance. But clay images such as the idiosyncratic Hanumān whose burning of Lanka is annually celebrated in Sonepur are quintessential examples of folk art. Even roof tiles in western Orissa may bear images that have an aesthetic as well as apotropaic role. The folk theater of Orissa uses ingenious props and masks, inextricable as objects from their performative context. Orissa is known for its rich textiles, which range from the most costly and elegant to those still in use by villagers. Finally, there are anomalous forms such as *dokra* bronzes produced by Hindu professional artisans for tribal buyers.

Forced to come up with a definition that fits such diverse examples, we are likely to put this in negative terms: *not* elite or high art, *not* belonging in an art museum but in an anthropology museum, and even more unsatisfactory alternatives. Let us try to think of positive defining characteristics.

One criterion frequently used in America is that the artist is self-taught, as for instance, Grandma Moses. She is set apart from those painters before the early twentieth century who were trained in academies. The United States is rife with individualistic artists of this kind, whose free treatment of human anatomy and depiction of space was facilitated by their lack of indoctrination with the rules of any art school. South Asia, where the equivalents of Grandma Moses are busy producing images according to patterns taught by their mothers, has fewer isolated "originals" of this kind. One now famous self-taught artist is Nek Chand of Chandigarh, who used his position as an employee of the Public Works Department to create a secret rock garden from a wide range of discarded objects, an enterprise in which he had no major model, although parts draw upon the *sanjhi* tradition of Haryana and the Punjab, in which broken plates are used along with other forms to create goddess images on walls. If Nek Chand is our model, however, it is hard to find many South Asian examples. And many folklorists would question whether such an individual is not the antithesis of folk art, embedded in a community.

A second criterion for folk art in use in the West is the nonprofessional status of the artist. This would sound very odd in China, where the amateur painter, of high social status, is regarded as the model of "genius," superior to the mere professional. In South Asia, nonprofessionalism characterizes many rural mural painters, such as the women of Orissa or Madhubani or the men of the Rathva and Worli tribes; likewise, women's floor decoration is executed gratis. Such images are produced as part of events in the life cycle, whose forms follow inherited ritual patterns. By this token, however, the potter and painter castes, which earn a living by their products, would be omitted.

A third common connotation of folk art in English is its low socioeconomic context. If this means that the maker is poor, it would embrace some odd bedfellows even in the West, for example, the American black slave and Vincent Van Gogh (whose paintings began to command high prices only after his death). In India the makers of Gupta sculpture or Chola bronzes were not necessarily well-to-do. Many cultures have sayings to the effect that art and wealth are rarely sisters. Turning to the patron, however, we can more readily draw a line between works produced for the elite and for the "folk." Folk images would require less time to make as well as less expensive materials; as a result, these are less long-lasting. In many of India's painting traditions, the same families of craftspeople produce objects for various markets, tailoring the product to the price. Thus the same workshop of *pata* painters in Orissa may make rough, cheap images on old newspaper for sale in the bazaar and large, elaborate pictures of the same basic subject commissioned by maharajas and business people. Admitting this anomaly, we will return to patronage as part of a definition.

But first let us consider the definitions of folklorists and attempt to apply these to the visual arts. A criterion often invoked, although problematic even applied to verbal texts, is that folklore is oral rather than written. Are we to define folk art as transmitted orally rather than by the written word? In fact, the teaching of most painting and sculptural traditions inevitably involves practical demonstration, even when complex theoretical and technical texts exit. Thus much of the Sanskrit *Śilpa Śāstra* literature appears to have been composed post facto and to have been used by artisans to validate their religious status rather than as a guide in making their great temples. If we substitute visual models for written ones, that is, the use of other images, then we must admit that inherited sketchbooks and aides-mémoires are used not only by court painters and stone carvers but also by the women of Madhubani and the *chitrakāras* of Orissa.

Progressive folklorists have devised ontological definitions for folklore: patterns of words (tales, proverbs, etc.) that enjoy a multiple existence (that is, are repeated by two or more people) and that also vary in each telling. Here "folk" is taken to be any group sharing one or more characteristics. Variation in detail characterizes pots and terra-cottas that show small irregularities of hand throwing and final decoration; likewise handmade stone sculpture or Mughal jade carvings also repeat iconographic types and vary in the same way. The social inclusiveness of this definition may reflect a twentieth-century American egalitarian ideal: we are all "folk" or would like to think we are, in the same way that virtually all Americans describe themselves as middle class. Moving into a premodern period even in the West, such inclusiveness is harder to accept.

What of the indigenous Indian terms? The modern *lok-kālā* has been devised as a literal equivalent of folk art in Hindustani (similarly *lok-fan* in Urdu), and hence it tells us little about South Asia. A more promising distinction originates in Indian musical theory, between *marga* (mainstream), and *deśi* (localized). This seems at first to differentiate between the broadly similar temple-building codes of North or South India, as opposed to the *devra* shrines of western Rajasthan or the *bhūta* shrines of Karnataka. It is by no means an absolute distinction, however, for the contemporary temples of the Hoysalas in Karnataka are equally distinct from those of the Later Chalukyas in the same state, or of the Kakatiyas in Andhra. Among the courts of western Rajasthan by the nineteenth century, many localized painting styles developed, whereas the *paḍh* was used in more uniform guise throughout the same region. In pluralistic India, the marga seems often an illusion, a prescriptive ideal. This distinction once led Ananda Kentish Coomaraswamy to assert that Mughal painting, however technically refined, was a deśi, "byway," from the Rajput mainstream (Coomaraswamy 1936, 7). In this the great pioneer of the study of South Asian art revealed his own distaste for Mughal art and the assumption that deśi means "inferior."

In fact, such an assessment of quality is a frequent implication of the term "folk art." In the past "folk" was usually equated with inferior, except perhaps by the ethnographer who developed particular affection for a particular group and its products. But particularly in the second half of the twentieth century, the balance has often been reversed. Folk images may today be described as vital, as opposed to effete fine art, and as providing a "wider, deeper, richer view of human beings" (Glassie, 1993, 5). In India, both Gandhian ideals, promoting the use of hand-spun *khādī* cloth, and more recent "ethnic chic" in dress accentuate this reevaluation.

Can we conceive of an objective criterion in the object itself, not dependent upon the origin of maker or buyer or upon a constructed ideal framework of tradition? Here another indigenous term comes to mind, *jungli,* meaning wild. This term is widely understood in many languages of South Asia, sometimes used pejoratively as deśi was, sometimes describing with admiration a quality of Dionysian, gutsy energy. It characterizes the work of many nonprofessional artists, as well as objects made for villagers before the machine age. These qualities are promoted by the use of inexpensive, rough, and ephemeral materials. For the traditional art historian, such a visual quality is satisfactory as a criterion residing in the image itself—its use of asymmetry, wobbly lines, geometrical human bodies, and unmixed colors. Concepts such as jungli and deśi need to be explored throughout the many languages of South Asia.

In the background of any definition of folk art lurk several alternative terms that require brief consideration. "Popular art" describes objects made for the masses. Today, in many societies, these are likely to comprise machine-produced things, from comic books to mill cloth, which would normally not be classified as folk. Yet in China, where printing has been in use for over a millennium, it is possible to group together handmade embroidery and popular prints that have long decorated the kitchens of the populace.

In India, as in many other parts of the world, handicraft is usually assumed to be a necessary characteristic of folk art. Thus the National Handicrafts and Handlooms Museum in New Delhi constitutes the largest repository of folk arts of all kinds. It is worth noting, however, that "handmade" would also describe the stone sculpture and court painting of the National Museum of Art in New Delhi. Handicraft is not a sufficient criterion for folk art.

Our difficulties have been compounded by the loaded term "art," sometimes equated only with the elite or with objects that have an exclusively aesthetic function. "Folk art" may derive from a more basic use of this component, in which art is equivalent to skill, as in "artful dodger." In this case, surely, it is legitimate to admit that folk art may be judged by aesthetic standards. To assume that these are unknown to the humble makers and users is unwarranted. It is this dimension that distinguishes the folk arts within the larger rubric "material culture." That term encompasses the social contextualization which may indeed add to our understanding of all art. But it focuses upon practical function rather than the appearance of the object. To call something a work of art (folk or fine) entitles us to look long and hard at it.

A frequently invoked characteristic, but far from a necessary one, was implicit in the first words of Stella Kramrisch's major catalogue, *Unknown India—Ritual Art in Tribe and Village*. This title was in fact an oxymoron, for the exhibition it accompanied made these forms widely known in North America. Much current research on folk art is fueled by a sense of social and intellectual outrage that the subject has been overlooked. There is also concern that modernization may change and replace the traditional object with machine-made or mechanical products, a fear already voiced at the beginning of the twentieth century in the groundbreaking study of the craftsmen of Sri Lanka by Coomaraswamy. It is indeed worth recording change as it occurs today and attempting to reconstruct that in the past, although this is rarely easy, due to fragile materials and lack of written documentation. Nor need we wring our hands over change of the kind that surely has been going on for millennia, in our quest for specious authenticity.

In short, it seems impossible to construct a definition of folk art that will fit every culture or even every South Asian genre that is considered in this volume. It may be healthy to think of ourselves as The Folk rather than displacing the term to some romantically imagined Other, but we will probably want to exclude forms produced by and for the Global Village or for specific elite, urban communities, although even these have been taken seriously by American folklorists. The subaltern social status of those who use these objects, the production of objects largely by hand, and the fact that they do have an aesthetic dimension, which Indians have termed deśi or jungli, are widely shared, almost necessary criteria.

Perhaps as important as what we consider is how we study it. We must pay particular attention to the social role of makers and users of folk art and to their interaction as members of a community. Along with the artifact itself and its individual creator, we must examine the way in which traditions are passed on among the makers and at the same time permitted to alter. The objects must be considered not only in terms of technique and practical function but also in terms of appearance and aesthetic choice. It is useful to identify ourselves in the process of our study, recognizing that our own ethnic background, academic discipline, and taste color our view of culture. Finally, while the methods of art history would encourage the scholar to look carefully at a single work, often designated a masterpiece, the folk image, however high its aesthetic status, also benefits from wide comparative study. This may simply acknowledge the multiple existence of most types, the products of a single artisan or of a community. Comparison may also, like that of the folklorist, range fruitfully across diverse cultures.

References

Berliner, Nancy Zeng. 1986. *Chinese folk art: The small skills of carving insects*. Boston: New York Graphic Society.

Clifford, James. 1988. *The predicament of culture: Twentieth-century ethnography, literature, and art*. Cambridge, Mass.: Harvard University Press.

Coomaraswamy, Ananda Kentish. 1907. *Medieval Sinhalese art*. Broad Campden: Essex House Press. 2nd ed., New York: Pantheon, 1986.

———. 1936. The nature of "folklore" and "popular art." *Quarterly Journal of the Mythic Society* 27(1–2): 1–12.

Cort, Louise. 1984. "Temple potters of Puri." *Res* 7/8: 33–41.

Das, J. P. 1982. *Puri paintings*. New Delhi: Arnold Heinemann.

Fischer, Eberhard, Sitakant Mahapatra, and Dinanath Pathy. 1980. *Orissa: Kunst und Kultur in Nordost Indien*. Zürich: Museum Rietberg.

Glassie, Henry. 1993. *Turkish traditional art today*. Bloomington: Indiana University Press.

———. 1997. *Art and life in Bangladesh*. Bloomington: Indiana University Press.

Hall, Michael D. 1988. *Stereoscopic perspective: Reflections on American fine and folk art*. Ann Arbor: University of Michigan Press.

Jain, Jyotindra, and Aarti Aggarwala. 1989. *National Handicrafts and Handlooms Museum, New Delhi*. Ahmedabad: Mapin Publishing.

Jones, Michael Owen. 1987. *Exploring folk art: Twenty years of thought on craft, work, and aesthetics*. Ann Arbor: UMI Research Press.

Kramrisch, Stella. 1968. *Unknown India: Ritual art in tribe and village*. Philadelphia: Philadelphia Museum of Art.

Williams, Joanna. 1994. *The monkey with the flaming tail*. San Francisco: San Francisco Craft and Folk Art Museum.

JOANNA WILLIAMS

SEE ALSO

Calendar Art; Card Games; Carpets and Carpet Weaving; Comic Books, India; Craft; Embroidery; Faience; Floor Designs; Folk Art, Orissa; Folk Painting; Godboxes, Painted; Handloom Weaving; Image-making, Metal; *Jāmdānī*; Jewelry and Adornment; *Kāñthā; Kolam;* Masks; Material Culture; Metal and Metalworking; Metalwork, Bangladesh; Mithila Painting; Museums and Folklore, Bangladesh; Narrative Scroll Painting; Painting; *Paṛ; Paṭa Citra;* Pottery; Quilting and Piecing; Recycling; Tattooing; Tiles and Tilemaking, Terra Cotta; Toys; Vehicle Painting

FOLK ART, ORISSA

The state of Orissa is home to a great number of folk and popular art traditions, in painting, carved wood, metalworking, textiles, and other media. The most well-known of these traditions is that of the *paṭacitra*s, or paintings on cloth. These devotional paintings are associated with temples to the god Jagannātha, especially the famous temple in Puri, in which the "triad" of deities, Jagannātha, his brother Balabhadra, and his sister Subhadrā, are worshiped. Traditional artists, known as *citrakāras,* who live in the vicinity of the temples, paint paṭacitras and sell their work to pilgrims. The paintings are characterized by strong line and bright color. Common themes are Jagannātha and incidents from the life of Kṛṣṇa.

Other devotional art forms are related to the paṭacitras. Paintings on silk of deities and village scenes, in the style of the paṭacitras, have become common. Artists carve and paint small wooden statues of the triad for use in home shrines. Pilgrims can also find brightly painted portable wooden shrines whose doors open to reveal small wood statues of the Jagannātha triad. Dowry boxes, used for holding the wife's valuables, are often decorated with paṭacitras.

A long-standing folk art tradition in Orissa is that of palm leaf etching. Though production of the palm leaf manuscripts that long served as books in Orissa has virtually ceased, the tradition continues in etchings sold to pilgrims and tourists. The booklike format has changed to a series of leaves sewn together to form a rectangular surface. The artist etches a design into the surface of the palm leaves. Then lampblack or ink is rubbed over the surface and wiped away, revealing the line drawing, which might depict a deity or illustrate an incident from the life of Kṛṣṇa. Erotic pictures are also common.

Another folk tradition with a long history is that of the *ganjīfā* playing cards. A typical set for the *daśāvatāra* ("ten incarnations") game includes 120 individually painted, circular cards in 10 suits, one suit for each incarnation of Viṣṇu. Picture cards depict the *avatāras*.

Orissa is home to several wall painting traditions. In Ganjam district, colorful ritual murals are painted on the walls of temporary shrine rooms. Śiva or the goddess Mangalā, in the center of the mural, is surrounded by other deities and many smaller figures. The tribal Saoras paint ritual pictographs on the walls of their houses, and tribal Santals paint decorative pictures on walls.

Textiles produced in Orissa include sārīs, scarves, and other woven items using the ikat technique, in which threads are tied with dye-resistant material and dyed before weaving. The village of Pipili is famous for its brightly colored appliqué textiles, which range from wall hangings to patio umbrellas.

Near Puri, artists create molded and painted papier-mâché masks representing various deities. Carved and painted wooden masks are also common. Silversmiths in Cuttack produce fine filigree work, both jewelry and small figures. Craft workers in the tribal areas of the state use the lost wax technique to cast bronze human and animal figures and utilitarian items. Additional craft objects produced in Orissa include soapstone carvings of deities, carved and painted wooden animals and toys, and lacquer boxes. The prevalence and popularity of these and other craft objects highlight the rich diversity of the folk arts of Orissa.

References

Cooper, Ilay, and John Gillow. 1996. *Arts and crafts of India.* London: Thames and Hudson.

Das, J. P. 1982. *Puri paintings*. Atlantic Highlands, N.J.: Humanities Press.

Das, J. P., and Joanna Williams. 1991. *Palm-leaf miniatures: The art of Raghunath Prusti of Orissa*. New Delhi: Abhinav Publications.

Fischer, Eberhard, and Dinanath Pathy. 1996. *Murals for goddesses and gods: The tradition of Osakothi ritual painting in Orissa, India.* New Delhi: Indira Gandhi National Centre for the Arts; Zürich: Museum Reitberg.

Glassie, Henry. 1989. *The spirit of folk art: The Girard collection at the Museum of International Folk Art.* New York: Harry N. Abrams.

Mahapatra, Sitakant. 1991. *Tribal wall paintings of Orissa.* Bhubaneswar: Orissa Lalit Kala Akademi.

Patnaik, Durga Prashad. 1989. *Palm-leaf etchings of Orissa.* New Delhi: Abhinav Publications.

Rossi, Barbara. 1998. *From the ocean of painting: India's popular paintings 1589 to the present.* New York: Oxford University Press.

Von Leyden, R. 1949. Ganjifa: The playing cards of India. *Marg* 3(4): 36–56.

BERNARD CESARONE

SEE ALSO

Card Games; Folk Art; God-boxes, Painted; Museums and Folklore, Bangladesh; *Paṭa Citra*

FOLK DRAMA, AFGHANISTAN

Wartime events culminating in the dominance of the Ṭālibān regime in Afghanistan in the 1990's caused the emigration, de-professionalization or death of traditional performers of music and drama whose livelihood could no longer be sustained in wartime conditions or whose activities were subsequently forbidden outright by the Ṭālibān, who regarded them as unIslamic. In western Afghanistan, from which most of the following discussion derives, folk actors and musicians were assigned by general opinion to a marginalized, endogamous group (called *jat*) along with certain other marginalized service professions (barbers, blacksmiths). The degree of endogamy of this category of persons was probably exaggerated in the public mind, however, as was its homogeneity. Different professional groups within the category have their own terms for themselves, traditional histories of their family or group, specialized features of language use, and other cultural features distinguishing one so-called *jat* group from another. What survives of these specialized groups' cultural contribution in light of the last twenty years of profound disruption remains to be seen. The folk drama traditions discussed here were current in the valley of Herat in the 1960's through the 1970's, and are documented in some systematic detail due to the pioneering research of Hafizullah Baghban.

The most robust drama tradition at the time of Baghban's research was farce, in which personality types or stereotypes (clergy, tax collectors, governors, landlords, pederasts, quarrelsome wives, etc.) were satirized, sometimes with improvised language connecting the play's topic to current local events and personalities. The folk actors of Herat called themselves *Magad* and their private ethno-professional dialect (a patois of Persian with additional specialized vocabulary) *Magadī*. They shared a kinship network with lineages of musicians and barbers. They resided in certain neighborhoods of Herat city and as clusters of families in certain surrounding villages, from which they traveled locally to perform.

Their usual performance venue was city and rural celebrations in private homes, such as weddings and circumcisions. Thus while the drama itself was construed purely as entertainment, of a slightly disreputable but highly enjoyable sort, its context remained to some degree a ritual one. The host would commission the performance, for a certain troupe at a certain fee. The players would take up a collection from the audience to augment the fees paid by the host family. The actors had some choice of which to perform of the traditional plays they had in repertoire, though hosts could also request specific plays if they had preferences. Plays and roles within them could be improvisationally adjusted to praise and criticize local figures (e.g. for generosity or tight-fistedness), a component of performance humor that was much appreciated by the audience and somewhat to be dreaded by its objects. Besides the rite-of-passage performance contexts, this performance tradition also was reported as street entertainment in the Persian culture area from late medieval up to recent times.

The all-male troupes in the Herat area sent varied numbers of actors to perform depending on the size of performance the host was willing to pay for. A minimal Magad performance might be two men staging a *chūb-bāzī* ("stick play," a kind of choreographed mock combat with staves) or a solitary clown doing routines with the audience, in conjunction with music by a duo of *sāz-dohol* (*sāz* being a double-reeded oboe-like wind instrument with a very penetrating, nasal sound; *dohol* being a large wooden-framed drum struck with a drumstick). More elaborate performances included plays by half a dozen or more actors using named, orally scripted plots on various topics. The leader of the troupe, simultaneously lead actor, business manager and director, is often the buffoon in his role assignment. Actors work up in role assignments over their careers, from female and child roles through the stereotypic male authority figure roles, to the role of the critical adversary, the underdog buffoon.

Baghban's extensive anthology of play scripts organizes plots by categories: Arranged Marriage ("The Four Daughters"), Polygamy, Domestic Relations and Divorce ("The Old Women's Play," "Ahmadak the Well-digger"), Liberated Women ("The Ladies' Play"), Supernatural Power in Humans ("The Fakirs' Play"), Supernatural Power in Dolls and Magic Objects ("The Seven-Colored Loom"), The Contest of the Feeble and Robust ("The Wrestlers' Play"), Contest of Human and Animal ("The Hyena's Play"), The Contest of Have and Have-Not ("Amirjan the Boy-Lover"), Contest of Employer and Employee ("Ahmadak the Well-digger"), Criminal-Victim Dichotomy ("The Thieves' Play"), National and Ethnic Dichotomy ("The Hindus' Play"), and Peasant-Nomad Contest ("The Shepherds' Play"). Popular titles were shared among troupes and performances could be elaborated or truncated depending on players' preference and audience response.

The house courtyard or similar open space was the performance space, the performance being held in the round with minimal props. Plays taking place after dark would be minimally illuminated by kerosene lanterns, villages almost never being electrified. The male audience would sit or stand at ground level around the performance space, women sitting or standing on adjacent flat roofs or in a designated space at ground level. Costuming also was improvised from a minimal collection of troupe equipment and host family-provided garments and objects. Humor, both physical and verbal, was extremely broad and frequently obscene.

Baghban traces the earliest, scattered reports of indigenous popular theater in the region to Greeks interacting with Persian imperial armies, beginning with Xenophon in 401 B.C.E. Scholars find in scanty surviving texts mention of the presence of clowns and jugglers at the Sassanian court in Iran, 300-650 C.E. While the early Islamic period on the Iranian plateau is poor in records of drama, by the Safavid period, portrayals of court players are to be found in occasional miniatures. John Chardin, in his seventeenth century. Persian travelogue describes street farce performed with and without masks, in conjunction with juggling and "a thousand stories." Present-day western Afghanistan (Khorassān) was part of a cultural continuum with what is now Iran. Western observers used the Persian term for these street performers, *lūtī*, which is cognate to one of the common terms for the marginalized service-performer group in contemporary Balochistan (*lūṛī* or *lūṭī*), which some scholars trace to the ethnic-tribal designation of a particular out-migrating ethnic group originating in Sindh as early as the fifth century C.E. Specifics about the historical development and formal diversity of this entirely oral art form over time are, however, elusive.

In drama as in other cultural matters, it is not safe to treat local practice, however locally claimed now, as unique to its place of occurrence, and contemporary national-political boundaries often do not delineate cultural territories. Baghban's comparison of the practices of the buffoon (e.g. whiteface masking in flour-and-egg make-up, long hat and goatskin costume, wool and cotton whiskers, mix of farce, puppetry, and juggling in improvised performance) reported in eighteenth and nineteenth century Iran and still in the Herat area in 1975 confirms the regional spread of this tradition.

Baghban mentions puppetry as a component of the Magad repertoire and regards it as ancient in the region, not necessarily derived from Far Eastern traditions (e.g. Javanese, Chinese) as other western scholars have inferred. Baghban cites classical Persian poets' metaphorical and direct references to puppets and dolls, and their allusions to preIslamic performance traditions, as evidence of common knowledge of the antiquity of puppetry traditions in the area.

Baghban also gives limited examples of duo farces performed informally by pairs of women at home ("The Co-Wives' Play," which is a rendition of the laments of a first wife as the engagement and marriage of her husband to a second wife go forward). Also observed in the region, but not yet formally studied, are forms of improvisational masking or mumming using bits of local dress and sheep or goat skins for costume, by local groups of young boys. Some of these performances are connected with seasonal events including the spring New Year (Naw Rūz), in which the boy troupes go door to door in their village neighborhood, begging and putting on a simple play or skit. In one example, put on after the evening meal for this author and fellow travelers by boys from a transhumant pastoral group near whom we had camped in Ghoriān east of Herat, one of the themes depicted appeared to be the death, healing, and successful resurrection of one of the characters, a very ancient theme also found in European mumming repertoires and in "rain plays" reported from Kurdish Iraq in the middle of the twentieth century.

Recent developments in public performance include an urban theatrical form of mixed music and drama, rather similar to western vaudeville, called *nanderī,* represented by two troupes in Herat in the 1970's, one sponsored by the government, one organized by a local entrepreneur/performer, each with their own small theater. Unlike the case of traditional street and village theater, the *nanderī* audience was effectively limited to men; though each theater provided a small screened seating space for women to attend, few did.

References

Baloch, N. A. 1982. Prehistoric to early historic period; Developments under Islamic civilization. In *Folk music of Sind,* ed. G. M. Allana. Jamshoro, Pakistan: Institute of Sindhology, University of Sindh, pp. 1–16.

Baghban, Hafizullah. 1976 (1978). *The context and concept of humor in Magadi theater.* 4 vols. Indian University Dissertation. Ann Arbor: University Microfilms.

Sakata, Hiromi Lorraine. 2002. *Music in the mind: The concepts of music and musician in Afghanistan.* 2nd ed. Washington, DC: Smithsonian Institution Press.

MARGARET A. MILLS

SEE ALSO

Dom; Balochi Oral Tradition; Theater and Drama

FOLK ETYMOLOGIES

Folk etymologies are stories, often quite brief, that purport to explain the origin of a word through reference to the linguistic form of the word itself. In South Asia, folk etymologies are usually concerned with the origins of the proper names of people, kin groups, castes, and places. Rural and urban, literate and illiterate people tell folk etymologies, although the tellers seem more often to be men than women. The contexts of the telling of these short tales vary. They may be imparted to begin a historical narrative (such as the history of a community), to prove a connection (as between a deity and a local place), or to validate a caste's claim to a higher status than it is commonly accorded. Sometimes folk etymologies are told simply to demonstrate the teller's grasp of erudite information. Some etymological tales are well known by people over a wide area; others are known only by people who live in a specific locality or who belong to a particular group.

A particularly famous Sri Lankan folk etymology was first reported in print by the merchant sailor Robert Knox, prisoner of the Sinhalese king for almost twenty years (1659–1679) and author of a lengthy description of the island, published after he escaped and returned to England. It was told to account for the name of Sri Lanka's capital, Colombo.

> On the West [is] the City of Colombo, so called from a Tree the Natives call Ambo [*amba*] (which bears the Mango-fruit) growing in that place; but this never bare fruit, but onely [*sic*] leaves, which in their Language [Sinhalese] is Cola [*kō̱la*], and thence they called the Tree Colambo: which the Christians in honour of Columbus turned to Columbo. (Knox 1966[1681]:2)

The pattern of this etymology, which ties a place name to a local natural feature, is a common one.

Another common etymological pattern invokes a local occurrence involving an important personage—such as a king, a monk, a priest, or a deity—which yields the place's name. This example, again from Sri Lanka, was collected from Sinhalese-speaking pottery makers in a Kurunegala District village called Rukmale. The name is said to have come because at the temple where King Walgambutta died there were trees (*ruk*). The monks who meditated under the trees to honor the king could see only the tree's flowers (*ruk mala*), and so the name Rukmale.

Yet a third pattern associates the name being explained with a desired quality. In a Tamil-speaking village on Sri Lanka's east coast, the anthropologist Dennis McGilvray was told that the Mukkuvar caste name derived from the Tamil word *mukkiyam* (importance), making them the "important people." Pauline Kolenda provides a reverse etymology of this type—one built on what a caste would like to be called—from southern India when she reports of a group of toddy tappers who, claiming higher, *Kśatriya* status, alleged that they should be called Nadar, meaning "Lord of the Land" (from the Tamil word *nāḍu*) rather than the low-caste name, Shanan, by which they were actually known. Similarly, in a Pakistani village, Saghir Ahmad was informed by members of the Doogal *qom* (ranked lineage) that they were really higher-ranked Gujars but were called Doogal because of an ancestor known as a "double talker," as *dū-gal* means "two-talk."

Folk etymologies are usually linguistically unlikely, and standard etymological dictionaries of South Asian languages often suggest quite different origins for the same words. However, the persistence of folk etymologies in South Asia suggests that, rather than being simply dismissed as false linguistic history, they should be taken seriously in their own right. Viewed collectively, common themes emerge. In contrast to the European tradition of naming new places after old ones, South Asian folk etymologies repeatedly tie place names to specifically local features. Consistent with the ritual power attributed to words in general and names in particular in South Asia, the folk etymologies also show a serious regard for the power of names to convey the character of what is named and an attempt to control the message that is so conveyed. This suggests an active discourse of resistance, in which people employ the very symbols used to define a hierarchical society (royalty, sacred persons, purity of fruits and flowers) to reinvent and so improve upon their own names (and character) and the names of the places with which they are associated.

References

Ahmad, Saghir. 1977. *Class and power in a Punjabi village*. New York: Monthly Review Press.

Knox, Robert. 1966 [1681]. *An historical relation of Ceylon*. Dehiwala, Sri Lanka: Tisara Press.

Kolenda, Pauline. 1985. *Caste in contemporary India: Beyond organic solidarity*. Prospect Heights, Ill: Waveland Press.

McGilvray, Dennis. 1994. Personal communication.

Lewis, J. P. 1924. Folk etymology: Place-names and traditions in the Matale District. *The Ceylon Antiquary and Literary Register* 9: 135–142; 10: 100–113.

Winslow, Deborah. 1984. The onomastic discourse of folk etymologies in Sri Lanka. *Social Analysis* 16: 79–90.

DEBORAH WINSLOW

SEE ALSO
Myth

FOLK LITERATURE

The concept of folk literature is best understood by defining each of its terms separately. The "folk" are any group of humans who share a common community, set of beliefs, attitudes. Generally, "folk" refers to nonelite communities, but recent research by folklore scholars extends this category to include elite groups. A folk group can be a caste group, Sanskrit-trained priests, the workers in a particular factory, members of a particular religious group or cult, women of a particular social stratum, or government bureaucrats. Each individual belongs to many folk groups, and these groups all have their own literature.

The word "literature" derives from the Latin root *littera,* letter of the alphabet, also implying that which is both learned and written. While the derived words "literate" and "literature" are now taken to imply the ability to write and that which is written, respectively, the Latin origin does not preclude unwritten knowledge. Hence, the literature of the folk includes oral or written verbal statements of their knowledge of the world in which they live, both materially and spiritually. It is the stories, songs, proverbs, myths, and epics of the folk, whether they be factory workers telling tales about broken machinery or women singing about their overbearing mothers-in-law, or caste members telling the origin myths of their caste and its status.

Much folk literature, such as stories, songs, and proverbs, remains oral knowledge even today. Other folk literature is written, either in inexpensive pamphlets containing songs, ritual stories, or episodes of epics, or in published collections by folklore scholars, often in the form of massive compendiums. Throughout Indian history, scholars have at various times collected the literature of the folk into scholarly volumes, as in the medieval Indian work by Somadeva, the *Kathāsaritsāgara,* the "Ocean of Streams of Stories," a volume which contains some 350 tales, fables, and anecdotes. Nowadays, modern university scholars as well as publishers for a wider readership undertake similar tasks.

Folk literature is invariably found in the many dialects and languages of South Asia; as the knowledge of the folk, it is generally distinguished from the more prestigious Sanskritic literature to which only high caste males previously had access. Nor is it in the Arabic of the Qur'ān or the Pali of the Buddhists. Whatever the language of their "great books," the folk use their mother tongues as the primary medium for folk literature.

Nevertheless, there is a continual exchange of ideas between the literature belonging to "great traditions," as scholars have termed them, and the literature of the folk, or "little traditions". This exchange allows us to suggest the timings of origins; for example, stories of many goddesses do not appear in the Sanskrit literature until after 500 C.E., suggesting that these were late additions borrowed by literate scholars from the folk traditions of their region. These newer accretions may have been traditions from regions recently conquered or may have been ideas and beliefs that only slowly were found acceptable by the elite male gatekeepers to the Sanskrit canon. Further, there is a tendency to identify the Sanskritic (or other classical language) version of a story or song as the "original" or "ur-text." Hence, many scholars consider the *Rāmāyaṇa* of Valmiki, written in Sanskrit around 200 B.C.E. to be the first *Rāmāyaṇa,* when, in fact, our knowledge of the development of story traditions suggests that this is the time that a popular oral vernacular tradition was recomposed in a prestigious language. Recently, scholars have begun to talk of "many *Rāmāyaṇas*," of which Valmiki's is only the most famous and the oldest written record.

It is important to remember that the number of speakers of any vernacular language (Tamil, Hindi, Bengali, Marathi, Malayalam, Kannada, Telegu, plus myriad dialects) have at any time far outnumbered the speakers of Sanskrit or Arabic or Pali or any other prestigious religious or legal language. Hence, the stories of the folk often reach a wider audience than texts of the so-called great traditions and there is a continual exchange between the folk and great traditions.

Any community has many kinds of folk literature, each filling different expressive niches in that community. Women sing birth songs in their courtyards, while men tell stories of local heroes around campfires at the edge of village lanes; the women pass on the meanings and rituals of childbirth, while the men's stories reflect what it means to be male in their society or how to contest local power structures. Older women teach *vrat kathā,* stories of rituals, to their daughters and daughters-in-law while men enact famous religious tales like the *Rāmāyaṇa* on verandahs, using costumes and props and having audiences in the hundreds. In different ways, these stories reflect the values of their localized communities and describe the proper roles of men and women, as well as members of different castes, within it. For example, women of a low-caste group may tell *vrat kathā* that glorify women who are poor and often hungry and who work outside their homes, while women of high caste groups are likely to tell similar *vrat kathā* that glorify secluded women able to offer the most prestigious foods to the gods. Oral epics tell of local or regional gods and goddesses and are often tied to specific rituals. Requiring extensive knowledge of performance styles as well as content, these are usually performed by professional (though often illiterate) singers. Through epics, larger regional communities construct a world view that is often at odds with the acclaimed "great traditions."

Oral folk literature, not being fixed by writing and the demands of publishers, is highly innovative, responding to the specific situations of each telling and to current events. An oral epic sung in the early 1970s in northern India, for example, refers to the war in Bangladesh, while the same epic sung ten years earlier speaks of a war with China. Tellers are responsive to their audience—eliminating or adding elements such as obscenities or local referents depending upon their judgment of their hearers. Hence, folk literature as performed is highly politicized, though often in subtle ways.

The various kinds of folk literature reflect different aesthetics: some are short and pithy, such as proverbs or jokes, while others are long and sung or chanted, such as oral epics. The aesthetic rules and standards for each genre may define the rhyme, alliteration, meter, framing, formulas, and presentation styles, among other poetic devices. For example, some song genres have a narrative style, with little repetition and parallelism; others are highly repetitive, perhaps being little more than the repeating of the names of a god or goddess. The aesthetic standards for each genre are known by the community and largely adhered to.

One form of aesthetic alteration and change is parody, that is, the transfer of the aesthetics of one genre (whether meter or melody or alliterative rules) to another genre. Often, the result is a humorous comment on the original, although it may also be resistant to or reflective of the borrowed original. Through processes such as parody, folk literature is constantly responding to new aesthetic demands.

Folk literature retains its oral qualities in the shift to audio recordings, so that a multitude of small recording companies across South Asia now produce tape cassettes for local distribution. Often specializing in popular local genres and performers whose audiences are more often rural than urban, the ease of making inexpensive audio recordings has aided the transfer of folk traditions to a more modern, popular culture.

Modern urban communities have their own folk literature, perhaps stories of the failures of new technology or songs that incorporate the ills of urban society or jokes that focus on confused teenagers in urban colleges. While the content of these new pieces of folk literature may differ from that of more traditional folk literature, the role of folk literature in discussing or marking critical social issues remains the same. Nor do modern urban societies lack folk literature because the "folk" are now literate; rather, folk literature remains a vital part of all human societies, even if transmitted via e-mail rather than word-of-mouth.

References

Appadurai, Arjun, Frank J. Korom, and Margaret A. Mills, eds. 1991. *Gender, genre, and power in South Asian expressive traditions*. Philadelphia: University of Pennsylvania Press.

Babb, Lawrence A., and Susan S. Wadley, eds. 1995. *Media and the transformation of religion in South Asia*. Philadelphia: University of Pennsylvania Press.

Blackburn, Stuart H., and A. K. Ramanujan, eds. 1986. *Another harmony: New essays on the folklore of India*. Berkeley: University of California Press.

Flueckiger, Joyce Burkhalter. 1996. *Gender and genre in a north Indian folk community*. Ithaca, N.Y.: Cornell University Press.

Lopez, Donald J., ed. 1995. *Religions of India in practice*. Princeton: Princeton University Press.

Marcus, Scott. 1989. The rise of a folk music genre: Biraha. In *Culture and power in Banaras*, ed. Sandra Freitag, 93–116. Berkeley: University of California Press.

Redfield, Robert, and Milton B. Singer. 1954. The cultural roles of cities. *Economic Development and Cultural Change* 3(1): 53–73.

Singer, Milton B. 1980. *When a great tradition modernizes: An anthropological approach to Indian civilization*. Chicago and London: University of Chicago Press.

Tawney, C. H., 1968 [1880]. *The Kathā Sarīt Sāgara, or Ocean of the streams of story*. Delhi: Munshiram Manoharlal.

SUSAN S. WADLEY

SEE ALSO

Balochistan: Oral Tradition; Brahui Folk Literature; Cassettes; Chapbooks; *Dāstān;* Epic; Folk Literature, Sinhalese; Folktale; Folktale, "Tale Type"; *Jātaka* Tales; *Kathāsaritsāgara; Kerāmat; Mangal* Kāvyā; Narrative Classification; Pañcatantra; Proverbs; *Qiṣṣa;* Riddle, Balochi; Riddle, Nepali; Sindh; Song; Story Literature, Persian; Story Literature, Sanskrit; West Bengal

FOLK LITERATURE, SINHALESE

Prior to the arrival of Buddhism in the third century B.C.E., Sinhalese literature would have been a strictly folk oral literature. The society of the Anuradhapura period was predominantly rural and agricultural, and the people were likely not well educated. Whatever literature that was produced in this early mission period would have been aimed at the newly converted, unlettered masses who were mainly listeners rather than readers.

There was a shift of literary interest from Pali, the language of Buddhist texts, to the courtly Sanskrit poetry around the twelfth century C.E. Former folk elements were gradually replaced by artificial, pedantic, and more elaborate rhetoric and ornate features borrowed from Indian Sanskrit literature. However, the folk tales, poems, songs, and theater did not disappear completely, as they had been deeply embedded in the folk culture. Buddhist monks, who were the undisputed custodians of literature and language, never neglected the aesthetic needs of the masses. In the long history of Sinhalese literature, not only the monks but also lay authors have made valuable contributions to both classical and folk traditions.

As in any other folk literature, most Sinhalese folk poems and songs come to us anonymously and unwritten; they prevailed through the centuries in oral tradition and only recently have been collected and published. Oral traditions are often less restricted by stereotyped forms or literary rules than are written traditions. As a result, we see in Sinhalese folk literature a variety of themes, forms, rhythms, rhymes, meters, and styles. Contemporary Sinhalese folk literature may be categorized as follows:

1. humorous and didactic tales
2. tales of religious nature
3. tales of the origins of gods, kings, and places
4. poems, songs, and ballads associated with daily life
5. poems and songs associated with dances and rituals
6. folk drama.

The origin of some Sinhala folk tales may be traced to Sanskrit, Pali, Tamil, and some other Indian sources. Popular *Jātaka* (recounting previous lives of the Buddha) tales and episodes of the *Rāmāyaṇa* and the *Mahābhārata* also exist in the Sinhala folk tradition. Adventures of heroic kings, originally recorded in the Pali chronicles, also have found a place in the folk repertoire. Tales known as *gamakatā* (village tale) are indigenous, representing a realistic picture of the Sinhala villager. These tales also illustrate a moral point or a proverb.

In the long history of Sinhala literature the folk element predominated. The scholarly ornate epic poems never integrated well with the unpretentious folk tradition. The village folk, however, have enjoyed listening to some great religious collections of stories, such as the Sinhalese version of the *Book of Jātaka Tales,* since they were rendered in a style that could be understood equally by the scholar and the ordinary villager. The bulk of the existent folk literature was produced on secular as well as religious themes and subjects between the sixteenth and nineteenth centuries.

UDAYA MEDDEGAMA

SEE ALSO
Folk Literature; *Jātaka* Tales

FOLK MUSIC

The pervasiveness of folk music in South Asia has long been recognized by scholars who have written about the extraordinary diversity of the subcontinent's music, variegated through regionalism, ethnic multiplicity, and countless foreign influences. Indeed, much of the abundant verbal folklore of the region is performed along the continuum from speech to chant to song, and many everyday activities, as well as most special events, take place within a musical context. This reflects a widely held belief in music's auspicious properties.

From a Western-trained musicological viewpoint, indigenous nomenclature does not provide terms for classifying many of the common varieties of musical genres found throughout South Asia. Classical music is generally referred to as *śāstriya saṅgīt,* the music of the treatises (from the Sanskrit *ṣāstra,* "treatise," and *saṅgīt: sam-* "with"; *gīt,* "song") or *rāgdāri saṅgīt,* music based on *rāg,* the melodic modes of South Asian classical music. The term *saṅgīta,* however, in the thirteenth century Sanskrit treatise, *Saṅgīta Ratnākara* (The Ocean of Music and Dance) was used to indicate song, instrumental music, and dance. Dance is no longer regarded as being a necessary part of saṅgīt. Folk music is generally referred to as gīt (song), with the prefix *lok* (of the people). Further distinctions are sometimes made, for example, *ādivāsi gīt* (the songs of the aboriginal peoples), *bhakti gīt* (devotional songs), and *filmī gīt* (Indian film music). There are numerous Western performance categories for which there are no equivalent indigenous terms, such as the English categories of instrumental folk music and epic and romantic ballads. Some of these English terms are commonly used by South Asians to classify their traditions. English terms such as "classical" and "semiclassical," the former in place of śāstriya or rāgdāri saṅgīt, and the latter to refer to some of the genres that exist between the classical and the folk, such as *ṭhumrī, jāvalī,* etc., which are usually performed in concerts. Indeed, the boundaries between folk and classical, as well as other categories such as tribal, devotional, semiclassical, light classical, popular, film, and others, are highly permeable and in a constant state of flux. For example, filmī gīt borrow heavily from folk musics as well as classical and Western styles. Likewise, folk melodies have often inspired classical *rāg* (melody patterns), which are sometimes named for a tribe, region, or town, as in *rāg Ahīr* (melody named after a herder tribe), *rāg Kāṇḍa* (melody named after Karnataka state) and *rāg Jaunpurī* (melody named after the town of Jaunpur). Similarly, many folk songs exhibit rāg-like characteristics and often have a comparable modal basis.

The oppositional terms *deśī* and *mārga* are often used in music classification. In general the term "deśī" is understood to refer to regional folk music, defined as nonclassical, traditional (that is, pre-media influenced), and predominantly rural music. Folk music is contrasted with classical music, which is supported by a theoretical base and learned through the traditional master-disciple path (*mārg*) of tutelage, referred to as *gūrū-śiṣya* (from Sanskrit, for Hindus) or *ustād-shāgird* (from Urdu, for Muslims). Folk music is also contrasted with other distinct types of traditional genres, such as theatrical music (*nāṭyasaṅgīt* in Maharashtra and the music of *yakṣagāna* in Karnataka) and liturgical chanting of the Vedas and the Qur'ān, as well as the popular commercial music of mass media.

Roughly 80 percent of the population in South Asia still lives in villages, although the boundaries between rural and urban are always in a state of flux. Similarly, the boundaries between rural and urban musics have constantly been mediated, increasingly now through radio and television, the prolific Indian film industry, and the recently flourishing audio- and videocassette industries.

Musical Style

It is difficult to characterize all of South Asian folk music, but some stylistic features are quite common. Vocal music predominates throughout South Asia, and singers generally perform together in near-unison melodies that make frequent use of repetition. Vocal melodies seldom exceed an octave and can have as few as three or four notes. A stringed melodic instrument, flute, or harmonium may follow to embellish the vocal melody in a style called heterophony. Percussion instruments generally accompany, using cyclical patterns especially in recurring units of three, four, or seven beats. While the drone is always present in classical music, it appears in only some folk music traditions. Folk melodies sometimes follow the same alternating bipartite structure as classical compositions, in which the first section (*sthāyī*) is in a lower register, followed by a second section (*antarā*) in a higher. The first section

Drummers from the Halakki Gowda tribal community perform at an annual dance ceremony. Karnataka, India. © Mimi Nichter

then returns as a refrain for conclusion or transition to a subsequent verse in the antarā.

In contrast, the outdoor music of percussion and oboe ensembles occupies a unique position as a purely instrumental folk genre. The oboes play drones and continuous heterophonic melodies using circular breathing techniques, and curved trumpets may provide sporadic elephantine blasts unrelated to the tonality of the oboe melody, while the percussionists play interlocking rhythmic patterns.

Performers

"Folk" in the indigenous terminology does not distinguish between the music of lay musicians and that of those for whom music is a vocation, whether full time, part time, or seasonal. The music of the former is sometimes described as functional, since it is performed by individuals and communities to satisfy their own needs and responsibilities. It is not usually performed for an audience and is not generally recompensed, whereas vocational musicians perform for others and are compensated in cash or kind for their performances. Such vocational musicians develop special expertise through training and practice, though not always of the formal kind implicit in the gūrū-śiṣya model. Among the many vocational groups of musicians are *Laṅgā, Maṅgaṇiyār,* and *Ḍholī* in Rajasthan and *Ḍom* in many parts of North India, as well as their counterparts in South India, *Pāṇan, Pulluvan,* and *Malayā,* who often exhibit great technical virtuosity and musicianship, usually far in excess of that of lay performers. Although there are occasions when both may perform together, the distinction between the music performed by lay performers and that of the vocational is a useful way of classifying South Asian folk music, as this influences the interactional dynamics of the performance event.

Nonprofessional Performers

Music of the more than fifty million non-Hindu aboriginal tribals of the region has received relatively little attention from scholars, and like most research on folk music, the available publications have tended to focus more on the texts of tribal songs than their melodies or performance contexts. Cylinder recordings of tribal music in South India were made by Edgar Thurston during the end of the nineteenth century as part of the Ethnological Survey of India. This survey resulted in his monumental *Castes and Tribes of Southern India and the Deccan* (1909). Continuing in the survey methodology, A. H. Fox Strangways made cylinder recordings of tribal, folk, and classical musicians in many parts of India in 1910, which he described and notated in his *The Music of Hindostan* (1914). Both these cylinder collections are now housed in the British Library National Sound Archive in London. Arnold Bake (1899–1963) also recorded and filmed many tribal examples in the course of his survey documentation made during the 1930s, copies of which are archived at the University of London, the University of California at Los Angeles, and the Archives and Research Centre for Ethnomusicology in New Delhi. His student Nazir Jairazbhoy continued in the same survey mode; his work resulted in a series of narrated BBC broadcasts later published as *A Musical Journey Through India 1963–64*. Recent research includes that of Babiracki on the music of the Muṇḍā tribals in eastern India and Wolf on the Koṭās of the Nilgiri Hills. Though highly diverse, tribal music often exhibits more melodic range and freedom than that of the mainstream population, and even includes some harmony among some northeastern tribes, such as the Nāgas. Monodic pentatonicism (single melody based on a five-note scale) and small-range melodies with small intervals also exist. Another distinguishing feature is that tribal men and women often join together to dance and sing, in lines as well as circles, sometimes extemporizing sung verses antiphonally between the sexes or between members of different villages. Such cross-sexual interaction rarely occurs in nontribal village life, where men and women usually perform in segregated groups.

The majority of the rural population in South Asia is, however, nontribal. Hindu women are especially noted for their vast repertoire of songs, often sung in groups during life-cycle celebrations such as the many stages of weddings: during the application of henna to the hands of the bride, the arrival of the bridegroom at the bride's house, and the departure of the bride for the groom's house, for example. They also sing songs asking for divine protection during observances marking various stages of pregnancy—such as at the seventh month—for celebrations after the birth of a child, for the first menstruation, for invoking blessings during household rituals, and for special calendrical festivals. Women sing songs alone or in small groups while performing domestic work, as in the Maharashtrian *ovī,* grinding songs. Such songs may contain sarcastic lyrics aimed at in-laws, particularly the mother-in-law, who has a great deal of power over the young bride, or they may be romantic or devotional. The gender boundary in such songs is sometimes permeable in the sense that male vocational singers often appropriate these women's songs, transforming them in order to utilize them for entertaining broader audiences or for other commercial gain.

Village women and men also sing in sex-segregated groups while engaging in circle dances at festive occasions, sometimes rhythmically clapping or beating sticks together or against the hands and sticks of the other dancers, as a danced form of music making. In recent times men and women sometimes dance together, as in the *rās* stick dance of Gujarat. Certain women's genres were originally intended for the ears of other women alone. For example, Punjabi women amuse themselves, unobserved, by creating satirical verses about their in-laws and even their own husbands, especially during weddings and festivals, such as *Baisākhi* at harvest time. In this genre, called *giddhā,* one or two women take turns singing and miming the text in dance. This example expresses a young bride's frustration at having to veil her face each time her husband's father appears:

> I will grind red chilis fine with my new pestle
> And throw them in my father-in-law's eyes to blind him.
> Then I won't have to cover my face in his presence.

There are many such satirical and rude insult songs, called *gālī,* sung by women during weddings and the ludic spring festival, *Holī.* While most of the women's repertoire of songs is concerned with the home and the family, the men's repertoire consists primarily of occupational songs about fishing, rowing, and other manual labor, devotional songs, and festival songs. Since women often work in the fields with men, agricultural-cycle songs of planting, transplanting, and harvest are sung by both sexes. Such songs are often in call-and-response form, in which a leader or series of leaders first sings the verse to be repeated by the others. Radios and cassette players are beginning to replace such self-created music with the consumer music of mass media, just as mechanization is replacing the traditional work activities of fishermen and other occupational groups in some places.

Vocational Performers

Vocational musicians may be full-time, part-time, or seasonal professionals. Many supplement their livelihoods by farming or rearing animals; in addition, some also practice hereditary trades such as barbering. Most instrumental music is played by specialist musicians, usually hereditary, whose patron families or temple and shrine duties are inherited from their forebears. The traditional instrumental ensemble consists of one or two double reed or multiple reed aerophones (regionally named *shahnāī, nāgasvaram,* and *mohorī*) and a variety of membranophones (drums with skin heads) such as the double-headed *ḍholak/ḍhol/tavil,* paired kettle-drum *nagāra,* and *daf* frame drums, often adding curved or S-shaped horns (*kombu*). They perform at weddings, festivals, and other auspicious outdoor occasions, and also for temple and shrine rituals. Such groups provide the auspicious (*maṅgal*) music needed by all walks of society, in tribal and nontribal villages, towns, and cities from Afghanistan to Nepal, from Sri Lanka to Bangladesh, for processions in weddings, festivals, and other public functions. In many instances, they are now being replaced by Western-style marching bands with brass, woodwinds, electronic keyboards, and most recently by audiocassette recordings.

Among the vocal traditions are hereditary bards such as *cārans* and *bhāṭs* who have been supported by patron families for generations to recite genealogies and sing ballads and heroic poetry praising the patron and his ancestors. Others include wandering mendicants, bards and minstrels, snake charmers, musicians associated with acrobats, actors, puppeteers, and other street entertainers who find patronage in both rural and urban contexts.

Narrative and Theatrical Genres

The performance of folk narrative often involves musical elements in the way the storyteller's voice is manipulated, using devices such as heightened speech, chant, song, or all three. He or she may also play an instrument to echo or embellish the text melodically or rhythmically, or just to provide a drone. One or more partners may join in the vocal and instrumental activity. Small hand cymbals, often played extremely well, pellet bells (hollow metal balls containing rattling pellets, like the dancer's ankle bells, *ghuṅghrū*), variable-pitch drums (e.g., *cawaṇḍgā* and *uḍukkai*) and the one- or several-stringed lutes (*ektār*) are the most prevalent form of accompaniment, but bowed fiddles (*sāraṅgī, rāvanhatta*), sometimes with pellet bells attached to the bow for rhythmic emphasis, and even wind instruments may elaborate the performance of narrative, as in the Baluchistani and Rajasthani *narḥ* players who intone words directly into their notched flutes. Often such storytelling is part of a larger ritual. One form of ritualized storytelling of the Tamils in southern India and northern Sri Lanka is the *viḷ pāṭṭu* (bow song). In the performance of epic stories concerning such local deities as Shasta, two lead singer-players use jingling sticks to strike the string of a six-foot-long bow, which has a dozen bells hanging below, while a chorus of singers strike hand drums and the bow's brass or clay pot resonator. Recently, women's viḷ pāṭṭu groups have become especially popular. The form has been adapted for telling Christian and contemporary stories and was even used in Sri Lanka to disguise the intent of political meetings and to communicate secret messages among Tamil Tiger separatists.

Most forms of folk theater make use of music's power to attract audiences and transport them to another realm of experience. They usually perform stories from the epics *Rāmāyaṇa* and *Mahābhārata,* and the Purāṇas, as well as from local legends. The voices of singing actors and actresses are most typically accompanied by at least one drum, small hand cymbals, and often a harmonium (free-reed hand-pumped keyboard organ introduced by English missionaries in the late nineteenth century) or wind instruments suited to the typically outdoor performance setting.

Devotional Music

Each of the many religions of the region also has its own devotional songs, constituting one of the most widespread forms of music found throughout South Asia. The *bhajan* (from Sanskrit, "to serve, adore") or *kīrtan* (from Sanskrit, "to praise") is the most prevalent form of Hindu devotional song. It is sung in praise of Hindu deities and may be performed alone by a specialist *kīrtankār* who illustrates stories with bhajan. Most often, however, bhajan are sung by a chorus of nonspecialists led by a specialist singer in leader-chorus fashion. Such groups are usually accompanied by drums, cymbals, wooden clappers, and often the harmonium. Bhajan singing often continues throughout the night as participants seek ecstatic experiences in a process that is believed to be a means for the soul to achieve salvation from rebirth.

Many bhajans sung today were composed by saint-singers from the *bhaktī* (devotion) religious revolution which began more than ten centuries ago in Tamil Nadu. Beginning with the Ālvār and Nāyanmār saints, the devotional movement spread north, west, and east, especially through the songs of singer-saints such as Jñyāneśwar (thirteenth century C.E.), Nām Dev (thirteenth century), and Tukārām (seventeenth century) of Maharashtra, Mīrābai of Rajasthan (fifteenth century), Kabīr Dās (fifteenth/sixteenth century) and Tulsidās (sixteenth/seventeenth century) of Uttar Pradesh, Purandara Dāsa of Karnataka (sixteenth century), and Caitanya of Bengal (fifteenth/sixteenth century). These wandering saints sang in temples, religious shrines, and other settings in order to communicate with ordinary people, so that the songs gradually permeated rural society and strongly influenced its folklore. Unlike many forms of folk music, these song texts, transmitted orally as well as through print, include the name of the author in the final verse as a signature. Hindu *sagun bhajans* glorify the names and virtues of the gods and goddesses, while *nirgun bhajans* ponder the formless aspects of divinity. Sikhs, Jains, Christians, and Muslims have their own equivalents of devotional bhajan as well, since the phenomenon of adoration through music, either communally or individually, is pan-South Asian.

The comparable Muslim genre is *qawwālī* (songs sung in praise of Allah, the Prophet Muḥammad, his son-in-law, ʿAlī and his descendents, and the martyrs Ḥasan and Ḥusayn). Qawwālīs also include praise of Sufi saints and the genre called *ghazal* with its mystic/romantic song texts in Urdu and Persian. Like bhajan, qawwālī performances provide a pathway to ecstatic union with the Divine, and may display a high degree of influence from classical music. In contrast to bhajans, however, qawwālīs are nonparticipatory, as members of the ensemble are largely limited to specialist singers. Although both bhajan and qawwālī typically follow a leader-chorus pattern, frequently with refrain, qawwālī is characterized by individual spontaneity, with melodic and sometimes textual improvisation. Qawwālī sessions are led by one or more qawwāl (singer), a professional and highly skilled musician respected for his knowledge of mystic poetry. Hand clapping is prominent among the responding chorus members, along with the same instrumental accompaniments used in bhajan singing, but without hand cymbals and with such instruments as the stringed *bulbultaraṅg* (a board zither with typewriter keys originally from Japan) and clarinet.

In contrast, Muslim communal singing occurs especially among women during Sunni celebrations of the birthdays of the Prophet and his wife Bībī Fāṭima and during Shīʿa observances of the death of Ḥasan and Ḥusayn, the Prophet's grandsons. In a unique pocket of Arab-influenced Muslims, Mappila Muslim women of North Kerala clap a steady beat while singing narrative responsorial religious songs called *mālā* (garland) in a musical style reminiscent of their ancestors from the Persian Gulf. These songs are traditionally sung during evenings at home and recount such historical events as the Battle of Badr and the Mappila uprising of 1921. In addition to the liturgical chanting of ritual texts and singing of devotional songs, many of the regional folk cults make use of music's suggestive and sensory powers in consciousness-altering ceremonies for inducing trance and ecstatic states. One example is the Manipuri shaman (male *maibā* and female *maibī*), who goes into trance for healing and divination while singing and playing the *penā*, a horsehair-stringed fiddle.

Modern Performance Contexts

Regional and national folk festivals conduct competitive public events for musical forms found throughout South Asia; international tours result for the most favored performers. Many rural music and dance forms have thus become folklorized and are performed not only in staged folk festivals but also in classicized versions in dance and music concerts. Commercialized versions of these folk forms use orchestral settings, electronic instruments, and special effects for "Bollywood" (Bombay's film industry) or the regionalized cassette boom.

Government patronage of folk music in India has been highly centralized since independence and consists mainly of the activities of the Sangeet Natak Akademi (SNA; Academy of Music, Dance, Song, and Drama) in New Delhi and its satellites in each state. The central SNA conducts field research and sponsors the annual Republic Day parade in New Delhi to which folk artists are invited from each state. It also publishes books and a journal, sanctions a small percentage of time on the state-controlled national and local television and radio networks for folk and folkloric genres, and presents national awards for leading figures in the field, including performers and scholars. Lok Virsa Institute for Folk Heritage in Islamabad, Pakistan, fulfills a similar function and also issues cassette and video recordings of folk music.

Co-optation of folk music to convey messages of political propaganda and social welfare (population control, sanitation, and health), following the practice of sharing life management skills in some folklore forms, has been found to be an effective means of communication by the central and state government offices of publicity. Regional song and drama divisions commission live performances of theatrical forms, including puppetry, which incorporate music's persuasive powers to communicate the state's messages.

State-run as well as private museums throughout South Asia display folk musical instruments, some with archives of audio recordings and related materials. The SNA and its ancillaries have such exhibits and collections, as do many privately owned museums such as the Raja Dinkar Kelkar Museum of Musical Instruments in Pune, Maharashtra, and the Karnataka Janapada Trust near Bangalore, Karnataka, which also sponsors publications and performances.

Conclusion

Due to the relative isolation of many regions, stylistic differences in South Asian folk music have developed over time and have served to identify the regional affiliation of the performers. Within regions, the social and functional identity of performers is further distinguished, in part through musical means. As in other forms of expressive culture whose traits change and evolve over time in response to the environment, music thus provides socially necessary information on ethnic and societal identity, as well as meaningful commentary on the human condition.

References

Allana, Ghulam Ali, ed. 1982. *Folk music of Sind*. Jamshoro, Pakistan: Institute of Sindhology, University of Sind.

Babiracki, Carol M. 1991. Musical and cultural interaction in tribal India: The Karam repertory of the Mundas of Chotanagpur. Ph.D. diss., Department of Music, University of Illinois at Urbana.

Baily, John. 1988. *Music of Afghanistan: Professional musicians in the city of Herat*. Cambridge: Cambridge University Press.

Blackburn, Stuart H. 1988. *Singing of birth and death: Texts in performance*. Philadelphia: University of Pennsylvania Press.

Bryce, Winifred. 1964. *Women's folk-songs of Rajputana*. Delhi: Ministry of Information and Broadcasting, Publications Division.

Capwell, Charles. 1986. *The music of the Bauls of Bengal*. Kent, Ohio: Kent State University Press.

Chandola, Anoop. 1976. *Folk drumming in the Himalayas: A linguistic approach to music*. New York: AMS Press.

Deva, B. Chaitanya, and Josef Kuckertz. 1981. *Bhārud, Vāghyāmuralī and the Daff-gān of the Deccan: Studies in the regional folk music of South India: A research report*. 2 vols. and cassette recording. Munich: E. Katzbichler.

Fox Strangways, A. H. 1914. *The music of Hindostan*. Oxford: Clarendon Press.

Frasca, Richard Armando. 1990. *The theater of the Mahābhārata: Terukkūttu performance in South India*. Honolulu: University of Hawaii Press.

Hansen, Kathryn. 1992. *Grounds for play: The Nautankī theatre of North India*. Berkeley: University of California Press.

Henry, Edward O. 1988. *Chant the names of God: Musical culture in Bhojpuri-speaking India*. San Diego: San Diego State University.

Jairazbhoy, Nazir Ali. 1988. *A musical journey through India, 1963–64*. Book and 3 audiocassettes. Los Angeles: University of California at Los Angeles, Department of Ethnomusicology.

———, and Amy Catlin. 1991. *The Bake restudy in India, 1938–1994: The preservation and transformation of performance in Tamilnadu, Kerala, and Karnataka*. A video monograph. Van Nuys, Calif.: Apsara Media for Intercultural Education. Color, 1/2", 60 min.

Karacaudhurī, Amalendubikāśa. 1984. *Tribal songs of northeast India: With special reference to Arunachal Pradesh (A field study from December 1977 to May 1981)*. Calcutta: Firma KLM.

Mishra, Mahendra K. 1989. *Folksongs of Kalahandi*. Bhubaneswar: Mayur Publications.

Parmar, Shyam. 1977. *Folk music and mass media*. New Delhi: Communications Publications.

Prasad, Onkar. 1985. *Santal music: A study in pattern and process of cultural persistence*. New Delhi: Inter-India Publications.

———. 1987. *Folk music and folk dances of Banaras*. Calcutta: Anthropological Survey of India.

Qureshi, Regula Burckhardt. 1986. *Sufi music of India and Pakistan: Sound, context, and meaning in Qawwali*. Cambridge: Cambridge University Press.

Rāya, Sukumāra. 1988. *Folk-music of eastern India: With special reference to Bengal*. Shimla: Indian Institute of Advanced Study.

Sakata, Hiromi Lorraine. 1983. *Music in the mind: The concepts of music and musician in Afghanistan*. Kent, Ohio: Kent State University Press.

Slobin, Mark. 1976. *Music in the culture of northern Afghanistan*. Tucson: University of Arizona Press.

Tingey, Carol. 1990. Nepalese *pancia baja* music: An auspicious ensemble in a changing society. Ph.D. diss., Department of Music, University of London.

Thompson, Gordon Ross. 1987. Music and values in Gujarati-speaking western India. Ph.D. diss., Department of Music, Ethnomusicology Division, University of California at Los Angeles.

Thurston, Edgar. 1909. *Castes and tribes of southern India and the Deccan*. Madras: Madras Government Press.

Wolf, Richard Kent. 1997. *Of God and death: Music and ritual in everyday life*. Ph.D. diss., University of Illinois at Urbana-Champaign.

Yusuf, Zohra, ed. 1988. *Rhythms of the lower Indus: Perspectives on the music of Sindh*. Karachi: Department of Culture and Tourism.

AMY CATLIN

SEE ALSO

Bake, Arnold Adriaan; Balochistan: Oral Tradition; Bow Songs (Vil Pāṭṭu); Brass Bands; Cassettes; *Dom;* Film Music; Herders' Field Songs; Holī; *Kāfī; Mahābhārata; Ovī;* Popular Music; Purāṇa; *Qawwālī; Rāmāyaṇa;* Saints; Song; *Tarannum;* Thurston, Edgar; Tribal Music, Nilgiris; *Yakṣagāna*

FOLK MUSIC, NEPAL

Music is very important in Nepal and has been stressed alike in religion, education, and entertainment, as well as everyday life. Hindu priests, Buddhist monks, as well as common people make music both to please their deities and to appease malevolent supernatural spirits. Minstrels play music to entertain their patrons; common people play music to enliven their tedious work activities and enrich their festivities or leisure; and lovers use music to express their innermost desires more aesthetically and powerfully.

The diversity of musical contexts and ethnic groups in Nepal, and their perpetual interaction and mutual influence, have created a diverse range of musical traditions, thus making it difficult to present Nepali music as one unified musical system. Nevertheless, *rāga* and *tāla,* South Asian musical concepts defined below, are considered the essence of music by almost every ethnic group. Musicians are taught these concepts and learn their skills through formal training by a guru skilled in music, or through informal observation and practice.

Rāga is the expressive mood of music. It is considered a coloring agent of mind or generator of feelings and emotions. Rāga evolve from *mūrchanā* (scales) and *jāti* (derivative scales) and have the power to invoke unique musical-psychological feelings. They may be associated with various Hindu deities, regions, seasons, times, scientific and aesthetic elements, and magical properties. Attesting to the power of the rāga, Nepali legends record that the singing or playing of *Dīpak Rāga* once caused an unlit lamp to burn and the singing of the *Rāga Megha Malhār* brought down rain. Many folksongs, ballads, epics, dances, and dramas are named after specific *rāga,* such as *Mālasirī Gīt* (Mālasirī song), *Danasirī Karkhā* (Dhanasirī Karkhā ballad), *Ghaṭu (Ghaṭu* Epic*), Karuwā Nāca (Karuwā* dance) named after the rāga Mālasirī, Dhanasirī, Ghāṭu, and *Kaharawā,* respectively.

Tāla, or meter, is an essential component of the rāga. A given tāla has a fixed number of beats arranged in distinctive groupings determined by stress and quality. The tāla is thus a point of departure for the music's rhythm and, as such, is normally played on the drums. Within a given tāla, two performers (the singer or instrumentalist and drummer) may vary their rhythms to some extent, but they must coincide on the first beat of each tāla segment. The most popular instrument for the tāla in Nepali folk music is the *mādal,* a barrel-shaped drum with parchment stretched over both ends which is played with bare hands.

The Constitution of Nepal (1962) has provided equal status for every caste and the freedom to choose any profession. Nevertheless, in Nepali life the traditional musical castes are still looked down upon, and many of these castes still perform their age-old profession. One example of a musical caste is Damāī (derived from the *damāhā,* kettledrum), who prefer to be called Nagarchī (a player of *nagarā,* a large kettledrum mainly used in temples and palaces), and who earn their living both as musicians and tailors. The *damāi bājā* (caste-based instrumental ensembles) are hired by almost all ethnic groups to perform festive music, and they are also regularly employed by temples. In western Nepal, Damāī are also called *Ḍholi* (derived from *ḍhol,* two-headed laced drum) and *Huḍke* (a player of *huḍko,* an hourglass drum). Huḍke also perform folk ballads, epics, and dance-dramas. Because of their special talents, Huḍke are considered superior to their fellow Damāī and march in front of them on auspicious occasions.

The Gāine consider themselves descendants of the mythical celestial musicians, *Gandharvas*, and prefer to be called by this latter name. Until the mid-nineteenth century, they were court musicians and messengers and were not allowed to adopt any other professions. Their only job was to entertain and inform the court and the people by composing and singing hymns, ballads, and other songs. Today they are reduced to mendicants who entertain their patrons in bazaars and private homes by singing to the accompaniment of their primary instrument, the *sārañgī* (stringed instrument similar to fiddle). Drawing upon their vast repertoire, they entertain their patrons according to their interests: singing a combination of *maṅgala* and *stuti* (religious songs); lyrical *jhyāure* songs; *sabāi* and *karkhā* (social and historical ballads), political and satirical songs; and even mimicking the cries of animals and birds to entertain any children in the audience. The Gāine usually begin with preselected songs of their choice, but often sing also upon request from patrons in the audience.

The members of the musical castes of western Nepal, *Bādī* and *Bhāñnda,* entertain their patrons with song and dance. Unlike the practice of other musical castes, Bādi and Bhāñnda women also participate in the performance. Due to their seminomadism, their music has a heterogeneous origin and is even influenced by Indian commercial films, radio, and television.

Among the Newari-speaking castes of the Kathmandu Valley, *Kusle* are tailor-musicians. Being descendants of Kāpālika (a sect of Śaivism in Hindu religion), they are also called Jogī (practitioners of yoga) and function as priests and temple caretakers. *Jyāpū* (farmers) and *Kasāī* (butchers) have distinct musical traditions and are hired by other castes to perform ritualistic and festive music, dance, and drama. *Kulu,* however, are drum makers only.

Nepali folk music employs a number of instruments of indigenous origin. It has also been enriched by instruments from the Middle East and the West. More than a hundred specimens of instruments have been collected by the Royal Nepal Academy Musical Instrument Museum. (Some instruments, however, seem to have a much shorter history than others.) The standard, widely distributed, Nepali folk instruments may be classified according to both the Indian classification system and the Hornbostel-Sachs *Systematik,* developed by Erich von Hornbostel and Curt Sachs, the founders of modern organology.

The first group of Nepali folk instruments is the *tāla vādya,* or chordophones or string instruments, where the music is produced by stretched strings that are plucked, bowed, or hit. The instruments in this category are *ārbāio* (lute), *sāraṅgī* (fiddle), *tuṅnā* (long-necked lute), *murcuṅgā* (metal Jew's harp), and *bināyo* (bamboo Jew's harp).

The second group is the *suśir vādya,* or tubular or wind instruments. These include *muralī* (bamboo, wood, or metal flute played straight outward, as in a recorder), *bā̃surī* (bamboo, wood, or metal flute played out to the side), *karnāl* (trumpet), *narsiṅhā* (S-shaped trumpet which provides a pulsating, droning bass with high pitch), *śahanāī* (shawm), and *śaṅkha* (conch shell).

The third group is the *avānāddha vādya,* or membranophones, where the music is produced by hitting a skin stretched over a hollow object. Single-headed membranophones include *nagarā, damāhā,* and *ṭyamko* (kettledrums of descending size); *ḍamphu* (frame drum); *khaijaḍi* (frame drum, preferably made of lizard's skin with or without jingling bells along the edge); and a pair of *tablā* (drum): the *dāyāṃ* (right drum) for treble and the *bāyāṃ* (left drum) for bass. The double-headed membranophones include *ḍhol* and *mādal* (barrel drums); *ḍamaru* (rattle drum); *ḍhyāṅgro* (frame drum); and *huḍko* (hourglass drum). Especially among the Newari-speaking communities of Kathmandu Valley, dozens of drums are used for different purposes.

The final group of instruments is the *ghana vādya,* or idiophones, in which the music is produced by striking solid objects. The instruments in this category include three varieties of jingling anklets (*chāmp, ghuṅghuṅru,* and *paiñjarī*), five different types of cymbals (*jhyālī, jhāl, jyāmṭā, kartāl,* and *mujurā*), and the *ghanṭī* (handbell).

The *pance bājā,* a musical ensemble, is comprised of members of a single caste, *Damāī.* The Damāī are hired by various castes, ethnic groups, and government and nongovernment organizations to play as an ensemble, especially at auspicious occasions, and hence, their ensemble is referred to as a national ensemble. The pance bājā (literally, an ensemble of five types of instruments) comprises five kinds of wind and percussion instruments. These instruments are a pair of karnāl or narsiṅhā trumpets; a pair of śahanāī where one, the *rāgī śahanāī,* plays the melody and the other, the *surai śahanāī,* accompanies with a drone; three kettledrums where a pair of bigger drums are considered *bhāle* (male) and *pothī* (female), and the third smaller one is callled *ṭyāmko;* the *ḍholak* two-headed laced drum; and jhyālī cymbals with a large central bass. Since the ensemble is formed by a distinct caste group, it is also called *damāi bājā.* For example, among Newars of Kathmandu Valley a similar ensemble is composed of members of the *Kusle* caste, and their ensemble is called *kusle bājā.* Kusle serve only Newars, whereas Damaī serve various castes and ethnic groups of Nepal, including Newars.

Especially in urban areas, as an indication of modernization, the *naumatī bājā* (the instruments of Indo-Persian origins named after a famous musician, Naubat Khan) and *bacchai bājā* (Western musical instruments) are replacing or subordinating the traditional pance bājā. The former have not limited themselves to modern music but also play Nepali folk music, just as the pance bājā is not limited to traditional music and even plays discotheque music. Hence, these ensembles are an excellent source for studying continuity and change in Nepali folk music.

References

Bhattarai, Harihar P. 1985. Folklore studies in Nepal. *Himalayan Culture* 3(1): 10–14.

Helffer, Mireille. 1965. *Musician castes in Nepal.* Paris: Musée de l'Homme.

Hoerburger, Felix. 1975. *Studien zur Muzik in Nepal* (Studies of Nepali music). Regensburg: Bosse Verlag.

Lienhard, Siegfried. 1984. *Song of Nepal: An anthology of Nevar folksongs and hymns.* Honolulu: University of Hawaii Press.

Varya, Tanka V. 1985. *Nepal: The seat of cultural heritage.* Kathmandu: The Educational Enterprise.

HARIHAR P. BHATTARAI

FOLK PAINTING

No matter how diligently we attempt to catalogue South Asia's folk painting traditions, the researcher (or even the casual visitor) will still be likely to stumble upon one more village with a localized ritual art form, or yet another community whose vocation is to produce paintings on order for patrons of various kinds. Among the many surfaces that may be decorated with pigments are walls (*pithora* murals by Bhīl tribals in Gujarat); cloth (*paṛ* scrolls used by itinerant storytellers in Rajasthan, Gujarat, and Andhra Pradesh); paper (Kālīghāṭ souvenir paintings from Calcutta); and glass (reverse painting in the Thanjavur style).

One useful way of classifying folk painting is to divide it into three categories: domestic mural or floor paintings, often executed by women and ritually renewed at regular intervals; paintings made for use by wandering storytellers; and paintings produced at temples as religious souvenirs for pilgrims to take home with them. Not all traditions fit neatly into these pigeonholes, and some fit into more than one. For example, the *jādū paṭ* is a paper scroll carried by traveling showmen in Bengal; they use its pictures to demonstrate to tribal villagers the rewards in the afterlife of good and evil deeds performed here on earth. However, the particular occasion that draws the showman to a village is a death in one of its households. The first frame of his scroll depicts a man or woman without eyes; only when the eyes of this figure are painted on in the presence of the grieving relatives is the soul of the deceased believed to be liberated. Thus, the itinerant showman (who often illustrates his own scrolls) not only entertains his customers, but performs an essential ritual function in village society.

In considering the first category, that of ritual domestic art, we may make a few generalizations. These paintings are usually undertaken in relation to some festival or life-cycle event (a wedding, the birth of a son); in Orissa, they may be the visible record of a woman's vow (*vrat*), for the duration of which she has promised

Babhruvahana Fights the King of the Nāgas: An Illustration to the 14th Book of the *Mahābhārata*. Pinguli, 19th century, Maharashtra, India, © Asian Art Museum, San Francisco

the deity to fast, prepare special foods for her family, and renew the mural designs regularly. In such cases, the artist is clearly an "amateur," since she is executing the mural gratis, for the benefit of her own family. This distinction also holds true for the ephemeral threshold designs (variously termed *kōlam, rangolī,* and *alpanā* in different regions of India). Rendered in rice flour, lentils, colored powders, or a solution of lime and water, these intricate diagrams are believed to protect the home from danger and to welcome auspicious deities into it. They are effective only when made by the women of the house. In contrast, certain women in a village or community may become specialists in wall painting and be paid in cash or kind to decorate the homes of their neighbors. Responding to a severe famine in 1964–1965, the central government encouraged women of the Madhubani district in Bihar to create versions of their lively mural compositions on paper. This modification of their tradition proved salable in urban centers and meant that some of the women became entrepreneurs; it also resulted in male family members taking up what had previously been a strictly female ritual art form.

The Citrakathis of Maharashtra produce paintings used as storytelling props. They illustrate episodes from the Hindu epics (the *Rāmāyaṇa* and *Mahābhārata*) and the Purāṇas on pieces of paper that they then paste together back to back. They recite these legends to musical accompaniment, turning the laminated sheets over when they arrive at the appropriate juncture in the tale. The paintings, which measure roughly twelve by eighteen inches, are transported in cloth bundles (*pothī*) by the peripatetic Citrakathis. Known centers of production for these vigorous and colorful paintings include Paithan and Pinguli (Maharashtra). Elements of their artistic style recall the leather shadow puppets of the neighboring state of Karnataka.

Puri (Orissa) and Nathadwara (Rajasthan) are two great centers of Hindu pilgrimage. Construction of the present temple of Jagannātha at Puri was begun in the twelfth century, and the tradition of hereditary artists who serve the deity may be almost as ancient. Known as Citrakāras, these artisans execute ritual paintings for the temple, produce souvenir pictures for purchase by pilgrims, and paint murals at monasteries and other locations. When subsidiary temples to Jagannātha (a form of the god Kṛṣṇa) were established at other sites in Orissa, Citrakāra families followed; in this way, the artisan clans spread throughout the region. Like the majority of Hindu craftsmen in India, they are Śūdras, belonging to the lowest caste category (*varṇa).*

The most important temple duty performed by the Puri Citrakāras is painting substitute images of the Jagannātha triad. Jagannātha is worshiped along with his brother Balabhadra and sister Subhadrā; the icons of the three deities are really carved wooden posts, with rudimentary arms and legs and large, staring eyes. During a period of fifteen days in the month of Jyeṣṭh (May/June), the wooden images undergo repairs; at this time, the gods are said to be "ailing," and temple visitors are prevented from viewing them. Artists from preeminent Citrakāra families are delegated to supply surrogate icons, in the form of paintings representing the triad. At other times, the Citrakāras are called to paint murals in the temple and to decorate the carts for the annual cart festival (*ratha yātrā*).

The majority of paintings produced by the Puri Citrakāra community are souvenir images called *jātrīpaṭi* (pictures for pilgrims). Ranging in size from minuscule (half an inch square) to large (two by three yards, or more), they may be painted either on paper or on specially laminated cloth. Cheap likenesses of the triad of deities are portrayed roughly, on old newspaper, while large cloth hangings may be meticulously rendered. Favorite subjects for the large-format images are the Jagannātha temple, depicted in vertical section so that the triad is visible inside. Arranged in panels above and around this schematic temple are depictions of the ten avatars (descents into bodily form) of Viṣṇu and episodes from myths about them, shrines and temples in Puri, and festivals celebrated in the town. Sometimes the entire town of Puri is shown enclosed in a conch-shaped outline—the conch is an attribute of the god Viṣṇu.

By the mid-twentieth century, the Orissan Citrakāras had virtually ceased practicing their hereditary vocation. Rapacious middlemen had made it impossible for them to earn their livelihood by their traditional craft. Then, in 1952, a Polish woman named Halina Zealey mounted a social-service campaign to revive the art of Puri painting. She succeeded in interesting both the government and foreign nationals in the plight of the Citrakāras, and when she left Orissa after only two years, they were already well on their way to recovery. Nowadays, the state once again hosts a thriving community of traditional artists.

At Nathadwara, in Rajasthan, another Kṛṣṇa temple attracts pilgrims from across India (and from the expatriate community abroad). Its primary icon, known as Śrī Nāthjī, was brought from Braj in the late seventeenth century and established in what was then a small village near Udaipur. Soon, artisan families began migrating to Nathadwara in order to serve the needs of the temple and its pilgrims. Members of three distinct caste groups dwell in separate quarters of the town. Although historically Śūdras, the Nathadwara artists claim Brahman status and have been fairly successful in moving up in the caste hierarchy. As in Orissa, the women play an important role in image making.

Nathadwara artists furnish many images of Śrī Nāthjī for sale to pilgrims, since sectarian rules dictate that only hand-painted (not printed) images can be worshiped in the devotee's home shrine. Better known than these small images on paper, however, are the large-scale cloth hangings called *picchavāīs* ("that which is placed behind"), produced in nearly all of the Nathadwara artist ateliers. These painted hangings are a ritual necessity in the temple, for they constitute theatrical backdrops for Śrī Nāthjī's many *līlās* (playful activities performed by the god Kṛṣṇa). Thus, for the festival of Śarad Pūrṇimā, the picchavāī will portray milkmaids dancing with linked hands; they will appear to hold Śrī Nāthjī's raised and lowered hands, too, as though they were dancing with the statue.

Picchavāīs made for use in Nathadwara's main temple never depict Śrī Nāthjī. Instead, a large rectangular opening is left in the hanging so that it may be fitted around the relief stele of the god. Śrī Nāthjī does appear on most other picchavāīs, however. In some cases, the image on the picchavāī may be the only focus of devotion for those subsidiary temples or private shrines that do not possess a stone or metal icon of Kṛṣṇa.

The painters of Nathadwara were formerly involved in complex patronage relationships with the Śrī Nāthjī temple and with the ruler of Mewar (the princely state to which Nathadwara's high priest owed political allegiance). Hence, it is difficult to characterize them as folk painters. Perhaps they were folk artists when they worked for nonroyal pilgrims, and courtly artists when they executed commissions for the high priest of the temple or for the Mewar ruler. Nowadays, their major patrons are businessmen, who commission works for sale in major urban centers; for this reason, perhaps they ought now to be referred to as "export artists."

Certainly, not all genres of folk art fit into these three major categories. An example of a vital art form that does not is Indian playing cards (*ganjīfā*). Manufactured by artist communities throughout India (including those of Maharashtra and Orissa), these small, usually round, cards of laminated paper come in sets of one hundred or more (up to 360 cards per set). They are minutely painted in the style of the region where they are produced (von Leyden 1980). Specialized genres like the playing cards point up the richness and diversity of South Asia's numerous folk and popular traditions.

References

Ambalal, Amit. 1987. *Krishna as Shrinathji.* New York: Mapin International.

Dalmia, Yashodhara. 1988. *The painted world of the Warlis: Art and ritual of the Warli tribes of Maharashtra.* New Delhi: Lalit Kala Akademi.

Das, Jagannath Prasad. 1982. *Puri paintings: The chitrakāra and his work.* New Delhi: Arnold-Heinemann.

Fischer, Eberhard, and Haku Shah. 1970. *Rural craftsmen and their work: Equipment and techniques in the Mer village of Ratadi in Saurashtra, India.* Ahmedabad: National Institute of Design.

Harle, J. C., and Andrew Topsfield. 1987. *Indian art in the Ashmolean Museum.* Oxford: Ashmolean Museum.

Huyler, Stephen P. 1987. Rural wall painting of Orissa: A study of four villages. In *Facets of indian art,* ed. Robert Skelton et al. New Delhi: Heritage.

Jain, Jyotindra. 1984. *Painted myths of creation: Art and ritual of an Indian tribe.* New Delhi: Lalit Kala Akademi.

———, ed. 1998. *Picture showmen: Insights into the narrative tradition in Indian art.* Mumbai: Marg Publications.

Joshi, O. P. 1976. *Painted folklore and folklore painters of India.* Delhi: Concept Publishing.

Lyons, Tryna. 1997. Women artists of the Nathadwara school. In *Representing the body: Gender issues in India's art,* ed. Vidya Dehejia. New Delhi: Kali for Women.

Maduro, Renaldo. 1976. *Artistic creativity in a Brahmin painter community.* Research Monograph Series, no. 14. Berkeley: Center for South and Southeast Asia Studies, University of California.

Mode, Heinz and Subodh Chandra. 1985. *Indian folk art.* Bombay: Taraporevala.

Nagarajan, Vijaya. 1993. Hosting the divine: The *kolam* in Tamilnadu. In *Mud, mirror and thread: Folk traditions in rural India,* ed. Nora Fisher. Ahmedabad: Mapin.

Rossi, Barbara. 1998. *From the ocean of painting: India's popular paintings 1589 to the present.* New York: Oxford University Press.

Skelton, Robert. 1973. *Rajasthani temple hangings of the Krishna cult from the collection of Karl Mann.* New York: The American Federation of Arts.

Talwar, Kay, and Kalyan Krishna. 1979. *Indian pigment paintings on cloth.* Historic Textiles of India at the Calico Museum, Ahmedabad, vol. 3. Ahmedabad: Calico Museum.

Von Leyden, Rudolf. 1980. *Ganjifa: The playing cards of India.* London: Victoria and Albert Museum.

Williams, Joanna. 1996. *The two-headed deer: Illustrations of the Rāmāyaṇa in Orissa.* Berkeley; University of California Press.

TRYNA LYONS

SEE ALSO

Calendar Art; Card Games; Floor Designs; Folk Art; Folk Art, Orissa; Mithila Painting; Narrative Scroll Painting; *Paṛ; Paṭa Citra; Ratha Jātrā;* Vehicle Painting

FOLKLORISTS

See Balochistan, Oral Tradition; Benfey, Theodor; British Folklore (in South Asia); Brown, William Norman; Chaube, Pandit Ram Gharib; Colonialism and Folklore; Crooke, William C.; Elwin, Verrier; Frere, Mary Eliza Isabella; Grierson, George A.; Kothari, Komal; Mackenzie, Colin; Natēṣa Śāstri, Pandit Sangēndi Mahālinga; Nationalism and Folklore; Penzer, Norman Mosley; Ramanujan, A. K.; Sen, Dinesh Chandra; Tagore, Rabindranath; Thurston, Edgar

FOLKTALE

The terms for narrative genres in South Asia vary by language, region, and community. Nevertheless, we can analytically distinguish some broad characteristics and categories of folktales. "Folktale" as a term refers to a variety of oral prose narrative traditions in South Asia, told in prose, not sung, although some folktales may include sung rhymes or verses, usually for special effect. Hence the speech style of the teller of a folktale is conversational and relatively unmarked. This distinguishes the folktale from the folk epic, which is sung and usually has major portions in verse.

Stories, or folktales, as one woman from the Kangra valley in North India recently stated, "are about love.... They are about deluded infatuation, possessive attachment, and nurturing affection" (Narayan 1997, 3). Folktales contain cultural wisdom to be passed on to further generations, while being continually responsive to the settings and times in which they are told. They tell of social and cosmological relationships, as they create new relationships between tellers and audiences. Folktales are not necessarily used to teach, but even those told for entertainment often contain biting commentaries on social situations and incorporate and substantiate key cultural beliefs. Other tales, especially those used in religious contexts, are explicitly didactic, whether they be women's tales associated with rituals, known as *vrat kathā,* or tales told by a gūrū to teach his disciples the ways of the world.

In South Asia, there are three major categories of folktales that correspond to the named folktale genres in some regions. First, there are tales with named characters. These are most likely to have kings and queens as their heroes and heroines. The main character(s) are generally named in the first line, as in "There was once a king named Vikramaditya." Often these tales are considered both mythological and true, and sometimes have an opening frame or formula that marks the truthfulness of the tale. One such frame, used in a village on the Gangetic plain, starts, "An elephant in a tree, a peddler in a bazaar . . . dried cow dung sinks, the grinding stone rises. . . . From now on my talk goes straight." After stating the impossible, the teller then makes an overt claim for the truthfulness of what follows.

These tales form part of that category of literature that Hindus mark as *ithihas* (history). Both men and women tell these kinds of tales, although male tellers predominate, and the focus of men's and women's tales of the same event is often different. Further, these tales with named characters are likely to be longer than those with unnamed characters, and have more convoluted and multifaceted plot structures. Many of them have counterparts in Sanskrit or Persian literature, and many are available in inexpensive chapbooks in the markets or, more recently, have been produced for an urban market as comic books. Some of these stories are also found in other narrative genres, such as epic, ballad, narrative songs, or folk dramas.

A second category of folktale includes those with unnamed characters. Here other identities, for example, caste or occupational markers, are most salient. Lacking the explicit concern for "truth," no opening frames are found. Rather, a typical opening to such a tale is "There were once four friends, a woodcutter, a priest, a goldsmith, and a barber," or "There was once a man with no children. He was very rich, and his wife was virtuous." These stories focus on unlikely events or the use of magical accessories, such as a snake stone, all the while marking out key cultural concepts and social relationships. The endings of these tales are usually abrupt, often framed by "the tale of [name of teller] is over."

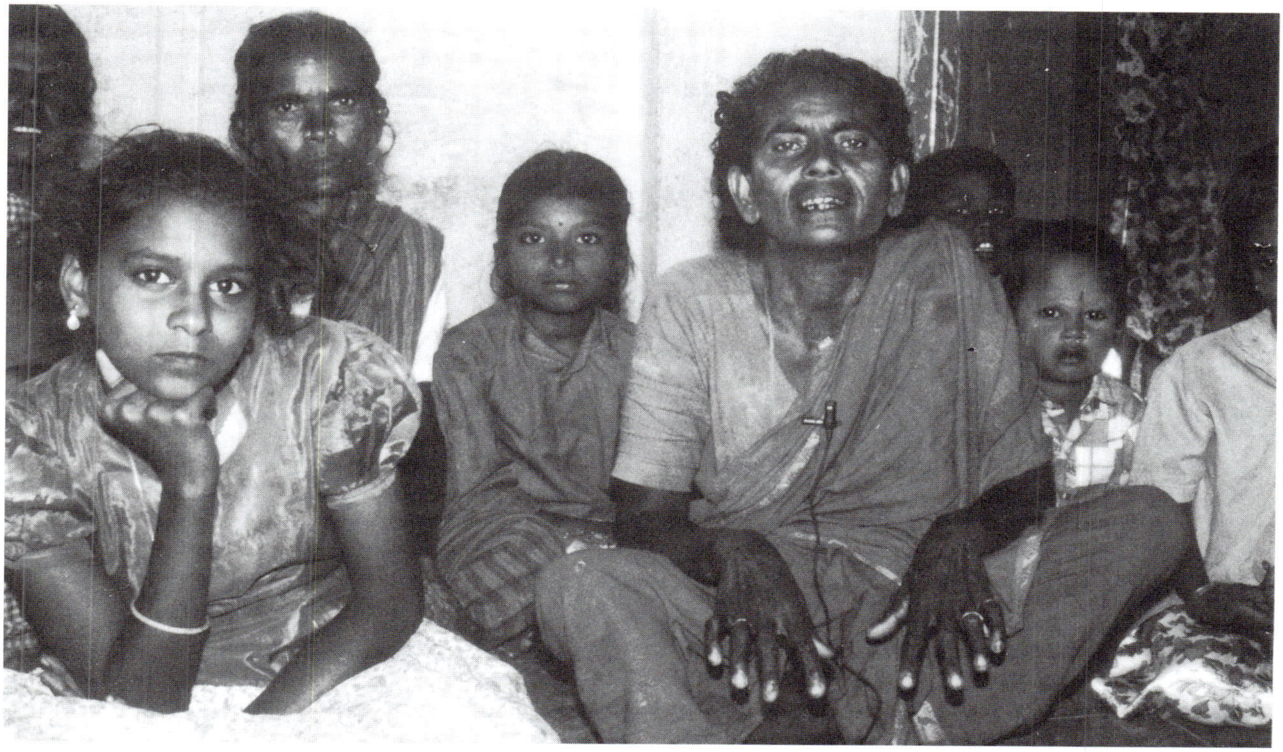

Telling of a folktale. Tamil Nadu, India, 1995. © Stuart Blackbum

These tales are more likely to be short than long and are told by men, women, and children. Not considered myth or "truth" or history, they are often humorous and deal with both extraordinary and everyday events. It is uncommon for these tales to be published for a general public, though many are found in schoolbooks or in compilations for other special audiences. In nineteenth-century compilations, these tales are more likely found in collections made by women of women's tales than those made by men of men's tales.

A third category of folktale is that of ritual tales. Most Hindu rituals have an explanatory tale that elucidates the rules for that ritual, how it came about, and how humans have benefited from performing it. Often called vrat kathā, these ritual tales are told or read from cheap pamphlets when the relevant ritual is performed. Many of these ritual tales have no named human characters, but a few, perhaps borrowed from other kinds of tales, do have them. Pamphlets containing the tale for a specific ritual, or for all the rituals of a month or year, are commonly found in the markets. These are the most widely available and read published folktales and are the only printed tales found in many homes.

Despite the fact that men and women may tell any of these tales, there are some differences in context and content. Men's tales are told outside of the home, whether around a neighborhood fire on a winter's evening or in a gathering on a verandah. Male tales tend to focus less on domestic topics and issues and involve caste and political issues, including warfare. Women's tales are told inside the home, often around a hearth or inside a cool room on a hot summer's day, and focus on issues of family and kin. Whereas men are more likely to tell tales marked as historical truth, women tell more ritual tales.

Another key facet of folktales is their intertextuality, the shifting of themes and motifs between tales and between tale genres and other forms of folklore. Hence a "historical" tale about Harischand will be referenced in women's folk songs about being a proper wife or will become the answer to a riddle. Or a tale about an oil presser and a king may be incorporated into an oral epic where it merges into a much more complicated plot structure. Further, many tales may form a larger connected corpus through the use of a frame story, a story that contains another story within it that allows the teller to link one tale to another as the frame story itself proceeds.

Several kinds of tales associated with particular cultures or religions are prevalent throughout the subcontinent or in various regions. One style of Persian tale, the *qiṣṣa* or *dāstān,* both words meaning "story," is particularly popular in northern India, sometimes incorporated into the categories discussed above, sometimes standing more markedly distinct. The tales marked as qiṣṣa include stories of demons, fairies, dragons, and ghosts, as well as romance. The genre being especially popular in vernacular printed form, qiṣṣa narrators were popular professionals in the late nineteenth and early twentieth centuries, while the qiṣṣa tales became popular plots for folk theater.

The Jātaka tales of the Buddha's early births are another set of religious tales that remain current in both oral and written versions. Here moral teachings are woven into entertaining tales. Equally well known are the Pañcātantra or animal tales that heavily influenced narrative traditions in the Middle East, Europe, and Southeast Asia. It is probable that both the Jataka tales and the Pañcātantra tales have always coexisted in elite written versions and vernacular oral and written versions, from their earliest writing down, as they do today.

The oral narrative traditions in South Asia are enormous and continue to develop as new social themes and issues lead to new tales or new versions of old tales responsive to current social crises. While a shift to print and other new media no doubt exists, the plethora of folktales provides endless fodder for new variations.

References

Blackburn, Stuart. 2001. *Moral fictions: Tamil folktales from oral tradition.* Folklore Fellows Communications 284. Helsinki: Academia Scientiarum Fennica.

Mills, Margaret. 1991. *Rhetorics and politics in Afghan traditional storytelling*. Philadelphia: University of Pennsylvania Press.

Narayan, Kirin. 1997. *Mondays on the dark night of the moon: Himalayan foothill folktales*. New York: Oxford University Press.

Pritchett, Frances. 1985. *Marvelous encounters: Folk romance in Urdu and Hindi*. Riverdale, Md.: Riverdale Co.

Steel, Flora Anne, and Richard Carnac Temple. 1884. *Wide-awake stories*. London: Trubner and Co.

Stokes, Maive. 1880. *Indian fairy tales*. London: Ellis and White.

Temple, Captain R. C. 1962 (reprint). *The legends of the Punjab,* Vol. 2–3. Patiala: Language Department, Punjab University.

Thompson, Stith, and Jonah Balys. 1958. *Types of Indic oral tales*. Folklore Fellows Communications 80. Helsinki: Suomalainen Tiedeakatemia.

Zvelebil, Kamil V. 1987. *Two Tamil folktales: The story of king Matanakama and the story of peacock Ravana*. Delhi: Munshiram Manoharlal.

SUSAN S. WADLEY

SEE ALSO

Balochistan: Oral Tradition; Chapbooks; Comic Books; Fortune-tellers; Frere, Mary Eliza Isabella; *Jātaka* Tales; *Pañcātantra;* Story Literature, Persian; Story Literature, Sanskrit; *Vrat Kathā*

FOLKTALE, "TALE TYPE"

The concept of "tale type" defined by American folklorist Stith Thompson (1947, 415) as a "traditional tale that has an independent existence" was developed by the Finnish school of comparative folk narrative research in the early twentieth century. It is based on the assumption that tales originate in a singular act of storytelling by a gifted individual, who combines narrative raw materials, or subunits, subsequently termed "motifs." A motif is understood by Thompson as "the smallest element in a tale having a power to persist in tradition," and three classes of motifs are differentiated: actors, items, and incidents. Only in rare cases do motifs exist independently, and they usually represent elements of a tale. On the other hand, tales surviving in the long course of diffusion tend to develop along uniform lines, so that their essential form may be reconstructed by analyzing the common narrative elements from a large body of texts that are basically identical in content. The analysis of tales containing both an essentially identical structural frame as well as a similar stock of motifs constitutes the deduced tale type. Although the concept of tale type has been disputed over the past decades, it still represents the most practical way to systematize large amounts of traditional narrative units from a given geographical or ethnic area.

The theoretical foundation for the concept of tale type arose within the European Romanticists' search for primordial folk forms, constituting one of the primary goals of the geographical-historical school, or Finnish school, in folk narrative research. In its present form, the concept was devised by the Finnish scholar Antti Aarne and further developed by Thompson in his effort to map a macrocultural area labeled "Indo-European" within a wider world tradition. In Thompson's view, a tale type is a unit defined purely by content. His definition disregards most other methods of analysis or interpretation, which address narrative structure, performance, or meaning.

The concept of tale type has been developed and usefully applied by empirical research. In order to establish tale types, large numbers of tales originating from various regions and periods were abstracted and analyzed, eventually leading to the establishment of certain content elements, which, in their specific order, constitute the type. This method has been practiced in a number of exemplary monographs by scholars following the method of the Finnish school, such as Aarne, Jan-Øjvind Swahn, and Warren E. Roberts.

The basic theoretical assumptions for documenting a tale type are as follows: Tales are recorded in versions, each version representing a single written or verbal articulation of a given tale. Since versions of any given text by necessity deviate from each other, even if only in single words or phrases, each version is a potential variant. (Practical use tends to restrict the term "variant" to those versions incorporating particular elements and deviations not represented in the majority of versions establishing the actual tale type.) When variants of a certain tale type occur in larger numbers in specific regions, the term "oicotype" (ecotype) is employed (essentially equivalent to the term "redaction" for literary texts).

In the latest revision of Aarne/Thompson's international catalogue, *The Types of the Folktale* (1961), tale types are organized into three major groups: animal tales, ordinary folk tales, and jokes and anecdotes; a smaller fourth group includes formula tales, with a residual fifth category of unclassified tales. All three of the major groups are further subdivided. Ordinary folk tales include (a) tales of magic, (b) religious tales, (c) *novelle* (romantic tales), and (d) tales of the stupid ogre. At the end of various further subdivisions stands the actual tale type, which may belong to any one out of three categories: (1) regular tale type, identified by a cardinal number ranging between 1 and 2400 and supplied with a fairly detailed analysis and extensive documentation of published occurrences or references to archived texts; (2) subtype, identified by a cardinal number and additional letter, indicating a relationship to the regular type, which might range from constituting a variant to a loosely connected similar tale type; (3) irregular type or subtype with additional (one or more) asterisks, indicating that the relevant tale types at the time of the last revision were not yet regarded as being sufficiently well documented to be accepted as regular tale types.

A tale type is established by the tale's existence in a considerable number of versions, fixed by Thompson as three in any specific smaller tradition area. Alternatively, it would suffice for a tale type to be recorded in singular versions in different tradition areas. A tale type, in some cases, may be as short as a single motif. If it is longer and more complex, then it may be divided into several episodes. Certain tale types may also occur together in larger narrative units, usually termed "conglomerates." A number of specific tale types regularly, or even exclusively, appear in conglomerates of variable content. Conglomerates differ from cumulative tales or chain tales, which are defined by their formula structure involving the repetition of certain actions.

The concept of tale types implies that one can characterize any narrative, incorporating motifs, episodes, or sequences, believed to belong originally or substantially to another tale type, as being contaminated by extraneous elements. The reality of narrative performance, on the other hand, testifies to the fact that tale types are but an analytical construct. The idealized tale type is encountered very rarely and is extremely unlikely to be met with in the case of spontaneous storytelling. Tellers do not tell tale types; they always tell tales. These tales are generated by the combination of large and small narrative units, with the tellers adjusting content appropriately to fit the immediate context in which they are performing. In this respect, the concept of tale type is inadequate for analytically addressing the large amount of improvisation, variability, and creativity practiced in the art of actual storytelling.

In the present day, the search for an ideal original form from which all other documented versions derive has largely been abandoned in favor of other topics of analysis concerned with local varieties, context, and meaning. Besides the fact that the establishment of tale types rarely corresponds with narrative reality, any attempt at analyzing and establishing "pure" tale types has serious flaws since tales always convey ideas related to specific cultural contexts. If a tale is performed in a different cultural context, elements extraneous to the new context are bound to be adapted. Thus the content of identical tale types is bound to differ in different communities, though scholars might not recognize them due to the distortion of essential elements by narrative acculturation. On the other hand, the combination of narrative elements in regionally static tale types is also determined by local cultural concerns.

Due to agreement among scholars of the geographical-historical school "that India itself demanded special consideration" (Thompson 1961, 5), there is a certain preference for tale types analyzed from Indian tradition in Thompson's index. In several instances, it has since been demonstrated that tale types that the index documented as existing solely in India have been found to be prevalent also in other regions. In several instances, such as 951A ("The King and the Robber") and related subtypes, detailed analysis proves the supposed Indian original tale type to be identical with previously abstracted subtypes from other regions and thus only representing an Indian oicotype. We should question the particular emphasis given to Indian texts, especially since this was so clearly tied to Thompson's notion of an "Indo-European" cultural area in which India possessed the pride of origin. Most of the narrative data analyzed by Thompson and his collaborators were collected in the colonial era, and many of the tales are of unclear origin, revealing a history of cross-cultural influences from the Near East (especially Iran), Europe, and other parts of Asia.

References

Aarne, Antti. 1908. *Vergleichende Märchenforschungen* (Comparative Folktale Research). Helsinki: Finnische Literaturgesellschaft.

Beck, Brenda F. 1987. Frames, tale types and motifs: The discovery of Indian oicotypes. In *Indian Folklore*, ed. Peter J. Claus, Jawaharlal Handoo, and D. P. Pattanayak, 1–51. Mysore: Central Institute of Indian Languages.

Ben-Amos, Dan. 1980. The concept of motif in folklore. In *Folklore studies in the twentieth century*, ed. Venetia J. Newall, 17–36. Wood Bridge: D. S. Brewer; Totowa, N. J.: Rowman and Littlefield.

Georges, Robert A. 1983. The universality of the tale-type as concept and construct. *Western Folklore* 17(1): 21–28.

Holbek, Bengt. 1990. Variation and tale-type. In *D'un conte... à l'autre. La variabilité dans la littérature orale* (One story to another. The variability in oral literature), ed. Veronika Görö-Karady, 471–484. Paris: Éditions du Ventre National de la Recherche Scientifique.

Jason, Heda. 1972. Structural analysis and the concept of the "tale type." *Arv: Scandinavian Yearbook of Folklore* 28: 36–54.

———. 1989. *Types of Indic oral tales: Supplement*. Folklore Fellows Communications, vol. 242. Helsinki: Academia Scientiarum Fennica.

Mode, Heinz. 1960–1961. Types and motifs of the folktales of Bengal. *Folklore* (Calcutta) 2(4): 201–205.

Roberts, Warren E. 1958. *The tale of the kind and the unkind girls: Aa-Th 480 and related tales*. Berlin: De Gruyter.

Swahn, Jan-Øjvind. 1955. *The tale of Cupid and Psyche*. (Aarne-Thompson 425, 428). Lund: CWK Gleerup.

Thompson, Stith. (1947) 1977. *The folktale*. New York: Holt, Rinehart and Winston; repr. Berkeley and Los Angeles: University of California Press.

———. 1955. *Narrative motif-analysis as a folklore method*. Folklore Fellows Communications, vol. 161. Helsinki: Academia Scientiarum Fennica.

———. 1955–1958: *Motif-index of folk-literature*. 6 vols., 2nd ed., rev. and enl. Bloomington: Indiana University Press.

———. 1961. *The types of the folk-tale. A classification and bibliography: Antti Aarne's Verzeichnis der Märchentypen (FFC 3)*. Trans. and enl., 2nd rev. Folklore Fellows Communications, vol. 184. Helsinki: Academia Scientiarum Fennica.

Thompson, Stith, and Warren E. Roberts. 1960. *Types of Indic oral tales*. Folklore Fellows Communications, vol. 180. Helsinki: Academia Scientiarum Fennica.

ULRICH MARZOLPH

SEE ALSO
Narrative Classification

FOLKTALE, NEPAL

The orally transmitted prose narratives of common people are termed *lokakathā* or *dantyakathā* in Nepali. The terms *kathā, kahānī, kissā,* and *āhān* are also sometimes used. Nepali folktales are thought to express the thoughts, feelings, hopes, and fears of the common people, and many of the tales center on folk heroes or the realm of the supernatural.

Folktales share many characters, stories, and other elements with other folklore genres, such as proverbs, songs, and ballads. For example, the proverb *Mukundasenle muluk māreko jasto* ("One should not be like Mukunda Sen in battle") recalls the story of the sixteenth-century king of Pālpā who declared war on many kingdoms at once without a proper strategy, and hence lost most of the wars. This proverb is used to refer to any person who takes on too many tasks at once and therefore fails to accomplish any specific goal.

In the imaginative world of Nepali folklore, birds and beasts, as well as rivers, forests, and mountains, may take on human characteristics such as the power of speech. Some stories, generally classified as fables, explain the mythological origins of natural phenomena, such as why the River Kālī is black (*kālī* is both the name of a Hindu goddess and the word for "black") and why the River Setī is white (*setī*); why one river flows deeply and makes a hissing sound, while another river hastily changes its course; why the *uttis* tree is straight, slender, and grows on cliffs, whereas the *lālīgurāns* tree is crooked with spectacular flowers; and why monkeys do not steal at night, and tigers will not enter cowsheds.

In Nepali villages, folktales are often told by elders to children, as they sit around the fireplace in the winter, or upon a shaded platform in the summer, when the daily household chores are done. Alternatively, when villagers gather under the big banyan tree on the hot sunny days, the elders narrate various folktales. They might ask young people who the most virtuous king was and then give a name of a king and tell a story to justify the point. The subject of the tale can vary from kings and queens to ghosts and supernaturals to village tricksters. In general, the objective of the performance is to entertain and educate youths on norms, values, and survival skills in the society. Generally, all the tales start with the phrase, *ekā deśmā* (literally, "In a certain land"), followed by the introduction of the central character. For example, *ekā deśmā eutā rājā thie* or *ekā deśmā eutā syāl thiyo* ("In a certain land there was a king," or "In a certain land there was a jackal"). Then the narrator proceeds with the tale, often concluding with a rhyme:

Bhannelāī phulko mālā.
Sunnelāī sunko mālā.
Yo kathā vaikuṇṭha jālā.
Bhanne belāmā tāttātai āijālā.
(A garland of flowers to the narrator.
A chain of gold to the audience.
Let the tale go to heaven,
and may it return anew at the next performance.)

Folktales also serve devotional purposes, particularly those that center upon gods, goddesses, and other supernatural spirits. Sacred folktales such as *mahātmya* and *vrata kathā,* whose stories are recorded in the *purāṇas* (classical Hindu texts) are performed during certain astrological periods for festivals and other special functions. For instance, *Swasthānī Vrata Kathā* is performed during the month of Māgha (January–February) and deals with power and compassion of the goddess Swasthānī, emphasizing that faith in her and good conduct can make a poor person prosperous and a prosperous person poor. *Tīj Vrata Kathā* relates to the penance of Pārvatī in order to get her desired husband, Lord Śiva, and is told on the festival of *Tīj*. In this festival, celebrated on the third day of brighter moon in the month of Bhādra (August–September), the Hindu women honor Lord Śiva and Pārvatī through worship, song, dance, and vrata kathā performance with the belief that their blessing will prosper conjugal life. *Satya Nārāyaṇa Vrata Kathā* deals with truthfulness and good conduct and can be told on any auspicious occasion. The narrators of these *vrata kathā,* who are generally learned persons, tell of the benefits accrued to those individuals with *vrata* (piety) who have sponsored such ceremonial storytelling in the past. The stories, narrators, hosts, and audiences are all venerated during these performances.

Whether or not the story is devotional, there is a common belief in Nepal that the event of the storytelling should be completed. If not, the goddess of tales, Vāgīwarī, will be displeased, and as a result, some misfortune may befall the narrator or audience. Some tales recount such misfortunes. For example, once a king was fond of stories, but he used to fall asleep before the stories were completed. The goddess of tales considered this habit an insult. She appeared in his faithful minister's dream and warned that she would put a needle in the king's food, fell a tree to crush him, and send a cobra into his bedchamber to kill him. She also warned the minister not to disclose her intention. Otherwise, he would be transformed at once into a stone. The minister saved the king from the needle and tree. While he was saving the king from the cobra, the king noticed his minister's presence in his bedchamber, and, flying into a rage, he ordered him to be hanged. The minister preferred a noble death and told all the events to the king and turned at once into a stone.

Folktales are the most studied genre of Nepali folklore. However, almost all the studies by native and foreign scholars alike are either limited to collections of texts or general classification of tale types. Thus, there is much room for advancement in analysis and interpretation of Nepali folktales, especially with regard to the context of performance events.

References

Bhattarai, Harihar P. 1985. *Folklore studies in Nepal.* Himalayan Culture 3(1): 10–14.

Department of Culture. n.d. *Some folktales of Nepal*. Kathmandu: Department of Culture.

Jest, Corneille. 1993. *Tales of the turquoise: A pilgrimage in Dolpo.* Translated by Margaret Stein. Kathmandu: Mandala Book Point. (Original: *La turquoise de vie*. Paris, 1985).

Lall, Kesar. 1978. *Lore and legend of Nepal*. Kathmandu: Ratna Pustak Bhandar.

Sakya, Karna, and Linda Griffith. 1980. *Tales of Kathmandu: Folktales from the Himalayan Kingdom of Nepal.* Brisbane: House of Kathmandu.

Sharma, M. M. 1978. *Folklore of Nepal*. Delhi: Vision Books.

Vaidya, Karunakar. 1978. *Nepalese folk stories and legends.* Kathmandu: Purna Book Stall.

HARIHAR P. BHATTARAI

SEE ALSO

Purāṇa; Satya Narāyana Vrat Kathā; *Vrat Katha*

FOOD AND FOODWAYS

The various diets of South Asia center around rice and bread and share an emphasis on aromatic spices and seasonings. Turmeric, cumin, coriander, asafetida, tamarind, aniseed, fenugreek, rock salt, and curry leaves are some of the common spices that flavor the *dal*s, curries, vegetables, relishes, pickles, and chutneys that accompany the staple dishes. Barley, maize, millet, rice, sorghum, and wheat are the staple grains in different parts of South Asia. Lentils and pulses provide an important source of protein.

Regional cuisines vary in both their ingredients and methods of cooking, reflecting local climates and crops as well as community tastes and taboos. In the wheat belt of North India, breads (*capati, paraṭha, nān, roṭī*) substitute for, or complement, rice. North Indian and Pakistani cuisines include fragrant *biryānī*s (rice with saffron) and *pūlau*s (pilaf), savory lamb, goat, and vegetable curries, enriched with ghee or cream and often studded with almonds or dried fruits. Clay ovens (*tandur*s) are used for baking breads and roasting meats. South India's cuisine is dominated by rice. Coconut, chilies, and mustard seeds are common seasonings in South Indian cooking, which is known for its Udipi cuisine of *iḍli*s (steamed rice dumplings), *dōsa*s (pancakes made of a rice and black gram batter), and *sambhar* (a lentil soup). In Sri Lanka, rice is also the staple, and fish curries are popular, as they are in Bangladesh, Bengal, and the coastal states of Kerala and Goa.

Cooking mediums also vary regionally: pungent mustard oil is commonly used in Bengal and Bangladesh, while coconut and sesame oils are preferred in the south, and peanut oil in the west. Rich and flavorful *ghee* (pure butter fat with milk solids removed), considered ritually pure and auspicious, is widely used for cooking, especially on ritual and festive occasions, but has been increasingly replaced by the less costly *ḍālḍa* (vegetable oil) for everyday cooking.

The virtues of vegetarianism are preached by several South Asian religions—Hinduism, Jainism, and Buddhism—but vegetarianism is most strictly adhered to by Jains and some orthodox Hindus. Jains, steadfast adherents to the doctrine of *ahiṃsā* (nonviolence), believe that a *jīva* (soul) exists in even the most microscopic forms of life, and thus they are particularly attentive to rules governing diet and food preparation. Among their food prohibitions are meat, eggs, potatoes, and onions. Other Jain food customs include boiling and straining drinking water and eating before sunset. Many Buddhists are also vegetarian, though unlike the Jains, some Buddhists do eat eggs. Strict, orthodox Hindus avoid onions and garlic in addition to meat. In their rituals, several tantric sects deliberately partake of traditionally prohibited foods, notably meat (*mamsa*), fish (*matsya*), and alcohol (*madya*), in order to transcend the boundary distinctions of mind and body. Many South Asians include meat (chicken, goat, lamb) and eggs in their diet, although Hindus eschew beef and Muslims, pork. Muslims look to the Qur'ān and Sharīʿa for dietary regulations, one of which requires that food animals be ritually slaughtered.

Tea and coffee, both imports to South Asia, became popular during colonial times and now provide daily opportunities for socializing during midmorning tiffin (a light midday meal) and afternoon tea. Sweets and snacks usually accompany tea. Tea preparation ranges from the green, cardamom-spiced tea of Kashmir to the yak-butter tea of Nepal to the peppery *masāla* tea of Rajasthan. Coffee is more popular in South India. Other favorite drinks are the frothy *lassi,* made from buttermilk (served sweet or salty); *limbu-pāṇī,* a thirst-quenching drink made with lime juice, water, sugar, and salt, especially in the hot season; and the seasonal mango and sugarcane juices.

The midday meal is the main meal of the day. A typical meal may include dāl or sambar (lentil preparations), one or two vegetable dishes, a meat or fish curry (in nonvegetarian homes), a yogurt-based salad (*raita*), and some condiments (pickle, chutney, lime wedge, salt), all arranged in small portions around a mound of rice. Meals are typically eaten in silence while sitting on the ground near the home hearth. Great effort is made to ensure the purity of the kitchen, the cook, and the preparation of foods: washing is required before and after eating; some cooks will wear special pure clothing (such as silk) while cooking; food is not to be tasted as it is prepared (because saliva pollutes); animals are prohibited in the kitchen; and menstruating women are not allowed to participate in food preparation. Meals are prepared and served by the women of the household on disposable leaves or stainless steel or brass *thāli*s (round plates). There is a specific ordering of the placement of foods on a thāli, just as there is a specific order in which to eat foods; this ordering is region-specific and reflects the classification and cultural values assigned to foods and their preparation.

In homes of pious Hindus, prepared food is first offered to the household deities, whose shrine is typically found in the kitchen area. Tradition also dictates that guests, pregnant women, infants, and the elderly should eat first, and husbands before their wives. Many Hindus follow the custom of facing the auspicious direction of east or north while eating; some also observe the habit of sprinkling their thāli with water while saying a prayer of thanksgiving before eating. Food is eaten with the right hand, the left hand reserved for unclean activities; drinks are not common with the meal, though water is drunk at the end of it. Leftovers are considered polluted (having come in contact with a person's saliva) and are given to dogs and crows.

The Indian Āyurvedic tradition recognizes a direct correspondence between foods and their physiological effects. Āyurveda identifies six different tastes, each of which exerts a particular influence on one of the three humors of the body (phlegm, bile, wind): these are sweet, sour, salty, bitter, pungent, and astringent. Ideally, a balanced meal should contain all six flavors. Variety in texture is also important, and a healthy diet includes foods of these five types: chewed, licked, sucked, drunk, and *bhōjya* (food which may be eaten without mastication). Foods are also classified according to their intrinsic qualities as *sattvik* (purity-inducing), *rajasik* (passion-inducing), or *tamāsik* (lethargy-inducing); they are also indicators of types of people, for it is believed that passionate persons tend to eat more rājasik foods, and those of greater spiritual and intellectual purity eat more sattvik foods. Sattvik foods are considered conducive to purity of mind and body and include foods that are fortifying as well as tasty, such as milk and milk products, rice, wheat, barley, green gram, fruits, and many vegetables. Sattvik foods promote serenity and calm, and are appropriate for religious fasts. Most people eat what are considered rājasik foods, that is, foods that produce the energy and passion of humankind; rājasik foods are bitter, sour, salty, and pungent. Rājasik foods like meat, eggs, onion, and mangoes excite the senses and heat up the body. Tamasik foods are characterized as cold, stale, and spoiled, promoting sloth and impeding spiritual development and the purification of mind and body.

The emphasis within these classification systems of taste, texture, and quality is on preserving health of mind and body through a balanced diet. The diet often needs to be manipulated to achieve this balance, and in trying to remedy an imbalance (which may display itself as a physical or mental illness), one has to take into account the season as well as an individual's personality and health. In the winter and monsoon months, foods classified as "hot" like jaggery (unrefined brown sugar), dates, radish, mustard, jackfruit, and bitter gourd can provide one with the stamina to fight the cold and damp, whereas cooling foods like bananas, sugarcane, and honey are preferred in the summer. The digestive system is considered most active in the winter and weakest in the summer and rainy seasons; thus one is advised to adapt one's eating habits to the season. Hot foods are prescribed to counteract colds, but should be avoided by pregnant women; cool fools are prescribed for dysentery and fever. The hot-cold classification is quite widely used to regulate diet and health in South Asia, though what is considered hot or cold may vary from region to region. There are many folk beliefs about the curative powers of different foods and spices, in which the method of preparation is as important as the ingredients if the remedy is to be efficacious.

Foods are ranked in a hierarchical order within Hindu communities, as are cooking techniques, although the ranking varies from region to region. Ghee, cow's milk, roots, fruits, and vegetables rank among the purest foods, while meat, intoxicating beverages, water stored in an animal skin, garlic, and onions are traditionally ranked low because they are inherently impure, conducive to impurity, or difficult to digest. Those of higher caste rank and ritual status are expected to maintain and protect their status by avoiding foods that may compromise their purity.

There is a dominant ideological ranking that is reflected in the practice of commensality and food exchange in South Asia; the scholarly literature on food in South Asia has predominantly concerned itself with Hindu commensality issues in discerning how food transactions reflect caste ranking. To simplify a rather complex system, the general rule of thumb is that a Hindu takes cooked foods (more susceptible to pollution) from someone of higher or similar rank. Foods cooked in ghee (*pakka* foods) are considered superior to *kaccha* foods—those that are boiled, steamed, or fried (in something other than ghee). Raw foods are easily purified and pakka foods are less vulnerable to pollution; both can be exchanged more widely among different castes. Food exchanges reflect social and ritual relationships. Respect and humility are often demonstrated by eating someone's leftovers or, in some cases, by drinking the water in which someone's feet have been bathed. These practices are particularly evident in the relationship between a devotee and his or her god, and to a lesser extent between disciples and their gūrū, and wives and their husbands.

In Hindu temples, devotees receive as *prasāda* (the grace or blessing of the deity) a spoonful of the *pañcāmṛtā* (milk, honey, yogurt, ghee, and sugar) that has been used to bathe the deity. In temples and homes, deities are offered food and meals (*naivedya*) by devotees; the food offered to the deity is transformed into prasāda and is distributed to devotees. It is believed that gods and goddesses enjoy certain foods more than others and the naivedya offered to the deities often reflects their personal preferences; For example, Gaṇeśa's favorite food is *modak* (sweet balls), Śiva prefers white foods, Kṛṣṇa enjoys sweets, *khīr* (rice pudding) is a favorite of Gauri, and Rāma is said to like *pānaka* (a drink made of jaggery, ginger, and cardamom). Sacrifices of goats or chickens are also made to some deities who have a taste for blood. In some communities, animal sacrifices have been replaced by the offering and breaking of coconuts or watermelons. In Muslim communities, animals are sacrificed on the festival of *Bakra* *ᶜId (ᶜId-ul-Aẓḥa)* during the month of the Ḥajj and commemorate Abraham's submission to God in agreeing to sacrifice his son.

Foods play an important part in the life-cycle rituals of all the communities of South Asia. *Dohada* are the foods that satisfy the special cravings of pregnant women. Special diets, designed around the hot-cold classification of foods rather than their nutritional value, are popularly prescribed for menstruating or pregnant women, and lactating mothers. Among Hindus, the ritual of first feeding (*annaprasana*) takes place when infants are six months old, when they are typically fed a spoonful of rice gruel enriched with milk, ghee, and honey. Before undergoing the rite of initiation (*munj, upanāyana*), a young Hindu boy takes his last meal with his mother. After being initiated as a Buddhist novice, a young monk begs his first food from his mother. The first fast (*roẓa khushā'ī*) of a young Muslim undertaking his or her first *Ramaẓān* fast is marked with a special breaking-the-fast feast.

Marriages are marked with great feasting (and in some communities, with a period of fasting by the bride and groom). Certain foods, in particular rice, meant to symbolize the fertility of the union, are used during several of the marriage ceremonials. At the marriage feast, the bride and groom together pour ghee, a symbol of prosperity, onto the rice of each guest. Various customs are observed when a bride enters her marital home for the first time: in some communities, the first thing she touches are the cooking utensils, and in some regions, the bride knocks over a container of rice on entering the home to ensure its overflowing prosperity. Muslims mark the signing of the wedding contract as well as the consummation of the marriage with feasts.

Menstruation and death both invoke prohibitions in food and food processes. In Hindu and Jain households, menstruating women may not cook, and in many homes they eat alone. Among Hindus, no food or drink may be taken by any relatives of the deceased until the body has been cremated; during the mourning period, the family is fed by friends. The deceased are provided with food in the form of rice balls (*piṇḍa*s) during the twelve days after death and on annual memorial days (*śraddha*s); the mourning period as well as śraddha rites are concluded with a special feast traditionally served to Brahmans.

Festivals and fasts crowd the many calendars of the various South Asian communities. Every festival is marked by some special regional food preparation; favorites are *jālebīs, laḍḍus, halvā,* and khīr or *payasam. Besan* flour, rice flour, rose water, and cardamom are among the ingredients used in the preparation of festival sweets; sweets made from milk products of the venerated cow are also savored on auspicious days. The popular South Indian winter solstice festival is called *Poṅgal* after the boiled rice dish flavored with jaggery that is cooked and shared during this festival. One notable North Indian "food festival" is that of *Annakuta* ("mountain of food"), celebrated in honor of Lord Kṛṣṇa in the month of Kārtika at harvest time; during this festival mounds of foods are prepared and presented in Kṛṣṇa temples. Fasting (*upavāsa*) and abstinence from food are prescribed by several different religious traditions within South Asia and serve as rites of purification, penance, or preparation. Besides individual, supererogatory fast days (prescribed for particular weekdays, lunar days, months, etc.), some of the more well-known prescribed periods of abstinence include: Ramaẓān, the ninth month of the Muslim lunar year, during which Muslims abstain from food and drink between sunrise and sunset; the Hindu period of *caturmasa* (four months) and the three-month "rain retreat" (*Vassa*) of Buddhists, marked by restrictions in diet and other austerities; and *Paryushana,* a fast observed by all Jains. Many of these fasting periods conclude with a great feast (for example, *Ramaẓān* concludes with the feast of *ᶜId-al-Fiṭr*), or with the gift of food, as in some Hindu fasts that end with the feeding of a specified number of Brahmans (*paṅkti*).

Hospitality and charity are values enjoined and greatly praised by all the religious traditions of South Asia. The gift of food (*annadāna*) brings merit, and the traditions of Buddhism, Jainism, and Hinduism each have communities of ascetics dependent on the hospitality of householders for their food. It is a widespread practice that no guest may leave a house unfed, no matter how bare the larder; and offering a sweet to a newly arrived guest is a customary way to sweeten his or her welcome. Gifts of food are given on special auspicious occasions (festivals, weddings, initiations, etc.) to guests, relatives, servants, priests, or teachers. Traditionally, a cow was considered the greatest gift, bringing prosperity and sustenance in the form of milk, ghee, and yogurt. More common gifts are coconuts, rice, bananas, and sweets. According to the *Mahābhārata,* sesame is a superior gift that brings everlasting merit; thus sweets prepared with sesame are popular in some communities. The coconut, a popular offering in temples, is considered bounteous, and, like the cow, a symbol of fertility and long life. The banana rivals the coconut as a food offering; it is one of the "great fruits" (*mahāphala*), and since it grows in clusters, it is symbolic of fecundity and prosperity. Rice is also symbolic of fertility and abundance, and is offered both husked and unhusked, raw and cooked. Mangoes, a treasured delicacy during their limited season, are symbols of wealth and auspiciousness; mango leaves are commonly used to garland thresholds on festival and auspicious occasions. During women's household festivals, married women guests receive gifts of food such as rice, coconuts, cucumbers, and gram associated with prosperity and fertility. Guests who are served a full meal are offered *tambula* at the conclusion. Tambula, a packet of spices and condiments wrapped in betel leaf, is believed to aid digestion; it is popularly known as *pān supārī. Supārī* is chopped betel nut, which may be chewed alone, and pān is the betel leaf that wraps a customized selection of aromatic condiments. The pān leaf is smeared with lime paste (*cunam*) and then filled with one's choice of such ingredients as camphor, supārī, cloves, fennel, cardamom, cinnamon, or perfumed tobacco. Many folk beliefs are associated with tambula; among them are magical powers, curative powers, and the enhancement of sexual desires.

Food has more than nutritional value in South Asia; food and food transactions carry with them moral, social, economic, and symbolic values, all of which factor into one's diet and eating habits. What one eats, how one eats, and with whom one eats, reveals information about one's caste, rank, status, and social relationships. Eating with someone can convey and strengthen political and social alliances; eating is used to maintain boundaries (of caste, class, clan, gender) as well as break them. Boundaries traditionally marked by strict rules governing food transactions are increasingly being crossed, especially in urban centers where the proliferation and popularity of coffee shops and roadside vendors make it more difficult to observe ritual rules about what one may eat and with whom. However, despite these changes, food continues to carry complex cultural markers in South Asia, and South Asian folklore is particularly rich in its use of food metaphors in proverbs, parables, and folk songs to convey values, relationships, and, in particular, sexual attraction and consummation.

References

Achaya, K. T. 1994. *Indian food: A historical companion.* Delhi: Oxford University Press.

Banerji, Chitrita. 1991. *Life and food in Bengal.* New Delhi: Rupa & Co.

Khare, R. S. 1976a. *Culture and reality: Essays on the system of managing foods.* Simla: Indian Institute of Advanced Study.

———. 1976b. *The Hindu hearth and home.* Durham. N.C.: Carolina Academic Press.

———, ed. 1993. *The eternal food. Gastronomic ideas and experiences of Hindus and Buddhists.* Delhi: Sri Satguru Publications.

Khare, R. S., and M. S. A. Rao, eds. 1986. *Food, society & culture: Aspects in South Asian food systems.* Durham. N.C.: Carolina Academic Press.

Marriott, McKim. 1968. Caste ranking and food transactions: A matrix analysis. In *Structure and change in Indian society,* ed. Milton B. Singer and Bernard Cohn. Chicago: Aldine Publishing.

MARY MCGEE

SEE ALSO
Dohada (Pregnancy Cravings); Fish and Fishing; Foodways, Bangladesh; Foodways, Pakistan; Hospitality; Hot/Cold; Jain Folklore; Jainism; Medicine, Ayurveda; Muslim Folklore, Sri Lanka; Navānna/Nabānna; *Ponkal;* Ramaẓān/Ramadan; Tabarrak; Turmeric

FOODWAYS, BANGLADESH

Bengalis are proverbially rice and fish eaters. However, Bengal has been host to numerous ethnic in-migrations which have had an impact on food habits as well. Rice forms the principal cereal at lunch and dinner and might also be served at breakfast—usually in the form of *pāntā-bhāt* (leftover rice to which water has been added), or as *muṛ, khai,* or *cin̐ṛā,* that is, puffed, popped, or flattened rice. Ground into flour, rice is also made into various forms of breads, cakes, fritters, and crepes.

Full meals feature plain boiled rice; a thick soup of *masuri ḍāl* (red lentils); a *bhartā* (vegetables, boiled or roasted, then mashed and seasoned with mustard oil, onions, and chilies); a vegetable *bhāji* (dry curry, cooked uncovered in an iron wok [*kaṛāi*] with onions, chilies, turmeric, salt, garlic, and oil), or a vegetable curry (a stew of mixed vegetables cooked in a covered pot); and a fish or meat dish. Apart from the more common vegetables and greens, Bengalis enjoy eating various roots and flowers such as banana, sweet pumpkin, and *sajnā* or drumstick flowers.

Bengalis are fond of a variety of river fish, ranging from inch-long *kecki* to three-feet-long *rui.* The favorite fish of Bangladesh is the *iliś* or *hilsa* that might be cooked with a minimum of spices in a spicy mustard gravy, or simply deep-fried. The most expensive fish is the *rui,* which is sent as a gift to the bride's house along with sweet curds and sweetmeats on the day of the *lagan* or *holud* (ceremony during which the bride-to-be is rubbed with turmeric and other spices). Dry fish is also popular, especially in the hot weather, when fresh fish spoils easily, and in the hill tracts of Chittagong. Perhaps most used—to lend flavor to an otherwise bland dish—is the small *cin̐ṛi* (shrimp), which blends well with a number of vegetables. Lobsters and crayfish are popularly cooked with coconut milk, which is also used in other dishes in the coastal districts.

While most meat curries are similar to North Indian or Pakistani meat curries, Bangladesh has developed certain meat dishes not found elsewhere in the subcontinent. Bengali *kormā,* for instance, is a meat curry cooked with "white" spices, that is, garlic, ginger, and onion. *Rejālā,* which also uses the same spices, has, in addition, turmeric and green chilies. Bengali spicy meat curries tend to use fairly large amounts of red chilies, cumin, and bay leaves in addition to ginger, onions, and garlic. Mustard oil was normally used for cooking some decades ago; now it is generally reserved for bhartā. For meats and special dishes, ghee (clarified butter) is used, though in considerably less quantity than before, partly due to health considerations, but mainly because ghee is expensive for many urban-dwelling families.

Apart from plain boiled rice, *khicuṛi,* a preparation of rice and a variety of lentils, is very popular on rainy days since the ingredients are conveniently stored at home and since it is associated with warmth. Plain *polāo* (rice pilaf) and various types of meat and chicken polāo—attributed to Turkish and Mughal influence—are served on special occasions. Dhaka cooking has added a spicy rice and meat dish called *tihāri,* which uses mustard oil instead of ghee and a generous sprinkling of green chilies.

Mughal influence, dating back to the sixteenth century, has led to certain dishes such as the *biryāni,* a pilaf in which rice and goat meat are steamed together, and *murgh musallam,* a roast chicken that is cooked along with a large amount of fried onions and garnished with slivered almonds and raisins. Halwa (Bangla hāluẏā)—rich sweets made of semolina flour, yellow gram, eggs, carrots or gourds, to which generous portions of ghee or oil and sugar are added—may also be attributed to this influence.

The British, Portuguese, Armenians, and Greeks who entered the Bengali region at various times after the seventeenth century have also gradually influenced some of the food, particularly in Dhaka and the coastal region of Khulna. Most Bengali women, for instance, know how to make an egg custard, a jelly of ripe guavas, and a variety of spicy tomato sauces. Armenians and Greeks are believed to have brought the *śirmal* and *bākarkhāni,* two types of flaky Dhaka breads, one rich and moist with ghee, the other baked until dry. *Vindaloo,* a spicy meat curry cooked with oil and vinegar, popular in the Khulna region, has been attributed to the advent of the Portuguese.

Bengalis are fond of sweet yogurt, made with browned milk, and milk-based sweets made with curds. Popular sweets include the *sandeś,* a form of sweetened cottage cheese, and *rasagollā* and *camcam,* which are yogurt or cottage-cheese sweets cooked in a heavy sugar syrup. Milk-based sweets, made by professional sweetmakers called maẏrā, are usually purchased in shops. In the past maẏrā would be hired to prepare sweets at home on the occasion of weddings.

Most Bengali women make various types of oil-based pickles with unripe mangoes and olives, as well as sweet preserves of fruits and vegetables. Homemade snacks include moẏā, (balls made with puffed rice and molasses) and *piṭhā* (cakes made with rice powder). Piṭhā range from simple fritters to the elaborate *naksi piṭhā,* made in fancy shapes. Many piṭhā are seasonal, being made only when fresh rice has been harvested and molasses made from date palm juice is available. Tea is the popular hot drink. It is almost always consumed with milk and sugar. Meals are normally rounded off by serving a preparation of betel leaf and areca nut slivers.

In most middle-class homes, cooking is done by wives and mothers. In urban areas, families sit together to eat, but in villages, as well as in less well-to-do families, women serve the food and eat after everyone has finished. Pork and alcohol are *hārām* (forbidden) for Muslims. Bengal Hindus eat fish, poultry, and goat meat, but not beef. Food is an important part of social and religious life in Bangladesh, with special foods being associated with different ceremonies and functions. During Ramadan, for example, most households will serve dried dates, *muṛi,* Bengal gram (soaked overnight and cooked with onions and other spices), fritters made of lentil flour, bananas and other seasonal fruits, *dai baṛā* (lentil dumplings in yogurt), *caṭpaṭi* (boiled potatoes in a spicy tamarind sauce), *jelabi* (batter swirls fried and soaked in sugar syrup), *samosā* (pastry with meat or vegetable filling), and *halim* (a porridge made of different lentils, wheat, meat and spices). While these dishes are eaten throughout the year, they form the staple *iftāri* (food for breaking the fast).

On Eidul Fitr, apart from different types of halwa, *polāu,* meat dishes and *kabāb,* different preparations of vermicelli will always be served. Vermicelli is also prepared on Eidul Azha, though on this occasion, meat preparations are also included. On the occasion of Shab-e-barat, when prayers last throughout the night, different types of halwa are prepared along with some form of bread—either flaky *parāṭhā* or *çapāti* made from rice or wheat flour—for eating at home or for distribution to neighbors and relations. Food also forms an important part of *milād* (gatherings celebrating the birth of the Prophet Muḥammad but extending to gatherings where passages from the Qur'ān are read and accounts of the Prophet's life narrated or the Islamic way of life discussed), with sweets or food being served to the congregation. Food is also served on the occasion of Muḥarram observances at the Shiite *imāmbārā* (literally, house of the *imām* or leader, where Shiites congregate for devotional gatherings), ranging from sweets to substantial meals.

Certain foods are also associated with weddings. At most Muslim marriages, for example, *biryāni* or *murgh polāu* will be served on the day of the wedding or, for less well-to-do families, plain *polau* with a chicken *kormā* and a goat curry. On the *lagan* or *holud* ceremony, various forms of piṭha will be served. On this occasion, the bridegroom's family will send sweet yogurt and a large fish, which will be cut up and the pieces fried and served to guests along with other dishes.

Food is also part of the *aqiqā* or Muslim naming ceremony. One goat for a girl and two goats for a boy are ritually slaughtered and the meat cooked and served to guests. The child's parents do not eat the meat. Animal sacrifices are also made for boons asked or received, and the meat prepared and served to beggars and orphans. Common acts of piety (especially observed following someone's death or performed on the occasion of someone's death anniversary) include, among Hindus, feeding Brahmans and, among Muslim, feeding beggars.

Apart from social and communal functions, food is also associated with the national identity. Piṭha ceremonies, for example, are held in December in a manner reminiscent of days when there was only one paddy harvest in winter. Similarly, celebrations of *Pahelā Baiśākh,* the first day of the Bengali year, include eating fried hilsa with *pāntā-bhāt,* the traditional food of Bengalis who do not have a refrigerator. Though nowadays most middle-class families can afford a refrigerator, Pahelā Baiśākh is a celebration of things seen as traditionally Bengali. Hence, the inclusion of pāntā-bhāt on the Bengali New Year's Day.

References

Banerji, Chitrita. 1993 [1991]. *Life and food in Bengal.* New Delhi: Rupa.

Kabir, Siddiqua. 1982. *Bangladeshi curry cook book.* Dhaka: Taj Publishing House.
Rahman, Hakeem Habibur. 1949. *Dhākā Pachās Baras Pehle* (Dhaka fifty years ago). Lahore: Kitab Manzil.

NIAZ ZAMAN

SEE ALSO
Food and Foodways; *Tabarrak*

FOODWAYS, PAKISTAN

Foodways are a major medium of health management, religious observance, and local and ethnic self-identification, as well as aesthetic experience, demonstrably affected by local ecology. In Pakistan, bridging the boundary of the subcontinent with Central Asia, the distribution of certain items can be seen to articulate physical and cultural geography. The use of chilies (*Capsicum* sp.) as condiments is pervasive in the east and south, more moderate in the Northwest Frontier, and virtually nonexistent in the northern Karakorum Mountains. Wheat breads are the staple in much of the country, supplemented by maize in some ares (Punjab and the northern mountains) and, until recently, by barley bread in areas too elevated for wheat cultivation. Only a few areas, such as Sialkot and Gujranwala in the Indus Valley, have rice as the staple, though it is sold and eaten everywhere. *Lassī,* a drink made with yogurt and water with or without salt and seasonings (black pepper, mint) is widely enjoyed with meals, and in some places is a main source of animal protein during the milking season. Pulses (*dāl*) and vegetables, generally cooked with oil and various curry seasonings, typically complete the meal.

While certain regions, especially Balochistan and the North-West Frontier Province (NWFP), are famous for meats in specific roasted, stewed, or grilled forms, meat-eating is to varying degrees seasonal, and daily meat consumption requires some affluence. Punjabis prefer goat meat, while Peshawar people (in the NWFP) favor the meat of fat-tailed sheep. *Karāhīgosht* (variously seasoned pot-roasted meats in oily sauces), *tikka* (grilled pieces of meat, often marinated), and *caplī kabāb* (seasoned ground meat patties, fried) are NWFP specialities. A Balochi specialty is *sajjī,* lamb roasted on spits arranged vertically around an open-pit fire. Across the mountain areas, where winters are cold and dry, slaughtering is concentrated in late autumn, culling the herds for better winter management on limited fodder supplies and supplying meat for the winter. According to the region, meat is either hung in a cold, dry storage room (as in the Karakorum Mountains) or sun-dried with a surface treatment of salt, into a jerked meat called *landī* in highland Pashtun areas of NWFP and Balochistan. The fall slaughtering season in the northern mountains is also the season for weddings, when large amounts of meat are consumed. Meat consumption in these areas is concentrated in the months of winter, while supplies last and before the weather warms too much for preservation. Food ideology supports this pattern, designating meat "hot" in the traditional hot/cold food typology, and therefore unsuitable for summer eating.

Lahore and Gujranwala are centers for Punjabi cuisine. Traditional Punjabi diet has featured *saag,* mustard greens, and certain seasonal wild plants, which are boiled and pulverized in a mortar, seasoned with chilies and other spices, cooked on a slow fire, and eaten with maize bread and fresh buffalo-milk butter. Meats are also cooked with a variety of local vegetables in oily, spicy combinations.

Around Manchar Lake on the Indus River, near other major waterways, and in the coastal areas of Sindh and Makran, fish are important in the local diet. The rice-growing areas of the Indus Valley favor souplike preparations of dāl (various pulses, especially *masūr,* lentils) served with boiled rice, for the evening meal.

Doudo, a wheat-noodle soup with a broth based on locally produced dried whey concentrate (*shūt* in Khowār language), is unique to the northern mountains. Other dishes based on dried fruits and nuts (especially apricots, apricot kernels, almonds, and walnuts) are also particular to high mountain cuisine. The northern areas had a very ancient tradition of grape wine and mulberry brandy-making, now discouraged by Islam but not wholly forgotten.

Wheat bread being the staple in much of the country, four basic cooking techniques account for a wide variety of breads, collectively called *nān* in Urdu. The *tandūr* is a beehive-shaped clay oven, preheated by firing with wood or brush, in which flat sheets of simple flour and water dough (*capātī*) bake while stuck to the hot clay walls and are then peeled off and removed through a hole in the top. The *tandūr* can also be used to bake thicker types of bread, as well as certain kinds of baked meats, which are placed in covered pans and left in the hot ashes. The same covered-pan technique is used for thick breads baked in the open cooking hearth by some groups. Wakhi and Burosho (Hunza) people of the northern areas produce a thick whole-wheat loaf (*mistīkī* or *pittī*) similar to European bread by this hearth-cooking technique. Other forms of bread (*capātī, rotī*) common in many areas are made with or without oil added to the dough, and cooked on a flat or convex griddle (tauah). The tauah is now generally made of steel, a basic product of village and town blacksmiths, but is still occasionally made from stone in a few areas such as Chitral, and northeast Balochistan, and from baked clay in Bahawalpur. Various forms of fried breads (*parātha, celpāk*) are served, often as festival breads or special snacks, in different locales. *Kāk* is a Balochi bread specialty, a simple flour and water dough which is cooked by preheating a good-sized (1 kg. or more) stone in the fire, then wrapping the dough around it, setting the dough-wrapped stone on other stones near the fire, and turning it steadily until it is evenly cooked.

A wide variety of sweet dishes are eaten, from rice-flour and farina puddings to pastries and fried sweets, to more esoteric regional specialties such as boiled-down fruit juices made into a fruit leather coating nutmeats (a Chitrali sweet), or malted-wheat flour-based sweet pastes or halvās (called *ṣ́oṣ́p* in Khowār), important in spring New Year observances. Sweets are an important part of festival cuisine, both for personal rites of passage (weddings, circumcisions, and births) and for religious and seasonal holidays. They are usually offered as a snack or party food with tea, not as dessert after a full meal.

Tea (*cāī*), usually black tea strongly brewed, with milk and sugar, is the staple and omnipresent social beverage all over the country. Some regional varieties include Kashmiri cāī, brewed from green tea with a special technique of pouring the tea back and forth to aerate it, so that it develops a distinctive pink color, then reheating it with milk and sugar or nonsweet spicy seasonings. Tea with milk and salt, rather than sugar, is the traditional beverage of the northern mountains from Baltistan to Chitral, continuing the Himalayan form of tea cosumption. Green tea served with sugar or hard candies is common in parts of the NWFP and standard in Afghanistan. Tea, like other classes of edibles, is divided into "warming" (black, with milk) and "cooling" (green, with sugar only) forms in regions where both forms are used. Ideally, the whole culinary universe can be scored for degrees of cooling or warming properties and manipulated to promote physical health according to the conceptual system operating widely over Muslim South Asia, derived from Galenic humoral theory and from ancient Indian concepts of food and body balance.

References

Khare, R. S., and Rao, M. S. A., eds. 1986. *Food, society and culture: Aspects of South Asian food systems*. Durham, N.C.: Carolina Academic Press.

Mills, Margaret. 1996. Foodways in a Karakorum community: Notes toward a handbook of Pakistani cuisine and food customs. In *Studies in the popular culture of Pakistan*, ed. William Hanaway. Islamabad: Lok Virsa.

KHALID JAVAID AND MARGARET A. MILLS

SEE ALSO

Fish and Fishing; Food and Foodways; Hospitality; Hot/Cold; Ibex and Goat; Medicine, Āyurveda

FORTUNE-TELLERS

The fortune-teller is one of the most recurrent characters in almost all kinds of folk narratives of South Asia. In folk tales this character may appear in the form of

- the court astrologer in a king's court (almost invariably a Brahman)
- a holy sage, or mahatma (great person), *sādhū, siddha, sant, swāmījī, bābā fakīr,* Buddhist monk, etc., with the most usual Hindi adjective used for him being *trikālajnāni* ("knower of the three times: past, present and future")
- a tribal male soothsayer, called a *kōyavādu* in Telugu folk narratives
- a tribal female soothsayer, or *erukalasāni*
- a bird, usually a parrot
- a supernatural being, such as a *yaksha* (male) or *yakshiṇi* (female)
- an article, such as a supernatural mirror, devised and employed by a *māntrik,* or sorcerer, witch, or black magician
- the ghost of an ancestor who may appear either in a dream or during waking state
- *ākāṣavāṇi* ("sky voice"), or *adrisyavāṇi* ("invisible voice").

The abundance of this character in folk narrative makes it an archetype.

Fortune-telling, as a folk or indigenous knowledge system, and fortune-tellers as folk performers of various kinds, are ubiquitous in contemporary South Asian societies. One of the most frequent forms of fortune-telling, astrology, can be categorized under the various ways it is calculated; but, in effect, it is also based partly on intuition. Strictly speaking, astrologers cannot be consulted as fortune-tellers unless there is a system of maintaining a record of the exact place, date, and time of birth, and many folk communities do not do this. Still, members of such communities throughout the subcontinent have developed ways of remembering astrological details of a child's birth through customs such as naming babies according to the star under which it was born. Such communities consult astrologers right from the time of naming the baby, and continue throughout a person's life. Although this method, within the norms of professional systems of astrology, may be regarded as spurious, it continues to be a way through which astrologers retain folk communities as clients.

Folk communities consult an astrologer for inquiries other than that of personal fortune, too. These inquiries are usually about an appropriate time to begin occupational activities such as plowing, grazing expeditions, buying an animal, fetching clay for pot-making and so on; an auspicious time for marriage; or prospects of good rain, good harvest, or good trade. There is often an annual fortune-telling session on the New Year day in each village when the village astrologer predicts "prospects" for all the occupational activities of the village. But purely intuition-based fortune-tellers, variously called yogis, sādhus, *sant*s, mahatmas, *bairāgi*s, *swāmījī*s, fakir, *siddhā*s, *upāsakā*s, *avadhūtā*s, *bābā*s, etc. are consulted by all communities, irrespective of caste and religion. Their fortune-telling ability is considered to be part of the spiritual powers possessed by them. In the literary tradition, Patanjali's *Yogasūtrā* include aphorisms that discuss how to acquire the supernatural power of knowing happenings in the past, present and future.

Spiritual fortune-telling practices exist in the oral tradition also. In Kerala and other parts of the country, for example, *nādījyotisham* is a prevalent system of fortune-telling. A *nādījyotisha* practitioner is believed to possess and use books called *Nādīgranthās,* in which lives of all human beings are recorded with their names. The consultant needs only to go to the page where the client's life is described and read it out for him. It is believed that the fortune-teller has both the books and the knowledge of how to locate the required page.

Hastasāmudrikam (palmistry) is part of a larger system of fortune-telling called *sāmudrikam* (body feature reading). This includes the reading of such features as moles, facial features, the size and shape of different limbs, whorls of hair or folds of the skin on different parts of body, and numbers of fingers and toes. Beliefs falling under this category are also found elaborately mentioned in the texts of different folk epics. The *Bīrappakatha* and *Mallammakatha* epics performed by *Oggukatha* performers, for example, contain a long song listing the features of the body of a woman that indicate an auspicious future. Palmistry also exists independently of the larger traditions of reading body features, and many palmistry-based fortune-tellers do not go on to reading other parts of the body at all. There is no special community with either palmistry alone or entire body feature reading as its traditional occupation, but the members of communities associated with officiating at rituals and supernatural practices have been the most commonly known fortune-tellers using these methods, and almost all performer castes have fortune-telling functions included in their traditional occupations.

Sorcerers and practitioners of black magic (*māntrikā*s and *tāntrikā*s) are also consulted as fortune-tellers. The fortune-telling abilities of these practitioners of the supernatural, too, are believed to be part of their occult powers, but specifically these "nocturnal" or "black" practitioners are believed to use spirits of the dead or other spirit powers as media to learn about the past and the future. One of the most well-known spirits is *Karna-piṣāci,* the "ear spirit" or "voice-spirit." The practitioner uses gestures of hearing the invisible by cupping one of his or her ears with his or her hands, during the fortune-telling session.

Praṣna paddhati ("question method"), often considered a part of astrology, is in fact part of numerology. In this system, fortune is believed to be associated with the mystical features of different numbers. Most of the professional numerologists in the subcontinent are Muslims, giving strength to the belief that this system of fortune-telling migrated to the Indic subcontinent from Arabic countries. Fortune-tellers whose work is based on praṣna paddati make a few computations beginning with the time of questioning by the client, a number chosen at random at that time, numbers associated with objects like flowers, chosen at random by the client, and the number which results from a roll of dice or cowrie shells thrown by the client. The resulting number is used to reach the description of a fortune listed sequentially under different numbers in a written or printed book or retained in the memory of the fortune-teller. This method is believed to have a historical connection with the *raml* system of fortune-telling prevalent in pre-Islamic Arabia.

Another method based on the time of questioning by the client is called *svarayōga*. In this, the fortune-teller bases his fortune-telling on the direction and other features of the breath exhaled from his client's nostrils. Some Muslim fortune-tellers who use the raml and other methods also claim to derive their supernatural power through inspiration acquired by chanting specific prayers from the Qur'ān or specific *ᶜilms* (spells and sequences of mystical syllables).

Fortune-tellers using parrots, found mostly in southern India, are often migrants from Maharashtra. These fortune-tellers go around the streets announcing their presence, or wait along footpaths or in front yards of busy buildings like temples or offices. Usually wearing a Maharashtrian cap, the parrot astrologer carries a cage of parrots and a bag of cards, a book, and a few remedies for misfortune, such as stones or talismans. The fortune-telling begins by inviting the parrot to pick a card at random from the pack, each card having some figure of a popular god or goddess of the Hindu pantheon pasted on one side and a number associated with a particular fortune on the other side. The fortune teller "reads" the figure and the fortune in a peculiar Marathi dialect mixed with syncretic forms of other South Indian languages in a catchy shrill voice and emphatic pronunciation. For "elaboration" upon the reading he "consults" the book he carries with him. Usually clients are offered "remedies" for evil eye or other misfortune, first in the form of a prescription and later from the various objects in the bag. Parrot astrologers quite often use dice-throwing, numerology, and palmistry, too, if that is desired by the client.

Tribals are a popular category of fortune-teller among the nontribal population of Andhra Pradesh. The male tribal fortune-teller is usually referred to as *kōyadora* (lord of the Kōya community) or a *koṇḍadora* (hill lord). Kōyas and Koṇḍareḍḍis are tribes to which many, though not all, of the tribal fortune-tellers belong. The male tribal fortune-teller uses sevaral different methods for fortune-telling, the most common being "hearing the voice of the god/goddess of the hill." He "hears" the voice usually through the sound of his single-string instrument, which has a dried, hollow gourd as a resonator. Another method is to "read" the drawings on a palm leaf, which the client picks by placing a small, pointed iron rod at random between two palm leaves within a bunch. The figures drawn on the palm leaves include the gods, the sun, the moon, and various animals and birds, trees, and geometric shapes. The tribal fortune-teller has even more remedies for the evil eye and other misfortunes than does the parrot astrologer. The tribal fortune-teller affects the accent, intonation, archaic forms, and rough voice "typical" of tribals. Deliberate use of this language gives the impression that it is the technical vocabulary of fortune-telling. If the client has difficulty understanding, the fortune-teller will translate.

The female tribal fortune-teller is called *erukalasāni* or *sōdavva* in Telugu and *koravanji* in Kannada and Tamil. *Eruka* in Telugu means knowledge and *sōdi* is an old Dravidian form for "something said." Erukala and Korava are the names of the tribes to which these women are said to belong. Erukala speak a southern Dravidian language and may have originally inhabited the Nilagiri Hills. But today Erukala and Korava fortune-tellers have spread to different parts of Andhra Pradesh, Karnataka, and Tamil Nadu, and the families in these states are cut off from each other. Thus, Koravanjis of Tamil Nadu and Erukalasānis of Andhra Pradesh are different in their costume and the details of their fortune-telling performance. But there are several features common to both.

Both the Erukalasāni and Koravanji use three main methods of fortune-telling. One, only rarely used, is palmistry. The most frequent methods are speaking in the *vāg* ("voice" or "speech") of the mother goddess and calling the gods, goddesses, or ancestors of the client into the sodī. The sodī is the ritual space of fortune-telling that the tribal woman creates by drawing lines with a magical stick in a heap of rice offered by the client in a bamboo basket. The Erukalasāni then becomes possessed by the spirit and swings in a trance, switching from time to time from her own voice to that of the spirit's voice. The coconut-leaf basket and the stick are the distinctive props of Erukalasāni fortune-telling performance. The language and voice of the Erukalasāni share features with other tribal fortune-tellers, such as a deliberately maintained strangeness in vocabulary and a heavy mixture of tribal dialect.

Using spirit possession for fortune-telling is found throughout all of southern India in village-level rituals if a person becomes possessed by a god or goddess. In many of these rituals, possession of a priest-medium is a regular event, but almost any occurrence of spirit possession, even among devotees in the audience, can turn into fortune-telling as the people make use of the "opportunity" to communicate with a supernatural presence. The *rangam* ritual during the *Bonalu* festival of Hyderabad and Secunderabad and the *kāmika* ritual during festivals of the god Mailaralinga in southern Andhra and Karnataka are formalized ritual events based on this kind of fortune-telling. At some locations these have become weekly spirit possession sessions on a specific day of every week to which throngs of devotees come.

P. NAGARAJA

SEE ALSO
Divination; Oggu Kathā

FRERE, MARY ELIZA ISABELLA (1845–1911)

Mary Frere, the eldest daughter of Bartle Edward Frere and Catherine Frere, is the author of an extraordinary collection of folktales called *Old Deccan Days, or Hindoo Fairy Legends, Current in Southern India,* first published in 1868. Frere was born in Britton Rectory, Gloucestershire, and privately educated at Wimbledon. At eighteen, she accompanied her mother to India, where she lived for three years. During this time, as she traveled in southwestern India with her father, the Governor of the Bombay Presidency, the young Frere collected stories from her āyāh (maid) and traveling-companion, Anna Liberata deSouza. The book is remarkable not only for Anna's lively stories, but also for its methodology, respect for detail, and adherence to what we now call the ethics of ethnography. Frere's book started a flood of collections of Indian folklore by numerous authors over the next seventy years. Unfortunately, very few of these authors matched her attention to ethnographic detail.

The twenty-four tales in the collection are preceded by several layers of narrative in the following order: Bartle Frere's "Introduction," a brief section called "The Collector's Apology," by Mary Frere, and the third and longest, an autobiographical reflection by Anna DeSouza. Transcribed by Mary Frere, this last section is "The Narrator's Narrative," in which Anna tells us about events and choices in her life and about her relationships with her mother, grandmother, and children.

In her preface to the third edition (1881), the author outlines the routes they traveled as the collection was being made, details of the camps they lived in, and the process by which the stories were recorded. Frere writes, "As she [Anna] told me a story, I made notes of what she said, then wrote it down, and read it to her, to be certain that I had correctly given every detail" (xi). Further, in the "Collector's Apology," she tells us that, although both the tales as well as Anna's story had been altered as minimally as possible, ". . . half the charm, however, consisted in the Narrator's eager, flexible, voice and graphic gestures" (xix). Spellings are retained in accordance with Anna's preference for pronunciation, while with regard to "interpretations and geography," Frere says, "Where it is possible to identify what is described, an attempt has been made to do so; but for other explanations, Anna's is the sole authority: . . . " (xix). At a time when cultural generalizations were sought for their presumed value in colonial governance, Frere, on the contrary, cautioned that "These few legends, told by one old woman to her grandchildren, can only be considered representative of a class" (xix). Regarding the "legends," Frere tells us that the object of collecting them had been not only "for amusement," but for the preservation of a fast-disappearing oral tradition.

It is this remarkable understanding of the breadth and moral importance of "context," a key issue in contemporary folklore studies, that makes *Old Deccan Days* a pioneering ethnography. Indeed, Georgina Frere, Mary's younger sister, writes in a little-known biographical note: " . . . the work at that time was a new departure in Indian folk lore literature. . . ." It was reprinted by John Murray four times and translated into many Indian and European languages.

Mary Frere remained a lover of the arts all her life. As a young woman, she played on the amateur stage many of Shakespeare's tragic heroines; she also wrote a short, critically well-received pastoral play in 1869 called *Love's Triumph*. Her poetry was occasionally published in the *Spectator*. When her father was posted to South Africa as high commissioner in 1877, Mary pursued her interest in local cultures and communities there, apparently endearing herself to the inhabitants of the many Dutch and English farmhouses she lived in. As Georgina notes of her sister, she always retained ". . . a very human interest in her fellow creatures. . . . " Once the Frere family returned to England, Mary focused her intellectual energies on the study of the Old Testament, and learned Hebrew. In 1906, she had the opportunity to go to Jerusalem. She stayed in Palestine for eighteen months, and in Egypt for four months, and acquired some rare Samaritan manuscripts while in Nablus. She bequeathed these manuscripts along with her Jewish collection to Girton College, Cambridge, which today holds them in the Mary Frere Hebrew Library. Mary Frere never married. She died at St. Leonards-on-Sea in 1911.

References

Frere, Georgina. N.d. "Biographical Notice." In *Catalogue of the printed book and of the Semitic and Jewish MSS in the Mary Frere Hebrew Library, Girton College, Cambridge,* ed. Herbert Loewe, v–xii. Cambridge: Girton College, 1916.

Frere, Mary. 1868. *Old Deccan days, or Hindoo fairy legends, current in Southern India*. London: John Murray.

Lee, Sidney, ed. 1912. *Dictionary of national biography,* vol. 2. London: Smith, Elder and Co.

LEELA PRASAD

SEE ALSO
Folklorists

G

GAMBHĪRĀ

Gambhīrā is a ritual form of masked dance performed in the Malda region of West Bengal and, formerly at least, in nearby villages of what is now Bangladesh. The name seems to derive from an old term for the inner sanctum of a Śaivite temple and, more generally, connotes depth of feeling and profundity of meaning. Though now performed on various occasions, the dances were traditionally part of a series of ceremonies honoring Śiva and Śakti performed in the four days leading up to *Caitra Parva*.

The oldest items in the repertoire, perhaps dating back to the seventh century C.E., are solo dances representing and invoking various aspects of *śakti,* including Kālī, Narasiṃhī, Cāmuṇḍā, Mahiṣāsuramardinī, Jhāntakālī, and Ugracaṇḍā. These dances are extremely energetic and are marked by rapid shifts of weight, sudden drops to the knees, and the flailing of arms and pointing of fingers. The masks used for these *śakti* dances are traditionally made of *dimiri,* or margosa wood, and are thought to provide a conduit for visitation. The possession of the male dancer by an aspect of *śakti* is facilitated by the driving rhythms of the *ḍholak* drum and cymbals accompanying the dance. The possession of the performer is said to provide a model for the erasure of the duality between the worshipper and the worshipped, the individual and the cosmos. The performance of Jhāntakālī, in particular, is associated with exorcism. The dance has been deployed to ward off smallpox and cholera as well as the effects of black magic, and *gambhīrā* performers have traveled as far as Delhi to partake in healing ceremonies.

Recently, possession has been de-emphasized, although it still can occur. Since the early twentieth century, papier-mâché masks have also been made and are often deployed in scenes from Purāṇic legends that have been added to the repertoire, along with such non-masked features as a dance depicting traditional fishing methods.

Reference

Ghosh, Prodyot. 1979. Gambhira: traditional masked dance of Bengal. *Sangeet Natak: Journal of the Sangeet Natak Akademi* 53–54: 14–25.

JOHN EMIGH

SEE ALSO

Exorcism; Song, Bengal

GAMES AND CONTESTS

See Afghanistan; *Aṅkeḷiya; Balī Khelā; Baṇgānī* Ball Games; Bicār Gān; Bull-pulling Competitions; *Buzkashī;* Card Games; Cockfighting; Games and Contests, Bangladesh; *Holī; Jallikaṭṭu*; Kamsāle; Maldives; Martial Art Traditions; *Mushā'ira*; Riddle, Balochi; Riddle, Nepal; *Silok*; Song, Bengal; *Tamāśa*; Tibet; Toys; Verbal Dueling

GAMES AND CONTESTS, BANGLADESH

Folk games may be traced to various origins including religion, folk beliefs, chants and charms, legends, animal tales, festivals, dance, and song. For the vast majority of the rural population of Bangladesh, folk games are both a physical and mental outlet. Games can stimulate the intellect and promote physical health. Though some involve simple bodily gestures and postures, most of these games have definite rules. Apart from intellect, knowledge, patience, and tactics, games also express the creative abilities of the predominately illiterate inhabitants of rural Bangladesh. Items used in traditional games are simple and locally available, such as dried lumps of earth, hay, straw, sticks, tree branches, leaves, jute stalk, seeds, fruit, stones, dust, plants, rope, and coconut. Since most are found in nature, expenses are minimal. Fantasy and realism go hand-in-hand in games. Games also have produced a significant amount of folk literature, especially in the form of children's rhymes.

The term *khelā* may be applied to a wide variety of play activities, sports, games, and contests, which may be classified into the following nine groups (although some games may belong to more than one group):

(1) games of strength and strategy involving the body
(2) outdoor games, including games played in fields, fire games and water games
(3) household games
(4) games of intellect, including riddles and rhyming games
(5) games with animals
(6) games involving game pieces or pawns
(7) kite games
(8) seasonal and ceremonial games

All these games are inseparable from the physical and sociopolitical conditions in which the rural people live.

Games of strength include *balī khelā* (wrestling), *lāṭhi khelā* (stick game), *ḍheṅki khelā* (husking machine game), and *nārkel khelā* (coconut game). Some of these games may initially have been devised as strategies for self-defense as well as for attacking enemies. *Kusti* (wrestling) and *lāṭhi* (stick games) are, no doubt, variations of martial arts. Other games involving the body include *kānāmāchi khelā* (blindman's buff) and *lukocuri* (hide-and-seek).

Outdoor games are innumerable and varied and played in various settings, from courtyards to open fields and from ponds to riverbanks to treetops. Outdoor games, mainly played by boys, include *kānāmāchi* (blindman's buff), *cil o haṁs haṁs* (kite and duck), *cor cor* or *pālān ṭukṭuk* (robbery and pursuit), *phāṅd pātā* (trap making), *bhāluk nāc* (bear dance), and *lāṭhi khelā* (stick game). Water games include *naukā bāic* (rowing) (the most popular), *māch dharā khelā* (fishing), *pānijhuppā khelā* (frog jumping contests), and *sāṅtār khelā* (a swimming game). Games involving fire include *cuṅgā khelā* (a game with gun powder inside pipes usually made of bamboo). Games played in fields divided into blocks are *pākhi śikār khelā* (a bird hunting game), and *rumāl khelā* [a handkerchief game].

Two other outdoor games that are among the most popular in Bangladesh are *dariẏabāndhā* and *hādu-du*. Like most outdoor games in Bangladesh, they are played in teams. Dariẏabāndhā (also called by various names in different districts of Bangladesh) is a game between two teams of six to eight players, played in a field divided into six or eight blocks. Hādu-du is a rhyming game between two teams of six to ten players, played in a field divided into two big squares.

In outdoor games played in teams, the system of choosing players for the teams is quite interesting. First, two team leaders are selected, as are a pair of code words, such as *dhān* (paddy) and *kāun* (a crop similar to paddy) or *phul* (flower) and *phal* (fruit), *latā* (vine) and *pātā* (leaf), etc. Each player is free to decide whether he will be *dhān* or *kāun*. A player then goes in front of the two leaders and asks them to choose between *dhān* and *kāun*. The leader who first utters *dhān* gets all the *dhān* players as his teammates, the rest going with the second leader as *kāun* players.

Alternatively, players may be invited to a team by a leader reciting rhymes, such as this rhyme from the Mymensingh district which invites the *phul* players:

ejid bhejid, khejid khā.
parjāpati uire jā.
istishaner bishti phul
āire āmār golāp phul. (Islam 1992, Page 7. Translated by Mohammed Nurul Huda)

Ejid Bhejid, Khejid [proper names] eating.
Butterfly going flying.
Station's rain flower,
Come, O my rose flower.

In *hādu-du* a player has to recite rhymes without taking a break in a bid to keep his *dom* (long continued breath), as in this example:

āmār kheur mārli
kothāẏ giyā gārli
śiẏāl śakune khāẏ
gandhe parān jāẏ.

You've killed my player
Then buried him where
Fox and vultures devour (the carcass)
I can't stand its bad odour. (Islam 1992, Page 3. Translated by Mohammed Nurul Huda)

Clashes occur at times between the contending groups, who may reach a compromise after reciting rhymes such as the following from the Comilla district:

ek paẏsār tāgā
mahardamā lāgā
ek paẏsār kiśmiś
mahardamā diśmiś. (Islam 1992, Page 8. Translated by Mohammad Nurul Huda)

One penny cotton rope
Starts the lawsuit.
One penny Kishmish
The lawsuits dismiss.

Other games of intellect include *āgdum bāgdum* and *nākṭānā khelā* (nose-pulling game), and *dhāṅda khelā* (riddle games).

Household games include *putul khelā* (playing with dolls) and *topabhāti khelā* (rice-cooking game). Household games are often devised for home entertainment, and many of these games also involve rhyming. Most of the indoor games center around the young children in the family. Some of the most interesting indoor games are *āgdum bāgdum, ikri mikri, lukocuri,* and *tāi tāi,* all of which produce beautiful nursery rhymes. In āgdum bāgdum, young children sit in a circle touching their knees and utter rhymes referring to legendary *āgdum* (frontline soldiers) and *bāgdum* (sideline soldiers). In ikri mikri, children sit in a circle with their knees crossed and rapidly repeat rhymes. Lukocuri is a form of hide-and-seek, and in tāi tāi, children rhyme while clapping their hands.

Games with animals include *kumīr kumīr khelā* (crocodile game), *bānarer khelā* (monkey game), *morager laṛāi khelā* (cockfights), *garu dauṛer khelā* (cattle races), *sāper khelā* (snake game), *bulbulir khelā* (nightingale game), *ṣāṅṛer khelā* (bullfights), and *kabutarer khelā* (pigeon game). Games played with game pieces or pawns include *chatriś guṭi khelā* (thirty-six-pawn game), *joṛ bā bejoṛer khelā* (game played with pieces of an odd or even number), and *mon kāṛākāri khelā* (game of catch with a small *mon* fruit). Finally, *ghuṛir khelā* is one among many kinds of kite-flying games. *Mānuṣ ghuṛi* (human kite) was a parody form of *ghuṛi* (kite game) with which the rural people mocked the British colonial rulers. For this reason, mānuṣ ghuṛi was banned by the British rulers of the then Indian subcontinent.

Seasonal and ceremonial games include *dhopbāri khelā,* which is the game of beating drums in celebration of the New Year. *Hādu-du* (described above under games of intellect), also known as *kābādi,* has been declared the national game of Bangladesh. It is now played as a regional game among the South Asian countries, and, very recently, has been added to the Asian Games.

References

Ahmed, Wakil. 1381 Bengali year. 1974. *Banglar Loksangskriti* (Folk Culture of Bengal). Dhaka: Bangla Academy.

Islam, Samiul. 1992. *Bāṅglādesher Grāmeen Khelādhulā* (Folk games of Bangladesh). Dhaka: Bangla Academy.

Khan, Shamsuzzaman (ed.). 1987. *Folklore of Bangladesh*. Vol 1. Dhaka: Bangla Academy.

———. 1992. *Folklore of Bangladesh*. Vol 2. Dhaka: Bangla Academy.

Pathan, Mohammad Habibullah. 1395 Bengali year. 1988. *Narshindir Laukik Kheladhula* (Folk games of Narshindi). Dhaka: Bangla Academy.

Sengupta, Sangkar. 1976. *Bangaleer Kheladhula* (Games of the Bangali). Calcutta: India Publishing House.

Sur, A. K. 1999. *Folklife of Bengal*. Calcutta: Best Books.

Badiuzzaman (ed.). 1982. Loksahitya [Folk Literature]. Vol 12. Dhaka: Bangla Academy.

MOHAMMAD NURUL HUDA

GAṆEŚA

Gaṇeśa is a Hindu deity worshipped throughout India. The name Gaṇeśa (as well as its near equivalent Gaṇapati) means "the lord of the Gaṇas." The Gaṇas are followers of Śiva, and Gaṇeśa, as Śiva's son, is chief (*pati*) among them. His other name is Gajānana, "the elephant headed one." Gaṇeśa is also known as Mahākāya ("the large-bodied"), Lambodara ("the pot-bellied"), Ekadanta ("the single-tusked"), Vighneśvara and Vighnarājendra ("the lord of obstacles"), Piḷḷaiyāra (Tamil: "a young elephant") and Vināyaka (chief leader). Iconographically, Gaṇeśa is shown sitting or standing and, occasionally, in a dancing posture. Of his four hands, the upper right hand may hold a lotus or a hatchet (*paraṣu*), while the upper left hand holds either a goad (ankuśa) or a noose (pāśa). Alternatively, either of these hands may also hold his own broken tusk as a weapon. The lower right hand usually holds his favorite food, a sweet called *modaka*. He wears a serpent for a sacred thread. His ample belly and plump gait convey a serene happiness. His vehicle, the mouse, sits near his feet.

Although the myth of the birth of Gaṇeśa appears in most of the Purāṇas, the antiquity of Gaṇeśa remains a matter of controversy. One claim is that he is the Gaṇapati of the *Ṛg Veda* verse, *"Om, Gaṇānām twā Gaṇapatim Havāmahe,"* ("We invoke you, the chief of the Gaṇas, the most knowledgeable among the knowledgeables"). However, this prayer is thought to refer to Bṛhaspati, the priest of the gods. Renou (1937) identifies the god with tusk and elephant head in the Maitrāyaṇī Saṃhitā as Rudra, the slayer of the elephant demon, rather than Gaṇeśa. More recently, Dhere (1981), on iconographic and other evidence, concludes that the worship of Gaṇeśa was prevalent around 200 B.C.E., if not earlier, in India and Afghanistan. He equates the elephant-headed deity in Afghanistan, Piluṣāra, with Gaṇeśa. The worship of Gaṇeśa was certainly very wide spread in the past as it is now, and his images have been found in Tibet, Nepal, Bali, Afghanistan, Myanmar, Java, and Japan, besides India. Although there is no concrete evidence about an elephant cult or a totem in prehistoric India, many scholars take Gaṇeśa to be a non-Aryan tribal deity, absorbed at some stage into the pantheon of the Indo-Dravidians. Chattopadhyay (1973) has suggested that Gaṇeśa may

A man bows down in devotion to an elephant in front of a large temple. Elephants are worshipped as the deity Gaṇeśa. Karnataka, India, © Mimi Nichter

have been the leader of a tribe called Mūṣikas. A rare epithet of Gaṇeśa, Vrātapati, suggests that he may have been the chieftain of the ancient tribe of Vrātyas. Mahayana Buddhists adopted Gaṇeśa as a tantric deity and developed special *sādhanā*s (tantric procedures) for his worship.

Although several sources deal with the origin myth of Gaṇeśa, there are considerable variations. The most commonly accepted version is as follows: Once, in Śiva's absence, Pārvatī decided to have a bath. She removed the unguents from her limbs and from it created a young son. She gave him life and put him at the door to guard her privacy, with instructions to admit no one. The guardian took the command literally and refused to let Śiva in on his return. The furious Śiva beheaded him in the ensuing argument and battle. When Pārvatī found this out, she was overcome with grief and anger and asked Śiva to restore her son, threatening to destroy the universe if this was not done. Śiva agreed and sent his Gaṇas in search of a new head. The Gaṇas found an elephant, chopped off its head, and brought it to Śiva, who revived the young man by placing the elephant head on him. He then named him the chief of his Gaṇas and accepted him as his own son. Another variation of this tale is that when Śiva removed Gaṇeśa's head, he replaced it with the head of the demon Gajāsura, whom he had just slain. In a third variation of the myth, Pārvatī once made a figure with elephant head and human torso. She then put it into the sacred river Gaṅgā, her co-wife, when the figure assumed enormous proportions and covered the whole universe. The gods called him Gāṅgeya (Gaṅgā's son) and made him the leader of the Gaṇas, called Vināyakas.

The most striking feature of Gaṇeśa is his elephant head. Courtwright (1998) explains the elevation of the elephant to godhood by referring to the great importance attached to the animal in Indian mythology and also the status the animal carries. As proof, he quotes the association of the elephant with clouds and storms, the use of the animal as a vehicle of gods and kings, and the elephant as a symbol of fertility. The elephant's graceful movement and its ample form link it to erotic imageries. Like *Vināyaka*s, the malevolent aspect of Gaṇeśa, the elephant is capable of bringing destruction when maddened in rut. In fact, an elephant is an emblem of the cosmos itself, containing all the dichotomies within him.

According to the *Gaṇeśapurāṇa,* Gaṇeśa is the representation of *Ōm,* the sacred syllable that represents Brahmā (the creator god) and the three *guṇas*. Born out of Brahmā, Prakṛti gives rise to three guṇas (qualities or facets of all things): *satva, rajas* and *tamas*. Satva signifies knowledge and happiness, rajas embodies attachment, and tamas leads to lack of knowledge and sorrow. Gaṇeśa's vehicle, the mouse, is time itself, because, like the mouse, time incessantly nibbles away at all living things. Gaṇeśa has a malevolent, as well as his usual benevolent, character. As Vighneśvara, the lord of obstacles, he can remove but also create obstacles for human beings. The *Yājnavalkyasmṛti* mentions spirit possession by Vināyaka, the son of Pārvatī, The *Mānavadharmasūtra* classes Vināyakas as deities who place obstacles in the way of people and cause seizures, nightmares, and paranoia. It then details the ritual called *vināyakakalpa* to propitiate them. The Buddhist text *Vināyakasūtra* identifies Vināyaka as one of the two sons of Śiva who commanded two thousand malevolent children of Śiva. In recent times, however, Gaṇeśa is worshipped at the beginning of all ritual occasions because of his special attribute as remover of obstacles.

Gaṇeśa worship takes the form of household prayers and *pūjā*s, calendrical rites, pilgrimages to places especially sacred to Gaṇeśa, and the annual public festival called *Gaṇeśa Caturthī*. The pūjā he is given on this day is the sixteen-part pūjā (*Śodaṣaopacārapūjā*) like that given to any other deity. In addition, he is also offered the *durvā* grass (a bent grass, *Panicum dactylon*) especially favored by him, and his favorite sweet, the *modaka*. Gaṇeśa Caturthī is held on the fourth day in the month of Bhādrapada (September). It is celebrated with great gusto in contemporary Maharashtra. Clay images of the god are made and worshipped for one-and-a-half, five, seven, ten, or eleven days at home, depending on the family or neighborhood practice. Large images are installed in public places. On the final day called Ananta-Caturdaṣī, these images are taken in a great procession for immersion into the sea or river.

The cult of Gaṇeśa prospered mainly between the fifth and the ninth centuries C.E. Its followers, known as Gāṇapatyas, take Gaṇeśa to be the sole and ultimate creator of the universe, including the gods and all living things. Two *upa-purāṇas* deal especially with Gaṇeśa: the Gaṇeśa and Mudgala Purāṇas. Translations of these in regional languages are regularly read by many Hindus, especially Maharashtrians.

In 1894, B. D. Tilak, the famous Brahmin nationalist, politician, journalist, and Hindu revivalist, gave the Gaṇeśa festival a political dimension in Maharashtra. Tilak galvanized the people against the British and produced a new unity among Hindus. The festival rivalled the Muslim practice of Muḥarram held with the same gusto as the Gaṇeśa festival.

References

Chattopadhyaya, Debiprasad. 1973. *Lokāyata: a study in ancient Indian materialism*. 3d ed. Delhi: Peoples Publishing House, pp. 143–144.

Courtwright, Paul B. 1988. The Gaṇeśa festival in Maharashtra: some observations. In *The experience of Hinduism,* Eds. Eleanor Zelliot and Maxine Berntsen. Albany: State University of New York Press, pp. 76–94.

Dhere, R. C., 1990. Vighnadevatānce Viṣva. In *Lokasāhitya: Śodha and Samīkṣhā* (in Marathi). Pune: Shri Vidya Prakashan, pp. 86–90.

Getty, Alice. 1971. *Gaṇeśa,* 2d Ed. Delhi: Munshiram Manoharilal.

Heras, H. 1972. *The problem of Gaṇapati*. Delhi: Indological Book House.

Renou, Louis. 1937. Note sur les origins de Gaṇeśa. *Journal Asiatique,* 229: 271–274.

JAYANT BHALCHANDRA BAPAT

SEE ALSO
Gods and Goddesses

GAVARĪ

Gavarī (a local pronunciation of Gauri) is a forty-day religious performance cycle of groups self-identifying as Bhīls and Mīnās (*ādivāsīs* or tribals) of Udaipur and adjacent districts in southern Rajasthan enacted during the rainy season (July-August). The ritual cycle honors Gaurī, an alternative name for Pārvatī, who is believed locally to be the daughter of a Bhīl. The origin of Gavarī, Bhīls say, lies in the kidnapping of Pārvatī and her consort Śiva by the demon Bhasmāsur. Viṣṇu interceded on their behalf by appearing in the form of Mohinī, a woman even more beautiful than Pārvatī. Bhasmāsur, distracted by Mohinī's beauty, was tricked into destroying himself. But before his death, the demon elicited a promise from the deities that his name be remembered for all time. Gavarī is the Bhīl fulfillment of this pledge. Bhasmāsur is one of the major performers, readily identifiable to local observers by his distinctive costume, large round mask, and continuous counter-circumambulation of the performance arena.

Annual performances of the multi-episode dramatic cycle rotate between villages; a village performs only once every eight or ten years, but hosts several performances by other village troups each year. Only Bhīls perform, but other *jāti* (local caste groupings) contribute food, money, and related products and services, and attended performances. Gavarī is an expensive and time-consuming undertaking; the male performers (numbering between twenty and one hundred, depending on the size of their village) require special clothes and ornaments for the performance period. These are not removed until the conclusion of Gavarī. The performers are absent from their own villages for over a month, so farming, labor, and income responsibilities fall on wives, children, and the elderly, who remain at home.

Gavarī begins within a few days of Rakṣābandhan, the Hindu festival that honors obligations between brothers and sisters; the theme of the brother-sister bond is prominent in many of the Gavarī episodes. During Gavarī, performers travel daily to other villages into which their sisters and other female kin have married. They perform various episodes for five to six hours during the day, and on two occasions perform episodes and related rituals throughout the entire night.

All the roles are played by males, including those of *raī* or female deities. During the entire cycle, performers abstain from liquor and sex, from wearing shoes, and from eating green vegetables. They consume only one meal a day, consisting of lentils and rice, at the end of the performance. During the last performance of the 40-day cycle, the performers break their fast with a ritual meal of vegetables, served to them in the performance arena by their sisters in the hosting village.

The six or seven episodes of a day's performance blend secular, folk, and Hindu epic characters with references to local daily life and bureaucracies. All Gavarī episodes, despite the occasional interjection of comedic characters and diversions, end with the solemn and dramatic appearance of gods and goddesses, which often prompts performers and observers to fall into possessed states.

The Gavarī performance cycle enacts religious imagery and marks social and economic connections between rural Bhıls and other local castes and classes.

It is therefore what anthropologists call a total social phenomenon—one in which religious, economic, political and aesthetic aspects of society are brought into play simultaneously.

References

Chauhan, B. R. and D. S. Chelawat. 1966. Bhil Gauri. *Tribe* 3(3): 5–25.

McCurdy, David W. 1964. A Bhil village of Rajasthan. Ph.D. diss. Department of Anthropology, Cornell University.

MAXINE WEISGRAU

SEE ALSO

Goddesses, Hindu; Gods and Goddesses; Theater and Drama

GĀZĪR/GĀJĪR GĀN

Gājīr (gāzīr) gān are sung narratives of the exploits of the Bengali folk saint known variously as Jindā Pīr, Gājī Sāhib, or simply Gājī. He has a large following, both Hindu and Muslim, in the greater Dhaka, Faridpur, Mymensingh, Jessore, and Khulna districts of Bangladesh, as well as southern parts of West Bengal in India, especially the Sundarban forest belt. He is worshipped mostly in the form of a small mound, but occasionally portrayed in human form, on horseback and carrying an *āśā* (metallic staff with supernatural power) and a whip. His Muslim legends portray him in conflict with Dakshiṇ Rāy, the god of tigers and the most widely worshipped folk deity of the region, while Hindu legends portray him as his equal and friend.

Performance texts, in rhymed metrical verse—some oral and traditional, others composed by known authors—relate stories of Gājī's birth to royal parents, early miracles in connection with his renunciation of his worldly status, and the honor accorded him by tiger, crocodile, and supernatural devotees. These tales include remarkable associations of Muslim and Hindu elements. For example, in the city of Sonapur, built by seven woodcutter brothers who are Gājī's devotees, a golden mosque is constructed with the aid of the goddess Gaṇgā. Angels decide that Gājī should marry Cāmpā, the daughter of the Hindu King Mukuṭ Rāy. The god Śiva says that Gājī's brother Kālu should serve as marriage broker to the Hindu king, who rejects the suit. A battle ensues in which Gājī, with tiger devotees, besieges Mukuṭ Rāy's city, whose defense is aided by the Hindu deity Daksiṇ Rāy. Eventually Gājī prevails and marries. In a second major exploit, Gājī and Kālu journey to the underworld, from which they retrieve their elder brother Julhus and his wife Pañcu-tulā.

Other oral tales recount not Gājī's own heroic exploits but those of other heroes whom he sponsors and supports as a patron saint. Still other tales in which Gājī does not figure at all are also designated gājīr gān on account of performance and stylistic similarities. Of nineteen such related texts, two concern a historical figure (Shuja or Shoja, brother of the Mughal Emperor Aurangzeb) and his associates; six are on the romantic adventures of royalty; five others concern love relations (two of them illicit: one incest, one adultery); two concern outlaws turned saints; and one is about trapping of elephants. The tales of illicit love in particular are uncommon in devotional contexts.

Gājīr gān performances are generally sponsored by wealthy rural patrons for purposes of propitiating the saint (for example, to obtain a child or blessings for existing children). The all-male *gājīr gān* troupe includes a lead narrator (*gāyen, gāine* or *bayāti*), his assistant (*titli gāyen*) and four or five musicians playing harmonium, *ḍhol* and/or *khol,* and *kartāl* and/or *juṛi*. The musicians sing choral refrains with the assistant. The *gāyen,* who may be either Hindu or Muslim, is usually a full-time performer and often a healer as well. Other performers also engage in farming or trade for income. The gāyen are not greatly respected, and in Chittagong district especially, many are forced to give up their profession in their mature years.

Performances are staged in courtyards or, occasionally, in fields away from habitation if religious opposition is strong. Performers sit on the east and south sides of the square performance space, which is adorned with Gājī's staff (*āśā*) and whip emblems and a winnowing tray containing rice, mango leaves, and other ritual offerings, which vary regionally. The gāyen's characteristic dress also varies regionally, and by the particular performer. A pre-performance ritual conducted by the gāyen dedicates the performance space and the offerings and blesses the spectators.

Performances begin around 9 A.M. or after 8 P.M., with a *bandanā* (cycle of praise songs) saluting Hindu deities, Allah, the Prophet, various *pīr*s (saints), and Gājī himself. Either the sponsor has elected the episode to be performed, or the gāyen may negotiate with the audience after the bandanā to choose which episode to perform. Some of the narrative is in verse, with choral refrain and musical interludes. The gāyen dances while singing, often depicting the sung action. Improvised prose passages also render narrative, dramatizing events by manipulating clothing and simple props. The titli gāyen may interject comments or queries, take part in sword fights, or crouch over to represent a throne. Other sections are narrated in declaimed verse, with musical accompaniment. Performances last four to six hours. Donations are collected at points when characters in the story are in need or making offerings to Gājī. Those who donate are blessed by the gāyen who wields Gājī's power to do so. The secularization and eventual disappearance of the performance repertoire in some regions, such as Chittagong, is seen by some scholars as the result of pressure from religious fundamentalists who reject the veneration of a combination of deities and saints like that found in the narratives most concerned with Gājī Sāhib.

References

Basu, Gopedrakrishna. 1966. *Bāṅglār Laukik Devatā*. Calcutta: Dey's.

Haque, Khondaker Reajul, ed. 1995. *Bangla Academy Folklore*. Vol. 66: Gājīr Gān. Dhaka: Bangla Academy.

Sen, Sukumar. 1994. *Islāmi Bāṅgla Sāhitya*. Calcutta: Ananda Publishers.

SYED JAMIL AHMED

SEE ALSO
Saints; Śiva; Song, Bengal

GENDER AND FOLKLORE

Issues of gender permeate the folk traditions of South Asia. Every piece of folklore is gendered by its performer's identity, while the content of every item reflects, comments on or challenges the gender constructions of the community and norms of the performer. Whether an item of folk art, such as a Mithila painting from the Madhubani region of northern Bihar, a women's song performed at puberty rites in southern India, a male singer's epic story of Rajasthani heroes, or a *hijra's* song at a child's birth in the Delhi suburbs, a gendered analysis—of both performer and performance—is necessary. This essay begins with the gender divisions that influence performance and then turns to the ways in which gender is constructed and challenged in the content of performances, whether that performance is a painting on a wall or a song.

Both the performance of folk items, including where and by whom a genre is performed, and its content are constrained by ideas about the proper roles of male and female, especially as captured in the terms "public" and "private," designating respectively male access to spaces outside of the domestic realm and female access to spaces within the domestic realm. A. K. Ramanujan noted that these categories are not merely imposed by western scholarship, but are present in the literary traditions of southern India. In Dravidian poetry, the terms *akam* and *puram* refer, respectively, to the domestic realm and the public realm. Akam, meaning interior, house/home, heart, refers more broadly to tellers, tales, and events tied to the home, the hearth, and the inner circle of kin relations. Puram, meaning exterior/outside of the house, refers more broadly to tellers, tales, and events connected to the world outside of the house, whether temple, verandah, or wider circles of kin. When applied, as Ramanujan does, to folklore, akam implies women's folk events taking place within the house, perhaps even at the household hearth, simplified speech, and less complex tales or songs often without named characters. Puram, in contrast, implies male public events, formal speech patterns, and lengthy complex tales filled with named people and places. Ramanujan acknowledges a continuum between akam and puram, and notes that some tales actually move from one pole to the other, starting as a kin-based event interior to the house and ending as epic histories of war. When applied to folk events, whether tellers, language or content, the intricacies of the designations of akam/puram become complicated, but they nevertheless are categories that emerge as relevant to analysis again and again.

Folk performances in South Asia are heavily influenced by the gender roles current in any one community, roles that largely mandate the physical separation of males and females, especially on occasions where folk performances occur, whether for ritual or for pleasurable purposes. In northern India, Pakistan, and Bangladesh, these rules of gender segregation are loosely termed *purdah* (female seclusion), a term derived from the Persian for curtain. Purdah is marked by restrictions on speech and movement, and ultimately marks the segregation of male and female work, leisure, and ritual activities.

Rules on speech demand that married women not speak to certain males (though these rules differ by religious community), especially those who are older and unrelated. Muslim women are more likely to be able to speak to affinal relatives resident in their own households, though they are banned from speech with those outside, while Hindu women often are restricted from interactions with any male in her husband's household and community who is older than her husband. In connection with these rules, most South Asian women do not sing or tell stories when adult males are present. Folk art, which may or may not be constructed inside or outside of a home, presents different issues because, once produced, it is accessible to males belonging to that household or community.

Restrictions on movement are found throughout South Asia. Depending on religion, caste, and class, women after reaching adolescence are often forbidden access to certain areas. In Rajasthan, this could be the male portion of the traditional house or *haveli;* in south India, certain village locales would be off limits to women not resident there; in many communities in northern India, married women can only leave their homes for women's ritual functions or when escorted by men to places such as a doctor's clinic, and then must be heavily veiled to prevent their being seen by the men of the community.

The result of these kinds of restrictions is that, traditionally, men and women have formed very separate groups for both ritual functions and leisure activities. In a marriage ceremony, the Sanskritic rituals organized by the family *purohit* (Brahman priest) and the focus of male concern are complemented by women's songs, whether sung concurrently or before and after key Sanskritic ritual events. Likewise, births, especially of sons, are celebrated by female-only song fests where mother and baby are lauded and female kin acknowledged for the roles that they play in birthing. Yet the actual naming ceremony of the child is performed by the family purohit, an event with males as its primary focal point. Given that life cycle events are intricately interwoven with intimate kinship relations (the addition of a family member through birth or marriage, or the loss of a family member through marriage or death) and also because they involve women as well as men, life cycle rituals normally take place in the interior of the house (the exception being parts of funeral rituals).

Other women's events take place within the interior of the house—in a courtyard, inner room, or cooking area. For a typical Hindu women's song fest, for example, men would be barred from the courtyard, which becomes the gathering place of women and girls, safely secluded from male vision and hearing by high mud (now brick) walls.

In contrast, male events are predominantly in public spaces, whether an epic singer performing on his patron's verandah or a men's 24-hour *kirtan* (an event marked by the singing of devotional songs) set up alongside a road or major lane. Throughout northern India, events such as the *Rām Līlā*, the enactment of the popular Hindu epic *Rāmāyaṇa* performed in many communities throughout the days leading up to the fall festival of *dasahra,* are organized and performed solely by men. The Rām Līlā is held in a public space such as a verandah or tent set up for the purpose, with the women allotted a small portion of the audience space and clustering there, usually leaving long before the men, who might well stay most of the night. Similar spaces are sometimes set aside for women at other folk epic performances.

One parallel event held in villages throughout north India every spring is the Holī bonfire at the time of the Holī festival. Here, male and female segregation is blatant. For weeks before the event, boys and young men gather wood and trash to build a bonfire on the edge of the village. Late in the evening on the day before Holī, the village men and boys gather around the fire that is lit by a low ranking Brahman. Either then or early in the morning, the men circumambulate the fire, those of highest caste rank going first, shouting "Jai jai holika Māta" ("Victory to Mother Holī") and roast fresh barley stalks over the fire, seeds of which are tossed in the four directions to bring auspiciousness throughout the coming months. After the men depart and the fire dies down, a young girl or boy is sent from each village house to retrieve a few coals from the main fire and bring them back to the courtyard, where the women have built a small fire out of cow dung cakes and a few sticks. There the women's fire is lit, and the women roast their stalks of barley, toss their barley grains, and sing devotional songs. Only young boys are able to attend both performances.

In these parallel male and female performances of the same core event, we see the ways in which gender norms are acted out in the actual event itself, we see gender performed. Not only is gender noted in these gender-specific folk functions, but gender is actually constructed and affirmed by expected behaviors found in these folk performances. For example, men's song fests in rural north India are often marked by competition among singers and drummers, with the competitive element being central to some events. While children of both sexes play riddle games, some male performances actually focus on riddling (*jhikri*) and other competitive question and answer formats (some *kavali* require respondents to answer a question sung to them by the previous singer; the best answer wins). Muslim men's poetic cum musical traditions retain this competitive spirit. The *mushā'ira* public performances by male (usually Muslim) poets begin with the least adept poet and end with the most adept; where one is placed for performance marks one's status.

When north Indian village men have a song fest, they arrange themselves as if on a stage, with the main performers facing an audience of onlookers. Only the best singers, harmonium players, and drummers are allowed to perform, and if a visiting group of men is present, their best may be pitted against the best of the host locale. The men perform with various drums, a harmonium, *cimta* (steel tongs), large cymbals, and even an old glass bottle struck with a stick, seeking, it would appear, to make as much clamor as possible. Their songs are usually narrative in quality, with few chorus lines and little opportunity for the onlookers to join in. Often the singer will use a text written in a notebook, composed himself or heard and noted down for future use. Other male events, such as the singing of *phag,* songs of Holī, or *dank,* a healing ceremony for snake bite that involves snake possession, require two groups of men who alternate in singing verses of a song, again creating a form of competition between groups.

Women's song fests in the same locales are focused on the making of community, on bringing together women who are otherwise separated and segregated in their individual houses. These events allow women who seldom see each other to meet and gossip, thus creating an ethos of sharing rather than of competition. Tight clusters of women pass the drum from one to another, with numerous women leading the singing as the afternoon or night progresses. The songs are highly repetitive, often a four line stanza followed by a four line chorus which all present can join in on. The stanzas themselves change little from verse to verse, allowing the listeners to join in easily after hearing the first line. The songs thus have a circular quality that draws in the audience rather than excluding it. In north India, such events usually end with individual women dancing, with the hostess expected to dance first. But even with this focus on the individual dancer, competition is muted as the group encourages all to dance, not just those who are good dancers. Further, in conscious reference to the silencing of women, the women's events often use only drum and perhaps small cymbals, thus preventing the sound of the women's function to float over the walls into the public domain. The modern exception is that nowadays some groups use microphones and loudspeakers to send women's voices throughout the community.

This distinction between men's public space and women's inner or private space also differentiates many of the genres of folklore into those performed by men and those performed by women, albeit with some variation across South Asia. For example, folk epics are performed by men as public events, whether *Ālhā* in north central India, *Gūrughlī* in Afghanistan, or *Palnadu* in Andhra Pradesh. Sometimes the singer may have a female assistant, as in Rajasthan, where the wife of the singer of *Pābūjī* or *Devnarayan* (epics sung before a larger painted scroll of the epic itself), fully veiled, works with her singer-husband by lighting the portion of the scroll that he is currently singing about. She is, however, silent. Other primarily male genres include *barahmasi* (songs of the twelve months), as well as *ghazal* and *thumri,* both related to classical traditions. Within the realm of storytelling, men are more likely to tell *qissa,* stories with named heroes and heroines than are women, who often tell *vrat katha,* stories associated with folk rituals aimed at gaining some desire, such as a son, success in school examinations, a long-living husband, etc. While men, too, perform *vrat* (fasts) and tell or read the related stories, especially those of certain days of the week or the month, the *vrat katha* is largely understood as a women's genre. Moreover, Muslim women in places like Hyderabad, Andhra Pradesh, have comparable stories that are also performed in conjunction with fasting to obtain some desire. Called *kahānī* (story), these Muslim counterparts of the *vrat katha* are sold as cheap pamphlets to be read or are told by a knowledgeable woman at the ritual.

Some folk genres are specifically those of women: these include, for north India, *lori,* the songs of childbirth; *varna* and *varni,* the songs of groom and bride; *gali,* the songs of abuse performed before the kin of the groom; and *bhat,* songs to honor the mother's brother who brings clothing for his sister's child's wedding. In the south, there is an additional set of women's songs and stories associated with girl's puberty rituals, a folk event not found in northern India. Other north Indian women's songs include *savan* and *malhar,* both connected to the rainy season when daughters hoped to visit their parents.

In some instances, the associations of genre with gender are shifting with urbanization and modernization that have contributed to alternations in traditional gender practices. One site for such changes is marriages. Traditionally, the marriage procession from groom's house to bride's would be composed only of males. The band brought with the male procession plays as it nears the bride's house, with the men of the *barat* (marriage procession) dancing erotically as it nears her door. Nowadays in urban areas, women join the marriage procession and the dancing that accompanies it.

Folk healing is another setting where complicated gender rules dominate. Women often deal with curing and providing of protection to their household members. Whether Hindu or Muslim, these often involve warding off the evil eye, for example by putting lampblack on a babies' eyes and asafoetida (a bitter smelly gum resin used in South Asian cooking) on its feet. A Hindu woman might also burn sacred cow dung under the cot of a child who is sick to ward off evil spirits. Muslim women might whisper prayers over someone that they are trying to protect, blow into the person's body (as when a son is leaving home to travel somewhere), or burn the seeds of *isfand* (rue) to ward off evil spirits or evil eye. Thus, for regular, daily protection and health, Hindu and Muslim women care for their kin themselves. But when more serious illnesses or crises occur, professional healers are sought out, and these are almost always men. Muslim professional healers use written amulets as protection and cures, rather than relying on the oral prayers used by women. Only rarely are these professionals women. A related form of folk healing is possession by a guardian spirit in order to provide information to those seeking help. Here, the gender divide seems less clear, as both men and women become possessed in order to cure others.

Shifts related to the commercialization of traditional folk art forms are taking place. For example, Bengali women belonging to families of traditional painters have recently begun painting *pat*s, Bengali story scrolls that are also performed by the painter before his or her patrons. Here, as both performers and painters, women have moved into a public arena previously denied them, thus marking a change in the public arenas in which women may participate, as well as increasing the popularity of this art form with urban audiences. In a reverse pattern, however, men have begun to play significant roles in the women's painting traditions of the Mithila region of northern Bihar. Mithila paintings created by women were traditionally found behind the mud walls of courtyards and on the walls of inner rooms such as those used for childbirth or marriage rituals. Beginning in the 1960s, with encouragement from Delhi officials of the Handicrafts Board, women began making paintings on paper for sale in India and abroad. As this lucrative work expanded, men have begun to paint, although their themes are less likely to be the traditional ones of household prosperity and more likely to be public events. For example, a series was being completed on the events of September 11, 2001 in summer of 2002. In a comparable example, in Tamil Nadu men are now making *kolam,* the auspicious designs before a house entrance, in order to enter competitions in which monetary prizes are awarded. Men have taken on women's traditions because of the economic incentives involved, and have also transformed those traditions to more clearly represent their concerns.

There are also professional folk singers, both male and female. Many of these were patronized by kings and their courts, whether Moghul or Rajput. The female professionals, still in existence, are associated with the courtesan traditions found in India and Pakistan, where skill in music and dance was a requirement for success. Often termed *tawā'if* or *nācnī,* these women singer/dancers stand out in their Hindu or Muslim communities in that they perform before men. Notably, the songs of both male and female professionals often cross the gender-specific genre divides, so that a male court singer might sing women's song genres and a female courtesan might sing songs normally associated with men.

There are numerous other professional folk performances in which again only the male performs. Two, now renowned, groups of male professional singers and musicians are the Langas and Manganiyars from western Rajasthan. Noted for their superb musical abilities, they traditionally performed for rural patrons in villages throughout the desert regions now bordering Pakistan. Most recently they have brought their music to festivals in Europe, the United States, and Japan. Another group of professionals are the *bhat,* the puppeteers of Rajasthan, who both make and perform with their puppets (*kathputli*). Although even today women never perform, they have begun to aid in making puppets for sale in urban and international markets, though directed by the men and restricted to certain tasks such as sanding the wooden heads, which are carved by men, and doing the finishing details such as sewing on lace and ribbon. Likewise, male puppeteers in both southern Andhra Pradesh and Kerala perform with leather shadow puppets, produced primarily by men.

Another group of professional folk singers and performers is the *hijra,* transgendered individuals found throughout India who perform at births, weddings, and other auspicious occasions. Renowned for their potential curses, *hijra* seek out auspicious events where, dressed as women, they sing and bless the occasions. Themselves impotent and marked by sexual ambiguity, the *hijra* bring great auspiciousness to those occasions in which sexuality and fertility are celebrated (births and marriages). Their curse is equally powerful, so families seek to accommodate their demands when they arrive, unannounced, at the door.

South Asia's many tribal groups have different gender norms than the Hindu/Muslim patterns discussed above, and resulting differences in performance. For example, among the Mundas in the Jharkhand region, women have significantly more public mobility than their Hindu neighbors. When a communal dance is held in the village dancing grounds, men and women both dance, though separately. Men begin the event with instruments and song, and women have the option of rejecting the singers or song by refusing to participate, in which case that singer/group is humiliated and must retire, giving way to another group. Once dancing begins, women form a line for dancing, with men dancing in a loose group in front. When such events are for the local community only, the women are in fact performing before either natal or affinal kin. At larger festivals, men from other communities attend in order to seek out brides, with the women again having the option of rejecting suitors. There are some occasions when Munda women do perform separately from the men, such as singing *gali* (songs of abuse, also sung by Hindu and Muslim women) to the groom's kinsmen at a wedding. Munda women also rarely play instruments.

Among some Gond groups in Madhya Pradesh, a different togetherness exists: like the Munda, Gond men and women dance at the same time on the dancing ground, but each sex dances to a different meter, so that in fact the drum beat and music for each group is distinct, marking musically a separation that is not present visually.

The gender divides that exist in folk performances throughout South Asia create special problems for those hoping to study them. It is difficult for female researchers to have access to male performers, at least in some settings, and even more difficult for male researchers to have access to female performers, especially in communities where stringent purdah restrictions are imposed. Thus it is not surprising that our knowledge of women's folklore in South Asia has expanded enormously with the increasing numbers of female researchers in the past thirty years.

Gender also permeates the content of folklore in South Asia, along the lines of akam and puram. Whether an Afghan man telling a tale, a Pashtun (northern Pakistani) or Tamang (Nepali) woman telling her life story as a lament, a low caste Hindu male epic singer, or high caste Hindu women singing gali (songs of abuse) to their bride's groom and his party, gender is ever-present as a theme. Women's folklore tends to be focused on themes of intimacy, love, familial relations, and household prosperity, all the while emphasizing the crucial roles that women play in the latter. Men's folklore tends to emphasize larger political themes, and is less concerned with the intimacy of family life.

Both men's and women's folklore, however, sometimes upholds and reinforces traditional values, as when a Mithila man in northern Bihar paints a groom leading his crying bride away from her family. In other instances, gender norms are challenged, as when a Brahman woman from the same Mithila region paints of the enormous burden of work that women carry while the men sit around performing rituals. Likewise, women from Rajasthan tell the *dasa mata* stories that ultimately prove that women are responsible for their household prosperity and well-being, while low caste male singers of the north Indian oral epic Dhola tell of warring kings whose battles are ultimately resolved by their women or goddesses, because "men fight with swords, and women with magic." Women's abuse songs, sung at marriages, have long been a source of challenge to traditional gender norms, while new songs continually bring challenges to old norms. Two examples capture the difference between male and female concerns with marriage and daughters-in-law. Women now sing of the dominance of the "newly English-language educated" daughter-in-law who should be subservient to her mother-in-law, but who in fact reverses the roles, forcing the mother-in-law to grind the grain and cook the bread, jobs that should be the younger woman's. Men's songs of marriage, in contrast, are likely to focus on issues of dowry and the costs of the alliance that fathers must make for their daughters, immediately taking their concerns out of day-to-day family relationships and into the realm of economics and politics.

Oral traditions, whether composed or sung by men or women, frequently challenge the norms and values found in Sanskritic literature, almost always written by men. Numerous examples relate to the popular Hindu epic, the *Rāmāyaṇa,* particularly around the role of the hero-god Rāma's wife, Sītā. For example, Usha Nilsson writes of women's songs from eastern Uttar Pradesh which, in line with Ramanujan's akam pole, focus on human fragilities, tensions among kin, and "Rama's insensitivity to Sita's needs and wishes," especially when she is banished to the forest while pregnant. Nilsson comments on the role that barrenness plays in women's songs about the *Rāmāyaṇa,* where Rama's mother is childless for some years, noting that barrenness is a cause of great anxiety to South Asian women. She also notes the importance to women of suspicions of a woman's misbehavior, a key theme in the Rāmāyaṇa that leads to Sītā's banishment when Rāma believes that she might not have been chaste while kidnapped by the demon Rāvana. It is not surprising that these two themes, prominent in women's lives, are articulated in women's songs. Women also use songs about the Rāmāyaṇa to assert their spiritual powers, as women do in *vrat kathās* such as those for *dasa mata:* when the queen mother (of Rāma) speaks of how she became pregnant, she remarks, "I got Rāma as the fruit of my penance" (Nilsson 2001:143); it was her women's work that brought her a son, not her husband's actions. Likewise, in the north India epic *Dhola,* the childless king gets a son only when his wife catches hold of the feet of the gods and forces them to give her the boon of a son; again, women are credited with doing the penances necessary to gain a son. Unfortunately, they are also blamed when there is no son.

Both men's and women's folk songs also question Sītā's relationship with Lakśman, her younger brother-in-law, an often-charged relationship in South Asia due to the practice of levirate, whereby the widow of the older brother marries the younger brother. Since Lakśman is Sītā's younger brother-in-law, itself a joking relationship in part based on the potentiality of a marriage, Sītā and Lakśman's relationship is culturally sensitive and hence often questioned in folklore, where that which cannot otherwise be stated is articulated. In one woman's song Lakśman approaches Sītā as a lover and is rejected, while in a man's song Rāma turns himself into a parrot in order to spy upon Sītā and Lakśman, only to discover no wrong-doing. Finally, in many folk *Rāmāyaṇas*, Sītā is given powers denied her in authoritative male versions, including having Sītā herself kill the demon Rāvana.

The themes in the *Rāmāyaṇa* are echoed again and again in the folk traditions of South Asia, of whatever religion or ethnic/caste group; women's traditions, in particular, focus on kinship roles and women's ritual powers, while male traditions are more likely to question masculinity and the male world of politics and money. In some instances, traditional norms and values of gender are challenged, so that women's folklore is important in articulating new and changing roles for men and women. Some activist groups use modified traditional folk songs to articulate new visions of the world, one example being the feminist folk songs produced on a tape cassette by the women's journal, *Manushi*. Thus, the content of South Asian folklore as well as its performance is gendered along the continuum of akam and puram, domestic and private, though with great variation and nuance as we move across the religious and ethnic landscape that makes up South Asia.

References

Appadurai, Arjun, Frank Korom and Margaret Hills, eds. 1991. *Gender, genre and power in South Asian expressive traditions*. Philadelphia: University of Pennsylvania Press.

Babiracki, Carol M. 1997. What the difference? Reflections on gender and research in village India. In Gregory F. Barz and Timothy S. Cooley, eds., *Shadows in the field: New perspectives on fieldwork in ethnomusicology.* Oxford: Oxford University Press, pp. 121–136.

Flueckiger, Joyce B. 1997. "There are only two castes: men and women": Negotiating gender as a female healer in South Asian Islam." In *Oral tradition 12*(1): 76–102. Special Issue: South Asian Oral Traditions, edited by Gloria Goodwin Raheja.

Grima, Benedicte. 1992. *The performance of emotion among Paxtun women: "The misfortunes which have befallen me."* Austin: University of Texas Press.

Hall, Kira. 1995. *Hijra/Hirin: Language and gender identity.* Unpublished doctoral thesis, Department of Linguistics, University of California, Berkeley.

Huyler, Stephen P. 1994. *Painted prayers : Women's art in village India.* Rizzoli

Jain, Jyotindra. 1997. *Ganga Devi: Tradition and expression in Mithila painting* Ahmedabad: Mapin.

Lee, Christopher. 2002. *Banaras, Urdu, poets, poetry*. Unpublished Ph.D. diss., Department of Anthropology, Syracuse University.

Maggi, Wynne. 2001. *Our women are free: Gender and ethinicity in the Hindukush.* Ann Arbor: University of Michigan Press.

March, Kathryn S. 1997. Two houses and the pain of separation in Tamang narratives from highland Nepal. *Oral Traditions 12*(1): 134–172. (Special edition on South Asian Oral Traditions, edited by Gloria Goodwin Raheja.)

Mills, Margaret Ann. 1991. *Rhetorics and politics in Afghan traditional storytelling*. Philadelphia: University of Pennsylvania Press.

Narayan, Kirin. *Mondays on the dark night of the moon*. New York: Oxford University Press.

Nilsson, Usha. 2001. Grinding millet but singing of Sita: Power and domination in Awadhi and Bhojpuri women's songs." In Paula Richman, ed., *Questioning Ramayanas: A South Asian tradition*. Berkeley: University of California Press, pp. 137–158.

Ramanujan, A. K. 1986. "Two Realms of Kannada Folklore". In Stuart H. Blackburn and A. K. Ramanujan, eds., *Another harmony: New essays on the folklore of India*. Berkeley, University of California Press, pp. 41–76.

Raheja, Gloria Goodwin and Ann Grodzins Gold. 1994. *Listen to the heron's words: Reimagining gender and kinship in north India*. Berkeley: University of California Press.

Richman, Paula, editor. 1991. *Many Ramayanas: The diversity of a narrative tradition in South Asia*. Berkeley: University of California Press.

Saeed, Fouzia. 2001. *Taboo! The hidden culture of a red light area*. Karachi: Oxford University Press.

Singh, Mani Shekhar. 1999. *Folk art, identity and performance: A sociological study of Maithil painting*. Ph.D. diss., Department of Sociology, University of Delhi.

Wadley, Susan S. 1975. *Shakti: Power in the conceptual structure of Karimpur religion*. The University of Chicago Studies in Anthropology Series in Social, Cultural and Linguistic Anthropology, No. 2. (Reprinted in 1986 by Munshiram Manoharlal, New Delhi.)

Wadley, Susan S. ed. 2002. *Beneath the banyan tree: Ritual, remembrance, and storytelling in performed north Indian folk arts* (exhibition catalog). Syracuse, N.Y.: Lowe Art Gallery and the South Asia Center, Syracuse University.

SUSAN WADLEY

SEE ALSO

Āl; *Bihishti Zewar;* Birth Songs; *Cait Parab;* Character Stereotypes; Circumcision; Courtship, Afghanistan; Credit System; Dance; Dowry and Bridewealth; Epic; Epic, Nepal; Fish and Fishing; Floor Designs; Folk Music; Goddesses, Hindu; Gods and Goddesses; *Hijra* (Transvestite) Performances; *Kahānī;* Kalasha; *Kathak* Dancers; *Koṭahaḷuva Gedara;* Lament; Life Cycle Rituals; Malignant Spirits, Nepal; Mammā; Marriage Ceremonies; Mithila Painting; *Mu'jizāt Kahānī; Ovi; Parī;* Sufi Folk Poetry; *Tīj* Songs; *Tiruvātira;* Toys; Witches and Sorcerers; Witches, Nepal

GEOMANCY

In geomancy, or divination from the earth (from the Greek *manteia,* meaning prophesying, the gift of prophesy, divination), one starts from the assumption that natural earthly places possess a cosmic order dependent on space and time. If one alters a place at a particular point in time by, for example, building a temple or house, this is an intrusion into this order and therefore threatening.

The geomancer, who in many societies also exercises priestly functions or may even be an architect or possess prophetic gifts, has the task of finding out which powers, predominantly either good or bad, will prevail, and with how much intensity, at the time of the intrusion. He predicts how the constellation of powers will influence the intention and purpose of the intrusion.

For example, if a house is to be built, the geomancer has to establish whether the powers specific to the place are beneficial or an obstacle and whether they will influence the people wishing to occupy the house positively or negatively. A homeowner strives for harmony, satisfaction, and happiness for himself and his descendants, and therefore wants to know from the geomancer whether or not the intention to lay out a site at a given point in time is in harmony with the local constellation of powers. The geomancer guarantees happiness and satisfaction for humans wishing to live, pray, and bury their dead in a structured place.

It is Chinese geomancy that is best documented in the academic literature. In China, the art of geomancy is called *feng shui,* literally "wind and water." The geomancer determines the "life breath," that is, the specific power of a place. Although geomantic techniques and methods differ at any one time and change over time, one usually starts by assuming the existence of a "life breath" of some sort or other. This is also the case with any form of geomancy which, as a method of divination, is dependent on geometry, arithmetic, or algebraic systems, or when a terrestrial and cosmic concentration of rays can be found using modern apparatus at a sacred site of antiquity. Sacred places are frequently revealed by natural features—an unusual tree, the confluence of two rivers, springs, mountains, unworked stones, or caves. However, not every place where, for example, two rivers flow together is holy. Only the geomancer can recognize cosmic models of order and determine the suitability of the site for a particular purpose. In the Indian science of *vastu,* the equivalent to the Chinese *feng shui,* the correct placement of the house is most important. For the inhabitants of a house to live in harmony, the geomancer has to find out a perfect layout. For selecting the site and starting the construction an auspicious day has to be chosen by an astrologer. If the construction of the house, for example, is started in the end of August, the inhabitants will suffer from desease. Generally, it is said that the site or the house should be rectangular or square. Entrance doors should face toward the north or northeast, and the kitchen should face northwest or east. Likewise, each room is connected with one specific direction. Plants around the building have to be planted with care, as human beings should live in the peaceful company of and in harmony with natural vegetation. Plants such as tamarinds or cotton, for example, should not grow near human dwellings, otherwise the property will be damaged by weapons or eye diseases will occur. Neem trees or mango trees are allowed to exist near inhabited areas. Generally, there should be no trees at all opposite the main entrance. In the southwest, the south, and the west there should be trees that are bigger than the house. In the north and east there should be trees that do not grow, bigger than the house. Flowers should grow in the north, in the northeast, or in the east of the house; roses should be planted in the southeast, and medical plants in the northeast.

In contrast to China, the state of knowledge in academic literature concerning geomancy in India is meager, not because geomancy plays a marginal role in India, but because the geomancers treat their knowledge as a secret. In India, geomancy always goes together with a relationship between macrocosmos and microcosmos. Every earthly place has its heavenly equivalent. The geomancer must use divinatory methods to recognize this relationship and ensure that the immanent cosmic harmony that governs relations between heaven and earth is maintained and not disturbed. Then, and only then, can a person living in an artificially altered place, for example, a town, temple, or dwelling, be in harmony with himself and his environment.

An example from South India will make this clear. Geomancers in this region are architects, town planners, or various types of artisans (*ācāri*), called Viśvakarma Brāhmans. Viśvakarma Brāhmans are men who work in stone, wood, metal, or clay. They stand in close contact with terrestrial and heavenly powers, possess at times priestly functions, and are feared by society as magicians. Their task is to create boundaries for space and time which, in themselves, are infinite.

Whether building a temple or dwelling house, setting up an icon, or planning towns and irrigation systems, the architect and geomancer must not only preserve and recognize the order that is immanent in the site but also rearrange the site in conformity with this order and, indeed, in harmony with the recognized cosmic order. An architect therefore not only erects buildings and lays out towns, he is also a demiurge helping to shape the cosmos. In this way, it lies in his hands whether or not people are granted the luck they strive for and the harmony they hope for. Besides performing numerous rituals in which he takes over the status of a priest, the geomancer also applies a numerical calculation system, called *aiyāti kaṇitam* in Tamilnadu. Every place on earth indicates not only a firm spatial relation between microcosmos and macrocosmos (each earthly place has its heavenly equivalent) but also a relation in time; that is, each place has its own sound and rhythm, which is equally to be found in heaven, for example, among particular heavenly bodies or *nakṣatra*. Through aiyāti kaṇitam and through his reckonings, therefore, the geomancer takes account of human beings (in the case of a dwelling), the deity (in the case of a temple or icon), the site on which the dwelling, temple, or icon is to be placed, and the one (or more) nakṣatra to which they are related.

In this respect, astrological calculations carried out by the geomancer himself are also incorporated into an extremely complex calculation system. The essential thing—the actual statement as to whether one is to expect good or bad–is the remainder, in other words, what is left over through multiplication and division. In the *Maitrāyaṇiya Sāhitā* (I.6.12), there is a story in which the leftovers of the food offered to the gods are linked with progeny, movement, infinity, and procreations.

S. Kramrisch writes (1946, 45): "If something is complete in itself, perfection, nothing is left over, there is an end of it. So the remainder is the germ and material cause for what subsists. It is the concrete reality of a thing." Through the interpretation of the remainder in his calculation system, the geomancer can turn what for humans is something indeterminate, lying in the future, into something determinable and determined, something concrete, which for him is to be recognized in the present and therefore is no further threat. Happiness, harmony, and peace are assured.

References

De Groot, J. J. M. 1963 (1903). *Sectarianism and religious persecution in China: a page in the history of religions.* Taipei, Taiwan: Literature House.

Freedman, M. 1966. Chinese lineage and society. *London School of Economics Monographs on Social Anthropology.* (33): 118–154.

Kramrisch, S. 1947. *The Hindu temple.* 2 Vols. Delhi. Motilal Banarsidass.

Link, H. K. 1993. *Das Unbegreifbare begreifbar machen. Sudindische Baumeister gestalten einen sakralen Platz. Anthropos* 88: 194–201.

March, A. L. 1968. An appreciation of Chinese geomancy. *Journal of Asian Studies* XXVII (2): 253–267.

Needham, J. 1956. *Science and civilization in China.* Vol. 2. Cambridge: Cambridge University Press.

Ronan, C. A. and J. Needham 1978. *The shorter science and civilization in China.* Vol. 2. Cambridge: Cambridge University Press.

HILDE K. LINK

SEE ALSO

Divination; Goddesses, Place, and Identity in Nepal; Sacred Places

GHAZAL

Ghazal is the predominant poetic form of Urdu literature and, by extension, a musical rendering of the same. Ghazal as a poetic form originated in Arabic literature, but was cultivated far more extensively in Persia, where it became the favored literary genre. Reaching a zenith in the work of Sa'adi (d. 1292) and Hāfiẓ (d. 1390), the Persian ghazal acquired the formal and aesthetic features that persist to the present in the ghazal as cultivated in other languages. Formally, the ghazal consists of concise couplets, in strict meter, using a double end-rhyme (*radīf* and *qāfiya*), in the scheme *aa ba ca da,* etc. The couplets need not be thematically related; rather, each couplet is taken as a discrete entity—like a flower in a garland, to use a familiar simile. Most ghazals deal with familiar, interrelated themes: mystical devotion, philosophical rumination, ridicule of Islamic orthodoxy, metaphorical celebration of madness and inebriation, and above all, unrequited love, as narrated from the male persona. These stock themes, together with standardized symbols and metaphors, compensate for the fragmentary nature of the ghazal as a poem and heighten the epigrammatic condensation for which individual couplets are prized.

The Persian ghazal was cultivated extensively in Indo-Muslim society until the eighteenth century, when it was replaced by the Urdu ghazal, which adhered largely to the conventions of its predecessor. The Urdu ghazal gained wide popularity in India and continues to be avidly cultivated and enjoyed there and in Pakistan—much more so, it might be said, than any poetic genre in the West. Ghazal is the quintessential expression of refined Urdu culture; while intimately linked to the traditional urban Muslim elite, it is appreciated by a considerably broader spectrum of Urdu speakers, and one even occasionally hears of poets who are illiterate. As Urdu is intelligible to Hindi-speakers, the Urdu ghazal has long been popular among interested Hindus, as well as among Muslims for whom Urdu is a second language. Ghazal (or *gajal*) is also a fairly widespread genre in Hindi folk and popular literature, and, to a lesser extent, in Gujarati and Marathi. Hindi ghazals, particularly as disseminated in published anthologies of Hindu devotional songs, generally adhere to the rhyme-scheme of the Urdu ghazal, while not maintaining its strict meter, its conventional imagery and diction, or its Muslim orientation.

Ghazal, with its strict meter, flowery diction, romantic themes, and extended end-rhymes, lends itself well to musical rendering. Accordingly, in South Asia, as in Iran, Turkey, and elsewhere, ghazals have long served as the basis for a number of musical genres. In India and Pakistan, most of these renderings exhibit certain shared textual-melodic features. Typically, the rhyming ("a") lines of each couplet are performed to a fixed melodic refrain (in classical and light-classical parlance, the *sthāī* or *asthāī*). The nonrhyming lines are sung to a melody that is higher in range and more florid in character and may be extended, in some genres, by melodic improvisation. A degree of suspense is generated in anticipation of the completion of the end-rhymes, whose arrival often elicits cries of approbation from listeners.

Ghazals in India and Pakistan are performed in a variety of subgenres. In a *mushā'ira* (poetry reading), poets often chant their ghazals in a simple melodic style called *tarannum.* More distinctly musical is the frequent usage of different ghazals as song texts in *qawwāli,* a Muslim devotional folk-song form. Qawwāli is generally performed by an ensemble of four to ten instrumentalists and singers (almost invariably male), archetypically in the courtyard of a Muslim saint's shrine. Qawwāli is ideally intended to transport the listener into mystical ecstasy. Accordingly, it is generally fast and rhythmic, and often features virtuoso improvisations by the lead vocalist(s). Qawwāli has also found a place in film music, and since the 1970s, stage performances and commercial recordings of artists like the Sabri Brothers and Nusrat Fateh Ali Khan have become widely popular among Urdu speakers of all social classes.

In the North Indian province of Awadh (Oudh), ghazals came to be widely cultivated in the nineteenth century as a light-classical vocal genre, benefiting from the attention of professional singers (especially courtesans) and the rise of a land-owning incipient bourgeoisie which was replacing the Mughal aristocracy. The light-classical ghazal used classical *rāg*s (melodic modes), *tāl*s (meters), and instrumentation (especially the *tabla* [drum-pair] and *sārangi* [fiddle]), while stressing sophisticated textual-melodic improvisation (*bol banāo*) on the nonrhyming lines. In the first half of the twentieth century, with the definitive shift from feudal to bourgeois fine arts patronage, the light-classical ghazal was to some extent stigmatized by its associations with courtesan culture; nevertheless, both the ghazal and individual singers like Begum Akhtar (d. 1974) successfully negotiated the transition from court and courtesan salon to the public concert hall. The light-classical ghazal, however, declined after the midcentury decades.

By this time, ghazal had become a popular subgenre of film music, especially as sung by "playback" vocalists like Talat Mahmood. The film ghazal, unlike its light-classical counterpart, was entirely precomposed, featuring orchestral interludes rather than tabla solos in between couplets. It was also populist, rather than elite, in character. Nevertheless, by the 1970s, the film ghazal's popularity was waning, partly because of the decline of Urdu in India and also because the genre's sentimentality and leisurely melodies were incompatible with the trend toward action films and disco-influenced songs.

In the mid-1970s a simplified form of the light-classical ghazal was popularized by the Pakistani singers Mehdi Hasan and Ghulam Ali. Indian vocalists like Jagjit Singh further developed this style, which features simple Urdu texts, simple melodies, slow tempi, silky, nonpercussive accompaniment, and a generally languid and sentimental ambiance. Capitalizing on the advent of cassettes and the tastes of a newly self-conscious middle class, the new pop ghazal became the first music genre to achieve mass popularity independently of cinema.

As a musical genre, ghazal has penetrated folk culture in the form of qawwāli, and via its inclusion in folk theater forms like the *nauṭanki* theater genre of North India. The film ghazal, as a form of commercial popular music, also reached a mass audience. For its part, the modern crossover ghazal, with its aristocratic air, appears to be enjoyed primarily by the middle classes, while seen as elitist or dull by the poor. In India the popularity of all forms of ghazal, literary and musical, has been affected by the decline of Urdu as a language.

References

Manuel, Peter. 1988. A historical survey of the Urdu gazal-song in India. *Asian Music* 20(1): 93–113.

———. 1993. *Cassette culture: popular music and technology in north India*. Chicago: University of Chicago.

Qureshi, Regula. 1969. Tarannum: the chanting of Urdu poetry. *Ethnomusicology* 13(3): 425–468.

PETER MANUEL

SEE ALSO

Cassettes; Film Music; *Mushā'ira; Nautaṇki; Qawwāli; Tarannum;* Song; Sufi Folk Poetry

GHOSTS

Hindus and Buddhists commonly refer to ghosts as *bhūt* or *pret,* or use the conjunct expression *bhūt-pret*. Ghosts are regarded as disembodied souls (Hindi: *ātmā*) of the dead who have become stuck in a transitory or liminal existence. These souls have been unable to complete the transition into official ancestors (Hindi: *pitṛ*).

People who die suddenly or unexpectedly, especially in gruesome or violent manners through accidents or by murder, often become ghosts feared by the living. Due to ardent unfulfilled desires from a previous human incarnation, or because of an inauspicious death, many souls become trapped as ghosts. Ghosts frequently torment the living and may seek revenge for previous misfortunes. Even miscarriages and abortions produce much fear of ghostly reprisal among the living.

Ghosts are classified into numerous categories, which vary both linguistically and regionally. The expressions bhūt and pret, or their closely cognate forms, however, are used in many South Asian languages as generic terms for ghosts, and have also been incorporated into several tribal languages. Moslems often use the Urdu expression *jinn*.

In northern India, specific expressions are used to label different kinds of ghosts: *bhavānī* is the ghost of an unmarried female and *marī* is a female ghost, often regarded as coming from an impure or Untouchable caste. A *brahm* is the ghost of a Brahman and perceived as quite powerful and dangerous. The *maruā* is the ghost of a young child, an aborted fetus, or the result of a miscarriage.

Many people also divide bhūt-pret into two general groupings. There are *ghar kā pret,* literally ghosts of the house, and *bāhar kā pret,* meaning ghosts from the outside. Ghosts of the house come from the family or its lineage members, and they tend to bother or possess living blood-relatives or in-laws. Such ghosts usually attain ancestor status through special pacification, but in some cases continual long-term appeasement is required. Outside ghosts are often strangers to those whom they afflict. Typically, they are removed by exorcists (Hindi: *ojhā*) and again placed outside the home, where they are, at times, cast onto strangers in some public setting.

Demons and other malicious beings are often considered as different forms of bhūt-pret. Common expressions include: *rākshas, piśāc, daity, gaṇ, yaksh,* and *asur,* terms also used in many Sanskrit religious texts. Such entities may be regarded as ghosts, but they can also signify various kinds of trouble-causing beings who are not necessarily considered disenfranchised wandering souls.

References

Crooke, William. 1979. *The popular religion and folklore of northern India.* 2 Vols. New Delhi: Munshiram Manoharal.

Freed, Ruth S. and Stanley A. Freed. 1993. *Ghosts: life and death in north India.* (Anthropological Papers of the American Museum of Natural History, no. 72). Seattle: University of Washington Press.

Gough, E. Kathleen. 1959. Cults of the dead among the Nayar. In *Traditional India: structure and change.* Milton Singer, ed. 240–272. Austin: University of Texas Press.

Hopkins, C. Washburn. 1986. *Epic mythology.* Delhi: Motilal Banarsidass.

Stanley, J. M. 1988. Gods, ghosts, and possession. In *The experience of Hinduism: essays on religion in Maharashtra,* ed. E. Zelliot and M. Berntsen, 26–59. Albany: State University of New York Press.

DANIEL J. COHEN

SEE ALSO

Bhūta; Bhūta Kōla; Cosmology, Hindu; Exorcism, Spirit Possession and Mediumship; Supernatural Beings; Turmeric

GHŪL

A *ghūl* is a supernatural figure in the folktales of Afghanistan. The term, originally Arabic, is also a loanword in English, "ghoul." The ghūl in Persian is a solitary monster of uninhabited desert places and ruins who ambushes travelers and, in the absence of fresher rations, chews on bones in isolated cemeteries. Female ghūl sometimes appear as shape-changers, luring male travelers by appearing in the guise of beautiful women. Male ghūl are stupid and generally readily defeated by a hero's deceptive strategy; the male ghūl, unlike the *dib,* does not abduct human or supernatural females or figure as the major adversary of a human hero on a quest.

Reference

Massé, Henri. 1954. *Persian customs and beliefs.* New Haven: Human Relations Area Files.

MARGARET A. MILLS

SEE ALSO

Supernatural Beings

GINĀN

Derived from *jñana,* the Sanskrit word for "knowledge," the term refers to one of nearly one thousand religious songs or hymns recited by members of the subcontinent's Nizari Ismā'īlī Muslim community (popularly known as Khojas or Aga Khanis). A ginān may vary in length from four to eight hundred verses, and usually employs one of the poetic forms and meters typical of the folk song traditions of Gujarat, Sind, and Punjab. The entire genre of the ginān is meant to be sung in a variety of prescribed of *rāga* and folk tunes. Indeed, the singing of ginān, alongside the performance of ritual prayers, is one of the mainstays of the worship service whenever the community meets in the *jamā'at khāna* (house of congregation), not only in the subcontinent but also in areas of Africa, Europe, and North America to which Isma'īlīs of South Asian origin have immigrated in recent times. In the role it plays in the community's religious life, the ginān is reminiscent, on the one hand, of the *pada* and *bhajan* of the north Indian *bhakti* and *sant* traditions and, on the other, of Islamic Sufi poetry in the regional languages.

Community tradition attributes the composition of these hymns to preacher-saints (called *pīr* or *sayyid*) of Iranian ancestry, who are believed to be responsible for spreading the precepts of Ismā'īlī Islam in South Asia between the thirteenth and early twentieth centuries. Like much medieval Indian devotional poetry, the genre of the ginān seems to have originated primarily as a tradition of oral literature that was committed to writing (initially in an exclusive alphabet called *Khojkī*) only late in its history, probably around the seventeenth century. Although much of the information we possess about the reputed authors of these religious poems is hagiographic in nature and may not be corroborated by historical or philological evidence, the compositions are clearly didactic in tone. They provide guidance on a variety of doctrinal, ethical, and mystical matters for the edification of the followers of the *Satpanth,* "the true path," the local Indic term used in the literature to refer to Nizari Ismā'īlī Islam. Conspicuous in the hymns, from a thematic point of view, is the strong emphasis on interior religion, personal religious experience, and the efficacy of an inner mode of worship against the mindless performance of rituals. Equally significant as a theme is the role of love as a force on the mystical journey undertaken with the direction of the spiritual guide or *Imām*.

In composing these devotional songs, the Ismā'īlī preacher-saints, like several of their Sufi contemporaries, adopted an approach that stressed the expression of Islamic concepts in terms of the indigenous religious and cultural milieu of their audience. For example, the Ismā'īlī concept of the *Imām* (spiritual leader and guide) is explained by establishing an ostensible correspondance with the Vaisnavite Hindu concept of the *avatāra* (earthly incarnation of the deity Vishnu as a saviour). Consequently, in the contemporary period, neoconservative Islamic groups have attacked the ginān literature for its "syncretistic" and supposedly "un-Islamic" character. The community has responded by replacing vocabulary and concepts likely to be construed as "Hinduistic" with those having a greater resonance with the Perso-Arabic Islamic tradition.

References

Asani, Ali, 1997. Authorship and authority in the Ismaili Ginans. In *Essays in medieval Ismaili history and thought,* ed. F. Daftary, pp. 265–280. Cambridge: Cambridge University Press.

———. 1992. The Ismaili *Ginans* as devotional literature. In *Devotional literature in South Asia,* ed. R. S. McGregor, pp. 101–112. Cambridge: Cambridge University Press.

———. 1991. The *Ginan* literature of the Ismailis of Indo-Pakistan: Its origins, characteristics and themes. In *Devotion divine,* ed. D. Eck and F. Mallison, Groningen Oriental Series vol. VIII, pp. 1–18. Groningen and Paris: Egbert Forsten and Ecole Francaise d'Extreme-Orient.

Shackle, Christopher and Moir, Zawahir, 1992. *Ismaili hymns from South Asia. An introduction to the Ginans*. SOAS South Asian Texts No. 3. London: School of Oriental and African Studies, University of London.

ALI ASANI

SEE ALSO
Islam; Saints; Song; Syncretism

GIRAU

Islam forbids the taking of interest on loans, which is regarded as usury, but allows for the lending of real property in return for money, as an exchange of usufruct. Thus in Afghanistan, in *girau,* a common form of traditional lending arrangement avoids interest payment while still benefiting the lender. The borrower turns over to the lender a piece of real property, such as a house or a piece of land, for a set period, usually seven years, and gets in return a sum of money. Each uses the other's property for the stated period, at the end of which, either the real property owner returns the same amount of money that was borrowed and receives his property back, or the money lender keeps the property that secured the loan. Although this arrangement allows the money lender to derive profit from the use of the borrower's property without resorting to the collecting of interest, historically it represented some danger for small landowners. Although a good number of Afghan farmer-land owners in recent decades have been small farmers, the climatic cycle of Afghanistan includes periodic droughts during which such small farmers have mortgaged land under girau to make ends meet, and then been unable to accumulate enough surplus to redeem the property in the time period.

The principal lenders have been larger landowners or urban merchants with surplus capital. The communist regime in Afghanistan tried to eliminate girau by decree in 1979, as one of their first major reform efforts, but contrary to the government's expectation, this decree became a focal point of protest and armed resistance to the government. For one thing, the decree simply declared all girau arrangements null and void, with real property to be returned to the debtors, but the government did not have the capital required to replace the traditional lending institution with other forms of rural credit. Also, because Islam recognizes the sanctity of private property, the decree was criticized as simple robbery of the money-lending parties in the voided contracts. Thus, the central government's attempt to eliminate a traditional credit form, which they regarded as exploitative of the non-moneyed population, backfired and became a focal point in the Islamic critique of the communist government's policies and a basis for *jihad* or holy war.

References

Ferdinand, Klaus. 1962. Nomadic expansion and commerce in central Afghanistan: a sketch of some modern trends. *FOLK* 4, pp. 123–159.

Olesen, Asta. 1983. The Saur revolution and the local responses to it. In Forschungen in und iiber Afghanistan. ed. S. W. Breckle and C. M. Naumann, pp. 131–147. Hamburg: Mitteilungen des Deutschen Orient-Instituts.

MARGARET A. MILLS

SEE ALSO
Credit System; Jajmāni

GLASS

The earliest true glass in the subcontinent, in the form of a red-brown bead, has been recently discovered at the site of Harappa dating to the Late Harappan Period around 1730 B.C.E. More widespread use of glass is seen in black-colored bangles and beads dating to the Painted Grey Ware period (1100–800 B.C.E.) in northern India and Pakistan. During the Early Historic period, beginning around 300 B.C.E., there is a significant increase in the use of glass for making black, yellow, green, and blue bangles and beads. These ornaments were produced at major settlements throughout the subcontinent and traded to Southeast Asia as well as Africa.

During the colonial period, a flood of European glass beads, bottles, and lamp fixtures undermined most of the local industries. After the independence of India and Pakistan, many of the traditional glassworking areas have been revived, and the ancient techniques continue to be practiced alongside more modern processes. For example, Hyderabad in Sindh, Pakistan, is famous for glass bangles as well as layered glass inlay for jewelry, and Muradabad, near Delhi, is now one of the largest glassworking areas of northern India.

Glass is primarily different from a glaze in that it is made without an underlying body of quartz or terracotta. Other differences between glazes and glass are apparent in their overall physical structure and chemical composition. The preparation of good quality glass requires the preparation of a frit (semivitrified silica) mixed with colorants, followed by the cooling and regrinding of the frit to homogenize the mixture, and finally, the melting of the powdered frit to produce a molten glass. In antiquity, glass was more opaque due to many tiny bubbles and impurities; modern glass contains lead and other additives to create clear and uniform colors. Using metal tongs, hooks and blow pipes, the molten glass can be made into beads, bangles, vessels, flat sheets, or mirrors. After forming, the glass must be annealed and cooled slowly to relieve stresses and avoid cracking.

Today, the most important common ornaments made of glass are bangles and beads, which are cheap enough to be available to most people. More valuable beads and bangles are coated with gold or mercury to produce brilliant gold and silver-colored ornaments. The wearing of many glass bangles is customary for women widely across the subcontinent. For Hindus, glass bangles are ritually broken, and not worn again, when a woman is widowed. Glass is extensively used for decoration of jewelry as a glaze, as in the famous *minakari* ornaments of Rajasthan and South India. Mirror work is also used in architecture: in the interiors of rooms, a single candle is reflected in thousands of mirrors, brightening the room, and on the exteriors of buildings, the mirrors sparkle in the bright sunlight. Embroidery with mirror work is also an important part of folk costume, creating glistening movement in the darkness of night or dazzling displays in the daylight. In folk traditions of northern India and Pakistan, ground glass mixed with glue is used to coat kite strings in order to cut the string of an opponent during kite festivals. Bottles and lamp fixtures are also made of glass.

References

Basa, Kishore K. 1992. Early glass beads in India. *South Asian studies: Journal of the society for South Asian Studies* 8: 91–104.

Glover, Ian, and Julian Henderson. 1995. Early glass in south and south east Asia and China. In *South east Asia, China: Art, interaction and commerce*, eds. R. Scott and J. Guy, 141–170. London: University of London.

Sen, S. N., and M. Chaudhuri. 1985. *Glass and India*. New Delhi: Indian National Science Academy.

Singh, R. N. 1989. *Ancient Indian glass: Archaeology and technology*. Delhi: Parimal.

JONATHAN MARK KENOYER

SEE ALSO

Bangles; Beads; Faience; Material Culture

GOA

Goa, the twenty-fifth state of India, is one of the more recent states to join the Indian nation. It was first granted the status of a territory within the Indian Union in 1961 following 451 years of Portuguese colonial rule. Goa was fully integrated into the Indian Union as a separate state in 1987. It has an area of 3701.2 square kilometers and an estimated population of 1,168,622, with a literacy rate of approximately 77 percent. Panjim, the capital of Goa, was first used as a port city by the Portuguese until it became the capital in 1843.

Despite the Portuguese attempt to link Goa to Lisbon phonetically and etymologically, the most explicit reference to the name Goa occurred in the twelfth century. The name Goa derives from the pastoral and cattle (*gō-*) herding communities of Gōpa, who gave their name to the river Gomati and created such names for the territory as Goparashtra, Gaurashtra, Gomantak, and Goa. According to the People of India series (1993), they are most likely the ancestors of the present-day Gauḍa of the Western Ghats.

Goa remained a Portuguese colony from 1510 to 1961. The arrival of Vasco de Gama in 1498 led to the downfall of the Adil Shahi dynasty reigning at Bijapur and the establishment of an intricate trade network between the ports of Lisbon, East Africa, and the west coast of India. With the capture of Goa by Affonso d'Albuquerque, the Portuguese created a center for an empire that was largely cast "in a military and ecclesiastical mold." As the first Viceroy of Goa, Albuquerque embellished the seaport of Panjim with Portuguese architecture, Portuguese governors, and a long wall on the eastern side of the state of Goa for added protection against invading Muslims. Throughout Portuguese colonial rule, a large number of Goans were converted to Christianity and induced to adopt Portuguese surnames, language and literature, dress and food, as well as other aspects of Portuguese culture. In addition, the Inquisition of 1560 further reinforced the Portuguese philosophy that "the religion of the king is the religion of the subjects." Despite conversion, many of these Goan Christians continued to practice the caste system as well as their own *varṇa* hierarchies within Christianity. During this same period, many Goans resented the Portuguese destruction of local idols, temples and mosques, and as a result, resisted forced conversions. However, this resistance often led to their being denied access to land, education, and employment. Consequently, many of these Hindu Goans, as well as a smaller number of Catholic Goans, became involved in both international and internal migration as a way to seek new employment opportunities and religious freedom. With the 1867 Civil Code put into practice by the Portuguese, any new Hindu or Muslim conquests were given equal status as full citizens of Portugal.

With growing political consciousness and organization taking place throughout India during the late eighteenth and early nineteenth centuries, and the subsequent independence of India from the British in 1947, Goans all over India united forces to fight against Portuguese rule. Such organizations as Rancour Patriota, United Front of Goa, the Goan People's Party, and the Quit Goa Organization came into existence for the purpose of increasing public awareness of and resistance to Portuguese rule. These struggles ultimately led to the liberation of Goa in December 1961.

According to the 1991 census of Goa, one-third of the indigenous population are Roman Catholic, while Hindus make up 63 percent of the population and Muslims the remainder. A small percentage of the population are tribal Kunbis or Gauḍas, who are either Hindu or Catholic. The Christians of Goa are largely concentrated in the coastal areas of Goa, while the Hindus live mainly in the areas adjacent to the states of Maharashtra and Karnataka, although large numbers have recently migrated to the coastal villages. One Goan Catholic community has reconverted to Hinduism. Goans, in general, are rice eaters (85 percent) and non-vegetarian (75 percent); their diet consists of a variety of fish and meats as well as fruits and vegetables. Thus, Goan culture today is very much a mix of the different influences that shaped its complex history.

The principal languages spoken in Goa are English, Konkani, and Marathi. By state referendum held in 1967, Konkani—using Devanagari script—was given the status of the official language (alongside English) over Marathi. Konkani is also written in Roman script, but only by the Catholics. Goan Muslims speak Urdu, Marathi and Konkani and use both the Devanagari and the Perso-Arabic script. In addition, many Goans speak Hindi as well as Portuguese.

Goa is located between the states of Maharashtra and Karnataka. Its geography has been described as a "tropical paradise." Bordered on its Western side by the Arabian Sea, it is known for its long stretches of beaches dotted with palm groves and its green countryside. The eastern side of Goa is hilly, and forms the northern edge of the Sahyadri Mountain range. The Mandovi and Zuari rivers are the principal rivers running through the state. Goa's climate is humid, with an annual rainfall between 2800 and 3500 mm.

The economy of Goa today is dependent on the export of iron ore and manganese, the production of cash crops such as coconuts and cashew nuts, and expanding tourism. In addition, the fishing industry is a large part of the Goan economy; it provides employment for many Goans, feeds the majority of the population, and supports tourism in Goa, which has been growing rapidly in the last ten years. With 105 miles of coastline and Portuguese architectural monuments visible throughout the state, Goa is fast becoming a popular place for internal as well as international tourists. In addition, the yearly festival of St. Francis Xavier, a Catholic saint who came to Goa in 1542 as part of the Portuguese colonial endeavor, brings together both Catholic and Hindu Goans as well as other Goans from all over the world to celebrate the "life and miracles of the Apostle" as well as the unique history and culture of Goa.

References

Boxer, C. R. 1963. *Race relations in the Portuguese colonial empire 1415–1825*. Oxford: Clarendon Press.

da Fonseca, Jose. 1986 (1878). *Sketch of the city of Goa*. New Delhi: Asian Educational Services.

Mascarenhas-Keyes, Stella. 1993. International and internal migration: The changing identity of Catholic and Hindu women in Goa. Gina Buijs (ed.) *Migrant Women*. Oxford: Berg Publishers.

Singh, K. S., ed. 1993. *People of India: Goa,* Volume XXI. Bombay: Anthropological Survey of India, Popular Prakashan Pvt Ltd.

PAMILA GUPTA

SEE ALSO
Festival of St. Francis Xavier

GOD-BOXES, PAINTED

Portable wooden shrines, sometimes referred to as god-boxes, are produced in several different regions of South Asia. Some of the boxes resemble diminutive temples; their pair of hinged doors open to reveal the deity inside, just as the doors of a real temple sanctuary are thrown open for worshippers to experience *darśan* (ceremonial viewing). Traditional artists in Orissa make simple shrines of this type. Purchased by pilgrims as miniature, take-home versions of the temple of Jagannātha at Puri, the brightly painted boxes are surmounted by an abbreviated *śikhara* (temple spire). Inside are tiny, carved replicas of the Puri triad (Jagannātha, Balabhadra, and Subhadrā).

Another tradition with a long history is the storytelling box. A reference in early Buddhist literature notes that peripatetic picture-showmen made use of a boxlike device with panels. In the performative tradition of the Telangāna region of Andhra Pradesh, masked storytellers narrate the legends painted on the sides of a large wooden box before opening its front doors to display the fearsome, fanged goddess inside. Less is known about the fabricators and itinerant narrators of a group of boxes associated with the Tirupati temple (Andhra Pradesh). The structure of these small shrines is more complex than that of the goddess-boxes; at least three sets of doors, one inside the other, bear narrative sequences.

At Basi (near Chittor, Rajasthan) a group of hereditary craftsmen manufacture storytelling boxes called *kāvaṛ*s. Male and female artisans work together, building and painting the boxes in family workshops. The artists are periodically visited by their patrons, the *kāvaṛiya bhāṭ*s, who take up temporary residence at Basi and direct the crafting of the boxes they have commissioned. Each storyteller's route takes him to regions where different local deities are worshipped; hence, his narrative requirements are specific. He may even instruct the artist to include the portraits of villagers who have paid him well for his storytelling. The box, which can range from one to five feet in height, has an intricate system of hinged, interlocking wooden panels. The panels are designed to be opened and closed in a particular fixed sequence that accords with the order of invocations and myths the narrator recites from memory.

The kāvaṛ is not merely a mechanism for telling stories. Kāvaṛiya bhāṭs refer to it as a "travelling and wandering temple" that enables worshippers to get the same benefits (with less expense) that they would by making a pilgrimage to a "stationary" religious establishment. After the bhāṭ recounts the legends portrayed on its panels, he opens the innermost doors of the box, displaying the deities in the sanctuary. The viewers are then urged to place a generous contribution in the "secret drawer" at the bottom of the kāvaṛ.

A parallel tradition evolved in Bhutan, where equally complex god-boxes called *tashigomangs* were formerly produced in the service of the Buddhist religion. Even today, itinerant showmen (*maṇip*) rent the boxes from monasteries and carry them to markets and fairs. There they extend the numerous painted panels of the tashigomang while reciting Buddhist prayers and legends. The storytellers apparently used to manufacture the shrines themselves, although they no longer do so. Constructed of wood, the tashigomang takes the form of a three-tiered *stūpa,* housing as many as two hundred clay images and embellished with silver, gilding, and gems. Perhaps the expense involved in fashioning these luxury items meant that only monasteries could afford to commission them; the boxes were then rented back to the maṇip families who had made them.

References

Aditi: the living arts of India. 1985. Washington, D.C.: Smithsonian Institution.

Harle, J. C., and Andrew Topsfield. 1987. *Indian art in the Ashmolean Museum*. Oxford: Ashmolean Museum.

Mode, Heinz, and Subodh Chandra. 1985. *Indian folk art*. Bombay: Taraporevala.

Montmollin, Merceline de. 1992. *bKra shis sgo mang* of Bhutan: on a specific tradition of shrines and its prolongation in the Museum of Ethnography in Neuchâtel (Switzerland). In *Tibetan Studies: Proceedings of the 5th Seminar of the International Association for Tibetan Studies,* Vol. 2, ed. Shōren Ihara and Zuihō Yamaguchi. Narita: Naritasan Shinshoji.

TRYNA LYONS

SEE ALSO

Darśan; Gods and Goddesses; Mandecculu; Narrative Scroll Paintings; Shrines; Stūpa; Worship

GODDESSES, HINDU

The goddess in Hindu traditions is imagined in a variety of ways: a compassionate mother, an ideal consort, a model devotee, a fiery independent warrior who is not associated with any god, a local guardian or protector, or an unconventional, passionate lover. In almost all manifestations, however, she is seen as the wielder of special powers and as benevolent bestower of grace to her devotees. Hindu iconography, particularly as it developed around Purāṇic mythology, frequently depicts the image of the goddess alongside her consort-god—an image that reflects the much-idealized "auspicious couple" in Hindu theology—but it is just as common to find imagery and lore that project an independent, all-powerful goddess. Historical research on goddess worship in Hindu traditions locates the emergence of a "Great Goddess" in Sanskrit textual traditions such as the *Dēvī Mahātmya* and the later *Dēvī Bhāgavata Purāṇa* which depict her as a single, omniscient deity who controls the cosmic principles of *śakti* (power), *māya* (illusion), and *prakṛti* (manifest universe). The mythologies and worship traditions associated with the many Hindu goddesses, however, are too richly diverse to be contained under a single rubric. Hindu goddesses are no doubt worshipped for their cosmic roles—establishing *dharma,* combating evil, and achieving *mokśa,* or liberation from the cycle of births and deaths. But Hindu goddesses are equally invoked for remedies to the very specific and localized problems of their worshippers—such problems as might fall in the realm of healing, marriage, property dispensation, familial relations, offspring, travel, and material benefits.

While Vedic and post-Vedic Sanskrit literature (such as the epics of the *Mahābhārata* and the *Rāmāyaṇa*) privilege Sarasvati, Pārvati, and Lakśmi (and to some extent, Durga and Kāli as distinct goddesses but also as "aspects" of Pārvati), lived Hindu experience recognizes and celebrates numerous goddesses with their own genealogies, legends about their powers and deeds, forms of worship, and visual representation. Thus scholarship on contemporary goddess worship among Hindus has concluded that the goddess is imagined both as "Dēvī," a transcendent, all-encompassing feminine force or *śakti* of the universe, both maternal and warrior-like, and as many goddesses with unique identities and regional sway who may or may not resemble each other. Oral and written vernacular literatures, local politics, social order and gender relations, and worship traditions interweave in myriad ways to make goddesses distinctive. In fact, Durga, Pārvati, Kāli and Lakśmi, the very goddesses who enjoy a prominent place in the Sanskrit literature that catalyzed the rise of the goddess tradition, are uniquely characterized in sectarian traditions or in local sacred geographies.

Historical studies of goddess worship in South Asia agree that the *Dēvī Mahātmya,* a widely popular fifth-sixth-century C.E. text, part of the *Mārkaṇḍēya Purāṇa,* has been seminal to the "crystallization of the Goddess tradition" (Coburn 1984). This text clearly formulates the idea that it is a feminine source that generates, sustains, and nourishes the universe. Integrating earlier myths about goddesses in a richly layered narrative, the *Dēvī Mahātmya* creates a mythology of an all-powerful Dēvi who is neither the consort of, nor the śakti of any particular god. In one of the three central episodes narrated in the *Dēvī Mahātmya,* Dēvī, identified as Durga, is created when the gods, furious at being unable to kill Mahiśāsura (a powerful buffalo demon who is protected by a boon of immortality) emit a collective brilliance that becomes a beautiful goddess. Armed with individual gifts of emblems and weapons from the various gods, and the vehicle of a lion, the invincible goddess proceeds to vanquish Mahiśāsura. In the first episode of the *Dēvī Mahātmya,* on the other hand, this warrior-goddess is personified as profound sleep, or *yōganidra* (yōga of sleep) that has overcome Viṣṇu. Brahma, seated in a lotus in Viṣṇu's navel, is assaulted by two demons, Madhu and Kaiṭabha. Unable to rouse Viṣṇu from his slumber, Brahma invokes Durga, and she responds by withdrawing from Viṣṇu's body. Awakened, Viṣṇu is thus enabled to fight and win the battle by slaying the demons on his thighs. According to Thomas Coburn (1996) Durga is hence both delusion itself, but also the remover of delusion whose agency is required for action. The third episode in the text returns Durga to the battleground, this time rescuing the gods and the universe from the demons Śumbha and Niśumbha in a bloody battle that powerfully displays Dēvī's cosmic status. Herself the generator of śakti, she also reabsorbs the seven śaktis that have emanated (to aid her in battle) from seven gods after she wins the battle.

The many liturgical contexts of the *Dēvi Mahātmya* indicate also the pan-regional popularity—and the dazzling varieties—of Durga worship. For many Hindus, the festival of Navarātri (during autumn) is especially significant when, for nine nights and ten days, the goddess is worshipped in her many forms (as Durga, Kāli, Pārvatī, Lakṣmī, Saraswati, or as the seven śaktis). In areas of the former Vijayanagara empire of the mid-thirteenth to fifteenth centuries, such as in Mysore and in Śṛingēri, South India, Navarātri celebrations index the coming together of traditions of imperial display, regional discourses about identity, and centuries of goddess worship. The state government continues the tradition of the royal procession of Mysore kings even today. In Tamil Nāḍu, Durga is among several other goddesses who are at the center of women's festivities during Navarātri. These festivities include the artistic display of dolls representing Purāṇic motifs, women's devotional singing on the goddess during evening get-togethers, the exchange of special foods, and the tracing of *rangōli*/*kōlam* designs in house-fronts. In eastern India, especially in Bengal, Durga Pūja is virtually the locus of cultural identity. Here, Durga is identified with Pārvatī or Uma, wife of Śiva, who returns to her natal home once a year with her children, Gaṇeśa, Kārtikeya, Lakṣmī, and Saraswati. The festival is celebrated with the pomp and poignancy befitting the occasion of a daughter returning to her natal home. Thousands of temporary shrines with clay and straw images of Durga (typically depicting the slaying of Mahiśāsura) and her children are erected prior to the festival, and worshipped daily, gifts and visits are exchanged, schools are closed, and posters, music, and bustling trade proclaim the festival, which concludes on the tenth day with the images being immersed in water. The goddess is bid a moving farewell with departure songs and travel-related gifts marking her "return" to her marital abode in Kailāsa. Many regional goddesses are associated with Durga or with Pārvatī (the two frequently are thought of as one), although they retain their regional identity strongly (Examples are Vindhyāvāsini and Śerāṅvali in Northern India.)

Pārvatī, whose name means "born of the mountains," is identified in literary traditions as "Dēvī," and is a classic example of a familial goddess. Known primarily by her identity as the wife of Śiva, the powerful ascetic god in the Hindu pantheon of gods, Pārvatī is frequently depicted in Purāṇic mythology as the reincarnation of Uma who commits suicide when her father, Dakśa, insults Śiva by not inviting him to a much-publicized sacrifice that he is performing. The self-immolation has given her the name of "Sati." In one rendering of the story, Śiva, enraged, vanquishes Dakśa, and wanders about the earth with Sati's corpse until his grief begins to disturb the cosmos. Viṣṇu, in order to protect the cosmos, follows him and cuts away Sati's corpse bit by bit until Śiva realizes that he has nothing left of her and calms down. The places where Sati's corpse is supposed to have fallen on earth are sites of Pārvatī temples or *Śakta Pīthās*, which are frequently identified with local goddesses. Śiva and Pārvatī are depicted in popular conceptions with their two sons; Kārtikeya, and the elephant-headed god, Ganeśa. The Śiva Purāṇa also recounts the story of the terrorizing demon, Tāraka, who could be killed only by a child of the unmarried ascetic Śiva. Sati, heeding the appeals of the gods, reincarnates as Pārvatī to woo Śiva, and is born to the king of the Himālayās. Pārvatī wins Śiva's love through rigorous penance, and their first son, Kārtikeya, kills Tāraka, fulfilling Sati's promise to the gods.

Pārvatī's uncompromising devotion to Śiva, despite her differences with him, makes her a model devotee among Śiva worshippers. Her domestication of his searing ascetic nature is a prominent theme in Purāṇic stories. The image of the phallic *linga* and the female *yōṇi* iconifies the theme of the coupling that is necessary for the generation of the universe. As such, Pārvatī provides a creative outlet for Śiva's energy; she is the female half of Śiva in his form as Ardhanārīśwara (Lord who is half-woman); she is Śiva's śakti, or embodied power. Worship traditions centering on Pārvatī invoke her fertility and her power to ensure a happy family life. In Karnataka, Hindu women and girls perform a *vrata* (ritual fast) known as *Bhīmanamāvāsya vrata* on the last day of the ritually inauspicious month of Asada (June-July), and pray for "good husbands" or for the happy continuation of their married lives. The vrata derives its name from Jyōtirbhīmēśvara, a form of Śiva. The *vrata-kathā* recounts the plight of a young, innocent, Brahman girl whose poor parents accept money to marry her off to the corpse of a dead prince so that his soul can go to heaven. The hapless bride and her dead husband are abandoned amidst a torrential downpour in a small temple in the forest on a dark *amāvāsya* (new moon) night. Her wails resound in the heavens, and the exemplary couple, Śiva and Pārvatī, come down to the temple, where Pārvatī makes the Brahman girl perform the Bhīmēśvara Pūja. The dark night is illumined by the lamps, and in this ambience, the auspicious month of Śrāvaṇa is born. Pārvatī helps revive the dead prince, and the girl becomes a *sumaṅgali* (an auspicious married woman). The ritual involves the worship with earthen lamps representing Pārvatī and Śiva. In parts of North India—Rajasthan, Bihar, and parts of Uttar Pradesh—as well as in Nepal, the women's festival of Tīj in July-August celebrates Pārvatī's reunion with Śiva made possible by a hundred years of Pārvatī's penance. Tīj is marked by a fast that women and girls undertake for good husbands. In Rajasthan, Tīj is famous for its canopied procession carrying the covered image of Pārvatī, known as Tījmāta, its colorful song and dance traditions, and the exchange of new clothes, finery, and special foods between women. The *Vāmana Purāṇa* recounts how Pārvatī, challenged at being referred to as the "dark one" by Śiva, acquires a golden skin after performing rigorous austerities, and thus becomes Gouri ("the golden one"). She is thus worshipped as Gouri in the festivals of Gaṇgaur in Rajasthan and Gouri Pūja (at the time of the Gaṇeśa Chaturthi) in Karnataka, Maharashtra, and Andhra Pradesh.

While Purāṇic mythology, particularly the *Dēvī Mahātmya,* traces Pārvatī, Kāli, and Durga to a composite identity that is sometimes simply referred to as "Dēvī," their cosmic roles and their relationships to ṭiva—who is their consort—reinforce their distinctiveness from each other as goddesses. Regional custom also locates these three goddesses within their own spheres of worship and story. If Pārvatī is perceived as a familial goddess who harnesses Śiva's generative potential and wander-hungry nature, Kāli—whose name comes from *kāla* or "time" in Sanskrit—is "of the wild" and unbridles Śiva's destructive energy, even frequently provoking it in contests of dance and in confrontations over territory. It is he who is called on to calm her. Typically, Kāli's iconography depicts her with her tongue lolling out, almost bare-bodied, but festooned in human skulls and corpses, bloodthirsty, dancing frenziedly atop the prostrate body of Śiva, inhabiting cremation grounds and battlefields, and riding a *prēta* (ghoul): the complete and exuberant antithesis of Pārvatī's family-bound identity. The *Linga Purāṇa* narrates how Pārvatī, at Śiva's request, summons Kāli out of herself to destroy Dāruka, the demon who is granted a boon that he would be slain by none but a woman. As David Kinsley (1987) notes, Kāli thus emerges as Pārvatī's fury personified. The *Dēvī Mahātmya* similarly recounts the battle circumstances of Kāli's "birth." Infuriated at being harassed by the two demon generals, Canda and Muṇḍa, during her war against the demons Śumbha and Niśumbha, the goddess Durga (who herself emerges from Pārvatī's wrath) creates Kāli, who leaps from her darkened brow to slay the generals. At another time, Durga calls on Kāli when she is being overwhelmed by an immortal demon called Rakhtabīja who multiplies himself with every drop of blood he sheds. Kāli vanquishes him by sucking out all his blood, or as in other versions of this story, by spreading her tongue so wide that the battle is fought on it.

Although Kāli's Purāṇic personality is vivified by such deeds, her place in Hindu worship traditions has varied widely, with the apparent paradoxes in her identity contributing to her metaphysical richness. In the *Śakta Āgamas*, (goddess-oriented scriptures that detail a wide range of modes of worship), Kāli is śakti personified, and worship of her through Tantric rites is believed to elicit the deepseated śakti present in the worshipper. Kāli's exuberant expressivity, unpredictability, naturalness, and ability to generate and destroy have led to the conceptualization of her as divine mother who both embodies and transcends all aspects of creation. On new moon day, in Kāli temples across Madras, many women make special offerings to her, petitioning her for a long and healthy life and for progeny. It is not an uncommon sight to see groups of women with jars of milk (or grains) making pilgrimages to her shrines. Worship of Kāli is accentuated at these temples during Śivarātri. The power and energy associated with Kāli is rendered in dramatic form in performance traditions like the *Mutiyeṭṭu* in Kerala. And yet, while the Kāli who is the center of these worship, performance, and pilgrimage traditions bears some resemblance to the Kāli of the Purāṇas mentioned above, the precise correspondence is in fact blurred, making Kāli share a greater kinship with other goddesses popular in the region or locality. In Bengal, Kāli worship has acquired a cultural centrality, occupying a revered place in the annual and daily worship of the goddess that is characteristic of the region. A large measure of this cultural adoration of Kāli in Bengal is attributed to the influence of the poetry of Ramprasad Sen (1718–1785) and later to that of Kamalakanta Bhattacharya (1769–1820). In a literary genre known as *Śakta padavali,* which Sen initiated, he composed more than three hundred poems to Kāli, in which he depicted her as compassionate mother. While these depictions did not necessarily seek to overturn Kāli's "older" iconography, they transformed the primarily martial Kāli into a maternal one who could be cajoled, adored, chided, appealed to, and worshipped in a range of identifications familiar to a well-established *bhakti* tradition that, in fact, had similarly conceived Kṛṣṇa in Bengal. Today the prolific circulation of *Śyāma Sangīt* (songs to Śyāma, "the Black goddess,") and the annual festival of Kāli Pūja, which occurs a few weeks after Durga Pūja, signify the popularity of Kāli in the daily religious imaginary of Bengali Hindus. But in the nationalist consciousness of a Bengali male elite in the late eighteenth and late nineteenth centuries, the worship of Kāli was the target of political critique, cited not only as "idolatrous" but also as counterproductive to a nationalist conceptualization of Indian womanhood. A study of the differences in class and gender-based responses to Kāli in Bengal provides a suggestive glimpse into a region's social and political history. Because of Kāli's powerful, war-winning mythology, her body-centered iconography, and her rebuttal of patriarchy, Kāli worship has been accorded a niche—albeit a problematic one because of its contextual innocence—in New Age goddess spirituality.

Not part of the Durga-Pārvatī-Kāli triad is the goddess Lakṣmī who similarly occupies a high, if not more ubiquitous, pan-regional status. Worshipped by Hindus and Jains as the goddess of wealth and fortune, Lakṣmī, or Śri (auspiciousness), as she is known among the Śri Vaiśnava community, is also believed to grant liberation from the cycle of birth and rebirth. For Jains, and Hindus from the merchant classes, Diwāli, the festival of lights, is marked by the performance of a special Lakṣmī pūja, when new account books are opened. Almost unrivalled in her ubiquitousness, a figure of Lakṣmī noticeably adorns almost every home, business, or store.

As Viṣṇu's beloved consort, she is represented as dwelling on his chest, but in popular iconography, she also appears independently, bejeweled and radiant, seated or standing on a red lotus, flanked by white elephants (symbols of royalty and fertility), with a shower of gold coins cascading from one hand which is the *varada hasta* (boon-endowing hand) gesture, while the other is in the *abhaya hasta* (fear-banishing hand) gesture. Her other two hands typically carry lotuses. The lotus is Lakṣmī's classic symbol, suggesting her spiritual autonomy, fertility, and purity. *Varamahālakṣmī vrata* performed by South Indian Hindu women during the auspicious season August-September is an invocation to the bounteous and beneficent aspects of Lakṣmī. David Kinsley traces Lakṣmī's earliest appearance in literature to the *Śri Sukta,* a hymn to Śri, or the goddess, a possible addition to the *Ṛg Veda,* and in coinage and architecture going back to the third century B.C.E. Shrines to Lakṣmī became immensely popular with the establishment by the tenth century of the Śri Vaiśnava community in South India. Śri Vaiśnavas generally agree that Śri is ". . . a mediator between human beings and Viṣṇu in the matter of salvation, but the community is split on the issue of her equality to Viṣṇu" (Narayanan 1996, 90). Perhaps the most well-known story about Lakṣmī is narrated in the *Viṣṇu Purāṇa* (but also in the *Padma* and *Bhāgavata Purāṇas*), where we are told of how she emerges from the ocean when gods and demons churn it, competing for the nectar of immortality. She chooses Viṣṇu for her consort. Depictions of Lakṣmī vary with variations in Viṣṇu's forms; for example, as consort of Narasimha, she appears seated on his lap.

While purāṇic stories emphasize the inseparability of Śri and Viṣṇu, temple traditions and towns have their own repertoire of narratives and festivals that in fact, vivify the couple's relationship by embellishing it with romantic details, episodes of quarrel, and negotiation. Pamphlet literature sold in the temple towns of Tirupati and Tirumala, the home of the famous Śri Venkatēśwara temple, recounts in several variations a legend in which the sage Bhrigu insulted Viṣṇu after being kept waiting by him. Viṣṇu's apologetic attitude toward the sage angers Lakṣmī, who stomps off to earth. Seeking her, Viṣṇu ends up courting a local king, Ākāśa Rāja's adopted daughter, Padmāvati (from "Padma," lotus) who has been discovered in a piece of land that was being ploughed. (The allusion to Sītā, also born of the furrow, is of course, unmistakable, recalling Viṣṇu's incarnation as Rāma.) On the eve of the marriage, the gods "replace" Padmāvati by Lakṣmī. Padmāvati and Lakṣmī seem to become synonymous with each other in various tellings of the legend, and thus the Śri Venkatēśwara image on Tirumala Hill bears on his chest "two" goddesses; Padmāvati and Lakṣmī. They are also known as Bhudēvī (goddess of the earth), and Srīdēvī (goddess of wealth). A temple at the foothills of Tirupati is dedicated to Padmāvati, and legends recount either that the temple marks the spot where she performed penance, or the spot where she chose to stay after a quarrel with Venkatēśwara.

Goddess traditions continue to emerge, creatively widening the arena of worship, performance, and architectural expression. Narayanan reports that following the composition of a song called *Aśṭha-Lakṣmī Ślōka* ("Prayer to the Eight-Lakṣmīs") by a leading Vaiśnava theologian in 1970, and the subsequent release of an audiocassette in the 1980s containing this song and a prayer on the thousand names of Lakṣmī, the worship of Aśṭha-Lakṣmī became immensely popular. While the "eight Lakṣmīs" do correspond to aspects of Lakṣmī extolled in earlier prayers, Narayanan notes that the ". . . emergence of these eight in precisely this combination . . . " and the invention of aspects like "Primeval Lakṣmī" and "Lakṣmī worshipped by elephants" is new (1996, 104). In 1974, a temple dedicated to the Aśṭha-Lakṣmīs was built in Kovalam Beach in Madras, in which there are small shrines to each of the eight Lakṣmīs, and a ninth to the images of Śri and Viṣṇu. Items and manuals of worship enhance the growing devotion to the Ashta-Lakṣmīs.

In the everyday social and religious imaginary of Hindus, Sītā occupies a shifting position in the continuum between "epic heroine" and "goddess." Although she is mentioned in Vedic literature as a goddess associated with agricultural fertility, Sītā's prominence has been shaped primarily by Valmiki's *Rāmāyaṇa,* and particularly by the emergence and popularization of many regional *Rāmāyaṇa*s. Temples to Rāma invariably depict her by Rāma's side, underscoring her characterization as an "ideal wife," and yet this marital relationship has elicited the most diverse and passionate range of responses over the centuries. Scholars have for long assumed that the centuries-old *Vālmiki Rāmāyaṇa*'s duty-bound and husband-worshipping Sītā provided a mythological role model for Hindu women. And indeed for many Hindus, she is an ideal, a *pativrata,* or a satī. However, the woman-authored South Indian *Rāmāyaṇa,* known as the *Atukuri Molla Rāmāyaṇamu,* written in Telugu in the sixteenth century by Atukuri Molla, a young girl of the artisan community, is a brilliant example of the many other expressive traditions that have time and again revealed the cracks in this assumption. Even while the duty-oriented, exiled prince Rāma (the hero of the *Rāmāyaṇa*), who wages an epic war against a demon to win back his abducted wife, Sītā, is popularly worshipped by Hindus, his heroism has nevertheless been critiqued in retellings and performances of the story that challenge Rāma's decision to put Sītā repeatedly to the test. Just as song traditions based on the *Rāmāyaṇa* story in Andhra Pradesh reveal an "interior" *Rāmāyaṇa* oriented toward women's experiences not dealt with by the martial hero-centered epic, a few exclusively Sītā temples embody not Rāma's heroism, but Sītā's suffering, culminating in her final rejection of Rāma and her return to Earth. The Sītā temple near Kuradzai village in Satara district, and the one near Raveri in Yeotmal district, both in Maharashtra, mark places where Sītā is believed to have wandered, abandoned, and to have given birth to her twin sons. Such a Sītā is celebrated as a gentle mother, as an emblem of independence, and as a representative of women's experiences in a patriarchal society.

References

Atukuri Molla. 1968. *Atukuri Molla Rāmāyaṇamu.* Madras: Vavilla Ramaswami Sastrulu and Sons.

Brown, Mackenzie C. 1990. *The triumph of the goddess: the canonical models and theological visions of the* Dēvi-Bhāgavata Purāṇa. Albany, New York: State University of New York Press.

Caldwell, Sarah. 1999. *Oh terrifying mother: sexuality, violence and worship of the goddess* Kāli. Oxford University Press: Delhi.

Coburn, Thomas. Devi: the great goddess. In *Dēvi: goddesses of India.* Hawley and Wulff, eds. 31–48.

———. 1984. *Dēvi Mahātmya: the crystallization of the goddess tradition.* New Delhi: Motilal Banarsidass.

Dhal, Upendra Nath. 1978. *Goddess* Lakśmi: *origin and development*. New Delhi: Oriental Publishers and Distributors.
Erndl, Kathleen M. 1993. *Victory to the mother: the Hindu goddess of northwest India in myth, ritual, and symbol*. New York: Oxford University Press.
Hawley, John S. and Donna M. Wulff. 1996. *Dēvi: goddesses of India*. Berkeley: University of California Press.
Hess, Linda. 1999. Rejecting Sīta: Indian responses to the ideal man's cruel treatment of his ideal wife. *Journal of the American Academy of Religion,* 67: 1–32.
Kinsley, David. 1986. *Hindu goddesses: vision of the divine feminine in the Hindu religious tradition*. Berkeley, California: University of California Press.
Kishwar, Madhu. 1998. Yes to Sīta, no to Rām: the continuing popularity of Sīta in India. *Manushi* (Jan-Feb): 20–31.
Lalye, P. G. 1973. *Studies in Dēvi Bhāgavata*. Popular Prakashan: Bombay.
McDermott, Rachel. 1995. Bengali songs to Kāli. *Religions of India in Practice*. Prentice.
———. The western Kāli. In Dēvi: *goddesses of India*. Hawley and Wulff, eds. 281–313.
Narayana Rao, Velcheru. A ramāyana of their own: women's oral tradition in Telugu. In *Many ramāyanas: the diversity of a narrative tradition in south Asia,* Paula Richman, ed. Berkeley: University of California Press. 114–136.
Narayanan, Vasudha. Sri: Giver of fortune, bestower of grace. In Hawley and Wulff, eds. Dēvi: *goddesses of India*. 87–108.
Pintchman, Tracy. 1994. *The rise of the goddess in Hindu tradition*. Albany, New York: State University of New York Press.
Richman, Paula. 1991. ed. *Many ramāyanas: the diversity of a narrative tradition in south Asia*. Berkeley: University of California Press.

LEELA PRASAD

SEE ALSO

Bhagavati Rituals of Kerala; Buffalo; Ellamma; Floor Designs; Gavarī; Gender and Folklore; Goddesses, Place, and Identity in Nepal; Māriamma; *Muṭiyēṯṯu; Navarātri; Pēranṭālu; Purāṇa*; *Śākta* Song; Śiva; Tulsi (Basil); West Bengal

GODDESSES, PLACE, AND IDENTITY IN NEPAL

Every god and goddess in Nepal, whether of Hindu, Buddhist, or local religious pantheons, has a name and an address in a particular place or temple. Thus, in the broader sense, all goddesses are goddesses of local and regional identity by virtue of their particular manifestations. But some have more highly valorized or explicitly conceptualized associations with local places. Associations of places with specific deities, especially goddesses, are a prominent aspect of worldview constructions and ritual expressions. Towns and villages in the Kathmandu Valley of Nepal often define their autonomous identities through an affiliation with a primary central resident goddess, called *grāmadevatā,* or through boundary goddesses, called *mātṛkā,* who surround the territory. A national goddess, or *rāṣ ṭradevatā,*

Mandala painting of the eight Asta Matrka goddesses with Bhairava at the center.

may be associated with national identity in relation to larger groups of towns or villages. Deities can acquire this "national" status because they are often tutelary lineage goddesses, or *kūladevatā,* associated directly with a royal family. Royal lineage kūladevatā may take the role of central grāmadevatā and/or rāṣ ṭradevatā and frequently receive extensive ritually prescribed service and patronage from all members of the kingdom as decreed by a ruler.

Construction of personal identity is also linked with ideas about the place (*sthāna*) and residence of these goddesses. Potential multiple meanings of these goddess-associated places range from one's personal place in life or existence to geographic places such as the home, community, or nation.

Grāmadevatā, central resident goddesses, of a *grāma,* (village, town, or settlement), usually reside in the center of the defined area. In some instances the name of the deity is the name of the community; for example, the town Harasiddhi, is named after the goddess Harasiddhi Māī. These goddesses are affectionately called "queen of the town" or "mother." Grāmadevatā are given great respect, and in local mythology are directly associated with local community identity because of their founding of the town or their arranging of the physical landscape to facilitate human habitation, for example, by draining water to form a fertile valley or establishing fresh drinking water sources. At the same time, they may be identified with classical South Asian Hindu goddesses such as Durgā, or female Buddhas.

Village goddesses provide a bridge between the universal values of the "great" traditions, and local ideas of the origin, preservation, and well-being of the community. For example, Vajrayoginī, one of the female Buddhas and supreme goddesses of Tantric Buddhism, is the patron goddess of Sānkhu, a town in Nepal. According to popular oral tradition based on a Buddhist *avadāna* (origin text), *Maṇiśaila Mahāvadāna,* Vajrayoginī not only creates the landscape by draining a lake with her sword, but also pronounces who the first king will be. He is Śankhadeva (one of the previous lives of Buddha). She instructs a Buddhist priest in the origin and construction of a town named Śankhapur (now Sānkhu) that should be built in the shape of a conch shell, *śankha,* with water surrounding it on all sides. It should contain eight neighborhoods, *twā;* eight Buddhist residential monastic communities, *vihāra;* eight dance platforms, *dabu,* for performing her dances; roads in eight directions; four gates; a cremation ground in the north; and two sets of Aṣṭa Mātṛkā (eight mother goddess) shrines both outside and inside the town.

Associated with a primary Buddhist goddess, Vajrayoginī, by Buddhist residents, and with a primary Hindu goddess, Khadgayoginī (a form of Durgā Bhavānī), by Hindu residents, this goddess is the focus of an annual town festival, *deśa jātra,* in which everyone participates, including people living in nearby regions extending beyond marked boundaries of the town. In a large palanquin procession, the community carries the sword-bearing Khadgayoginī, together with her husband, Svayambhū Buddha, and two children (lion and tiger), from their "married home" in a hillside Buddhist monastery above the town, to her maternal home, in the heart of Sānkhu. This goddess is at the very heart of the place, and ritual choreography reconstructs her ordered relationship to the geographical physical space and to the people living there.

Besides Vajrayoginī, protective goddesses of other historical kingdoms in Nepal include Tripurāsundarī of Bhaktapur, the Bhagavatī of Palāncok, and Taleju in Kathmandu and Pātan, all of whom are identified with Durgā. These particular goddesses were lineage goddesses, or kūladevatā, for Hindu kings who sought legitimation of their rule from the spiritual energy and power or *śakti* of such goddesses. Kings instituted ritual practices and dedicated lands to families whose respective lineages subsequently became responsible for maintaining the ritual traditions that have continued to the present. One such ritual includes a living goddess in the form of a prepubescent girl, who embodies Kumārī. From at least the fifteenth century to the present, the Hindu King of Nepal must receive a *tika* blessing from the living goddess Kumārī to renew his political authority and well-being each year. Failure to do so bodes disaster for king and country. Living Kumārīs are specially chosen high-caste Buddhist girls who embody the goddess Kumārī, who is understood to be Buddhist, or the Hindu goddess Durgā, according to the respective beliefs of her worshippers. Community participation and representation in such rituals frequently defines the center and/or boundaries of the original kingdom; thus, contemporary re-creation of ancient sacred spaces is often a popular venue for public assertion of a historical local identity autonomous from later hegemonic or oppressive authorities and their imposed boundaries.

Protective boundary goddesses, mātṛkā, usually found in groups of seven, eight, or nine, are also goddesses of places. In the Kathmandu Valley of Nepal, configurations of the eight Aṣṭa Mātṛkā and the nine Nava Durgā goddesses surround and protect regions, towns, neighborhoods and individual homes, defining both sacred and geopolitical spaces. These spaces are defined and regularly marked by Hindu and Buddhist ritual pilgrimages to shrines, and by goddess dance rituals based on the geometrical arrangements of shrines. The mātṛkā goddesses are distinct from, yet potentially related to, the central goddess of the town, grāmadevatā, who is distinguished from them by the singular honorific title of *Māju* or *Māī,* "respected mother" rather than the plural, mātṛkā. Both a central goddess and her set of associated mātṛkā provide protection to the town; the one from within and the others from without, with the mātṛkā helping to define the place and its central goddess.

Primarily the defenders of towns, mātṛkā are sometimes identified directly as guardians of places (*lokapāla*), directions (*digpāla*), or lands (*kṣetrapāla*), and they may also be worthy of blood sacrifice due to their potentially ferocious natures. Newar Buddhists in the Kathmandu Valley also associate mātṛkā with human qualities and emotions, and, by visiting three groups of eight Aṣṭa Mātṛkā shrines, they strive to master each of the twenty-four human qualities in their own persons.

Mātṛkā goddesses usually emanate themselves in aniconic unhewn stones located in fixed open-air shrines called *pīṭha,* but their essence can also be temporarily extracted from their permanent shrines and placed into water-filled vessels that can be carried in processions around towns or to other locations. The vessels, called *pātra,* may be clay or copper pots, or possessed masked dancers who temporarily embody the deity.

Especially in these dancing anthropomorphic forms, they take on human-modeled family relationships. In the *Pacali Bhairava* and *Bhadrakālī* dance of Kathmandu, for example, the eight Aṣṭa Mātṛkā goddesses are the daughters; the elephant-headed god Gaṇeśa is their brother; two protective deities, Simmā, Lioness, and Dumbā, Tiger, are junior rival siblings; while the great Tantric god, Pacali Bhairava, is Āju, the Grandfather, and the great Tantric goddess, Bhadrakālī, is Ajimā, or the Grandmother. In order to make them temporarily more accessible to worshippers once every twelve years, the families of gods and goddesses must be brought to life and "pulled" out of their permanent rock shrine, pīṭha, in a birth ritual performed by a Buddhist Tantric priest, Vajrācaryā, who installs them into the human dancers.

The gods and goddesses are embodied in male human dancers who first engage in Tantric initiations and training to attain *siddhi,* the supreme power of Tantric wisdom, at cremation grounds near the pīṭha permanent shrine location. The siddhi acquired is carried with the dancers in swords, *khadga*. The sword of the central "grandparent" deity is exchanged with that of the King of Nepal in a ceremony called "wisdom of the sword" or *khadgasiddhi,* which recharges the king and his sword with the siddhi (wisdom) and śakti (power) of the god and goddess family. According to historical chronicles, the city of Kathmandu was built in 724 C.E. in the shape of a sword with the shrines of this grandfather-grandmother god and goddess couple forming the sword hilt, and the shrines of their eight daughter goddesses, mātṛkā, outlining the sword's blade.

After completing the cycle of dance performances, the family of deities are fed "death rice," symbolically "killed," and mourned by the community while their masks are returned in a large community funeral procession and cremated downstream from the same pīṭha shrine with unhewn stones from which they were ritually born. Group goddess dances such as this are still found in old Kathmandu Valley towns and are taken on ritual pilgrimage performance tours under local and royal joint sponsorship. But the separate groups of goddess dancers never cross paths or perform at the same time in the same site, an index of both their autonomous identity and regional affiliation with places.

Other pilgrimage site goddesses of place include the set of sixty-four open-air shrine sites, *chatuhṣaṣṭhi pīṭha,* where pilgrims worship the goddess at the locales of the scattered sixty-four body parts of the Purānic Hindu goddess, Sātī Devī, the wife of Śiva, who threw herself on a fire sacrifice to preserve her husband's honor. Other deities and grāmadevatā may also have pīṭha shrine pilgrimage locations, and often eight Aṣṭa Mātṛkā shrines may be called pīṭha as well.

Pīṭha tend to be permanent sunken open-air stone shrines, from which gods and/or goddesses may be invoked. But such shrines may also be inside a temple, for example, the grāmadevatā Harasiddhi Māī functions as the central goddess of a town named Harasiddhi, and her stone slab pīṭha is on the second floor of her centrally located temple. Her affiliated pantheon of gods and goddesses, embodied in ritual dancers, are invited to "come down" from this pīṭha location. Some gods and goddesses may also be bound and transferred from an origin site at a sacred mountain, tree, or river to a permanent pīṭha location for the convenience of community worship and regular control.

Personifications of the earth and physical landscape as a goddess or female being can be found in literature as early as mentions of Pṛthivī in the *Ṛg Veda* (second millennium B.C.E.), and Bhūdevī in later Brāhmanas and Purāṇas. From the earliest Buddhist literature onward, the Buddha calls "Earth," who appears in the form of a goddess to bear witness to his enlightenment, with his "earth-touching gesture," *bhūmisparśa mūdrā*. Contemporary idioms such as Bhārata Mātā, "Mother India," also link the idea of a unified sacred landscape to a notion of regional or national identity.

Strong personal identification with one's birth home and land is pervasive in South Asia and is related to the identification with the living divinity of the landscape itself. In Nepal, the special goddess of the crossroads and intersections, called Cwasā Ajimā, is witness to life's major liminal transitions of birth and death. At birth, the afterbirth is offered to this goddess, and in death, the clothes of the recently deceased are left at her side. Even in sickness, she receives an offering of a dough image likeness of sick individuals with the illness transferred away from the real person in order to consume the cause of the suffering. By removing the impurities associated with childbirth, sickness, and death, Cwasā Ajimā ensures that individuals are symbolically linked to the physical landscape of their community through time.

Svasthānī

The Goddess Svasthānī, whose name literally means "One's Own Place," is found exclusively in Nepal. Besides providing origin stories of sacred geography and the pantheon, the sacred text, *Svasthānī Vrata Kathā,* includes popular narrative stories about the Goddess Svasthānī and other gods, goddesses, humans, and non-humans who benefit from worshipping her. The manuscript text itself, existing in many "editions" copied, compiled, and elaborated over many generations by members of each family that owns a copy, is the primary object of worship in households throughout Nepal.

In this religious narrative, the wife of Śiva, Pārvatī ("Mountain," i.e., Himalayas), is the daughter of Himālaya Rāja (King Himālaya). The Himalayas are her own place, *svasthāna,* and those who hear these *vrata kathā* stories see the setting as the Himalayas or Nepal. The goddess gives the vrata or ritual vow of Svasthānī to all creatures to overcome suffering and to obtain well being and reunification, especially of families and spouses. Individual families recite the text together each year in a month-long ritual, with family members taking turns reading. In a large month-long annual public vrata performance, women from around the Kathmandu Valley practice vows of fasting, abstinence, and ritual observances, while staying on the banks of the Sālinadi River, in Sānkhu, the primary pilgrimage site from the *Svasthānī Vrata Kathā* story. The fruits and blessings of their month-long vrata are extended to the recipient of one's own choosing and to the king and the nation of Nepal. The meaning of "own place" extends from one's own place in life (and how to improve it) to place in the community, to place in the Himalayas. Therefore, Nepal equals svasthāna.

Nepalese living outside Nepal also recite *Svasthānī Vrata Kathā* as a way of contemplating who they are, their place of birth, where they are, and their own ideal, true place; and of symbolically recreating or improving that place wherever they are.

Svasthānī texts were written, copied and recited by Kathmandu Newar traders while living in remote areas of Nepal and in Tibet. Nepalese living in Burma, Hong Kong, the United States, and elsewhere continue to recite it and observe Svasthānī Vrata in their new homes. Thus, goddesses of place, including Svasthānī in the form of a sacred text, are also portable and may ultimately facilitate movement of people from one place to another, while simultaneously remaining connected to an original place through the symbolic re-creation of sacred geography in the diaspora.

Likewise, the essence of goddesses of place may be ritually transferred from a permanent shrine seat (pītha) into a pot of water collected from prescribed sacred river confluences or *tīrtha*s. Subsequent movement of the vessel through the community or to distant locations distributes the energy and power of the goddess through space to a wider territorial place. Hence, local gods and goddesses of homes, towns, and specific regional places also become universalized. Kees Bolle summarized this phenomenon:

> The family deity [*kūladevatā*] is what he is because he is local. . . . He is *essentially* a local deity, but at the same time universal. When a family moves, they take their god along, or, more accurately, . . . God too moves. . . .[U]nless one understands the primacy of the *place,* the nature of the sacred in most of Hinduism remains incomprehensible, and the plurality and variety of gods continues to form an unsolvable puzzle. *God is universal because he is there.* (Bolle 1969: 128–129).

References

Anderson, Mary. 1971. *The festivals of Nepal*. London: George Allen and Unwin.

Bolle, Kees W. 1969. Speaking of a place. In *Myths and symbols: Essays in honor of Mircea Eliade,* eds. J. Kitagawa and C. Long. Chicago: University of Chicago Press, pp. 127–139.

Gutschow, Neils and Axel Michaels, eds. 1987. *Heritage of the Kathmandu Valley*. Sankt Augustin: VGH Wissenschaftsverlag.

Iltis, Linda. 1985. The Swasthani Vrata: Newar women and ritual in Nepal. Ph.D. diss. University of Wisconsin-Madison.

———.1994. Women, goddesses, and Newar representations of geopolitical space. In *Anthropology of Nepal: Peoples, problems and processes,* ed. Michael Allen. Kathmandu: Mandala Book Point, pp. 349–357.

———. 1996. Women, pilgrimage, power, and the concept of place in the Swasthānī Vrata. In *Change and continuity: Studies in the Nepalese culture of the Kathmandu Valley,* ed. Siegfried Lienhard. Torino: CESMEO, pp. 303–320.

Naraharinath, Yogi. 1966. *Devamālā Vamśāvalī*. Mṛgasthali, Nepal: Śrīpīramanata Kshiprānātha Yogirāja.

Slusser, Mary. 1982. *Nepal Mandala*. Princeton, N.J.: Princeton University Press. *The Kauṭilīya Arthaśāstra*. Trans. R. P. Kangle. Bombay: Bombay University Press, 1965.

Toffin, Gérard. 1993. *The palace and the temple. [Le Palais et le Temple: La fonction royale dans la vallee du Népal]*. Paris: C.N.R.S. Editions.

Vajrācaryā, Varṇavajra 1962. *Maṇiśaila Mahāvadāna*. [Supreme Origin of the Gemstone Mountain.] Banepa, Nepal.

Zanen, Sj. M. 1986. The Goddess Vajrayoginī and the Kingdom of Sānkhu (Nepal). In *L'espace du temple: Les sanctuaries dans le royaume,* J.C. Galey, ed. *Puruṣārtha,* Vol. 10, Paris: EHESS, pp. 125–166.

LINDA ILTIS

SEE ALSO

Buddhism and Buddhist Folklore; Geomancy; Goddesses, Hindu; Gods and Goddesses; Nationalism and Folklore; Shrines; *Vrat Kathā*

GODS AND GODDESSES

In the study of South Asia, the term "god," or "gods," is used to translate or gloss indigenous terms for a variety of beings. But terms of Sanskrit derivation, especially the word *deva,* pl. *devāḥ,* find their way into designations of deity in most South Asian languages. For this reason, a discussion of the folklores of South

Asian gods can become a laboratory for methods derived from the history of religions, including Sanskrit and Indo-European studies (as it first did in the work of Max Müller, and later of Georges Dumézil), comparative religions (particularly Christian and Muslim folklores in South Asia), and, in this vein, even comparative theology (often implicit in scholarly discussion). Such studies tend all too easily to elitist, purist, and "trickle-down" views of South Asian folklore, but certain folklorists in reverse often mention "Sanskrit," "Christian," or "Muslim" as equivalents to "contamination" of folklores presumed to have been originally non-Sanskritic or pre Christian / Muslim. While scholars of varying persuasions have sought to keep such "influences" conceptually apart, South Asian folklores about divinity have often been subtle in weaving these strands together and maintaining narrative and cultic tensions between them.

Sanskrit *deva,* with such Indo-European cognates as Latin *deus* and French *dieu,* is usually derived from the Vedic verbal root *div* (to shine), and the nominal *div* (day; brightness, sheen). In classical Hinduism it also resonates with derivatives of the root *div,* (to play). Gods thus "shine" or "play;" the feminine form *devī* can mean "she who plays." The word *devatā,* (deity), has the same derivation, but it can have more technical uses, as in identifying the deity of an image or *mantra* (incantation), or referring to deities in classes. Both terms are used commonly in the plural, and, unless incremented adjectivally (as in *Mahādeva* "Great Deity" for Śiva), only rarely refer to the highest divinity or reality.

Buddhists and Jains also classify "gods" of high cosmic realms, although they regard these beings as nonetheless still caught up in reincarnation and thus inferior to the enlightened human. Jews deny the existence of all gods except Yahweh, and Muslims deny that there are gods other than Allah. Christians accept the God of the Old Testament, but believe Jesus to be the son of God as well as his messiah.

In the earliest Vedic hymns, *devas* as a class are lower than deities called *asuras*, a term that soon comes to designate "demon," the gods' opponents. Terms like *Puruṣa* (primordial "Man"), *brahman,* Śakti (designating the goddess), Īśvara (designating Śiva), and Bhagavan (designating Viṣṇu) refer to a supreme reality or divinity higher than "the gods," while other semidivine-to-demonic beings such as *yakṣas*, *gandharvas*, *apsaras*, and *rākṣasas* range below them.

The *Veda* speaks of thirty-three gods: either eleven for each of the three worlds, or the combination of eight Vasus, eleven Rudras, twelve Ādityas, and two Aśvins. The thirty-three also have their wives, and the actual number of Vedic deities is far greater. The *Upaniṣads* speak of fractional gods. In popular Hinduism, the

The goddess Mahishasuramardini (Kālī) at Harihareshwar. Maharastra State, India, © Dr. Jayant Bapat

count has risen to thirty-three *crores* (one crore equals ten million) of gods (three-hundred and thirty million). Early European reactions to the iconography and mythology of Indian gods developed a virtual folklore about them as "much maligned monsters."

Classification

Sanskritic typologies have rooted themselves into the representation of folk traditions by both villagers and scholars. Most prominent is the threefold classification of *grāmadevatā* (village deity), *kuladevatā* (family deity or clan deity), and *iṣṭadevatā* (personal divinity). Individuals may worship three different deities under these headings, or there may be overlap.

Village deities are mostly female, with their temples typically at village centers and boundaries. Their primary ties are to the village's land and its fertility, and with the health of the villagers and their livestock. Festivals to village deities typically involve an idealized representation of the "whole" village. They are patronized by leading members of the landed dominant caste or castes and enlist ritual service castes (potters, washermen, barbers, untouchables, and others) whose members have traditional rights to undertake specific festival tasks. A village will have many deities, and often the designation of village deity extends to several of them. A woman who marries into a village will adopt the new village's deity, but she may also maintain festival ties with her natal village deity. This inclusive village-deity-festival complex is most typical of southern and eastern India. In North India, one finds inclusive village festivals such as Holi (not performed in South India) and Navarātri or Dasarā (which have southern variations), but they are not performed for village deities. North Indian villages do, however, have both female (for example, Śakti Mātā, Śitalā) and male (for example, Thākur Dev, Dharma Thākur, Bhairava) village deities.

Family deities, worshiped especially at life cycle rites by members of male lineages within a caste, can have temples both within and outside a village, the latter approached on pilgrimage or vows. While most are female, many are male. Legends about such deities often link them with ordeals: *satī* (widow self-immolation) for females; other violent deaths for males. A woman takes her husband's family deity. A dominant caste's family deity may take on characteristics of a village deity if village members of such a caste draw villagers from other castes into its worship.

A personal divinity is the deity one "chooses" to worship individually in matters bearing on both personal desires and ultimate salvation. Such deities tend to be those high in the *bhakti* or devotional pantheon: Viṣṇu or his *avatāras*; Śiva; the great goddess (known under names like Pārvatī, Durgā, Mahālakṣmi, Bhagavatī, and Kālī); and in more regional settings, Śiva and Pārvatī's (or in Bengal, Durgā's) children Gaṇeśa (most popular in Maharashtra) and Skanda-Murukaṉ (most popular in Tamilnadu and Śri Lanka under the name Kataragama). Viṣṇu, Śiva, and the goddess may have temples in one's village, but their full worship entails pilgrimage to their interregional and pan-Indian temples. They have both royal and ascetic forms. The former, often linked with royal dynasties and regional territories and histories, tend to be in or near royal capitals. The latter often have their temples on mountains or in other remote places.

Deities of all these types, insofar as they are worshiped in the sanctum of a temple, may have attendant deities (*parivāra devatā*) at temple entrances, corners, and boundaries, with varied guardian functions such as "field-protector" (*ksetrapāla*), "gate keeper" (*dvārapālaka*), and "deity of (who neutralizes) the impure residue of offerings" (*nirmālyadevatā*). Such subordinate deities may also have their own temples and may be family deities. In Tamil, such deities are called *kāval teyvam* (guardian deities). A Sanskritic term for folk deities in general is *kṣudradevatā* (small divinities).

Vernacular traditions also use specially derived terms for gods, for instance: the Tamil word *cāmi* (from the Sanskrit *svāmin,* "lord"), or the Tulu *bhūta* (from the Sanskrit word for "ghost", or "element"). *Nāth* (Sanskrit, *nātha,* "lord"), *thākur* (god), and *bābā* (dad) are terms used in North India for male gods. *Śakti* (power), as well as various terms for mother (*mātā, māī* in the North; *ammaṉ, amma* in the South) are terms used for goddesses. Such terms are also used for holy personages, such as saints and royalty.

Fluidity and hierarchy

Vernacular traditions also make further classifications. Bow song (*villuppāṭṭu*) performances at festivals in southernmost Tamilnadu enact "god stories" (*cāmi katai*) about figures of two types: "birth stories" (*piṟanta katai*) about gods and goddesses of "divine descent" (*teyva vamcam*) or "divine birth" (*teyva piṟavi*), and "death stories" (*iṟanta katai*) about "spirits who were killed" (*iṟantuppaṭṭa vātai*) or "cut-up spirits" (*veṭṭuppaṭṭa vātai*). In Tulu *pāḍdana*s, *dēvaru* and bhūta are fluid categories. Although the former is higher, many deities (for example, Jumādi) are called both, and there can be mobility, as when a caste claims the higher status for a deity (for example, Kordabbu) in conjunction with seeking higher status for itself. In the Rajasthani *Pābūjī* epic, lists of all the gods and goddesses (*sarva devī deva*) invited to weddings include the pan-Indian deities Gaṇeśa, Kṛṣṇa, Śiva, Hanumān, and the goddess Jagadambā; the regional deities Vemātā (goddess of destiny), Rāmdev, and Black Bhairu (a form of Bhairava); the *bhomiyo* (a local hero deified after being slain rescuing cattle); and a dutiful son unjustly slain in the *Rāmāyaṇa* by Rāma's father.

In such cases, two intersecting, yet also contending, principles can be observed: the divine is both fluid and hierarchical. Inanimate objects can be divine. As a poem by the Vīraśaiva poet Basava puts it with scorn, the pot, stone, and comb are gods. Animals—notably the cow and monkey—are deities in certain contexts. Among living humans, divinity may be attributed to husbands, wives, kings, saints, and in some contexts virgins. There are also deified dead, such as *satī*s and heroes worshiped on hero stones over much of India, and the "cut up spirits," bhomiyo, and some but not all bhūtas mentioned above. Muslim saints (*pīrs*), martyrs (*śahīd*), and warriors (such as Muttāl Rāvuttaṉ in Tamilnadu) are deities in Hindu folk traditions, as are some deified British soldiers and adventurers, (such as Veḷḷaikkāracāmi (White man god), represented in southern Tamilnadu by boots and a chair, who receives guardian-deity-type offerings of liquor and cigars. Heroes and heroines of several regional folk epics, some of whom are incarnations of Sanskritic deities and heroes, receive cults as gods after their deaths. Vedic and classical *deva*s figure as gods of the directions, senses, elements, and other natural forces. Pan-Indian bhakti deities—Viṣṇu. Śiva, and the goddess—know no restrictions on the forms and places (including the human heart) in which they appear, and each has many regional *avatāra*s (incarnations or descents) in folk cults beyond the classical ten avatars of Viṣṇu. For example, the deity known as Khaṇḍobā, Mallanna, and Mailāra in Maharashtra, Andhra Pradesh, and Karnataka respectively is an incarnation of Śiva. Such fluidity is also a feature of the classical Hindu pantheon, in which the divine can be found in the innermost self of all beings—epigrammatically, "from Brahmā to a blade of grass."

Although it is both a popular commonplace and a prominent, though not pan-Hindu, philosophical teaching that divinity is indivisible, and thus the same in all its fluid manifestations, hierarchy is also inherent to all its cultural and textual formulations. Brahmā is not the highest deity and has few temples (the exceptions are at Lake Pushkar in Rajasthan and more controversially in the worship of the folk deity (bhūta) Bermeru, identified by some with Brahmā, in South Kanara). The highest deity, with such rank influenced by sectarian affiliation and the choice of one's "personal divinity," is either Viṣṇu, Śiva, or the Goddess, each with designations appropriate to recognition of their cosmic supremacy: Bhagavān or Puruṣottama for Viṣṇu, Mahādeva or Paramaśiva for Śiva, Mahādevī or Paraśakti for the Goddess. The hierarchy descends through all the forms mentioned above, down to the "small divinities."

It is probably most accurate to think of several reinforcing principles, rather than just one, as sustaining such hierarchy. Purity and impurity constitute one axis. The highest divinities receive worship with vegetarian food from Brahman priests; and lower divinities receive both vegetarian and nonvegetarian offerings from non-Brahman priests; and the lowest receive impure offerings (liquor, drugs, violent forms of blood sacrifice) in ritual contexts that may enlist participation or involve symbolic representation of untouchables and outsiders. The highest deities have corresponding benign and fierce forms. Another tendency is to find Sanskrit "textuality" at the higher end and regional or local vernacular "orality' at the lower. Another is found in bhakti, which introduces hierarchical principles of time (only bhakti deities in their transcendent aspects are immortal and can thereby bestow salvation; mortality begins with Brahmā), yogic detachment (such gods intervene only when awakened from their meditations), cosmic lordship (they rule as royalty), and encompassment (all deities are forms of them). A scale of forms extends to the "little divinities," who also have their royal courts and inverse modes of encompassment, for instance, through rituals of possession rather than yogic meditation.

References

Babb, Lawrence A. 1975. *The divine hierarchy: popular Hinduism in central India.* New York: Columbia University Press.

Fuller, C. J. 1992. *The camphor flame. Popular Hinduism and society in India.* Princeton: Princeton University Press.

Hiltebeitel, Alf. 1989, ed. *Criminal gods and demon devotees. Essays on the guardians of popular Hinduism.* Albany: State University of New York Press.

Macdonell, Arthur A. [1898] 1974. *Vedic mythology.* Delhi: Motilal Banarsidass.

Mitter, Partha. 1977. *Much maligned monsters. A history of European reactions to Indian art.* Chicago: University of Chicago Press.

Sontheimer, Gunther-Dietz. 1989. *Pastoral deities in western India.* Anne Feldhaus trans. New York and Oxford: Oxford University Press.

ALF HILTEBEITEL

SEE ALSO

Bandara Cults; *Bhakti; Bhūta;* Bow Song (*Vil Paṭṭū*); Buddhism and Buddhist Folklore; Dasarā; Fairs and Festivals; Epic; Goddesses, Hindu; Hanumān; Heroes and Heroines; Holī; Jainism; Kataragama; Kṛṣṇa; Mailāra/Mallanna/Khandobā; Muslim Folklore; Myth; *Navarātri; Pābūjī;* Pāḍdana; *Pattini, Pēraṇṭālu;* Pilgrimage; Rāma; Rituals; *Satī;* Śiva; Skanda; Supernatural Beings

GONDHAḶA

Gondhaḷa is a song and dance performance in honor of either the goddess known as Bhavānī or Ambābaī, both epithets of the consort of Śiva, or of Reṇukā, the mother of Paraśurāma. Until recently, gondhaḷa constituted the secular component of important rites of passage, particularly marriage and initiation ceremonies (investing with the sacred thread), among the Deśastha Brahmins and Marāthās. The tradition dates back over a thousand years and was observed by the Cālukya and Kadaṁba kings. It appears to have its root in the worship of Bhūtamāta, the mother goddess of ghosts and goblins. Gondhaḷa is traditionally performed by men of the Gondhaḷī caste who trace their origin from Tuljapur and Mahur, the towns known for their shrines of Bhavānī and Reṇukā. However, the Gondhaḷīs have spread over many parts of Maharashtra, Andhra, Karnataka, and Madhya Pradesh.

The performance starts with homage to the goddess by the host. The Gondhaḷīs bring a *divtī* (lamp) and a *budhlī* (oil container). Once the lamp is lighted, the performance goes until the host lets the flame extinguish. Four men of the Gondhaḷī caste usually take part, the chief among whom is called a *nāika*. There are an assistant singer-storyteller and two musicians who play the *sāmbaḷa* (two-sided drum) and the *tunṭuṇe* (a drone with one to three strings). As befits any Hindu theatrical performance, the nāika invokes Gaṇeśa, along with various regional deities, to seek blessings for the gondhaḷa. A well-known invocatory verse is:

> Oh Gaṇeśa, Come to gondhaḷa;
> 33 Crore Gods, come to gondhaḷa
> Gaṇeśa from Wai, come to the gondhaḷa
> Rivers Kṛṣṇa and Koynā, come to the gondhaḷa
> Lakṣmī from Kolhapur, come to gondhaḷa
> Bhavānī from Tulajapur, come to gondhaḷa
> Śivābāī from Junnar, come to gondhaḷa
> The seven seas, the nine lākha stars, come to gondhaḷa
> Mother earth, heavenly father, come to gondhaḷa
> All the devotees, all the others, come to gondhaḷa

In the main part of performance, the nāika skillfully weaves Purāṇic myths and secular heroic legends into songs, interspersed with prose. To maintain interest, he often talks about the important individuals present in the audience, including the host, and spontaneously weaves their names into his singing.

The Gondhaḷīs possess a large repertoire of poetry and literature of their own. Marathi saints like Jnaneśwara, Ekanātha, and Nāmdeva have also written many poems for Gondhaḷīs.

The gondhaḷa was an easy, natural, and effective medium of instruction. During the heyday of Marāṭha and Peśwā rule, the Gondhaḷīs served a useful role in uniting people through their *powādā*s (ballads) and inspirational performances.

Reference

Dhere, R. C. 1988. The *Gondhaḷī:* Singers for the Devi. In *The Experience of Hinduism,* Eds. Eleanor Zelliot and Maxine Berntsen, pp. 174–189. Albany: State University of New York Press.

JAYANT BHALCHANDRA BAPAT

SEE ALSO

Dance; Goddesses, Hindu; Song; Worship

GOPĪ CAND

The legend of King Gopī Cand is part of popular North Indian religious lore, spanning the subcontinent from Punjab in the west to Bengal in the east. Gopī Cand's story is sung and recited by bards of the Nāth caste, also called Jogīs, and performed as a play (*nauṭaṅkī*) by traveling drama troupes. In several well-known versions of the legend from Western India, Gopī Cand is identified as the ruler of Gaur—an ancient Bengali kingdom that fell to Muslim invaders in the thirteenth century. Attempts to link Gopī Cand with an historical Bengali dynasty have been inconclusive, but we know that, by the early seventeenth century, the legend of this king who turned yogi was well established and accepted as history, in Bengal and elsewhere.

As with many oral traditions, each performed version of the Gopī Cand legend differs, even within a single village, and regional variations are significant. Nonetheless, a basic plot structure common to all renditions of the tale is readily summarized: An extraordinarily beautiful only son is born to a widowed queen who has some connection with a powerful Nāth guru. Gopī Cand's mother is sometimes a yogic adept in her own right, sometimes a devotee of Śiva, but always a religiously determined woman and a pushy mother. In most versions her brother is identified as another renouncer-king, Bharthari, whose capital was Ujjain in Malva (part of today's Madhya Pradesh).

Gopī Cand's mother knows he will die unless he becomes an initiated yogi. If he takes the path of yoga, she tells him, his body will become immortal. But the young king enjoys his worldly pleasures and resists his mother's advice. When she introduces him to his future guru, he rejects him aggressively. In one common version, he throws this guru down a well and buries him in manure.

Eventually, however, Gopī Cand realizes his error and willingly gets his ears cut—the sign of initiation for Nāth yogis. His guru then sends him to beg from his former palace and call his queen "Mother"—always a melodramatic highlight of the story. In the Panjabi, Rajasthani, and Hindi versions, an episode follows where the former king visits his sister, with highly traumatic results for both of them. In almost every version, the yogi-king is captured and abused by low-born, magic-wielding, female enemies. After defeating predatory women and eluding loving ones, Gopī Cand's yoga is fulfilled, and he becomes immortal.

British colonial folklorists Sir Richard Temple (1963) and Colonel G. A. Grierson (1878; 1885) recorded, transliterated, and translated versions of the tale of Gopī Cand—in Punjabi and Eastern Hindi respectively—in the late nineteenth century. About a hundred years later, Ann Grodzins Gold (1992) recorded and translated a Rajasthani Nāth bard's performance. Kathryn Hansen (1992) has studied Hindi dramas of the Gopī Cand legend. Printed pamphlet versions of dramatic texts and Nath hagiography are readily accessible, as are cassette recordings of Gopī Cand's tale.

In popular lore, but not included within the epic tales, Gopī Cand and his uncle Bhartharī are paired as immortal companions still wandering the earth. Thus they appear in the signature lines of hymns (*bhajan*s) and are recalled in proverbs such as,

"As long as sky and earth shall be,
Live Gopī Cand and Bharthari."

(*Jab tak ākāsh dharatī,*
tab tak Gopī Cand Bharthari).

References

Gold, Ann Grodzins. 1992. *A carnival of parting: the tales of King Bharthari and King Gopi Chand as sung and told by Madhu Natisar Nath of Ghatiyali, Rajasthan.* Berkeley: University of California Press.

Grierson, G. A. 1878. The song of Manik Candra. *Journal of the Asiatic Society of Bengal* 3: 135–238.

Grierson, G. A. 1885. Two versions of the song of Gopī Cand. *Journal of the Asiatic Society of Bengal* 54(1): 35–55.

Hansen, Kathryn. 1992. *Grounds for play: the Nautanki Theatre of northern India.* Berkeley: University of California Press.

Temple, Sir Richard. 1963. The Legend of Rājā Gopī Cand, as Played at Jagādhrī in the Ambālā District. In *The Legends of the Punjab.* Vol. 2. Patiala: Department of Languages, Punjab.

ANN GRODZINS GOLD

SEE ALSO
Epic; Folklorists; Nāth; *Nauṭaṅkī;* Rajasthan

GORAVA / GORAMMA

*Gorava*s are wandering devotees and active traditional bearers of the Mailāra (or Mailāralinga) tradition, which is found in many parts of Karnataka. Mailāra is believed to be a manifestation of Lord Śiva, incarnated for the purpose of slaying the two dreaded demon brothers, Mallasura and Manikasura. Male devotees are called goravas, while female devotees are called *goramma*s. They are initiated into a particular sect of goravas by a ritual process called *Hore Horuvudu.* Goravas are easily recognized by their unique costumes, consisting of one or another of various symbolic representations of the Mailāra legend: a black woolen coat, a fur cap, a turban, a *damaruga* (hand drum), a necklace of cowrie shells, or a *doṇi* (oblong begging bowl).

The goravas and gorammas are not restricted to a particular caste. They are initiated into the tradition by Wodeyars, a priestly class within the Kuruba community, a pastoral caste of Karnataka. This initiation rite is hereditary in many families, and it is believed that if these devotees are not initiated to the traditional service of Mailāralinga, their families will be troubled mentally and physically by the power of the deity.

There are different varieties of goravas, classed according to the kind of service (*sēve*) they render to the deity. *Divatige goravappa* hold burning torches in front of the deity. *Doṇi goravappa* are so called because they receive alms from other devotees in the distinctive metal or wooden bowl called a *doṇi*. Other instruments carried by the doṇi goravappa are the *damaruga* (hand drum), flute, *gante* (small bell), stick, turban (*pīṭa*), and trident. *Cāṭi goravanna* lash themselves with whips in the service of the deity. These devotees believe they are horses, representing the mount of Mailāra. According to legend, Manikasura, the younger demon brother, after having been vanquished by Mailāra, was blessed by Mailāra forever to be his *vahana* (mount). The devotees believe that the deity will be pleased with them, too, if they act as horses and lash themselves; *Cabaku goravappa*s are another group who lash themselves with a whip as a service. *Kambali goravappa*s wear long black woolen coats similar to that said to have been worn by Mailāra. *Couri goramma* are women who perform the duty of fanning (*couri seve*) the deity. *Elecenci goramma* offer betel-nut to the deity Mailāralinga. *Pawaḍada goravappa* render their service to the deity by piercing iron tridents through their cheeks and wrists, and pass leather threads of a quarter inch diameter through the holes they drill in their legs. These devotees, also called *Kancavīra*s, are from *Harijan,* the once untouchable caste (Maadiga). *Sarapali goravappa* render their service by breaking iron chains in front of certain temples of goddesses associated with the Mailāra tradition. Yet other goravas enact a sort of dance around meal bowls in which they appear like dogs and bark, or dance like horses and eat roasted rice (*manḍakki*), bananas, and other foods favored by horses. These *gorava*s who enact animals are called *nayi* (dog) *gorava*s and *kudure* (horse) *gorava*s.

These groups of *gorava*s can be found mainly in cult ritual centers such as *Mailāra* and *Devaragudda* of northern Karnataka. In southern Karnataka, Mailāralinga tradition is influenced by another important folk tradition, the cult of *Mādēśwāra.* Like followers of Mādēśwāra, the Goravas in these areas wear a fur cap and carry a flute and wear a long coat. They are also called *karaḍi* (bear) *gorava*s. The *Vāghyā / Muraḷī* in Maharastra and Mallappolu of Andhra Pradesh are similar groups of devotees of *Khandoba* and *Mallaṇṇa,* as Mailāralinga is known respectively, in those two states.

References

Sontheimer, Gunther-Dietz. 1989. *Pastoral deities in western India.* Anne Feldhaus, trans. New York and Oxford: Oxford University Press.

Sontheimer, Günther-Dietz. 1989. Between ghost and god: a folk deity of the Deccan. In *Criminal gods and demon devotees: essays on the guardians of popular Hinduism,* ed. Alf Hiltebeitel, 299–337. Albany, N.Y.: State University of New York Press.

M. N. VENKATESHA

SEE ALSO

Gurav; Mailāra / Mallanna / Khandobā; Self-sacrifice; Vāghyā / Muraḷī

GOVINDEVJI, TEMPLE OF

The Temple of Govindevji is a huge seven-story red sandstone temple, built by Raja Man Singh of Amer in 1590 in Vrindavan, Uttar Pradesh. Govinda Deva is the patron deity of Jaipur, the capital city of Rajasthan in Northwest India. This image of Kṛṣṇa was originally discovered in the mid-1500s by Rupa Goswāmi, one of the six Goswāmis who were disciples of Caitanya Mahaprabhu, the founder of the Gaudiya Vaiṣṇava sect in Bengal. The life-size black marble deity of Lord Kṛṣṇa as a cowherd was brought to Jaipur by the Maharaja Jai Singh in 1735 in a great exodus of deities from Vrindavan due to fear from the widespread destruction wrought by the Mughal emperor Aurangzeb. Since the deity's arrival in Jaipur, Govinda Devji has been considered the ruler of the city, with the devout Vaiṣṇava kings acting merely as instruments for the deity.

The temple was built in the city palace garden grounds, just facing the Chandra Mahal, the main palace. This was so that the mahārāja could have the divine sight (*darśan*) of the deity every day. Now the temple is accessed via side gates through which thousands of Kṛṣṇa devotees enter to perform *pūja* (worship) daily. The public gets *darśan* of Śrī Śrī Radha-Govindevji seven times a day for periods lasting from half an hour to an hour, the times varying with the seasons and special festivities. The first period (*jhānki*), Mangalā, around 4:30 a.m., shows the Lord still in his night clothes. This is followed by Dhūp, Shringāra, and Rāj Bhog, the lunchtime offering at noon. At these *darśan*s, the Lord is seen in full opulence, dressed in fine, glittering silks and facy turbans or crowns, and adorned with garlands, sandalwood paste, and jewels. The temple is closed while the deities of Govinda and his consort, Radha, rest from 12:30 p.m. until around 6 p.m. There are three evening services: Gwāl, Sandhya, and Sen, when the Lord again dons his night clothes, lasting from 6 p.m. till around 9 p.m., after which the temple closes for the night.

A bustling and colorful place of worship, Govindevji's is a sacred space for the performance of prayer. Performance at the temple can be divided into three major genres. First, there is the formal religious performance of ritual worship by the priests (*pujārīs*) and workers (*sevaks*) in the temple, which follows a strict daily schedule. Second is the informal everyday performances of devotion (*bhaktī*) practiced by devotees throughout the day. Lastly, there are unique performances by ritual specialists and professional dancers and musicians that take place on particular occasions, usually in conjunction with religious festivals. These three aspects of worship at the temple are the very essence of what makes the temple such a vibrant and salient feature of people's lives in Jaipur, regardless of caste, gender, class, education, and even religious affiliation.

Every morning the priests bathe and prepare for the morning worship. The priests touch, bathe, apply elaborate sandalwood paste designs, dress, decorate, and garland the deities. They make food offerings, say prayers, and offer the daily worship (*āratī*) during the jhānkīs. This consists of waving auspicious lights of camphor first, then ghee wicks, and, finally, waving a conch shell filled with water from a distance around the deities. The sacred water is then splashed onto the assembled devotees. The priests also distribute *tulsī* (basil) leaves, flowers, perfumed cotton swabs, and sandalwood paste from the deity to the public as they circumambulate the temple.

In addition to the main priests, there are many other devotees (sevaks) who help in the daily worship (*sevā* or pūjā). Some are cooks; others string garlands of rose, jasmine, marigolds, and even lotus flowers; still others sew the deities' clothes. Some serve the blessed food (*prasād*) to the temple-going public, the poor, and religious mendicants. One family has been in charge of lighting the temple and sweeping for generations. Still another has volunteered to watch over the devotees' shoes as they go barefoot into the temple.

The people of Jaipur are so devoted to Radha-Govinda that many have developed their daily routine around the deities' schedule. Many devotees have vowed not to eat or drink before they have darśan of the Lord. During some special religious months (*Phālguna* and *Kārtik*), thousands of devotees attend the early morning services, often walking for miles at 4 a.m. Some come to all seven jhānkīs; others attend one in the morning and one at night. Some stay for hours at a time; still others come whenever they can.

The singing of devotional prayers (*bhajan*s and *kīrtan*s) is the public's main activity. Specific songs are sung according to the time of day and the season. Instruments are played during the most significant kīrtan of the day, that of *Sandhya Āratī* at around 6:45 p.m. The leader of the kīrtan has been coming every night for the past forty-five years without fail, but due to asthma, he often lets his apprentices take over the lead during the one-hour kīrtan. Men play drums and cymbals, while women sing along. Devotees, male and female, will often dance in front of the deities, usually twirling around and around in the typical folk style of Rajasthan.

Religious storytelling and listening are part of the daily worship. Formal lectures on scripture by local and traveling Brahmins are piped out to the congregation over a public address system, while the more intimate, yet no less ritualistic, storytelling by women is done just after the Mangalā services in small groups of five to twenty women huddled in a circle around the main storyteller. Usually, the stories describe situations in which a woman fasted for a particular goal. The stories are told according to the day and season.

The third type of performance at the temple is done by professional musicians and dancers in front of the deities and thousands of gathered devotees, usually for special festivals. A four-day festival in March is celebrated during the springtime festival of colors, *Holi*. For three hours in the afternoon, an offering (*hāzrī*) of dance and devotional singing takes place. *Kathak* dancers, mostly from the Jaipur area, accompanied by singers and musicians, take turns performing devotional and technical dance items. Classical and folk singers also perform. The performers are both male and female, and though most of the performers are Hindu, some of the musicians are Muslim. All the main performers are presented with a flower garland, a special blockprinted cotton cloth, a basket of blessed food (prasād) and, sometimes, a humble monetary offering by the son of the Goswami of the Govindevji Temple. The performances end with all the dancers twirling and showering the audience with flowers. In recent years the event has become so popular and the temple grounds so crowded, that TV screens have been installed in the circumambulation path (*parikramā*) so that everyone can see the performance.

MEKHALA NATAVAR

SEE ALSO
Dance; *Darśan;* Worship

GRIERSON, GEORGE A.

George A. Grierson (1851–1941) was born at Glenageary in Dublin County, Ireland. He was a student of mathematics at Trinity College in Dublin where he came in contact with Professor Robert Atkinson. Grierson was deeply influenced by Atkinson's erudition on India and studied Sanskrit and Hindustani with him. Grierson entered the Indian Civil Service, went to Bengal in 1873, and served as a civil servant until 1898. Concurrently, he pursued his research in Indian languages, literature, and folk traditions. Between 1877 and 1933, his publications, ranging from notes to books, grew to about three hundred in number and covered many disciplines: literature, languages, lexicography, folklore, translations, and religion. In addition, he also published about seventy reviews. Grierson was the recipient of twenty-nine honors including honorary degrees and a knighthood in 1912.

His magnum opus is the *Linguistic Survey of India* (1898–1928). European indologists at the Congress of Orientalists at Vienna in 1886 moved a resolution for a systematic inquiry into the spectrum of Indian languages. The government of India received the proposal favorably, and eight years later it entrusted Grierson with the project of organizing the survey. After consultation with various provincial governments, the Indian government decided to exclude from the survey Hyderabad, Mysore State, Madras State, and Burma.

The *Survey* contains information on 723 linguistic varieties (179 languages and 544 dialects) and consists of approximately 8000 pages in nineteen books in eleven volumes. The survey includes three specimens for each linguistic variety: a translation of the biblical Parable of the Prodigal Son, a piece of folklore or a passage in narrative prose or verse recorded directly from the mouth of a native speaker, and a standard list of words and test sentences. The survey also provides linguistic and social information about minor and major speech communities in India. It gives a schematic view of the people's history and their habitat, a grammatical sketch, pronunciation (through phonetic transcription in Nagari and Roman scripts), a genetic grouping of the languages, and literature and bibliography wherever possible. This survey is unique in its size and coverage and has proved to be the substructure of much research, particularly in linguistics and folklore. More recently, the survey has provided valuable insights into the study of transplanted varieties of Hindi and Bhojpuri outside the Indian continent.

As Grierson himself made clear, the survey was meant to be a collection of linguistic facts; theoretical discussions, wherever present, were only incidental to the genetic categorization of the languages. Through the collection of linguistic data, Grierson captured grassroots traditions, alternative and diverse perspectives, experiences, and expressions of folk traditions. Being interested in folklore, he published on folk songs, birth customs, omens, folktales, folk etymologies, and folk epics. He frequently communicated with the journal *Folklore* and contributed to *Indian Antiquary* and the *Journal of the Gypsy Lore Society,* of which he became president (1928–1930). His book *Bihar Peasant Life* (1885) contains an enormous body of data and has been mined for scholarly perspectives on material and non-material nomenclatures and customs.

References

Gupta, Asha. 1970. *George Abraham Grierson aur bihari bhasha sahitya*. Delhi: Atmaram and Sons.
———. 1984a. *Dr. Grierson ke sahityetihasa*. Delhi: Atmaram & Sons.
———. 1984b. *Madhyayugina Hindi kavi, anveshaka Dr. Griyarsana*. Delhi: Atmaram & Sons.
Thomas, F. W., and R. L. Turner. 1942. George Abraham Grierson 1851–1941. In *Proceedings of the British Academy,* 28: 283–306. London: The British Academy.
White, Edith M. 1936. Bibliography of the published writings of Sir George A. Grierson. In *Bulletin of the School of Oriental Studies* 8(2–3): 291–318. London: The School of Oriental Studies.

SURENDRA K. GAMBHIR

SEE ALSO
Colonialism and Folklore; Folklorists; Herders' Field Calls

GŪGĀ

Gūgā is a Rajput prince and hero who has been deified because of his powers to control snakes. His cult is most prominent in Rajasthan, Punjab, Harayana, and western Uttar Pradesh. He is believed to have ruled in the Bagar region of Rajasthan in the twelfth century.

Gūgā's story is told as an oral epic, performed by *jogi* and other religious specialists throughout the region. In the epic, Gūgā's birth is attributed to the powers of Guru Gorakhnāth, leader of the *Nāth jogi* (The *Nāth jogi* follow a form of tantrism developed in Bengal, but spread throughout North India by their renowned leader, Gorakhnāth.). From Gorakhnāth's blessing, Gūgā gained, even prior to his birth, the ability to control snakes.

Born to a barren woman who is a devotee of Gorakhnāth, Gūgā is believed by some to be a reborn disciple of Gorakhnāth. Gūgā subdues the snake Basak (Vasuki) from his mother's womb. Meanwhile, his mother's sister bears twin sons, also from the boon of Gorakhnāth. When he is twelve years old, a marriage is arranged with a princess from a faraway kingdom, but his mother refuses to allow it, desiring a closer alliance. She imprisons Gūgā, only to have him escape with the aid of Gorakhnāth. Some time later, the twin cousins seek their share of the kingdom and enlist the aid of the great Hindu king of Delhi Prithvīrāj. Despite having only five hundred soldiers to Prithvīrāj's nine hundred thousand, Gūgā is able to defeat Prithvīrāj with the aid of Gorakhnāth's fourteen hundred disciples. His cousins flee, and he follows, eventually beheading them. Gūgā's mother is furious at the loss of the twins whom she had nursed in childhood and banishes Gūgā, who goes to live with Gorakhnāth. At the end of twelve years, he starts to secretly visit his wife. When his mother discovers this, she begs him to return, but Gūgā rejects her plea, saying that he will never return to a mother who had banished him. He then implores Gorakhnath to allow him to commit *samādhi* (voluntary live burial). Gūgā and his magical blue horse disappear into the earth.

Several versions of this epic were collected by Richard Temple in his *Legends of the Punjab*. Other British scholar/administrators like Crooke and Tod also noted his presence as a key figure in rural religious life. In some versions of the story, Gūgā converts to Islam before his death. Hence he is also known as Gūgā Pīr (Saint Gūgā), Ẓahīr Pīr (the manifest saint), or Bagarvālā (the one from Bagar).

Gūgā's story is most commonly told at the rituals surrounding his birth celebration on the ninth day of the dark half of the Hindu month of Bhādon (August-September). This ritual is included in the yearly cycle of many villages in northwestern India. His chief shrine is in Bikaner District, Rajasthan, and an elaborate fair takes place here on his birth date. Gūgā is usually depicted riding on a blue horse, holding the standard of blue and yellow flags by which he is commonly represented. His ritual involves use of a *cābuk* (iron whip) and the standard representing him. In addition to the oral epic associated with him, Gūgā appears in snake possession rituals in the region, such as *ḍank,* where he is invoked to control the snake possessing a victim.

References

Crooke, William. 1926. *Religion and folklore in northern India*. London: Oxford University Press.
Lapoint, Ellwyn C., 1978. The Epic of Guga: A north Indian oral tradition. In *American studies in the anthropology of India*. ed. Sylvia Vatuk, 281–308. New Delhi: Manohar Books.
Temple, Sir Richard. 1963. *Legends of the Punjab*. Patiala: Dept. of Languages.
Tod, James. 1972. *Annals and Antiquities of Rajasthan*. Vol III. ed. W. Crooke. Delhi: Motilal Banarsidas.

SUSAN S. WADLEY

SEE ALSO
Epic; Pīr; Saints

GUJARAT

Gujarat is one of the twenty-six States and six Union Territories of India, and is situated on the west coast. Gujarat has an international boundary with Pakistan in the north; its internal boundaries in the northeast touch the state of Rajasthan, in the east, Madhya Pradesh and in the south, Maharashtra. On the west, the Arabian Sea washes its long coastline. Gujarat came into being as a separate linguistic state in 1960 with its boundaries aligned with the region where the language Gujarati is spoken.

Geographically, Gujarat comprises three separate regions: Kutch (Kacheh), with its desert in the north; Saurashtra and its hills, rivers, and forest areas and sea in the west, and the plains of north and central Gujarat, with their mountain ranges in the east and in the south.

Rivers of all sizes flow through its many hills and mountain ranges. Because of uneven rains ranging from 40 cm to 150 cm, several dams have been built to irrigate the land. More dams are under construction at present, including the controversial Sardar Sarovar Dam, popularly known as the Narmada Project.

The long coastline of Gujarat has several big and small ports, facilitating sea trade with far-off countries dating back to ca. 3000 B.C.E., beginning with the port of Lothal, the Indus Valley Civilization settlement, where evidence is found of its trade with Egypt, Mesopotamia, and, perhaps, Assyria. During historical times, the adventurous seafaring people of Gujarat traded from ports of Khambhat, Dwarka, Bharuch, Surat and as far as Surparak (Sopara). They also traded with countries such as Greece and Rome in the west, those of Africa in the southwest, and with Java, Sumatra, and Borneo in the southeast. Many people from these countries came to Gujarat, as did a few from other parts of the country, and merged with the mainstream of the local people. Others who followed were the English, the French, the Dutch, and the Portuguese.

The physiography of the land had its effect on the history and life of the people as well. The population became heterogenous, multiracial and multireligious. The religions followed by the people are Hinduism, Islam, Christianity, Zoroastrianism, Judaism, Jainism, and, now, Neo-Buddhism.

The people of Gujarat not only worship gods but also trees, serpents, animals, and so on. Each village, each group and each family, has its own ancestral god or goddess, who is worshiped with elaborate rituals, which involve the chanting of holy *mantras*.

The tribals have their own culture, which reflects their religious beliefs and practices: fairs, festivals, rituals, performing arts, oral epic traditions, and devotional songs. In addition to the tribal populations, the long coastline has a sizable seafaring people called Kharvas who have their characteristic folklore and performing arts.

The ethnic groups one finds today in Kutch and Saurashtra are the remnants of the ancient people who came to Gujarat and settled down permanently. Mers, Kathis, Ahirs, Kolis, Kharvas, Sidis, and others have not only distinctive physical features but also their costumes, religious beliefs, folktales and styles of decorating their houses. The material and design they use for decoration also reflects their ancestral traditions.

This mosaic of ethnic and religious groups finds expression in the performing arts, architecture, and folklore, all influenced, more or less, by mainstream life in Gujarat. People generally speak Gujarati with its regional variations.

Gujarat was never a single political entity in ancient times. At various times in its history its three geographical regions were ruled by different dynasties from outside the state. These regions were then called Anarta, Surashtra, and Lata; their borders changed in conjunction with political changes.

During the Chaulukya or Solanki dynasty (942–1244 C.E.) these different regions were gradually brought under one rule by sagacious, enlightened, and tolerant rulers. During this period, trade flourished and, with peace and prosperity, literature, arts, and architecture reached their zenith. It was truly called the Golden Period of Gujarat.

Ahmedshah was the first independent Muslim ruler of Gujarat who founded the city of Ahmedabad in 1410 C.E. and made the city his capital. Muslims established their independent kingdom in some parts of Gujarat. With the end of Muslim rule came that of the British, which ended in 1947 when India became independent under the leadership of Mahatma Gandhi.

For the purpose of folklore, the three geographical regions of Gujarat need to be regrouped into further subregions: north Gujarat, which has some cultural, religious and social affinities with the neighboring states of Rajasthan and Madhya Pradesh in the east and with Maharashtra in the south; the eastern hill areas where the tribals broadly called the Bhils live; the hills and forests in the south inhabited by tribals mainly called Gamits who have their subgroups as do the seafaring Kharvas who occupy the coastal areas of the state.

Among the common performing arts, the *rās* and the *garbā* are the most ancient folkdance forms prevalent in Saurashtra, Katch, and Central Gujarat. Rās is a circular dance performed by males, striking small sticks (*ḍānḍiā*) against those of their partners. Garbā is danced by women clapping their hands. They go round an earthen pot called a *garbo* (literally, "womb"), which has tiny holes and a lit earthen lamp placed inside, symbolizing the eternal light of the Goddess Amba. During the *Navarātri* (the festival of nine nights), the whole of Gujarat echoes with singing and dancing, the beating of the drums, striking of the sticks and clapping of hands. Besides the *rās* and *garbā,* there are also local versions of dance and music.

Bhavāī is the popular open-air form of dance-drama played traditionally by people belonging to the Targala caste, to propitiate the Goddess Amba. In Saurashtra, there is a variation of Bhavāī performed by a caste called Vyās. During Navarātri festival, other castes also perform Bhavāī as a ritual offering.

The play begins with a pilgrimage (*jatar*) from a ritually marked circular spot called *cacara.* Musicians sit near the edge of this circle, and spectators squat on the ground around them. In earlier times, the arena was lit by burning torches made out of rags soaked in oil. The main characters of the play dance through a passage left open by the spectators to reach the cacara. They hold in their hands small torches (*kaka*) for self-illumination.

Each geographical region of Gujarat is rich in its folklore, folk dances, folk drama, folk arts and folk crafts. Various fairs and festivals are held year-round, some of them at village temples to honor the memory of holy men.

Saurashtra region has a rich and varied heritage of oral literature, tales, and lyrics sung on popular or religious festivals. A caste known as Bhāṭs or Barots maintain the hagiological accounts of their patrons in the form of epic songs. Oral traditions of storytelling are maintained in Saurashtra by a caste known as Gadhavis or Cārans, and in central Gujarat by the caste known as Bhāṭs or Barots. *Bhajan*s of numerous saint-poets, marriage songs, and lullabies are sung by peoples of all castes.

Corresponding to the oral epics of Rajasthan like the *Pābūjī* and the *Bāgadawat,* Gujarat also has Bhili epics known as *Rathor Varta* and *Devanārāyan.* In the nontribal oral epic traditions, Gujarat has epics like *Pāṇḍavāla* and *Rāmāvāla.*

The tribals lead a community life, and the whole village participates in the various social and religious festivities.

The folklore of the Kharvas (fisherfolk) of the west coast region, particularly of the southern coastline, have rich sea songs reflecting their beliefs, customs, trials and tribulations, and secular and religious fairs and festivals.

In Kutch, there is a tradition—developed initially by Muslim artists—of popular paintings found on the walls of the palaces of the former rulers. The Kacchis also have a long oral tradition of storytelling. They have their own form of *rās* called Kacchi *rās* in which the dancing pairs not only strike the sticks in their hands against those of their partners' while posing heroic stances, but also roll themselves and circle on the floor in tune with the rhythm of a big drum.

References

Patel, Madhubhai. 1974. *Folksongs of South Gujarat.* Baroda: Indian Musical Society.

Caufield, Catherine. 1997. The holiest river. In *Masters of illusion: the world bank and the poverty of nations.* New York: Henry Holt & Company.

Thompson, Gordon R. 2000. Gujarat. In *South Asia: the Indian subcontinent. The Garland encyclopedia of world music,* Vol. 5, ed., Alison Arnold. New York: Garland Publishing, Inc.

GOVERDHAN PANCHAL

SEE ALSO

Bhajan; Bhavāī; Devnārāyaṇ; Fish and Fishing; *Jātrā/Yātrā; Navarātri; Pābūjī;* Rajasthan; *Rāsa Līlā*

GURAV

Guravs are the traditional temple priests in the Śiva, Devī (Pārvatī), Gaṇeśa, Hanumāna, and Grāmadevatā temples in Maharashtra and parts of Karnataka, Andhra, and Madhya Pradesh. In the patron-servant system (known as Balute in Maharashtra), Gurav is the ninth *Balutedāra* out of a total of twelve village service providers. The function of the Gurav is to manage and maintain the temple and also act as the temple priest. The other occupations of the Gurav include making and selling leaf-plates and selling flowers and Bel leaves (*Aegle marmelas*) used in the worship of Śiva. The Guravs also play music for patrons. In the Goa and Konkan areas of Maharashtra, one of the duties of the Gurav in many temples is to solicit omens from the idol and to seek answers to specific questions on behalf of a devotee. This shamanistic ritual is still followed in several temples of the region. In Goa, the Guravs are also family priests to Devadāsis, the traditional female temple dancers.

There are several endogamous castes and subcastes amongst the Guravs; the main castes are Śaiva Gurav, Liṅgāyata Gurav and Konkaṇī or Bhāvika Gurav. Among the Śaiva Guravs there are three divisions: Nagari, Nīlakaṇṭha, and Swayambhu Guravs. Hugāra, Jīra, and Malgara are the main subdivisions among the Liṅgāyata Guravs. Like all those belonging to the Liṅgāyata sect, the Liṅgāyata Guravs wear stone Lingam (Śiva's icon) around their necks. The Liṅgāyatas in Maharashtra claim to have come from Karnataka and say that their ancestors migrated to Maharashtra when, after the death of Basava, the founder of Liṅgāyatism, they were persecuted in Karnataka. The other Guravs in Maharashtra have no connection with Karnataka. They speak only Marathi and are not aware of the original caste to which they

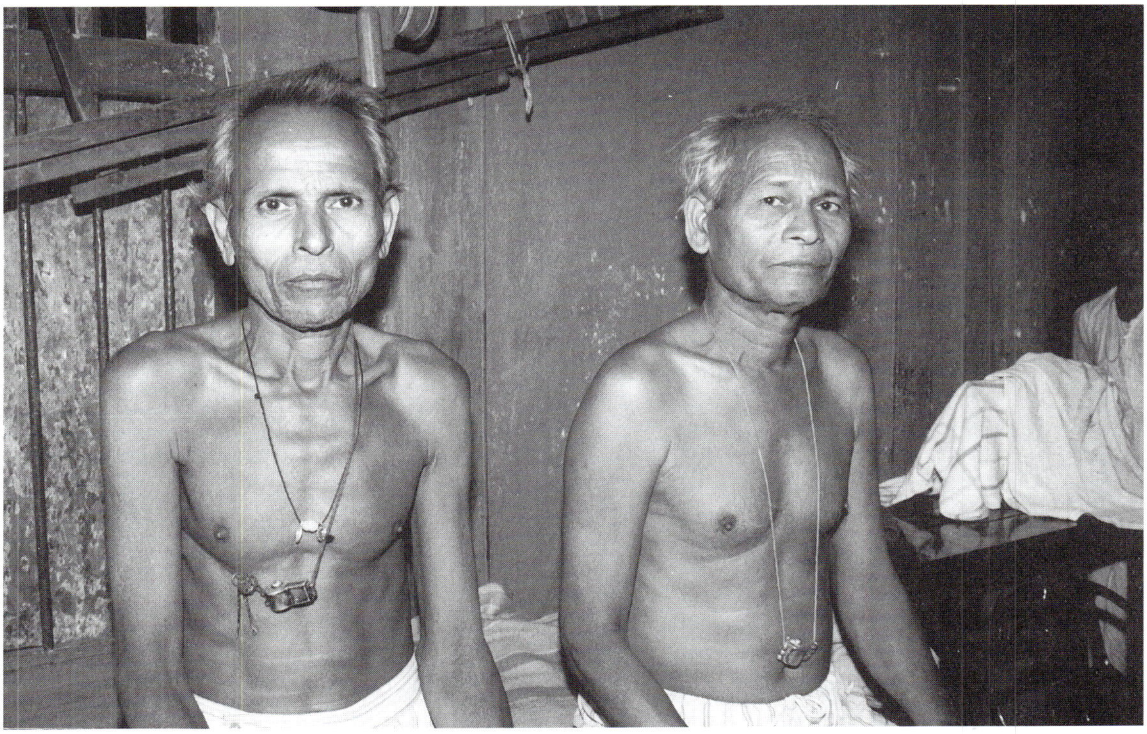

Lingayat Guravs with linga around their necks. Note: no sacred thread. Maharashtra State, India, © Dr. Jayant Bapat

once belonged. They live mainly in the Konkan region and also the border areas of Maharashtra and Karnataka. The priests of the Liṅgāyatas known as Jaṅgamas, also act as temple priests in Maharashtra. Liṅgāyatas are strict vegetarians and, being strongly Śaivite, they refuse to be grouped with other caste Hindus. They also claim to be superior to other Guravs because of their devout Śaivism.

The Bhāvika Guravs are concentrated mainly in the Konkan. They function as priests for the shrines of village gods and goddesses called *Grāmadevatās*, which are little more than crude constructions on the outskirts of villages. Not many are literate, nor do they have secular education or training in rituals. They usually belong to the Kuṇbī caste and often make animal sacrifices to their deities during folk festivals.

The Śaiva Guravs are considered superior to all other Guravs by Maharashtrian society. They are usually literate and have a secular education. Since the beginning of the nineteenth century, they have called themselves Śaiva Brahmins, and they claim to be descendants of Sudarśana, the son of the famous sage Dadhīcī. The story of Sudarśana is described in the forty-fourth chapter of the *Jnānasaṃhitā* of the *Śivapurāṇa*. Using the Sudarśana myth, the Śaiva Gurav have produced five *Jātipurāṇas* (clan history books) in support of their claims to brahminhood. These Purāṇas describe why, in spite of being Brahmins, the Śaiva Guravs are forbidden Vedic knowledge and practice of the Vedic rituals. The myth states that Sudarśana was cursed by Śiva for a folly he committed on the auspicious Śivarātri day, and, as a result, Śiva took away his Vedic rights. He, however, gave Sudarśana the first right to his *pūjā*. Pūjā is a worship ritual comprised of as many as sixteen separate acts. These actions vary from bathing the icon, dressing it up, offering flowers and food, and chanting in praise of god. Gurav pūjās are usually simpler and consist only of bathing the icon and offering some flowers. Śiva also gave Sudarśana the right to his *Nirmālya,* the offerings made to Śiva by other devotees.

Early in the nineteenth century the Śaiva Guravs took their claim to brahminhood to the *Śaṅkarācārya* of Sringeri, who accepted their claim to brahminhood. The *Śaṅkarācārya* is an ascetic office holder at one of the four seats (*pīṭhas*) established in India by the first *Śaṅkarācārya* in the seventh century. The *Śaṅkarācāryas* may be asked to pronounce upon in social and religious disputes within Hinduism. Although not binding, their opinions are highly respected. The Śaiva Guravs also fought and won their case for their brahminic status in secular courts during the colonial period. In spite of this, however, the other Maharashtrian Brahmins classify the Śaiva Guravs as *Śūdras* but grant them custodianship of the Śiva temples. The other brahmins also accept the Śaiva Guravs' right to Śiva's first pūjā of the day and the keeping of the Nirmālya for their own use.

Guravs have their counterparts in Karnataka, Madhya Pradesh, and Gujarat. In Karnataka, they are called Goravās, in Gujarat, Tapodhan Brahmins, and in Madhya Pradesh, the Guravs. Those from Madhya Pradesh claim that they migrated there from Maharashtra and Karnataka. The etymology of the word "Gurav" is unclear. The Guravs claim that it is the plural of the Sanskrit word *gūṛū*. In the distant past, they say they were highly educated in Śāstras and were considered gurus to Śaivites, and hence the name.

The denial of brahminhood to the Śaiva Gurav temple priests seems to be confined to Maharashtra only. In other parts of India, Śiva temple priests are accepted as Brahmins, albeit of a lower social and ritual status than the rest.

References

Bapat, Jayant Bhalchandra. 1993. The Gurav temple priests of Maharashtra, *South Asia,* XVI: 79–100.

Bapat, Jayant Bhalchandra. 1998. A Jātipurāṇa (clan history myth) of the Gurav temple priests of Maharashtra, *Asian Studies Review* 22(1): 63–77.

Enthoven, R. E. 1920. *Tribes and castes of Bombay,* vol. 20. Bombay: Government Printer, p. 27.

JAYANT BHALCHANDRA BAPAT

SEE ALSO

Gorava / Goramma; Purāṇa; Shrines; Worship

GŪRŪ NANAK, LIFE STORIES OF

Gūrū Nanak (1469–1539), a native of Punjab, was the first Gūrū of Sikhism, a religion followed by two percent of the Indian population today. Popular hagiographic narratives called *Janamsākhī* relate anecdotes about the life events, deeds, miracles, and travels of the Gūrū. Such tales probably began to circulate within his lifetime and continued to evolve for centuries after his death. They are a vital part of Punjabi culture, in which similar story cycles were already associated with Sufi masters. Due to the paucity of historical sources, these collections of anecdotes are traditionally accepted as "biographies" of the great teacher.

At least six distinct *Janamsākhī* sequences can be recognized, the most popular of which is reputedly written by Bhai Bala, who, according to this source, was an inseparable companion of the Gūrū. The *Purātan Janamsākhī* is considered to be a more rational account of the Gūrū's life. The fifty-seven paintings of the B-40 *Janamsākhī* at the India Office Library in London illustrate many Gūrū Nanak stories.

Nanak's contempt for worldly riches and status, especially caste barriers, is demonstrated by several *Janamsākhī* episodes. He chooses the home of a poor low-caste carpenter, Lalo, instead of that of a rich man. When invited to the rich man's feast he squeezes blood out of his host's bread, thereby exposing the exploitative basis of the man's wealth. In turn, milk issues from Lalo's bread, proving the wholesomeness of a poor man's labor.

Janamsākhī anecdotes usually portray Nanak as a nonconformist, rejecting external forms of worship such as rituals, pilgrimages, temples, and mosques in both Hinduism and Islam. He travels to several holy sites and challenges prescribed behavior, engaging in arguments with members of the establishment. On a visit to Mecca, the Muslim holy city in Arabia, Nanak falls asleep with his feet pointing towards the holy shrine. An angry *mullā* (religious teacher) awakens him and insists that he change position. "Then please point my feet in a direction where God is not," Nanak says. The holy shrine miraculously moves to stay aligned with his feet! In another story, Nanak, a Hindu by birth, watches fellow Hindus bathing in the holy river Ganges, pouring water toward the east in order to send water to their dead ancestors in heaven. Nanak starts pouring water towards the west instead. He claims that he is watering his fields back in the Punjab, hundreds of miles away, surely an equally plausible action.

The *Janamsākhī*s recount Nanak's famous declaration: "There is no Hindu and there is no Muslim." He wears the composite garb of both Hindus and Muslims, and his constant companion is Mardana, a humble Muslim minstrel. It is therefore popularly believed that Nanak's fundamental mission was to reconcile the tenets of Hinduism and Islam. However, his own writings in the *Adi Granth,* the sacred book of the Sikhs, do not bear this out. Instead, like many others in the Hindu Sant tradition, Nanak preached inner devotion to a formless God. Nevertheless, although Gūrū Nanak stories are not an official part of the sacred scriptures of Sikhism, they have served to transmit the values and conventions traditionally associated with the great Gūrū.

References

Hans, Surjit, ed. 1987. *B-40 Janamsakhi Guru Baba Nanak Paintings*. Amritsar: Guru Nanak Dev University.

Jagdev, Santokh Singh. 1994. *Bed time stories-2* (Guru Nanak Dev Ji). Birmingham, England: Sikh Missionary Resource Centre.

McLeod, W. H. 1989. *The Sikhs: history, religion, and society*. New York: Columbia University Press.

Singh, Harbans. 1969. *Guru Nanak and origins of the Sikh faith*. Bombay: Asia.

Singh, Mala. 1969. *The story of Guru Nanak.* New Delhi: Hemkunt.
Thursby, Gene R. 1992. *The Sikhs.* Leiden: E. J. Brill.

AMITA VOHRA SARIN

SEE ALSO
Punjab; Saints; Sikh Folklore; Sikhism

GŪRUGHLĪ

Gūrughlī is the title character of a Central Asian epic cycle. A group of these related heroic tales of various lengths, numbering between thirty-two and fifty-two separate segments (*shākh*) or branches, are widely performed among the peoples of Central Asia in Turkistan, including northern Afghanistan. Gūrughlī tales, also popularly referred to as Gūrghulī, are most likely part of the ancient epic traditions of Turkic-speaking peoples of Central Asia. At present, Gūrughlī epic tales are equally popular among Turkic and Tajik (Persian-speaking) inhabitants of Central Asia and are performed in both Turkī and Tajik languages.

Studies of Gūrughlī epic tales indicate that stories may have been composed in the land of Tūrān, the ancient name for the region of Eastern Turkistan (modern Xinjiang, People's Republic of China), western Turkistan (former Soviet Central Asia), Afghan Turkistan, and part of ancient Khurāsān and Ariana (eastern Iran and northwestern Afghanistan), which were contiguous territories with common borders. Central Asian Turks speak many related languages and dialects including Uyghur, Turkmen, Āzarī, Uzbek, Kazāk, Kyrghyz, and Tatar. Tajiks, who regard themselves as descendants of the ancient Indo-Iranians and speak Tājīkī (a type of Persian), share much with Turkic peoples in their culture as well as areas of habitation.

Gūrughlī epics are structurally and thematically very similar to the great Kyrgyz national epic of *Manās,* the hero whose thousand-year anniversary was celebrated by the newly independent state of Kyrgyzstan in August 1995. The principal character is Gūrughlī (literally, "born in the crypt or grave"). Gūrughlī's adopted son, Āwāzkhān, a child of a fairy (*parī*) mother from the mythical Qāf mountains, is the other main hero of these tales. Gūrughlī is a product of immaculate conception attributed to the mystical powers of a man who impregnates the sister of Ahmadkhān, one of the Khāns, or leaders, of Turkistan. Ahmadkhān's sister dies while pregnant, is buried, and the child is born in the grave or crypt. The infant Gūrughlī suckles a mare from the herd of his maternal uncle, Ahmadkhān, and is later found by herders and named Gūrughlī.

Once grown, Gūrughlī enters the dramatic world of fabulous epic deeds in the land of Tūrān. Gūrughlī stories are generally narrated in free verse accompanied by *dambura* (two-string lute) during long winter nights in gatherings of men in public guest houses (*qoshkhāna*). The telling of these long stories continues all night for many nights and the audience often eagerly and impatiently awaits hearing the incredible and heroic actions of Gūrughlī as he moves from one branch (*shākh*) of the tale to another. The reciters of these epics (*Gūrughlī khwān*) rest during the day and perform at night. They exact material rewards from their audience by abruptly stopping their recitation at cliff-hangers in the tale and setting down their musical instruments. The storytellers are further rewarded by offers of gifts at the conclusion of their particular repertoire of Gūrughlī.

The telling of Gūrughlī epics does not begin, like other imaginary fables in this region, with "Once upon a time, there was . . . ." Instead, people assume the historicity of Gūrughlī, and recitation often begins more ceremoniously, preceded by the singing of popular couplets known as *falak*. Undoubtedly, these stories are the products of popular or folk imagination. Unfortunately, to date, no real effort has been made in Afghanistan to document their full range; however, there have been some efforts to document Gūrughlī in Tajikistan and Uzbekistan.

Examination of the Gūrughlī stories indicates that their initial composition may have preceded the arrival of Islam in Turkistan. However, like other aspects of Central Asian cultural traditions, over the ages, these stories were also Islamicized and turned into a vehicle for the transmission of religious and moral instruction, especially targeted at the masses of nonliterate Muslims. Therefore, the content of Gūrughlī narratives must have undergone considerable change throughout history. However, Gūrughlī tales have, without a doubt, always reflected significant popular sentiments, societal norms, attitudes, and religious beliefs and values, as well as powerful psychological trends, emotions, mores, and local customs.

References

Aimoq, Faizullah. 1980. *Khalq Durdonalari.* [Pearls of the people] Kabul: Dowlati Matba'a (Government Press).
Qawim, Abdul Qayum. 1975. Gūrughlī. *Adab,* 1–126. Kabul: Ministry of Education Press.
Reis Nia, Rahim. 1998. *KOR OGHLU in the legend and history.* Tehran: Donya Publishers.
Shahrani, Enayatullah. 1973–76. Gūrughlī. *Folklore* 2, 135–156; 3, 80–83; 4, 54–59; 5, 59–73, 6, 64–69; 7, 77–80. Kabul: Dowlati Matba'a (Government Press).
———. 1996. The Tales of Gūrughlī. *Critique and Vision: An Afghan Journal of Culture, Politics and History* 3, 99–115. Los Angeles: Parkhash-Ahmadi Press.

ENAYATULLAH SHAHRANI

SEE ALSO
Afghanistan; *Chahārbaytī;* Epic; *Parī*

H

ḤADĪTH

An Arabic word meaning "talk, discussion, narrative," the term *ḥadīth* is generally used to refer to the brief accounts that record the sayings and actions of Muḥammad, the prophet of Islam, and his companions. Structurally, each ḥadīth consists of the *matn* ("text") containing a first-hand report of what the Prophet said or did, and an *isnād* ("a chain of transmitters"), which guarantees the accurate transmission of the report from the actual eyewitness. Depending on the number of isnād and the reliability of the various transmitters involved, as well as its contents, a ḥadīth may be classified into several categories of authenticity, ranging from *ṣaḥīḥ* ("sound") to *ẓa'īf* ("weak"). The concept of isnād as an object of study indicates a critical theory of oral transmission in early Islamic history. Those ḥadīth considered to be authentic were compiled in the ninth century into two major canonical collections, both called *Ṣaḥīḥ,* one by Bukhārī (d. 870) and the other by Muslim (d. 875).

The importance of the ḥadīth as a genre of Islamic religious literature stems from its association with the prophet Muhammad, whom Muslims revere as a paradigm for exemplary human conduct in this world. As an embodiment of the Prophet's *sunna* ("custom, habitual practice"), the ḥadīth guide the faithful as they seek to emulate aspects of the Muhammad's behaviour and lifestyle, even in everyday matters such as personal hygiene, courtesy and dress. One hears such ḥadīth quoted conversationally, or sees them written in certain mass media such as an adult literacy advocacy poster from the Muslim Sisters of Afghanistan in 1995 quoting the ḥadīth, "Seek knowledge even though it be in China." In this case, the Arabic verse is also glossed in Persian, "Knowledge is the duty of every Muslim." Since they often shed light on the context in which Quranic verses were revealed to the Prophet or the manner in which these verses should be understood, the ḥadīth are also significant tools in the exegesis of the Islamic scripture. In the sphere of Islamic jurisprudence, the ḥadīth are second only to the Qur'ān in importance as sources for establishing the legal and social norms for society.

Among the Muslim intelligentsia of medieval India, study of ḥadīth literature and the so-called "science of ḥadīth" were especially significant since for them adherence to Muḥammad's way of life was crucial to maintaining the religious identity of the Muslims in a milieu in which they were a minority. Not surprisingly, medieval India was home to many prominent scholars of ḥadīth, who compiled collections and treatises that were influential and popular in the regions of the Islamic world beyond the subcontinent. In the modern period, as well, various Muslim reformers, as they reacted to the impact of colonial rule, modernization and westernization on South Asian Muslims, also focused on ḥadīth to re-examine the practice of Islam. For example, Shāh Walīullāh (d. 1762), first to advocate socio-political reform of the Indo-Muslim community, placed a renewed emphasis on the ḥadīth as a source of authority and guidance. Also noteworthy in this respect are the so-called *Ahl-i ḥadīth* ("the People of Ḥadīth") who, in the nineteenth century, with their extreme emphasis on ḥadīth as a "concealed" form of divine revelation, became involved in a polemical war with the religious establishment and its conservative stance on the ḥadīth as well as pro-western modernists, such as Sayyid Aḥmād Khān (d. 1898), who were skeptical about the authenticity of many ḥadīth.

References

Azami, Muhammad M. 1992. *Studies in Ḥadīth methodology and literature*. Plainfield, In.: American Trust Publications.

Goldziher, Ignaz. 1971. *Muslim studies (Muhammedanische Studien)* 2. S. M. Stern (Ed.); C. R. Barker and S. M. Stern (trans.). New York: State University of New York Press.

Graham, William A. 1977. *Divine word and prophetic word in early Islam*. The Hague: Mouton.

Juynboll, Gautier H. A. 1996. *Studies on the origins and uses of the Islamic Ḥadīth*. Brookfield, Vt.: Variorum.

———. 1983. *Muslim tradition*. Cambridge: Cambridge University Press.

ALI ASANI

SEE ALSO

Islam

ḤĀL

The custom of giving and receiving the latest news, between a male traveler and the persons he encounters on his way or on return to his village or camp, is called *ḥāl* in Balochistan, a linguistic and cultural area now divided among the states of Pakistan, Afghanistan and Iran. In the most elaborated form of the exchange, the traveler gives all his news in detail and in return is told in detail about the situation in the locale of his arrival, in a strict sequence. Topics may commence with current market prices of grain and other commodities, then any tribal or intertribal conflict, including casualties if any, epidemics, weather conditions, availability of fodder for cattle, etc. No reference is ever made to women in men's formal ḥāl exchanges, however.

If the visitor has come for some important personal purpose, he is not expected to reveal it in his ḥāl-giving. Ḥāl is a public affair, taking place in a guest room or reception area, often with local men and any other visitors present. Ḥāl is also given and received by two or more travelers who meet on the road. After exchanging *salām* (greetings of "Peace!"), they dismount from their riding animals if they are mounted, sit down and go through the ḥāl exchange. After the ḥāl is exchanged, a visitor is given water, tea and biscuits, which nowadays replace the dates and milk products of the past as initial hospitality refreshments. He then joins the general conversation. Food is prepared and served to him, and only after the meal is he asked his business, or if he is a stranger, asked to introduce himself. If he has come to take refuge from pursuit, he is assured of safety since the protection of a *mayār* or *bāhoṭ* (refugee) is a sacred duty to every Baloch.

The order of ḥāl giving and receiving depends on status. When traveling in a group or joining one, the first right to give and receive ḥāl is that of a tribal chief, religious leader (*mulla* or *sayyid* [descendant of the Prophet]); thereafter, those of noble birth, then the eldest person in the gathering, and so on. No formal ḥāl giving is expected from a person of low social status. Men may closely calculate their relative age, one saying "We are the same age but [I am a few days older and therefore] I reserve the right of *che habar* (lit. "What news?", the term for ḥāl giving/receiving) from him."

Ḥāl exchanges vary in length and form across Balochistan. In Makran, toward the coast, ḥāl, though considered necessary to proper conduct, is most often kept short and formulaic. When two persons meet or one enters a space from outside, the outsider is first greeted with the simple Muslim salutation, "salām" ("peace"), and welcomed ("*washsh ahtē*", "you are welcomed"). He responds, "*Washshnām bey*" ("May you have a good name"). Then the person who has the right to ask for the news invites others to ask ("*Marda che habar begirit*", "Ask the man for the news"). Then they all say with one voice, "*Che habar taī int*" ("*Che habar* is your right"). The chief or elder then asks the person to furnish the news: "*Aḥwāl kon*." The visitor simply says, "*Salāmatī o heyr int, to aḥwāl kan*." ("There is peace and tranquility; you give the news"). The representative of the host replies, "*Drāhī o heyr int*" ("There is health and peace"). After that all join them in repeatedly asking, "*Joḍey?*" ("Are you in good health?"), "*Tayārey?*" ("Are you OK?"), "*Mardum o ālam joḍ ant?*" ("Are your relatives and other people in good health?"), etc. This formulaic exchange is one of many locally patterned polite greeting routines to be found across South Asia. Balochi women's greeting routines can also be quite long and repetitive. They greet each other in chorus, with questions about health, welcoming formulas, and queries about the well-being of each other's families. Women also have the custom of *ḥāl pursī* ("asking the news"), going on visits to inquire about mutual family concerns and affairs, but this is less formal than men's ḥāl custom.

The most elaborated ḥāl is currently found among the Eastern Baloch of Dera Bugti and Mari areas, and those living in the Punjab and Sind. Hosts decide whether to elicit a full ḥāl in detail or simply fulfill the formalities. Brief forms may be preferred when there are strangers present and the parties do not want to recount detailed information in their presence, or when there is a concern that the visitor's news may be disturbing to the host, or to someone sitting with them.

Notwithstanding variations, ḥāl survives as a sacred social norm in all of Balochistan, at least among middle aged persons and elders. If a person is not asked for ḥāl, it is quite demeaning of his person and status. Yet ḥāl has almost disappeared among the youth of the Makran coast, under the influence of the state education system, the increase in national and international mass media access, and the market economy, including labor migration to Pakistani urban areas, the Gulf States and elsewhere.

References

Baluch, K. B. M. 1976. *Searchlights in Baluchi and Baluchistan.* Karachi: Royal Book Company.
Janmahmad. 1982. *The cultural heritage of Baluchistan.* Karachi: Royal Book Company.

SABIR BADALKHAN

SEE ALSO
Balochistan: Oral Tradition; *Hujra*

HANDLOOM WEAVING, BANGLADESH

Handloom weaving has survived over the centuries in Bangladesh through a process of specialization, diversification, and adaptation. References go back to the third century B.C.E. At the time, regional varieties included *kṣauma* (a coarse linen mixed with cotton), *dukūl* (pure and fine linen), *patrona* (a wild silk) and *kārpāsik* (a pure cotton fabric).

Textiles were important in the spice trade to the coastal ports in South and South East Asia, as well as in the overland trade to Samarkand, Bukhara, and Istanbul. By the sixteenth century, the finest variety of muslins (fine white cotton) included *cahārkhāne* (muslin with checks produced by twisted yarn), *ḍuriya* (muslin with stripes), and *jāmdānī* (muslin with woven-in designs).

In response to export demand, handloom weaving became highly specialized by location, techniques, and occupation. Dhaka became a flourishing town because of its trade in plain and embroidered muslins, such as *cikan* (muslin with fine white filigree emboridery) and *kaśīdā* (white cotton fabric embroidered with *mugā* silk). Jāmdānī varieties were known by their designs such as *pānnā hājār* (a thousand diamonds), *terchā* (diagonal), *bagnoli buṭi* (tiger's claws) or their colors, such as *nīlāmbarī,* a midnight blue dyed with indigo.

Cotton was cropped twice a year. The finest cotton, *photī,* was grown along the banks of the Meghna river. It was spun into very fine yarn by Brahman women using a hand spindle known as tākoẏā. *Bhoga* cotton, a medium variety, was spun on a *carkā,* or spinning wheel, for medium fine cloth. Specialization of techniques was evident in the process of cleaning cotton, winding yarn, starching warp threads, washing the finished cloth, and repairing torn threads in the loom. Each process required simple techniques and an occupational division defined by caste, gender, and age.

Jāmdānī was produced in lengths of one yard by twenty yards and measured in Portuguese *covid.* Two weavers sat on pitlooms, threading intricate geometric designs with separate spindles for each floral motif. The spindles (*māku*) were made traditionally from shell and later from tamarind wood.

Young women carries yarn at sellur spinning workshop.

Although export demand declined by the early nineteenth century, the handloom tradition did not fade away. Weaving clusters specialized in *sari* (the traditional long, wrapped cloth garment worn by women), *dhuti,* and lungi (types of sarong with either cotton stripes or checks worn by men).

In 1851, exhibits of Bengal's cotton handlooms were very popular in the Grand Exhibition held in London, and in 1857 John Forbes Watson compiled an extensive collection of textile samples from all over India, including Bangladesh, for replication in the U.K. Four bound volumes of these samples are still preserved in the India Office Library.

During India's independence struggle in the nineteen forties, Mahatma Gandhi campaigned for the use of *svadeśī* (meaning literally, "self-reliance") goods, promoting the use of handspun and handwoven cloth instead of British imports. This provided an impetus to the production of cotton-bordered saris in weaving centers in Tangail, Dhaka, and Pabna, *khaddi* (cotton cloth made from handspun yarn) in Comilla, lungis (men's sarongs) in Rupganj, jāmdānī in Dhaka, and silk in Rajshahi.

Weaving techniques have changed little over time. Simple pitlooms made with bamboo and string heddles continue to be used for jāmdānī, while Tangail saris are made on jacquard looms. It is only in the last twenty years that Chittaranjan and power looms have been introduced for some varieties.

Among the ethnic communities women use backstrap looms for their sarongs and scarves. The designs, woven horizontally, are different in each community. Every Chakma woman is expected to weave a catalogue of designs known as an *alam*.

The war of liberation from Pakistan in 1971 led to the destruction of many weaving villages and dislocation in supplies. This disrupted production, but in the last decade handloom fabrics have been revived through credit and marketing support and cotton yarn imports. Handwoven cottons have become important items for domestic and export trade. Of particular note is the production of Grameen cotton checks, which are used by the export garment industry.

Reference

Hossain, Hameeda. 1988. *Company weavers of Bengal: East India Company and the organization of production in Bengal in 1750–1813.* Delhi: Oxford University Press.

HAMEEDA HOSSAIN

SEE ALSO

Carpets and Carpet-Weaving; Craft; Embroidery; *Jāmdānī; Kāñthā;* Material Culture, Bangladesh; *Swadeshi*

HANUMĀN

Commonly referred to by outsiders as the "monkey-god," Hanumān is the simian helper of Rāma, hero of an epic tradition popular throughout South and Southeast Asia. His name comes from Sanskrit, meaning "one having a prominent jaw." Other common epithets include Māruti, or "son of the wind-god," and Āñjaneya, "son of Añjanī". He is also a deity of great importance in contemporary Hinduism. His muscular form, with monkey-like face and curved tail, bearing a mace and a mountain peak, is a ubiquitous popular icon. Hanumān is often worshiped in conjunction with Rāma (the seventh incarnation [*avatāra*] of the preserver-god Viṣṇu), but also independently, as a complex figure who fulfills a variety of functions and transcends sectarian divisions.

The early history of Hanumān's cult is obscure. The presence of ceramic monkey figurines at sites associated with the Harappan civilization (ca. third millennium B.C.E.) and of a single hymn (10:86) in the *Ṛg Veda* (ca. 1200 B.C.E.) in which the goddess Indrāṇī complains of an aggressive *vṛṣākapi* (male monkey) usurping offerings intended for Indra have been taken by some scholars as indications of a pre-Aryan cult of a simian *yakṣa*, or fertility deity, that was gradually assimilated by Brahmanical tradition. In literature, Hanumān first appears in the Sanskrit epic *Rāmāyaṇa* attributed to the poet-sage Vālmīki (ca. fourth century B.C.E.), as a prominent leader of a forest-dwelling race of talking monkeys (Sanskrit, *vānara*) who ally themselves with the exiled Rāma. The fifth book, *Sundara kāṇḍa* ("The Beautiful Story") recounts Hanumān's mission to the island of Lanka in search of Rāma's abducted wife, Sīta, and his burning of the capital of its demon-king, Rāvaṇa. Later, Hanumān plays a prominent role in the war to recover Sīta, functioning as a healer when he brings a mountain of herbs from the Himalayas to revive Rāma's wounded brother Lakṣmaṇa. He then accompanies the victorious Rāma back to Ayodhya, where he receives the boon of immortality; an epilogue includes an account of his birth and childhood.

Hanumān's extraordinary powers (immense strength, flight, shape-shifting, and physical immortality) coupled with his single-minded devotion to Rāma must have captured the imagination of audiences, and his role expanded in later retellings of the Rāma story. This is especially the case in regional-language epics composed from about the tenth century onward under the influence of the devotional or *bhakti* sensibility.

Although few surviving images of Hanumān predate the twelfth century, his worship by villagers as a protective boundary-guardian (*dvārpāl*), by Śaiva ascetics as an immortal *yōgī,* and by wrestlers as an exemplar of martial arts may reflect ancient practices only loosely assimilated to the Rāma tradition. Notable is the widespread identification of Hanumān (attested from the twelfth century in Sanskrit *purāṇas*) as one of eleven incarnations of the powerful and often destructive deity Rudra/Śiva. In this role he is sometimes associated with local mother goddesses. One folktale cycle popular in southern and eastern India recounts Hanumān's descent to the netherworld to rescue Rāma and Lakṣmaṇa from the subterranean demon Mahirāvaṇa. These and other stories suggest a shamanic or trickster role, as does the widespread invocation of Hanumān in rites of exorcism and healing. A few variants of these tales involve sexual encounters (as in the Southeast Asian *Rāmāyaṇa* tradition), in contrast to the dominant Sanskritic view of Hanumān as a strict celibate exemplifying the patriarchal and yogic ideology of semen-retention.

Shrines to Hanumān have proliferated in recent times and draw large clienteles, especially on Tuesdays and Saturdays, when worshipers seek protection from malefic planetary influences. Both literary and oral traditions emphasize the divine monkey's role as an efficient intermediary and intercessor, and devotees also cite his embodiment of the complementary principles of *śakti* and bhakti—power and devotion—as well as the simplicity of his worship (often through recitation of a short prayer, such as the Hindi *Hanumān cālīsā*) in explaining his popularity. At once comic and cosmic, subhuman and supernatural, Vaiṣṇava and Śaiva, militant and contemplative, Hanumān plays a growing role in Hindu practice.

References

Aryan, K. C. and Aryan, Subhashini. 1975. *Hanumān in art and mythology*. Delhi: Rekha Prakashan.

Lutgendorf, Philip. 1994. My Hanumān is bigger than yours. *History of Religions* 33: 211–245.

———. 1997. Monkey in the middle: the status of Hanuman in popular Hinduism. *Religion* 27: 311–332.

Nagar, Shanti Lal. 1995. *Hanumān in art, culture, thought and literature*. New Delhi: Intellectual Publishing House.

Wolcott, Leonard T. 1978. Hanumān: the power-dispensing monkey in north Indian folk religion. *Journal of Asian Studies* 37, 653–661.

PHILIP LUTGENDORF

SEE ALSO

Bhakti; Exorcism; Gods and Goddesses; Martial Art Traditions; *Rāmāyaṇa*

HERDERS' FIELD CALLS

Clearly the most distinctive oral performance genre of the Bhojpuri-speaking region in eastern Uttar Pradesh and western Bihar is the *kharī birahā*. It is a "holler," or "field call," or, as defined by Bartis, "a vocal performance intended to project information or emotions over long distances." (1975). In the field or at home a man may intone the kharī birahā by himself, perhaps to alleviate boredom, enjoy the pleasure of singing, or alleviate fatigue. If he is with caste brothers, such as at a wedding, his companions will chime in on the last word of a line. Singers are members of the local herding castes, the Gaṛeriyā shepherds and more numerous Yādav (Ahir) cowherds.

The kharī birahā consists of two to five lines of doggerel verse with spontaneous interjections like *Are!* (roughly, "Hey!" or "Oh!"). In its most common form the first line or two is chanted on the tonic and adjacent tones of the scale. In the second portion the melody rises to a higher range and is sung as loudly as a man can sing. The last part of the last line is sometimes repeated. The forcefulness of the kharī birahā performance—a good one is an athletic feat—is in keeping with the strongman image of the Yādav caste. Given its distinctive scale and loudness, it is a unique expression of caste identity.

Although it shares its name with the *birahā,* also associated with the herding castes, the kharī birahā's form bears little similarity to that of the birahā, which is characterized by a small but forceful unison male chones, accompanied by a *ḍholak* drum and distinctive *kartāl* (pairs of iron rods clanging together) interspersed with the leader's solos. The oral performance genre most like the kharī birahā is that called *dohā* (rhymed couplet), performed by members of the Laṅgā community, a caste of musicians in desert Rajasthan, and recorded in 1978 by Professor Nazir Ali Jairazbhoy. The musical form of the dohā shares two important features with the kharī birahā. First, it is a solo performance. Secondly, in the rendering of each couplet one portion will be sung on a high tone relative to the singer's range and held for a length of time at full intensity, clearly demonstrating the field call function of the genre. But the scale of the dohā differs from that of the kharī birahā; its first portion is not chant-like, and the final lines of the dohā are sung in a highly elaborate melisma, unlike the kharī birahā.

Kharī birahās largely concern two kinds of subjects—religious and philosophical matters, and heterosexual love. In the first published collection of kharī birahās in 1886 the great linguist George A. Grierson (1851–1941) translated forty-two songs. More than half concerned religion, and of these, eight dealt with the Rāma story. Others of this type were about Kṛṣṇa, Śiva, mother goddesses, and Dih Bāba, the village guardian spirit. Ten of Grierson's collection described matters of sex and love, four of those regarding women's breasts. Kharī birahās in Edward Henry's 1988 collection are mostly concerned with topics from Hindu mythology and philosophy, primarily Vaisnava devotional religion.

Kharī birahās were still being sung, by young as well as old men, in 1990 in Ghazipur District, Uttar Pradesh. One of the more widely sung kharī birahās there has this text:

> Oh, when Lakṣman was hit by the poison arrow
> Rām took him on his lap and started to cry
> Oh, who will ever return with me to Ayodhyā
> Should in the morning Lakṣman die?

References

Bartis, P. T. 1975. An examination of the holler in North Carolina white tradition. *Southern Folklore Quarterly* 39: 209.

Grierson, George. 1886. Some Bhojpuri folksongs. *Journal of the Royal Asiatic Society* 18: 207–67.

Henry, Edward O. 1981. *Chant the names of God: village music of the Bhojpuri-speaking area of India*. Cambridge, Mass. Rounder Records 5008. Compact disk.

———. 1988. *Chant the names of God: music and culture in Bhojpuri-speaking India*. San Diego: San Diego State University Press.

———. 2002. Melodic structure of the Kharī Birahā of north India: a simple mode. *Asian Music* 33(1): 105–24.

EDWARD O. HENRY

SEE ALSO
Grierson, George A.; Song

HEROES AND HEROINES

The terms *hero* and *heroine* encompass many types of human and superhuman beings in South Asian cultures, including some who are simply admired, some who are venerated and perhaps approached for help or intercession, and some who are literally worshiped as deities. The nature of a hero's or heroine's enduring power is somewhat conditioned by the religious traditions of the followers. In the Hindu context, the Sanskrit word *vīra* (Hindi, *vīr*), which means "hero" and also "man," conveys the idea that the hero is a paradigmatic or perfected man. The most evident marker of this status is death in battle, a glorious demise earned by virtuous and admirable living. Through violent death, heroes metamorphose into divinities who protect and promote the welfare of devotees. Iconic and aniconic memorials to Hindu heroes are found throughout India. Many of these are stelae on which are carved relief images of equestrian heroes or heroes displaying weapons, usually clubs. The memorials often become shrines attended by descendants.

Occasionally the reputation of a hero spreads and he attracts devotees from diverse caste backgrounds. The story of his life and apotheosis is recited or sung by worshipers and may eventually expand into a full-blown folk epic like Pābūjī and Devnārāyaṇ in western India. Heroic epics are generally performed by professional singers from low- and middle-ranked castes, but they may attract patronage from higher castes, particularly if the epic is Sanskritized and the hero identified as an incarnation of a Sanskritic deity such as Viṣṇu or Śiva.

Heroes are normally considered to have transcended the general class of ancestors (*pitṛ*), who are worshiped jointly. Many are described as having attained liberation from rebirth (*mokṣa*) or having become residents of a warrior heaven (*vīrgati*). Because they were once human, heroes, as compared with deities, are considered particularly accessible to devotees. Some hero shrines attract priests who perform ritual veneration or shamans who become possessed by heroes and cure various ailments and afflictions. The shrines are particularly active during annual festivals.

Heroes who are worshiped are often homologized to or identified with guardian deities such as Bhairava, Kṣetrapāla, and various directional deities (*dih*s). Like Bhairava, who is often presented as having two forms, one light and one dark, some are said to have a dark, fierce nature while others are said to have a light, peaceful one. This split in the warrior persona, which is often illustrated in folk and Sanskrit epics, reflects the inherent tension in the role of the warrior-chief (*Kṣatriya*), whose nature must be violent enough to wage war, yet subdued and wise enough to rule as a good king.

Women who fought in battle and who subsequently died on their husbands' funeral pyres are worshiped as ancestral *satī*s rather than as heroines (*vīrāṅganās*). Throughout India the satī, whose image is found on commemorative stelae that resemble hero stones, or sometimes on the hero stones themselves, is considered the hero's inevitable counterpart. In south India are found many narratives in which women who have become satīs or suffered other types of violent death become goddesses. Better known examples include the Kōmaṭi goddess Kanyakamma and Kaṇṇaki, heroine of the Tamil epic *Cilappatikāram*. Other women who have sometimes been categorized as heroic are certain ascetics, gurus, *bhaktas* (devotees of deities), and *devadāsī*s (temple dancers).

Muslims who die sacrificial deaths in battle are often venerated as martyrs (*shahīd*s). Some of these are also revered as *pīr*s (teachers). The pīr achieves that status either because of his success in interpreting the Qur'ān and converting people to Islam or because of the example he provides by sacrificing himself to preserve or promote Islam. Among the most famous of the pīrs are the so-called *panch pīr,* or "five pīrs," who are worshiped as a group; the names and identities of individual members change from place to place. Some Muslim pīrs are worshiped as vīrs by Hindus and some vīrs are regarded as pīrs by Muslims. Like the vīr's memorial stone, the pīr's tomb (*dargāh*) often becomes a busy local shrine or even a well-known pilgrimage place.

In Buddhist tradition, hero veneration begins with devotion to Gautama Buddha, who is regarded in Theravada Buddhism as a man who conquered attachment and thereby achieved liberation. Throughout south Asia other *buddha*s and *bodhisattva*s are also venerated as heroic beings. The tantric tradition in Nepal teaches that men seeking liberation as adepts are heroes, vīrs, who defy convention in order to transcend dualism. In Sri Lanka, certain historical kings are given special veneration during the annual Heroes' Day festival. Prominent in village folklore are legends of Duṭṭhagāmiṇi, Parākramabāhu, and Kīrtti Śrī Rājasinha, three of the Sri Lanka's most famous monarchs.

In Jainism, heroic or martial virtues are often transformed to accord with the doctrine of nonviolence. Jain lore contains numerous stories about violent warriors who are converted to Jainism and become advocates of nonviolence. The word *Jain* refers to a follower of a *jina,* a spiritual conqueror who battles and ultimately defeats attachment to worldly desires.

References

Babb, Lawrence A. 1996. *Absent lord: ascetics and kings in a Jain ritual culture.* Berkeley: University of California Press.

Blackburn, Stuart H., Peter J. Claus, Joyce B. Flueckiger, and Susan Wadley, eds. 1989. *Oral Epics in India.* Berkeley: University of California Press.

Hansen, Kathryn. 1992. "Heroic Modes of Women in Indian Myth, Ritual, and History: The Tapasvinī and the Vīrāṇganā," *Annual Review of Women in World Religions,* vol. II: *Heroic Women,* ed. Arvind Sharma and Katherine Young. Albany: State University of New York Press.

Holt, John Clifford. 1991. *Buddha in the Crown: Avalokiteśvara in the Buddhist Traditions of Sri Lanka.* New York: Oxford University Press.

Roy, Asim. 1982. "The Pīr-Tradition: A Case Study in Islamic Syncretism in Traditional Bengal," *Images of Man: Religion and Historical Process in South Asia,* Fred W. Clothey, ed. Madras: New Era Publications.

LINDSEY HARLAN

SEE ALSO

'Alī; Ancestor Worship; Buddhism and Buddhist Folklore; Dargāh; *Devnārāyan;* Draupadī; Epic; Fāṭima; Gods and Goddesses; Gūrū Nanak, Life Stories of; Imām Ḥusayn; Jainism; *Kāfī; Pābūjī; Panch Pīr; Pīr;* Saints

HIJRĀ (TRANSVESTITE) PERFORMANCES

Hijrā, also spelled *Hijidā* or *Hidjrā,* is the most commonly used Hindi label for eunuchs, hermaphrodites, impotent men, transvestites, transsexuals, and women with male characteristics, some of whom act as passive homosexual prostitutes. Growing their hair long and plucking all facial hair, they dress in female attire and wear jewelry and makeup. They live as women, yet have the freedom of men; thus they bridge the worlds of men and women. Historically, they were the guards of the king's harem, moving unrestricted in the company of men and women, often acting as spies, messengers, or as tutors for the concubines. Hijrās are ritual specialists and have continued to play a variety of important roles in Indian society for several thousand years.

Though some Hijrās are Muslim, many are castrated male devotees of the Mother Goddess, Bahucharā (often called Besarā Mātājī). Empowered by the Goddess, who is the bestower of life or death, Hijrās are known for their mysterious power to bless and curse, particularly in cases involving fertility, making them at once auspicious and dangerous. They dance, sing, and play drums during life cycle rituals such as weddings, the birth of a child, and sometimes to celebrate the tonsure of the child. They can be seen begging in the marketplace and are represented on the Indian screen.

Hijrās are perhaps the most conspicuous guests at an Indian wedding. Welcome or not, they seductively dance their way into the procession and ceremony, singing erotic love songs loudly. Hijrās dance flirtatiously, often teasing men in the wedding party, even coercing their amused, yet embarrassed, male audience to participate. They entertain the guests and family, and bless the newlyweds to ensure their fertility. Family members offer rupee notes, circling the money around the couple three times in a ritual gesture before dropping the money on top of the drum or harmonium. Depending on the length and quality of the entertainment and on the affluence of the families involved, wedding income can vary drastically.

Although Hijrās may receive a higher income at weddings, it is with the birth of a child, specifically a male child, that the Hijrā is associated. Acting in the role of a scapegoat, the Hijrā, believed to possess increased physical vigor and power due to castration, blesses the infant, transferring "her" strength to the child and warding off evil influences. Several days after the birth of a child, a small group of Hijrās, draped in colorful saris or wide skirts and, often, stuffed bras, appear at the newborn's house, singing in a chorus. Songs may include an invocation of God for the gift of a son, describing the joy and feeling of prosperity felt by the Lord and all the family members and relatives. They bless the child with a long, healthy, and wealthy life. Holding the child and singing songs that mention the relatives of the child in an order that reflects the family hierarchy, the Hijrās provoke each one to make a monetary offering. To the accompaniment of a chorus of raspy voices and a two-headed drum *(ḍholak),* the Hijrās dance with bells on their ankles, miming the final stages of pregnancy, sometimes stuffing a pillow under their saris, and imitating the cradling of an infant. They then examine the genitalia of the child to see if there are any defects, as that would indicate that the Hijrās could claim him as their own. In addition to money, they are offered a sari, a blouse piece, some jaggery sugar, and some wheat.

Especially during springtime festival of *Holī* and during the festival period in the fall which begins with *Navarātri* and ends with *Dīvālī,* the Hijrās go begging in the streets, dancing and singing from store to store. Clapping their hands loudly, they wiggle their way ungracefully through the crowds. Shopkeepers are intimidated into giving them money, for if the Hijrās are dissatisfied with the offering, they have been known to cause a commotion in front of the store and to shout obscenities. They may even threaten to lift up their skirts, indecently exposing whatever is left of their mutilated genitalia. Rather than ruin their business, most merchants give the expected few rupees, and in exchange, receive the blessing that they will prosper in the next year. Some merchants even work out a weekly or monthly contract with their local group of Hijrās.

Ancient Sanskrit plays utilized Hijrās or cross-dressers as comical characters. This tradition is presently represented in popular Indian cinema, where either real Hijrās or impostors are employed to play light, humorous roles, in stark contrast to the very masculine heroes and very feminine heroines portrayed.

References

Anderson, Christopher. 1977. Gay men in India. Unpublished manuscript. University of Wisconsin, Madison.

Eliade, Mircea. 1987. *The encyclopedia of religion.* (Androgynes, Castration, Gender Roles, Sacred Prostitution, and Virginity.) New York: Macmillan Publishing Company.

Nanda, Serena. 1990. *The Hijra of India.* Belmont, Calif.: Wadsworth Publishing Company.

Salunkhe, G. 1976. The Cult of the Hijaras. *Illustrated Weekly of India,* August 8, pp. 16–21. Bombay: Times of India.

MEKHALA NATAVAR

SEE ALSO

Ali; Birth Songs; Dīvālī/Dīpāvalī; Gender and Folklore; *Holī; Navarātri*

HIMACHAL PRADESH

Himachal Pradesh—"the land of the abode of snow"—is a state cross-cut with mountain ranges, dividing inhabitants into distinct cultural regions. Although an administrative unit, it is a cohesive group in name only; the diversity of peoples in the state makes it impossible to speak of its folklore in general terms.

Among the districts represented in Himachal Pradesh are Una, Hamirpur, Bilaspur, Solan, Sirmaur, Kangra, Mandi, Shimla, Chamba, Kullu, Kinnaur and finally Lahul and Spiti. The state government has attempted to promote Pahari "of the mountains" as the state language. However, Pahari itself is distinctively shaped by regions, and is a conglomeration of partially mutually intelligible dialects: Kangri, Chambiali, Kullui and so on. Furthermore, in Kinnaur, Lahaul and Spiti, Tibeto-Burman languages are spoken.

Himachal Pradesh can thus be conceptualized as representing an intersection of cultural features shared with the plains—particularly Punjab—and those associated with Tibet. While Kinnaur, Lahaul and Spiti are strongholds of Tibetan Buddhism, Tibetan refugees are also present elsewhere in the state, particularly in Kangra (the Dalai Lama's government in exile is based in Dharmasala, Kangra). Hinduism is practised in other areas, with strong regionally based traditions. Muslims are represented mostly by the nomadic, buffalo herding Gujjar tribe. Enclaves of Sikhs are also found here.

Mountains are often associated with sacred centers in South Asia, and Himachal Pradesh is sprinkled with pilgrimage sites. Festivals associated with the calendrical cycle also draw pilgrims and tourists from other regions of India. Popular festivals include the Kulu Dassera celebrations (in October), pilgrimages to the Goddess Jwalamukhi in Kangra (April and October) Śivrātri celebrations in Mandi (February), the Renuka fair by the lake in Sirmaur (November), and ritual dances celebrating Tibetan New Year, Lossar, in the monasteries of Lahaul, Spiti and Kinnaur (February).

The present state of folklore scholarship in Himachal Pradesh is far more descriptive than analytical. Popular collections and travelogues are the norm. At this time there is ample scope for further ethnographic research in this area.

References

Ranchan, Som P. and H. R. Justa, 1981. *Folktales of Himachal Pradesh.* Bombay: Bharatiya Vidya Bhavan.

Seethalakshmi, K. A. 1972. *Folktales of Himachal Pradesh.* New Delhi: Sterling Publications.

Mian Goverdhan. 1992. *Festivals, fairs and customs of Himachal Pradesh.* New Delhi: Indus Publishing House.

Sharma, Dr. Gautam 'Vyathit'. 1984. *Folklore of Himachal Pradesh.* New Delhi: National Book Trust.

KIRIN NARAYAN

SEE ALSO

Central Himalayan States; Pilgrimage; Tibet

HINDUISM

See Cosmology, Hindu; Fate, Hindu; Goddesses, Hindu; Mythology, Hindu; Shrines, Hindu; Syncretism

HĪR/RĀNJHĀ

The tale of Hīr and Rānjhā is one of many popular romances from the Punjab and northwestern India, part of a longstanding oral tradition with roots in the Persian *masnawī* (rhymed narrative poems, often on romantic or Sufi themes) and Punjabi *vār* (ballads of praise). Surviving written versions of *Hīr/Rānjhā* date to the sixteenth and seventeenth centuries, and new versions are still being composed. The language of the earliest written Punjabi versions of *Hīr/Rānjhā* is challenging even for native speakers; many recent editions of different versions of the story include Urdu or modern Punjabi translations and commentary.

In its most basic form, it is the tale of the love of Rānjhā, who leaves his family after being cheated out of his inheritance, and Hīr, the beautiful daughter of a village chieftain. Rānjhā secures a job tending

Hīr's family's cattle, which allows the couple to meet secretly. But when Hīr's family members hear gossip about her scandalous behavior, they marry her to another man against her wishes. Rānjhā and Hīr manage to meet secretly (in some versions, Rānjhā disguises himself as a Hindu *yogī* so that he may visit Hīr). When Hīr's relatives find out that she still loves Rānjhā, they promise to allow Hīr to marry him (she had steadfastly refused to consummate her first marriage). In some versions of the story, such as Damodar's (ca. sixteenth c. CE) and Muqbal's (1746), the two lovers marry and live happily ever after in Mecca. In Waris Shah's celebrated 1766 version, Hīr's family poisons her, and Rānjhā dies heartbroken when he hears the news.

This romance remains popular in both the Pakistani and Indian Punjab. There are several film versions of the romance, inexpensive chapbook editions are sold in many markets, and many musicians include sections of the story in their repertoire. The tale of Hīr and Rānjhā (particularly Waris Shah's version) is championed by both Pakistani and Indian Punjabis as an emblem of a shared Punjabi culture. For some, the romance is simply a poignant love story; others take Hīr's longing for Rānjhā as an allegory for the soul's quest for god, a motif found throughout Punjabi Sufi poetry, especially in the works of the poet Bullhe Shah (1680–1758).

The many versions of the story, composed and transmitted by Hindus, Muslims and Sikhs, are a rich source of information on cultural and religious attitudes, practices, and beliefs of the rural Punjab, particularly conceptions of communal identity. In Waris Shah's *Hīr,* for example, the characters identify themselves not in terms of "Hindu" or "Muslim," but along more complex caste, class, and sectarian lines. Waris Shah draws a marked contrast between his own involvement in Chishti Sufism and the practices of a peasant such as Rānjhā. Rānjhā's religious practice centers primarily on the Five *Pīrs* (*Panch Pīr,* a group of five saints referred to in much medieval Indian literature), and he is sharply critical of the bookish, legalistic Islam propagated in mosques. When Rānjhā is initiated as a yogī, no one seems to find it odd that he should be joining an ostensibly Hindu group. Instead, the story emphasizes a stark contrast between institutional, corrupt, soulless religion (that of both the mosque and the yogī's order) and the sincere faith of villagers such as Hīr and Rānjhā. The romance seems to evoke nostalgia among many twentieth century Punjabis for what they recall as more peaceful times before the communal lines between "Hindu" and "Muslim" were so sharply drawn; Amrita Pritam began a famous 1947 poem with the line "Today I call upon Waris Shah," requesting that the poet add a new page to the romance, reflecting the horrors of partition and a Punjab whose five rivers flowed with blood.

References

Singh, Gurcharan. 1978. *Warris Shah.* New Delhi: Sahitya Akademi.

Swynnerton, Charles, ed. and tr. 1963[1903]. The love story of Heer and Ranjha. In *Romantic tales from the Punjab, with Indian nights entertainment,* 1–37. Patiala: Department of Languages, Punjabi University.

Temple, R. C., ed. and trans. 1981[1884]. The marriage of Hīr and Ranjha. In *The legends of Panjab,* Vol. 2, 507–580. Islamabad: Institute of Folk Heritage.

Waris Shah. 1966. *The adventures of Hir and Ranjha,* edited with an Introduction and Notes by Mumtax Hasan, trans. C. F. Usborne. Karachi: Lion Art Press Limited.

———. 1978. *The love of Hīr and Ranjha,* trans. Sant Singh Sekhon. Ludhiana: Old Boys' Association, College of Agriculture.

ROBIN RINEHART

SEE ALSO

Chapbooks; Epic; *Panch Pīr;* Punjab; Sufi Folk Poetry

HOBSON-JOBSON: THE ANGLO-INDIAN DICTIONARY

First published in 1886, *Hobson-Jobson: The Anglo-Indian Dictionary* was compiled by Henry Yule and A. C. Burnell. Due to Burnell's death in 1882, most of the entries were written by Yule, who was nevertheless careful in the preface to give credit to Burnell's having "contributed so much of value, so much of the essential." Although the work purports to be a dictionary of "Anglo-Indian," it includes entries on many words from other Asian countries, notably China, as well as some from as far afield as Madagascar, the Caribbean, and the East Indies. The name derives from the supposed British rendering of the cry "Yā Hassan, yā Husayn", to be heard during processions for the Shī'ī festival of Muḥarram. Although the work pays particular attention to such anglicizations, it by no means restricts itself to them.

The scholarship involved is formidably wide-ranging; apart from citations from Indian sources (in Sanskrit, Hindi, Urdu and Persian), the authors draw on Greek, Latin, French, German, Italian, Chinese, and Arab sources, as well as contemporary anecdotes, jokes, and so forth. Despite occasional errors, it is remarkable for its general accuracy and for the extraordinary range of information that it conveys, much of which is unavailable elsewhere. In common with most lexicographical works of the nineteenth century, its main interest is in establishing correct etymologies. Many of the articles are enlivened by a sometimes exasperated humor, usually at the expense of other scholars who have, in the authors' opinion, misunderstood something (for example a quite hilarious entry on "Jack" (fruit).)

The dictionary's value to students of folklore is substantial. First, it contains a great deal of data on the quotidian life of India during and prior to the authors' lifetimes. There are numerous entries on, for example, foods, articles of clothing, religious festivals, castes, professions and means of livelihood, social and religious hierarchies, and the like. Second, it provides a vivid picture of the preoccupations of the British in India during the period in which the book was being compiled and written (the 1870s and 1880s). Numerous entries mention the Ilbert Bill "giving natives magisterial authority in the provinces over Europeans" as well as its predecessor, vulgarly known as the "Black Act" of 1836, and this appears to be an indication of the anxiety felt about the bill by the Anglo-Indian community. Further, the length and detail of some entries would seem to be there, at least in part, as an explanatory justification of British rule (for example, the long and very circumstantially detailed entry on "Suttee" (*satī*)). However, the work also looks back with some nostalgia on an India that was less modified by the British presence, and in which "the old travelers entered more fully and sympathetically into native tastes."

Reference

Yule Henry, and A. C. Burnell, 1996 [1902]. *Hobson-Jobson: The Anglo-Indian Dictionary;* facsimile reprint of the second edition (1902). Hertfordshire, U.K.: Wordsworth.

DICK DAVIS

SEE ALSO
British Folklore (in South Asia); Colonialism and Folklore; Muḥarram; Sātī

HOLĪ

The festival of *Holī* is celebrated all over India during the month of Phālguna (February-March), lasting a week from the day before full moon day (*Pūrṇimā*) to the fifth day after the full moon. The word "Holī" may have come from the Sanskrit word "Holika," the demoness who is symbolically burned on this day. In the purānic story dealing with the myth of Holī, Prahlāda is a devotee of the god Viṣṇu and hence disliked by his demon family. Prahlāda's father, Hiraṇyakaśipu, persuades his sister Holikā to sit in an oven with Prahlāda, his own son, on her lap so that Prahlāda will be burned, but not Holikā, since she has the boon that fire will not harm her. Viṣṇu, however, protects Prahlāda and Holikā gets burned instead. Other names by which the festival is known include Horī, Holī-Dulhendī, Holī-Dhurendī (North India), Śimgā (Maharashtra), Simgo (Goa), Dolyātrā (Bengal and Orissa), Phāga (Madhya Pradesh), and Kāmadahana (South India).

In most places, the festival's main event consists of lighting a huge pyre of wood and other combustible materials in the village square. The collection and heaping of these materials begins several weeks prior to the main event. Much of the wood is taken from, rather than given by, the people. On the full-moon night, the pyre is lit by a light brought to the venue by a child or an untouchable. A Brahmin then performs a *pūjā*. The *Bhaviṣya Purāṇa* enjoins physical contact with a *Cāṇḍāla* (an untouchable) on this day. The fire lit, bands of youth roam around the streets, dancing, singing bawdy songs, throwing colored water on themselves and onlookers, and uttering obscenities. Next morning, after the fire dies down, many villagers bathe in water heated on the hot coals. The fire is then extinguished by offering milk, ghee, and water, and a pūjā is again performed by a Brahmin. The ashes are smeared on the foreheads of the participants and the remains of the fire thrown away into a river or tank.

There are many variations to these customs in different parts of India. In Bengal, the Dolyātrā begins with the worship of Kṛṣṇa and Agni, the fire god. *Kumkum* (the auspicious red dye) is then thrown on the people gathered, usually in the village square. A human effigy made of straw is then burned in public. The Caitanya sect in Orissa celebrates the festival with a procession of the idol of Lord Kṛṣṇa through the town. In south India, Holī is associated with the burning of Kāma, the god of love, by Śiva. It is therefore customary to site the Holī in front of a Śiva temple.

The North Indian festival is accompanied by wrestling competitions held on the full moon day. On that day, the women fast all day, cook, clean their houses, and then visit the pyre with their children and make offerings of turmeric, ghee, and decorated cowdung cakes. *Urid dāla* (the white split pea lentil) is waved around the children and then thrown into the fire to ward off evil spirits. They then return home for a meal. After the meal, it is the women who get very aggressive and boisterous and play *phāga* games, which include singing of ribald songs. Many consume alcohol and *bhāṅga* (a drink made out of intoxicating leaves). Some dress as men and perform phallic dances. These boisterous activities are continued on the next day of Dulhendī (Dhurendī). Women race through the streets and beat all men who come within their range, especially the village officials. Elders prefer to hide on this day for the fear of being humiliated by women. Colonel Todd, the nineteenth century British administrator based in Western India, described the Rajput kings celebrating Holī for up to forty days: dancing, consuming alcohol and other intoxicating substances, and uttering obscenities in public.

The Holī is a festival of norm reversals. The observances and customs attached to Holī deviate markedly from Śāstric (religiously prescribed) and everyday behavior. The Holī behavior, which includes contact with untouchables, soldiers in Indian armed forces smearing their superiors with color (*gulāla*), the uttering of obscenities in public, and north Indian women drinking in public and beating men, has attracted the attention of many researchers. McKim Marriott (1966) calls the festival a "precise inversion of the social and ritual principles of routine life." He argues that in the normally strict segregated Hindu society, a reversal even for a day allows each villager "to play his routine role afresh with renewed understanding." Donald Miller (1973) on the other hand sees Holī as "a momentary escape for those most affected by the vexatiousness of society resulting from their structured and restrictive roles." Where Marriott sees a festival of renewal, Miller sees a seething hostility of the subalterns coming out as if it were a day of revenge.

The *Bhaviṣya Purāṇa* has explained this festival by referring to the myth of the demoness Dhuṇḍhā, who used to enter villages and molest children. The villagers once lit big bonfires to scare her, and they beat drums and shouted obscenities to successfully drive her away. On the other hand, the *Viṣṇupurāṇa* and the *Bhāgavatapurāṇa* state that the demoness Putana, who tried to kill the newborn child Kṛṣṇa by offering him her breast immersed in poison, is the one burned on the day of the Holī. The public utterances of obscenities are explained in these Purāṇas by the fact that the ruling constellation on Holī day is Phālguni, whose presiding deity is Bhagā, the female sex organ. The utterance of obscenities in the name of Bhagā is in fact worshipping it. *Horī* is a folk musical genre sung all over north India in *Rāga* Kāfi. The accompanying words describe the observance of Holī revelries by Kṛṣṇa, Rādhā and other *gopi*s (female cowherds), the female devotees.

References

Christian, Jane M. 1982. The end is the beginning: a festival chain in Andhra Pradesh. In *Religious festivals in south India and Sri Lanka*. Ed. Guy Richard Welbon and Glenn Yocum. Pp. 243–267. New Delhi: Manohar Publications.

Marriott, M. 1966. The feast of Love. In *Kṛṣṇa: myths, rites and attitudes*. Ed. M. Singer. Pp. 200–212. Honolulu: East-West Center Press.

Miller, D. B. 1973. Holi-Dulhendi: licenced rebellion in a north Indian village. *South Asia* 3:90–94.

JAYANT BHALCHANDRA BAPAT

SEE ALSO

Fairs and Festivals; *Lāvaṇī;* Prahlāda Nāṭaka; *Pūjā; Purāṇa; Tiruvatira*

HOOK-SWINGING

The act of hook-swinging is one of a number of mortificatory practices offered as religious devotions in parts of South Asia to please the deity, to pay back a vow, or to compel the deity's succor. The practice consists of piercing the skin with one or more iron hooks and suspending the penitent from a beam, pole, or cart, while moving it either up and down, over a rough surface, or in a circular rotation. Despite repression of such acts of penance by the British colonial administration, they continue unabated in some areas of South Asia and the diaspora.

References

Fuller, E. F. 1993. Pierced by Murugan's lance: the symbolism of vow fulfillment. In *The psychoanalytic study of society: essays in honor of Alan Dundes*, ed. L. B. Boyer, R. M. Boyer and S. M. Sonnenberg. Vol. 18, 277–298. Hillsdale, N.J.: Analytic Press.

Oddie, Geoffrey A. 1995. *Popular religion, elites and reform: hook-swinging and its prohibition in colonial India, 1800–1894*. New Delhi: Manohar.

Tarabout, G. 1986. *Sacrifier et donner à voir en pays Malabar: les fâtes de temple au Kerala (Inde du Sud): étude anthropologique*. Paris: École Française d'extrême-orient.

SARAH CALDWELL

SEE ALSO

Bhagavati Ritual Traditions of Kerala; Bihar; Self-sacrifice

HOSPITALITY

The importance of hospitality in South Asian culture is evident from the high place it is accorded in the normative literatures, the narrative traditions, and in the everyday and ritual practices of the region. In Hindu culture, *ātithyā*, the Sanskrit term for hospitality, derives from the conjunction of two words, "*ā*" meaning "without" and "*tithi*" meaning "specific date." Hence, *ātithī* is one who comes without prior notice—a guest. The well-known Hindu adage from the *Taittirīya Upaniṣad, ātithī dēvo bhava* ("guests are like gods") epitomizes the revered status that hospitality occupies in Hindu social and ritual practice. Hence, in the devotional realm, the sixteen prescribed acts of worship that form the core of *pūjā* center around a model of hospitality in which deities are supreme guests. They are invoked, invited, seated, offered water to wash and bathe, given clothes, incense and ornaments, fed lavishly, paid homage, and bade farewell. On the other hand, devotees themselves are seen as worthy of honors reserved for guests. Pilgrim centers provide facilities, often free of charge, for lodging, bathing and eating. The pilgrimage center of Tirupathi in South India epitomizes the institutionalization of hospitality through its many lodging halls, free food facilities, subsidized transportation, and other services. Many legends are told of how Annapūrna, the goddess of food, personally ensures that pilgrims to her temple in Hornad, Karnataka, are fed whenever they want.

In Hindu prescriptive literature, such as the *Manu Smṛti* (*Laws of Manu,* dated roughly between 200 B.C.E and 200 C.E.), hospitality is regarded as one of the five important sacrifices a Hindu householder must fulfill every day as part of his religious duties: "He who does not so sacrifice lives not, though he breathes" (trans. Buhler [1886] 1969). Vedic and post-Vedic literature treats with remarkable specificity the rules of conduct to be observed by hosts and guests in accordance with given social situations, elaborates on the consequences of lapses in hospitality, and often suggests ways in which such breaches can be redressed. For example, the *Āpastamba Dharmasūtra,* a Sanskrit treatise on conduct, specifies, "If a brahmana that has not studied the *Veda* comes to the house of a brahmana, the latter should offer him a seat, water and food, but need not rise to receive him" (Kane 1974, 753). The rites and responsibilities of hospitality are believed to extend into other worlds also, as in the annual *śrāddha* ritual for the propitiation of ancestors, in which deceased ancestors are "invited" and "fed." This annual meal is believed to constitute their daily meal in the "other" world.

Islamic traditions are also famous for their attention to the performance of hospitality. Muslims say, "The guest is the friend of God" (Persian, *Mihmān dūst-e khoda ya*), to which those of modest means may add, laughing, "*Agar khar dāra, balā ya*!" (If he has a donkey [to feed], it's a disaster"). In practice, and in stories, the host should provide three days of food and lodging, without asking any questions about the guest's plans. On the third day, the guest is expected to state the specific purpose for which he has come, so that it can be addressed, or depart. More formally, *adab* (conduct) literature is an example of normative discourse that, among other things, prescribes the exact mode of behavior—physical and verbal, external and internal—that Muslim guests and hosts are expected to cultivate. Mughal court culture included extravagant feasting and hosting, both of which were considered indices of personal wealth, social and aesthetic refinement, generosity, and a publicly displayed adherence to "Muslim brotherhood and its egalitarian ethos." In fact, an important symbol of hospitality in Muslim culture is the *dastar-khwan* (Persian, "table cloth," sometimes with verses printed at the borders) that is laid on the floor and used for eating together from common dishes. Another popular gesture that symbolizes the reciprocity underlying hospitality, associated primarily with Muslim traditions of hospitality, but shared by other South Asian communities, is the offering of the areca nut-betel-leaf preparation, *pān*.

Khare traces contemporary social hospitality in India to a complex interweaving of older Hindu, Mughal, and colonial British forms of hospitality. Social life among the British in India, especially in the nineteenth century, governed by the British class system and by imperial power structures, dictated norms of socializing among the British, and between the British and the Indians. A distinctive "Raj hospitality" emerged with cultural vocabulary and categories such as *bobajee* (corruption of Hindi, *bāvarchi,* or cook) and *bobajee-khāna* (kitchen), *burra-khāna* (big dinner or evening party), *dolley* (complimentary tray of fruits, sweets etc.), *dastūr* (literally, "custom;" also, bribery), *phal-phul* (gifts to British officials), and *nazar* (customary gift from "inferior" guest to superior host as in a royal audience).

The medium for expressing hospitality in South Asia ranges from lavish food offerings and shelter to guests to the performances of services like oil baths and massages, from verbal etiquette to stylized entertainment. Depending on the social occasion and the context, the performance of hospitality is regulated by the gender, rank, class, and caste of hosts and guests as well as by finer permuations of insider-outsider statuses that characterize guest-host relationships. Life-cycle celebrations like marriages can involve many elaborate meals for hundreds of guests over several days and entail careful assessment and negotiation of guest-host relationships. The risk of social impropriety is heightened in these celebrations because, often, the statuses of individuals attending large gatherings are difficult to determine. Weddings, which are often general communal invitations in Muslim villages and urban neighborhoods, also figure ubiquitously in folktales as places where people reconnoiter (as stranger-heroes or interlopers), or as huge royal weddings of seven days' duration. Storytellers end Afghan Persian folktales that culminate in such marriages with the following traditional closing formula:

> For seven days they illuminated the city,
> They beat the drums with sticks and the sticks with drums,
> They gave the Hindus raw food and the Muslims, cooked,
> But I didn't get even one burnt bit off the bottom of the pot.

Muslim votive offerings (*naẕr*) include some form of hosting the saint whose blessing is sought, inviting him or her to partake of the food, symbolically, and thus bless it before it is distributed as charity to neighbors, shrine visitants or passers-by.

Not even gods are exempt from the duties of proper hospitality, as Hindu myths and folk narratives, which are replete with stories of hosts and guests illustrate. The *Kaṭha Upaniṣad* narrates the much-famed tale of Yamā, the god of death, who has to propitiate the young Brahman boy, Naciketas, by giving him three boons as recompense for having kept him without food for three days in his house. Narratives, a staple in *bhakti* (devotional) traditions, recount how a god or a sage appears disguised as a guest to "test" the faith of a devotee with little means. A well-known motif in folk narrative, on the other hand, centers around the test set by an inimical host for a guest who is a holy personage: the host deliberately offers prohibited food (usually meat and wine to a renunciant) but when the food is revealed, discovers that it has been miraculously transformed into food that is acceptable to the guest.

Muslim folktales often have a royal hero, disguised as an indigent, receive hospitality and guidance from a poor old woman or other marginal person who then helps the hero on his quest. Sometimes the host/helper is a dangerous female supernatural whose breast the hero must sieze and suck (thus forcing the hospitality issue and making him her foster child) before she has a chance to attack and kill him. Other Hindu stories, real-life and fictional, illustrate the internecine nature of host-guest transactions, which are never simple social formulas, but are linked in complex ways to caste rules, ritual prescriptions, and moral injunctions.

Hospitality has usually been relegated to the position of a "sub-phenomenon" of larger social systems in South Asian scholarship. Given its pervasiveness as a cultural imperative with sociopolitical implications, and its representation in normative literature, it is important that hospitality be viewed, not as arbitrary acts of social or religious largess, but rather as a complex social system in its own right intricately connected to other socio-cultural systems.

References

Aklujkar, V. 1992. Sharing the divine feast: evolution of food metaphor in Marathi sant poetry. In *The eternal food: gastronomic ideas and experiences of Hindus and Buddhists,* ed. R. S. Khare, 95–115. New York: State University of New York Press.

Breckenridge, C. A. 1986. Food, politics and pilgrimage in south India, 1350–1650 A.D. In *Food, society and culture: aspects of south Asian food systems,* eds. R. S. Khare and M. S. A. Rao, 21–53. Durham: Carolina Academic Press.

Buhler, G. 1969. *The laws of Manu*. New York: Dover Publications.

Burton, David. 1993. *The Raj at table*. London: Faber and Faber.

Hankin, Nigel. 1994. *Hanklyn-Janklin*. New Delhi: Banyan Books.

Jamison, Stephanie W. 1996. *Sacrificed wife, sacrificer's wife: women, ritual and hospitality in ancient India*. New York and Oxford: Oxford University Press.

Kane, P. V. 1968. *History of the Dharmasastras*. Poona: Bhandarkar Oriental Institute.

Khare, R. S. 1991. Indian hospitality: some cultural values and social dynamics. In *The cultural heritage of the Indian village,* eds. Brian Durrans and T. Richard Blurton, 45–61. London: The British Museum.

Metcalf, B., Ed. 1984. *Moral conduct and authority: the place of Adab in south Asian Islam*. Berkeley: University of California Press.

O'Flaherty, Wendy. 1981. *The Rig Veda: an anthology*. New York: Penguin.

Prasad, Leela. 1998. Scripture and strategy: narrative and the poetics of appropriate conduct in Sringeri, South India. Ph.D dissertation, University of Pennsylvania, Philadelphia.

Toomey, Paul. 1994. *Food from the mouth of Krishna: feasts and festivities in a north Indian pilgrimage centre*. Delhi: Hindustan Publishing Corporation.

LEELA PRASAD

SEE ALSO

Ancestor Worship; Food and Foodways; *Ḥāl; Ḥujra*

HOT/COLD

Hot/cold is a conceptual framework widely adhered to throughout South Asia. Within Asian medical systems, hot/cold descriptors are used to denote the qualities of people, plants, animals, minerals, places, times, seasons, celestial bodies, foods, medicines, stages of development, gender-based proclivities, and bodily sensations as well as symptoms and types of illness. Symptoms are recognized as signs of internal heat and cold manifest in myriad forms, related to various humoral imbalances. To the lay population, hot/cold reasoning guides behaviors ranging from folk dietetic practice to bathing habits, domestic health care to the interpretation of how medicines work, evaluations of the qualities of soil to deliberation about the use of various types of fertilizers.

Significant intra- as well as interregional variation exists in the classification of specific items and phenomena as hot/cold; there is more of a pattern in the way the framework is employed than in the specific rules for its application. Consensus is greatest for items involved in rituals. For example, Hindu rituals follow a logic that demands particular types of offerings representing hot/cold qualities matching the characteristics of a deity or the intent of a particular sequence in the ritual.

Hot/cold may refer to either selective qualities or the overall qualities of an item being described. A point of comparison may be implicit (rice is cool in relation to wheat) or explict when an index object is noted in conversation. For example, particular colors and tastes are widely associated with states of hot/cold (e.g., red: hot, white: cold), but these attributes may be eclipsed by others, such as body sensation, which are more immediate (e.g., burning sensation: hot) as well as subject to personal interpretation.

Hot/cold reference is often relational, hot-cold constituting a continuum along which one item may be described in relation to others within a common domain (e.g., milled rice: hot, parboiled rice: cold; beer: cool, rum: hot). A point of comparison may be implicit (rice is cool in relation to wheat) or emerge as an anchor point in conversation. Items tend to be classified within domains (vegetables, meats, liquor, medicines), each domain analogous to an octave on a musical scale. Thus, a grain such as wheat may be classified as hot, as may a meat such as chicken and an oil such as mustard seed oil. Each may be thought of as hot in relation to other members of a class, but their qualities may not be seen as identical, although each may be described as causing a heating effect on the body if consumed in excess.

The hot/cold conceptual framework constitutes an excellent example of an interpretive "model of" serving as a "model for" (Geertz 1973) practice. At issue is when the model is invoked. Research in South Asia suggests that predispositions toward hot/cold reasoning are embodied through a complex of practices, especially those associated with pregnancy and delivery, child care, and illness. South Asians do not spend their lives strictly abiding by rules of healthy living underlain by hot/cold conceptualization. They do, however, follow practices influenced by hot/cold reasoning at times associated with states of vulnerability. Hot/cold reasoning is further employed to explain new phenomena (e.g., how birth control pills work), and it serves as a guide for experimentation. A flexible, user-friendly conceptual framework, hot/cold facilitates communication between expert domains of knowledge such as astrology, Ayurveda medicine, and exorcism wherein associations between the hot/cold properties of stars, spirits, and bodily states may be drawn. Hot/cold also provides specialists with a widely understood reference point enabling communication with laypersons unable to grasp the complex relationships underlying expert practice.

References

Beck, Brenda. 1969. Color and heat in a South Indian ritual. *Man* 4: 553–572.

Babb, Lawrence. 1973. Heat and control in Chhattisgarhi ritual. *Eastern Anthropologist* 26: 11–28.

Geertz, Clifford. 1973. *The interpretation of cultures*. New York: Basic Books.

Nichter Mark. 1986. Modes of food classification and the diet-health contingency: A South Indian case, edited by R. S. Khare and M. S. A. Rao. In *Food, Society and Culture*. Durham: Carolina Academic Press.

Wandel, Margareta, Padmi Gunawardena, Arne Oshaug and Nils Wandel. 1984. Heating and cooling foods in relation to food habits in a southern Sri Lanka community. *Ecology of Food and Nutrition* 14: 93–140.

MARK NICHTER

SEE ALSO

Exorcism; Food and Foodways; Medicine, Āyurveda; *Pūjā*

ḤUJRA

In Pashto-speaking areas the term *ḥujra* [Arabic: room, cell] refers to a separate room(s) or house maintained for male guests. The ḥujra provides a site for hospitality, which is one of the main tenets of the Pashtun tribal code (*paṣhtūnwalī*). It is used in villages for daily gatherings and special occasions such as marriages and circumcisions. The ḥujra also serves as public space for meetings between senior members of several villages, clans, or tribes, and for meetings of village elders for decision making on issues of tribal law, both social and criminal. The ḥujra may be maintained by a village collectively or by a powerful member of a village (a *khān* or *mālik*); the prestige of the person(s) who maintains the *ḥujra* is directly proportional to the number of guests. In Pashtun sex-segregated society, the ḥujra provides a focal point for social life of the often interrelated village males as well as male guests. Women guests are taken into the women's quarters of the village homes.

Pashtun etiquette is observed within the ḥujra; older men sit in the best places, while younger men sit elsewhere or stand on the room's perimeter, bringing tea and food as needed. Conversation is serious and the silences dignified when senior men (*spīn–ẓhīray,* literally, "white-bearded") are present; when they leave, the younger men are free to laugh, joke, make music, and have fun. Traditionally, younger men sleep overnight in the ḥujra, both before and after marriage.

A ḥujra was traditionally constructed of simple materials such as local stone and mud. The basic piece of furniture was one or more simple rope-strung wooden beds (*chārpāy*) set along the walls, usually with bolsters or cushions for more comfortable seating during the day; quilts were added in cold weather. During warm weather, the beds were moved outside and both eating and sleeping took place in the open air of the ḥujra veranda or the ground in front of it. Today, the custom of maintaining a village ḥujra is gradually declining, as attached sitting rooms are added to individuals' homes. Increasingly, radios, cassette players, and televisions with VCRs and satellite-dish antennae are playing a role in the entertainment of guests.

References

Ahmed, Akbar S. 1980. *Pukhtun economy and society: traditional structure and economic development in a tribal society*. London: Routledge, Kegan Paul.

Lindholm, Charles. 1982. *Generosity and jealousy: the Swat Pakhtun of northern Pakistan*. New York: Columbia University Press.

WILMA L. HESTON

SEE ALSO

Hospitality

I

IBEX AND GOAT

Now a rare, high-mountain animal due to hunting and habitat loss, the ibex, an ungulate with long back-curving, ridged horns, appears to have been the object of long-standing religious and aesthetic interest from the western Himalayas and Hindu Kush westward. Ibex and ibex horns were commonly represented on Bronze Age painted pottery from the Iranian plateau. The small surviving non-Muslim (Kalasha) population of the Hindu Kush in northwest Pakistan, numbering between 2000 and 3000, still practices a polytheistic religion in which the ibex is regarded as a sacred animal. While ibex are the herds belonging to deities who inhabit the high mountains, domestic goat herds (maintained by men exclusively) are regarded as the pure animals appropriate for religious sacrifice and cared for with concern for ritual purity and religious observance.

Though Muslims do not venerate the animals, ibex horns are still to be seen decorating local Muslim shrines and mosques in Afghanistan and northern Pakistan. Chitrali Muslims from Northern Pakistan, among others, hold that ibex meat is pure and exceptionally healthful, because of the animal's diet of high-mountain plants, and it is said not to shrink when cooked like all other meat, but actually to expand and become more plentiful. They say the ibex are the goats of the *parī* (mountain spirits), who protect them and punish humans who prey on them unduly. One hunter in the Ishkoman Valley of Pakistan who by his mid-forties (in 1990) was reputed to have killed more than three hundred ibex, is also quite bald and his neighbors, among whom male-pattern baldness is rare, say with laughter that the parī have taken his hair in revenge for his killing so many of their goats. In Quetta, Pakistan, in 1995, this author met a Baluchi street entertainer who played a bowed spike-fiddle. He had constructed for himself a small wooden, jointed figure of an ibex mounted on a cylindrical platform in such a way that a hidden string attached to the wrist end of his fiddle bow caused the ibex to dance in time to his bowing.

References

Dupree, Louis. 1973. *Afghanistan.* Princeton, NJ: Princeton University Press.

Jettmar, Karl. 1975. *Die Religionen des Hindukusch.* Stuttgart: Verlag W. Kohlhammer.

Loude, Jean-Yves, and Vivian Lievre. 1988. *Kalash Solstice.* G. Romaine and M. Intrator, trans. Islamabad: Lok Virsa.

Maggi, Wynne. 2001. *Our women are free: gender and ethnicity in the Hindukush.* Ann Arbor: University of Michigan Press.

Mills, Margaret. 1996. Foodways in a Karakorum community: notes toward a handbook of Pakistani cuisine and food customs. In *Studies in the Popular Culture of Pakistan,* ed. William Hanaway, Islamabad: Lok Virsa.

MARGARET A. MILLS

SEE ALSO

Kalasha; *Parī;* Shrines, Muslim

IMAGE MAKING, METAL

Metal image making is the casting of devotional and ritual figures in several kinds of copper-based metal alloys. Often referred to generically as bronzes, these classical and folk images are more often made of brasses or bell metals. Very few centers continue to produce metal images in the classical tradition that is in accordance with traditional dictates of form, iconography, and materials found in Hindu scriptures. Those that do are found primarily in South and Northwest India at locales such as Swamimalai (Tamil Nadu) and Chamba (Himachal Pradesh). Rural artisans throughout India produce so-called folk, popular, ethnic, or tribal images according to their own local and regional traditions. These images frequently represent local versions of Hindu deities or deities and figures unknown in the classical Hindu repertory. Even when they portray standard Hindu deities with standard attributes, the proportions and processes are free of scriptural dictates.

Producers in the high classical mode, such as the renowned Sthapatis of Swamimalai (Tamil Nadu), are caste Hindus established in permanent workshops. Although their situations vary widely, the artisans who make folk images are more likely to be itinerant, work in family units including women and children, and remain outside the caste system. For both, it is difficult to make a living solely through image making. Nearly all image-makers cast other kinds of objects as well (rice measuring bowls, utensils, lamps, tribal jewelry, and so on). Many take on additional occupations to supplement their income.

Production Techniques

The most common method for making metal images is lost wax, or *cire perdue,* casting using several copper based alloys. Bronze properly refers to a mixture of copper and tin; a 10 percent tin content is common. High tin bronze is called bell metal because of its sonorous quality. Brass, often confused with bronze, is an alloy of copper with zinc. In folk metalwork, the mix is not usually well controlled since its source is scrap metal—even scrap aluminum may be used. Artisans select alloys in part for their cost, working properties and melting temperatures. However, metals in India have esthetic and ritual properties as well. When the patron so specifies, temple images may be cast in modern versions of the five-metal (copper, brass, lead, silver, and gold) or eight-metal (gold, silver, copper, zinc, lead, tin, iron, and mercury) alloys prescribed by the scriptures. The more precious metals may be included as a small drop or bead rather than a true amalgam.

Other materials needed in quantity for metal image making are beeswax, resins, and oils for the model; clays and their tempers (such as sand, rice husk, or jute) for the mold; and fuel (wood, coal, coke, or dung) for the kilns. The tool kit can be extremely simple. Itinerant casters travel with what they can carry on their backs and build their furnaces on the spot with materials at hand. Established artisans invest in permanent, sometimes elaborate, furnaces and a range of specialized tools.

In the process, a wax or resin model of the image is encased in a clay mold. The mold is then heated until the clay is baked hard and the wax melts. The wax is poured or burned out and leaves behind a hollow impression of the image. Molten metal is then poured into the hollow of the mold and set to cool. When the metal hardens the mold is broken. After the mold is broken away, a classical image can be finished with inlay, incision and polishing. A folk image is usually complete as cast.

If the wax model is solid, the resulting image will be a solid piece of metal. However, for technical and economic reasons, larger classical pieces and most folk images are hollow cast. In this process the image model is a skin of wax over a prepared clay core, often just the head and torso—hands, ears, limbs, and decorations can be solid wax. When the wax is replaced with metal, the clay core remains inside, lending weight and support to the metal surface.

Image makers in the rural and tribal areas of central and eastern India (especially Madhya Pradesh, Orissa, Bihar, and West Bengal) practice a distinctive variant of hollow casting called wax thread work. The model is made of wax or resin threads wrapped around the clay core. The crucible is attached directly to the mold and the whole placed in the kiln metal side down. The wax or resin burns and vaporizes through the walls of the mold. When pulled from the fire, the mold is inverted so that the metal flows directly through to the hollow impression within. These images have a characteristic surface and wiry decoration quite unlike work elsewhere in India.

Sand casting is a less common technique for image making found primarily in the north, especially Rajasthan, Himachal Pradesh and Utter Pradesh. Not mentioned in texts, or used in medieval casting, it can be considered a small-scale, manual system of mass production. The "sand" is actually a preparation of fine sand or clay and a binder such as resin or molasses and oil. The model image, usually of brass, makes a hollow impression in the center of a sand filled frame into which molten metal is poured.

History of Craft

South Asia has a long if broken tradition of lost wax casting dating back to the Indus Valley civilization of the third millennium B.C.E. But until recently the study of folk bronzes and contemporary image production has taken place apart from the art historical study of classical images. A nineteenth-century, colonial interest in India's crafts produced the first brief reports on metalworking and metalworkers that included image-makers. The pioneering work of Ruth Reeves and Meera Mukherjee in the 1960s represents the first of a series of systematic ethnographic studies that continue to the present. The National Handicrafts and Handlooms Museum in New Delhi, by presenting working demonstrations by contemporary metalworkers as well as its collections, has done much to promote the study of the craft in India.

The craft is changing even as it is being recorded. In response to a shrinking market and rising production costs, metal workers have had to alter their products and clients or go out of business altogether. Those that survive frequently do so because they have been organized into handicraft cooperatives with an urban and international market. In this market, lay subjects such as tribal figures in "typical" roles or animals removed from their original cultural meaning are more popular than religious images. A few artisans have become well-known artists, designated Master Craftsmen by the Indian government, and participate in the Festival of India and its successors around the world. Most, however, remain anonymous and in precarious economic circumstances.

References

Aryan, Subhashini. 1994. *Folk bronzes of Rajasthan*. New Delhi: Lalit Kala Akademi.

Handicrafts Survey Monograph on Dokra Artisans of Dariapur (Burdwan). 1973. *Census of India 1961, West Bengal and Sikkim, Volume XVI, Part VII-A(4)*. Delhi: Manager of Publications, Government of India.

Dallapiccola, A. L., ed. 1984. *The sacred and the profane: bell metal casting in the folk art of India*. Heidelberger Akten der von-Portheim-Stiftung, Neue Serie Nr. 1. Heidelberg: Völkerkundemuseum der von-Portheim-Stiftung.

Jain, Jyotindra and Aarti Aggarwala. 1989. *National Handicrafts and Handlooms Museum, New Delhi*. Ahmedabad: Mapin.

Mallebrein, Cornelia. 1993. *Die anderen Götter: Volks- und Stammesbronzen aus Indien*. Ethnologica (Cologne), n.F, Bd 17. Cologne: Rautenstrauch-Joest-Museum für Völkerkunde; Heidelberg: Braus

Mukherjee, Meera. 1978. *Metalcraftsmen of India*. Calcutta: Anthropological Survey of India.

Reeves, Ruth. 1962. *Cire perdue casting in India*. New Delhi: Crafts Museum

LEE HORNE

SEE ALSO

Craft; Metal and Metalworking; Metalwork, Bangladesh

IMĀM ḤUSAYN

Imām Ḥusayn was the grandson of the Prophet Muhammad and the third Imām of the Twelver Shīʿī Muslims, and the son of Muḥammad's daughter Fāṭima and his cousin ʿAlī b. Abu Tālib, the first Shīʿī Imām. In the years following the death of his father and elder brother Ḥasan, Ḥusayn—as the only remaining grandson of the Prophet—constituted a threat to the legitimacy of the Ummayad Caliph, Yazīd b. Muʿāwīya. Fearing Ḥusayn, Yazīd tried to force Ḥusayn to offer an oath of fealty. Knowing that his oath would strengthen what he considered to be an illegitimate and unjust government, Ḥusayn refused. Instead, along with his closest friends and relations, he set out for the city of Kufa in Iraq. Before reaching their destination, he and his companions were slaughtered by forces sent by the Caliph Yazīd at the Battle of Karbalā. Shīʿī Muslims, and the vast majority of Sunnis, consider Ḥusayn a symbol of the heroic resistance of good against evil. The anniversary of his martyrdom, commemorated during the first ten days of the lunar month of Muḥarram, is the occasion for important ritual performances. For the Shīʿī community, the mourning of Ḥusayn's death on the tenth of Muḥarram (ʿĀshūrā) is emblematic of faith in Islam itself. Their yearly mourning for Ḥusayn is rooted in their love for Muḥammad. Muḥammad is the beloved of God; therefore, if one loves God, it is essential that one also love his Prophet. Similarly, anyone who loves Muḥammad must also love those whom he loved. Thus, love for the Prophet and his immediate household (*ahl al-bayt*), which consists of ʿAlī, Fāṭima, Ḥusayn, and Ḥasan, is essential to Islam. These five persons make up the *Panjatan Pāk* (Five pure ones) who are symbolized by the *panjah*—the image of the human hand on which each finger represents one of the members of this holy family, also called the "Hand of Fāṭima." For the Shīʿa, it is not enough to remember Ḥusayn's heroic sacrifice at Karbalā, he must be mourned as the murdered grandson of the Prophet and the last of the *Panjatan Pāk*. The remembrance of his death should provoke grief like that felt over the loss of a treasured loved one. Although most fervent in the Shīʿī community, devotion to Ḥusayn in South Asia extends beyond it into the Sunni and even the Hindu community, which has produced poets who have honored Ḥusayn in verse.

References

Ayoub, Mahmoud. 1978. *Redemptive suffering in Islam*. The Hague: Mouton.

Schubel, Vernon. 1993. *Religious performance in contemporary Islam: Shiʿi devotional rituals in South Asia*. Columbia: University of South Carolina Press.

VERNON JAMES SCHUBEL

SEE ALSO

ʿAlī; Fāṭima; Muḥarram

INDIA

See Andhra Pradesh; Assam; Bihar; Central Himalayan States; Goa; Gujarat; Karnataka; Kashmir; Kerala; Madhya Pradesh and Chattīsgaṛh; Maharashtra; Punjab; Rajasthan; Tamil Nadu; Uttar Pradesh; West Bengal

ISLAM

In recent years, western folklorists taking a phenomenological approach to the study of belief and religious subjects have come to reject any simple dichotomy between "orthodox" or "canonical" and "folk" or "vernacular" religion. Believers, it is argued, do not divide their beliefs and practices in this manner. At the level of enactment in everyday life, all religion may be considered "vernacular". Yet among Muslims, there is a venerable and vigorous tradition of critique of religious practice along similar lines, rejecting local beliefs and practices as *khorāfāt* (Arabic/Persian: ridiculous tales, superstitions). Locally distinctive elaborations of religious practice are ubiquitous throughout the world's Muslim communities, their credibility waxing and waning among Muslims with varying degrees and kinds of religious education. A grounding principle of Islam is the universal set of basic requirements for practice and belief. These "five pillars" or duties of all Muslims are

(1) to bear witness that Allāh is the one God and Muhammad is his Prophet,
(2) to pray the ritual prayer (*ṣalāt* or *namāz*) five times a day when not disqualified by ritual impurity,
(3) to fast in daylight hours during the month of Ramaẕān each year, unless ill or traveling,
(4) to give the annual *zakāt* property tax (about 2 percent) as alms in support of needy Muslims,
(5) once in life, to make the pilgrimage to Mecca (*ḥajj*) if able to do so with lawful savings, and without hardship to ones family.

There are also five canonical tenets of belief:

(1) the oneness of God (Allāh),
(2) angels as agents of divine revelation and help,
(3) prophecy and revealed sacred books, culminating in the Qur'ān revealed to Muhammad,
(4) the last judgment and resurrection of the dead, when the righteous enter heaven and the unrighteous, hell,
(5) Divine decree (predestination), as a mystery which nonetheless enables human moral and spiritual choice.

It is in reference to these grounding principles that local Islamic practice is undertaken, and debated.

While belief in angels is specifically mandated for all Muslims, and *jinn* are mentioned in the Qur'ān as a class of creatures created by Allāh from fire (just as humans were made of earth), local beliefs in other categories of supernaturals are accommodated by verses in the Qur'ān which allude to the fact that no human can know all that God has created. Thus, the *dēv* and *parī* of pre-Islamic Iranian origin, *preta* and *bhūta* of Hindu and Buddhist tradition, the *gwāt* ("air spirits") of the Makrān coast of Pakistan, and others are supernaturals of varying powers and origin which can affect human lives, and are managed by local spiritual practices. There are also local categories of human practitioners who can manage these forces for good or ill. Acts of sorcery (Persian *jādū*) can be at the root of certain kinds of human misfortune (such as impotence, infertility), as can evil eye, the not-always-intentional effect of the envious or admiring gaze of a human or spirit.

Protection techniques vary. In the Iranian plateau and adjacent areas of South Asia, fumigation with the burning seeds of wild rue (Persian *isfand*) is a common women's domestic practice when supernatural interference is feared, and an activity of religious mendicants or other poor men or children, who receive a few coins from Muslim shopkeepers for passing through the bazaar swinging a small burning censor in the entry ways of shops. For evil eye, the simplest form of wearable protection is a bead or other round object, often blue in color. *Ta'wīẕ* (Arabic and Persian) are protective charms which may contain particular words or verses of the Qur'ān, and/or magical alpha-numeric charts or formulas or other graphic designs, written on paper or inscribed on metal objects and worn on the body. Paper *ta'wīẕ* may be folded and encased in a bright bit of cloth or a small metal container, usually rectangular or triangular in shape. Other ways of delivering the protective or curative power of written *ta'wīẕ* include burning the paper on which the inscription has been written and inhaling the smoke (*dūdī*, "smoky ones"), or writing the formula in water-soluble ink on a piece of paper or directly on the surface of a china saucer, adding water to dissolve the inscription, and drinking the water. Such written *ta'wīẕ* invoke and extend the third tenet of faith, the written Sacred Word as powerful in the world. Specialized books used by practitioners provide the written and drawn formulas for addressing particular problems. Other *ta'wīẕ* components or techniques may not directly quote scripture, nor even the "mystical" mathematics of "magical squares", whose arrays of letters and numbers (Arabic/Persian *abjad*) invoke the mysterious patterns of order in the universe. Local non-written forms of protective charms include knotted strings (e.g. in seven colors of thread) or special types of stones, salt, sand, sugar or other materials which are infused with power by having prayers or other "holy words" breathed on them in prescribed ways, or plant materials particular to the locale (heads of wheat from the first harvest anointed with butter, sprigs of juniper). Besides vulnerable persons, such as childbearing women, children and the ill, valued domestic animals, important household objects or components and tools (e.g. the stable, the master pillar or doorway of the living space, the butter churn) may also be protected by charms with a variety of ways of invoking sacred power.

Craftsmen may refer to special books of prayers and procedures for the success of their work. One such, the *Kesb Nāma* (Book of Professions), written in Pashto verse and published in Peshawar for sale in Pakistan and Afghanistan, gives mythic or legendary histories for the founding of the listed professions, and procedures and prayers for blessing phases of production for potters, carpenters, blacksmiths, washermen and barbers, all more or less marginalized craft groups in South Asia. Such books identify each craft's spiritual origin in the acts of an angel, a prophet and/or a particular Sufi *pīr* (in parallel with legitimating stories in Hindu caste *purāṇa* literature). The *Kesb Nāma* recently reported in use by Olesen in Afghanistan and Rye and Evans in Pakistan also stipulates prayer texts and procedures (including manipulations of consecrated protective objects or substances) to be used at designated phases of production, as in pottery (lifting the clay, firing the kiln, opening the kiln, etc.). Attribution of a craft to a Sufi order's founder or other religious authority sanctifies the craft and affirms its purity over latent or overt caste-related ideas of low status and impurity which underlie the social marginalization of some professions, even in supposedly caste-free Muslim contexts.

Richard Eaton has argued that "folk" or popular Islam in the Subcontinent is characterized above all by the importance of the *pīr / murīd* relationship of Sufi saint and disciple. Sufism, Islamic mysticism, highly personalistic and charismatic in its emphasis on devotion to God through devotion to a spiritual master, was the active force of Muslim missionizing in South Asia, giving rise to a wide spectrum of orally performed devotional poetry and song in local languages, derived both from Arabo-Persian and from indigenous poetic genres. Yet music and song are problematic in orthodox Islam, because poets' and false prophets' exciting recitations can lead the faithful into improper enthusiasms, making the whole range of local devotional music and song vulnerable to critique and to occasional suppression. The spectrum of accepted practice, however, is wide. While recitations of praise for the Prophet and for God may be generally approved, at the other end of the spectrum are eulogies and funeral laments (the latter usually the province of women) which may be condemned. Lament is a particular problem as it may be taken as protest against God's decision to take the person's life. A wide variety of love poetry may be performed either in a worldly reference frame, or as mystical metaphor for the devotee's love and longing for God, the staple theme of Sufism.

Votive rituals (*naẕr*) are another very widespread, generally female devotional practice, as much criticized in some quarters as treasured in others. The sponsor (generally female) of such a vow articulates a wish or a need, addressed to a saint or other venerated figure who is considered to have intercessory power. An initial offering of charity food, specified items (often sweets) ritually prepared and dedicated with prayers, may be distributed to neighbors, the poor, shrine visitants or religious persons. A specific vow may, on the other hand, only require the offerant to pledge such an offering, in the event that her wish is fulfilled. If she is answered, generally her naẕr becomes an annual commemorative event, by preference in the Islamic month of Safar (among Afghans). Tales attached to vow rituals attest the negative consequences of neglecting the pledge. Such offerings may be distributed from home, or a local or more distant shrine, or from the mosque or prayer hall. Daughters or daughters-in-law may join forces with a mother who has been fulfilling an annual naẕr pledge, adding their own wishes and then their own offerings in subsequent years. The particular vows are offered primarily on behalf of kin: to bear a child, to heal an illness, to bring a family member safely through school examinations or home from a journey, to find a child a good spouse, or even to protect against a communal misfortune such as a drought or warfare.

A woman may "retire" her naẕr after some years, perhaps after twenty years, or when her last child is wed, or at some other milestone she has stipulated. Naẕr as a practice has obvious parallels in Hindu votive (*vrāt*) rituals; particular Muslim naẕr may include ritual narration of the origin story of the ritual in the actions of some Muslim supplicant and a sacred helper, parallel to the Hindu *vrāt kathā*. Naẕr, though a form of supererogatory alms-giving (and thus perhaps meritorious as an extension of the idea of zakāt, the fourth "pillar" of Muslim duty), is strongly criticized by more "orthodox" Muslims as "bargaining for blessings", or as second-guessing God, who distributes blessings and trials to believers in the best possible way at all times. *Islām* literally means "submission" to God's will, the proper attitude of believers.

Other, very local practices also elaborate on basic Islamic principles in ways that orthodoxy questions. Among Shī'a Hazāra in Afghanistan, the dying may ask an eldest son to "recover" or make up for them the prayers or fast-days they have missed while too ill to participate in worship. While both daily prayer and the 29 or 30 days of the annual Ramaẕān fast are among the five pillars of the faith, the ill are exempt from these duties. People can make up for themselves any fast days missed due to illness, travel or ritual impurity (such as menstruation), but the merit (or obligation) is not "transferable" between persons in this way in orthodox thought.

References to Islamic ideas and personages abound in popular culture not itself deemed "religious" by Muslims. In Dari (Afghan Persian)-language folktales, the opening formula that designates the tales themselves as fiction, "lies", also invokes God: *Yakī būd, yakī nabūd, be ghayr az khodā kasī nabūd,* "Once there was, once there was not, there was/is no one other than God." A common folktale motif has the successful hero or heroine induce a potentially dangerous supernatural (*dēv* or *bārzangī*) to swear "by the Truth of the Prophet Solomon [who bound the jinn] and by Mother's milk" not to harm them. The 100th Name of God or the Ring of Solomon may be a magical weapon bestowed on a folktale hero by a supernatural sponsor. Ablutions, ritually necessary for prayer, may be directly or inversely included in magical procedures in folktales.

Historical figures such as Amīr Ḥamza, the Prophet's uncle and a hero of the early Islamic campaigns in Arabia, or the notoriously tyrannical Umayyad governor of Basra and Wasit, Hajjāj b. Yūsuf, figure as heroes or villains in fantastically elaborated multi-episodic adventure tales (*qiṣṣa*). The Caliph 'Alī, the Prophet's cousin and son-in-law, or the legendary, immortal wandering prophet Khiẕr, or even Adam himself leave their marks on the landscape: rock outcroppings in central Afghanistan are the bones of dragons slain by 'Alī, Adam's footprint is to be seen on Adam's Peak in southern Sri Lanka (Serendib), where, by Muslim legend, Adam and Eve first landed when they were expelled from Eden.

Nineteenth-century South Asian Muslim religious reformers' writings such as the still very widely-read *Bihishti Zewar* and the less well-known *Majālis un-Nisā* take particular issue with the vernacular devotional practices of women. These reformist efforts, emanating from such places as the Muslim Deoband College, seem in general to have been conceived as representing the view from urban centers where formal education was more available, and aimed through education to abolish vernacular practices common in more rural communities as well as among unschooled urbanites. Yet paradoxically, some late twentieth century Afghan reformers, themselves accused of provincialism, ignorance, and localism by other Muslims, have seen more educated urban populations (in Kabul, Mazar-i Sharif, Herat) as hotbeds of apostasy, with purdah (female modest dress and seclusion) and female education as particular points of contention.

In the hands of extreme reformists such as the Deoband- and Arab Wahhābī-inspired Afghan Ṭālibān, the spectrum of acceptable social practice may be considerably narrowed in the name of religion, yet resistant effects have also been evident. Naw Rūz (the solar New Year, celebrated at the vernal equinox), a Central Asian spring festival which was canonized as the climax of the Zoroastrian religious feast cycle, was and is an important festival moment for Shī'a and Isma'īlī Muslims from Iran to Pakistan's Northern Areas. It is the dramatic national pilgrimage occasion at Mazar-i Sharif, the shrine to 'Alī in northern Afghanistan, attended by Afghan Muslims of all sects. The Sunni Ṭālibān sought to suppress Naw Ruz celebrations (among other practices) as un-Islamic. In March 2002, the year of the Ṭālibān's departure from Afghan rule, the festival with its many themes of purification, rebirth, renewal, reunification of families and the solution of quarrels, was reported celebrated with renewed fervor in Kabul. In another such example of re-emergent tradition, the *gwāt-i leb* healing trance traditions of the Makran Coast of Pakistan, formerly practiced publicly by both Sunni and minority Ẕikrī Muslims, became more private, domestic, female ceremonies under reformist pressure, only to re-emerge in recent years as a public ceremony in the Ẕikrī neighborhood of Lyari in Karachi, where Ẕikrīs claimed the ceremonies as part of a distinctive ethno-cultural heritage.

References

Baghban, Hafizullah. 1972. Islamic folklore: annotated bibliography. *Folklore forum* Bibliographical and Special Series, No. 9.

Denny, Frederick M. 1987. *Islam and the Muslim community*. San Francisco: Harper Collins.

Eaton, Richard M. 1978. The profile of popular Islam in the Pakistani Punjab. *Journal of South Asian and Middle Eastern studies* 2,1: 74–92.

Frembgen, Jürgen, 1993. *Derwische: Gelebter Sufismus*–Köln: DuMont Buchverlag.

Martin, Richard C. 1982. *Islam in local contexts. Contributions to Asian studies* 17. Leiden: E. J. Brill.

Metcalf, Barbara D. 1990. *Perfecting women: Maulana Ashraf'Ali Thanawi's Bihishti Zewar, a partial translation and commentary*. Berkeley: University of California Press.

Mills, Margaret. 1991. *Rhetorics and politics in Afghan traditional storytelling*. Philadelphia: University of Pennsylvania Press.

———. 1995. Muslim folklore and folklife. Azim Nanji (ed.) *The Muslim almanac: A reference work on the history, faith, cultures and peoples of Islam:* 371–377. Detroit: Gale Research.

Minault, Gail. 1986. *Voices of silence: English translations of Khwaja Altaf Hussain Hali's Majalis un-Nissa and Chup ki Dad*. Delhi: Chankya Publications.

Olesen, Asta. 1994. *Afghan craftsmen: The cultures of three itinerant communities.* London: Thames and Hudson.

Poladi, Hassan. 1989. *The Hazāras*. Stockton, Calif.: Mughal Publishing Co.

Pugh, Judy. 1986. Divination and ideology in the Banaras Muslim community. Katherine Ewing (ed.) *Shariat and ambiguity in South Asian Islam*. Berkeley: University of California Press.

Roy, Asim. 1983. *The Islamic syncretistic tradition in Bengal*. Dhaka: Academic Publishers.

Rye, Owen, S. and Clifford Evans. 1974. *Traditional pottery techniques of Pakistan*. Washington, DC: Smithsonian / Islamabad: Lok Virsa.

Sakata, Hiromi L. 2002. *Music in the mind: The concepts of music and musician in Afghanistan,* 2nd ed. Washington, DC: Smithsonian.

Sultana, Farhat. 1996. *Gwat* and *Gwat-i Leb:* spirit healing and social change in Makran. Paul Titus (ed.) *Marginality and modernity: Ethnicity and change in post-colonial Balochistan:* 28–50. Karachi: Oxford University Press.

MARGARET A. MILLS

SEE ALSO

'Alī; Amīr Ḥamza; *Bhānd Paṭhar; Bhūta; Bihishtī Zewar; Dēv;* Dṛṣṭi; Ginān; Kerala; Lament; Life Cycle Rituals; *Majlis;* Maldives; *Marṣiya; Mātam;* Mosques; *Muḥarram;* Muslim Folklore; Muslim Folklore, Sri Lanka; Nauḥa; *Parī;* Sacred Places, Afghanistan; Saints, Muslim; Sufi Folk Poetry

J

JAIN FOLKLORE

Most Jains dress, speak, and celebrate births and marriages in ways similar to their local Hindu counterparts. However, even shared practices take on a Jain color or interpretation. For *Śvetāmbar*s (one of the three largest Jain sects) the celebration of the new year (*Dīvāḷī*) is joined with the celebration of *Mahāvīr Nirvāṇ,* which is the spiritual successor of the most recent *Jina* (*tīrthaṅkara* or Jain saint, literally, "one who makes fords"). Thus, alongside the annual worship of Lakṣmī (the Hindu goddess of wealth) during *Dīvāḷī,* there are dramatic reenactments of Mahāvīr's life, the worship of Gautam Svāmī (Mahāvīr's closest disciple), decorations on Mahāvīr's and Gautam Svāmī's images, and a tour of all Jain temples in the city. Very little research has been done on Jain folklore, especially with the sect of *Digambar* Jains, but from what we know, Jain folklore centers on food preparation, religious storytelling, decorative arts, and the magical properties of religious objects.

Perhaps the most significant and widespread identifying feature of being Jain is food. It is so central, in fact, that the complex food restrictions and beliefs are often used as a way to demarcate a boundary between Jains and non-Jains. First and foremost, because of their understanding of nonviolence, Jains are strict vegetarians, although they drink milk and use other dairy products. Their understanding of nonviolence is extended to plants and seeds, some of which they also do not eat. Jain normative texts give long lists of forbidden foods; these have been logically extended to include newer foods. Illustrative of the Jain preoccupation with food and food restrictions are the restrictions against roots and tubers, including onions, garlic, potatoes, and carrots (the former two restrictions are shared by some Hindus), as well as specific daily observances: no food after dark, no green foods, no vegetables during the annual festivals of *Paryuṣaṇ* and *Daśalakṣaṇa Parv* (which celebrate the coming together of the whole Jain community at the end of the rainy season).

While the dishes cooked reflect the cuisines of the regions in which the Jains live, the food practices are markedly Jain. Because of the concern that one's food be completely pure and that it be produced under the strict procedures of Jain cooking, virtually all food is made at home, demanding of Jain women (who do the bulk of food preparation) that they be scrupulously careful to remove—alive—every bug or imperfection from the legumes, grains, spices, vegetables, and fruit that make up the cuisine. Few families use the new and prestigious prepared foods—not even flour or ground spices—preferring to monitor the foods' ethically sound production at home. Jain homes have filters (at least for drinking water) to filter out the larger living creatures that might be in the water. Jain food rules are a rallying point for reformist Jains who claim Jain unity in the face of serious Jain sectarian disputes.

Jain folk narratives tell of virtuous women (the *Mahāsatī*), fasts, and the lives of the *Jina* (and relatives or disciples closely associated with that Jina). *Mahāsatī* narratives tell how women retain their Jain faith under persecution and thus gain great religious merit. Fasting narratives illustrate the merits and worldly gains from the fast while showing the piety of the first performer of the fast. Much of the actual performance of fasts today derives from these popular and well-known narratives. For example, the contemporary beliefs about the efficacy of the *Navpad Oḷī* fast are based on the tangible gains of wealth and good health expressed in the *Śrīpāl Rājā no Rāso* (King Śripal's Rāsa) (a popular seventeenth century retelling of the older *Śrīpāl* story) which women read during a nine-day fast performance. The story of Śrīpāl and his wife, Mayṇāsundarī, centers on how her firm adherence to Jain praxis both cures his leprosy and leads him to garnering overwhelming good fortune. Also, when fasts are broken, they are done so first with sugarcane juice, in imitation of the fast breaking of Ādināth, the first Jina in this era. These fasting narratives, then, seem both to reinforce beliefs about religious justification for fasting and to recreate the actual experiences of the virtuous through imitation.

The Jina's life narratives are generally restricted to events celebrating some moment of the Jina's life. For instance, during the *Kalpa Sūtra* (ca. 4th c. B.C.E.) recitation in the *Paryuṣaṇ* ceremony, the birth of Mahāvīr is celebrated. In this ceremony, the privilege of performing the venerations is auctioned to the highest bidders, who then perform (or have children perform) the garlanding of the fourteen symbols of the dreams that Mahāvīr's mother dreamed upon conception. When the dream symbols are all garlanded, the narrative of the birth of Mahāvīr is told and everyone in the crowd breaks open coconuts to feed one another. All then rush forward to rock the newborn Mahāvīr in his cradle—a ritual act very similar to the celebration of Kṛṣṇa's birth. Many Jains believe that rocking the cradle helps a woman conceive, although the ritual also carries general good luck since unmarried men and women and married men also rock his cradle. The story itself is recounted in normative texts; yet the performance includes certain folkloric elements as well: devotional songs based on folk narratives of the life of Mahāvīr, the practice of veneration of the dreams, special foods prepared for the festival, and special decorations of the Mahāvīr images.

While *Digambar* Jains reject the practice of decorating Jina images—they do decorate their guardian deities—the *Śvetāmbar Mūrtipūjak* Jains decorate the Jina with armor, crowns, and earrings, silver foil, flowers, and gems. These decorations (*aṅgī*) are both a folkloric expression of how a Jina's glory might look and the normative accepted value of the glorification of the Jina. This glorification of the Jina is the rationale behind the grand parades at the installation of an image and the decorations and other folkloric celebrations surrounding Jain worship. There is a popular narrative in which Marudevī, the mother of Ādināth, sees her son in all his glory and instantly attains omniscience; seeing the Jina's glory helps Jains gain knowledge.

The canopies and backdrops hung behind the Jina images are often covered with couch-work embroidery, usually made by Jain laywomen. These canopies are sometimes embroidered for women who have completed extreme fasts such as those lasting thirty-one days. The embroidery usually represents the fourteen dreams that the Jina's mothers have upon conception of a Jina, pilgrimage site maps, the Jina's assembly hall (*samavasaraṇ*), or the narrative of a particular fast. The cloth dusters that Śvetāmbar mendicants use to sweep the areas on which they sit and to protect insects, and that serve as a key symbol of their renunciation, include inside them—although they are not visible except when the mendicants check the dusters for insects—small pieces of embroidery, usually representing the eight auspicious symbols: the *svastika, śrīvatsa* (an auspicious mark found on the chest of the Jinas), *nandyāvarta* (an extended svastika), throne, water jar, a pair of fish, banner, and mirror. Almost every temple has a series of pilgrimage map paintings, which are representations of various pilgrimage sites for Jains containing stylized depictions of the temple, the images, and the path one walks to the temple. These same paintings are reproduced and can be found in many Jain homes. Jain paintings of the Jina's assembly hall and of the cosmos are a major part of the illustration tradition.

The patterns Jains make with rice as offerings at the temple each day are the most common Jain drawings. Though the normative texts direct one to draw a svastika with three dots and a curved line above it, the drawings in the temples are of a wide variety of designs including the eight auspicious symbols and variations on the svastika. (The svastika is a traditional symbol of good fortune in Hinduism, which Hitler used to symbolize Aryan rule.) For special events, more complicated drawings are made with several colored powders, too. Hand-drawn powder designs (*raṅgolī*) are drawn outside the home, around plates for special guests, and around the plate with the food for a person breaking a long fast. Within the community, there are contests for the young men and women for the best representation of a Jain theme—drawings of the life of a Jina, the eight auspicious symbols, and episodes in the virtuous lives—which are extremely popular. The winning entries are displayed at community events.

Several materials associated with Jain worship take on magical, protective properties for Jains. *Vāskep* powder (a mixture of sandalwood, camphor, and saffron powders), used by mendicants to bless devotees, is also used for its protective powers associated mostly with travel. People about to travel might recite the *Navkār Mantra* (three times, usually) and then put vāskep on their heads. The water that runs off the Jina's images after their bathing worship (*prakṣāḷ*) is believed to have protective powers; many Jains dip their finger in this water and dab it on their eyelids, and women put some on the part of their hair. Vials are filled with prakṣāḷ and brought home to bless sick or vulnerable people. This milky water is sometimes paraded to the bathing ritual's sponsor's house, where it is left in the house shrine overnight to help a woman conceive a child.

In sum, though Jains are primarily a religious group, they are also a culturally distinct group, as can be seen in their folklore. While some of their practices have arisen in direct response to the demanding philosophy of the Jain religion, most are Jain articulations of virtue, beauty, and magic.

References

Carrithers, Michael, and Caroline Humphrey, eds. 1991. *The assembly of listeners: Jains in society*. Cambridge: Cambridge University Press.

Cort, John E. 2001. *Jains in the world: religious values and ideology in India*. New York: Oxford University Press.

Granoff, Phyllis, ed. 1990. *The Clever Adulteress: A Treasury of Jain Literature*. New York: Mosaic.

Mahias, Marie Claude. 1985. *Délivrance et convivialité: Le système culinaire des Jaina* [Deliverance and Conviviality: The Cooking System of the Jains]. Paris: Éditions de la Maison des Sciences de L'Homme.

Pal, Pratapaditya, ed. 1994. *The peaceful liberators: Jain art from India*. Los Angeles: Los Angeles County Museum of Art.

Reynell, Josephine. 1985. Honour, nurture and festivity: aspects of female religiosity amongst Jain women in Jaipur. Ph.D. dissertation, Anthropology Department, Cambridge University.

Stevenson, Mrs. Sinclair. [1915] 1984. *The heart of Jainism*. New Delhi: Munishiram Manoharlal.

M. WHITNEY KELTING

SEE ALSO

Dreams; Floor Designs; Food and Foodways; Jainism; Kṛṣṇa; Painting; Pilgrimage

JAINISM

Jains are a religious group concentrated in western and southern India. The religion itself dates from at least the time of the Buddha, when Jainism's most recent *Jina* (saint), Mahāvīr, walked the earth revitalizing the Jain faith. Though there are several sects within Jainism, three—Digambar, Śvetāmbar Mūrtipūjak, and Sthānakavāsī—are the largest and most influential. Jainism accepts a four-fold congregation of male and female mendicants and male and female laity. Mendicants and laity are in periodic contact, though less so in the Digambar sect because of the relative scarcity of Digambar mendicants.

There are several debates among these various groups, but, for the purpose of this essay, two are most significant. The debate between Digambars and Śvetāmbars over whether Mahāvīr renounced clothing or whether he was only detached from clothing affects how the two groups worship and whether or not the male mendicants wear clothing. While Śvetāmbar Mūrtipūjak Jains decorate their images with armor, flowers, and gems, Digambar Jains reject this practice as both inappropriate (by showing a Jina wearing clothing) and violent (by offering flowers that have been plucked from the plants). The Sthānakavāsīs, though they base their theology in Śvetāmbar tradition, reject the worship of Jina images and do not have temples as Digambar and Śvetāmbar Mūrtipūjak Jains do. Sthānakavāsī worship centers around the mendicant rest halls, where laity gather to meet with mendicants, hear lessons, perform ritual expiations, and sing.

Jainism has an agglomerative history, with a few periods of "purification" usually leading to schisms within the religion. Temple practice—though rejected entirely by Sthānakavāsīs—has been encouraged and revitalized by the mendicant community. The Jain orthodoxy has been remarkably supportive of lay practice, focusing on giving orthodox interpretations of practices rather than repudiating them. The long history of converting narratives and supplying Jain alternatives to popular non-Jain practices shows that this is a longstanding approach of Jain leadership in response to lay pressures. That these texts and practices lie outside the normative tradition does not mean they are inevitably discordant with orthodoxy; rather, regional and folk practices behave something like a fulcrum between the lives of Jains and the philosophies and prescriptions of the normative texts.

There are two major regions of Digambar Jain communities, one in Rajasthan and Delhi, and the other in southern Maharashtra and Karnataka. Śvetāmbar Jains are clustered in a belt stretching from Jaipur to Bombay (including southern Rajasthan and all of Gujarat). (There are Jains all over India and in every major city, as well as relatively large groups in England, North America, East Africa, and Japan, but these are the two most influential regions.) Jain worship includes aspects of regional folk culture that are woven into the ritual culture. For example, while rās-garbā dance and music are common to many Gujaratis, the Jain formal ceremonies from that region have thoroughly integrated this dance and music tradition into an expression of Jain devotion.

Jain devotional hymns (*stavan*) are sung to a combination of different melodies with rās-garbā melodies dominating the Śvetāmbar Mūrtipūjak repertoire followed by Hindi Film song melodies. The formal ceremony texts (*pūjā*), which are a part of the folklore genre of the Gujarati *raso* (a form of heroic ballad similar to the Rajasthani *ḍhoḷa*), are sung to a variety of rās-garbā and *bhajan* melodies. Dance is a central part of the formal pūjā performances as each section of the text's singing is accompanied by a seated version of rās-garbā. (One section is also accompanied by standing dance.)

In Rajasthan, Jain worship is linked closely to Rajasthani narratives of martial heroes and lineage goddesses, while in Gujarat one finds links to the model of the great merchant patron. In south India, Digambar worship draws on models of sacred kingship, especially in the centrality of the reenactment of the royal anointment ceremony. This is reflected in the importance of the Digambar Ādipurāna (the story of the first Jina's children, Bāhubali and Bharata), which challenges the Hindu narrative *Mahābhārata*. The largest Jain festival, the Digambar Mahāmastakā bhiṣeka, is a celebration of the Bāhubali narrative marked by the grand-scale anointment of the immense Bāhubali statue in Śrāvaṇbelgola.

Devotional singing is central to daily worship as well as to the more formal Jain ceremonies and celebrations. The songs (*stavan* or, in Hindi, *bhajan*) are performed by both laity and mendicants, though the performance of singing is dominated by women. The songs are often collected into small volumes sold at pilgrimage sites and local Jain bookstores. Temple and meeting halls maintain a stock of the more popular collections for believers to borrow while performing worship. Because of the rejection of temples and temple images, singing comprises the bulk of Sthānakavāsī devotionalism. Likewise, in all pilgrimage sites the female mendicants gather and sing devotional songs; like male mendicants, they are not permitted to make material offerings. These songs have obvious Jain lyrics set to folk melodies (religious bhajan, dance music, birth and marriage songs), film melodies, and a small selection of melodies considered to be Jain in origin. These melodies are mixed freely in song performances.

Dance, too, forms a part of Jain daily and formal worship. For example, Śvetāmbar Mūrtipūjak women's singing collectives (*maṇḍaḷ*) accompany their singing performances with dance. This seated dance derives from the western Indian rās-garbā dance style. A few other dances accompany Jain worship: the yak-tail broom dance (as part of the eight-fold offerings), the lamp dance (done for holidays, but also seen as an extension of the lamp offering), and the winnowing basket dance (performed at fast-breaking gatherings).

An identifying feature of Jain religious practice, and one not specifically indicated in the normative textual tradition, is the practice of auctioning off the constituent parts of a particular ritual or the privilege of performing the entire ritual. The bids come in the form of measures (*maun*) of ghee. These measures are now fixed at one and one-half rupees per measure (considerably less than the usual price of ghee today). The bids come in increments of four or six rupees, varying to keep the numbers odd (5, 11, 15, 21, 25, 31...), which is seen as a gesture towards the unlimited desire for giving. (An even number would indicate a completeness to a bid that might thus look stingy.) The bidding itself is interspersed with bidding songs sung (usually spontaneously) by the women present during the bidding. The bidding songs celebrate the goodness of giving money to the Jain religion and are sometimes pointed urgings towards particular bidders from whom the community expects a larger bid.

After any religious event, the sponsoring family distributes small gifts (often sweets, fruits, coins, or small steel dishes), a practice called *prabhāvana* (appreciation). It is a way of marking one's appreciation of the good acts of those who attend these events. It is one of the duties of all Jains to show affection to all who believe in Mahāvīr with a feast for all Jains (*sādharmik vātsalya* or *svāmīvātsalya*). This feast identifies all the members of the community while they share in one of few congregational celebrations and is often celebrated on the day after the end of the festivals of *Paryuṣaṇ* (for Śvetāmbars) or *Daśalakṣaṇa Parv* (for Digambars). *Paryuṣaṇ* includes an eight-day recitation of the *Kalpa Sūtra,* narrating the lives of the Jina, and a program honoring Mahāvīr's mother's fourteen dreams (signaling a *Jina's* birth) and Mahāvīr's birth itself. *Daśalakṣaṇa* includes a ten-day recitation of the *Tattvārtha Sūtra,* accompanied by daily homilies by Digambar laymen. Both festivals end with the public expiation of the year's sins and the exchange of apologies with all other Jains in the community. This displays respect for and identification with one's community.

The celebration of fellow believers is the normative reason for the worship of the guardian deities as well. Both Digambar and Śvetāmbar Jains have a lively worship of Jain guardian deities (*śāsan devatā*). These gods and goddesses are portrayed in the temples, often in association with a particular Jina, and are worshipped for assistance in worldly endeavors (which the Jina themselves transcend). The popularity of certain deities is regionally specific (like Cakreśvarī in Pālītāṇā or Kūṣmāṇḍinī in Śravaṇabelagola) and some guardians have achieved a widespread following (such as Bhairav—especially Nākoḍā Bhairav—for Śvetāmbars and Padmāvatī for Digambars). One group of Śvetāmbars (Khartar Gacch) also has an elaborate worship of four mendicant saints who are believed to have magical powers (the *Dādāguru*). Digambar Jains focus their worship on three goddesses: Padmāvatī, Jvālāmālinī, and Kūṣmāṇḍinī, while Śvetāmbar Jains focus on Cakreśvarī, Ambikā, and Padmāvatī. There are many folk narratives connecting each of these goddesses with her particular Jina. There are fewer guardian gods who have a serious following. Those who do include: Bhairav, Maṇibhadra, Bhūmiya, and Ghaṇṭākarṇ Mahāvīr (a Jain form of the Hindu god, Hanumān), who is rising in popularity.

The distinction between popular and normative religion is misleading in the case of Jain religiosity. For example, the devotional songs are often written by the mendicants to existing folk melodies and then incorporated into the active repertoires of laywomen, whose singing groups travel to Jain households to perform ceremonies written by Jain mendicants, perhaps to counteract the practice of hiring Hindu priests for household ceremonies. The interweaving of these worlds and the (sometimes cautious) approval of this practice by the orthodox mendicant community and the normative textual tradition make popular–normative distinctions extremely problematic.

References

Babb, Lawrence. 1996. *Absent lord: ascetics and kings in a Jain ritual culture*. Berkeley: University of California Press.

Cort, John. 1987. Medieval Jaina goddess traditions. *Numen* 34: 235–254.

———. 1991. Śvetāmbar Mūrtipūjak Jain scripture in a performative context. In *Texts in context: traditional hermeneutics in south Asia,* ed. Jeffrey R. Timm, pp. 171–193. Albany: State University of New York Press.

Dundas, Paul. 1992. *The Jains*. London: Routledge.

Jaini, Padmanabh. 1979. *The Jaina path of purification*. Berkeley: University of California Press.

Kelting, M. Whitney. 1996. *Singing to the Jinas*. New York: Oxford University Press.

Laidlaw, James. 1995. *Riches and renunciation: religion, economy, and identity among the Jains*. Oxford: Oxford University Press.

Reynell, Josephine. 1987. Prestige, honour and the family: laywomen's religiosity amongst Svetambar Murtipujak Jains in Jaipur. *Bulletin D'etudes Indienne* [Bulletin of Indian Studies] 5: 313–359.

Sangave, Vilas. 1980. *Jaina community*. Bombay: Popular Prakashan.

Zydenbos, Robert. 1994. Jaina goddesses in Kannada literature. In *Studies in south Asian devotional literature,* eds. Alan Entwhistle and Françoise Mallison. 135–145. New Delhi: Manohar.

M. WHITNEY KELTING

SEE ALSO

Bhajan; Dance; Ḍholā; Fairs and Festivals; Film Music; Folk Music; Food and Foodways; Gods and Goddesses; Hanumān; Kalpa Sūtra; Song; Syncretism

JAJMĀNI

To most people, the "*jajmāni* system" represents a conception of Indian village economy determined by ritual rules laid down 2,500 years ago in the Dharma Śāstras. The term jajmāni itself comes from the Hindi term "*jajmān*," which derives from the Sanskrit term *yajamāna,* "the one who provides the sacrifice." It stands in semantic opposition to the term *purohita,* "one who performs the sacrifice." Indeed, many people cite this etymology to support a belief that the ancient doctrinal norms for relations between a sacrificer (especially a royal donor of a sacrifice) and a sacrifier (the priest who performs the sacrifice) is the origin of and model for every kind of patron-client, if not every kind of economic relationship, throughout the entirety of rural Indian history. Yet, despite a near universality of references to the Indian jajmāni system, the term should be recognized as the mark of an orientalist fiction that has never existed in India.

So dominant has jajmāni become as a metaphor for Indian economy that only specialists are aware of other kinds of patron-client relationship between families, such as those between landlords and landless laborers, relationships between corporate villages and state authorities, and various contractual, commercial relationships. To this day, graduate students taking courses in economic anthropology are offered descriptions of the jajmāni system as representing the totality of the Indian economy.

By "jajmāni system," writers refer to a putative division of labor and economic distribution in which landowning castes of families called jajmāns exchange shares of crops grown on their land in return for ritual and economic services from landless castes of families. Remarkably, this conception of village economic life became prominent only during the last sixty years: there is an early reference in Wilson's (1855) *Glossary of Judicial and Revenue Terms,* but the first reference to jajmāni in the social sciences occurs in William Wiser's (1936) book, *The Hindu Jajmāni System*. Interest in traditional village economies has a deeper history, however, in nineteenth century studies of Indian village communities. It has also been powerfully influenced by Henri Hubert and Marcel Mauss's (1898) interpretation of sacrifice in classical India and by A. M. Hocart's (1950) comparative analysis of caste.

Wiser and Mauss have had, perhaps, the greatest influence on anthropological studies of village economy under the rubric of jajmāni, steering inquiry into economic and ritual aspects of the system respectively. Different authors have debated the merits of the system as beneficial or exploitative of landless clients in the system. Other authors have explored the extension of ideas about the sacrifier-sacrificer relationship to all patron-client relationships within Indian villages. An excellent review of jajmāni literature through the 1960s may be found in Kolenda (1967). Increasingly, however, anthropologists have found themselves straining to fit all kinds of village economic exchange within the Procrustean bed of jajmāni. Many researchers discovered that only some of the exchanges that take place between landholders and clients are determined by custom rather than through price-setting mechanisms of the market place. Others found that patron-client exchanges took place in cash rather than kind. Still others discovered that patron-client relationships were not confined to single villages. Historians, to be sure, have explored the complexity of India's economy for decades. But it has only been during the last few years that anthropologists have begun to consider the implications of this complexity and reflect more carefully on data from contemporary ethnographic studies. The result has been a growing recognition of the misleading nature of the jajmāni concept and the development of a more sophisticated understanding of Indian economy.

References

Perlin, Frank. 1983. Proto-industrialization and pre-colonial south Asia. *Past and Present* 98: 30–95.

———. 1994. The invisible city: monetary, administrative, and popular infrastructures in Asia and Europe, 1500–1900. Aldershot, Hampshire, U.K.: Variorum; Brookfield, Vt.: Ashgate.

Wilson, H. H. 1855. *A glossary of judicial and revenue terms,* London: W. H. Allen.

Wiser, William H. *The Hindu Jajmāni system.* 1988. New Delhi: Munshiram Manoharlal.

DAVID RUDNER

SEE ALSO

Credit System (Women's Private Banking in Rural India); *Girau*

JALLIKKAṬṬU

Jallikkaṭṭu is one of several types of "bull-fights"—or, more technically, tauromachy—found in Tamil Nadu. Besides jallikkaṭṭu, there are *mañciviraṭṭu* and *erutukaṭṭu,* and each has several subtypes. Jallikkaṭṭu is the most important and is more fixed by rules than the other types. It also requires greater preparations of the playing ground.

The term jallikkaṭṭu (or *callikkaṭṭu*) literally means "tying a small coin," which refers to a form of tauromachy in which a coin or badge is tied between the bull's horns and has to be pulled away, as, for example, in the *Course à la Cocarde* in the south of France and in the Tamil form called mañciviraṭṭu. However, this form of play is not found in jallikkaṭṭu; hence, the reason for applying the word jallikkaṭṭu in this instance remains unclear. During a jallikkaṭṭu, the bull is brought into the *uḷvāṭi,* a small roomlike enclosure from which he is released on to the playing ground (*vāṭi* or *vāṭivācal*) after all ropes, including the noseband, are taken off him. Right on the threshold of the uḷvāṭi, two tree-trunks, called *aṇaimaram* ("protective trees") are fixed upright into the ground; they serve the catchers as a hideout from which they will jump on the bull, the moment it leaves the uḷvāṭi. The aim of the game is that the catcher—a single man for each bull—should remain on the beast, with one hand grasping a horn and the other arm slung aroung the animal's hump, over a certain distance, demarcated on the starting point by the aṇaimaram, and at the farthest point by a string of neem and mango leaves tied over the playground. In great jallikkaṭṭus, up to 350 or 400 bulls are released one by one.

Jallikkaṭṭus are very common between Tañjāvūr and Tiruccirāppaḷḷi in the north and Tirunelvēli and Rāmanātapuram in the south, a region centered around the city of Madurai and populated for the most part by the *Mukkulattār* castes (literally, "those belonging to the three lines," the Kaḷḷar, Maṟavar, and Akampaṭiyar), who are the main participants in this ritual sport.

The bulls that take part in jallikkaṭṭu, are reared only for this purpose; they are not used for any other work. Normally, a family or a group of people (sometimes a whole village together) raises a jallikkaṭṭu bull in fulfillment of a vow made to a village deity. The performance of a jallikkaṭṭu is considered to be a sort of offering (very often, a substitute for ancient blood-offerings). The deities mostly concerned are *Karuppaṉ, Muṉiyāṇṭi* and *Kāḷiyammaṉ,* but nowadays, jallikkaṭṭus are also performed for other gods during the annual temple festivals. (There is even a region with a large Christian population—mostly converts who formerly belonged to the *Mukkulattār*—where for three generations jallikkaṭṭus and Mañciviraṭṭus have been performed for Saint Anthony.)

There are two Jallikkaṭṭu seasons a year, the first starting on *māṭṭuppoṉkal,* and going on for about three months, during which jallikkaṭṭus are performed mainly for male deities, and the second in the Tamil month *āṭi* (July/August) during the festivals for Kāḷiyammaṉ and other female deities.

Jallikkaṭṭu rarely occurs in literature, but there is a group of folk-stories (*katai*) in which they figure importantly. One story, which tells the life of the regional hero Aḻakattēvar, a legendary character who lived about seven generations ago in villages to the west of Madurai, is virtually centered around jallikkaṭṭu. The story tells of the establishment of a new marriage-relation between families in two nearby villages. This relation lasts over three generations, during which the customary cross-cousin marriages take place between the families, until, one day, a girl refuses to marry her customary fiancé, Aḻakattēvar. This is almost like abrogating the dharmic order of the world; hence, the problem must be solved. The solution is found by holding a jallikkaṭṭu: the girl announces that she is willing to marry the man who will subdue all her seven bulls. Aḻakattēvar does so and finally gets his traditional bride; order is reinstituted. In many episodes of this story, jallikkaṭṭu is brought into close connection with the village deity Karuppaṉ and is clearly defined as a kind of offering.

Today, the term jallikkaṭṭu is often used for the cow and bullock races which take place in almost all Tamil villages on *māṭṭupoṅkal* day, but which have nothing in common with the real sport.

References

Dumont, Louis. 1986. *A south Indian subcaste: social organization and religion of the Pramalai Kallar.* Delhi: Oxford University Press.

Muttaiya, A. 1981. Maturai vaṭṭārattil callikkaṭṭum mañcivirattum. Thesis, Madurai Kamaraj University.

Niklas, Ulrike. 2000. Callikkaṭṭu—Embracing the Bull, Tamil Style. In *Newkolam,* vols. 5–6, July 2000. http://www.fas.nus.edu.sg/journal/kolam/index.htm.

ULRIKE NIKLAS

SEE ALSO
Buffalo; *Poṅkal*

JĀMDĀNĪ

Jāmdānī is a muslin of Bengali origin, with designs woven in on the loom. It was popular in the Mughal court of the sixteenth and seventeenth centuries and by Aurangzeb's reign (1658–1707) was included in a yearly tribute of cloth, *malbus khās* (royal clothing) paid by Bengal. Mughal noblemen wore robes made of jāmdānī as well as jāmdānī girdles called *patka.* Jāmdānī, along with other types of muslin, was exported to Europe until the mid-nineteenth century when weavers found it impossible to compete with European manufactured goods.

In the seventeenth century the royal workshops that supplied the Mughal court were located around Dhaka, as were the factories that supplied the East India Company in the eighteenth century. The short staple cotton that provided yarn for jāmdānī weaving was indigenous to the region. The air, too, had the necessary high moisture to prevent the fine yarn from breaking. Jāmdānī weaving continues to be concentrated round Dhaka today. Because of its close association with Dhaka, *jāmdānī sāṛī* are also known as *Ḍhākāi sāṛī.*

Woven on a pit loom (constructed so that the worker sits upright with his or her legs in a dug-out pit below the loom), jāmdānī weaving requires two craftsmen working together. The *kārigar* (master craftsman) sits on the right side of the loom, while the younger *hāgrid,* (from the Persian *shāgird,* apprentice), sits on the left. Motifs are worked into the fabric with the help of a smooth, pointed instrument called *kāṇḍul.* Short lengths of yarn are ranged across the warp and worked into the weaving.

The cost of jāmdānī depends on the yarn as well as the number and intricacy of the motifs. The finer the yarn, the more costly the fabric. Older jāmdānī were made of yarn of higher thread counts. Today, however, the yarn used is coarser, ranging from 40 to 80 counts. Traditionally, jāmdānī sāṛī were made of cotton yarn; jāmdānī are now being made increasingly in what is popularly termed half-silk—with the warp of silk and the weft of cotton. *Korā*s, or unbleached jāmdānī sāṛī with multicolored motifs, are popular, as are *sāṛī*s in a dark-blue or black field with motifs worked in silver and gold.

References

Sayeedur, Muhammad. 1993. *Jamdani.* Dhaka: Bangla Academy.

Taylor, James. 1840. *A sketch of the topography and statistics of Dacca.* Calcutta: G. H. Huttman, Military Orphan Press.

Watt, George. 1987 [1903]. *Indian art at Delhi, 1903: being the official catalogue of the Delhi exhibition, 1902–1903.* Reprint Edition. Delhi: Motilal Banarsidass.

Whitechapel Art Gallery. 1988. *Woven air: the muslin and kantha tradition of Bangladesh.* London: Whitechapel.

NIAZ ZAMAN

SEE ALSO
Handloom Weaving

JĀRĪ GĀN

The term "jārī gān" comes from the Persian word "zārī," meaning lamentation, and from the Bengali word "gān," meaning song or song recital. *Jārī gān* signifies an important class of Bengali narrative songs that are closely associated with the elegies of the festival of Muḥarram (first month of the Islamic lunar calendar), a time when Shī'a Muslims commemorate the deaths of their martyrs. The repertory of jārī gān also includes a wide range of other themes from Islamic lore. The underlying themes are so universal that, in Bengal, Sunni Muslims and even Hindus, Buddhists, and Christians enjoy the recitals.

The central themes of jārī songs concern the battle of Karbalā that occurred near the Euphrates River in 680 C.E. during the first ten days of the month of Muḥarram. The tragic incidents of this battle constitute the thematic material of sermons, chants, and pageantry during the Muḥarram festival worldwide. In the Bengali celebrations, poet-singers trained in the jārī gān style of extempore singing relate the Karbala episodes, telling how Ḥusayn, a grandson of the Prophet Moḥammed and the leader of a small band of Shī'a Muslims, was besieged in the desert by the army of a jealous Caliph and how they all perished. The women were taken captive, and it is said that the Muḥarram festival and its literature developed from their annual mourning rituals.

Although the characters and places of the Karbalā stories come from another culture and a distant region, they have been naturalized by jārī gān bards to reflect the world of the rural people among whom they mostly sing. Thus, Bengali audiences hearing the Karbalā events relive them as if they occurred in their own fields and homes.

The expression "jārī gān" also connotes a diffuse repertory of narrative themes that range from Biblical parables, such as that of Abraham and Isaac (Muslim: Ibrahim and Isma'īl), or of Joseph (Yūsuf) and his wicked brothers, to romances in which noble descendants of the Prophet are sent by Allah to convert Hindu princesses. Other jārī gān tales are imported from Perso-Arabic poetry, such as the story of "Isuf-Jolekā" (Joseph and Zulaykha) and "Laẏlā-Majnu" (Laila and Majnun). Many other tales are sung that have little to do with lamentation, but are nevertheless referred to as jārī gān.

Some time after the seventeenth century, when the Muḥarram festival was introduced in Bengal, jārī gān recitals expanded into a form of mass entertainment which by the nineteenth century attracted rural audiences in the thousands. The program of these performances could span as many as seven or eight nights and included several groups of jārī singers in sequence or paired in poetic dialogues. A night's program might also include popular songs other than the featured jārī gān songs to relieve the monotony of lengthy narrations.

A typical jārī group consists of a chief singer known as a *baẏāti* (maker of couplets) and his *dohār* (repeaters), generally a group of ten or twelve men. The dohār give emphasis to a phrase of poetry sung by the baẏāti by repeating it in chorus, or they sing refrains in rapid give-and-take with the baẏāti. They may interpolate songs borrowed from other repertories to give variety to the recital.

The baẏāti may alternate his metric singing with passages of dramatic declamation. He may talk to the audience or pose difficult questions during his recital for the baẏāti of a rival group to answer, a popular source of entertainment that is thought to have been adapted from Hindu competitions of poetic wit known as *kabi gān* (poet-songs). Jārī gān recitals in some districts of Bengal include *jārīnāc* (jārī-dance) in which the dohār dance in various formations.

Jārī gān singing is generally accompanied by instrumental music. A baẏāti may accompany himself by beating on a small drum, plucking a *dotārā* (a stringed instrument native to Bengali folk music), or playing on a fiddle. Often a small but lively band of musicians plays on local instruments, echoing sung phrases, maintaining rhythms, or playing softly in the background to emphasize a particular mood.

The standard verse form for jārī songs is the *paẏār* poetic meter inherited from ancient Indian epic poetry. Each line contains fourteen syllables; the second line of each couplet rhymes with the first one. The baẏāti interprets this meter in a chant-like tune with a compelling rhythm. An exceptionally talented baẏāti adds rhythmic and melodic variety, emphasizing the mood of his poetry without sacrificing the clarity of his words.

Before embarking on his chosen narrative, the baẏāti devotes as many couplets as he wishes to an invocation to Allah, and he often honors people and places as well. Without breaking the meter, he announces the subject of his story, which he may repeat at the narrative's conclusion, along with his name and even his address. In the course of his singing, the baẏāti may include witty philosophical and social commentary as well as jibes at rival singers.

In modern times, jārī gān singing survives mostly as entertainment in country fairs or in festivals of folk songs. Jārī gān songs can also be heard on commercial recordings, on the radio, and occasionally on television. A few women have become baẏāti, and many serve as dohār and instrumental accompanists. In 1971, jārī gān songs were composed to inspire Bangladeshis in their War of Liberation. The jārī gān style of performance is sometimes used to propagate ideas on such topics as family planning, proper nutrition, and hygiene. Although these non-jārī uses represent deviations from traditional jārī gān recitals, they testify to the popularity, resilience, and cogency of the jārī gān form.

References

Dunham, Mary Frances. 1997. *Jarigan: Muslim epic songs of Bangladesh*. Dhaka: University Press, Ltd.

Jasīmauddīna. 1968. *Jārīgāna*. Dhākā: Kendrīya Bāmlā-Unnayana-Borda.

Rahman, S. M. Lutfor. 1986. *Bangladeshi Jarigan*. Dhaka: Mrs. Anawara Rahman.

MARY FRANCES DUNHAM

SEE ALSO

Muḥarram; Song, Bengal; Story Literature, Persian

JĀTAKA TALES

The 547 *jātaka* ("birth stories") preserved in Pali recount how the aspiring *bodhisatta* (Sanskrit *bodhisatva*, "enlightened being"), in his previous animal and human incarnations, perfected various forms of spiritual and moral behavior [*pāramitās:* loving-kindness (*metta*), perseverance (*viriya*), even-mindedness (*upekhā*), morality (*sīla*), wisdom (*paññā*), and above all, selfless-giving (*dāna*)], which culminated karmically in his final rebirth as Prince Siddhattha, wherein he was finally prepared to experience enlightenment, to attain *nibbāṇa*, and to become the Buddha of our contemporary cosmic time and space. Regarded as *buddhāvacanā* ("sayings of the Buddha"), but not considered to be canonical literature per se, the jātaka may be the most popular form of all Buddhist literature among the religious laity of South and Southeast Asian Theravada Buddhism. Certainly the most accessible if not the most didactic, the jātaka offer tangible illustrations to the laity of what they, too, might achieve: if not enlightenment in this lifetime, at least favorable rebirths and progress along the path to eventual enlightenment in the future. Jātaka are an essential component of literature studied within the curricula of Buddhist schools, often function as pericopes for monks delivering sermons to the laity, and are often illustrated on *poya* (full-moon) holidays in the form of *pandal*s (hexagonal or octagonal panels of framed, almost cartooned, pictures encircled by variegated electric bulbs forming a rather spectacular marketplace display).

Historically, the jātaka are also an extremely important constituent of Buddhist temple art and cultic practice. They dominate the visual liturgies painted in nearly every surviving late medieval Sinhalese Buddhist temple in Sri Lanka and are illustrated in bronze reliefs at the bases of important *stūpa* at Pagan, Burma, and at northern Thailand stūpa complexes as well. They have also provided substantial inspiration for classical vernacular poetry written in Sinhala, Burmese, and Thai through late medieval times. The *Vessantara Jātaka,* for instance, the best known and longest of all jātaka, comprising the story of the Buddha's penultimate rebirth as a prince who willingly gave away all of his wealth (as well as his family) in resolute pursuit of the perfection of giving, was sculpted in detail in central India at the great Bharhut stūpa (reliquary) as early as the second century B.C.E. Later depictions are found at the Sanchi stūpa in the first century B.C.E. and in south India at Amaravati from the first through the third centuries C.E. The *Vessantara* was also painted in detail at the Ajanta cave complex in the fifth century. In Sri Lanka, it was painted in no less than seven important temples, royally refurbished during the eighteenth century Sinhala Buddhist cultural rennaisance. It also was the basis for the seventeenth century epic poem *Vessantara Jātaka Kavyaya* and was the subject of one of the most successful dramas ("Vessantara") in the history of modern Sinhalese theater in the twentieth century.

Each jātaka opens with a verse (*gātha*) drawn from one of the four *nikāya*s (sections) of the *Suttapiṭaka* (doctrinal "basket of discourses" of the Pali canon) and is followed by a brief preface giving the specific instance in which the story was purportedly told by the Buddha to his followers. The Buddha then proceeds to recall a signficant event, or series of events, in one of his manifold previous lives in which he behaviorally realized the existential verity of the doctrinal quotation first cited. This consistent pattern has led some scholars to surmise that the jātaka are, essentially, a popularized commentary on aspects of the Buddha's *dhamma* (teaching), intended to make his teachings on *sīla* (moral behavior) and *karma* accessible to a wider audience than one consisting only of monastic incumbents. Having told the illustrative tale to reaffirm a paradigm of moral behavior, the jātaka ends with the Buddha identifying the characters in the story, including himself, with some of those in attendance.

References

Cowell, E. B. 1895–1913. *The Jataka; or stories of the Buddha's previous births.* 6 vols. London: Luzac and Co. (for The Pali Text Society).

Gatellier, Marie. 1991. *Peintures murales du Sri Lanka: Ecole Kandyan XVIII–XIX siecle.* [Mural Paintings from Sri Lanka: the Kandyan School in the 18th and 19th Centuries]. 2 vols. Paris: École Française d'Extrême-Orient [French School of Asian Studies].

Gombrich, Richard and Cone, Margaret. 1977. *The perfect generosity of Prince Vessantara.* Oxford: The Clarendon Press.

Jones, John Garret. 1979. *Tales and teachings of the Buddha: The Jataka stories in relation to the Pali canon.* London: George Allen and Unwin.

JOHN CLIFFORD HOLT

SEE ALSO
Buddhism and Buddhist Folklore; Stūpa; Vessantara

JĀTRĀ/YĀTRĀ

Jātrā (from Sanskrit *yātrā,* meaning procession or journey) is a folk dramatic genre that incorporates music and dance and is performed primarily in the eastern Indian states of Bengal and Orissa. The jātrā season begins in the autumn and continues until the monsoons begin in June. It is usually performed on an open-air stage with the audience seated on all sides. Although, traditionally, jātrās had an all-male cast, women are now gaining access.

The origin of jātrā is variously attributed to the *Nāṭya Śāstra* (second century C.E.) and the rise of Vaisnavism, particularly as practiced by Śrī Caitanya (sixteenth century). Whatever the origin, the jātrā evolved and diversified through the centuries from mythological stories based on the lives of Kṛṣṇa, Rāma, Durgā, and Śiva, through historical tales, to the political *svādēśī* (Independence) jātrās, based on Gandhi's nonviolent movement and themes of untouchability. With the introduction of Western theater into Bengal by the British, the jātrā became a vehicle for political protest and social reform and finally fell into disrepute. Recently, however, jātrās have again gained in popularity and been revived, with the Orissan jātrās primarily focusing upon mythological themes in rural settings and the Bengali jātrās on sociopolitical themes in urban and semiurban settings.

References

Chattopadyaya, Nisikanta. 1976 [1882]. *The Yatras: or. the popular dramas of Bengal*. Calcutta: Rddhi. [London: Trubner & Co.]

Chowdhury, Santi P. 1978. *Bengal's theatre-in-the-round. Times of India Annual,* 4–48.

Dash. Dhiren. 1976. *Jatra-the-theatre*. Bhubaneswar: Kwalitv Press.

———. 1979. *Jātra: people's theatre of Orissa. Sangeet Natak: journal of the Sangeet Natak Akademi,* 52: 11–26.

———. 1981. *Jātra The People's Theatre of Orissa*. Bhubaneswar: Sneha Press.

Raha. Kironmoy. 1978. *Bengali theatre*. New Delhi: National Book Trust.

Sarkar, Pabitra. 1975. Jatra: the popular traditional theatre of Bengal. *Journal of South Asian Literature*. 10: 2–4, 87–107.

Vatsyayan, Kapila. 1980. *Traditional Indian theatre: multiple streams*. New Delhi: National Book Trust.

RATNA ROY

SEE ALSO

Pilgrimage; Theater and Drama

JEWELRY AND ADORNMENT

The great diversity of jewelry and adornment in the subcontinent reflects the complex social hierarchies and religious beliefs of urban and rural populations. Although many of the ornament styles present in the subcontinent have parallels in other regions of the world, unique styles of body ornament are distinctly South Asian in character and can be traced to the prehistoric and early historic periods.

During the late Upper Paleolithic and Mesolithic periods (before 10,000 to 6000 B.C.E.), cave paintings in central India depicted male and female figures wearing earrings, necklaces, bangles, belts, leg and ankle ornaments, hair ornaments, horned headdresses, and masks made of hanging beads or strings. Mesolithic burials with antler and bone ornaments suggest that most of these early forms of adornment were made of perishable materials such as bone, antler, shell, and plants. Body painting or tattooing may also be represented in some of the rock paintings.

In the earliest Neolithic burials at Mehrgarh, Pakistan (ca. 7000 B.C.E.), children as well as adults were buried with elaborate ornaments, including bracelets made of beads or circlets of shell, beaded anklets, necklaces, hair ornaments, and waist ornaments. Somewhat later, around 4000 B.C.E., painted terra-cotta figurines provide strong evidence for the use of pigments in ritual and decorative ways: henna-colored hair, eyes outlined with black pigment, and vermilion powder painted in the central part of the hair. With the rise of cities during the Indus Valley Civilization (2600–1900 B.C.E.), there was an explosion of new ornament styles and newly created raw materials used in ornaments. This dramatic change can be associated with the need for more distinctive ornament styles to differentiate the many different ethnic communities and occupational classes living in the cities and villages. Numerous styles of bangles and ankle ornaments are created from both natural and artificial materials. Finger and toe rings, stud earrings, and possible nose ornaments are seen for the first time in the Indus cities. A conical form of hair ornament as well as red carnelian pendants that may have been worn in the center of the forehead have also been recovered. These ornaments were made from precious metals such as silver, gold, copper or bronze, as well as from semiprecious stones, shell, ivory, terra-cotta, glazed faience, and decorated steatite.

Today, the symbolic meaning of ornaments is quite complex and varies by ethnic community. In most communities, however, ornamentation is used to enhance sensual beauty, to protect the individual from evil, and to control or enhance the power of the wearer. The wearing of ornaments begins with childhood and ends with death, when most people's ornaments are removed. During each stage of life, different forms of ornaments are worn, depending on the social class, religion, and economic status of the individual.

Children's jewelry is often quite functional and serves to protect the child during illness and physical development. Teething amulets are tied around the wrist of infants, and anklets with bells help the mother keep track of a child's movements. Amulets tied around the waist or arms protect the child, and ears are often pierced to cure fever and other childhood illnesses. In the Punjab, mothers often pray for a son and vow to adorn him with silver bangles and anklets for five years, after which the ornaments will be given to a holy person or donated to the tomb of the saint. Protective amulets may continue to be worn into old age, even though they soon become overshadowed by other forms of jewelry or clothing. Girls begin to wear distinctive jewelry quite early on, especially in communities that practice child marriage, even though this practice is officially banned. Boys are often dressed as girls to confuse the evil spirits who prey on male children. Eventually, as they pass into puberty, boys tend to retain only bangles, earrings, and necklaces, depending on the specific social class or ethnic community.

In adulthood, the differences between men's and women's ornaments are generally defined by specific social or ethnic communities. In some societies men do not wear earrings or bangles, while in others, these are the norm. Men in South Asia rarely wear nose rings or nose studs, both of which are distinctively female ornaments. Among Hindu communities, women, who are considered the embodiment of *śaktī* (the female principle), often wear bangles, anklets, nose rings, earrings, etc. to protect the major orifices and extremities, and to control the power that can emanate from these parts of the body. The control and protection of these powers is something that is particular to women and not men. For example, the nose is a very important channel for life-sustaining air, but only women wear nose ornaments to protect this part of the body. Bangles protect the woman's own body, but by wearing bangles, especially iron, a woman also protects her husband, and thereby the rest of her family, from evil powers. Forehead ornaments are worn to enhance beauty, but also have a symbolic connection to the third eye or spiritual power. When a woman's husband dies, all of her ornaments are removed or broken, and she is only allowed to wear a few protective amulets.

Perhaps the most important function of ornaments is that they serve to define a person's social and economic status and reinforce ideology. Jewelry worn by women is particularly important as insurance against hard times and unsupportive husbands. Much of a woman's jewelry is obtained during marriage rituals from relatives or from the husband's family, either as a dowry or as bride wealth. The styles of ornaments identify a woman's religion and ethnic affiliation, with distinctive ornaments being worn by different classes of Muslims, Hindus, Jain, Sikh, Christian, and other communities. When these ornaments are worn, anyone who is familiar with the symbolism can identify the caste, class, and religion of a woman without ever speaking to her. This is also the case with ornaments worn by men. This form of nonverbal communication helps to reduce conflict in urban centers by informing strangers about a person's affiliations.

Over and above all of these symbolic and functional reasons, people wear jewelry and adornment for the joy and beauty of ornamentation. The sound of ankle bells or clinking bracelets is a common theme in poetry, evoking the long-awaited approach, or departure, of a lover.

References

Alkazi, R. 1983. *Ancient Indian costume*. New Delhi: Art Heritage Books.

Brijbhushan, Jamila. 1979. *Masterpieces of Indian jewelry*. Bombay: Taraporewala.

Coomaraswamy, Ananda. 1913. *Arts and crafts of India and Ceylon*. London: T. N. Foulis.

Jarrige, Catherine. 1988. *Les figurines humaines au Baluchistan* [Human Figurines of Baluchistan]. In *Les Cités oubliées de l'Indus*, ed. J.-F. Jarrige, 65–70. Paris: Musée National des Arts Asiatiques Guimet.

Kenoyer, J. Mark. 1992. Ornament styles of the Indus tradition: Evidence from Recent Excavations at Harappa, Pakistan. *Paléorient* 17(2): 79–98.

Mathpal, Yashodar. 1984. *Prehistoric rock paintings of Bhimbetka central India*. New Delhi: Abhinav Publications.

JONATHAN MARK KENOYER

SEE ALSO

Bangles; Beads; Dowry and Bridewealth; Dress; Punjab

JEWISH FOLKLORE

Two Jewish communities in South Asia are the Cochin Jews and the Bene Israel Jews. These communities differ in their culture and religious practices.

Cochin Jews

While their faithful adherence to "high tradition" Judaism marks the Cochin Jews of Kerala off from their Hindu, Muslim, and Christian neighbors, a variety of folk practices and beliefs serve as cultural bridges between them and their Malayali cultural milieu.

The Cochin Jews invest much creativity in articulating an origin legend that stresses roots in both Jerusalem and Cranganore, the traditional capital of the Chera dynasty, known as Shingly in medieval Jewish geography. The Cochin Jews claim they arrived in Cranganore directly from Jerusalem, fleeing the Roman sack of the city in 70 C.E., and were warmly welcomed by the Maharaja. Three hundred years later, the Maharaja, whom the Cochin Jews refer to as Cheraman Perumal, gave a copper plate charter (which scholars date from the beginning of the eleventh century) to the leader of the Jews, Joseph Rabban, granting him proprietary and taxation rights over Anjuvannam, which the Jews claimed was an independent principality. The Maharaja and Joseph Rabban became archetypes of Hindu–Jewish relations in Kerala, celebrated in Malayali wedding songs which state that "every bridegroom is Joseph Rabban."

Women's religious life shows some Malayali influence, especially of the matrilineal Nayar nobility. For example, the synagogue's *parohet* (curtains before the Holy Ark) are made from women's festive *mundu* (sarongs), a display of the esteemed position of women in this community. During their most distinctive celebration, *Simhat Torah* (the autumn festival of "rejoicing in the Torah"), scores of mundu decorate the synagogue, a reflection of the royal Nayars' matrilineality.

Mystics also serve as bridges between the Jews and their neighbors. One in particular, Nehemia Mota (d. 1631), has become the center of a local saint cult. His tomb in Jew Town is revered by Hindus, Muslims, and Christians as well as Jews, and Nehemia Mota functions as a "village god," efficacious in settling disputes, in intercessionary healing, and in the fulfillment of vows (especially by women). Similarly, neighbors believe that water from the synagogue's *miqveh* (ritual bath) and oil from its *ner tamid* (eternal light) have a powerful healing quality.

The Cochin Jews reflect Indian social structure in being divided into endogamous subcastes. The earliest division, documented from the sixteenth century on, was between those who purported to be *meyuhasim* (Jews with attestable descent from Israel) and a group they derided by referring to them as *meshuhrarim* (manumitted slaves). In all likelihood, the former were Sephardic immigrants, and the latter were indigenous Jews. Under Portuguese colonial influence, this legal distinction was racialized, and the two groups became known as "White" and "Black" respectively, with a subgroup of *gerim* (converts) and meshuhrarim attached to each, resulting in four subcastes.

Bene Israel Jews

Unlike the Cochin Jews who have maintained contact with Jews elsewhere, the isolated Bene Israel of Mumbai (former Bombay) did not maintain strong traditions of Judaic learning and observance to set them apart from their Hindu and Muslim neighbors on the Konkan coast of Maharashtra. The origin of the Bene Israel is unknown, but their oral history tells of an Israeli shipwreck off Navgaon, on the Konkan coast of Maharashtra near modern Mumbai, in which seven men and seven women were washed ashore and became the ancestors of all Bene Israel. Thus cut off from world Jewry, the Bene Israel are said to have been "lost" Jews who preserved only vestiges of Judaism. They refrained from labor on *Shabbat* (Saturday), and thus were known as *shanwar teli* (Saturday oil-pressers). They circumcised male infants on the eighth day. They retained the rudiments of *kashrut* (Jewish dietary laws), and they would recite the *Shema* (the credo of Judaism) on occasions when prayer was appropriate. They retained some festival practices, but not the narrative structure of the holidays. Like the Cochin Jews, the Bene Israel had subcastes, the Gora (White) and Kala (Black). The larger Gora group claimed descent from the shipwrecked couples, and the Kala were either converts or the offspring of concubinage.

It was because of their tenacity in their attenuated Judaism that they are said to have been "discovered" by David Rahabi, whom they say was the brother of Moses Maimonides (twelfth-century Judaism's intellectual giant), but who may have been instead an eighteenth-century merchant from Cochin. Rahabi is reputed to have brought three young Bene Israel to Cochin for instruction in Judaism; they later returned to the Konkan region as religious leaders. Over the next two centuries, Bene Israel made the remarkable transition into the modern, urban Jews of Mumbai. In the process they discontinued many "Indianized" practices.

Today, pregnancy, birth, and circumcision practices among the Bene Israel evidence a high degree of acculturation to Maharashtrian culture. For example, during the seventh month of pregnancy a woman with five fresh fruits on her lap, accompanied by her husband, will customarily board a small boat from which a coconut is tossed into the water. Returning home, the *malida* rite is performed, a ritual using parched rice, fruit, flowers, and myrtle. The woman is bedecked with green bangles, and a dinner party is held. Seclusion, special foods, baths, and amulets follow the birth. Circumcision (*brit milah*) is a defining Judaic rite, and the Bene Israel augment the ceremony with such localized practices as a palanquin procession, gifts of ornaments, sugar cakes, citrons, and myrtle.

References

Isenberg, Shirley Berry. 1988. *India's Bene Israel: a comprehensive inquiry and sourcebook*. Berkeley: Judah L. Magnes Museum.

Johnson, Barbara C. 1986. The emperor's welcome: reconsiderations of an origin theme in Cochin Jewish folklore. In *Jews in India*, ed. Thomas A. Timberg, 161–176. New York: Advent.

Katz, Nathan. 1990. The ritual enactments of the Cochin Jews: the powers of purity and nobility. *Journal of Ritual Studies* 4(2): 189–225.

Katz, Nathan and Ellen S. Goldberg. 1993 [1988]. Jewish "apartheid" and a Jewish Gandhi. *Jewish Social Studies* 50(3–4): 147–176.

Kehimkar, Haeem Samuel. 1937. *The history of the Bene-Israel of India*. Tel Aviv: Dayag Press.

NATHAN KATZ

SEE ALSO
Judaism

JHUMUR JĀTRĀ DRAMA

Jhumur jātrā is a secular musical drama based on folk romances that is popular in rural areas over most of Bangladesh. Jhumur jātrā is performed by both amateur and professional troupes that include actor-singers and musicians. An entire professional orchestra may include harmonium, two cornets, clarinet, flute, synthesizer, a pair of *juṛi, ḍhol, ḍholak,* bām̐yā-tabla, and a pair of *ḍugi*-tabla. According to Mohammad Jaffar Mollah, a "master" (director) of an amateur troupe from Madan Hat village in Natore district, jhumur jātrā is so named because of the abundant use of songs in jhumur rhythm (a cycle of eight beats). Jaffar Mollah's amateur troupe is drawn from his relatives, mostly Muslim farmers.

They usually perform during the months of Āśvin, Kārtik, Agrahāẏaṇ, and Pauṣ (mid-September to mid-January) when harvesting is over and there is ample free time. Professional troupes may comprise both Hindus and Muslims.

Amateur troupes usually perform jhumur jātrā in the outer courtyard of rural homesteads, whereas professionals perform in public spaces. The performance space is a square platform some eighteen inches high and about twelve feet on each side. About four feet away from the corners of the platform stand four bamboo posts to support a canopy. Kerosene or electric lamps, hung from the posts, light the performance space. A ramp runs down from the stage to a passage leading to a greenroom (*sāj-ghar*) beyond the audience space. Spectators sit on all four sides of the central platform, the men separated from the women. The positions of the musicians (*ẏantrī-dal* or *bājiẏār*) and choral singers (*dohār*) vary. In one performance observed by the author in Madan Hat, Natore, in December 1994, musicians playing harmonium, bām̐ẏā-tabla, flute, and juṛi sit on the ground adjacent to the ramp, while the five choral singers sit on the opposite side away from the ramp; at another performance musicians playing harmonium, ḍholak, and juṛi sit together with six choral singers adjacent to the ramp. Unlike the amateur troupes, at least some major professional troupes have no choral singers. A larger group of musicians may sit divided into two groups, wind instruments on one side, percussionists on the other. In both amateur and professional performances, a prompter sits at the corner nearest the ramp, together with a stagehand who manages props, rings a bell to signal act changes, and blows a whistle to mark entrances of characters.

The popular plays are known by name, and some few are published in standard Bengali, in mixed prose and verse. Subject matter most often involves the separation and eventual reunion of lovers, and all plays have a proliferation of characters, scenes, and interspersed songs. For example, one typical, unpublished play is *Nachimaner Banabās* which relates the magically mediated birth of a son to a childless royal father, the separation of that young hero and his pregnant bride, the birth of their son whose smiles scatter rubies and whose tears are pearls, and the family's eventual reunion. The play has forty-five songs, forty-three scenes, and thirty-two characters.

Performances may begin with a patriotic song presented by four or five female performers or female impersonators, or with a broadly addressed bandanā (song of salutation). The bandanā may also be addressed broadly to Allah, the Prophet, various other Islamic religious-historical figures, some Hindu deities, key geographical locations, and all the Hindu and Muslim spectators. Dances by women are included in some plays and not in others; female parts are also sometimes taken by men.

Scenery and props are minimal and highly schematic. For example, a teacher sitting on a chair and students sitting on the ground represent a school, and a king sitting and couriers standing represent a royal audience hall. A ship may be represented by two oarsmen rowing "oars" made of bamboo poles as they sing and slowly walk the bare stage. In turn, flying on the back of a bird is represented by one performer being covered with a white cloth, bending forward from the waist, and waving his hands like wings while another performer sits on his back. Costume is colorful and similar to historical jātrā drama styles. Animals are represented with masks, such as the popular tiger, with a papier-mâché mask and a jumpsuit of imitation leopard-skin fabric.

Historical developments in jhumur jātrā are reflected in the presence or absence of features in contemporary plays. Plays reflecting the style of the mid-nineteenth century lack act or scene divisions, and yet include choral singers, female impersonators, bandanā addressed to Nirañjana (the "Stainless One," a Hindu concept of deity), figures venerated by Shiite Muslims, and Brahmanical deities. The presence of act divisions, the appearance of the *vivek* character, and the absence of choral singers bespeak an early twentieth-century style. Post-Partition (after 1947) changes include the presence of actresses and the absence of bandanā.

SYED JAMIL AHMED

SEE ALSO

Jātrā/Yātrā; Song, Bengal; Theater and Drama

JIHĀD POETRY

The successful coup d'etat initiated in April 1978 by Afghan Marxists inspired a widespread popular resistance, one manifestation of which was the production of anti-Marxist poetry. Poets representing different ethnic and linguistic groups in Afghanistan produced their own compositions, the vast majority of which were recited and sung locally but neither preserved nor widely disseminated. A fraction of the resistance poetry did receive a more permanent form and broader popularity, however, thanks largely to the common availability of portable tape recorders. The poetry most widely distributed via tape cassette was that produced in the Pakhtu (Pashtu) language by Afghan refugees living in Pakistan. According to informant reports, tape cassettes began to appear in local markets in Peshawar, Quetta, and other centers of refugee concentration in the months following the Marxist takeover. The poems on these cassettes usually featured a single vocalist (often the poet himself), a harmonium, a tabla, and a *rabāb* (lute) or other stringed instrument.

The poems produced in the early period of the resistance tended to reflect traditional Pakhtu poetic forms, such as the *qaṣīda* (a type of ode), and its themes are of the sort associated with the famous seventeenth century poet Khushhāl Khān Khattak. Thus, one finds in this poetry professions of the poet's willingness to die in battle to defend honor; sardonic denunciations of the immorality of the enemy; invocations of ancestors who won glory in war; satiric rebukes of those tribes and ethnic groups perceived as unwilling to take up arms; and finally, exhortations to all listeners to live up to their cultural legacy by rushing to the field of battle. According to eyewitnesses, cassettes produced and sold in Pakistani bazaars were carried back inside Afghanistan and were avidly played during the period when many tribes and groups were deciding how to respond to the change in government. These reports indicate that the message of these poems, couched as it was in a familiar and powerfully evocative idiom, provided an effective counterweight to heavy-handed Marxist propaganda broadcast over Kabul radio and enunciated by newly appointed government officials.

Following the Soviet invasion of December 1979, the taped verse produced by Afghan refugees in Pakistan began to move away from heroic and exhortatory themes to a more sober and meditative poetry that is in some ways reminiscent of the mystical religious verse of another seventeenth century Pakhtu poet, Rahman Baba. Instead of the defiant exhortations to honor and bravery that characterized the first stage of resistance poetry, one finds in this second stage laments for the absent beloved (in this instance, fallen friends and kinsmen) and dark ruminations on the evil represented by communism, the Soviets, and their "puppets" in Kabul.

While Islam was repeatedly invoked in the earlier poetry as one of those enduring values that must be defended, the ethical pivot of the first poems was honor. In this later poetry, Islam became the ethical center, and the reasons for this seem to be several. First and most importantly, it is clear that poets (in many cases, the same poets who had earlier produced heroic verses) were responding to the reality that people were being killed on an unprecedented scale. In the first poems, death was still in the future and served primarily as a rhetorical device—that which a man faced in the affirmation of his honor and the attainment of renown. Later, however, death became a pervasive reality, and poets felt the need to affirm its meaning by referring to the Islamic belief that those who die in the path of jihād, or religious struggle, will be rewarded with eternal residence in paradise.

A second factor in the changing nature of poetry was that warfare bore little resemblance to the heroic combat depicted in early poems. Thus, while poets in the first stage of the resistance romantically depicted men with swords rushing into battle and facing the enemy in hand-to-hand duels, many of those who died when the fighting became severe did so as a result of bombardment, helicopter strafing, artillery shelling, and other impersonal means of destruction. Likewise, the casualties of war were not always warriors. Women, children, and the elderly received no immunity from the mechanical engines of war unleashed following the Soviet invasion, and the disparity between this brutal reality and the heroic vision of warfare as an enterprise of eager and able-bodied young men helped to create a sense of dissonance that undermined the credibility and relevance of earlier poetic conceits.

Taped cassettes featuring poems of martyrdom and loss continued to be produced for a short time in the early 1980s. However, the popularity of these tapes was small in comparison to the earlier heroic poetry, and fewer and fewer new tapes appeared in the bazaar. One probable reason for this is that it became increasingly difficult to summon up original poetic responses to the demoralizing reality of ongoing death, destruction, and exile, particularly when the war dragged on year after year. According to some informants, including poets, however, a more sinister reason for the disappearance of poetry was that the Islamic political parties who took control of the resistance after the Soviet invasion actively suppressed independent poets, particularly those who were inclined to cast a satiric eye on the corruption and hypocrisy of party leaders.

Whether or not this accusation is true, it is the case that from the mid-1980s on, new cassettes became scarce in the marketplace, and poetry in general returned to its roots as an individual pursuit, with poets keeping the recitation of their verses within a narrow circle of family and friends. The only exception to this rule was poetry produced by the political parties themselves. All of the parties had active propaganda departments and published poetry periodically in their many newspapers and magazines. For the most part, these poems were panegyric odes to fallen martyrs (almost exclusively commanders and other party loyalists) and generic praise poems for the Prophet Ṃuhammad.

References

Edwards, David B. 1993. Words in the balance: The poetics of political dissent in Afghanistan. In *Russia's Muslim frontiers: new directions in cross-cultural analysis,* ed. Dale F. Eickelman, 114–129. Bloomington, Indiana: University of Indiana Press.

Grima, Benedicte. 1992. *The performance of emotion among Paxtun women: "the misfortunes which have befallen me."* Austin: University of Texas Press.
Shalinsky, Audrey C. 1993. Women's roles in the Afghanistan jihad. *International Journal of Middle East Studies* 25(4): 661–675.
———. *Long years of exile.* 1993. Lanham, Md.: University Press of America.

DAVID B. EDWARDS

SEE ALSO
Afghanistan; Cassettes; Muslim Folklore and Folklife; Refugee Lore

JINN

The belief in spirits called *jinn* is ubiquitous among the Muslim peoples of Central and South Asia. Originating in pre-Islamic Arabia, this belief was incorporated into Islam by the Prophet Muḥammad, who affirmed the existence of the jinn. When Islam spread outside of Arabia, it took with it the belief in jinn and other supernatural beings. In the Qur'ān, Islam's sacred text, the jinn are mentioned along with angels (*malāika*), and demons (*shayāṭīn*), as three categories of beings created by God in addition to "mankind." The Muslim belief in the jinn is therefore based on the highest religious authority. The jinn have been the subject of theological treatises and appear in various folk traditions from Morocco to India. In the famous *1001 Nights,* they appear in English as genies.

Jinn are considered to be elemental creatures, made of "unsmoking" fire. They are incorporeal, but capable of assuming human or animal form. They have the ability to fly and are endowed with many other magical powers. Some jinn are "believers" and obedient to Allah's will. These jinn, it is said, flocked to Muḥammad's side with "open ears" whenever he disclosed God's revelation to the people (Qur'an lxii. I). Other jinn are in the service of *Iblīs* (Satan) and are the harbingers of misfortune, sickness, and death. These jinn roam at night, haunt houses, possess people, cause insanity, and lead people astray. Only the most devout Muslims are safe from such jinn attacks. Those who are jinn-afflicted must seek the assistance of holy men, who are able to neutralize the effects of the jinn.

References

Ashur, Mustafa. 1993. *The Jinn in the Qur'an and the Sunna.* London: Dar al-Taqwa.
Westermarck, Edward. 1978 [1933]. *Pagan survivals in Mohammedan civilisation.* London: Macmillan.

H. SIDKY

SEE ALSO
Islam; Muslim Folklore and Folklife; Supernatural Beings

JUDAISM

There were approximately thirty-five thousand Jews in India in 1947, at the time of Independence. By 2001, emigration, primarily to Israel, had reduced their number to about six thousand, but there were about fifty thousand Israelis of Indian origin. There are three major Jewish communities in India: the Cochin Jews, the Bene Israel, and the Baghdadis. The Cochin Jews have resided on the Malabar coast in Kerala for at least a millennium and possibly two. They were well positioned in Malayali society and have adapted Hindu religious symbols and have practices within the framework of Judaic law (*Halakha*). The Bene Israel of Mumbai (formerly Bombay) and the Konkan coast of Maharashtra were "lost" Jews who lived as an oil-pressing caste (*shanwar teli*), preserving vestigial Judaic practices. These practices led to their "discovery" and, ultimately, to their transformation into modern, urban Jews. The Baghdadis are Arabic-speaking Jews from the Middle East who settled in port cities—primarily Mumbai, Calcutta, and Rangoon—at the beginning of the British era. They identified more with British than Indian culture, from which they remained aloof; consequently, their religious practices have evidenced little Indian influence.

"In order to understand our community," Cochin Jews say, "you must see three things: *Simhat Torah* (the autumn festival of "rejoicing in the Torah"), *Pesah* (the spring festival that commemorates the Exodus of the Jews from Egypt), and a wedding." Indeed, in these three celebrations it is most clear how symbol and ritual complexes were borrowed from their Hindu neighbors, within the constraints of normative Judaic practice.

During Simhat Torah, the synagogue's Torah scrolls are displayed on a temporary Ark and are carried in more processions—both within and without the synagogue—than elsewhere in the Jewish world. After returning the scrolls to the permanent Ark, the temporary Ark is ritually demolished; the entire ritual is set to the accompaniment of locally composed Hebrew songs. These singular behaviors reflect Hindu temple festivals in which the *murthi* (image of the deity), the analog to the Torah scrolls, is displayed publicly on a cart (like the temporary Ark), taken on a royal procession (as in the additional Torah processions), and then destroyed (as in the dismantling of the temporary Ark). None of these borrowings violate Judaic law, and they serve to integrate the "foreign" Jewish community into a traditional Hindu culture.

During Pesah, ascetic themes predominate. The Judaic avoidance of leavening (*hamets*) is exaggerated. Homes are repainted, wells emptied and scrubbed, pains are taken to ensure that all food is especially "pure," and Gentile friends are avoided during the eight days of the festival. This ascetic Pesah reflects the brahmanic valuation of purity and is a mechanism by which the Jews attain high-caste status.

Jewish weddings in Cochin are as elaborate as in any Hindu community, sometimes lasting two weeks. Brides affix the *tali,* a necklace symbolic of a married woman's status and power. Women sing folk songs in Malayalam that liken the bridegroom to Joseph Rabban, who, according to local traditions, was a Jewish prince under whose leadership the Jews were granted autonomy in 379 C.E. by a monarch called Cheraman Perumal. As in Hindu weddings, the bride and bridegroom are treated as royalty.

The most distinctive religious practices of the Bene Israel revolve around Eliahu Hanabi (Elijah the Prophet), patron and protector of the community. Eliahu is said to have visited the village of Khandala on the Konkan coast, where markings on some rocks are said to be scratches from the prophet's chariot wheels. Eliahu is revered throughout the Jewish world, and many intriguing folk traditions about him developed, but nowhere is he so revered as among the Bene Israel.

Khandala is the favorite pilgrimage site for the Bene Israel, who journey to the site to fulfill vows. Pilgrimage to a cave associated with Eliahu near Haifa in Israel, and performing the malida rite there is another important identity marker for the Bene Israel as an *edah* (ethnic group). The malida rite is named for a parched rice mixture, similar to ones used ritually by both Hindus and Muslims in Maharashtra. The malida mixture, along with a variety of fruits, flowers and myrtle, are blessed in Hebrew, and songs to Eliahu are chanted in thanksgiving. The rite is performed only on auspicious occasions.

While the Cochin and Bene Israel Jews express their sense of belonging by adapting Hindu symbols and behaviors in their religious traditions, the Baghdadi Jews use their religion to draw boundaries between themselves and their Indian milieu. Since they aspire to be accepted as European, the Baghdadis have increasingly distanced themselves from their Bene Israel co-religionists in Mumbai. For example, despite initial amity and cooperation, the Baghdadis eventually would not count Bene Israel for their *minyan* (prayer quorums), nor eat meat slaughtered by their *shohetim* (ritual slaughterers), and, ultimately, barred them from their synagogues and cemeteries. They have preserved the traditions and liturgical styles of their "home" synagogues in Basra or Damascus, and, compared with the Cochin Jews and the Bene Israel, their religious practices evidence very little borrowing from Indian culture.

References

Isenberg, Shirley Berry. 1988. *India's Bene Israel: a comprehensive inquiry and sourcebook*. Berkeley: Judah L. Magnes Museum.

Johnson, Barbara C. 1985. "Our community" in two worlds: the Cochin Paradesi Jews in India and Israel. Ph.D. dissertation, Department of Anthropology, University of Massachusetts.

Katz, Nathan. 2001. *Who are the Jews of India?* Berkeley: University of California Press.

Katz, Nathan, and Ellen S. Goldberg. 1993. *The last Jews of Cochin: Jewish identity in Hindu India*. Columbia: University of South Carolina Press.

Kehimkar, Haeem Samuel. 1937. *The history of the Bene-Israel of India*. Tel Aviv: Dayag Press.

Roland, Joan G. 1989. *Jews in British India: identity in a colonial era*. Hanover, N.H.: Brandeis University Press, distributed by University Press of New England.

Timberg, Thomas A., ed. 1986. *Jews in India*. New York: Advent.

NATHAN KATZ

SEE ALSO

Fairs and Festivals; Jewish Folklore; Life Cycle Rituals: Marriage; Processions; Song; Syncretism

JUNJAPPA

Junjappa is a popular deity and cultural hero of Kāḍugollas, a Kannada speaking tribe in transition from pastoralism to agriculture, living in Tumkur, Chitradurga, and Bellary Districts in South Central Karnataka. The tradition of Junjappa includes ritual performances in the form of daily worship in temples, annual religious fairs called *Jātres,* and an elaborate narrative epic, the *Epic of Junjappa,* about the deity performed by religious minstrels called *gaṇeyavaru* (singers who play on an unusually long (three-foot) bamboo flute, called a *gaṇe*). Although Junjappa is a cultural hero of the Kāḍgollas, people of many other castes worship him. The belief that he has the power to cure deadly snake and scorpion bites is widely held, and people of all castes come to his temples for this reason.

Junjappa is represented in different forms: sword, gaṇe, stone, termite mound, serpent, *lingam* (a phallic representation of the god, Śiva), and as a warrior sitting on a bronze horse. Priests of Junjappa use the sacred gaṇe as a representation of Junjappa during divination sessions.

The temple of Junjappa is a round thatched hut, the traditional form of a Kāḍugolla house. Simply structured jātres are performed annually at important traditional centers, such as *Bēvinahaḷḷi* and *Hāgalawāḍi* villages in Tumkur District, and *Dummi* village in Shimoga District. The devotees bring *ghī* (clarified butter) from their houses and pour it in the lamppost set up for this purpose; the lamp burns for one month during the *Dīpāvaḷi* festival time (October). Devotees who have been cured of snake or scorpion bites offer figures of snakes and scorpions made of gold, silver, or copper plating as a fulfillment of committed vows (*parake*).

The staunch devotees of Junjappa are called *Kāṇikeyavaru*. Following the sacred bull of Junjappa (called *Junjappa Basava*), they go to *Kāḍugolla* settlements (*haṭṭis*) while carrying an image of Junjappa in the form of a brass-plated snake. This image is tied to a gaṇe and decorated with colored cloth and peacock feathers. The devotees collect offerings in the form of money called *kāṇike* to be passed on to the temple of Junjappa.

The length of performance of the *Junjappa Epic* varies from half an hour to fourteen hours, the variability depending on which and how many of the episodes of his life that are sung. In the men's performance, one person sings the epic and another person plays a gaṇe. Men might sing for the sheer pleasure of it, and some renowned singers might be invited to other villages to sing. Male priests usually sing portions the epic and play the gaṇe as a prelude to their divination activities. Women, in groups of two to four or more, also sing the *Junjappa Epic* on various occasions, such as during processions, or as a form of prayer when sitting up all night attending a person sick with a serious disease. Women do not accompany their singing with a gaṇe, and men and women do not perform together. Men's and women's performances are, in fact, quite different in both text and delivery styles. The men's narrative is more prosaic and formulaic, whereas the women's narrative is more poetic and rhythmic.

The epic of Junjappa is a story of three generations of a cow-herding family: Junjappa, his father Kenguri Mallegowḍa, and grandfather Dēvara Dayamāra. The stories of the father and grandfather closely resemble one another. Both of them were dedicated cowherds when they were forced to get married, but they did not stay with their wives. The two brides, Chinnamma and Kambakka, faced many hardships as they were tortured by the other family members before finally joining their husbands and begetting children.

The grandfather, Dēvara Dayamāra, and Kambakka died from hunger and thirst deep in a mountain forest. Their son, Kenguri Mallegowḍa, was nurtured by his paternal aunt and, at a later stage, by Honnahaṭṭi Alēgowḍa of an agricultural caste. He and Chinnamma had three sons, Junjappa, Māraṇṇa, and Mylaṇṇa, and one daughter, Mārakka. Following Kenguri Mallegowḍa's death, Chinnamma suffered much at the hands of family members.

Junjappa's story consists of four parts: his supernatural birth (it is believed he was born through his mother's backbone), his adventures, his death, and his post-death adventures causing the destruction of his enemies and performing miraculous cures for his worshipers. Major points of the epic include his battles against the local chieftains, called Pāḷayagars, belonging to the Mēsabēḍa (hunter) community in connection with the grazing of his cattle, winning eight different battles with the help of his trusted and ferocious bull, Baḍamyla, and his mild brothers, Māraṇṇa and Mylaṇṇa, and his conflicts with his jealous maternal uncles. The uncles invite Junjappa to dinner, forcing his sister Mārakka to serve him poisoned food against her will. Even though he knows his uncles' strategy, Junjappa is bound by tribal custom and etiquette to consume food given by his sister, and so chooses death rather than refuse his sister's offering. Before dying, though, he burns his uncles' settlement. And as a result of his tragic death, Junjappa was deified.

References

Blackburn, Stuart. 1985. Death and deification: Folk cults in Hinduism. *History of Religions*. 24(3): 255–74.

Paramashivaiah, J. S. 1979. *Daksina Karnātaka Janapada Kāvya Prakāragalu* (Genres of folk poetry of southern Karnataka). Mysore: Prasaranga, University of Mysore.

Shankaranarayana, T. N. 1982. *Kādugollara Sampradāyagalu Mattu Nambikegalu* (Customs and Beliefs of Kāḍugollas). Mysore: Prasaranga, University of Mysore.

Shankaranarayana, T. N. 1991. "Three Folk Epics," *Encyclopedia of the folk culture of Karnataka*. Madras: Institute of Asian Studies.

T. N. SHANKARANARAYANA

SEE ALSO

Dīvālī/Dīpavālī; Epic; Heroes and Heroines; Karnataka

K

KĀFĪ

Kāfī constitute a genre of Muslim mystical songs popular in Pakistan, based on regional folk melodies, and referring to heroes and heroines of well-known and beloved regional romances. The heroines of the tales typically symbolize the soul, seeking union with the eternal Beloved. The meetings, separations, and trials of the heroic couple symbolize different facets of mystical experience in ways that appeal to a popular audience. The kāfī poetic form is said to derive from the Arabic *qaṣīdāh,* a monorhyme ode. The kāfī is always meant to be sung, with the first or second line used as a refrain.

Major Sufi poets of Punjab and Sindh, such as Sheikh Farīduddīn Maśud Ganj-ī Shakār, Shāh Husain, Bulleh Shāh, Shāh Abdul Latīf, and Sachal Sarmast, all composed kāfī with wide appeal to common people that are still performed today. While kāfī became associated with one particular musical mode in the Hindustani *raga* system, in Pakistan today kāfī may be sung in any mode. True to its folk roots, kāfī is not knitted to one particular musical style, though it is usually sung solo. Famous contemporary singers include the female singers Pathana Khan and Abida Parveen. Pathana Khan uses harmonium, *sarangī,* and *tabla* as in classical Hindustani tradition, whereas Abida Hussein's ensemble includes various folk drums and percussion, harmonium, and keyboard.

In Sindh, where kāfī is the most popular musical form, dervishes (*faqir,* religious mendicants) accompany kāfī with *yaktaro* (a one- or two-stringed plucked lute providing drone and rhythm) played with one hand and wooden clappers (*chappar*) in the other, dancing as well while singing and playing their own accompaniment. Groups of dervishes singing and dancing in chorus in this manner perform the songs as devotional offerings dedicated to the *murshid* (Sufi guide or teacher) in his presence or at his *dargāh* (court).

References

Abbasi, Muhammad Yusuf. 1992. *Pakistani culture: a profile.* Islamabad: National Institute of Historical and Cultural Research.

Abbasi, Tanveer, ed. 1989. *Sachal Sarmast.* Khairpur, Sind: Sachal Chair, Shah Abdul Latif University.

Baloch, N. A. 1973. *Development of music in Sind.* Hyderabad: Sind University Press.

Nizami, Khaliq Ahmad. 1973 [1955]. *The life and times of Shaikh Farid-u'd-din Ganj-i-Shakar.* Reprint, Delhi: Idārah-i Adabiyat-i Dihlī.

Puri, J. R., and Shangari, T. R., eds. and trans. 1986. *Bulleh Shah: the love-intoxicated iconoclast.* Amritsar: Radha Soami Satsang Beas.

Sakata, Hiromi Lorraine. 2000. Devotional music of Pakistan. In *Garland encyclopedia of world music, Vol. 5: South Asia: The Indian Subcontinent,* pp. 751–761.

LORRAINE SAKATA

SEE ALSO

Dargāh; Folk Music; Islam; Sufi Folk Poetry

KALASHA

The Kalasha are a community of about 3000 people who live in three small finger valleys of the Hindukush: Rumbur (Kalasha *rukmu*), Biri (*biriu*), and Bumboret (*mumoret*), near the town of Chitral in Pakistan's Northwest Frontier Province. They speak Kalashamun, an Indo-Aryan language similar to Khowar, the language of Chitral. In this region, where all neighboring people celebrate a common faith in Islam (despite sectarian, cultural and linguistic diversity), the Kalasha still actively practice their indigenous religion. For this reason (and perhaps because the valleys themselves are such a nice place to be), Kalasha culture has received more than its share of enthographic attention. The Kalasha are widely recognized throughout Pakistan, as pictures of Kalasha women dancing in their elaborate and beautiful dresses and headdresses grace many tourist brochures and posters. Despite their academic and popular notoriety, and despite the increasing pressure of tourism (as well as being a popular destination for college boys from the Punjab, the valleys are host to many international tourists, especially those traveling around South Asia on as little money as possible), most Kalasha lives are turned inward, dedicated to family, community, work, and the practice of a religion that weaves all this together. They tell good stories, and like to sing and dance at their many festivals. They make good wine and cheese. They are a people of tremendous generosity, at once humble and proud.

Kalasha people, like most people carving their lives in narrow valleys throughout the Hindukush, practice a mixed economy that combines transhumant pastoralism (mostly goats, but also a few cattle and sheep) with small-scale agriculture. Through creatively utilizing the range of resources available in their narrow valleys, the Kalasha are able to craft a living in an otherwise difficult environment. An elaborate system of canals moves water from the river in the center of each valley to the hillsides where Kalasha women cultivate corn, wheat, barley, walnuts, and fruit trees and grow small vegetable gardens. Water mills in each village operate all year, so women grind grain for their staple food, *tasili,* a flat corn or wheat bread made by spreading batter onto a convex griddle. Men are almost entirely responsible for the care of livestock and for the resulting dairy production.

Men's role as primary pastoralists leads them on a seasonal transhumant migration that begins in June when they take their herds from winter stables near the villages to spring pastures at about 9,000 feet. The high pastures are located above the upper tributaries of the river that runs through each valley. Women and girls accompany men on the first day of the yearly trek to help coax and carry the young animals. All women thus have some experience of the high pastures, and so can join men in waxing poetic about the beauty and freshness of the mountains. Men remain in the high pastures all summer, making cheese and butter (and eating a whole lot). They graze their flocks in still higher pastures as the summer sun uncovers tender alpine meadows at 12,000 feet, returning in autumn to lower pastures as these recover late in the season. Finally, as winter edges near, snow urges them back to the villages where the animals will be fed on fodder (collected and dried by women the previous summer) and taken to graze in the nearby holly oak forests until the next spring.

Pastoralism is prestigious, because goats have social, ritual, and economic importance. The size of the family herd is an important marker of wealth and status, and merit feasting continues to be one of the primary avenues through which men compete with one another for status within the community. Goats are offered in sacrifice on important ritual occasions or purification ceremonies, and the sacrifice of many goats is necessary for the proper funerals of both men and women. Finally, the many types of goat cheese that men produce are a source of culinary delight and the staple protein food.

Kalasha villages are built up the steep hillsides, each house made of stacked shale and heavy timbers. One family's dirt-packed roof becomes the balcony of the family living above. Each household shares a central fireplace, with beds lining the walls of the house, and cooking pots kept in a special area in the back. In the summertime, the cooking and socializing are done on the front porch. In contrast to their Muslim neighbors, Kalasha social life is quite open. There are no walls around family compounds. It is easy to see what is going on in other houses, and doors are rarely closed.

Kalasha society is organized into patrilineal clans. Kalasha have a rich oral tradition concerning the history of the various lineages. Marriage between clan members (or between those related within three generations on their mothers' side) is strictly forbidden. Girls are usually given in marriage when they are quite young. Bridewealth is exchanged, a process that takes place over many years. Young wives grow up moving between their natal household and their husband's household. In-laws develop intense economic and emotional ties. Yet this bond is frequently severed, because Kalasha culture accords a young woman the right to elope (*alashing parik*) with another man when she reaches adolescence. Her new husband's family must pay her former husband's family twice the bridewealth her former husband's family had given her natal family. The negotiation of bridewealth and orchestration or prevention of elopements are a major political arena in which Kalasha "big men"(*ghona muc*) and village elders demonstrate their authority and political finesse. The social and emotional intrigue of these dramatic, divisive events is a compelling topic of conversation for everyone, small children to the very old.

A hundred years ago, people with similar (though distinct) religious and cultural practices populated the high mountain valleys of the Hindukush, an area known to Muslims as *Kafiristan*—Land of the Non-Believers (obviously not an indigenous term). In 1895, British representatives, hoping to create a buffer between British India and Russian expansion in Central Asia, drew the famous Durand Line on a map, separating the North-West Frontier from Afghanistan, and also (quite accidentally) separating the Kalasha from other "Kafir" groups. The following winter, the Amir of Afghanistan, Abdur Rahman, led his army into Kafiristan, slaughtering and relocating tens of thousands of non-Muslim people, and forcibly converting the rest to Islam. The genocide took only 40 days. "Kafiristan" was renamed "Nuristan"—Land of Light. The Kalasha fell under British protection, and so were spared the Amir's religious zeal. It is a cruel irony that the Kalasha, who were apparently peripheral to Kafiristani culture and were looked down on by the "true Kafirs" of Kafiristan, are now the only living representatives of this once dramatic and varied cultural region. The Nuristanis themselves appear to have embraced Islam with commitment and enthusiasm.

Central to Kalasha cosmology are the concepts of *ónǰeṣṭa* and *prāgata* which have been glossed in English as pure and impure. The world of Kalashadesh is divided into things and places that are ónǰeṣṭa, and those that are prāgata, and there is much concern about the separation of the two, and endless discussions about the transgressions of the boundaries beteen them. The English glosses "purity" and "impurity" are misleading because these words commonly involve judgments about sexuality, cleanliness, and relative worth in the eyes of God. In Kalasha thought, the concepts do not imply moral judgments, nor are they tied to honor, shame or prestige. Kalasha do not rank one another, or rank their patrilineal clans (*kam*) in terms of relative purity. So in contrast to many other South Asian communities, ideas about purity do not organize and legitimate class hierarchies. The concepts are, however, highly gendered.

Men are explicitly associated with the ónǰeṣṭa; women with the pragata. The most fully ónǰeṣṭa places include the important ritual altars at all times, the goat stables during the purest time of winter, and the altar to the goddess Jestak located in the back of every family house. The most prāgata things or places include death, the *bašāli* or menstrual house, and especially menstrual blood and the blood of parturition (a euphemism for both these kinds of blood is simply "prāgata"). Sexual intercourse itself is not prāgata, unless it happens at an inappropriate time or place. All Muslims are considered prāgata, and Kalasha people and places are defined as ónǰeṣṭa against the surrounding Islamic identity in which they are embedded. The point of most Kalasha rituals and customs is to avoid the "mixing" *mišāri hik* of ónǰeṣṭa and prāgata things and places, since it is the careful separation of the two that fosters prosperity and fertility.

I am often asked if Kalasha culture will "survive". For hundreds of years they have withstood tremendous pressure to convert to Islam, and how to maintain their religious identity is a topic of compelling concern. Yet, currently the birth rate of Kalasha far outstrips the handful of people who become Muslim each year. Their culture is dynamic, and new ideas seem to be easily assimilated. And young Kalasha people clearly take pride in their culture. Still, I suppose I can only respond to this question as most Kalasha people do, "Who knows? I hope so. I hope so."

References

Jettmar, Karl. 1975. *Die religionen des Hindukusch.* Stuttgart: Verlag W. Kohlhammer.

Loude, Jean-Yves and Vivian Lievre, 1998. *Kalash solstice.* G. Romaine and M. Intrator (trans.). Islamabad: Lok Virsa.

Maggi, Wynne. 2001. *Our women are free: gender and ethnicity in the Hindukush.* Ann Arbor: University of Michigan Press.

Parkes, Peter, 1994. Personal and collective identity in Kalasha song performance: the significance of music-masking in a minority enclave. *Ethnicity, identity, and music: the musical construction of place:* 157–183. Martin Stokes (ed.). Oxford and Providence: Berg.

———. 1997. Kalasha domestic society: Practice, ceremony, and domain. *Family and gender in Pakistan: domestic organization in a Muslim society:* 25–63. Ed. Hastings Donnan and F. Selier. New Delhi: Hindustani Publishing.

WYNNE MAGGI

SEE ALSO

Dowry and Bridewealth; Gender and Folklore; Ibex and Goats

KALPA SŪTRA

Kalpa Sūtra (Sanskrit), or *Kappasuttaṃ* (Prakrit), a Jain hagiographical text used in lay ritual, is attributed to Bhadrabāhusvāmin (fourth century B.C.E.), but was probably compiled several hundred years later. It is not to be confused with other Jain and Vedic texts of the same name. The *Kalpa Sūtra* is part of the Canon (*Āgama*) of the Śvetāmbara sect (literally "White-Clad," whose monks wear white robes, as opposed to the Digambara sect, literally "Sky-Clad," whose monks practice ascetic nudity). The edifying legend of Kālaka is sometimes appended and read with the *Kalpa Sūtra* during the annual eight day celebration of Paryuṣaṇā.

The *Kalpa Sūtra* begins with biographies of twenty-four *Tīrthaṃkaras* (literally, makers of "Fords," soteriological paths or dispensations), starting with the detailed legendary biography of the twenty-fourth Tīrthaṃkara Mahāvīra, followed by brief formulaic biographies of the preceding Tīrthaṃkaras: the twenty-third, Pārśva; the twenty-second, Ariṣṭanemi; a collective biography of the next twenty; and the first Tīrthaṃkara, Ṛṣabha, the legendary founder of civilization. The *Kalpa Sūtra* describes the Five Auspicious Events (*Pañca Kalyāṇaka*) in the lives of each

Tīrthaṃkara: conception, birth, initiation, attainment of omniscience, and final liberation (death).

By far the most attention is given to the life of Mahāvīra (sixth century B.C.E.). The *Kalpa Sūtra* describes, in vivid and repetitive detail, his descent into the womb of the Brahmin woman Devānandā, and his mother's seeing of the fourteen Great Dreams which, in the Śvetāmbara Jain tradition, accompany the conception of either a Tīrthaṃkara or a Cakravartin (Universal Monarch). Devānandā's Great Dreams are listed in order: an elephant, an ox, a lion, an anointment, a garland, the moon, the sun, an ensign, a jar, a lotus lake, a sea, a celestial abode, a heap of gems, and a flame.

Since it is not customary for a Tīrthaṃkara to be born of a Brahmin womb, the god Śakra (Indra) intervenes, ordering his general, Hariṇegamesī, the antelope-headed Lord of Miscarriage, to exchange Mahāvīra's embryo with the undistinguished embryo of Triśalā, a woman of the Kṣatriya (warrior) caste. The Great Dreams are likewise taken away from Devānandā and given to Triśalā. The Great Dreams, their interpretation, and their joyful reception by Triśalā's household are then fully and vividly described. The embryo transfer episode, unique to Mahāvīra, has sometimes been considered a sixth Auspicious Event (*Kalyāṇaka*), although few now remember the heated medieval debate over this issue. The embryo transfer is rejected by the Digambara sect of Jainism.

The embryo transfer and the Great Dreams, although found in other texts, are given their most detailed description in the *Kalpa Sūtra,* and are featured in many illustrated manuscripts of this text. The *Kalpa Sūtra* also briefly describes the birth-baths (*janmābhiṣeka*) given to the Tīrthaṃkaras by the gods. These birth-baths are today ritually reenacted by Mūrtipūjak Śvetāmbara Jains (those who worship images) in a ceremony called the *Snātra Pūjā*. An abbreviated form of the Snātra Pūjā begins every daily pūjā (worshipping ceremony). The Five Auspicious Events (minus the embryo transfer) are celebrated in the *Pañca Kalyāṇaka Pūjā,* frequently performed in temples. The Great Dreams are reenacted once a year on the fifth day of the eight day celebration of Paryuṣaṇā (commemorating Mahāvīra's life and messages), during which icons of the Dreams, usually made of precious metal such as silver, are suspended from a platform. Laymen bid money for the honor of swinging these images, the proceeds going to the temple treasury. Monks (*muni*s) and nuns (*sādhvī*s) do not participate in this ritual, called the *Svapna Darśan* (Dream Viewing), because it concerns reproduction and the worldly life, which they have renounced.

The *Kalpa Sūtra* is intended to be read only by monks. However, according to legend, 980 years after Mahāvīra (perhaps 453 or 466 C.E.) the practice began of reading the account of the life of Mahāvīra aloud from the *Kalpa Sūtra,* in the original Ardhamāgadhi Prakrit and in vernacular paraphrase, to the assembled laity during the celebration of Paryuṣaṇā. Events in the life of Mahavira are sometimes reenacted as they occur during the course of this reading. For example, an empty cradle may be rocked to represent Mahāvīra's nativity. Interpretation of the Great Dreams and other topics from the *Kalpa Sūtra,* are discussed in lectures.

Although only monks ordinarily recite the *Kalpa Sūtra* during Paruṣaṇā, under unusual conditions others may perform this role. For example, because monks are ordinarily prohibited from overseas travel, Jains outside of India are forced to rely on lay teachers, most of whom are male.

The *Kalpa Sūtra* continues to be popular among the Śvetāmbara Jain laity. It has been retold, with variations, in Gujarati and other South Asian languages, and translated into English, many times. The illustrated manuscript tradition lives on in deluxe editions suitable for gifts. *Kalpa Sūtra* stories are retold in books and videos, and in Jain homes.

References

Bauer, Jerome H. 1998. Karma and control: the prodigious and the auspicious in Śvetāmbara Jaina canonical mythology, Ph.d. diss., University of Pennsylvnia.

Jacobi, Hermann, trans. 1983. *Jaina Sūtras, part I: the Ākārāṅga Sūtra, the Kalpa Sūtra.* Sacred books of the East, ed. Max Müller, vol. XXII. Rpt, Delhi: AVF Books Distributors.

Lalwani, K. C., trans. 1979. *Kalpa Sūtra of Bhadrabāhu Svāmī.* Delhi: Motilal Banarsidass, 1979.

I especially wish to thank the Pennsauken Jain Society for their generous assistance in preparing this article.

JEROME H. BAUER

SEE ALSO

Dreams; Jain Folklore; Jainism

KAMSĀLE

Kamsāle is a martial and ritual dance form of southern Karnataka practiced by male initiates of the cult of Male ("Mountain, of the Mountains") Mādēśwara ("Great Lord"). The word *kamsāle* is derived from the Sanskrit term *kamsatalya,* meaning a bronze cymbal. Those who use this instrument in the dance are called *kamsāleyavru* (or *kamsāle gudda,* or *dēvara guddalu*). The songs, derived from the epic-cycle of Male Mādēśwara, are sung by the group's leader, who is their religious leader (*guru*) as well as dance master. The dancers answer his songs with a chorus.

Among the Male Mādēśwara is a group of devotees called *kamsāleyavaru,* who come from the lower castes, especially the shepherd caste, and vow to live a life of devotion to the god Male Mādēśwara. Parents pledge their eldest or youngest son to the group in hopes of relief in times of family crisis. When the boys are ten to fifteen years old, they are officially initiated into the practice, either at the house of a gūrū, or at the Mādēśwara shrine on Mādēśwara Beṭṭa (mountain). They are thereafter called *dēvara guddaru* (god's disciple), and treated as sons of Lord Mādēśwara, and are no longer children of their birth parents. Although they are allowed to marry, as members of the group, they are expected go into the streets every Monday as itinerant mendicants, performing the kamsāle.

Kamsāle is a group dance, similar in many ways to stick-dances (*kōlāta*) found in most parts of South Asia. Instead of sticks, the participants hold in one hand a sharp-edged bronze cymbal, called a *gari,* while in the other, they hold a smaller, bowl-shaped bronze instrument called a *battalu*. Attached to the cymbal is a short rope decorated with metal bells. These musical instuments can double as a formidable weapon (the gari) and shield (the battalu). During the dance, the instruments are moved around the body of the dancer in skillful patterns in such a way that the dancer executes a complex choreography, alternating series of offensive and defensive maneuvers. This practice is also said to develop skill with swords.

The main musical elements in the dance are the rhythmic clang that results when each dancer in turn strikes his gari against another dancer's battalu and the songs led by the dance master. While the performance could be viewed as merely a dance associated with a religious cult, many traditional groups regard it as a martial art (*bīsu*) and fuse a combative ethic to that of their religious practice. As their guru, the group leader instructs his disciples in both the religious tenets of the Mādēśwara cult and teaches them the songs (called, in this context, *kamsāle kathe*) of the life of Mādēśwara that exemplify aspects of their devotion. During performances, he leads the singing as his disciples dance.

References

Keshavan, Prasad K. (Trans. by C. N. Ramachandran and L. N. Bhat) 2001. *Male Madeśhwara a Kannada oral epic as sung by Hebbani Madayya and his Troup*. New Delhi, India: Shitya Akademi.

Nallur, Prasad, ed. 1998. *Jaanapada Karnataka* (A collection of folk articles from different writers) Bangalore, India: Karnataka Janpada and Yakshagana Academy.

Ramakrishna, H. A., and H. L. Nagegowda 1998. *Essentials of Karnataka folklore*. Bangalore, India.

S. A. KRISHNAIAH

SEE ALSO

Folk Music; Karnataka; Martial Arts Traditions; Pilgrimage

KĀÑTHĀ

Kāñthā is a form of quilting indigenous to Bengal. Kāñthā—also called *khetā* or *keñthā*—are made from old cloth, discarded *sāṛī, dhuti* (a white sarong-like garment worn by men), and lungi (a patterned sarong-like garment also worn by men), and range from utilitarian quilts to exquisitely embroidered heirlooms. In Bihar and parts of West Bengal, India, kāñthā are also referred to as *sujni*. Depending on the thickness required, three to seven sāṛī may be layered and quilted with the simple running stitch that typically produces a rippled effect. Traditionally, thread drawn from the colored borders of sāṛī was used to embroider motifs or border patterns imitative of sāṛī borders.

Kāñthā serve primarily as bed pallets and as light wraps for the cool monsoon nights and mild winters of Bengal. Small kāñthā are used as swaddling clothes for babies. Depending on their size and use, kāñthā range from *lep kāñthā* (winter quilts) and *sujni kāñthā* (spreads and coverlets) to one-foot square *rumāl* (handkerchief) kāñthā. Other kāñthā articles include the *āsan* (a spread for sitting on during *pūjā,* or for guests to sit on), the *bayton, bostāni,* or *gatri* (types of wrappers used for clothes and other valuables), the *ārśilatā* (a wrap for mirrors or toilet articles), the *durjani* [wallet], the *dastarkhān* (a floor spread for dining seated on the floor), the *gilāph* (an envelope-shaped kāñthā to cover the Quran), and the *jāinamāz* (prayer rug).

By far the vast majority of kāñthā are utilitarian, with the quilting being done simply to hold the layers of cloth together. Many old kāñthā dating from the nineteenth century, however, manifest an ingenious use of stitchcraft. Varying the simple running stitch, the needlewomen created a variety of effects: ripples, expanses of color, pointillistic designs, and textures that appear woven. Thus, from being a quilting stitch that simply holds the several layers of cloth together, the running stitch was transformed into a variety of forms, among them stitches known today as the *chātāi* or *pāti* (mat) stitch and the *kāityā* (bending) stitch. Occasionally, as in sāṛī border patterns, the running stitch is used in a manner similar to weaving by varying the length of the stitch to match the design.

Kāñthā are an example of thrift, where old cloth is put together to make something new. However, they are also symbolic of prosperity, security, and fertility. The use of old cloth has always had a magical purpose, particularly that of warding off the evil eye. It is significant that motifs found in the kāñthā are also common to the *ālpanā,* which are drawings made on the ground on occasions of marriages and semireligious ceremonies known as *brata,* which are observed to celebrate the changing seasons, and to promote the well-being of the husband, prosperity, fertility, and happiness. Common motifs used in these ceremonies include the lotus flower—sacred to the goddess Lakṣmī—other floral and leaf motifs, and feminine articles such as the vermilion pot and the *kājal-latā* (a container for kohl), combs etc. Kāṅthā made as gifts often contain these symbolic motifs suggestive of prosperity, security, marriage, and fertility.

Despite their variety, most kāṅthā tend to follow a similar basic pattern that has its focal point in a central lotus motif. The lotus symbolizes Lakṣmī, goddess of beauty, wealth, abundance, and also is associated more generally with being female. Around the lotus are concentric circles of undulating vines or sāṛī border patterns. In the four corners of the kāṅthā—or in the four corners of the square containing the central lotus—are embroidered tree-of-life motifs or *kalkā* (cones) pointing towards the central motif. The empty spaces between the central and corner motifs are filled with motifs drawn from nature and the homestead or with scenes from real life or legends. Apart from floral motifs, recurrent motifs are the curvilinear *svastika* (a traditional symbol of good fortune in Hinduism, inverted by Hitler to symbolize Aryan rule), kitchen utensils, ornaments, elephants, tigers, horses, peacocks, boats, palanquins, and *rath* (the carriage of the gods). Scenes from Hindu mythology juxtapose secular scenes of dancing, hunting, and boating. The areas left without motifs or scenes are quilted with the rippling kāṅthā stitch.

Other types of kāṅthā include the *pāḍ tolā kāṅthā,* which are embroidered entirely with *sāṛī* border patterns, and the *lāhārī kāṅthā,* in which thick yarn is used for close pattern darning. In the most intricate of pāḍ tolā kāṅthā, there is no space between the border patterns so that the entire kāṅthā seems a piece of woven cloth.

While most kāṅthā are the work of illiterate women, some of the best kāṅthā contain proverbs, blessings, and even captions of motifs and scenes in Bengali lettering. Thus, in one kāṅthā, the kāṅthā maker blesses her son-in-law: "*Sukhī thāko*" (Be happy). Some kāṅthā are autographed, usually indicating the relationship the needlewoman bore to the person for whom she was making it. A few have the name of the person for whom it was being made. One exceptionally beautiful and finely stitched kāṅthā in the Gurusaday Museum, Thakurpukur, West Bengal, shows various scenes, including rows of British soldiers, and contains the name of the maker—Manadasundari—as well as the name of her father.

While the utilitarian kāṅthā has never ceased to be made, political upheavals, the availability of manufactured articles, and changing tastes led to a decline in richly embroidered kāṅthā beginning in the 1940s. In recent years the interest in ethnic arts and crafts has encouraged a kāṅthā revival in Bangladesh and West Bengal. In Bangladesh, in tribute to Jasimuddin, the poet who celebrated the kāṅthā, the term *nakśi* (pictorial) kāṅthā, in his poem *Nakśi Kāṅthār Māt* (1929), became prevalent in order to distinguish the embroidered kāṅthā from the utilitarian one.

References

Dutt, Gurusaday. 1990. *Folk arts and crafts of Bengal: the collected papers*. Calcutta: Seagull.

Kramrisch, Stella. 1968. *Unknown India: ritual art in tribe and village*. Philadelphia: Philadelphia Museum of Art.

Whitechapel Art Gallery. 1988. *Woven air: the muslin and kantha tradition of Bangladesh*. London: Whitechapel.

Zaman, Niaz. 1993[1981]. *The art of kantha embroidery*. 2nd rev. ed. Dhaka: University Press.

NIAZ ZAMAN

SEE ALSO

Crafts and Development, India; Dṛṣṭi; Embroidery; Floor Designs; Quilting and Piecing.

KARMA

Karma (Sanskrit) and *Kamma* (Pāli) mean "action" or "deed" in classical South Asian religious thought, the law according to which actions have consequences in this or some subsequent lifetime. Karma is the force behind *saṃsāra,* the transmigration of souls in a cycle of death and rebirth.

The origins of the idea of Karma/saṃsāra are uncertain; however, the Jains have preserved an extensive and ancient karma literature, leading some to speculate that the idea was developed by "heterodox" sects such as the Jains and Ājīvikas. Karma and rebirth are important to contemporary Hindu, Buddhist, Jain, and Sikh doctrines, and compete with other ideas as a folk explanation for misfortune and evil in South Asia.

Fundamental to the classical doctrine of karma/saṃsāra is the hypothesis of amnesia, according to which a person has control over his or her own destiny, but cannot know what actions taken in a previous life may account for present misfortunes. In some traditions, this amnesia may be partially, or fully, overcome, and past lives recalled (for example, salvation according to Jain doctrine is accompanied by a state of omniscience, and many edifying stories of karma and its fruition are told from a literally omniscient point of view).

According to some traditions, the karma/saṃsāra doctrine is nontransactional, involving no transfer of merit: a person's fortune, good or bad, is earned by oneself, not by another. However, in most South Asian religious traditions (except Jainism), the possibility of merit transfer through ritual transactions such as feeding the ancestors, or by the grace of a deity, is admitted in theory (and even popular Jainism seems to admit this in practice).

The doctrine of karma is widely diffused in South Asian folk culture, although some tribal communities seem to be unaware of this Sanskritic idea complex (and other South Asians accept karma but reject saṃsāra). Karma is accepted by most adherents of South Asian religions outside of South Asia, and the word has entered European languages. Karma / saṃsāra competes and coexists with a variety of other explanatory traditions, such as fate, the position of the planets, ghosts, gods or demons, witchcraft, ritual errors, natural events, etc. Generally a misfortune will be first attributed to natural causes, then perhaps to witchcraft or ritual errors, then to the will of God, and, lastly, to the fruition of karma. Although karma is generally the explanation of last resort, it is also the last to be abandoned.

Karma is closely connected with dharma, often translated as "duty," "Sacred Law," or "what is expected." Because the general principles of dharma can be known, the past is, in principle, knowable, and the future is, in principal, controllable. This contrasts with other explanatory traditions, such as witchcraft or ritual errors, which tend to explain particular events in the present or recent past in terms of particular errors made unintentionally by oneself or maleficent actions taken by others, causing undeserved suffering. According to the doctrine of karma, suffering is in some sense deserved; however, in popular religion, amelioration, and ultimately salvation, is possible by means of austerities. In the popular Jain view, karma (conceived as a substance) is believed to be burnt off by austerities such as rigorous fasts; Hindu performance of *vrat*s (vows accompanied by fasts) may serve the same function. Disciplined action taken with the right intention may overcome the effects of (intentional or unintentional) past acts.

Popular Buddhism, in contrast, tends to focus more on the performance of meritorious acts which lead to good karma for future fruition, for oneself and for others, especially family members. In many popular traditions (for example southeast Asian and Sri Lankan Buddhism) the theory and practice of merit transfer are well developed (for example, in texts such as the "Blessings of Ordination"). Hindu ritual feeding of ancestors was apparently reinterpreted as transfer of merit, rather than transfer of physical substance. Charitable action to earn merit (*pūṇya*) is also important in popular Jainism, although no formal doctrine of merit transfer has been developed. In popular Hinduism, transfers of merit are more likely to accompany transfers of substance (exchanges of food or sex).

Devotional or *bhakti* types of religiosity have transformed the classical karma doctrine. In popular Hinduism, vrats (vows with fasting) are usually accompanied by a pūjā, in honor of a deity, who is requested to destroy one's sins and grant one a boon. Karma is not denied, but it is qualified: a deity intervenes in the karmic process with a dispensation of grace. In popular Mahāyāna Buddhism, Bodhisattvas may intervene on one's behalf. In popular Jainism, the tutelary deities accompanying the Tīrthaṃkaras (Jain saviors) may legitimately grant this-worldly boons, but no formal Jain theology of grace exists. Even so, the devotional behavior of Jains is often indistinguishable from that of their Hindu neighbors. In the Sikh tradition, although karmic causality is admitted, more emphasis is placed on the grace of God, obtainable by anyone in this life.

In Tamil folk culture, karma is qualified by fate, or "headwriting" inscribed on everyone's forehead by God, preordaining all one's acts and fortunes. This headwriting is also influenced by the deeds of relatives, transferred from generation to generation in the blood, and perhaps from person to person in shared food. Headwriting determines when and how karma will come to fruition, and is thought to be generally immutable, although occasionally it may be changed by the grace of God, after the completion of vows and sacrifices.

References

Doniger O'Flaherty, Wendy, ed. 1980. *Karma and rebirth in classical Indian traditions.* Berkeley: University of California Press.

Keyes, Charles F., and Daniel, E. Valentine, eds. 1983. *Karma: an anthropological inquiry.* Berkeley: University of California Press.

Neufeldt, Ronald W., ed. 1986. *Karma and rebirth: post classical developments.* Albany: State University of New York Press.

Sharma, Ursula. 1973. Theodicy and the doctrine of karma. *Man* 8: 347–364.

JEROME H. BAUER

SEE ALSO

Ancestor Worship; *Bhakti;* Buddhism and Buddhist Folklore; Fate, Hindu; Jainism; *Vrat Kathā*

KARNATAKA

Karnataka is the name currently used to denote one of the southern states of the Indian Republic. Under British rule, and even after Independence up until 1973, the state was called Mysore. In ancient records the term Karnataka had been used to denote a particular geographical area of south India; in works of art the term has also been used in the context of music and the language. Karnataka is the eight largest state in the Indian

Woman of the Halakki Gowda community wears her traditional black beads. Women in this community say the beads help them when they carry heavy headloads. Karnataka, India, © Mimi Nichter

union today. It has the population of 44,977,201 with 2 revenue districts and 175 taluks. Its capital is Bangalore.

Karnataka is bordered on the north by Maharashtra, on the east by Andra Pradesh, on the southeast by Tamilnadu, on the southwest by Kerala, and on the west by the Arabian Sea. It is encompassed by the river systems of Krisna in the north and Kaveri (or Cauvery) in the south.

The attractive and lush green coastal area abounds in coconut, cashew, Areca gardens, green fields, and thick forests. The western Ghats, hills rising steeply from the narrow coastal belt, are thickly jungled and, except for a few important passes, maintain an effective separation between the cultures to their east and those to their west within the state. The forest area extending from the ridges of the western Ghats toward the plain in the east is known as Malenadu ("mountain country"). It narrows down to 2 kilometers in some places and extends to 10 kilometers in other places. The eastern Ghats less dramatically define the eastern border of the state. The highest peaks in Karnataka are in the Sahyadri portions of the western Ghats, with Kudremukha at 1,892 metres high. On the southeastern border of the state, the Biligiri Rangana Betta mountains are the highest in the eastern Ghats, rising as high as 1,737 metres. The broad plain between the western and eastern Ghats delineate the broad cultural regions of Karnataka's major language, Kannada, divided into northern and southern parts by the Tungabhadra river.

The etymology of the word Karnataka has been hotly debated. Most scholars agree that the final ending in the word Karnataka is derived from the Dravidian word *nāḍu,* meaning a country. The initial syllable, *kār,* is more problematic. As an adjective, *kār* means black, and some scholars see the name as a reference to a tract of black soil. Some other scholars interpret the prefix as *kāru,* which means big and expansive or wide-ranging, although other scholars dispute this, saying that the prefix *kāru* means an elevated region above sea level. Some of the districts of the state are endowed with black soil; it is also true that some of the districts rise above the sea level. But which one of these connotations was responsible for the formation of "Karnata" remains a matter of contention.

The Saravati, Aghanasini, Netravati, Varahi, Payasvini, Seetha, and Suarna are some of the important rivers that originate in the western Ghats and flow toward the west. They are the main sources of hydroelectric power generation for Karnataka. The Krisna river, which originates in Maharastra, flows through Karnataka before entering Andhra Pradesh, where it is joined by the Tungabhadra. The Kaveri, which originates in Coorg (now spelt Kodagu) district, has been greatly helpful for agricultural production in the districts of Mysore and Mandya and flows toward the southeast into Tamil Nadu.

In many parts of the state we find the cultivation of coconut, areca-nut, plantain, mulberry, rubber, and other cash crops; sugarcane and paddy are the main crops in the areas enjoying irrigation facilities. In northern Karnataka cotton is grown. Ragi, maize, and other grains are also grown in the state. Karnataka is famous for some of its woods, such as sandalwood and teakwood, as well as cash crops such as cashew nut, cardamom, and citrus fruit. Sheep, goats, cattle, buffaloes, and pigs are the common domestic animals.

Karnataka has been inhabited by humans for as long as 400,000 years. Many areas of the state have been identified as the habitat of Paleolithic cultures. Races hailing from diverse areas and periods from prehistoric times to the present day are found throughout the state. The Arabs, Persians, and people from elsewhere in south Asia came during the seventh and ninth centuries. Additional Muslims and people of other west Asian origins came during the twelfth century. The Portuguese, French, Dutch, and British communities established contacts with Karnataka around the forteenth century. Lingayats and Vokkaligas constitute the major castes. Brahmins, Bunts, Pujaris, Buddhists, Jains, Parsis, Christians, Kodavas, and Muslims are also living in the state.

Karnataka is the homeland of a number of languages and cultures: the Tuluva occupy the coastal belt, while the Kodagu-speaking Kodava inhabit the mountainous region of Coorg (Kodagu). No doubt other, smaller languages and cultures existed in the region but have now disappeared or have been absorbed by the dominant Kannada language, and to the extent their culture differs from that of the mainstream, they are still recognized as tribes. Examples are the Koraga, Malekudiya, and Maila of Dakshina Kannada District; the Palliyan, Kurumba, Kaniya, and Irula in the forested mountain regions of Kodagu, Bangalore, and Mysore districts; and the Golla (or Yadava) and Kuruba inhabiting the drier grasslands on the plains.

Political History

The Kadambas of Banavasi (fourth through sixth centuries A.D.) and the Gangas of Talakadu (third through tenth centuries A.D.) are the ancient dynasties who ruled over the northern and southern parts of Karnataka, respectively. Calukyas of Badami marked the ascendency of Karnataka in Indian political history. The period of Rastrakutas (700–900 A.D.) constituted a brilliant epoch in the political history of Karnataka. Vikramaditya VI was the most distinguished ruler of the Kalyana Chalukyas, who started the Calukya-Vikrama era in 1076 A.D. Hoysalas of Dorasamudra ruled Karnataka in the eleventh and twelfth centuries, until Mallikkafur, the general of Alla-ud-din Khilji, invaded Karnataka. The Vijayanagara empire (1336–1650) was the last, greatest, and most glorious empire of Karnataka. Harihara II, Devaraya II, and Krisnadevaraya were the illustrious kings of that great empire. After Vijayanagara, Bahmani Sultans ruled Karnataka until 1686 A.D. The Mysore Vodeyar family ruled much of the southern region of the state from the fall of the Vijayanagara Empire until British rule, for a relatively short period from 1776 to 1799, during which the Muslim general Hydar Ali and his son Tippu Sultan ruled over the Mysore dominions.

From the beginning of the nineteenth century until Independence in 1965, Karnataka was under British rule. After Independence, the Kannada-speaking areas were brought together under the name Mysore State, which was subsequently changed to Karnataka on November 1, 1973.

Classical Arts

Painting provides one of the most continuous records of Karnataka's artistic culture, beginning with rock paintings that have been discovered throughout the state dating from 10,000 to 1,000 B.C. Karnataka's classical style, unique in technique, begins with the painting from Badami and Ellora, which differed only slightly from those of the famous Ajanta caves. In the seventh century A.D. Vijayanagara paintings gave rise to variations in style and composition of common subjects. The paintings of Mysore, which are now seen as traditional for Karnataka, show a unique mixture of late Vijayanagara, Muslim, and Western influence.

Karnataka is probably most famous for its sculpture. An outstanding work is the monolithic Gommata at

Sravanabelagula of the Ganga period. Installed in 972 A.D., the statue is fifty-seven feet high. The temples at Banavasi, Aihole, Pattadakallu, Ellora, and Lakkaundi are the best representatives of early styles of Karnataka architecture, but those at Belur and Halebidu temples are more widely associated with the state's highly decorative style and extraordinarily luxurious display of narrative representation. Vijayanagara architecture is known for its vast enclosures, granites, and lofty towers over the entrances. The Muslims initiated the Deccan school of the Indo-Saracenic style. They introduced domes, enpolas, arches, and minars. Vidhanasudha at Bangalore, the biggest granite structure in modern India, is a wonderful contemporary building of Karnataka.

With 26,887,837 people using it as their mother tongue, the Kannada language in the state and has a literary history of about 1,500 years. Tulu and Kodagu, are the other two major indigenous languages. The oldest writing in Kannada is the Halmidi inscription of 450 A.D. The oldest available literary work in Kannada is *Kavirajamarga* (850 A.D.) by Srivijaya, followed by Pampa's (b. 902 A.D.) two great epics, *Adipurana* and *Vikramarjina Vijaya.* During the later half of the twelfth century, under the influence of a major anti-Brahmanical reform movement called Vīraṣaiva, and the writings of Basavanna (1131–1167), Allama Prabhu and Akkamahadevi, a new form of poetry called *vacana* became a powerful instrument of social change. Epic poetry reached its peak with Kumaravyāsa's epic, *Karṇāta Bhārata Kathamanjari* (ca. 1430), popularly known as *Kumaravyāsa Bhārata.* The fourteenth century witnessed a *bhakti* movement with the devotional songs of Purandaradasa (ca. 1484–1564) and Kanakadasa (1508–1606). Both have contributed much to Karnataka music.

The modern age of Karnataka literary output began with the national struggle for freedom and a renaissance of the arts. Masti Venkatesha Iyangar, K. V. Puttappa, D. R. Bendre, and K. Shivarama Karanth are among the great Indian writers of the twentieth century. T. P. Kailasam and Sriranga helped shape Indian theater. Niranjana and A. N. Krisna Rao brought Marxism to Kannada literature. In recent years, Dalit (Untouchable) writers have made their mark. These writers sympathize with downtrodden and oppressed classes. The experience and feelings of the common man, which had remained outside the realm of literature in classical times, are finding its place in modern literature with a resurgence of interest in folk forms.

PURUSHOTHAMA BILIMALE

Folklore

The state can be divided into four folklore regions, two of which are defined by their distinctive regional languages and cultures, while the other two are delineated by their geography and their unique historical influences. The four regions are:

- Tuluva, the Tulu-speaking area of the coastal plain
- the district of Kodagu
- the northern portion of the broad plain that lies on the eastern side of the western Ghats in northern Karnataka
- southern Karnataka.

Although each region of Karnataka has a wealth of folklore, the folklore in some regions has been studied more broadly than that in others.

The Tuluva region is most distinctive, having its own language and culture and an agricultural system based in monsoon paddy cultivation. It also supports large fishing and trading communities among the ports and villages on the Arabian Sea. *Bhūta* worship, along with the region's main ritual celebration, the *bhūta kōla*, and the *pāḍdana* oral narrative song tradition, is unique within Karnataka, but similar in many ways to the *teyyam* ritual traditions and *tor̲r̲am* songs of Kerala, the neighboring state to the south. Tuluva's spectacular *Siri Jātra,* during which hundreds of women simultaneously undergo spirit possession, and its long oral epic tradition, the *Siri Pāḍdana,* also have many similarities with the bhūta kōla traditions. It is sometimes argued that even the distinctive form that the *Yakṣagana* theater tradition takes in this region is due to the influence of the costuming found in bhūta kōlas, but other scholars point out that the *Yakṣgana* found in this region is very similar to that in other Kannada-speaking areas, especially the Malnad. The cock fight and buffalo racing (*kambala*) are both popular sports unique to this region.

Another folk tradition is *karangolu,* a kind of harvest dance during which the members of several Harijan communities paint their bodies white, wear anklets, and dress themselves with leaves. They go from house to house and receive alms from villagers and landlords in return for their singing and dancing. A somewhat similar tradition called *mādira* is performed by a community called the Nalke, who dance at bhūta kōlas. During the mādira the dancers wear normal dress and their songs and dances are more sophisticated than the karangolu. Both the karangolu and the mādira have similarities with the *suggi kuṇita,* which is a harvest dance found in the Kannada-speaking area to the north, and with other dance traditions in Malnad.

A popular tiger dance called *pilita veṣa* is performed during major religious celebrations by amateur troops who go from house to house dancing for alms, and is an every-changing, dynamic composite of many forms. Its core probably stems from a form of animal dance (a tradition shared with Kerala) combined with influences from Maratha and Muslim immigration during the time of Śivajī in the seventeenth century. The central performer, wearing only a minimal lioncloth, covers his entire body with yellow (turmeric) and black (charcoal) in an oilbased paint and dances an imitation of tiger movements, while other characters, dressed in western clothes and faces painted white, represent hunters. They are led by a character called *dōre* (lord, king) and attempt to "shoot" the tiger with antique rifles. In this contest the tiger is always supposed to win and escape. The symbolism represented by the characters and actions of the performance has many possible interpretations.

The Kodagu region, too, has its own language. The main body of distinctive Koḍagu culture pertains to a single caste, the Koḍavas (often called Coorgs), who are regarded as the original inhabitants. They are primarily a farming community and own most of the cultivated rice fields. Much of what the Koḍavas see as distinctive about their musical traditions is probably an elaboration of forms found in common with the "tribal" communities (Irula, Kurumba, Manseru, Muggeru, [Mēra], Malekuḍiya, and others) along the slopes of the western Ghats. Most of the other communities found in the region see themselves as immigrants—consisting primarily of speakers of Kannada, Tulu, and Malayalam—who retain the identity and traditions of their home cultures.

The distinctive folk traditions of the Koḍavas stem mostly from a single form of circle-dance singing. Of this, there are male and female variants. Men perform varieties of dance that include songs (*pāṭü*) accompanied by a drum (*duḍi*). The basic form is the *boḷkoṭ* or "lamp dance." Variant song traditions are known individually either by the occasion on which they are sung (such as the *pūttari pāṭü* at the new rice ceremony), or by the implements involved (a stick-dance using two three-foot long sticks, a sword-dance, a whisk-dance, a dance during which deer antlers are carried, etc.) Other songs are sung in relation to the worship of particular local deities and are named after the deity, such the Mandakkana pāṭü to the goddess Mandakkana. Women also perform circular dances around a lamp, the most famous being the *umattāṭa* dance, which may be performed for any festive occasion (Ṣaṣti, Dīpāvalī, Ugādi, Sankrāndi, and throughout the auspicious harvest months of Suggi and Wasanta), in which the women dance around a special lamp (*dīpa*). The women's dance perhaps has its origin in the form called *tummattāṭa,* performed at a girl's first menstruation.

Northern Karnataka is most famous for its several forms of open-air theater forms: *doḍḍāṭa,* a distinctive local variety of *yakṣagaṇa,* and *parijāta āṭa*. While the former utilizes numerous stories drawn from the Mahābhārata and Rāmāyaṇa, the later is confined to a single story concerning the origin of the *parijāta,* a flowering tree that blooms during the night and then loses its beautiful scent the next morning. According to tradition, the tree was stolen from god Brahma's heaven by Lord Kṛṣṇa for one of his wives, Satyabhama, which engendered the jealousy of his other wife. Only Kṛṣṇa himself could settle their disputes. The story derives from a few lines in the early Sanskrit text, expanded somewhat in the Mahābhārata, and then later greatly elaborated in *bhakti* literature. In the theater form, much of the action is derived from a variety of additional sources focusing on both intra- and inter-gender rivalries. Other folk performances include *vīragāse,* a dance performance by devotees of Śiva, accompanied by narrative singing of the *Dakṣayajṇa* (the sacrifice of Dakṣa), who pierce their cheeks with pointed iron spears; Kalgi and Tura songs (*lāvaṇi*), which challenge male chauvinism and are often sung competitively by women; and Gondal, a ritual performed mainly by Marathi immigrant communities for appeasing *ganas* (retinue of spirits) of Śiva and Ammanavaru, a form of the mother goddess.

In south Karnataka the most famous ritual performance is called *sōmana kuṇita,* or "mask dance." The huge, round masks depict—or embody, as images—both the character and the nature of the specific village deities. The *sōma* deities are believed to be the spirits of warrior heroes and virtuous women who have died before fulfilling life's desires, as well as local manifestations of the mother goddess. During ritual celebrations the masks are decorated with mango leaves, flowers, and cloth. Animals are sacrificed to them and they are then carried in procession by possessed priests who dance to the frenzied tune of musicians playing percussion and wind instruments.

South Karnataka also has its local form of yakṣagana, called Mūḍalapāya āṭa (southern style). Although perhaps not as sophisticated in costuming, this style is famous for its vigorous music and movements. Several epic traditions such as the Male Madeṣwara and Manteswāmi epics are more prominent in south Karnataka than they are elsewhere in the state, and the principal pilgrimage place associated with the heroes of these epics are located within the region. *Kamsāle,* a unique form of ritualistic dance and martial art using cymbals as shields, is practiced by the devotees of Madeṣwara is also found widely here.

All of the folk forms from many regions of the state may be witnessed at once during the Dassara procession in Mysore City.

References

Caldwell R. 1875 (1956). *A comparative grammar of the Dravidion or south Indian family of languages* Madras.

Kamath, Suryanath U., Chief Editor. 1983. *Karnataka State Gazetteer.* Part II. Bangalore: Government of Karnataka.

Kassebaum, Gayathri Rajapur, and Peter J. Claus. 2000. Karnataka. In *South Asia: the Indian subcontinent. The Garland encyclopedia of world music, volume 5.* Alison Arnold, editor. New York: Garland Publishing, Inc.

Saletore, B. A. 1936. *Ancient Karnataka vol. I. History of Tuluva:* Poona; Oriental Book Agency.

PETER J. CLAUS

SEE ALSO

Bhūta; Bhūta Kōla; Cockfighting; *Kamsāle; Mādēśvara* Epic; Manteswamy; *Pāḍdana;* Siri; *Teyyam; Tōṟṟam; Yakṣagāna*

KASHMIR

Kashmir has had the misfortune for much of its history to be on the borders of aggressive competing empires. Early accounts of Kashmir do not necessarily refer to the area today defined by the disputed boundaries of the Indian state of Jammu and Kashmir, and the ceasefire line that demarcates an Āzād (or "free") Kashmir claimed by Pakistan. Pre-nineteenth-century references to Kashmir often mean primarily the valley of Kashmir, which is drained by the Jhelum river and surrounded by high mountains. While the people of Kashmir experienced some isolated periods, the mountains did not prevent their participation in the overland trade routes of Asia, known as the "Silk Road" in later times, nor did they prevent conquest by foreign armies. Kashmiri folklore thus draws from a very rich background of ethnic and religious heritages. Written and oral records include an eleventh-century C.E. collection of stories called the *Kathāsaritsāgara* (The Ocean of the Streams of Story), as well as tales from the periods of the Mughal emperors (sixteenth through eighteenth centuries), Afghan adventurers (eighteenth century), Punjabi Sikh rulers (nineteenth century), and the Dogra Maharajas (1846–1947). In 1846 the British created the kingdom of Jammu and Kashmir, which was then ruled by local Dogra maharajas until Independence in 1947.

The collection and translation of Kashmiri oral tales was a popular pastime for British administrators and their family members in the nineteenth and early twentieth centuries. James Hinton Knowles, a British missionary, published the earliest collections of Kashmiri folktales in English, the 1885 *Dictionary of Kashmiri Proverbs and Sayings,* followed by his 1888 *Folk-Tales of Kashmir.* Knowles was familiar with the contemporary methods of scientific collection, and he used a comparative method, making his field work particularly useful for other folklorists. George A. Grierson, most famous as a colonial linguist, published *Hatim's Tales* in 1923, combining the original transcription and translation of tales told in Kashmir at the end of the nineteenth century with his own translation of them. After Independence, the regional study of folklore in India and Pakistan is reflected by the Kashmiri tales in collections such as *Folktales of Kashmir* (1989) and the Kashmiri selections included in *Folktales of India* (1987). While this brief survey has focused on folklore published in English, there are also collections in local languages (Dube, 1969). While the bulk of collections in the past have shared the nineteenth-century paradigms of the "folk" and ideas of "authenticity," contemporary scholars such as Sadhana Naithani are collecting tales that portray the British folklore collectors themselves through "rumors" or other narratives of colonial relationships. For example, Naithani recounts indigenous "rumors" about George A. Grierson's official activities, and urges folklorists to search for such oral narratives about the colonized as relatively new materials for folklorists throughout South Asia.

References

Beck, Brenda E. F., Peter J. Claus, Praphulladatta Goswami, and Jawaharlal Handoo, eds. *Folktales of India.* Chicago: University of Chicago Press, 1987.

Dube, Bisanadasa. Bidhamata de likha: Dogari loka kattham. In *Ramanagar [Zila Udhamapura]: Bandaralata Sahitya Mandal,* 1969. [in Dogri]

Grierson, George A. *Hatim's tales.* London: J. Murray, 1923.

Jaitly, Jaya, ed. 1990. *Crafts of Jammu, Kashmir, and Ladakh.* Ahmedabad: Mapin.

Islam, Mazharul. *A history of folktale collections in India, Bangladesh and Pakistan.* Calcutta: Panchali Prakasan, 1982.

Knowles, James Hinton. *A dictionary of Kashmiri proverbs and sayings.* New Delhi: Asian Education Services, 1985 [1885].

Naithani, Sadhana. An axis jump: British colonialism in the oral folk narratives of nineteenth-century India. *Folklore 112*(2001): 183.

Roy Chouudhury, Bani. *Folk tales of Kashmir.* New Delhi: Sterling Publishers, 1989.

Saraf, D. N. 1987. *Arts and Crafts, Jammu and Kashmir.* New Delhi: Abhinav Publications.

MICHELLE MASKIELL

SEE ALSO

Bhānd Paṭhar; British, Folklore about; Colonialism and Folklore; Crafts; Grierson, George A.; *Kathāsaritsāgara*

KĀṬAMA RĀJU

Like many of India's long oral narrative traditions, the epic (*katha*) of the Kāṭama Rāju is usually regarded by Western scholars as an epic, but is often identified by Indian scholars as a ballad cycle. The former designation emphasizes the unity of the piece while the latter stresses the characteristics of its performance through a number of segmented narrative traditions about a single hero and members of his family (patrilineage and their in-laws). Both terminologies recognize that the narrative consists of partially independent story traditions normally delivered through sung poetic verse often accompanied by instrumentation, prose commentary, and elaborated through dance, entertaining skits (often of a humorous nature) and other theatrical features.

The Epic and the Golla

The *Kāṭama Rāju Katha* is closely associated with the Golla (also called Yādava), community of Andhra Pradesh, and most of its versions are in the language Telugu. All of the performing communities have a strong connection to the Gollas and some are regarded as a subsection of Gollas. In its most elaborate present-day forms, the ballad cycle can be thought of as a narrative genealogy of the Gollas, and Kāṭama Rāju, the epic's hero, as their caste champion. Acknowledging Kāṭama Rāju as one of their own, and having the ballad cycle performed for them, identifies a local community as a Golla community. Although the epic takes its name from its main hero, the goddess Gangamma (or Yādava Gangamma), the paramount deity of the Gollas, is the presiding figure and the epic is normally performed as a mode of worshiping her.

The performing traditions are numerous, as are the modes of delivery and the castes that perform them. The largest and most famous of the performances in Andhra is that of the Māḍiga, a Harijan community which, in some regions of Andhra, is allied with Gollas as a "left-hand" caste. In their capacity as performers of the Kāṭama Rāju epic and rituals, they are called Kommawarlu (*komma,* "horn," has the same double meaning in Telugu as it does in English). Another performance form is that of the Ālu Gollas, called a *mande ecca,* by which term the performers derive their name, Mandecculu. Another form mentioned in the literature, but not yet fully researched or described, is that of the Golla Suddalolu (or Suddala Gollalu) performers of the Nellore and Chitoor Districts. The Suddalolu are Pūja Golla by caste. They use a *kalamkārī* painted cloth during their recitation. More recently, during fieldwork in 1992, I encountered a performance by Teljīralu (or Teracīra Bhaktulu) of Telangana, who also use a kalamkārī erected above a small plot of ground made sacred by the drawing of a *paṭnam* consisting of colored powders. The ritual, along with the epic recitation, is described as a *gollana,* which means simply "tent". In the southern portions of Andhra Pradesh, along the borders with Karnataka and Tamil Nadu, the Piccakoṇḍlu (known as Helava in Karnataka) perform the *Kāṭama Rāju Katha* for their Telugu-speaking Golla patrons, but can also perform it in Kannada and Tamil. The Piccakoṇḍlu distinguish their performance by the type of instrument they use: normally a bell, but also sometimes a goatskin bagpipe (*śruti*).

The *Kāṭama Rāju Katha* may be said to unite the identity of the dispersed Golla communities. By sponsoring its performances and supporting the performers, Gollas not only remind themselves of their lineage, but inform their neighbors about their identity and glorious past in both an entertaining and grandiose way.

The Stories

The first portion of the epic consists of a series of references to Kāṭama Rāju's ancestors. In a typical performance there is only mention of their names accompanied by a claim that the story of their deeds is too long to narrate. The central core of the story focuses on the lives of Kāṭama Rāju's father, Peddi Rāju, and mother, Peddamma, who are childless until Kāṭama Rāju is born to them as a boon. The narrative then proceeds to describe a feud between Peddi Rāju (or, in some versions, Kāṭama Rāju) and another king, Vāliketuva Rāju, in which Peddi Rāju is killed along with many other Golla heroes. When Kāṭama Rāju, only seven years old at the time, goes to retrieve his father's body from the battlefield, he encounters the goddess Gangamma, the patron goddess of the Gollas, who falls in love with him and wants to marry him. He refuses, and the insulted Gangamma devises many ways to "conquer" him and force him to marry her. Kāṭama Rāju manages to evade her wiles and eventually proceeds to the battlefield where he is confronted by her brother, Pōtu Rāju, a demon who feeds on the bodies of dead warriors; he overcomes Pōtu Rāju.

Although some Gollas trace their tradition of offering a goat to Pōtu Rāju on the last day of their annual Sankrandi festival to the battle, others trace it to an incident where Gangamma steals a young goat belonging to Kāṭama Rāju and his followers as they cross a river during their migration south (see below). She gives it back to them only if they promise to make an offering: "Either a large he-goat now, or a small one annually at Sankrandi." They choose the latter.

Another important portion of the epic relates Kāṭama Rāju's migration south to the area around Nellore and his subsequent feud with the king of that region,

Nallasiddhi, and his consort, Kundamadevi, whose pet parrot causes enough noise to disturb the Golla's herd. One of the Golla heroes shoots the parrot with an arrow, but before it dies it manages to fly back to the palace where it relates the incident. Angry, Kundamadevi sends hunters to kill some of the Golla's cattle. Feeling that this was a heinous act (killing cattle is against Hindu law), Kāṭama Rāju refuses to pay grazing tax to the king, which leads to a terrible battle wherein Kāṭama Rāju kills Nallasiddhi.

Other episodes relate the lives and battles of Peddi Rāju's four brothers and their children. The full ballad cycle contains stories related to yet earlier ancestors, going back to the ancient time of the first Yadava lineage mentioned in the Vedas and classical epics. This lineage includes (according to the Gollas) Lord Kṛṣṇa. Episodes from the Mahābhārata are also included in some versions.

Research on the history of the story content of the Kāṭama Rāju ballad cycle has only just begun. The epic is sometimes attributed to Śrināthuḍu, a legendary fifteenth-century high caste Telugu poet who is supposed to have composed the epic of Palnāḍu as well. There appears to be considerable variation between the different oral reported versions; few of them appear to have been collected in full, and none of them have been systematically compared either to one another or to the literary text. Although regarded as an historical account of the heroic deeds of their ancestors, there is little or no independent documentation, outside the epic literature, of the existence of the heroes whose names appear in the story.

References

Narayana Rao, Velcheru. 1986. Epics and ideologies: six Telugu folk epics. In *Another harmony: new essays on the folklore of India,* edited by Stuart Blackburn and A. K. Ramanujan. Berkeley: University of California Press.

———. 1989. Tricking the Goddess: Cowherd Kāṭamarāju and goddess Gaṅga in the Telugu folk epic. In *Criminal gods and demon devotees: essays on the guardians of popular Hinduism,* edited by Alf Hiltebeitel. Albany: University of New York Press, pp. 105–121.

Subba Rao, Tangirala Venkata. 1978 and 1986. *Kāṭama Rāju Kathalu* (In Telugu.) Hyderabad: Andhra University Sahitya Akademi.

PETER J. CLAUS

SEE ALSO

Epic; Mandecculu

KATARAGAMA

Kataragama is, at once, a god and a place (*gama* means "village") where the god resides. Kataragama, as a god, refers both to the Sinhalese version of the Hindu war god Skanda, second son of Śiva, and to the autochthonous South Indian god Murukan with whom Skanda has long been merged. Skanda, of course, has a multitude of other names including Subramaṇiya, Kumaraṉ ("the Prince"), Vēlaṉ ("he of the lance"), and Āṟumukaṉ ("six-faced"), and was known in the ancient Sanskrit *purāṇās* as Kārttikeya (or Kumāra Kārtika). In both India and among Sri Lankan Tamils, Skanda as Murukan has been associated with *bhakti* (devotional) religiosity. For the Sinhalese, however, Kataragama is one of the four "warrant" (*varam*) or protector gods of the Kandyan kingdom, which controlled the central highlands of precolonial Sri Lanka (or Ceylon) from the late fifteenth century until 1815.

In form and personality, Kataragama is very much the virile, bellicose lover of ancient South Indian lore. Six-faced and twelve-handed, a vanquisher of *asura*s (demons), Kataragama wields a lance (*vēl*), rides a peacock, and is most famous and popular, in myth and modern lore, for his love affair with the half-god, half-deer, Vedda goddess Vaḷḷi. (The Vedda are both the mythological first inhabitants of Sri Lanka, and a contemporary caste.) Kataragama is first mentioned in a Sinhalese context in the eighth century *Mahāvaṃsa,* but only briefly and as a god of the Tamils. By the fourteenth century, however, according to Obeyesekere, inscriptions cite him as one of four guardian deities; by the sixteenth century his fame had spread widely enough that he was named in the Siamese *Jinakālamāli,* written in 1516. Captain Robert Knox (1606–1720), an English East India Company sailor captured in 1660 by the King of Kandy, Rajasingha II (r. 1635–1687), also noted the god's importance in the Kandyan kingdom.

Kataragama, the site, has attracted considerable scholarly attention because of its multivocalic appeal to a variety of ethnic groups and religions. Sinhalese Buddhists, Tamil Hindus, Muslims, and Christians all make pilgrimages to Kataragama, a fact of no small interest for a nation rent by decades of interethnic civil war. Kataragama is located in the jungles of southeastern Sri Lanka on the same longitude as Mount Kailāsa. The god's presence in this remote spot is explained by two myths. As told there, the first describes a duel of wits between Skanda-Kataragama and his brother, the elephant-headed god Gaṇeśa, to win a golden mango from their mother, and Siva's consort, Umā. The goddess tells them she will bestow the mango on the first of them to race around the world. Skanda-Kataragama rushes to do so on his peacock, but Gaṇeśa wins the contest by more sagely circling his parents. Skanda-Kataragama, enraged, flies from India to Kataragama. The second myth recounts how the Vedda girl, Vaḷḷi, catches Skanda-Kataragama's eye. Frightened, however, by his godlike appearance, she runs away. Skanda-

Kataragama's brother, Gaṇeśa, ever the cleverer sibling, devises a plan to win her affections for his brother. He appears to Vaḷḷi as a wild elephant, propelling the frightened girl into Skanda-Kataragama's willing arms. It is the consequences of this myth that are acted out every year at Kataragama's *ăsala perahăra* (procession), fifteen days during which the god is brought from his temple to visit the temple of his lover, Vaḷḷi, while ignoring the temple of his legitimate wife, Tēvānī Amma. The festival is famous for displays of ecstatic devotionalism (including dancing, fire walking, and self-torture) and ends with the water cutting ritual (*diyakapīma*) in which impurity is washed away.

References

Gombrich, Richard, and Gananath Obeyesekere. 1988. *Buddhism transformed: religious change in Sri Lanka.* Princeton: Princeton University Press.

Link, Hilde. 1997. Where Valli meets Murukan: "landscape" symbolism in Kataragama. *Anthropos* 92: 91–100.

Obeyesekere, Gananath. 1978. The fire-walkers of Kataragama: the rise of *Bhakti* religiosity in Buddhist Sri Lanka. *Journal of Asian Studies* XXXVII, no. 3: 457–476.

Wirtz, Paul. 1972. *Kataragama: the holiest place in Ceylon.* Translated from the German by Davis Berta Pralle. Colombo, Sri Lanka: Lake House.

Zvelebil, Kamil V. 1991. *Tamil traditions on Subrahmanya-Murugan.* Madras: Institute of Asian Studies.

MARK P. WHITAKER

SEE ALSO

Buddhism and Buddhist Folklore; Firewalking, Sri Lanka; Gods and Goddesses; Pilgrimage; Processions; Sacred Geography; Skanda; Sri Lanka, Sinhala; Veddas [Văddo]

KATHĀ

Kathā, a generic word meaning "story," is used in a number of North Indian vernacular languages. However, ethnographic research suggests it has a technical sense in indigenous genre theories in terms of true and fictional narratives. That is, kathā is often understood as "that which is true" as opposed to *kahānī* (another term meaning "story") for "that which is made up." Roma Chatterji has found that this basic dichotomy extends to a number of storytelling realms in Purulia, West Bengal. Thematic, internal features of the text usually signify the distinction between kathā and kahānī. As she explains it, "Time is given different values in these two genres. In kathā the consequences of each action reverberate throughout of cosmic universe, relating the different *yuga*s (ages) to each other. This kind of causality through *karma* is absent in the kahānī, or, if present, is so only as an afterthought, as an explanation for the circumstances in which the *dramatis personae* are placed" (50). I have elaborated this idea in terms of indigenous distinctions made between the sacred and profane realms in which stories are told in Goalpara, West Bengal.

The distinction is not isolated to West Bengal. Susan Wadley has found a similar division in Karimpur, Uttar Pradesh, where kahānīs "are often humorous and are peopled with typical or foolish earthly beings" (314). On the other hand, she writes, kathās are usually mythological stories "recited or read in conjunction with a particular ritual form, the fast (VRAT)." The fact that kathā is used for "vows" or "fasts" is clear in Bengali as well, where the term *brata kathā* is used for stories told during women's household rites held on such occasions. Kirin Narayan has found this distinction in Kangra, Himachal Pradesh, as well, where her collaborator and storyteller, Urmila Devi, reserves the term kathā for women's rituals. Kahānī is used solely for secular stories told by anyone at any time.

References

Chatterji, Roma. 1985. Folklore and the formation of popular consciousness in a village in the Purulia District of West Bengal. Ph.D. Dissertation, University of Delhi.

Korom, Frank J. 1992. To be happy:" narrative, ritual play and leisure in an annual Bengali religious festival. Ph.D. Dissertation, University of Pennsylvania.

Narayan, Kirin. 1997. *Mondays on the dark night of the moon: Himalayan foothill folktales.* New York: Oxford University Press.

Wadley, Susan. 1978. Texts in contexts: oral traditions and the study of religion in Karimpur. In *American Studies in the Anthropology of India,* ed. Sylvia Vatuk, 309–341. New Delhi: American Institute of Indian Studies.

FRANK J. KOROM

SEE ALSO

Epic; Karma; Myth; *Vrat Kathā*

KATHAK DANCERS

The word *kathak,* from the Sanskrit word *kathā,* or "story," refers to both the classical dance style of North India and to the caste of dancer/musicians who have been performing and teaching this dance style for hundreds of years. Males of the Kathak caste were professional storytellers who enhanced their recitations with song and dance in order to attract wider audiences as they wandered from town to town. Though some Kathakārs claim to come from Uttar Pradesh, most have their roots in the desert of Rajasthan, where they served the local feudal lords, dancing and playing the drum for festivals and special occasions. The Rājās of the princely states in Rajasthan were great patrons of the arts and employed Kathaks in their courts to entertain them and teach the women of the harem. In search of adventure and new patronage, kathak performers migrated to different major cities where they developed their own styles. Thus, there are two major and one minor schools of kathak: the Jaipur, the Lucknow, and the Benares Gharānā.

Over the centuries, kathak has developed into a sophisticated and complex dance style that takes many years of rigorous training to master. Dancers are also expected to perfect the arts of music, both vocal and instrumental. In the past, male pupils often lived with the guru's family, providing them with personal services such as cooking, cleaning, and massaging in exchange for knowledge. Since the 1950s, dance schools have replaced, for the most part, the tutorial apprenticeship method of transmission with group classes in an institution where students can pay a fee or receive a government scholarship to learn dance. The young dancers, who are now of any caste, gender, and class, continue the tradition of showing respect for their gurus by touching their feet and offering services to them.

Before the 1920s, in addition to males born into the *paramparā,* or hereditary line of succession, traditional kathak was performed by *tawā'ifs*, or courtesans. These professional women were expert in the arts, and often studied with male Kathaks. After forcing these women to become mere prostitutes in their cantonments, the British Colonialists referred to these artists in a derogatory manner, calling them *nautch,* or dancing girls. The connection of dance with prostitution and lack of morals continues to haunt female kathak dancers even today. Perhaps it is due to this stigma that women of the Kathak caste adhere to strict purdah practices of veiling and neither study the dance style nor perform on stages or in the company of non-kin males, though they are adept singers, drummers, and folk dancers and may be employed by their female Rajput superiors to entertain them.

During the Indian Nationalist movement, women from educated, urban, elite backgrounds began to study and promote the classical dances of India in an attempt to bolster national pride in their cultural heritage. At the turn of the century, the majority of male dancers still belonged to the hereditary caste of dancers/musicians, but the woman entering and even dominating the field were no longer courtesans, but educated, elite women living in urban centers. Unlike their mostly uneducated and impoverished male teachers, these women were able to compete in the modern market, presenting their material in elegant Hindi and English, with the financial and familial support needed to succeed.

MEKHALA NATAVAR

SEE ALSO

Colonialism and Folklore; Dance; *Nāca; Nauṭaṅki*

KATHAKAḶI

At the historical moment of its emergence in the late sixteenth and early seventeenth centuries in Kerala, *kathakaḷi* was given its present name meaning, "story play." It refers to the performance of dance-dramas written in often florid Sanskritized Malayalam. Kathakaḷi was created from such existing traditions as the martial art (*kaḷarippayattu*), Sanskrit temple drama (*kūṭiyāṭṭam*), the devotional dance-drama sacred to Lord Kṛṣṇa (*kṛṣṇāṭṭam*), and ritual performances (*teyyam, mūṭiyēṯṯà*). At first plays were based on the *Rāmāyaṇa,* later the *Mahābharata,* and then the purāṇas, often stories about Kṛṣṇa from the *Bhagavata Purāṇa*.

On a bare stage, using only a few stools and occasional properties, three groups of performers create kathakaḷi performances: actor-dancers, percussionists, and vocalists. With a few exceptions, companies of actor-dancers are all male. They use a highly physicalized performance style embodied through years of training. The characters they play are kings, heroines, demons, demonesses, gods, animals, and priests, along with others drawn from everyday life. Each role is easily identifiable to local audiences as a particular character type, with its own inherent characteristics, by the codified makeup and elaborate, colorful costumes.

The actor-dancers create their roles by using a repertory of dance steps, choreography, a complex language of hand-gestures (*mudrās*). They literally "speak" their character's dialogue with their hands and use pliable face and eye expressions to portray the internal states (*bhāva*) of the character. The percussion orchestra consists of three types of drums (*ceṇṭa, maddaḷam,* and *iṭekka*), each with its own distinctive sound and role in the ensemble. The drums and brass cymbals keep the basic rhythmic cycles around which the dance-drama is structured. The two onstage vocalists keep the basic time patterns on their cymbals and sing the entire text, including both third-person narration and first-person dialogue, in a vocal style in which elaboration and repetition are common characteristics. Performances traditionally begin at dusk, and it can take all night to perform what would be equivalent of thirty pages of written dialogue and soliloquy.

Kathakaḷi drama texts in written tradition, known as *aṭṭakatha* ("enacted story"), consist of third-person metrical verses (*ślōkas*) which, often composed completely in Sanskrit, narrate what happens in the ensuing dialogue/soliloquy portions of the text—*padams,* composed as dance music for interpretation by the actors. Padams, usually in the first person with a mixture of Sanskrit and Malayalam, typically have three parts: the *pallavi* (refrain), *anupallavi* (subrefrain), and *caraṇam*

A Young girl dances the Indian classical dance. Kathakali, India, © Mimi Nichter

(literally, "foot"). Ślōkas and padams are set to specific musical modes (*rāgas*) appropriate to mood and context. *Padams* are set in specific rhythmic patterns (*tāla*) and tempos (*kāla*).

Over the years, kathakaḷi literary texts have been added to or subtracted from by lineages of performers and patrons who pass on to succeeding generations their techniques, styles, and conventions of performing particular plays. In keeping with the *rasa* aesthetic, which encourages elaboration of all performative modes to enhance the pleasure of aesthetic delight, performative interpolations (*iḷakiyāṭṭam*) have been added in performance. Lasting up to an hour, the best known are opportunities for senior performers to display one or more aspects of their virtuosic abilities, such as the choreographic *tour de force* of Arjuna's interpolation in *Kālakēya Vadham* in which he describes the sights of Devaloka, or the histrionic display of inner emotional turmoil demanded of the actor playing Nala in *Naḷa Caritam* when he enacts the wrenching turmoil of his decision to leave Damayanti to the mercy of the wild forest. What distinguishes aṭṭam from the literary text is that they are not sung, but simply enacted without repetition by the actor or actors onstage at the time through action and hand-gestures.

Many kathakaḷi plays still in the active repertory have been "edited" for performance to shorten them to three-to-four hour performances. It is commonplace to attend all-night performances of three shortened plays, each focusing on scenes of most interest to connoisseurs, or the performance of a single shortened play. Since 1930, when the best known Malayali poet, Mahakavi Vallathol Narayanan Menon, founded the now well-known Kerala State arts school, the Kerala Kalamandalam, kathakaḷi has been adapted both by practitioners from within the tradition and by Malayali, Indian, as well as Western artists and entrepreneurs from without. These experiments have included shaping and marketing kathakaḷi for tourist audiences, writing and staging new plays based on traditional epic and purāṇic sources, transforming kathakaḷi techniques and choreography into modern forms of Indian stage dance and dance-drama, writing and staging new plays based on nontraditional sources or current events, such as the 1987 leftist production of *People's Victory,* which pitted the personified hero (World Conscience) against the personified villain (Imperialism), and adapting non-Hindu myths or non-Indian plays for kathakaḷi style productions, such as the story of Mary Magdalene, the Buddha, Faust, the *Iliad,* and *King Lear.*

References

Jones, Clifford R. and Betty True Jones. 1970. *Kathakaḷi: an introduction to the dance-drama of Kerala.* New York: Theatre Arts Books, 1970.

Namboodiri, M. P. Sankaran. 1983. Bhava as expressed through the presentational techniques of Kathakaḷi. In *Dance as cultural heritage,* Vol. I. New York: Congress on Research in Dance.

Rajagopalan, L. S. and V. Subramanya Iyer. 1975. Aids to the appreciation of Kathakaḷi. *Journal of South Asian Literature* 10(2–4): 205–210.

Zarrilli, Phillip B. Forthcoming. *When gods and demons comes to play: Kathakaḷi dance-drama in performance and context.* London: Routledge.

———. 1992. A tradition of change: The role(s) of patrons and patronage in the Kathakaḷi dance-drama. In *Arts patronage in India: methods, motives and markets,* ed. Joan L. Erdman. New Delhi: Manohar Publishers, 91–142.

———. 1984. *The Kathakaḷi complex: actor, performance, structure.* New Delhi: Abhinav Publishers.

PHILLIP B. ZARRILLI

SEE ALSO

Dance; Kerala; Kṛṣṇa; *Mahābhārata;* Martial Art Traditions; Nationalism and Folklore; *Purāṇa; Rāmāyaṇa; Teyyam*; Theater and Drama

KATHĀSARITSĀGARA

Kathāsaritsāgara, or "An Ocean of Streams of Stories," is a Sanskrit work by Soma, usually called Somadeva or Somadevabhaṭṭa. An immense work of some 22,000 stanzas, the *Kathāsaritsāgara* is, as the author himself says, "a compendium of the essence of the *Bṛhatkathā,*" another poetical work of the early centuries A.D. by Guṇāḍhya (composed in Paiśācī Prakrit, a once widely spoken dialect of Northern India). Since no manuscript of this Paiśācī work has yet come to light, the character and content of the *Bṛhatkathā* are known primarily from the compendium of Somadeva.

Somadeva states that he made his compendium for the diversion of Queen Sūryavatī of Kashmir. From the few details he gives concerning the royal house, with additional help from Bilhaṇa's *Rājataraṅgiṇī* (a history of the kings of Kashmir), the date of the composition of the *Kathāsaritsāgara* can be placed between 1063 and 1081 A.D. It is one of the very few classical Sanskrit works whose date of composition can be so closely determined.

The importance of the *Kathāsaritsāgara* lies not only in its greatness as a literary work, but especially more in the inestimable value of its contents. It contains the bulk of the story literature of ancient India, otherwise preserved in many separate works of uncertain date and unknown authorship. Thus, it contains, among countless others, the entire *Pañcatantra,* the *Vetālapañcaviṃśati* ("The Twenty-five [Tales] of a Vampire"), the legend of Purūravas and Urvaśī, and a summary of the entire story of King Nala and Damayantī, only five cantos of which, in the version found in the *Mahābhārata,* are generally familiar.

Throughout the *Kathāsaritsāgara* are themes that recur again and again in Indian literature, as, for example, the motif of the "craving of a pregnant woman" (called *dohada,* "two-heartedness"), which is particularly common in Buddhist and Jaina tales. Other motifs, such as that of the "magical articles," have numerous correspondences in literature outside India as well.

Many of the stories in the *Kathāsaritsāgara* are of Buddhist origin, as, for example, the story of King Śibi, whose piety is tested by Indra in the form of a falcon. Others are of demonstrably Hindu origin, as the story of the elephant, the hare, and the moon, reflecting the Hindu belief in a hare in the moon. Yet others are ultimately of non-Aryan or even non-Indo-European origin, so that the whole collection brings together many streams of many diverse sources, as exemplified in the title, "An Ocean of Streams of Stories."

The frame story of the *Kathāsaritsāgara,* like that of *Pañcatantra,* dramatizes in mythical or legendary form the vagaries of oral transmission and of transformation of the oral tales to writing. In the opening section called *Kathāpīṭha* ("Pedestal of the Stories"), it is alleged that the *Bṛhatkathā* was first told by the god Śiva to his wife Pārvatī. It was overheard by Śiva's attendant Puṣpadanta, who told it to his wife. When, by a circle of retellings, it came back to Pārvatī, she was angered, thinking that her husband had told her an *old* story. She cursed Puṣpadanta to become a mortal along with Mālyavat, another attendant who spoke on his behalf. The curse upon Puṣpadanta ends when he relates the story to a certain Kāṇabhūti, living in the forest also under a curse.

The curse upon Mālyavat, Puṣpadanta's intercessor, is to end when, after hearing the story from Kāṇabhūti, he makes it known to the world. Mālyavat, in his earthly form as the poet Guṇāḍhya, attempting to make the poem known to the world, sends the 700,000 couplets to King Sātavāhana. Puffed up with his newly acquired knowledge of Sanskrit, the king rejects it as composed in the lowly Paiśācī dialect. Disheartened by the rejection, Guṇāḍhya burns the poem, except for 100,000 couplets that his two assistants especially liked. Upon hearing of the conflagration, the king arrives at the scene and accepts the remaining portion, whose fame subsequently spreads from the royal city to the whole world.

The stories are full of charm and cleverly told, often with masterly touches. In one incident King Sātavāhana, while playfully splashing his wives with water, betrays his imperfect knowledge of Sanskrit grammar, specifically regarding the coalescence of vowels at word-junctures. Misunderstanding his chief wife's request, he pelts her with sweetmeats (*modakaiḥ*) instead of ceasing to cast handfuls of water (*mā udakaiḥ*) at her as she had requested.

The stories are held together rather loosely in a series of encapsulations of one in another (frame structures), each being introduced by some character or event in the foregoing, so that the initial story becomes somewhat difficult to retain in mind, as one proceeds from one subsidiary story to another until the initial or main story is again picked up and resolved.

The *Kathāsaritsāgara,* in sum, is an almost inexhaustible treasure trove, not only for the folklorist in search of new themes or old ones told afresh, but also for the general reader who wishes to read stories with quickly moving action, yet with a sustained level of human interest and charm.

Reference

Somadeva. 1968[1924]. *The Ocean of Story, being C. H. Tawney's translation of Somadeva's Kathā Sarit Sāgara (or Ocean of Streams of Story).* Reprint Edition. Delhi: Motilal Banarsidass.

WALTER HARDING MAURER

SEE ALSO

Buddhism and Buddhist Folklore; Dohada (Pregnancy Cravings); Nala and Damayantī; Pañcatantra; Śiva; Story Literature, Sanskrit

KERALA

Hemmed in between the mountain ranges of the Western Ghats and the Arabian Sea, the modern state of Kerala, which defines nearly 360 miles of India's southwest coastline and rises steeply to the crest of the Ghats, largely corresponds to a cultural region known under that same name for more than two millennia. Though open to significant military and cultural incursions from the rest of India through its mountain passes, and to prolonged interregional and international trade relations through its coastal ports, the basic fact of Kerala's well-delineated geographical boundaries has helped define it as a distinctive culture area throughout its history.

Culturally speaking, the region's closest affiliation is with the Tamil country, over the mountains to the east, for ancient Kerala chieftains and bards were full partners in the early Tamil literary culture that produced the corpus of ancient Tamil or Caṇkam literature of the early centuries, C. E. These chieftains were known as the Cēralas, or Cēras, from which the modern name Kerala is derived. Despite the subsequent divergence of Kerala speech from ancient Tamil and toward the modern language of Malayalam, with an accompanying infusion of Sanskrit and Brahmanical literary influences, both the common language and folklore of Kerala preserve many linguistic, stylistic, and thematic patterns that reach back to this shared Dravidian literary heritage. At the folk level, there have also been considerable cultural interactions between Kerala and neighboring coastal Karnataka to its north, the region traditionally known as Tulunad (now Dakshina Kannada District of Karnataka). For instance, the striking similarities and overlap between the worship of popular deities knowns as *teyyam*s in northern Kerala and *bhūta*s in Tulunad form just one example among a whole complex of cultural features shared between the regions.

Historically, aside from ancient Caṇkam literature and some later Sanskrit works attributed to Kerala writers, the earliest firm documentary evidence of developed cultural life from within Kerala itself is found in inscriptions which commence in the nineth century, C.E. These already chart the language's divergence from the neighboring Tamil, and writers in the local language began in the following centuries to develop Kerala's noteworthy literary culture. The degree and extent of political centralization, and hence the nature and development of cultural life in this formative medieval period, are matters of considerable historical debate, particularly around the existence of the so-called Second Cēra Empire.

What is certain is that by the twelfth century, Kerala was fragmented into a number of shifting, feuding chieftaincies that characterized the region's political life down to the coming of the European colonial powers. During the colonial period, while the Portuguese, Dutch, French, and British struggled in sequence to dominate Kerala's coastal trade, the main indigenous powers to emerge were the Zamorins based in Calicut in the north, the rulers of Cochin in central Kerala, and the Travancore kingdom, based in Trivandrum in the south. In the mid-eighteenth century the Muslim kings of Mysore repeatedly invaded Kerala and sporadically controlled northern Kerala, commonly known as Malabar, until the British defeated them in 1792. The British took over direct control of Malabar, which they administered as part of the Madras presidency, leaving Cochin and Travancore as independent states. After Indian Independence, Travancore and Cochin became a single political entity in 1949, and British Malabar was subsequently added to this unit on linguistic grounds, to form the modern state of Kerala in 1956.

Throughout its premodern developments, the tenor of Kerala culture was shaped within the wider influences operative throughout south India. The basic cultural matrix was defined through the "Hinduism" typical of Dravidian south India: the early Caṇkam traditions of warrior chieftains, ancestors, and indigenous deities being worshipped through dance-possession, memorial stones, and blood rites yielded to the mode of emotional devotion or *bhakti* dedicated to increasingly Brahmanical and Sanskritic deities. This bhakti movement commenced in the Tamil country in the sixth and seventh centuries C. E. and by the tenth century was consolidated into the growth of large structural temples as political and religious institutions. This new Hindu mandate effectively effaced the considerable influence of Buddhism and Jainism that had held sway at various points in south Indian history down to this time.

The temples of Kerala, though structurally more humble than their Tamil counterparts, and usually in wood, rather than stone, became the centers of medieval Sanskritic learning and artistic culture in the region. Controlled by Brahmans, who were either local intelligentsia or were brought into Kerala by chieftains from elsewhere, these temples and their attached theaters and compounds were the fora in which Kerala's rich repertoire of performing arts developed, often as a way of mediating the language and styles of classical Sanskrit into vernacular forms more accessible to the local (higher caste) populace. The temple-servant castes, known collectively as *Ambalavāsi*s, had key roles as performers, authors, scholars, and innovators in creating dance and dramatic traditions like *kūṭiyāṭṭam, kṛṣṇāṭṭam, rāmanāṭṭam, cākyārkūttà, mohiniyāṭṭam,* and the most famous, *kathakaḷi*.

A rigidly enforced and highly differentiated caste system, however, excluded the religious culture from a majority of the people. The result was that there were different strata of lower-caste shrines and temples that developed their own performative and festival genres and their own modes and liturgies of worship. These were partly imitative and partly disjunctive of their higher-caste counterparts. Often these latter traditions evolved around dance in elaborate costume and makeup, with rites of possession by local deities and ancestral spirits that recalled the earlier Caṇkam traditions. Performance forms, such as *teyyam, muṭiyēttà, Dārikavadham* and *pāmpin tuḷḷal,* exhibit different constellations of these features, overlaid with varying degrees of Sanskritic language and ritual. Also typical of the region's folk worship, is the prominence given to local goddesses. Often identified as incarnations of the Sanskritized goddess Bhagavati, they have exerted a considerable pressure for acceptance even in the pantheons of Brahmanical and upper-caste temples and domestic shrines. At farthest remove from the temples, the thick forests of the Western Ghats have been home to numerous tribal communities whose cultures have intergrated with and contributed to that of the lowland, settled agriculturalists, particularly, but not exclusively in the lower strata of the caste-spectrum.

Finally, as a legacy to its cosmopolitan maritime trading culture along the coasts, Kerala has been home to communities of immigrant Jews, Muslims, and Christians along its coasts since medieval times. While the small Jewish community has migrated almost in its entirety to Israel, the latter two have grown through conversion and intermarriage during the medieval and modern periods into powerful and substantial minorities. Though the Syrian Christians claim their settlements were founded by St. Thomas, their presence can be reliably confirmed only back to the seventh or eighth centuries, C.E. While much in the Christians' folk traditions has undoubtedly developed from the surrounding cultural matrix, the wider South Indian affinities of their predominant performance forms, such as *caviṭṭunāṭakam* and *mārgamkaḷi,* clearly derive from the substantial proselytizing activity of European missionaries. The Kerala Muslims, known as Mappilas, trace their cultural origins from the conversions and intermarriages with Arab traders on Kerala's coast (from the eighth century, C.E.), rather than from the Persian and Central Asian sources of most Islamic cultures in South Asia. They developed their own Arabicized dialect of Malayalam (called *Arabi-Malayāḷam* or *Māppiḷa-Bhāṣa*) in both literary and popular registers, the latter being much closer to the standards of spoken Malayalam, as used in their well-known war-songs (*paṭa-pāṭṭu*). This linguistic and cultural development of Christian and Muslim communitites in Kerala has thus woven their traditions of folksongs, performance genres, and literature, as synthetically creative strands, into the cultural fabric of the region. Linguistically and culturally fully integrated into Kerala society, these communities' traditions of folksongs and literature have contributed another interesting strand to the cultural fabric of the region.

Though there are numerous surveys of Kerala's folklore in Malayalam, most of the scattered works in English tend to be devoted to particular genres or forums of performance. The only attempt at a fairly comprehensive survey of folk genres is by the Kerala Sangeetha Nataka Akademi (1978).

References

Choondal, Chummar. 1980. *Kerala folk literature*. Trichur, Kerala: Kerala Folklore Academy.

Kerala Sangeetha Nataka Akademi. 1978. *Nadodi drissyakala soochika: folk arts directory*. Trichur: Kerala Sangeetha Nataka Akademi.
Logan, William. 1989 [1887]. *Malabar*. Madras District Manuals. New Delhi: Asian Educational Services.
Narayana Panikkar, K. 1991. *Folklore of Kerala*. Folklore of India Series. New Delhi: National Book Trust, India.
Padmanabha Menon, K. P. 1982–1986 [1922–1937]. *A history of Kerala*. Vols. 1–4. New Delhi: Asian Educational Services.
Parameswaran Nair, P. K. 1967. *History of Malayalam literature*. New Delhi: Sahitya Akademi.
Raghavan, M. D. 1947. *Folk plays and dances of Kerala*. Trichur: The Rama Varma Archaeological Society.
Sreedhara Menon, A. 1967. *A survey of Kerala history*. Kottayam: National Book Stall.
Sreedhara Menon, A. 1978. *Cultural heritage of Kerala: an introduction*. Cochin, Kerala: East-West Publications, Ltd.
Tarabout, Gilles. 1986. *Sacrifier et donner à voir en pays Malabar: les fêtes de Temple au Kerala (Inde du Sud)*. Paris: École Française d'Extreme Orient.

RICH FREEMAN

SEE ALSO
Bhagavati Ritual Traditions of Kerala; *Bhūta; Cavițțu Nāțakam*, Christianity, Kerala; *Dārikavadham*; *Kathakali*; *Muțiyēțțu; Ōņam*; *Pāmpin Tuḷḷal*, *Teyyam*; *Tiruvatira*; *Tōṟṟam*

KERĀMAT

Kerāmat (miracle, generosity) are written in prose narrative form; they are religious legends and memorates, or supernatural experiences that the narrator has personally experienced in his or her immediate environment. In Bangladesh they are connected primarily with the Muslim faith, especially with belief in the charisma of saints (*pīr*), but they also include Hindu legends. The legends are usually single-episode tales passed down from generation to generation, narrating supernatural experiences and historical and miraculous deeds attributed to Sufī saints. Kerāmat memorates differ from legends in that they relate the personal supernatural experiences of the narrator or other present-day followers.

A common explanation for the miraculous powers of saints is that by controlling their *nafs* ("earthly soul", that is, greed, hunger, desire, anger) through *sādhanā* (meditation), they realize in themselves the Supreme Being and can see or know things beyond their time and space. The power to predict future events is exhibited in a kerāmat legend, summarized as follows:

> In the Bengali year 1283, 14 Kartik, a devastating cyclone and tidal wave occured in Bengal. Through his intuitive power, Pāglā Miā (a great saint) came to know of the cyclone before it started. The day before the cyclone, Pāglā Miā took a fishing trap (*chai*) and fixed it to a large banyan tree. The people all laughed at him since the day was clear and there was no sign of water. How could any fish be trapped? The people ridiculed Pāglā Miā. But the next day the cyclone came. His prophecy came true. Many people died, and a lot of fish were trapped in the *chai*.

The miraculous powers of legendary saints continue to be demonstrated to those who visit their *mājār* (shrines containing the tomb of an important holy man). The following kerāmat memorate was told by Maulana Lakman Al-Husseini Junus Miā in Fadikchary, Chittagong district:

> When I was studying at Fadikchary Madrassa (religious school), there was a friend of mine among the students. One day he suddenly died, and his younger brother was also struck by a dangerous fever and died. The whole family was crying over the body. Then one disguised person (a stranger) informed them: Jia-ul Haq Māijvāndāri (the living saint) told you to go to Māijvāndār Sharif (an important Sufi religious center and temple site in the Chittagong), to the *mājār*. Hearing this we started for Māijvāndār with the body. After *Jamā* (Friday prayer), the *Milād* (the celebration of the anniversary of the Prophet's birthday) was organized. Jia-ul haq Māijvāndāri was there. In the final prayer, called *Munājāt* (prayer in which one can make personal requests), the Imām (prayer leader) uncovered the body before the *Pīr* (saint). Then the *Pīr* looked at the body and uttered, 'You, rise up!' Suddenly and miraculously, the dead body rose up in front of the followers. I can never forget it!" (Harvilahti and Jahangir 1994).

As the above passage demonstrates, the tradition of composing and remembering kerāmat is still very much alive among the followers of saints in Bangladesh, reflecting their religious views, beliefs, and social customs.

References

Harvilahti, Lauri and Salim Jahangir. December 1994. Tape-recorded interview with Maulana Lakman Al-Husseini Junus Miyā of Fadikchary, Chittagong.
Triningham, J. Spencer. 1973. *The Sufi Orders in Islam*. Oxford University Press: London.

SHAFIQUR RAHMAN CHOWDHURY
AND LAURI HARVILAHTI

SEE ALSO
'Aql and Nafs; Folk Literature; Islam; Legend; *Maulid;* Pīr; Saints; Sufi Folk Poetry

KESAR

Kesar, or Gesar, is the hero of the great Tibetan and Mongolian epics. His name may ultimately derive from the title of the Roman Caesar. His life and deeds are the subject of numerous heroic and shamanic traditions performed in prose, verse, song, and dance among the ethnic groups of the mountain ranges that form the natural and cultural boundaries between south and central Asia.

The essential elements of the story found in the written epics are: divine or, at least, supernatural birth; humiliation in childhood, usually at the hands of an evil uncle; trickster personality with king- and clown-like manifestations; the winning, loss, and eventual regaining of his kingdom and favorite queen; the destruction of his enemies and ultimate establishment of his rule as ideal king.

While the regional versions of *Kesar* contain modified forms of these basic elements, they also vary considerably from the literary epics and from one another. As Matthias Hermanns has observed, "The familiarity with the Tibetan Gesar saga prompted them to create their own folk epics." Although early philological studies viewed the regional versions of Kesar as awkward descendants of Tibetan or Mongolian epic poetry, more recent anthropological field work has shown the importance of the folk Kesars as expressions of the cultural autonomy of mountain societies with long histories of political independence.

The center of the ancient indigenous versions of the Kesar saga appears to have been in the westernmost area of Tibetan cultural and linguistic influence on the basis of ethnographic, historical, and archaeological materials. In a recent study of a version in the Burushaski language, from the former princely state of Nager (Karakorum, Pakistan), Jettmar, H. Berger and H. van Skyhawk showed that underlying the story of Kesar are autochthonous themes of great antiquity, reaching back to the time of Buddhism in the Karakorum and Hindu Kush region. Especially interesting in this regard is the perception of woman as ambivalent and potentially dangerous to her sexual partner, not unlike the flesh-eating *ḍākinī* of Tantric Buddhism.

A great variety of themes and performance situations distinguishes the regional versions of *Kesar*. A general division into eastern (Lamaist, shamanic) and western (Muslim, heroic) traditions of Kesar emerges on comparing, for example, a Lepcha (Sikkim) with a Burushaski (Hunza-Nager region), and a lower Ladakhi (Muslim, heroic) with an upper Ladakhi *Kesar* (Lamaist, shamanic). Within this framework, the Balti versions represent a middle point: Kesar remains an infidel Buddhist, but his wife is a pious Muslim; he loses the numinosity of a divine birth, but gains stature as a human hero; the use of magic becomes a secondary means to achieve his goals: cunning and presence of mind are his foremost characteristics; his ultimate victory is not over the demonic kings of the four quarters, thus establishing righteousness in a chaotic world, but over a neighboring king who attacks his fortress, robs him of his queen and his riches, and thus destroys his honor as a warrior. Although in the Balti versions, Kesar is an infidel, his saga was read in the royal houses of Shigar, Baltistan, as a model for Balti princes. As in the Ladakhi versions, songs are numerous in some Balti versions but, in contrast to the Ladakhi versions, there are no passages taken directly from the Tibetan epic.

While the Ladakhi versions are often lengthy—some requiring three evenings to perform—the westernmost versions (Burushaski, Shina) are prose narratives without song or dance that can be performed in two to three hours. Again, the Balti versions represent a middle point: some are lengthy, some brief. In the Balti versions, Kesar remains a Buddhist; in the Nager version, he becomes a Twelver Shī'a; the Hunza version makes no mention of his religion.

Gesar, the hero of the Tibetan epic, is known to Tibetan immigrant groups in Nepal, and his deeds are still sung by the Drogpa nomads of the eastern part of the Manang District of the Annapurna Himal. Though he is said to be known to the Sherpas, Thakalis, and Tamangs as well, thus far there has been no confirmation of independent traditions of Kesar among these ethnic groups. Though unknown in Garhwal, Kesar can be found in Lahul and Spiti, where he has come to be identified with Bhīma, the Pāṇḍava. However, there have been no systematic studies of folk versions from Nepal, Lahul, and Spiti. If extant, such traditions are known only to the specialists on the ethnic groups concerned. There is no evidence of traditions of Kesar among the people of the plains of South Asia.

References

Berger, Hermann, Karl Jettmar, and Hugh van Skyhawk (eds.) 1996. *Libz Kisar von Nager: Ein Folksepos in Burusaski.* In *Asiatische Forschungen. Monographienreihe zur Geschichte, Kultur und Sprache der Volker Ost- und Zentralasiens.* Wiesbaden: Otto Harrassowitz.

Hermann, Silke. 1991. *Kesar-Versionen aus Ladakh.* In *Asiatische Forschungen,* vol. 109, Wiesbaden [Otto Harrassowitz].

Hook, Peter Edwin. 1995. Kesar of Layul: a central Asian epic in the Shina of Gultari. In *Studies of popular culture in Pakistan,* ed. W. Hanaway. Lahore: Sang-e-miil Publishers.

Samuel, Geoffrey. 1992. Gesar of Ling: The origins and meaning of the east Tibetan epic. In *Proceedings of the Fifth Seminar of the International Association for Tibetan Studies,* ed. Shoren Ihara and Zuiho Yamaguchi, pp. 711–721. Narita: Naritasan Shinshoji.

HUGH VAN SKYHAWK

SEE ALSO
Epic; Tibet

K͟H͟VĀJA K͟H͟IZ͟R

K͟h͟vāja K͟h͟iz͟r is a hero of Islamic story tradition. In Arabic, *k͟h͟vāja* is a term of respectful address, and *k͟h͟iz͟r* means "green." This hero is sometimes compared to the figure of Melchizedek. He is widely believed to have been mentioned in the Qur'ān, though his name does not appear there. He is identified in folk tradition as the "one of Our servants" (Qur'ān 18:65–82) whom God sent Moses to visit when God wished Moses to be humbled by learning the limits of his own merely human understanding. K̲h̲iẓr is also supposed to have gone with Alexander to seek the Water of Life; for one reason or another (in different stories, through either happenstance or trickery), K̲h̲iẓr drank the Water while Alexander did not. Thus he alone will live until Judgment Day.

K̲h̲iẓr is a guide; he wanders the wilderness, helping those who are lost and astray. Wearing green robes, he is especially associated with water and fertility. In South Asia, he is an important figure in the story cycle of Amīr Ḥamza and in much qiṣṣa literature as well; he is also frequently imported into folktales when a powerful white-magic figure is required. He enjoys God's special blessing, and has a sort of freelance saintly status that sometimes becomes quite exalted. In one Ḥamza version, he is elevated to the rank of "Ḥaẓrat" (a title otherwise reserved in this version), and given as a brother Ḥaẓrat Ilyās (Elias); most interestingly, they are both given an even more powerful mother called Bībī Āṣifa Bāṣafā (Lady Asifa the Pure).

Reference

Pritchett, Frances W. 1991. *The romance tradition in Urdu: adventures from the dastan of Amir Hamzah.* New York: Columbia University Press.

FRANCES W. PRITCHETT

SEE ALSO
Amīr Ḥamza; Islam; Muslim Folklore; Saints

KĪRTANA

A *kīrtana* is a temple performance that is part of *bhakti* tradition. It involves telling popular Purāṇic stories about the deeds of gods and, at the same time instructing people about moral and spiritual conduct and the observing of social norms. A kīrtana performance is an important element in temple culture.

In Maharashtra the performer is known variously as *Haridāsa* (Servant of Hari or Viṣṇu), *Kīrtanakāra,* or *Kathekarī* (storyteller). He usually wears a long white robe reaching his knees, a shawl over his shoulder, a *dhoti,* and either turban or *pagḍi* (the nineteenth-century Brahmin headgear in Maharashtra) on his head. He uses either cymbals or iron tongs in his left hand to maintain rhythm in his narrative. A good kīrtanakāra is able to sing well in the classical tradition and knows the Sanskrit language, the Vedas, the Purāṇas, and the

six Darśanas, besides being conversant with Hindu and Indian history, literature, poetry, and even contemporary politics. He is accompanied by an assistant singer, a harmonium player and a *tabla* (drums) player.

A kīrtana performance consists of two parts: *pūrva-raṅga* (initial section) and *uttara-raṅga* (post-section). The former deals with the exposition and explanation of a complex theological issue, while the latter explicates the topic further by introducing concrete examples in the form of stories from Purāṇas, the *Rāmāyaṇa,* the *Mahābhārata*, and historical sources. The performance ends with an *abhaṅga,* a devotional song composed by famous saint poets such as Tukaram or Namdev. A favorite with many performers is the song *Heci Dāna Degā Devā* ("Please God, Grant the Boon that will Ensure that I will Never Forget You"). The *prasāda* (food offerings) left after the offering to the god are distributed to the gathered devotees who make small donations to the kīrtanakāra during *āratī* (a ritual waving of the lamp). In hundreds of temples in Maharashtra, the birth of the residing deity is celebrated with a kīrtana.

The mythical sage Nārada is credited as the originator of kīrtana, and Sant Namdev is thought to be the first kīrtanakāra of Maharashtra. D. B. Tilak, the Marathi nationalist, recognized in kīrtana a powerful tool for the freedom struggle against the British and persuaded many kīrtanakāras to weave the message of liberty into their performances. Many kīrtanakāras, such as Dandekar, Paranjape, Tambe-Shastri, Patawardhanbuva, and Khadilkar, did this so successfully that they were imprisoned by the British for spreading disaffection against the state. In the postindependence period, kīrtanakāras such as Sant Gadge Baba have used kīrtana effectively to fight untouchability, blind faith, and caste-politics.

Reference

Dandekar, G. N. 1988. The last kirtana of Gadge Baba. In *The experience of Hinduism,* Eleanor Zelliot and Maxine Berntsen, eds. pp. 223–251. Albany: State University of New York Press.

JAYANT BHALCHANDRA BAPAT

SEE ALSO
Bhakti; Govindevji, Temple of; *Laḷita; Pūjā*

KOHOṀBĀ KANKĀRIYA

Kohoṁbā Kankāriya is a ceremony of the central region of Sri Lanka held in honor of the Twelve Gods (a collection of deities whose precise identification varies by locale). The texts of the *Kankāriya,* recited in Sinhala, describe the myriad of deities and malevolent beings who are invoked in the ritual, including stories of their birth, powers and territories. In the Kankāriya the most important of these are the three Malaya kings: Malaya, Saňdaliňdu, and Kitsiri; the *Kohombā* deities (who are sometimes identified with the three kings); the various *Banḍāra* ("chieftain") deities, and the *yakā* ("demon"), Kaḍavera. The painted wooden plaques of the Kohoňbā deities, which are housed in deity shrines, depict them dressed in the traditional garb of the Kandyan aristocracy.

Usually conducted in the post-harvest season as a rite of thanksgiving, the Kohoňbā Kankāriya is a general purpose ceremony, which is also performed to ensure success in other worldly matters, such as the healing of illnesses, the building of a house, or the resolution of a court case. Though today the ritual is rarely performed due to the decline of the local deities, the lack of qualified performers, and the considerable expense of the ritual, it is still occasionally staged as a cultural performance for state functions and, more rarely, on behalf of a family or village.

The ritual traditionally took place over the course of about seven days. Incorporating dancing, drumming, singing and comic drama, the Kohoňbā Kankāriya is loosely structured on the myth of Vijaya and Kuvēni, the founding myth of the Sinhala people. Vijaya, a foreign prince who has been banished from his homeland in India, arrives on the island and falls in love with Kuvēṇi, an indigenous demoness. After living with him, and bearing his two children, Kuvēṇi is betrayed by Vijaya who, as the king of Lanka, is compelled to abandon her to marry a princess of royal lineage. In anger over her abandonment, Kuvēṇi curses Vijaya and his successor, King Paṇḍuvas. Vijaya dies and Paṇḍuvas becomes afflicted with various illnesses. The protector gods of the island, seeing him in distress, devise a scheme to bring a healer from India to cure him. They send the demigod Rāhu, in the guise of a boar, to trick King Malaya into coming to Lanka. After his arrival on the island, Malaya is told of the king's plight, and, after performing several rituals, the king cures Paṇḍuvas and the curse is ended.

In the Kankāriya ritual, the elaborate costume of the dancers, which includes an intricate silver headdress adorned with shimmering *bō* leaves, is said to include half of the ornaments worn by King Malaya. The Kohoňbā Kankāriya is performed in a hall built especially for the ceremony. The emblems and weapons of the Twelve Gods are placed in two altars, adorned with flowers and palm leaf decorations, situated at opposite ends of the hall. The sequence of events in the ritual is highly structured, beginning with the consecration of the dancer's ritual cloths, and ending with the shooting of a plaintain flower. The ritual traditions of the three Kandyan regions (Kurunegala, Kegalle, and Kandy) essentially follow the same structure, though differing in some details. The lead ritual performer has some leeway in editing and expanding parts of the ritual to showcase his skills and those of his fellow dancers and drummers.

Though the Kohoňbā Kankāriya has been in decline over the last several decades, it continues to be performed in abbreviated versions as a display of Sinhala cultural heritage. While the ritual texts have receded in importance, dancing and drumming have been given greater emphasis. Some dances derived from the ritual are now performed on stage in concerts of Kandyan dance, a secular form popularized by the Sri Lankan government. At the University of Kelaniya, where mostly female students study for the bachelor's degree in Kandyan dance, knowledge of the Kankāriya texts and the ritual acts is required, though performance of the ritual remains an exclusively male domain.

References

Godakumbara, Charles. 1955. Popular cults. In *Sinhalese literature*. Colombo: Colombo Apothecaries.

Reed, Susan. 1991. The transformation of ritual and dance in Sri Lanka: Kohoňbā Kankāriya and the Kandyan dance. Ph.D. thesis, Department of Anthropology, Brown University.

Walcott, Ronald. 1978. Kohombā Kankāriya: an ethnomusicological study. Ph. D. thesis, University of Sri Lanka, Vidyodaya.

SUSAN A. REED

SEE ALSO

Banḍāra Cults; Buddhism and Buddhist Folklore; Dance; Sri Lanka, Sinhala

KOLAM

Kolam is a type of women's folk art—in the form of designs, drawings, and paintings—passed on from mother to daughter, sister to sister, or aunt to niece, articulating visually the creation of sacred space and time, and marking thresholds of space—households, domestic shrines, and temples as well as time—dawns and dusks, new moons, and winter solstices in Tamil Nadu. In front of the thresholds of most Tamil households, women draw the kolam daily with their right hands dipped into ground rice flour (wet or dry) or colored powders; the powders are rubbed off throughout the day by the feet of passersby as well as by those who cross the threshold of the particular household.

Tamil women say there are six major reasons why the kolam is created: 1) to create a space of auspiciousness, goodwill, and luck; 2) to show the presence of the woman householder; 3) to welcome the goddess Lakṣmī, the goddess of wealth, prosperity, and alertness, and to banish the goddess Mudevi, the goddess of poverty, misery, and laziness; 4) to show that the household is in a state of overflowing abundance and not in

Pondy kolam. Pondicherry, India, © Richard Rapfogel

misery; 5) to feed a thousand souls—ants, insects, and birds; and 6) to absorb the ill effects of the evil eye.

The kolam inaugurates the beginning of activities, the initiation of ritual events, the start of a new day. It provides the finishing touch to a fresh ritually cleansed space, whether on the threshold of a house, at the base of a domestic shrine, or during a temple festival. It is a visual sign of *mangalam,* or auspiciousness. It is a form of ritual prayer embedded in an aesthetic, a kind of visually drawn prayer.

The kolam is also an emblem of household cleanliness, a marker of good housekeeping in the Tamil world. It purifies, orders, and wipes clean through adornment the spaces where it is drawn. Hospitality to guests, goddesses, and animals is one of the central raison d'etres of the kolam's existence. It is as if these paintings on the ground, drawn by women's hands, provide a space of protection and honor for the person whose feet graze the kolam. The kolam acts as an open invitation to welcome the goddess Lakṣmī, the goddess of wealth and prosperity, into the household and simultaneously creates a space where Mudevi, the goddess of misery, poverty, and laziness is kept at bay.

One of the preeminent reasons for the making of the kolam is to protect and honor the household's *dharma,* or morality. It is important for a household to feed a thousand guests as one of its first actions of the day. Because that is considered physically and economically impossible to do, the kolam, made of rice flour, is used to feed a thousand souls, including ants, insects, birds and other small creatures throughout the day. The kolam also absorbs the ill effects of the evil eye of passersby as well as those in the household by attracting, catching, and holding the eyes of the passersby.

To draw a kolam, a woman may spend anywhere between a few minutes to a few hours, depending on her mood, and the state of the household that the kolam reflects. If, for example, there had recently been a death in the family, then, the kolam will not be drawn for a certain number of days, depending on the type of kinship relationship that existed between the household kin and the person who had died. If, on the other hand, there has been a birth or a wedding, the kolam will be bordered in *kavi,* or ochre red, to show the mood of auspiciousness and abundance of the household. The white of the rice flour and the red of the kavi powder together create a sense of sacred space, marking places that divinity is invited to occupy. To prepare the space on which a kolam is drawn, the ground, floor, or shrine area is doused with a mixture of fresh cowdung and water or plain water and carefully swept clean to create a canvas of freshly moistened brown or reddish earth.

The kolam is created with hand-ground rice flour, store-bought stone powder, or colored powders. Primarily an ephemeral aesthetic form, the kolams are visible as designs that adhere to the ground usually for a day or more. Yet, depending on the preparations of the materials used and the location, the kolam can last anywhere between one hour to a couple of months. Rice is the goddess Lakṣmī, a sacred substance, and therefore flour made from ground rice is the most common and preferred material to use. If the kolam is created with dry rice flour and is located in front of the threshold of the house, then its existence on the ground will be ephemeral. The dry rice flour drawings are made by holding a small amount of dry rice flour between the thumb and forefinger. The thumb is pressed hard against the forefinger, thereby controlling the flow of the dry rice flour onto the ground. If the kolam is created with wet rice flour and is in front of a household shrine where it will not be rubbed off as easily, then it can endure for a couple of months. Here, rice is ground fine into a powder, wetted in water, and then is dipped into with a cloth. The cloth, in turn, is squeezed between the thumb and first two forefingers, a tripod of pressure through which the rice flour is controlled. The lines are thick and bold, the white of the wet rice flour emerging slowly over a period of a couple of hours as it dries.

There are two major types of kolam—geometric and figurative. The geometric type includes smaller focussed patterns based on a straight or curved line, circle, square, or a triangle, which are then repeatedly elaborated over an expanding space, ultimately contained by a boundary of a large square or circle. Interestingly, kolam variations extend to the subcaste level among the Brahmins; square (or *katta*) kolams are usually made by the Iyer subcaste of the Tamil Brahmin women and concavely curved squares are made by the Aiyangar subcaste, especially those from the town of Srivilliputtur in southern Tamil Nadu. The unusual labryinth design (*shulli* or *pulli kolam*) is one of the most popular among non-Brahmin women and the design type that has attracted the most attention in the western scholarly literature. One line continually crossing itself is like a continuous snake twisting and turning around a graphically laid-out series of dots. Sometimes more than one line is crossed with another, but, like a maze, or a puzzle, it still gives the illusion of one line. Although Chettiar and other high-caste non-Brahmins also tend to create the katta kolams for ritual occasions, the pulli kolams are the staple designs of everyday life.

In the recent past, the caste-based designs were more rigidly maintained, and rarely did a woman of one caste cross from the border of one caste set of designs to another. But over the past ten to fifteen years, due to the popularity of chapbooks bought in the bazaars and local markets, most of them produced in large cities like Madras and Madurai, certain designs are no longer the prerogative of distinctive caste styles. Rather, there is a marketplace in the popularity of kolams, and it shifts from year to year.

What is commonly referred to as the "color" kolams involve densely packed lavish applications of brightly colored figurative kolams. These require a different artistic and stylistic creativity, reminiscent of some of the wall paintings and art found in magazines and other popular literature. These cross caste, class, and even, surprisingly, religious boundaries. The designs range from figurative designs that include common motifs such as the lotus, temple bells, musical instruments, dancers, peacocks, etc. The figurative and even the geometric traditions have recently expanded their repertoire of designs enough to attract a few young Muslim and Christian women and some men to widely popular kolam competitions held throughout Tamil Nadu.

And now, increasingly, the kolam chapbooks found in the local markets display secular and non-Hindu themes, including musical instruments, Islamic mosques, and Christian churches. Women increasingly emphasize the kolam as an integral part of Tamil rather than Hindu culture, saying again and again, the kolam is a Tamil, not a Hindu, art. It belongs to everyone who is Tamil.

References

Archana, Shastri. 1981. *The language of symbols: a project on South Indian ritual decorations of a semi-permanent nature.* Madras: Crafts Council of India.

Beck, Brenda. 1976. The symbolic merger of body, space and cosmos in Hindu Tamil Nadu. *Contributions to Indian Sociology.* 10(2): 213–245.

Huyler, Stephen. 1994. *Painted prayers: women's art in village India.* New York: Rizzoli.

Layard, I. 1937. Labyrinth ritual in South India: threshold and tatoo designs. *Folklore* 48: 115–186.

Layard, I. 1993. Hosting the Divine: The *kolam* in Tamil Nadu. In *Mud, mirror and thread: folk traditions in rural India.* ed.

Nora Fisher, pp.192–203. Santa Fe: Museum of International Folk Art.

Layard, I. 1988. Tamil Panpattil Kolangal [*Kolams* in Tamil Culture] 4. Ph. D. dissertation, Madurai Kamaraj University, Madurai.

VIJAYA NAGARAJAN

SEE ALSO

Dṛṣṭi; Floor Designs; Gods and Goddesses; Tamil Nadu

KORDABBU

Kordabbu is the name of a deified hero in the Tulu-speaking region of Karnataka. There is an epic-length song (*pāḍdana*) about his life and deeds, and his spirit is worshiped in a distinctive village-level cult. (See Claus 1989a for a description of the cult, and 1989b for a synopsis of the song.) In life, Kordabbu was devoted to his masters, but immoderate in his behavior. Even as a child, he incurred the anger of Brahmans, and later in his life he was feared by the corrupt authorities, who then tricked him into imprisonment at the bottom of a well.

Although born of the "untouchable" Mundala caste, his deified spirit is highly esteemed and widely venerated by villagers of all castes. He is particularly renowned for recovering lost articles, and for his adherence to his devotees' requests, if also often excessive in carrying them out through the violent deaths of those he punishes.

In rituals (*bhūta kōla*s) he is accompanied by a female spirit, Tani Maniga. The *Kordabbu Pāḍdana* explains that Tani Maniga, a woman of the Muggeru caste, through her spiritual powers, rescued Kordabbu from imprisonment in the well. Tani Maniga is a name that appears in other pāḍdanas as well, and this incident forms the basis for linking Kordabbu's pāḍdana with those of other Tuluva heroes (*bhūta*s).

References

Claus, Peter J. 1989a. Behind the text: performance and ideology in a Tulu oral tradition. In *Oral epics of India,* eds. Stuart Blackburn, Peter J. Claus, Joyce Flueckiger and Susan Wadley, 55–74. Berkeley: University of California Press.

———. 1989b. Kordabbu. In *Oral epics of India,* eds. Stuart Blackburn, Peter J. Claus, Joyce Flueckiger and Susan Wadley, 231–235. Berkeley: University of California Press.

PETER J. CLAUS

SEE ALSO

Bhūta; *Bhūta Kōla*; Heroes and Heroines; *Pāḍdana*

KOṬAHAḶUVA GEDARA

Literally meaning "short cloth house," *koṭahaḷuva gedara* is the Sinhalese Buddhist term for a girl's first menstruation ceremony. Like most rites of passage, koṭahaḷuva gedara has a tripartite structure, with sequential stages of separation (sequestration), transformation (a ritual bath), and reincorporation (her return to public life as a mature woman). "Short cloth" generally is understood to refer to the short skirt worn by a young girl; after the first menstruation ceremony, she gives her old skirts to the washerwoman and wears only the long woman's skirt from then on.

Upon first noticing the onset of menstruation, *loku venevā* (becoming big), the girl informs an adult who acts quickly to isolate her, either in a closed room or behind a curtain rigged for the purpose. The *killa* (pollution) of first menstruation is considered especially strong and harmful to men. Stories are told of dire misfortune befalling fathers who see their newly menstruating daughters.

As the girl is being installed in her temporary quarters, other family members consult an astrologer. Often they include her father and *māmā,* mother's brother and father's sister's husband, either of which is a potential father-in-law because of preferential cross-cousin marriage. The astrologer compares astrological tables with the time of onset to determine an auspicious day and time for the girl's bath, the kind of bath water (such as river water enriched with turmeric and sandalwood), and the direction the girl should face during the bath. The astrologer also advises on diet and may use the girl's birth horoscope in conjunction with the time of onset to make predictions about her future and that of other members of her family.

During her isolation, the girl is never unaccompanied because loneliness and menstrual blood attract demons. Items known to repel demons—limes, iron, a kitchen pestle—are placed near her. She may use a toilet pot inside or, covered in a sheet and clutching an iron key, be allowed to go out to the latrine. She does not bathe, eats little, and if her confinement (usually three to ten days) is long, may become thoroughly miserable, despite frequent visits from girlfriends and female kin.

Finally, the day and hour of the bath arrive. The washerwoman (*redi năndā*) comes to lead the girl, shrouded in a white cloth, out the back door to a river, well, or bathing enclosure in the yard. Facing the astrologically determined direction, the girl gazes at a tree branch with milky sap (connoting fertility and cooling) while the washerwoman pours pots of water over her. The earthenware bathing pot is then smashed and the girl, head covered and dripping wet, is led to the front door of her home. At the threshold, the washerwoman lifts the cloth and the girl gazes into a basin of water (to absorb more pollution) and then halves a coconut using an iron knife to distract demons and repel *ăs vaha,* or "evil eye," and—because the tufted end of the coconut is male and the other, female—to predict the balance between the girl and her husband in marriage. Finally, the girl is led into the house, this time through the front door, where she assures herself a prosperous future by circling a mat containing auspicious items symbolizing, primarily, abundance: sweets, basic foods (such as, rice, onions, sugar, salt), money, and a comb and mirror (associated with goddesses), as well as two burning oil lamps, which she extinguishes.

The girl is led away to be dressed in all new clothes and then returns to be presented anew to assembled relatives and guests. They give her gifts as she bows before each individually. The girl's old clothes and sleeping mat, sweets, and money are given to the washerwoman. Guests are feasted in a celebration that may last throughout the day. The girl is now marriageable, but early marriage is rare and she usually returns to her normal schoolgirl life.

In Sri Lanka, similar ceremonies are found among Muslims, Christians, and Hindus. Indeed, one local washerwoman may be called to attend them all. But while the ritual is common, its significance varies, reflecting differing notions of womanhood. Buddhists and Hindus emphasize the danger posed by the girl's ritual pollution; Christians do not attribute pollution to her but say that, as a pure virgin, she must be protected from the evil eye and bathed because the Virgin Mary cares about cleanliness; Muslims emphasize the girl's marriageability and give her gifts of household items. Consumerism has increased in recent years and koṭahaḷuva gedara ceremonies generally have become more elaborate as families demonstrate their own achievements with expensive wedding-like celebrations for their daughters.

References

Alahackoon, H. W. 1893. Ceremonies observed by low-country Sinhalese: a girl attaining the age of puberty or maidenhood. *Modern Literary Review: Notes and Queries for Ceylon* n.s. I(5): 153–55.

Buckley, Thomas, and Alma Gottlieb, eds. 1988. *Blood magic: the anthropology of menstruation*. Berkeley: University of California Press.

Gennep, Arnold van. 1960. *The rites of passage*. Trans. Monika B. Vizedom and Gabrielle L. Caffee. Chicago: University of Chicago Press. (Original: *Les rites de passages*. Paris, 1909.)

Gough, E. Kathleen. 1955. Female initiation rites on the Malabar Coast (Curl Bequest Prize Essay for 1953). *Journal of the Royal Anthropological Institute* 85: 45–80.

Leach, Edmund R. 1970. A critique of Yalman's interpretation of Sinhalese girl's puberty ceremonial. In *Echanges et communications: Mélanges offerts à Claude Lévi-Strauss à l'occasion de son 60ème Anniversaire*. [*Exchanges and communications: A collection offered to Claude Lévi-Strauss on the occasion of his 60th birthday.*] Jean Pouillon and Pierre Maranda, eds. Hague: Mouton, 819–828.

Stirrat, R. L. 1975. Compadrazgo in Catholic Sri Lanka. *Man* n.s. 10: 589–606.

Winslow, Deborah. 1980. Rituals of first menstruation in Sri Lanka. *Man* n.s. 15: 603–25.

Yalman, Nur. 1963. On the purity of women in the castes of Ceylon and Malabar (Curl Bequest Prize Essay for 1961). *Journal of the Royal Anthropological Institute* 93: 25–58.

DEBORAH WINSLOW

SEE ALSO

Astrology; *Dṛṣṭi;* Gender and Folklore; Life Cycle Rituals: Puberty; Sri Lanka, Sinhala

KOṬHĀRĪ, KOMAL

Komal Koṭhārī (b. March 4, 1929) is an international authority on Rajasthani folk traditions, whose expertise extends across multiple genres and regions of India. Although his academic training and early work was in Hindi literature, he soon developed an interest in folk forms of poetry and story, and, after becoming the secretary of the Rajasthan Academy of Dance, Drama, and Music, he began to study and collect folk musical instruments. In 1960, together with Vijaydān Detha, and with few resources, he founded Rūpāyan Saṃsthān, the Rajasthan Institute of Folklore, in the village of Borūnda in western Rajasthan.

Their vision was to explore all aspects of folk life in this single village. Setting out to develop a comprehensive understanding of the people's lives, they examined not only narratives, epics, songs, riddles, music, drama, and crafts but also religious beliefs and practices, caste composition, economics, government interactions, village power structures, community desires for development, agricultural practices, land and water use, and much more. They published some of their findings in the journal *Lok Saṃskṛti,* which they co-edited for many years. In 1962, researchers started coming to Borūnda seeking their expertise and assistance, and, since 1971, a steady stream of foreign scholars from Europe, America, Asia, and Australia have come, bringing resources that allowed the institute's research to expand across Rajasthan.

Koṭhārī specifically pursued the study of folk music and instruments, oral epics, and folk gods and goddesses, but moving beyond and through these studies, he explored traditional ways of understanding and ordering the world. In addition, he studied the processes by which oral knowledge is learned, remembered, and passed from generation to generation outside formal educational systems. He has been particularly interested in the documentation, preservation, and development of folk music, working with traditional musicians to develop the inherent musical potential of their instruments and organizing a number of camps for children to cultivate an awareness of their own musical traditions.

Koṭhārī has brought these traditions to the attention of the world by taking folk musicians, singers, and dancers abroad to perform. The first sponsors of these programs were ethnomusicologists working with the institute, and the initial interest was academic, but the performances soon shifted to the public arena, providing additional forms of patronage for traditional musicians in a changing world. This exposure has generated a number of collaborative commercial recordings and films released in Europe, Japan, and India.

Researchers in multiple fields, performers and artists, photographers and filmmakers, regularly come to consult with Koṭhārī at his home in Jodhpur (the location of the institute's video and audio archives), and he continues to organize performances, to participate in national and international conferences, and to pursue the work of collecting, preserving, disseminating, and analyzing a wide variety of folk traditions. Musical instruments remain his major focus—how they are made, their musical potential, the ways they govern singing style and rhythmic patterns, how people are taught to play them, and more. Puppetry, sung epics, storytelling, traditions surrounding the devotional saints Mīrābāī and Kabīr, and many other projects also continue to engage his attention. He has received innumerable awards, including the high honor of being named a fellow of the Indian National Academy of Dance, Drama, and Music.

References

Koṭhārī, Komal. 1972. *Monograph on Langas: a folk musician caste of Rajasthan*. Borunda: Rupayan Press.

———. 1977. *Folk musical instruments of Rajasthan: a folio*. Borunda: Rupayan Sansthan.

———. 1982. The shrine: an expression of social needs. In *Gods of the byways: wayside shrines of Rajasthan, Madhya Pradesh and Gujarat*, eds. Julia Elliott and David Elliot, 5–31. Oxford: Museum of Modern Art.

———. 1989. Performers, gods, and heroes in the oral epics of Rajasthan. In *Oral epics in India*, eds. Stuart H. Blackburn, Peter J. Claus, Joyce B. Flueckiger, and Susan S. Wadley, 102–117. Berkeley: University of California Press.

———. 1994. Musicians for the people: the Manganiyars of western Rajasthan. In *The idea of Rajasthan: explorations in regional identity*, Vol. 1, eds. Karine Schomer, Joan L. Erdman, Deryck O. Lodrick, and Lloyd I. Rudolph, 205–237. Columbia, Mo.: South Asia Publications.

———. 1995. Patronage and performance. In *Folk, faith, and feudalism: Rajasthan studies*, eds. N. K. Singhi and Rajendra Joshi, 55–66. Jaipur: Rawat Publications.

NANCY M. MARTIN

SEE ALSO

Dance; Folk Music; Folklorists; Rajasthan; Shrines

KṚṢṆA

Kṛṣṇa ("dark one," "black") is one of the incarnations of Viṣṇu and is regarded by some sectarian movements to be the principal manifestation of this supreme deity. One of the most popular gods in the Hindu tradition, Kṛṣṇa is the focus of extensive devotional literature in Sanskrit and the vernacular and is celebrated in folksongs, narratives, sculptures, painting, and the performing arts.

Origins

The *Chāndogya Upaniṣad* (ca. seventh–sixth century B.C.E) mentions a Kṛṣṇa Devakīputra (Kṛṣṇa, the son of Devakī), but there is very little information added. Inscriptional evidence indicates that worship of Vāsudeva (another name of Kṛṣṇa) was popular around the second century C.E.; grammarians from the fourth century B.C.E. use the names of Kṛṣṇa and various episodes from his life to illustrate rules. It is believed by western scholars that many hero figures have merged over the centuries to emerge as the composite "Kṛṣṇa Vāsudeva." The Jain tradition speaks of Kṛṣṇa as a cousin of a *tirthaṇkara* called Nemi.

Iconography

Kṛṣṇa is generally portrayed as a chubby child or as a slim, young adult with a smiling visage. He wears a peacock feather in his diadem and a yellow cloth around his waist. Literature and paintings depict Kṛṣṇa as blue in color, and while there is no single explanation for it, two interpretations are popular: "Kṛṣṇa" means "black," but since that color may suggest anger, he is portrayed in a more aesthetically appealing blue. Others prefer a more metaphoric explanation: the blue form represents a cloud laden with life-giving rain. The dark clouds are harbingers of life for parched crops; so too is Kṛṣṇa's grace said to be life-giving for the soul thirsty for salvation. Just as the coming of rain is unpredictable, so too is the shower of Kṛṣṇa's mercy.

Kṛṣṇa's life in Text and Ritual

The *Viṣṇu Purāṇa* (circa fourth century C.E.), *Bhāgavata Purāṇa* (circa nineth century C.E.), parts of the *Mahābhārata*, like the *Harivaṇśa* and the *Bhagavad Gīta*, as well as vernacular texts composed between 400 B.C.E. and 1200 C.E. give a composite picture of Kṛṣṇa. Devakī and Vasudeva, parents of Kṛṣṇa, are imprisoned by the ruler Kaṃsa because of a prophecy that his nephew, Devakī's eighth child, will kill him. Kamsa slays all of Devakī's children at birth. However, when Kṛṣṇa is born in Mathura (modern Uttar Pradesh), on the eighth night of the dark half of Āṣāḍha (August 15–September 14, a date which became fixed and accepted in the last thousand years or so), Vasudeva is miraculously able to transport his divine son to a nearby village of Braj/Vraja. Hindus from many parts of India mark his birthday by fasting and later by feasting to celebrate the divine descent (*avatarana*).

Kṛṣṇa is raised by a cowherd couple, Yaśoda and Nanda, and several medieval devotional songs and lullabies in Tamil and Hindi extol the maternal affection of Yaśoda. The childhood adventures of Kṛṣṇa include his killing numerous demonic agents who have been sent by his uncle to trace and destroy him. Other stories portray him as a mischievous, adorable child who loves and steals butter (a popular motif in sculpture and classical Bharata Nāṭyam dance) and as one who relentlessly teases the cowherd girls. He subdues the snake Kaliya, and in another story, he persuades the cowherd community not to worship Indra with food offerings. When Indra shows his anger by sending forth thunderstorms, Kṛṣṇa lifts the Mountain Govardhana as an umbrella to protect his friends. The themes of subduing Kaliya and being victorious over Indra are prominent in temple sculpture in medieval India, especially Belur (Karnataka). Mīrā, the fifteenth-century princess-poet, uses the epithet "lifter of Mount Govardhana" frequently in her poems, and followers of Caitanya commemorate this event with a big feast.

As a teenager, Kṛṣṇa is the alluring lover, dancing the moonlit nights away with the cowherd girls. Kṛṣṇa and his cowherd girlfriends playfully throw colored powder and waters on each other, drenching their world with color, a ritual enacted with abandon all over northern India in the festival of Holī. Their dances are re-created by many communities in India; the *rās līlā* dances in the state of Gujarat are particularly renowned. Tamil classics, starting with the *Cilappatikāram* (ca. fourth century C.E.), and devotional poems (seventh–ninth century C.E.) speak of Kṛṣṇa doing a circular dance (reminiscent of a *maṇḍala*) with his friends. These texts also identify Kṛṣṇa's cousin Nappiṉṉai as his beloved; he is said to have conquered seven bulls to make her his bride. Sanskrit texts like Jayadeva's *Gīta Govinda* (twelfth century C.E.) identify Rādhā (a person who becomes prominent only at this time period) as his lover; their rapturous physical union becomes an important way of depicting the union between a human soul and the divine in later devotional poetry and classical dance, especially in Bharata Nāṭyam and Odissi. In his adolescence, Kṛṣṇa is summoned to Mathura, and in fulfilment of the prophecy, kills Kaṃsa. In some Bengali traditions, Kṛṣṇa and Rādhā are permanently separated and this *viraha* (separation) reflects the condition of a human being separated from the divine one.

As a young adult, Kṛṣṇa marries the princesses Rukmiṇi and Satyabhāma. Telugu oral tradition and the Kuchipudi dances native to the Andhra area extol the beauty, grace, and vanity of Satyabhāma, as well as Kṛṣṇa's love for her. After defeating Narakāsura ("the demon of hell") with the help of Satyabhāma, he marries thousands of other princesses. The victory over Narakāsura is celebrated in many parts of southern India during the festival of Dīpāvalī ("necklace of lights"); the fireworks celebrating the festival are supposed to emulate the missiles used by Kṛṣṇa in his war. He defeats Narakāsura at dawn and the victory of light over darkness becomes the major theme in the celebration of Dīpāvali.

The *Mahābhārata* presents the mature Kṛṣṇa as a comrade of the Pāṇḍavas and their common wife Draupadi. He miraculously saves Draupadi's honor when Duhśāsanah tries to disrobe her in the Kaurava court. This incident is frequently recalled in classical Bharata Nāṭyam dances; the audience is reminded that, just as he came to the rescue of Draupadi, so too will he give salvation to anyone who seeks refuge in him. In the *Mahābhārata,* Kṛṣṇa is famous in his role as a peacemaker between the Pāṇḍavas and Kauravas and as a counselor to Arjuna just before the epic war. Kṛṣṇa becomes the charioteer of his cousin Arjuna and advises him of righteousness and duty at a time of moral crisis. The conversation between Kṛṣṇa and Arjuna has been revered as the *Song of the Lord* (*Bhagavad Gīta*) by Hindus for over two millennia. Kṛṣṇa eventually witnesses the death of his clan, the Vṛṣṇis; he finally relinquishes his mortal body when a hunter called Jaras ("old age") hits him with an arrow.

While Kṛṣṇa is generally perceived to be either the eighth or ninth incarnation of Viṣṇu, several traditions like those of Caitanya think of him as the supreme reality who descends to earth as Rāma and others. To some extent, most Hindus accept his supremacy among the incarnations of Viṣṇu by considering him to be the "full" descent of the deity. His preeminence is seen in other millenial narratives; many Tamil poets (eighth–nineth century C.E.) say, at the end of the eon, he lies down on a banyan leaf in the waters of chaos. He is portrayed as a baby sucking his toe—vulnerable, yet supreme, with the universe inside his belly.

Sanskrit and vernacular poets, both male and female, have sung extensively about Kṛṣṇa. Periyāḻvār (eighth century C.E.) was one of the first poets to adopt the stance of Yaśoda and compose songs of maternal affection for Kṛṣṇa; Āṇṭāḷ (eighth century C.E.) and Mira express their romantic feelings and passion for him.

Sūrdās's poems portray a variety of moods and attitudes and Purandaradāsa's songs to Viṭhala, a manifestation of Kṛṣṇa enshrined in Pandharpur, are popular all over south India.

It is important to note that the tone of the songs addressed to Kṛṣṇa are substantially different from those to Rāma. While Rāma is addressed with love and respect, devotees usually tease Kṛṣṇa about his unconventional behavior. Moreover, poets like Āṇṭāḷ sing erotic songs, seeking a rapturous physical and spiritual union with him, but because Rāma is perceived to be married only to Sīta, and is faithful to her, he is not the focus of romantic songs. These songs have played a significant role in the history of music and dance in the Indian subcontinent.

While Kṛṣṇa is worshipped in a generic form in many parts of India, in some places like Pandharpur (Maharashtra) and Nathdwara (Rajasthan), the regional manifestations are renowned. *Śrīnāthji,* the name given to Kṛṣṇa in Nathdwara, is decorated and dressed in different clothes several times a day and devotees delight in the diverse forms of adornment (*alaṅkāra*). In the temple town of Puri, in Orissa, Kṛṣṇa is known as *Jagannātha* ("lord of the world") and is worshipped with his brother Baladeva and his sister Subhadra. The Kṛṣṇa temples at Udipi (Karnataka) and Guruvayur (Kerala) are also renowned.

Kṛṣṇa-devotion has been made popular outside India primarily through the efforts of Bhaktivedanta Prabhupada (1896–1977) who belongs to the Caitanya tradition. Prabhupada is recognized as the founder of the International Society for Kṛṣṇa Consciousness (ISKCON), a community with hundreds of branches across the world.

References

Haberman, David L. 1994. *Journey through the twelve forests: an encounter with Krishna.* New York: Oxford University Press.

Hawley, John Stratton. 1983. *The butter thief.* Princeton: Princeton University Press.

Hawley, John Stratton. 1981. *At play with Krishna.* Princeton: Princeton University Press.

Miller, Barbara Stoler. 1977. *Love song of the dark lord.* New York: Columbia University Press.

Precadio-Solis, Benjamin. 1984. *The Kṛṣṇa cycle in the Purāṇas: themes and motifs in a heroic saga.* Delhi: Motilal Banarsidass.

Singer, Milton B, ed. 1966. *Krishna: myths, rites, and attitudes.* Honolulu: East-West Center Press.

VASUDHA NARAYANAN

SEE ALSO

Bhāoyāiya Song; *Dīvālī/Dīpāvalī;* Draupadī; Gods and Goddesses; *Holī; Mahābhārata; Navarātri; Purāṇa; Rāsa Līlā*

L

LĀLAN FAKIR

Lālan Fakir (*fakir*, Sufi mendicant; Bangla, *phakir;* Arabic, *faqīr*, poor), also known as Lālan Sām̐i or Lālan Śāh, lived in the nineteenth century (d. 1890) in the village of Cheuriya in what is now Kushtia District, Bangladesh. He is widely considered the best of all the Bengali folk poets of the Bāul religious tradition. Lālan is also celebrated as a folk hero who epitomizes the folk culture of Bengal common to both Hindu and Muslim communities.

Lālan's early life is shrouded in legend. His songs give evidence that even his contemporaries were puzzled about his religious affiliation and that one of the reasons he intentionally concealed his parentage was to avoid being labeled Hindu or Muslim. According to the earliest and most commonly cited biographical accounts, Lālan was born to Hindu parents, contracted smallpox while on a pilgrimage, and was left for dead. He was then found by a Muslim, according to some accounts by his guru Sirāj Sām̐i, who nursed him back to health. This story, however, cannot be uncritically accepted, since an obituary published just two weeks after Lālan's death in the journal *Hitakari* states that it is unverifiable. In the 1960s, another legend began to circulate, giving Lālan Muslim parents. This account appears to be fabricated in order to claim him for Islam. What is known for certain is that Lālan achieved widespread fame during his lifetime as a guru and composer of songs. His disciples—said to number ten thousand—were spread all over Bengal. He spent the latter part of his life in Cheuriya where he died on 17 October 1890, purportedly at the age of 116, and was buried on the site of his *ākhṛā* (ashram) without religious ceremony.

Lālan composed approximately five or six hundred songs, each consisting of three or four rhymed verses with the last verse concluding in a signature line (*bhaṇitā*) in which Lālan's name and usually that of his guru, Sirāj Sām̐i, appear. He probably was illiterate and composed his songs orally; they were later written down in notebooks by his disciples. Like the songs of other Bāul poets, Lālan's songs are passed down orally from guru to disciple and from one singer to another. The versions sung by *Lālan-panthī fakir*s (*fakir*s in Lālan's lineage), who are specially trained by their gurus to sing Lālan's songs, are accurately preserved, differing little from those in the oldest notebooks. Lālan's songs are unequaled for their high poetic quality, scintillating imagery, simplicity, and dry wit. Their felicitous use of words from the Kushtia dialect as well as colorful folk sayings and proverbs give many of them a racy, colloquial flavor, as in the refrain and last verse of "*Uparodhe dekho re bhāi ḍheki gelār mato*" (Look, brother! Being forced to work is like swallowing a husking machine):

> Look, brother!
> Being forced to work
> is like swallowing a husking machine —
> it doesn't go down.
> It tears open your throat.
> You end up dead.
>
> Whatever people desire
> let them do it!
> Let them do it!
> Let them do it!
> What's all the fuss?
> Lālan asks: Does a fruit taste sweet
> when it's kicked till it's ripe?
> (Mitra 1980: 257; trans.)

References

Cakravarti, Sudhīr. 1992. *Brātya lokāyat Lālan*. Calcutta: Pustak Bipani.

Caudhurī, Ābul Āhsān. 1992. *Lālan Śāh*. 2nd ed. Dhaka: Bangla Academy.

———. ed. 1974. *Lālan Smārak Grantha* (Lālan commemorative volume). Dhaka: Jātīya Grantha Kendra.

Dāś, Matilāl, and Pīyūṣkānti Mahāpātra, eds. 1958. *Lālan-gītikā* (Lālan's songs). Calcutta: Calcutta University.

Das Gupta, Shashi Bhusan. 1969. *Obscure religious cults*. 3rd ed. Calcutta: Firma K. L. Mukhopadhyay.

Jhā, Śaktināth. 1995. *Phakir Lālan Sāṁi: deś kāl ebaṃ śilpa* (Fakir Lālan Sāṁi: His country, time, and art). Calcutta: Saṃbād.

Mitra, Sanatkumār, ed. 1980. *Lālan Phakir kabi O kābya* (Lālan Fakir: The Poet and his Poetry). Calcutta: Pustak Bipani.

Rushd, Abu. 1991. *Songs of Lalon Shah*. Dhaka: Bangla Academy.

Salomon, Carol. 1991. The cosmogonic riddles of Lalan Fakir. In *Gender, genre, and power in South Asian expressive traditions,* eds. Arjun Appadurai, Frank J. Korom, and Margaret A. Mills, 267–304. Philadelphia: University of Pennsylvania Press.

———. 1995. Bāul Songs. In *Religions of India in practice*, ed. Donald S. Lopez, Jr., 187–208. Princeton: Princeton University Press.

CAROL SALOMON

SEE ALSO

Bangladesh; Baul Song; Song

LAḶITA

Laḷita is an old Marathi folk play genre that observes the rules of *Nātyaśāstra,* a Sanskrit treatise that prescribes rules of drama, dance, and music. The purpose of Laḷita is to convey moral and spiritual teachings of Dharma through role-playing. The main players include the *sūtradhāra* (the organizer), the *naṭī* (the actress), a clown, some bards, the *copdāra* (lawman) and the *pātīla* (village chief). Other motley characters who confront the audience are the *rājbhāta* (royal bard), the *gāvabāata* (village historian), the *jaṅgama* (a Śaivite mendicant), a pilgrim from Varanasi, the king, the queen, and so on. The highlight of the theatrical form is a play upon words and humorous critique of cultural differences. The characters expound their viewpoints on various subjects from their own vantage points and in their own language and vocabulary. The differences among them and the mutual unintelligibility in the theatrical space create much mirth among the audience, who is familiar with such religious and social confusion in real life.

The language of laḷita is a mixture of Hindi, Urdu, and Marathi. It has been suggested that this may be due to the laḷita possibly being a north Indian import. It may also have been influenced by the Muslim culture of the Adilshahi kings. *Hāsya* (mirth) is the main *rasa* (sentiment) in the laḷita. The humor is circumstantial, produced by puns, mixing of languages, clowning, and double entendre. In a purposefully long-winded way, the laḷita tells many stories of spiritual and moral value.

Laḷita, as a folk theatre form, is performed by itinerant troupes hosted either by the whole village or a single patron. The latter part of laḷita consists of a *kīrtana* performance (songs of praise accompanied by musical instruments) and is called *uttara-raṅga* (post-section). This part ends with the *kīrtanakāra* (singer) stressing the importance of moral and spiritual values of the Purāṇic story he has elaborated. *Āratis* (ritual praise) to various gods are then performed, followed by distribution of the *prasāda* (offerings). This later part of the kīrtana is also called the laḷita in Maharashtra.

JAYANT BHALCHANDRA BAPAT

SEE ALSO

Kīrtana; Nāca; Nauṭanki; Rāsa Līlā; Tamāśa; Theater and Drama; *Vidinātakam; Yakṣagaṇa*

LAMENT

Lamentations are expressive performances that communicate acute feelings of sorrow over the death of a relative or a beloved. In South Asia it is mainly women who display these states of high emotion during funerals. Even where such behavior is normally proscribed, as is the case in Islamic law (*shar'īat*), women utter high-pitched, undulating wails to dramatize their bereavement.

The kinetic and vocal expressions of lamentation cut across religious, ethnic, and caste lines. Throughout South Asia, as soon as a death occurs, women huddle on the ground near the body in tight clusters. Arms around each other, they sway, moan, and weep together, sometimes resting their heads for comfort on their partners' shoulders. Lamenters also may beat their chests, pull their hair, strike their foreheads against each other, wound themselves, and often faint.

Without instrumental accompaniment, lamenters address the dead from the viewpoint of their particular kinship ties to them. In the folk taxonomies of the Afghān, Pashtun, Punjābī, Tamil and Toda communities, for example, dirges are classified according to relational categories. Those that deplore the loss of fathers, mothers, husbands, brothers, sisters, sons, and daughters are given special intensity.

Laments differ from ordinary speech in that they are usually sung in rhythmic, formulaic lines or rhyming verses, punctuated with audible sobbing. Whether orally transmitted or improvised on the spot, laments communicate grief through poetic devices such as metaphor and hyperbole; the Tamil term for these dirges, *oppāri,* for instance, means "comparison." By means of images of receding landscapes and uprooted vegetation or through tropes that evoke a sense of absence, they contrast the happy past before death with the desolate present. The emotional pitch of these laments is sustained throughout the funeral. During the ensuing wake, dirges of the Toda tribe from South India often praise the wealth, character, and accomplishments of the deceased person. In the Punjab, lamenters may deny the tragedy altogether or express their desire to die and reunite with their beloved. Sometimes Pashtun and Tamil mourners accuse the dead of abandoning them.

When the funeral procession departs for the burial grounds, lamentation breaks out with renewed intensity. As women are often not allowed to follow the procession, this may be their last opportunity to see the deceased. After the cremation or burial, some Hindu traditions forbid weeping since it may persuade the dead to linger instead of proceeding to the hereafter. Among most castes of Tamilnadu, however, laments recur at stated intervals until the funeral cycle is completed, ten or sixteen days later. Yet their themes shift, expressing less lamentation for the dead than the sorrow of the bereaved.

Because laments provide such a distinctive code for expressing grief, South Asian women also resort to them in other situations of loss. At the marriage of daughters, for instance, North Indian village women may lament the coming separation; when sons or brothers neglect them, they might bemoan their sudden destitution. Traditional laments may even be sung in times of national crisis to communicate discontent to government authorities, making women, according to Indian anthropologist Veena Das, "the special interlocutors between the worlds of kinship and politics" (1990a:29).

References

Das, Veena. 1986. The work of mourning: death in a Punjabi family. In *The cultural transition: human experience and social transformation in the Third World and Japan,* eds. Merry I. White and Susan Pollak, 179–210. Boston: Routledge and Kegan Paul.

———. 1990a. Introduction. In *Communities, riots and survivors in South Asia,* ed. Veena Das, 1–36. Delhi: Oxford University Press.

———. 1990b. Our work to cry: your work to listen. In *Communities, riots and survivors in South Asia,* ed. Veena Das, 345–398. Delhi: Oxford University Press.

Egnor, Margaret T. 1986. Internal iconicity in Paraiyar "crying songs." In *Another harmony: new essays on the folklore of India,* eds. Stuart H. Blackburn and A. K. Ramanujan, 294–344. Berkeley: University of California Press.

Emeneau, Murray B. 1971. *Toda songs.* Oxford: The Clarendon Press.

Grima, Benedicte. 1992. *The performance of emotion among Paxtun women.* Austin: University of Texas Press.

Kieffer, Charles. 1975. *Les formules de lamentation funèbre des femmes à Caboul: āwāz andāxtan-e zana.* In *Mélanges linguistiques offerts à Émile Benveniste,* 313–323. Paris: Collection Linguistique, Société de Linguistique de Paris.

Vallikkannan, K. 1990. Songs of mourning. In *Encyclopedia of Tamil literature,* ed. G. John Samuel. Vol. 1, 456. Madras: Institute of Asian Studies.

ISABELLE NABOKOV

SEE ALSO

Angạy; Complaint; Death Rituals; Gender and Folklore; Islam; *Jārī Gan; Majlis; Mārphatī* and *Murśidī* Songs; *Marsiya; Mātam; Nauḥa;* Song; Wedding Songs

LANḌAY

Lanḍay literally meaning "short" in Pashto, is an unrhymed couplet with nine syllables in the first hemistich and thirteen in the second. This form of folk poetry is also known as *ṭapa* or *miṣr'a,* especially in eastern dialects of Pashto. The final syllable ends in *-īna, -ūna, -āna,* or *-āma.*

Although each *lanḍay* is an independent unit, it can be grouped with others, usually by subject matter such as a particular historical event or folk romance, and sung as a sequence either by a single singer or by different people, sometimes competitively. Pashtuns usually consider this to be the quintessential Pashto verse form. Although commonly called a woman's form of verse, men also compose it, sometimes speaking in a woman's voice. Traditionally sung during work in the fields or at home, these couplets are included in chapbooks of this genre alone or along with other genres of folk poetry.

The subject matter of the *lanḍay* is as broad as the Pashtun culture itself and includes love and honor, social tragedies, legendary and historical events, the natural and the spiritual world, and departures, exile, and reunions. The short and pithy nature of *lanḍay* makes it an ideal form in which to express sarcasm or ridicule. In general, the poet's pen name is not included, thus giving women anonymity and an opportunity to express feelings about sexuality.

References

Darmesteter, James. 1888–1890. *Chants populaires des Afghans.* (Popular songs of the Afghans) Paris: Imprimerie nationale.

Heston, Wilma. 1996. Rhyme and repetition: Pashto poetry as song. In *Studies in Pakistani popular culture,* eds. William L. Hanaway and Wilma Heston. Lahore: Sang-e Meel and Lok Virsa.

MacKenzie, D. N. 1958. Pashto verse. *BSOAS* 21: 319–333.

Shaheen, Selma. 1984. *Rohī sandare* (*ṭape*) [Pashto songs (tappas)]. Peshawar: Pashto Academy.

WILMA L. HESTON

SEE ALSO

Afghanistan; Gender and Folklore; North-West Frontier Province; *Paṣhtūnwalī;* Song

LĀVAṆĪ

The term *lāvaṇī* generally designates a song form found in Maharashtra, Karnataka, Tamil Nadu, and Uttar Pradesh. Since its characteristics vary from region to region, the present discussion will focus on the *lāvaṇī* of Maharashtra. The *Marāthī lāvaṇī,* one of the best known genres of popular vocal music in Maharashtra, is based on a wide range of topics including love (by far the most common); descriptions of persons, places, and events; and spiritual views on life. While reflecting pan-Indian perspectives, many of the songs also contain names of Maharashtran places, castes, musical instruments, deities, and customs not generally mentioned in the more classical genres of Indian music. Their poetic form is generally strophic with one or more stanzas (*kaḍva* or *cauk*) and, in many cases, a refrain consisting of words (*dhruvapad* or *dhrupad*) or vocables (sometimes called *jhīl*). End rhyme and, to a lesser extent, internal rhyme often connect the final syllables of lines and syllables within a line, respectively. In poetic style most lāvaṇīs are lyric, that is, they are full of vivid, concrete imagery and rich descriptions readily understood by the masses. This contrasts sharply with the relatively abstract compositions of classical music.

As a written tradition, the lāvaṇī is almost four centuries old in Maharashtra. The oldest lāvaṇīs date sometime after 600 C.E. when an anthology of 315 lāvaṇīs by Manmathaśivaling, called the "Paramarahasy" collection, was composed. Whether or not these lāvaṇīs were actually sung is unclear. However, even in the absence of musical notations and musical theory, one can trace a continuous musical history for lāvaṇī that reaches back two or more centuries when the royal courts of the Marāṇhā Empire (and particularly the Peśvās) generously patronized its exponents. With the British defeat of the Peśvā regime, this kind of patronage declined, although some musicians continued to receive support in the princely states up until the time of Indian Independence. Others turned to the general public for their livelihood, and their descendants continue to perform for this group even today.

In Maharashtra, at least four distinct musical traditions may be identified. In *sangīt bārī,* a tradition arising from the courtesan tradition practiced in many parts of India, women sing and dance erotic lāvaṇīs for the entertainment of male patrons. These women come mainly from the Kolhāṭī caste, but include other castes and Muslims as well. In *ḍholkīcī bārī* men and/or women from a variety of religions and castes (mainly Māng, Mahār, and Marāṭhā) sing lāvaṇīs on various subjects before and during a drama to entertain mixed audiences of men, women, and children. In the *utpāt maṇḍalī* tradition men of all castes from Paṇḍharpūr and the surrounding area, led by a family of Brāhmaṇ priests, sing erotic lāvaṇīs for themselves during the saturnalian festival known as Holī. Finally, in the *nāradīya kīrtankār* tradition, male preacher-singers from the Brāhmaṇ caste perform lāvaṇīs on a variety of subjects, ranging from spiritual views on life to profane love as a means of drawing their congregation of men, women, and children to God.

In order to enhance the meaning of the text, lāvaṇī singers rely on various kinds of artistic expression. For example, the women of saṅgīt and ḍholkīcī bārīs use body movement and facial gestures to make the meaning of their erotic lāvaṇīs more explicit and personal for their male patrons. Singers in dramas and religious discourses rely on the plot or spoken message to provide a specific context to lāvaṇīs that might otherwise appear too abstract or out-of-date.

A genre of popular music, lāvaṇīs are songs set to a simple, modal tune (*cāl*) and short rhythmic cycle (*tāl*) lasting four, six, or eight beats. Stanzas within a single lāvaṇī usually have the same melodic form, and when a refrain is present, its melodic form completes the stanza. Brief musical improvisations occur mainly in the beginning and between divisions, and are generally based on vowels rather than solfege or dance mnemonics.

Monophonic in texture, lāvaṇīs consist of a melody performed by a solo singer throughout, or by a solo singer periodically alternating with either a secondary supporting singer or unison chorus. The melody is supported by a drone or melodic accompaniment and a rhythmic accompaniment maintaining the *tāl.* In all of the traditions except ḍholkīcī bārī, the *peṭī* (hand- or foot-operated harmonium) supports the melody while the *tablā* (pair of drums) maintains the tāl. In ḍholkīcī bārī, the Maharashtran *ḍholkī* (double-headed drum) and *tuṇtuṇe* (kind of plucked chordophone) are more characteristic, supplying a rhythmic accompaniment and reiterating drone, respectively; this texture is often thickened by adding the tablā and peṭī. In some traditions, cymbals and ankle bells provide an additional layer of rhythmic accompaniment.

References

Deva, B. Chaitanya and Josef Kuckertz. 1981. *Bhārūḍ Vāghyā-muraḷī and the Ḍaff-gān of the Deccan: Studies in the regional folk music of South-India*. 2 vols. Munchen-Salzburg: Musikverlag Emil Katzbichler.

Rao, Kristin Olson. 1985. The Lāvaṇī of Maharashtra, a regional genre of Indian popular music. Ph.D. dissertation; University of California, Los Angeles.

KRISTIN RAO

SEE ALSO
Folk Music; *Holī;* Maharashtra; Song

LEGEND

Legends and myths are always someone else's. When we call a story a legend or a myth, we imply that it is largely untrue. For the people who tell these stories as their own, however, the stories are fact and not fiction. Nonetheless, not all facts need be true in exactly the same sense. Even those people who own the stories often distinguish legends from myths, and both from more mundane history, though their ways of drawing the distinctions may not correspond at every point to the ways an external observer would draw them.

Modern folklorists usually define legends as stories set in real, historical time about important cultural and political heroes. Myths, on the other hand, are stories set in nonhistorical time about the origin of things, about how culture, society, and nature came to be the way they are. Both legends and myths may incorporate supernatural interventions by gods, demons, and animals, as well as all sorts of miraculous events, but these elements are more prevalent in myths. The implicit aim of myths is often to define the basic cultural concepts and values of the society, while the implicit aim of legends is often to either affirm or question existing social and political institutions.

The closest common Sanskrit equivalents to the terms, "myth" and "legend" are *kathā* and *carita* (also *caritra*), and close cognates exist in other languages. Both these terms may refer to almost any story, whether it be fiction, myth, legend, or even roughly historical. Nonetheless, the term *carita* is more likely to be used for stories we would call legends. More literally, *carita* means "deeds" or "adventures." Traditional South Asian authors do make one important distinction that corresponds roughly to the modern distinction between myths and legends. Stories about the saints and heroes of earlier *yuga* (ages) correspond roughly to myths, while stories about the saints and heroes of the present *Kālī Yuga* correspond to legends. The myths about the avatars of Viṣṇu (except Buddha and Kalkin) and about the heroes of the *Mahābhārata* all take place in earlier yuga. The legends about saints such as Śaṅkarācārya, Kabīr, and Caitanya, or about royal heroes such as Vikramāditya, Pṛthvīrāja, and Pābūjī all take place in the still current Kālī Yuga.

Legends about Kālī Yuga saints are curiously absent in early Sanskrit literature. Vedic Brahmins believed that religious truth is eternally embodied in the *Vedas*, texts that have no human authors. The appeal to the authority of the lives of historical saints first becomes important in legends about the heterodox religious leaders Buddha and Mahāvīra. The most powerful stimulus to the writing of saints' legends, however, was the rise of the *bhakti* movement in vernacular languages. Beginning in Tamilnadu in the seventh century, this movement slowly spread northward, until by the sixteenth century, it had become dominant throughout the subcontinent.

Important collections of legends about saints include the *Periyapurāṇam* about the Nāyaṉmārs of South India; the *Śūnyasampādane* about the Vīraśaivas of Karnataka; Mahipati's *Bhakti-vijaya* about the Vārakarī saints of Maharashtra; Anantadās's *paracaī* about various saints of North India; the Sikh *janam-sākhī* about Gurū Nānak; the *vārtā-sāhitya* of the Vallabha sect; and Kṛṣṇadāsa's *Caitanya-caritāmṛta* about the Bengali saint Caitanya. By the late medieval period, even traditional Sanskrit theologians such as Śaṅkarācārya and Rāmānuja had acquired their own hagiographies, mostly written in Sanskrit.

Secular legends, or historical romances, grew up around the adventures of kings, queens, princes, and princesses. Such legends appeared in Sanskrit at an early date. Indeed, the main stories of the *Mahābhārata* and *Rāmāyaṇa* are thought to have originated from legends of this sort and only later became more mythical in character. A few Sanskrit texts such as Bāṇa's *Harṣa-carita* and Bilhaṇa's *Vikramāṅkadeva-carita* come close to entering the category of historical narrative but also display many legendary elements. Throughout South Asia there also exist a large number of traditional historical romances told in vernacular languages. These include the stories of Ālhā, Aṇṇaṉmār, Lorik and Candā, Ḍholā, and Pābūjī.

In English, the word "legend" denotes a loosely defined type of story, part history and part fiction. No word exactly equivalent to "legend" is found in Sanskrit or modern South Asian languages, but South Asian literature is full of stories that can be called legends. These are the kathā and carita that tell stories about the saints and heroes of the Kālī Yuga. In at least this over-arching sense, the concept of legend can help us to distinguish such stories from other kinds such as myths.

References

Blackburn, Stuart H., et al., eds. 1989. *Oral epics in India*. Berkeley: University of California Press.

Reynolds, Frank E., and Donald Capps, eds. 1976. *The biographical process: studies in the history and psychology of religion*. The Hague: Mouton.

McLeod, W. H. 1980. *Early Sikh tradition: a study of the Janam-sakhis*. Oxford: Clarendon Press.

Mahipati. 1982 [1933]. *Stories of Indian saints: an English translation of Mahipati's Marathi Bhaktavijaya*, trans. J. E. Abbott and N. R. Godbole. Delhi: Motilal Banarsidass.

Pritchett, Frances W. 1985. *Marvelous encounters: folk romance in Urdu and Hindi*. Delhi: Manohar.

Smith, John D. 1991. *The epic of Pabuji: a study, transcription and translation*. Cambridge: Cambridge University Press.

DAVID N. LORENZEN

SEE ALSO

Ālhā (Ālhā-Ūdal); Amīr Ḥamza; *Aṇṇanmār Katai; Bhakti* Saints; *Ḍholā;* Folk Literature; Gūrū Nanak, Life Stories of; *Kathā; Kerāmat; Mahābhārata;* Material Culture; *Mu'jizāt Kahāni;* Nationalism and Folklore; Pābūjī; Rāmāyaṇa; Saints

LIFE CYCLE RITUALS

Life cycle rituals, such as naming, weddings, or funerals, move an individual from one stage of life to another. Also called "rites of passage" or "life crisis rites," they give social and moral meaning to biological processes of birth, maturation, and death. They affect the organization of society by adding or removing members and transforming key relationships. As Arnold van Gennep explained in his classic 1908 study, *The Rites of Passage,* such rituals are varied but universal human customs. An individual going through a life cycle ritual separates from one stage of life, makes a ritual transition, and then becomes incorporated into his or her new social status.

Every life cycle ritual has individual, social, and magical significance. It not only changes the position of an individual; it also includes references to moral organizing principles, such as "duty" (*dharma*) or "honor" (*'izzat*). A ritual is also very likely to include some customary folk blessings, such as waving of lamps, anointment with turmeric, or preparation of special foods, intended to promote the general well-being of all concerned.

General Patterns

Hindu and Islamic texts provide idealized schemes of life stages, but Buddhist scriptures do not. Among Hindus, life cycle rites are called *samskāra*s, and the four idealized stages of life, *āśrama*s. The classic Hindu prescription moves a person from student to householder, thence on to the status of hermit, and finally, renunciant. This scheme is not fully observed in practice, but it is a source of inspiration for some life cycle rituals. For example, at a wedding of a "twice-born" caste boy, it is not unusual to see him set off on his student life only to be summoned back by the father of the bride, who playfully begs him to marry the bride and assume the responsibilities of a householder. Folk custom thus uses the great literary traditions as one among many ideological or moral threads in the life tapestry it weaves.

The immense variability of custom among different south Asian groups and regions includes four major ritual patterns. These are based on the four predominant linguistic, geographical, and historic influences of the region—central Asian, northern, southern, and Himalayan.

The central Asian pattern is found mainly among peoples of Afghanistan and parts of Pakistan who speak Turkic or Iranian languages. Some are tribal groups occupying rugged, mountainous areas. Muslim customs show little Hindu influence if any.

The northern pattern is characteristic of Muslim or Hindu groups living in the northern, northwestern, or central plains and valleys of the subcontinent (including some, but not all, groups in Nepal) and speaking Indo-European languages. Marriage is the most elaborately celebrated life cycle rite. Girls often are married before they mature, and female puberty ceremonies are rarely, if ever, performed. Bride-giving families have a perpetual obligation to give gifts at life cycle rites and other times.

The southern pattern is found among Muslim, Hindu, or Buddhist populations who occupy southern India, Sri Lanka, and the area extending northeast through Orissa and Bihar into West Bengal and Bangladesh. With its mix of Dravidian and Indo-European languages, the area has ancient historic ties to southeast Asia and to scattered tribal groups. Families linked by marriage are less clearly ranked than in the north, and ritual gift-giving obligations between them are more variable. Weddings may or may not be elaborate events, depending on the strength of lineage or clan organization and other factors. The southern pattern includes the performance of some type of girl's puberty ceremony.

The Himalayan pattern is found among speakers of Tibeto-Burman languages in the Himalayan region and some historically related tribal groups. Examples are Sherpa, Newar, Tamang, and Limbu of Nepal. Their customs derive in part from Chinese and southeast Asian folk traditions and Tibetan Buddhism, combined with some animistic practices, such as shamanistic spirit possession. Animal sacrifice and beer (offering and drinking) are commonly found as parts of rituals. Some groups have Hindu influence or affiliation, while others show little or none. Death rituals tend to be elaborate. The presence of polyandry and other forms of polygamy often are associated with relatively relaxed sexual practices that contrast starkly with central Asian, northern, and southern values emphasizing female chastity. Female puberty rites are very important to some (for example, Newars) but nonexistent in other groups.

Scholarly Studies and Surveys

The most detailed ethnographic reports to date on life cycle rituals of northern India are those of R. and S. Freed (1980) and Vatuk (1975) and, on south India or Sri Lanka, those of Srinivas (1965) and Good (1991). For Bangladesh, Aziz and Maloney (1985) provide details on birth and early stages of life. Afghanistan and Pakistan reports are less detailed, except for the work of Dupree (1973). Ethnographies covering life cycle rituals of Tibeto-Burman language speakers include those of Fürer-Haimendorf (1964) and Nepali (1965). Ethnographic studies supplement wide-ranging folklore surveys by Thurston and Rangachari (1909) or other authors of *Castes and Tribes* volumes and, more recently, N. N. Bhattacharyya (1975). While folkloric surveys demonstrate the extent and possible historical connections of specific practices, ethnographies show how customs fit in with family and social life.

Specific Life Cycle Rituals

A summary description of the most widespread south Asian life cycle rituals follows. Each group has its own emphases and preferences, elaborating some and minimizing others for various reasons, both cultural and economic.

Pregnancy and Birth Rituals

The rituals immediately preceding and following birth are more relevant to the status of the mother or the family than to that of the child, who is not recognized as a person until formally welcomed in by the family. Common practices include the following:

Before birth a Fifth- or Sixth-Month Ritual is performed by Hindus of both north and south and a Ninth-Month Ceremony takes place in some Himalayan groups such as the Limbu. Just before the child receives its first drink of breast milk, there may be a Nipple-Washing Ceremony. The "First Milk Feeding" is a ritualized occasion among southern groups and Bengali Muslims, and in Sind in Pakistan. Northern Hindus, including Hindus of eastern Nepal, and many Muslims (of both north and south) conduct rituals on the sixth day after a birth. The intent of these rituals is to remove the impurity that an infant is thought to accumulate in the womb.

All groups seem to consider a house in which a birth occurs to be polluted to some extent. One effect of this sense of pollution is to separate the mother and/or the whole family from the rest of society while it goes through a transition, incorporating a new member. Purification allows the family to reunite with society at the end of a customary period of separation.

Establishing an Infant's Social Identity

One of the first gestures of fully accepting a newborn is the public announcement of his or her birth. This often is done differently for girls and boys, with grander celebration, singing, and dancing for the latter. Naming is done very differently by different groups. It may be a casual process or a formal rite.

Childhood Rituals

After being incorporated into his or her family, a child may go through one or more other life cycle rites before marriage. Typical customs include the "first solid food," in which Hindu children may receive their first taste of rice as part of a ritual celebrated sometime within the first year. Though not universally done, its significance as a folk rite is profound. It represents the child's first ingestion of rice, which is not only an important staple, but also a substance considered emblematic of family unity in many folk rites.

Other rituals include:

First haircut. Another childhood rite is the first haircut. Its significance is to remove all remnants of birth pollution, marking the end of babyhood and the beginning of the childhood stage of life.

Ear-piercing is done in many northern and southern areas for both boys and girls, but its present social significance is minimal.

Circumcision. Muslim boys in all regions are circumcised between the ages of seven days and ten years in the ceremony of *Musalmani karna* (literally, "to make a Muslim"). At least one Hindu caste, the Pramalai Kallar of Tamilnadu, circumcises its boys.

Religious initiation. Hindus and Buddhists may require their boys or young men to go through formal initiations before they begin religious instruction. For Hindus of the so-called twice-born castes, this initiation, the *upanāyana,* is considered to be a second birth for the boy. The equivalent Buddhist rite, or *Upasampadā,* puts a boy through certain steps of "going out" from the worldly life by having his head shaved and changing into the yellow robe. There is a widespread Muslim ritual, *bismillah khani,* for young boys and girls about to begin religious instruction.

Puberty Rituals

There are numerous female puberty rituals, especially in the southern parts of south Asia, where the first menstruation is considered to be an auspicious occasion. For some groups, religious initiation ceremonies serve as male puberty rites paralleling those for females.

Marriage

There is great variation in the form and function of the marriage ceremony within the subcontinent. First marriages of virgin girls and boys are usually more complex than remarriages of either one or both partners. The typical northern or southern wedding may take one to three days; or it may be drawn out for several months or even years. In northern areas marriage involves detailed, lifelong gift-giving and ritual service obligations on the part of families who have given brides in marriage to others. Dealing fairly in accordance with their status and honor and attending ceremonial events in a proper way maintains a whole family's reputation.

Wedding rituals generally serve to: (1) establish the agreement between the two families; (2) prepare the bride and groom for their union; (3) formally unite the marital pair; and (4) celebrate the consummation of the marriage. The wedding also may serve as the occasion when the daughter of the family receives her inheritance.

For all Hindus marriage is considered essential to reaching full adult status. However, it is not until the consummation ceremony that a person is considered fully married and, thus, an adult.

The northern and southern wedding ceremonies—at least, for groups having patrilineal descent—are generally similar, with the addition of a customary marital pendant (*tāli*) in the south. A woman actually may wear two marital pendants, one from her natal family and one from her marital family. Women of both bride's and groom's parties participate actively in southern weddings.

Families in Afghanistan conduct a wedding according to the widespread Muslim formula, starting with betrothal and moving on to engagement, wedding, and consummation rites. The wedding itself takes about three days and is paid for by the groom's family, who traditionally offer "bridewealth" to the bride's family. The women of each family participate actively in each stage, going back and forth to each other's houses. This is different from the prevalent north Indian pattern, in which it is men who go back and forth to conduct negotiations and perform rites. Some Afghan groups (Turkoman) with central Asian ties may celebrate weddings with simulated bride capture.

A standard, three- or four-day Muslim wedding in the south includes numerous folk rituals similar to those of nearby Hindus; including garlanding, preliminary application of turmeric paste to the face (and sometimes other parts of the body) of the bride and groom, and, in south India, tying of the *tāli*.

In the Himalayan region among speakers of Tibeto-Burman languages, there also is much variation in wedding ritual, and divorce seems to be simpler there than elsewhere. The Tamang of central Nepal have only minimal wedding rites. The Sherpa conduct marriage preliminaries and associated rituals over a period of years, but child bearing may occur without social stigma before completion of the cycle. At her true wedding the Sherpa woman receives as dowry her share in her natal family's property. This remains hers for life, irrespective of the success or failure of the marriage, and thus her wedding establishes her as a legally independent, propertied individual. In cases of polyandry, the Sherpa woman and her two husbands, who are nearly always brothers, go through the wedding at the same time, with the bride seated between the two grooms.

Death Rituals

Death is of course the final transition out of the life cycle, and all human societies have some standard way of arranging the social exit of the individual, just as they have ways of admitting new members at birth. One parallel between death and birth in south Asia is the customary sense of pollution that surrounds a family that has lost a member, especially an adult member. All observe some conventional period of mourning, variations depending on the status of the deceased. (Funerals for adults, for example, are always more extensive than those for children.) Returning from mourning to a normal condition of integration with society requires purification ceremonies and a ritual meal. The exact family affected depends on the type of kinship system a group has.

The period of mourning is the ultimately "inauspicious" time, and Hindus tend to distinguish it from auspicious times. They do so by such actions as moving counterclockwise (rather than the more usual and auspicious clockwise direction) when circumambulating a grave or funeral pyre, or by using specific numbers (one or four) in the ritual. The bereaved family and chief mourner severely restrict their activities during the mourning period.

Among Muslims it is the universal custom to bury the dead, and readings from the *Qur'ān* are part of each stage of the funeral. The family of the deceased is under certain restrictions. For a specific number of days (usually two or three) there is no fire in the family hearth, and the family is fed by near relations.

A Himalayan Hindu or Buddhist funeral includes either burial or cremation, according to each group's custom. The Tamang of Nepal, for example, cremate their dead during a three-day funeral period, but the Limbu bury theirs in rock slab compartments. The Tamang's final death ritual is to remove charred bones from the funeral pyre, pulverize them and re-burn them. The Buddhist Sherpa have elaborate funeral rites (with cremation) supervised by a lama. At the funeral they too pulverize bones of the deceased, mixing the powder with clay and other substances to make small figures.

There is great concern throughout the subcontinent with the danger posed by ghosts. Individuals who die by suicide or murder, sexually mature individuals who die without consummating a marriage, or women who die while pregnant may receive special funeral treatment and postmortuary rites to prevent their ghosts from returning to torment the living.

When a northern or southern Hindu woman loses her husband, she may be expected to go through a rite of passage to establish her in her new status as a widow. The woman's glass bangles are broken. In some places she receives from her brother a replacement set of silver bangles.

Themes in Life Cycle Rituals

For any one family, group of families, or caste, life cycle rituals tend to form a coherent, interconnected set of activities. There are certain foods, typical blessings, and, possibly, special colors or numbers and specific people considered necessary to each rite. For example, the number five tends to have auspicious connotations. Items or actions required for inauspicious events, such as funerals, may be forbidden for auspicious ones, such as weddings, especially among Hindus. Each group thus develops its typical ritual style. A clear example is the (south Indian) Coorgs' use of ritual acts they designate as *mangala* for multiple auspicious occasions moving a person from one status to another, establishing a new "social personality." The style of a family's life cycle rites is based on many deeply held beliefs and wishes about the nature of the cosmos and humanity's place in it.

In addition to the style of the ritual act itself, the social aspect of a life cycle rite reflects the basic values of a people and the structure of their family life. These ceremonies provide the most important opportunities for activation of familial gift-giving obligations and repayment of social debts incurred on previous occasions. Gifts or services offered in one event are remembered and reciprocated in others. Seen as a series, these events span whole lifetimes, of course, and the work of one generation has implications for generations to follow.

Another social aspect of life cycle rituals has to do with intercaste relationships. In large parts of the region the services of specific castes such as priests, midwives, messengers, musicians, cleaners, or grave-diggers are still required for life cycle ceremonies. Payments in kind for these services, given along with cash compensation, are customary.

Ideas of purity and pollution are important for an understanding of life cycle rituals in much of south Asia. A family going through a transition, especially a birth or a death, and possibly also the maturation of a daughter, often is required to maintain some kinds of social and religious isolation because of its presumed impure or polluted condition. The end of the period is marked by purification rites of some sort.

Life cycle rituals relate to long-term purity concerns. This is because these ceremonies affect not only individuals but also their whole family lines, assumed to include past, present, and future generations. Ceremonies have to be done with the utmost care, so as to protect the living from danger and to preserve the integrity of the family as a whole.

References

Aziz, K. M. Ashraful, and Clarence Maloney. 1985. *Life stages, gender and fertility in Bangladesh.* Dhaka: International Centre for Diarrhoeal Disease Research, Bangladesh.

Bhattacharyya, Narendra Nath. 1975. *Ancient Indian rituals and their social contents.* Delhi: Manohar Book Service.

Dupree, Louis. 1973. *Afghanistan.* Princeton, New Jersey: Princeton University Press.

Freed, Ruth S., and Stanley A. Freed. 1980. *Rites of passage in Shanti Nagar.* Anthropological Papers of the American Museum of Natural History [New York] 56 (part 3): 323–554.

Fürer-Haimendorf, Christoph von. 1964. *The Sherpas of Nepal; Buddhist Highlanders.* Berkeley and Los Angeles: The University of California Press.

van Gennep, Arnold. 1960. *The rites of passage.* Trans. by Monika B. Vizedom and Gabrielle L. Caffee. Chicago: The University of Chicago Press.

Good, Anthony. 1991. *The female bridegroom: a comparative study of life-crisis rituals in South India and Sri Lanka.* Oxford: Oxford University (Clarendon Press).

Hanchett, Suzanne. 1988. *Coloured rice: symbolic structure in Hindu family festivals.* Delhi: Hindustan Publishing Corp.

Nepali, Gopal Singh. 1965. *The Newars: an ethno-sociological study of a Himalayan community.* Bombay: United Asia Publications.

Srinivas, M. N. 1965. *Religion and society among the Coorgs of South India.* Bombay: Asia Publishing House.

Thurston, Edgar, assisted by K. Rangachari. 1909. *Castes and tribes of southern India.* Madras: Government Press, 7 vols.

Vatuk, Sylvia. 1975. Gifts and affines in North India. *Contributions to Indian Sociology* (NS) 9(2): 155–196.

SUZANNE HANCHETT

SEE ALSO

Birth Songs; Circumcision; Courtship, Afghanistan; Death Rituals; Dohada (Pregnancy Cravings); Dowry and Bridewealth; Ghosts; *Koṭahaḷuva Gedara;* Lament; Muslim Folklore, Sri Lanka; Names and Naming Practices, Balochistan; Naming Ceremonies; Puberty Rituals; Turmeric; Wedding Songs

LIFE HISTORY AND PERSONAL EVENT NARRATIVE

While we all experience life as individuals, we do so in dialogue with others and as persons who sustain our very sense of self in relationships. We are, consequently, both social beings and historical beings because the events of a life history and the collective order and disorder of social history are entwined processes. The collection of life histories, therefore, can be a key method for soliciting data on social and cultural topics that do not have as their central issue the life of an individual per se, but the lived and experienced society and culture, a lived social history. However, because social history is rooted in the actions of individuals, the self-narrative may also reveal the teller's understanding of his or her role in events, his or her motivations, assessment of experience, and understanding of agency and responsibility for life. Often this self-awareness is more an ongoing argument than a purely harmonious interaction, and a life story recalls a complexity of voices arguing alternative perspectives. A life history is, then, in a sense, a "still-life" of this complexity. Arranged for presentation to an audience, it expresses an argument uttered for a purpose, and so preserves traces of co-respondents, the person or persons the individual is addressing, and the counter interpretations that the telling is designed to confront. In anthropological writing, life histories of South Asians have been used as a "de-Orientalizing" device designed to preserve such points of view by allowing the ordinary person to speak and to explain him- or herself, rather than to be spoken about and characterized by the anthropologist.

What are the cultural and social factors that determine a person's sense of self? When informants describe themselves, they may provide answers from a variety of perspectives. For example, there are the person's own interpretations of who he or she is, which are set in the context of groups and relationships. There are always multiple dimensions to such views—my self as "wife," my self as "writer," my self as "father"—these being markers of the public me. But informants also tell of their dreams, their sense of accomplishment and failure, expressing the inner voice of a private self, which is nonetheless intertwined with their public self and is expressed in cultural terms of estimation. A second perspective is the interpretations others offer of who an individual is. A reputation is an expression of how others view one's self, and, when individuals find it important to inform each other about themselves, they often describe their personal sense of what their own reputation is. A third perspective might focus on the interplay between these two views. After all, each tries to influence what others think of him or her. And what others think of someone—or at least what the subject thinks they think—affects his or her sense of self.

A life story may also be solicited in a variety of ways, each leading to different self-descriptions. If an informant is asked to begin by recalling his or her first dream or goal, the life story will emphasize personal agency, decisions made, and the consequences that followed. If asked to relate what it was like growing up in one's parents' household, a different kind of life story emerges, one that might emphasize individuation. Yet again informants may want to describe what troubles them and will couch their stories in terms of issues and events that distress them.

There is, therefore, no single way for an individual to express who he or she is. There are multiple ways that are often in dialogue with each other, and among these ways there exists a tension between self-interests and the interests and views of others. The Indian psychoanalyst Sudhir Kakar labels this tension the "fusion/separation psychological polarity"—where "fusion" refers to the degree to which the individual is embedded in social relations, and "separation" the degree to which the individual acts independently from others. He considers this polarity a basic feature of the Indian psyche and central to how Indians believe they should act.

A perennial problem for every individual is how, satisfactorily, to mediate this tension. All societies offer a preferred solution: in the United States, we come down more on the side of the individual and self-interest, while in India, society comes down more on the side of groups and the interest of others, holding to the ideal that the individual should subordinate his or her desires and live in harmony with others, especially with family and caste. However, a society's solution always creates its own psychological problem; for Americans, the problem is how to have meaningful relationships; for Indians, it is how to gain enough control over decisions affecting one's life to avoid the despair that comes from living only for others.

Age also affects the manner of a person's understanding of life because at different ages the individual is integrated into society in different ways and is engaged with different tasks and issues. Mines has found that young Tamil adults sometimes describe others as having important control over them, but, by age fifty, Tamils—both men and women—begin describing themselves as the only one responsible for their lives. They say that how a person's life has turned out is a result of his or her own actions; for every action there is a consequence, this being a karmic idea. Once Tamils have fulfilled the tasks society asks of them—namely, getting married, raising and marrying off children, and working—they depict themselves as freer to pursue goals and interests of their own.

Gender, another major dimension of a person's sense of self, affects the manner in which Indians understand and describe their lives; men and women see life from different vantage points. Poor men speak of their struggles with poverty, work, ill health, and lack of food. Men of better means tell of desiring control over their own lives and of seeking to live lives of honor and respect. A few seek preeminence, striving to be seen as first among others, as patrons and commanders. Recognizing their eminence, followers may refer to such persons as "big-men/women." Women usually do not figure prominently in Indian men's discussions of who they are. By contrast, Indian women speak of trying in early adulthood to live as dutiful daughters and daughters-in-law and of the subsequent painful realization that things will not work out well for them if they live their lives only to fulfill the expectations of others. Like men, they describe realizing that they alone are responsible for their own lives; again, a karmic idea. Men figure prominently in women's life stories, especially fathers, husbands, and sons, reflecting the dependence Indian women have on men and the determinant role men play in their lives. Life is not easy for women, and society's constraints on women seem greater than they are for men.

A linked set of studies in anthropology has endeavored to conceptualize the person in Indian society and to assess the role that the individual as agent has played in South Asian history. From the 1960s to the 1980s, this debate was dominated by the structuralist and culturalist interpretations propounded by Louis Dumont at the Sorbonne and McKim Marriott at the University of Chicago. These scholars, each in his distinct way, argued that Indian culture does not recognize the individual. For these theorists and their followers, cultural recognition of the individual is a Western peculiarity; "individualism" and its accompanying emphasis on freedom and happiness certainly are. But, then, how is one to explain Indian history? For Dumont, a structuralist, a religious notion of hierarchy is the essential causal idea that determines the form of Indian society, and society is given primacy over the individual actor. Structure replaces events as the cause of society's continuity. It is the order of society that is valued, not individual affairs. In final analysis, then, Dumont's interpretation ignores agency and is ahistorical; the form of Indian society is changeless. Similarly, ignoring India's history of world involvement, Marriott argues for an Indian "ethnosociology"—that Indian society must be understood only in its own pristine cultural terms, and actions should only be interpreted as logical outcomes of such indigenous Indian understandings. He, therefore, gives priority to culture over the individual actor, and like Dumont, offers an ahistorical interpretation of Indian society. For Dumont and Marriott, culture speaks through the person, who is *its* agent. But the person is not an actor who is capable of creating meaning.

Beginning in the 1980s with the "subalternists," South Asianists, seeking to overcome the formulas of Orientalism which had remained embedded in structural and ethnosociological inquiry, have made history and agency key features of their analysis. In this context, the individual's role in history becomes a locus of investigation. Life history and event narratives have become central features of interpretation. Subaltern approaches, which look to the narratives and actions of ordinary persons to explain the dynamics of historical processes, have been particularly influential. Letting, when possible, ordinary persons speak for themselves has enriched Indian history, demonstrating that historical process is composed of a complexity of contesting viewpoints and processes, and that ordinary persons are capable of understanding the conditions of their own actions, of acting intentionally and with reason. Life history and event narratives also sometimes reveal the "agentive moment," when an individual intentionally constructs a new understanding of the self in relationship to society. Such an agentive moment is observed when the individual describes pioneering a fresh sense of self sustained in a new kind of social grouping or in one that conjoins new and old cultural, social, and conceptual spaces in novel and innovative ways.

Despite the importance of their contribution to social theory, the subalternists have been criticized for interpreting the individual as an autonomous actor. As a corrective, Douglas Haynes and Gyan Prakash, among others, propose that agency be understood and analyzed in the field of power relations and at the intersection of social institutions and individual action, arguing that agency embodies the interplay between structures and forces beyond individual control and the resistance and invention of individual actors. Life histories, then, reveal that individuals act not as autonomous actors, but as interactors, who create their sense of self in dialogue with others within a social field that they themselves affect. In the words of Charles Taylor, they are dialogical interactors.

References

Dumont, Louis. 1970. *Homo Hierarchicus: the caste system and its implications.* Trans. By Mark Sainsbury, Louis Dumont, and Basia Gulati. Complete Revised English Edition. Chicago: University of Chicago Press. (Original: *Homo Hierarchicus: Le systeme des castes et ses implications.* Editions Gallimard, 1966)

Freeman, James M. 1979. *Untouchable: an Indian life history.* Stanford: Stanford University Press.

Grima, Benedicte. 1992. *The performance of emotion among Paxtun women: "the misfortunes which have befallen me."* Austin: University of Texas Press.

Haynes, Douglas and Gyan Prakash. 1991. *Contesting power: resistance and everyday social relations in South Asia.* Delhi: Oxford University Press.

Kakar, Sudhir. 1981. *The inner world: a psycho-analytic study of childhood and society in India,* 2nd ed. Delhi: Oxford University Press.

Karlekar, Malavika. 1991. *Voices from within: early personal narratives of Bengali women.* Delhi: Oxford University Press.

Mandelbaum, David. 1973. The study of life history: Gandhi. *Current Anthropology* 14(3): 177–206.

Marriott, McKim. 1989. Constructing an Indian ethnosociology. *Contribution to Indian Sociology* (n.s.) 23(1): 1–39.

Mines, Mattison. 1994. *Public faces, private voices: community and individuality in South India.* Berkeley: University of California Press.

O'Hanlon, Rosalind. 1988. Recovering the subject *Subaltern Studies* and histories of resistance in colonial South Asia. *Modern Asian Studies* 22(2): 189–224.

Taylor, Charles. 1991. The dialogical self. In *The interpretive turn: philosophy, science, culture,* ed. David R. Hiley, James F. Bohman, and Richard Shusterman, 304–314. Ithaca: Cornell University Press.

Trawick, Margaret. 1991. Wondering lost: a landless laborer's sense of self. In *Gender, genre, and power in South Asian expressive traditions,* ed. Arjun Appaduarai, Frank J. Korom, and Margaret A. Mills, 224–266. Philadelphia: University of Pennsylvania Press.

Wadley, Susan S. 1994. *Struggling with destiny in Karimpur, 1925–1984.* Berkeley: University of California Press.

MATTISON MINES

SEE ALSO

Gender and Folklore; Karma; Person

LITERATURE

See Brahui Folk Literature; Folk Literature; Folk Literature, Sri Lanka; Story Literature, Persian; Story Literature, Sanskrit

M

MACKENZIE, COLIN

Born in Scotland in 1754, Colin Mackenzie first became interested in India through research on Hindu mathematics. Securing a position in the army of the East India Company, Mackenzie arrived in Madras in 1783 at age thirty. There he was soon transferred to the Army Engineers and sent out to survey areas of the Deccan newly acquired by the Company. After the defeat of Tipu Sultan in 1799, Mackenzie's supervisors, impressed with his detailed and accurate maps, commissioned him to map and fix the boundaries of the newly conquered territories. The resulting *Great Survey of Mysore,* as it was known, was extraordinarily rich and detailed. For this project, Mackenzie and his Indian assistants not only surveyed and produced maps of the geographical features of most of South India, they also gathered information and historical documents on local political structures, land tenure systems, economic products, religious institutions, cultural practices, and belief systems. Company officials in London were initially wary of the expense and broad scope of Mackenzie's survey, which was not completed until 1809. However, by 1810, they had formally recognized Mackenzie's skills and contributions by making him Surveyor-General of Madras. In 1815 he was promoted to the new post of Surveyor-General of India, a post he held until his death in 1821 at age sixty-eight.

Mackenzie's goal in his surveys of Mysore and elsewhere was to provide the East India Company with a fuller historical, economic, and social understanding of India. To do so, he and his assistants traveled widely, interviewing inhabitants about local ways and histories, and collecting documentation of all sorts of the present and past functioning of the area. In the process, they collected thousands of local tracts, literary manuscripts, and copies of historical inscriptions and produced over two thousand drawings of local peoples, costumes, and places. Of particular interest to the survey teams was information on political institutions and people of power in local societies, although they also collected genealogies, caste histories, and origin myths. All of these types of information had both general and particular practical interest to Mackenzie. On the one hand, the survey would broaden understandings of the world: at the same time, it would help facilitate the application of British rule in India. The Company agreed on these dual goals initially and gave Mackenzie special funds to purchase materials and documents. After Mackenzie's death, however, the utility of his collection came to be doubted, as many of the documents contained unverifiable or jumbled versions of the past. Later surveyors in the nineteenth century were advised to focus on statistical rather than historical materials.

References

Dirks, Nicholas B. 1994. Guiltless spoilations: picturesque beauty, colonial knowledge, and Colin Mackenzie's survey of India. In *Perceptions of South Asia's visual past,* eds. Catherine B. Asher, and Thomas R. Metcalf, 211–232. Delhi: American Institute of Indian Studies.

Mackenzie, W. C. 1952. *Colonel Colin Mackenzie: first surveyor-general of India.* London.

Mahalingam, T. V., ed. 1972. *Mackenzie manuscripts: summaries of the historical manuscripts in the Mackenzie collection,* Vol. I. Madras: University of Madras.

Robb, Peter. 1998. Completing 'Our stock of geography,' or an object 'still more sublime': Colin MacKenzie's survey of Mysore, 1799–1810. *Journal of the Royal Asiatic Society 8,* no. 2 (July): 181–206.

ABIGAIL MCGOWAN

SEE ALSO

Colonialism and Folklore; Folklorists

MĀDĒŚVARA EPIC

Consisting of some fifteen to thirty thousand lines, the *Male Mādēśvara Kathe* (or *Kāvya*) is one of the longest oral epic traditions in the Kannada language. Like many epics of India, the *Mādēśvara* (also spelled *Mahādēśvara*) is in the form of a narrative cycle. It is traditionally divided into seven segments, or *kavatlu* (or *sālu*). However, unlike India's many warrior-hero epics, this one narrates the life of a saint, Maleya Mādēśwara, who is believed by his followers to be an incarnation of Iśvara (Śiva). The epic cycle describes the miracles performed by the saint, which caused people to follow him and spread the worship of Śiva.

Regarded as a god, *Maleya Madeśvara* is enshrined in a temple situated in the midst of the hills called Mādeśvara Beṭṭa, which are located in Kollegal Taluk, Karnataka, and the adjacent areas of Tamil Nadu. His devotees, called *dēvara gudda,* come mainly from the lower castes: Shepherds (*Kuruba*), Washermen (*Madwāla*), Hunters (*Parivardavaru*), and Peasants (*Vakkaligas*) in the southern districts of Karnataka (Mysore, Mandya, and Bangalore) and the northern districts of Tamil Nadu (Salem, Coimbatore, Satyamangalam). Most scholars feel that Mādēśvara himself was born of a *Harijan* (untouchable) caste. His appeal among the lower classes of society is no doubt due to the belief that Lord Śiva himself chose to be incarnated as a Harijan. The fact that though he was god, he was not given recognition in the *Vīraśaiva Mattha*s (monasteries) implies that religious reform was desperately needed even within Vīraśaivism, itself born of a populist Hindu reform movement in the twelfth century.

Although devotees sing only portions of the ballad cycle at any one time, independent of its chronological sequence, it is said to be comprised of seven segments, or sālus. This is the way it was compiled by P. K. Rajashekara in his influential two-volume *Maleya Mahādēśvara Kāvya,* published in 1973, which was the first written edition of the text. The seven episodes in the cycle are:

Tālugathe. Mādēśvara first appears as a *jangama* (saint) and performs a miracle in front of a married couple, who become his first devotees. Mādēśvara travels to Suttūru, a *Vīraśiva Mattha,* (a center of religious learning). The chief of the maṭṭha bars his entry until Mādēśvara performs many miracles to prove his religious powers.

Śravana kavatlu /sālu (Killing a Demon). After returning from the Suttūru Maṭṭha, Mādēśvara returns to a life of solitary meditation. One day he meets a demon named Śravana at Bankapur, in the Mysore region. With his many powers the demon had conquered many deities, enslaving them in his palace. Śravana insults Mādēśvara by asking him to make sandals. Mādēśvara prepares the sandals, but places explosives in them; when Śravana wears them they explode, killing him and freeing the gods from the demon's service.

Junjēgowdana kavatlu/sālu (the *Junje Gowda* episode). Mādēśvara visits Junje Gowḍa, a wealthy leader of the shepherd caste whose followers are devotees of the god Birēdēvaru. There he performs miracles and convinces Junje Gowḍa of his religious power. Finally Junje Gowḍa accepts Lord Mādēśvara as his god and invests all his wealth to build temples in the Mādēśvara hills.

Sānkammana kavatlu/sālu (the *Sankammas*' episode). Sanakamma is a beautiful lady, but childless. She is a devotee of Mādēśvara, but her husband, Nīle Gowḍa, is very cruel. One day before going on a long journey, her husband undresses her, ties her up, and blindfolds her. Mādēśvara comes to the door of her house and, to test her devotion, begs religious alms. Sanakamma says that she is naked and has been tied up, but if he could release her and bless her with children, she would donate to him. Performing a miracle, Mādēśvara gives her wealth and causes her to beget children. Sanakamma agrees to make her children disciples of Mādēśvara. When Nīle Gowḍa returns home he becomes suspicious and challenges her, but in every test she reflects upon Lord Mādēśvara and passes. Finally, Nīle Gowḍa also becomes a devotee.

Bēvina kāli kavatlu/sālu (the Bēvina Kāli episode). Bēvina Kāli, a devotee of Lord Mādēśvara, becomes rich by his grace, but she refuses to give him alms. Mādēśvara destroys all her wealth with his magic power.

Dēvamma kavatlu/sālu (the Dēvamma episode). Dēvamma is an evil woman, who invites saints (*jangama*) to her house and poisons their food. Mādēśvara visits her and, as usual, she offers poisoned food, but Mādēśvara gives it to her son who consumes it and dies. Mādēśvara causes her to realize that poisoning food is both dangerous and evil; he later brings her son back to life and they both become devotees.

Saragurappana kavatlu/sālu (Saraguru Madappa episode). A woman named Rāmavve has only one son, Saraguru Madappa. Mādēśvara asks her to allow her son to become his disciple. At first she refuses to give her son because she is a devotee of the god Biligiri Rangayya. Mādēśvara causes her son to die by snakebite and then appears in the guise of a jangama (saint) to bring him back to life. Both Rāmavve and her son become his devotees, and Saraguru Madappa is put in charge of giving massages to Mādēśvara.

References

Ramchandran, C. N., and L. N. Bhat, trans. 2001. *Male madeshwara: a Kannada oral epic*. New Delhi: Sahitya Akademi.
Rajashekara, P. K. 1973. *Maleya Madēśvara*. 2 vols. Mysore: P. K. Rajashekara.
Shanakara Narayana, T. N. 1991. Mahādeśvara. In *Encyclopaedia of the folk culture of Karnataka*. vol. 1., edited by Krishnamurthy Hanoor. Madras: Institute of Asian Studies.

S. A. KRISHNAIAH

SEE ALSO
Epic; Saints; Śiva

MADHYA PRADESH AND CHATTĪSGAṚH

Madhya Pradesh (literally "middle" or "central" "state" in Hindi-Urdu), with an area of 308,245 square kilometers, and Chattīsgaṛh (literally "thirty-six forts" in Hindi-Urdu), with an area of 135,191 square kilometers, together comprise about 14 percent of the entire area of India. Madhya Pradesh was formed after independence by combining twenty-nine former princely states and pieces of British India, previously known as "The Central Provinces and Berār," with some of those formerly included in the "Eastern States Agency." Bhopāl, the major city of the old Muslim state of the same name, became the capital of an expanded and reorganized Madhya Pradesh in 1956. Today, Bhopāl is a thriving administrative-industrial municipality of over one million people.

Chattīsgaṛh, a distinct geographical and cultural region formerly included within southern and eastern Madhya Pradesh, became a separate state in the year 2000, with its capital at the important rail and road junction of Raipur, a city of about half a million persons.

The geography of Madhya Pradesh is varied and complex. It includes fertile valleys, such as that of the Mahānadī (literally "great river" in Hindi-Urdu), broad plateaus, rugged, hilly tracts, semi-arid regions, and extensive forests. Chattīsgaṛh is essentially a broad, fertile plain, drained by the Mahānadī and Seonāth rivers. Much of the area is still forested, but forests continue to give way rapidly to agriculture.

The principal language of Madhya Pradesh is Hindi-Urdu, its "western" and "eastern" branches divided roughly by the 80-degree longitudinal, which passes through the middle of the state. There are also several dialects of the two branches spoken in Madhya Pradesh, such as the western dialects of Bundelī and Braj Bhāṣa, and the eastern dialects of Āwadhī, Baghelī, and Chattīsgaṛhī. The dominant language of the new state of Chattīsgaṛh is the Chattīsgaṛhī dialect of Hindi-Urdu, but the southern-most district of Bastar includes numerous tribal languages such as Gondī, Koya, and Halbī.

The linguistic variety of Madhya Pradesh and Chattīsgaṛh, taken as whole, is consistent with extraordinary social and cultural diversity throughout the region. The many distinct geographical niches have hindered easy population movement and communication over the centuries, resulting in the development of small pockets of distinctive linguistic and cultural entities. Some of the major geographical-cultural subregions are Mālwā in the west, Bundelkhaṇḍ in the north, and Maṇḍlā, Chattīsgaṛh, and Bastar in the south. Bastar, a former princely state, was included in Madhya Pradesh in the 1956 reorganization as a southeasterly administrative appendage famous for a rich diversity of folk cultures. With the formation of the new state of Chattīsgaṛh, Bastar was divided into two districts, Bastar proper in the north and Dantewāḍa in the south. Together they comprise an area of about 39,000 square kilometers, and constitute the southern-most districts of Chattīsgaṛh. They are home to many "tribal" peoples, such as the Muria, Hill Māṛīā, and Bison Horn Māṛīā Goṇḍs, Parjās, Koyās, and Bhattrās.

The history of central India is long and complex. The region served as the locus of interaction between coastal areas as well as between north and south. Mālwā, in particular, was always important as a crossroads between west coast ports in Gujaerāt and Mahārāṣhṭra, and cities of the Gangetic plain, such as Allahābād, Vāranasī, and the ancient city of Pātaliputra (the modern Paṭnā, in Bihār). Mālwā formed the principal administrative element in the old loose confederacy known as "Madhya Bhārat" (literally, "Middle India").

Contemporary Madhya Pradesh includes many important industrial centers, such as Indore, Gwalior, Ujjain, and Bhopāl. Particularly significant is the Bhārat Heavy Electricals factory at Bhopāl, with over 15,000 employees. Tourism is also a major and growing economic activity. Famous attractions include the imposing first century B.C.E. Buddhist *stūpa* at Sānchi near Bhopāl; the eleventh century C.E. temples at Khajurāho in Bundelkhand, with their spectacular erotic carvings; the Hindu pilgrimage center at Ujjain; the Gwalior fort; the "Marble Rocks" near Jabalpur; and the hill station at Pacmaṛhi.

Agriculture continues to be the main source of livelihood for the vast majority of the state's population. The principal subsistence crops are rice, wheat, and sorghum, with rice concentrated mostly in the east, and wheat and sorghum in the west. All three crops are grown in many areas, and in some years surpluses are produced, which then become partial cash crops. Important commercial crops are cotton, edible oil seeds, and sugarcane. Ubiquitious on the rural scene are cattle and water buffalo, which are used for traction, milk, hides, and dung, this last an important fuel in many areas and sometimes also a fertilizer.

Chattīsgaṛh is particularly well known for its rice production, but other crops are grown as well, and there is some industry, most notably the major steel plant at Bhilai, west of Raipur. Tourism is not well developed, but the waterfalls, hills, and forests of Bastar and Dantewāḍa constitute good potential for tourism, especially if they are protected in the future. Wildlife is abundant in this area, and includes many varieties of birds, monkeys, leopards, hyaenas, boar, wild bison, deer, antelope, and other animals.

The peasant farmers of Madhya Pradesh and Chattīsgaṛh live in densely nucleated villages in most regions, their houses constructed of timbers and sun-baked earth, and, increasingly, of red brick baked in local kilns. House sizes vary, and, in most areas, consist of the traditional central courtyard surrounded by a set of rooms and verandahs. As in most of rural India, the social structure is dominated by patrilineal, patrilocal institutions and the caste system. Although there are substantial Muslim populations in some districts, Hindus constitute the vast majority in both states, and Hinduism dominates the rich ceremonial life.

As in most of India, major festivals such as Divālī and Holī are celebrated, and during the fall and winter months especially, a series of fairs or *melā*s, with both religious and commercial functions, are held. Some of these center on a religious town, such as Kāṛtik Purnimā at Ujjain in Madhya Pradesh, or the spectacular Kumbh Melā, held there once every twelve years, and Māgh Purnimā at Rājim, near Raipur in Chattīsgaṛh. Other melās are local, organized at the village level.

Folk explanations of ritual detail are provided by means of songs and recitations. The *Mahābhārata* and *Rāmāyaṇa* epics are the source of many narratives that serve as the underlying rationale for the performance of ceremonies. The singing of hymns in characteristic *bhajan* style in homes and temples constitutes an important means of transmission of ceremonial knowledge from one generation to the next. Itinerant bards and locally organized dramatic performances frequently are also agents of cultural transmission.

Consistent with Hindu traditions, domestic ceremonies receive great emphasis. Particularly important are weddings, which vary in ritual detail and elaborateness by region, caste, and social class. Most marriages are arranged by the parents of the bride and groom and take place at the home of the bride, though there are exceptions, as among the Goṇḍs, where the performance is at the home of the groom. Weddings provide an important context for the singing of bawdy folksongs, usually by female relatives of the bride.

In Chattīsgaṛh, and in some regions of Madhya Pradesh, village drama is an important folk tradition, with local playwrights and actors taking great pride in their productions. Everywhere, rural people maintain a plethora of folk traditions within various social and ritual contexts. An interesting example is the institution of the *gotul,* or adolescent dormitory, among the Goṇḍs of Bastar, which perpetuates local traditions of folk dancing and singing that are famous throughout India.

References

Babb, Lawrence A. 1975. *The divine hierarchy: popular Hinduism in central India*. New York: Columbia University Press.

Census of India. 1981. *General population tables.* Series 1, Part 2A, Volume 1. New Delhi: Registrar General, Government of India.

Mayer, Adrian C. 1960. *Caste and kinship in central India.* Berkeley: University of California Press.

Schwartzberg, Joseph E., ed. 1992. *A historical atlas of South India.* New York: Oxford University Press.

Spate, O. H. K. 1967. *India and Pakistan. a general and regional geography.* New York: E.P. Dutton & Co.

EDWARD J. JAY

SEE ALSO
Bhajan; Candainī (Lorik-Candā); Dīvālī/Dīpāvalī; Holī; Melā; Tribal Folklore, Central India

MAHĀBHĀRATA

The Sanskrit epic text known as *Mahābhārata* is the longest metrical work of literature known in any language. In its vulgate form it consists of approximately 100,000 verses, most of them of thirty-two syllables each, and it has been calculated that it is eight times as long as the *Iliad* and the *Odyssey* put together. However, this enormous bulk took many centuries to achieve. The text makes reference to a shorter version of itself—24,000 verses—which is said to have been composed first, and recent scholarship suggests that the earliest form of the work may have been considerably shorter even than that. In particular, Mary Carroll Smith has proposed that the most ancient core of the text still survives within the existing vulgate, consisting of the approximately 2,000 verses in irregular *triṣṭubh* meter which are scattered throughout the work.

The origins of the *Mahābhārata* probably go back to the middle of the first millennium B.C.E., or slightly earlier. This was the period when Gautama the Buddha and Mahāvīra, the founder of Jainism, were formulating their doctrines, both of them rejecting the brahmin-dominated world view of the *Vedas*. The *Mahābhārata,* too, shows clear signs of heterodoxy, but it is not expressed in such a way as to present a direct challenge to prevailing orthodox opinion. Rather, it seems that the differences of viewpoint spring principally from differences in social background. The *Mahābhārata* was in origin a product of the Kṣatriya class, presenting Kṣatriya mythology and ideology, whereas the Vedas had always been the domain of the Brahmins. In choosing to absorb, rather than to reject, the *Mahābhārata,* Brahmanism was opening itself to a new mythology, a new set of gods, and a new world view. The process of absorption was a part of the emergence of the new religion generally called Hinduism. The massive inflation of the *Mahābhārata*'s text that was involved did not reach completion until about the fifth century C.E., involving as it did numerous lengthy additions to the story, major didactic sections, and much else beside.

The central narrative of the *Mahābhārata* concerns dynastic problems affecting the Kuru rulers of ancient North India. As the result of complex events in previous generations, the throne of Hāstinapura is disputed by two sets of cross-cousins: the five Pāṇḍavas, who are "partial incarnations" of various deities, and the hundred Kauravas, who are demonic in character. The leader of the Kauravas, Duryodhana, attempts to have the Pāṇḍavas killed in a house fire, but they escape; then, with their joint wife Draupadī, they set off to found a new capital, Indraprastha. Duryodhana is still not satisfied. With the help of his uncle Śakuni, he engages the Pāṇḍava leader Yudhiṣṭhira in a crooked gambling match in which the Pāṇḍavas lose everything and are exiled in the forest for twelve years. When this term, and an additional one year of living incognito, are completed, they return, only to learn that Duryodhana still refuses to restore their kingdom to them. Kṛṣṇa acts as peace negotiator, but without success, and both sides prepare for a mighty war.

Before battle is joined, Kṛṣṇa, who is acting as charioteer to the third Pāṇḍava brother, Arjuna, explains to him in the *Bhagavad Gītā* why it is right to take part in such a bloody war. Then the war itself starts. It lasts for eighteen days and results in terrible loss of life. In the end, the Pāṇḍavas are victorious, in part at least thanks to various underhanded tricks suggested to them by Kṛṣṇa. But any joy in victory is swiftly turned to grief when the three surviving Kauravas slip into the Pāṇḍava camp at night and massacre all the Pāṇḍavas' allies.

Years later the Pāṇḍavas decide to retire from the world, and they begin to climb Mount Meru, the way to Heaven. On the way, all but Yudhiṣṭhira himself fall to the ground, and on reaching the summit Yudhiṣṭhira discovers that Heaven is full of his enemies. He prefers, instead, to stay with his brothers, even though he sees that they are suffering hellish torments. At this point, he learns that what he has seen was illusory, and he and his brothers are reunited in Heaven.

In recent centuries the story of the *Mahābhārata* has not been able to compare for pan-Indian popularity with that of the other great epic narrative, the *Rāmāyaṇa*. Indeed, there is a widespread superstition that to read the entire *Mahābhārata* is to invite severe misfortune. Yet it has never completely lost its power over the imagination, as was demonstrated in the late 1980s when it was turned by Doordarshan (the Indian national television service) into an enormously protracted serial watched by equally enormous audiences. In addition, there exist numerous more traditional genres of performance.

It is useful to make a distinction between those traditions that make occasional use of (generally episodic) narrative material from the *Mahābhārata* in much the same way as they would use material from any other source and traditions that explicitly focus on the *Mahābhārata* narrative itself and make some attempt to convey a notion of that narrative as a whole, perhaps by treating it as a "cycle" of connected stories. As might be expected, the former type of tradition is widespread throughout India. Traditions of dramatic representation making regular use of episodes from the *Mahābhārata,* for example, include the *sāng*s of Haryana, the *jātrā*s of Bengal, the *yakṣagāna* tradition of Karnataka, and the shadow puppet tradition of Andhra Pradesh known as *tōlubommalāṭa*. Other styles of performance involve narrative singing, often with interspersed spoken commentary or explanation: in Haryana, episodes may be performed by groups of men in *bhajan* style; in Maharashtra and Gujarat, solo singers perform in a style known as *kīrtan* to the accompaniment of drum, harmonium, etc.; in Andhra Pradesh, the *harikathā* tradition presents a more elaborate and Sanskrit-influenced variation on the same pattern. All of these performance types normally take place at night and offer their audiences a mixture of entertainment and religious experience.

In addition to traditions such as these, which simply draw piecemeal on the *Mahābhārata,* however, there exist in at least four regions of India more complex traditions in which something approaching a "cycle" of *Mahābhārata* narratives is performed, generally in a ritual context. What is more, though the regions in question are geographically very far apart—Tamil Nadu, Madhya Pradesh, Rajasthan, and Garhwal in the hills of northern Uttar Pradesh—it is clear that there exists some form of relationship between them other than a common ultimate indebtedness to the Sanskrit *Mahābhārata:* certain narrative elements are held in common between a number of them for which no parallels are known among pan-Indian written sources. Thus, for instance, the Rajasthani, Garhwali, and Tamil traditions all refer to Arjuna marrying a princess of the underworld in the course of his efforts to provide for the funeral rites of his dead father Pāṇḍu (in the Rajasthani and Garhwali versions Arjuna has to fetch back the hide of a rhinoceros for these rituals); similarly, the stories from Rajasthan, Madhya Pradesh, and Tamil Nadu refer to Kṛṣṇa testing Karṇa's fabled generosity as he lies dying. However, scholarly investigation of these traditions is still at an early stage, and it is not as yet possible to begin to account for such parallelisms.

References

Hiltebeitel, Alf. 1988. *The cult of Draupadī*. Vol. 1 *Mythologies: From Gingee to Kurukṣetra*. Chicago: University of Chicago Press.

Leavitt, John. 1991. Himalayan variations on an epic theme. In *Essays on the Mahābhārata,* ed. Arvind Sharma, 444–474. Leiden: E. J. Brill.

Sax, William S. 1991. Ritual and performance in the Pāṇḍavalīlā of Garhwal. In *Essays on the Mahābhārata,* ed. Arvind Sharma, 274–295. Leiden: E. J. Brill.

———. *Dancing the self: personhood and performance in the Pandav Lila of Garhwal*. Oxford: Oxford University Press.

Smith, John D. 1980. The two Sanskrit epics. In *Traditions of heroic and epic poetry*. vol. I. ed. A. T. Hatto, 48–78. London: Modern Humanities Research Association.

———. 1987. Formulaic language in the epics of India. In *The Heroic Process: Form, Function and Fantasy in Folk Epic,* ed. Bo Almqvist, Séamas Ó Catháin, Pádraig Ó Héalaí, 591–611. Dublin: Glendale Press.

———. 1990. Worlds apart: orality, literacy and the Rajasthani Folk-*Mahābhārata. Oral Tradition* 5(1): 3–19.

Smith, Mary Carroll. 1972. The Core of India's Great Epic. Ph.D. diss. Harvard University.

Zoller, Claus Peter. 1994. The Paṇḍuan, an Oral Mahābhārata from the Garhwal-Himalayas. Unpublished typescript.

JOHN D. SMITH

SEE ALSO

Aravān; Draupadī; Epic; *Jātrā/Yātrā;* Kṛṣṇa; Marionettes; *Pāṇḍav Līlā; Rāmāyaṇa;* Shadow Puppetry; *Yakṣagāna*

MAHARASHTRA

Maharashtra is India's third largest state in size (307,607 sq. km.) and population (78 million). Its capital is the international industrial city and port of Bombay (Mumbai), with a population of over eight million. Maharashtra is unified by a common language, Marathi, and a shared pride in the history of Maratha nationhood dating back to the seventeenth-century Maratha leader Sivaji. Several folk etymologies for this state's name exist, but "the great nation," is its most probable meaning.

Situated on the west coast of India, Maharashtra is bounded by the Arabian sea to the west, Gujarat in the northeast, Madhya Pradesh to the north, Andhra Pradesh to the southeast, and Karnataka and Goa to the south. The state has three main geographic areas marked by particular physical features. The Konkan is a coastal strip along Maharashtra's west coast, known for its coconuts, fishing, rice paddies, and beautiful beaches. The region known as Desh is a part of the Deccan Plateau, separated from the Konkan by the Sahyadri mountain range (Western Ghats). Flowing eastward from the Ghats across the Desh are the rivers Godavari, Bhima, and Krishna. Other significant rivers include the Tapi, Wardha, and Wainganga. Major pilgrimage sites are found in these mountains and along these rivers. The third major region is that of the thickly forested and fertile Vidarbha in the northeast.

Although the most industrialized state in India, and the one enjoying the highest standard of living, Maharashtra nevertheless derives 70 percent of its economy from agriculture, its principal crops being rice, jowar, baira, wheat, and pulses. Other contributions come from the production of chemicals, pharmaceuticals, and textiles, and from the well-known motion-picture industry based in Bombay (India's "Bollywood").

Significant social groups within Maharashtra include the Marathas, Brahmans, and Mahars. Marathas, traditionally landowners, agriculturists, and warriors, make up about 50 percent of the population. The largest Brahman groups are the Desasthas (the ritual priests of this region), Konkanasthas (Chitpavans), and Karhades. The Mahars, the largest caste of untouchables (now known as "scheduled castes" or "Dalits") in Maharashtra (9 percent of the population), are considered the original inhabitants of the area. Predominantly servants and agricultural laborers, the Mahars form a significant proportion of the Neo-Buddhist population of Maharashtra, following the example of the great Mahar statesmen, B. R. Ambedkar (1892–1956), who converted to Buddhism rather than die a Hindu. Many Hindu Mahars are fervent participants in the regional Varkari cult, and, traditionally, Mahars have been temple attendants for the goddess Mariai, a task now assumed by the Mangs, another Scheduled Caste. Maharashtra is also the home to many other religious and ethnic groups, including Muslims, Parsis, Sikhs, Bene Israel Jews, Portuguese-Goan Christians, Jains, and Armenians. Tribal groups in this state (some 5 percent of the population) include the Bhils, Gonds, Warlis, Kolis, Katkaris, and Agaris.

Acting as a cultural bridge between the Dravidian South and the Indo-Aryan North, Maharashtrian culture and language combine elements of both these cultural and linguistic groups. Marathi, an Indo-Aryan language derived from the Prakrit language Maharashtri, includes many loan words from Dravidian languages. Other related languages and other major dialects spoken within the state are Ahirani, Varhadi, Konkani, and Kolhapuri. Maharashtri Prakrit, the premier vehicle for early Prakrit poetry and the chosen language for nonelite characters in many classical Sanskirt plays, maintained close ties in its form and content with regional folk poetry and folksongs. Marathi literature made its debut with the Mahanubhava cult founded by Chakradhar (1194–1276). The Mahanubhavas, devotees of Kṛṣṇa, traditionally have led ascetic lives, been anticaste, and eschewed Brahmanical orthodoxy and Sanskrit, which led them to develop a rich Marathi literature.

The folklore of Maharashtra is particularly influenced by two major themes: the martial history of the Marathas and the waves of Hindu devotional (*bhakti*) movements that developed in medieval times. The Mahanubhavas' devotional influence is overshadowed by the better-known Varkari Panth, whose devotions center on Vithoba, a form of Kṛṣṇa, with his main shrine in Pandharpur. During the annual pilgnmage to Pandharpur in the Hindu month of Asadha (June-July), devotees sing *abhangs* (devotional songs) composed by such poet-saints from this tradition as Jnaneshvar, Namdeva, Janabai, Eknath, Tukaram, Chokhamela, and Ramdas. Other regional folk song traditions include the *keliya* (playful songs), *gavlan* (songs about Kṛṣṇa and the Gōpis), *bharud* (folk dramas weaving bhakti and Vedantic philosophy), *laliṭ* and the *gondhaḷ*. *Gondhaḷis*, devotees of the goddess, are invited to perform gondhaḷs by patrons celebrating an auspicious occasion such as a marriage or thread ceremony. A typical gondhaḷ weaves storytelling and song with humor, history, and praise. Sometimes the bardic gondhaḷis sing *pavadas*, heroic folk ballads detailing the achievements of a warrior and his battles.

Various Hindu dynasties ruled over this region, ending with the Yadavas in 1294, who were defeated by the Muslims. Under the leadership of the hero Sivaji, Maratha forces challenged the Muslims and the Maratha Empire was established, later to be presided over by the Peshwas until the colonization of India by the British. From this memorable martial period in Maratha history come many pavadas. Other wandering mendicant performers include *vagyas* (male performers) and *muralis* (female dancers), devotees of the regional deity Khandoba (associated with Śiva), whose main shrine is in Jejuri near Pune. Khandoba's *rakṣa bhakti* cult blends together martial and devotional themes.

One of the best-known forms of folk entertainment in Maharashtra is the *tamāśa*. Typically performed at fairs and festivals by a small troupe made up of dancers, musicians, singers, and a jester, a tamāśa combines song, dance, and drama with social commentary and political satire to illustrate traditional themes (such as Kṛṣṇa's dalliance with the Gōpis) as well as to address socially relevant issues. *Lāvaṇīs*, romantic ballads, form part of the tamāśa repertoire.

Within the folk culture of women, *ukhanas*, *kahānīs* and *ovīs* abound. Riddles (*ukhanas*) designed to disguise the forbidden utterance of a husband's name are a popular pastime during all-women gatherings. *Ovis* are the mill-grinding songs and lullabies of women that recount the joys and sorrows of their domestic life. *Kahānīs*, or *kathas* are the stories associated with particular festivals and fasts. Women's festivals such as *Bhondla, Mangala Gauri, Mahālakṣmi,* and *Nāga Paṇcami* are occasions for sharing such traditions, as well as for participating in games and dances such as the popular *pirugadi,* a dance with many variations in which two women hold hands, spinning as fast as they can.

The most popular festival in Maharashtra, which has now spread to other parts of India as well, is the ten-day festival of Ganesh (Gaṇeśa), the elephant-headed god who is the remover of obstacles. Celebrated for ten days in the month of *Bhadrapada* (August-September), this family festival was transformed into a public demonstration of patriotism by the nationalist Bal Gangadhar Tilak (1856–1920). The festival of *Dasera* or *Vijayadaśamī* also has particular significance in Maharashtra, where many observe the *Simollangham,* or the crossing of boundaries by walking to the outskirts of the town commemorating the expeditions of Maratha warriors. Other popular festivals include *Gokulastami,* the birthday of Kṛṣṇa; *Dīvāḷī,* the festival of lights; *Makar Sankranti* (winter solstice); *Holī Pūrṇimā* (or *Shimga*) and *Ranga Paṇcamī,* celebrating the coming of spring; *Gudi Padva* (New Year's Day); *Pola* (Bullock Day); and *Rakṣa bandana,* a brother-sister festival. Hindus in Maharashtra observe their festivals according to a luni-solar calendar. The year begins on the first day of *Caitra* (March-April). The months begin with the first day of the waxing moon and end with the full moon. In addition to Pandharpur, Jejuri, and the *samadhis* (graves) of various saints, there are many other pilgrimage sites in Maharashtra, among which are the *astavinayakas*, eight places sacred to Ganesh; two of the twelve *jyotirlingas* of Siva, at Bhimasankar (Pune District) and Tryambakesvar (Nasik District); and three and a half of the 108 *satī* or *shakti pithas* of the Goddess, represented by Mahālakṣmi at Kolhapur, Bhavani at Tuljapur, Renuka at Mahur, and Saptasrngi (the half) at Vani near Nasik. The great *Kumbha Mela* festival celebrated every twelve years on the banks of the Godavari in Tryambakesvar attracts hundreds of thousands of pilgrims, while the ancient rock-caves and temples at Ellora and Ajanta, Karla, Khaheri, Bhaja and Elephanta draw a new breed of pilgrim-tourist. While Vaiṣṇavite sentiments are particularly evident in Maharashtra due to the enthusiastic Varkari Panth, there are strong pockets of Śaivite and goddess worship as well particularly in rural areas. Devotion to the three-headed Dattatreya (a combination of Brahma, Viṣṇu, and Śiva) is a specialty of Maharashtra, and worship of the monkey deity Maruti is also strong.

MARY MCGEE

SEE ALSO
Bhakti; Fairs and Festivals; Gaṇeśa; *Gondhaḷa; Laliṭa; Ovi; Tamāśa*

MAILĀRA / MALLANNA / KHANDOBĀ

Mailāra is the chief deity of an old and important folk religious tradition in many parts of Karnataka, Maharashtra, and Andhra Pradesh. Mailāra is also known as Mailāralinga in Karnataka, Khaṇḍobā in Maharashtra and Mallaṇṇa, and the Malikārjuna of Srisailam in Andhra Pradesh. Although at present the deity has devotees from all castes, in medieval Kannada literature (twelfth Century) Mailāra is referred to as a *ṣudra daiva,* a deity who has a following only among low castes (Ṣudras). Despite attempts to uplift the status of this deity to the level of such classical deities as Viṣṇu and Śiva, the god's character remains primarily that of a pastoral deity in form and content.

Mailāralinga is believed to be an incarnation of Śiva, who came down to earth to rid the world of two dreaded demon brothers, Mallāsura and Manikāsura. After slaying the demons he stayed on earth in the form of a *swavambhulinga,* (a self-emerging round stone). In each of the languages of the three states there is a vast repertoire of stories and song-cycles recounting the deity's life and deeds. Although variable in each of the regions, all include elaborate renditions of the story of killing the two demons as well as of the god's marriages to two wives, one high born, and one from the pastoral castes or forest tribes.

Although there are many pilgrimage centers in each of these three states, the town of Mailara of Hoovinahadasali Taluk of Bellare District in Karnataka is considered by many to be the most important one in this tradition. Devaragudda of Ranebennur Taluk in Dharwar District is another important center of Mailāralinga tradition in Karnataka. Pial and Jejuri of Maharashtra and Ailoni and Komaralli of Andra Pradesh are important centers of Khaṇḍobā and Mallaṇṇa cults, respectively.

Anadur-khandoba with shivalinga in foreground. Maharashtra State, India, © Dr. Jayant Bapat

In Karnataka, a group called Woḍeyārs are regarded by many followers to be teachers (gurus) in this tradition. Their origin is linked to the sage Gomuni, the brother of Kapila Muni, a legendary saint, who is believed to have discovered the swayambhulinga of Mailāra on the earth and to have explained the story of Mailāralinga to his disciples for the first time.

Goravas and Kancavīras are two important sects and active tradition bearers among the followers of Mailāralinga. While Goravas are mainly minstrels, Kanchavīras perform various acts of self-mutilation as a form of religious service to the deity by piercing their cheeks and hands with iron tridents and passing thick leather thongs through their legs as a ritual identification with the deity's legend and to appease the demons who were killed by the deity. Goravas are primarily of the shepherd castes (Kuruba or Kuruva), while Kanchavīras are recruited from Harijan castes.

The tradition of Mailāralinga includes both narrative and ritual performances. The dramatization of the god's myth includes a reenactment of the deity's marriage, the slaying of the demon, Mallāsura, and other episodes of the god's legend. During one annual festival, there is a form of divination during which a Gorava, in a state of trance and sitting on top of a six-meter long bow implanted in the earth, is believed to be possessed by the deity and speaks a prophecy in the form of a riddle. That statement is interpreted by the cult's experts and used by followers to predict rainfall and crop yields for the coming year. Although this ritual lasts only a few minutes, hundreds of thousands of people gather every year to witness it. The festival itself is regarded as the most important ritual event of the annual ritual cycle, which enacts the victory of the deity over the demons.

References

Sontheimer, Gunther-Dietz. 1989. *Pastoral deities in western India.* Anne Feldhaus, trans. New York and Oxford: Oxford University Press.

———. Between ghost and god: a folk deity of the Deccan. In *Criminal gods and demon devotees: Essays on the guardians of popular Hinduism,* ed. Alf Hiltebeitel. Albany, N.Y.: State University of New York Press, 299–337.

M. N. VENKATESHA

SEE ALSO

Gorava/Goramma; Gurav; Self-sacrifice; Śiva; *Vāghyā/Muraḷī*

MAJLIS

Majlis (Arabic, "gathering, assembly," pl. *majālis*) is a religious ritual in which Shī'a Muslims commemorate Imām Ḥusayn's martyrdom at the battle of Karbalā in Iraq in 680 C.E. Imām Ḥusayn (grandson of the Prophet Muḥammad) and some seventy male followers died fighting against the much larger forces of the reigning Caliph, whose succession to Muslim leadership they disputed. Zaynāb, Ḥusayn's sister, courageously grieving and recounting the martyrdom story even as she and the other women were taken captive to Damascus, initiated the Shī'a lamentation traditions, further developed in Safavid Persia. During majālis, South Asian Shī'a reconnect themselves with Imām Ḥusayn through recitations, mourning chants and hymns, and self-mortification.

Particularly after the sixteenth century, with the establishment of some Shī'a-ruled states in South Asia, Shī'a Muslims arrived in South Asia from Shī'a Persia as political refugees, merchants, scholars, literati, invaders, administrators, and bureaucrats. They brought their Ḥusayn mourning rituals, which then became modified by regional social and cultural influences. South Asian majlis ceremonies utilize garlands, candles, incense, and brightly hued cloth. Inspired by Hindu practices, South Asian Shī'a arrange home shrines as well as special buildings where they hold majālis. Such holy areas (*imāmbārgāh* or *imāmbārā*) house banners (*'alams*), which represent the battle flag held by Ḥaẓrat-i 'Abbās (Imām Ḥusayn's half-brother) and which sometimes feature a miniature replica of Imām Ḥusayn's shrine at Karbalā, and perhaps even a small statue of his horse Duldul (or Zuljinnah) standing in worship and sorrow before his master's tomb.

Typically, a South Asian majlis begins with readings from holy texts, followed by mourning hymns. A preacher delivers a sermon outlining religious precepts and duty and concluding with a poignant martyrdom account, bringing the audience to anguished tears. Participants then stand to perform mourning chants accompanied by blows to the chest. Finally, congregation elders lead salutations to the martyrs and Imāms (Shī'a leaders, successors to the Prophet) and prayers. At more elaborate majālis, introduction of an *'alam* banner recalling 'Abbās's martyrdom or a white horse representing Imām Ḥusayn's mount inspires even more distraught grief and extreme self-flagellation, with men beating their backs raw with flails and women rapidly striking their heads with their fists. When the formal part of the majlis is over, attendees settle down, spirits cleansed and refreshed, to enjoy quiet conviviality and refreshments.

Because of Shī'a women's seclusion (*purdah*) from unrelated males, majālis are sex-segregated. Males practice mourning routines at their neighborhood majālis and then display their group's distinctive chants and self-flagellation styles during the related public processions, often entering other imāmbārgāh along their route to put on brief exhibitions. Women hold their majālis in private shrines or in public *Ḥusaynīyyah* halls when men are not using them. Considered more soft-hearted and compassionate than males and less occupied with income-generating activity, Shī'a women devote much time and feeling to majlis participation during the more than two-month annual mourning season. Men's mourning is more dramatic and bloody, signaling their readiness to follow Imām Ḥusayn's example.

In contrast to orthodox Sunni Muslims, Shī'a believe that the Prophet's family and their descendants, including the twelve Shī'a Imāms, possess spiritual power that enables intercession with God. Through recitations, weeping and self-flagellation, and donations, believers show their loving devotion to Imām Ḥusayn and his cause. They hope to gain favor with the martyred saints who will then help them in this world and the next.

Besides their spiritual and religious aspects, majālis are arenas for construction of self, community, and world view. They are significant in cultural, social, and political life. More able to provide mourning space and fund performances and meals, the wealthy benefit from the political legitimacy gained through majlis sponsorship and the resulting consolidation of supporters. Shopkeepers and artisans profit from the demand for ritual paraphernalia.

In past centuries, rulers of Shī'a states in South Asia sponsored elaborate mourning rituals, which often became community-wide events with Sunni and even non-Muslim participation. Today, due to their emotional content and potential for social bonding and exhibiting community identity and pride, mourning rituals can lead to clashes between Hindu and Muslim, Sunni and Shī'a, and even between competing male flagellant groups. When Muslim–Hindu conflict escalated in the years leading to the 1947 partition between India and Pakistan, the spectacular Shī'a mourning practices and colorful public processions took on implications of sectarian separation and fostered violence. Since Shī'a consciousness has flowered internationally following the 1979 Iranian Revolution, and religious fundamentalisms have flourished, South Asian Shī'a majālis participation has promoted Shī'a identity, Shī'a religious and cultural practices, and Shī'a social ties in opposition to Indian Hindus and Pakistani Sunnis.

MARY ELAINE HEGLAND

Majlis Performance Forms

In majlis performances, amateur and professional reciters chant a purposeful sequence of commemorative and elegiac poetry in a richly expressive variety of musical genres that gradually move from slow melodic elaborations embellished by a vocal drone to fast-paced rhythmic phrases reinforced by chest beating. Formal assemblies also include a sermon and narrative poetry recited in a special dramatic style of oratory. Majlis poetry is mainly in Urdu, some of it composed by renowned poets. The musical settings combine both classical and folk elements of Northern Indian music. Of the five hymn forms in the majlis, two use classical melody while two reflect folk or popular song tradition.

The majlis sequence is as follows. First, there is *soz,* a short lament, usually expressing one emotion intensely and concisely. It is a chanted by a soloist with a group providing a sung drone or support for the soloist. Second is *salām,* a salutation or eulogy, often reflective or didactic in character, consisting of couplets with a refrain. It may be chanted as is soz, or without group participation. Occasionally, the order of soz and salām is reversed. Third is *marṣiya,* an elegy or heroic narrative, often highly dramatic, consisting of six-line strophes. It is chanted, usually by the group in unison. The chanted marṣiya may be followed by a marṣiya poem in the style of formal oratory. Fourth is *hadīs,* an address or dramatic narration, sometimes omitted in a short majlis. Fifth is *nauḥa,* a dirge, simple, highly expressive and lyrical in character. Its form is that of couplets or strophes, usually with a refrain, sung solo or by a group. Sixth is *mātam,* a dirge, simple, highly expressive but passionate, even martial in character. It is accompanied by chest beating on the part of the standing audience, and concluded by responsorial calls invoking the martyrs to continuous chest beats. Seventh is *zyārat,* a salutation of the martyrs and Imāms in Arabic, a type of litany chanted by a leader of the majlis; it is the standard conclusion of the formal assembly. Finally, there are *nāra* or *salavāt,* responsorial calls or benedictions, which conclude every majlis.

References

Cole, J. R. I. 1988. *Roots of North Indian Shī'ism in Iran and Iraq: religion and state in Awadh, 1722–1859.* Berkeley: University of California Press.

Hasnain, Nadeem, and Abrar Husain. 1988. *Shias and Shia Islam in India.* Delhi: Harnam.

Hegland, Mary Elaine. 1997a. Flagellation and fundamentalism: (trans)forming meaning, identity and gender through Pakistani women's rituals of mourning. *American Ethnologist* (in press).

———. 1997b. A mixed blessing: *The Majales*—Shī'a women's rituals of mourning in Northwest Pakistan. In *Mixed blessings: gender and religious fundamentalism cross culturally,* eds. Judy Brink and Joan Mencher, 179–196. New York: Routledge.

———. 1997c. The power paradox in Muslim women's *Majales:* Northwest Pakistani mourning rituals as sites of contestation over religious politics, ethnicity, and gender. *Signs: Journal of Women in Culture and Society* (in press).

Hollister, John Norman. 1953. *The Shī'a of India.* London: Luzac.

———. 1989. *Islam and Shia's faith in India.* Delhi: Taj.

Pinault, David. 1992. *The Shiites: ritual and popular piety in a Muslim community.* New York: St. Martin's Press.

Qureshi, Regula Burckhardt. 1981. Islamic music in an Indian environment: The Shī'a Majlis. *Ethnomusicology* 25: 1, 41–71.

———. 1990. Musical gesture and extra-musical meaning: words and music in the Urdu Ghazal. *Journal of the American Musicological Society* 43(3): 472–496.

Rizvi, Saiyid Athar Abbas. 1986. *A socio-intellectual history of the Isna 'Ashari Shī'is in India.* Canberra: Ma'rifat.

Schubel, Vernon James. 1993. *Religious performance in contemporary Islam: Shī'i devotional rituals in South Asia.* Columbia: Unversity of South Carolina.

REGULA BURCKHARDT QURESHI

SEE ALSO
Mātam; Muḥarram; Ta'ziya

MALANG

The term *malang* has different meanings from one region of Afghanistan to the next. At times the word is used to refer to *madārī* (stage-magicians), *faqīr* (either beggars or holy-men), *qalandar* (religious mendicants and Sufis), *jādūgar* (sorcerers), *charsī* (hashish addicts), *dīwāna* (possessed madmen), and, finally, *palang dar libās-i malang* (literally, "leopards in malang clothing," that is, impostors and charlatans). In Afghanistan, as in Pakistan and Muslim India, the term is consistently applied to Muslim mystics and mendicants who are not directly attached to any religious orders. Occasionally, however, certain *malang* may claim to be Sufi—some may even belong to one of the many organized Sufi *ṭarīqāt,* or orders of mysticism, that have grown up around indigenous customs and traditions. But the majority of *malang* operate as "freelance" holy men.

The malang is an exclusively male role. These practitioners, who are believed to be endowed with magical powers to both harm and heal, comprise an ill-defined and heterogenous collection of people. Malangs are immediately recognizable by their distinctive dress and accoutrements: a long robe, chains, and bead necklaces, a wooden or metal bowl called *kaj-kol* that they hang over their shoulder, and a staff called *'aṣā*. Malangs sometimes carry an ornamental metal axe, both to signify their victory over supernatural beings and to provide personal protection.

Malangs practice a variety of ecstatic techniques with clear affiliations with shamanism. They are believed to acquire their powers through the control they exercise over supernatural entities called *jinnd* (from the Arabic *jinn,* meaning a demon or spirit). Some malangs acquire their powers over jinnd after spontaneously suffering "supernatural madness," a state known as *jalālī shudan*. Yet others undergo several years of tutelage under a practicing malang, after which they acquire their powers through the performance of a special initiatory ceremony.

Those who are afflicted by supernatural madness may be seen to be conversing with spirits, which only they can see and hear. Such men may wander naked, roaming the hills and countryside as if in a state of intoxication. These individuals display symptoms that Western clinical psychologists might diagnose as psychotic or schizophrenic, but which Afghans attribute to supernatural influences. Indeed, these "holy madmen," who are thought to have been touched by the hands of God, are honored, feared, and held in awe. They are said to possess magical abilities to cure sickness, foretell the future, cast spells, and counteract harmful magic. The psychological crisis that impels such persons to choose "the company of spirits, over the fellowship of humans," as Afghans put it, seems similar to that described for neophyte shamans in Siberia and elsewhere. It may be assumed that in traditional Afghan society the malang role provided a socially useful outlet for otherwise disruptive personalities.

Men who wish to acquire the powers of a malang through instruction from an established practitioner generally apprentice themselves for several years. In return for gifts, personal services, and money, a master-malang will impart his knowledge to a disciple by familiarizing him with the way of the spirits (teaching him how to harness the powers of some and contend with others), explaining to him the uses of medicinal plants, and tutoring him in the performance of healing rituals. When the teacher deems his pupil ready, he gives his *izin,* or "permission," for him to prepare to "master the demons," (*taskhīr-ī afrīd*), and so, finally, to obtain preternatural powers for himself.

Initiation involves a combination of physical seclusion (*khilwat*), the recitation of ritual formulae (*ẕikir*), and fasting (*rawẕa*). Although the ritual is known as the "forty-days recitation" (*chilla neshastan*), or more commonly, "the completion of the formulae" (*qaṣīda pukhtan*), the number of days required for its completion, referred to as *waẕīfa,* varies from twelve to forty, depending upon the powers the initiate hopes to achieve. Initiation takes place in a cell, in a mosque, in a cave, or on a mountainside far from human settlement. Of all of these places, a cave is regarded as most suitable because, it is said, that it was while meditating in a cave that the Prophet Muḥammad received the divine revelations of the Qur'ān.

When the initiate and his master have chosen the appropriate site for the ritual, the master instructs his pupil to draw seven circles on the ground, one within the other. When he performs the ẕikir, the initiate must sit at the center of the innermost circle. Such circles are believed to be barriers against spirit invasion; for each one of the seven, the initiate has been taught special formulae which, when recited correctly, simultaneously force particular jinnd into submission and protect the initiate himself from supernatural harm.

During ẕikir, the initiate recites, a stipulated number of times without interruption, passages from the Qur'ān, magical formulae, or simply the name of Allah. Such recitation, it is said, compels the jinnd to materialize before the initiate, who is instructed to look down but also to focus his peripheral vision on the boundaries of the outermost circle. Here, it is said, the spirits first appear. The jinnd, it is said, manifest themselves to the initiate, beyond the outermost circle, in the form of wild beasts, dwarfs, and giants. Some of these horrifying apparitions simply sit and stare at him, while others taunt him, trying by means of tricks and illusions, to have him leave the safety of his circles. To repulse these spirit hordes who clamor to cross his magic circles, the initiate must continue unwaveringly to chant the appropriate formulae. It is said that even a momentary pause may allow the spirits to breach the magical barriers and kill him.

As the initiate continues his recitation, he passes through various mental states, during which he may feel himself to be dying, burning in flames, or wasting away. These illusions are said to be created by the malicious jinnd. This is reminiscent of the recurrent motif of agony, death, and rebirth described in the ethnographic literature on shamanism elsewhere in Asia.

Each time the initiate encounters a particular rank of jinnd and is able to withstand its supernatural assaults, it is said that he has succeeded in enslaving that particular spirit. Subsequently, he will be able to use the powers of this spirit in his shamanic practices. Enslaving the more powerful jinnd entails for the initiate a longer period of recitation and a greater psychological ordeal.

Malangs who successfully complete the more dangerous phases of the initiation rite and are able to command exceptionally powerful jinnd are said to have the ability to appear in people's dreams, to fly, and to be present in two places at the same time. Such individuals are referred to as *qudp,* a word that roughly translates into "axis" or "pole." In Sufi circles this term (literary, *quṭb*) is used to designate a spiritual leader. But in reference to an Afghan malang, the term implies an individual with immense occult powers, a potent link to the supernatural world. The concept of qudp is remarkably similar to the "Axis Mundi," the "Sacred Pole," the "World Pole," or the "Cosmic Tree" frequently associated with shamanistic beliefs elsewhere. As Hultkrantz has noted, in the shamanic context, the "axis" or "pole" are ideograms that represent the link between the natural and the supernatural worlds.

Prior to the 1978 Communist coup in Afghanistan and the resultant departure of large numbers of people from the country, one could find malang roaming the city streets and rural areas, dispensing charms, curing disease, and performing other services for the benefit of their clients. The present-day status of Afghan malang, whose numbers have been on the decline since the 1950s, has not been researched.

References

Dupree, Louis. 1973. *Afghanistan*. Princeton: Princeton University Press.

Hultkrantz, Ake. 1978. Ecological and phenomonological aspects of Shamanism. In *Shamanism in Siberia,* ed. Mihaly Hoppel, 27–58. Budapest: Academiai Kiado.

Shah, Ikbal Ali. 1928. *Afghanistan of the Afghans*. London: Diamond Press.

Sidky, M. H. 1990. Malang, Sufis, and Mystics: An ethnographic and historical study of Shamanism in Afghanistan. *Asian Folklore Studies* 49: 275–301.

M. H. SIDKY

SEE ALSO

Character Stereotypes; Conjuring; *Jinn;* Muslim Folklore; Spirit Possession and Mediumship; Shamanism, Islam

MALDIVES

The Republic of the Maldives, (*Divehi Raajje,* "Island kingdom"), comprises a 500-mile north-south archipelago of almost two thousand low-lying islands and islets that form part of a series of nineteen coral atolls lying to the west below the southern tip of India. Approximately two hundred of these islands are inhabited. Many of the islands, with the coral lagoons that surround them, are exquisitely beautiful. Some are small enough to conform to the stereotype of the sun-drenched desert island, containing nothing but white sand and a few coconut palms. Many of the islands rise only a few metres above sea level, and the Maldivian government is an active lobbyist against global warming: even small rises in sea level would have very serious consequences for the islands.

Overview

The rapid growth of the tourist market since the 1960s has meant that it is now possible to reach the Maldives directly by international air travel. But in the past, travellers usually reached the islands by sea from the southwest coast of India, from Sri Lanka, or after crossing the Indian Ocean. The treacherous submerged coral reefs surrounding the atolls have been responsible for countless shipwrecks, and we owe most of our rare early accounts of the islands to visitors who arrived there quite unintentionally.

Divehi is the national language of the Republic of the Maldives. It is an Indo-European language, related historically to Sinhala, the language of Sri Lanka. Divehi today uses a script that was invented by an Arab Muslim traveller in about 1200, and is written right-to-left with Perso-Arabic numerals acting as consonants, and vowels being marked with diacritics more or less in the style of the Indian Devanāgarī script used for Hindi (but with different signs). Thus, the script appears, superficially, Semitic. Pre-1200 C.E. copper-plate grants and inscriptions are in an earlier and quite different script, historically related to the Sinhala script. There is ample archaeological evidence in the Maldives archipelago of a long Buddhist history before 1200, strongly influenced by Sri Lanka. Today the Republic of the Maldives is a Sunni Muslim state; no non-Muslim may be a Maldivian citizen. Maldivian religious and political authorities have in the past preferred to focus attention exclusively on the Islamic history of the Maldives, which is, after all, responsible for most of its present culture and traditions. However, the Buddhist prehistory of the islands, which has sometimes been viewed almost with chagrin, is becoming more interesting to a new generation of archaeologists and historians. For example, several Maldivian mosques face East, not towards Mecca, a fact that becomes comprehensible only when it is realized that some mosques are built on premodern foundations.

The Lakshadweep (formerly, "Laccadive") islands to the north of the Maldives are part of the same undersea volcanic structure as the Maldives, a geological feature first correctly described by Charles Darwin (1889). The people of the Lakshadweep islands speak a variant of Malayalam, the language of Kerala in India. They are also Sunni Muslims, probably by conversion from Hinduism by mainland Muslims from Kerala, rather than by Arab Indian Ocean travellers, as in the case of the Maldivians. But curiously, the Keralan Nair system of matrilineal descent still survives among sections the Lakshadweep people. This combination of Malabar-style matrilineality with a fundamentally Muslim patriarchal ideology is unexpected. At the present time, matrilineality is on the decline in the islands.

The island of Maliku ("Minicoy" in atlases), exactly between the Lakshadweep islands to the North and the Maldives to the south, is culturally a special case. During its early history, it was part of the Maldives, and Divehi is still spoken there. In fishing and other traditions the island is closely aligned with the Maldives. But in the eighteenth century, a Maldivian Sultan ceded the island to Keralan rajas, and it is today part of India.

Folk Traditions

A century ago, the distinguished archaeologist H. C. P. Bell witnessed a number of sports in the Maldives, including hand-to-hand combat with swords, shields, and quarterstaffs. Another recreation he witnessed was stick dancing *(dandijehun),* in which men tapped tiny sticks to create a pleasing rhythm. Chess is widely enjoyed, and sports popular in more recent times include a game of wrestling tag *(bai bali),* a lacrosse-like game played with a small stick *(mandi),* a baseball-like game that has been played for over four hundred years *(thin mugoali),* and the ubiquitous soccer and cricket.

Drumming has a long history in the Maldives, and the virtuoso drum *(beru)* performance was sometimes integrated into royal processions and celebrations. Perhaps the most popular traditional song and dance performance in the Maldives today is the *bodu beru,* which often takes place as the high point of the festivities following the circumcision of a young boy. To the accompaniment of drumming and clapping, a singer chants in Arabic or Divehi, and dancers, both young and old, gradually work themselves into a rapt frenzy of free-form dancing that ends abruptly. Sometimes, some of the dancers fall into a trance state. The lyrics of these songs usually concern familiar folk themes of love and loss. Although the *bodu bern* has traditionally been sung and danced only by men, some women are beginning to participate.

A rare dance form probably introduced from the Middle East about four hundred years ago is the *thāra.* The external form of this dance is similar to the *bodu bern,* with lines of men sitting on the ground beating hand drums, while others dance and sing in Arabic. However, the thāra dance is distinguished by the violence that sometimes characterizes its wilder forms, which are banned by the Maldivian government. At the peak of a dancing frenzy, the dancer may stab himself in the back of the neck with an iron spike. Such practices are perhaps to be compared with the head-wounding of the Keralan "oracle men" *(velicapada)* and other forms of ecstatic self-wounding known from South Asia.

Another song tradition in the Maldives is that of the *raivara,* a slow lament cast in a strict metrical pattern, sometimes in difficult coded languages. These are sometimes sung by fishermen returning at the end of the day, or used by mothers as lullabies.

Many Maldivian people are convinced of the existence of various spirits *(jinni),* and such forces as the evil eye. A person capable of cursing another is termed a *ravābīneza,* and even a compliment from such a person can be dangerous. A form of astrological magic whose practitioners are called "*fanditha* men" is still practiced in the islands. These practices are strongly influenced by similar Indian traditions; for example, the heavens are read on the basis of twenty-eight star constellations, which correspond to the India *naksatra* groups. Hussain (1991: 103–110) has published photographs of a fanditha's astrological almanac. Magical fanditha practices, such as gaining the love of another's wife *(varithoihi),* jinni exorcism, or communicating with the dead, are all services offered by different fandithas. Their practices also include the treatment of a wide range of illnesses, and the Maldivian government sanctions such traditional healing practices through granting licences to fanditha. As one might expect in an archipelago of tiny islands, traditional medical practice *(divehi bais)* draws on the use of sea creatures of various kinds. For example, the white innards of the sea-cucumber are pasted onto a broken arm; this sets hard in the sun and provides an effective bandage and splint. In the eighteenth century, Bontius (1769: 206) recorded that "sweet-smelling rush . . . is carefully cultivated in the gardens by the Maldivian women, and is highly beneficial against female disorders, in baths and fomentations." However, Islamic prophetic traditions of healing are also common: Forbes and Mi (1980: 19) show a photograph taken on Fedu Island, Addu Atoll, of a young girl with a *sura* from the Qur'ān pasted to her forehead to cure a headache.

In Maldivian villages, one of the most enjoyable evening activities is telling stories. These range from tales about jinnis and other supernatural beings to accounts of seafaring, health and sickness, and animal fables. A rich fund of such folk tales exists, and in recent years, efforts have begun to record and publish them.

Today, organizations such as the Esjehi Gallery in Male are working to preserve and promote Maldivian artistic and creative traditions through providing a platform for the exhibition of craft work, as well as documenting the islands' history in the face of rapid modernization.

References

Amin, Mohamed (ed.) 1993. *Spectrum guide to Maldives*. Nairobi: Camerapix Publishers International.

Balla, Mark, and Bob Willox. 1993. *Maldives & islands of the East Indian Ocean*. 2nd ed. London: Lonely Planet Publications.

Bell, Bethia N., and Heather M. Bell. 1993. *H. C. P. Bell, archaeologist of Ceylon and the Maldives*. Denbigh: Archetype Publications.

Bontius, James. 1769. *An account of the diseases, natural history and medicines of the East Indies. Translated from the Latin of James Bontius, physican to the Dutch settlement at Batavia, to which are added annotations by a physician*. London: T. Noteman.

Darwin, Charles. 1889. *The structure and disposition of coral reefs*. 3rd ed. London: Smith Elder.

Farook, Mohammed. 1985. *The fascinating Maldives*. Malé: Novelty Printers & Publishers.

Forbes, A., and Fawzia Ali. 1980. The Maldive Islands and their historical links with the coast of Eastern Africa. *Kenya Past and Present,* 12, 15–20.

Hussain, Ali, ed. 1988. *Finiashi: heard in the Islands*. Vol. 1. Vol. 6: Novelty Printers & Publishers. Vol. 5 of *Finiashi* was published in 1990.

———. 1991. *Mysticism in the Maldives: eyewitness accounts of supernatural encounters* Male: Novelty Printers and Publishers.

Reynolds, C. H. B. 1993. *Maldives*. Vol. 158, *World Bibliographical Series*. Oxford: Clio Press.

Seth, Pepita (1998). *The divine frenzy*. Kapil Jariwala Gallery, 4 New Burlington Street, London W1X 1FE.

Singh, K. S., K. P Ittaman, V. K. Tandon, and V. M. Shamsuddin, eds. 1993. *Lakshadweep*. Vol. XXVII, *People of India*. Madras: Anthropological Survey of India and Affiliated East-West Press.

DOMINIK WUJASTYK

SEE ALSO
Dṛṣṭi; Jinn

MALIGNANT SPIRITS, NEPAL

Belief in ghosts or malignant spirits (*bhut*) is widespread in South Asia and takes many forms. Malignant spirits occupy a position in the cosmology intermediate between gods and human beings. People in North India and Nepal believe that those who die unnatural deaths or who die before their time (by drowning, in childbirth or while pregnant, or by some other accident), or for whom proper funeral rites are not performed, or who die leaving no heirs to perform these rites, become bhut. Some bhut are deliberately malignant; others become malignant if provoked or disturbed. Bhut are usually active at dusk or at night. They are afraid of fire, and a lighted torch can be used to protect oneself from them. They are condemned to wander the earth without rest; some people believe however that the bhut exists as such only until it has completed the natural span of human life.

Two examples of the great variety of malignant spirits found in the cosmology of the Tharus of Chitwan, in Nepal, illustrate these concepts. Tharus believe that under certain conditions, a married woman who loved her husband deeply becomes, if she precedes him in death, a bhut known as *curaini*. She becomes a curaini if the funeral rites have not been properly carried out or if they had never been performed. The curaini goes in search of the husband after death; if she finds him, she will appear to him in the form of his wife and ask him to come with her. If the husband, recognizing the bhut for what it is, refuses to go with her, the curaini can either kill him through her śakti (power), or she may ask him to perform the proper funeral rites.

The curaini may also seek out a young man sleeping alone and, appearing to him in the guise of a beautiful woman, seduce him. This unnatural liaison eventually leads to the man's death through progressive emaciation, and he becomes the curaini's companion in the afterlife. If the man can recognize the curaini for what she is however, he can escape her stratagems by seeking out her resting place and destroying her there. He does so by tying a string around her waist at night; she must leave before morning, and he follows the string to her hiding place as it unwinds behind her. During the day, the curaini changes her shape to look like a piece of wood or bone; if this object can be found and destroyed, the curaini is destroyed with it. In Champaran in India, one of H.H. Risley's correspondents for his ethnographic researches observed that "Stories are related of *kitchin*'s [the term used in Champaran for the Tharu curaini] abode in the family of young men, serving as their wife, giving birth to living children and disappearing after years and months when detected."

The second example concerns male ghosts. A man who dies accidentally—by falling out of a tree, for example—becomes a bhut known to Chitwan Tharus as *martuki*. Such a bhut will haunt the place where he died; he blocks human traffic, and his touch means death. An example of a martuki is the spirit of a flautist who, because the funeral rites were not properly performed, haunts the place where his body was cremated or buried. Such a martuki, by playing his bamboo flute, uses the power of the music to draw people to the spot, where he causes them to lose consciousness. If he wishes to kill his victims, he continues to play; if he ceases, they are able to recover. In this example, the bhut is not particularly malevolent; rather, he is capricious.

Reference

Guneratne, Arjun. 1999. *The shaman and the priest: ghosts, death, and ritual specialists in Tharu society.* Himalayan Research Bulletin 19(2): 1–12.

ARJUN GUNERATNE

SEE ALSO

Bhūta; Supernatural Beings

MAMMĀ

A large, ape-like creature that appears in Brahui prose tales from Balochistan, Pakistan. It is known for its physical strength and resemblance to humans and believed to have been numerous in the past. The animal is reported to be still alive, but rare, in the Pab mountains of the Jhalawan area of Balochistan. A mammā was reported to have appeared in various parts of Quetta City by night in about 1980. In folk stories, the *mammā* leaves the mountains to abduct young girls and carry them back to his cave where he licks their palms and the soles of their feet, rendering them permanently unable to flee. In one such story, a mammā abducted a girl from a village, but she managed to catch and hold the leg of a sheep passing the mouth of the cave. The shepherd, who was searching for the sheep, became aware of her presence. The shepherd quickly brought other villagers and they killed the mammā and rescued the girl. Mothers use the threat of mammā kidnapping to intimidate their children. Though other animals appear frequently in Brahui poetry and song, it is interesting that the mammā only appears in prose narrative.

Reference

Sabir, Abdul Razzak. 1993. Description of animals and birds in Brahui literature. In *Studies of symbolism and iconology,* vol. VII, pp. 143–158. Tokyo: Wako University.

ABDUL RAZZAK SABIR

SEE ALSO

Brahui Folk Literature; Supernatural Beings, Nepal

MĀNAS KATHĀ

The *Mānas Kathā* is another name for an original retelling of the Rāma narrative, the epic poem *Rāmcaritmānas* (Holy Lake of Rāma's Acts), composed in ca. 1574 C.E. by the poet-saint Tulsidas of Banaras (ca. 1532–1623), that has become a revered and beloved text to much of the Hindu population of northern and central India. A work that challenges the categories of "folk" and "classical," the *Mānas* (as devotees commonly abbreviate its name) is a literary masterpiece cast in a folk idiom: rhythmic and rhyming popular meters of the rustic Avadhi dialect of Hindi. Already popular by the close of the sixteenth century, it was disseminated to a world without print reproduction or widespread literacy through genres of oral performance that significantly interpreted and enlarged on its text: recitation, singing, exposition, and dramatic enactment.

Such performance is anticipated in the text, which repeatedly styles itself a *kathā* or "oral narration" to be uttered, sung, and heard, and which is ingeniously structured as a series of four interwoven dialogues that themselves frame and comment on the familiar Rāma saga. The *Mānas* was championed by ascetics of the Rāmā-worshiping Rāmanandī order (who rose to prominence during the decline of the Mughal empire in the eighteenth century) and by resurgent local rajas and merchants. By the mid-nineteenth century the *Mānas* became, (in a British observer's words) "the Bible of North India," popular "from the court to the cottage . . . appreciated alike by every class of the Hindu community, whether high or low, rich or poor, young or old." (Growse 1891;1v) Its fervent devotional mood and syncretic philosophy (combining Vaiṣṇava and Śaiva, nondualist *advaita* and devotional *bhakti* elements) made it, in the nineteenth and twentieth centuries, the preferred scripture for middle-class people seeking a mainstream Hindu identity in response to colonial and modernist critiques.

Contemporary *Mānas* performance includes private and public recitation, often accompanied by elaborate rituals (as when 108 Brahmans chant the epic during an annual nine-day festival in downtown Banaras) and folk singing in which the text is set to seasonal modes such as *caitī* and *kajlī* (folksongs popular in the spring and rainy seasons, respectively). In kathā performance, a specialist known as a *vyās, kathāvācak,* or *rāmayaṇī* delivers a rambling, extemporaneous sermon on the epic that may include song and humor as well as anecdote and interpretation. Such discourses may also feature question and answer sessions, in which listeners raise "doubts" (*śaṅkā*) for the expounder to resolve. The autumn cycle of outdoor *Rāmlīlā* plays that sequentially reenact the Rāma story may have started in Banaras during Tulsidas's lifetime but have proliferated to include innumerable village and urban productions. Ranging from nine to thirty-day pageants performed by local amateurs, these plays generally incorporate, but also freely elaborate on, *Mānas* verses and have undoubtedly constituted a prime medium for transmission of the epic to new generations of admirers. Newer media now serve as well: since the early 1980s, sung renditions of the *Mānas* have been widely available on audiocassette, and a 1987–1988 serialization on Indian television (Doordarshan), loosely based on the Tulsidas epic, created a national sensation.

References

Growse, Frederic Salmon, trans. [1891] 1978. *The Rāmāyaṇa of Tulasīdāsa.* Cawnpore: E. Samuel. Reprint ed., New Delhi: Motilal Banarsidass.

Lutgendorf, Philip. *The life of a text: performing the Rāmcaritmānas of Tulsidas.* Berkeley and Los Angeles: University of California Press, 1991.

PHILIP LUTGENDORF

SEE ALSO
Bhakti; Kathā; Rāma; *Rāmāyaṇa;* Rāmāyaṇa, TV Production; *Rām Līlā;* Vyās

MANCALA

Mancala, an Arabic term, is used by game scholars as a generic designation for all the varieties of a popular board game played throughout a region from Africa to the Philippines. The South Asian board is usually twelve to twenty-four inches long, with two rows of cup-shaped "pits" and two larger cavities at either end for storing captured pieces. Ordinary boards are usually made of wood, sometimes painted an auspicious yellow and decorated with designs. More rarely, one finds ornately carved boards, or ones made of precious metals. At the other extreme, an effective temporary "board" can also be scratched in the earth, and temples in many parts of southern India have mancala playing surfaces carved in stone floors. Playing pieces are usually tamarind seeds or coral tree seeds, but cowrie shells or small pebbles are also used.

The various games are played by taking the pieces from one pit and distributing them in a given direction, one by one, in the following pits. As the play continues, the pits accumulate different quantities of pieces. Variations in rules, which are equivalent to different games—each with a distinctive name—that can be played on the board, determine how the pieces are moved and when a player has won (see Claus 1987 for details). The number of players is generally two, but there are also solitaire forms and forms for three or more players. All are games of skill, highly competitive, and associated especially with women. Frequently, there are seasonal restrictions on the play of the game—in Tulunāḍu, for example, the game cannot be played during the time when the seed beds have been set out for the first (monsoon) rice crop. There are also proscriptions as to who may play together; in Tulunāḍu, to use the same example, sisters should never play this game together. Gambling, a common dimension of the game in some parts of the world, is generally proscribed in South Asia except when mancala is played by men.

Mancala games are especially popular in the southern regions of South Asia (see Claus 1987 for details). There one finds elaboration of the board and the greatest variety of games played on it. Reference to the game is found in verbal folklore, and its play is occasionally seen in rituals and ceremonies. For example, in the Tulu-speaking region of coastal Karnataka, the game, called *cenne maṇe* (beautiful—or auspicious—board), is the central motif of the tragic Siri legend and the associated spirit possession rituals of the Siri cult.

The Telugu term for the board itself is *vāman guṇḍi,* and several games are played on it. The board is usually made of wood and painted with turmeric paste, associated with auspiciousness and prosperity. Playing the game is said to bring rain and increase the fertility of the crops. There are several folktales in Telugu that relate that Rāma and Sīta, hero and heroine of the *Rāmāyaṇa* epic, played the game together.

Mancala is played throughout Tamilnadu under a variety of names: *pannānkuri* (fourteen pits); *pallānkuri, pāntinkuri* and *kāśi* (the Tamil name for the sacred city of Benares). The game is sometimes played during marriage ceremonies between the newly wed husband and wife, with female onlookers from both parties actively encouraging and advising the play of one or the other player. Whoever wins the game is said to prosper more in the marriage.

In Kerala the game is commonly played among children, where it is called *nikkikkaḷi,* or "licking game." It is generally played on the ground, by scooping out two rows of seven holes and using tamarind seeds, pebbles, or other small objects as playing pieces. The game gets its name from the fact that, upon reaching an empty pit, a player "licks" (wipes) that pit with his hand before taking the seeds in the next pit. The loser must "lick" with his hand all of the empty pits.

In Sri Lanka, one of the games, called *olinda deliya* (game of the licorice tree seed), is closely associated with the goddess Pattini. Other terms for various games are *puhumuti* (ashpumpkin peel), *walak pussa* (empty hole), *kotu baendum* (tying-up holes), and *dara mutu* (row of pearls).

References

Claus, Peter J. 1987. Mancala (*cenne*) in Tulu myth and cult. In *Indian folklore II,* eds. Peter J. Claus, D. P. Pattanayak, and J. Handoo. Mysore: Central Institute of Indian Languages Press.

Claus, Peter J. 1986. Playing *cenne:* the meanings of a folk game. In *Another harmony: new essays on the folklore of India,* eds. Stuart Blackburn and A. K. Ramanujan, 265–293. Berkeley:University of California Press.

Murray, H. J. R. 1952. *A history of board games other than chess.* Oxford: Oxford University Press.

PETER J. CLAUS

SEE ALSO
Siri

MANDECCULU

The Mandecculu are performers belonging to the Ālu Golla community. They perform a narrative ritual called *manda heccu* ("increasing the herd") in the homes of those of the other subdivisions of the Golla herding community. The main performers are men, although the troupe usually travels in a group including one or more female relatives, some of whom may accompany the men in the singing. The ceremony is performed in honor of a recently deceased person, and is regarded as both a purificatory rite and a social obligation.

The storyteller uses a wide array of brightly painted figures to animate his formulaic, invocatory narrative. The performance lasts between four and six hours, and takes place in front of the house of the deceased person. The stories that are sung are part of the long and complex oral epic called the *Kāṭamarāju Katha*, which traces the lineages of the Golla heroes. The *Kāṭamarāju Katha* is an expression of self-identity—a story that the Gollas tell about themselves. The performance of the epic allows the Gollas to situate themselves in history through the biographies of their deified ancestors.

The Ālu Gollas own the rights to use the votive figures in the death rituals they perform for their Erra Golla sub-caste patrons. The performers are the officiating priests and the authorized storytellers in the death rites.

The Manda Heccu Figures

The fifty-three figures that typically make up a *manda heccu* performance set acquire their visual and emotive significance when viewed as a whole. The list is fixed, as is the order of their appearance in the performed narrative. The figures are very light, brightly painted, and modeled with a paste of tamarind seed, gum arabic, and sawdust over a softwood inner core. The mixture is secured in place with little strips of old cotton cloth pasted over the figures, and the whole is coated with a layer of white zinc oxide. The images are carefully wrapped in layers of cloth and carried around in two large cane baskets woven specially for the purpose. They include animal and bird figures: a parrot, a tiger, two dogs, and a single-horned cow. The rest (besides the two milkmaids) are figures of the heroes and their wives.

The heroes are identified on the basis of color (for instance, green is the color for Gangirāju, blue for Simhādrirāju; Pōlrāju is shown in white with a beard), or through physical features such as height (Erraṇṇa is shown taller than all others). A further distinction is maintained between the five important heroes (like Kātamarāju and Peddirāju) who are seated on raised *pīthams* (pedestals, "thrones") and the lesser ones who simply stand on flat platforms. The women are placed against wooden backgrounds and, in general, play a more passive role: calm, fearless, and stoic they stand in contrast with their able-bodied, alert, and adventuresome spouses.

Gangamma is the patron deity who is appeased at the end of the ceremony. She is summoned (through song, formulaic verse, narrative, and ritual) to reside in a special figure so that she may protect the storyteller as he steps forth to perform the ameliorative rites in the patron household. It is believed that this rite, when appropriately performed, removes impurities from the patrons and transfers them to the *manda heccu* priest (storyteller). The priest can absolve and absorb the impurities only if he has the power of the goddess residing with him at the time. This practice is deeply and profoundly predicated on a belief in the efficacy of the Gangamma image.

Bargaining and Worship

The complex bonds of inherited rights and mandatory obligations that exist between patrons and storytellers are most clearly disclosed during the bargaining about payments that follows the narrative part of the ritual. After the images are all out of the baskets, the storytellers ask for the material possessions of the deceased person "in whose name they took out the images" (i.e., performed the ameliorative rite), claiming those possessions are rightfully theirs. This may include a silver bracelet, steel utensils, clothes, and a goat, depending upon the status of the family. In the beginning, the claims are made through a formalized, punctilious mode of discourse, but when there are no signs of an agreement being reached, both narratives of self-identity (patron and priest) become mutually aggressive, manipulative, and bitterly contested.

The figures, in the meantime, are left standing outside. They are now filled with the presence of the divine beings who were summoned (through appropriate ritual and narrative) to reside in them, and they now ask to be properly venerated. The storytellers will not allow them to be worshiped, and no offerings can be made until an agreement is reached. The patrons dislike the state they find themselves in: they are anxious to placate the wandering soul of their deceased relative, and they are equally afraid of invoking the wrath of their patron deities who wait to be venerated at the doorstep. All of this serves to hasten the negotiations, and when agreement is reached, the images can be worshiped and appeased. They are then wrapped up in small pieces of cloth and carefully returned to their assigned places in the two cane baskets.

It is this sacred status of the images in the lives of the Mandecculu that has allowed them to maintain their essential services and defy commodification. Thus, although the figures of Gangamma and the Golla heroes are the only material assets that the Mandecculu truly possess, their profound belief in the endowed nature of these images gives them a power that is much greater than (and not attributable to) issues of mere materiality alone.

Until very recently, the manda heccu sets were made solely for the storytellers by traditional artist families (*Nakāśi*s), and their possession of them has been an integral part of their identity. Today they are also being sold as individual pieces (as "dolls" and "toys") in secular and urban contexts.

References

Narayana Rao, Velcheru. 1986. Epics and ideologies: six Telugu folk epics. In *Another harmony: new essays on the folklore of India,* edited by Stuart Blackburn and A. K. Ramanujan. Berkeley: University of California Press.

———. 1989. Tricking the goddess: cowherd Kāṭamarāju and goddess Gaṇga in the Telugu folk epic. In *Criminal gods and demon devotees: essays on the guardians of popular hinduism,* edited by Alf Hiltebeitel. Albany: University of New York Press, 105–121.

Thangavelu, Kirtana. 1998. Itinerant images: embodiments of art and narrative in Telangana. In *Picture showmen: insights into the narrative traditions in Indian art,* edited by Jyotindra Jain. Mumbai: Marg Publications, 90–99.

KIRTANA THANGAVELU

SEE ALSO
Death Rituals; Goddesses, Hindu; Kāṭama Rāju; Worship

MAṄGALKĀVYA

Maṅgalkāvya is a homogeneous genre of medieval Bengali narrative verse meaning "auspicious poetry." These texts form the bulk of Middle Bengali literature (1400–1600 C.E.) and they have often been termed epics because of their length, internal structure, and thematic content, which invariably evokes a great deal of martial imagery. Sukumar Sen has suggested that the composition and recitation of maṅgalkāvyas emerged during the "dark centuries" (1400–1600 C.E.) of Bengali history when the incursion of Islam disrupted the social, cultural, and religious patterns of the region. Out of the crisis situation, new, localized deities began to be worshipped by Hindus, leading to the need for narratives explaining their origin and justifying their worship.

The deities of this indigenous Bengali pantheon were numerous (for example, Dharma, Manasā, Caṇḍī,) and many maṅgalkāvyas were written about them. Usually the name of the deity preceded the word "*maṅgal*" to provide a name for the particular text; hence, *dharmamaṅgal* or *manasāmaṅgal*. Further, many recensions and versions of the narratives for each deity exist today, some in fragments and others complete. We can thus speak of the poetry for each of the medieval Bengali deities as a subgenre of maṅgalkāvya. Unfortunately, not a great deal of attention has been paid to these texts by Western students of folklore. Complete translations in European languages do not exist, but a number of critical editions of these texts have been published in Bengali.

Although each subgenre has a unique characteristic, they all conform to a basic maṅgalkāvya type; that is, all of the plots unfold in a predictable manner, focusing on the specific deity's attempt to establish his or her worship on earth. The texts generally begin with a number of invocations to the divine pantheon, a cosmogonic section drawing on the mythological *purāṇa* literature as well as other (such as tribal) sources, an introduction to the deity in whose honor the text has been composed, the birth of the hero or heroine, and the ordeals the main character must go through in order to establish the deity's worship. Aside from this basic structure, the texts take interesting and often fantastic turns.

It is often said that this corpus of literature reflects the folk religion of medieval Bengal and provides us historical glimpses into the social dynamics of the period. The texts also play an important role in contemporary worship, even though they are rarely recited in their entirety today. Nevertheless, fragments of the texts are performed in numerous ways during worship, providing a core of local knowledge for the average devotee who has no understanding of the medieval scenario.

References

Bhattacharya, Asutosh. 1943. *An introduction to the study of medieval Bengali epics*. Calcutta: Calcutta Book House.

Raychaudhuri, Tapan. 1978. Medieval Bengali culture: the nonelite elements. In *Mass culture, language and arts in India*, ed. Mahadev L. Apte, 142–151. Bombay: popular Prakashan.

Sanyal, Hitesranjan. 1982. *A study of a few Mangalkavya texts*. Occasional Paper No. 52. Calcutta: Centre for Studies in Social Sciences.

Sen, Sukumar. 1979 [1960]. *History of Bengali literature*. New Delhi: Sahitya Akademi.

Smith, W. L. 1980. *The one-eyed goddess: a study of the Manasā Maṅgal*. Stockholm: Almqvist and Wiksell.

FRANK J. KOROM

SEE ALSO

Epic; Folk Literature; *Purāṇa*

MANTESWAMY

Manteswamy (Manteswāmi) is a folk saint hero of Southern Karnataka. In his name, a religious tradition has developed in Mandya and Mysore districts that includes rituals in the form of daily worship, annual fairs, and a narrative tradition of the epic performed by a group of minstrels. Manteswamy is believed to be an incarnation of Lord Īśvara (Śiva), and has a large number of followers among the untouchable castes and also from some other communities, including Muslims. There is not much evidence to establish Manteswamy as a historical figure, but it cannot be completely ruled out.

Manteswamy is believed to have moved from a Vīraśaiva center (a community in the northern part of Karnataka that emerged because of protest against the Brahman caste under the leadership of the renowned religious teacher and poet, Basawēśāra, in the twelfth Century C.E.) towards the south. There, he established his religious center and selected disciples to propagate his teachings, testing the integrity and sincerity of his disciples by punishing those who opposed him and protecting those whom he liked. Today, Manteswamy's religious centers are situated at Chikkallūru, Kappadi, Boppagowḍanapūra, and Maḷavaḷḷi.

The minstrels of Manteswamy are called *nīlagāraru* or *līlegāraru*. They wear distinctive costumes and are initiated in a specific method of sung narrative performance. They perform in a group of four, in which a chorus of three follows the lead singer, and are accompanied by a musical instrument called *tambūri* (a four-stringed instrument). The chorus uses musical instruments called *gaggara* (hollow brass anklets containing metal beads that make a rhythmic sound when the instrument is moved) and *ḍamaru* (a double-headed, hourglass-shaped drum with beaded strings, which strike the drumheads when the instrument is rotated).

The epic of Manteswamy consists of the following four parts: 1) *Dārege Doḍḍavāra Sālu;* 2) *Rāchappāji Sālu;* 4) *Siddappāji Sālu;* and 4) *Chikkallūru Sālu*. The word "Sālu" literally translates as "chapter," but here means a section of the oral narrative that can be sung alone in performance. In this epic, Manteswamy is called *Dārege Doḍḍavaru,* which means "a great man on the earth."

The first part of this epic describes the journey of Manteswamy from the Vīraśaiva Cultural Center in the north to the southern part of Karnataka. There is also a description of how he is identified as a saint-hero, how he finds his first important disciple, Rāchappāji, and how he succeeds in finding a suitable place to settle down.

The second part of the epic deals with how Manteswamy tests and initiates his second important disciple, Siddappāji. There is also a description of how Manteswamy wants to end his life by being laid on a golden cradle and buried in a deep well. The Kings of Halagūr, who belong to the Pānchāla (smith) community, refuse to help dig this well initially, but are defeated and subdued by Manteswamy's miraculous powers. This episode is more widely known as "*Halagūru Pavada*" (Miracle of Halagūr).

In the epic's third part, Rāchappāji helps the King of Mysore win a battle against the Chieftain of Kārugahaḷḷi; afterwards, the king becomes his devotee. In the last part, Siddappāji moves from Boppagowḍanapūra to Chikkallūru. With his miraculous powers, he wins over seven arrogant sages. Both disciples, *Siddappāji* and *Rāchappāji,* were buried in the deep well alongside their mentor, Manteswamy.

The Manteswamy tradition has been in existence for the past six centuries. It is a liberal tradition, which incorporates the characteristics of both Śaiva and Vīraśaiva cults. The annual fairs honoring Manteswamy are held during January and March at Boppagowḍanapūra and Malavaḷḷi, the two religious centers where the monasteries connected to this tradition are situated and which are headed by the religious leaders of the Kṣātriya community. Siddappāji's annual fair is held at Chikkallūru; Rāchappāji's is held at Kappaḍi. During the annual fairs, unpeeled fruit and coconuts are offered to Manteswamy. Religious practices, such as *maṇḍe sēve* (shaving the head) and *uruḷu sēve* (circumambulating the temple in a prostrate position), are also offered as fulfillment of the devotees' vows at the fairs.

The epic suggests that Manteswamy might have been a person of a lower caste who faced opposition from the upper castes and won a place of prominence for himself by his miraculous powers as well as through the deeds of his disciples. Although J. S. Paramashivaiah has made an extensive study of this epic tradition, it is still worthy of further study.

References

Paramashivaiah, J. S. 1979. *Dakshina Karnataka Janapada Kavya Prakaragalu* (Genres of poetry of southern Karnataka). Mysore: Prasaranga, University of Mysore.

Shankaranarayana, T. N. 1991. Three folk epics. *Encyclopedia of Karnataka folk culture,* ed: Krishnamurthy Hanur. Madras: Institute of Asian Studies.

T. N. SHANKARANARAYANA

SEE ALSO

Epics; *Gurav;* Heroes and Heroines; *Kamsāle; Mādēśwara* Epic; *Mailāra;* Saints, Hindu

MĀRPHATĪ AND *MURŚIDĪ* SONGS

In Bangladesh, folk songs have been influenced by Islamic, Buddhist, and Hindu religious traditions. Both *mārphati* and *murśidī* songs show the influence of Sufism (Muslim mysticism) on all levels of Bangla society, from illiterate devotees and adherants of "popular" Islam to the urban elite. The Bangla word *mārephat* or *mārphat* (Arabic *ma'rifa*) means "secret spiritual knowledge." In Sufi terminology it pertains to *al-'ilm al-ladunni* or *al-'ilm bāṭinī,* the inspired or hidden supreme knowledge of oneself acquired through both rigorous ascetic exercises and through *sādhanā* (meditation). Especially popular amongst Sufis in Bangladesh, mārphatī songs explain the mysteries of creation of the world, the universe, and the body, and thus teach methods for discovering the Supreme Being (*Paramātmā* or *Gāuchul ājam*). In the Sufi tradition, the *murśid* (Arabic, *murshid,* spiritual leader) transmits this secret knowledge, or *nūr* (light), to the heart of the *murīd* (initiate), during the *bayāt* (initiation). They are sung by professional singers or festival participants at *khānakā* (Sufi hospices), *mājār* (shrines), or concert halls, during *'urs* festivals, organized folksong concerts, and various other occasions.

Bangladeshi mystic poets and folksingers compose mārphatī songs. The songs transmit knowledge derived from sacred Muslim texts such as the Qur'ān and *hadīth;* the *Rāmāyaṇa* and *Mahābhārata* (Hindu epics); and from realizations of saints (*Pīr*) achieved through sādhanā. In creating mārphatī songs, Bangladeshi folk poets and folksingers are greatly influenced by the thoughts and ideas of earlier Arabo-Persian philosophers and poets such as Rūmī (d. 1273 C.E.), Ḥāfeẓ (d. 1111 C.E.), or Imām Ghazalī (d. ca 1400 C.E.). Thus, in mārphatī songs we find a harmonizing of Arabian, Persian, and Indian philosophy.

The songs' central theme is that the universe and human body are synonymous and that the Supreme creator is equally manifest in every person. Sufis believe that one who truly knows himself knows the Supreme Being. The ultimate goal of the devotee is union with the eternal Supreme Being. Sufis also believe that human life does not have to end with physical death. Through uniting with the Supreme Being, one can exist for eternity.

This theme is also evident in *murśidī* songs, which center on the Sufi spiritual guide known as *murśid* or *pīr*. The concept of pīr or murśid came to Bengal with the advent of Sufism from Persia, Central Asia, and Northern India. These saints preached in the midst of the common people and thereby disseminated this concept. The Hindu Vaiṣṇavas (those who worship Viṣṇu) call the spiritual leaders *guru,* and the Bāuls of Bangladesh, call them sām̐i. The murśid teaches his disciple (*murīd*) how to search and discover the supreme being in the body through deep meditation or ascetic exercises.

Murśidī songs are sung in praise of the murśid. In the songs, the murīd expresses his respect, devotion, and love for his murśid. Metaphors are frequent, as is evident in the following passages:

> Oh, *murśid,* show me the path,
> I have lost my path
> Do not leave me alone

and,

> Oh, benevolent and benign *murśid*
> Take me in your boat

In the last passage, like a boatman who helps passengers to cross the river, the murśid helps his murīd to cross the metaphorical river and to reach the ultimate destination, union with the Supreme Being.

Murśidī songs are related to laments as far as the melody and style are concerned. The instrument used for accompaniment is called the *sārindā*. This wooden, stringed instrument symbolizes the human soul detached from the Supreme Being when it enters the body. When man comes to this physical world he weeps, and throughout his life he weeps in longing to unite with the Supreme Being, as does the sārindā. Thus, the Sufis find similarities between the wooden sārindā and human body.

References

Hai, Muhammad Abdul. 1987. Folk songs of East Bengal. In *Folklore of Bangladesh*, vol. 1, ed. Shamsuzzaman Khan, 295–300. Dhaka: Bangla Academy.

Schimmel, Annemarie. 1974. *Mystical dimensions of Islam.* Chapel Hill: University of North Carolina Press.

———. 1980. *Islam in the Indian Subcontinent.* Leiden: E. J. Brill, Köln.

SHAFIQUR RAHMAN CHOWDHURY
AND LAURI HARVILAHTI

SEE ALSO

Hadīth; Islam; Lament; *Mahābhārata;* Music; Pīr; *Rāmāyaṇa;* Saints; Song; Song, Bengal; Sufi Folk Poetry; *'Urs*

MĀRIAMMA

Māriamma, the goddess of smallpox, is also known as Māri and Māriyammaṉ in Tamil Nadu, Māramma in Karnataka, and Marīāī in Maharashtra, all terms derived from the Sanskrit *mārī,* meaning "plague, pestilence, epidemic pestilence personified." In Kerala she is known as Vasūrimāla, in North India as Śītalā, and in Andhra Pradesh the goddess of smallpox has various names, such as Gangamma and Poleramma. Sometimes cholera is attributed to her as well. Today she is worshipped in connection with all ills, especially those caused by excessive body heat and those resulting in skin eruptions and damage to the eyes.

Characteristic for the smallpox goddesses are:

1. The belief that the goddess is the illness. While she graces the patient with her presence, she is worshipped in the home.
2. The goddess is hot. She/the patient is cooled with cool foods and margosa leaves, and anything that could anger her is avoided, especially the frying of food and sexual union.
3. Her festivals take place during the hot season. Cooling and heating substances are used in the rituals: water, margosa leaves, butter, blood, and fire. Dalits (members of "untouchable" castes) participate in the festival.

There are various myths associated with Māriyammaṉ. The most popular one involves Reṇukā. A minor lapse in Reṇukā's steadfast devotion to her husband, Jamadagni, leads to her beheading by her son, Paraśurāma. He also beheads a woman of the leatherworker caste into whose arms Reṇukā runs for shelter. Paraśurāma revives his mother, but gets the heads mixed up. The woman with Reṇukā's head and the leatherworker's body becomes Māriyammaṉ, the other woman Ellaiyammaṉ. However, in Karnataka and Andhra Pradesh, Reṇukā's head is worshipped as Ellamma, while her body is the goddess Mātaṅgi or Bhūdevī. This and another myth give rise to a folk etymology of her name from the Tamil *māṟu,* "to change," referring to the change in her body. In another myth Māriyammaṉ is a Brahman. She is married to a Paṟaiyar (a Dalit-caste man) who pretends to be a Brahman. When she finds out the truth about her husband, she kills herself by fire. Her husband is beheaded and serves as a model for the buffalo sacrifices to the goddess. Variants of this myth are known in Gujarat in association with the goddess Meladī and with cholera. Māriyammaṉ causes the pox with her pearls, which she received from Śiva. In the myth of Vasūrimāla the pearls are drops of Śiva's sweat, which cause smallpox on Kālī. The pox pearls are compared to eyes, and Māriyammaṉ is called the "Hundred-eyed" and "Thousand-eyed."

Often the head of the smallpox goddess alone receives worship. In Tamilnadu the main festival procedure involves an obscure wedding of the goddess to a tree trunk with three branches, a battle and death of her tree-husband, widowhood of the goddess and reestablishment of her auspicious state, tied loosely to the theme of Durgā's victory over the buffalo demon. The worship of the goddess with sacrificial offerings of, for example, animals, flour lamps, salt, silver eyes, hook swinging, dressing in margosa leaves, marking the body with red and black dots, walking over hot coals, and carrying a pot with hot coals, is in gratitude for her healing and restoration of the harmony that illness disrupts.

References

Aiyappan, A. 1931. Myth of the origin of smallpox. *Folklore* 42: 291–293.

Beck, Brenda E. F. 1981. The goddess and the demon. A local South Indian festival and its wider context. In *Autour de la Déesse Hindoue.* ed. Madeleine Biardeau, 83–136. Collection Puruṣārtha 5. Paris: École des Hautes Études en Sciences Sociales.

Hiltebeitel, Alf. 1982. Sexuality and sacrifice: convergent subcurrents in the firewalking cult of Draupadī. In *Images of man: religion and historical process in South Asia,* ed. Fred W. Clothey, 72–111. Madras: New Era Publications.

Meyer, Eveline. 1986. *Aṅkāḷaparamēcuvari: a goddess of Tamilnadu, her myths and cult.* Stuttgart: Steiner Verl. Wiesbaden.

Whitehead, Henry. 1976. *The village gods of south India.* Delhi: Sumit Publications.

EVELINE MASILAMANI-MEYER

SEE ALSO

Ellamma; Exorcism; Folk Etymologies; Goddesses, Hindu; Gods and Goddesses; Sacrifice; Sītalā; Spirit Possession and Mediumship

MARIONETTES

South Asia has long had puppets of many kinds. The string puppet, or marionette, almost certainly developed among itinerant bards, whose repertoire of storytelling performance forms includes a variety of props—cloth paintings (*paṛ*), scroll paintings, god-boxes, statuettes, and leather puppets. Marionettes are generally of two types, string puppets and rod puppets, although sometimes both strings and rods are used on a single puppet. The local varieties of these two kinds of puppets throughout India are numerous.

In Rajasthan, sometimes held to be the home of South Asia's marionette traditions, there are many different itinerant groups of puppeteers, or *puṭlivāla*s. One group, for example, called *kathapuṭli* ("Story-Puppet") Bhats, uses string puppets to enact the saga of various heroes and heroines. Another, the Naths, performs the story of Amar Sing Rathod, a famous snake charmer. Performances blend moralistic tales and religious themes with the life histories of heroes. Popular story lines are the lives of renowned Naths, such as Champa Nāth Gulab, Nāth Zehri, and Hīra Lāl, and those of the *Jōgi*s (snake charmers). Both of these groups also serve as genealogists for their patron castes. A woman of the puppeteer's family sings the story, while other members form the chorus. The puppeteer plays a humming reed instrument called a *bōli,* which he holds in his mouth throughout the performance. He is the story's true narrator, interpreting what the puppets say through the *bōli.* The puppets are made of mango wood. Black strings tied to the puppet's headgear connect the puppet to puppeteer, who manipulates the puppet from above the stage.

In West Bengal there are marionette troupes who use rod and glove puppets. Puppetry here is called *putulī nāc* or *tārer putuli.* Of the hundreds of families who used to perform in the remote district of West Bengal there are now only twelve to eighteen, scattered in different places. During eight months, the puppeteers perform in villages, moving from place to place. The other four months they spend in agricultural fields as laborers. The major themes of the marionette plays are drawn from episodes of the *Rāmāyaṇa* and *Mahābhārata,* as well as the locally popular stories of Satyavān-Sāvitrī, Hariścandra, Lālan Fakir (a famous saint of the Bāul tradition), and folk tales and historical legends of the heroes of West Bengal.

In the Dumka district of Bihar State there is a rather unique marionette tradition among the Santal, a tribal group. The art is called *cadar-badar,* but there are also variant styles known as *cand-badani* or *cadari-badari.* In this art, miniature, three-to-four-inch dolls are made out of soft wood. The puppets are fixed in a row with threads and plates to a single wooden plank, connected to a lever system for manipulation. Opposite this row of moveable puppets are figures of men depicted with instruments. The plank of puppets is decorated with cloth, making it a kind of decorated stage which hanging on a bamboo pole. During a performance, this pole is placed in front of the people, and the puppeteers pull the strings and sing. When the manipulator pulls the strings downward, the assembled puppets in the canopied stage seem to dance as men of the performing group dance with tribal instruments: the *mādal* (drum), *tamak* (a kettle drum), *banam* or *sarinda* (both bowed instruments), and *kām̐sar* (cymbals). Bells (called *jhunkae*) are tied to the legs of dancers. Troupes travel from door to door during the Navarātri festival season, performing during the daytime. Each day a performer may earn as much as 150 rupees in payments of grain. In the past, other Santal clans knew cadar-badar, but today this art is practiced only by the Murmu clan.

Although several different puppet performance traditions existed in Assam several centuries ago, that which is currently popular, called *putula nāc,* is said to have been introduced from West Bengal by Śaṅkar Dev in the fifteenth century as a medium to propagate Vaiṣṇavism. In those days royal family members were the patrons who invited artists to perform at rituals. Since the days of Śaṅkar Dev, the art of puppetry has declined. Today, there are only some thirty-five traditional families in Assam dependent on the art of puppetry.

Water puppets, a form of puppetry unique in South Asia to the region of Assam, Tripura, and southern Bengal, is also found in Southeast Asia. In upper Assam water puppet plays are performed to celebrate the festival season after the crop is harvested and when there are floods and much of the land is submerged under water. The puppets are made out of bamboo roots and soft wood, which is very light and easy to carve and manipulate. The wood is wrapped with cloth.

The instruments used in the puppet traditions of eastern India are similar to those in Rajasthan. A wind instrument like the bōli, called a *peppa,* is made out of bamboo strips fixed in a plantain leaf bit. In the Rajasthani tradition the bōli-playing interpreter stands at the back of the stage, whereas in Assam, the interpreter stands in front.

The puppets of Assam have three to five strings. The philosophy behind the number three is connected to the concept of the three *guṇa*s (*sātvika, rajas,* and *tamas*), or the balanced qualities of nature within each human life, of which God is the manipulator. This belief is still prevalent in Assam. However, some puppets are now being made with three, five, seven, and sometimes even eleven strings. Puppet traditions have also recently been influenced by the *Chau* (masked theater/dance) traditions of Assam and West Bengal. Like the puppets of Karnataka, many of the Assamese puppets lack legs.

Usually the *khol* (a percussion instrument) player sits in front of the stage with the other musicians, along with the *sūtradhār,* who sings and narrates the story and conducts the performance. There are two groups of musicians, called *gāyan* (lead singer) and *bāyan* (chorus). A cymbal player, to maintain the rhythmic pattern, completes the troupe. Behind the screen six to eight people manipulate the wooden puppets. The main text used is the Assamese Kandali *Rāmāyaṇa,* recited in song and accompanied by prose commentary. Sometimes the sūtradhāra starts the first line of the song, and the rest of the chorus and poetry is sung by the gāyan and bāyan groups.

Puppeteers of Maharashtra come from the region called Pinguli, in the Kudal District. Artists belong to the Thaker community and are not only puppeteers but also storytellers, performing with pictures painted on handmade paper in a unique style called *citrakathā.* Besides marionettes, they use leather shadow puppets and glove puppets. As in all traditions, they narrate *Rāmāyaṇa* and *Mahābhārata* stories.

The marionette form of Maharashtra is unique in its stage structure and wooden puppets. The puppets are like mini-dolls made of soft wood. Traditionally, one man stands behind the stage and manipulates the puppets. His assistants, who correspond to his dialogue and support the lead singer through singing and dialogue, are positioned between the manipulator and the percussionist. They have a traditional musical instrument called *vātavādya,* which is also used in leather puppet performances. In earlier days artists used a traditional percussion instrument called *gummat,* a clay pot with one end covered by Iguana hide and the other end open. Today artists use more pan-Indian *tabla-dagga* or *dhōlak* (both percussion instruments) during performances. The themes of the puppet play are, as usual, drawn from *Rāmāyaṇa* episodes.

In Karnataka, puppet techniques vary from region to region. Traditional stage light for the puppet show is from an oil wick, or country lamp, which sheds a dim light. Since the revival of this art, electricity has come into vogue in the shape of low-voltage bulbs. The performer controls the puppets by strings tied to each doll or by the rod through the puppet's hand called *nārāc.* From above the stage, the manipulator's techniques are unseen because the upper part of the stage is covered with a black screen. The puppet's entry is generally from either the left or right wing, but sometimes from above the stage. Stories selected for the performance are from the *Rāmāyaṇa* and the *Mahābhārata* or *Bhāgavata Purāṇa* and, often, use texts (*prasanga*) of the *yakṣagāṇa* (a south Indian form of dance theater) plays. The instruments accompanying puppet shows in Karnataka are the *maddale* (two-headed hand drum), *mukhavīne* (wind-pipe instrument), and *tāla* (cymbals). The lead singer sings the major songs, and each puppet manipulator speaks the dialogue of a character. Marionette performers are traditionally of the Viśvakarma, or smith caste, but today the troupes will take all interested artists with no bar of caste or community.

Generally, string puppets are manipulated from above the stage. The head strings are three thin black strings tied to an iron ring, worn by the manipulator on his head like a crown. The puppeteer bends forward and controls the movement of rods or the strings' stick with both hands. The puppeteer stands behind the curtain or in a concealed scenery and dances along with the dolls, creating the fantasy that the puppets are really obedient to a master or controller. In the Nagamangala area (Mandya District), many string puppets have no legs or feet, yet "dance" very flexibly.

In Coastal Karnataka the puppets are made by the Gudigāra caste, whereas in the northern and southern parts of Karnataka, the Ācāri or Jinagār make them. Traditional puppets here are made out of soft wood, such as jackfruit wood, or papier-mâché and painted according to the nature of the character. The roughly carved portions are later shaped by cloth padding. Rich costumes and appropriate jewelry enhance the attraction of a puppet's appearance. Puppets are designed according to the *yakṣagāṇa* or the regional *bayalāta* (a form of *yakṣagāṇa* performed in an open-air theatre) conventions. Costumes of the puppets are similar to the regional *yakṣagāna* actors and are made out of gold and silver-colored ornaments. Demon characters are painted reddish, with bulging eyes and long teeth, similar to the iconography of the ferocious mother goddesses in village temples. Divine characters' colors are yellow and green, while the face of jester characters is jet black.

The earliest reference of puppetry available in Tamil Nadu is in the *Śilappadigāram* text of the first or second century C.E. There is also reference to the shadow theater or leather puppetry in the same text. Today, the string puppets of Tamil Nadu are called *bommalātam,* and are especially prevalent in Tanjavur District. Puppeteers use both string and rod techniques in manipulating the puppets from above the stage. The Tamil puppets are the largest, heaviest, and most articulate of all Indian marionettes. The puppet may be as big as four-and-a-half feet in height and weigh from four to ten kilograms. The wood puppets have joints at their shoulders, elbows, hips, knees, ankles, and wrists. As in Karnataka, the strings from the puppet are tied to an iron ring fitted to the main puppeteer's head and the puppets have three or five strings attached to the ring. Made out of a wood called *kalyāna murungai* by the artists themselves, Tamil puppets are comparatively poor in ornamental and decorative motifs. The music of the Tamil puppet shows is similar to that of *terukkūttu* folk theater performances.

Nōkuvidya pāvakali is one kind of puppetry performed by the Vela community during the *Ōnam* festival session in Kerala state. Both men and women of a family take part in the performance, which today can be seen in only a few remote villages in Kottayam and Alleppy districts. It is still performed by only two families, and even they have almost stopped performing during the last several years. The leading manipulators of these puppets are the women, accompanied by men singing and beating an hourglass shaped drum called a *duḍi.* The puppet is fixed to a plank placed atop a colored bamboo pole. The bottom end of the pole is placed between the nose and upper lip of the manipulator. Balancing this pole, the manipulator pulls the strings in rhythm with the drum beat. The several puppet characters derive from both mythology and contemporary life.

Today, many marionette artists all across India have given up the profession due to lack of patronage. Many of them have moved into the city and engaged in work as day laborers in order to have the safety of a steady income. In some urban areas, puppeteers are still able to attract tourists with their performances, and they also perform on invitation. All too frequently, puppeteers are turning to film music for entertaining their audiences instead of using traditional musical accompaniment. Traditionally, the puppeteers were nomadic, moving from one district to another, but in recent years, most of the artists have settled down in one place.

References

Ashton, Martha Bush and Bruce Christie. 1977. *Yakshagana: a dance drama of India.* New Delhi, India.

Bhaskar Kogga Kamath (Trans. N. T. Bhat). 1995. *Story of Kogga Kamath's Marionettes.* Udupi, Karnataka, India: Regional Resources Centre.

Birendranath, Datta. 1999. *Puppetry in Assam past and present.* Tezpur University, India: North Eastern Archival Centre for Traditional Art and Folklore.

Karanth, Shivaram. 1975. *Yakshagana.* Mysore University, India.

Krishnaiah, S. A. 1988. *Karnataka Puppets.* Udupi, Karnataka, India: Regional Resources Centre.

Interview with Komal Kothari (Folklore Scholar) at Bangalore. 8 October 1992.

Interview with Kamala Devi Chattaophadyaya (Craft Counsil Director, New Delhi). 1981. New Delhi.

Interview with Prof. K. S. Haridas Bhat at Udupi. January 1998.

S. A. Krishnaiah

SEE ALSO
Chau; God-Boxes, Painted; Lālan Fakir; *Navarātri;* Ōṇam; *Paṛ;* Shadow Puppetry; *Terukkūttu; Yakṣagāna*

MARRIAGE CEREMONIES

Wedding rituals in south Asia range from ostentatious to nonexistent. For the majority of communities in northern and southern India, Pakistan, and Bangladesh, a series of twenty-five or more different marriage rituals may continue over several months or even years. One Delhi State report claims that, "... More time and money were spent on this rite of passage than on any other" (Freed and Freed). In the Himalaya region and parts of Sri Lanka, on the other hand, couples may produce children, their families interrelating as 'in-laws', with minimal concern about wedding ritual.

Hindu rites considered to unite the pair are: the formal offering of the bride to the groom (*kanyadān*); presentation of agreed-upon dowry or other gifts; blessings from important relatives; and either 'Seven Steps'—usually taken by the couple around a sacred fire or ritual pole—or other rituals in the presence of a sacred fire. Ancestral spirits generally are present in symbolic form at the ceremony. In southern India the Hindu bride's marital pendant, called *tāli,* may be tied by her husband, his father, his mother, or some other individual, according to caste custom.

In a north Indian wedding the gifts often described as dowry are given to the groom's father after completion of formal wedding rites:

> A substantial portion of the goods ... are clothing and personal effects for the bride herself, usually including several pieces of gold or silver jewellery which will remain her private property. There are also household furnishings.... Finally, there are sets of clothing ... for the groom and members of his extended family and close kindred (Vatuk 1975: 161–162).

A standard, three- or four-day Muslim wedding (*nikah*) consists of the reading of the required words and signing of the marriage contract by the groom. (The groom's mother ties a marital pendant in one south Indian community.) In the Pakistan Punjab the bride and groom each make three formal visits to the house and village of the respective parents-in-law. On the third visit to her in-laws' home, the bride is told to cook *khichṛi,* a dish made with rice and lentils. This is the signal that she is to take up her household duties.

After a girl's puberty ceremony in the dry zone of northern Sri Lanka her children are considered to be legitimate if their father is of the correct subcaste; and any woman who cooks for a man is considered to be his wife for the time being. The Vedda, a tribal people of Sri Lanka, traditionally consider a couple to be married after the woman gives the man a waist-string of her own making and the man presents food gifts to her father and a lock of his own hair to the woman herself. The only wedding celebrated traditionally by the matrilineal Nayar of Kerala is a group marriage between a group of Nayar girls and a group of Nambudiri Brahman boys, whom they may never see again once the ceremony is finished.

References

Eglar, Zekiye. 1960. *A Punjabi village in Pakistan.* New York and London: Columbia University Press.

Freed, Ruth S., and Stanley A. Freed. 1980. *Rites of passage in Shanti Nagar.* Anthropological Papers of the American Museum of Natural History [New York] 56 (part 3): 323–554.

Leach, E. R. 1960. The Sinhalese of the Dry Zone of Northern Ceylon. In *Social structure in Southeast Asia,* ed. George Peter Murdock, pp. 116–126. Chicago: Quadrangle Books [Viking Fund Publications in Anthropology, No. 29].

Vatuk, Sylvia. 1975. Gifts and affines in North India. *Contributions to Indian Sociology (NS)* 9: 2, pp. 155–196.

SUZANNE HANCHETT

SEE ALSO

Brass Bands; Courtship, Afghanistan; Dowry and Brideprice; Life Cycle Rituals; *Oggu Katha;* Veddas [Văddo]

MARSIYA

A *marsiya* is an elegy, but in Urdu, unless otherwise qualified, the word refers to the poems that commemorate the martyrs Imām Ḥusayn (the grandson of the Prophet Muḥammad) and his companions, who lost their lives at Karbalā (in Iraq) at the hands of their Umayyad enemies in 680 C.E.

Like much of early Urdu poetry, the first Urdu marsiya were written in the sixteenth century in the Shī'a sultanates of Bijapur and Golkonda in South India, and only quite a bit later are examples also found in North India. These early poems are not restricted to any one formal structure, nor do they show any preference in terms of meter. They are uniformly not very long and were meant to be chanted or sung, singly or in chorus, indoors or outdoors in a procession. But by the beginning of the nineteenth century, the formal practices preferred by the poets at Faizabad and Lucknow in North India came to be the defining model. Now, a marsiya is invariably written in a six-line stanza form called *musaddas,* the rhyme scheme in the stanza being: *aaaa bb.* One example is the following stanza from the renowned poet Dabīr, describing the terrible day of the battle:

> The birds, like fabled phoenix, have become rare;
> The beasts dejected sit by the burning river;
> Though not a wing flaps in the desolate air,
> That prince among the faithful alone stands there.
> No shadow, hot the sun, what cruel heat!
> No drop of water, and the thirst is great! (Ali 1973:270)

Metrical choices in marsiya are limited to a few medium-length meters. These preferences clearly reflect the needs of the highly dramatic, declamatory style used by marsiya reciters. Further, whereas the early marsiya were not organized around topics, the established practice now is to devote each marsiya to just one hero/martyr or to a single incident.

As established by Mīr Babar 'Alī, Anīs (1802–1874), and Mirzā Salāmat 'Alī, Dabīr (1803–1875), the great marsiya writers of Lucknow, a marsiya now consists of several clearly discernible sections such as *cihra* (prologue), *sarāpā* (physical and spiritual qualities of the hero), *rukhsat* (departure for battle), *jang* (battle), and *shahādat* (martyrdom). The poet carefully organizes his verses in such a manner that the grief-filled sections (*mubkī*) do not overwhelm the exultant (*ghair-mubkī*) parts, and carefully alternates between the two to work toward a final, cathartic moment of abject lamentation, after which the poem ends with a few lines of prayer, ultimately leaving the audience with a sense of grace.

The text of a marsiya reaches its audience in a gathering of devout mourners (*majlis-i 'azā,* or simply, *majlis*). These gatherings may occur at any time, but particularly during the month of Muharram (first month of the Islamic lunar calendar), the month of the Imam's martyrdom. A majlis may be held at home, in an *Imāmbāṛa* (a hall or building specifically dedicated to the purpose of mourning the Imāms), or in some other public place. At these more public gatherings, the marsiya is declaimed either by the poet himself or—as is more common now—by some informally trained marsiya reciter. While the audience in either instance is mostly male and Shī'a, both educated and uneducated, the reciter simultaneously seeks two goals of equal importance: to make the audience exult in the courage and virtue of the martyrs and come out with exclamations of delight, as well as grieve over their cruel deaths and sob and weep.

References

Ali Ahmed, ed. and tr. 1973. *The golden tradition: an anthology of Urdu poetry.* New York: Columbia University Press.

Anis, Mir Babbar Ali. 1994. *The battle of Karbala: a Marsiya of Anis.* Translated by David Matthews. New Delhi: Rupa.

Naim, C. M. 1983. The art of the Urdu Marsiya. In *Islamic society and culture,* eds. Milton Israel and N. K. Wagle, 101–116. New Dehli: Manohar.

Sadiq, Muhammad. 1984. *A history of Urdu literature*. 2nd ed. Dehli: Oxford University Press.

C. M. NAIM

SEE ALSO
Lament; *Majlis; Muḥarram*

MARTIAL ART TRADITIONS

Martial arts have existed on the South Asian subcontinent since antiquity. Two archaic traditions, the Tamil (or, more broadly, Dravidian) heroic tradition and the Sanskrit *Dhanur Veda,* have influenced the history, development, subculture, and practice of extant South Asian martial arts such as the *kaḷarippayaṯṯu* of Kerala and *varma adi* of Tamil Nadu.

From the early Tamil *Sangam* "heroic" (*puṟam,* "exterior") poetry we learn that from the fourth century B.C.E. to 600 C.E. a warlike, martial spirit predominated across southern India, and each warrior received regular military training in target practice and horse riding, and specialized in the use of one or more of the important weapons of the period, including the lance or spear (*vel*), sword (*vāl*) and shield (*kedaham*), bow (*vil*) and arrow. War was considered an honorable sacrifice, and memorial stones were erected to fallen heroes, kings, and warriors, whose manifest power could be permanently worshipped by one's community and ancestors. This tradition can be witnessed today in the propitiation of local medieval martial heroes in the *teyyams* of northern Kerala and the *bhūta kōla* of coastal Karnataka.

The Sanskrit Dhanur Vedic tradition was considered one of the traditional eighteen branches of knowledge. This tradition also encompassed all fighting arts from empty-hand grappling techniques to use of a variety of weapons, but as reflected in the name (*Dhanur Veda*), chief among them all was expertise at bow and arrow which were considered the supreme and purest form of martial practice. Much of our knowledge about the Dhanur Vedic tradition is recorded in the *Mahābharata* and *Rāmāyaṇa,* whose vivid scenes describe how princely heroes obtain and use their humanly or divinely acquired skills and powers to defeat their enemies by training in martial techniques under the tutelage of great gurus like the Brahmin master Droṇa, by practicing austerities and meditation which give the martial master access to subtle powers in combat, or by receiving a gift or a boon of magical powers from a god. There is Bhīma who depends on his brute strength to crush his foes with grappling techniques or use of his mighty mace, and then there is the "unsurpassable" Arjuna who uses his subtle accomplishments of focus and powers, acquired through meditation, to conquer his enemies with his bow and arrow. One late encyclopedic textual compilation of Dhanur Vedic techniques is in several chapters (249–252) of the *Agni Purāṇa,* which focus on the specific mental and technical preparation of the martial artist, with emphasis on techniques of mastery with bow and arrow. Martial accomplishment was circumscribed by ritual practices and achieved by combining technical practice with training in specific forms of yoga and meditation, including repetition of sacred formulas (*mantra*), so that the practitioner achieved self-control, mental calm, and the single-point concentration necessary to face combat, possible death, and access to specific powers applied in combat.

Practice of a martial art was traditionally a way of life. Informed by assumptions about the body, mind, health, exercise, and diet implicit in indigenous Ayurvedic and Siddha system of medicine, rules of diet and behavior circumscribed training and shaped the personality, demeanor, behavior, and attitude of the long-term student so that he ideally applied his knowledge of potentially deadly techniques only when appropriate. Expertise demanded knowledge of the most vulnerable "death" spots (Sanskrit, *marman*) of the body for attack, defence, or for administration of health-giving hands-on massage therapies. Consequently, martial masters were also traditional healers, usually physical therapists and bone setters.

Historically, each region of the subcontinent had its own particular martial techniques, more or less informed by the Dhanur Vedic and Sangam traditions. Among those traditions still extant are Tamil Nadu's *varma adi* (striking the vital spots) and *silambam* (staff fighting); Kerala's *kaḷarippayaṯṯu*; North India's *muṣṭi* (wrestling) and *daṇḍi* (staff fighting); and Karnataka's *malkambha* (wrestler's post). Of these, Kerala's *kaḷarippayaṯṯu* (literally, "exercises practiced in a special earthen pit [*kaḷari*]") encompasses the greatest number of distinct practices and forms of knowledge.

Martial traditions and techniques have been integrally related to a wide range of South Asian performance genres that display and enact the heroic ethos and deeds of epic heroes and gods. This relationship is most evident in Kerala where *kaḷarippayaṯṯu* techniques have influenced the training and/or performance of many other forms, including folk dances (stick dance [*kōlkali*] and sword play [*vēlakali*]), ritual performances such as *teyyam,* the dramatic ritual enactments of the killing of the demon Darikan by the goddess Kali in the ritual theater form called *muṭiyeṯṯu;* Christian dance-dramas (such as *caviṭṭu nāṭakam*); devotional dance-dramas enacting the life history of Lord Kṛṣṇa (*Kṛṣṇāṭṭam*); and *kathakaḷi* dance-drama.

References

Alter, Joseph S. 1992. *The wrestler's body: identity and ideology in North India*. Berkeley: University of California Press.

Ashton-Sikora, Martha Bush and Robert P. Sikora. 1993. *Krishnattam*. New Delhi: Oxford & IBH Publishing Co.

Gangadharan, N., trans. 1985. *Agni Purana*. Delhi: Motilal Banarsidass.

Hart, George L. 1975. *The poems of ancient Tamil: their milieu and their Sanskrit counterparts*. Berkeley: University of California Press.

Mujumdar, D. C. 1950. *Encyclopedia of Indian physical culture*. Baroda: Good Companions.

Raj, J. David Manuel. 1977. The origin and historical development of Silambam fencing: ancient self-defense sport of India. Ph.D. dissertation, Department of Physical Education, University of Oregon.

Staal, Frits. 1993. Indian bodies. In *Self as body in Asian theory and practice,* ed. Thomas P. Kasulis, Roger T. Ames, and Wimal Dissanayke. Albany: State University of New York Press, 59–102.

Subramanian, N. 1966. *Sangam polity*. Bombay: Asian Publishing House.

Zarrilli, Phillip B. 1992. To heal and/or to harm: the vital spots in two South Indian martial arts, *Journal of Asian Martial Arts,* 1(1): 36–67; 1(2): 1–15.

———. 2000. *"When the body becomes all eyes": paradigms and discourses of practice and power in Kaḷarippayaṯṯu, a south Indian martial art*. 2d ed. New Delhi: Oxford University Press.

PHILLIP B. ZARRILLI

SEE ALSO

Bhūta Kōla; Caviṭṭu Nāṭakam; Chau; Dance; *Hanumān; Kamsāle; Kathakaḷi; Muṭiyeṯṯa; Ōṇam;* Tamil Nadu; *Teyyam*

MARTYRDOM

Martyrdom—self-sacrifice for God's sake—is an important part of Islamic discourse. A *shāhid,* literally, "witness," Arabic for "martyr," is essentially a witness for the faith. The word is derived from *shahada,* which refers to the Islamic creed that there is but one God and the Muḥammad is his prophet, the recitation of which is one of the five duties of Islam. One who is witness for Islam and submits even unto death thus is a shāhid.

The martyr who dies during the time of *jihād* (spiritual struggle) is rewarded at the final judgment, the *qīyāmat*. Then, all humans will come forth from their graves to be judged by God. The martyr goes to paradise and is spared the agonies of hell.

Since *jihād* does not refer only to wartime, but to any spiritual struggle, including the struggle to purify oneself or strengthen the Muslim community, anyone who dies during such a struggle can be considered shāhid. For example, a woman who dies in childbirth can be considered a martyr. However, such usages are generally secondary to the most important martyrdom, that of one who is slain for Islam. Such a person is buried in regular clothes without the customary washing or shrouding, because the person's martyrdom itself brings purity.

The first martyrs in Islam were those who fought with Muḥammad during the early battles with the Meccans. Shī'a Muslims have especially emphasized martyrdom as an essential component of their beliefs. They commemorate the martyrdom of Ḥusayn, the son of 'Alī and Muḥammad's grandson, on the first ten days of Muḥarram, with pageants that reenact his death. These include processions of mourners who flagellate themselves (*ta'ziya*). For the Shī'a, the supreme example of martyrdom is Ḥusayn's death at Karbalā, Iraq, at the hands of those who usurped the true leadership of the Muslim community.

In any situation of jihād, martyrdom stories circulate among Muslims. Often the stories considered most inspirational include prayer requests that God allow individuals to be shāhid, or examples of people who somehow knew in advance that they would be martyred. There are numerous examples from the Afghanistan War (1979–1987), including:

> One night a man had a dream that his head was carried in his hands as he approached God at the *qīyāmat*. So he went to the *mullah* (religious leader) to ask what the dream meant, and he was told that he would be *shāhid* the next day, and to prepare by putting on good clothes and purifying himself carefully. He did as the *mullah* had advised, and the next day, his head was blown off (Shalinsky 1994, 138).

The Muslims telling the story believe that at the time of the *qīyāmat,* the man's head will be returned. He will carry it before God as a visible sign of his martyrdom. Afghans from all ethnic groups during the time of the war kept photos of martyrs and displayed them as mementos. Occasionally, these were printed as booklets or circulated as part of publications by the *mujāhidīn* (jihād participants) for the Afghan resistance.

References

Ayoub, Mahmoud. 1987. Martyrdom in Christianity and Islam. In *religious resurgence: contemporary cases in Islam, Christianity, and Judaism,* eds. Richard T. Antoun and Mary Elaine Hegland, 67–77. Syracuse: Syracuse University Press.

Shalinsky, Audrey C. 1994. *Long years of exile: central Asian refugees in Afghanistan and Pakistan.* Lanham, Md.: University Press of America.

AUDREY C. SHALINSKY

SEE ALSO

Islam; *Jihād* poetry; Muḥarram; *Ta'ziya*

MASKS

There is evidence in the Mesolithic and Upper Paleolithic cave paintings of central India that masks have been used in South Asia since ca. 15,000 B.C.E. and possibly much earlier. Dancing figures—some clearly wearing animal masks and carrying bows and arrows and others wearing what seem to be more abstract masks—appear, for example, in the rock art of Bhimbetka and Ladi-ki-Karar in Madhya Pradesh. While the dating of these images remains tentative and the function of the masks highly conjectural, entoptic designs accompanying some of the masked figures indicate that trance ceremonies may have been involved and suggest dances of exorcism and renewal.

Clay masks have been found at Mohenjodaro, and what seems to have been an actor's terra-cotta mask was unearthed at Chirand and dated from the third-fourth centuries B.C.E. Masks of various materials—gourds, wood, leaves, clay, and papier mâche—are still used by the *ādivāsi* (tribal) peoples of India in agricultural, fertility, and curing ceremonies, frequently evoking connections to the animal and chthonic realms. Similar ceremonies have been developed with great vigor in the Himalayan regions in which Buddhism supplanted and incorporated elements of the animistic Bon religion under the influence of the remarkable religious teacher Padmasambhāva. Thus, in Tibet, Sikkim, Bhutan, Nepal, Ladakh, and Arunachal Pradesh (as well as in related traditions found in Mongolia and parts of Siberia), seasonal performances by the lamas of Buddhist monasteries feature horrific masks of Yāma and his deathly cohorts, ferocious Bodhisattvas with the power of conquering or containing the forces of death and disease, and comic old monks. In Tibet, the more secular operatic form of *lāmho* is introduced by the black masks of "hunters" that seem to hark back to an earlier hunting and gathering culture and features the mask of the ferocious queen Lāmho herself. One of the most elaborate uses of masks in South Asia is in the *sanniya yakuma* (also called *thovil*) curing ceremonies of Buddhist Sri Lanka, in which a series of eighteen sickness-causing demons and their leader, Mahā Kola Sannīya, are summoned; their influence over the afflicted patient is then countered by a company of ritual specialists using masks, trance, showmanship, and humor. A more secular masked form in Sri Lanka is the *kolam,* also featuring animal and elaborate demon masks.

The various interlocking and competing strands of Hinduism have also frequently deployed masks. Particularly of note is the use of *śakti* masks, representing the more active, feminine aspects of divine power—often for exorcistic purposes—in southern and eastern India. These forms seem to have blossomed first in the seventh century C.E., as Tantric Śaivism rivaled and eventually eclipsed Buddhism in these regions. A particularly old and well-preserved form of śakti masked dance is *gāmbhīra,* performed in the Malda region of West Bengal. Other instances of śakti mask usage, often associated with exorcistic pratices and especially performed at the time of the spring festival of *Chaitra Parva,* can be found scattered through West Bengal, southern Bihar, Orissa, and Andhra Pradesh, as well as in several sites in southern India. Of particular note is the interaction of this tradition with *ādivāsi* traditions of masking (as in the *mukha khel* traditions of West Bengal and *Mahākālīpyakhan* of Nepal) and the expansion of these hybrid traditions to include the portrayal of Purāṇic tales and stories from the *Mahābhārata* and *Rāmāyaṇa,* as in the *bhawada* tradition danced by the Konkana people living on the border between Gujarat and Maharashtra and the masked *chau* (also transliterated as *chho*) dances of West Bengal that deploy a wide variety of papier and cloth mâché masks to portray humans, gods, demons, and animals. In Seraikella, Bihar, a variant of this tradition was refined under royal patronage in the 1930s, and the repertoire was expanded to include metaphysical themes incorporating anthropomorphic masks for such characters as Night, the Moon, and a Boatman and his wife ferrying across life's treacherous waters.

The *Rāmāyaṇa* has been especially receptive to the use of masks and mask-like puppets (sometimes called *probhā,* or halos, in Orissa) worn over the entire body of the actor. Usually, the deployment of masks is confined to the animal and demonic characters in the epic. Thus, the ten-headed Rāvana and his demonic family and followers as well as the monkey army led by Sugrīva and Hanumān are frequently portrayed with masks; these range from the relatively simple papier-mâché helmet masks of the *deśīa nāṭa* dance theatre in the Koraput region of Orissa to the elaborately decorated cloth and metal masks used in the vicinity of Varanasi. A similarly selective use of masks for animals and demons in the portrayal of other Hindu myths may be found in such widely separated forms as the venerable *bhaona* tradition of devotional plays in Assam and the *kṛṣnattam* of Kerala, which features beautifully carved and painted masks for Jambhavān and Narakasura.

In the rock art of India—as well as Europe and Africa and in cultures as widely separated as ancient Egypt and the northwest coast of America—masks have proven particularly apt in portraying theriomorphic beings. An elephant-headed masked figure is featured in a 1,000 B.C.E. rock painting in India, where the elephant-headed Gaṇeśa is to this day similarly portrayed; as the god of propitious beginnings, he is often summoned at the start of Indian plays. Even more striking are the wooden and papier-mâché masks used to represent the man-lion avatar of Viṣṇu, Narasimha: examples of Narasimha masks are found in the modern *gāmbhīra* repertoire, and in many other forms of ritual theatre such as the *Prahlāda nāṭaka* of Orissa, the *kuchipudi* repertoire of Andhra Pradesh, the *bhāgavatamēla nāṭaka* and *terukkūttu* of Tamil Nadu, and the *yakṣagāna* repertoire of Karnataka. Animal masks continue to be used in secular dances, as well, including those deployed with two person animal costumes (*kola*) in wedding celebrations and festive holidays in the Ganjam hills of Orissa and the deer and tiger masks used in Kashmiri *bhānd paṭhar*.

Still, masks are relatively rare in secular contexts in South Asia, and masks representing the human face, as in the *chhau* tradition and in the old comic monks of Himalayan traditions, are very much the exception, not the rule. Masks were used in the pan-Indian Sanskrit theatre tradition, but, there too, seem to have been used sparingly and mostly for animals and demons. Instead, the play of human emotions on the face was elaborated under the *rasa/bhāva* system of empathetic responses triggered by specific emotional displays. This exaggeration of facial displays has also found its way into the folk theatre traditions, often abetted—in teyyam, in kathakali, in yakṣagāna, and in many other forms—by an elaborate use of highly stylized makeup, sometimes referred to as a pliant mask.

References

Asian Traditional Performing Arts Project. 1983. *Dance and music in south Asian drama: Chhau, Mahakali Pyakhan, and Yakshagana*. Tokyo: The Japan Foundation.

Emigh, John. 1996. *Masked performance: the play of self and other in ritual and theatre*. Philadelphia: University of Pennsylvania Press.

Fantin, Mario. 1976. *Mani-Rimdu, Nepal: the Buddhist dance drama of Tengpoche*. New Delhi: The English Book Store.

Ghosh, Prodyot. 1979. Gambhira: traditional masked dance of Bengal. *Sangeet Natak* 53–54: 14–25.

Goonatilleka, M. H. 1978. *Masks and mask systems of Sri Lanka*. Colombo: Tamarind Books.

Kapferer, Bruce. 1981. *A celebration of demons*. Bloomington: University of Indiana Press.

Lorblanchet, M. ed., 1992. *Rock art in the Old World*. New Delhi: IGNCA

Pani, Jiwan. 1986. *World of other faces: Indian masks*. New Delhi: Ministry of Information and Broadcasting.

Vatsyayan, Kapila. 1980. *Traditional Indian theatre: multiple streams*. New Delhi: National Book Trust.

Venu, G. 1990. *Puppetry and lesser known dance traditions of Kerala*. Folklore Series, no. 1. Trichur: Natana Kairali.

JOHN EMIGH

SEE ALSO

Bhānd paṭhar; *Chau;* Gāmbhīra; *Mukhos Nāc; Prahlāda Nāṭaka; Terukkūttu;* Theater and Drama; *Yakṣagāna*

MASKS, SRI LANKA

In the Asian region as a whole, masking and related practices, their forms and concepts, are based on a variety of ritual and cultural experiences. Similarly, in Sri Lanka, masking practices relate to the folk religions and folk dramatic traditions of the Sinhalese people. These masks must be studied in their dance contexts, which include: demon and god rituals and use in ritual processions; folk dramas (social events with ritual overtones); and professional displays during village celebrations. The most common mask types are confined to the first two categories. One exemplary demon ritual, which involves a variety of masks, is the healing ritual *Sanni Yakuma* (also called *Daha-aṭa Sanniya*). *Kōlam,* a dance-drama traditionally confined to the southern and western coastal belt of the island, involves a cycle of fully masked dance episodes, containing over one hundred masked characters representing demons, mythological figures, humans, and animals.

Sri Lankan masks are not generally used as protective devices, except for the *Garā* demon mask that at times is hung at the entrance of a newly built house in order to ward off the evil eye. The Buddha, the Buddha-aspirant (*Bōdhisattva*), and the pantheon of Buddhist deities are not symbolically portrayed through masks, nor are mask collections housed in Buddhist temples. There is no evidence of royal patronage being accorded to mask making.

It is not known exactly when and how masks first were used in Sri Lanka. However, the history of masks in Sri Lanka does not appear to be very long. *Ves-muhuṇa,* the Sinhalese word for "mask," does not appear in the ancient inscriptions or in the classical Sinhala literature. The oldest extant masks are not more than two or three hundred years old. Archaeological evidence of purely incidental value is provided by two terra-cotta figurines from circa thirteenth–sixteenth century C.E., yet, in all probability, these display facial distortion as a stylistic device of the folk sculptural traditions, rather than representing masks. The Văddo (Veddas) people, the indigenous hunter-gatherer society of Sri Lanka, have not used masks, although their rituals retain costumes and other structural similarities with those of the Sinhalese cults.

Sri Lankan masks may also be classified according to their form and the position in which they are worn. These types include: elaborately dressed masks hollowed from within, which cover the entire head of the wearer; tall masks, not hollowed, but which cover the face; masks that cover only half the face; and (4) mask-like gadgets or elements.

Kōlam masks display a rich variety and exquisite craftsmanship. They are basically of three kinds: human (royalty, officials, ordinary villagers, etc.); supernatural (demons and mythical beings); and animal (lions, bears, etc.). Human masks are either naturalistic but somewhat formalized, realistic (intensely individualized), or caricatures.

Sri Lankan masks are made entirely of wood, except for one or two types of masks made out of animal hide. Metal, clay, and other materials have not been used. The commonest wood is a variety of *nux vomica* (*vel kaduru*) which also yields strychnine. The wood is soft and does not crack in the process of carving. Moveable components are at times attached or mortised. The color combination of the mask depends on the mask type, and on the age, sex, and social position of the intended wearer.

References

Goonatilleka, M. H. 1978. *Masks and mask systems of Sri Lanka*. Colombo, Sri Lanka: Tamarind Books.

Höpfner, Gerd. 1969. *Masken aus Ceylon* (Masks of Ceylon). Berlin: Museum für Völkerkunde.

Sarachchandra, Ediriweera. 1966. *The folk drama of Ceylon*. 2nd ed. Colombo, Sri Lanka: Department of Cultural Affairs.

Sharma, Ram Karan, and Bhagawan Das, eds. and tr. 1985. *Agniveśa's Caraka Saṃhitā*. Varanasi, India: Chowkhamba Sanskrit Series Office.

M. H. GOONATILLEKA

SEE ALSO

Daha-Aṭa Sanniya; Dance; Rituals; Sri Lanka, Sinhala; Theater and Drama; Veddas [Văddo]

MĀTAM

Mātam is a word of Arabic origin that in both Persian and Urdu indicates actions of mourning or funeral-lamentation for the deceased. In Shī'a Islam the word designates observances (whether weeping or acts of self-mortification) performed annually during the month of Muḥarram (first month of the Islamic lunar calendar) in honor of the Imām Ḥusayn ibn 'Alī and the other martyrs of the battle of Karbalā (Iraq, 680 C.E.). More specifically, the term denotes the action of striking oneself as a gesture of ritual mourning—either with the bare hand (as indicated by the Persian phrase *sīneh-zanī* [chest beating]) or with a dagger, flail, or chains (as for example in the flagellation known as *zanjīr-zanī*). Bare-handed mātam is much more common than the use of weapons. Mātam is performed during *majālis* (pl. of *majlis* [liturgical gatherings held throughout Muḥarram]) and the great public processions of 'Ashura (the tenth of Muḥarram, the day on which Ḥusayn died in battle). Shī'a justifications of mātam cite the example of Zaynab, Ḥusayn's sister, who survived Karbalā and is said to have held the first majlis in lamentation for the Imām while she was kept a prisoner in Damascus. Shī'a informants interviewed by this author in Hyderabad (India) offer as reasons for mātam the desire to identify empathetically with the Karbalā martyrs ("We want to feel Ḥusayn's sorrow," as one young man put it) and the hope of earning *Ṣawāb* (religious merit) as a reward for strenuous mourning. Popular tales assert that the grieving Lady Fāṭima (Ḥusayn's mother) is invisibly present at every majlis; acts of mātam assure her that she is not alone in mourning the slain Imām.

Among the most enthusiastic performers of mātam are the mātami *gurūhān* (Shī'a men's associations), which sponsor many of the majālis and processions held in Hyderabad. Each guild boasts a characteristic style and rhythm of mātam; some groups favor one-handed breast-beating, others, a two-handed stroke; some an overhead sweep of both arms, others, a windmill slap to the chest with an accompanying twist of the torso. Regardless of style, mātam is consistently performed in a communal liturgical setting rather than in private: participants beat their chests in unison and in time to the chanting of *nauḥajāt* (pl. of *nauḥa,* dirges in honor of the Karbalā martyrs). Poets affiliated with each Hyderabadi guild compose fresh lyrics annually to be recited during Muḥarram. The following verses are excerpted from an Urdu nauḥa composed by Najm Effendi for a guild named Parwāneh-yi Shabbīr, meaning "the moths of Ḥusayn," a title that recalls the moth/flame imagery of Sufi mystical poetry, with the candle-flame symbolizing Ḥusayn's quality of luminous attractiveness for believers; Shī'a exegesis identifies "Shabbīr" as an ancient Syriac variant of the Imām's name. The text is printed in a chapbook published by Parwāneh-yi Shabbīr:

> Truly, within these breasts, our hearts are lamentation-shrines for Ḥusayn . . .
> No one before has ever seen or heard of such mātam for any sultan . . .
> For thirteen hundred years there has been wondrous mātam.
> Praise, o give praise, to the beloved splendor of Ḥusayn;
> We are the lovers of Shabbīr, the moths of Ḥusayn.
>
> May this effort be acceptable;
> perhaps through this means pardon and forgiveness will be attained.
> Najm, you, too, join these moths and say:
> Praise, O give praise, to the beloved splendor of Ḥusayn;
> We are the lovers of Shabbīr, the moths of Ḥusayn.

Another Parwāneh-yi Shabbīr nauḥa states:

> In our eyes, even now is that time when Ḥusayn staggered and fell bleeding.
> On the battlefield, there resounded the complaint and cries for help of one afflicted.
> Even if streaks of blood now flow from our breasts, may our hands never cease:

Let this mātam continue on behalf of the one who was wronged, for as long as Fāṭima's cry comes forth.
This mātam is a prayer for Fāṭima:
how could this mātam ever cease?

These verses warrant comparison with a nauḥa composed for another Hyderabadi Shī'a guild, the Anjuman-i Ma'ṣūmīn [the association of the "sinless ones"]:

O young men of lamentation . . .

truly, till the gathering of humankind on the Day of Resurrection there will continue from breasts the sound of mātam.

Such verses focus less on the past historical event of Karbalā and more on the present-day Shī'a congregation that recalls this event. These poems hold a mirror up to participants, inviting them to contemplate themselves as they perform the characteristically Shī'a ritual of mātam. In South Asia as elsewhere in the world, Shī'a populations define themselves as those Muslims who are outstanding in their loyalty to the Prophet's family, to Ḥusayn and to his descendants the Imāms. Breast-beating and group lamentation during Muḥarram give witness to this loyalty in a way evinced by no other people, in a way that marks Shī'a Muslims as distinct from all other communities. Mātam, then, can be said to contribute to Shī'a communal identity.

Such at least is the ideal as represented in the texts chanted by the mātami gurūhān. In practice, however, there is some blurring of communal boundaries in the religiously syncretistic environment of Hyderabad's Old City neighborhoods. During Muḥarram some Hindus visit Shī'a shrines to venerate the relics on display; and at least a few prominent Hindu families in the Old City sponsor majālis and invite the most popular Shī'a mātami gurūhān to come and lead the mixed Hindu–Muslim congregation in the performance of mātam.

References

'Alī, Mīr Aḥmad, ed. 1989. *Karbalā wāle: Nauḥajāt-i anjuman-i Parwāneh-yi Shabbīr* [Mourners of Karbala: lamentation poems of the association of the moths of Ḥusayn]. Hyderabad: Maktab-i Turabia.

Anonymous. n.d. *Du'ā-yi Fāṭima: Muntakhab-i nauḥajāt* [Fatimah's prayers: a selection of lamentation poems]. Hyderabad: Anjuman-i Ma'ṣūmīn.

Pinault, David. 1992a. Shī'a Muslim men's associations and the celebration of Muḥarram in Hyderabad, India. *Journal of South Asian and Middle Eastern Studies* 16(1): 38–62.

———. 1992b. *The Shiites: ritual and popular piety in a Muslim community*. New York: St. Martin's Press.

———. 2001. *Horse of Karbala: Muslim devotional life in India*. New York: Palgrave.

DAVID PINAULT

SEE ALSO

Chapbooks; Fāṭima; Islam; Lament; *Majlis; Muḥarram; Nauḥa*

MATERIAL CULTURE

Material culture refers to the physical objects that are created by humans. Modern studies of material culture have changed significantly from the early collections of tools, clothing, and ritual paraphernalia in the eighteenth and nineteenth centuries, to a focus on the interplay of the different variables that affect the creation of material culture. These factors include the environment and available raw materials, technology and the organization of production, socioeconomic organization, and ideology and belief systems. Material culture is a key element for personal identity as well as community and national identity. Because material culture encompasses every aspect of human society, both past and present, methodologies and theoretical frameworks for its study are varied.

Historically, material culture studies began with pure description of different types of objects and then moved to evolutionary and diffusionist perspectives. In the evolutionary approaches, classification was based on the number of components of which an object was comprised. Simple objects such as a sharpened stick for digging or throwing were placed at one end of the classification, and more complex objects with attachments and ornamentation were placed at the opposite end. Diffusionist approaches assumed that certain aspects of material culture originated in one area of the world and spread to the rest. The movements could be traced by comparing similar objects and relating the numbers of components or stylistic attributes. In a later development, historical particularists focused on the unique material objects of individual culture areas to understand independent trajectories. Initial attempts at a universal classification of objects and the indiscriminate use of diffusionary models have proven to be relatively meaningless and have not helped to understand variation within or between cultures. Subsequently, the study of material culture has become fragmented into many different subfields with very different methodologies and goals.

Ethnographers tend to collect, classify, and describe objects collected from living communities by using a wide range of methodologies that are developed for a limited culture and that are later adapted for broad cross-cultural comparisons. Functionalist and structural approaches concentrate on the role of material culture in serving basic human needs as well as its function in maintaining socioeconomic and political order. More recently, popular culture studies have begun to look at the role of material culture in defining such topics as personal identity, ethnicity and globalism. Many of these more recent ethnographic approaches have moved from the study of the objects themselves to a study of what those objects mean and how their production or reproduction reflect social, economic, and ideological aspects of a society.

Archaeological research relies totally on material culture that is preserved in the archaeological record. This body of data represents a distinct but incomplete record of prehistoric or archaeological cultures. Ethnoarchaeologists study specific aspects of modern material culture to understand how the patterning of material culture that would be preserved archaeologically can help us to understand social, economic, and political aspects of earlier societies. A material science approach is used by specialists who are interested in the ways in which materials are transformed through various technological processes among specific communities today or in antiquity, including, for example, the processes for producing glazed ceramics or coloring stone.

In the study of material culture it is often useful to compare and contrast objects from different regions over time. The variations in shape and decoration represent different contextual levels of a culture, individual variation, community or assemblage variation, and on a larger scale, variation between cultural traditions. Cultural traditions are "persistent configurations of basic technologies and cultural systems within the context of temporal and geographical continuity" (Willey and Phillips 1958, 37).

In order to compare material culture in a meaningful and reproducible way, it is necessary to classify and order material culture, but there is no absolute classification system because each classification system must be designed to address specific questions or problems. However, all good classification systems employ two complementary approaches, taxonomy and systematics. Taxonomy is the system of concepts and terms used to classify objects: jar, pot, bowl, and dish. Systematics is the method for creating units; for example, a jar is taller than it is wide and has an open or restricted orifice. The different variables that are used to characterize objects are usually referred to as attributes. This term, and the concept itself, are a part of taxonomy, while the way in which attributes are grouped or identified is a part of systematics. Five basic attributes that can be used to understand an object include: (1) form (shape and size); (2) style (decoration); (3) technology of manufacture; (4) raw materials; and (5) function (utilitarian and/or symbolic). These attributes vary in importance, depending on the cultural context and the type of object being produced. In South Asia, the type of wood used in prayer beads is generally more important symbolically than is the shape. In contrast, shape may be more important than material in the production of the pipal leaf or mango shape in textiles, gold ornaments, clay, or wood.

Another approach to material culture, coming from the field of archaeology, has tried to understand the factors that lead to standardization of production and style, as well as the potential for control of crafts that are used to reinforce and legitimize social order. Kenoyer has proposed a four-category classification of craft professions that produce material culture based upon two cross-cutting axes: the local versus nonlocal availability of raw material and the simple or complex character of the technologies involved. The local raw material and simple technologies include: woodworking, handformed and low-fired terra-cotta ceramic production, and house building. The nonlocal material and simple technologies include: stoneworking and flint knapping. The local raw material and complex technologies include: stoneware bangle production, other elaborated ceramic industries, and elaborate woodwork. The nonlocal raw material and complex technologies include: agate bead manufacture, seal production, and metalworking. The more complex technologies tend towards increased standardization, while the other categories show a higher degree of regional variation.

Political and economic control of craft production may include control of technological know-how, labor, access to raw materials, distribution, and consumption. In general, cross-cultural research has shown that political elites of chiefdoms patronize the production of luxury goods manufactured with raw materials that are nonlocal, rare or difficult to obtain, and are transformed through massive investment of labor in the form of simple technologies. On the other hand, many state-level societies show a radical shift, sponsoring the production of ornaments and status signs whose raw materials are relatively common or easy to obtain but require very elaborate technologies. These studies of material culture can be applied to nonarchaeological contexts as well, but in living crafts, a host of other factors that normally are not preserved archaeologically must be accounted for. These include the status associated with specific materials or their production, and the socioritual and economic value of specific materials. These values often translate into the ranking of specific crafts as well as the social and ritual status of craft communities.

The social dimensions of production and exchange are continuously being negotiated as communities struggle to survive competition, and improve their economic as well as ritual status. The legitimization of social status and ranking among craft communities is often provided through folk stories and origin myths. Stories that explain the origin of specific materials can be found in the early Vedas and Purāṇic texts. For example the sacred conch shell was created when the god Śiva destroyed a powerful demon and cast his bleached bones into the sea. Hindu and Buddhist traditions generally link the different crafts communities to mythical events, while Muslim communities often rely on historical associations. For example, Hindu shell bangle workers in Bengal trace their craft to the sage Agastya Muni who created a specialized saw from the sacred *khus* grass in order to make shell bangles for the goddess Pārvatī. Muslim agate bead makers in Khambhat trace their origins to the Abyssinian saint Bawa Ghor, who brought Islam to Gujarat and destroyed the temple of the goddess who controlled the agate-mining areas.

These stories are important sources of information on changing social and religious dimensions of material culture. The conch shell was first used in ritual contexts of the Indus Valley Civilization (2600–1900 B.C.E.). It was then borrowed and incorporated into late Vedic culture (roughly 1800–800 B.C.E.) and has come to be a distinctive symbol of various Hindu deities. Buddhist rituals incorporate the conch shell as an important symbol and use conch shell libation vessels and conch shell trumpets. Even Muslim mystics in many parts of Pakistan and India use the conch shell trumpet in ceremonies associated with specific saints. Each of these communities has specific stories to validate the use of shared material culture symbols such as the sacred conch shell, but it is not always possible to sort out the origins of these accounts.

Due to a reaction against positivist approaches to the study of culture, many anthropologists and folklorists shy away from the systematic and quantitative study of material culture. In their work, material culture is viewed qualitatively without rigidly defined parameters. On the other hand, specialized studies of specific types of material culture, such as textiles, masks, and jewelry, do implement standard methodologies for classification and analysis, generally borrowing from standards in commerce and the fields of history and archaeology.

References

Akbari, Nasreen, and Rosemary Crill. 1997. *Colours of the Indus: costume and textiles of Pakistan.* London: Holberton.

Appadurai, Arjun. 1990. Disjuncture and difference in the global cultural economy. *Public culture* 2(2): 1–24.

Gould, Richard A., and Michael B. Schiffer, eds. 1981. *Modern material culture: The archaeology of us.* New York: Academic Press.

Grassi, Letizia. 1997. Sacrality, myth, objects: techniques of fabrication and semiotical, anthropological interpretations of carpets and jewels from Pakistan. In *Semiotics around the world: synthesis in diversity* ed. Irmengard Rauch and Gerald F. Carr, pp. 281–82. Berlin: Mouton De Gruyter.

Hodder, Ian. 1982. *Symbols in action: Ethnoarchaeological studies of material culture.* Cambridge: Cambridge University Press.

Kenoyer, J. Mark. 1992. Harappan craft specialization and the question of urban segregation and stratification. *Eastern anthropologist* 45(1–2): 39–54.

Lechtman, Heather, and Robert S. Merrill, eds. 1977. *Material culture: styles, organization and dynamics of technology.* St. Paul, Minn.: American Ethnological Society.

Saeed, Fouzia. 1988. *Traditional furniture of D. I. Khan.* Islamabad: Lok Virsa.

Sharma, R. S. 1983. *Material culture and social formation in ancient India.* Delhi: Macmillan India.

Smith, Cyril S., and M. Kranzberg. 1975. Materials in history and society. *Material science and engineering* 37(1): 1–39.

Willey, George R., and P. Phillips. 1958. *Method and theory in American archaeology.* Chicago: University of Chicago Press.

JONATHAN MARK KENOYER

SEE ALSO

Carpets and Carpet-Weaving; Crafts; *Dāsara;* Dress; Faience; Fish and Fishing; Folk Art; Food and Foodways; Glass; *Mandecculu;* Metal and Metalworking; Toys; Wedding Videos

MATERIAL CULTURE, PAKISTAN

Pakistan's territory encompasses a highly varied geography, from the severe Tharparkar deserts of the southeast and the arid Makran coast to the west, the rich irrigated Indus Valley agricultural lands of Punjab and Sindh, to the semi-arid highlands of Balochistan, the wooded southern slopes of the Hindukush/Karakorum mountain ranges, to the highest semi-arid valleys and alpine pastures north of passes reaching over 12,000, and the permanent snows of some of the highest peaks in the world, including Nanga Parbat and K-2. This range of ecological zones supports a number of distinctive cultures. As elsewhere, however, ecological resources only begin to explain the distribution of craft skills and material culture styles. Yet there is also continuity, in that certain elements can be traced to the oldest layers of regional style, dating from the Indus Valley civilizations, including Mohenjo Daro and Harappa (ca. 2600–1700 B.C.E.). Shapes of pottery and design motifs attested from this most ancient period are still produced today; a contemporary wooden cart in Lok Virsa, the National Folk Heritage Museum in Islamabad, closely resembles the style of cart preserved in small models of fired clay from Mohenjo Daro. The *borendo,* a shepherd's three-holed clay flute, can be similarly dated and is still played. The more recent Buddhist culture of the Gandhāra region (north central Indus Valley to

Afghanistan) is represented still in certain surviving motifs in embroidery and woodwork from the Swat region. Consciously or unconsciously, certain items of Pakistan's folk art derive from and evoke these ancient civilizations. The major contemporary crafts of Pakistan are variously developed in different regions.

Woodworking

Woodworking includes carving, turning, inlaying and lacquering. It is used for storage boxes, vessels, furniture, and architectural decoration in Sindh and Multan. Doors, windows, and house pillars are carved to display householders' wealth especially in Swat, in the Peshawar are Potohar, and certain parts of the Punjab (Chiniot) and Sindh (Shikarpur). Elaborate carving is used to decorate mosques in Swat and Indus Kohistan, and to some extent in the Northern Areas, especially in pillars, capitals and trim. Religiously inspired decorative carving also distinguishes the homes and ritual sites of the non-Muslim Kalasha people living in three valleys near Chitral. Wooden blocks are also carved in complex floral and geometric patterns for use in woodblock printing of textiles in Sindh and Punjab.

Weaving and Textile Decoration Techniques

Varieties of woven products include fabrics such as *khes, pattu, sūssī, khadar,* and *lungī*; flat-weave floor coverings known as *darī, pilasī, felasī, sharma,* and *pilesk.* Prominent textile dyeing and printing styles include the elaborate, multi-staged block print and resist-dye techniques (*ajrak*) of Sindh and Multan, as well as tie-dye and so-called wax-painting. Free-hand "wax" painting on cloth, using an adhesive of linseed oil and lime to attach dry powdered colors, is a Peshawar City tradition that seems to derive its fluid floral and scenic motifs from Chinese influence. Blocks are also used to transfer the gum for border designs on some more tribal-style women's garments. Distinctive needlework styles are claimed by almost every region and ethnic group: bright, mainly monochrome satin-stitch counted-thread styles on shawls and dresses from Hazara and Swat in the north; fine-cross-stitch on women's caps and wedding dresses from the Northern Areas (Hunza and Nagyr) and Chitral; *kacca thanka* ("raw stitch"), an open running stitch, monochrome for men's wear, polychrome for women, from Multan, Dera Ghazi Khan, and Dera Ismail Khan; locally distinctive, multicolored mixed-stitch techniques on dress fronts from Makran, upland Balochistan and Dera Ghazi Khan; gold-thread work on women's dresses, men's hats and shoes for both sexes characteristic of certain Pashtun tribes; pieced quilts and more recently, appliqué techniques (both called *rillī*) used for bedcovers and throws from Sindh; mirror work in various styles on men's caps, women's dresses, furnishings and decorative pieces from Balochistan to Sindh and the Tharparker desert, and still other distinctive styles of the Makran coast and the Cholistan desert. Two distinctive regional styles of embroidery on leather are *tilla* in Punjab and the Northwest Frontier Province, in which paper cut-outs are created (*okair sāzī*) and pasted to the leather as patterns, which women then embroider, and the Sindhi and Balochi silk-thread chain-stitch embroidery (*thal*) done by men using a small awl. Gun and cartridge belts, holsters, gun covers, formerly also sheathes for swords and daggers, and small personal articles are all made from leather, decorated or undecorated, in the Northwest Frontier Province, Balochistan and Sindh. Recently, large numbers of Afghan refugees resident since about 1980 have introduced Afghan Pashtun, Hazara and Turkic embroidery styles into the Pakistani needlework scene, but this is part of an ongoing process of cultural transmission. A substantial population of Afghan Hazara refugees have been settled in and around Quetta for more than a hundred years. Prior to the Afghan wars of 1978–2001, certain groups of Pashtun nomads routinely pastured their flocks in Pakistan in winter and in the Afghan highlands in summer, taking back and forth with them materials for trade as well as their own handicraft traditions.

Basketry and Straw Weaving

Traditions are widespread, using wild grass (*mazrī*) in the Northwest Frontier Province and Balochistan, wheat straw or types of palm leaf (*pīsh*) as available, and also willow in some areas. Utility items include floor mats, construction matting for walls and underlayment for earthen roofs, sturdy willow carry baskets for transporting fruits and other materials to market and home, small and large baskets for serving and storing bread, hand fans, winnowing fans and sieves, and fine decorative baskets. Sandals and entire summer shelters are made of woven palm fronds by certain semi-nomadic groups in Balochistan, who also produce a great quantity of hand-twined palm-fiber rope for use and sale.

Leatherwork

Leatherwork besides the embroidered Balochi forms mentioned above, include shoes and sandals (*cappal*) in many distinctive designs. Shoes, like styles of dress, decoration, caps and turbans, are ethnic and regional group markers and in the past, shoe types were said to change every twenty years. Now regional styles find their way into markets at the center and go through phases of national fashion. Shoes may be decorated or undecorated. The curled-up toes characteristic of some styles are most radically curled in the North-West Frontier tribal areas, more moderately in Potophar and down the Indus valley.

Papier Maché

Papier maché is said to have been brought from Iran to Kashmir long ago. It now flourishes there, used for small objects such as boxes, dishes and vases with floral and animal designs derived from miniature paintings. Other styles exist in Multan and Punjab as well.

Jewelry

Jewelry throughout the country is a medium of women's self-expression as well as their main form of personal savings. Made by male craftsmen and widely sold in bazaars in cities and major towns, jewelry sets are a basic component of personal property contributed to the bride both by her own family and that of the groom. Women may receive other gifts of jewelry from their husbands during their married life. Every large village or small town has its own jewelers and regional styles vary, but generally rural and tribal people favor heavy silver designs, while urban people and the wealthy prefer fine gold work, often with gemstones. Certain groups (Pashtuns and Balochis for example) make elaborate glass beadwork, the design of which (unlike the silver and gold work) is in women's own hands.

Ivory and Bone Carving

Now mostly confined to camel bone, in Multan and Lahore, ivory and bone carving includes furniture inlays, small carved models and decorative objects, plus jewelry (beads, pins and earrings).

Traditional Metalwork

Metalwork in brass, copper, silver and bronze includes plates and trays, drinking glasses, local traditional forms such as the Punjabi bronze *cenna,* a wide, flat bowl tapered inward at the mouth, the *sīnī*, a widely-used large copper tray used for serving foods family-style, the copper *khuza* or water-jug, the *cāīnak* (tea kettle), the Central Asian-derived samovar (a charcoal-burning urn for boiling water), and all sizes of *daig* (a stew or rice-pot, broader at the bottom than at the mouth) and *kerāī* (round-bottomed sauté pan), Two major styles of metalwork center on Peshawar (with Central Asian influence) and Lahore/Punjab, respectively. Decorative techniques include embossing, engraving, *citrāī* (a shallow surface scratching), *sīāh kalam* ("black pen work") which first coats brass with a black paint then scratches designs through to the metal; some enameling, and inlays of mixed metals. Molding is relatively new; the traditional shaping techniques of beating sheet metal are ancient and ubiquitous.

Pottery

Pottery of local types exists in most regions except Swat and the Northern Areas (Baltistan, Karakorum and Hindukush), where stone vessels were used for cooking, and stone, wood and basketry for storage, until itinerant Gujar people from the Punjab brought their pottery to the area for trade. Sindhi and Punjabi pottery is historically interesting for its connection to ancient forms and styles. Gujarat was historically famous for very fine bowls; some *kāghazī* ("paper-thin") unglazed ware still comes from Ahmedpur Sharqiya near Bahawalpur, though the artisans have mostly turned to other trades. Taxila is the center for polychrome painted ware, while there is another, monochrome painted ware tradition around Larkana and Hyderabad in Sindh. Blue glazes on white come from Multan and Hala. Peshawar's *pabbī* wares have green or blue glazes.

References

Baloch, N. A., ed. 1966. *Traditional arts and crafts of Hyderabad Region, Pakistan*. Karachi: Mehran Arts Council.

Cousin, Francoise, 1981. Some data on block-printing in Sind. *In* Hamida Khuro, ed., *Sind through the Centuries*. Karachi: Oxford University Press, pp. 228–236.

Frembgen, Jürgen W., 1998a. *Stickereien aus dem Karakorum*. München: Staatliches Museum für Völkerkunde.

———. 1998b. Innovations in traditional crafts: Nager and Hunza in the 20th century. *European Bulletin of Himalayan Research* 14, pp. 3–17.

———. 1998c. Religious folk art as an expression of identity: Muslim tombstones in the Gangar Mountains of Pakistan. *Muqarnas, An Annual on the Visual Culture of the Islamic World,* vol. 15. pp. 200–210.

Gardezi, H. 1986. *Crafts of the Punjab,* Vol. 1: *Murree Hills*. Lahore: Sang-e Meel.

Haider, Sajjad, n.d. *Tilework in Pakistan*. Islamabad: Lok Virsa.

Khuro, Hamida, ed., 1981. *Sind through the centuries*. Karachi: Oxford University Press.

Mills, Margaret, 1994. The esthetics of exchange: embroidery designs and women's work in the Karakorum. *In* A. Giese and J. Ch. Bürgel, eds., *"God is beautiful and He loves beauty": A Festschrift for Annemarie Schimmel,* pp. 331–345. Bern and New York: Peter Lang

Riazuddin, Akhtar. 1988. *History of handicrafts: Pakistan-India,* Islamabad: National Hijra Council.

Rye, Owen S., and Clifford Evans. 1990. *Traditional pottery techniques of Pakistan*. Washington and Islamabad: Smithsonian Institution Press/Lok Virsa.

Saraf, D. N. 1987. *Arts and crafts: Jammu and Kashmir, land, people, culture*. New Delhi: Abhinav.

Schienerl, Peter W., 1983. Muslim tombs and cemeteries: their importance for jewelry research. *Ornament* 7: 1, pp. 10–13.

Srinavasan, Doris, 1996. Swati textiles: how long has this been going on? *In* William Hanaway and Wilma Heston, eds., *Studies in the popular culture of Pakistan*. Islamabad and Lahore: Lok Virsa/Sang-e Meel Publishers, pp. 15–60.

von Oppen, Renata. 1992. *Art on wheels*. Karachi: Ferozsons Ltd.
Yacopino, Felicia, 1977. *Threadlines*. Islamabad: Ministry of Industries, Govt. of Pakistan.
Yousuf, Mahrukh, 1990. *Folk motifs of Pakistan*. Islamabad: Lok Virsa.
———. 1991. *Catalogue of the collection of woodworks of Pakistan in the archives of Lok Virsa Museum*. Islamabad: Lok Virsa.

KHALID JAVAID AND MARGARET MILLS

SEE ALSO
Bangles; Beads; Dress, Pakistan; Foodways, Pakistan; Glass; Jewelry and Adornment; Tiles and Tile-making, Terra Cotta; Toys

MAULID

Maulid refers to the celebration of the birth of a holy person, especially the Prophet Muhammad; it also refers to elegiac poetry celebrating the Prophet's birth. In most parts of the Muslim world this term is used to refer to the annual celebrations of the birth anniversaries of Sufi saints, which take place at their tombs. This term is seldom used for saints' festivals in South Asia—the *'urs* being the more common celebration, commemorating the saints' death anniversaries and their union with God at death. Instead, in South Asia, maulid refers specifically to the birthday of the Prophet Muhammad on the twelfth night of Rabī' al-Awwal (also the date of his death—in fact, the maulid is sometimes referred to as *Bara Wafat,* literally, "Twelve Death").

Particularly in the Sunni community, the maulid of the Prophet or *'Īd Mīlād-i Nabī* is celebrated with great festivities. Processions with floats, songs and illumination are common facets of maulid celebrations. Some commentators have argued that the growing popularity of 'Īd al-Mīlād processions in the Sunni community is a response to the popularity of Shī'ī processions—providing an analogous visible Sunni act of pious allegiance. The earliest forms of commemoration of the Prophet's maulid involved poetry and honored the Prophet's birth, miracles, and death. They specifically referred to miraculous events surrounding his birth—for example, the fact that the Prophet was born circumcised. It is still considered a day of great spiritual power and an occasion for the possibility of miraculous intervention.

'Īd al-Mīlād-ī Nabī has been the focus of controversy within the Muslim community. Wahhābis and certain other puritanical Muslim groups have viewed the commemoration of the Prophet's birthday as *bid'a* (religious innovation) and, thus, an unacceptable Islamic practice. They point out the unseemliness of festive celebrations on this date. More specifically, they are uncomfortable with the degree to which the Prophet is raised to a miraculous supernatural status in the poetry of the maulid and the common belief that the Prophet attends the recitation of maulid in a spiritual form—in their view, this borders on shirk (polytheism, "assigning partners to God"). Some modernist Muslims, for example Sayyid Ahmad Khan, have shared some of the criticisms raised by Wahabis about the "superstitious" nature of the maulid, but in general they have been fond of 'Īd al-Mīlād-ī Nabī. They have redefined it as an opportunity to celebrate the social and ethical achievements of the Prophet Muhammad. The late dictator of Pakistan, Zia al-Haqq, used the occasion of the 'Īd al-Mīlād-ī Nabī in 1979 to enact a series of penal laws based on the sharī'ah (Islamic law).

References

Sharif, Ja'far. 1921. *Islam in India or Qanun-i Islam*. London: Oxford University Press.
Schimmel, Annemarie. 1985. *And Muḥammad is His Messenger: the veneration of the Prophet in Islamic piety*. Chapel Hill: University of North Carolina Press.
Von Grunebaun, G. E. 1992. *Muhammadan festivals*. London: Curzon Press.

VERNON JAMES SCHUBEL

SEE ALSO
'Urs

MEDICINE, ĀYURVEDA

Āyurveda is an Indian system of medicine estimated to be over two thousand years old. Largely consistent with Brahmanic values, Āyurveda is associated with such classical texts as the *Caraka Saṃhitā, Suśruta Saṃhitā,* and *Vagbhata Ashtanga-hidaya.* Literally, the science of longevity (*ayu:* life/longevity; *veda:* knowledge/wisdom), Āyurveda is a humoral system of medicine organized around three humors (*tridoṣa: vata, pitta, kapha*) associated with discrete life processes and complexes of vital activities co-occurring within the body. Central to Āyurveda is a system of correspondences derived by analogical reasoning on the basis of astute observation of the body as well as of domains of experience ranging from the movement of the sun and moon to weather patterns, the growth of plants, and the behavior or animals. Within Āyurveda, the body is perceived to be an organic microcosm subject to the same universal principal as an all-encompassing macrocosm. A physiomorphic conception of the body-mind pervades Āyurveda, lending itself to a holistic approach to healing.

Health, according to Āyurveda, is largely an outcome of proper digestive processes. One's health, humoral status, and digestive processes are subject to

An Āyurvedic compounder pours a medicinal wine, arishta. kerala, India, © Mimi Nichter

body constitution (*prākriti*) and age, habit and habitat, lifestyle, and work. Maintaining the integrity of one's digestive processes requires the adjustment of diet and the monitoring of body signs indicative of excess or deficiency. The importance of digestion is highlighted in the *Caraka Saṃhitā,* where a person's role in feeding the gastric fire (*jathara agni*) is compared to that of the Brahman priest who tends to the sacred fire where sacrifices are made to the gods.

Within Āyurveda, disease is interpreted both as an imbalance of bodily humors and a hunger associated with a state of deficiency or excess. *Kayacikitsa*—measures taken to remove factors causing illness and restoring humoral equilibrium—focus on *pathyam* (diet and lifestyle compatible to health) as well as proactive health in the form of *ojus* production. Ojus constitutes the quintessence and purified product of the digestive process responsible for controlling multiple bodily processes. *Samṣodhana* is a division of Āyurveda associated with the removal of causative factors of illness and entails bodily purification and acts of elimination (for example, *vamana:* emetics; *virecana:* purgatives). Āyurveda has an extensive pharmacopeia and offers the afflicted a wide range of both curative and palliative (*praṣamana*) regimens, including treatments to reduce mental disturbance and fear (*prayaṣitta*).

Āyurveda, as practiced in India (and elsewhere in South Asia), has been subject to significant modification, (re)interpretation, and experimentation over the centuries. "Classical" Āyurveda is currently practiced by *vaidya* (practitioners) who have either been trained through apprenticeship or as students in colleges of "*Ṣudda*" (pure) Āyurveda which operate in several different states of India and Sri Lanka. A growing movement within Āyurveda is the "integrated school," which incorporates the biomedical study of anatomy and physiology and employs biomedical knowledge and research methods to search for equivalences that explicate Āyurvedic principles.

Āyurvedic medicine is growing in popularity in India, and there is presently a boom in the commercial production and sale of both traditional and modern Āyurvedic products. While traditional products take the form of medicinal wines (*aristha, asava*), decoctions (*kṣyia*), medicinal oils (*tyla*), ghee preparations, and medicinal powders (*curna*), modern products are often marketed with English names and distributed in pill, capsule, syrup, and injection form. While the Āyurvedic system of medicine is based on a careful contextual assessment of one's person, not just one's illness, Āyurvedic medicines are increasingly being sold on the open market as a commodity fix for a wide range of health problems with instructions that mimic those of biomedical products.

MARK NICHTER

SEE ALSO

Food and Foodways; Hot/Cold

MELĀ

The word *melā* denotes a meeting, an assembly, mixing, concord, associating with, or gathering together. Melā, in the popular sense, thus refers to a large gathering or a congregation of people usually assembled at religious fairs and festival. A number of melās are held during auspicious periods at pilgrimage centers and temples throughout North India. During such astrologically determined periods, the power of sacred places is greatly enhanced, attracting hundreds or thousands or pilgrims, religious groups, and religious mendicants. While mendicants (*sādhus*) engage pilgrims in religious discourses, pilgrimage priests (*paṇḍas*) conduct special rituals for pilgrims. Most important are *pitṛtarpaṇa* (feeding the ancestors) *snāna,* (ritual bathing) and *darśana* (seeing the divine). One of the most famous melās is the *Kumbha melā,* which is held every twelve years under the sign of Aquarius at such places as

Allhabad and Haridwar. The religious nature of melās is complemented by both economic exchange and entertainment. Thus, for example, the well-known melā at the pilgrimage center of Puṣkar in Rajasthan is held during the month of Kārttika (October-November) and includes a huge camel, oxen, and horse fair, as well as staging of folk theater, camel-racing tournaments, Ferris wheels, and magic shows.

Reference

Bhardwaj, S. M. 1973. *Places of pilgrimage in India.* Berkeley: University of California Press.

ADITYA MALIK

SEE ALSO

Ancestor Worship; Fairs and Festivals; Pilgrimage; Sacred Places; *'Urs;* Worship

METAL AND METALWORKING

The use of metal in the subcontinent has a very long history and from the very earliest times, the color of different metals, and presumably their symbolic value, may have played a more significant role in their use than utilitarian functions usually associated with metals. The oldest use of metallic ores is found during the Palaeolithic period, dating more than 10,000 years ago, where oxidized iron in the form of red and yellow ochre or black hematite was used for cave paintings. Natural stones with laminations of ochre forming triangular patterns were used in what is thought to have been a shrine at the site of Baghor, Madhya Pradesh, India at around 11,000 years ago. Early terra-cotta female figurines dating to around 4000 B.C.E. reveal the use of red ochre (iron ore) to decorate the central part of the hair, and in later times vermilion (mercuric sulfide) was used to make a red dot in the middle of the forehead and the central part of hair as a sacred symbol of purity and power. Even today, Hindu women continue to use the *tika,* or dot on the forehead, to symbolize ritual purity or as cosmetic decoration.

The earliest metal object is a copper bead on a burial necklace from the pre-ceramic levels at the site of Mehrgarh, Pakistan, dating to around 6500 B.C.E. Probably made from native copper, a reddish metal, this bead appears to have been used as an ornament or amulet. Among the earliest gold objects are tiny beads from the site of Jalilpur, Pakistan, dating to before 3500 B.C.E. Many other early uses of metal have been documented, and, in all cases, metals were first used as decorative or symbolic objects. Even in later times, when the functional properties of various metals were fully understood and exploited, the color and symbolic properties of metals continued to play an important role in the production of ornaments, images, tools and utensils. South Asia is one of the only regions of the world where pure gold and silver foil is used extensively for the decoration of food or as a component of medical preparations and is consumed by people from all walks of life. Copper was first used to make functional tools such as pins and blades beginning in the 5th to 4th millennium B.C.E. at the site of Mehrgarh. The beginnings of copper alloys, comprising tin bronze and arsenical bronze, are not well dated, but both types of alloys are reported from numerous sites of the Indus Valley Civilization beginning around 2600 B.C.E.

Historically, the important metals used in the subcontinent include gold, silver, copper, tin, iron, lead, mercury, zinc, and nickel. After the discovery of aluminum and platinum, these metals have also become important in the production of both ornamental and functional objects. Alloys comprised of two or more metals have also play a significant role in the symbolic and utilitarian technologies of the subcontinent, and, in many cases, South Asia has been at the forefront, producing new alloys, such as crucible steel (Damascus steel or *wootz*), which were later replicated in other regions of the world.

The social status of metalworkers in the subcontinent has undergone significant modifications and subdivisions during the past two thousand years. In the early texts, such as the *Ṛg Veda* and later *Rāmāyaṇa* and *Mahābhārata,* smiths occupied a position of importance and were grouped with the third *varna,* the Vaiśya. During the later Mauryan period (3rd century B.C.E.) and Gupta period (3rd century C.E.) many of the occupational Vaiśya communities were regarded as mixed castes and grouped with the fourth varna of Ṣudras. However, metalworkers continued to be ranked higher and remained in this status until the eleventh and twelfth centuries C.E., after which they became relegated to a lower status of Vaiśya, which was basically equal to Ṣudras. In modern times, metalworkers in different parts of the subcontinent hold varying status, depending on their ethnic affiliations and the specific activities they engage in. For example, tribal ironworkers, such as Agaria and Asur, are ranked lower than Lohar from Bihar, while goldsmiths, such as the Sonar of the Punjab, take the sacred thread of Vaiśya castes and are considered semi-clean by the highest Brahman caste.

Gold

Gold is the most highly valued metal of the subcontinent, and the earliest evidence for gold ornaments is found during the Chalcolithic period of the Indus Valley region, fifth to fourth millennium B.C.E. All of the early gold ornaments that have been tested are comprised of gold with silver, and, in some cases, copper alloy that must have been intentionally added. Several hoards of gold jewelry, probably hidden by rich merchants or elites, have been found in the Indus cities of Mohenjo-daro and Harappa, as well as in smaller settlements such as Kunal, Lothal, and Allahdino. During the Indus Civilization, elaborate gold ornaments were not buried with the dead, but were kept in circulation, an indication that gold's economic value was well established. This perception of gold continued in the Early Historic Period. In the Arthashastra (3rd century B.C.E.) a kingdom was considered prosperous if it had sufficient gold reserves from which it could purchase grain or support armies when needed. Written sources attest to the early use of gold punch-marked coins, but the oldest preserved gold coins date to the Mauryan period around 300 B.C.E. and continued to be used up through the Mughal period.

The legendary sources for gold in the northern subcontinent were of great interest to early Greek and Roman writers, resulting in stories of ants the size of small dogs that mined the gold into anthills from which it could be collected. These animals were, in fact, marmots that dug burrows into the underlying sandy gold-bearing layers and are still to be seen in the high mountain valleys of Baltistan. Even today, the Soniwal tribe (literally, gold people) wash gold dust from the Indus and other rivers in Northern Pakistan and India. Even though there are major sources of alluvial gold along the Indus and many of the peninsular rivers of the Deccan, throughout history, large quantities of gold have been imported into the subcontinent from central Asia, Southeast Asia, Africa, and other adjacent regions. At present, with the high consumption of gold by the burgeoning middle class, large quantities of the ore are imported—or more often smuggled—into Pakistan and India. The high consumption of gold in South Asia is due to its pervasive use in all aspects of life. Thin sheets of gold leaf are pounded out, using leather booklets and a heavy metal or stone mallet. Gold leaf is used to decorate sweets, festival foods, and betel nut, and it is commonly used in medicinal preparations. Gold powder is sprinkled over the hair or on the face as a form of decoration. Fine threads of gold are woven into cotton or silk cloth, and gold-wound yarns are used for elaborate embroideries. Gold is used for decorating all manner of utilitarian and ritual objects from swords to the images of deities, and small amounts of gold are alloyed with other base metals to increase their ritual purity. Gold is considered to be a pure substance that cannot be polluted, and in Hindu rituals it is usually associated with the sun god Surya or the god of fire Agni.

The most widespread use of gold is seen in ornaments worn by men, women, and children and even as decoration on animals and vehicles. Because of gold's economic importance, gold ornaments function as a form of wealth and status. Women are given gold ornaments as a part of their dowry, and these ornaments are passed on from generation to generation, often being remelted to create new styles of ornaments. People who cannot afford pure gold or solid gold commonly use gold alloys or gilded ornaments, and even the poorest classes wear ornaments made of colored lac or plastic that imitate this highly valued metal.

Silver

Silver metallurgy can be traced to the Indus Valley Civilization, around 2600 B.C.E., where the metal was used to make seals, beaded necklaces and pendants, utensils, and containers that were identical to ceramic pots and jars. At present, silver is less valuable than gold, but in the prehistoric period it may have been more valuable, due to the rarity of native silver deposits and the difficulties in separating silver from ores that also contained other minerals such as lead. Today, silver is widely used in the manufacture of jewlery, utensils, and furniture, and silver foil is widely used for the decoration of foods and condiments. All classes of people use silver, but it is more commonly used as an ornament among lower economic classes, who store their wealth in the form of heavy anklets, belts, buttons, and necklaces. Due to the fact that silver tarnishes and turns black with oxidation, it is not usually made into threads and woven into cloth.

Silver coinage has been used since around 400 B.C.E., with the invention of punch-marked coins that were made in rectangular-to-circular shapes and stamped with symbolic designs. The low percentage of lead in some silver coins indicates that cupellation, a process of purification, was carried out with great perfection during the early historic period and that the use of copper alloying was also practiced to economize the use of silver and to create a stronger and more wear-resistant metal. As with gold coins, silver was used until quite recently for coinage and even today, ritual amulets and commemorative coins or pendants are made of pure silver.

Copper

Copper was one of the earliest metals used in the subcontinent to produce a wide range of objects, including ornaments and ritual objects, utensils, tools, and weapons. Occupational specialists who make objects from pure copper (Hindi, *tamba* or *tama*) are generally distinguished from artisans who make objects from copper alloys such as bronze (Hindi, *kansi*) or brass (Hindi, *pital*). Copper-working areas are common at many of the earliest sites of the Indus Valley civilization, and copper workers are attested to in the early literary sources. Hindus generally consider copper to be a pure metal, and it is used extensively for the preparation of ritual containers and utensils for use in household shrines and temples. Copper vessels and utensils are also used in domestic contexts where ritual purity is maintained. Throughout the historical period, permanent legal documents and land grants were often inscribed on rectangular copper plates that were buried or stored in temples. Even today, pure copper is used for a wide array of ornamental and ritual objects that are produced using much more difficult techniques of manufacture than is necessary for other copper alloys. Due to the fact that pure copper is very difficult to cast, most objects are produced through a labor-intensive process of heating and hammering, followed by chiseling, chasing, or lathing.

Pure copper objects that are used in temples or domestic contexts include water vessels, spoons or ladles, plates, cups, and glasses. Copper is used to make tridents, snakes, and other ritual paraphernalia, such as small sheets of pure copper decorated with stamped designs or sacred words. Many medicinal treatments require the wearing of pure copper against the skin, and it is not uncommon to see people wearing copper rings, bangles, amulets, and earrings alongside gold or silver jewelry. Because of the toxic accumulations that result from chemical reactions produced by acidic foods, pure copper cooking vessels are always coated with a protective coating of tin or nickel.

Copper Alloys

During the prehistoric period, copper was alloyed with tin or arsenic. Arsenical bronze is harder and more brittle than tin bronze, but it also may have had a distinctive color because many ornaments and nonutilitarian objects were made with arsenical bronze during the Harappan period (2600–1900 B.C.E.). Arsenical coppers are no longer produced, due in part to the dangers in smelting and the common availability of iron and steel.

At present, the major alloys produced in the subcontinent include bronze (copper and tin), brass (copper and zinc), and a variety of alloys made by combinations of more than two metals. The amount of alloy determines the taste, brittleness, color, and sound of the metal. Usually, bells and gongs are made from tin bronze with a small amount of lead to improve the flow for casting. Ritual images and complex ornamental fixtures are often made with similar compositions of copper, tin, and lead. In some cases, tiny amounts of gold and silver are added to create a five-metal alloy. Iron is also sometimes added to such complex alloys, primarily for its symbolic or ritual properties and not for any known structural benefit.

Brass is quite common throughout the subcontinent, and because it is easy to cast, many complex images and ornamental pieces are made with this alloy. In domestic contexts, brass is used to make plates, cups, bowls, glasses, and serving utensils. Although brass is ritually less pure than copper, it is still used to make a wide range of ritual objects.

Unlike goldsmiths and silversmiths who can be found in large cities as well as in small villages, copper workers generally live in segregated villages or urban neighborhoods. Historically, copper-working centers were located near major sources of the metal or along major trade routes. A similar distribution pattern is seen for bronze-working and large scale brass-production centers. Copper, bronze, and brass objects that were produced in these widely dispersed workshops were traded throughout the subcontinent by middlemen or sold at annual fairs.

Due to the fact that metal can be easily recycled and old metal objects are available throughout the countryside, many communities of itinerant metalworkers move along annual circuits to scavenge broken vessels and utensils. Votive figurines, toys, utensils, and containers of various shapes and sizes are produced for personal use and also for a wide array of consumer groups. The object to be cast is usually formed with beeswax or resin around a clay core and then covered with a clay mold. Casting is achieved by melting the wax and pouring molten metal into the hollow spaces enclosed by the mold. Generally, the metal is melted in closed crucibles that are attached to the mold. The metal is a mixture of copper, brass, and bronze in differing proportions. More recently, with the increasing availability of recycled aluminum, this nontraditional metal is commonly mixed with the copper alloys or cast by itself. Because of their mobility and the fact that they scavenge metal and rework it, the social status of these itinerant communities is generally lower than the permanently settled artisans who work only with pure metals or standardized alloys. The distinctive styles of cast utensils and figurines produced by these communities are often referred to as a folk craft and set apart from the classical metal casting.

Iron

Iron has a long history in the subcontinent, and, though its introduction is often attributed to external sources, current research suggests that the earliest iron objects result from indigenous technological developments during the Painted Gray Ware period around 1200 to 800 B.C.E. in the northern subcontinent. In these early sites, the oldest iron objects appear to be ornaments such as bangles and pins. Even today, the most basic form of ornament, an iron bangle or ring, is used to indicate the marriage status of a woman or man. Eventually, utilitarian tools and weapons, such as axes, arrowheads, and blades were produced, and the *Mahābhārata* epic, which is thought to correspond to the Painted Gray Ware period, has numerous references to iron tools, weapons, and armor.

The economic importance of iron production may have had a significant impact on the location of major cities in the Ganga-Jamuna region during the Early Historic period, 600 to 300 B.C.E. In fact, some of the most powerful early city-states—Mathura, Ujjain, and Rajgriha—are strategically situated near the major iron-producing regions of north India. The manufacture of iron is much more labor intensive than copper metallurgy, and it requires more fuel for smelting and transforming the iron bloom into a workable piece of metal. In the long term, however, iron came to be much more economical to produce because of a large labor force, boundless forests, and rich iron depostits. After the initial use of iron in ornamental objects, this common metal rapidly replaced bronze tools and weapons because of its hardness and versatility. Iron can be forged, melted, joined, and cast into tools and weapons that are much lighter and stronger than copper or bronze. When wrought iron is repeatedly worked in charcoal fires, the build-up of carbon-rich layers results in carburization, a process that is attested to in metal objects dating to around 600 B.C.E.

Massive production of iron begins as early as 200 C.E. and is represented by the famous iron pillar of Delhi. This pillar weighs approximately six tons and was made by forge-welding wrought-iron blooms that each weighed approximately thirty-five kilograms. Because of unknown processes of manufacture, this iron pillar does not rust and has been the focus of numerous technological studies. Some scholars believe that the use of stone hammers resulted in a fine silica coating that effectively seals the iron surfaces and protects them from oxidation. Iron tools made with stone hammers by Agaria and Asur metalworkers of Central India are also reported to be rustproof. The pillar is 7.2 meters long and has a diameter between 30 and 40 centimeters. A popular practice among tourists is to stand with one's back to the pillar and reach backwards to try and touch ones hands around the pillar. One belief, common among teenage tourists, is that if you can accomplish this feat you will be married within the year.

Traditional iron-working communities include settled ironsmiths, or *lohar,* who live in villages or towns throughout the subcontinent, and tribal iron smelters, who live in isolated hamlets and remote villages in Central India. The settled lohar generally process only commercial iron and steel. Most of these smiths are men, but some women are involved in smithing, especially among the more mobile or itinerant iron workers. Among the Gadulia Lohar, a semi-nomadic community in Western India, the men and children are involved in collecting old scrap iron while the women do much of the actual smithing.

In contrast to the lohar castes, two major tribal communities of Madhya Pradesh, the Agaria and the Asur, are closely associated with ironsmelting and, in the past, were involved with ironsmithing as well. Tools and weapons made by the Asur and the Agaria were less prone to rust than those made by the lohar or village ironworkers. While this factor may be attributed to the use of stone hammers or anvils in the past, the Agaria and Asur are also thought to have magical powers that are used to secure good iron while smelting. In the past, both men and women were involved in the processing and smelting of iron ore, but due to changing economic conditions and exposure to outside communities, this traditional lifestyle has disappeared.

Steel

Steel is a form of iron that has varying percentages of carbon interlayered with the iron to create a hard but resilient material. Carburization of iron to produce steel is relatively easy to achieve when using carbon-rich charcoal during the forging process, but the artisans of ancient India were able to produce a form of high carbon steel that was created in a crucible without any forging. Crucible steel is thought to have originated in the subcontinent and represents one of the most difficult and most advanced techniques of metalworking. The earliest evidence for crucible steel in the subcontinent is around 200 B.C.E., but recent studies suggest that it may be even earlier. Specialized ceramic crucibles that could hold molten metal were created, using locally available clays and charred rice husks. A mixture of wrought iron and steel was sealed inside of these crucibles, along with other secret ingredients, and heated in high temperature furnaces for several days. The resulting ingots of high-carbon steel were hammered out to make a variety of weapons, tools, and armor. This type of steel was being produced extensively in the subcontinent and was traded to the Near East, Africa, and Central Asia. One of the important markets for Indian steel was in Damascus, where it was reworked into swords and armor that was then sold further to the west. European merchants and crusaders came to refer to this steel as "Damascus steel," when, in fact, it was Indian steel.

References

Bhardwaj, H. C. 1979. *Aspects of ancient Indian technology.* Delhi: Motilal Banarsidas.

Dani, A. H. 1991. *History of northern areas of Pakistan*. Islamabad: National Institute of Historical and Cultural Research.
Das, M. P. N. 1960. *Coins of India through the ages*. Madras: Government Museum, Madras.
Elwin, V. 1942. *The Agaria*. Oxford: Oxford University Press.
Figiel, L. S. 1991. *On Damascus steel*. Atlantis, Fla.: Atlantis Arts Press.
Jarrige, J.-F., and R. H. Meadow 1980. The antecedents of civilization in the Indus valley. *Scientific American* 243(2): 122–133.
Kenoyer, J. M., and H. M.-L. Miller 1997. Metal technologies of the Indus valley tradition in Pakistan and Western India. The emergence and development of metallurgy Ed. V. C. Pigott. Philadelphia: University Museum.
Lahiri, N. 1995. Indian metal and metal-related artefacts as cultural signifiers: an ethnographic perspective. *World Archaeology* 27(1): 100–115.
Leuva, K. K. 1963. *The Asur: a study of primitive iron-smelters*. New Delhi: Bharatiya Adimjati Sevak Sangh.
Lowe, T. L. 1989. Refractories in high-carbon iron processing: a preliminary study of the Deccani wootz-making crucibles. *Ceramics and civilization IV: Cross-craft and cross-cultural interactions in ceramics* Ed. P. E. McGovern and M. D. Notis. Westerville, Ohio: The American Ceramic Society, Inc., 237–251.
Mughal, M. R. 1974. New evidence of the early Harappan culture from Jalilpur, *Pakistan. Archaeology* 27: 106–113.
Mukherjee, M. 1985. *Metalcraftsmen of India*. Calcutta: Anthropological Survey of India.
Pal, M. K. 1978. *Crafts and craftsmen in traditional India*. New Delhi: Kanak Publications.

JONATHAN MARK KENOYER

SEE ALSO
Crafts; Image-making, Metal; Metalwork, Bangladesh

METALWORK, BANGLADESH

In Bangladesh, metalwork is a folk craft since it is essentially done by the use of hand-operated tools. Metelwork products embody creativity, individual expression, and aesthetic values of a high order. The demonstration of human skill is exceedingly varied both in form and design. From the standpoint of use, the metalwork of Bangladesh falls into three broad types: utilitarian, decorative, and functional/decorative.

The metals commonly used in metalwork in Bangladesh are *tāmā* (copper), *kā̃nsā* (bell-metal, a bronze alloy), *pital* (brass), and *lōhā* (iron). Because of its bright color and the polish that it takes, kā̃nsā is in much demand for ornamental purposes. *Sonā* (gold), because of its cost, is prohibitive for the metalworker and is restricted to the jeweler. *Rupā* (silver), the most beautiful and adaptable for all hand processes, is also costly, but not prohibitive for the skilled metalworker who uses it in filigree work.

Three traditional methods of making metal objects are: (1) *pitāi kāj,* beating; (2) *ḍhālāi kāj,* casting; and (3) *cādar kāj,* brazing. The first two methods seem to have been known and practiced in Bengal from early times. Pitāi kāj is the forging of metal or the controlled shaping of metal by the force of hammering; ḍhālāi kāj is the act of shaping an object by pouring molten metal into a previously formed mold; and cādar kāj is the shaping of available ready-made sheet metal. The beating method is generally the technique followed by blacksmiths, bell-metalsmiths and brass-smiths, and that is why this method is also known as smithing: In smithing, the object is shaped by hammer blows rather than mechanical means.

There are three kinds of casting: open-mould, *cire-perdue* (French: "lost wax"), and sand casting. In open-mould casting, clay is used as a mould, and the mould is useable for only one casting. Open-mould casting is practiced at Dhamrai in Dhaka District. The *cire-perdue* process is widely prevalent in Bangladesh, especially in Dhaka City. Sand casting is the best known and most frequently used casting process in the Indian subcontinent, since it is the method best suited for high quality mass production. In Bangladesh most of the brass articles are sand-cast. Brazing differs from smithing in that forging is not employed at all, though the brazier may shape objects by hammer blows. Since the brazier works with prefabricated metal sheets, what he basically needs is a solid, hollowed-out surface on which to beat his vessels into shape. Blacksmithing is universally practiced in Bangladesh with no characteristic regional variations. Almost every village, town, or city has at least one *kāmārśālā* (smithy). Blacksmiths beat iron into various agricultural implements, household utensils, and tools used by different craftspeople, and they also repair damaged ones.

Utilitarian metalwork in bell-metal and brass has flourished over the centuries in rural centers, since the people who have traditionally used metal household objects live mostly in villages. However, these centers are located in close proximity to towns, so that products can be easily transported beyond the local market. All the important sites of decorative and functional/decorative metalwork are located in urban centers, especially in Dhaka and Chittagong, because of the concentration of prospective customers in cities.

In the British period (1757–1947) the artistic excellence of metalwork in East Bengal (the area now constituting Bangladesh) was demonstrated in gold and silver filigree, in silverplate, in architectural ironwork, and, occasionally, in brass sculptures of deities. Since 1947, there has been a major shift from the previous order and style of metalwork. This shift has taken place in two successive phases: the Pakistan period (1947–1971) and the Bangladesh period (1971 onwards).

By 1951 about 700,000 Muslims had migrated from India to East Pakistan (now Bangladesh) after the partition of British India in 1947. There were skilled metalworkers among them, the best ones being from Moradabad in northern Uttar Pradesh, one of the greatest centers of decorative metalwork in the Indian subcontinent. Muslim metalworkers from India brought with them the techniques of decorative metalwork in copper and brass. Most of the highly skilled Hindu goldsmiths and silversmiths left for India in the late 1950s. As a result, after the partition of British India in 1947, the artistic excellence of metalwork began to shift in the area now constituting Bangladesh from gold, silver, and iron to copper and brass. The Pakistan period witnessed the production of a wide variety of copper and brass wares in the major cities of East Pakistan, especially in Dhaka and Chittagong where the non-Bengali metalworkers mostly settled. Their products included wall-plates, trays, jugs, mortars, *aptābā* (water ewers), *surahi* (tall-necked water containers), *pāndān* (boxes made to contain the spices, betels, nuts, and tools associated with betel chewing), *ātardān* (perfume flasks), *chāidān* (ashtrays), *dhupdān* (incense-burners), *kalamdān* (pen-boxes), *kālidān* (inkwells), *surmādān* (kohl bottles), *ogoldān* (containers for rinsing), *pikdān* (spittoons), *momdāni* (candlesticks), *phuldāni* (flower-vases), *golābpāś* (rose-water sprinklers), *cilumci* (basins), *bālti* (buckets), *sarata* (nutcrackers), tiffin-carriers (Anglo-Indian lunch boxes), caskets, wallets, lamp stands, polycandelons, lanterns, table tops, door knockers, and door panels.

Utilitarian metalwork has been affected by industrialization, especially since the period after 1971 when Bangladesh became an independent country. Tedious and labor-intensive methods of beating or casting metal into the required shapes of household utensils and other humble items of utility, while still widespread, are being displaced by machinery in factory conditions of mass-production. Consequently, rural demand for handmade objects of bell-metal and brass, though still substantial, is being replaced by a market in machine-produced fancy and cheaper substitutes in aluminum, stainless steel, porcelain, plastic, and glass. But the trend is just the opposite with decorative and functional and decorative metalwork, which continues to thrive in urban centers with human ingenuity and creativity. While urban demand for utilitarian metalwork has almost been exhausted, urban demand for decorative and functional/decorative metalwork has developed partly from the compulsions of fashion, but mostly from varied needs. With industrialization and urbanization a larger and more wealthy middle class has progressively emerged. Middle-class patrons of decorative and functional/decorative metalwork long for decorative items to demonstrate their taste but need them to work in urban, modern settings.

Today decorative and functional/decorative metalwork is booming in and around Dhaka City. The Bengali metalworkers, rather than those from Uttar Pradesh, are in the forefront of the new movement of metalwork in Bangladesh. Sirajul Islam and Mohammad Manik Sarkar are chasing big bell-metal plates (*thālā*), brass water vessels (*kalsi*), and other bell-metal and brass domestic utensils familiar to Bengali people. The *kalsī* now represents a dominant symbol of Bengali culture. Siraj, who is considered to be a great engraver by his peers, was the first to choose bell-metal vessels for intricate decoration in Bangladesh. "It is very difficult to engrave a pattern on a bell-metal surface, but once the pattern is engraved, it looks superb," he said. Unlike their non-Bengali masters, Siraj and Manik are chasing human figures, animals, and medallions featuring Hindu gods and goddesses. They are also applying the *padma* (lotus) and various Bengali floral patterns in greater profusion as decorative motifs. The flowers are now more naturalistic and elaborate. Even though human figures and animals have come into use for decoration, purely nonfigural representation, with the geometric order explicit in the overall design, and the practice of engraving wall-plates with verses from the Qur'ān also continue, as in the Pakistan period.

Wall plates and planters are generally of larger size than in the Pakistan period, and are elaborately and delicately chased. Designs are sometimes produced on the surface by incision and then inlaid with colored lacquer. The method of decorating large planters is different. Such objects are filled with a hot mix of linseed oil, brickdust, and resin to provide stability to the thin sheet metal and then hammered from the front in an embossing technique that gives the appearance of repoussé (as if hammered from the inside).

Nakshiwala Babul, another outstanding Bengali metalworker, has abundantly shown that even utilitarian objects can be designed in a surprising variety of pleasing shapes to fulfil the purposes for which they are intended. He has produced a wide variety of brass candlesticks (*momdāni*) and betel nut boxes (*pāndān*), brass flower vases (*phuldāni*) with floral and linear designs against colorful backgrounds, and wall plates with scenes of rural houses, boats, coconut trees, and the palanquin or the bullock cart in which the Bengali bride is seated. In all, Bengali metalworkers have succeeded in integrating their products into Bengali culture.

While rural metalworkers, with the exception of some hired workers, are craftspeople by hereditary profession, most urban metalworkers are craftspeople by independent choice. Rural metalworkers still maintain traditional forms and designs. Not restrained by tradition, urban metalworkers are constantly endeavoring to shape or design their products in the direction of market-driven innovation.

References

Birdwood, G. C. M. 1980. *The industrial arts of India.* London: Chapman and Hall.

Glassie, Henry H. 1997. *Art and life in Bangladesh.* Bloomington: Indiana University Press.

Ghose, Benoy. 1981. *Traditional arts and crafts of west Bengal.* Calcutta: Papyrus.

Gupta, G. N. 1908. *A survey of the industries and resources of eastern Bengal and Assam for 1907–1908.* Shillong: The Eastern Bengal and Assam Secretariat Printing Office.

Mukherjee, Meera. 1978. *Metalcraftsmen of India.* Memoir No. 44. Calcutta: Anthropological Survey of India, Government of India.

Pal, M. K. 1978. *Crafts and craftsmen in traditional India.* New Delhi: Kanak Publications.

Reeves, Ruth. 1962. *Cire perdue casting in India.* Crafts Museum Series, ed. Ajit Mookerjee. New Delhi: Crafts Museum.

Untracht, Oppi. 1968. *Metal techniques for craftsmen: a basic manual for craftsmen on the methods of forming and decorating metals.* New York: Doubleday.

Firoz Mahmud

SEE ALSO
Metal and Metalworking

MITHILA PAINTING

Mithila art is a women's tradition, the product of women of the Brāhmaṇ and Kāyasṭa communities of the North Bihar region known as Mithila; the participation of other castes and genders came later with the commercialization of the art in the 1960s. The art is also sometimes known as Madhubani art after the district capital town nearest the handful of villages (Jitwārpur, Rāntī, and Rasīdpur) that most successfully entered the international folk art market. However, since the art originated in women's rituals common throughout the larger region, it is more appropriately called Mithila art.

Mithila women like to say that when Lord Rām came to Mithila to pull the bow of Śīva and win the princess Sītā, the town was beautifully painted, evidence of the antiquity of the art. These descriptions in the *Rāmćaritmāṇas* of Tūlsidās, written in 1633, may testify to practices three to four centuries ago. What is certain is that in the 1930s when W. G. Archer, then a government official, was touring the region after a devastating earthquake, he discovered the lovely art on humble mud homes broken open by the force of the quake; he published his photographs in several articles in the art magazine *Marg*. Many observers felt that this art had the potential of providing income for women of this deeply impoverished region if transferred to paper. In 1966 the Handloom and Handicraft Export Corporation (HHEC) and the All India Handicrafts Board (AIHB) began distributing paper and paints and providing the infrastructure to market the art internationally. Within a few years, Mithila art was widely known throughout the world, a great deal of income flowed into a few villages, and a handful of women artists achieved international fame.

Mithila art began, however, as a ritual art painted on the interior walls of the family compound. The compound, consisting of four small houses arranged in a rectangle around the courtyard, with a covered platform in the center, was the family temple as well as the home of Brahmans and Kayasthas. The western house invariably housed the family shrine and the cooking hearth; the southern house (*kōhbarā ghar*) was the site of the meeting of bride and groom and consummation of their marriage. These two houses, plus the walls of the inner courtyard, were a kind of sacred gallery for glorious paintings of goddesses, gods, and various designs, often quite abstract, largely drawn from nature.

Mithila art was imbedded in a social environment in which objects and images had specific powers and functions, and interacting with them changed something: one's body, one's future, other people's responses. As women, the domains in which they could act were limited by *purdah,* but tremendous powers resided in the household with them. Whether as a daughter worshipping Gauri to bring a husband like Śīva, or as a wife worshipping *kula devī,* the lineage goddess, and incarnating her to bring offspring to her husband's family, there were powers which women controlled. Mithila art was a powerful visual discourse of Brahman and Kayastha women; it was reflexive, about themselves, their powers as women, and their mystical connection with the goddesses, Bhagavatī, Gaurī and Kula Devī, who sometimes stood distinct from, and sometimes shared identity with living women.

The most puzzling and powerful of the ritual signs was found in the kōhbarā ghar; this is the *kōhbar* or *puren* that dominates the walls. There is a Brahman and a Kayastha version. We might think of these as visual tropes that can be interpreted. There is an invariant combination of elements: always, a bride and groom; Gaurī on the elephant; parrots, snakes, sun, moon and bamboo; and—at center stage, dominating all—a vast growth of lotus coming up from a pond. Sometimes the lotus leaves have feminine faces. In the Kayastha version there is a stem or shoot emerging, with a face on it.

This cluster of visual symbols is polyvocalic. The associations with nature are obvious enough. Mithila is dotted with ponds clogged with vegetation and other forms of life that function as natural symbols for women of Mithila. When asked why they paint puren or kōhbar on their wedding chambers, they say, "Because, just as a seed dropped in a pond produces many lotus, so should the bride and groom produce many offspring." It is a metaphor from nature; not seed and field, the more classic Indian metaphor for fertility, but seed and pond. So, women paint their own fertility in extravagant fecundity on their walls, perhaps to transfer these powers to the *kanyā,* the virgin bride.

Puren appears again in childbirth, not as art, but as nature in the actual organ, the placenta. The word for placenta, *narpuren,* means "lotus leaf of the navel." The infant emerges from the pond-like womb attached to a long cord, much like the long cords that connect lotus leaves to the bottom of the pond. At the end of this cord is the narpuren, wet and shrunken with the baby extruded.

There are many, many associations of ponds with feminine powers and fertility in Mithila culture. Those ponds are also associated with divine feminine powers. In almost every village there is a temple or shrine to a local goddess that is discovered at the digging of the local pond; Bhagavatī manifested herself in the form of an irregular stone. This is her most powerful manifestation, because she comes unbidden, not in humanly made images. In every lineage the living wives, all themselves called *Devi* (goddess)—Sita Devi, Ganga Devi, Baua Devi—incarnate her to provide the next generation of the lineage.

Another of the kōhbara ghar images is *bāns,* bamboo. There is a tremendous variety of abstract portrayals of bamboo. Stands of bamboo dot the region, each clump arising from a single root. These bamboo are a visual metaphor for the patrilineage and the patrilineal extended family, also arisen from a single root. The word for the maximal lineage, *mūl,* means "root." Bans also is one of the ranked grades of Brahmans, which means "good family." And *bansāvalī* means "genealogy." So a verbal pun, *bans* and *bāns,* appears on the walls as a visual pun, the patrilineal family shown as a stand of bamboo.

Another mysterious feminine power is present: *nainā yogīni,* who must be painted on all four walls of the nuptial chamber. Her name means "eye goddess"; her role is to protect from evil, but she herself is a little dangerous. The women say she is there to give the bride magical control over her husband; they seem to mean both keeping his romantic interests focused on her and giving her influence over his actions. Commodification of Mithila art began in the late 1960s when, for the first time, a portion of women's work was disengaged from its embeddedness in the patriarchal structure and its needs. The impact of this disengagement was generally different from the one most commonly celebrated, as for instance, "With availability of paper, the women painters of the area for the first time experienced freedom from the constraints of making of ritual-bound, static, magical images in the fixed medium of wall-painting. They could now paint whatever they liked, on any scale" (Jain 1997, 9). Rather, the power of the ritual art, when it came off the walls, died on the paper. These papers were not ritual spaces, and no sacred work was done in their precincts. Commodified and on paper, the art could not be about ensuring a bride's fertility, nor about forging identities with the goddesses, not about protection from evil. The paper art became a commodity in the international folk art market. The scale of paintings was more fixed than ever, not by a whole wall, but by the 22 inches by 30 inches that were the standard dimensions of the paper. The artist had to scale down her work to these unrelenting rectangles. They were sold to *Mleccas* (foreigners), whose tastes, moreover, now had to be deciphered and accommodated. What, then, to put on these blank white spaces? The nudging of market forces and the good will of those bent on helping the women find a market directed the development of a handful of professional painters in creating personal styles that found favor in the folk art market.

Women searching for themes turned themselves into objects that could become art. They were asked to portray their lives, express a unique viewpoint. Mithila painters began to paint scenes from their lives. The vast majority of these works depicted moments from the cultural system established for women: *mohuak,* eating the first meal with the new husband; worship of Gaurī at the wedding; *otāngar,* the ceremonial pounding of rice by eight Brahman men; *saptapadi,* the seven steps around the sacred flame; the bride being carried to the groom's house. But these were not efforts at unique visions, and they were very far from self-expression as that term is commonly meant. The development of "projected individualism" has been slow. Very few went as far as Ganga Devi toward autobiographical painting; she portrayed scenes from her own terminal illness with breast cancer before her death in 1991 and earlier painted her impressions of life in New York City. Nevertheless, women began to reflect on and externalize their lives in art.

In addition to objectifying women's lives, at least one village, Jitwarpur, has become a kind of permanently staged "Mithila village." It has been the site of at least three films and many photo shoots for a variety of books. Residents turn their village into a movie set with extravagant paintings on every wall and lane.

Finally, inevitably, the commodification of Mithila art has produced a few celebrities. India is proud of these women and has bestowed honors on them. They include Sita Devi of Jitwarpur, Ganga Devi, and Baua Devi.

References

Brown, Carolyn Henning. 1996. "Contested meanings: Tantra and the poetics of Mithila art." *American Ethnologist* 23(4): 717–737.

Jain, Jyotindra. 1997. *Ganga Devi; tradition and expression in Mithila painting.* Grantha Corporation.

Vequaud, Yves. 1977. *The women painters of Mithila: ceremonial paintings from an ancient kingdom.* London: Thames and Hudson.

CAROLYN BROWN HEINZ

SEE ALSO

Folk Art; Gender and Folklore; Goddesses, Hindu

MOSQUES

A mosque (from the Arabic word *masjid,* meaning "place of prostration") serves as a house of worship for Muslims. The conceptions underlying mosque design are simple, as they are related to its primary function. For a space to serve as a mosque it should be sufficiently sheltered from the elements, capable of accommodating a community of worshipers, and egalitarian in nature, allowing each member of the community to pray as an equal under God. While Muslims pray individually on most days, on Fridays and festival days men pray communally in the mosque.

A set of standard features aids prayer within the mosque. Many mosques contain a fountain or other water source for the ritual washing which precedes prayer. Inside the mosque, the *qibla* wall orients the act of prayer towards the black stone of the *Kaaba* in Mecca. The qibla is marked by the presence of one or more *miḥrāb,* or niche articulations, set into the wall. Among the most ornamented features of the mosque, the miḥrāb is often framed by decorative patterns and inscriptions selected from the Qur'ān. In many mosques used for communal prayer on Fridays, a *minbar,* or stepped pulpit, stands just to the right of the main *miḥrāb* and is often equally ornate.

Relation to Classical Prototypes

The very first mosque was the Prophet Muhammad's house in Medina, a modest mud brick structure with a courtyard surrounded by a colonnade of palm trees. As Islam spread in the centuries following Muhammad's death, the form of the mosque, based roughly on the prototype of the Prophet's house, developed into a number of standard regional types. For instance, the oldest mosques built in the central Islamic lands were configured to form what is generally termed the "Arab" or "hypostyle" plan, a square or rectangular courtyard surrounded on three sides by colonnades or arcades, and by a larger covered area for prayer on its qibla side. The stylistic varieties which developed throughout the expanse of the Islamic world testify to the mosque's flexibility, for the absence of specific symbolic or liturgical requirements left the mosque readily adaptable to diverse geographic and cultural environments.

In South Asia, the presence of distinct regional architectural styles played a significant role in dictating the appearance of mosques. The mosque, as it was developing in the broader Islamic world, was successfully fused with local trends in religious, imperial, and vernacular architecture. Likewise in South Asia, through such processes, the standard repertoire of mosque ornamentation—calligraphy, vegetal and floral motifs, arabesques, and geometric patterns—took on distinctly local flavors at the hands of local craftsmen. For more than a millennium, South Asian mosques have been informed by the architecture of Islamic lands further west; yet, even when a foreign model figured in the conception of a mosque, the mosque was ultimately expressed through local decorative idioms in local materials.

A landmark structure, the gateway added to the Quwwat al-Islam Mosque in Delhi by 'Alā ud-Din Khalji (r. 1296–1316), the third ruler of Delhi's Khalji dynasty, represents this adaptive process most vividly. For his gateway, known as the 'Alā'i Darwāza, 'Alā ud-Din sought inspiration from the architecture of his Turkic Afghan forebearers, most notably by importing the technology to construct "true" voussoired arches, one of the features most characteristic of Islamic architecture. However, like the Muslim patrons in India who ruled previously, 'Alā ud-Din enlisted Hindu stone masons to construct and decorate his monuments using locally quarried materials, and effectively translated the brick and tile architecture of his homeland into finely carved red sandstone and white marble. Repeatedly in South Asia, the interaction between local craft and imported technologies resulted in the creation of dynamic, hybrid styles. In later centuries, the South Asian mosque was infused with new forms as well as new ideological paradigms; these included visual expressions of imperial power and colonial rule, and—most recently—modernity.

Varieties of the South Asian Mosque

Excavations at Muslim sites in South Asia, such as Banbhore in Sindh, reveal simple hypostyle mosques dating from as early as the eighth century. In keeping with a long-standing practice of recycling building materials, many of the oldest mosques in South Asia were configured from stones previously used in other struc-

Wood and stone mosque near Gulmith, Hunza, Pakistan, © M. Mills

tures. In the earliest stages of the Muslim conquest, materials appropriated from pre-existing sites were sometimes conspicuously displayed as trophies of Islamic victory; however, the incidence of these cases has been exaggerated in the rhetoric of early Persian mythical histories, one of which describes the Ghaznavid Sultan Mahmud (d. 1030) laying down the idol of the Somnath Temple at the threshold of the Mosque of Ghazni. The archaeological record, on the other hand, reveals that reuse in South Asian mosque architecture was most often driven by pragmatism rather than intolerance.

A fully realized mosque architecture began to be formulated only in the final years of the twelfth century, as the Ghurid rulers of the Delhi Sultanate enlisted the skills of local stone masons in their new constructions. At that time, the mosque was a fundamentally new building type in South Asia. Indigenous religious structures, the principal type of which was the temple, served to shelter idols and were frequently covered in figurative sculptures, practices anathema to the ideals of Islam. In addition, the temple was not designed for congregational worship, and therefore could not fulfill the mosque's most basic requirement. Nonetheless, over the course of six centuries the two architectural systems were synthesized, allowing local materials and craftsmanship to fit the needs to Muslim worshipers.

The history of Islamic architecture in South Asia is most often centered around the dynasties which ruled the Indian subcontinent previous to British rule, a period traditionally divided into three phases: the Delhi Sultanates (1206–1526), the Regional Sultanates (1336–1686) which seceded from Delhi's centralized rule to form independent provinces, and the Mughal dynasty (1526–1785). Due in part to the selective survival of imperially-sponsored monuments, our knowledge of mosque architecture is disproportionately based upon grand-scale and luxurious structures. The archaeological record reveals that mosques were patronized on many sub-imperial levels in the pre-modern period; some employed fine craftsmanship and materials, while others were built from recycled or semi-permanent materials in a make-shift manner.

Many types of rural, village, and neighborhood mosques are built today throughout South Asia. For the most part, they are constructed on a small scale in vernacular styles, employing materials available locally, ranging from mud brick and bamboo to corrugated steel and concrete. The use of vernacular forms was not limited to small-scale or rural projects, however. Repeatedly, in the past eight centuries, the imperial mosque has borrowed the language of vernacular and domestic architecture. The most dramatic example developed under the independent sultans of Bengal (1336–1576), where the conditions in the low-lying delta area (which historically included the modern state of Bangladesh) largely determined the forms of vernacular architecture. Mosques adopted locally available materials—red clay bricks formed from the alluvial silts—as well as local architectural forms which had evolved in response to Bengal's extreme climatic conditions. A unique style resulted, bearing the distinctly curved form of the region's bamboo and thatched-roof hut—translated into brick and stone, and monumentalized to serve a community of worshipers.

In the last three centuries, the mosque has been infused with European concepts and increasingly modern forms and materials. In the eighteenth and nineteenth centuries, mosques such as those built under the Nawabs of Oudh (1732–1856) shared motifs with the revival styles popular in European architecture at the same time. More recently, since the progressive dissolution of the Western colonial empires, the new nation states of South Asia have increasingly engaged in mosque building projects at all levels of patronage and on several scales. As in the past, many of these projects represent attempts by governments and private patrons to express their state's sovereignty and national identity. The state-sponsored Shah Faisal Mosque in Islamabad (1978–1986) combines a massive tent of concrete with a predominant symbol of the traditional mosque, tall pencil-thin minarets. Its particular combination of forms defines Pakistan as both modern and Islamic, representing once again an act of architectural innovation through adaptation. The construction of modern—and now post-modern—mosques continues the legacy of architectural synthesis which has characterized South Asian mosques for nearly a millenium.

Anna Sloan

Mosques in villages, provincial centers, and wayfarers' roadside rest stops can take a variety of forms, from a simple floor of swept clay, surrounded by a peripheral marking of stones, or a simple platform of poured concrete for the use of travelers along a roadside, up to elaborated buildings using local materials and crafts, and decorative styles. Modest local mosques in Balochistan are of mud brick with stubby elevations at the two ends of the front façade; some are accented with tile decorations, or more modestly, recycled automobile headlights set into the mud-brick façade. Mosques in mountain Afghanistan and Pakistan, like shrines, may be decorated with the horns of wild goats (ibex, markhor), recalling the ancient pre-Islamic beliefs involving those animals, which were regarded as pure beings.

Not all prayer spaces are covered, and not all roofed mosque buildings were intended to accommodate congregational prayer. The chip-carved wooden mosques of Pakistan's Swat District, Baltistan and Northern Areas have received some attention from local and European material culture scholars. In the Hunza River valley in northern Pakistan, the oldest surviving wooden mosques are small buildings, not adequate themselves to hold more than a few people at prayer, but may be built adjoining a dedicated outdoor space for congregational prayer. These flat- or lantern-roofed wood-framed mosques characteristically do not have minarets, though the more elaborate ones may have a "tower" or skylight structure, wood-framed and often hexagonal, over the central aperture of the lantern-roof. A loudspeaker mounted on the roof may now amplify the call to prayer.

The lantern roof, itself the trademark feature of Karakorum regional vernacular architecture dating from pre-Islamic times, rests quadrilaterals of hewn wood beams in progressively smaller dimensions one on top of another, rotating 45 degrees in each course, and diminishing to a small aperture at the center of the roof. The beams themselves may be decorated with paint or flour designs. This "lantern" roof beam structure is supported by an open square of wooden pillars, themselves anchored in another open square of soleplate beams at the floor level. This structure is reputed to be relatively earthquake-resistant in this highly earthquake-prone zone, because of the wooden members' ability to "work" and slide over one another when shaken. Unfortunately, the wooden mosques of northern Pakistan, among the most elaborated expression of this local architectural aesthetic, are being replaced as they age in many areas by poured concrete structures with simple painted wooden trim, while the old wooden buildings' carved components are aggressively bought up by dealers in folk art objects for export sale.

Mosques in smaller communities and neighborhoods are built and maintained by charitable individuals and/or donated labor of groups in the congregation. The prayer leaders attached to them may be local volunteers or *mullā*s hired by the community for the job, paid by annual donations of a share of each family's harvest or other income. Besides their primary purpose as dedicated focal points for congregational prayer, mosques have served a variety of other social functions. They are gathering places for the male members of the community. (Women tend to pray the daily prayers at home, and attend shrines for personal devotion and attendant socializing. In larger mosques, a separate space may be designated for women's congregational prayer.) For men, reading aloud or recitation of Sufi or other religious literature may supplement the prayer service, and community members may gather to discuss and decide local affairs. Mosques also serve, together with shrines and the guest houses of village notables, as formal sites of sanctuary for those seeking asylum when pursued by enemies. Thirdly, mosques serve the general purpose of safe lodging for religious travelers, or for travelers in general in villages where no other guesthouse is available.

While shrines are more likely to figure in folk narrative than mosques, there are remarkable scenes in some stories, enacted against the backdrop of the idea of the mosque as sanctuary and ritually pure space. In an Afghan variant of the Silence Wager folktale, recorded by this author in Herat in the 1970's, a married woman pursues a thief who has robbed her house and traveled with the goods to another town where he is staying in the mosque. She pretends to be an available woman and lures him on (sexual activity would itself be an offense to the mosque space), giving him a false name, *Bibi Kojāberīnom* (Lady Where-Shall-I-Pee), which she says he should use to summon her. When he calls to her surreptitiously in the middle of the night, the other travelers who overhear him assume he is asking where he should urinate in the mosque, another desecratory act, and they beat him and throw him out. In the morning, she gathers up her family's stolen property and triumphantly goes home to her feckless husband.

References

Asher, Catherine. 1992. *The architecture of Mughal India*. Cambridge: Cambridge University Press.

Dani, A. H. 1989. *History of northern areas of Pakistan*. Islamabad: National Institute of Historical and Cultural Research.

Fischer, Klaus. 1978. *Dächer, Decken und Gewolbe Indischer Kultstätten und Nutzbauten*. Wiesbaden: Franz Steiner.

Frishman, Martin and Hasan-Uddin Khan (eds.) 1994. *The mosque: History, architectural development, and regional diversity*. London: Thames and Hudson.

Glassie, Henry, 1997. *Art and life in Bangladesh*. Bloomington and Indianapolis: Indiana University Press.

Khan, F. A. n.d. *Banbhore*. Karachi.

Marzolph, Ulrich. 1984. *Typologie des Persischen Volksmärchens*. Beirut and Wiesbaden: Franz Steiner.

Michell, George (ed.) 1984. *The Islamic heritage of Bengal*. Paris: Unesco, 1984.

Welch, Anthony and Howard Crane. 1983. The Tughluqs: Master builders of the Delhi sultanate. *Muqarnas* 1: 123–166.

MARGARET A. MILLS

SEE ALSO

Architecture, Bengal; Islam; Muslim folklore

MUHĀJIR

Muhājir, sometimes translated in English as "refugee," "emigrant," or "exile," is an important concept in Islamic discourse. *Muhājir* in the Qur'ān, Islam's sacred text, refers to those righteous followers of the Prophet Muḥammad who were persecuted by the people of Mecca and who then emigrated (made *hijra* [a spiritual journey]) to Medina where they formed part of the fledgling Muslim state. After a difficult struggle against the Meccans, considered *jihād* (spiritual struggle), the Muslims eventually returned in triumph. In its Islamic context, muhājir implies spiritual movement in addition to physical migration; one leaves home or one's previous level of existence for God's sake.

Using Muḥammad's and his followers' migration to Medina as a paradigm for exemplary behavior has meant that for Muslims in different locations, leaving one's homeland in the face of persecution becomes a sacred and obligatory act. When a government perceived as illegitimate and non-Islamic comes to control a region, that area becomes *dar al harb* (the land of war). If they cannot practice their religion, to change that government, good Muslims must undertake jihād, struggle peacefully, and use violence if necessary. In such situations, taking the family to a place of refuge, becoming muhājir, is an intrinsic part of the struggle. Because of Muḥammad's example, there is hope for an eventual triumphant return.

In the late 1940s, at the time of the partition of colonial India into the independent states of India and Pakistan, muhājir refugees from India crossed the border to settle in the newly created *dar al Islam,* the place of peace and refuge: Pakistan. Over the decades since that time, these muhājir groups have argued that they are subject to discrimination and have set up their own political parties beside others organized along ethnic or ideological lines. In addition, the war against the Marxist government in Afghanistan (1978–1987) together with the 1979 Soviet invasion of that country resulted in Afghans from many different ethnic groups arriving as muhājirīn in Pakistan.

References

Edwards, David. 1990. Frontiers, boundaries and frames: the marginal identity of Afghan refugees. In *Pakistan: the social sciences' perspective,* ed. Akbar S. Ahmed, 61–99. Karachi: Oxford University Press.

Masud, Muhammad Khalid. 1990. The obligation to migrate: the doctrine of Hijra in Islamic law. In *Muslim travellers: pilgrimage, migration, and the religious imagination,* eds. Dale F. Eickelman and James Piscatori, 29–49. Berkeley: University of California Press.

Shalinsky, Audrey C. 1994. *Long years of exile: central Asian refugees in Afghanistan and Pakistan*. Lanham, Md.: University Press of America.

Thomas, Raju G. C., ed. 1992. *Perspectives on Kashmir: the roots of conflict in south Asia.* Boulder: Westview Press.

AUDREY C. SHALINSKY

SEE ALSO
Islam; Refugee Lore

MUḤARRAM

Muḥarram is the name of the first month of the Islamic lunar calendar. The term is also used to refer to the ritual commemorations for the martyr Ḥusayn ibn ʻAlī, grandson of the Prophet, who was brutally killed in battle on the tenth day (*ʻāshūrā'*) of this month in the year 680 C.E. While ʻāshūrā' was already a sacred day of fasting for Hebrews (Leviticus 16.29) prior to the birth of Islam, the month of Muḥarram took on a new significance after Ḥusayn's death. The month developed a special cosmological and historical significance for the Shīʻī community, who hold that the spiritual lineage and political office of the Prophet should have passed down through his familial line.

The earliest record of a commemoration for Ḥusayn during the month of Muḥarram is from the tenth century. Ibn al-Athir wrote that, during the Persian Buwayhid Dynasty, mourners with blackened faces circumambulated Baghdad while beating their chests. At that time the event was a public procession. After 1500 C.E. Shah Ismaʻīl I declared Shīʻī Islam as the state religion of Persia and staged performances gradually took shape to complement the public processionals.

The staged performances grew out of processional observances occurring during the first ten days of Muḥarram. Reactualizations of the historical events culminating in Ḥusayn's martyrdom first took place at locations where large numbers of people could gather. Ritual battles took place at crossroads in front of an audience, while tableaux of dismembered martyrs slowly moved past the viewers on wheeled platforms. During the sixteenth century a private tradition of martyr narration also began to flourish. The stories of the suffering martyrs were adapted from Vāʻiz Kāshifī's text, *Rawḍat al-Shuhadā'* (The Garden of Martyrs), a Persian literary work. The text was retold by professional poets for private patrons, hence the name *rawẓah khwānī* (garden recitations). These two traditions—public performance and private recitation—existed separately for nearly 250 years, but fused in the mid-eighteenth century. The important element in the observance was participation. An audience member could not just observe passively, but was expected to show emotion by weeping and to experience the suffering of Ḥusayn, in order to identify completely with the martyr. Many aspects of these original Muḥarram observances continue to be practiced in South Asia after being modified to suit local contexts.

Although death rituals for Ḥusayn are observed throughout the subcontinent, the manner of observance differs from place to place. This is due to a number of factors, ranging from centuries of interaction between Hindus and Muslims to differences in urban versus rural practices. Moreover, ideological differences between the Sunnī and Shīʻa throughout South Asia have led to a continual need for the modification of performance practices associated with the rite. Nevertheless, many practices in Pakistan, India, and Bangladesh today bear close resemblance to the Iranian practices. Rituals still center on public processions and private recitations of narrative. For the Shīʻa of South Asia, Muḥarram is still a sober event, even though it incorporates some practices—such as flagellation—often perceived to be inappropriate behavior by their Sunnī counterparts. However, the bulk of South Asian Shīʻī practices associated with Muḥarram conform to the Persian theological paradigm of identification with Ḥusayn. It should also be noted that the Sunnī observe the anniversary in many parts of South Asia as well, but understand it more as a quiet commemoration of an unfortunate incident, rather than as a soteriological necessity. Such differing interpretations often end up in communal violence between the Sunni and Shīʻa.

Identification is achieved through public processionals involving the display and burial of *taʻziya*s (model mausolea) and *majālis* (private gatherings) designed for the recitation of *marṣiya*s (dirges performed for ritual mourning). The development of marṣiya composition in South Asian vernaculars innovates upon the rawẓah khwānī tradition of Iran. Such a dialectic between the public and private observances is not condoned by some orthodox clerics, since some of the public aspects of the event are not to be found in scriptural or exegetical references. Nonetheless, the interface between public and private continues to function on the level of popular practice. The anthropologist Keith Hjortshoj notes that religiously learned men in Lucknow consider the public processional rituals, firewalking, and states of possession, which seem so prevalent on the streets of India during Muḥarram, to be virtually meaningless without the majālis. This may well be, from the clerical point of view, but the great amount of activity found on the streets also contributes to the mourning and leads to identification with Ḥusayn from the public practitioner's point of view.

During the ten days of observance, a participant will attend different majālis to hear recitations of marṣiyas concerning the historic events of each day. There will be intense weeping and breast beating (*mātam*). After a majlis one can engage in public processions, followed by attendance at yet another mourning session, all in one day. These mourning sessions are generally segregated, with women either attending their own sessions or set apart spatially from the men. Thus, the individual experiences the suffering of the martyr through both types of observances, without any incongruity. The "drama" of Ḥusayn's passion is reactualized through a variety of intersecting pious acts performed by the community of believers.

The annual drama of Ḥusayn's passion culminates on *'āshūrā,'* when the public and private observances converge. On this day neighborhood processions move the *ta'ziyas* towards predesignated graveyards, symbolizing the plains of Karbalā, the place in southern Iraq where Ḥusayn was killed and where his actual tomb was constructed. These structures are then buried during the noonday hour, the legendary time of Ḥusayn's last breath. In some parts of South Asia, and elsewhere in the world where East Indians have settled, the ta'ziyas are immersed in rivers, oceans, or sanctified tanks of water, following the Hindu custom of deity immersion (visarjan).

The communal rituals around the death of Ḥusayn during Muḥarram are the focus of what some scholars now call the "Karbalā paradigm." It is a force as vital and potent today as it was during the first few centuries after the original incident, for the Shi'a understand Ḥusayn's death as an event without parallel in human history, and the annual reactualization of his suffering is the central Shī'ī ritual observance of the year. Indeed, every aspect of a pious Shī'ī Muslim's religious life revolves around the remembrance of the event and is ordered by it. Through Shī'ī ritual observances reactualizing this event, individuals experience the suffering of Ḥusayn and also participate in a communal phenomenon that not only lends to a localized ethnic identity, but to a broader religious one that ideologically unites all practicing Shī'a throughout the world.

References

Chelkowski, Peter J. 1979. Ta'ziyeh: indigenous avant-garde theatre of Iran. In Ta'ziyeh: *ritual and drama in Iran*. ed. Peter J. Chelkowski, pp. 1–11. New York: New York University Press.

Cole, Juan. 1988. *Roots of north Indian Shi'ism in Iran and Iraq: religion and state in Avadh, 1722–1859*. Berkeley: University of California Press.

Fruzzetti, Lina M. 1981. Muslim rituals: the household rites vs. the public festivals in rural India. In *Ritual and religion among Muslims in India,* ed. Imtiaz Ahmad, pp. 91–112. New Delhi: Manohar Publications.

Hjortshoj, Keith G. 1977. Kerbala in context: a study of Muharram in Lucknow, India. Ph.D. diss., Cornell University.

Korom, Frank J. 2002. *Hosay Trinidad: Muḥarram performances in an Indo-Caribbean diaspora.* Philadelphia: University of Pennsylvania Press.

Naim, C. M. 1983. The art of the Urdu Marsiya. In *Islamic society and culture: essays in honor of Aziz Ahmad,* eds. Milton Israel and N. K. Wagle, pp. 101–116. New Delhi: Manohar Publications.

Pinault, David. 1992. *The Shiites: Ritual and popular piety in a Muslim community*. New York: St. Martin's Press.

Qureshi, Regula Burckhardt. 1981. Islamic music in an Indian environment: The Shi'a majlis. *Ethnomusicology* 25: 41–71.

Schubel, Vernon James. 1993. *Religious performance in contemporary Islam: Shi'i devotional rituals in South Asia.* Columbia, S.C.: University of South Carolina Press.

FRANK J. KOROM

SEE ALSO

Imām Ḥusayn; Jārī Gān; *Marṣiya; Majlis; Mātam; Ta'ziya*

MU'JIZĀT KAHĀNĪ

Mu'jizāt kahānī (miracle stories) are used in rituals performed by Muslim women in South Asia. Because these stories are connected with figures associated with Shī'ī piety—one of the Imāms, or important women in Shī'ī piety like Zainab and Fāṭima—they are particularly popular among Shī'ī women. They are, however, read by Sunnī women as well. Mu'jizāt kahānī are written in simple Urdu and are readily available in inexpensive paperbound editions. These stories are similar to Persian *sufra* stories, also used in rituals, and also to *vrat kathā* (stories told or read by Hindu women in connection with vows and fasts).

The recitation of a kahānī is usually linked to the making of a *mannat* (vow) in which one seeks the intercession of a spiritual figure—such as the Prophet Muḥammad's daughter Fāṭima—and makes the intention *(niyyat)* to arrange a reading of a particular kahānī once that request is granted. People make mannat for a variety of reasons; for example to find lost objects, to derail an unwanted arranged marriage, or to find work for one's unemployed husband.

Following the fulfillment of the mannat wish, one arranges for a reading of the story before a group of women. An air of ritual propriety and sanctity is observed because the reading of the story evokes the presence of the spiritual person at the center of the story. Following the recitation of the story blessed sweets are distributed to the guests.

Perhaps the most famous and popular kahānī is *Bībī Fāṭima kī Kahānī* (The Kahānī of Lady Fāṭima). Like other miracle stories, it consists of a frame story and interlocking miracle stories. The frame story concerns the wife of a goldsmith whose son falls into a kiln and dies. She falls unconscious from grief and encounters a veiled woman who tells her that her son has been restored through the intercession of Fāṭima and that she must return and hear the story of Bībī Fāṭima and distribute sweets. She awakes to find her son alive, but discovers that no one in her village will take the time to read the story. Distraught, she wanders into the wilderness where she again encounters the veiled woman, who recites the story. This story concerns a Jew who invites Fāṭima to his daughter's wedding, hoping that she and her father, Muḥammad, will be ridiculed for her obvious poverty. At first she hesitates, but when she decides to go, she is given a miraculous gown and retinue from Paradise that is so beautiful that all of the wedding guests are struck dead with awe upon her arrival. Fāṭima, however, intercedes with God so that they are resurrected, and the Jewish bride and all of her guests accept Islam. After reading this story the woman vanishes, and the wife of the goldsmith returns to her village to find the houses of the people who refused her burned to the ground.

This story emphasizes the importance of allegiance to and respect for the family of the Prophet, and the danger of ignoring it. Like other kahānī, it focuses on the concerns of women and has strong female characters. Thus the kahānī provide an important opportunity for the expression of Muslim female piety.

Reference

Schubel, Vernon. 1993. *Religious performance in contemporary Islam: Shi'i devotional rituals in contemporary Islam.* Columbia: University of South Carolina Press.

VERNON JAMES SCHUBEL

SEE ALSO
Legend; *Vrat Kathā*

MUKHOS NĀC

Mukhos nāc is a form of masked performance by Hindus and Muslims in Natore and Rajshahi districts of Bangladesh. In Natore, Hindu devotees of the goddess Kālī perform it in the two to four weeks prior to *Caitra Saṃkrānti* (vernal equinox), or more recently, in the months of Baiśākh and Jaiṣṭha (mid-April to mid-June), because, the performers say, fruits and grains are more plentiful then.

The performances are held in the evening, in the outer courtyards of Hindu homes. Performers arrive and ask permission to perform. The troupe includes three musicians (*bāyen*) playing two *ḍhāk* and one *kāṁsī*, a like number of choral singers (*dohār*) who also play a harmonium and a *khol,* plus dancers. Dhāk and kaṁsī music introduces the dancers, wearing only *dhuti* (loincloth), who arrive from outside the courtyard and perform a brisk warm-up number called *Hāṅṭu Khela*.

The dancers retire to don costumes and masks. The *Bāṛi Gananā* (literally, "reading the homestead") song and dance sequence follows, in which the troupe master calls the character of the astrologer to divine which evil spirits haunt the household. A disciple enters, singing, with the astrologer's books, and a comic interlude follows in which the disciple usurps the astrologer's signs of office (umbrella, baton, brahminical cord) and attempts to take his place. The astrologer and disciple then conduct the "reading of the homestead" to determine which episodes should be performed to exorcise particular evil spirits present. Three or four episodes are performed, with donations collected from the audience at certain points. A dance of Śiva and Kālī to bless all present concludes the performance. Finally, the master and a priest offer ritual worship to Śiva and Kālī in accordance with Tantric practice. The troupe may hold performances in two or three different homesteads within a single night.

The repertoire of episodes of one representative troupe in Natore includes dances relating to the *Rāmāyaṇa* epic, including those of Hanumān, Rāma's monkey companion and devotee; the vulture Śakuni; Rākṣasī the Ogress; and Rāvaṇa abducting Sītā: Other topics include that of Narasiṅgha, the man-lion incarnation of Viṣṇu; the Tiger and the Hunter; the Old Man and Woman; the Tooth Cleansing of the Mad Woman; Śiva and Gāurī, his wife; and finally, Śiva and Kālī. Hanumān wears a predominantly white mask, a wig, suit of jute fiber, and a tail. Śakuni wears a brown mask, black wig, a skin-tight brown-dotted suit, and a pair of wings. Rākṣasī wears a pink mask with a broad grin and large eyes, a *sārī* (worn wrapped like a *ghāgrā* long skirt) and blouse, and in both hands carries branches with leaves. Rāvaṇa wears a gray or green mask, although sometimes a mask with ten heads (one life-size and the others miniature). Narasiṅgha wears a white mask, black wig, and a skin-tight black-and-white striped suit. The Hunter wears a blue mask, carries a bow and arrow, and speaks Hindi, rather than the local common language, Bangla, while the Tiger's mask is yellow with red and blue-black spots. The Old Man, Old Woman, and Mad Woman wear pink masks. Śiva (also called Hara) wears a white mask and tiger pelt, while Gaurī's mask is yellow, and she wears a sari. *Kālī*'s mask is blue with a large, blood-red tongue protruding.

Masks in Natore district are made from calabash or margosa timber covered with cotton fabric permeated with clay and tamarind paste, polished with bamboo, and painted with synthetic enamel paint. Masks in Rajshahi are made of clay (the small ones, for example, of Sītā) or fig wood.

SYED JAMIL AHMED

SEE ALSO
Dance; Masks; Theater and Drama

MULLĀ NAṢRUDDĪN

Mullā Naṣruddīn is a prominent fictional protagonist of humorous prose narratives known throughout the whole area of Islamic cultural influence. While Mullā Naṣruddīn's fame peaked in twentieth century Turkish folklorism, the development of the narrative repertoire focusing on him goes back many centuries. The oldest layer of anecdotes dates from a stock of stories about the stereotype fool Juḥā, documented in Arabic literature since the ninth century, some of which reappear as Mullā Naṣruddīn stories. The largest body of anecdotes is formed by humorous stories about Khvāja Naṣruddīn (Hoça Nasreddin), allegedly a minor cleric (Persian *Mullā*) in thirteenth- and fourteenth-century Anatolia, documented in Ottoman Turkish literature since the sixteenth century. While early tradition relied on either manuscript or oral ways of transmission, the introduction of printing in Near and Middle Eastern countries in the nineteenth century resulted in the enlargement of the narrative repertoire as well as translations into virtually every language of the Muslim world. In late twentieth century South Asia, Mullā Naṣruddīn was most prominent in Muslim areas, mainly Afghanistan, Pakistan, and Muslim communities in India.

In South Asia, the character is traditionally given his Persian title, Mullā. He is documented in oral tradition as well as popular literature, and above all in large numbers of cheap booklets (chapbooks) in the Persian and Urdu languages. For future research, it should be kept in mind that Mullā Naṣruddīn is not indigenous to non-Islamic areas of South Asia, where other local or regional trickster characters prevail. In India, for example, these are the Emperor Akbar's wise court-fool and companion Birbal or the (occasionally wise) fool Muladeva, both of whose narrative repertoire is partly interchangeable with Mullā Naṣruddīn's. On the other hand, the Indian broadcast of a nationwide television serial in Hindi in the early 1990s, with the popular actor Raghuvir Yadav performing as Mullạm, resulted in enhancing Mullā Naṣruddīn's popularity all over South Asia.

References

Marzolph, Ulrich. 1992. Naṣr al-dīn Khōdja. *Encyclopaedia of Islam,* vol. 7, fasc. 129–130. Leiden, pp. 1018–1020.

———. 1995. Mulla Nasroddin in Persia. *Iranian Studies* 28, 3–4. 157–174.

———. 1996. Nasreddin Hodscha. *666 wahre Geschichten.* Munich: Beck.

ULRICH MARZOLPH

SEE ALSO

Chapbooks; Character Stereotypes; Muslim Folklore and Folklife

MUNAZIRA

Munaziras are Sindhi disputations in verse composed in the form of fictional dialogues between two parties competing in excellence. Each party disputes the arguments of the other, asserting its own superiority. The compositions are also called *jherras*, or quarrels. However, the parties do not quarrel because of any animosity; they fondly engage in controversy, each arguing its superiority over the other.

A munazira, in its scheme in presentation and technique in argumentation, resembles a short drama in verse, in which at least three characters—the two main parties in the dispute and the arbitrator—play their parts. The plot is deliberately contrived so that nonhuman characters such as birds and other animals, or inanimate objects like trees, minerals, untensils, and seasons can be personified and play roles.

The technique of dialogue basic to the munazira composition generally opens with a prologue containing praise of God, followed by the mention of the two parties and the circumstances under which the dispute has arisen between them. The parties may be abstract ideas personified (love and reason, youth and old age, knowledge and wealth), family characters (husband and wife, mother-in-law and daughter-in-law), items of clothing (cap and turban, trousers and loin-cloth), metals (iron and gold), smoking items (*bidi,* the local cigerette and hubble-bubble), animals (horse and bullock, camel and horse), beasts (jackal and lion, pig and porcupine, frog and lizard, frog and catfish), birds (parrot and crane, swan and crane), insects (dragon-fly and mosquito), trees (*kandi* and *jaar*), seasons (winter and summar), or male and female (dog and bitch, he-chameleon and she-chameleon). Lately, some modern parties have been joined in disputation, such as car and jeep.

The party that has the weaker case is usually the aggressor, and begins to speak first, asserting its superiority or recounting the weakness of the opponent. The arguments are hot and spirited, but the controversy remains verbal, seldom leading to the use of physical force. As the parties almost exhaust their arguments, a third character is introduced. He is the referee, or arbitrator, to whom the parties agree to refer their case, or to whom one party appeals to adjudicate. Often, someone passes by and offers his advice in setting the matter. Sometimes a partisan intervenes and the dispute begins between the partisan and one of the original parties. One who intervenes without any reason is usually ridiculed.

In munaziras, the folk poet has maintained a high standard of achievement in development of theme as well as style of expression. He shows remarkable talent in initiating, developing, and terminating the arguments. The setting provided, physical as well as social, is natural, and the language employed, whether standard or dialect, is effective. The speech attributed to each party is appropriate to its stature and character. The folk poet is a keen observer and a natural critic who, through his treatment of the theme, holds a mirror to mankind, depicting the trifling nature of the disputes, the aggressive behavior of a party, or the just or partial attitude of the arbitrator.

The fertile mind of the folk poet sometimes brings in odd parties to dispute, for example:

She-Frog and Camel

As the camel walking leisurely had almost trampled it to death, the she-frog was high on her heels in anger:

She-Frog: You fool! how you walk haughtily
With deaf ear, ugly nose, closed eyes!
Camel: Don't you taunt me thus, I am alert!
With clean food, fresh grass green.
While you with tummy like a tombstone,
Bald head, without hair!

(She-frog lept onto the he-lizard and complained against the haughty camel:).

She-Frog: He is calling me names!
Be thou the witness and judge!
He-Lizard: Dear me! With thy slim nose and slender stomach
A perfect bride thou art!

(With tributes paid, she turned and shouted at camel:).

She-Frog: Get thee gone!
You long neck and heedless head!
Camel: For long you took to the roadside,
flirting with every passer by,
And yet you found not a spouse
Better than the he-lizard, ah!

He-Lizard and She-Lizard

He-Lizard: Keep not distance, be nearer to me!
She-lizard: Thy wife I am, be patient with me with people around.
You would hug me now and then again.
He-lizard: I hold you dear in great affection!
I like the way you strut about
Slim and soft, smart in action!
She-lizard: Behave yourself!
I am not from the street.
I am of noble descent, with manners and means.

Reference

Baloch, N. A., ed. 1961. *Munazira*. Sindhi Folklore Project, Book X, Hyderabad, Pakistan: Sindhi Adabi Board.

N. A. BALOCH

SEE ALSO

Games and Contests; Sindh; Verbal Dueling

MUSEUMS AND FOLKLORE, BANGLADESH

In the early nineteenth century, British scholars first initiated the study of folklore in Bengal. They were interested not only in oral traditions of the natives but also in antiquities. In 1907 Rabindranath Tagore published a book under the title of *Loksāhitya,* which is a compound of *lok* and *sāhitya* meaning folk and literature respectively. Tagore used this title for his work as it contained a series of articles on folk literature. Eventually loksāhitya became the term for folklore. As Bengali scholars were involved in collecting and publishing oral traditions, they considered the term loksāhitya appropriate for the study of folklore. Because of their language-centered and literature-oriented bias they continued to retain the term loksāhitya even though it was not compatible with the term folklore. However, the English word *folklore* came into use in Bangladesh and found its way into the Bengali dictionary after the Bangla Academy had realized the limitations of the term loksāhitya in encompassing all the other genres of folklore. Some well-known folklorists were so much obsessed with the vernacular term that they tried hard to resist the adoption of the foreign word; they argued that all the genres including those of folk literature could safely be accommodated under loksāhitya. As the new generation of folklorists quickly got rid of the vernacular term without any prejudice, the older folklorists finally capitulated.

When the Dhaka Museum was formally inaugurated on 7th August 1913, H. E. Stapleton, Secretary to the Executive Committee of the Museum, observed:

> The object of our meeting to-night is to celebrate the initiation, under the auspices of his Excellency, of the Dacca Museum—a Museum which we trust will ultimately serve as a centre of the collection of antiquities from all parts of the Presidency. Mere collection however of records of the past is far from being the aim of the Committee of the Dacca Museum; and in the present paper we endeavor to illustrate the way in which historical facts tend to pass into the folk-lore of the people and how necessary it is to collect and study the folk-lore if we are to hope to interpret rightly the history of the country.

Although Nalini Kanta Bhattasali, the first curator of the Dhaka Museum, enriched the folklore of Bangladesh through his writings on Bengal history, art and, archaeology, the Museum refrained from collecting objects of folk art during his curatorship (1914–1947). In fact, in the prepartition period, appreciation of Eastern Bengal's heritage in the Dhaka Museum was almost totally confined to archaeology and natural history. It was not that the authorities of the Dhaka Museum dismissed objects directly relating to folklore as unworthy of inclusion in the collections, but that they were actually unable to acquire such objects for lack of both funds and space.

The industrial revolution in Britain, with its attendant mechanization and cheap methods of production, affected the rural arts and crafts of Bengal so fiercely that many craftsmen, especially weavers, were forced out of work. Having seen the plight of the craftsmen, Rabindranath Tagore was under the impression that the artistic traditions of handmade objects were in the process of becoming extinct. In 1915 he was the first Bengali to realize the immediate necessity for the collection of objects of folk art, and he began collecting such objects himself to set an example for others. Dinesh Chandra Sen and Gurusaday Dutt, two highly cultivated and vigorous collectors of folk art emerged. They both strongly believed that folk art, as an expression of community life, was distinguished from the academic, self-conscious and cosmopolitan expression that constituted the fine and decorative arts of the elite.

Gurusaday Dutt was born at Birasri in Sylhet, Bangladesh, on 10 May 1882. In January 1932 he organized the Rural Heritage Preservation Society of Bengal. He viewed folk art as the art of the common people for the expression of collective order and harmony. He articulated the folk art tradition of Bengal in a nationalist discourse at a time when there were serious efforts by both politicians and intellectuals to impose a synthetic Indian tradition on the rich diversity of the regional idioms in British India. The folk art exhibition that Gurusaday organized in Calcutta in March 1932, the lectures that he delivered in Calcutta and London, and the articles that he published on folk art created among educationists and art critics a lively interest in Indian art in general and in the folk art of Bengal in particular. His work eventually led to the opening of the Asutosh Museum of Indian Art in 1937 by the Calcutta University, and here special importance was given to the folk art of Bengal.

While Dinesh Chandra Sen donated his large collection to the Asutosh Museum of Indian Art, Gurusaday Dutt was the first to think in terms of a museum devoted exclusively to the arts and crafts of rural Bengal. Before his death, Dutt presented his entire collection to the Bengal Bratachari Society to establish a museum at Bratacharigram in the district of 24-Parganas. This museum became known as the Bratachari Janasiksha Pratisthan Museum (now the Gurusaday Museum of Bengal Folk Art). The collections of both Dinesh Chandra Sen and Gurusaday Dutt, now held by those two museums, include numerous objects from Bangladesh.

In the 1960s the Dhaka Museum began collecting objects of folk arts and crafts by purchase. As the financial situation improved considerably in the early 1970s, the Museum enriched the collections. Soon after the emergence of Bangladesh the Dhaka Museum Board of Trustees submitted to the Government a scheme for the National Museum of Bangladesh. Under this scheme the Department of Ethnography and Decorative Art was created in 1972. Since then the Museum has been collecting objects of ethnographic interest as well as of folk arts and crafts on a regular basis.

There has been great interest in folklore research in Bangladesh since the establishment of the Bangla Academy in Dhaka on 3 December 1955. In accordance with a proposal made by Shilpacharya Zainul Abedin, the Government of Bangladesh, in July 1975, established the Bangladesh Folk Arts and Crafts Foundation with the following principal objectives: (1) to set up a folk art museum and an artisan village at Sonargaon; (2) to undertake and manage such projects to promote folk arts and crafts; (3) to institute and maintain training centers for artisans; (4) to conduct research pertaining to folk arts and crafts; and (5) to publish both scholarly and popular works. The Foundation came under bitter criticism shortly thereafter, as its overall outlook became more commercial than creative. Critics argued that folk artists, instead of being trained, should be allowed to work in accordance with their inherited traditions and free will. They argued further that better tools and materials as well as financial support should be provided by the Foundation.

While the Bangladesh National Museum has a large collection of objects pertaining to folklore, not less than ten museums are exclusively or substantially devoted to the collection of such objects. These include the Dhaka University Sociology Department Museum and the Dhaka University Geography Department Museum (both established in the Pakistan period, that is, prior to 1971), the Folk Heritage Museum of the Bangla Academy in Dhaka (established on 24 July 1969 and formally inaugurated on 31 August 1978), the Chittagong University Museum (started on 13 June 1973), the Bangladesh Folk Art Museum at Sonargaon (established by the Bangladesh Folk Arts and Crafts Foundation on October 26, 1976 and formally inaugurated on September 25, 1981), the Museum Wing of the Tribal Cultural Institute, Rangamati (established on July 1, 1977), the Research Wing of the Upajatiya Cultural Academy at Birisiri (established in 1977), the Hasan Raja Museum at Sunamganj (established by the descendants of Dewan Hasan Raja in 1977), the Lalan Museum at Chheuria in Kushtia (established by the Lalan Academy in 1979), and the Varendra Academy Collection at Rajshahi. While all these museums are contributing significantly to the study of folklore, folklore has been recognized as a separate academic discipline at the Rajshahi University and a scheme for the establishment of an institute of folklore in Dhaka has been under active consideration by the Government.

Folklore research according to modern concepts in Bangladesh has remained slow until now, though the country is exceptionally rich in living folklore. The Bangla Academy has so far played the most important role in enhancing the analytic and technical capabilities of active folklore scholars by an international exchange of ideas. It acquired a huge corpus of recorded oral traditions, sponsored three national folklore workshops, organized fieldwork, undertook research, and published a large number of books covering all genres of folklore. *Art and Life in Bangladesh,* a work based on fieldwork conducted by Henry Glassie from 1987 to 1996 under the auspices of the Bangla Academy, has been a major breakthrough because of the author's direct contact with artisans and first-hand knowledge of their creations.

References

Glassie, Henry H. 1997. *Art and life in Bangladesh.* Bloomington and Indianapolis: Indiana University Press.

Mahmud, Firoz and Habibur Rahman. 1987. *The museums in Bangladesh.* Dhaka: Bangla Academy.

Mahmud, Firoz. 1993. *Prospects of material folk culture studies and folklife museums in Bangladesh.* Dhaka: Bangla Academy.

———. 1998. A short history of the Bangladesh National Museum, *Bangladesh Jatiya Jadughar 85th Foundation Anniversary Celebration.* Dhaka: Bangladesh National Museum.

FIROZ MAHMUD

SEE ALSO

Bangladesh; Folk Art; Nationalism and Folklore; Sen, Dinesh Chandra; Tagore, Rabindranath

MUSHĀ'IRA, URDU

Urdu, with 150 to 200 million speakers worldwide, is the national language of Pakistan and is widely spoken in northern India and in pockets of Urdu culture in South India as well. Urdu is also the defining language of the Indo-Pakistani Muslim diaspora, particularly in Great Britain and the United States, where it continues to be used in a significant number of radio and television programs, newspapers, and, in a few places, in schools.

The Urdu *mushā'ira,* public recitation of poetry, is the central sociocultural event in the Urdu-speaking world. In the West the full range of live cultural performances include the opera, ensemble concerts and solo musical recitals, ballet and other forms of dance, theater, and the occasional poetry reading. Among the majority of Urdu speakers—given the tendency in much of the Islamic world to devalue music, dance, and reality theater—cultural performance tend to focus primarily on an aural embellishment of "the word," i.e., poetry. The mushā'ira is the dominant medium for the oral presentation of poetry. In the mushā'ira, poetry can be recited either in pure declamatory recitation, or in a rendition which makes some degree of use of the musical elements of melody and rhythm.

The mushā'ira is governed by a traditional procedural *adab* (etiquette). There is a *sadr* (president) whose responsibility includes inaugurating the event, introducing the poets, echoing and repeating phrases and lines that please him (although women poets currently participate in mushā'iras, the president is invariably male), uttering exclamations of praise for the poet's best achievements, and remaining conspicuously silent when warranted. In traditional mushā'iras, the poets would sit on the floor in a large room (often in a provincial or imperial court). They would sit on either or both sides of the sadr in a partial circle on a large carpet at the front of the audience. A candle was passed from poet to poet, and each poet would recite individualy. The order usually proceeded from those of lesser stature to those most senior and revered poets. The contemporary mushā'ira, transplanted to the auditorium, places the poets on a raised stage with a microphone replacing the candle.

The style of recitation can range from *taḥt-ul-lafẓ,* the declamatory style, to *tarannum,* a kind of melodic chant often rendered with a haunting mastery of phrasing, pitch, ornament, and rhythm. Since the *ghazal* is the dominant poetic genre recited at a mushā'ira, a few words about its structure are appropriate.

The ghazal is the most popular genre of lyric poetry in both Persian and Urdu and is the quintessential expression of Indo-Muslim cultural sensibilities. The single most distinguishing feature of the ghazal is its capacity for poetic compression. Formally, the ghazal consists of a series of couplets sharing a common rhyme scheme and meter but usually not related in content. Each couplet, or *she'r,* must contain a complete thought, and in the best ghazal this thought is expressed in a manner that creates internal and external resonances, overtones, and echoes that richly enhance the elemental thought itself. In a single couplet, the ghazal poet must achieve the complete statement of an idea that would be expressed in a longer poem in other cultures. Most ghazal have at least five couplets, and a few have as many as fifteen or more.

The first line, or *miṣrā',* establishes the meter for each succeeding line, and the rhyme-scheme for the second miṣrā', as well as the second miṣrā' of each succeeding couplet. The rhyme pattern of the ghazal consists of a double rhyme, which has as its components a true rhyme, or *qāfia,* as well as a repeated rhyme, or *radif.*

The rhyme scheme of the ghazal may be represented as a^1x, a^2x; b, a^3x; c, a^4x; and so forth, with *a* and its derivatives representing the true rhyme, *x* the repeated rhyme, and *b, c,* and so on, the non-rhyming ends of the first lines of each succeeding couplet. A translation of verses from a famous Urdu ghazal by Mirza Ghalib (1797–1869) illustrates this effect:

The world is but a bauble for children's play before me	a^1x
It is a constant spectacle night and day before me	a^2x
Though the hand cannot move, there's life left in the eyes	b
Let the goblet and the flask of wine now stay before me	a^3x
He works with me, drinks with me, shares my confidence	c
The evil you would speak of Ghalib do not say before me	a^4x

The first couplet is called the *maṭla'*, and with its two rhyming lines, introduces the ghazal. The last couplet is called the *maqṭa'*, and concludes the ghazal, usually with the *takhallus̱*, or pen-name of the poet.

What is most remarkable about the contemporary mushā'ira is the involvement of the poet and the audience in an exceptionally dynamic interaction, even in a large auditorium. The audience not only manifests vocal, sometimes thunderous verbal praise, for pleasing images, conceits, and rhymes, but also—in following in each stanza the progression of the poet's thought and using the meter, rhyme scheme, and rich tradition of recurring imagery and themes—anticipate, often vocally, the poet's final choice of rhyming words.

BRIAN Q. SILVER

SEE ALSO
Ghazal; Tarannum

MUSIC

See Brass Bands; Film Music; Folk Music; Folk Music, Nepal; Popular Music; *Tarannum;* Tribal Music, Nilgiris

MUSLIM FOLKLORE AND FOLKLIFE

The last several decades of western folklore theory have taken as a grounding concept the idea that some body of shared expressive culture ("folklore") establishes and constitutes social groups ("folk," "community," etc.) Yet by no means all of the orally or informally learned, consensually shared knowledge and practices we might call "folklore" are seen by their practitioners as proprietary to a particular group. Rather, much of traditional culture has a "natural" or "given" quality, such that its practitioners may assume it to be universal until contact with other groups and their traditions casts this assumed universality in doubt. Concepts of difference and reflexive awareness of alleged or real cultural practices taken as distinctive to one group rather than another are included in what Richard Bauman has called the "social base of folklore." Interplay between a sense of universality or naturalness and a sense of communal identity or distinction is abundantly evident in the customs and expressions associated with religious affliation, as in folklore in general. Local religious views and practices, assumed to be canonical or universal, exist alongside beliefs and observations, positive and negative, about the distinctive qualities of the group or its members.

"Muslim identity" thus becomes a topic in the folklore of Muslims as well as their non-Muslim neighbors. In a predominantly Muslim population or a Muslim state such as Afghanistan or Pakistan, the differentiations (including negative stereotypes) most prominently expressed may be between different varieties of Muslims (Sunnī, Shī'a, Isma'īlī, Ẕikrī, etc.). Conversely, local practice and belief statements may invoke commonalities across religious boundaries: Jews and Muslims may claim or disclaim common spiritual heritage and practices such as dietary laws, or Muslims may share local or major pilgrimage sites with Buddhists (as at Kataragama in Sri Lanka), Jews, Hindus, etc. The repertoire of belief within and across communities accommodates both solidarity and divisiveness, even violent action. The negotiations of solidarity and difference occur in everyday conversation as well as in more elaborated performance events. A Muslim intellectual in Dhaka equated Bangladeshi Hindu and Muslim religious gatherings in a statement of solidarity: "We visit their *pūjā* (worship ceremonies) and they come to our *'īd* celebrations (religious feasts)."

Another inclusionary formulation of a kind, reported from Bangladesh, is the idea that the deities of Hinduism are in fact the 120,000 unnamed prophets said in the Qur'ān to have been sent to all peoples, but which the Hindus have subsequently mistaken for gods. A female Muslim, a popular Sūfī healer practicing in Hyderabad, Andhra Pradesh (India), commented to a daily gathering of Hindu and Muslim women (and a few men) clients, and to a western woman ethnographer who was present, "There are only two castes (*jātī*), men and women," a remark that was greeted with smiles and nods by both Hindu and Muslim clients.

In a more ambiguous inclusionary claim, a Jewish rabbi in Herat, Afghanistan, is alleged to have invited a Sunni Muslim religious teacher (*ākhund*) to share a waterpipe with him, pointing out that under Muslim law, Jewish food hospitality is fully permissible (*ḥalāl*)

to Sunnis, perhaps more so than Shī'a Muslim hospitality because the Shī'a unduly venerate other spiritual leaders subsequent to the Prophet and are therefore apostates (an allegation on which Sunnī-Shī'a hostilities have been based). Inclusionary principles of popular Islam may also be articulated as jokes. Hospitality to strangers of all kinds is a universal Muslim value, articulated in the saying, "The guest is the friend of God" (in Darī Persian, *Mihmān dūst-i khodā ya,*) to which a Muslim of modest means may add, in rhyme, *"Agar khar dāra, balā ya!"* ("But if he's got a donkey with him, it's a disaster!")—because the donkey will also have to be fed.

While considering religious themes, one must bear in mind that social identity is experienced not just in one cultural dimension, but in several at once. Ethnic and gender differences, while recognized, may be subsumed under categories of religious solidarity or difference, such that the ethnic (or gendered) "other" is accused of not being a "proper" Muslim, since ethnic/racial identity is not a legitimate category of distinction in Islamic thought (ideally and ultimately all persons are equal before God). What is perceived by outsiders as ethnic tension may be articulated (and experienced) by participants as sectarian: Shī'a Hazāra against Sunnī Pashtun in Afghanistan; mutual allegations of religious malpractice among Sunnīs such as (predominantly Pashtun) Ṭālibān ideologues vis-à-vis "liberal" Tājīk and Uzbek, all self-professed Sunnī Muslims. Some Hazāra assert that if a Hazāra converts from Shī'a to Sunnī Islam, she or he ceases to be Hazāra, but becomes Tājīk, a Persian (Darī)-speaking Sunnī.

Legends of origin of ethnic groups often centrally concern Islam: Qays, the legendary ancestor of all the Pashtuns (now comprising several major tribal divisions and two or three dialect groups), is said to have journeyed to Mecca where he received Islam directly at the hands of the Prophet, making all Pashtuns true and original Muslims equal (*sīyāl*) to the Arabs the Prophet brought to Islam. Among craftsmen, Persian-speaking Musalli threshers now in Afghanistan claim royal (*shāhī*) descent in Punjāb, prior to their displacement and migration into eastern Afghanistan, and they also say that they were converted to Islam by the Ṣūfī saint Shams-i Tabrīz, whose shrine is in Punjāb.

Libelous legends, some of global distribution, also find a place in Muslim folklore and undergird stereotypes. The so-called "Blood Libel," well known from European tradition (as in the Prioress's Tale in Chaucer's *Canterbury Tales*) asserts that Jews use the blood of kidnapped, murdered boys in religious rites. Versions of this legend were in active circulation in Afganistan in the 1970s, asserting that Jews and possibly Christians preyed on Muslim boys for ritual purposes. "What they do when the lights are turned out" summarizes a libelous legend that has been directed variously against (godless) Russians and Shī'a and Isma'īlī Muslims by other Muslims. The legend asserts that the libeled group indulges in a pseudo-religious ritual in which the lights are turned out in a room and everyone gathered there has sex promiscuously with whomever comes to hand, including parents, siblings, etc.

Certain evening ceremonies that are distinctive, respectively, to Hazāra Shī'a and Isma'īlī local practice may have been targeted by this legend. The Hazāra *shao-i 'īd-i mordā* ("Festival Eve of the Dead," an all-souls observance) is a night ceremony held on the eve of the two great Muslim annual feasts, *'īd ul-fitr* and *'īd ul-azha*. At night, candles (representing souls) are burned and a special sweet, malted-wheat-flour dish, *halwā-yi samanak,* is distributed to neighbors, mullās, and *sayyids* (descendants of the Prophet). Butter is sprinkled on the fire to comfort the souls of the dead, with a short dedicatory verse. An animal may be sacrified and cooked as part of the food distribution, and Qur'ān recitations are offered. A moving component of funeral rites as practiced by Isma'īlī Muslims in the Hindukush mountains is also an evening ceremony, including recitation of devotional poetry by famous Isma'īlī poets such as Ṇāsir-i Khosraw. It takes place in the home of the deceased, attended by male and female family and friends of all ages and illuminated by a single ceremonial oil lamp. Light symbolism connected with the idea of the soul, well developed in Muslim mystical thought, is evident in both these ceremonies.

Another slander directed against Hazāra Shī'a Muslims by their detractors alleges the practice of sexual hospitality, "wife lending" (*kuru-bastān*), in which a host is said to lend his wife to a male guest. This appears to be a distortion of the practice of *mut'a* or *sīgha,* temporary, contractual marriage, which is legal under Shī'a jurisprudence but not under Sunnī law.

A more localized, migratory legend is told as a slanderously humorous origin story about various identified saint's tombs (*zīyārat*) located in different places in Afghanistan and Pakistan. It is said that the local people were so desirous of securing the blessing (*barakat*) that goes with having a saint buried in their community that they killed a visiting Sūfī saint who had a strong reputation as a healer and built him a shrine.

A rich vein of Muslim lore is anti-clerical humor. While anti-clerical Muslims assert that mullās are more prone to greed and lust than lay people, and tell many jokes and folktales to demonstrate that, the clergy themselves may assert in their own defense that the Devil (Iblīs) puts extra temptation in their way because the corruption of a clergyman is more of an achievement than that of an ordinary citizen. One well known joke concerns a layman who tries to rescue a mullā who has fallen into a flooded stream, shouting, "Give me your hand!' with no response from the floundering mullā. A passerby says, "Don't you know he's a mullā? You have to say, '*Take my* hand' or he won't do it!" Another joke describes a layman who sees a mullā walking down the road with all four of his wives ranged out in front of him. The layman says, "Mullā, Sir, don't you know that in Islam the wives walk behind the husband?" The mullā replies, "That was Islam before land mines."

The *jihād* (religious struggle) of Afghanistan has also yielded more serious oral history and personal experience narratives that give insight on Muslim values and viewpoints. One oral history narrative exemplifies innocent piety and sincerity in the person of an elderly *mujāhid* (Islamic fighter) who was delivering a donated cow to some fighters on the front lines, as food on the hoof. When the cow was struck by a Russian shell and had to be hurriedly ritually slaughtered in order to be lawful (*ḥalāl*) food, the old man declined to eat the meat, because to him the cow was a *shahīd,* a religious martyr, killed by the enemy. Yet he also declined to tell the other fighters his reservations, lest they be deprived of rightful and needed food.

A miraculous personal experience narrative told to this author by a mujāhid in Herat, Afghanistan, concerned his own close escape when out one night distributing clandestine "night letters" (*shab-nāma,* resistance literature). He desperately dropped the incriminating papers into a dry roadside irrigation ditch at the sight of an oncoming police patrol jeep, whereupon the ditch suddenly filled with an unscheduled flood of irrigation water, washing away the evidence before the patrol arrived to search him. This experience confirmed for him, he said, that he was on the right side.

References

Anderson, Jon W. 1984. How Afghans define themselves in relation to Islam. In M. Nazif Shahrani and Robert L. Canfield, eds, *Revolutions and rebellions in Afghanistan*. Berkely, Calif: Institute of International Studies, University of California, pp. 266–287.

Ashraf Alī Thānawī, Maulānā. 1991 [1906]. Edited and translated by Barbara D. Metcalf. *Perfecting women: Maulānā ashraf 'alī thānawī's bihishti zewar*. Berkeley: University of California Press.

Altāf Ḥusain, Ḥālī Khwāja. 1986 [1874]. Majalis un-nissa. In *Voices of silence: English translation of Hālī's "Majalis un-Nissa" and "Chup ki Dad."* Edited and translated by Gail Minault, pp. 31–137. Delhi: Chanakya Publications.

Bauman, Richard. 1971. Differential identity and the social base of folklore, *Journal of American Folklore 84: 31–41.*

Edwards, David, 2002. *Before Taliban: genealogies of the Afghan jihad.* Berkeley and Los Angeles: University of California Press.

Flueckiger, Joyce. 1997. "There are only two castes, men and women," negotiating gender as a female healer in South Asian Islam. *Oral Tradition* Special Issue: *South Asian Oral Tradition* (Gloria Raheja, ed.) 12(1): 76–102.

Mills, Margaret. 1991. *Rhetorics and Politics in Afghan Traditional Storytelling.* Philadelphia, Penn.: University of Pennsylvania Press.

———. 1995. Muslim folklore and folklife. In Azim Nanji, ed., *The Muslim Almanac: a reference work on the history, faith, cultures and peoples of Islam.* Detroit, Mich.: Gale Research, pp. 371–377.

———. 2000. Seven steps ahead of the devil: A misogynist proverb in context. In Pasi Enges, ed., *Telling, remembering, interpreting, guessing: a festschrift for Prof. Anniki Kaivola-Bregenhōj on her 60th birthday.* Joensuu: Suomen Kansatietouden Tutkijain Seura, pp. 449–458.

Olesen, Asta, 1994. *Afghan craftsmen: the cultures of three itinerant communities.* London and New York: Thames and Hudson.

Poladi, Hassan, 1989. *The Hazāras.* Stockton, Calif.: Mughal Publishing Co.

MARGARET A. MILLS

SEE ALSO

'Alī; *'Aql* and *Nafs; Baiṭhak; Bhānd Paṭhar;* Circumcision; *Dev;* Divination, Balochi; Hospitality; Imām Ḥusayn; *Jihād* Poetry; *Jinn; Malang;* Maldives; Mullā Naṣruddīn; Muslim Folklore, Sri Lanka; *Parī; Qalandar;* Sacred Geography, Afghanistan; Shamanism, Islam; Shrines, Muslim; Sufi Folk Poetry; *Tabarrak;* Vehicle Painting

MUSLIM FOLKLORE, SRI LANKA

Muslims represent eight percent (1.5 million) of the total of 18.7 million Sri Lankans estimated in 1997, making them the island's third-largest minority after the Tamils. Within that broad category, one must distinguish the small number of Sri Lankan Malays (descendants of eighteenth century soldiers and princely exiles from the Dutch East Indies) as well as Bohras and Memons (Gujarati-speaking trading communities) from the predominant Tamil-speaking Muslim community known otherwise as the Sri Lankan Moors. Roughly one-third of the Moors live as paddy farmers in the Tamil-speaking eastern zone of the island in towns such as Mutur, Kattankudy, and Kalmunai, while the remaining two-thirds are dispersed in the Sinhalese majority areas in the central and western zones of the island, including major urban concentrations in Colombo and Galle. A key source for research on Sri Lanka's Muslims is Goonetileke's exhaustive *Bibliography of Ceylon (Sri Lanka),* augmented by other works after 1978, including especially Mahroof et. al., 1986 and Shukri, 1986.

Various Names and Clan Structure

From the beginning of the colonial period in the early sixteenth century, the Muslims of Sri Lanka were designated by the term "Moor" (*Mouro*, "Moroccan") which the Portuguese applied to Muslims throughout their African and Asian empire, as well as by such familiar European terms as "Mohammedan" or "Mussalman." In Tamil, the preferred term today is "Muslim"; the older term *Cáĺakar* (Sonagar, Jonagar), which originally denoted West Asians, especially Arabs or Greeks, is falling out of fashion. The Sinhalese have traditionally called them *Marakkala minissu* ("boat people") or *Hambankāriya* (possibly from the Malay *sampan*, "boat," or from Tamil *cāmān*, "goods"). In common English parlance, both "Moor" and "Muslim" are used interchangeably today to refer to indigenous Tamil-speaking orthodox (Sunni) Muslim Sri Lankans.

With the advent of Islam in the Arabian Peninsula in the first half of the seventh century, trade across the Indian Ocean was increasingly dominated from the eighth century onward by Arab Muslim merchants from ports on the Red Sea and the gulf. The medieval Hindu and Buddhist kingdoms of South India and Sri Lanka allowed these Arab merchants—many of whom acquired local wives by whom they fathered Indo-Muslim progeny—to establish port settlements in places such as Calicut, Kayalpattinam, and Colombo. As a result of this simultaneous pattern of Muslim coastal settlement, there is a good deal of shared tradition and common social structure between the Māppiḷas of northern Kerala, the Marakkāyars of the Tamil Nadu coast, and the Moors of Sri Lanka. All three groups—Māppiḷas, Marakkāyars, and Moors—follow, or at least prefer, some form of matrilocal marriage and household pattern, and many of them recognize some type of matrilineal descent, a fact that makes them distinctive, although not unique, in the typically patrilineal Muslim world. The nature of the Sri Lankan Moorish matrilineal system is best documented for the east coast Moors of the Batticaloa and Amparai Districts, where a system of exogamous ranked matriclans, matrilocal residence, and de facto pre-mortem matrilineal transmission of houses and lands to daughters through dowry is followed by the Tamil Hindus as well. Matrilocal marriage is widespread among Sri Lankan Muslims elsewhere on the island, but not formal membership in matrilineal clan groups. Additional evidence of long-term connections between the coastal Muslims of Tamilnadu and Kerala and the Moors of Sri Lanka is found in the fact that all three groups share a set of distinctive Tamil kinship terms for parents and elder siblings, which are not found among other South Indian Muslims (McGilvray 1989; 1998a).

The Sri Lankan Moors are mainstream Sunni Muslims who observe all of the five orthodox "pillars of Islam:" creed (*kalima*), prayer (*salāt*), pilgrimage (*hajj*), alms (*zakāt*), and fasting during the month of Ramadan. Like Muslims of the south Indian coast and Southeast Asia, the Sri Lankan Muslims adhere to the Shāfi'ī school of Islamic jurisprudence, which distinguishes them from the Indian Muslims of the Deccan plateau who are mostly Hanafī. Unlike Muslims in many parts of India, the Sri Lankan Moors are not internally stratified by hereditary caste-like divisions. There are, however, certain highly respected families with the title of Maulānā who are Seyyids (patrilineal descendants of the Prophet's family) who dispense blessings and embody saintly power. The only hereditary profession among the Moors is that of barber/circumciser (Ostā, from Arabo-Persian *ustād*, master), a lower status group that marries within itself.

Muslim households in Sri Lanka tend to be found in enclaved neighborhoods in the towns and in distinct Muslim villages in the countryside, interspersed between Sinhalese and Tamil settlements. A few Muslim towns, such as Beruwala and Akurana, have a reputation for affluence generated by gem trading, but the vast majority of Muslims on the island are of lesser means, earning their living from weaving and mercantile trade or, especially in the Mannar, Trincomalee, Batticaloa, and Amparai regions of northern and eastern Sri Lanka, from rice farming. Because of their great concern for female modesty, the Muslims tend to ensure that their homes provide some degree of visual seclusion for wives and daughters. By the beginning of the twenty-first century, most Sri Lankan Muslim women who formerly wore a sari and blouse had begun to wear an Islamic outer gown (*abayah*) and an embroidered head covering that frames the face (*hijāb*). Marriages are usually arranged, giving consideration when possible to the Dravidian preference for cross-cousin matches, which is found among the Tamils and the Sinhalese as well.

Foodways

Muslim cooking incorporates the widespread Sri Lankan preference for coconut milk, rather than ghee, as the basis for curry gravies and sauces. Meals are based on boiled rice as well as rice flour dishes such as *piṭṭu* (steamed rice flour mixed with grated coconut in a bamboo tube) and "stringhoppers" (Tam. *iṭiyappam*), which are steamed patties of rice-batter vermicelli. There is a popular belief that Muslim curries are hotter and spicier than those of the Tamils or Sinhalese, and the Muslim love of meat, especially beef, is believed to lend a "heating" and energizing quality to their food. In addition to *biriyani* (a sweetly spiced meat and rice dish), the Muslims have given Sri Lankan cuisine one of its most popular desserts, *vaṭṭilappam* ("*wattalappam*"), which is a cocoanut milk custard sweetened with jaggary. In some Muslim communities in the central and western parts of the island, it is customary for guests at domestic celebrations such as weddings to share food from a large circular brass tray, but elsewhere individual servings are the norm.

Rites of Passage

Sri Lankan Muslim rites of passage bear a resemblance to those of the Tamils, but the variations are fascinating. To promote fertility, both Muslims and Tamils present pregnant women with plump steamed tarts (*koḻukkaṭṭai*), each containing another smaller ("child") tart within, auguring a healthy childbirth. A pregnant woman is regarded as being "heated" until her child is born, at which time her body suddenly becomes "cool," temporarily requiring "heating" foods. The danger to the mother and child posed by lurking ghosts and demons is guarded against by carrying some object of iron on the body at all times. After the twelfth day, the most severe postpartum restrictions are lessened, but it is not until the fortieth day, when the baby's head is shaved for the second time, that the Muslims consider the birth pollution (*muĺukku*) to be entirely gone. In accordance with local Islamic practice, on or before the fortieth day, the wife of the Muslim circumciser (*Ostā māmī*) is called to the house to ritually incise (but not to surgically remove) the clitoris of baby girls.

Later, when these girls reach puberty, the traditional custom—now largely abandoned by Moorish families out of hightened Islamic concern for the modesty of women—had been to conduct a celebration of their first menstruation. Parallels with the puberty ritual for Hindu girls, which is still celebrated by Tamil families today, included seclusion of the Muslim girl and a diet of "cooling" foods. After a week of light-hearted "turmeric play" in which unsuspecting relatives were doused with the "cooling" yellow spice, a group of the girl's female cross-cousins would bathe her with scented soap and lead her, dressed in a fancy sari, into the house to glimpse auspicious ritual objects (e.g., a mound of turmeric paste and a flaming wick, or a decorated water pot). The Moors, unlike the Tamils, also administered a sip of *pāl paḻam* (mashed banana, milk, and sugar) to the girl, just as modern Moorish brides and grooms still do today. This illustrates the strong "wedding" symbolism found in both Muslim and Tamil puberty rituals.

While the minor genital operation on infant girls is conducted secretly, and the Muslim girl's puberty rite is nowadays virtually extinct, the circumcision of Muslim boys between the ages of nine and twelve continues to be celebrated publicly by Moorish families with lots of fanfare and public hospitality. Nuptial metaphors are evident in the popular name for the ceremony (*cunattu kaliyāṇam,* "circumcision wedding") and in the nickname given to the boy himself (*cunattu māppiḷḷai,* "circumcision bridegroom"). Earlier generations would have dressed the boy in a bright woman's sari and glittery mirrors, while today he might wear fashionable western trousers and movie-star dark glasses. After a procession to the mosque for prayers, the boy returns to his home where food and refreshments are offered to the guests. The operation is often performed on a cohort of several Muslim boys together, both to save money and to provide moral support among a set of chums. After reciting the *takbir,* the standard Islamic invocation before slaughtering an animal—and while women of the family loudly warble *kuravai* ululations (the high-pitched warbling sound produced by women while flapping the tongue against the roof of the mouth) from an adjacent room—the hereditary Muslim barber-circumciser (*Ostā māmā*) swiftly removes the boy's foreskin with a razor. During the week of convalescence that follows, the severed foreskin itself is carefully kept on tray of ashes under a paddy mortar, later to be safely disposed of by burial or by being cemented into a wall crevice in order to prevent it being used in hostile sorcerery (McGilvray 1994).

Weddings

Sri Lankan Muslim weddings, like those of the Tamils, take place in the house of the bride. Because Muslims everywhere on the island tend to be matrilocal, the wedding house itself later becomes the home of the married couple—as a key part of the bride's dowry. Before the wedding, a formal Islamic marriage contract is signed at a private *nikāh* ceremony at the groom's house, at which a nominal amount of *mahr,* or Islamic brideprice, is also pledged. All subsequent wedding rituals occur at the bride's house, usually around midnight, starting with the arrival of the groom's party bearing the wedding sari and the gold *tāli* necklace in a special wooden box. Compared to the Tamils, there is greater seclusion of women at a Moorish wedding; in fact, the Moorish bride never makes a public appearance before the guests. The crucial rituals of the bride's father handing a few strands of his daughter's hair to the groom, followed by the groom's tying of the wedding *tāli* (which among the Muslims is often a massive gold necklace), and the couple's sipping of a mixture of mashed bananas and milk (*pāl paḻam*), all take place privately in the bridal chamber.

Burials

Funeral customs among the Sri Lankan Muslims emphasize the Islamic injunction for a swift burial.

Same-sex relatives of the deceased conduct the bathing of the corpse, purifying it with perfume and camphor, and wrapping it in a plain white cloth, before a procession of men briskly carries it in a reusable palanquin (*cantakku*) to the mosque for final prayers and thence to the Muslim cemetery for burial on its side in the grave, facing Mecca. Post-mortuary rituals and concerns about death pollution are generally less elaborate among the Muslims than among the Tamil Hindus, although Islamic rules require a 130-day period of seclusion (*iddā*) for widows before they are permitted to remarry. A sequence of domestic post-mortuary prayer-feasts (*kattam*) are held, culminating with the fortieth day *kattam,* which often includes gifts of food to the poor.

While the souls of most ordinary Muslims pass quickly to heaven, the spirits of exceptionally holy persons, especially charismatic Sūfī teachers, are believed to remain closely associated with their buried but undecayed corpses, which are often venerated in public tomb-shrines (*dargāh*) or in a sarcophagus within mosque buildings. All across the island, these deceased Muslim saints (*auliyā*) are worshipped and given offerings for their ability to protect local places and to solve problems for devout believers. This highlights the fact that many orthodox Sri Lankan Muslims also follow Sūfī mystical teachings to some degree, and their most widespread religious devotion has been to Sūfī saints popular in south India as well. Often in association with the worship of these saints one finds groups of Sūfī initiates who share the saint's spiritual lineage (*tarīqa*) and are organized under the leadership of a *sheikh* or *kālifā*. The most ecstatic of these are the *Bāwās,* mostly members of the Rifā'i order, whose distinctive *ẕikr* (ecstatic devotional practice) is to stab themselves with iron spikes and whose initiation rituals involve a symbolic burial and rebirth.

Well-known saints include Shaykh Muhiyadeen Abdul Qādir Jīlānī (d. C.E. 1166), popularly known in Tamil as Mohideen Āṇṭavar ("Lord Mohideen"), Persian-born founder of the Qādiriyya Order whose popularity extends throughout the South Asian Muslim world. He is believed to have visited the popular cave-mosque of Daftar Jailani at Kuragala near Balangoda, Sri Lanka, while on a pilgrimage to Adam's Peak. A second devotional figure popular with Sri Lankan Moors is the sixteenth-century saint Shāhul Hamīd, sometimes referred to in Sri Lanka as Mīrān Sāhib, whose tomb-shrine on the Tamil Nadu coast at Nagoor attracts Muslim pilgrims from both south India and Sri Lanka to witness the saint's death anniversary festival (*kantūri*). Several physically empty but spiritually filled "branch office" tomb-shrines, including one at Kalmunai in eastern Sri Lanka and one in Singapore, celebrate Shāhul Hamīd's death anniversary with flag-raising and *kantūri* celebrations timed to coincide with those at Nagoor.

Recent History

In precolonial and colonial times, the Muslims of Sri Lanka actively participated in the production and enjoyment of literature written in Arabic-Tamil, a genre that phonetically represents Tamil sentences using the letters of the Arabic alphabet. Close economic ties between Sri Lankan Muslims and their Tamil-speaking trading partners on the south Indian coast permitted an active exchange of works written in this hybrid literary genre, However, in the mid-twentieth century, with memories of the bloody 1915 Sinhalese riots against Muslim shopkeepers still vividly in mind, Sri Lankan Muslim leaders came to view their Tamil linguistic heritage as a political liability in an era of Sinhalese nationalism. After independence in 1948, the Moors strategically allied themselves with the island's Sinhalese majority parties, extracting political favors for the vulnerable Muslim minority in the face of Tamil charges of cultural betrayal. When in the 1980s and 1990s the Tamil separatist guerrillas of the LTTE (Liberation Tigers of Tamil Eelam) launched attacks on government fortifications and Muslim mosques in the eastern region, and expelled Muslims from the Jaffna peninsula, many Muslims found themselves unexpectedly caught in the middle of a civil war. Despite this, in regions such as the east coast where Moors have lived for centuries alongside Tamils, there still remains hope that interethnic relations can be healed over time.

References

Goonetileke, H. A. I. 1970–1983. *A bibliography of Ceylon (Sri Lanka)*. 5 vols. Zug, Switzerland: Interdocumentation Company AG.

Ismail, Qadri. 1995. Unmooring identity: the antinomies of elite Muslim self-representation in modern Sri Lanka. In *Unmaking the nation: The politics of identity and history in modern Sri Lanka,* edited by Pradeep Jeganathan and Qadri Ismail, Colombo: Social Scientists' Association.

Mahroof, M. M. M. 1991. Mendicants and troubadors: toward a historical taxonomy of the faqirs of Sri Lanka. *Islamic Studies* 30:501–516.

———. 1994. Community of Sri Lankan Malays: notes toward a socio-historical analysis. *Journal Institute Muslim Minority Affairs* 14, nos. 1–2:143–155.

Mahroof, M. M. M., M. M. Marina Azeez, H. M. Z. Farouque Uwise, and M. J. A Rahim. 1986. *An ethnological survey of the Muslims of Sri Lanka from earliest times to Independence*. Colombo: Sir Razik Fareed Foundation.

McGilvray, Dennis B. 1988. Village Sufism in Sri Lanka: an ethnographic report. *La transmission du savoir dans le monde musulman peripherique*. Lettre d'information 8, Programme de recherches interdisciplinares sur le monde musulman peripherique. Paris: Ecole des Hautes Etudes en Sciences Sociales.

———. 1989. Households in Akkaraipattu: dowry and domestic organization among the matrilineal Tamils and Moors of Sri Lanka. In *Society from the inside-out: anthropological perspectives on the South Asian household,* edited by John N. Gray and David J. Mearns, New Delhi, Newbury Park, and London: Sage.
———. 1994. Sexual power and fertility in Sri Lanka: Batticaloa Tamils and Moors. In *Ethnography of fertility and birth.* 2nd ed. edited by Carol P. MacCormack. Prospect Heights: Waveland Press.
———. 1997. Tamils and Muslims in the shadow of war: schism or continuity? *South Asia* 20:239–253.
———. 1998a. Arabs, Moors, and Muslims: Sri Lankan Muslim ethnicity in regional perspective. *Contributions to Indian Sociology* 32, no. 2:433–483.
———. 1998b. *Symbolic heat: gender, health, and worship among the Tamils of south India and Sri Lanka*. Ahmedabad: Mapin.
Shukri, M. A. M., ed., 1986. *Muslims of Sri Lanka: avenues to antiquity*. Beruwala, Sri Lanka: Jamiah Naleemia Institute.
Uwise, M. M. 1990. *Muslim contribution to Tamil literature*. Kilakarai, Tamilnadu: Fifth International Islamic Tamil Literary Conference.

DENNIS MCGILVRAY

SEE ALSO

Gender and Folklore; Life Cycle Rituals; Muslim Folklore and Folklife; Tamil Folklore, Sri Lanka

MUṬIYĒṮṮU

Muṭiyēṯṯu is a ritual dance drama performed in the central districts of Kerala, South India, as an offering to the goddess Bhagavati, also known as Bhadrakāḷi, a local form of the pan-Hindu goddess Kāḷi. The all-night performance may only be conducted by males of the Mārār and Kuṟuppu (matrilineal temple-serving) castes during annual festivities at Hindu temples dedicated to the goddess. *Muṭiyēṯṯu* is a complex dramatic form that evokes, presents, and worships the goddess in a variety of artistic media, including rice-flour painting, song and drumming, costumed possession-performance, and ritual practice. A full-length drama in seven scenes enacts the story of the goddess's destruction of a fierce male demon, Dārika. *Muṭiyēṯṯu* is said to have healing properties and may be performed to cure outbreaks of pustulant fevers such as smallpox and chicken pox.

Muṭiyēṯṯu enacts the traditional story of the vanquishing of the demon Dārika by a violent form of the mother goddess Bhagavati. In the preliminary ritual, an elaborate colored powder image of the goddess (called *kaḷam)* is drawn, worshipped, and then wiped out by the priest, dissolving the image in a mass of colored powders, which are finally distributed to the faithful as *prasādam* (blessed food or offerings). This rite is accompanied by the performance of songs and instrumental music, leading up to the spectacle of the *Muṭiyēṯṯu* drama proper. The goddess Bhadrakāḷi (always enacted by a mature male actor of the appropriate caste) appears, sporting fearsome makeup, elaborate headdress, and colorful costume. Singers and an orchestra of percussionists tell the tale while the actors act it out. The actor playing Bhadrakāḷi is ritually empowered with the spirit of the goddess before her shrine and is possessed by her at least once during the performance itself, causing the actor to lose consciousness. Two comic scenes intervene while the actor playing Bhagavati takes a rest. The goddess then resumes her search for the demon Dārika, and a lengthy battle scene ensues. The drama culminates in the death of Dārika at daybreak by symbolic decapitation (removal of the headgear). At the conclusion of the drama, Bhagavati blesses children from the audience, waving them before the sacred oil lamp, and the *guruti* ritual is performed, representing blood sacrifice (though now, by law, done only with vegetable products).

Despite regional differences in style, Muṭiyēṯṯu always has seven characters: Śiva, Nārada, Dārika(n), Kāḷi (Bhadrakāḷi), Kōyimbaṭa Nāyar, Kūḷi, and Dānavēndran. Kūḷi and Dānavēndran vary in prominence according to the troupe style, but the other roles are fairly constant in makeup, dialogue, and characterization. The action takes place in seven scenes, starting with the sage Nārada's recital to Lord Śiva of the infractions of Dārikāsura, the demon king. The action unfolds in an unvarying pattern, showing Dārika's ferocity; Kāḷi's birth, *pūja* (worship), toilette, and search for Dārika; the entrances of the comic characters Kōyimbaṭa Nāyar and then Kūḷi; the fight between Kāḷi and Dārika, each accompanied by his respective sidekick (Kūḷi and Dānavēndran); and the final triumph of Kāḷi over Dārika.

The text of Muṭiyēṯṯu (the story of *Dārikavadham,* or the death of Dārika) is transmitted orally from uncle to nephew (nowadays, often, father to son) in matrilineal families trained to perform this art; the story is not found in full form in any of the Sanskrit *purāṇa*s (mythological texts). Training is done at home during the monsoon season and takes about ten years to complete. The majority of performances take place in the Ernakulam District of central Kerala, as well as in the bordering areas of Trichur, Idukki, and Kottayam Districts. Eight troupes currently perform Muṭiyēṯṯu, comprising three different styles and family lines. The three main styles of Muṭiyēṯṯu performance are centered in Koratty, Pazhur, and Muvattupuzha. Muṭiyēṯṯu performances always take place in the months between Dhanu (December-January) and Mēṭam (April-May), concentrating in Mīnam (March-April).

Muṭiyēṯṯu bears some resemblance to the better known *Kathakaḷi* drama, in its use of stage, curtain, orchestra, mime, and costuming. The language of Muṭiyēṯṯu includes Sanskrit, *Maṇipravāḷam* (a literary mix of Sanskrit and Malayalam), medieval Tamil, and colloquial Malayalam. The exclusively ritual context of performance, emphasis on curing and possession, rituals of blood sacrifice following the performance, and strictly oral transmission of technique and text reflect Muṭiyēṯṯu's roots in ancient south Indian folk culture.

References

Caldwell, Sarah. 1999. *Oh Terrifying Mother: sexuality, violence, and worship of the goddess Kali*. Delhi: Oxford University Press.

Choondal, Chummar. 1981. *Mudiyettu: study in folk theatre*. Trichur, Kerala: Kerala Folklore Academy. (In Malayalam.)

Venu, G. 1984. Mudiyettu: ritual dance-drama of Kerala. *Quarterly Journal of National Centre for the Performing Arts* 13(4): 5–12.

Vidyarthi, Govind. 1976. Mudiyettu: rare ritual theatre of Kerala. *Sangeet Natak* 42: 41–63.

SARAH CALDWELL

SEE ALSO
Bhagavati Ritual Traditions of Kerala; *Dārikavadham;* Floor Designs; Gods and Goddesses; *Kathakali;* Kerala; *Pūja*

MYTH

Myths are cosmogonic narratives, stories about the beginnings of things. Their characters are superhuman: gods, demons, powerful animals, divinities of all kinds. All South Asian religions have their myths. Some Muslim myths depict fantastic versions of the lives of Moḥammed and his family, while others deify local saints. Hindu myths describe gods, demons, their battles and their capacities for both destruction and creation. Christian myths, Jewish, Jain, Buddhist, Sikh, Parsi, and tribal myths, all find expression in the oral, performative, and textual traditions of their respective religions. In more recent decades the popular media have transmitted myths through comic books, radio, cinema, and television.

Hindu mythology is the largest and oldest corpus in South Asia, dating back as far as the *Ṛg Veda* (ca. 1200 B.C.E.). Major mythological texts, known as *Purāṇa*s, were composed in Sanskrit (others were composed in Tamil) between 300–1400 C.E. These compositions are generally thought to be literary renderings of oral mythologies already in circulation at the time. Myths have continued to be part of both textual and oral traditions in all South Asian languages since that time. In addition to purāṇic tales of the major gods of the Hindu pantheon, local mythologies continue to be told and created. Such myths are often unknown beyond a specific village, town, or region. Such myths may be hagiographies of local gods. They may tell the origins of temples or describe the supernatural origin of local caste groupings. Tellers of local myths often link their myths to pan-Hindu myths through yet other myths, all passed down orally in evening stories to children and visiting folklorists.

South Asian Muslim myths depict the life of Moḥammed and of the many local saints entombed throughout the subcontinent. In India, many of these myths contain intertextual references to Hindu myths, as the fluid and syncretic tendencies of folk religion and folk stories would predict. For example, Asim Roy describes how Bengali Muslim mythic texts bring Hindu gods such as Kṛṣṇa into the Islamic fold as earlier prophets, while other texts take Moḥammed's birth to be part of a specific divine plan to denounce Hinduism, and some myths pit Moḥammed in physical battles against the likes of Indra.

South Asian myths have been grist for many analytic mills. Structuralists, for example, have studied myths as expressions of unconscious mental structures that influence the form of all human institutions, including social structure, marriage, art, and religion. Many psychological approaches take myths, like dreams, to be generated from deep-seated psychological and psychosexual desires or dilemmas, dilemmas that the myths help to resolve. One kind of functionalist approach to myth focuses on myths as "charters" or models for behavior. Humans, according to this view, model their own actions and values on those of mythological characters. Myths are in this way ethical and moral texts according to which people may measure, as well as design, their own action in the world.

Myth is commonly contrasted to history. Both endeavor to relate past events, yet while the latter is said to deal in facts, the former is said to deal in fictions. Still, the pragmatic truths of myths are unquestionable. Telling myths is a kind of action in the world, and myths take their historical reality not from content but from their use in social contexts. Accordingly, some folklorists, historians, and anthropologists have focused on the pragmatic use of myths in social, political, and historical situations contemporary to their tellings and use myths to get at local discourse about social realities, such as gender relations and political relations. Mohammed battling Indra is a mythic telling of the historical struggle to convert. Many Hindu *purāṇa*s tell historians about sectarian divisions within Hinduism as the same myth is told from different points of view: A Vaiṣṇavite myth will subordinate Śiva to Viṣṇu, while the same story told from a Śaivite point of view will demonstrate Śiva's superiority. Himalayan villagers tell different versions of the basic creation myth, versions that point to gender politics. The stories men tell tend to see a male principle as the creative principle of the universe, while some of the stories women tell see the female principle capable of creation without the male. The *Rāmāyaṇa,* a South Asian epic filled with mythological material, will be told one way by women, another by Jains, another by South Indians and another by Hindu nationalists.

Myths thus tell us not only about gods, saints, and cosmogony. They also tell us something about social orders, morality and ethics, human psychology, as well as about social history and discourse.

References

Appadurai, Arjun, Frank Korom and Margaret Mills. 1991. *Gender, genre, and power in South Asian expressive traditions.* Philadelphia: University of Pennsylvania Press.

Blackburn, Stuart. 1988. *Singing of birth and death: texts in performance.* Philadelphia: University of Pennsylvania Press.

Doniger, Wendy, trans. 1975. *Hindu myths: a sourcebook translated from the Sanskrit.* New York: Penguin.

Obeyesekere, Gananath. 1984. *The cult of the Goddess Pattini.* Chicago: University of Chicago Press.

Roy, Asim. 1983. *The Islamic syncretistic tradition in Bengal.* Princeton: Princeton University Press.

Sax, William S. 1991. *Mountain goddess: gender and politics in a Himalyan pilgramage.* New York: Oxford University Press.

Zimmer, Heinrich. 1946. *Myths and symbols in Indian art and civilization.* Princeton: Princeton University Press.

DIANE MINES

SEE ALSO

Goddesses, Hindu; Gods and Goddesses; Heroes and Heroines; *Kohaṁba Kankariya*; Sacred Places; Syncretism; *Terukkūta*;

MYTHOLOGY, HINDU

"Mythology," a Greek-derived English word, does not do justice to the various genres in which Hindus tell stories about their gods, speculate upon the beginnings of the cosmos, and formulate their view of the meaning of human life. No single genre covers all of these topics. Mythology is treated in all of the sacred texts, not only in the *Ṛg Veda* (whose mythology was made famous in Europe by Max Müller in the nineteenth century) and the Epics and *Purāṇa*s, but also in lawbooks, medical texts, court poetry, and philosophical texts such as the *Upaniṣad*s. Nor do Sanskrit texts hold a patent on this body of stories; each region, each language, each village, each temple has its own tellings both of stories that appear, with infinite variations, throughout India, and of stories particular to one place. Indeed, no written texts hold the key to Hindu mythology, since the themes are told to children by women who may not know how to read, and they are perpetuated in nonverbal forms, such as paintings on house walls, statues in roadside shrines, embroidery on clothing, Hindi films, and comic books.

Certain overarching patterns may be discerned in classical Hindu mythology during several broad historical periods. In the *Ṛg Veda* (c. 1000 B.C.E.), the gods (led by Indra, king of the gods, and Agni, god of fire) were aligned through sacrifice with humans, together against the *asura*s (the enemies of the gods in heaven) and the *rākṣasa*s (the enemies of humans, more particularly of the sacrifice). The three worlds of heaven, earth, and the intermediate space or ether constitute an enclosed sphere, the Egg of Brahmā (*brahmāṇḍa*), with the sky the top half of the shell and the earth the bottom (the sun, in the middle, is the yolk). After death, according to the Veda, humans go to a fairly happy afterlife in a heavenly world ruled by Yama. In the *Brāhmaṇa*s and *Upaniṣad*s (c. 900–600 B.C.E.), another postmortem option is presented—an alternative to life in heaven: Some people can manage to escape altogether from the worlds of heaven and earth, the worlds of the gods and humans, into an indescribable state of release (*mokṣa, nirvāṇa*).

In the second period, that of the epics (the *Mahābhārata* and the *Rāmāyaṇa,* c. 300 B.C.E. to 300 C.E.), the sacrificial relationship was challenged by the possibility that demons or humans might amass individual ascetic power (*tapas*) and thus become the enemies of the gods. The demons (*asura*s) now ruled not in heaven but in the underworld, which became the third world (replacing the now redundant and insignificant "ether"). Hell now became a new alternative to life in heaven: A human at death could be reborn, as a result of his or her amassed record of good and evil actions (*karma*), in heaven or in hell, or, as in the *Upaniṣad*s, one could escape altogether. But in the third period, that of the classical *Purāṇa*s (c. 500 to 1000 C.E.), the great gods Śiva and Viṣṇu (in his various *avatār*s (incarnations), such as Kṛṣṇa and Rāma) and the Goddess in her various forms (Devī, Pārvatī, Kālī) inspired a religion of mutual loving devotion (*bhakti*) between deity and devotee. The heaven in which the gods of *bhakti* reign breaks open the world-egg to create an infinitely expansible heaven in which all devotees, even women and the lowest castes, could dwell forever.

References

O'Flaherty, Wendy Doniger. 1975. *Hindu myths: a sourcebook.* Baltimore: Penguin.

O'Flaherty, Wendy Doniger. 1988. *Other peoples' myths: the cave of echoes.* New York: Macmillan.

WENDY DONIGER

SEE ALSO

Cosmology, Hindu; Gods and Goddesses; Hinduism; Purāṇa

N

NĀCĀ

Nācā (from Hindi *nāc,* "dance") is a professional performance style of dance-drama in central India that includes song, dance, and spoken conversation. The nācā is performed by all-male troupes, consisting of eight to ten performers, some of whom are musicians and others, actors. There may also be a side-stage narrator. Female parts are played by male actors in female dress (and this is often a point of humor). Full-time itinerant professional troupes may travel long distances, or nācās may be performed by local semi-professionals. Certain troupes perform only one narrative tradition (such as those that perform the Chattisgarhi epic *Candainī*), while others have a more expansive repertoire drawn from the *Rāmāyaṇa* and *Mahābhārata* traditions, *purāṇas*, and local legends. The inclusion of costuming, musical accompaniment (harmonium, drum (*tablā* or *ḍholak*), cymbals, and ankle bells) and minimal dance distinguish the genre from other narrative, professionally performed, genres in Chattisgarhi performances.

The occasions for nācā performances may be religious or civic festivals or family rites of passage such as birth celebrations, but their primary purpose is entertainment rather than ritual or devotion (in contrast, for example, with *rāmlīlās*). Patrons may be wealthy shopowners, landowners, or caste headmen; sometimes a community-wide collection may support the performances. Performance spaces are public, such as a village center or urban neighborhood crossroads, and audiences, unrestricted by age, caste, or gender, are drawn from an entire village or urban neighborhood and may number several hundred people.

In the Chattisgarh region of central India, the genre of nācā as narrative performance that includes costume and dance is said to have developed in the 1970s in direct response to the spread and pervasive presence of movies and, in the early 1980s, to the ubiquitous video halls. Today, television is the most immediate competition for audiences. However, the nācā performance style remains popular, particularly in rural areas.

The nācā is part of a constellation of genres that share a configuration of dance movement, song, and dramatic narrative that take different regional manifestations and names. Other performance genres in this constellation are north Indian *nauṭankī, khyāl,* and *svang;* the eastern Indian genre of *jātrā;* the *tamāśā* of Maharashtra; and the *burrakatha* of Andhra Pradesh. In the nācā, dance movements are simple and unchoreographed or unstylized (in comparison to the highly stylized hand movements, for example, in *kathakaḷi*). Dramatic elements are dominant: there are no "pure" dance interludes. This primacy of narrative contrasts with the more classical forms of dance-drama such as kathakaḷi and *yakṣagāna,* which are dramatic but give "primary or equal emphasis to dance when enacting . . . dramatic story" (Zarrilli 1990, 308).

References

Flueckiger, Joyce Burkhalter. 1988. "He should have worn a sari": a "failed" performance of a central Indian oral epic. *The Drama Review* T117: 159–169.

Gargi, Balwant. 1966. *Folk theater of India.* Seattle: University of Washington Press.

Swann, Darius L. 1990. Introduction to Part 4: the folk-popular traditions. In *Indian theatre: traditions of performance* ed. Farley P. Richmond, Darius L. Swann, and Phillip Zarrilli. Honolulu: University of Hawaii Press.

Zarrilli, Phillip B. 1990. Introduction to Part 5: dance-dramas and dramatic dances. In *Indian theatre: traditions of performance* ed. Farley P. Richmond, Darius L. Swann, and Phillip Zarrilli. Honolulu: University of Hawaii.

JOYCE BURKHALTER FLUECKIGER

SEE ALSO
Candainī (Lorik-Candā); Dance; *Jātrā/Yātrā; Kathakali; Nauṭaṅkī; Rām Līlā; Tamāśā; Yakṣagāna*

NĀGA

Nāga is the Sanskrit word for cobra, serpent, or hooded serpent. One of the most ancient symbols of fertility throughout the world, in South Asia the serpent evokes intense fear and fascination, vividly portrayed in worship and mythology. Nāgas are powerful gods, capable of both curses and blessings. Capriciously quick to vengeance, they are considered dangerous. As guardian spirits, they are protectors of land and family, violently punishing offenders while blessing loyal worshipers with fertility and prosperity. The nāga, with raised hood, is usually depicted as half-human, half-serpent. It may be three-to-seven-thousand-headed (*Mahābhārata* 1.2162; 5.3622). Nāgas are also known as *sarpa* (serpent), *pannanga,* or *uranga* (creeping creatures), and in Tamil and Malayalam of South India, *pāmpu* (serpent).

In Hinduism village serpent gods, often perceived as spirits rather than living serpents, are worshiped in the form of iconographic representations or unhewn stones, water pots, or small dwellings, and serpent maidens. Nāgas are associated with ancestors, trees and anthills, along with goddesses and gods of the forest and mountains. Their worship is directed towards goals of immortality, fertility, the womb, and curing children's diseases, snake bite, and famine. Household, lineage, village and temple worship, and lore take a diverse range of forms, varying by region, caste, and class, combining variously with the worship of other gods and goddesses.

Nāgas are common accountrements of major Hindu gods, coiled around the Śivalingam or Śiva's neck (as the serpent king Vāsuki); depicted as Ananta (infinity) or Śēṣe, the serpent upon whom Lord Viṣṇu rests; or as weapons in the hands of the fierce goddess Kāḷi. In South Asian tantrism, the serpent is Maṇi Nāga (jewel-serpent) or Kundalīni, the life force, or *śakti,* motivating birth and rebirth. Hindus believe that the entire globe is supported upon the raised head of a giant nāga, and many housebuilding ceremonies involve propitiation of nāgas.

The great pan-Indian Hindu epics, the *Mahābhārata* and the *Purāṇa*s, are filled with stories about serpents. The most famous is the story (*Mahābhārata* I.20.1–23.4), in which Kadrū, the mother of a thousand serpents, and Vinitā (mother of the eagle-god, Garuḍa) and Ārjuna, vie for the sacred *soma,* the nectar of immortality. This episode is followed by the destruction of the serpents (*sarpavināśana,* I.20.15). In other contexts the powerful nāga is represented by the kings, Vāsuki, Tārkṣya, and Śēṣe. Nāgas are reputed to live in the underworld, Pātāla, ruled by the king, Vāsuki, where nāgas are said to possess great wealth in jewels.

Also prominent in the *Mahābhārata* and *Purāṇa*s are mythologies concerning nāga kings and ascetics attracted to the wiles of seductive serpent maidens (*nāga kaṇya* or *nāgini*s), half-human, half-serpent beings whose liaisons forged grand alliances between kingdoms. Famed for their beauty, the charms of seductive nāgini (serpent maidens) aroused even the passions of ascetics. Whether pictured alone or as consorts to the male nāga, serpent maidens represent a powerful force in Indian mythology for their courage and magical charms. The serpent has been such a potent and mysterious symbol of sexuality and fertility worldwide that Freudians claimed it to be the archetypal universal symbol, representing the male phallus. In South Asia, however, and perhaps elsewhere, this is not the case. Nāgas often represent female fertility spirits of an unattached (that is, not a consort) variety, fostering fertility, prosperity, and energy accrued through sexual abstinence. The serpent is associated with the goddess in Kannada, Tamil, Malayalam, and Telugu areas of South India, as well as in many parts of the north, where females play pivotal roles in worship. In much of North India, as well as parts of the south, it is Nāga Rāja, the nāga king, associated variously with Śiva, Viṣṇu and local gods, who is worshiped.

Although there is no direct evidence of worship, mention of the serpent is present in Vedic mythology. In the *soma* sacrifice of the Vedas, the life-energy is represented as serpent, a form of Nature (*prākṛiti*) conquered by the eagle, constituting a symbol of the cycles of time. These cosmic oppositions are also present in the combat between Indra and the cosmic serpent Vṛtra, a serpent dragon force connected to release of the rains from the clouds, an ancient motif. The worship of termite mounds in village rituals, usually associated with nāga worship, may also be related to the cosmogony of primordial mounds and with the world-tree which separates and unifies heaven and earth (Irwin 1982). Like the snake that was used by the gods to churn the oceans in order to obtain immortality-granting soma, the world-tree sets in motion the cosmic life cycle. In the *Ṛg Veda,* the chariot of the sun is said to be drawn by a nāga. In the Vedas, the serpent is also represented as an *āsura,* or anti-god, which worships Varuṇa. Buddhist and Jain religious art and literature also portray serpents as worshipers of the new religions. The Buddha is sheltered by the serpent, Muchilinda, and nāgas are door guardians in the portals of Buddhist shrines.

Today, the nāga is widely worshiped in India and Nepal in a ritual called *Nāg Panchami.* In Nepal, Nāg Panchami commemorates the fight between Garuḍa and the nāgas. In Uttar Pradesh, a male family head draws serpent figures on the wall, while in Bihar, women offer fried grains and milk. In the Punjab, Baski Nāga is worshiped. Thought to have been widespread throughout India, nāga worship achieves special importance in Kashmir, Nāgaland, and Kerala, where serpents are associated with local gods and goddesses and the genealogies of kings. A race of nāgas is considered to be the original inhabitants of Kerala; serpents are genii of trees and forests, worshiped in sacred groves by non-Brahman castes. Nāgas are believed to have been associated with the ancient Dravidians, who may have been a serpent-worshiping people indigenous to the region before the arrival of Brahmans.

In Kerala, the popular Paraśurāma myth claims that after being given most of the land, Brahmans were soon overcome by serpents and retreated, allowed to return only under the condition that they worship the serpents of the land. This myth charters the worship of serpent spirits in sacred groves (*kāvu*) performed by non-Brahman castes today, while Brahman serpents have been moved to temples. People say that the nāgas were a powerful group of warriors with which the Brahmans found it impossible to live; as such, they may have been a race of Dravidians that could not be overpowered. The existence of three major Kerala Brahman serpent temples supports this view. Members of the famous Maṇṇarśāla Mana claim that their large, forested grove was a refuge for the serpent Takṣaka (*mayāḷam*). Family priests claim that Brahman serpent worship temples were created to bring together the Aryan (Sanskritic) and Dravidian. Uniquely Dravidian elements at the Brahman temple, Mannarśāla, include a female priestess, large wooded serpent groves, and the performance of serpent songs by "untouchable" priests (*Puḷḷuvas*). However, the male Nāga Rāja, associated with Śiva or Viṣṇu, is the primary god of the temple.

The worship of serpent spirits in outdoor shrines is a common form of popular worship in South Asia, where non-Brahmanic rituals such as Kerala's *pāmpin tuḷḷal,* performed by "untouchable" Puḷḷuvas, propitiate both local and Brahmanic forms of serpents. Symbolic elements include the water pot (a symbol of the womb), active roles of both married and unmarried women, and ritual diagrams of serpents on floors and walls in colored or white powders (usually rice paste), symbolizing powerful transformations promoting fertility, health, and prosperity. Also commonly included is the elaborate recitation of local and pan-Indian serpent mythology. Wherever they occur, serpent worship and lore combine a complex fusion of diverse elements implicating a long and enduring history in South Asia.

References

Bhattacharyya, Asutosh. 1965. The serpent as a folk-deity in Bengal. *Asian Folklore Studies.* 24(1): 1–10.
Fuller, Mary. 1944. Nāg-Panchami. *Man in India* 24(2): 75–81.
Irwin, John C. 1982. The sacred anthill and the cult of the primordial mound. *History of Religions* (21)4: 339–360.
Knipe, David. 1967. The heroic theft: myths from the Ṛg Veda IV and the Ancient Near East. *History of religions* (6)4: 328–360.
Neff, Deborah L. 1987. Aesthetics and power in Pāmbin Tuḷḷal: a possession ritual of rural Kerala. *Ethnology* 26: 6371.
O'Flaherty, Wendy. 1980. *Sexual metaphors and animal symbols in Indian mythology.* Chicago: University of Chicago Press.
Sinha, Binod Chandra. 1979. *Serpent worship in ancient India.* London: East-West Publications.

DEBORAH L. NEFF

SEE ALSO
Animals; Gods and Goddesses; Kerala; *Pāmpin Tuḷḷal*

NALA AND DAMAYANTI

The story of Nala and Damayanti is one of the most beloved stories from India. The earliest written version is from the *Mahābhārata,* where it forms an interlude in the epic battle represented there. But the core story is found in women's *vrat kathā,* in the epic *Ḍholā,* acted out in Yakṣagāna performances, in Jain didactic texts, as well as being told in many of India's languages as a popular story.

The core story contains themes of gods versus humans, of fate, of love, and sometimes of passion. Nala is a human and a king—a quintessential human, but one also devoted to the gods. Here is the essence of the Sanskritic version: Nala was the most beautiful of human beings and the best of kings. Damayanti was equally beautiful. A golden goose, captured by Nala, tells Damayanti of his wonderous being. Falling in love, she pines for her love, growing thin and pale. So her father arranges for a *svayambār* (ceremony where a bride chooses her husband) and sends an invitation to Indra, king of the gods. When the gods learn that Damayanti intends to garland Nala as her chosen husband, they transform themselves into images of Nala, but Damayanti is able to distinguish the true Nala because of signs of his humanness (he has a shadow, the garland around his neck is wilted, he perspires). The gods return to heaven in anger, only to meet Kālī on the road. Kālī is determined to punish Nala for taking Damayanti for himself and is able to enter his body when he forgets to wash a tiny spot on his toe. Possessing Nala, Kālī forces him to gamble away his fortune and kingdom, after which he and Damayanti are banished to the forest. There Nala is unable to protect his wife and, through the curse of Kālī, abandons her despite his love. Damayanti eventually makes her way back to her father's kingdom, while Nala, misshapen and bowed, cursed with leprosy, takes refuge in another kingdom as a charioteer. Unable to find Nala, Damayanti's father sends the coded message, "Beloved gambler, where have you gone? You who are so kind, why are you unkind to your wife?" When Nala responds to the message, Nala and Damayanti are reunited, but only after Nala learns the secret of numbers from his patron and banishes Kālī forever from his body. After a final game of dice, Nala regains his kingdom. Thus ends the great story of misfortune.

In other versions, the god Sanicār, whose curse is feared by Hindus but can be alleviated by mustard oil, plays the role of Kālī and brings destruction to Nala. In women's versions, it is Nala's own act of destruction of the necklace of the goddess Dasa Mātā that brings overwhelming sorrows to Nala and Damayanti. But in all its various renditions, the roles of fate versus human action, of humans versus the gods, of wifely virtue and possible male wrong-doing, and of the triumph of good fortune over misfortune are questioned, thus contributing, through these essential questions, to the longevity and variety of this story.

References

Buck, William. 1987. *Mahabharata.* New York: Meridan Book.

Shulman, David. 1994. On being human in the Sanskrit Epic: The riddle of Nala. *Journal of Indian philosophy* 22(1): 1–24.

Unni, N. P. 1977. *Nala episode in Sanskrit literature.* Trivandrum: College Book House.

Van Buitenen, J. A. B., trans., *The Mahabharata,* vol. 2. Chicago: University of Chicago Press.

SUSAN S. WADLEY

SEE ALSO

Ḍholā; Gender and Folklore; *Mahābhārata; Vrat Kathā*

NAMES AND NAMING PRACTICES, BALOCHISTAN

Traditional personal naming practices and beliefs (onomastics) can be intricate, displaying both local and general features of identity management in relation to other social institutions. The complexities of the topic vary by region, language, ethnic group, and religion. For example, a Baloch child (in western Pakistan, southern Afghanistan, or southeastern Iran) is given the first name (*nām*) at any time within the first six days after birth. Naming may be postponed until the sixth or seventh day, as is normal practice in two tribes, Mari and Bugti, or for special reasons, for example if a woman has a live birth after several stillbirths, or finally has a son after several daughters. In such cases, the child is hidden from all except the mother and the midwife, and its name and sex are kept secret until the sixth day (*shashigān*). On the sixth day, in normal practice, the mother and child are bathed, an animal is sacrificed and the meat distributed among the village people, and the sex and name of the baby are announced. Evil forces are believed prone to attack the newborn within the first six days of life, but after that the risks are reduced. In some parts of Balochistan, according to custom, if a couple has several daughters and no son they give a male name to their youngest daughter and make her wear male dress in the hope of confounding the evil forces and clearing the hurdles for the birth of a son in future.

There are heavy names (*grānen nām*) and light names (*subakken nām*). A heavy name does not let the child grow strong and s/he passes from one illness to another. If such illness occurs, a religious person (*mullā*) or a specialist in reading *fāl* (a fortune-teller) is asked to consult a book of talismans or astrology, to establish if the name is unsuitable for the child. If so, he finds a new name through the book and is given some money as *shugrāna* (thanksgiving) "to the book." A name may be changed several times in hope of finding one that is in harmony with the spirit of the person. In one recent case, a schoolteacher had his name changed five times in childhood and adulthood, from Bashīr (birth name) to Jānmahmad (name given at circumcision) to Bashshām (grandfather's name, given to him after the former's death) to Abdulmajīd (name given by a spirit healer when he fell seriously ill in his thirties, after his graduate studies), and back to Jānmahmad (dictated by another spirit-healer). In the same village, a woman has gone through similar multiple name-changes in her thirty years of life.

The Baloch used to give temporary names after birds, trees, expressions of joy, etc., to a newborn child. A boy was then given an elder's name at circumcision. As the circumciser was cutting off the prepuce, the father or a male relative would loudly announce the new, adult name of the boy. A girl's name, on the other hand, was changed on the night of her *nikāh* (finalizing the marriage contract), when she entered society as a woman. Before reading the *nikāh,* the new name was announced and was used in the marriage contract. Now, permanent names are given to babies and are regularized when the child enters school. If, for healing or other matters of belief, a religious person proposes a name change, or if a grandparent dies and a child's parents decide to give his or her name to one of their children, an animal is sacrificed for food distribution or sweets are distributed by a poorer family, and the new name is announced in public. It was and is inauspicious ("not good," *sharr na int*) to change a name without any *herāt* (food or sweets distribution).

Temporary names might include, for boys, *Pullo* ("flower-like"), *Kauro* (from *kaur,* "acacia-like"), *Gazzo* ("tamarisk-like"), *Diluk* ("little heart"), or *Murādak* ("little wish"), or for girls, *Shātul* ("ring-dove"), *Kapot* ("wild pigeon"), *Tūtuk* ("little parrot"), *Guluk* ("little rose"), *Sharruk* ("little good one"), or *Muruk* ("little pearl"). Traditionally, Baloch use single-word names or two-word compound names (especially those with reference to God or the Prophet Muhammad), attaching the name of the father as a second name if specification was needed (*Alla-Dād-i Sēhakk,* "Alla-Dād son of Sēhakk," or *Māhikān-i Gangozar,* "Māhikān daughter of Gangozar"). Diminutive names ending in *ū* demonstrate contempt or designate low social status of a person, and are attached to names of low-caste persons or used as nickname formations for those one dislikes. Diminutive names ending in *o* or *u* are used for girl children before marriage. Diminutives ending in *uk* (meaning "little one") demonstrate affection, usually in children's names. Diminutives in either form are disrespectful if used for elders.

If a son dies in a family and another son is born soon thereafter, it seems a compensation from God, and he may be named *Badal* ("exchange"). There is no such custom for girls, whose loss is not seen as so important as that of a son. Sons and daughters are named after their deceased grandparents, the eldest son having first claim to use the names of his parents for his own children. After naming a child for his father or mother, a father calls him or her *manī pit/māt* ("my father/mother"), with a sense that the child embodies the spirit of the deceased parent, perhaps to become a protector of the father in old age as the deceased parent was in his childhood. If a child named after a grandparent dies, that name is not passed on to any other child. Apart from inherited names, parents try to choose a name that no one else is using at a given time in the immediate community, though some parents may "borrow" an auspicious name from a successful living person, which the other family will to some extent resent.

For a number of years after marriage, the wife may avoid speaking the name of her husband, calling him *manī mard* ("my husband") until they have a child, after which she calls him "father of so-and-so." There is a danger of loss of affection if she calls him by name before they have children. She may start calling him by name after several years, only when the husband has agreed (after discussion, usually after at least one child's birth) to give her a share of his *chullē sawāb* (heavenly reward "of the hearth," which he hopes to obtain by giving alms and feeding the poor or guests at his hearth; The share of this *sawāb* offered to wives is usually one third). Paradoxically, husbands might also tease or playfully try to force their wives to speak their name; if a wife does so too early in the marriage, other women may tease her as one who flirts or calls attention to herself (*laṛī kant*).

Because of satellite television networks, other mass media and school books, and the presence of outsiders, Balochi onomastics are changing drastically. "Sophisticated names" borrowed from film and televison stars and political or sports personalities are replacing more traditional names for men and women that referred to landscape, calendar (day names and month names commemorating one's birth), or natural phenomena (gems, flowers, etc.), or invoked auspicious status ("king," "chief," "lady," etc.). A child is now given a permanent name at birth, with no changes except in case of later serious illness, with the intervention of a religious person or spirit healer. If a child has a name not found in Pakistani books or not related to a religious figure, a schoolteacher may change it to give the child a "more modern name," to avoid embarrassment in hospitals or other official settings, or in travel outside of Balochistan for any reason. Voter name lists and lists from hospitals (with ages specified) show these striking changes, especially with names drawn from television.

Reference

Badalkhan, Sabir. 2000. Language contacts in Balochistan and its impact on Balochi onomastics. In Jahani, Carina and Agnes Korn, eds., *Proceedings of the International Symposium on Linguistic Contact in Balochistan in Historical and Modern Times*. (Uppsala, August 17–20, 2000).

SABIR BADALKHAN

SEE ALSO
Divination, Balochi; Person

NAMING CEREMONIES

Bestowing a name on an infant is one of the first ways of recognizing it as a member of a family and community. Some cultures may wait to be sure the child lives for a while before they name it, or they may feel that it is bad luck to name it too soon. If the child is unwanted, naming also may be delayed.

People in the Himalayan region seem to name their infants very soon after birth. The Limbu of eastern Nepal allow a mother to name an infant immediately after birth, but they do not conduct purificatory rituals until the third (for a girl) or fourth (for a boy) day of life. Among the Sherpa, where women often give birth in their parents' homes, the father's family comes to name the baby several days after the birth. His party brings a prayer flag and some beer. The privilege of naming is reserved for a kinsman or friend of the father, who smears butter on the baby's head and mouth and ties a scarf to the central house post.

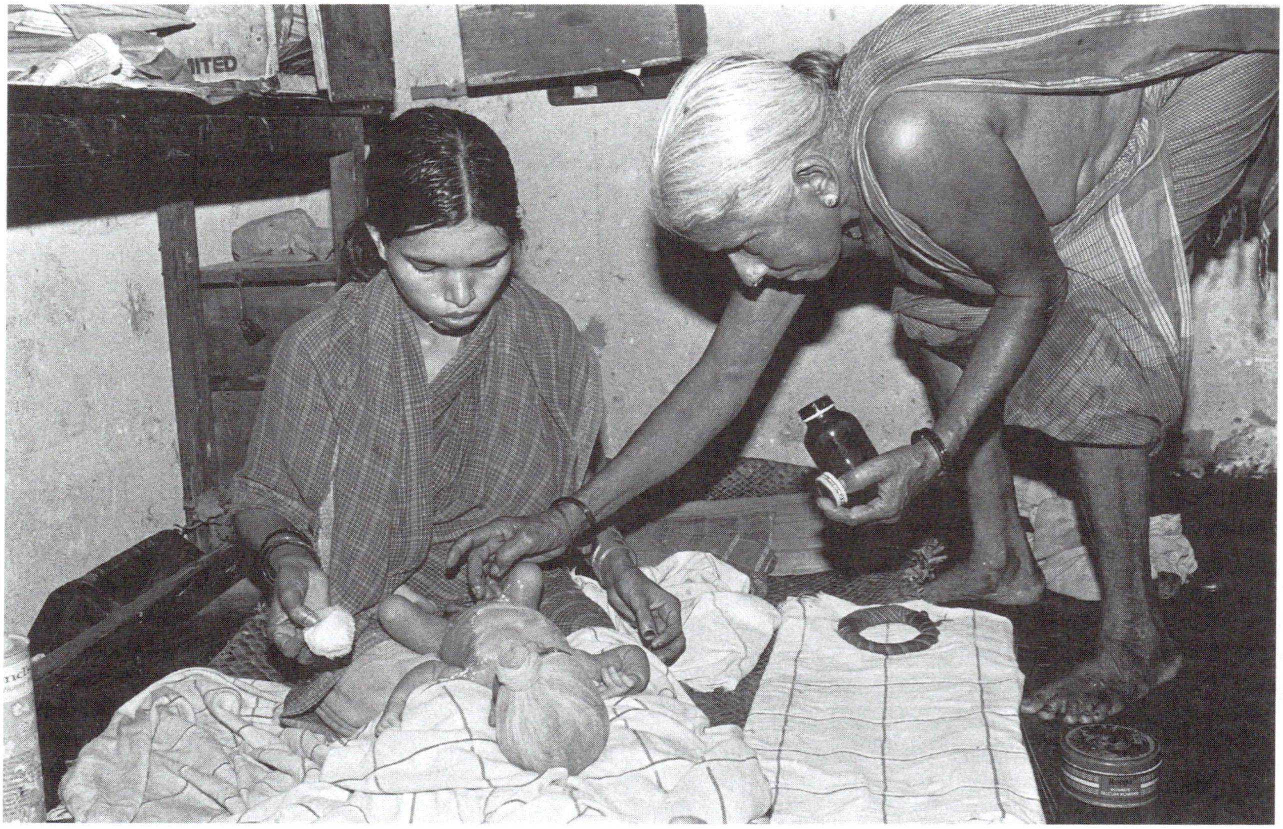

A grandmother puts āyurvedic oil on the umbilical cord of a newborn to prepare the baby for the naming ceremony, © Mimi Nichter

Like many other Hindu groups, the Newar of Nepal provide a horoscope name before the birth pollution period ends, but this is not the name that will be used to address the child, which is given later. This group has no formal naming ceremony.

In Delhi State it is common practice to have a Brahman provide a name ten days after birth. In Karnataka State, Hindu families customarily bestow a name on the eleventh day after birth in the *nāmākarana* ritual, which is celebrated by many Hindu families throughout the subcontinent. In one Uttar Pradesh study, Hindu families were found to have no formal naming rituals. The name actually used is decided informally after several months of family and neighborhood discussion. The only restriction in the selection of a name is to avoid the name of any living adult family member, since there would always be some people who would not feel free to address the child for fear of violating etiquette that restricts use of elders' names. In the Telangana area of Andhra Pradesh, Hindus name a child on the twenty-first or thirtieth day after birth, when the elders announce the name to an assembled group of men and women. Muslims in this region name a child on the seventh day.

The Muslim naming ceremony is *ḥaqīqa; hakika* or *akika* (also spelled *aqiqah*). A sacrifice of two large animals is required for a boy or one large animal for a girl. Most Bangladesh families find it too expensive to conduct this rite, but it is widely celebrated in Pakistan. One Afghan custom is to perform an official naming ceremony on the third day after birth, when a mullā whispers "God is great" in the infant's ear four times. Among some Afghan nomads, the paternal uncle names the infant.

References

Dube, S. C. 1955. *Indian village*. London: Routledge & Kegan Paul Ltd.

Freed, Ruth S., and Stanley A. Freed. 1980. *Rites of passage in Shanti Nagar*. Anthropological Papers of the American Museum of Natural History [New York], vol. 56, p. 3, 323–554.

Luschinsky, Mildred Stroop. 1962. The life of women in a village of North India; A study of role and status. Ph.D. dissertation. Cornell University.

SUZANNE HANCHETT

SEE ALSO

Life Cycle Rituals; Names and Naming Practices, Balochistan; Person

NARRATIVE CLASSIFICATION

Systematic arrangement is an indispensable prerequisite for any analytical or comparative research relying on large bodies of narrative data. While classification primarily serves the need to present material for further interpretation, it is itself a way of interpreting the materials considered. Though there has been much dispute as to the feasibility of various proposed systems, the only classification of folk narrative applied on a large scale for comparative purposes is the system established by the so-called Finnish School, following the geographical-historical dispersion theory. Its practical result is the compilation of indexes of narrative tale types and motifs in geographic and/or ethnic tradition areas worldwide.

The discourse about different systems of classification touches on a number of sensitive issues of folk narrative theory, including the debates on genre, context, and meaning as described by Ben-Amos. However, practicable models of classification have only been developed for traditional narrative genres similar to those thoroughly investigated in the European literatures. Morphological and structural studies, on the other hand, have advanced the understanding of basic mechanisms at work in folk narrative, yet they have contributed little to practical problems of genre and subgenre classification.

In a historical perspective, the early nineteenth century collectors of folk tales, such as the Grimm brothers, were aware of the fact that certain tales might be rooted in older tradition and be disseminated over wide geographic areas. The German indological scholar Theodor Benfey, originally commenting on the Sanskrit fable collection *Pancatantra,* was to postulate the influential theory that all or at least most of the folk tales extant in the West were of Indian origin and had migrated to the Western world by various means. Benfey's "Indian theory" was basically right insofar as the literary works he scrutinized were concerned; as a general statement, however, it was later proved to be false and misleading. Still, it encouraged folklorists to consider questions of origin and migration / diffusion in great detail, ultimately proposing the diametrically opposed theories of polygenesis (origin of one story in more than one place) versus monogenesis of folk tales. The quest for the primary origin of folk tales also resulted in comparative studies coinciding with large-scale collections of folklore data in late nineteenth century Europe. For both purposes, large bodies of narrative data had to be systematized, and this eventually required a solid classification system.

While it was not the first or only system proposed, the classification system established by the Finnish folklorist Antti Aarne at the beginning of the twentieth century proved to be most influential until the present. Primarily working on the narrative data in Finnish archives, Aarne organized traditional folk tales into three main categories: animal tales, ordinary folk tales, and jokes and anecdotes. This general structure is divided and subdivided into smaller categories and units in such a way as to group tales with similar contents and/or common protagonists closely together, and each tale is given a specific number. Aarne's system was translated and adapted to large amounts of narrative data by the American folklorist Stith Thompson, eventually accommodating several thousand tales. Thompson also was to develop a classification of folk narrative by motifs, systematizing smaller narrative units, that were the components of complex tale types. While Thompson's classification of tale types includes the "Folk-Tale of Europe, West Asia, and the Lands Settled by These Peoples" (1961; 7), his motif index attempts a theoretical classification of motifs covering the whole world.

As for the classification of South Asian narrative, research has almost exclusively concentrated on the Indian subcontinent. This concentration no doubt resulted from the impact of Benfey's "Indian theory," and research was facilitated by the fact that in the colonial era a considerable number of translations of narratives was available to the European reader without specialized knowledge in Indian languages. A first and very interesting attempt at classifying "Modern Indian (Aryan) Folk-Tales" is appended to Steel and Temple's 1884 collection, *Wide-Awake Stories*. The survey divides the incidents of the folk tales under consideration into four classes: " (I.) into those connected with the Actors; (II.) with the *Progress* of the tale; (III.) with the Means necessary to insure the progress of the tale; and (IV.) Miscellaneous incidents. Each class is divided into major and minor heads and sub-heads." (Steel and Temple, 1884, 390). Though the survey is very interesting in that it anticipates aspects of later structural studies, it passed without notice at its time of publication.

Within the framework of the Aarne/Thompson classification systems, only India, Pakistan, and Ceylon (Sri Lanka) are represented in a satisfactory way. The Aarne/Thompson classifications mainly rely on two basic works of analysis in whose compilation Thompson himself cooperated, a motif-index (Thompson and Balys, 1958) and an index of tale types (Thompson and Roberts 1960), both essentially drawing on the same body of folk tale collections. In addition to this, classical works of narrative literature in translation were considered, such as the *Pancatantra,* the *Tripiṭaka,* the compilation of *Jātakas* and Somadeva's *Kathāmsaritsāmgara.* Laurits Bødsker, in his survey of Indian animal tales, avoided the arbitrariness of the

Aarne/Thompson classifications by simply numbering the tales sequentially. In order to facilitate comparison with the Aarne/Thompson systems, however, he mentioned tale types and motifs where applicable.

Another attempt at classification of South Asian narratives has recently been prepared by Heda Jason. Jason, while essentially offering a supplement to the previous catalogues of Indian narratives, also analyzes the texts' ethnopoetic genres according to a system she devised for Jewish culture. While Jason is confident that her system "proved to be usable for Indian high culture, too" (1989, 13), her ensuing self-criticism amounts to pointing out a large number of shortcomings, which eventually might bring into question the general feasibility of her system. The Indian scholar K. D. Upadhyaya, in a short paper, classified Hindi oral folk tales under six headings: didactic tales, religious tales, love stories, tales of entertainment, local legends, and myths. However, no attempt has been made to subdivide these categories or to classify any body of narratives according to the proposed scheme.

As for other South Asian countries, Persian (*Darī*) folk tales of Afghanistan, though they have not been classified anywhere, comply largely with Persian narratives from Iran surveyed by Marzolph in a separate catalogue. The classification adopted there, with a few minor adaptations, follows the Aarne / Thompson system of tale types. Future attempts at classifying South Asian narratives face several obstacles: First, no serious large-scale collection of narrative data in any of the South Asian tradition areas is known to be available. Second, existing classifications exclusively rely on texts published in translation, mostly in English. Since translations invariably influence the original wording to the point of falsification, the sources scrutinized up to the present are questionable for classificatory purposes. Third, folk narrative research so far has studied South Asian narrative culture largely from a Western point of view. The available text material mainly dates from the British colonial period. It has been collected under colonial premises with the highly biased general aim of procuring comparative data for Western research. Fourth, while various recent studies in context and performance have pointed out the prevalence of indigenous systems of classification, few attempts have endeavored to classify larger bodies of narrative in that way. Fifth, any attempt at classifying folk narrative has to consider the totality of existing narrative texts. Various genres, such as myths, legends, and jokes, have been excluded from tale-type classification while being considered, to a certain extent, in motif classification. And finally, it should be remembered that classification evolves on empirical grounds. Boundaries between genres, tales, communities, languages, and religious concepts are likely to be of a transitory nature. While classification serves a need in systematic presentation, there will always be exceptions to any rule.

References

Azzolina, David. 1987. *Tale-type and motif-indexes. An annotated bibliography,* xxi–xxxix. New York: Garland.

Ben-Amos, Dan. 1992. Do we need ideal types (in folklore)? Nordic Institute of Folklore, *Papers,* vol. 2. Turku: Nordic Institute of Folklore.

Bødsker, Laurits. 1957. *Indian animal tales: a preliminary survey.* Folklore Fellows Communications, vol. 170. Helsinki: Academia Scientiarium Fennica.

Flueckiger, Joyce B. 1996. *Gender and genre in the folklore of middle India.* Ithaca, N.Y.: Cornell University Press.

Jason, Heda. 1989. *Types of Indic oral tales.* Supplement. Folklore Fellows Communications, vol. 242. Helsinki: Academia Scientiarium Fennica.

———. 2000. *Literary motif, content type and ethnopoetic genre: a manual for compilation of indices & a bibliography of Indices and Indexing.* Folklore Fellows Communications 273. Helsinki: Academia Scientiarum Fennica.

Marzolph, Ulrich. 1984. *Typologie des persischen Volksmärchens.* Beiruter Texte und Studien, vol. 31. Beirut: Deutsche Morgenländische Gesellschaft.

Sydow, Carl Wilhelm von. 1948. Popular prose traditions and their classification. In *Selected Papers on Folklore,* 127–145. Copenhagen: Rosenkilde and Bagger.

Steel, F. A. and R. C. Temple. 1884. A survey of incidents in modern Indian (Aryan) folk-tales. In *Wide-Awake Stories. A Collection of Tales Told by Little Children, between Sunset and Sunrise, in the Punjab and Kashmir,* 386–436. Bombay: Education Society's Press; London: Trbner, Co.

Thompson, Stith. [1947] 1977. *The folktale,* ch. 4. New York: Holt, Reinhart and Winston. Reprint; Berkeley, Los Angeles: University of California Press

———. 1950. Types and classification of folklore. In *Funk and Wagnall's standard dictionary of folklore, Mythology and Legend.* ed. M. Leach. vol. 2, 1138–1147. New York: Funk and Wagnalls Co.

———. 1961. *The types of the folk-tale. A classification and bibliography.* 2nd rev. Folklore Fellows Communications, vol. 184. Helsinki: Academia Scientiarium Fennica.

Thompson, Stith, and Jonas Balys. 1958. *The oral tales of India.* Bloomington: Indiana University Press.

Thompson, Stith, and Warren E. Roberts. 1960. *Types of Indic oral tales.* Folklore Fellows Communications, vol. 180. Helsinki: Academia Scientiarium Fennica.

Upadhyaya, K. D. 1965. The classification and chief characteristics of Indian (Hindi) folk-tales. *Laographia* 22: 581–587.

ULRICH MARZOLPH

SEE ALSO

Benfey, Theodor; Folk Literature; Folklorists; Folktale, "Tale Type"; *Pañcatantra*

NARRATIVE SCROLL PAINTING

South Asia has a rich array of performance traditions in which scroll paintings are used in storytelling events.

The paintings illustrate religious narratives embedded in ritual contexts. The scrolls from these traditions are sacred objects. Believed to be mobile shrines, they are ritually consecrated, properly venerated, and periodically appeased. When not in use, they are rolled up and kept away from the common domain. The performances mostly take place at night and continue until the early hours of the morning. Examples of such painted scrolls are found in Rajasthan, Gujarat, Andhra Pradesh, West Bengal, Maharashtra, Orissa, Nepal, and Bangladesh.

The storytellers who own the scrolls are hereditary professionals who travel from village to village. Often they are priests, genealogists, and marriage brokers to the communities they serve. In most instances, these roles are embedded in traditional caste relations.

The relationships between the painters of the scrolls and the narrators of the stories vary between the traditions. For example, in Bengal and Gujarat, the storyteller is also the painter, but in Rajasthan the storyteller (*bhopo*) commissions the paintings from the members of the Joshi community. In another instance, the *Nakāśis* of Telangana are painters to the storytellers of more than one caste.

The scrolls' subject matter varies among the traditions but, in general, they illustrate stories from the epics, the *Pūrāṇas*, and local legends. The scrolls from Bengal and Orissa illustrate local versions of episodes from Hindu mythology; those from Rajasthan illustrate the exploits of local heroes (Pābūjī and Devnārāyaṇ); those from Gujarat illustrate Jain themes; and the *yama-paṭas* from Andhra Pradesh and Tamil Nadu illustrate the journey to heaven and punishments to sinners in hell. The scrolls from Telangāna in Andhra Pradesh narrate legends about the origins of particular castes and the deeds of its legendary heroes.

These are sacred stories: there is religious merit to be gained from their ritual telling and re-telling. They are narrated for different reasons: caste myths tell of caste origins and identities; yama-paṭas warn about the consequences of evil doings; the Pābūjī epic cures camel diseases; and a *paṭa* is commissioned to atone for the sin of killing a cat or dog, or cursing a Brahman. These performances are also modes of entertainment.

The pictorial narratives are intimately linked to the theme, size, and format of the scrolls. In some traditions the scrolls illustrate a single story (Telangana, Santhal *jaḍu paṭas*), while scrolls in other traditions illustrate several stories (Garoḍa scrolls of Gujarat). The pictorial narrative of some scrolls is divided into discrete panels; in other traditions, the stories merge into one another with no simple chronological or linear order to the narrative (*paṛs* of Rajasthan).

The pictorial narratives are also intimately connected to performance contexts. The visual, verbal, and performed narratives are interwoven in ways that confirm and reify one another. Some traditions use several scrolls in a performance (Bengal paṭas), while others use only one scroll for the entire duration of a telling. Some paintings are unrolled all at once and placed on display throughout the length of the performance (Rajasthan paṛs); others are held and unrolled scene by scene (Garoda scrolls of Gujarat or the paṭas from Bengal). Some traditions have a fixed narrative repertoire of stories that are illustrated (Pābūjī or Telangāna scrolls), whereas in other traditions new themes are contantly being added as older ones are discarded (Bengal paṭas). In all cases, however, the performance is marked by elaboration and improvisation. The oral traditions use prose, verse, music, dance, and song. Often, there is ritual possession that takes place during the performances.

Numerous literary references testify to the widespread popularity of this tradition of painting and storytelling in India. The earliest dates to the second century B.C.E. Brahmanical, Jain, and Buddhist source literature contains many references to the art of painted scrolls (*paṭa citras*) which were exhibited in ancient times to educate and entertain viewers. Classical Sanskrit literature has references to yama paṭas. Despite the literary evidence for the enduring popularity of this genre, we have no material evidence of narrative scroll paintings prior to the fifteenth century because cotton cloth, on which the images were painted, does not preserve well. Moreover, these paintings were considered sacred objects. When they were no longer usable, they were deconsecrated and then ritually destroyed. Until very recently, these paintings were never sold.

The scroll paintings from Nepal illustrate Buddhist and Hindu themes. The Hindu scrolls (*paubhas*, *toranas*, or paṭas) deal with pūrāṇic episodes. They are long, narrow scrolls (usually 20 × 2 feet) and are kept rolled up when not in use. They are associated with a particular deity and brought out and displayed in temples on special festival days. They are painted on coarse cotton cloth and often have inscriptions along with the portraits of the donors who commissioned the painting.

In Rajasthan, the scrolls are called paṛs. They are large panels that illustrate the stories of Pābūjī and Devnārāyaṇ. The storytelling event is called *parbanchana,* literally a "reading," or telling, of the scroll. The scrolls are conservative in style and content. The Bhopas (storyteller priests) perform at night; the event is a ritual of commemoration (*jāgrata*) in which the audience also participates. When scrolls are to be discarded, they are ritually deconsecrated and the deities on the painted scroll are asked to leave the painting. The scrolls are then immersed in a lake in the same way that the bones of a dead person are consigned to the waters.

The Garoḍa storytellers of Gujarat narrate sacred legends with the help of a *tipānu* (scroll painting). The stories are taken from the epics, the Pūrāṇas, and from the subjects of the yama paṭa tradition. The tours of the itinerant storytellers are called *jātrā*s (pilgrimages); the paintings are mobile shrines that house the deities. The Garoḍa scrolls are painted on paper and held by the teller as he recites the story.

In Bangladesh, *ghazir paṭa*s narrate the lives of Muslim great men, saints, and early preachers who were responsible for the Islamization of the land. The most popular of the *ghazi* ballads is that of Ghazi Kalu. His name is associated with princess Campavati, who may have been a Hindu princess who succumbed to his piety and virtue and converted to Islam. Other such themes from West Bengal are *Cand Ghazi* and *Sona Ghazi*. There are also Buddhist *paṭa*s in Bangladesh with scenes of *Jātaka*s and *āvadana* tales, but it is not known if they are used in performance contexts.

The paṭas of West Bengal illustrate stories of Kṛṣṇalīla, Mānasamangala, Rāmayaṇa, Caitanyaḷila, and Śitala worship, as well as secular and topical themes. The traditions of *cakshudana paṭa, jādu paṭa*s, and *jam paṭa*s (hell scrolls) are popular in this region among the Santhal people. Besides the long scrolls, West Bengal has a tradition of illustrating narrative paintings in sets called *couka pāta*s (square paṭas). The earlier paṭas were painted on cotton cloth, but paper has increasingly become the norm. The storyteller (pātua) is most often the painter of the scrolls. The songs are drawn from a traditional repertoire, although new themes are constantly added. The storyteller holds the scroll and narrates the story frame by frame. In Bengal today, many of the paṭa performances are considered to be secular entertainment; there are fewer castes now who feel obliged to patronize ritual performances.

In Telangāna, the tradition is still deeply embedded in the caste system. The scrolls from this tradition are the largest in size among the known examples of Indian pigment painting on cloth. The scrolls are both horizontal and vertical in format. They are considered ritual objects. The storytellers are itinerant professionals, and an elaborate system of caste obligations links them to their respective patrons. The painters of the scrolls are called Nakāśis. The scrolls, painted on cotton cloth, illustrate caste myths and tell the stories of legendary heroes. As in many other traditions, the performances are held at night. Andhra Pradesh also has scrolls of the Yama paṭa tradition that display scenes of punishments meted out in hell for sinners.

The *citrakathi* tradition of storytelling from the Paithan region of Maharashtra uses the paintings as visual aids in the performance, but instead of a single long scroll, they use a series of loose leaf folios bound together in a set called a *potis*. These paintings are done on paper, and the themes are taken from the epics and *pūrāṇa*s.

Today the tradition of picture storytelling competes against the entertainment provided by television, video, film, and the Internet. The roles of storytellers are increasingly those of secular entertainers. The caste nexus that once characterized these traditions is being loosened. Meanwhile, the traditions have moved into urban domains and are adapting to the demands and formats of new audiences.

References

Coomaraswamy, Ananda. 1929. Picture showmen. *Indian Historical Quarterly* 5, no 2: 182–187.

Dallapicolla, A. L. 1998. Paithan paintings: the epic world of the Chitrakathis. In Jyotindra Jain, ed., *Picture showmen: insights into the narrative tradition in Indian art*. Mumbai: Marg Publications, pp 66–73.

Jain, Jyotindra. 1998. *Picture showmen: insights into the narrative tradition in Indian art*. Mumbai: Marg Publications.

Sen Gupta Sankar. 1973. *The paṭas and patuas of Bengal*. Calcutta: Indian Publications.

Sharma, Shiv Kumar. 1993. *The Indian painted scroll*. S. K. Sharma.

———. *Painted scrolls of Asia: Hindu, Buddhist and Lamaistic* New Delhi: Intellectual Publishing House, 1994.

Singh, Kavita. 1998. To show, to see, to tell, to know: Patuas, Bhopas and their audiences. In Jyotindra Jain, ed., *Picture showmen: Insights into the narrative tradition in Indian art*. Mumbai: Marg Publications, pp. 100–115.

Smith, John. 1991. *Epic of Pabuji: a study, transcription and translation*. Cambridge, Eng: Cambridge University Press.

Thangavelu, Kirtana. 1998. The painted pūrāṇas of Telangana: a study of a scroll painting tradition from south India. Ph.D diss., University of California, Berkeley.

KIRTANA THANGAVELU

SEE ALSO

Devnārāyaṇ; Folk Art; Folk Painting; *Jātaka* Tales; *Jātrā/Yātrā; Pābūjī; Paṛ*

NAṬĒŚA ŚĀSTRI, PANDIT SANGĒNDI MAHĀLINGA

A prolific and erudite writer in English, Sanskrit and Tamil, Pandit S. M. Naṭēśa Śāstri (1859–1906) left a legacy for Indian folklore that is perhaps best evident in his impressive four-volume *Folklore in Southern India* (1884–1893), published by Bombay's Education Society Press and Trubner. Naṭēśa Śāstri's work is significant because it was published at a time when British 'collectors' dominated the publication of Indian folkore—although, of course, we know today that many Indians facilitated the difficult processes of collection and translation, and in many instances, even made collections possible. By 1893, Śāstri had been elected a member of the council of the British Folklore Society. The range and thoroughness of Pandit Naṭēśa Śāstri's scholarship should have earned him a prominent place in the historiography of Indian folklore, but surprisingly, critical assessment of his work and biographical information about him remains pitifully scanty.

A native of Tiruchirapalli district in Tamil Nadu and born to Mahālinga Iyer and Akhilāṇḍēśwari, Naṭēśa Śāstri lost his mother early in life and was brought up by his grandmother and his stepmother (whose kindness he acknowledges in the brief autobiographical preface to his third volume of *Folklore in Southern India*), in the villages of Lālguḍi and Kulitalai (nearby Sangēndi being the ancestral village). After studying in Kumbakōṇam College and Chennai Government College, he joined the Government Archaeological Survey in 1881 where he assisted Robert Sewell in his archaeological research. We know from Sewell's writings (especially in 1884) that Naṭēśa Śāstri was an insightful translator of medieval Tamil inscriptions. Later, Śāstri worked in public offices such as the Survey of India, Inspector General of Registration, and the Jail Superintendent's office, in Ārcoṭ, Tiruvallur, Mysore, and Udhagamanḍalam, as well in parts of the former Bombay Presidency. Besides numerous articles on South Indian folkore. Śāstri authored *Dravidian Nights Entertainment* (1886), a translation of the Tamil romance, *Madanakāmarājakadai,* that comprises a frame story into which are woven a series of sub-stories. Other notable books relevant to foklore study include *Medieval Tales of Southern India* (1897), *Tales of Tennalirāma* (1900), *Hindu Feasts, Fasts and Ceremonies* (1903), and *Indian Folk-Tales* (1908). His four-volume collection, *Folklore in Southern India* (1884–1893), contains tales recounted by his stepmother and grandmother and those collected during his service in various parts of South India. The collection displays Śāstri's fluency with several languages and folk idioms.

In 1888, he co-edited a collection called *Tales of the Sun, Or, Folklore of Southern India* (the subtitle recalls the title of his own four-volume book) with Mrs. Georgiana H. Kingscote, wife of Colonel Howard Kingscote of the Oxfordshire Light Infantry. We have no information about the origins or the nature of this joint authorship, and neither Kingscote's fiction—she wrote over 60 novels under the pseudonym of Lucas Cleeve—nor her virulently racist manual written for British mothers posted in India, *The English Baby in India and How to Rear It* (1893) mention this acquaintance. However, Kingscote's preface to the joint folktale collection informs us that Naṭēśa Śāstri "... not only corrected the errors of [the] tales, but allowed [Kingscote] to add to them many that he had himself collected ..." (v–vi). A comparison of Naṭēśa Śāstri's own previously published works indicates that Śāstri contributed at least 25 of the 26 tales of the co-edited collection. Kingscote claims to have added other tales, which she says she recorded from her "native servants" who in turn had got them from "old women in the bazaars" (v). The volume contains notes by other folklorists like "Mr. Cowper Temple, Mr. Clowston and others," and it is not entirely clear what editorial leverages were assumed by whom. The collection in fact is worth scrutinizing for the vexed issue of collaboration in colonial folklore and anthropological ventures.

Naṭēśa Śāstri wrote on a variety of literary, religious, and philosophical subjects in Tamil and English and is recognized by critics such as P. G. Sundararajan ("Chiṭṭi") as a pioneer in Tamil fiction at the turn of the century. He wrote six novels between 1902 and 1903. Characters and incidents in his Tamil novel, *Tinatavālu* (reprint 1980) are believed to resemble sketchily those in his own life. Naṭēśa Śāstri knew eighteen languages, translated a Persian noval and Shakespeare into Tamil, collected and published Telugu and Tamil folklore in the *Folklore Journal, The Indian Antiquary, Madras Christian College Magazine* and *Theosophical Studies* rendered Vālmiki's *Rāmāyaṇa* in short story form, and edited and translated Sanskrit poetic drama, notably Viśākadatta's *Mudrarākśasa.* His other work includes a manual based on śāstric elucidations for sanitary science, as well as a Tamil translation of the Sanskrit poetical composition *Ātmavidya Vilāsa* of Sadāśiva Brahmēndra, the eighteenth century *bhakti* saint-composer. By the age of 47, Pandit Natēśa Śāstri had established an impressive record in folklore, archaeology, numismatics, and literature—a record that would have enriched scholarship even further had it not been for his tragic death after being struck by a panic-stricken horse in a temple procession in Triplicane, Madras.

References

Anonymous. 1959. Note on Naṭēśa Śāstri in *Kalai Kalanjiyam*: Vol. 6 (Tirun Paricai), 1st edition, p. 286. Chennai; Valarchi Kalagam.

Anonymous. 1908. Pandit S. M. Natesa Sastri. In *Men and women of India.* Reprinted in *Indian folk-tales.* Naṭēśa Śāstri, Madras: Guardian Press.

Kingscote, Mrs. H. and Naṭēśa Śástri, S. M. 1890. *Tales of the sun, or, folklore of southern India.* London and Calcutta: W. H. Allen & Co.

Naṭēśa Śāstri, S. M. 1886. *Dravidian nights entertainment: Being a translation of Madanakāmarankadai,* Madras: Excelsior Press.

———. 1884–1893. *Folklore in Southern India.* Vol I–IV. Bombay: Education Society Press, & London: Trubner.

———. 1888. Some specimens of South Indian popular erotic poetry. *The Indian antiquary* 253–259.

———. 1897. *Medieval tales of southern India.* Madras: Madras School Book and Literature Society.

———. 1900. *Tales of Tennalirāma: the famous court jester of southern India* Madras: G.A. Natesan and Co.
———. 1903. *Hindu feasts. fasts and ceremonies.* Madras: M. E. Publication House.
———. 1905. *Sukha Sandarśana Dīpikai: a handbook of sanitary science based on Hindu Śāstrās* Madurai: Tamil Sangam.
———. 1907. *Muttira Rākśasam.* Madras; Guardian Press.
———. 1908. *Indian folk-tales.* Madras: Guardian Press.
———. n.d. *Sadāśiva Brahmendra Ātmavidya Vilāsa: An exposition of the science of the soul* (text and trans.) Madras: The Brahmavādin Press.
Sewell, Robert. 1884. *Archaeological survey of southern India: list of inscriptions and sketches of the dynasties of South India* Madras: University of Madras Press.

LEELA PRASAD

SEE ALSO
Colonialism and Folklore; Folklorists

NĀTH

As a group name, *Nāth* may refer to an ascetic sect—renunciatory or *nāga Nāth*s—as well as to a hereditary caste—*grihasthī* or householder Nāths. "Nāth" means "master" in Hindi and the Nāths are understood to be masters of yogic powers. Most scholars treat the terms "Nāth" and "yogī" as interchangeable when dealing with the sect and its teachings; one common designation for the householder castes is *jogī,* a vernacular version of yogī. A yogī is an adept, a practitioner of yoga—from a Sanskrit root meaning "yoke," carrying implications of self-discipline as well as union.

As applied to renouncer members of a religious sect *(sampradāy)*, the category "Nāth" may cover any number of loosely organized associations of renouncers who share certain orientations and practices and who worship Śiva. Nāga Nāths are celibate ascetics whose traditions must be passed on through recruitment and guru-to-disciple transmission. Theoretically, this recruitment has nothing to do with birth-given caste status (*jāti*) but rather draws upon individual decisions to follow a particular path to divinity.

Householder Nāths, found in India and Nepal, are castes whose group identity is rooted in renunciation. Several nineteenth-century British sources attribute low rank and bad reputation to Jogī castes. In general, their image appears to be strongly associated with wandering minstrel-beggars and low-status weavers. A number of Jogī groups are converts to Islam. While members of Nāth castes usually own property and raise families, they retain emblems of identity (such as ochre-colored turbans) as well as certain professions (such as temple service, magical cures, knowledge and performance of hymns and epics concerning Nāth gurus) linking them with their renunciatory heritage. Their death rites are the most distinctive feature of the Nāth caste, setting them apart from other Hindu villagers. Nāths bury their dead near their homes, rather than cremating them outside the village, as is the custom for most other Hindu castes. How did castes of married yogīs come to exist? Oral histories tend to formulate the transformation explicitly as a process of degradation. Householder Nāths are fallen ascetics whose ancestors couldn't resist the blandishments of women and domestic life.

The origins of Nathism dissolve in the mists of a presumed selective merging of Buddhist and Hindu esoteric, ascetic meditation techniques with yoga philosophy that took place somewhere in the 10th or 11th century. A shadowy but imposing figure looming in those mists is Gorakh Nāth (also Goraksa Nāth)—who probably lived, but whose biography is totally overlaid with myth and magic. Although some locate Gorakh's birthplace in Northwestern India and his lore certainly flourished in Punjab and Rajasthan, most cultural historians agree that the real Gorakh lived not later than 1200 C.E. and that he came originally from Eastern Bengal.

There exist numerous and conflicting stories of the origins and guru-to-disciple lineages of the early Nāth gurus. One popular version has Gorakh Nāth a disciple of Macchendra Nāth (also Matsyendra Nāth, Mina Nāth) who obtained his knowledge directly from divine Lord Śiva (known as the Adi-Nāth or original Nāth to yogīs). Great magical feats are told of the legendary "nine Nāths," enumerated differently in different sources, but usually including the better known figures of Bhartharī (also Bhartṛhari), Carpati, Gopī Cand, Gorakh, Jalandhar, Kampha, and Macchendra Nāth. Guga, often worshipped as a deity able to cure snake bites, is another important figure in North Indian Nāth lore.

Nathism is associated with esoteric yoga based on complete control over physiological, mental, and emotional functions. But as Nāth teachings spread within popular Hinduism, both their content and mode of transmission changed. From secret instructions transmitted from guru adept to select disciple, Nāth ideas passed into folklore, publicly performed. There, these teachings are strongly associated with the "perfection of the body" (*kayā siddhi*) and the quest for immortality. Purveyors of Nāth stories all over India are often members of Nāth or yogī castes. What makes this lore distinctive is that it is about renouncers, but plays largely to householders.

Nāth yogīs in popular oral traditions have in common a particular, visible lifestyle outside the domestic and social realms of marriage, work, and caste. Nāth emblems of identity include a begging bowl, a deer-horn instrument, a "sacred thread" made of black wool, iron tongs, wooden sandals, a body smeared with sacred ash, and thick crystal earrings. The earrings are especially important. For Nāths, full initiation is marked by cutting the disciple's ears, and this cut is said to allow a yogī to bring his senses under control. Thus another name for Nāth is *Kanphatā* or "split ear." Nāth figures are represented as dedicated to meditation or divine recitation. All yogīs sit by a campfire—understood as an ascetic act in a tropical climate—with lowered eyelids and repeat divine names. When ordered by the guru to do so, they go into villages, towns, or castles and beg for alms.

An obvious cause-and-effect relationship exists between the lifestyle and miraculous capacities of yogīs. The primary conditions for, if not the sole sources of, yogīs' miraculous powers are their ascetic practices or ardor (*tapas*), often simply construed as unbroken meditation by the campfire. The ability to pursue such activity single-mindedly is in turn grounded in detachment from the worldly snares of women and wealth. Powerful Nāths possess the capacity to perform miracles: they can bring the dead to life and turn rocks to precious metals. Nāths frequently play minor parts in regional tales, epics, and legends where they are not the central heroic figures, but rather assist such heroes in various ways. Thus the renouncer Rūpa Nāth aids the Bagaṛāvat Brothers' war efforts in Rajasthan's martial epic of *Devnārāyan,* while in the Punjabi romance of *Hir Ranjha,* the frustrated lover Ranjha seeks initiation from a Nāth guru so he can pursue his beloved in disguise.

In folkloric representations of Nāths, both a high evaluation of world renunciation, and an appreciation of the sacrifices entailed by acting on that evaluation, are transmitted for the edification and entertainment of householders. The stories provide a kind of interface between two distinguishable, though intricately linked, social and religious universes.

References

Bouillier, Véronique. 1989. *Des prêtres du pouvoir: les yogī et la fonction royale* [Of the priests of power: yogis and the royal function]. *Purusārtha* 12: 193–213.

Briggs, George Weston. 1973. *Gorakhnāth and the Kānphata Yogīs*. Delhi: Motilal Banarsidass.

Gold, Ann Grodzins. 1992. *A carnival of parting: the tales of King Bharthari and King Gopi Chand as sung and told by Madhu Natisar Nath of Ghatiyali, Rajasthan*. Berkeley: University of California Press.

Gold, Daniel, and Ann Grodzins Gold. 1984. The fate of the householder Nath. *History of Religions* 24(2): 113–132.

Mahapatra, Piyushkanti. 1972. *The folk cults of Bengal*. Calcutta: Indian Publications.

Vaudeville, Charlotte. 1974. *Kabīr*. Oxford: Clarendon Press. (See especially Chapter 4, "Kabīr and His Times," pp. 81–119.)

ANN GRODZINS GOLD

SEE ALSO

Ālhā (Ālhā-Udal); Devnārāyan; Gopī Cand; Guga; Hīr Rānjhā; Pābūjī

NATIONALISM AND FOLKLORE

A number of scholars have pointed out that the study of folklore often develops concurrently with the formation of a new nation-state. This has been the case in European countries such as Finland and Hungary, and the notion applies equally well to the countries of South Asia.

Although a number of British and indigenous researchers and collectors published materials on folklore many years prior to the culmination of the freedom movement, it was only towards the end of the nineteenth century that a strong emphasis was placed on folk materials as an emblem of regional and national consciousness. Intellectuals involved in the push for independence felt that creating an awareness of folklore and folklife would revive regional pride and foster a concrete sense of national identity. Moreover, the events surrounding the struggle for freedom also created new folklore in the form of ballads and legends about freedom fighters. Often these genres focused on regional figures who were inivolved in some sort of local conflict, but in a few extraordinary cases, hagiographies concerning pan-Indian figures such as Mahatma Gandhi emerged to provide inspiration for all Indians.

While many proponents of folklore for the sake of nationalism worked locally and had only a regional impact, some, such as Rabindranath Tagore (1861–1941), had a greater influence due to their national and international fame. Consequently, their message spread to other areas of the subcontinent. Because Tagore traveled abroad, he was exposed to freedom movements in other parts of the world as well. For example, his journey to England between 1878 and 1880 exposed him to the colonial plight of the Irish, and when he returned to Calcutta, he took up the cause of freedom wholeheartedly.

Upon returning to England in 1890, Tagore came to realize that the freedom movement had to be grounded in "tradition." By this he meant the linguistic and cultural climate of the Indian people. Realizing the vast diversity within the nation, he attempted to focus his efforts on Bengal. Tagore was deeply concerned about the alienating effects that urbanization had on his fellow Bengalis, and he attempted to remedy the situation by reuniting country and city residents. By doing so, he hoped that essential moral and ethical values would be rediscovered and a clearer sense of identity would result through the propagation of local traditions. As he wrote, "The soil in which we are born . . . is the soil of our village, the mother earth in whose lap we receive our nourishment from day to day. Our educated élite, abstracted from this primal basis, wander about in the high heaven of ideas like aimless clouds removed from this our home" (Kripalini 1980, 155). However romantic this sentiment might be, many Indian intellectuals felt the same way. Romanticism, then, served a clearly defined political purpose for those involved in the freedom movement.

It is with such ideas in mind that Tagore and others began establishing societies and journals for the purpose of reviving self-perceived tradition. Central to this notion was the development of a canon of national literature to be based on folk genres. To this end, Tagore, along with other prominent literary figures, founded the Bengali Literary Society in 1894. Their journal published samples of numerous genres collected by fieldworkers in the region and did much to infuse a strong sense of identity and unity into the local population. Efforts such as this were not limited to Bengal, however, for similar movements sprang up in virtually every part of the country, providing inspiration for freedom fighters in their own languages.

One thing that must be kept in mind is that the majority of those who were responsible for the indigenous development of folklore studies were highly educated individuals who were provided with the finest British education. Their models and theories thus reflected current trends advocated by researchers in Europe. In other words, "folklore," as understood by this class of urban intellectuals, was conditioned by the works of British scholars and civil servants who had been collecting in India for many decades before the freedom movement took shape. Tagore himself was influenced by the folkloric writings of British researchers such as Harry Acworth, James Tod, William Crooke, Herbert Risley, and others who devoted a lifetime to studying Indian folk culture, albeit for imperialistic purposes. The indigenous concept of "folklore," therefore, was based on foreign models, and contrived vernacular terms were coined to create parallels to the English term.

Since Independence, a number of national institutions have been established in each of the South Asian countries to document, collect, and publish the collective folklore of each respective nation. These official institutions still advocate a strong nationalistic stance in an effort to maintain national unity in the face of rising communalism and regionalism. Very few academic institutions with folklore departments exist in South Asia, but as the discipline continues to develop into a mature field of inquiry, we may see a profusion of indigenous theories that will ultimately enrich our overall understanding of the relationship between politics, ideology, and folklore.

References

Amin, Shahid. 1984. Gandhi as Mahatma: Gorakhpur District, Eastern U.P. 1921–2. In *Subaltern Studies III,* ed. Ranajit Guha, 1–61. New Delhi: Oxford University Press.

Haque, A. S. Zaharul. 1981. *Folklore and nationalism in Rabindranath Tagore.* Dacca: Bangla Academy.

Islam, Mazharul. 1982. *A history of folktale collections in India, Bangladesh and Pakistan.* Calcutta: Panchali Prakashan.

Korom, Frank J. 1989. Inventing traditions: folklore and nationalism as historical process in Bengal. In *Folklore and historical process,* eds. D. Rihtman-Auguštin and M. Povrzanović, 57–84. Zagreb: Institute of Folklore Research.

Kripalini, Krishna. 1980. *Rabindranath Tagore: a biography.* Calcutta: Visva-Bharati Publishing Department.

Narayan, Kirin. 1993. Banana republics and V.I. degrees: rethinking Indian folklore in a postcolonial world. *Asian Folklore Studies* 52: 177–204.

FRANK J. KOROM

SEE ALSO

Colonialism and Folklore; Crooke, William C.; Dance; Goddesses, Place, and Identity in Nepal; *Rāmāyaṇa,* TV Production; Tagore, Rabindranath

NAUḤA

Nauḥa (Arabic, dirge) is genre of mourning chant of Shī'a Muslims widely performed during the month of Muḥarram (first month of the Islamic lunar calendar) to commemorate the martyrs of the battle of Karbalā (Iraq, 680 C.E.). Poems in Urdu, and also occasionally Punjabi and other South Asian languages, are recited to simple but poignant melodies that follow the strophic and metric form of the verses. The term nauḥa designates a specific hymn genre, most usually set to a poem in *ghazal* form, but is also used to refer to mourning chants in general. Metric accents may be added to the chanting by regular chest beats (*mātam*). Nauḥa recitation is primarily associated with the mourning assembly (*majlis*), where a soloist is supported by one or two vocal supporters. Women and young girls also chant nauḥa informally at home, while men form chanting groups or "societies" (*anjuman*). These societies recite nauḥa with *mātam* in Muḥarram processions and may also include rhythmic flagellation with chains. Historically, and to this day, nauḥa embodies for Muslims the power of beautiful sound to move listeners to tears.

References

Qureshi, Regula Burckhardt. 1981. Islamic music in an Indian environment: The Shī'a Majlis. *Ethnomusicology* 25(1): 41–71.

———. 1990. Musical gesture and extra-musical meaning: Words and music in the Urdu Ghazal. *Journal of the American Musicological Society* 43(3): 472–496.

REGULA BURCKHARDT QURESHI

SEE ALSO

Ghazal; Majlis; Mātam; Muḥarram

NAUṬAṄKĪ

Nauṭaṅkī is a popular secular theatrical form, once widely circulated among the Hindi and Urdu-speaking villages and towns of northern India. A principal medium of entertainment before films and television, *nauṭaṅkī* combines sophisticated folk singing and drumming, erotic dancing by female artists and transvestites, and dramatic recitation of a large repertoire of stories. It belongs to the class of "traditional" theatre forms that originated in premodern rural contexts, e.g. the *jātrā* of Bengal, *tamāśā* of Maharashtra, *bhavāī* of Gujarat, *khyāl* of Rajasthan, *sāṅg* of Haryana. Most of these forms absorbed urban influences during the colonial period and have assumed significance in regional identity formation since Independence. Although it possesses certain linguistic and musical affinities with *rās līlā* and *rām līlā,* the Hindi-language devotional theatrical forms, nauṭaṅkī is distinguished from these sectarian performances by its syncretistic Indo-Muslim character. Itinerant troupes of professional actors and musicians carried nauṭaṅkī stories across a wide terrain, serving to mediate various aspects of knowledge and ideology as they moved between centers of local culture and more peripheral areas.

Earlier known by the generic term *svāṅg* ("mime," "impersonation"), nauṭaṅkī was probably named after a legendary princess whose tale became prevalent in a distinct musical style in the Punjab and United Provinces in the nineteenth century. To the romance of *Princess Nautanki* were added stories such as *King Gopichand, Devotee Prahlad, Truthsayer Harishchandra,* and *Devotee Puranmal* to form an early corpus. Legends based on romances of Arabic, Persian, or Indo-Islamic origin, such as *Laila Majnun, Shirin Farhad,* and *Benazir Badre Munir* are also evident from the earliest period. The libretti of these dramas, entitled *sāṅgīt*s, were among the first Hindi and Urdu texts to be printed, and copies of them are preserved in the India Office Library and other archives. In the early twentieth century, martial legends from the Ālhā cycle and tales of Rajput chivalry such as *Amar Singh Rathor* joined the core of common plots. Social dramas based on contemporary life appeared around 1920, and new stories continue to be composed, some borrowed from popular films (*Jai Santoshi Ma*), others based on current figures (*Phulan Devi*).

Performance contexts include fairs, religious festivals, weddings, and other celebrations. Troupes may be sponsored by an individual patron or booked for one or more ticketed performances. Troupe personnel include a wide range of castes, among which artisan groups tend to dominate. Audiences are drawn from the semi-urban working class as well as agriculturalists. Women and children do attend performances, although they are discouraged from doing so. Merchant groups based in commercial centers have historically been influential patrons.

Earlier, the entire dramatic portion of the performance was composed of songs and recitative. Later, prose passages and comic skits were interpolated within the main text. An evening's show is generally introduced by a prologue of dance items and comedy. Nauṭaṅkī singing and drumming on the *nagārā* (kettle drums) follow a highly conventionalized format. Prosodic patterns (poetic meters) such as *dohā, caubolā, dauṛ,* and *bahr-e tavīl* underlie the recurrent rhythmic and melodic motifs. Other meters and song types employed range from *ṭhumrī, dādrā,* and *holī* to several types of *lāvanī, śer,* and *ṭheṭar kī dhun* (tunes from Parsi theatre). Spectator participation and encouragement spur the actor-singers to display their vocal skills, executed by prolonging notes in the high register or improvising with florid melismatic passages. A number of distinct Hindustani *rāga*s (melodic types) and *tāla*s (rhythm cycles) are brought into service, although performers may not be cognizant of the nomenclature employed by classically trained musicians.

Stylistically, nauṭaṅkī is divided between two broad traditions associated, respectively, with Hathras and Kanpur. A commercial center in a rich agricultural region, Hathras became the home of a number of *akhāṛā*s, or lineages of folk poets, towards the end of the nineteenth century. Chief among these poets was Indarman, who founded the foremost akhāṛā, which became particularly famous under the leadership of his disciple, Natharam Sharma Gaur. Natharam was a popular actor in both female and male roles, a stage director, and a poet, and he dominated the field until about 1920. Several other important Hathras akhāṛās, such as that of Muralidhar, also flourished in this period, creating the atmosphere of rivalry that stimulated development of the popular art. Kanpur, a military and manufacturing center, began to develop its own brand of nauṭaṅkī around 1910, particularly under Shrikrishna Khatri Pahalvan, who was active as troupe organizer, actor, author, and publisher. His influence extended for forty years or more, during which time nauṭaṅkī absorbed traits of both Parsi theatre and Bombay cinema. Female singers are also said to have entered the nauṭaṅkī stage first in Kanpur. More recently, women have assumed managerial control of a number of companies in the Kanpur area.

With the advent of mass media such as films and television, the performance tradition of nauṭaṅkī began to decline. Live shows, in which songs and dances based on Hindi films predominate, still occur in the countryside of Bihar and Uttar Pradesh. Sāṅgīts continue to be published from Hathras and Kanpur as well as a host of small presses located across north India. Several veteran artists have received national and regional honors. Gulab Bai, an actress from Kanpur, was awarded a Sangeet Natak Akademi prize in 1984. Giriraj Prasad, an exponent of the Hathras style of singing, has made archival recordings for the Sangeet Natak Akademi. All-India Radio has recorded and broadcast a number of nauṭaṅkī artists from its station in Mathura. Other artists have entered the commercial cassette recording industry, which has made available several dozen nauṭaṅkī plays in abbreviated versions. Among films based upon nauṭaṅkī, the most well-known is *Tīsrī Kasam* (The Third Vow), starring Raj Kapoor and Waheeda Rahman, based upon a short story by Phanishwarnath Renu. Dramatists such as Habib Tanvir, Anuradha Kapur, and Urmil Thapaliyal have adopted nauṭaṅkī performance features into their modern productions or made successful adaptations of traditional nauṭaṅkī stories for urban audiences.

References

Gargi, Balwant. 1966. *Folk theater of India*. Seattle: University of Washington Press.

Hansen, Kathryn. 1992. *Grounds for play: the Nautanki Theatre of North India*. Berkeley: University of California Press.

Hansen, Kathryn. 1983. Indian folk traditions and the modern theatre. *Asian Folklore Studies* 42(1): 77–89.

Hansen, Kathryn. 1983. *Sultana the dacoit and Harishchandra:* two popular dramas of the Nautanki tradition of North India. *Modern Asian Studies* 17(2): 313–331.

Richmond, Farley P., Darius L. Swann, and Phillip Zarrilli, eds. 1990. *Indian theatre: traditions of performance*. Honolulu: University of Hawaii Press.

Vatsyayan, Kapila. 1980. *Traditional Indian theatre: multiple streams*. New Delhi: National Book Trust.

KATHRYN HANSEN

SEE ALSO

Ālhā (Ālhā-Udal); Bhavai; Gopi Cand; *Jātrā/Yātrā; Prahlāda Nāṭaka; Rām Līlā; Rāsa Līlā; Tamāśa;* Theater and Drama

NAVĀNNA/NABĀNNA

Navānna, meaning, literally, "new rice," is a festival in which the freshly harvested rice is offered to the village gods and goddesses before it is consumed by the people. It is a ceremony celebrated in many parts of India, wherever paddy is the most important crop. People celebrate the festival in accordance with the harvesting time of that region. It is celebrated in South Bihar and Orissa and West Bengal in the month of September-October. In Chattisgarh and Bundelkhand region of Madhya Pradesh and also in Himachal Pradesh, it is celebrated after Dīpāvalī (November). In Tamil Nadu, the new rice ceremony is called *Ponkal* and the festival is held on the first day of the Tamil month Tai (January-February), when the sun begins its journey northwards, which also coincides with the beginning of the rice harvest.

In the tribal areas of Western Orissa, celebration of Navānna is the most significant festival of the year, celebrated in all villages, by everyone, irrespective of age, gender, caste, and creed. People in this region celebrate the occasion during the month of September (Bhadrava), on an auspicious day determined by the village priest (*jhānkar,* or *jāni*), between the third day and the thirteenth day in the fortnight of the waxing moon (*sukla pakshya*).

On the day of *Navānna,* the jhānkar goes to a selected field to get the new paddy. After reaping paddy from the field, he collects some *kurei* leaf (Sanskrit, *kutaja patra*) from the *kutaja* tree (*Holarrhena antidysenterica*) and comes to the temple (*guḍi*) of the village goddess.

The women of the village paint their houses with *ratā māṭi* (red soil), wash all the clothes, utensils, and materials of the household, and decorate the walls with paintings. Then the new rice is husked from the paddy and boiled along with milk and sugar to prepare a new-rice dish called *nuāchoul,* which is offered on a *kurei* leaf to the goddess by the jhānkar, acting on the part of the whole village. The jhānkar also makes a kind of porridge, called *jokhā,* out of new rice, milk, and sugar, which is regarded as a festive food. This, too, is then offered to the goddesses. The villagers then worship their tutelary deity and ancestral spirits (*ḍumā*) in their respective houses, in a similar fashion. The head of the family conducts the worship and ritual in his house.

Each member of the family is served nuāchoul on a kurei leaf, and it is eaten with both reverence and satisfaction. Generally, this meal is taken at an auspicious time (*māhendra belā*) and preferably before noon. All the members of the family wear new clothes. Later they prepare other festive foods and distribute them among the neighbors.

Younger people, irrespective of age, gender, and caste, pay obeisance (*juhār*) to the village elders. Young boys and girls gather and perform folk dances accompanied by music, songs, and games.

The second day of Navānna is called *bāsi*. The day is celebrated by drinking liquor and communal feasting. The first day of Navānna is considered sacred *(sātwika),* while the bāsi is considered passionate *(rājasika).*

References

Das, K. B. and L. K. Mahapatra. 1993. *Folklore of Orissa*. New Delhi: National Book Trust.

Parmar, Shyam. 1981. *Folklore of Madhya Pradesh.* New Delhi: National Book Trust.

MAHENDRA KUMAR MISHRA

SEE ALSO
Calendrical Ceremonies and Rites; *Dīvālī/Dīpāvalī;* Madhya Pradesh and Chattīsgaṛh; *Ponkal;* Tribal Folklore

NAVARĀTRI

Navarātri ("nine nights") is a festival celebrated primarily in honor of Durgā and to a lesser extent, Rāma, in many parts of India. Religious texts speak of two periods of Navarātri, coninciding roughly with the spring and autumn equinoxes. The autumn Navarātri is the only one known by this name now, and the celebrations lasting nine nights and ten days (*Dasara*) start on the first day after the new moon in the month of Aśvina (Tamil: *Puraṭṭāci;* circa September 15 to October 14). It is a time of ritual military exercises, patronage of performing arts, and worshipping Durgā either in consecrated dolls and images or in the form of young virgin girls. While the Goddess Durgā (Sanskrit: "inaccessible") is worshipped in many parts of India, the goddesses Sarasvatī, Lakṣmī, and Durgā are all worshipped in Tamilnadu and Karnataka. Durgā's martial victory over the buffalo demon Mahiṣa is particularly remembered, and she is worshipped for military success by royal families and warriors. In Uttar Pradesh and other parts of northern India, the story of Rāma from the epic *Rāmāyaṇa* is enacted during the nine nights, and on the tenth day, Rāma emerges victorious from his battle with Rāvaṇa.

Origin

Although Durgā is praised by Yudhiṣṭhira and Arjuna in the *Mahābhārata,* the full story of Durgā as the slayer of the buffalo demon is found in the *Devī Mahātmya* (circa ninth-tenth century C.E.) which is part of the *Markandeya Purāṇa,* and the *Devi Bhāgavata Purāṇa* (circa sixth century C.E.). First century terra-cotta representations of a four-armed goddess riding a lion and slaying a buffalo found in Nagar, Rajasthan, may indicate the prevalence of this story and Durgā worship in the centuries prior to the Common Era. Apparently, the demon Mahiṣa was undefeated, and the gods Brahmā, Viṣṇu, and Śiva combined their energies to create Durgā. She manifested herself as a beautiful warrior, took a different form for nine days, and ultimately killed the demon. Theological discourses sometimes identify Mahiṣa with the potent power of ignorance and lust in human beings.

Modes of Celebration

Historical narratives including accounts by western travellers during the time of the Vijayanagara empire in South India (circa fifteenth century C.E.) give us details of the celebrations in the royal courts. Both these and Sanskrit texts speak about the importance of animal sacrifices, especially a goat or buffalo, to Durgā. People of all castes celebrate *Navarātri,* and regional differences are more important than caste differences. In the twentieth century, royal celebrations have been replaced in popularity by domestic and neighborhood festivities. In West Bengal, people from local communities consecrate and worship enormous images of Durgā, take the goddess in a procession, and, on the tenth day, submerge her in water. Concerts, recitation and fairs mark the ten days. Married daughters return to their natal homes for the celebrations. The beneficent and fecund Devi (goddess), represented by a flame, is worshipped in Gujarat. A lamp is kept in a clay pot (*garbhī,* "womb") with several holes, and women dance around it through the nine nights. Dances representing the *rās līlā* of Kṛṣṇa and his cowherd friends are also popular in Gujarat, and among Gujarati people in the diaspora. The fertility theme is reinforced in other rituals. In many parts of India, nine plants, kept in a pot of water, are placed over a bed of mixed grain, and the pot is worshipped as the creative energies of the goddess. The sprouted grain is immersed in a local river or lake. In Maharashtra and other states, Durgā or Lakṣmī is invoked to reside in a jar of water, and this filled jar is worshipped as a symbol of the Goddess's life-giving propensity. Following texts such as the *Skanda Purāṇā,* women from Punjab and Uttar Pradesh invite nine virgin girls under the age of nine to their houses, honor them, and give them gifts of clothing.

The story of Durgā and Mahiṣa is enacted in Tamilnadu and Bengal, with effigies and human beings playing the key roles. In Ramnagar (near Benares, Uttar Pradesh), the story of Rāma is acted out by prepubescent boys in celebrations known as the *Rām Līlā* (the joyful sport of Rāma). While the religious dimension of the festival in Tamilnadu, Karnataka, and Andhra Pradesh focusses on the worship of the goddesses Lakṣmī, Sarasvatī, and Durgā (representing wealth, wisdom, and physical strength), ritually, it is a celebration where women take on leadership roles. The ceremonies revolve around a nine-day domestic "festival of dolls" (Tamil: *kolu;* Telugu: *bommala koluvu,* or "a courtly display of dolls;" Kannada: *gombe puje,* or "worship of dolls"). Although generally celebrated by Brahmins and merchant/business communities, it is also practiced by a cross-section of other castes. The dolls are made of clay, wood, and metal and include religious and secular figures. They are placed on seven or nine steps covered with white cloth. For the nine days the area is treated as the family shrine, and the dolls are considered to be consecrated. Parks, schools, stores, and scenes from everyday life may also be arranged on the floor. While the origins of the festival can be traced to the invocation of divine beings into goddess images and the display of traditional mythological themes, secular dolls have been exhibited at least for the two centuries. Social themes have gained in prominence in postcolonial India and serve to raise people's consciousness on issues such as India's independence movement and even family planning. The displays are put up by the entire family, with women deciding the main themes. During the nine days, women visit each other's houses, receive the auspicious *kumkum* (red powder applied on the forehead by married women) and turmeric seeds (markers of a married state), sing or play classical music, especially songs to Devī.

References

Coburn, Thomas B. 1984. *Devi Mahatmya: The crystallization of the goddess tradition.* Delhi: Motilal Banarsidass.
Kane, Pandurang Vaman. 1958. Durgotsava. In *History of Dharmaśastra,* Vol. V, Pt. 1, 154–187. Poona: Bhandarkar Oriental Research Institute.
Ostor, Akos. 1980. The festival of the goddess. In *The play of the gods: locality, ideology, structure, and time in the festivals of a Bengali town.* Chicago: University of Chicago Press.
Schechner, Richard, and Linda Hess. 1977. The Ramlila of Ramnagar. *The drama review* 21(3): 51–81.
Sivapriyananda, Swami. 1995. *Mysore royal dasara.* New Delhi: Abhinav Publications.

VASUDHA NARAYANAN

SEE ALSO
Bhagavati Ritual; Buffalo; *Dāsara;* Goddesses, Hindu; Rām Līlā; *Rāmāyaṇa*

NEPAL

Who will see the peacock's dance in the jungle?
(Nepali proverb)

The kingdom of Nepal began to emerge 220 years ago, when the king of Gorkha, one of many petty hill states, embarked on the conquest of his neighbors, successfully conquering the Newari cities of the Kathmandu Valley in 1769. That king, Prithvi Narayan Shah, described his kingdom as "a flower garden of four castes and thirty-six subcastes" *(cār varṇa chattis jātko phūlbārī),* an impression that figuratively conveys Nepal's ethnic distinctions and cultural diversity. Despite an area of only 55,000 square miles, Nepal's twenty million inhabitants form dozens of distinct ethnic groups. More than thirty-five different languages, many of which have multiple, mutually unintelligible dialects, are spoken.

Well-known ethnic groups include Newar, Sherpa, Rai, Limbu, Sunuwar, Dhimal, Santal, Yolmo, Tamang, Gurung, Thakali, Raji, Chantel, Magar, Chepang, Tharu, and Raute. Geographically widespread are the "Brahman-Chetris," as Nepali-speaking castes throughout the kingdom are euphemistically called—a synecdochal designation that conveniently ignores the majority, who are of ritually impure castes. Other groups, particularly those along the Tibetan border, are most often identified by their area of residence—as residents of Dolpa, Mustang, Manang, Mugu, or Humla—while other groups along the Indian border tend to be identified by their language—as Maithili, Rajbangsi, or Bhojpuri speakers. Lowland languages tend to belong to the Indo-Aryan family, while languages of the hills tend to be Tibeto-Burman, a distinction that roughly correlates with Hindu or Buddhist religious practices, although clear distinctions between the two are often blurred.

Nepal's folk traditions overlap with those of India and Tibet, but due to the long geographic isolation of Himalayan communities, and the particular success of Nepal as a nation at keeping out both colonialists and missionaries, each group within Nepal maintains distinct, extensive, diverse, and complex folklore traditions. Unfortunately, both the orally transmitted knowledge and the material culture of common people, as opposed to that of various sorts of specialists (particularly religious and political authorities), have been neglected topics of research. There are many topics, including children's games (*keṭākeṭīkokhel*), riddles (*gau khāne kathā*), nursery rhymes (*bālakbitā*), jingles and clichés (*tukkā*), insults (*mānhani*), dream omens (*sapanāko apasabya*), gestures (*hāwabhāwa*), jokes (*ṭhaṭṭā*), gambling and betting methods (*jūwā khelnu, bājī thāpnu*), or the extraordinary social satires published and performed for the festival of Gai Jātrā (an annual festival occurring every spring), for which no published studies exist.

Work done on more standard components of "folklore" systems consists primarily of collections of legends, proverbs, and songs, few of which have been translated into English, in Nepali and local languages. Collections of stories that have appeared in translation, like those published in Nepali, present the material wrenched from its social context, with little regard for the caste, ethnicity, gender, or status of the sources, and inevitably "polished" into elegant literary texts that conceal their oral origins. Without information on informants and their social situations, much

Katmandu pagoda–detail of temple guardian sacred animals, representing levels of consciousness. Katmandu, Nepal, © Anthroarcheart.org

of this material is reduced to curious tales and fragments of seemingly bizarre knowledge, curiosities that contribute little to our understanding of Nepal's peoples or their cultures. But elements of folk tradition can contribute significantly to the ways that Nepal's cultures are understood and how they are changing. For Nepalese folklore studies to advance significantly, there is a strong need for a well-documented folklore archive in Nepal; such a store of information would contribute significantly to Nepalese cultural, religious, linguistic, and historical studies, as well as help preserve a rich cultural heritage. A crucial proposal for a comprehensive Nepal Encyclopedia (*Nepāl jyānko*) languishes at the Royal Nepal Academy for lack of official funding, as successive governments show little concern for the country's heritage, conflating "modernity" and "development" with an abandonment of the past.

Folk speech is one area with a great deal of collected material; however, little systematic analysis has been done to explain its social and contextual meanings. Even without exhaustive studies or thorough inventories, well documented collections could contribute much to an understanding of Nepalese culture, for elements of folklore can reveal, for example, sweeping principles of Nepalese social organization, such as gender hierarchies or embedded caste tensions, as well as contrasts between social expectations of different ethnic groups. For example, the prevailing practice among Nepali speakers, but not among speakers of Tibeto-Burman languages, of a woman never uttering any man's name, not even her husband's (as revealed in the common Nepali proverb: "When co-wives are angry, they use their husband's name"), succinctly demonstrates the lower social status of women in these groups, even as it records the practice of polygamy. Other common proverbs, such as "If you have no other work, daughter-in-law, go scratch the calf," or "The father and mother-in-law order the daughter-in-law, the daughter-in-law orders the dog, the dog wags its tail," succinctly reveal prevailing principles of family hierarchies, in which daughters-in-law find themselves at the bottom in patrilocal households.

Other common sayings, such as that to sneeze while eating indicates that you've been touched by an untouchable (so that someone should immediately sprinkle you with water before you resume the meal), reveal embedded caste prejudices. Stereotypes of castes such as that all Brāhman (priests) are greedy, Ṭhakurī (royalty) ostentatious, Magar (a western Nepal group who eat pork) filthy, and Newar (often found as traders throughout the kingdom) untrustworthy, are also topics well represented in many Nepali proverbs. A few examples include:

Yogurt where? A Brahman there!
If bananas are supplied, a Brahman's big-eyed.
A Ṭhakurī brags with what he wears, a Magar brags with how he fares.
In a pig's stomach, the Magar's stool; in a Magar's stomach, the pig.
Never a father offend or a Newar befriend.
By a Ṭhakurī guaranteed, a staff of reed. [That both break when put to the test.]

In a similar fashion, elements of a folk psychology begin to emerge from the emotions revealed in many folk lyrics, even without much direct evidence of their particular contexts of expression. The Khas (Matwālī Chetri of Western Nepal) have a tradition of song competitions between young men and women, in which the first lines are parts of a standard repertoire, the second line improvised. From such songs, we discover the value of romantic and illicit love in a society often represented as lacking it and a more flirtatious orientation than the doctrines of arranged marriage would suggest:

Horses and sheep bring salt from Talakhar;
without a lover there's no pleasure, neither near nor far.

Take the buffalo up the ridge, there it will find grass at that place;
when my mind turns to you, the tears stream down my face.

The Karnali flows so quietly, the Bheri noisily churns;
my heart loses its rhythm, when to you it turns.

Many anthropological and religious studies conducted within Nepal do contain numerous bits of folklore, but these fragments are often widely scattered within each publication, and overshadowed by the researcher's theoretical concerns. The material is rarely identified by the genre of folklore it may represent, making it difficult to locate. However, for any particular community, the ethnographic literature does offer the best starting point. Of particular note are the exemplary works of John Locke, with their thorough and accurate presentation of detail documenting traditional monastic organization and religious observances of Newars of the Kathmandu valley.

Folk medicine and studies of shamans are two areas of Nepalese studies in which somewhat more progress has been made than in other genres of folklore. A series of anthropological studies based on an appreciation of local medicinal beliefs and shaman oral traditions all demonstrate the close connections between language, belief, and sociocultural practices. The careful documentation of context found in these works shows that meaningful social worlds are created and maintained through minute details, and that, conversely, such details must be understood within that context if their meaningfulness is to be preserved.

Indigenous urban architecture of the Kathmandu Valley is another area that has been well documented, even as its subject rapidly disappears under the onslaught of "modernization." Also of note is the documentation of ethnic music, an area of study that has recently made considerable progress. An internationally sponsored department of music devoted to practice, preservation, and performance of traditional repertoires has been created, linked to Kathmandu University. Possibly this program will provide a model for the urgently needed conservation and encouragement of other areas of Nepal's threatened cultural heritage.

References

Bennett, Lynn. 1983. *Dangerous wives and sacred sisters: social and symbolic roles of high-caste women in Nepal.* New York: Columbia University Press.

Crooke, William. 1986 [1884]. *Introduction to the popular religion and folklore of Northern India.* rev. ed. London: Archibald.

Desjarlais, Robert R. 1992. *Body and emotion: the aesthetics of illness and healing in the Nepal Himalayas.* Philadelphia: University of Pennsylvania Press.

Diwas, Tulsi, ed. 1975. V. S. 2032. *Nepālī Lokkathā* (The folk tales of Nepal). Kathmandu: Royal Nepal Academy.

Fīrer-Haimendorf, C. von. 1964. *The Sherpas of Nepal: Buddhist Highlanders.* London: John Murray.

Gellner, David N. 1992. *Monk, householder, and Tantric priest: Newar Buddhism and its hierarchy of ritual.* Cambridge: Cambridge University Press.

Höfer, András. 1981. *Tamang ritual texts.* 1*: Preliminary studies in the folk religion of an ethnic minority in Nepal.* Wiesbaden: Franz Steiner Verlag.

———. 1994. *A recitation of the Tamang Shaman in Nepal.* Bonn: Wissenschaftsverlag.

Holmberg, David. 1989. *Order in paradox: myth, ritual and exchange among Nepal's Tamang.* Ithaca, N.Y.: Cornell University Press.

Josi, Satyamohan. 1958. *Chūnākh (ukhānko)* [Chūnākh (of proverbs)]. Kantipur: Saraswati Press.

Lall, Kesar. 1991. *Gods and mountains: the folk culture of a Himalayan kingdom,* Nepal. Jaipur: Nirala Publications.

Levy, Robert I. 1991. *Mesocosm: Hinduism and the organization of a traditional Newar city in Nepal.* Berkeley: University of California Press.

Lienhard, Siegfried, ed. 1984[1974]. *Songs of Nepal: an anthology of Nevar folksongs and hymns.* rev. ed. Honolulu: University of Hawaii Press.

Locke, John K. 1980. *Karunamaya: the cult of Avalokitesvara-Matsyendranath in the Valley of Nepal.* Kathmandu: Sahayogi Prakashan.

———. 1985. *Buddhist Monasteries of Nepal.* Kathmandu: Sahayogi Prakashan.

Maskarinec, Gregory G. 1998. *Nepalese Shaman oral texts.* Cambridge: Harvard University Press.

Oakley, E. S., and Tara Dutt Gairola. 1935. *Himalayan folklore: Kumaon and West Nepal.* Allahabad: Superintendent, Printing and Stationary, United Provinces.

Oppitz, Michael. 1991. *Onkels tochter, keine sonst* [Uncle's daughter, no one else]. Frankfurt am Main: Suhrkamp.

Ortner, Sherry B. 1978. *Sherpas through their rituals.* Cambridge: Cambridge University. Press.

Pignède, Bernard. 1966. *Les Gurungs: une population himalayenne du Népal* (The Gurungs: A Himalayan People of Nepal). Paris: Mouton.

Shrestha, Hari, ed. 1974. VS 2031. [*Nepālī lok gīt* Nepali Folk Songs]. Kathmandu: Royal Nepal Academy.

Stone, Linda. 1988. *Illness beliefs and feeding the dead in Hindu Nepal: an ethnographic analysis.* Lewiston, N.Y.: E. Mellen.

Toffin, Gérard. 1984. *Société et religion chez les Néwar du Népal* (Society and Religion of the Newar of Nepal). Paris: Editions du Centre National de la Recherche Scientifique.

GREGORY G. MASKARINEC

SEE ALSO

Ballad, Nepal; Caste and State, India and Nepal; Dance, Nepal; *Dhāmī;* Epic, Nepal; Folk Music, Nepal; Folktale, Nepal; Goddesses, Place, and Identity in Nepal; Malignant Spirits, Nepal; Riddles, Nepal; Shamanism, Nepal; *Silok;* Song, Nepal; Supernatural Beings, Nepal; *Tukkā; Ukhān;* Witches, Nepal

NORTH-WEST FRONTIER PROVINCE

The North-West Frontier Province (NWFP), created by the British in 1901 from parts of the Punjab, is Pakistan's third-largest province in population and its smallest in area.

Pashto, an Indo-Iranian language, is the NWFP's most commonly spoken home language (sixty-eight percent in 1982); its speakers are Pashtuns or, in Hindustani and English usage, Pathans; "Afghan" is sometimes applied to Pashto speakers whether from Pakistan or Afghanistan. Pashto is divided into two major dialect divisions, soft and hard; Pakhtu and Pakhtun indicate hard-dialect pronunciation for the language and its speakers, respectively. Adjacent to the NWFP are the seven Federally Administered Tribal Areas (FATA), which are culturally and linguistically Pashtun (almost one hundred percent) and sometimes with quite distinctive dialects.

Hindko, an Indo-Aryan language, is the NWFP's second most commonly spoken home language (eighteen percent in 1982, when Pakistan's census first recognized it as a separate language rather than grouped with Punjabi). It is the majority language in Hazara District and in the merchant community of the old city of Peshawar, the NWFP's capital. In Chitral, the NWFP's largest district in area, at least eight languages (Khowar, Yidgha, Phalura, Kalasha, Dameli, Eastern Kativiri and Kamviri/Shekhai, and Gawar-bati), are spoken; in the NWFP's second-largest district, Kohistan ("Land of Mountains"), different varieties of Kohistani predominate. Gujari speakers (Gujars) are found in scattered communities of the NWFP; originally pastoral nomads, they are now often transhumant or settled agriculturists. The Summer Institute of Linguistics' studies provide brief histories of the speakers of languages they have surveyed for shared vocabulary; the remarks on bi- and multilingualism afford insights into paths for transmission of oral cultural phenomena between linguistically distinct populations where Pashto and Urdu are the common second and sometimes third languages. In Peshawar, the Persian-speaking communities date from at least the nineteenth century; the influx of refugees from Afghanistan in the 1980s and 1990s has greatly augmented the number of Persian speakers in the NWFP.

The Pashtun culture has been the most extensively examined of the diverse linguistic groups within the NWFP. Its tribal society with a code of conduct (*pashtūnwalī*) where high value is given to honor (*nang*) and revenge (*badal*), hospitality (*melmastiyā*) and rights to refuge (*nanawāta*), and the patrilineal society with the rivalry for inheritance between patrilateral male cousins (*tarbūr*) that has been extensively examined by anthropologists. For Swat, a princely state until 1969, Barth's pioneering work and Lindholm's later study provide a detailed picture of the Yusufzai Pashtuns. The Durand line, drawn by the British between Afghanistan and Pakistan, resulted in some tribes having traditional territories in both countries. Similarly, within Pakistan, some tribes live both in the settled areas and the tribal areas (FATA). Akbar Ahmed compares the economy, society, and cultural values of the Mohmand tribe living in both the tribal and the settled regions.

Except for the Kalasha, relatively little attention has been given to non-Pashtun communities of the NWFP by Western scholars. The mountain ranges such as the Hindukush, where many non-Pashtun communities exist, form the focus of publication series and conference proceedings, which help to fill this gap. Hindko has been treated as a western dialect of Punjabi, and hence its speakers have received little attention as a distinct community.

Collections

Thorburn, a British civil servant, collected two ballads of the Marwat tribe, and fifty translated and condensed short tales which he classifed as (a) humorous and moral, (b) comic and jocular, and (c) fables. He comments that the best storytellers were itinerant low-caste professionals (*dums*) traveling with music instruments (*rabāb* or *sarinda*). Darmesteter's collection of folk verse from areas now in Pakistan includes religious, romantic, and martial narratives ("ballades") as well as other forms of verse. Malyon's ten folktales were collected from Pashto hard-dialect regions.

Pakistan's Folk Heritage Institute, Lok Virsa, has published a variety of volumes for the NWFP. Hamdani's martial tales include forty-one Pashto texts followed by Urdu versions and comments on sources; the tales range from a story about the early days of Islam to several about Pashtun heroes in the British period; versions of six of Hamdani's tales were among the fourteen sung verse narratives translated by Heston and Nasir. Ghazanvi's thirty-one romantic tales are organized by regions within and adjoining the NWFP; some stories are deeply rooted in Pashtun tradition and found in both folk and literary forms; others relate to events in the more recent past and are not from the Pashto traditions. Bukhārī's collection includes folk songs in Pashto, Hindko from four regions, Gujari, Kohistani, and Pashto of Pawindas (nomads) with Urdu translations. Hamdani's Hindko *chārbaita* collection with Urdu translations includes notes about the poets who wrote the verses and performance of them; Lok Virsa also recorded an audiocassette of the singing of some verses in this collection.

Proverbs were one of the earliest forms of collected oral literature in Pashto. More recently, the Pashto Academy published two large volumes of proverbs collected by M. N. Tair; the 1975 volume contains over six hundred pages of Pashto proverbs with Urdu translations. Ample anecdotal evidence since the nineteenth century illustrates the importance of being able to quote a particular Pashto proverb (*matal*). Bartlotti's study includes extensive examples of the uses of proverbs for negotiating Pashtun values, particularly in the context of Islam. Mukhtar Alī's Collection of almost three hundred Hindko proverbs includes accompanying explanatory comments.

Oral Transmission

In Pashtun areas, the traditional locus for the transmission of poetry, whether narrative or lyric, is the *hujra*. Talented amateurs sing informally accompanied by their friends. For other occasions, professional musicians are hired. Baily's video recording shows a typical hiring of a singer and accompanists in a Peshawar bazaar, their transport to the festive site, and the enthusiasm of the guests who fire weapons and dance spontaneously. The best-known Pashto dance form is the *aṭaṇ;* costumed groups perform at cultural festivals and have been filmed by Lok Virsa.

The gender-segregated nature of Pashtun life has left few records of women as either audience or storyteller. Housing arrangements in purdah-observing families often permit women to hear a performance done for men while remaining unseen by them. Informal networks, especially of kinship, as well as the employment of women as teachers of the Qur'ān and reciters of religious poetry provide other avenues for transmission. Women have their own songs for special occasions, which they sing in their own domain, often playing a type of tambourine (*tambal*) as a rhythmic accompaniment; female professional female musicians may also be invited to perform. Grima's study of Pashtun women's performance of life-story narratives draws attention to the ethnopoetic use of language in a particular cultural environment.

The development of audiocassette technology in the 1980s expanded the potential audiences for narrative and nonnarrative singing of Pashto poetry; a variety of forms are available in bazaars through the NWFP. Heston (1991) examines the relationship between printed verse and audiocassettes for folk poets in the NWFP. Audiocassettes of folk songs and *ghazal*s in Hindko have been produced by Pakistan's Folk Heritage Institute as well as commercial companies in the NWFP and Karachi.

Local TV stations have Pashto programs that have included the retelling of folk narratives as well as singing various forms of verse; probably the most popular Pashto songs are ghazals. Pakistan's movie industry produces films in Pashto; a number of early films were about romantic or martial folk heroes and became available as videocassettes.

Printed Popular Literature

Among the NWFP's languages, only Persian and Pashto have a written tradition before Pakistan's independence. For some NWFP languages, standard alphabets still need to be devised. Narrative Pashto folk petry has been printed in chapbooks since the nineteenth century and continues to flourish. Some tales, such as the originally Arabic Layla and Majnun, the originally Persian stories of Bahram and Gul-andam and of Shirin and Farhad, and the tale of Gul and Sanobar are well documented in other languages of South Asia. Other short tales, generally in prose, include stories of Mullā Nasir-al-din and tales from the Arabian Nights. In addition to narrative verse, Pashto chapbooks include other forms such as the tappa and chārbayta. Different versions of the romance of Yūsuf (Joseph) and Zulaykha are perhaps the most frequently retold of Pashto romances; various sections of the Karbalā story (in verse) as well as the adventures of Amīr Ḥamza (usually in prose) are also found in Pashto chapbooks. Some devotional chapbooks are comprised entirely of the verses labeled *na't* or *hamd*. Except for a few chapbooks in Persian, no NWFP language except Pashto has yet been popular enough for chapbook printing.

Religious Observances

The NWFP is ninety-nine percent Muslim and observes the Islamic holidays and most rites of passage celebrated elsewhere in Pakistan; the only significant religious community in the non-Abrahamic tradition is the Kalasha. Although the Pashtuns are predominately Sunnī, Peshawar has a Shī'a community with Muḥarram rituals that include parades through the city streets and recitations of religious poetry in languages including Pashto, Hindko, Persian, and Urdu. At Sūfī shrines throughout the NWFP, informal singing of Sūfī poetry can be heard; the tomb of the classical Pashto Sūfī poet, Rahman Baba, on the outskirts of Peshawar, has frequent gatherings; his verses are popular throughout the province and can be heard on TV and cassette tapes.

Material Culture

Except for the Kalasha community, the prevailing dress for both men and women in the NWFP is the *kamīz-shalwar* common elsewhere in Pakistan. For men, the colors are usually browns, grays, and blues, and grays; cool weather brings the addition of a sleeveless woolen vest and the flat woolen hat with a rolled brim (*pakol*) sometimes referred to in the U.S. as a mujāhidīn cap. Other headwear includes a flat-topped brimless cap with rows of stitching often of the same color around the side; the turban, mentioned in folk poetry and proverbs, is also worn, particularly in less urbanized areas. In colder weather, a wool blanket worn like a shawl, wrapped over the shoulders and perhaps also the head, is traditional in rural areas where it has not been replaced by a Western jacket.

Women's kamīz-shalwars are of more varied color and patterns depending on the occasion and income of the wearer; in rural and tribal areas they tend to be looser and made from heavier fabrics. Outside the house, a shawl (*tsador*) of about three by six feet is worn over the head and often pulled up to partially cover the face. The shawls vary in fabric and decoration according to the occasion. In conservative families, outside the house, a woman may be covered from head to toe by a *burqa,* often in blue or gold; a loose mesh insert over her eyes permits her to see without being seen. The NWFP burqas are often tightly pleated so that the wearers are said to resemble a shuttlecock.

Swat and Hazara are known for their *phūl-kārī* shawls which are traditionally satin-stitched geometric or stylized floral patterns, usually in bright colors. Swat's wooden furniture, pillars and doorways are deeply carved and blackened. These handicrafts are being replaced by modern manufactures, but museums in Pakistan are preserving fine examples of both.

Pashtuns are skilled in hand working of metals; men's love for their guns appears in both classical and folk poetry. Pashtun skills in copying imported weaponry have been noted for over a century.

Pashtuns active in transport have contributed to the colorful painted trucks, often with added metal medallions, that ply the roads from Afghanistan to Karachi. In Peshawar and smaller cities, the three-wheeled motor-rickshaws that function as taxis have appliques of plastic material on the top and sides protecting the passengers and adding color to urban streets; in more rural areas where two-wheeled horse-drawn tongas are used, they too often have some painted, stitched, or riveted decorative elements.

References

Ahmed, Akbar S. 1980. *Pukhtun economy and society.* London: Routledge Kegan Paul.

Akbar, Mohammad. 2000. North West Frontier Province, In *South Asia, the Indian subcontinent,* Alison Arnold ed. (The Garland Encyclopedia of World Music, Vol. 5). New York: Garland.

Baily, John. 1990. *The making of Amir: an Afghan refugee musician's life in Peshawar, Pakistan: a study guide to the film.* Watertown, Mass.: Documentary Educational Resources.

———. 1985. *Amir: an afghan refugee musician's life in Peshawar, Pakistan.* United Kingdom: Royal Anthropological Institute and National Film and Televisions School. Videorecording.

Barth, Fredrik. 1959. *Political leadership among Swat Pathans* (Monograph on Social Anthropology, No. 19, London School of Economics). London: Atalone Press; reprinted with corrections, 1965.

Bartlotti, Leonard N. 2000. Negotiating Pakhto: Proverbs, Islam and the construction of identity among Pashtuns. Ph.D. diss., University of Wales, 2000.

Bukhārī, Fÿrigh. 1974. *Sar-haddī ke Lok Gīt* (Frontier Folk Songs). Islamabad: Pakistan National Council of the Arts.

Darmesteter, James. 1888–1890. *Chants populaires des Afghans.* Paris: Imprimerie nationale.

Decker, Kendall. 1992. *Languages of Chitral. Sociolinguistic Survey of Northern Pakistan,* Vol. V. Islamabad: National Institute of Pakistan Studies and Summer Institute of Linguistics: High Wycombe (England).

Ghazanvi, Khatir. 1978. *Sar-ḥaddi-Rūmānī kahāniya* (Romantic Tales from Frontier). Islamabad: Institute of Folk Heritage.

Grima, Benedicte. 1992. *The performance of emotion among Paxtun women: the misfortunes which have befallen me.* Austin: University of Texas Press.

Hallberg, Daniel. 1992. *Pashto, Waneci, Ormuri.* Sociolinguistic Survey of Northern Pakistan, Vol. I. Islamabad: National Institute of Pakistan Studies and Summer Institute of Linguistics: High Wycombe (England).

Hamdani, Raza. 1978. *Chārbaita.* Islamabad: Lok Virsa.

———. 1981. *Razmiya Dāstānen.* (Razmia Dastanain [epics]) Islamabad: Lok Virsa.

Heston, Wilma. 1991. Footpath Poets of Peshawar. In *Gender, genre, and power in South Asian expressive traditions,* edited by Arjun Appadurai, Frank J. Korom, and Margaret A. Mills, 305–343. Philadelphia: University of Pennsylvania Press.

Heston, Wilma, and Nasir, Mumtaz. 1988. *The bazaar of the Story-tellers.* Islamabad: Lok Virsa.

Lindholm, Charles. 1982. *Generosity and jealousy: the Swat Pakhtun of Northern Pakistan.* New York: Columbia University Press.

Maggi, Wynne. 2001. *Our women are free: gender and ethnicity in the Hindukush.* Ann Arbor: University of Michigan Press.

Malyon, F. D. 1912. *Some current Pushto folk stories.* Memoirs of the Asiatic Society of Bengal, Vol. 3, Calcutta. English

translation only reprinted as *Pushto folk stories*. Islamabad: Institute of Folk Heritage, 1980.
Mukhtar 'Alī "Nayyar". 1974. *Mahatalā̱n: Hindko zarbulmasāl*. Peshawar: Maktabah-yi Hindko zabān.
Proceedings of the second international Hindukush Cultural Conference, edited by Elena Bashir and Israr-ud-Din, 1996. Karachi: Oxford University Press.
Rensch, Calvin, Sandra J. Decker, and Daniel Hallberg. 1992. *Languages of Kohistan.* Sociolinguistic Survey of Northern Pakistan, Vol. I. Islamabad: National Institute of Pakistan Studies and Summer Institute of Linguistics: High Wycombe (England).
Rensch, Calvin, Calinda E. Hallberg, and Clare F. O'Leary. 1992. *Hindko and Gujari.* Sociolinguistic Survey of Northern Pakistan, Vol. 3. Islamabad: National Institute of Pakistan Studies and Summer Institute of Linguistics: High Wycombe (England).
Tair, Mohammad Nawaz. 1975, 1981. *Rohī Matalīna (Pashto Proverbs).* Vols. I and II. Peshawar: Pashto Academy.
Thorburn, Septimus Smet. 1978. *Bannu: or, our Afghan frontier.* Lahore: Sang-e-Meel reprint of London: Trübner 1876 edition.

WILMA L. HESTON

SEE ALSO

Atan; Badala; Chapbooks; *Dom;* Dress; Ghazal; *Hujra;* Kalasha; *Laṇḍạy;* Mullā Naṣruddīn

NUMEROLOGY

According to Euclid, "Number is the multiplicity of assembled units" (*Elements 7*) in which the unit is not a number, but the principle of counting. Consequently, with numbers, one is dealing with designations for quantities in the form of words or signs abstracted from objects. In contrast, numbers used in folklore are almost always bound up with sense perception or with the objective, as, for example, planets or human beings. Everything that the universe contains, as well as the universe itself, is linked to a specific or individual numeric value. This numeric value indicates, first of all, a quantity. However, in elaborate folk numerological systems this quantity also refers to a hidden quality, contained in sense perception. Culture-specific theories and the procedures derived from them serve to determine the numeric value and the quality of the sense perception that goes along with it, so that human beings can adjust their behavior to this otherwise hidden quality in relation to the relevant object or in contexts in which the object is an effective factor.

In folk numerological systems, numbers are ciphers belonging to the symbolic expression of a culture's understanding of the world. They open insights into the cultural view of the nature of things and simultaneously allow statements concerning the mutual relationship of objects to be derived from them. With the aid of culture-specific techniques, they help the individual to determine his personal relationship with one or several significant others.

As a rule, the literature concerning numbers or mathematics gives general information about the theory, history, origins, and creative processes of systems of numbers, but, for the most part, it does not take sufficiently into account the cultural background or the embeddedness of numbers in the religious and cosmological ideas of each culture.

In India number is embedded in a cosmic whole and is the symbolic counterpart of the Universe. Numbers aer linked with colors, metals, gems, planets, etc. and have not only a spatial but also a temporal dimension.

By numerology one can get information about a person's life, habits, psychological qualities, or special talents, and one can see clearly which obstacles keep the person from reaching his or her destination. Further, numerology can tell the best time for any kind of plan to be put into effect or how to chose a partner. Numerological systems in India connect microcosm and macrocosm. To determine the influence of planets on a person's behavior, the digits in the day, month, and the year of that person's birth are added, along with the numerical value of the person's first name. Zero has no numerological value, it is *sunya,* emptiness. Zero is abstract; numbers are concrete.

Indian numerology has only nine numbers. Even numbers are solar and male; uneven numbers are lunar and female. Numbers are connected with nine heavenly bodies—sun, moon, Mars, Mercury, Jupiter, Venus, Ketu (the ascending moon), and Rahu (the descending moon)—who have special patterns of behavior. Sun, for example, is equal to number one: royal, domineering; moon is number two: attractive, feminine; Jupiter is number three: spiritual, friendly; Rahu is number four: impulsive, irritable; Mercury is number five: sensible, intelligent; Venus is number six: slow, soft; Ketu is number seven: intuitive, dreamy; Saturn is number eight: wise, resentful; Mars is number nine: belligerent, strong-willed.

Indian numerology is always connected with astrology. The astrologer is able to understand the individual's past, present, or future situation. Numerology deals with general aspects of a person, such as behavior or character. All people with the numerologoical value two, for example, have the same character. For a numerological analysis three kinds of numbers have to be taken into consideration: the psychological number, the number of fate, and the number of name. The psychological number indicates how the individual is regarding himself, which wishes or needs are predominant. The number of fate indicates the individual's social field and, finally, the number of name indicates the individual's vibration in life. The relationship of these three numbers decide whether or not a person can life in peace and harmony. The numbers themselves have to be in harmony to each other.

Each number's quality depends on the planet the number is connected to. To calculate the psychological number it is necessary to know the day of birth, for example, 14th of April. The digits of the number 14 are 5, so the psychological number is 5. To calculate the number of fate one would add the day, month and year of birth, for example, 14th April 1961 $= (1+4+4+1+9+6+1) = 26$. The digits of that number are $2+6=8$. That means the number of fate is 8. To calculate the number of name one assigns a number between 1 and 9 to each letter. $A = 1$, $B = 2 \ldots H = 8$, $I = 9$, $J = 1$, $K = 2 \ldots Q = 8$, $R = 9$, $S = 1$, etc. The number of the name Kumar Raja is: $(2+3+4+1+9)+(9+1+1+1) = 31 = 4$. So the number of name is 4.

All the names a person has must be considered, and, to make any statements about the relationship between the numbers, connected with planets. Planets always influence the individual's life. In the example mentioned above, we have calculated the numbers 5 (psychological number), 8 (number of fate) and 4 (number of name). The next step would be to consider the different planets' qualities connected with the calculated numbers. Five represents Mercury, who is sensible and intelligent; eight representents Saturn, who is wise and resentful; four represents Rahu, who is impulsive and irritable. This can tell a lot about a person's character and whether or not that character is a good match with another person.

For numerological analysis, as mentioned above, the connection with the heavenly bodies plays the important role. Sun (number one) and Saturn (number eight) are said to be mother and son, but also enemies. So, in analysing a suitable marriage, it is not advisable for partners to marry if one person has the number of name one and the other person the number of name nine.

Numerology in India also plays an important role in ayurveda and architecture. In ayurveda numbers are connected with the biological humors of *vata* (air), *pita* (fire), and *kapha* (water), as well as with the three *gunas* ("what binds"): *sattva* (intelligence), *rajas* (energy), and *tamas* (substance). South Indian architecs use a numerological system called *ayadi ganidam,* which deals with the prediction of gain and loss for the inhabitants of a house. Microcosm and macrocosm are connected by means of special division calculations. The remainder reveals the inhabitants' luck.

References

Ascher, M. 1991. *Ethnomathematics: a multicultural view of mathematical ideas.* Pacific Grove: Brooks/Cole Publishing Company.

Crump, T. 1990 *The anthropology of numbers.* Cambridge: Cambridge University Press.

Davis, P. J. and R. Hersch. 1983. *The mathematical experience.* London: Pelican Publications.

Euclides. *Elements* 7, Definition 1. In Hubertus Busard, ed. 1983. *The first Latin translation of Euclid's elements commonly ascribed to Adelard of Bath.* Toronto: Pontifical Institute of Mediaeval Studies.

Hardy, G. H. 1940. *A mathematician's apology.* Cambridge: Cambridge University Press.

Hardy, G. H. and E. M. Wright. 1945. *An introduction to the theory of numbers.* Oxford: Oxford University Press.

Hurford, J. R. 1975. *The linguistic theory of numerals.* Cambridge: Cambridge University Press.

HILDE K. LINK

SEE ALSO

Medicine, Āyurveda

O

OGGU KATHA

The *oggu katha* is a narrative form traditionally performed by a *Kurma Pujārulu* or *Ogguwāru,* a person who holds the office of priest in the Kurma (or Kuruva, Kuruba, or Kurma Golla) community of the Telangāṇa region of Andhra Pradesh. *Oggu* is the Telugu name of a two-headed hourglass-shaped drum (Sanskrit, *ḍhamaru*), often associated with the god Śiva. *Katha* is the Telugu word for story, epic, or any long narrative performance. The narrative performed is the story of the god Mallaṇṇa, an incarnation of Śiva. In the performance, the oggu is held by the lead singer; one other singer and three musicians (one playing a large drum called a *ḍōlu* and two playing small cymbals) accompany him. The performance intersperses a two-part dialogue between the lead singer, who takes the part of Mallaṇṇa, and another male singer, who assumes the role of Ratnāṇgi, one of Mallaṇṇa's wives, with a repertoire of traditional songs in which these two are joined in the choruses by the musicians. The songs belong to the Mallaṇṇa (Mailāra) story cycle.

Traditionally, the *oggu katha* is performed at the time of marriage of members of the Kurma caste. The families construct a marriage *pandal* (a decorated stall) and draw an elaborate floor design—called a *paṭṇam*—with colored powders. During this time, the Ogguwāru performs the story of Mallaṇṇa's (Mailāra's) marriage to Ratnāṇgi, and only after it, are the bride and groom seated in the pandal and their marriage performed. The oggu katha thus serves to entertain the wedding guests as well as being a ritual remembrance of the god's marriage. Furthermore, since the Kurmas believe they are the descendants of the marriage of Mallaṇṇa and Ratnāṇgi, each marriage is seen as a reenactment of that auspicious event.

Stories of Mallaṇṇa and Bīrappa (guru of the Kurma) are told at the time of any death in the community. Telling of the stories is believed to aid the dead in finding their way to Kailāsa, the abode of Śiva, and therefore also Mallaṇṇa, an incarnation of Śiva.

In the form and context described above, oggu katha is restricted to the Telangana region of Andhra Pradesh. In a wider area, oggu kathas—particularly the Mallaṇṇa Kalyāṇa, or "Marriage of Mallaṇṇa" episode—are also performed at Mallaṇṇa temples during the annual *jātra.* At some locations (particularly Komarelli), Mallaṇṇa *jātra* has become extremely popular, with hundreds of thousands of people of all communities attending every year. At this time, the oggu katha is directed to a more general audience, and much of the specific Kurma ritual is omitted. Probably derived from this, the oggu katha has, in recent times, begun to be performed at secular gatherings by people other than Kurmas outside of the restricted context of Kurma caste ceremonies and temple occasions. Furthermore, oggu performers are adding stories other than those of Mallaṇṇa to their repertoires. Even more recently, political parties and government agencies have begun to utilize the tremendous popularity of oggu katha performances to propagate their political messages, governmental programes, agendas, and ideologies.

References

Sontheimer, G.-D. 1997. *King of hunters, warriors, and shepherds: Essays on Khandob,* ed. Anne Feldhaus, Aditya Malik, and Heidrun Brückner. New Delhi: Manohar.

Rama Raju, B. 1991. *Glimpses into Telugu folklore,* Jānapada Vijnāna Prachur aṇalu, Hyderbad.

BITTU VENKATESWARLU

SEE ALSO

Floor Designs; *Gorava/Goramma; Mailāra/ Mallaṇṇa/Khaṇḍobā;* Song

ŌṆAM

Ōṇam is the harvest festival celebrated in Kerala, on India's southwest coast, over a number of days during the month of Ciṅṅam (August–September), that culminates on the day of the lunar asterism called *Tiruv–Ōṇam,* after which the festival is named. Of Kerala's three major traditional Hindu festivals—the others being *Viṣu* and *Tiruvātira*—Ōṇam is the one that has remained as the most significant festival representing the region's identity at a popular and official level. This is probably not unrelated to its being sponsored by the state government in 1961, despite its Hindu background, as the festival for regional integration between Kerala's Hindus and its sizeable Muslim and Christian populations.

Ōṇam is a time when Malayalis, as the people of Kerala are called, are supposed to return to their natal or ancestral homes for feasting on traditional items of Kerala cuisine, donning new clothes, and exchanging gifts. Seen as a time for the reaffirmation of familial and regional ties around the native Kerala cuisine, clothing, and lifestyle, this is especially important, given the large proportion of Malayalis who have migrated outside Kerala, nationally and internationally. For Hindus, however, this is also the time for a complex of rituals and various folk arts and performances connected with the mythological background of the festival.

Mythologically, Ōṇam is associated with the events around an incarnation of the god Viṣṇu who took the form of the dwarf Vāmana in order to vanquish and relegate to the underworld the formerly generous demon-king of Kerala known as Mahābali, or simply Bali. Ōṇam celebrates the few days each year when Mahābali is allowed to return to his people and briefly reestablish the kind of bounty and prosperity that were characteristic of his former rule. The myth has been variously interpreted by scholars as a collective memory of Dravidian society before the Sanskritic order of caste was brought to Kerala, or of the old kings of Kerala before the coming of the Brahmans, or of the rivalry between the communities worshipping Viṣṇu as against Śiva, or of the convergence of all three.

There is a rich corpus of folk songs (*ōna-pāṭṭà*) sung on the occasion of these festival days which can be found scattered through collections by Malayali folklorists. The historical roots of the festival seem to reach back to a fusion of Viṣṇu worship from the adjoining Tamil country with the pan-Indic mythology of the Sanskrit *Purāṇa*s.

Ritually, the main acts of worship consist of preparing special conical earthen images of the deity (representing either one of Viṣṇu's incarnations or Mahābali himself) along with beautifully intricate designs of flowers (*pūkkaḷam* or *attappūvà*) that women prepare on the ground.

A variety of competitive games (like the ball game *tala-pantà*) and even quasimilitant contests (like the massed boxing match *kāyyaṉkaḷi*) were traditionally played in different regions of Kerala on Ōṇam. Various (mostly laboring) castes also had, and have, performance genres that they might perform especially in the Ōṇam period, in their own and others' (particularly patrons') house-compounds and temple precincts. Enormously varied from region to region and caste to caste, these performances may include: massed singing accompanied by rhythmic clapping (*kai-koṭṭi-kkaḷi*) or by the clacking of paired staves (*kōl-kaḷi*); martial arts and fencing performances (such as *parica-kaḷi*); and singing as the costumed impersonation of deities, like the *teyyam,* Ōṇattār, in northern Kerala. Finally, there are varieties of women's games, activities like swinging and the songs accompanying it (*ūññāl-pāṭṭu*), and group dances, with special varieties of song accompanying each of these.

However, there has been no adequate folkloric description or analysis of these genres to date in English.

References

Census of India. 1961. *Ōṇam: A festival of Kerala.* Part 8B Monograph Series I. New Delhi: Government of India.

Hospital, Clifford. 1984. *The righteous demon: A study of Bali.* Vancouver: University of British Columbia Press.

Padmanabha Menon, K. P. 1986 [1937]. *Ōṇam.* In *A history of Kerala.* Vol. 4, 286–306. New Delhi: Asian Educational Services.

RICH FREEMAN

SEE ALSO
Kerala; *Teyyam*

OVĪ

Ovī is a Marathi song genre traditionally sung by women at work on the grindstone. Generally of four lines, the ovī has been sung by women for a thousand years, and for almost that long has been adopted for religious texts. Although the grindstone is no longer much in use in Maharashtra, the ovī may still be found among older women, in some rural areas, as a lullaby and a swing song, and recently in the women's movement. The most popular religious text in Maharashtra, the *Dnyāneśvarī,* was written in ovī form in the thirteenth century C.E. The use of the ovī for women's work song *and* for sacred writing illustrates the interrelationship of folk and literary forms in Marathi.

The first mention of ovī is in an early twelfth century C.E. work on grammar and genre by Someśwar, and,

Traditional image of Dnyaneshwar writing in *ovi* form. Sketch by Sudhir Waghmare

significantly, it credits the ovī to women. Both the saint-poets and the later more intellectual "pandit poets" wanted to write popular Marathi texts, poems, and songs, and so the ovī or its lengthened version, the *abhanga,* is found in the thirteenth century commentary by Dnyāneśwar on the *Bhāgavad Gītā* (the most beloved of all Marathi religious texts) and in Eknāth, Rāmdas, Tukarām, Mukteśwar, and Cridhar's work as well. But while the classical literary use of the ovī has ceased today, and the grindstone is no longer found in most Marathi villages, some versions of the ovī continue, true to its origin as an expression of women's lives.

The ovī metre usually consists of four lines, with five to twelve syllables in each line and, almost always, a short, sharp, final line. The first three or the first and third lines are rhymed irregularly, and this flexibility, combined with its rhythm, has made the ovī extraordinarily popular. The first serious collection, published by Sane Guruji in Marathi in 1940, consisted of over 2500 ovīs, chiefly sung by Brahman women. The themes of these ovīs tell us the range of women's interests: sister-brother (246 ovīs); mother-child (524); daughter (281); experiences of joy and sorrow (605); stories of Gods and Purāṇic references (284); holy places and cities (Bombay as well as the Maharashtrian religious center of Pandharpur) (163); history and nationalism (65); vows, festivals, etc. (68); descriptions of nature (76); proverbs (66); and miscellaneous (129). Note the wide-ranging interests of women, expressed in song as they work!

The only collection of any size is by Guy Poitevin and Hema Rairkar (1993) and is located at the American Resource Centre for Ethnomusicology, New Delhi. Several dozen of these ovī, translated into English, are compiled in a book intended to record the inner feelings of women in order to help enable self-help programs. The authors found "not a single song of the millstone which expresses delight or pride in being a woman" (34). These songs typically criticize the mother-in-law, some the idea of dowry. Poitevin and Rairkar do, however, record some of the ovīs related to the *Mahābhārata* and the *Rāmāyaṇa* that identify ordinary women with epic heroines. Other collections (in Marathi) of ovī are less pessimistic about women's lives.

Ovīs may be religious, celebrating a God, such as this ovī about Kṛṣṇa cited by R. C. Dhere (1982):

Peacock feathers in his crown;
forest garlands 'round his neck;
let's remember the Dark One from Gokul!
(787)

In Sane Guruji's (1976) collection, an ovī celebrates the beloved Maharashtrian saint-poet Tukarām of the seventeenth century as well as his village:

Go to Dehu,
forget the body!
Let's sing ovī to Tukarām.
(224)

Although traditional ovī may go the way of the grindstone, at present they are used to reflect contemporary themes and concerns. A very common counting ovī (often sung by girls while swinging), begins "My first ovī..." and continues to ten. It has been found by Georg Amshoff in the songs of the women's movement:

My first ovī is
for women's freedom!
Let's keep fighting
for women's freedom!

Any number of verses may be added spontaneously in this context.

Another ovī, originally sung by Daya Pawar as a protest against government inaction during Maharashtra's 1970s drought, has been adopted by the current (1995) "Stop the Narmada Dam" movement as its hymn and includes this verse:

I am building a dam; I am pounding my death.
The day sinks down, my life sinks with it
I cover my little one—with a basket.

The ovī has had many varied and creative uses since it was first recorded as a woman's song and then used in religious works meant for the common people. The grinding of grain at home is a thing of the past, but the rhythm and simplicity of the ovī and the popularity of the religious works in ovī mean this folk form will be used for generations to come in new ways.

References

Amshoff, Georg. 1995. From songs in the house to songs of social change. Paper presented at the Sixth International Conference on Maharashtra Studies, Moscow.

Dhere, R. C. 1982. Ovī. In *Bharatiya Sanskrutikosh* (Encyclopedia of Indian Culture), ed. Pandit Mahadevshastri Joshi, et al. Vol. l, 2nd ed. 786–790. Pune: Bharatiya Sanskruti Kosh Monoal.

Poitevin, Guy and Hema Rairkar. 1993. *Indian peasant women speak up*. Trans. from the French by Michel Leray. Hyderabad: Orient Longman.

Sane Guruji. 1976 [1940]. *Stri jivana* (Songs of women). 2nd ed. Pune: Indrayani Sahitya.

ELEANOR ZELLIOT

SEE ALSO

Gender and Folklore; Maharashtra; Song

P

PĀBŪJĪ

The very limited historical evidence suggests that Pābūjī was a real person. According to the records of Marwar (Jodhpur, Rajasthan), he was a minor ancestral figure in the ruling Rāṭhoṛ Rajpūt family. It seems probable that he lived in the early fourteenth century C.E. and was based in the remote desert village of Koḷū. He was "a brigand who lived by his wits and his weapons" (Smith 1991, 82). He seems to have achieved deification quickly. We know that he was served by *bhopo*s (folk-priests) as early as the early sixteenth century C.E. In present-day Rajasthan he is widely worshipped, in particular by rural Rajpūts and by Rebārī shepherds and camel herders; he is believed to be an *avatāra* (incarnation) of Lakṣmaṇa, brother of Lord Rāma, and is appealed to in cases of sickness (of humans or of livestock) and other such misfortunes. Since at least the early nineteenth century the chief form of communal worship has been the ritual performance of an epic narrative relating the god's deeds on Earth. This is the traditional work of bhopos of the Nayak caste, an "unclean" scheduled caste, who travel in pairs from village to village to perform. A typical pair will be man and wife—bhopo and *bhopī*—though all-male performances also occur. In a suitable public spot, the bhopo erects a *paṛ,* a large narrative cloth-painting on which are depicted the heroic deeds performed by Pābūjī. The paṛ is the ritual center of the performance and functions as the temple of the deity. The epic is performed through the night, in alternating sections of *gāv* (song) and *arthāv* (declamatory speech). Bhopo and bhopī sing the *gāv* together, while the bhopo provides accompaniment on a *rāvaṇhattho,* a spike-fiddle. Sometimes he also dances, swirling his red robe and setting his ankle-bells jingling. The *arthāv* recapitulates the story, and, during it, the bhopo points with the bow of his fiddle to the relevant scenes on the painted paṛ behind him; his bhopī may hold a small lamp to illuminate them in the darkness.

The story tells how Pābūjī's niece Kelam was married to the snake-god Gogo Cauhāṇ. Pābūjī promised Kelam as a wedding gift that he would fetch camels from the demon-infested land of Laṅkā. After being taunted by her new in-laws, Kelam insisted that this promise be fulfilled, and after sending his brave Rebārī companion Harmal ahead as a spy (a favorite episode among Rebārī audiences), Pābūjī succeeded in bringing the camels. On the way home he was seen by the princess of Umarkot, who fell in love with him. A wedding was arranged and took place, but before the ceremony was complete, Pābūjī insisted on riding off to rescue the cattle of his protegee, the lady Deval, which had been stolen by the wicked Jindrāv Khīṉcī. Pābūjī now faced Khīṉcī in battle, and at a blow from Khīṉcī's sword, he ascended to Heaven in a palanquin. His nephew Rūpnāth later avenged him by beheading Khīṉcī.

Reference

Smith, John D. 1991. *The Epic of Pābūjī: A study, transcription and translation.* Cambridge: Cambridge University Press.

JOHN D. SMITH

SEE ALSO

Bhopo; Epic; Lakṣmaṇa; Narrative Scroll Painting; *Paṛ;* Rajasthan; Rāma

PĀḌDANA

*Pāḍdana*s (from the Dravidian root *pāḍ-*, "to sing") are a genre of sung narratives in the Dravidian language, Tulu. The genre, a major one for the Tuluva people, consists of several closely related singing traditions.

The individual songs—perhaps over two hundred in total—range in length from less than one hour to as many as twenty hours of recitation, with most taking about two to four hours to sing. Scholars have variously classified them as epics, ritual songs, or even (broadly) ballads, depending on the context or purpose in which they are sung. The major subject of the songs is the deeds of the local deities classed in Tulu as *bhūta* and *daiva*. Some of the songs—particularly those sung in a ritual context—are little more than a catalogue of the deities' activities, while others, dealing more with the lives and tragic deaths of devotees, have a stronger narrative content and are more lengthy.

Although the common term for this group of songs is pāḍdana, under that label there are at least two distinct traditions, or subgenres. These two subgenres are sometimes distinguished by the terms pāḍdana and *sandi,* but often a terminological distinction is not made, or the terms are used somewhat indiscriminately. Pāḍdanas, or *naṭṭina pāḍdana,* "planting songs," are normally sung by women; sandis are ritual songs, usually sung by men. The latter tradition-set (what is sometimes called sandi, ritual songs) are sung by three different castes of professional bardic caste performers, the Pambadas, the Paravas, and the Nalkes. There are numerous stylistic and compositional differences between the songs of women singing in the fields and the ritual songs of men. The songs of the women's fieldsong tradition are, in comparison to the ritual traditions, long—even epic-like—with very strong narrative qualities. The ritual songs of the Nalkes and Paravas also tend to be fairly long and strongly narrative, but among the Pambadas, the songs are often so highly abbreviated it is difficult to follow the narrative sequence.

The earliest collection of pāḍdanas was done by several members of the Basel Mission in the nineteenth century. A collection of these was published in Tulu using a modified Kannada script under the title *Pāḍdanolu* in 1886. The *Indian Antiquary* published a large number of these texts in both transliteration and translation over the years 1894–1898. In more recent times, several scholars have published collections in Kannada prose. In German, Heidrun Brückner's *Texte und Rituale der Tulu-Volksreligion an der Wesküste Südindiens,* a major study of the Pambada ritual tradition, includes the transliteration and translation of many pāḍdanas. Several articles by Peter J. Claus (1975, 1979a and b, 1989, 1991) contain transcriptions and translations or summaries of major pāḍddanas from both ritual and fieldsong traditions. A number of unpublished tape recorded collections are also known to exist, the major one being that of the Tulu Lexicon, housed at present in the Regional Resource Centre for Folk Performing Arts, Udupi, Karnataka, India.

References

Brückner, Heidrun. 1995. *Texte und rituale der Tulu-Volksreligion an der Westküste Südindiens.* Wiesbaden: Harrassowitz (Neuindische Studien).

Burnell, A. C. 1894–98. The devil worship of the Tuluvas. *Indian Antiquary,* 23, seq.

Claus, Peter J. 1975. The Siri myth and ritual: A mass possession ritual of South Indian. *Ethnology* 14: 47–58.

———. 1979a. Spirit possession and mediumship from the perspective of Tulu oral traditions. *Culture, Medicine and Psychiatry* 3: 29–52.

———. 1979b. Mayndala: A myth and cult of Tulunad. *Asian Folklore Studies,* 38(2): 95–129.

———. 1989. Behind the text: Performance and ideology in a Tulu oral tradition. In *Indian oral epics,* ed. Peter J. Claus, Stuart H. Blackburn, Susan S. Wadley, and Joyce B. Fleuckiger. Berkeley: University of California Press. 55–74.

———. 1991. Kinsongs. In *Gender, genre, and power in South Asian expressive traditions,* ed. Arjun Appadurai, Frank J. Korom, and Margaret Mills. Philadelphia: University of Pennsylvania Press.

PETER J. CLAUS

SEE ALSO

Bhūta Kola; Epic; *Kordabbu;* Siri

PAINTING

See Folk Art, Orissa; Folk Painting; Mithila Painting; Narrative Scroll Painting; *Paṭa Citra;* Rock Painting, India; Vehicle Painting; Wall Painting

PAKISTAN

See Balochistan: Oral Tradition; *Kesar;* North-West Frontier Province; Punjab; Sindh

PĀMPIN TUḶḶAL

The Malayalam term *pāmpin tuḷḷal* could be translated as "the frenzied, jumping dance of serpents." The ritual to which it refers is also called *kaḷam eḻuttu pāṭṭu,* "floor drawing song," and *sarpa* (a Sanskrit term for serpent also used in Malayalam) *tuḷḷal.* Pāmpin tuḷḷal is an elaborate Hindu ritual *(pūjā)* performed in Kerala in south India for the remedy of the curse of cobra (*pāmpu* or *nāgam*) deities, which is manifested in the form of infertility and other kinds of misfortune. The ritual is also performed for overall family prosperity, and benefits women in particular.

The performance is orchestrated by lower caste ("untouchable") Puḷḷuvas for middle class members of Nāyar, Iṛava, and, more recently, lower upwardly mobile Hindu castes. Patrons of the ritual performance belong to extended families called *taravāṭus*, numbering one to several hundred individuals. Like taravāṭu land, propitiating the taravāṭu gods is a shared responsibility, the actions of which contain abiding influence. Varying by region in Central Kerala, Puḷḷuva ritual specialists, paid to perform, and two female members of the patron kin group (*taravāṭu*) are responsible for the ritual's efficacy.

The all-night performance takes place in the courtyard of the most ancient and spacious house of the taravāṭu, with taravāṭu branches collectively responsible for feeding guests. Part of a longer three- to twenty-one-night sequence, the serpent gods (nāgams) are invoked through elaborate aesthetic media and song. Each progressively engaging stage of the ritual is punctuated with recitation of myth and incantation: "Oh God! My resort! If you have been polluted while practicing austerities or burnt by fire . . . come and speak truthfully to [us]." Ancient songs passed down in Puḷḷuva families (*tōṟṟam*) concern the origins of both the Nāgams and Puḷḷuvas, descriptions of ritual decorations, prayers for well being and *slōkam*s (verses) detailing ritual procedures. Other songs are more recent additions, redactions from the *Mahābhārata* and *Bhāgavata Purāṇa,* such as the story of Kadrū and Vinitā, the origin of Garuḍa, the curse of the King Parikṣit, and other stories related to serpent workship. These are sung to the accompaniment of the *kuṭam* (a stringed instrument made out of a clay pot used exclusively by the Puḷḷuva), *vīṇā* (a one-stringed lute made of lizard skin and a vine for a string) and *tāḷam* (hand cymbals), played by Puḷḷuva men and women.

The centerpiece of the ritual is a large (often sixteen-foot-square) colored floor drawing (*kaḷam*) created on the ground by Puḷḷuva ritual specialists with colored medicinal powders. The deities arrive when two women of the patron group become possessed by the deities, following the invocation of the god:

> The girl who would dance is beautiful
> She arrives happily after her bath
> She has come holding a cluster of flowers from the
> arecanut tree . . .
> You shake, shake, shake my Nāgam
> You shake your hair and dance. . . .

The female Nāgam show their pleasure in the offering by dancing in the kaḷam and then erasing it in a sitting position.

The potential transformation of the deity's mood and, along with it, taravāṭu fertility and well-being, takes place during the trance sequence. The Puḷḷuvan orchestrates people's experience of the ritual through music, visual and olfactory art, dance, and song. Beliefs and experiences of serpents—in dreams, in the wild, and as spirits in ritual and myth—substantiate and empower the highly charged emotional *mise-en-scene.* Finally, through gifts of items such as rice, coins, and

cloth, the curses of snakes incurred by the taravāṭu are removed by the Puḷḷuvas.

Puḷḷuva priests today are increasingly refusing to accept the onus of taking on the sins of the taravāṭus; many are finding other forms of employment. Even so, pāmpin tuḷḷal continues to thrive in rural Kerala.

The distribution of pāmpin tuḷḷal is limited to Kerala state and is not found in similar form elsewhere. Although Brahmans are not involved in pāmpin tuḷḷal, another form of Nāga worship, *naga māṇḍala,* in southern Karnataka, is patronized by Brahmans and may be a cognate form. The central deity of that ritual, Nāga Bemmere, may also be cognate to the *naga bhūta* (serpent ghost or demon), a male guardian spirit worshiped along with the Nāga in outdoor serpent shrines in both Kerala and southern Karnataka, and propitiated during the final night of pāmpin tuḷḷal.

References

Jones, Clifford R. 1982. Kaḷam Eḷuttu: Art and ritual in Kerala. In *Religious festivals in South India and Sri Lanka,* ed. Guy Richard Welbon and Glenn Yocum. New Delhi: Manohar Publishing Company.

Natavar, Mekhala Devi. 2000. Tuḷḷal. In *South Asia: The Indian subcontinent.* Vol. 5 *The Garland encyclopedia of world music,* ed. Alison Arnold. New York: Garland Publishing, Inc.

Neff, Deborah L. 1987. Aesthetics and power in Pāmbin Tuḷḷal: A possession ritual of rural Kerala. *Ethnology* 26: 6371.

———. 1994. The social construction of infertility: The case of the matrilineal Nayars in South India. *Social Science and Medicine* 39(4): 47585.

———. 1994. Special status performers: Fertility and power in a Kerala serpent ritual. Ph.D. dissertation, University of Wisconsin, Madison.

DEBORAH L. NEFF

SEE ALSO
Animals; Dance; Floor Designs; Kerala; *Nāga;* Spirit Possession and Mediumship; Worship

PAÑCATANTRA

The *Pañcatantra* is a collection of eighty-four "animal fables" and "tales" divided into five books. First written down in Sanskrit, the work is accredited to a Brahman named Vishnusharman. The text is considered a *nītiśāstra,* a treatise or lawbook of *nīti.* The term nīti is difficult to translate because there is no precise equivalent in any European language; however, nītiśāstra can be defined as a "textbook of right, moral and wise conduct." Ethical conduct and political wisdom are the central themes the original author wished to convey to his audience, and he did so through prose narratives exemplifying patterns of proper behavior. The prose throughout the *Pañcatantra* is interspersed with precepts in verse form that draw on older sources of knowledge, displaying not only Vishnusharman's conceptual grasp of traditional Hindu thought, but also his marvelous ability to weave together numerous strands of story and verse into a coherent whole. Whatever Vishnusharman's epistemological sources of inspiration were, it is clear that he was very familiar with the literary, religio-philosophical, and jurisprudential works of his day.

The *Pañcatantra* is set within a frame story that is introduced at the beginning of the work. The overarching frame begins with an invocation to a host of deities and sages. It then goes on with the action of the narrative, which takes place in a city of "the south country." A king named Amarashakti lives there with his three foolish sons (Vasushakti, Ugrashakti, and Anekashakti). The king compares his sons to a cow that "neither gives milk nor calves," because they are ignorant of political science and are not of any use to him. The king meets with his ministers to decide on a method to teach his foolish sons the science of polity, and he is advised to summon the sage Vishnusharman for this purpose. The sage arrives and replies to the king's offer: "If within the space of six months I do not make your sons completely verst [sic] in the science of polity, then, Sir, you may (show me the door and) banish me" (Edgerton 1924, 2: 271). Upon hearing this, the king puts the three princes in Vishnusharman's care, and the teaching begins "under the guise of stories." It is for this purpose, according to the commentator, that Vishnusharman composed the five books titled "The Separation of Friends," "The Winning of Friends," "The Story of the Crows and the Owls," "The Loss of One's Gettings," and "Hasty Action."

Although there is this frame for the Pañcatantra's action, each of the five books is a separate dramatic unit with its own smaller frame story. Within each of these, then, there are a number of "emboxed" stories. Quite often there is a double emboxment. The result is a marvelous panoply of story within story within story, which Edgerton has termed a "Chinese net" (5). Through the gradual unfolding of each story, the task of educating the three princes is completed.

In 1908 the German Indologist Johannes Hertel postulated that the text was originally written in Kashmir, circa 200 B.C.E., and disseminated southward from there. He based this assumption on his interpretation of the earliest extant version of the Kashmiri text known as the *Tantrākhyāyika*. Hertel thought that the *Tantrākhyāyika* was the Ur-text, namely the original version of the *Pañcatantra*. The latest that this text could have been written is 570 C.E., since Khusrau, a Persian king of the Sassanian Dynasty between 531–579 C.E., commissioned a translation into Pahlavi during his reign. His order was carried out before 570 C.E., so the text must have been written between the two dates mentioned above.

Hertel retracted his antiquated date after convincing lines of argumentation were set forth by other Indologists. The proofs of the untenableness of Hertel's hypothesis forced him to change the date of the text to 300 C.E. However, Franklin Edgerton, the author of the critical edition of the *Pañcatantra,* refuted Hertel's claim about the Ur-text. Hertel eventually modified his claim by stating that the *Tantrākhyāyika* was the oldest extant version, not necessarily the "original." The dabate concerning the Ur-text has subsided, and scholars now feel that it is a moot question, since the original manuscript has not survived. Even though the dating of the Kashmir manuscript can only be regarded as speculation, we can be certain that the tales were already very old at the time of their first writing.

The *Pañcatantra* has a long and complicated history. Its range of diffusion spreads from Java in the East to Iceland in the West. Indeed, Hertel has recorded no less than two hundred versions in fifty languages in his magnum opus published in 1914. Moreover, the text was central to folkloristic theory in the nineteenth century, a time when interest in Indian literature and religion was revived during the "classical period of European Indology."

The two developments most critical to *Pañcatantra* studies were Sir William Jones' (1746–1794) discovery and declaration that Sanskrit was philologically related to Latin, and the public and academic fury caused by the debates between Max Müller (1823–1900) and Andrew Lang (1844–1912) over "solar mythology." But before their debate ensued, Theodor Benfey (1809–1881) had already written what many considered to be the first great classic in the field of comparative literature; his German translation of the *Pañcatantra,* published in 1859. The translation was based on the oldest extant version of the *Pañcatantra,* the aforementioned *Tantrākhyāyika,* and reached a wide audience in the German speaking parts of Europe. Shortly thereafter, German scholars, influenced by Müller's "Aryan connection," pursued the study of Sanskrit literature in general and the *Pañcatantra* specifically.

The *Pañcatantra* was already well-known outside of India before the nineteenth century. As mentioned above, the text was famous in Persia before the sixth century C.E. The original translation into Pahlavi did not survive, but Abdullah ibn al-Muqaffa did translate the Pahlavi text into Arabic in 750 C.E. Conservative estimates place the text in Europe by the eleventh century C.E. The earliest English relative of the *Pañcatantra* was written by Sir Thomas North in 1570 C.E. This work was based on the Latin version written between 1263 C.E. and 1278 C.E. by John of Capua.

The *Pañcatantra* also spread eastward into southeast Asia through the southern recensions of the text. A Middle-Javanese version known as *Tantri-carita* or *Tantra-wākya* has been dated as early as 1200 C.E. Later translations appeared in Malay through a Tamil intermediary in the eighteenth century. Balinese versions also exist, but these are only fragmentary. This southeastern stream has been heavily influenced by other sources, such as the Persian translation of the *Śukasaptati,* called *Tūtī-Nāma,* or the "Parrot Book." Further, it was often preceded by the frame story of the *1001 Nights,* resulting in a complex and interwoven narrative incorporating aspects of both Hindu and Muslim traditions.

References

Benfey, Theodor. 1859. *Pantschatantra. Fünf Bücher indischer Fabeln, Märchen und Erzählungen.* 2 vols. Leipzig: F. U. Brockhaus.

Brown, W. Norman. 1919. The Pañcatantra in modern Indian folklore. *Journal of the American Oriental Society* 39: 1–54.

Edgerton, Franklin. 1924. *The Panchatantra reconstructed.* 2 vols. New Haven, Conn.: American Oriental Society.

Hertel, Johannes. 1914. *Das Pançatantra: Seine Geschichte und seine Verbreitung.* Leipzig: B.G. Teubner.

Hertel, Johannes. 1915. *The Panchatantra. A collection of ancient Hindu tales. In its oldest recension, the Kashmirian, entitled Tantrakhyayika.* Cambridge, Mass.: Harvard University Press.

FRANK J. KOROM

SEE ALSO

Benfey, Theodor; British Folklore (in South Asia); Brown, William Norman; Story Literature, Sanskrit

PANCH PĪR

Panch Pīr refers to a list of five Sufi *auliyā* (saints) venerated by South Asian Muslims. It is likely that the term *Panch Pīr* originally refers to the *Panjatan Pāk* (Five Pure Ones) of Shī'ī Islam—Muhammad, his daughter Fāṭima, his son-in-law and cousin Imām 'Alī, and his two grandsons Imām Ḥasan and Imām Ḥusayn—who are also venerated by Sunnī Muslims. In the popular Ṣūfī tradition, this devotional allegiance to five holy individuals centers instead upon on a variety of lists of five Ṣūfī *pīrs*. For example, in his epic poem *Hīr-o-Rānjhā,* the Panjabi poet Waris Shah identifies the Panch Pīr as the prophet Khiẕr; the saint of the Chistī Sufi order, Bābā Farid Shakr Ganj of Pakpattan; Lal Shāhbāz Qalandar of Sehwan Sharif; Shaikh Bahā'ud-dīn Zakariyya of Multan; and Makhdum Jahāniyān Jalal Bukhari of Ucch. Within the epic, they perform a customary function of the auliyā' by collectively blessing the hero Ranjha. In Bengal, where the *Panch Pīr* tradition is particularly strong, the list often includes the Bengali saints Pīr Badr—the patron of sailors, Ghāzī Miyan, and Zinda Ghāzī, along with Bābā Farīd Shakr Ganj and Khiẕr. Other saints sometimes included in the Panch Pir are the Chistī pīrs (Sufi Masters)—Khwāja Qutb ud-dīn Baktiyār Kaki, Khwāja Mu'īn ud-dīn Chishti, and Nizām ud-dīn Auliyā; and Shāh Shams Tabrīz Multāni. There are several collective *dargāh*s of the Panch Pīr in South Asia which serve as sites of pilgrimage (*ziyārat*), including a very famous one in Sunargaon.

Along with the Shī'ī veneration of the Panjatan Pāk, the notion of the Panch Pīr also resonates with collective groups of five holy persons in indigenous South Asian religions, including the five Pandava brothers and the five chaste women (*panchsati*) in Hindu folklore and mythology, and the Buddhist veneration of the five *tathāgata*s. This resonance with pre-Islamic traditions has led some commentators to emphasize the syncretic aspect of this phenomenon, which is perhaps most evident in Bengal, where both Hindus and Muslims venerate the Panch Pīr with the aid of an image of a five-fingered hand on which each of the digits represents one of the five pīrs—a symbol analogous to the Shī'ī representation of the Panjatan Pāk in the form of a human hand. In Bengal both Hindu and Muslim sailors invoke the blessings of the Panch Pīr when going to sea. Perhaps for this reason it has long been a controversial practice among many Muslims; it was banned by the medieval emperor Sikander Lodi and remains a focus of criticism by certain *'ulamā* (Muslim clerics) today.

References

Abdul Latif, Sk. 1993. *The Muslim mystic movement in Bengal: 1301–1550.* Calcutta: K. P. Bagchi and Co.

Crooke, W. 1917. Panchpiriya. In *Encyclopaedia of religion and ethics,* Vol. IX, 600–601. New York: Charles Scribner's and Sons.

Rizvi, Saiyid Athar Abbas. 1986. *A history of Sufism in India,* Vol. I. New Delhi: Munshiram Manoharlal Publishers Pvt. Ltd.

VERNON JAMES SCHUBEL

SEE ALSO

Dargāh; Hīr/Rānjhā; Khvāja Ḵẖiẕr; *Pīr;* Pilgrimage

PĀṆḌAV LĪLĀ

Pāṇḍav līlā is the ritual drama or "play" (*līlā*) of the five Pāṇḍava brothers, protagonists of India's great epic, *Mahābhārata.* It is performed exclusively in the former kingdom of Garhwal, in the Uttarakhand region of the west central Himalayas. Performances usually occur in the winter months of Pauṣ and Māgh (December-February), though there are unconfirmed reports of summer performances. A pāṇḍav līlā can last anywhere from one day to several weeks and is collectively organized by a village at least once every generation and usually more frequently, sometimes even annually.

A typical performance begins when the Pāṇḍava brothers, their ally Kṛṣṇa, mother Kuntī, common wife Draupadī, and numerous other members of their "army" are ritually summoned to the dancing square and asked to descend upon villagers dancing their parts. These quasi-divine persons are believed to be actually present, therefore pāṇḍav līlā is considered ritually effective in ensuring bountiful harvests and good health, and especially in warding off hoof-and-mouth disease. Moreover, in Garhwal, as in Tamil Nadu, Draupadī is believed to be an incarnation of the goddess Kālī, and so pāṇḍav līlā performances are also considered forms of Kālī worship.

Initial invocations, chanted in the vernacular, are followed by dances accompanied by the *ḍhol,* a large two-headed drum, and either (in eastern Garhwal) the *damāūm,* a small single-headed drum or (in western Garhwal) the *bhāīṇā,* a brass gong, and occasionally the *raṇasingha,* or battle-horn. Male dancers sometimes wear skullcaps, trousers, and flowing skirts, all made of white cloth and colorfully embroidered. Female dancers always wear traditional dress: black woolen robes, white cotton cummerbunds and scarves, and heavy silver jewelry. Dances alternate with dramatic vignettes (*līlā*) and competitive oral recitations of *Mahābhārata,* chanted in the vernacular. Although published versions of *Mahābhārata* are readily available, competition between bards is normally settled on the basis of consensual memory and the reputation of the bards concerned.

The outline of *Mahābhārata* as represented in pāṇḍav līlā is fairly consistent with its well-known classical and popular versions, but in certain regions, special emphasis is placed on particular episodes. For example, in the Pindar River basin, a popular līlā has to do with the *śāmī* tree which guarded the Pāṇḍavas' weapons while they were in exile, and which they honored after the *Mahābhārata* war. In this līlā, a pine tree with no blemish is carefully uprooted and carried several kilometers to the dancing square, where it is joyfully erected. In the Nagpur area between the Mandakini and Alakananda rivers, the capture and death of Arjuna's son Abhimanyu is dramatized in the *cakravyeha līlā,* noteworthy for its length (up to several weeks in some cases). Here, performers utilize printed scripts, and, consequently, the oral tradition seems to be decaying. The only episode found throughout Garhwal is "The Rhinoceros," in which Arjuna stalks and slays a rhinoceros guarded by his son Nagarjuna, in order to obtain its hide for use in the ancestral rites for Pāṇḍu, his father. This episode (which is not found in Sanskrit versions of *Mahābhārata*) is so popular that, in many places, pāṇḍav līlā is metonymically referred to simply as "The Rhinoceros" (*gaiṇḍā*).

Episodes selected for ritual and dramatic representation in pāṇḍav līlā clearly emphasize martial and royal virtues. This is not surprising, because the tradition is strongly associated with Garhwali Rajputs, members of the Hindu warrior class (*kṣātriya varṇa*). All bards and most dancers are Rajputs. They consider themselves direct descendants of the Pāṇḍavas, and regard pāṇḍav līlā as a type of ancestor worship.

References

Sax, William S. 1991. Ritual and performance in the pandavalila of Uttarakhand. In *Essays on the Mahabharata,* ed. Arvind Sharma, 274–295. Leiden: E. J. Brill.

———. 1994. Who's who in pandav lila? In *The gods at play: līlā in South Asia,* ed. William S. Sax, 131–155. New York: Oxford University Press.

———. Forthcoming. Worshiping epic villains: A kaurava cult in the western Himalayas. In *Epics and the contemporary world,* ed. Margaret Beissinger, Jane Tylus, and Suzanne Wofford. Berkeley: University of California Press.

WILLIAM S. SAX

SEE ALSO

Ancestor Worship; Draupadī; *Mahābhārata*; *Śāmī*

PAṚ

A *paṛ* is a large narrative cloth painting used in Rajasthan as a form of portable temple. Traditionally, paṛs have been painted by members of the Josī lineage of the Chīpā caste living in Bhilwara and Shahpura, two towns in South east Rajasthan. Until recently, it appears that paṛs were produced only for use in ritual performances of the epics honoring the local hero-deities Pābūjī and Devnārāyaṇ. It seems likely that the tradition originated with mural paintings in temples: the paṛ of Devnārāyaṇ is still sometimes found painted around the walls of temples dedicated to him. During the twentieth century, paṛs were devised for other deities such as Rāma, Kṛṣṇa, the Goddess, and Rāmdev; these are used by Nāyaks and other low castes for ritual performance or worship. In addition, small versions of paṛs and fragments of paṛs have come to be produced in large numbers for the tourist market. Every paṛ for a given deity has essentially the same iconographic program: that deity's deeds are depicted in a large number of interwoven scenes, shown not in temporal sequence, but rather laid out as if upon a map.

References

Joshi, O. P. 1976. *Painted folklore and folklore painters of India: a study with reference to Rajasthan.* Delhi: Concept Publishing Company.

Smith, John D. 1991. *The epic of Pābūjī: A study, transcription and translation*. Cambridge: Cambridge University Press.

JOHN D. SMITH

SEE ALSO

Devnārāyaṇ; Epic; Narrative Scroll Painting; *Pābūjī;* Performance; Rajasthan

PARĪ

From the Karakorum mountains of Northern Pakistan across the Hindukush into Central Asia, Afghanistan, and Iran, local traditions variously recognize a category of supernatural called *parī*. In Avestan, the ancient Iranian scriptural language of Zoroastrianism, they are mentioned as *paraikā,* a category of benign minor supernaturals. In the western part of their range in recent times, they are most prominent in fictional folktales, as beautiful supernatural females who are the object of romantic quests and rescues by human male heroes. They also figure abundantly as supporting characters in the *Amīr Ḥamza Nāma* as it developed into an enormous, sprawling episodic romance in Urdu, derived from Persian. In folktales and fantasy romances, the abode of the *parī* is "the other side of Mount Qāf," the mountain that divides the human world from the worlds of supernaturals (*dev* as well as *parī*). There the *parī* have a kingdom, led by a king whose princess daughters travel by air to the human world, where they encounter humans and set them off on quests.

To the extent that belief in their actual existence remains active in the western part of the range, a few named *parī* figure as the objects of *naẕ* votive rites in Shī'a areas, but in some of these rituals they are assigned a relationship to the venerated members of the Prophet's family, to whom *naẕ* are more often dedicated.

The *parī* in the eastern part of the range (Karakorum mountains, Pamirs of Afghanistan) are still believed to be an active supernatural presence in the world. Those who interact with humans are no longer merely lovely female supernatural prizes, they are female and male, live in families with children, etc. They inhabit the high mountains, may also take up residence in individual stones or trees in areas of human habitation, and are encountered by humans primarily in two ways:

(1) Hunters operating at high elevations, where the *parī* live, may encounter them either while awake or asleep. The hunters' primary prey, the ibex or wild goat, is regarded as the livestock of the *parī*. Hunters' beliefs thus hold the *parī* to be custodians of their success in hunting, and capable of punishing physically or psychologically those who are disrespectful or wasteful of the resource.

(2) More immediately in village life, *parī* are believed to take an interest in human beings, especially young women and some young men, and to abduct them from time to time to attend *parī* weddings and other social events. The abduction may be physical, in that the possessed person is compelled to go to the place where the *parī* have summoned them, or psychological, in which case they lose consciousness and may need to be physically restrained to control their involuntary violent movements. During these periods of abduction, victims hear and see *parī,* interact with them and can sometimes report their words and appearance. One young Isma'īlī woman in the Ishkoman Valley of Pakistan who began to have *parī* problems in the late 1980's at about age 14, reported that one *parī* she saw looked like an older man with a beard like a Sunnī Muslim, sitting in a tree.

Cures for *parī* possession among Muslims are religious: whispering Muslim prayers into the ears of the possessed person, praying and blowing on them while they are possessed, or if the *parī* proves harder to dislodge, beating together with louder injunctions to leave. In northern Pakistan, although *parī* possession and epilepsy are described by the same term (in various languages) which translates as to "be frightened," they are recognized as susceptible to different therapies, epilepsy being treated with western style drugs if available.

Research with the non-Muslim Kalasha of Pakistan and on the history of non-Muslim religions in the Hindukush connects *parī* beliefs as presently found among the majority Muslims to the older religion, in which the high mountains are the abode of deities and the ibex are their flocks. Other aspects of local religious practice also reflect this older layer of belief, such as the use of juniper wood and juniper sprigs as purification materials, butter as a ritual food, and the designation of relatively ritually pure and impure, gendered zones in the traditional one-room Hindukush house which predominates in the area. Muslim beliefs about *parī* possession and healing techniques in the Karakorum are now formally similar to beliefs about jinn possession in Afghanistan, jinn being an order of creation recognized in the Qur'ān.

References

Jettmar, Karl. 1975. *Die religionen des Hindukusch.* Stuttgart: Kohlhammer.

Massé, Henri. 1954. *Persian beliefs and customs.* New Haven: Human Relations Area Files.

MARGARET A. MILLS

SEE ALSO

Amīr Ḥamza; Baiṭhak; Dēv; Ibex and Goat; Jinn; Kalasha; Shamanism

PARSI FOLKLORE

The Parsis are Indian followers of the Zoroastrian religion. They migrated from Persia to coastal Gujarat around 800 C.E., adapting to their new country over time. With the arrival of the British, the Parsis transformed themselves from rural farmers to urban entrepreneurs. Today they are a small but prominent community in Bombay with continuing ties to their ancestral towns and villages in Gujarat.

One story which is known throughout the Parsi community tells of their arrival and initial reception in India in the late eighth century. As the story goes, the Hindu ruler of Sanjan, who heard the Parsi request to immigrate to Sanjan, did not want newcomers to his land. To demonstrate his position he ordered a pitcher brimming with milk to be brought. He then likened the full pitcher to Sanjan—as the pitcher could not hold more milk, Sanjan had no room to accommodate newcomers. The senior-most *dastur* representing the Parsis drew a silver coin from his robe and carefully slipped it into the milk jug declaring, "We Persians will be like the coin in this milk. You won't even be aware of our presence." Not quite satisfied, the king asked the priests what their community could offer in return for permission to settle in his land, to which the *dastur* responded by dropping a pinch of sugar into the milk, saying "Your Highness, as the sugar sweetens the milk, so too we will strive to sweeten your lands with our earnest endeavors." Satisfied with this, the king asked them to give five assurances: (1) they must explain their religion, (2) they must give up speaking Persian in favor of Gujarati, (3) the men must not bear arms, (4) the women should wear the customary regional sari, and (5) they should hold their weddings at night.

The conditions set forth in this narrative may describe an undocumented historical event, or they may be a way the community accounts for Parsi acculturation. In any case, the story indicates some of the ways that they have adapted to their surroundings. These first steps towards adjusting to their new home were, however, tempered in important ways. Accepting these conditions did not amount to full assimilation—Parsis continued to wear the sacred woolen thread (*kusti*) and undershirt (*sudreh*), a practice still observed by some modern Parsis. From the earliest times until a century ago the observant wore a traditional skull cap, but today this practice has almost completely lapsed.

One important source of establishing a Zoroastrian identity early on in India was the *Shāhnāma,* the great Iranian epic of Firdawsi. The retelling of stories from this vast store has, in part, fulfilled a need to maintain cultural ties with their homeland, and it continues to shape their emerging Parsi identity. A strong sense of Indian national spirit does not cancel the Parsis' equally strong feelings of pride in their ancient Iranian heritage. In years past, separate schooling ensured an exposure to the *Shāhnāma,* and today these stories are received by Parsi children in much the same manner as they absorb the *Rāmāyaṇa* and the *Mahābhārata*.

The most important sources for the oral tradition of the Parsis are several types of songs sung in the distinctive dialect known as Parsi Gujarati. These include the *Monajāt,* songs of praise and devotion directed to Ahura Mazdā, or to the immortal Amesha Spentas (his six sacred creations), lullabies, wedding songs (sung by professional *goyen*), and songs of celebration. Monajāt and lullabies are typically sung by women. These have been recorded in notebooks by women and passed on to their daughters through generations. The contexts for these songs include the betrothal, the time when gifts are given to the bride, groom, or to a mother by her brother when her son or daughter is to be married, and finally, the song sung by the groom's party as they leave his house for the wedding ceremony. Some interesting details about wedding ceremonies can be learned from the wedding songs, for example, fresh *pan* (betel) leaves and flowers accompany a formal offer of marriage—the offer may be initiated from either family. According to the songs yogurt and fresh fish are the first gifts sent to the bride's family.

The lullabies in particular have been voiced and preserved by mothers. Above all, they emphasize how the family has prospered as a result of the child's birth. All auspicious things are equated with the birth, whether the newborn is male or female. One long lullaby touches on religious themes as it compares a male child to the light of the household. The light is metaphorically identified first with the grandparents, then with the parents, and finally with the infant.

Among the commemorative songs is one of particular importance for contemporary Parsis. The *Athash nu Gīt* ("Song for the Fire Installation") commemorates the construction of a fire temple at Navsari on the coast of Gujarat over a century ago. Performed on special occasions by commissioned goyen, the song takes four to six hours to complete. The lead singer is accompanied by three or four vocalists, but finding trained singers today is becoming increasingly difficult. Weddings serve as occasions for the most boisterous singing with male guests often joining in to accompany or displace the goyen. The wedding ceremony is a religious ritual, but this does not inhibit the flow of 'toddy' (a fermented drink tapped from the date palm) or whiskey that contributes to the festive atmosphere. The melodies of both commemorative songs and wedding songs are variations on Indian *rāga* melodies.

The relative scarcity of published data on Parsi folk cultural expressions cannot easily be explained.

Folklorists have yet to examine such areas as cooking and the transmission of recipes, sports (particularly cricket), humor, and religious festivals. The extremely high level of education achieved by the community as a whole, coupled with the dispersal of many in the Zoroastrian diaspora, may be leading to alterations in Parsi identity and a loss of their traditional lore. The rapid pace of urbanization and modernity—acutely felt by many Parsis—has diminished the traditional cultural loci for folklore. Conversely, new electronic forums have emerged in recent years which may compensate, even replenish, the community's ability to sustain and enrich its folklife.

References

Boyce, Mary. 1977. *A Persian stronghold of Zoroastrianism*. Oxford: Clarendon.

Choksy, J. 1989. *Purity and pollution in Zoroastrianism*. Austin: University of Texas Press.

Kulke, Eckehard. 1974. *The Parsees in India: a minority as agent of social change*. München: Weltforum Verlag.

Luhrmann, T. R. 1996. *The good Parsi. the fate of a colonial elite in a Postcolonial society*. Cambridge: Harvard University Press.

Parsiana. Ed. Jehangir Patel. Bombay: Parsiana Publications.

Wadia, Putlibai D. H. "Parsi and Gujarati Hindu nuptial songs." *Indian Antiquary* 19 (November, 1890), pp. 374–378; *Indian Antiquary* 21 (April, 1892), pp. 113–116; *Indian Antiquary* 22 (April, 1893), pp. 102–107.

The World Zoroastrian Organization http://www.w-z-o.org

Federation of Zoroastrian Organizations of North America http://www.fezana.org

Avesta–Zoroastrian Archives http.//www.avesta.org/avesta.html

TIMOTHY C. CAHILL

PARSIISM

Outlined here are some beliefs and practices of the Parsis, a small sect of Zoroastrians who emigrated from Persia to the west coast of India circa 800 C.E. in the aftermath of the Muslim invasion of Iran. Parsis follow and strive to preserve the ancient and authoritative teachings of Zarathustra, who lived in Persia in the latter half of the second millennium B.C.E. Yet it is clear that ethnicity, language, and a thousand-year residence in South Asia have also contributed to the formation of religious affinities which are unique to the Parsis.

The religion is ancient. Zoroastrian priests (*magi*) of ancient Iran were known to Herodotus in the fifth century B.C.E. Our oldest source for Zarathustra's teaching is a compilation of hymns called the Avesta ("The Injunction"), an oral composition of uncertain date (circa 900 B.C.E.?). It displays two linguistic strata of an otherwise unknown Eastern Iranian language; the first contains a kernel of seventeen hymns (*gāthā*) which are attributed to Zarathustra himself. Linguistic features point to a second stratum: the daily liturgical rite known as the "Act of Worship" (*yasna*) which incorporates the hymns, the whole being then piously preserved along with a burgeoning corpus of prayers and purification rites which came to form the canon. Like the *Ṛg Veda* (India's most ancient text), the hymns of the Avesta were memorized and preserved orally by members of a priestly class. The sacred texts were not committed to writing until the fifth century C.E.

The hymns are largely addressed of the one God, Ahura Mazdā, the eternal creator of the world and the source for all other beneficent divine beings. The divine being has an active agent, personified as Spenta Mainyu, who works in the world against an evil power known as Angra Mainyu. These two opposing spirits constantly strive to overcome one another both in the universe and in the soul of every Zoroastrian. The outcome of their battle is determined by a person's free will. Thus, Parsis believe that every individual bears sole responsibility for his or her own actions.

The realm of priest-craft is limited to the performance of rituals which still play a vital role in maintaining Parsi identity. Rules of purity form the basis for the liturgy; four types of purification apply to the laity, the most sacred lasting nine days. Zoroastrianism has no rules for fasting, nor does it encourage the ecstasy of mysticism. Parsi Zoroastrians have some important distinguishing characteristics such as strict endogamy and a refusal to accept converts. Moreover, despite the claim of some scholars—both traditional and modern—that early Zoroastrianism was dualistic, many Parsis are quite vehement in defending their faith as a strict monotheism.

Some years after their first settlement, the Parsis established their first fire temple (*agiari*) at Sanjan. The continuous maintenance of the fire—the main symbol for divine presence for Zoroastrians—is ensured by the priests who stoke it five times daily accompanied by chants from the Avesta. During their first few centuries on the subcontinent the newly arrived Zoroastrians lived in their own settlements in the state of Gujarat. According to the *Qissa-i-Sanjan* (Narrative of Sanjan) a Persian chronicle written in verse in 1600, the sacred fire was moved from Sanjan at the end of the fifteenth century due to a political upheaval. The fire was transferred to Navsari for a time and finally to Udvada in 1742. All three towns have acquired great religious and cultural prestige among the Parsis.

By the time the Mughal emperor Akbar conquered Gujarat in 1572 the Parsis had adjusted to their new environs in many outward ways while maintaining a strict adherence to their religious practices. Nevertheless, the distinct identity of the Parsis did not go unnoticed. Traditions record that Akbar invited the chief priest in Navsari, Meherji Rana, to Delhi to take part in religious debates held there. These discussions inspired Akbar to include many Zoroastrian concepts in shaping his own unique set of religious doctrines (the *Dīn-i-Ilāhī*), as well as adopting Zoroastrian names of the months and days incorporated into his new calendar.

Calculations of time were particularly important for Parsis since all rituals become effective only when performed at the correct moment. Contact with Iran via an ongoing correspondence (the "Persian *Rivāyats,*" 1478–1766) led to a controversy in the eighteenth century when it was discovered that the Parsi calendar was exactly one month behind the Iranian calendar. Certain Parsis decided to adopt the Persian calendar in June of 1745 while the majority of Parsis retained their traditional system. The resulting schism into two sects required separate temples and priesthoods, those following the former calendar, called "ancient" (*qadīm*), and those following the Iranian or "customary" (*rasmī*) one.

With the arrival of the British, many Parsis migrated to Bombay at the start of the nineteenth century from sites such as Surat, Broach, and Navsari. A key to this urbanization was a guarantee of religious freedom granted by the British East India Company, an important assurance to a people who continued to view themselves as refugees. The establishment of a fire temple and the construction of a *dakhma,* a roofless tower for exposing the deceased following funeral rites, were important factors in drawing rural Parsis to fast-growing Bombay. The city's prominence for the community can be seen in that it possesses four of the eight most sacred fire temples (*ātesh behrām*) in all of India, the others being found in Surat (two), Udvada, and Navsari.

Current sources of controversy within the community center around issues such as interfaith marriage, religious conversion, and ethnic identity, especially with respect to the religious heritage which Parsi Zoroastrians share with their Iranian co-religionists. An occult Zoroastrian sect called '*kshnūm*' also inspires debate. The "Kshnūmists," as they are popularly known, follow the teaching of Ustād Ṣāḥeb Behrāmshāh Howroji Shroff. Based upon the '*Ilm-e-kshnūm,* which involves a highly esoteric interpretation of Zoroastrian scriptures and rituals, the group affirms the validity of personal, intuitive responses to the Avesta. Included in this response is an understanding that the efficacy of the core mantras [recited verses] rests upon the sincerity with which they are recited. Such ideas have produced a mystical tradition of exegesis which many Parsis find compelling.

Another aspect of Parsi religiosity is a considerable involvement with various religious teachers of the Indo-Islamic tradition(s). Their response to these teachers met with official reprobation in the early nineteenth century and has continued to evoke the consternation of the orthodox. In recent times Parsis have looked to teachers such as Sai Baba of Shirdi, Meher Baba (himself a Parsi), and the contemporary Sai Baba of Puṭṭaparti for inspiration and reward. Visiting of Hindu and Muslim religious sites has also been commonplace, especially among women. A final observation regarding Parsi religiosity pertains to the question of differences, yet to be investigated, between rural Gujarati-speaking Parsis and the larger group of bi- or trilingual urban Parsis whose notions of their own religious identity have been shaped by a highly variegated pluralism.

References

Boyce, Mary. 1979. *Zoroastrians: their religious beliefs and practices*. London: Routledge, Kegan Paul.

Hinnells, J. R. 1987. Parsi attitudes to religious pluralism. In *Indian attitudes to religious pluralism,* ed. H. Coward. Albany: State University of New York Press, pp. 195–223.

Hodivala, Shahpurushah Hormasji. 1920. *Studies in Parsi history*. Bombay: (Includes a translation of the *Qissah-i Sanjan,* available online at:http://www.avesta.org/other/qsanjan.html.)

Menant, Delphine. 1977. *The Parsis in India*. 2 vols. Enlarged and annotated by M. M. Murzban. Bombay.

Modi, Jivanji J. 1986 [1922]. *The religious ceremonies and customs of the Parsees*. 2nd ed. Bombay: Society for the Promotion of Zoroastrian Religious Knowledge and Education.

TIMOTHY C. CAHILL

PAṢHTŪNWALĪ

Paṣhtūnwalī refers to idealized moral standards taken to be the code, particularly of honor, for the Pashtun of the Afghanistan-Pakistan borderlands. Its provenance, distribution, and precise content are unclear. The term appears to be unknown among western and southern Afghans, the so-called Durrani tribes between Kandahar and Herat, and it is not current among Ghilzai between Kandahar and Kabul, although Ghilzai are able to deconstruct the term to mean distinctively Pashtun ways. One folk etymology, probably influenced by efforts of the Pashtu Academy (Kabul) to record and regularize usage, relates the suffix *-walī* to the Afghan government designation for "governor" and "jurisdiction." In Pakhtu, *-wāl* also designates the inhabitants of a territory who are presumed to share customs and a character (*khūy*).

The term has some currency on the North-West Frontier of Pakistan, where British administrators took it to be a primitive or customary law in the unadministered Tribal Areas and tried to regularize it as part of the Frontier Crimes Regulation of 1901. From such efforts, analysts derive a set of "injunctions" to hospitality (*melmastyā*), asylum (*nanawātī*), revenge (*jang*, more specifically "fighting for honor"). To this list, Akbar S. Ahmed, a Pakistani successor to British officers on the Frontier and student of tribal society there, has added agnatic rivalry (*tarbūrwalī*) and protection of women. Such efforts amount to claiming the more formal status of law, and its prestige in the context of a bureaucratic state, for what is more properly a general morality locally called Pashtun honor (*nang-i-pakhtana*).

Collectivity and morality are key to these ideas. Their scope is public interaction, which ideally is structured as symmetry between persons. Contemporary Pashtun will compare Paṣhtūnwalī to the Golden Rule, but the indigenous reference is to "honor." Paṣhtūnwalī secures honor not only in the public and collective form of protecting those under one's charge (the male and political gloss that passed into the literature), but also in the form of respect extended to others that secures the independence of all. In this latter sense, Benedicte Grima has described how women are not just objects of honor, but are upholders and protectors of collective honor as well.

Comparatively, therefore, Paṣhtūnwalī is the interpersonal morality of a heroic society comparable to rule of law for a bureaucratic and bourgeois one. Its focus is honor, operationalized as independence rather than in societal institutions, and it refers not to individual rights but to obligations incurred to others in a context of intensely competitive, even agonistic, relations. Thus, it makes frequent reference to protecting landholdings (whose most solemn version is homeland, *waṭan*), house and women, guests and clients. Such obligations are intensely personal, which suggests analogies to tort (that is, individual responsibilities) law, although honor, not justice in some abstract sense as a social right is their reference.

Paṣhtūnwalī has been extended to include *jihād* (religious struggle) in Afghanistan, although the main thrust of Paṣhtūnwalī is self-help, which otherwise stands in contradiction to Islamic law in the keeping of religious specialists. Prior to the recent civil wars in Afghanistan, Pakhtun custom, generally, and Paṣhtūnwalī (as honor), in particular, were casually held to conflict with the letter, if not the spirit, of bookish Islam, as in the proverb: "There are things in Khost [a remote tribal district] that are not in the Book [Qur'ān] and things in the Book that are not in Khost." This is despite another commonly held belief that Pashtun custom (*rawāj*) is inherently Islamic, since Pashtun claim an ancestry that is wholly within the time of Islam and that reframes tribal customs as Islamic.

References

Ahmed, Akbar S. 1980. *Pakhtun economy and society.* London: Routledge and Kegan Paul.

Atayee, M. Ibrahim. 1979 [1958]. *A dictionary of terminology of Pashtun's tribal customary law and usages,* ed. A. Jabar Nadar, trans. A. Mohammad Shinwary. Kabul: International Center for Pashto Studies.

Berry, Willard. 1966. *Aspects of the frontier crimes regulation in Pakistan.* Durham, N.C.: Duke University Program in Comparative Studies on Southern Asia.

Grima, Benedicte. 1992. *The performance of emotion among Paxtun women.* Austin: University of Texas Press.

Steul, Willi. 1981. *Paschtunwali: Ein Ehrenkodex und seine rechtliche Relevanz* [*Paṣhtūnwalī*: A Code of Honor and Its Legal Relevance]. Wiesbaden: Franz Steiner Verlag.

JON W. ANDERSON

SEE ALSO
Afghanistan; North-West Frontier Province

PAṬA CITRA

One of the noteworthy religious folk art traditions in the state of Orissa is that of the devotional *paṭa citra,* or painting on cloth. These paintings are associated with the god Jagannātha, considered a form of Kṛṣṇa, and with the famous twelfth-century temple to Jagannātha in Puri, one of the principal pilgrimage sites in all of India. The "triad" of deities is worshiped in this temple: Jagannātha, his brother Balabhadra, and his sister Subhadrā.

Communities of artists known as *citrakāra*s, who live in the vicinity of the Jagannātha temple in Puri (and of other Jagannātha temples), paint the paṭa citras, which are purchased by pilgrims who visit the temple. The paintings made for pilgrims are called *jātrī paṭi*s. Besides producing paṭa citras a few citrakāras also have ritual painting duties inside the temple. A master artist may operate a studio, supervising family members and apprentices.

Characteristics

The artist begins work on a paṭa citra by gluing together two large sheets of cotton cloth, drying them in the sun, cutting them into smaller pieces (ranging from a few inches to several feet on a side), and polishing their surfaces. The citrakāra sketches a design on one of the surfaces, which is polished more finely than the other, and fills in the outlines with primary colors. Finer details are subsequently added over these areas of solid color.

Some formal characteristics of paṭa citras are a solid background color (often red), a standard palette of colors (usually red, blue, yellow, green, black, white, and pink), faces (except for those of the Jagannātha triad) in profile with extended noses and elongated eyes, and the inclusion of a double border with floral designs. Paṭa citras impress with their bright color and strong line. In recent years, a monochrome (black) style has also developed.

Themes

Several categories of themes appear in paṭa citras. A principal category relates to the Jagannātha triad. In one theme, the three deities are depicted as they appear in the inner sanctum. Variations on this theme show the deities in the different types of dress in which they are clothed in the temple, and portray scenes in which Jagannātha is equated with Kṛṣṇa or Viṣṇu. For example, Jagannātha, like Viṣṇu, rescues an elephant that was seized by a crocodile. Paṭa citras also depict scenes from the mythology of Jagannātha. For example, in the "journey to Kanchi" theme, Jagannātha and Balabhadra are shown on their way to a battle they fought for a devoted king. The traditional *baḍhiā* paintings provide a schematic map of the Puri temple precincts, filled with scenes from mythology or temple rituals.

Scenes from the Hindu epics and *purāṇa*s (mythological texts) comprise a second thematic category. For example, some paṭa citras depict the incident from the *Bhagavata Purāṇa* in which the young Kṛṣṇa lifted Mount Govardhana to protect his villagers from the storms of Indra; some depict the scene from the epic *Rāmāyaṇa* in which the hero-god Rāma goes into exile in the forest. A more recent type of paṭa citra is what Das (1982: 73) calls a "story painting," in which a central image, such as Kṛṣṇa and Rādhā embracing, is surrounded by scenes from the life of Kṛṣṇa or images of the ten incarnations of Viṣṇu. A third category of themes includes depictions of other deities, such as Śiva or Sarasvatī.

The declining paṭa citra tradition was revived in the 1950s by Halina Zealey, a Western woman who was staying in Orissa. She fostered the citrakāras' work by purchasing paintings and arranging exhibitions. Since then, the tradition has remained strong. Now the citrakāras' clients include not only pilgrims but also collectors from India and abroad.

References

Chandra, Sarat. 1991. The art and craft of Patta painting. *Arts of Asia* 21, no. 4: 139–145.

———. 2001. Beshas of the Puri Triad: A unique aesthetic tradition. *Arts of Asia* 31, no. 4: 80–96.

Das, J. P. 1982. *Puri paintings*. Atlantic Highlands, N.J.: Humanities Press.

Mohanty, Bijoy Chandra. 1980. *Patachitras of Orissa*. (Study of contemporary textile crafts of India). Ahmedabad, India: Calico Museum of Textiles.

———. 1984. *Pata-paintings of Orissa*. New Delhi: Publications Division, Ministry of Information and Broadcasting, Government of India.

Rossi, Barbara. 1998. *From the ocean of painting: India's popular paintings 1589 to the present*. New York: Oxford University Press.

BERNARD CESARONE

PAṬHKABITĀ

Paṭhkabitā, or roadside poetry, is a kind of Bangladeshi folk ballad that narrates incidents of real life. These poems are of limited length, not exceeding eight to sixteen pages, each page containing about twenty-five to thirty short lines. The poet first composes the poem orally for an audience and then sells its printed version. Paṭhkabitā is, indeed, a bridge between oral and written literary traditions. It may be called "folk" for two reasons: first, because it is composed orally, and second, because it is intended for an audience that chiefly belongs to folk groups. Such groups are composed of people of a particular region or tribe who have no formal education but do have artistic expressions unique to them. The stories it most often narrates are those of sentimental love, public issues, political incidents, adventures, and violence.

The paṭhkabitā's prologue praises Allah and introduces the poet to the audience. The incident is then narrated in rhymed verse, although strict meter and full rhyme are not followed. Most lines end with a half rhyme, such as "let" and "cot" as compared to the full rhyme of "let" and "get." In the epilogue, the poet emerges as a folk philosopher, providing solutions to the kinds of social problems addressed in the poem and appealing to the audience to follow the right path.

Perhaps the most interesting element of these verse stories is the poet himself, who composes and publishes his poems, as well as peddles them from one market to another, singing aloud the whole narrative for the spectators he attracts. Unlike the *Bāul* and other mystic poets, this poet is not indifferent to worldly concerns and is guided by pragmatic profit motives. Upon completion of his performance, he eagerly tries to sell the poem, even at very low prices just to make a sale. The poet follows the crowds, whether they be in buses, trains, steamers, *ferryghāṭ* (ferry landings), or railway junctions. Prized for its wit and humor, paṭhkabitā is of great interest to both urban and rural people. It is, indeed, a lively bridge between spontaneous folk poetry and modern urban literary poetry.

References

Ahmed, Wakil. 1381 Bengali year. 1974. *Bānglār Loksangskriti* (Folk Culture of Bengal). Dhaka: Bangla Academy.

Huda, Mohammad Nurul. 1986. *Flaming flowers: Poets' response to the emergence of Bangladesh.* Dhaka: Bangla Academy.

Islam, Mazharul. 1380 Bengali year. 1973. *Folklore Pariciti Ebang Loksāhityer Pothanpāthon* (Introducing Folklore and the Study of Folk Literature). Dhaka: Bangla Academy.

MOHAMMAD NURUL HUDA

SEE ALSO

Song, Bengal

PATTINI

Pattini (Tamil: *Kaṇṇaki*) is a goddess of Buddhists and Hindus in Sri Lanka. Pattini is the only major goddess of Buddhist Sinhalas, ranking as one of the most powerful deities. In some regions, she is classed as one of the four guardian deities of the island, along with Viṣṇu, Nātha and Kataragama. Though her popularity has waned in recent decades, the worship of Pattini was at one time prevalent in the western and southern coastal regions, in Sabaragamuva, and in the Eastern Province. In ritual texts, she is often referred to as Pattini of Navagamuva, the southwestern village where her main shrine is located.

Pattini is associated with disturbances caused by excessive heat. Her anger produces fire, drought, famine, epidemics, and infectious diseases such as smallpox and measles. The annual propitiation of the goddess is done to cool her anger, thus ensuring the blessings of the deity and the prevention of "heaty" conditions. In the southern region of Sri Lanka, the major rituals associated with Pattini are *gammaḍuva* ("hall in the village") and *aṅkeḷiya* ("horn game").

There are scores of texts related to Pattini, but the outline of her life story is recounted in similar fashion by Sinhala Buddhists and Tamil Hindus and in the epic South Indian Tamil poem, the *Cilappatikāram* (Tale of the Anklet) (probably composed in the period C.E. 500–800). Though many scholars view the ritual texts as derived from the Cilappatikāram, Obeyesekere (1984) has argued that while some aspects of the ritual traditions were thus derived, it is more likely that the epic itself was crafted from ritual traditions.

The basic story, as given in the Sinhala ritual texts, is as follows: born from a golden mango, Pattini marries Pālaṅga (Kōvalan), the son of a merchant prince. However, he falls in love with a beautiful courtesan, Madevi, and goes to live with her, spending all his wealth. After some time, Pālaṅga decides to leave Madevi and, destitute, he returns to Pattini. Pattini gives him her precious gem-studded anklet, and they leave for the city of Madurai, the city of the king of Pāṇḍi (in present-day Tamil Nadu). After many adventures, they come to the outskirts of Madurai, and while Pattini waits, Pālaṅga enters the city, planning to sell the anklet. While in the city, he is betrayed by a goldsmith, who claims he stole the anklet from the Pāṇḍi queen. For this offence, he is tortured and executed by the king without a trial. Pattini comes in search of him and resurrects him. She then confronts the king of Pāṇḍi and, in revenge for the death of her husband, casts out her left breast, destroying the king, the city, and its inhabitants with fire.

In southern Sri Lanka, the main body of Pattini texts in Sinhala is known as the *pantis kōlmura,* or "thirty-five ritual texts." These detailed texts, notable for their poetic quality, contain most of the ritual prescriptions related to the goddess. Indeed, the lament of Pattini over the death of her husband is considered one of the finest poems in Sinhala ritual tradition. The myths that recount Pattini's origins, including the prior lives of the goddess, are informed by a Buddhist ethos. Pattini offers alms to the Buddhas and aspires to become a Buddha herself, making a wish to be born as a male in a future life.

Reference

Obeyesekere, Gananath. 1984. *The cult of the goddess Pattini.* Chicago: University of Chicago Press.

SUSAN A. REED

SEE ALSO

Aṅkeḷiya; Buddhism and Buddhist Folklore; Self-sacrifice

PENZER, NORMAN MOSLEY

Penzer (1892–1960) contributed to South Asian folklore *The Ocean of Story* (1924–1928), an annotated and indexed edition of C. H. Tawney's translation of Somadeva's eleventh century C.E. *Kathāsaritsāgara.* Penzer's edition, reprinted in 1968, remains the standard source not only on Somadeva's work, but also on the lost *Bṛhatkathā,* a collection of folktales said to have been composed by Guṇāḍhya in Paiśācī, a variety of Prakrit, in the fifth century C.E., and which Somadeva retold in Sanskrit in the eleventh century.

A bibliophile of vast learning and varied interests, Penzer first produced studies of cotton and mineral resources of the British Empire. As joint secretary of the Burton Memorial Fund, he published a monumental *Annotated Bibliography of Sir Richard Francis Burton* (1923) and an edition of Burton's *Selected Papers in Anthropology, Travel and Exploration* (1924), but he disappointed those who expected from him a biography of the famous traveler and translator of the *Arabian Nights*. While reading Burton's papers, Penzer was captivated by a section of Charles Henry Tawney's translation of the *Kathāsaritsāgara*. As he reminisced in the "Retrospect" to his edition of Tawney's work, "it seemed almost as if Burton, with whom [he] had . . . become so intimate, was offering [him] the chance of giving to the public the Indian counterpart of his own great *Arabian Nights*." Without a knowledge of Sanskrit, but animated by "a deep interest in Oriental folklore," he proceeded to publish a ten-volume edition of the translation of the *Kathāsaritsāgara* that Tawney had published in two volumes in 1880–1884. Besides changes and additions to the translation contributed by L. D. Barnett, Penzer's edition features extensive commentary that runs from brief notes to long appendices, in which he examines the motifs and migration of stories, myths, and elements of material culture, with bibliographical references. Though secondary in nature, Penzer's work is a mine of information on various aspects of Indian and comparative folklore.

Penzer further published a retelling in English, illustrated with miniatures by P. Zenker, of the story of *Nala and Damayanti* (1926), which coalesces the versions in the *Kathāsaritsāgara,* the *Mahābhārata,* and other sources. He reprised four of the appendices to the *Ocean of Story*—on poison-damsels, the tale of the two thieves, sacred prostitution, and the romance of betel-chewing—in updated and expanded versions in *Poison-Damsels and Other Essays in Folklore and Anthropology* (1952).

Penzer oversaw for the Argonaut Press in the 1920s and 1930s the edition of a series of volumes of voyages and explorations, contributing himself a volume on the travels of Marco Polo (1929). Most notable among his other works are an annotated edition of a translation of *The Pentamerone of Giambattista Basile* by Benedetto Croce (1932) and an extensive, illustrated description and history of *The Harēm* in the grand seraglio of the Turkish sultans in Istambul (1936). His last years were devoted to studies of antique silver and of wine labels.

ROSANE ROCHER

SEE ALSO

Folklorists

PĒRAṆṬĀLU

Pērantālu is a Telugu word referring to deified women, either unwidowed or unmarried, who died in an unusual and extraordinary manner—such as by performing self-immolation (*satī*) or suicide, or by sacrificing themselves to protect walls of water tanks or newly dug wells—who were killed by their husbands or by thieves, or who died in an accident. A widowed woman, however, cannot become a pēraṇṭālu. Pēraṇṭālu also include children who were killed by thieves or wicked relatives, or who died in accidents and later exhibited miracles to the surrounding people. Such a spirit becomes a kind of village goddess. Women who become Pēraṇṭālu may come from several non-Brahman castes, and even from 'untouchable' castes, but they generally do not come from Brahman families, because Brahman do not worship pēraṇṭālu. Worshipping pēraṇṭālu is widespread in the Circar and Rayalaseema regions of Andhra Pradesh, south India, where there are as many as two hundred pēraṇṭālu temples. Tirupatamma, Erukala Nanchari, Sarojinamma, Balaravamma, Viramma, and Rangamma are some of the major pēraṇṭālu deities in Andhra Pradesh. A large number of pēraṇṭālu legends and myths are maintained in several folk performance traditions.

Pēraṇṭālu are of two kinds: *iṇṭi* (house) *pēraṇṭālu* and village (*vūri*) *pēraṇṭālu*. In several Telugu families ancestral women are worshipped, particularly when an important family ritual takes place. When the dead woman is worshipped only by her family she is called an iṇṭi pēraṇṭālu. When the deceased woman has shown miracles and attracts wider attention, she is subsequently worshipped by the whole village or even the region, and is called vūri pēraṇṭālu or pēraṇṭālu devata.

Pēraṇṭālu can be both malevolent and benevolant, but generally they are regarded as *challantitalli* (benevolent mother). Women like pēraṇṭālu more than they do the village goddesses because pēraṇṭālu protect women from widowhood. People believe that pēraṇṭālu can bestow children on barren women, find unmarried girls suitable husbands, and bless married women with perpetual unwidowhood. While most of the village goddesses are worshipped out of fears, the pēraṇṭālu are adored with love and devotion. Farmers worship pēraṇṭālu as guardians of their fields. They cook rice (*bōnam*) in front of a shrine, mix it with the blood of a sacrificed animal, offer it to the pēraṇṭālu, and then place it in their fields to ward off evil spirits and to increase their yields.

Thousands of people, especially those belonging to agricultural communities, throng to the shrines of pēraṇṭālu during the fairs and festival days (*jātara* and *tirunaḷḷa*) of the deities in the months of February, March, and April. Big fairs are conducted in these tirunaḷḷa days. People offer cooked rice (bōnam), and sacrificed goats, cocks, and rams in the name of pēraṇṭālu in front of the shrine to the village goddess, which is erected adjacent to every pēraṇṭālu shrine. The insignia of unwidowed women (*sumangali*), turmeric, vermilion (*kumkuma*), bangles, flowers, silver toe-rings (*mettelu*), and the *mangala sutra,* a sacred thread to which two small golden discs are fixed, are the main offerings to the pēraṇṭālu.

Inscriptional and literary evidence suggest that pēraṇṭālu cult traditions may not be over 400 years old. The pēraṇṭālu who are being worshipped today were deified not more than 200 years ago. It is possible that the entire structure of the cult is adopted from the tradition of worshiping village goddesses such as Mariamma, Ankamma, and Peddamma.

References

Census of India Vol. II Part VII B (10) Andhra Pradesh. *Fairs and festivals*.

Crooke. W. 1993. *Folklore of India*. New Delhi: Aryan Books International.

PULIKONDA SUBBACHARY

SEE ALSO

Fairs and Festivals; Goddesses, Hindu; Gods and Goddesses; *Mariamma; Satī;* Self-sacrifice; Worship

PERFORMANCE STUDIES

The study of performance in South Asian folklore is inseparable from the history of the concept in international folkloristics. Drawing on the pool of anthropological, literary, linguistic, and theater studies that coalesced into a performance-centered approach to folklore in the 1970s, performance studies in South Asia has produced a new literature that has changed the textual orientation of Indology. Although no sustained theory of performance has yet emerged, this new approach has demonstrated that the meanings of folklore are not confined to words but are encoded also in events, such as speech acts, behavior, music, song, and dance. Despite differing emphases, vocabularies, and conclusions, the numerous monographs published since 1970 have extended the definition and enriched our understanding of text, audience, and genre in South Asian folklore.

Nineteenth century and early twentieth century collections of South Asian oral literature followed contemporaneous collections elsewhere in their lack of attention to performance. An exception is R. C. Temple (1850–1931), who relished tracking down his Punjabi bards wherever he could find them, who (he said) published tales as they were told, and who included a transliteration of the performed texts. Even earlier, in her 1868 collection of tales, Mary Frere (1845–1911) anticipated folklorists' concerns of a century later when she included the voice of her informant, Anna Liberata De Souza, as "The Narrator's Narrative." Verrier Elwin (1902–1964), prolific folklorist of the mid-twentieth century, learned from his predecessors and "avoided bowdlerization as much as possible" (1944, xix) but still did not describe a performance event, except in the most general terms.

The major breakthrough in the study of folk performance in South Asia came from another quarter, the field of anthropology, in the writings of Milton Singer who conducted research on the so-called Great Tradition and Little Tradition in Madras city in the 1950s. Influenced by Robert Redfield, Singer explored several key concepts that performance-oriented folklorists came to discuss two decades later: events, communication, community, and media. He coined the term "cultural performances" to describe the musical concerts, weddings, and temple festivals to which his informants led the anthropologist in answer to his questions. Singer singled out these events not only because Hindus in Madras defined culture through them, but also because they represented discrete units of observation that enabled him to define the otherwise elusive object—"culture." Examining these events for their role in the development of civilization, Singer isolated three factors: location, performers ("specialists," he called them), and modes of communication. Location, or context, Singer observed, defined the institutional base of performance, its patrons and audiences. "Specialists" interested him because they were the living mediums through which culture was transmitted, from village to town to city, or vice versa. Performers were genres, he came close to saying, in that they defined themselves on the basis of their medium, whether dance, drama, song, or epic narration. For this reason, Singer reserved special significance for these media:

> I realized that the modes of communication—the "cultural media"—were themselves worthy of study, for it was these forms and not printed books that carried the content of belief and practice expressing the living outlook of a majority of the population. (1972, 76).

Singer also suggested that mass media, especially film, be added to the study of cultural performances. His final recommendation, which again anticipated the direction of performance studies in later decades, was that scholars study various performances of the *Rāmāyaṇa* in order to understand the complex exchange between folk and elite culture in Indian civilization.

More recent studies of narrative performance in South Asia have complicated the idea of "text," so central to earlier Indological scholarship. Documentation of different tellings of the "same" story (the Rāma story is a prime example) have rendered obsolete the idea of a fixed, single-author text. Similarly, any rigid distinction

Bow song performance or Muttupattan story. Tamil Nadu, India, 1978, © Stuart Blackburn

between oral and written texts has been undermined by studies of oral performances during which the performer reads or refers to written and printed books and manuscripts. This new knowledge of performed texts has led some to question basic terms; A. K. Ramanujan (1929–1993), for instance, rejected the use of "version" and "variant" because they imply a unitary, authentic text of which they are incomplete or discrepant imitations, and preferred the neutral term "telling." In what relation a performed text stands to a written text, however, is still a vexed issue, if only because the notion of a static, often ancient "text" is important in local communities who sing or hear stories. The Hindi text of *Rāmcaritmānas,* for example, is performed in several different settings, by different performers, who present alternative episodes and interpret them from various theological angles, yet each telling is said to be the text composed by Tulsidas in the sixteenth century. Whether as mental construct or physical aide-memoir, then, texts remain central to performance studies, and many writers recognize this force of narrative (Blackburn 1988). What we do know is that South Asian performed texts, or tellings, are rarely complete and never final; episodes encapsulate entire plots, and certain contexts demand that only a particular portion of the story be told.

A continuity between earlier Indology and performance studies of South Asian texts is a shared emphasis on epics. Other narrative genres, such as tales, legends, and myths, are unstudied from a performance perspective, although Kirin Narayan (1989) has analyzed tales told for religious purposes, and Ann Gold and Gloria Raheja (1994) have written about gender and tale-telling among women in Rajasthan. However, no other genre has attracted as much scholarly attention as oral epics, especially in India. Not all monographs on oral epics place performance at the center of analysis, but they all contribute to the ongoing debate over improvisation and memorization in performance. Although no systematic oral-formulaic study has been produced, several scholars have written in detail about formulaic composition, and the emerging consensus is that memorization is as important as improvisation in South Asian performances; what is missing in this debate are good definitions of improvisation and memorization (since a repeated phrase can be interpreted as both). A related omission in performance studies is formal analysis of language; John D. Smith's study (1991) of a Rajasthani epic is the only comprehensive treatment of this topic. The role of music in this controversy over compositional technique has also received insufficient attention, despite work by Regina Qureshi (1983) on *qawwāḷi* in North India, Edward Henry on wedding songs in Uttar Pradesh (1988), and Susan Wadley on epics (1989).

Following the lead of international folkloristics, theater studies have contributed significantly to the study of performance in South Asia with descriptions of choreography and performer training, as well as theoretical concepts. Phillip Zarrilli (1984), for example, has developed a concept of "scenario," while Richard Schechner (1976) has explored the transformations between everyday life, ritual, and theater. Anthropologist Bruce Kapferer (1983) has brought a dramaturgical perspective to bear on the analysis of exorcistic dance performances in Sri Lanka.

Irrespective of genre, performance studies in South Asia have expanded the notion of context to include more complex descriptions of audience and community. One major contribution is the point that audiences are not static receptors of performance since they shape the content of performance in many ways, including monetary donations and "voting with their feet." Several writers have drawn attention to the "contract" established between performer and audience, an unspoken agreement about what constitutes a successful presentation, including time of day, dress, delivery style, and music. The concept of audience is also plural since we know that invisible patrons influence events as much as do direct viewers, although analyses of the wider market in which performances are paid for and consumed have not yet been written. The concept of audience is also reflexive since listeners and auditors may become characters in performance. Distinguishing different types of audiences (immediate, overhearing, distant patrons, and so forth) has led to a discussion of the relation between community and performance as elaborated by Joyce Flueckiger (1996). Some performances, typically male, public singing of epics, encode regional, caste, or linguistic identities, and these community self-images may influence narrative content in a telling (Narayana Rao 1986; Joyce Flueckiger 1988). In arguing that performances activate identity, these studies underscore the force of Singer's idea of a "cultural performance." However, and despite the ethnographic orientation of many studies of South Asian performance, the reception and use of performed stories is still not well understood.

Finally, performance studies have opened new perspectives on genre classification in South Asian folklore. In international folkloristics, genres have been defined by evolutionary, functional, and textual criteria, but studies in South Asia indicate that genres are defined, at least in part, by performance features. South Asian folk genres are usually named by delivery style (*gīt,* "singing"); by medium (*tōlubommalāṭa,* "leather puppet dancing"); by instrument (*vil pāṭṭu,* "bow song"); by prop (*muṭiyeṯṯu,* "wearing the crown"; *paṛ vācaṉo,* "narrating the scroll"); by performative intent (*vrat kathā,* a "vow-story"; *tamāśa,* "spectacle"); or by formal feature (*ḍholā,* a specific meter). Many folk performers are similarly known by their instrument, for instance, *kamsāḷeyavaru,* "those of the metal-cymbals." For this reason alone, as evidence of indigenous concepts and systems of thought, genre classification and performance studies generally promise to yield fresh insights into broad cultural issues in the study of South Asia.

The full spectrum of performance genres is yet to be reported from South Asia, and many already reported (jokes and proverbs, for instance) are not well studied in performance. However, if one is willing to hazard a generalization, it would be that performances in South Asia are multi-media events (mixing written texts, singing, visual props, instruments, and spirit possession) in a public construction of local identities and histories.

References

Blackburn, Stuart. 1988. *Singing of birth and death: texts in performance*. Philadelphia: University of Pennsylvania Press.

Elwin, Verrier. 1944. *Folk-tales of Mahakoshal*. London: Oxford University Press.

Flueckiger, Joyce Burkhalter. 1988. He should have worn a sari. *The Drama Review*. 32(1): 159–169.

———. 1996. *Gender and genre in the folklore of middle India*. Ithaca, N.Y.: Cornell University Press.

Frere, Mary. 1967 [1868]. *Old Deccan days, or Hindu fairy legends current in southern India*. New York: Dover.

Gold, Ann Grodzins and Gloria G. Raheja. 1994. *Listen to the heron's words: reimagining gender and kinship in north India*. Berkeley: University of California Press.

Henry, Edward O. 1988. *Chant the names of God: music and culture in Bhojpuri-speaking India*. San Diego: San Diego University Press.

Kapferer, Bruce. 1983. *A celebration of demons: exorcism and the aesthetics of healing in Sri Lanka*. Bloomington: Indiana University Press.

Narayan, Kirin. 1989. *Storytellers, saints and scoundrels: folk narrative in Hindu religious teaching*. Philadelphia: University of Pennsylvania Press.

Narayana Rao, Velcheru. 1986. Epics and ideologies: six Telugu folk epics. In *Another harmony: new essays on the folklore of India,* ed. Stuart Blackburn and A.K. Ramanujan, 131–164. Berkeley: University of California Press.

Qureshi, Regula Burkhardt. 1983. *Qawwālī*: Making the music happen in the Sufi assembly. In *Performing arts in India: Essays on music, dance, and drama,* ed. Bonnie C. Wade, 118–157. Berkeley: Center for South and Southeast Asian Studies, University of California, Berkeley.

Schechner, Richard. 1977. *Essays on performance theory 1970–1976*. New York: Drama Book Specialists.

Singer, Milton. 1972. *When a great tradition modernizes: an anthropological approach to Indian civilization*. New York: Praeger.
Smith, John D. 1991. *The epic of Pābūjī: a study, transcription and translation*. Cambridge: Cambridge University Press.
Temple, R. C. The *legends of the Panjab*. 3 vols. Bombay: Education Society's Press; London: Trubner and Co.
Wadley, Susan S. 1989. Choosing a path: performance strategies in the north India epic dhola. In *Oral epics in India*, eds. Stuart Blackburn, Joyce Flueckiger, Peter Claus, and Susan Wadley, 75–101. Berkeley: University of California Press.
Zarrilli, Phillip. 1984. *The kathakali complex: actor, performance, structure*. New Delhi: Abhinav.

STUART BLACKBURN

SEE ALSO
Epic; Theater and Drama

PERSON

Marcel Mauss, the French sociologist, first offered a social history of the idea or category of the person. Mauss's work demonstrated that the meaning of the category of the person is culturally relative. His work, however, suffers from its evolutionary framework, which can be read as putting the Western idea of the fully individualized self as the height of progress, rather than as a different idea of the self. Louis Dumont, influenced by Mauss, argued that the person as a unique individual possessing all the rights, aptitudes, and qualities upon which the social order is naturally based is primarily a Western cultural idea, not an ontological being existing in all societies (1970, 8–11, 273–78). In India, he argued, society is primary and has those rights, aptitudes, and qualities. He correctly emphasized that the Indian person is constituted as a part of, and dependent upon, society, but, unfortunately, he also hypostatizes society and neglects the experience of Indians themselves.

More recently, McKim Marriott has argued that Hindu India does not conceive of "individuals," but rather of "dividuals," aggregates of fluid, fluctuating and transacting forces, and elements in the universe (Marriott 1979, 1980). Although Marriott rightly emphasizes that the person may have multiple identities in the process of daily life and that one's person changes as relationships with other change, his reduction of the person to psychophysical forces deprives the human person of what most characterizes it in Hindu quotidian understanding.

Anthony Carter, using interviews with Indians about what a person is rather than developing his own theory, presents a convincing argument for the Hindu conception of person and how one becomes a person (1982). According to Carter, the person (*vyakti*) is an individual possessing a human body through which he/she manifests her/his own independent personality (*vyaktitva*). Only a human can be *vyakti* because, unlike the gods, a *vyakti* has an earthly body, and although they share with animals the needs for food, sleep, and sexual activity, humans alone live according to *dharma* (moral principles and ethics). Unlike the gods and demons, human persons make moral judgements and live in the earthly world of *saṃsāra* of change, flux, desire, joy, and sorrow where such moral judgments are necessary for orderly social life. Thus, much Indian folklore concerns itself with the person struggling with the demands of kin roles and other kinspersons, as well as with the ubiquitous persons of scoundrels, fools, and clever tricksters. Daily, gurus use humorous tales about such folkloric persons to paint meaningful spiritual and morally didactic messages for their followers.

Unlike the Western person, who at birth is constituted with the potential to develop into a full personality through his/her individual experiences and choices, the Hindu person is in part already constituted by a *jīva* (soul) that has gone through previous births and carries with it traces of past lives and previous personalities that can effect present personality. Yet, the influence of the transcendental *jīva* is only partial; it is not identical with the earthly *vyakti*. Moreover, the particular conjuction of planets under which a person is born can affect one's present life and personality. Finally, a person's body is inherited from parents and ancestors and carries with it some of their qualities and features of social personhood. Thus, in folklore, Brahmans are often ridiculed for their inherent stinginess and gluttony.

Yet, not every Hindu is fully a *vyakti,* because not all have the ability to make mature moral judgments. In Hindu understanding, personhood is socially constituted through being embedded in a "web of relatedness" (Parish 1994) rather than individually constituted through the naturalized, psychological processes of separation and independence, as in the West. Thus, full, moral persons are those socially shaped, molded, and transformed by Hindu rites of passage (*saṃskāra*s). Of greatest importance among those, at least in the eyes of upper castes, are the sacred thread ceremony (*upanayana*) that separates males from childhood and requires them to live according to adult, ritual rules of *dharma* and the marriage ceremony *(śādī)* that invests both males and females with mature personhood and responsibility for creation and maintenance of a family. Finally, at the funeral ceremony (*mṛtyu saṃskāra*) when the soul *(jīva)* is separated from its body and its involvement with the living, the earthly person (*vyakti*) dies but the *jīva* remains to be reborn. Young children, not having passed through important rites of passage, are not cremated, but buried, just as holy men (*sanyāsī*s), having already had their funeral obsequies performed, are buried; neither are full persons.

The person's body is really two interpenetrating bodies: the gross or physical body *(sthūla śarīra)* and the interior, subtle body *(liṅga śarīra)*. Located in the subtle body is the *manas* (mind/heart), the center of reason and emotion, as well as of subtle and gross bodies. Mind and body are identical. Personality is not merely in consciousness but also in the body. Thus, characteristics of one's personality may be affected by contact with other persons or things, such as the soil on which one lives or by food exchanged with others, including the gods who give *prasād* (remains of offerings to the gods that transfer to human persons something of the divine essence). The wrestler's physical exercise of his gross body affects his inner subtle body and thereby creates a specific kind of moral person, just as austerities *(tapasya)* or the proper performance of one's *dharma* can create a person possessing great mystical power. Indumati, although a lowly courtesan, was able to perform a *satyakriyā* (an act of truth power), whereby she made the mighty river Ganges flow upstream because she was true to her *dharma* by serving alike members of all castes who paid for her services.

References

Alter, Joseph. 1992. *The wrestler's body: identity and ideology in north India*. Berkeley: University of California Press.

Beck, Brenda E. F., Peter J. Claus, Praphulladatta Goswami, and Jawaharlal Handoo, eds. 1987. *Folktales of India*. Chicago: University of Chicago Press.

Daniel, E. Valentine. 1984. *Fluid signs: being a person in the Tamil way*. Berkeley: University of California Press.

Carter, Anthony. 1982. Hierarchy and the concept of the person in western India. In *Concepts of person: kinship, caste, and marriage in India,* Harvard Studies in Cultural Anthropology, vol. 5, eds. Akos Oster, Lina Fruzzeti, and Steve Barnett, 118-142. Cambridge, Mass.: Harvard University Press.

Dumont, Louis. 1977. *Homo hierarchicus: the caste system and its implications*. Chicago: University of Chicago Press.

Karve, Iravati. 1961. *Hindu society: an interpretation*. Poona: Deccan College.

Marriott, McKim. 1980. *The open Hindu person and interpersonal fluidity*. Paper presented at the Meetings of the Association for Asian Studies (xerox).

———. 1979. *The open Hindu person and the humane sciences*. Unpublished Paper (xerox).

Mauss, Marcel. 1985 [1938]. A category of the human mind: the notion of person: the notion of self. In *The category of the person: anthropology, philosophy, history,* eds. Michael Carrithers, Steven Collins, and Steven Lukes, 1–25. Cambridge and New York: Cambridge University Press.

Narayān, Kirin. 1989. *Storytellers, saints, and scoundrels: folk narratives in Hindu religious teaching*. Philadelphia: University of Pennsylvania Press.

Parish, Steven M. 1994. *Moral knowing in a Hindu sacred city: an exploration of mind, emotion, and self.* New York: Columbia University Press.

OWEN M. LYNCH

SEE ALSO

Life History and Personal Event Narratives; Medicine, Āyurveda; Names and Naming Practices, Balochistan; Naming Ceremonies; Numerology

PILGRIMAGE

The practice of journeying to sites on earth where divine power is understood to be especially accessible to human beings, pilgrimage is presently, and increasingly, popular throughout South Asia, facilitated by ever-improving transportation. Every major South Asian religious tradition has its sacred geography, meaningful today and chartered in myth, popular oral traditions, and history.

Characteristics of pilgrimage shared among South Asian traditions and nations include heightened, sensual participation in religious life. Movement over actual kilometers, whether five or five hundred, is critical to pilgrimage, for what is important is not just visiting a sacred place but getting away from home. Practices at pilgrimage centers in most South Asian traditions involve the pilgrim in some combination of bathing, circumambulation, prostration, lighting of incense, offerings of food and flowers partially returned as blessings, musical performances, and other physically and aesthetically potent experiences.

Devotional singing and retelling miracle stories are common to every place of pilgrimage as well as to the pilgrims' road where such activities pass the time. Major pilgrimage centers are often sites for cultural performances, including folk theater and epic recitation, while pilgrimage fairs provide occasions and large audiences for such events.

Some Hindu and Jain texts recommend and elaborate on the practice of pilgrimage within the subcontinent, while Muslim scripture enjoins only the journey to Mecca, and Sikh teachings deride the value of visiting any sacred place. Nevertheless, at the level of "folk religion" or popular practice and belief, South Asian Hindu, Buddhist, Jain, Muslim and Sikh pilgrims have much in common. The South Asian concept of pilgrimage extends beyond literal travels on the surface of the earth. It becomes a symbol for other valued religious and spiritual practices, a quest for inner peace and truth.

Hindu Pilgrimage

The Hindu practice of pilgrimage is rooted in ancient scriptural charters. According to textual scholars, the earliest reference to Hindu pilgrimage in is found in the *Ṛg Veda* (ca. 1000 B.C.E.), where the "wanderer" is praised. Numerous later texts, including the epic

Shri Kalyanji. Diggi, Rajasthan, India, © Ann Grodzins Gold

Mahābhārata (ca. 300 B.C.E.) and several of the mythological *Purāṇa*s (ca. 300–1500 C.E.) elaborate on the capacities of particular sacred places and rivers to grant boons, including health, wealth, and progeny, as well as deliverance after death. Texts enjoin Hindu pilgrims to perform rites on behalf of recently deceased kin and ancestors. Genres of devotional literature in the regional vernaculars praise places, their gods, and their miracles.

The Sanskrit and Hindi word for a pilgrimage center is "tīrtha"—literally, a river ford or crossing place. The concept of a ford is associated with pilgrimage centers not simply because many are on river banks, but because they are metaphorically places for transit—either to the other side of particular worldly troubles or beyond endless cycles of birth and death. Pilgrimage is often advertised in classical Sanskrit texts as well as present-day vernacular tracts as an "easy" and populist practice.

The institution of pilgrimage is an integrating force among the linguistically and culturally diverse Hindu peoples of the Indian subcontinent. One widely recognized set of sacred centers are the "four places" (*cār dhām*) founded at sites in the four cardinal directions: Kedarnath in the North, Dvarka in the West, Puri in the East, and Rameshvaram in the South. A pilgrim who visits all four of these sites has circumambulated India. Other important pan-Hindu centers in the North include Ayodhya, Hardwar, Gaya, Prayag, Varanasi, and Vrindavan; in South India, renowned places include Cidambaram, the Minakshi temple at Madurai, the Ayyapan temple at Sabari Malai and Tirupati. At regional and local levels, there are thousands of places with deep religious significance for the devotees who visit them.

Most pilgrimage centers hold periodic religious fairs called *melā*s to mark auspicious astrological moments or important anniversaries. Fairs generate an increased influx of pilgrims, flourishing trade, and a profusion of artistic productions and cultural performances including dramas, epic recitations, and collective devotional singing.

Buddhist and Jain Pilgrimage

In the fifth century B.C.E., two so-called heterodoxies emerged in India in reaction to Brahmanical Hinduism: Buddhism and Jainism, both centered around the figures of their founding teachers: Siddhartha Gautama, the Buddha or "enlightened one" and Vardhamana Mahavira, the Jīnā or "conqueror." Buddhist and Jain pilgrimage centers exist throughout India today, and major Buddhist shrines flourish in Nepal and Sri Lanka. Within both traditions, pilgrimage centers commemorate the persons and lives of the founders, as well as their important followers. While many Buddhist shrines developed around relics of the Buddha's body, Jains have no reverence for physical remains.

After the Buddha's death, parts of his body were enshrined in *stūpa*s—the domed architectural form characteristic to Buddhism. Tradition has it that the Indian Emperor Ashoka (ca. 268–232 B.C.E.), after his conversion to Buddhism, established eighty-four thousand stūpas on the subcontinent. Pilgrims thought of enshrined relics as media through which they could deliver their prayers. However, the best known Buddhist pilgrimage centers in India are associated with signal events in the Buddha's life. Two places sacred to Buddhists today, drawing pilgrims from great distances, are Bodhgaya in modern Bihar, northeast India, where the historical Buddha is said to have achieved enlightenment under the Boddhi tree, and Sarnath in Uttar Pradesh, where he preached his first sermon. Notably both these sites are located on the outskirts of still more ancient Hindu places of pilgrimage—Gaya and Varanasi.

Power originating in one sacred place may be transferred to another site. For example, at the Buddhist temple complex of Anuradhapura in Sri Lanka, a branch from the Bodhgaya tree was miraculously established over two thousand years ago, and its worship has continued through the centuries. In Nepal, the land of the Buddha's birth, are many replicas of major Indian temples offering Nepalese Buddhist pilgrims goals that claim to confer blessings equal to those obtained on the more difficult journey to sites in India. Similar collapses of space are common in Hindu ideas about sacred centers. As in Hinduism, pilgrimage in popular Buddhist practice is often undertaken as a means of coping with the transitory, but acute, problems of worldly life, as well as out of religious emotion.

Jain teachers are called *tīrthankara*—literally "fordmaker"—indicating a close conceptual association between the persons of spiritual teachers and the salvation or passage across sorrows obtainable through pilgrimage. Distinctive to Jain shrines are stone images, often beautifully sculpted, of *tīrthankaras*. Of major significance to the Jain Digambara sect is Shravana Belgola, a small town in Karnataka. There stands a fifty-seven-foot-high colossal hilltop statue of Bahubali—an ascetic warrior. This spiritual hero is portrayed naked with vines twined around his arms and anthills and snakes about his legs. The statue dates from the late tenth century, but Sravana Belgola was sacred to Jain renouncers as early as the third century B.C.E., and is historically associated with the extreme ascetic practice of meditation until death.

Islamic Pilgrimage

A strong Islamic presence in India dates back to the eighth century C.E. Muslim scripture sanctions pilgrimage to Mecca—called "hajj." But in South Asia, as elsewhere, Muslims have for centuries practiced shrine pilgrimage—known as "ziyārat" or "visiting." Muslim shrines always revolve around a saint's tomb, but the cult of the saints begins during their lifetimes when a particular holy person gains a reputation for teaching, healing, and miracles. As shrines grow up around the tombs of deceased saints, living spiritual teachers may take up residence there, offering guidance, dream interpretation, and protective amulets to pilgrims. While a central tomb is common to all shrines, the more celebrated develop into large complexes called *dargāh,* meaning palace or royal court.

Tombs of the Chishti Sufi saints who flourished during the thirteenth and fourteenth centuries in India stand out today as places of pan-Islamic pilgrimage significance. The *dargāh* of Mu'īn al-dīn Chishī in Ajmer, Rajasthan—where the Mughul Emperor Akbar (1542–1605) made annual pilgrimages—is generally accepted as the most important among these and is venerated by many Hindus as well as Muslims. Like Hindu, Buddhist, and Jain pilgrims, Muslims may visit saints' shrines to seek a spiritual experience or to seek help with physical and worldly problems. Pilgrims pray to saints for cures, for good harvests, for children. Miracle stories and hagiographies constitute a body of living oral traditions connected with each shrine. Muslim shrines celebrate annual festivals, similar to Hindu *melās*. These mark the anniversary of the saint's death, and are known as "'urs."

Sikh Pilgrimage

The Sikh religion in India was founded in reaction to and in contradistinction to both Hinduism and Islam. Sikhism's founder, Guru Nanak (1469–1539), spoke against the practice of pilgrimage as a superficial one. Indeed, Sikhism teaches that the promised spiritual rewards of pilgrimage baths are to be gained only through meditation on the name of God. Although Sikh teachings vigorously deride the value of pilgrimage for purifying the soul, there is nonetheless a strong tradition among Sikhs of visiting places sacred to their own history.

Sikh shrines exist throughout India, Pakistan, and Bangla Desh, often in spots associated with the ten Sikh gurus' lives and travels. Sikh shrines are called *gurdvārā*—meaning the dwelling place of the guru, understood as God. Most celebrated among them is the *Darbār Sāhib* (Reverenced Court) at Amritsar in the Punjab—known widely in English as the Golden Temple. Unique features of Sikh temples include the enshrinement as divinity of their sacred book, the *Guru Granth Sāhib,* and the institution of the *langar,* or pilgrim's kitchen, where the needy receive free food.

Pilgrimage centers focus community identity. Recent history in India revealed a divisive potential here, when a politicized conflict that took place between Hindus and Muslims at the ancient pilgrimage center of Ayodhya culminated in December 1992 with the destruction of a mosque said to be built on the birthplace of the Hindu god Rama (*Rām janm bhūmi*). However, folk traditions surrounding many pilgrimage centers are notably syncretist in nature. After the devastating events in Ayodhya, communal riots afflicted many Indian cities with large Muslim populations. Ajmer, however, was peaceful, and popular living oral tradition has it that it was Hindu respect for the Muslim saint enshrined at the *dargāh* there, or even his visible and invisible power, that kept the peace.

References

Bhardwaj, Surinder M. 1973. *Hindu places of pilgrimage in India: a study in cultural geography*. Berkeley: University of California Press.

Currie, P. M. 1989. *The shrine and cult of Mu'īn al-dīn Chishtī of Ajmer*. Delhi: Oxford University Press.

Dundas, Paul. 1992. *The Jains*. London: Routledge. See especially "Pilgrimage and holy places," pp.187–194.

Eck, Diana L. 1982. *Banaras: city of light*. New York: Alfred A. Knopf.

Gaborieau, Marc. 1983. The cult of saints among the Muslims of Nepal and Northern India. In *Saints and their cults: studies in religious sociology, folklore and history*, ed. Stephen Wilson, 291–308. Cambridge: Cambridge University Press.

Gold, Ann Grodzins. 1988. *Fruitful journeys: the ways of Rajasthani pilgrims*. Berkeley: University of California Press.

Leoshko, Janice, ed. 1988. *Bodhgaya: the site of enlightenment*. Bombay: Marg Publications.

Morinis, E. Alan. 1984. *Pilgrimage in the Hindu tradition: a case study of West Bengal*. Delhi: Oxford University Press.

Schimmel, Annemarie. 1980. *Islam in the Indian subcontinent*. Leiden: E. J. Brill. See especially, "Muslim life and customs—saints and their tombs—mystical folk poetry," pp.106–149.

Shulman, David Dean. 1980. *Tamil temple myths: sacrifice and divine marriage in the South Indian Śaiva tradition*. Princeton: Princeton University Press.

Singh, Mehar. 1975. *Sikh shrines in India*. New Delhi: Publications Division, Ministry of Information and Broadcasting, Government of India.

Troll, C. W., ed. 1992. *Muslim shrines in India*. Delhi: Oxford University Press.

van Buitenen, T. A. B, trans. and ed. 1976. The tour of the sacred fords. In *Mahabharata,* vol. 2, pp. 366–455. Chicago: The University of Chicago Press.

van der Veer, Peter. 1988. *Gods on earth: the management of religious experience and identity in a north Indian pilgrimage Center*. London: The Athlone Press.

ANN GRODZINS GOLD

SEE ALSO

Dargāh; Fairs and Festivals; *Melā;* Sacred Places; Saints; *Ziyārat*

PĪR

Pīr is the term for a Sufi spiritual master. The fundamental institution of Sufism, or Islamic mysticism, is the relationship between pīr (master) and *murīd* (disciple). The Sufi tradition holds that there is an inner esoteric truth (*haqīqa*) underlying the exoteric practices of Islam. One attains this truth by journeying on the *tarīqa,* or interior path. This perilous spiritual journey requires a guide who has himself completed it—a pīr. A murīd must demonstrate abiding love for, and absolute allegiance to, his pīr and submit to him "like a corpse being prepared for burial." A pīr is essential for the Sufi path. According to the Sufi tradition, "he who has no pīr has Satan for a pīr."

Pīr-murīd is rooted in the longstanding tradition of personal allegiance in Islam. Since its inception, Islam has not only demanded allegiance to its message, as presented in the Qur'ān, but also allegiance to its messenger, the Prophet Muḥammad. Just as the early Companions gave allegiance to the person of Muḥammad, as the leader of the Muslim community, murīds give allegiance and obedience (*bai'at*) to their pīrs as his spiritual representatives. Each pīr traces his spiritual lineage through a chain of transmitters (*silsila*) that stretches back in unbroken succession to the Prophet, usually through his son-in-law and cousin 'Alī. When one becomes a murīd he joins the other disciples of the pīr in his *tarīqat* (Sufi order). Murīds meet individually and communally with their *pir* and engage in *z̲ikr* (the ritual remembrance of God) and other spiritual activities.

The Sufi path is rooted in the love of God and its corollary, love of the Prophet. Through intense love and devotion to their own spiritual masters, pīrs have achieved annihilation in the Prophet (*fanā fī-Rasūl*) and, through it, annihilation in God (*fanā fī-Khuda*). In the same fashion, murīds seek annihilation in the love of the Prophet, and the love of God, through the love of their own pīrs.

In South Asia, as in most other parts of the Muslim world, belief in pīrs is an essential element of popular Islam. Living pīrs share responsibility for the spiritual governance of the world with the great pīrs of the past whose *dargāh*s (tombs) are centers of *ziyārat* (pilgrimage). Because of their high spiritual status, many people believe that the very presence of a pīr imparts blessing (*baraka*) and that pīrs are capable of performing miracles (*karāmāt*). For this reason, many people visit pīrs for mundane reasons—to avoid bad marriages, to find jobs, or to be healed of illness.

Critics charge that the pīr-murīd relationship is easily corrupted by charlatans and opportunists. For example, they point out that many pīrs achieve their status simply on the basis of heredity. In some cases these "hereditary pīrs" have extensive land holdings and their "murīds" are the peasants who work their land. The pīr-murīd relationship has become a target of criticism by certain Islamic reformers, who see devotion to the pīr as *shirk* (worship of something other than God.)

References

Schimmel, Annemarie. 1975. *Mystical dimensions of Islam*. Chapel Hill: University of North Carolina Press.

Subhan, John A. 1970. *Sufism: Its saints and shrines*. New York: Samuel Weiser.

VERNON JAMES SCHUBEL

SEE ALSO
Kerāmat; Pilgrimage; Saints; Saints, Muslim; *Satya Pīr;* Sufi Folk Poetry; Ziyārat

PIRIT

The Sinhala word *pirit,* Pali *paritta* (protection), describes a popular ritual in which Buddhist doctrinal texts are recited as protection against disease and dangers. The truth of the textual utterance, a *saccakiriyā* (act of truth), generates magical powers that ward off ills. There are six parittas referred to in early Buddhist texts. They are the *Khandha paritta;* the *Ratana Sutta;* the *Karanīya Metta Sutta*; the *Dhajagga Paritta*; the *Angulimāla paritta,* and the *Aṭānāṭiya Sutta*. Each of them is associated with a specific incident where the Buddha invokes the power of truth, of loving compassion, of virtue, and of the "Three Jewels" (Buddha, Dhamma, Sangha) to overcome a danger. These parittas are today recited by monks in a ritual performance called a pirit ceremony.

Theravada Buddhism eschews magic and has few prescribed rituals for lay life. Pirit is the one Buddhist ritual, magical in function but performed officially by Buddhist monks and considered an integral part of Theravada Buddhist practice. During the ceremony, monks are conducted into a specially prepared "sacred" pavilion where they recite the *pirit* texts and, thereafter, distribute *pirit-p>an* (protective water) and *pirit nūl* (protective thread) to lay participants. The ceremony can be performed at any time for an event or crisis in the life of the individual or community. Its performance can be beneficial but its nonperformance is not harmful. This nonobligatory aspect of the ritual perhaps reflects the doctrinal position that rituals may be useful for daily living but are extraneous to an individual's quest for salvation.

References

de Silva, Lily. 1981. Paritta: a Buddhist ceremony for peace and prosperity. In Lily de Silva, *Spolia Zelanica,* vol. 35, part 6, Sri Lanka.

Dialogues of the Buddha. 1929. Translated by T. W. and C. A. F. Rhys Davids, Part. 111. London

Mahavastu. 1949. Translated and edited by J. J. Jones, vol. 1, London.

The Questions of King Milinda. 1963. Translated and edited by T. W. Rhys Davids, New York.

Der Paritta-Dienst in Ceylon. 1972. Von Peter Schalk, Lund.

RANJINI OBEYESEKERE

SEE ALSO
Buddhism and Buddhist Folklore; Buddhism, Sri Lanka

PONKAL

Ponkal, from Tamil *ponku,* "to boil up, foam," has three meanings: (1) *taipponkal,* the festival; (2) ritually boiled and unstrained rice; (3) a rice dish with sweet or spicy ingredients.

Ponkal is one of the most important festivals for the Tamil people. Celebrated on the first day of the Tamil month Tai (January-February), when the sun enters Capricorn and begins its journey northwards, it marks the end of the dark, rainy season. Coinciding with the beginning of the rice harvest, it is a day of thanksgiving.

The day before Ponkal, the last day of the Tamil month Mārkaḻi, is called Pōki, a name of the god Indra. On this day people discard their old pots and pans, old clothes, straw mats, and winnowing baskets, and clean and whitewash their houses. On Ponkal day, after an early morning bath, women decorate the freshly swept entrance to the house with an elaborate design (*kōlam*) of white or colored powder. In the courtyard or on the street each family sets up a fireplace, which consists of three or more bricks placed with enough space between them to fit the two new pots in which the rice will be boiled. The women decorate the bricks and the clay pots with a design of white lines and dots of the red *kunkumam* powder, and around the mouth of the pots, they tie fresh turmeric plants. Near this fireplace each family readies a small shrine to Piḷḷaiyār (Gaṇeśa). Piḷḷaiyār consists of a conical figure of cow dung, decorated with turmeric, kunkumam powder, and the grass sacred to the god. In front of the god are the usual *pūja* offerings spread out on a banana leaf: coconuts, bananas, betel, flowers, an oil lamp, incense, and for this occasion, some vegetables and a measure of paddy. Sugarcane sticks and turmeric plants frame the shrine. When the milk boils up, the eldest or the youngest member of the family pours some of the new rice into the pots, adds the sweet or spicy ingredients respectively, and when the rice boils, everyone present shouts "*ponkalōponkal*!" The women then take some rice from each pot, place it in front of Piḷḷaiyār, and offer it to him and the sun with a prayer. A feast follows.

The next day, called *Māṭṭupponkal,* "cattle-*ponkal,*" is dedicated to the cattle. Farmers and cattle owners wash the cows, bulls, and buffaloes, paint their horns in bright colors, and decorate their necks with new ropes and flower garlands and their bodies with colorful dots or impressions of the hand. Again, rice is ritually boiled, and this time is offered to the cattle. In some villages, bull races (*jallikkaṭṭu*) take place on one of the following days. Brave men try to lift off a cloth and money tied to the horns of the bulls, which charge, one after the other, through a path in the crowd.

Ponkal, traditionally an agricultural festival with cosmological implications, has been politicized and partially secularized into a specifically Tamil day. Political speeches and literary events are as much part of the festival today as are the greeting cards that show not only Ponkal scenes but also heroes and heroines from film and politics.

References

Beteille, Andre. 1964. A note on the Pongal festival in a Tanjore village. *MAN,* 64(89): 73–75.

Dumont, Louis. 1986. *A south Indian subcaste: social organization and religion of the Pramalai Kallar.* Delhi: Oxford University Press.

Good, Anthony. 1983. A symbolic type and its transformations: the case of south Indian Ponkal. *Contributions to Indian Sociology* 17(2): 223–244.

EVELINE MASILAMANI-MEYER

SEE ALSO

Calendrical Ceremonies and Rites; Food and Foodways; Games; Gaṇeśa; *Jallikkaṭṭu; Kōlam;* Plants; *Pūja;* Tamil Nadu

POPULAR MUSIC

Popular music includes musical genres whose style and evolution are closely associated with commercial mass media and commodity marketing. Popular music as a category can thus, in theory, be distinguished from traditional folk and classical genres that have evolved independently of the mass media. In South Asia, however, the folk and popular realms are often closely related and the distinctions between them blurred. The persistence and diversity of folk music genres and their coexistence with a vast commercial music industry have allowed for considerable interaction and mutual influence with popular music, and many genres share features of both categories.

The birth of Indian commercial popular music can be traced to the first decade of the twentieth century, when the Gramophone Company of India (later absorbed by EMI [Electrical and Musical Industries]) started marketing recordings of diverse indigenous classical, light-classical, and regional folk genres throughout the subcontinent. Although the recording industry thus got off to an early and lively start, until the 1930s, its impact was limited largely to the urban bourgeoisie who could afford phonographs and—from the 1920s—radios. The industry expanded with the advent of sound film in 1931, which led to the emergence of film music as a distinct genre of popular music, available to all those who enjoyed access to cinemas or radios. Film music soon came to marginalize other mass-mediated regional styles. In the early years of the genre, film songs were performed by singer-actors; since the mid-1940s, the norm has been for actors to mouth songs, which are separately recorded by professional "playback" singers. Commercial feature films almost invariably include five or six song-and-dance sequences, which audiences regard as essential and focal elements of the entertainment. Film music itself evolved as a syncretic genre, combining traditional instruments, modes, meters, and vocal style with modern and Western concepts of orchestration, harmony, and instrumentation. Although Hindi film remained the dominant model, regional-language cinema also flourished; songs in such films generally imitate Hindi film style while using local languages and introducing features of regional folk musics.

Although film music is a studio art form embedded in commercial cinema's fantasy world of glitter and luxury, it retains links to folk music. Film music directors have always borrowed folk melodies, even in the disco-influenced 1990s. For their part, folk musicians throughout the subcontinent borrow film tunes, setting to them new texts in regional languages and weaving them into the fabric of local genres. At the same time, films and film music have undoubtedly contributed to the decline of many folk genres, like traditional *nauṭaṇki* theater, whose audience has largely forsaken it for cinema, or like women's wedding songs, which are now often drowned out by loudspeakers blaring film music.

Despite the predominance of film music since the mid-1930s, the record industry—primarily EMI or its subsidiaries—continued to market a certain amount of music independent of cinema. This category included classical music, light-classical Urdu *ghazals,* and various folk or stylized folk genres that came to constitute incipient popular music idioms. From the mid-1970s, the dramatic spread of cheap cassette technology ended the monopolization of the music industry by EMI and the film world. The first "non-film" popular genre to flourish was a stylized and simplified form of the ghazal, which came to enjoy mass appeal among middle-class listeners throughout North India and Pakistan. The new ghazal style, as popularized by singers like Mehdi Hasan, Ghulam Ali, and Jagjit and Chitra Singh, generally employs simple, accessible Urdu, relaxed vocal improvisation on the first line of each couplet, and catchy refrains, over a leisurely, languid rhythmic background.

In the wake of the pop ghazal emerged a vogue of cassette-based Hindu devotional music styles. These have included a mainstream, ghazal-influenced, solo *bhajan* genre, as sung by vocalists like Anup Jalota and Pankaj Udhas, and a variety of stylized lesser genres associated with particular cults, deities, festivities, and rituals. Many of these combine traditional elements with film-influenced melodies and instrumentation.

In the early 1980s, more than three hundred cassette producers of various sizes sprouted up throughout the country, recording and marketing diverse regional musics to local audiences. Much of the cassette output has consisted of recordings of folk music in purely traditional style. A large proportion, however, has comprised relatively new subgenres explicitly associated with cassettes, often using film-style orchestration or other studio enhancements. In their evolutionary association with the mass media (especially cassettes), many such genres combine features of both folk music and commercial, syncretic popular music. Particularly popular among rural listeners are tapes of ribald songs, based on folk genres such as Braj *rasiya,* Haryanvi *rāgini,* and Maharashtrian *popat,* but produced especially for marketing on cassettes. In Gujarat, pop versions of indigenous *garbā* and *rās* have flourished in connection with the vogue of these social-dance genres. Punjabi popular music has been particularly vital, encompassing text-oriented songs of artists like Gurdas Man, and more Westernized forms of "disco *bhangra.*" (*Bhangra* is a traditional Punjabi folk dance.) The latter has evolved in a parallel fashion as a product both of South Asian Punjabis as well as emigrant Punjabi communities, especially in Great Britain.

Scholars and critics debate the ramifications of such developments and their relation to folk traditions. Some critics deplore the lewdness and triviality of the cassette output and denounce the common usage of film melodies in perceivably inappropriate genres (especially devotional music). In some cases, mass-mediated popular music can be argued to be flourishing at the expense of live performance. In many cases, however, it is unclear whether mass-mediated popular music is replacing or merely supplementing live performance; folk genres like narrative Bhojpuri *birhā* seem to be flourishing, both live and on cassette. Cassette dissemination also helps preserve genres like *qawwāli* (a Muslim devotional song genre), which are performed live less frequently than before. Most importantly, cassettes have revitalized regional music traditions and offered new mass-mediated alternatives to the otherwise hegemonic film music industry.

Reference

Manuel, Peter. 1993. *Cassette culture: popular music and technology in north India.* Chicago: University of Chicago Press.

PETER MANUEL

SEE ALSO

Bhajan; Cassettes; Film Music; *Gharal; Nauṭaṇki; Qawwālī*

POTTERY

Most pottery produced in South Asia is low-fired, unglazed terra-cotta made from alluvial clays that are abundant in the vast river valleys or near ponds. From about 6000 B.C.E. to the present, pottery has played an integral role in everyday subsistence and ritual activities.

The earliest terra-cotta ceramics have been recovered in excavations at the site of Mehrgarh, Pakistan, during Period Ib (ca. 6000–5500 B.C.E.). These early vessels were hand-formed bowls and pots, painted with red ochre pigment and fired at relatively low temperatures. It is quite likely that they were used for holding ritual offerings rather than serving as utilitarian vessels. During this same time, the first abstract terra-cotta female figurines were being made, also presumably for ritual purposes.

By 3500 B.C.E. ceramic production throughout the Indus Valley and the upper Ganga-Yamuna river system

A man from the potter caste carves a Ganeśa, or elephant god, which will be installed in a temple. Karnataka, India, © Mimi Nichter

had became more specialized, and a wide variety of shapes and forms had developed, which involved a combination of wheel-thrown and handcraft techniques. Various types of kilns were invented to fire pottery at higher temperatures to produce strong and durable utilitarian wares, as well as highly decorated symbolic wares. Firing of pottery with high oxygen levels in the kiln (oxidation firing) was practiced to produce red wares, and gray wares were made by making the fire smoky or with less oxygen (reduction firing). In central and south India, handcrafted pottery fired in bonfire kilns (some of which is called Black-and-Red ware) was being produced by farming communities who had limited contact with the cultures of the northwestern subcontinent.

These early ceramic traditions established the basic techniques of ceramic production that continue to be used throughout most of the subcontinent today. Various types of spinning devices are used, including the socketed wheel, the pivot wheel, and the kick-wheel. In addition to wheel throwing, pottery is handcrafted with coils, molded, or shaped with paddle and anvil. Often a combination of techniques is used to produce a single shape. While much of the everyday terra-cotta pottery is plain and undecorated, decorative techniques are used to distinguish special forms and the symbolic function of certain vessels. Slips made from red or yellow ochre are often applied to the body of the vessel, and black, brown, or white pigments are used to paint designs. Other colors are often painted after firing, such as green, bright yellow, bright red, or purple. Some pottery is burnished and highly polished, while other vessels are carved, incised, or coated with coarse slips containing sand, mica, or crushed pottery. Each of the decoration techniques has a different utilitarian or symbolic function.

In modern pottery production, men, women, and children are involved in different aspects of manufacture, with men often using the wheel, while women and children assist in clay and pigment preparation as well as in painting, figurine modeling, and molded pottery manufacture. The almost exclusive use of the potter's wheel by men throughout South Asia and many other parts of the world has puzzled scholars for decades. Some Muslim potters in the Punjab, Pakistan, say that it is the man's duty to work for the livelihood of the family and this is why the women do not use the wheel. Among many Hindu pottery communities, women are not even allowed to touch the wheel. Whatever the precise reasoning in each community, it is clear that men became the specialists who work the wheel to meet the demands of competitive mass production, while women continued to be involved in most other aspects of the process.

Pottery is used every day for cooking, storing, dispensing, and offering food. Porous terra-cotta is optimal for storing grain and other food stuffs without letting it mildew and is extremely effective for cooling water during the hot summer months. Evaporation on the exterior of the vessel helps to cool the water on the interior. This porosity, however, also allows bacteria to grow, and terra-cotta vessels on which cooked food is served are difficult to clean without firing them once again. These factors of hygiene may have contributed to the widespread belief that pottery used for eating is polluted and must be discarded. Disposable pottery is widely used for individual food service during religious festivals or feasts by both Hindu and Muslim communities. Water pots often have round bottoms or spouts so that the vessels can be tipped and the water poured, rather than dipping a cup in the vessel, which would result in pollution. Vessels that are used for cooking food can be used repeatedly so long as no one actually eats from the vessel. In fact, pottery for cooking milk and preparing yogurt are used over and over because the milk fats seal the pores, making the vessels less porous and more serviceable through the greater retention of liquids.

Pottery containers are used in most major rituals practiced by a wide range of religious communities. Among Hindus, globular pottery vessels are worshipped as a symbol of the goddess or *shakti,* possibly representing the womb, fertility, and prosperity. The Vedic sage Vasistha was born from a pot in which the semen of the god Mitra had fallen. The *Kumbha Mela,* one of the largest festivals of northern India, is held at four locations where the nectar of immortality spilled out of a golden *kumbha* (pot). In the Punjab, a pottery lid, symbolizing the bride's virginity, is broken under foot at the end of Muslim Rajput marriage ceremonies, and in Punjabi, the word for lid (*dakhan*) is often used in abusive language to refer to the hymen. At death a water-filled pot is perforated with a hole in the base and carried around the funeral pyre until the water has drained out. In some Muslim burials, a pot with a hole broken in the base is placed on the grave.

Glazed terra-cotta and porcelain ceramics became widespread in the subcontinent with the advent of Islam and the increased trade networks connecting the subcontinent to West Asia, East Asia, and later to Europe. Due to fears of pollution, strict Hindus avoid the use of glazed ceramics and prefer to use brass or bronze utensils, which can be ritually purified. However, glazed ceramic vessels are extensively used by communities that do not have strict pollution laws.

In traditional Hindu social hierarchy, potters have been relegated to the lowest castes, but, ironically, they are also seen as creators who transform mundane materials into usable, ritually pure objects through the use of fire. In modern South Asia, some potters have relatively high status and considerable wealth due to the popularity of their products in urban and international markets. The production of Western and East Asian forms of art pottery in terra-cotta, glazed terra-cotta, high-fired stoneware, and porcelain ceramics is now quite common throughout the subcontinent, for local as well as export purposes. These new developments add a new facet to the complex nature of pottery in the subcontinent and represent a new phase in the long history of this important tradition.

References

Dales, George F., and J. Mark Kenoyer. 1986. *Excavations at Mohenjo Daro, Pakistan: The pottery*. Philadelphia: University Museum Press.

Rye, Owen S., and Clifford Evans. 1976. *Traditional pottery techniques of Pakistan*. Smithsonian Contributions to Anthropology, No. 21. Washington, D.C.: Smithsonian Institution Press.

Saraswati, Baidyanath. 1978. *Pottery-making cultures and Indian civilization*. New Delhi: Abhinav.

Saraswati, Baidyanath, and Nab Kishore Behura. 1966. *Pottery techniques in peasant India*. Memoir, 13. Calcutta: Anthropological Survey of India.

Sinopoli, Carla M. 1991. *Approaches to archaeological ceramics*. New York: Plenum.

JONATHAN MARK KENOYER

SEE ALSO
Craft; Pottery, Bangladesh; Pottery, Sri Lanka; Tiles and Tile-making, Terra Cotta

POTTERY, BANGLADESH

Bangladesh occupies the world's widest delta. The land is flat, fertile, and layered with clay. This rich resource is exploited in 680 villages devoted to the manufacture of pottery. The largest villages, with three hundred families in the trade, lie in the western districts of Jessore and Rajshahi, but pottery-making villages are found throughout the country. Although Bangladesh is predominantly a Muslim country, pottery is predominantly a Hindu craft.

The potters divide themselves into workers of two kinds. Some make utilitarian vessels for carrying water and cooking; others make images (*mūrti*) for worship. In villages where both kinds of work are done, one in ten households contains a sculptor of mūrti. Because mūrti are made seasonally for worship (*pūjā*), few of the sculptors devote all their time to images, and they must fill slack time by making the vessels that others make.

In making useful vessels, men and women use different techniques. Men use the *cāk,* the wide hand-powered wheel that is found throughout the Indian subcontinent. Women combine molding in *pāṛā,* dishes turned by hand, with coiling and paddling. The range of utilitarian forms is wide and diverse, but two products can illustrate the technology. The *pātil* is a hemispherical bowl used to cook rice and curry. Men throw the rim of the pātil on the cāk, while women shape the bottom in a pāṛā and then paddle the parts together. The *kalsī* is a globular jar in which water is carried on the hip. Men throw the kalsī in two sections and then paddle them into unity. Women raise the kalsī in three different pāṛā completing the form with three applied coils. The vessels are slipped and then fired. The kiln, the *puin,* has a clay-firing chamber with a concave top on which pots are piled, then covered with rice straw and mud. The chamber is stoked with wood; the heat reaches 800 degrees centigrade, and firing lasts for two or three days, depending upon the thickness of the ware. If the fire is smothered, the pots will emerge blackened from the kiln, their surfaces mottled from silver to sooty black. If holes are poked through the cover, oxygen increases in the kiln, and the fired pots are buff in color. On both black and buff pots, the slip and the firing create variations in tone and sheen, adding, at much expense of labor, decorative qualities to useful objects.

Two main techniques are used in shaping images for worship. For small mūrti, clay is pressed into deep molds, and then the image is smoothed and painted. For larger images, a frame is constructed of wood. It is covered with rice straw, bound with twine into form, and then coated with clay. The final form is achieved by a blend of hand-modeling and molding. Molds are used for crowns, faces, and ornaments, while the body of the deity, the expressive hands, and ancillary forms, such as the *bāhan* (the vehicle of the deity) are shaped by hand. While the form is shaped, the sculptor consistently draws it away from the world and urges it toward the ideal; the deity sits in placid symmetry, in a moment of fecund youth; the parts fuse in unity. That unity is then confirmed by thick coats of bright paint.

The repertory of images is dominated by the goddesses who center veneration in Bangladesh: Durgā, Kālī, Sarasvatī, and Lakṣmī. Images often present the family of the Goddess: Durgā, calmly slaying the buffalo demon, accompanied by her daughters, Sarasvatī, the goddess of wisdom, and Lakṣmī, the goddess of wealth, and her sons, Gaṇeśa, the elephant-headed lord of beginnings, and Kārttikeya, the beautiful god of war. Other frequently represented deities include 'Sītalā, the goddess of smallpox, and Manasā, the goddess of snakes. The prime images of Vaishnavism are Rādhā and Kṛṣṇa, swaying together to the sounds of Kṛṣṇa's flute, and Gaurāṅga—the Bengali mystic Caitanya (1486–1533)—and his disciple Nitāi.

Parul Rani Pal making a kalsī. Kagajipara, Dhamrai, Bangladesh, © Henry Glassie

The sculptor of mūrti works on commission. His image is installed in a pavilion at a temple for pūjā. With prayer, the deity is invited to descend into the beautiful image prepared to receive her. She will remain so long as she is offered water and flowers, food and prayers of praise, incense and dancing lights. Worship lasts for one day in the case of Sarasvatī, a week in the case of Durgā. Then she departs, leaving no touch of power in the mūrti. It is now but a pretty shell, empty as the body is empty when the soul has flown. It is carried to the river, and, to the ululation of the women, sacrificed, returned to the water from which it came. Images for worship are not fired. They melt easily back into the water when worship is complete, and during worship they contain dampness—the moisture that would be eradicated by firing—so that the water in the body of the devotee can connect to the water in the mūrti, just as the soul present for this life in the body of the devotee can connect to the deity present for this pūjā in the body of the clay image and the wishes of the devotee can be fulfilled instantaneously.

From a distance, artistic traditions can seem to be the creations of anonymous performers, but within the community, the artist is never anonymous. Working at the pinnacle of the potter's trade, sculptors of mūrti serve the Hindu community and gain fame as artists. Babu Lal Pal of Khamarpara, Shimulia, and Ananda Pal of Kagajipara, Dhamrai, are great rural masters; the finest artist of modern times in Bangladesh is Haripada Pal, who works on Shankharibazar, in downtown Dhaka. Haripada Pal was born in 1947, in th village of Norpara, Shimulia. He was trained by his grandfather, Niroda Prasad Pal, and then traveled widely, perfecting his art before settling down in Dhaka to fill orders from temples throughout Bangladesh. Haripada Pal begins the creative process with a prayer that brings an image of the deity to his mind, and then, he says, concentrating intensely, he unifies with God. During his work, he believes, God flows through him and into the mūrti.

In contemporary Bangladesh, there is no decline in the demand for images of the deities. In a time of tension between Hindus and Muslims, brought on by the destruction of the Babri Mosque in Ayodhya, the pūjā have expanded in size and number as part of a resurgence of Hindu identity, and sculptors are busy in season. However, as a result of competition from factories that supply traditional forms in durable materials like plastic and aluminum, the need for utilitarian pottery is gradually declining, and potters have innovated in response. Trading the old cāk for a foot-powered wheel and replacing the wood-fired kiln with a gas-fired one, a few potters have modernized in order to ease their labor and reduce the workforce. They have also turned to the manufacture of decorative items for export and for sale to the urban middle-class market.

In Rayer Bazar, the old center for pottery in Dhaka city, while utilitarian forms are made in several shops and the master Lal Chand Pal continues to sculpt mūrti, three potters are creating new forms for new markets. Their leader is Maran Chand Paul. Born in 1946, he trained in his father's workshop, and was then educated at the Dhaka Art College. Maran Chand Paul specializes in fastidiously finished versions of traditional Bengali toys, especially horses and elephants, that are at once decorative and evocative of local identity.

While art theorists in the West create rankings among objects by raising the decorative above the useful, the masterpieces of the Bangladeshi tradition of *mṛtśilpa* (clay art) are, above all, useful. Some, shaped and burned, are used to ease labor. Others, shaped and unburned, are used to make connections with power. In the system of the Bangladeshi potter, the useful ranks above the merely decorative.

References

Glassie, Henry. 1997. *Art and life in Bangladesh*. Bloomington: Indiana University Press.

Jalal, Mohammad Shah. 1987. *Traditional pottery in Bangladesh*. Dhaka: International Voluntary Services.

HENRY GLASSIE

POTTERY, SRI LANKA

Pottery manufacture in Sri Lanka shares many of the features of pottery making elsewhere in South Asia. Most pottery is produced by people for whom it is their caste occupation. They use local alluvial clays and a technology, unique to the region, that combines wheel throwing with paddle-and-anvil finishing and outdoor pit-kiln firing. Three aspects, however, distinguish Sri Lankan potters. First, women, as well as men, are engaged in all stages of pottery production; second, because rural Sri Lankans have not fully abandoned open-hearth cooking or adopted metal pots, the demand for traditional terra-cotta kitchen pots has increased, not decreased; and, lastly, while Sri Lankan potters do produce vessels used in rituals, they do not make religious images as do other South Asian potters.

There are some Tamil- and Telugu-speaking potters with Indian-like traditions, but about 90 percent of Sri Lankan potters are Sinhalese Buddhists, and it is this caste group, named Baḍahăla, who are described here. More usually called *valan hadana minissu* (pottery-making people), the potters live in small, single-caste villages or hamlets attached to larger villages. Recent (1981) census occupation figures suggest that there are at least seven thousand Sinhalese potters in Sri Lanka today who are engaged in their craft.

The household is the unit of pottery production, and pottery usually is made in a small thatch-roofed shed behind the house. Using clay dug by hand from local deposits, often found in paddy fields, men and women form the pots on potter's wheels but remove them by cutting above the bottom, leaving only the thick side walls. The pots are then dried until they reach a leather-like stage. Then the potter inserts a hand through the pot mouth to hold an anvil stone inside the pot while using a moistened wooden paddle to beat the walls from the outside, a rhythmic motion in which the paddle and anvil meet each other on opposite sides of the pot wall. The beating thins and extends the walls to produce rounded bottoms, suitable for cooking on the three-stone kitchen hearth fires common in rural Sri Lanka.

If a more stable bottom is desired, such as for basins and food preparation pots used off the fire, the potter puts the pot back on the wheel upside down and adds a round base or "foot." Handles are added to lids in a similar manner. Finally, incised designs may be applied for decoration around the necks of water pots or to catch stones in the interior of rice-cleaning basins. The pots are then allowed to finish drying before they are fired overnight in shallow pit kilns. After firing, more elaborate decoration in white lime may be applied with a stick to water pots, although this is increasingly rare today.

The standard repertoire of pots produced in this manner includes two styles of water pots (*kaḷageḍiya*), footed basins of various sizes (*koraha*), shallow round-bottomed cooking pots (*ätiliya*), a dish with incised lines to remove stones from rice (*nâmbiliya*), and lids (*mūḍiya*). The largest sizes of cooking pots, such as those used for parboiling paddy, are now rarely made since metal replacements last longer and heat better. Also, large clay basins for bathing babies have been replaced by plastic ones.

Besides simple tools (wheels, paddles, anvil stones, and kilns), successful pottery industries require work space, clay, fuel, and customers. Contemporary variation in the Sri Lankan pottery industry can be explained by differential access to resources and markets. In the densely populated west coast, where space, wood, and clay are all scarce, many potters, with encouragement and training from the government's Department of Small Industries, have switched from manufacturing kitchenware to making smaller, more valuable items, such as fancy water pots, flower pots, and molded novelty items, which give a higher return for unit of input. In the mountainous Kandy area, where space and firewood are also at a premium but there is not the same easy access to urban buyers, the industry seems to be in decline. However, in central Sri Lanka, where clay abounds, biowastes from coconut estates provide cheap fuel, and households have ample work space, traditional pottery making is flourishing. Here, a few dozen communities produce pottery by the truckload, sending it to shops and marketplaces in neighboring districts.

There is little ritual associated with Sri Lankan pottery making, beyond mild prohibitions against talking while lighting a kiln and a preference that women, because of menstrual impurity, not make pottery for deity shrines. Pots are utilized at temples to carry water, prepare milk rice, and hold coconuts and palm flowers. Tiny clay basins, used as oil lamps, also are made for temples by Sinhalese potters, when requested. At one time, potters also produced a variety of temple drum. It had a large clay pot with painted designs, a large mouth at one end, and a small one at the other; the large mouth was covered with a stretched skin. Very few potters know how to make these drums today. Potters also supply pots for domestic rituals, including a new water pot for a newly menstruating girl's first bath, a set of pots to construct large lamps for weddings, and new sets of kitchen pots for every household at the New Year.

While the pottery tradition in Sri Lanka is an old one, it is not stagnant. Archaeologists have uncovered twelfth century C.E. tools that look very like modern ones, and potsherds dating back at least to the fifth century B.C.E. are found in many parts of the island. Nevertheless, Sri Lankan potters were quick to abandon floor-pivot wheels for new, chair-height ball-bearing ones introduced by the government in the 1950s, at which time they also adopted a new system of standardized sizes. More recently, potters in central Sri Lanka have begun making yoghurt pots for the first time, in response to the growth of the dairy industry, and potters in a few villages in different areas have begun to make the fuel-efficient clay stoves introduced by a British development group in the late 1970s. In the 1990s, a few individual potters started producing flat-bottomed yoghurt pots with a metal press, instead of a wheel and paddle.

In the long run, handmade pottery may be replaced by metalware and plastics, as has already happened to a large extent in India. But so long as rural Sri Lankans continue to use clay pottery to cook on open hearths, haul water from wells, and conduct their rituals, the potter's trade appears to be secure.

References

Crewe, Emma. 1988. *Sri Lankan potters: the socio-economic impact of the Sri Lankan national fuelwood conservation programme on stove producers.* Rugby, U.K.: Intermediate Technology Development Group.

Gunasekera, U. Alex, P. L. Prematilleke, and S. K. Roland, 1971. A corpus of pottery forms in Ceylon. *Ancient Ceylon: Journal of the Archaeological Survey of Ceylon* 1: 166–192.

Kirk, Colin. 1984. Tradition or transformation?: the Sinhalese potters of Ratmalagahawewa. In *Earthenware in Asia and Africa,* ed. John Picton, 1–27. London: School of Oriental and African Studies.

———. 1992. Perceiving agrarian change: past and present in Ratmale, a Sinhalese potter village. In *Agrarian Change in Sri Lanka,* ed. James Brow and Joe Weeramunda, 389–422. New Delhi: Sage Publications.

Ryan, Bryce. [1953] 1993. *Caste in modern Ceylon: the Sinhalese system in transition.* New Delhi: Naurang.

Winslow, Deborah. 1994. Status and context: Sri Lankan potter women reconsidered after fieldwork in India. *Comparative Studies in Society and History* 36(1): 3–35.

———. 1996. Pottery, progress, and structural adjustments in a Sri Lankan village. *Economic Development and Cultural Change* 44(4): 701–733.

DEBORAH WINSLOW

SEE ALSO

Craft; Pottery

PRAHLĀDA NĀṬAK

The *Prahlāda Nāṭak* is a miracle play based on the story of *bhakta* (devotee) Prahlāda, the son of Hiranyakasipu, an oppressive demon king in Hindu mythology in *Viṣṇu Purāṇa*. The plot involves Hiranyakasipu's acquisition of enormous power over gods, demons, and human beings through prayer and meditation to Brahma, the creator of the universe; the gods' consequent entreaty to Viṣṇu to stop the demon's rampage; Prahlāda's birth with divine powers to counter the king; reincarnation of Viṣṇu as half-man and half-lion (Nrsingha) to destory the evil and protect the good; and the coronation of Prahlāda on the throne.

Even as a child, Prince Prahlāda pays unflinching devotion to Viṣṇu, one of the trinity of Hindu gods, although the demons and their king worship Śiva, the god of destruction. When he reaches the age of twelve, in order to prepare him for the throne, King Hiranyakasipu orders the royal teachers to teach hymns of Śiva to the boy and divert his mind away from Viṣṇu. Immersed in his devotion to Viṣṇu, Prahlāda shows no change in his faith and after several months of futile *gurukula* (residential school) training returns to the palace with his teachers to display his knowledge of the scriptures. He sings songs of praise for Viṣṇu and remains loyal to his devotion, drawing the wrath of his father, who orders the teachers to take the boy back to school and make him learn the hymns to Śiva. The teachers return with Prahlāda, but finding him incorrigible, send him back to the palace the next day.

Assuming that Prahlāda has been converted overnight, Hiranyakasipu feels elated and congratulates the boy and the teachers, but he is soon disillusioned when the prince insists that Viṣṇu exists everywhere in all visible and invisible things. Angry with the prince's obstinate devotion to Viṣṇu, the king orders his servants to torture him until he changes his mind. Protected by Viṣṇu's grace and power, however, Prahlāda withstands the demons' vicious attacks unharmed.

Enraged, the king challenges him to prove Viṣṇu's omnipresence and threatens him with death unless he can show the omnipresent Viṣṇu in a pillar of the castle. Viṣṇu miraculously appears in the pillar to Prahlāda, who invites his father to witness the universal image of the god. When Hiranyakasipu approaches the pillar with his sword to kill Viṣṇu, the god appears as half-lion and half-man, and kills the demon. Because he dies in the hands of God, the demon ascends to heaven. Viṣṇu then destroys all the followers of Hiranyakasipu and places Prahlāda on the throne. Evil is destroyed, and peace is restored to the world.

Prahlāda *Carita* (balladic narrative) allegorically reinforces the paradoxical unity of the Hindu trinity of gods. Brahma, Viṣṇu, and Śiva exercise different powers and authorities, but manifest a single power, one that is understood through unconditional devotion (*bhakti*). Although Prahlada Natak is staged as a short drama, its narrative is often sung by ballad singers. The *carita* and the *natak* are based on the same story; they differ only in mode of presentation.

References

Chotaraya, Raja Ramakrshna. 1973. *Prahlada Nataka*. Bhagabana Panda, ed. Bhubaneswar: Samskrtika Vyapara Nidesanalaya.

Das, Pitambara. 1979. *Nrsingha Purana*. 8 vols. Cuttack: Dharmagrantha Store (n.d.). Mahapatra Trilochana. *Bhakta Prahlada: Pauranika Nataka*. Berhampur: Bani Bhandara.

SURA PRASAD RATH

SEE ALSO
Theater and Drama

PROCESSIONS

A procession is an ordered movement of a social group through space, usually on foot. Participants often carry objects indicating their social unity: a flag, a community deity or saint, royal regalia. Common South Asian processions include the procession of deities or saints around a village or city neighborhood or processions of community solidarity, such as Muslim saint celebrations called *'urs,* as well as secular processions of protest, such as "untouchables" (*Dalit*s) walking en masse through a Brahman neighborhood to assert their community inclusion, epitomized by Gandhi's march to the sea for salt.

Processions may be lineal, moving in a straight line across space to a particular destination, or circular, moving around a space or territory. Circular processions serve a double function. First, as processions, they define communities and their territories. Second, as circumambulations, they mark off interior spaces from exterior ones, thus serving to protect those interiors. For example, during some Hindu deity processions around neighborhoods and villages, actors throw ash or pumpkins to the exterior space beyond the procession route, actions which are intended to keep evil influences like ghosts and demons outside the protected interior enunciated by the procession.

Processions not only display gods, saints, and community solidarity. They also define communities and their territories. They define communities in two ways. First, who is allowed or invited to join a procession, in contrast to who is kept out, defines community inclusions and exclusions. Second, within those included in a community procession, the processual order may express and establish relations of rank within the community in question. Higher-ranking members of the community take leading or other important positions in the procession—and perhaps carry important paraphernalia—while lower-ranking community members take up the rear.

Processions also define community territory: As they move through space they also lay claim to space. For this reason, as well as for reasons of exclusion, whatever their ostensible motivation—whether religious festival or political protest—processions generally have political ramifications. It is no surprise that historically, as well as today, processions often instigate clashes. For example, in a village, a caste or other group that has been excluded from a village procession may include themselves by force, disrupting processual flow, and bringing out into the open—with arms and fists—disputes about who has power to define the village as a social unit. A Hindu procession may purposefully move through a Muslim neighborhood and set off community clashes, or vice versa.

Thus, processions may be expected to foster dispute in at least three dimensions: (1) those excluded from a procession may fight for inclusion, leading to skirmishes between communities; (2) those who think they should precede in line may force their way to the front, leading to skirmishes within the community; and (3) those whose territory is being crossed by another community may assert territorial control with violence. Historical and ethnographic studies of South Asia confirm all three.

The territorial and political ramifications of processions have both mythical and historical precedence in South Asia. Movement across space leads to rights over space. The *Ṛg Veda* (ca. 1200) praises Viṣṇu's great heroic strides: He took three footsteps to create the spaces of earth, heaven, and the distinction between the two. A later myth dramatizes these footsteps. Viṣṇu, in his dwarf incarnation, reclaims the earth as a territory for human occupation by tricking the ruling demon, Bali. The dwarf asks the demon to grant him just that bit of space he can stride in three steps. The demon is amused and so grants the dwarf his three steps, upon which the dwarf reveals himself as Viṣṇu , grows immense, and takes three strides that span heaven and earth.

As Viṣṇu claims mythical overlordship of heaven and earth with footsteps, so too have historical kings—Muslim, Buddhist, and Hindu—effected and pronounced their conquests in royal processions. In Hindu kinship, according to Ronald Inden, the *dig-vijaya,* "the conquest of the quarter," was a procession that established its performer to be "overlord of the four directional regions." In the *aśvamedha,* or "Horse Sacrifice," another ritual of kingship, a king would assert his control over a territory by releasing a horse to wander as far as it wished during the course of the year, followed by (and perhaps coaxed along by) a band of warriors ready to defend the horse against those whose territory it crossed. If they won their battles or continued unchallenged, the territory was considered that of their king.

References

Freitag, Sandra. 1990. *Collective action and community: public arenas and the emergence of communalism in north India.* Delhi: Oxford University Press.

Inden, Ronald. 1990. *Imagining India.* London: Blackwell Press.

Mines, Mattison. 1994. *Public faces, private voices: community and individuality in south India.* Berkeley: University of California Press.

Sax, William S. 1991. *Mountain goddess: gender and politics in a Himalayan pilgrimage.* New York: Oxford University Press.

Schubel, Vernon James. 1993. *Religious performance in contemporary Islam: Shi'i devotional rituals in south Asia.* Columbia: University of South Carolina Press.

DIANE MINES

SEE ALSO

Muḥarram; Ratha Jātrā; 'Urs

PROFESSIONAL PERFORMERS

Many of the folk traditions of South Asia are performed by folk professionals, specialists whose full-time job it is to enact their tradition at least during part of the year. Their relationship to the tradition they perform, to whatever professional organization or institution they belong, to their patrons, to the remuneration they receive, and even the paths that led them to their professions are extremely varied and are a complex topic for much-needed future research. Some, such as the *kamsāle* performer practice their art not only because they are devotees of the god Mādēśwara, but because their parents dedicated them to the deity as small child. Others, such as the *Mandecculu,* take up narrating the *Kātma Rāju Katha* as a profession because it is their caste tradition, although by no means do all of the members of their caste perform the art. Members of the Hijrā community, full-time "costumed" performers of a variety of different song and ritual traditions, have in common a sexual transformation: They are eunuchs, hermaphrodites, impotent men, transvestites, transsexuals, and women with male characteristics. The *yakṣagana* of coastal Karnataka attracts males of all ages and from all castes without exception; it is a low paying and seasonally arduous life. In some regions of Andhra Pradesh, however, troupes tend to restrict their membership to a single caste where some of the related forms of yakṣagana (such as *vithi nāṭakam, Cindu Bhagavatam,* and *Cencu Nāṭakam*) are all identified by the castes of the performers and the stories they enact are closely associated with either their own caste or the caste of their patrons. Even the internationally well-known North Indian dance form called *kathak* has its origins in particular lineages within a caste of professional itinerant Rajasthani storytellers who enhance their recitations with song and dance in order to attract wider audiences and wealthier patrons as they wandered from town to town. Today, *kathak* is regarded as a national dance form, and many young people of all castes and classes all over India study it.

The clear identification of performers as professionals associated with particular lineages or castes dates back to very early times in South Asia. Ancient texts of both southern (Dravidian) and northern (Indo-European) regions of South Asia make reference to professional bards. In the south the term used is *parava,* and the contemporary Tuluva caste of the same name perhaps continues this ancient tradition by reciting oral narratives called *pāḍdana*. In Sanskritic tradition, Veda Vyāsa is not only the reputed author of the Sanskrit epic, the *Mahābhārata,* but the one who arranged the ancient and sacred *Veda* into four parts. Although no longer a title limited to particular lineages or even castes, the contemporary *vyāsa*s see themselves as his descendants. The two streams of tradition are different in one respect: while the north Indian professional performers have always been granted a high status, their southern counterparts have historically been regarded as lowly untouchables. The reason for this difference is unclear.

Although it may not be usual for folklorists around the world to distinguish between traditions performed by professionals and ones done by everyone (or that at least *could* be done by everyone of a given gender, age, or region) in South Asia the distinction is often very significant. Performing a service for groups other than your own is something evaluated by criteria associated with the caste system. Even in regard to such ostensibly mundane matters as washing clothes, which everyone can do for oneself or for a family member, doing so for someone of another caste brings about a relationship with a strongly marked social value. While this value is usually negative, as is true in the case of Washermen castes, sometimes the relationship is positively valued and rewarded with high status, as is that of the Brahman priest. As discussed in the entry for "*Jajmāni* System," the value accorded to a particular relationship is by no means obvious and must usually be viewed within the larger social value system. In southern India in particular, performing castes tend to be regarded as being of a lower status than those for whom they perform. The Heḷavas of Karnataka (who are called Piccakoṇḍḷu in Andhra Pradesh) are a fairly typical example. Even though not all Heḷava families travel to villages of their patron castes to perform their duties (which include maintaining genealogies, singing songs about the lives of caste heroes, and performing certain rituals), the entire caste is stigmatized by this practice. Myths and stories describing how they came to perform for their patron castes apply to all members of it.

Although many professional performers are of castes whose position in the local caste system is associated with the performance they do, somewhat surprisingly, their role as performers is often not designated by their caste name. This is the case with, say, the Mandecculu of Andhra Pradesh (whose caste is called Ālu Golla), or the Tāgari Jōgalu of Karnataka and Andhra Pradesh who regard themselves as a section of the larger Kuruba (shepherd) caste. Sometimes, as in the case of both the Heḷavas and the Tāgari Jōgalu—both of whose performances are regarded primarily as rituals—the performers of the ritual tradition constitute an endogamous subsection of the larger caste. Sometimes the performance tradition is identified by an instrument used in the performance, as in the case of the Oggu Kathe—the *oggu* story—the oggu being an hourglass-shaped drum that represents a sort of "badge" indicating the performers' right (*hakku*) to perform. In the case of the Tāgari Jōgalu the identity badge is the skull of a ram (*tāgari*), which is affixed on the basket of images they carry.

However, it must also be said that many professional performers are not identified with a particular caste, but instead are recruited from a variety of castes (although usually of a similar rank) on the basis of devotion to a particular deity. This is the case of the *kamsāleyavru* (or *dēvara guddalu*) performers of Karnataka, who are dedicated by their parents to a life of itinerant performance in devotion to the god Mādēśwara, or the Gorava/Goramma performers, who travel from village to village singing songs of the Mailara ballad cycle on their annual pilgrimage to the large *jātra*s held in the name of Mailara/Mallanna/Khandoba. The terms *nāth* and *jogī* (or *yogī*) refer both to ascetic sects as well as to various hereditary castes. The term *nāth* means "master" and the Nāths are understood to be masters of yogic powers. While many live as homeless wanderers who have renounced caste membership, they usually belong to particular orders or sects, and trace their yogic practices through an intellectual lineage of gurus. Often, however, the term applies to any wandering minstrel-beggar whose attire is emblematic of a religious profession. Like others mentioned above, they may own property and be householders during much of the year. Their family shares the caste name of Jogi and the status associated with their performance.

Itinerancy

Many professional performers whose livelihood is derived solely from their performances are itinerant by necessity. If they serve a particular caste, a section of a caste, or a group of castes, they must travel to all of the locations to which that caste has dispersed. Often their itinerancy itself serves a multiplicity of functions in addition to merely that of reciting a caste myth or performing an essential ritual. Frequently these less obvious functions include maintaining the identity and coherency of a large, diasporic community, and conveying news of events and other matters of a social or political nature highly significant to its members. In many cases, too, itinerant performers carry medicines (and treat medical conditions), trade in animals and other goods, circulate information about eligible brides and grooms from surrounding villages, and are even equipped to make monetary loans, aggregate monies, and disperse winnings in a traditional form of lottery system called a "chit fund."

Most of the devotee-performers such as the Goravas and *kamsāleyavru,* whose itinerancy is the result of a religious vow, collect alms from the houses of devotees of all castes and carry offerings for the deity to major temple locations. On their return trip they stop at the same houses again, bringing *prasada* ("blessed offerings") and news of the region from the great crowds of pilgrims. Because their practice of begging is associated with their service and devotion to a deity, it is not regarded as "unclean," even if it does not accord them very high status. However, the term *khāndāni Vāghye,* which means "high born," to designate the status of lifetime devotion to Khandobā (the Maharastran equivalent of Mailara) would indicate that relatively low socioeconomic status does not necessarily correspond to high regard in a religious context.

Remuneration

In many cases, as Pulikonda Subbachary points out in his entry "Dependent Performing Castes," the relationship between performers and patrons cannot be understood in a commercial sense. Often the preferred or appropriate form of payment is food or uncooked grain. Sometimes patrons are obliged to give more extensive hospitality (room and board) for larger and longer performances. If the performers come on a regular periodic visit, or their performance is associated with life cycle ceremonies, they may be given an animal, such as a goat, a sheep, or a calf.

The nature of this relationship is not always easily understood by the outsider. Earlier anthropologists and folklorists often labeled the itinerant performers beggars, but this designation ignores the fact that the patron usually derives status or religious blessings from the visit of a Tāgari Jōgalu, Gorava, or one of the many other kinds of religious mendicants who need not even perform. Giving a performance—even a brief one—does oblige the patron to give more, but the reason may not be merely the added value of entertainment. In the case of a visit of a family's religious preceptor (*guru*), the food given by the host is a prop for the guest's "performance"—that is, the act of eating is the performance. Similarly, many performances, such as those of itinerant storytellers who carry "god boxes"—miniature temples—are themselves rituals in which a deity is invoked and it is to the deity the offering is made, even though this offering is kept by the performer and may be used to support their life of devotion.

Religious Duty and Entertainment

Although many professional performances have at their core some sort of religious duty that needs to be performed, almost all include entertainment and other functions. Interspersing humorous episodes in retelling the lives and exploits of a deity is not at all inappropriate in folk tradition, nor is the inclusion of the god's amorous adventures and the complications and intrigues these subsequently entail. In fact, both classical and folk Hinduism frequently use these sorts of themes and metaphors to express the deeper, more mystical means by which gods inspire the devotion (*bhakti*) of their followers.

Beyond the additional services performed by itinerants for their patrons (including acrobats, snake charmers, and others performing with animals), the female members of the performer's family sometimes provide sexual services to members of the patron households. When the Heḷava refer to themselves as *Reddi biddalu* ("the daughters of their Reddy patrons"), it is in reference to this service. While this may seem unconnected to their primary identities as professional performers, one must keep in mind that many temples have associated "temple dancers" and even some of the classical dance traditions of India derive from their performance. In many cases the temple dancers, like the female relatives of the itinerant performers, provide sexual services to temple patrons. This service is not regarded as inconsistent with their professional performance and the women are not necessarily regarded as prostitutes in the commercial sense of term as used today. Their sexual services are performed as a part of their performative dedication to god, and not as a kind of sideline.

Many of these additional practices are being discontinued today because of increasing commercialization and the spread of Western cultural norms. Itinerancy is giving way to a desire for a more settled lifestyle afforded by modern means of transportation. Indeed, traditional professional performers are rapidly disappearing in the face of new forms of entertainment and the use of modern media for religious storytelling (such as "TV Rāmāyaṇa").

PETER J. CLAUS

SEE ALSO

Acrobatics; Ali; Animal Performances; *Bhakti;* Dance; Dependent Performing Castes; God-Boxes, Painted; *Jajmānī; Jātrā/Yātrā; Kamsāle; Kathak* Dancers; *Kātma Rāju; Mādēśwara; Mailara/Mallana/Khandoba; Nāth; Oggu Katha;* Performance Studies; Rāmāyaṇa, TV Production; *Vāghyā/Muraḷī*

PROVERBS

Proverbs—terse, didactic, expressive, pithy, artistic, miniature, fixed phrases—abound in South Asian languages. The people of South Asia have proverbs in their linguistic repertoire to defy, warn, admonish, ridicule, rebuke, criticize, and confirm the moral code and social conventions, to smooth social friction, and to say yes and no. In almost all South Asian languages, innumerable proverbs are used in everyday speech. The fact that a large number have been collected and published in dictionaries indicates the richness and abundance of proverbial literature in the Dravidian and Indo-Aryan languages (among these dictionaries: Gundert 1896—Malayalam; Hermann Jenson 1897—Tamil; Hilton Knowles 1885—Kashmiri; John Christian 1891—Bihar; Kartha 1966—Malayalam; Kittel 1894—Kannada; Lazarus 1894—Tamil; Narottamdas Swami and Murlidhar Vyas Visharad 1849—Rajasthani; Percival—1843, 1846, 1894—Tamil and 1855—Telugu).

The proverbs of the South Asians reveal a vivid form of their life, morals, customs, traditions, and specific qualities. How the people of South Asia view proverbs can be seen in the metafolkloric Kannada proverb, "*gade vedakke samana*" ("the proverbs are equal to the Veda"). This "elder's genre" was defined more than two thousand years ago by the Tamil grammarian Tholkappiar as "an old saying containing depth of knowledge, brevity, clarity, and simplicity as its special characteristics, and it will come as a quotation in a given situation."

Proverbs, verbal symbolic interaction, are of three kinds: literal, image-motivated or metaphoric, and a combination of literal and metaphoric. In the literal proverb the general meaning is directly motivated, that is, directly derived, from the meanings of the component words. One example of a literal proverb is "Pride goeth before destruction" (Tiripuri proverb). In the image-motivated proverb the overall meaning is not directly derived from the component words but is linked with them through an image: "Where there is no horse, the ass is the leader" (Tamil proverb). A proverb that is both literal and metaphoric becomes metaphoric only when it is uttered in a particular context: "If pot and ghee both belong to others, why should a Brahman care for them?" (Magahi proverb).

Several scholars have observed the similarities between proverbs and riddles. Some proverbs are used as riddles or vice versa. This phenomenon occurs in both Tamil and Bengali. An example: "Can a person who could not walk lead the dance master?" (Tamil proverb); "A person who could not walk leads the dance master. Who is he?" (Tamil riddle). That proverbs can be the thumbnail sketches of folk tales is shown in the tale about the absent-minded man who put the lamb on his back and looked into the well.

The similarity between the Tamil and Marathi proverbs is well established through an account of the experience of Herman Jensen at Poona and Bombay. There, he came across two Marathi proverbs that are literally the same in Tamil and another one exactly the same as a Tamil proverb: "The dancing girl, who could not dance, said that the hall was not big enough" (Jensen 1897). This proverb is found all over India. Sathya Prakash Arya wrote about it as it appears in Northern India: "One who doesn't know or can't dance proficiently blames that the floor is uneven or crooked" (Arya 1984). A similar proverb with a different image is "The inexperienced thief, unable to steal, blames that the duration of the night is short." In the same context, even an obscene proverb can also be used: "Being ignorant of the correct technique and remaining unsuccessful and dissatisfied, [a man] blames that the woman's vagina is defective" (Arya 1984). Used in similar contexts with the same intent is the Tamil scatological proverb, "The king who rules over the country doesn't have a place to defecate."

As social beings, people have to interact with one another. Hence, there are a number of proverbs about the various kinds of relationships between a husband and wife, sisters, brothers, in-laws, and others. Some examples of family-related proverbs include: "At five, they are brothers, at ten, litigants." The relation between the mother-in-law and daughter-in-law is sarcastically depicted by an oppositional proverb: "If the mother-in-law breaks it, it is a mud pot. If the daughter-in-law breaks it, it is a golden pot."

South Asia is a region of caste-ridden societies, and caste as well as other kinds of ethnic slurs are innumerable. The caste system of India is based on the idea of inequality, that is, on the superiority and inferiority of different castes. Intragroup and intergroup proverbs ridicule a caste by mentioning a peculiar characteristic or exaggerating an abnormal feature. Brahmans are mocked with: "A man commits a sin if he does not beat a Brahman in this Age [*Kaliyuga,* a time of moral degeneration]" (Bengali) or "Even the simplest Brahman is crooked as a sickle" (Magahi). Few castes are excepted from ridicule in South Asia. The only reason one cannot find proverbs about Kṣātriyas in South Indian languages is because the four-tiered hierarchical caste system of the North is not prevalent in the South.

From the proverbs of South Asian people and their feudal society a conclusion can be drawn that they are conservative and past-oriented people: "Don't close the old canal and don't dig a new one." [Don't go against the tradition and create a new one.]

References

Arya, Satya Prakash. 1984. Proverb in Northern India. In *Indian and Japanese Folklore,* eds. Ramesh Mathur, Masahiro Manabe, 425–469. Japan: KUFS Publication.

Bedi, Sohindersingh. 1971. *Folklore of the Punjab.* New Delhi: National Book Trust.
Chaudhuri, Dulal. 1987. The Chakma proverbs: an ethnostructural introduction. In *Indian Folklore II.* Peter J. Claus, Jawaharlal Handoo, D. P. Pattanayak, eds., 69–77. Mysore: Central Institute of Indian Languages.
Choondal, Chummer. 1981. Proverbs in Malayalam. *Folklore,* 22 (9): 173–178.
Dundes, Alan. 1975. Proverbs and the ethnography of speaking folklore. In *Analytical essays in Folklore.* Paris: Mouton the Hague.
Fuchas, Mother. 1975. Culture and communication. *Folklore* XVI (11): 369–380.
Islam, Mazhurul. 1980. *Folklore: the pulse of the people.* New Delhi: Concept Publishing Company.
Jensson, Herman. 1897. *A classified collection of Tamil proverbs.* London: Trubner & Co.
Lazarus, John. 1894. *A dictionary of Tamil proverbs.* Madras.
Lourdu, S. D. 1980. *Tamil Palamoligal Oor Aaivu* (translation?). Unpublished doctoral dissertation submitted to the Madurai Kamaraj University, Madurai.
———. 1984. Proverbs in Southern India. In *Indian and Japanese Folklore,* eds. Ramesh Mathur and Masahiro Manabe. Japan: KUFS Publication. pp?
Niyogi, Tushar Kanti. 1974. A study of Tripuri proverbs. *Folklore* XV (1): 19–24.
Percival, P. 1874. *Tamil proverbs with their English translation.* Madras: Dinavarthamani Press.
Sharma, Nageshwar. 1975. Caste life as revealed in Magahi proverbs and sayings. *Folklore* XVIII (4): 113–118.
Taylor, Archer and Wolf Gand Mieder, eds. 1975. *Selected writings on proverbs.* FF Communication, No. 216.
Vanamamalai, N. 1974. Tamil parallels for Tripuri proverbs. *Folklore* XVI (3): 123–132.

S. D. LOURDU

SEE ALSO
Balochistan: Oral Tradition; Sindh; Stereotypes; *Ukhān*

PUBERTY RITUALS

Female puberty rituals are common among the populations (Hindu, Muslim, and Buddhist) of Sri Lanka, South India, Orissa, Bengal, and parts of Madhya Pradesh. Excepting the Newar of Nepal, most Tibeto-Burman speaking peoples do not have them. Puberty rituals are celebrated in Afghanistan or Pakistan among specific tribal groups only. Most communities that ritualize female puberty also encourage cousin marriage and tend not to have traditions of prepuberty marriage. Male puberty rituals are rare, although religious initiation serves as a transition to young adulthood for boys in some places.

Much of South Asian culture is characterized by an intense concern with female sexuality and a fear (or awe) of menstrual blood. Female sexuality is viewed as a potential threat to social order, insofar as caste integrity is thought to depend on sexual and reproductive purity. Puberty rituals serve to clarify a female's physical and social status vis-à-vis her natal relatives, her potential in-laws, and even her future descendants.

Puberty ritual. Madurai, Tamil Nadu, India, © Richard Rapfogel

The first menstruation is considered to be an auspicious occasion. Common ritual acts include bathing of the girl and isolating her for some time, after which she goes through a ritual reintegration into her family. The girl may receive fertility-enhancing blessings. In Sri Lanka a girl will have a new horoscope drawn up that supersedes her birth horoscope.

The puberty ceremony in some other areas involves a mock wedding, with the girl, seen as a bride, "marrying" an inanimate object, a baby, or another girl. In south India a girl may receive a marital type of necklace (*tāli*) during or after her puberty ceremony.

In southern Karnataka State the term for a newly matured Hindu girl is the same term as that used to refer to a new mother; and her lineage is considered to be "polluted" in the same way it is by a new birth or a death. Believing that a girl's first menstruation pollutes her kin group for eleven days, the Newar keep her in a dark room for that period, during which she eats no salt. Previously, she would have been wed (at the age of 4 to 11) to the god Narayan in a rite considered to be her most important marriage. Thus, she is in a sense already "married" by the time of her puberty rite.

The Kandyan Sinhalese regularly perform puberty rituals but may or may not have elaborate weddings. Their custom is to seclude a newly menstruating girl in a small hut. A male and female of the Washerman caste assist her with the purification necessary for her reentry into society. When she returns home, she is greeted by an uncle who is also a potential father-in-law.

A daughter's first menstruation is celebrated as a private, exclusively female, rite among Bangladesh Muslims, although Bengali Hindus tend to conduct puberty rites in a flamboyant manner. Among some Pashtun people in the Paktya area of Afghanistan, close female relatives share some brown sugar (*gur*) when a girl matures.

References

Bhattacharyya, Narendra Nath. 1980. *Indian puberty rites,* 2nd ed. New Delhi: Munshiram Manoharlal Publishers Pvt. Ltd.

Good, Anthony. 1991. *The female bridegroom; a comparative study of life-crisis rituals in south India and Sri Lanka*. Oxford: Oxford University (Clarendon Press).

Yalman, Nur. 1963. On the purity of women in the castes of Ceylon and Malabar. *Journal of the Royal Anthropological Institute* 93(1): 25–58.

SUZANNE HANCHETT

SEE ALSO
Koṭahaḷuva Gedara; Life Cycle Rituals; Muslim Folklore, Sri Lanka

PŪJĀ

A *pūjā* is a ritual performance that honors a being or an object and provides the context for the transaction between worshiper and deity in which a visual and substantive connection can occur. The most common expression in theistic Hinduism today, pūjās are done outdoors, in homes, temples, at natural sites, and within a devotee's mind and body. The external focus of a pūjā is a *mūrti* (form), which may be a respected living being, such as a teacher or guru; a stone, wood, or metal icon of a deity; an aniconic image, such as the Ganges River; plants; animals; the implements of one's profession or subsistence; or any form to which devotion and a relationship of dependence is to be demonstrated.

In practice, pūjās may vary widely in accordance with specific liturgies or ritual actions, the number and kind of officiants, and the kinds of offerings presented to the mūrti. The term itself is used to refer both to the simplest offering of a flower to an icon in a family pūjā room and to large-scale, multiday festivals at temple complexes. For instance, the *Navarātri,* or Nine Nights Festival, often called the Durgā pūjā, celebrates various qualities of goddesses in multipart ritual events and involves many kinds of ceremonial activities in addition to the pūjā rite performed at the mūrti in the temple sanctum. These large temple festivals often include ritual performances that link worshipers to the deity: the reenactment or recitation of sacred narratives such as the *Rāmalīlā* or *Rāslīlā,* a "car festival" (*rathajātrā*), the singing of songs, the taking of vows (*vratas*), ascetic practices, and other kinds of ritual behaviors. In the narrow sense, the liturgy at the icon is the pūjā. In the broader sense, celebrating the many forms of the goddess in various ways in the entire festival (*utsava*) is also called pūjā.

Pūjās can be classified in various ways, based on frequency, types of offerings, and dimensions or elaborateness of performance. The simplest pūjā is the daily event in the family worship room, where the single officiant (*pūjāri*) offers traditional substances, perhaps flowers, sandalwood paste, turmeric powder, water, incense, a lit oil lamp, or various foods while she/he recites *mantras* (verbal formulas) or prayers. Prescriptions and proscriptions set limits on performers and performance in this simple form of pūjā, as well as in its more elaborate forms. Ritual handbooks, sectarian treatises, purāṇic texts, and other sources specify the actions and offerings appropriate for different deities and occasions and outline behaviors that are enjoined or forbidden. Rules of purification must be followed by the pūjāri; for example, a woman in menses should not enter the pūjā room or temple, the pūjāri must have bathed, the offerings must be fresh and not have been used elsewhere, and chants and choreography must be done correctly. The actual form of a pūjā as a sequence of actions may draw more or less upon the Vedic or Brahminical tradition in defining who ritualists must be and which mantras must be used. But the diversity of pūjās in practice allows for formalism from other textual or ritual traditions, such as tantric or āgamic, or the creation of new forms. Theoretically, in certain sects of theistic Hinduism, anyone can be a pūjāri.

In the conservative Smarta Brahmin tradition, the standard daily pūjā done in the home or temple follows a sequence of sixteen actions (*ṣoḍaśopacārapūjā*) and enacts the receiving and taking care of the needs of a teacher, Brahmin, or deity as a guest. It begins with the purification and consecration of performers, implements, and place of the pūjā, a prayer for the removal of obstructions to success, and the statement of intent to perform the pūjā. Then, the deity is invoked as *prāṇa* (breath energy) into the icon, invited to be present, and offered a seat. The deity, now in the form of the mūrti, is greeted and offered water for cleansing and refreshing

Vilakka Puja. Madurai, Tamil Nadu, India, © Richard Rapfogel

the feet, the face, and the body. A beverage of honey and water is given to drink. Then, the deity is re-dressed in clean clothes; unguents, oils or sandalwood paste are applied to the body; flowers or garlands are draped on or set before the image; incense is burned; a lit flame is waved before the image; and the deity is treated to various cooked and raw foods (betel nut, rice, fruit, sweets). Devotees prostrate before the image to show honor and obedience; and, finally, the prāṇa of the deity, that has been focussed and localized in the image for the pūjā ceremony, is released into a more universal form. The pūjāri usually distributes the "leftovers" of the offerings to the devotees. The receiving back of these substances, which is called *prasāda* and treated as imbued with the energy of the deity, is a key form of interaction between devotee and deity in pūjā. As the pūjāri brings the offering tray with its burning incense and lit flame near, devotees hold their palms over it, and, with a wafting gesture, they bring the scent and light over their own heads to absorb the beneficial presence. They may then take a bit of the ash or colored *kumkum* powder and apply it to their foreheads or elsewhere, or ingest a bit. Prāsada in the form of food offerings may be consumed then or taken to others.

Pūjās are performed in a number of religious traditions in India, including Śaivism, Vaiṣnavism, Śaktism, Buddhism, and Jainism. The form and offerings may differ, as will the officiants, types of prayers or chants, the forms and understanding of the nature of mūrti as a focus of ritual attention, and the participation of devotees. In some pūjā ceremonies, a worshiper or pūjāri may be possessed by the deity invoked. In others, no actual presence is inferred, and the mūrti is a memorial. Consistent is the attitude of reverence and respect, the intent to honor by giving, and the creation and expression of an intimate relationship between worshipers and the deity, person, or object that is the focus of the pūjā.

References

Buhnemann, Gudrun. 1988. *Pūjā, a study in Smarta ritual.* Vienna: University of Vienna (Publications of the DeNobili Research Library).

Cort, John E. 1991. Mūrtipūjā in Svetambar Jain Temples. In *Religion in India,* ed. T. N. Madan. Oxford: Oxford University Press.

Courtright, Paul B. 1985. *Ganesa, lord of obstacles, lord of beginnings.* Oxford: Oxford University Press.

Fuller, C. J. 1992. *The camphor flame.* Princeton: Princeton University Press.

Oster, Akos. 1980. *The play of the gods*. Chicago: University of Chicago Press.

M. J. GENTES

SEE ALSO

Fairs and Festivals; Food and Foodways; Gods and Goddesses; Hospitality; Navarātri; *Rām Līlā; Rāsa Līlā; Ratha Jātra;* Worship

PUNJAB

Punjab (*panj-āb* "five waters"), adjoining provinces in India and Pakistan, was created when British India was partitioned in 1947. This partition resulted in changes in regional patterns of traditional culture within the area, with mass migrations of both rural and urban populations across the newly established border. Indian Punjab was reconfigured in 1966 with the creation of the states of Haryana and Himachal Pradesh. Punjabi is the majority language of both Punjabs; various dialects of Punjabi, with its related culture and significant numbers of speakers, extend to the Hindko-speaking city of Peshawar in Pakistan's Northwest Frontier Province, north into Jammu, south into Ganganagar district of Rajasthan, and east to Delhi.

An overview of folk traditions of Pakistani Punjab was produced by staff members of the National Institute of Folk Heritage, Lok Virsa, who traveled throughout the province, collecting oral literature and interviewing local residents about their customs for a volume edited in 1978 by Mazhar-ul-Islam. A 1971 overview of Indian Punjab by Sohinder Singh Bedi includes chapters on customs and traditions, fairs and festivals, oral literature, and folk music and dance; an appendix includes folk songs, short tales, riddles, and proverbs and poetry, some with Punjabi text.

A major nineteenth century collection of Punjabi oral literature was made by the soldier-administrator, Sir Richard Carnac Temple, in three volumes of fifty-eight tales (1884–1900). The tales are mainly in Punjabi and include English translations; each tale's title is followed by an identification of the story-teller and introductory material relating it to similar tales. Temple's prefaces to each volume include generalizations about the collected stories in the broader context of Indo-Aryan folk and classical literature and Indo-European folklore more generally; the third volume includes an index of names and motifs (for example, flying through the air, disguises, disgrace). Temple's papers, consisting of 240 volumes and six boxes of documents and papers, are now in the India Office Library and Records. The collection by Reverend Charles Swynnerton (1892, 1903) contains eighty-five tales in the first volume and twelve in the second; the preface includes a classification by tale type but no details about collection techniques or original texts. In 1908, Major J. F. A. McNair, in collaboration with T. L. Barlow, a British administrator in the Salt Range who had already contributed tales to the Swynnerton volumes, published an additional nineteen tales, collected mostly in a small village on the east side of the Indus River. Mulk Raj Anand (1974), in a preface to fourteen short tales remembered from his childhood, explicitly notes his own use of British collections. The twenty prose versions of folk romances by Duggal (1979) were first published in a Chandigarh weekly series.

Salt-range site of Amb, Pakistan, © Michael W. Meister

Punjabi popular literature began coming into print as chapbooks slightly earlier than these oral collections; most of these were printed in Lahore. Early Punjabi chapbooks of narrative verse (*qiṣṣa*) included romances of Hīr and Ranjhā (by five authors with at least thirteen printings between 1871 and 1883), Sassī and Punnūṉ (six authors with thirteen printings between 1862 and 1882), Mirzā and Ṣāḥibān, and Sohnī and Mahīnwāl. Other local qiṣṣas relate Dullā Bhattī's attempts at revenge against Emperor Akbar, the resistance of the

Hindu prince, Pūran Bhagat, to his stepmother's attempt to seduce him, and a series of adventures of Rāja Rasālu, which in some versions begins with the Pūran Bhagat tale; one version of the latter had at least twenty-five Lahore printings from 1867 through 1879. Some chapbooks, such as Layla and Majnūn (at least five printings by three authors from 1860 to 1877), Shīrīn and Farhād, and martial tales (*jang-nāma*) about events related to Karbalā, had sources in the Perso-Arabic tradition outside South Asia. Martial tales in verse also described events of more recent periods, such as the battles in Kabul and in Chitral. The tale of Yūsof (Joseph) and Zulayka, which was and is particularly popular, has had a series of Punjabi versions.

The early printings were in three scripts: the Arabic-based script used today in Pakistan, the Gurmukhi script associated with Sikhs, and the Devanagari script common in north India. In early printings, the popular story (qiṣṣa) in verse of Sassī and Punnūn̲ in the version by Hāshim had at least five Lahore printings during the 1870s: three in the Arabic-based script, one in Gurmukhi, and one in Devanagari. As chapbook printings continued, other qiṣṣa publications were added, including at least two Punjabi versions of Amīr Ḥamza's adventures, and contemporary local history (for example, verses on the brutal conduct of a local *nāẕim* [landlord]), autobiography (such as experiences as a laborer in Africa), and accounts of the substitution of trucks for tongas (*qiṣṣa moṭar lārī*). Tales of Sanskritic origin, such as Nala and Damayantī, and popular Hindi tales, such as Rūp Basant, were also published as Punjabi chapbooks.

Hanaway and Nasir documented Pakistan's chapbook literature as of 1990 and have over three hundred entries, partly or all in Punjabi and published mostly in Lahore. These chapbooks include traditional narrative verse of the previous century as well as tales about Shaykh Cillī and Mullā Nasīr al-dīn and collections of jokes. Chapbook collections of nonnarrative verse include popular Punjabi forms such as the *kāfī*, a poem of short stanzas, each followed by a refrain; the *dohṛa*, a rhymed couplet usually with a caesura in each line; the two-line *ṭappa* and the *māhiyā*, a rhymed couplet with the first line shorter than the last. Shārib (1994) has 232 māhiyās from a field collection; he includes the Punjabi text, Punjabi transcription, and Urdu and English translations. Punjabi chapbook publications also include the *sīharfī*, with verses beginning with successive letters of the alphabet, and the *bāramāh* with verses for successive months of the year. Chapbooks of religious nonnarrative verses include both the *na't* (praise) and the *nauḥa* (lamentation) as well as the *mātam* (mourning) associated with the Shia observances of Muḥarram.

Chapbooks in Urdu printed in Lahore include religious poetry and traditional qiṣṣas printed elsewhere in South Asia. Lahore chapbooks of charms (*'amaliyāt*), spells (*tilismāt*), amulets (*ta'vīẕāt*), and magic (*jādū*), collected by Hanaway and Nasir, are in Urdu, rather than Punjabi. In recent decades, film songs, mostly in Urdu, have added another genre to Lahore's chapbooks.

The poetry of Sufi mystics of Pakistani Punjab is popular at both folk and elite levels, and ceremonies at their shrines are an important part of cultural life. Certain poets are associated with particular forms of poetry, which can be heard sung at their shrines. The kāfī, for example, is particularly associated with Bulleh Shah (1680–1753), and the dohṛa with Shaykh (Bābā) Farīd (d. 1265), whose name is often included in his couplets. The tomb of Shah Ḥusayn (ca. 1538–1600 C.E.) in Lahore provides a focal point for his verses. Translations of the verses of Panjabi mystics can usually be found in articles and books about them.

Siraiki and Hindko became recognized as separate languages rather than Punjabi dialects in Pakistan's 1982 census. A 1917 collection of thirty-four stories has the romanized Siraiki/Multani text with an English translation; it includes tales of local events, among which one of the longest is "The Abduction of Lieutenant Grey." Shackle (1983) includes a few short Siraiki tales.

In addition to proverb collections, either all in Punjabi or in English without Punjabi texts, Bedi has Punjabi texts in all three scripts, together with English translations; the agricultural subject matter reflects the provinces' economic base until recent years.

The discussion of Indian Punjab's music by Middlebrook includes the dance-related secular *bhangṛa* and *giddhā* as well as Sikh devotional music. For Pakistani Punjab, Nayyar describes instruments, musicians, including both the hereditary musician (*mīrāṣī*) with its various subcategories and the non-hereditary musician, and secular and religious musical genres, which "are inextricably linked to poetry in the Punjab, and often take their name from the type of poetry being rendered with music" (771). The description by Sakata includes three important Sufi shrines in Punjab where annual death anniversary celebrations bring large crowds for the singing of poetry of the particular saints. Abbas examines from a linguistic point of view selections of Siraiki, Punjabi, and Urdu verse used in a religious context; the texts, which are given in romanized transcription and in translation, include portions of legends about Sassī and Punnūn̲ and Hīr and Ranjhā. The bhangṛa has become popular in Punjabi communities outside South Asia; in the videorecording by Tejaswini Ganti, DJs and cassette sellers discuss the growth of the bhangṛa's popularity in the New York City metropolitan area in the late 1980s.

Dhillon describes Punjabi folk dances of both men and women with songs, sketches of movements, and color photographs. He points out the growth of folk dance forms in Indian Punjab after 1947 and includes a bibliography as well as an extensive glossary of different dances and musical instruments used for accompaniment.

Indian Punjab is the only province on the subcontinent where Sikhs are in the majority. McLeod includes actual examples of modern bazaar prints in bright colors of Sikh personages; he compares them with the late nineteenth century woodcuts and lithographs from the J. Lockwood Kipling collection in the Victoria and Albert Museum and offers a popular view of Sikh history as illustrated by these prints. Indian Punjab shares with adjoining provinces a tradition of wall paintings both decorative and narrative. The devotional poster portraits described by Frembgen are from Pakistani Punjab; sometimes handpainted but mostly printed in Lahore, they are usually marketed at shrines, especially at the time of the shrine's death anniversary festivities.

Local pottery and textile traditions have long been known to travelers in Punjab. Certain areas have had specialties, such as the carpets of Lahore and the glazed tiles of Multan. Sharma examines the social setting for artisans in the century preceding partition. Kenoyer includes photographs of Harappan pottery and contemporary examples of similar shape but of different materials; evidence of weaving in the Punjabi region likewise appears in the Harappan period. Maskiell examines the context of *phulkārī* (flower work) embroidery from the colonial period to the present; her extensive bibliography includes useful sources for Punjabi history as well as for the embroidery itself.

Itinerant folk theater and mostly male, traveling entertainers have a long tradition in both Punjabs. For a few decades after partition, Lahore also developed a folk theater in which women were actively involved. Films in Punjabi are produced in both India and Pakistan; Mushtaq Gazdar's filmography list includes Pakistani films in Punjabi based on folktales such as Dulla Bhatti, Shaikh Chilli, Sassi Punnu, Gul Bakawali, and Heer Ranjha (sic); folk singers, dances, and dancers provide regional atmosphere in Punjabi films.

References

Abbas, Shemeem Burney. 1993. Speechplay and verbal art in the Indo-Pakistan oral Sufi tradition. Ann Arbor, Michigan: University Microfilm International. Revised version forthcoming as *The Female Voice in Sufi Ritual,* Austin: University of Texas Press.

Anand, Mulk Raj. 1974. *Folk tales of Punjab.* New Delhi: Sterling Publishers Pvt. Ltd.

Aryan, K. C. 1977. *Punjab murals.* New Delhi: Rekha Prakashan.

Barnett, L. D. 1961. *Panjabi printed books in the British Museum: A supplementary catalogue.* London: The Trustees of the British Musem.

Bedi, Kishan Singh, trans. [1962] *Agricultural proverbs of the Punjab.* Chandigarh: Public Relations Department, Punjab.

Bedi, Sohinder Singh. 1971. *Folklore of Punjab.* New Delhi: National Book Trust, India.

Blumhardt, J[ames] F[uller]. 1893. *Catalogues of the Hindi, Panjabi, Sindhi, and Pushtu printed books in the library of the British Museum.* London: Trustees of the British Museum. [Citations by *Panjabi* section column numbers.]

———. 1902. *Catalogue of the library of the India office, Vol II.-Part III: Hindi, Panjabi, Pushtu, and Sindhi Books.* London: Eyre and Spottiswoode. [Citations by *Panjabi* section page numbers.]

Dhillon, Iqbal Singh. 1998. *Folk dances of Panjab.* Delhi: National Book Shop.

Duggal, K. S. 1979. *Folk romances of Punjab.* New Delhi: Marwah Publications.

Eaton, Richard M. 1982. Court of man, court of god: local perception of the shrine of Baba Farid, Pakpattan, Punjab. In *Islam in local contexts,* ed. Richard C. Martin. Contributions to Asian Studies, Vol. 17, 44–61. Leiden: Brill.

Frembgen, Jürgen Wasim. 1998. Saints in modern devotional poster-portraits: meanings and uses of popular religious folk Art in Pakistan. *Res* 34 (autumn): 184–191.

Ganti, Tejaswini, producer, dir., ed. c.1955. *Gimme somethin' to dance to!* [videorecording]. New York University Department of Anthropology Program in Culture & Media. New York: Chutney Productions.

Gazdar, Mushtaq. 1997. *Pakistan cinema, 1947–1997.* Karachi: Oxford University Press.

Hanaway, William L. and Mumtaz Nasir. 1996. Chapbook publishing in Pakistan. In *Studies in Pakistani popular culture,* eds. William L. Hanaway and Wilma Heston, 339–615. Islamabad and Lahore.

Kang, Kanwarji Singh. ca. 1985. *Wall paintings of the Punjab and Haryana.* Delhi: Atma Ram.

Kenoyer, Jonathan M. 1998. *Ancient cities of the Indus valley civilization.* Karachi: Oxford University Press.

McLeod, W. H. 1991. *Popular Sikh art.* Delhi: Oxford University Press.

McNair, J. F. A. and Barlow, Thomas Lambert. 1908. *Oral tradition from the Indus.* Brighton: R. Gosden. Reprinted New York: Arno Press, 1977.

Maskiell, Michelle. 1999. Embroidering the past: Phulkari textiles and gendered work as "tradition" and "heritage" in colonial and contemporary Punjab. *The Journal of Asian Studies.* 58(2): 361–388.

Matringe, Denis. 1995. The Panjab and its popular culture in the modern Panjabi poetry of the 1920s and early 1930s. *South Asia Research.* 15(2): 221–140.

Mazhar-ul-Islam. 1978. *Lok Panjāb* (Folk Panjab). (in Urdu with Punjabi texts). Islamabad: Lok Virsa.

Middlebrook, Joyce. 2000. Punjab. In *South Asia: the Indian subcontinent,* ed. Alison Arnold. *Garland Encyclopedia of World Music,* Vol. 5., 650–657. New York: Garland.

Mir, Farina. 2001. The social space of language: Punjabi popular narrative in colonial India c. 1850–1900. Ph.D. diss. Columbia University, New York.

Nayyar, Adam. 2000. Punjab. In *South Asia: the Indian subcontinent,* ed. Alison Arnold, *Garland Encyclopedia of World Music,* Vol. 5, 762–772. New York: Garland.

Saeed, Fouzia, and Nayyar, Adam. 1991. *Women in folk theater.* Islamabad: Lok Virsa.

Sakata, Hiromi Lorraine. 2000. Devotional music. In *South Asia: the Indian subcontinent,* ed. Alison Arnold, *Garland Encyclopedia of World Music,* Vol. 5, 751–761. New York: Garland.

Seth, Mira. 1976. *Wall paintings of the western Himalayas.* New Delhi: Publications Division, Ministry of Information and Broadcasting, Govt. of India.

Shackle, C[hristopher]. 1983. *From wuch to southern Lahnda: a century of Siraiki studies in English.* Multan: Bazm-e-saqafat.

———. 1995. Between scripture and romance: The Yūsuf-Zulaikhā story in Panjabi. *South Asia Research:* 15(2): 189–220.

Shārib. 1994. *Māhiyā: Panjābī Lok Gīt* [Mahiya: Punjabi Folk Songs]. Lahore: Ferozsons.

Sharma, Harish C. 1966. *Artisans of the Punjab: a study of social change in historical perspective (1849–1947).* New Delhi: Manohar.

Skemp, F. W. 1917. *Multani stories.* Lahore: [Punjab] Government Printing, 1917.

Swynnerton, Charles. 1892. *Indian nights' entertainment or folk-tales from the upper Indus.* London: Elliot Stock. Reprinted: New York: Arno, 1977.

———. 1903. *Romantic tales from the Panjâb.* Westminster: Constable. Reprinted: Lahore: Qausain Goldmohur, 1976.

Temple, Richard Carnac. 1884–1900. *The legends of the Punjab.* Bombay: Education Society's Press. Reprinted: Patiala, Language Department, Punjab, 1962, and Arno Press, New York, 1977.

WILMA L. HESTON

SEE ALSO

Amīr Ḥamza; *Bārahmasā;* Chapbooks; *Hīr/Rānjhā; Kāfī; Mātam; Muḥarram;* Mullā Naṣruddin; Nala and Damayanti; Nauḥa; Popular Music; Qiṣṣa; Sikh Folklore

PURĀṆA

Purāṇa, Sanskrit "old," a class of mythological texts and story traditions, and a common word for "mythology," in various South Asian languages. Purāṇas generally treat a diverse range of topics, including cosmogony and the origin of human institutions such as ritual, caste hierarchy, the division of labor, etc. Also often classified as Purāṇas are the *Mahātmya*s, which proclaim the greatness of a particular pilgrimage place, auspicious time, deity, donation, etc. Purāṇas are as inclusive as possible, while Mahātmyas are more topical.

The classical Hindu Purāṇas contain passages which claim the status of "Fifth Veda" for the *Itihāsa-purāṇaṃ* consisting of the Itihāsa or Epics (*Mahābhārata* and *Rāmāyaṇa*) and the Purāṇas. This claim that the Purāṇas are *Śruti* or direct Vedic revelation is not generally acknowledged; the Purāṇas are usually considered *Smṛti* or revelation mediated by tradition. The Hindu tradition recognizes, in theory, eighteen *Mahā-* or Major Purāṇas and eighteen *Upa-* or Minor Purāṇas, although actually there are many more, and there is sectarian disagreement about which texts ought to be included in these lists, and which texts are designated by these traditional titles. The Mahāpurāṇas are not markedly different from the Upapurāṇas in content. Most Purāṇas are sectarian texts, promoting the (generally non-exclusive) worship of Viṣṇu, Śiva, or other deities. A traditional definition assigns to a Purāṇa five characteristics (*pañcalakṣaṇaṃ*): (1) cosmogony, (2) destruction and renovation of worlds, (3) genealogy of gods and patriarchs, (4) reign of the *Manu*s (semi-divine Patriarchs) over world-periods called *Manvantaras,* and (5) history, that is, the genealogies of the solar and lunar dynasties to the present day. Few Purāṇas actually conform to this definition, and discussion of these five topics comprises only a small percentage of the extant text of the Purāṇas, which concern also geography, laws of donation and propitiation of ancestors, caste and life-stage, consecration of images, and "anything else which exists on earth" (Rocher 1986: 29). One of the most popular Purāṇas is the *Bhāgavāta,* which concerns the life story of the Hindu deity and hero, Kṛṣṇa.

Western Indologists have held, and still hold, divergent views about the Purāṇic textual tradition. Some have held hypotheses of textual aggregation or deterioration, from eighteen ancient originals or from a single *Urpurāṇa* (original Purāṇa), and have attempted to reconstruct textual genealogies based on these assumptions. One Indologist, Vans Kennedy, has maintained the antiquity of the extant Purāṇas in their present form. Another, Edward Eden Pargiter, has attempted to reconstruct dynastic history using Purāṇic materials. Others have attempted to fix the dates and places of composition of these texts, although there is little consensus due to the heterogeneity of the Purāṇas.

Western scholars who assume a fixed textual tradition, like that of the Vedas, have often been frustrated by the actual practice of Purāṇic transmission. *Pandit*s (traditional scholars) contracted to copy Purāṇa manuscripts have been discovered to have filled in missing parts of the narrative with material of their own composition, including sometimes recent European history. These emendations, when discovered, have been considered fraudulent, casting doubt upon the authenticity of many of these texts and their tradition, in contrast to the Vedas and other texts which have been more reliably transmitted. However, such attitudes are foreign to the South Asian scholarly tradition. Literal translation is thought necessary for other branches of religious literature, but not Purāṇas, which may be freely paraphrased by the translators from a variety of textual and oral traditions, and published anonymously, in implicit recognition of the Purāṇas as a living tradition of authorless folklore/mythology, to be transmitted orally by bards and performed in other ways, and only secondarily to be written down and read. Even so, some Indologists, in India and elsewhere, continue the work of critically editing and publishing, and thereby fixing, Purāṇic texts.

Texts called Purāṇas are not limited to the classical Hindu religious tradition. There is only one Buddhist text with "Purāṇa" in the title, the *Svayambhūpurāṇa* (although one *Jātaka* calls itself a Purāṇa). However, many Digambara Jain texts are called "Purāṇas," for example the *Ādipurāṇa of Jinasena,* which concerns, among other topics, the origin of the caste system. The Jain tradition contains many similar texts called "*Carit(r)as*," which chronicle the deeds of the sixty-three Illustrious Persons of Jain Universal History, including Jain versions of the Rāma and Kṛṣṇa stories. These literary compositions do not conform to the pañcalakṣaṇaṃ definition of a Purāṇa, and, in most cases, their authorship is known, in contrast to the classical Hindu Purāṇas, which are generally attributed to the legendary sage Vyāsa, whose name means "Compiler."

Many purāṇic traditions are transmitted in languages other than Sanskrit, e.g. Tamil and Telugu. For example, caste Purāṇas, which treat the origin of a particular caste, are often recited, and written, in vernacular languages. There is great regional variation; for example, in Gujarat only Brahmins (priestly castes) and Baniyas (merchant castes) generally record their caste histories in (Sanskrit) purāṇic format, while in Andhra Pradesh, almost all of the castes have (vernacular) caste purāṇas.

Caste purāṇas serve as "origin myths" for particular castes, often legitimizing a caste's claim to a higher status, and resolving contradictions between the claimed status of a caste and its occupation. For example, in Gujarat a caste of wrestlers, the Jethimallas, have a text called the *Mallapurāṇa,* which supports their claim to be Brahmins (priestly caste), despite their occupation as wrestlers, on the grounds that Lord Kṛṣṇa himself taught their ancestors the martial art in order to protect the Brahmins' *dharma* (sacred duty) in the *Kali Yuga* (the present corrupt age). A Gujarati caste of coppersmiths, the Kansakaras, have a text called the *Kālikāpurāṇa,* which supports their claim to be a Kṣatriya (warrior) caste, despite their occupation as merchants and artisans, on the grounds that their Kṣatriya ancestors were tricked by a deity into requesting the boon of Vaiśya (merchant) occupation rather than their preferred warrior profession. The claims of both these caste purāṇas are contradicted by those of competing castes. Both of these purāṇas are written in deliberately archaized Sanskrit, in an apparent attempt by the mythographer to provide an ancient pedigree for his patron's caste. This process of archaization and Sanskritization is quite common in purāṇic literature (according to van Buitenen). The *Mallapurāṇa* claims to be part of a "classical" Mahāpurāṇa, the *Skanda Purāṇa,* while the *Kālikāpurāṇa* claims the title of a recognized Upapurāṇa, although it has nothing in common with the more generally recognized "classical" text of that name. This proliferation of local texts bearing a common "classical" title is characteristic of the purāṇic traditions.

In Gujarat the Kṣatriyas (warrior castes) do not have caste purāṇas in Sanskrit, but they may patronize a caste of professional genealogists and mythographers, for example the Vahīvancā Bārots, who keep meticulously accurate written genealogies (up to about seven generations) in books called *Vahīs*. These detailed, but selectively limited, records are situated within the traditional purāṇic genealogies of the solar and lunar dynasties, etc., to provide an appropriate mythological context for the caste genealogy, and the caste's claims to status mobility. These texts are jealously guarded by the mythographers as their professional property, and are not called purāṇas.

Bardic castes, both mendicant and non-mendicant, have transmitted purāṇic lore for millennia. The sagas ancestral to the Hindu epics, the *Mahābhārata* and *Rāmāyaṇa,* along with early purāṇic lore, were sung, to the accompaniment of music, by bards called *sūta*s, who performed in kingly courts, and *kuśīlava*s, who wandered from village to village, telling stories for alms. Mendicant Jain and Buddhist monks performed a similar role. In more recent times, the Rajput rulers of northwestern India have patronized a variety of bardic castes (for example, the Bhats of Gujarat), to legitimize their rule. This practice was apparently emulated by the "tribal" Gond rulers in central India, who patronize a bardic caste called the Pardhans, who are ethnically and linguistically distinct from the Gonds, speaking Marathi amongst themselves. A Pardhan family or group of families is attached to every Gond clan or sub-clan but they do not intermarry, and Gonds will not take food from Pardhans. Despite the ritually inferior status of the Pardhans, the Gonds depend on them for the transmission of their own mythology, in their own language. Gond mythology, as transmitted by the Pardhans, now incorporates elements of purāṇic Hinduism, an example of a process often called "Sanskritization."

Purāṇic stories are told and retold in a wide variety of ways, in the home by parents and grandparents, and by professional storytellers and performers of all kinds. Printed editions may be used to guide the storytellers, and vice versa; the Purāṇas are a continuously developing story tradition, which has formed the basis of popular Hinduism for more than a millennium. Purāṇic stories of the Hindu gods and goddesses continue to be popular, in India and abroad, and purāṇic themes are prevalent in South Asian cinema and other art forms. According to Milton Singer, "the very tissue of the culture is made from *purāṇic* themes" (Singer 1972: 76).

The term "Purāṇa" is so inclusive, and is used so variously, that it is almost impossible to generalize about the purāṇic traditions, with dichotomies such as "great and little traditions," "popular and official religion," "folklore and mythology," "folklore and literature," "Sanskrit and vernacular traditions," "folk Purāṇas and classical Purāṇas," or "oral and textual traditions."

References

Coburn, Thomas B. 1984. *Devī Mahātmya: The crystallization of the goddess tradition*. Delhi: Motilal Banarsidass.

Das, Veena. 1968. A sociological approach to caste Purāṇas of Gujarat. *Sociological Bulletin* 17: 141–64.

———. 1982. *Structure and cognition: aspects of Hindu caste and ritual*. Delhi: Oxford University Press.

Doniger, Wendy, ed. 1993. *Purāṇa Perennis: reciprocity and transformation in Hindu and Jaina texts*. Albany, NY: SUNY Press.

Fuerer-Heimendorf, C. 1951. The Pardhans: the bards of the Raj Gonds. *The Eastern Anthropologist*. IV (3–4): 172–84.

Purāṇaṃ (Half-yearly Bulletin of the Purāṇa-Department) 1959–Varanasi: All-India Kashiraj Trust.

Richman, Paula, ed. 1991. *Many Rāmāyaṇas: the diversity of a narrative tradition in South Asia*. Berkeley: University of California Press.

Rocher, Ludo 1986. *The Purāṇas*. Wiesbaden: O. Harrassowitz.

Shah, A. M. and R. G. Shroff. 1959. The Vahīvancā Bāroṭs of Gujarat: A caste of genealogists and mythographers. In *Traditional India: Structure and Change,* ed. Milton Singer. Philadelphia: American Folklore Society.

Singer, Milton 1972. *When a great tradition modernizes: an anthropological approach to Indian civilization*. New York: Praeger.

Van Buitenen, J. A. B. 1966. Archaicism of the *Bhāgavāta Purāṇa*. In Singer, Milton, ed., *Krishna: myths, rites and attitudes,* ed. Milton Singer. Honolulu: East-West Center Press.

Ziegler, Norman. 1976. The seventeenth century chronicles of marvar: a ṣtudy of the evolution and use of oral tradition in western India. *History in africa: a journal of method* 3:127–153.

JEROME H. BAUER

SEE ALSO

Caste Myths of Andhra Pradesh; Dependent Performing Castes; Gods and Goddesses; Jainism; *Jātaka* Tales; *Mahābhārata;* Myth; Rāmāyaṇa

PURDAH

See Gender and Folklore

Q

QALANDAR

Qalandar is a term generally applied to mendicants, ascetics, and itinerant Sufis in South Asia. The word is associated with the *qalandarī* movement, which first appeared in Khurasan in what is now Iran (fifth [Islamic] / eleventh [C.E.] century), and subsequently spread to the east and west. Qalandarīs were inspired by *malāmatī* Sufi beliefs originating in Nishapur (third [Islamic] / ninth [C.E.] century). Malāmatīs ("the blameworthy") professed the doctrine of hidden devotion, spurning communal religious activities as pretentious acts performed for the benefit of men rather than God. To conceal their spirituality, Malāmatīs devotees abstained from public rituals, making themselves despised or "blameworthy" in the eyes of people. Disregard for public opinion became their sign of devotion to God. In subsequent centuries, these beliefs took an antinomian turn, especially among the qalandarīs, who became notorious for eschewing religious scholarship and inviting public scorn by perpetrating outrageous sins to symbolize their disregard for public opinion and to prove their sanctity. Unlettered mendicants, outcasts, and sociopaths were naturally drawn to the qalandarī, adding to the movement's notoriety. By the seventh (Islamic) / thirteenth (C.E.) century, qalandarīs were to be found from Morocco to India. Qalandarī apparel was outlandish and varied geographically. South Asian qalandarīs wore a shawl, sashed at the waist, with iron rings around their necks, wrists, fingers, and genitalia, inserted through perforations in the skin, as a sign of penitence and chastity. Some groups shaved their heads, facial hair, and eyebrows. Their appearance and behavior often aroused public curiosity and sometimes hostility from religious authorities. Eventually, certain qalandarī groups evolved into distinct Sufi orders, while others were assimilated into preexisting tarīqas [orders]. Qalandarīs no longer exist, but the term employed to designate them is still in use.

References

Abd Allāh-i Anṣārī (d.1088). *Qalandar-nāma*. n.d. Tehran.

Trimingham, Spencer J. 1971. *The Sufi orders in Islam*. New York: Clarendon Press, 264–269.

H. SIDKY

SEE ALSO

Malang; Muslim Folklore and Folklife

QAWWĀLĪ

Qawwālī (from Arabic *qaul,* meaning "something said") primarily designates the vocal music of South Asian Sufism that is performed throughout Muslim centers of the Indian subcontinent. Group songs are performed by professional musicians for Sufi listeners at qawwālī or *samā* (listening) assemblies, which are held throughout the year but principally on the anniversary (*'urs*) of the numerous Sufi saints at shrines or wherever their devotees may gather. Mystical poems in classical Farsi, Hindi, and Urdu are sung strophically in a fluid style of alternating solo and group passages characterized by repetition and improvisation. The vigorous drum accompaniment on the barrel-shaped *dholak* is reinforced by handclapping, while the small portable harmonium, usually in the hands of the lead singer, underscores the song melody. A qawwālī performance normally begins with an instrumental prelude on the harmonium, while songs are preceded by an introductory verse sung as a solo recitative without drums.

By enhancing the message of mystical poetry and by providing a powerful rhythm suggestive of the ceaseless repetition of God's name (*ẕikr*), the music of qawwālī has a religious function: to arouse mystical love, even divine ecstasy—the core experience of Sufism. The qawwālī assembly is held under the guidance of a spiritual leader and is attended mainly by Sufi devotees though it is usually open to all who may come. In listening to the songs, devotees respond in accordance with social and religious convention, but also individually and spontaneously, expressing states of mystical love. The musicians structure their performance to activate and reinforce these emotions, adapting the performance to the changing needs of their listeners.

Musically, qawwālī shares general traits with the light-classical music of North India and Pakistan. The formal scheme combines metric group refrains and rhythmically free solo improvisations, including rapid coloratura (melodic) passages. There is an incessant repetition of salient text phrases, which build towards, or maintain, the state of ecstasy, and different verses and tunes are freely added within any one song. Qawwālī melodies derive from several sources: classical *raga*s, raga-like structures peculiar to the qawwālī tradition, and folk melodies; these melodies may be used within any one song to form several short tunes, with their many variations and melodic improvisations. In performance, emphatic enunciation and extremely rhythmic declamation are the most prominent features.

Qawwālī texts are richly metaphoric, drawing from Hindi as well as Farsi poetic idioms. Among a range of strophic forms, especially in Hindi poems, the predominant poetic genre is the *ghazal* with epigrammatic couplets linked by a strict rhyme scheme and a diverse range of Arabic-based poetic meters. In content, qawwālī poems focus on states of mystical emotion and on spiritual links to saints and the Prophet. Devotion to local saints is a central Sufi theme, especially at major shrines like that of thirteenth-century saint Nizamuddin Auliya in Delhi, whose main disciple, Amir Khusrau, composed a central repertoire of Farsi and Hindi poems in musical settings ascribed to him. He is also the patron of the original lineage of qawwālī performers, the *qawwāl bachche,* who have a hereditary attachment to the Nizamuddin Auliya shrine.

Due to its musical and performative appeal, qawwālī has been freely performed outside the religious context and adapted to various purposes, particularly by means of recording media, which also provide sonic documentation of these changes. Some such new settings are women's qawwālī and, most prominently, song contests (*muqābila*) between two *qawwāl* parties, one of them sometimes led by a woman in a battle of the sexes. Qawwālī also has come to carry political significance, especially in Pakistan, where it serves as an expression of national culture.

The two performers who have spread qawwālī internationally are both from Pakistan. Ghulam Farid Sabri (later called Sabri Brothers) and Nusrat Fateh Ali have used the rhythmic appeal and improvisational flexibility of qawwālī to make it a world music attraction, but their performances still retain the textual and musical integrity of qawwālī as a Sufi genre.

References

Qureshi, Regula Burckhardt. 1990. Sufi music and the historicity of oral tradition. In *Ethnomusicology and Modern Music History,* ed. S. Blum and P. Bohlman, 103–120. Urbana: University of Illinois Press.

———. 1994. Time, music and the Sufi Qawwali. *Journal of Musicology* 12(4): 493–528.

———. 1995a. Recorded sound and religious music: The case of Qawwali. In *Media and the transformation of religion in South Asia,* ed. Lawrence Babb and Susan Wadley, 139–166. Philadelphia: University of Pennsylvania Press.

———. 1995b. *Sufi music of India and Pakistan.* Chicago: Chicago University Press.

Sakata, Hiromi Lorraine. 1994. The sacred and the profane: Qawwali represented in the performances of Nusrat Fateh Ali Khan. *The World of Music* 36(3): 86–99.

REGULA BURCKHARDT QURESHI

SEE ALSO
Ghazal; Song; *'Urs*

QIṢṢA

The word *qiṣṣa* in Persian and Urdu (*kissā* in Hindi) means "story." While the term often refers to a group of Persian medieval oral narratives of heroic quest and romantic adventure, in Urdu and Hindi it has commonly been applied to a popular printed pamphlet (chapbook) genre. As a pamphlet genre, *qiṣṣa* literature goes back at least to the 1880s, to the time when printing presses first became cheap and widespread enough to be available to local entrepreneurs who sought only to satisfy local tastes. Such publishers usually obtained their texts of well-known stories from local amateur writers for lump-sum payments or (even more commonly) simply plagiarized them from each other, with or without minor cosmetic alterations. They printed them in small quantities, often in a sixteen-page format held together with two staples, adorned with vivid multicolored cover designs. Publishers scrapped old copies often and reprinted the best-selling stories frequently.

For these reasons, the history of Hindi and Urdu qiṣṣa publishing provides a valuable mirror of popular North Indian taste. The genre inherited its stories from both the *Arabian Nights* and the *Ocean of Story (Kathāsaritsāgara),* from other Arabic and Sanskrit literary sources, from Persian oral narrative tradition, from sophisticated Urdu literary works, and from medieval romance and folktale cycles. In general, it was greatly influenced by the Persian qiṣṣa or *dāstān* tradition. And in particular, many of its most popular stories were a legacy of Fort William College (1800) in Calcutta, which commissioned simple texts to help British civil servants learn Indian languages.

A number of the Fort William Urdu texts were qiṣṣa of the classic sort—quest stories full of marvelous adventures undertaken by noble heroes—like Mir Amman's famous *Qiṣṣa-e cahār darvesh* (also known as *Bāġh o bahār*). The simple prose style of these texts made them natural candidates for mass publication. Two other Fort William texts, *Siṅhāsan battīsī* (published in both Hindi and Urdu) and *Baitāl paccīsī* (published in Hindi), recounted the adventures of Raja Vikram, who had been a hero of Indian folk tradition for centuries; these also fit easily into the qiṣṣa genre. Other tales were gradually assimilated into the same category. "Hardy perennials" of the genre—most of them reprinted hundreds of times all over North India during the past century—have also included: *Chabīlī bhaṭiyārī, Qiṣṣa Ḍallā, Fasāna-e 'ajā'ib, Gul-e bakāvalī, Gul o Ṣanaubar, Qiṣṣa Ḥātim Ṭā'ī, Kesar Gulāb, Lailā Majnūn, Sārañgā Sadāvrīj, Sāṛhe tīn yār, Qiṣṣa totā mainā,* and *Triyā caritra*.

In general, qiṣṣas remain relatively close to the conventions and constraints of oral storytelling. They are organized paratactically and contain temporally ordered sequences of events; sentences begin with "Then." Changes of speaker are shown by introductory vocatives, as in, "O Parrot!," or explicitly noted by the narrator, as in,"Then the Mynah said," rather than indicated typographically. The authoritarian narrator is always present, but he "faces towards the story" and follows its logic as straightforwardly as possible.

Nowadays, the qiṣṣa genre seems to be moribund, with many old perennials vanishing from the bookshops. But some of the "hardy perennials" seem to be unkillable, and should not be written off prematurely.

Reference

Pritchett, Frances W. 1985. *Marvelous encounters: folk romance in Urdu and Hindi*. New Delhi: Manohar and Riverdale, Md.: Riverdale.

FRANCES W. PRITCHETT

SEE ALSO

Chapbooks; *Dāstān;* Folk Literature; *Kathāsaritsāgara*

QUILTING AND PIECING

As early as the sixteenth century, quilts from India, particularly Bengal, were being exported to Portugal, and then later, in the seventeenth century, to England. These Indo-Portuguese quilts—called variously "Bengalla quilts" and "Sutgonge quilts" after Satgaon, a former port on the Hoogly River, where they were made—were usually of white cotton and embroidered in *tussar* silk (a type of silk from silkworms that do not feed on mulberry) in natural yellow or fawn. The stitches used were the chain stitch and the backstitch. Images from the Old Testament and Greco-Roman mythology were juxtaposed with Indian themes and European scenes.

European-style quilts were also made in India for export to Europe. Made of white, cream, or fawn cotton material, these quilts were quilted with a fine backstitch. Motifs were usually floral or geometric, with the *kalkā* (paisley cone) being a current motif. Many of the quilts were fringed. Other trade quilts sent to England from India included whole-cloth quilts of mordant printed cottons and hand-painted chintz, all quilted with the running stitch.

Today, light quilts for personal use utilize old discarded cloth or scraps of cloth left over from clothes. Prominent among quilts using old cloth is the Bengal *kāñthā*. Old cloth is layered to achieve the desired thickness, so that kāñthā for use in winter are made with more layers than a light monsoon wrap. The cloth is then stitched through with small or large running stitches, depending on the skill of, or time available to, the needlewoman. Small kāñthā—called *gadlā* and *guḍrī* in other parts of India—are used to spread under children to soak up urine. The Bihar *sujnī* is similar to but simpler than the Bengal kāñthā. The Chapainawabganj Rajshahi region of Bangladesh produces a type of thick kāñthā, quilted with close rows of pattern darning, as well as a sujnī distinguished from both Bengal kāñthā and Bihar sujnī by being made of red cotton and worked in backstitch. It is possible that these sujnī were influenced by the quilts commissioned for the English market.

While many of the quilts are made of large stretches of cloth pieced together to form the requisite breadth, patchwork is also made from scraps of brightly colored cloth—occasionally new, but also older. In Gujarat, India, colorful patchwork is made from scraps of old clothing. Patches of cloth are cut into geometrical shapes and stitched onto a larger piece of cloth. Colorful appliqué work is also done in Bihar, India, on *kanat* (tents).

Sindh in Pakistan produces an intricate patchwork called *rilli*. Square pieces of cloth are folded several times and patterns—similar to paper-cut patterns—are cut out. These pieces are then appliquéd on to a larger piece of cloth with fine, almost invisible, stitches. Patterned pieces occasionally alternate with patches in a solid color. The entire quilt is then worked with fine running stitches, worked across the quilt in straight lines.

For colder weather, padded quilts are used throughout India. Called *razāi* and *lehāf* in north India and Pakistan, and *lep* in Bengali, these quilts use new cloth for the top and bottom and are filled with cotton padding. Specially printed razāi cloths are made for the tops of these quilts, and well-to-do families might use velvet and satin. Brightly printed cotton lengths are usually stitched by men who sell door-to-door when the cool weather arrives. The characteristic pattern for these padded quilts is a central medallion with borders. Fairly large stitches are taken through the layers with thick yarn. The stitching is usually just enough to hold the cotton padding in place and prevent it from shifting and lumping up.

Although readymade blankets have become popular in many parts of the subcontinent, the padded quilt continues to be the covering of choice in colder areas. American-style patchwork quilts, filled with polyfill, are also being made for export. In Bangladesh, where the kā̃thā has been revived, quilts are being made with kā̃thā embroidered tops but filled with polyfill—blending the old and the new.

References

Chattopadhyay, Kamaladevi. 1985. *Handicrafts of India*. New Delhi: Indian Council for Cultural Relations.

Irwin, John, and Margaret Hall. 1973. *Indian embroideries*. Ahmedabad: Calico Museum of Textiles.

NIAZ ZAMAN

SEE ALSO

Embroidery; *Kā̃thā*

R

RAJASTHAN

Rajasthan ("land of kings") invokes images of rolling deserts and heroic legends of its erstwhile princely rulers. These selective images of arid landscapes, Rājput political acumen, and heroic self-sacrifice in battle, while part of Rajasthan's contemporary cultural identity, obscure the state's economic, political, social, and ecological complexity.

The region of northwestern India that became the state of Rajasthan at Independence consolidated nineteen princely states ruled by Mahārājas and Mahārāṇās (the latter title used exclusively by the former rulers of Mewar, now Udaipur district) with areas under direct British rule. The resulting state has the second largest landmass in India, and the lowest population density (165 persons per square kilometer, half the all-India average). Roughly diamond-shaped, it is divided into two geographical areas by the Aravalli mountain range, one of the world's oldest mountain systems. Roughly two-thirds of the state lies in the arid, sparsely populated Thar Desert region that begins at the easternmost ridge of the Aravallis and extends westward to the Pakistan border. Areas to the south and east of the Aravallis have a more temperate climate than the desert region, generous (but unreliable) monsoons, and closer proximity to the state capital of Jaipur and New Delhi.

Although the Aravalli mountains are a natural watershed, containing many streams and rivers, these water sources are mostly seasonal and disappear a few months after the monsoon. Recently constructed canals deliver water to about one-half the net irrigated land; tube wells, tanks, and wells provide the balance. Recurrent monsoon irregularities cause extended periods of drought that periodically threaten the well-being of livestock and human populations. Most land holdings are small (under five hectares), and farmers rely on livestock for fertilizer and traction. Animal loss due to drought, or any other factor, has a devastating effect on household income for most of the state's small-scale agriculturalists. Both men and women in lower class rural households supplement agricultural income with day labor or migration to urban industrial sites or tourist centers. Deforestation in the Aravallis and changes in the Thar Desert ecosystem have compounded the effects of recurrent periods of drought in the past decade. Social forestry and other environmental protection programs are therefore a major strategy of both governmental and nongovernmental development organizations.

Rajasthan's population of 56.5 million has increased by 28 percent over the past decade. Although the number of towns and urban centers has grown substantially in the past three decades, nearly three-quarters of the state's population lives in rural areas and is primarily employed in agriculture, livestock, and forestry production. Wheat, millets, pulses, cotton, and sugarcane account for almost one-half of the state's income; animal husbandry and dairy production contribute an additional 10 percent.

Rajasthan's transportation infrastructure includes a growing network of paved roads and railroad and air travel systems. The state's industries include mining and processing of gypsum, mica, zinc, soapstone, asbestos, precious and semi-precious gems, and marble, as well as production of cement, chemicals, textiles, and handicrafts. Computer, Internet, and telecommunications enterprises are a growth industry throughout the state.

Tourism is a significant source of state income, accounting in some years for over 10 percent of total revenues and a wide range of related businesses and services. Many palaces of the former princely rulers have been converted into luxury hotels and museums, attracting hundreds of thousands of domestic and foreign visitors each year. Tourism in Rajasthan, however, as in

Durga shrine in Udaipur, Rajasthan, India, © Stephen Huyler

the rest of India, is unstable and unpredictable; national or global political events periodically interrupt the flow of tourist revenue. Despite the state's highly developed and profitable tourism infrastructure, economic benefits of tourism generally accrue only to state-controlled or elite-owned private enterprises, and rarely trickle down into underdeveloped rural areas.

The state's development is concentrated in its urban centers of Jaipur, Udaipur, Jodhpur, and Ajmer. Literacy and educational levels, electrification, access to public health facilities, and income levels all show a marked urban bias. Rajasthan's extensive system of rural development programs targets extension of educational, medical, and technological benefits to underdeveloped rural areas, but according to the 1991 census, 41 percent of rural households lacked safe drinking water, electricity, and toilets.

The status of women and children in rural areas is a significant indicator of inequitable development and social conservatism in Rajasthan. Adverse female sex ratios are documented throughout the state and are attributed in part to childbearing risks, although other factors of female discrimination throughout Northern India include male-biased differentials in nutrition, access to medical care, and increasing availability of fetal sex determination technologies.

Dowry, or pre-marriage payments from the bride's to the groom's family, is practiced by almost all caste and class groups in Rajasthan, and places additional economic and social pressure on families with female children. Rajasthan's female literacy rate of 44 percent, while showing improvement over the past three decades, is below the all-India rate of 54 percent; 80 percent of the thirty-five states reported in the 2001 Census have higher female literacy. The encouragement of schooling and literacy for female adults and children, particularly in rural areas, is a major agenda of the state's social activists.

Social conservatism in the form of *parda* (purdah, literally, "curtain" or "screen"), or female seclusion, is still observed by the women of some Rājput families and is echoed in the restrictions on public activity, modesty of dress, and acceptable behavior for girls and women of all castes and classes.

Most marriages in all caste and class groups are arranged by parents or other kin, and follow the Northern Indian norms of marrying outside one's village or town (exogamy), and marrying within one's caste group (*jāti* or caste endogamy). After marriage, girls live in the household of their husband's family (virilocal post-marital residence pattern) and become part of his multi-generational extended family. The life cycle, particularly of young women, turns on the significant event of marriage; anticipation combines with the sorrow young women experience at separating from their natal households and facing the uncertainties of their reception in their husband's home. These themes dominate the mournful songs sung by young girls during the wedding season as they walk through their own villages as protected daughters for the last time.

The population of Rajasthan reflects the religious and linguistic diversity of India. The official state language is Hindi, although most residents also speak one of eight local dialects of Rājasthāni as well. Approximately 90 percent of the population follows the Hindu religion; the major festivals and events of the Hindu calendar dominate the annual ritual cycle. About 8 percent of the state's population is Muslim; the balance is Jain, Sikh, Christian, or Buddhist.

The forty-five scheduled tribes (*ādivāsīs*) of Rajasthan, comprising approximately 12 percent of the total population, contribute greatly to Rajasthan's cultural diversity. The majority self-identify as Bhīls or Mīnās, although local designations of group affiliation vary within these two major categories. The multiple identities of Rajasthan's scheduled tribe populations are reflected in their religious practices, ritual cycles, and social patterns, which combine Hindu caste-based norms with localized myths, deities, and interpretation.

The contemporary history of Rajasthan is no less fascinating than its legends of the past. Rajasthan, like the rest of India, is striving for managed growth by protecting its natural resource base, developing its industrial infrastructure, and expanding opportunities and benefits to its diverse and dynamic population.

References

Census of India. 1991. Series 21 Rajasthan Provisional Population Totals.

———. 2001. Provisional Totals: India Part I.

MAXINE WEISGRAU

SEE ALSO

Bhopo; Dowry and Bridewealth; Gender and Folklore; *Kathak* Dancer; *Koṭhārī*, Komal; *Ramdev; Tējaji;* Tribalism and Tribal Identity; Wedding Songs

RĀM LĪLĀ

Rām līlā is the annual religious "play" (*līlā*) dramatizing the story of the divine king Rām (Sanskrit Rāma), performed throughout the Hindi-speaking region of north India in the autumn. It is one of a number of ritual dramatizations of the playful acts of various gods in their human incarnations: of Kṛṣṇa in *rās līlā* and *Kṛṣṇa līlā;* of the protagonists of the great epic *Mahābhārata* in *pāṇḍav līlā;* and of the god-king Rāma, hero of the Indian epic *Rāmāyaṇa,* in rām līlā.

The Sanskrit *Rāmāyaṇa* was composed by the poet Vālmīki, and is regarded as the archetype of Sanskrit poetry (*kāvya*). However rām līlā is based upon a later, vernacular version of the story, the folk *Rāmāyaṇa* of Tulasī Dās, written, in the last quarter of the sixteenth century, in Ayodhya and Varanasi (Banaras). It tells the story of Rāma, an incarnation of the god Viṣṇu, born in order to slay the evil Rāvaṇa, king of Lanka. After Rāma is unjustly exiled to the forest for twelve years, his beloved wife Sītā is kidnaped by Rāvaṇa, and so, along with his younger brother Lakṣmaṇa, Rāma leads an alliance of bears and monkeys to rescue her. In the course of doing so, he defeats and kills the wicked Rāvaṇa, and is finally restored to his rightful place as ruler of Koshala. The *Rāmāyaṇa* has usually been understood by Hindus as a straightforward tale of the triumph of good over evil, culminating in *rāmrājya,* "the (righteous) rule of Rāma." Several authors have noted the correlation between rām līlā performances and Indian nationalism.

A typical rām līlā dramatizes the principal events of Tulasī's *Rāmāyaṇa* over a period of days or weeks, normally culminating with Rāma's coronation on Vijayadasamī. Rām līlās are large, open-air productions, usually organized by urban or village committees. In larger towns and cities, neighborhoods may engage in de facto competition to produce the best rām līlā. Amateur actors and musicians receive their daily food, and sometimes also a stipend or final gift. Principal roles are played by Brāhmaṇ boys who are regarded as *svarūp*s, divine embodiments of the characters they represent; sometimes these roles become hereditary. Rāma represents the dispassionate calmness and self-control of the Brāhmaṇ; Lakṣmaṇa exemplifies the passionate aggression of the Kṣatriya; Sītā is the chaste, modest, and dutiful wife; and Hanumān the leader of the monkeys is Rāma's loyal devotee. Dialogue is minimal and usually supplemented by one or more reciters who chant passages from the *Rāmāyaṇa*.

In some rām līlās, the central event is not a dramatic performance but rather a procession incorporating grotesque effigies of demons and heroes. Elsewhere, a single episode is a focus for popular devotion, such as the sentimental reunion of Rāma with his elder brother when he returns to his capital city of Ayodhya after defeating Rāvaṇa, represented in the famous rām līlā at Nati Imli in Varanasi. The grandest and most famous rām līlā in India is patronized by the Maharaja of Varanasi, who takes part in the drama himself. It lasts one month and is enacted at a number of locations in a large area near the fortress-city of Ramnagar, upstream and across the river from Varanasi.

Historical information on rām līlā is scanty. Its existence is attested to by western travellers in the nineteenth century, but it must be far older than that. According to one influential but undocumented tradition, it was begun by Megha Bhagat, a disciple of Tulasī Dās, in Varanasi in about 1625 C.E. There is scattered evidence for rām līlā-like performances before the seventeenth century, and the great Mughal emperor Akbar is said to have attended such events. Swann concludes that there were plays based on Vālmīki's *Rāmāyaṇa* before the seventeenth century, and Hein asserts that rām līlā "took shape in North India between C.E. 1200 and 1500," and only later became associated with Tulasī's *Rāmāyaṇa.*

References

Gargi, Balwant. 1991. Ramlila. In *Folk theatre of India,* 91–113. Calcutta: Rupa and Co.

Hein, Norvin. 1972. *The miracle plays of Mathurā.* Delhi: Oxford University Press.

Kinsley, David. 1979. *The divine player: a study of Kṛṣṇa Līlā.* Delhi: Motilal.

Sax, William S., ed. 1995. *The gods at play: Līlā in South Asia.* New York: Oxford University Press.

Sax, William S. 1990. The Ramnagar *Ramlila*: text, performance, pilgrimage. *History of Religions* 30(2): 129–153.

Swann, Darius. 1990. *Rām Līlā* . In *Indian theatre: traditions of performance,* ed. Farley P. Richmond, Darius L. Swann, and Phillip B. Zarrilli, 215–247. Honolulu: University of Hawaii Press.

WILLIAM S. SAX

SEE ALSO
Kṛṣṇa; *Mānas Kathā;* Nationalism and Folklore; Rāma; *Rāmāyaṇa,* TV Production; *Rāsa Līlā*

RĀMA

Rāma, whose name in Sanskrit means "he who gives delight," is a legendary hero and ruler who, together with his three brothers, is believed by Hindus to have been an incarnation of the preserver-god Viṣṇu. He is considered to have lived on earth in the Tretā Yuga, or second age of the current cosmic cycle, often said to have been some 900,000 years ago. Rāma's deeds form the subject of a vast body of oral and written lore commonly designated by the Sanskrit term *Rāmāyaṇa* (The Deeds of Rāma), the title of an early and influential literary version attributed to the poet-sage Vālmīki (ca. fourth century B.C.E.). The literature encompassed by this term includes an estimated three hundred major works in virtually all the Indic languages, many of which reflect a *bhakti* or devotional attitude toward the hero and his consort Sītā. There are also numerous Buddhist, Jaina, and tribal Rāma narratives that depart significantly from the Vālmīki tradition, as do many Southeast Asian versions of the story. Related oral performance genres range from household tales, folksongs, and rituals to public performances by storytellers, bards, puppeteers, and the annual pan-North Indian cycle of *Rām līlā* plays.

Many versions of the story begin with the gods petitioning Viṣṇu to incarnate in order to slay the world-dominating demon Rāvaṇa, who has received the boon that he can only be slain by a human being. The hero and his brothers are then born to the three wives of Daśaratha, king of Ayodhya. As adolescents, Rāma and his brother Lakṣmaṇa accompany the sage Viśvāmitra into the forest to slay demons, and then visit the kingdom of Mithila, where Rāma performs a heroic feat and wins the princess Sītā as his bride. King Daśaratha's subsequent plans to install Rāma as heir-apparent are frustrated by his junior wife Kaikeyī, who demands the enthronement of her own son, Bharata, and Rāma's exile to the forest for fourteen years. Rāma calmly accepts this order and departs with Sītā and Lakṣmaṇa, despite Bharata's repudiation of his mother and the heartbroken king's death. During his exile, Rāma is drawn into a confrontation with the *rakṣasas*, a demon-like race, whose king secretly abducts Sītā to his island citadel of Lanka. While searching for her, Rāma forms an alliance with Sugrīva, king of a race of talking monkeys, whose lieutenant Hanumān leaps the ocean to Lanka and locates Sītā. Rāma's monkey allies then construct a causeway to the island and attack Rāvaṇa, whom Rāma himself at last slays. The years of exile having ended, the reunited Rāma and Sītā return to Ayodhya to reign as king and queen, initiating a long period of justice and prosperity. In some versions, an epilogue tells of Rāma's later repudiation of Sītā as a result of malicious gossip, the birth of their twin sons, and Rāma's ultimate death.

Although Brahmanical and elite interpretations of the Rāma narrative often emphasize themes of *dharma* (duty, morality) and *maryādā* (decorum, propriety) within a patriarchal and hierarchical social order, folk retellings may highlight other concerns. Thus, women's tales and songs stress the trials and triumphs of Sītā and other female characters, even of some (such as Lakṣmaṇa's wife Urmilā) who are barely mentioned in literary versions. Devotional retellings emphasize Rāma's accessibility and compassion, which often supersedes his dedication to dharma. Untouchable versions emphasize Vālmīki's reputedly low birth and the ability of Rāma's name to empower and purify anyone who repeats it. Children's stories focus on the sometimes humorous exploits of Rāma's monkey helper, Hanumān. Thus in contemporary India, multiple interpretations of the Rāma story continue to flourish, even alongside such "official" versions as the 1987–1988 serialization on national television, which created a sensation and led critics to warn of "homogenization" of the story. The variety of contemporary retellings lends credence to A. K. Ramanujan's assertion that the Rāma story is less a text than "a pool of signifiers" and "almost a second language of the whole culture area. . . ." (Richman, 45–46).

References

Goldman, Robert P., ed. 1984–1996. *The Rāmāyaṇa of Vālmīki, an Epic of Ancient India,* vols. 1–5 (vols. 6–7 in preparation). Princeton, N.J.: Princeton University Press.
Richman, Paula, ed. 1991. *Many Rāmāyaṇas: the diversity of a narrative tradition in South Asia.* Berkeley and Los Angeles: University of California Press.

PHILIP LUTGENDORF

SEE ALSO
Bhakti; Epic; Hanumān; *Mānas Kathā;* Rām Līlā; Rāmāyaṇa; Rāmāyaṇa, TV Production

RAMANUJAN, A. K.

A. K. Ramanujan (1929–1993) was born in the city of Mysore, Karnataka, graduated from high school there, and received his B.A. and M.A. degrees from Mysore

University in 1949 and 1950, respectively. He earned his Ph.D. in Linguistics at Indiana University in 1963, having joined the faculty of the University of Chicago a year earlier. For thirty-two years he taught at Chicago, where he was William E. Colvin Professor in the Department of South Asian Languages and Civilizations, the Department of Linguistics, and the Committee on Social Thought. In 1976 he received the Padma Sri, the prestigious cultural award from the Government of India, and in 1983 he received a MacArthur Fellowship. In 1990 he was elected to the American Academy of Arts and Sciences.

Throughout his life, Ramanujan lectured and wrote with originality about South Asian folklore, especially folktale. His first published article, in 1955, discussed Kannada proverbs; his first article in English, in 1956, reported a Kannada folktale he had collected from his own mother. In the 1970s and 1980s he published influential essays on an Indian Oedipus, a Kannada Cinderella, and on women-centered tales. His last two publications were collections of folktales from India in 1991 and from the Kannada language in 1997.

Far more than a collector and translator, Ramanujan always wrote from a theoretical position. Even in his first articles, written before his graduate work at Indiana, he questioned the extent to which Indic folktales did or did not fit into European typological categories. In his middle years he effectively dismantled the long-standing dichotomy between "Little Tradition" (folk culture) and "Great Tradition" (classical culture), as well as the simplistic separation of oral and written traditions in South Asia, and in his last essays, he explored the gendering of tales.

Ramanujan's inflence must also be judged to include his advocacy for the study of folklore. He inspired several doctoral dissertations on Indian folklore, and in the 1970s persuaded the Joint Committee on South Asia of the Social Science Research Council and American Council of Learned Societies to sponsor a long-term project on folklore as a source of indigenous cultural concepts. With his special ability to speak across disciplines and across regional specializations, he positioned folklore at the center of scholarship on India. Folklore has never been ignored in the study of South Asia, but Ramanujan was one of the first modern scholars of India to analyze it as a field of inquiry in its own right, not as derivative or grist for another mill. Most importantly, he brought to his analyses an unparalleled combination of precision and personal passion; he was, as he liked to say, both a student and a specimen of Indian folklore. His legacy will be that he demonstrated what others had only been able to state—that the study of South Asia is inseparable from the study of its folklore.

References

Ramanujan, A. K. 1983. The Indian Oedipus. In *Oedipus: a folklore casebook,* eds. Lowell Edmunds and Alan Dundes, 234–261. New York: Garland.

———, ed. 1991. *Folktales from India: a selection of oral tales from twenty-two languages*. New York: Pantheon Books.

———. 1997. *A flowering tree and other Indian oral tales from the Kannada region*. Berkeley: University of California Press.

STUART BLACKBURN

SEE ALSO
Folklorists

RĀMĀYAṆA

Most Rāma stories begin with his birth as a prince in Ayodhya, his marriage to Sītā, their banishment (along with Rāma's brother Lakṣmaṇa) to the forest where they live with hermits, destroy demons, and befriend the monkey king, Sugrīva, and his emissary, Hanumān. In the midst of these forest adventures, Sītā is stolen by Rāvaṇa, king of Lanka. Rāma and his allies are unable to find her until Hanumān leaps to Lanka, and discovers her alive, but in Rāvaṇa's captivity. The war against Lanka begins with the building of a causeway to the island, and it unfolds in a series of battles, in which his sons and brothers, and all his armies are slain by Rāma and Lakṣmaṇa. Finally, Rāma kills Rāvaṇa, places the dead king's brother, Vibhīṣaṇa, on the throne and returns with Sītā to Ayodhya, where he is crowned and rules righteously. Soon, however, a rumor that Sītā was unfaithful while in Rāvaṇa's palace forces Rāma to banish her to the forest, where she gives birth to two sons. In the end, Rāma is briefly reunited with his family, after which Sītā slips into the earth (whence she was born), and he ascends to heaven.

These events are told as tales, enacted as theater, paraded on television, printed in comic books, and sung in long epics, as well as summarized in a three-word Telugu proverb: "Built [the bridge], beat [Rāvaṇa], brought [Sītā]." More than a story with endless variation, the Rāma story is an ocean of stories and a moral code. Although it is largely a Hindu tradition, the story of Rāma so pervades the cultures of South Asia that it is known by many Muslims, Christians, Jains, and Buddhists as well. The story was told throughout premodern South Asia, but present-day textual production and performances occur almost exclusively in India, where since the 1980s, the Rāma story has been serialized on television, appropriated as a symbol of Hindu identity, and invoked to justify anti-Muslim riots. This politicization of the Rāma story, which is not a new or even modern development, demonstrates its potent social role and narrative variability.

The criss-crossed borrowings of these Rāma stories, the oral and written, the sung and seen, text and performance, are so densely entangled that it is difficult to pick out folk texts or elements. Vālmīki's Sanskrit poem (200 B.C.E.–200 C.E.) is often regarded as the original *Rāmāyaṇa,* although it is better understood as a cultural reference point than as an historical source. Vālmīki himself has entered folklore in legends about his life as a thief, his conversion, and his inspiration to compose his poem. Vālmīki's influence notwithstanding, there are several dozen Sanskrit Rāmāyaṇas, from different regions and centuries, with varying emphases. Moreover, each major Indian language boasts an influential literary text of the Rāma story. In Tamil, the long poem attributed to Kampan (12th century C.E.) is the basis for later southern Indian Rāmāyaṇa texts as well as for the contemporary shadow puppet performances in Kerala. In Bengal, the fifteenth century text composed by Krittivās has likewise exerted wide influence in eastern India. The politicization of the Rāma story is illustrated by Ekanath's *Rāmāyaṇa* in Marathi, which is often interpreted as a response to changing political conditions in the Deccan during the late fifteenth century. A century later, Tulsi Das wrote his famous Rāmāyaṇa in Hindi (*Rāmcaritmānas*), which remains popular over much of north India, and is enacted in the spectacular *rām līlā.*

Rāmāyaṇa scholarship, once largely confined to the influences and differences among these major literary texts, now analyzes their interaction with folk and oral tradition. Equally important are questions that assume Rāma stories cross linguistic boundaries. Some scholars, for example, have advanced the idea of a "folk stream" that flows beneath, and largely independently of the major texts, carrying motifs and episodes from one Indian language to another. An oral Rāma story in Gujarati, for instance, may owe as much to a similar story in Oriya as it does to a Gujarati literary text of the Rāma story.

Folk Rāmāyaṇas are performed in virtually every medium and genre known in South Asia. Folktales about Rāma and Sītā are common, especially among Indian tribal groups, which frequently cast the hero and heroine in roles scarcely imagined by literary texts. Rāmāyaṇa proverbs are told in every Indian language. A popular proverb in southern India challenges the central moral opposition of the story: "If Rāma rules or Rāvaṇa rules, what's the difference?" Rāmāyaṇa songs are particularly popular among women, who tend to sing episodes (the marriage of Rāma and Sītā, Rāma's birth and so on), introduce female characters unknown in the literary texts, and expand the roles of others. Rāmāyaṇa jokes (explaining that the present Congress Party are eunuchs reborn from the Rāma story), folk similes ("He eats like Rāma"), and riddles are widespread. Local legends all over the Indian subcontinent inscribe the Rāma story into local geography: Hanumān flew to Lanka from this mountain; Rāma and Sītā slept on this riverbank. In religion, Hanumān is widely worshiped in central and north India, while pilgrims in Maharashtra enter the forest in imitation of Rāma's famous exile. Professional epic singers and folk theater (*rām līlā, yakṣagāna, terukkūttu*) also perform long sections from the story. Finally, the Rāma story supplies the narrative for a variety of visual storytelling traditions that use scroll paintings, painted cards, and puppets. Although it is fair to say that folk drama in India relies more on the *Mahābhārata,* curiously, all six shadow puppet traditions in India draw heavily on the Rāma story, and two perform nothing else.

These performances and texts of the Rāma story produce enormous variation. One obvious example is that the major Rāma stories have three different conclusions. Many tellings, especially women's songs, conclude with the auspicious event of the marriage of Rāma and Sītā; some texts and performances are simply called "The Marriage of Sītā." Other tellings conclude the story with Rāma's coronation at Ayodhya, after he has defeated Rāvaṇa and rescued Sītā. The triumphant note in these texts and performances, however, is tempered by the revelation of shortcomings in Rāma's character. Still other tellings continue the story into the sequel (*Uttara Kāṇḍa*), in which Rāma acts on public rumor and banishes Sītā to the forest where she gives birth to twins, and is reabsorbed by the earth. The sorrow of this third conclusion recalls the legend which explains that pain and grief inspired the poet Vālmīki to compose his Sanskrit poem long ago. These three common conclusions to the Rāma story indicate its emotional range, from auspicious marriage to tragic separation. All are recognized as Rāma stories, none precludes the others, and each assumes audience knowledge of the others.

Another way to look at variation in Rāma stories is to consider tellings of the same episode. If anything like a "folk Rāmāyaṇa" exists, it might be found in folk versions of two controversial episodes: Rāma's meeting with Śūrpaṇakhā, and Sītā's relationship with Rāvaṇa. In the first, Rāma and Lakṣmaṇa mutilate Śūrpaṇakhā, Rāvaṇa's demon sister, because she declares her love for Rāma and (in order to win him) attempts to harm Sītā. Whereas devotional texts tend to emphasize the Śūrpaṇakhā's lust and Rāma's moral imperative, many folk texts soften Śūrpaṇakhā's character and hint at Rāma's attraction to her. Ethical divisions are similarly blurred by folk variations on the relationship between Sītā (a form of goddess Lakṣmī) and Rāvaṇa. Devotional tellings draw a firm line between her purity and his lust. In the Tamil literary *Rāmāyaṇa,* for example, a physical circle around Sītā forces Rāvaṇa to abduct her by ripping up and carrying off the ground beneath her (that is, without touching her). However, this moral opposition is questioned by many folk tellings in which Sītā is born as Rāvaṇa's daughter or harbors a secret desire for her captor (in some folk texts, even noble Lakṣmaṇa desires Śūrpaṇakhā). In these and countless other variations, folk Rāmāyaṇas challenge the idea that Rāma and Sītā are untouched by the emotions that cause their adversaries to desire them.

Yet another measure of variation in Rāma stories is their point of view. "Rāmāyaṇa" means something like the "way" or "story" of Rāma, and most texts center on the eponymous hero's birth, education, adventures, marriage, battles, coronation, and loss. Other orientations, however, are possible, and some texts begin with Rāvaṇa's birth and tell the story from his point of view. One particular folk Rāmāyaṇa, found in various forms all over India, places Hanumān at the center when he descends to the underworld to rescue Rāma and Lakṣmaṇa who are held captive there. Another role reversal occurs in a southern text when Sītā, as a goddess, slays the hundred-headed Rāvaṇa. In still other tellings, courageous and loyal Lakṣmaṇa overshadows his indecisive and morally flawed older brother.

Recognizing this multiplicity of Rāma stories—that there is no *the* Rāmāyaṇa—runs counter to two centuries of Indology, which reconstructed an authoritative Sanskrit text in the 1950s. Since the 1960s, field studies and translations of Rāma stories in oral performance, plus increased textual scholarship, has demonstrated that these folk Rāmāyaṇas are not deviations from literary texts but wellsprings of creativity in transmitting one of the great stories of world literature.

References

Blackburn, Stuart. 1996. *Inside the drama house: Rāma stories and puppet plays in south India.* Berkeley: University of California Press.

Lutgendorf, Philip. 1991. *The life of a text: performing The Ramcaritmanas of Tulsidas.* Berkeley: University of California Press.

Raghavan, V., ed. 1975. *The Rāmāyaṇa tradition in Asia.* New Delhi: Sahitya Akademi.

Richman, Paula, ed. 1991. *Many Rāmāyaṇas: the diversity of a narrative tradition in south Asia.* Berkeley: University of California.

———. 2000. *Questioning Ramayana: a south Asian tradition.* New York: Oxford University Press.

Smith, W. L. 1988. *Rāmāyaṇa traditions in eastern India.* Stockholm Studies in Indian Languages and Culture, 2. Stockholm: Department of Indology, University of Stockholm.

STUART BLACKBURN

SEE ALSO

Bhakti; Hanumān; *Mānas Katha; Rām Līlā;* Rāma; Rāmāyaṇa; Rāmāyaṇa, TV Production; *Vyās*

RĀMĀYAṆA, TV PRODUCTION

One of the most prominent and ubiquitous *Rāmāyaṇa* "texts" of recent times was the television serialization "Ramayan," produced and directed by Ramanand Sagar, that aired between 1987 and 1989 on India's then single-channel national television network, Doordarshan. Consisting of a main story in seventy-eight episodes and a sequel entitled "Uttar-Ramayan" (Sanskrit, *Uttara Rāmāyaṇa,* or "Epilogue to the *Rāmāyaṇa*") in twenty-six more, it kept millions of Indians riveted to television screens for a weekly hour on Sunday mornings over a period spanning more than two years.

Created by a self-styled devotee of the Tulsidas *Rāmcaritmānas,* the Hindi-language video epic attempted to promote, to an unprecedented simultaneous audience that eventually swelled to one hundred million, the theme of "national integration" advocated by Rajiv Gandhi's Congress (I) government. Its meandering and leisurely screenplay—in installments that were sometimes written not far ahead of the shooting schedule—drew on a variety of Sanskrit and regional–language *Rāmāyaṇa*s (prominently noted in the credits each week) as well as on oral traditions and the director's own inspirations. Its visual vocabulary derived from a century of mass-produced religious art: god-posters, comic books, and the mythological musicals of the Bombay film industry, but it used the small-screen format and slow pace of a TV serial to give viewers an unprecedented sense of intimate visual communion with epic characters. Although urban intellectuals bemoaned the serial's garish sets, slow pace, and melodramatic acting, the majority of viewers greedily devoured its hours of close-up *darśan* (visual communion) of a beaming, cherubic Rāma and tearful but brave Sītā, along with their entourage of family and friends.

Exploiting a new medium that permitted minute exploration of motivation and emotion, the serial advanced a number of striking interpretations that humanized traditional villains or advanced "progressive" messages (such as for communal harmony or against dowry). Broadly speaking, the director's endeavor was to utilize word and image deftly to smooth over controversial incidents (such as Rāma's and Lakṣmaṇa's mutilation of the demoness Śūrpaṇakhā, or Rāma's unchivalrous slaying of the monkey king Vālī) and to produce an unobjectionable epic that would resonate with the largest possible audience. By all accounts he succeeded. The public reception of the serial itself became a much-discussed phenomenon, as viewers surrounded weekly broadcasts with purificatory rituals and participatory performances, such as fasting, garlanding of television screens, *āratī* (ceremonial worship) of on-screen images with oil lamps, incense, and coconuts, devotional singing, and post-program distribution of sanctified sweets (*prasād*).

Images of the serial's actors quickly appeared in religious poster art, and the treatment of individual episodes became a subject of widespread public discussion and sometimes debate. Before the initial run of the serial ended in July of 1988, a public outcry (including a strike by sanitation workers in several northern states) resulted in an unprecedented court order to Doordarshan to schedule the Uttar Ramayan sequel. Some recent scholarship has forcefully argued that the airing of the serial contributed to an increase in communal tensions and to the rise during the 1990s of Hindu nationalist political parties.

References

Lutgendorf, Philip. 1990. Ramayan: the video. *TDR (The Drama Review)* 34(2) (T126): 127–176.

Rajagopal, Arvind. 2001. *Politics after television: religious nationalism and the reshaping of the Indian public*. Cambridge, U.K., and New York: Cambridge University Press.

PHILIP LUTGENDORF

SEE ALSO

Nationalism and Folklore; Rāma

RAMAẒĀN/RAMADAN

Ramaẓān is the ninth lunar month of the Islamic calendar during which daylight fasting is prescribed, also called *māh-i rūza* (month of fasting), *māh-i mobārak* (blessed month).

As the third of five obligatory acts of worship (*ibadāt*) known as the Five Pillars of Islam, the fast carries religious merit. It requires total abstention from food, drink, stimulants, medicine, and sexual intercourse from dawn until dusk throughout the month. Lying and wrong-doing are also to be avoided. Children; the ill, elderly, and insane; people travelling or fighting a *jihād* (holy war); women who are menstruatin or bleeding after childbirth; and lactating women whose milk may fail if they fast are all exempt.

Based upon lunar calculations, the month of Ramaẓān occurs eleven or twelve days earlier each year, so is not fixed to any season. The fast begins at dawn, "when it is light enough to distinguish a white thread from a black thread," and ends immediately after sunset. In many cities a cannon-shot would signal these times. Nowadays precise timetables are published.

A pre-dawn meal (*saḥarī*) precedes the daily fast. In cities in Afghanistan military bands used to patrol around before dawn to wake people up, a custom relating to the musical time-keeping of the *naubatkhāna* (time-keeping bands). At dusk, families and guests gather to break the fast (*'iftār*), sitting around a cloth spread with food and drink. The Prophet Muḥammad used to break his fast with fresh dates and water, so they are particularly favoured. Where dates are not readily available other local foods are popular. In Afghanistan when the fast falls in summer, a communal bowl of *dugh* is usually served. This cooling drink is made from watered yogurt (iced if possible) freshened with chopped cucumber, salt, pepper and mint.

The fast imposes a distinctive pattern upon daily life, and where the whole community is Muslim, a special atmosphere is created. Days are quieter than usual, businesses close early, people often sleep, restaurants are closed, and no one eats, drinks, or smokes in public. Nights are vibrant with social gatherings and solitary prayer vigils.

At night mosques are ablaze with light. Each evening congregations gather to hear a chapter of the *Qur'ān* recited. Readings are also organized in homes with invited guests. The very pious perform supererogatory prayers (*tarāwih*). The last ten nights of Ramaẓān are particularly holy, as the Qur'ān was revealed to the Prophet during one of these nights, usually taken to be the 27th of Ramaẓān. This Night of Power (*Lailat ul Qadr*) is "better than a thousand months," and angels mingle peacefully among us until dawn [Qur'ān 97: 1, 5]. Isma'īlīs pray throughout the night of prayer in religious meeting-places called *jamā' atkhāna*. Shī'as hold religious gatherings to commemorate the deaths of 'Alī and Imām Reẓa (21st of Ramaẓān) and 'Alī's birthday (22nd of Ramaẓān).

Popular entertainment is used to enliven Ramaẓān evenings. Theatrical shows, concerts, jugglers, and acrobats used to be commissioned to perform every evening, in public or privately operated entertainment venues, but the advent of television and videos has weakend live entertainment traditions, as has increased religious disapproval of such activities.

In Afghanistan, groups of boys traditionally went out on the evenings near the full moon looking for sweets, nuts, and dried fruit. If they were unlucky they would be showered with water. They advertised their arrival at a house singing traditional verses:

Ramaẓān yā rab, yā rab Ramaẓān
Ah salāmaleik māh-e Ramaẓān
Ramaẓān sī rūz mehmān-e mān ė

Ramaẕān qo'at-e imān-e mān e
(shouting) Baleh baleh baleh yā so'āl yā jawāb!
Yā sang-e panj man yā kuzeh āb!

Ramazan oh Lord, oh Lord, Ramazan
Greetings, month of Ramazan
Ramazan is our guest for thirty days
Ramazan is the strength of our religious faith.
Yes, yes, yes, either a question or an answer!
Either a five-*man* [forty-pound] stone or a jug of water!

Then followed verses describing the generosity of the houeholder, and the gifts the singers hoped to receive.

The 'Īd-e Ramaẕān (Arabic *'Īd ul Fiṭr*; Festival of Fast-breaking) falls on the first day of the next lunar month, Ṣafar. This used to be reckoned from the appearance of the new moon, but because some communities now use astronomical calculation, there is often a day's discrepancy in the date of the festival from one locale to another.

The celebration of the ending of the fast is marked by congregational midday prayers. The atmosphere is very joyous—people embrace one another when they meet, at home or in the street, and utter blessings, often give money to children and food to the poor. Among couples engaged to be married, the bridegroom will send *'Īd* gifts (often clothing) to his fiancée. Everyone visits relatives and friends to affirm mutual bonds of goodwill. New clothes are worn, and girls and women dye their hands with henna. People visit family graves to remember the dead—in Pakistan the graves are decorated with garlands.

Reference

Herklots, G. A. (trans.) 1998. *Islam in India of the Qanun-i-Islam: the customs of the Musalmans of India*. Delhi: Saujanya.

VERONICA DOUBLEDAY

SEE ALSO
Food and Foodways; Islam; Muslim Folklore and Folklife

RĀMDEV

Rāmdev, or Rāmdeo, is a folk hero/deity widely revered in Rajasthan, Madhya Pradesh, Gujarat, Punjab, and other parts of Western India, mainly by Meghvāls and other members of the scheduled castes.

Rāmdev is said to have been a Rajput of the Tanwar clan in Jaisalmer, Rajasthan, who lived in the fourteenth or early fifteenth century. Popular tradition holds that he was opposed to the caste system and other religious dogmas and was a miraculous and heroic figure. Like many of the other folk hero deities of Western India, such as Pābūjī and Gūgā, he is generally depicted on a horse, mounted as a warrior. Like Gūgā, he ended his earthly existence by taking *samādhi,* or entry into the ground, and is reputed to have proven himself before the Panch Pīr, a legendary group of five saints, well known in the folk traditions of North India. His miraculous powers were acclaimed within his lifetime and afterwards. Rāmdev has traditionally been revered by Muslims and Hindus alike and accepted by Hindu adherents as an incarnation of Kṛṣṇa. His worship remains tied to people of low societal status, although not exclusively so.

The worship of Rāmdev is similar to that of other folk hero deities in this area, in two key elements: the centrality of the story of the hero, including the narration of his quasi-historical life and the miracles associated with him, and the importance of the tomb or site of his samādhi.

The narrative of the hero-deities of Rajasthan and surrounding areas can take many forms, including oral epic, song, and performance. For Rāmdev it is composed mainly of *bhajan*s. These praise songs relate to the historical narrative of the hero and the miracles associated with him, both within his lifetime and since, all of which attest to his effective presence over time.

Like many of the cults of folk heroes of the area, such as Tejā and Gūgā, Rāmdev's worship centers around the site of his samādhi and yearly fairs, or *melā,* which commemorate his life and miracles. These fairs bring pilgrims from all over India to Rāmdev's samādhi site in Rāmdevra, Jaisalmer District, Rajasthan; similar smaller fairs also take place at the numerous small Rāmdev shrines scattered throughout the region. Such fairs combine pilgrimage with business, where cattle and other goods are bought, sold, and traded. The samādhi site is a prominent pilgrimage place and physical center for the cult, one which draws on both Hindu and Muslim traditions and is a focal point of worship, celebration, and community life. This practice relates to the general worship of saints', or *pīr*s', tombs in the Hindu and Muslim cultures of North India and Pakistan, a tradition that certainly was a formative influence in the development of Rāmdev worship.

The main Rāmdev melā (fair) takes place at his tomb in the bright half of the month of Bhadon (August/September). From the second to the eleventh day of this month, pilgrims arrive to receive *darśan,* sing the praises of Rāmdev and his miracles, and be touched by his miraculous nature themselves, as is done at pīr tombs throughout North India and Pakistan. Devotees can thus be struck with the light of the saint's presence, be healed, or find the fulfillment of their wishes. It is through this efficacy that Rāmdev and the other folk hero deities of Rajasthan touch and transform the lives of devotees with an immediacy not possible with more distant and higher-status divine personalities.

References

Binford, Mira. 1976. Mixing in the color of Rām of Ranuja: a folk pilgrimage to the grave of a Rajput hero-saint. In *Hinduism: new essays in the history of religions,* ed. Bardwell L. Smith, 120–142. Leiden: E. J. Brill.

Indian Pilgrimage: Rāmdevra. 1976. Mira Reym Binford and Michael Camerini. Madison, Wisconsin: South Asia Film Center. Color, VHS, 26 minutes.

Kothari, Komal. 1982. The shrine: an expression of social needs. In *Gods of the byways,* Anand, et al. Oxford: Museum of Modern Art.

ANNE MURPHY

SEE ALSO

Bhajan; Darśan; Gūgā; Heroes and Heroines; *Melā; Pābūjī; Panch Pīr; Pīr;* Shrines; *Tejāji*

RĀSA LĪLĀ

Rāsa līlā (also known as *rāsa-krīḍa*) is the name of particular *līlā* or "play" of the "circular dance" known as the *rāsa,* a special dance of divine love between the supreme divinity Kṛṣṇa and his divine cowherd consorts, the *gopīs*. The rāsa līlā, as it is described in the *Bhāgavata Purāṇa,* is treasured by the Caitanya (or Gauḍiya) school of Vaiṣnavism as the highest and most sacred revelation of God's love. In modern times, rāsa līlā can also refer to dramatic and musical performances of the many other childhood līlās of Kṛṣṇa that are performed in and outside of India.

The word "rāsa" indicates a certain ancient dance form, comprised of the circular formation of many female dancers, whose hands or arms are interlocked with one another in a chain-like manner, and around whose necks the arms of their male dance partners are placed. In the līlā of Kṛṣṇa's rāsa dance with the gopīs, however, it is Kṛṣṇa who, duplicating himself from the center of the rāsa circle by virtue of his mystic power, becomes the sole male partner for each and every gopī. While continuing to remain at the center of the *rāsa-mandala* or "circle of rāsa dance," Kṛṣṇa stands with his most favored gopī, who is understood to be the supremely loving goddess Rādhā. As the gopīs move in the circular dance, each experiencing the exclusive attention of Kṛṣṇa, they sing songs of love in harmony with Kṛṣṇa and in chorus. The percussive sounds of the bells on the gopīs' ankles and belts jingle, their bracelets clang to their rhythmic movements, and celestial beings shower flowers down, joining in with song and drumming from the heavens. The dance takes place in the paradisal forest of Vraja, in which the lotus flowers and full fruit trees and honey bees come alive during the enchanting night when this divine dance is performed under the full moon of the autumn harvest season.

The complete episode of the rāsa līlā, including the events that lead up to Kṛṣṇa's dance of divine love, is often referred to as the *rāsa līlā paṇcādhyāya,* the "five chapters of the rāsa līlā," comprising chapters 29 through 33 of the tenth book of the *Bhāgavata* text. Although the episode is found in less theologically rich and poetically elaborate forms within the *Harivaṇśa* and *Viṣṇu Purāṇa,* the *Bhāgavata* version has been the most celebrated and honored source of the rāsa līlā. Especially for the Caitanya school of Vaiṣnavism, for whom this episode is held as the most sacred and ultimate culmination of all other līlās of Kṛṣṇa, the *Bhāgavata* is the authoritative text.

Western and Indian scholars alike have viewed the amorous or even erotic imagery of the rāsa līlā allegorically or metaphorically as the soul's passion to be united with God, and some take it as a form of mystical eroticism. Still others fear its impassioned expressions as being degraded religion. The Vaiṣnava devotee, however, to this day, embraces the episode as the perfect picture of God's most intimate self, in the most profound revelation of selfless love.

In modern times, dramatic performances of Kṛṣṇa's various līlās are performed in two areas of India, and are called rās līla (Hindi form of rāsa). These performances open with the rāsa dance, acknowledging, indeed as a testimonial, that it is regarded as the ultimate līlā of Kṛṣṇa. In the village of Vrindaban, sacred to the devotees of Kṛṣṇa as Kṛṣṇa's spiritual center on this earthly plane, the rās līlā dramatic and musical performances are choreographed with young boys playing the parts of the gopīs and Kṛṣṇa. In contrast, in the state of Manipur, the dancers are young females playing the various parts. And in recent years, the members of the Hare Kṛṣṇa movement, who themselves have popularized the Kṛṣṇa līlās throughout the modern world since the late 1960s, have sponsored a worldwide tour of the Manipuri Dancers in their performances of the līlās of Kṛṣṇa.

Reference

Swann, Darius. 1990. Rās līlā. In *Indian theatre: traditions of performance,* eds. Farley P. Richmond, Darius L. Swann, and Phillip B. Zarrilli, 177–213. Honolulu: University of Hawaii Press.

GRAHAM M. SCHWEIG

SEE ALSO

Dance; Kṛṣṇa; *Purāṇas;* Theater and Drama

RATHA JĀTRĀ

Ratha Jātrā, meaning "Car Festival," is a central part of the annual festival in Hindu temples all over India, but it is most famous in the city of Puri, in the state of Orissa. Puri, also known as Śrīkṣetra, is famous for the Great Temple of Lord Jagannāth, Lord Balabhadra, and the Goddess Subhadrā (locally known as Śrīmandira). The *Ratha Jātrā,* also known as *Guṇḍīcā Jātrā,* is one of the most important festivals for all Hindus, not merely those from Puri, or even Orissa. Millions of pilgrims come from all over India to this sacred center during this festival every year. Though many scholars believe Lord Jagannāth is of tribal origin, a unique synthesis among all the sects of Hinduism is felt during the festival. It is believed that if a devotee gets a glimpse of Lord Jagannāth on the chariot during the festival, he or she will attain salvation (*mokṣa*) and be eternally free from rebirth (*punarjanma*).

Every year, Ratha Jātrā is celebrated on the second day of the bright moon fortnight (*śukla pakṣa*) in the month of Āsādha (June-July), during the rainy season. Formerly, once in every twelve years, the sacred spirits of the deities were installed in new idols made of wood carved from a sacred tree in a ceremony called *navakalevara* (new body). Now, however, this event falls in a year when the month of Āsādha occurs twice, consecutively, that is, when, instead of lasting a period from one new moon to the next, it is extended to include two lunar cycles.

The *Ratha Jātrā* celebrates the sojourn of the deities from their temple, Śrīmandira, to their aunt's place, Guṇḍīcā Mandira. Guṇḍīcā was the queen of the King Indradyumna of Avanti. Guṇḍīcā, who installed the deities in their temple in Puri, is considered to be the maternal aunt (*mausimā*) of these three deities. According to the tradition, the deities stay in the Guṇḍīcā temple for eight days, derive profound happiness from the love and hospitality rendered by their aunt, and then return to Śrīmandira on the tenth day.

The three main rituals of the festival are known as *Pahaṇḍibije, Cherāpāhaṃrā,* and *Bāhudā* (return) *jātrā*. During the first phase, Pahaibije, the three chariots are brought to the main gate of the temple, known as the Simhadvara, or "Lion Gate," because it is guarded by two magnificently carved stone lions. After the morning rituals, the deities are brought from the temple to their respective chariots. This sacred passage of the deities from the temple premises to the respective chariots is known as Pahaṇḍibije. The deities are decorated with crowns of flowers, or *tāhiā*. Lord Balabhadra, elder brother of Lord Jagannāth, is brought first, then the sister, Subhadrā, and at last Lord Jagannāth himself.

In the second phase, Cherāpāhaṇrā, the living heir of Gajapati King of Puri renders service to the deities by sweeping the platform of each car with a golden broom and sprinkling sandal water to sanctity the chariots. Then the chariots are pulled by the devotees to the Guṇḍīcā Temple.

The final phase, known as Bahudajātrā, celebrating the return journey of the deities from the Guṇḍīcā Temple to Śrīmandira, falls on the ninth day of the festival. When the three deities reach Śrīmandira, Lakṣmī, the Goddess of wealth and the consort of Lord Jagannāth at first does not open the Simhadvara Gate and allow them to enter, because she is unhappy for not being invited by Lord Jagannāth to accompany them to Guṇḍīcā Temple. However, with the intervention and request of the Gajapati King of Puri, Lakṣmī agrees to open the main gate and the deities resume their respective seats on the platform inside the sanctum sanctorium. It is particularly this return journey, the Bāhuḍā, in chariots (*ratha*), that is celebrated with the greatest pomp and joy during the Ratha Jātrā.

References

Das, K. B. and L. K. Mahapatra. 1993. *Folklore of Orissa*. New Delhi: National Book Trust.

Eschmann, Anncharlott, Hermann Kulke, and Gaya Charan Tripathi. 1986. *The cult of Jagannath and the regional tradition of Orissa*. New Delhi: Manohar.

Mohanty, Surendra. 1982. *Lord Jagannath*. Bhubaneswar: Orissa Sahitya Academy.

Patnaik, D. 1982. *Festivals of Orissa*. Bhubaaneswar: Orissa Sahitya Academy.

MAHENDRA KUMAR MISHRA

SEE ALSO

Calendrical Ceremonies and Rites; Folk Art, Orissa; Pilgrimage; Processions; Tribal Folklore, Central India; Tribalism and Tribal Identity: The Bhīls of Western Central India

RECYCLING

It is difficult to find words in the Indian vernaculars for the concept of utilizing discarded things for innovatively new purposes, but the practice has a long history in South Asia. Leaving aside Vedic philosophical speculations about the "recycled" nature of existence, we find quite early on in Indian history examples of materials reused to make functional ornamental objects. Soon after the introduction of tobacco into India in the sixteenth century, for example, exquisite examples of *huqqahs* (water pipes) made from discarded coconut shells, bamboo reeds, and clay began to appear. Cloth, glass, and paper were also reused for aesthetic purposes:

the Bengali *kāṅthā,* a type of symbolically embroidered cloth, utilized layers of old sari material; glass bangles (cūṛīs) and beads are made from remelted glass; and paper products were reused for a variety of items ranging from papier-mâché vessels and plates to canvasses for itinerant painters.

The ubiquitous nature of recycyling is most striking in the postindustrial period, when objects made of plastic, tin, and rubber become increasingly popular. In urban South Asia today, recycling activities range widely, from the simple collection and sorting of trash for ecological and economic reasons, to the artistic use of such materials to make new utilitarian objects such as tools, toys, and containers. In addition, some items are made simply for aesthetic reasons, as objects of beauty. This is not to suggest a strict division between functional and aesthetic recycling, for many of the items produced from reused materials operate on both levels. For example, in the rickshaws of urban Bangladesh, the metal panels of the carriage are most often made from sheets of falsely printed aluminum labels discarded by multinational corporations such as Coca-Cola, which are purchased at low prices in local markets. Rickshaw painters then create designs—both narrative and symbolic—for the vehicles' exterior surfaces, producing a vehicle that simultaneously pleases the eye and provides conveyance. Likewise, lamps made in Bankura, West Bengal, serve a dual purpose, since the makers consciously choose the colors of scrap metal that best serve their aesthetic inclinations.

Leisure is another realm in which recycled objects figure. As in other countries in the developing world, toys in South Asia are sometimes made from used materials. While one might think this practice is limited to chidren's play, it extends much beyond. In Pakistan and India, film projectors, slide viewers, kaleidoscopes, and other visual apparatus used to be made from scrap metal, old gears, and spectacle lenses. These objects are becoming harder to find now, due to the abundance of plastic. Nevertheless, the plastic is often old plastic, reheated at a low temperature and molded into the appropriate shape and size.

The availability and low price of raw, reused stuff has led a number of commercial brands in South Asia to utilize these materials for profit. However, the pervasive Hindu ideology of substance pollution has forced manufacturers to "mask" the recycled nature of their products in order to sell them as clean and new. Pollution ideology has also affected the way that workers in the recycling industry have been perceived. In general, recyclers come from the lowest strata of society, being marginalized for their involvement with impure substances.

Very little research has been done on this topic in South Asia from a folkloristic or anthropological perspective. Most of the attention paid to recycling in South Asia has come from urban planners and engineers who seek ways of using recycyling for urban renewal and waste management. The subject remains wide open for ethnographers to consider the artistic dimensions involved. It is clearly an area worth exploring in the future.

References

Gallagher, Robert. 1992. *The rickshaws of Bangladesh.* Dhaka: The University Press, Ltd.

Grothues, Jürgen. 1988. *Aladin's neue lampe: recycling in der Dritten Welt* [Aladins new lamp: recycling in the Third World] München: Trickster Verlag.

Korom, Frank J. 1996. Recycling in India: status and economic realities. In *Recycled, reseen: folk art from the global scrap heap,* ed. Charlene Cerny and Suzanne Seriff, 118–129, 190–192. New York: Harry Abrams, Inc.

Kramrisch, Stella. 1949. Kanthas of Bengal. *Marg* 3: 18–29.

Panwalkar, Pratima. 1990. Processus de recyclage du plastique a Bombay. [Processes of recycling of plastic in Bombay]. *Environnement Africain* [African Environment] 8: 153–157.

FRANK J. KOROM

SEE ALSO

Kāṅthā; Quilting and Piecing

REFUGEE LORE

Refugee lore provides a discursive space for the definition of displaced persons, and includes both lore of and about refugees. Within the lore of refugees, we see two further subdivisions. The first is the folklore from the home country that is still told by refugees in their new homes, and the second is an original body of folklore related to the experience of displacement, including migration narratives. Each of these genres of refugee lore plays an important role in the lives of refugees. This article focuses on the narrative components of this total body of lore, which may also include song, short verbal forms such as proverbs or jargon terms, material cultural (for example, foodways) or other customary practices.

Stories from home, which can be called "traditional lore" in that they were part of the oral cultural legacy of the home community, are treasured by refugees as links to their past. Collection of these stories by folklorists may be spoken of in terms of "salvage research," since it is assumed, and sometimes demonstrable, that this memorial knowledge becomes more selective or sparse through processes of forgetting with the passage of time in the new environment. This body of literature may be deployed by those striving to protect against cultural change and loss. Looking at the use of such folklore within Tibetan schools in India, for example, we can see that the stories are often used in children's textbooks to provide images of a "home" country that the children are likely never to have seen. Similar, less centrally organized efforts were undertaken in certain refugee-run schools for Afghan children in North-West Pakistan, where teachers produced and photocopied small booklets retelling stories and outlining traditional games remembered from their own home-country childhood for use in the schools.

Publication may create the assumption that there is an "authentic" body of folklore that is most in need of being saved, or officially taught to the next generation. This assumption overlooks the fact that texts are not the only sources of traditional folklore in exile communities. Refugees carry from their homeland a wide variety of traditional oral tales and memories, though only certain sets of folklore may be published. The process of selection or censorship that typically takes place in the act of producing texts affects the written presentation of traditional refugee folklore. The political situation of refugees may also act to censor voices in documented folklore that could be considered contrary to the group's strategic self-representation or that of their host nation, yet these alternative currents may continue to flow in oral registers and environments.

Folklore can help a community to explain the circumstances of their migration to a younger generation, as well as define present roles in their new location. As Kirschenblatt-Gimblett has demonstrated, different subgenres of narratives may thus relate to and be performed during different stages of geographical and social movement within a community. Stories about the refugee experience are rarely published as collections of refugee folklore; instead they are often found as personal accounts within the context of historical or sociological studies. Yet these tales are commonly told and exchanged in refugee communities, creating a sense of shared experience and strengthening the definition of the diasporic experience. For instance, the Partition of India and Pakistan remains a strikingly and sadly narratable set of events, prominent both nationally and in directly affected groups. These oral history narratives (narratives derived from witness accounts but not necessarily told by witnesses) depict the wholesale slaughter of trainloads of departing refugees in both directions (Muslims leaving India for Pakistan, Hindus and Sikhs leaving Pakistan for India).

As refugees address their new surroundings through lore, the surrounding communities also create images of the refugees in their own oral traditions. This lore about refugees may be glossily packaged, for example in the form of popular movies about Tibetan life and history, creating an idealized refugee community for easy Western consumption. Other narratives stress difference or negative stereotypes, as in commonly heard complaint narratives in northwest Pakistan, where up to 3.5 million refugees from Afghanistan's wars have been concentrated and have had major effects on local economic and social conditions. Initially welcoming of Afghans as fellow Muslim refugees (*muhājir*) fleeing religious persecution by a Marxist state, ordinary Pakistanis later commonly voiced complaints such as "We didn't have drug problems or theft problems until we let in all these Afghans with their guns and their heroin. They are all a bunch of bandits." In such cases, host fatigue (a folk concept invoked by refugee service providers) has set in to the degree that it visibly overrides some very strongly held local traditional values, including hospitality to strangers and support for fellow Muslims in the face of religious persecution. Yet most refugee groups large enough to affect local economic and social conditions face some degree of general distrust or dislike, framed in particular ways relating to local cultural terms and perceptions of the host community, including prior and newly-fledged stereotypes. While seemingly dissimilar, both types of folklore about refugees involve stereotypes, good or bad, and are an attempt on the part of the wider host community to project their own defining images onto the refugee community.

The processes of identity maintenance and formation that surround refugee folklore make this body of lore relevant to scholars working with a variety of issues. The folklore speaks of the placement of individuals vis-à-vis larger social institutions such as nations and international relief organizations, and hot issues such as ethnic conflict and migration policy. Studies of refugee folklore also necessarily deal with intersections of memory, history, group, and self within and across community boundaries. Thus, studies that address the importance of refugee lore scholarship in the broader scope of the social sciences provide academics with important new material for consideration.

References

Barth, Fredrik, ed. 1969. *Ethnic groups and boundaries.* Bergen, Germany: Universitetsforlagen; London: Allen and Unwin.

Kirschenblatt-Gimblett, Barbara. 1978. Culture shock and narrative creativity. In *Folklore in the modern world,* ed. R. M. Dorson, 109–122. The Hague: Mouton.

Korom, Frank. 1999. Tibetans in exile: A Euro-American perspective. *Passages* 1(1): 1–23.

Layoun, Mary N. 1995. (Mis)trusting narratives: Refugee stories of post-1922 Greece and post-1974 Cyprus. In *Mistrusting Refugees,* ed. E. Valentine Daniel and John Chr. Knudsen, 87–101. Berkeley: University of California Press.

Mills, Margaret. 1996. Family oral histories in the wider history of war: Afghanistan. *Suomen Antropologi: Journal of the Finnish Anthropological Society* 21(2): 2–11.

Mills, Margaret A., Sally Peterson, William Westerman, and Roberto Sanchez, 1990. Creative expression and the refugee experience. In *Reimaging America: The arts of social change,* eds. Mark O'Brien, C. Norris, C. Little and M. Schwarzman, 45–59. Philadelphia: New Society Publishers.

Shalinsky, Audrey C. 1994. *Long years of exile: Central Asian refugees in Afghanistan and Pakistan.* Lanham, Md.: University Press of America.

Thomas, Raju G. C., ed. 1992. *Perspectives on Kashmir: The roots of conflict in South Asia.* Boulder: Westview Press.

JACQUELINE H. FEWKES AND MARGARET MILLS

SEE ALSO
Muhājir

RELIGION

Folk religion comprises local religious practices that are generally unmediated by codified doctrine, text, or educated expert. Practitioners enjoy relatively direct participation in, and communication with, the divine and require no special scholarly or philosophical training. While the variety of folk religious practices in South Asia is extensive, oft-cited examples of such practices include Muslim saint worship; possession by gods and spirits, sometimes involving the communication of oracles and prophecies through human hosts; public processions of deities, saints, or sacred objects; animal sacrifice; and religious festivals of all kinds. The many "world" religions that South Asia hosts, including Buddhism, Christianity, Hinduism, Islam, Jainism, Judaism, and Sikhism, all have folk aspects, and often the folk religions borrow practices from one another across religious lines.

South Asian scholars have made many attempts to distinguish between folk religion and text-driven religious forms, effectively dichotomizing religion—and cultural forms more generally—into oppositions: great versus little traditions (Redfield, Singer); transcendental versus pragmatic religion (Mandelbaum); and the common classical versus folk. Implicit in these oppositions is a ranked valuation of the two terms: the "folk" term, invariably the second term in such oppositions, implies "low." Terms like Sanskritization (Srinivas) and Islamization reinforce the presumably lower position of the folk. These terms refer to processes whereby a social group—be it a caste, a village, or some other community—work to raise their social status and redefine and refine themselves by altering their local religious practices to fit great or transcendental forms. For example, a Muslim villager might send his children to Arabic school and reject local saints for worship exclusively in the mosque with an Imām. Hindu meat-eaters might turn to vegetarianism to mimic high Brahminical code, or non-Brahmans might hire specialized Brahman priests to mediate their relation with gods in their local temples. For some, the folk forms of their religion are not only thought inferior, but even heretical.

Many researchers have challenged both the easy dichotomization of religious forms and the unidirectional movement from folk to classical, from "low" to "high." Singer notes that the dichotomy between classical and folk suspiciously matches up with western academic categories of humanities (which studies "Great" literary traditions) and social sciences (which studies people—"folk"—where they live) and suggests the analytic category "cultural performance" to cut across the presumption. Marriott, responding to the concept of Sanskritization, coins "parochialization" to describe how the great becomes locally incorporated and pragmatically redefined. Ramanujan shows that great and little, classical and folk may be considered intimate partners: the "folk" grows into and feeds the "classical" as the "classical" grows into and feeds the "folk" in constant and dynamic interplays and intertextualities.

Folk religion is often said to be relatively syncretic or synthetic; that is, it takes its signs, symbols, forms, and meanings from a wide "cultural pool" (to borrow a phrase from Ramanujan). Muslims, Hindus, Jews, Christians, and Jains, if they live in close proximity, swim in a pool joined by common language, history, and ethnicity. They easily borrow and share religious practices and occasions. Ironically, it is in many cases the "world religion" in its classical form—the orthodox, the codified—that discriminates and excludes as it defines heresies and distinctions among its own folk, while it is the local, folk forms of religious practice that include, borrow, and share more globally with other religions.

References

Friedmann, Yohanan, ed. 1984. *Islam in Asia: South Asia.* Vol. 1. Boulder: Westview Press.

Mandelbaum, David. 1970. *Society in India.* 2 vols. Berkeley: University of California Press.

Marriott, McKim. 1955. *Village India: studies in the little community.* Chicago: University of Chicago Press.

Ramanujan, A. K. 1973. *Speaking of Siva.* Penguin.

———. 1991. Three Hundred Ramayanas. In *Many Ramayanas: the diversity of a narrative tradition,* ed. Paula Richman. Berkeley: University of California Press.

Redfield, Robert. 1955. *The little community: viewpoints for the study of the human whole.* Chicago: University of Chicago Press.

Singer, Milton. 1972. *When a great tradition modernizes.* Chicago: University of Chicago Press.

Srinivas, M. N. 1952. *Religion and society among the Coorgs of South India*. London: Oxford University Press.

DIANE MINES

SEE ALSO

Buddhism and Buddhist Folklore; Catholicism, Sri Lanka; Christianity, Kerala; Hinduism; Islam; Jainism; Judaism; *Kalasha;* Parsiism; Sikhism; Syncretism

RIDDLE, BALOCHI

The common Balochi word for riddle is *cāc* or, among eastern Baloch, *bujjārat*. Balochi is rich in riddles, some are very old and some are recently composed. Riddle composition is still a living art. Men, women, and children enjoy riddle contests, and in some families, such contests are arranged regularly. Although there are no particular occasions for riddle contests, winter evenings provide an ideal atmosphere as the nights are long and people spend time gathered around the fire. With the arrival of electricity in some towns and the introduction of television with satellite channels, oral tradition has given way to new entertainment. Until recently, people enjoyed riddle contests that had many famous poets compose riddles in rhymes and send them to rival poets. Makran people tell that once Mulla Bahadur, a renowned nineteenth century poet from Kolwah, sent a riddle to Mulla Fazul Rind, a famous poet from Mand. Mulla Fazul composed and sent another riddle in response to Mulla Bahadur. Mulla Bahadur's riddle goes:

Lab ba lab, sīna ba sīna, mekh dar sūrakh shud,
yakk safīdī bar mīāyad, pāk shud nāpāk shud.

Lips upon lips, chest upon chest, the nail
penetrated inside the hole,
a white [substance] came out, is it pure or impure?

To which Mulla Fazul replied,

Ast yakk fā'il o maf'ūle,
pahnād o takān yakk tūle,
Fā'il ki watā sāz kant
maf'ūl co kinjirā nāc kant.

There is a "doer" and a "done-to,"
both are equal in width and breadth,
when the doer tunes itself,
the done-to dances like a [dancing] prostitute.

The answer to both riddles is the millstone, the white substance being the flour.

Balochi oral tradition is replete with such examples. Poets are said to have used riddles for "coding" to describe the beauty of a woman or otherwise indirectly comment on some person if they wished to avoid having others understand. People recount examples with great admiration and enjoyment. Longworth Dames observed 100 years ago, "There is a great abundance of rhymed riddles and conundrums among the Baloches, and they are addicted to composing them on any unusual circumstance which attracts the attention of the unsophisticated hillman or shepherd" (Dames 1:195).

In what is still a fundamentally oral tradition, newly composed riddles portray electric bulbs, fans, TV sets, airplanes, cars, and so on. One says, *"Bārag int co sīmmā, dang jant co zīmmā."* ("Thin as a wire, stings like a scorpion," i.e. electric wire.) Simple Balochi riddles are in single lines, while others are small poems in a number of rhyming lines. Some examples: *"Taī pit pāgā bandīt bandīt na kuṭṭīt* ("Your father ties up the turban but it never ends [a path]); *"Taī māt shapā pacī pacī, suhbā hiccī neyst"* (Your mother bakes [bread] all night but in the morning nothing remains [stars]).

An example of a multiple line poem is:

Cill o cārdah ant nind ant,	They sit, forty and fourteen,
nakshīen kalāte band ant,	They build a colorful fort,
ā mard pa dilā ber byārīt,	The man who brings revenge
berā pa kalātā byārīt	Brings revenge to the fort.
	[bees and honey]

Some riddles are double entendres, appearing obscene or abusive until they are solved: *"Taī māt suhbā wābā pād kēt dastā harē kūnnā kant"* ("When your mother wakes up in the morning, she puts her hand in the donkey's anus" [the sack of dates she takes out every morning to feed the domestic animals]).

Riddles are also found in folktales, often as a "neck riddle," an intelligence test for the hero. By guessing the riddle he wins the princess; the other sages and heroes who fail are sentenced to death. In actual performance, two teams (including men, women, and children within the family or neighborhood) take turns telling a riddle, giving an answer, and if successful, countering with their own riddle. If they fail, they are told they must "give" a village, town, or country to get the answer. After this the first team can ask another riddle until the second team gives one correct answer. The losing team "gives" the town or city by naming it (e.g. "Take Panjgūr"), at which time the winners recite a formulaic phrase, e.g. (in Makran):

Jī jī pa Panjgūr. Alle kanīn, balle kanīn,
sī kucikkē julle kanīn,
lālahē anjagē pulle kanīn.

Praise be to Panjgūr. [nonsense words], I will make
it the cover of thirty dogs, make it the flower
[ornament] on the end of my brother's trouser string.

Then the winners give the answer before offering another riddle. Although riddles are a favorite test of wit for children and women, adult men also take part in these contests. Thus, a riddle contest may become family affair.

References

Dames, Longworth M. 1907. *Popular poetry of the Baloches,* 2 vol. London: The Folklore Society: [reprint: Quetta: Baluchi Academy, 1988].

Elfenbein, Josef. 1990. *An anthology of modern and classical Baluchi literature,* 2 vols. Wiesbaden: Otto Harrassowitz.

SABIR BADALKHAN

SEE ALSO
Tamāśa

RIDDLE, NEPAL

Riddles—traditional questions often imbued with metaphor demonstrating the cleverness of the questioner and challenging the audience—exist in Nepali intellectual life, although there is no single Nepali term to describe them as a genre. Nepali history and folklore provide many examples of heroes whose intelligence is tested by riddles and who, upon their success, are awarded prizes such as princess brides and villages. Perhaps to recall such traditions, riddles are commonly called *gāuṃ khāne kathā* literally "village-winning riddles."

As intellectually stimulating games, riddles are especially popular among Nepali children. If the answering party responds correctly, questioner and answerer switch roles, going back and forth in an extended game. If the answering party does not know the answer, then he or she jokingly promises a village to the questioning party. The questioner then announces that all the good things of the ceded village are his or hers, and all bad things remain with the loser.

One common riddle is "The Queen of the East visits the West. What is it?" Answer: the sun or the moon. *Jhyāṅgā,* a less common riddle, is the lyrical form of the village-winning riddle, in which children recite or sing the riddle. As in some Nepali folk songs, the first line of the Jhyāṅgā is a nonsensical play on words that rhymes with the second line. It sets an appropriate meter for the riddle that follows in the second line. For example:

Ekai ra muṭhī jirīko sāga tel-ghīule jhānana
Pūrvakī rānī paścima jāne, yo jhyāṅgā janana.

Fry a handful of *jirī* greens in oil or butter.
Try to solve the *jhyāṅgā* of the Queen of the East visits the West.

If the answering party cannot answer the riddle, he or she concedes:

Sānomā sāno kusume rumāl ālīmā sukāideu.
Timaro jhyāṅgā jānina maile, timīlenai phukāideu.

Put the small pink handkerchief on the ridge to dry.
Please solve your *jhyāṅgā* yourself, since though I have tried, I failed.

If the answering party knows the answer, then he or she recites:

Kururu garne narsine bājā, tāl dine ḍholakī.
Pūrvakī rānī paścim jāne jūn-ghamā holā kī?

The shawm goes *kururu* and the drum provides the rhythm.
We think that the Queen of the East who visits the West is the sun or the moon itself.

This stanza is recited or sung by the questioning party if the answering party fails to answer the riddle.

Deuḍā, dohorū, juhārī, and *roilā* are popular duets containing quizzes and riddles that boys and girls sing to express their love and to test the other's intelligence. Perhaps this tradition explains why *silok hœalne* is performed at weddings; the parties of the bride and the bridegroom sing duets in question–answer form. The bride's party asks:

Tulasīko lingo nau thāuṃ bāṅgo,
Kati ṭhauṃ lāyo carīle guṇḍ?
Tin tin carīko ke ho nauṃ?
Lāuñchauṃ artha ki choḍchau ṭhauṃ?

How many twists are there in the pole near the *Tulasī* [basil] plant?
How many places on the pole have the birds made nests?
Tell me the names of the birds.
Will you solve the riddle, or quit this place?

The bridegroom's party responds:

Tulasīko lingo nau ṭhauṃ bāṅgo,
Nawai ṭhauṃ lāyo carīle guṇḍ,
Tin tin carīka hīrā motī nāuṃ,
Lauñchauṃ artha choddainauṃ ṭhauṃ.

There are nine twists in the pole that is near the *Tulasī* plant,
and in all of those nine twists birds have made nests.
Diamonds and pearls are the names of those birds.
We have answered your questions and therefore will not quit this place.

Conundrums, or riddles based on puns or other wordplay, are popular among literate Nepalis. An example of a conundrum is *Bhandā cha, gandā sat ke ho?* (You say six, but when you count it is seven. What is it?) The answer is *cha* (six), the seventh consonant of the Devanagari script of the Nepali language.

A conundrum that is only one sentence long is also called *gāuṃ khāne kathā* (village-winning riddle), whereas a verse conundrum is called *kūṭpadya*. A *kūṭpadya* is thought to require more intellectual capacity and is more popular among educated Nepalis. One example is the following:

Kasale bigārcha bhana lohalāī?
Kasale bigārcha bujha lohalāī.

Tell me what [*kasa*] destroys iron?
Understand that rust [*kasa*] destroys iron.

Another conundrum, collected and translated by the author, is "How do you write *kapur* [camphor] with just one letter?" Answer: First write *ka* (the first consonant), and then *pur* (cover it).

Although the various subgeneric forms and functions of riddles have played a significant role in Nepali life, academicians have not recognized all of them. Most scholars recognize only *gāum khāne kathā* as a true riddle. Future studies of Nepali riddles promise to be a particularly fruitful area in Nepali folklore research and education.

References

Bhattarai, Harihar P. 1985. Folklore studies in Nepal. *Himalayan Culture* 3, no. 1: 10–14.

Pradhan, Kumar. 1984. *A history of Nepali literature*. New Delhi: Sahitya Akademi.

HARIHAR P. BHATTARAI

SEE ALSO
Silok; Tamāsá

RITUALS

See Ali; Ancestor Worship; Ankeliya; Aṇṇanmār Katai; Aravāṉ; Baithak; Bakshi; Bandara Cults; Baṅgāṇī Ball Games; Bāul Song; Bhagavati Ritual Traditions of Kerala; Bhakti; Bhakti Saints; Bhūta; Bhūta Kōla; Bow Song (Vil Pāṭṭu); Calendrical Ceremonies and Rites; *Cait Parab;* Circumcision; Daha-Aṭa-Sanniya; *Dārikavadham; Darśan; Dāsara; Dīvālī/Dīpāvalī;* Divination; *Dṛṣṭi;* Exorcism; Fairs and Festivals; Festival of Saint Francis; Firewalking, Sri Lanka; Games; Gavarī; God-Boxes, Painted; Gondhaḷa; Govindevji, Temple of; Gurav; Heroes and Heroines; Holī; Hook-swinging; Jallikkaṭṭu; Jārī Gān; Jātrā/Yātrā; Jhumur Jātrā Drama; *Kamsāle; Kohom̐ba Kankāriya; Kolam; Koṭahaḷuva Gedara;* Lament; Life Cycle Rituals; *Majlis;* Mancala; *Maṅgalkāvya;* Māriamma; Masks; Masks, Sri Lanka; *Melā; Muḥarram;* Muṭiyēṭṭu; Nāga; Naming Ceremonies; Navānna/Nabānna; *Navarātri; Oggu Katha; Ōṇam; Pāḍdana; Pāmpin Tuḷḷal; Pirit; Ponkal;* Processions; *Pūjā; Ratha Jātrā;* Sacred Places; Sacrifice; *Satī;* Satya Nārāyaṇa Vrat Kathā; Self-sacrifice; Shamanism, Islam; Shamanism, Nepal; Shrines, Hindu; Shrines, Muslim; Siri; Spirit Possession and Mediumship; Terukkūttu; *Teyyam; Tiruvātira; Vāghyā/Muraḷī; Vrat Kathā;* Water Lore; Wedding Songs; Witches and Sorcerers; Women's Songs; Worship.

ROCK PAINTINGS, INDIA

Prehistoric rock paintings are found in various parts of India, mostly in the provinces of Uttar Pradesh, Karnataka, Madhya Pradesh, Bihar, Orissa, Rajasthan, Kerala, and Andhra Pradesh. There are as many as thirty-six locations in these areas in which the picturesque rock paintings have been discovered. The main places retaining important rock paintings are Kāimur mountain range (Mirjapur in Uttar Pradesh), Vindhya Mountain range (Bhimbeṭkā), Mahādeo hill range, Charwardhan mountain range (Sinhanpur), Kabrā Ḍongar of the Rāigarh region, Panchamaḍhi mountain in Madhya Pradesh, Garjan Ḍongar (Sundargarh District), and Bikramkhol and Ushākoṭhi in Sambalpur District in Orissa. Rock paintings and engravings are also found in Maharashtra, Rāichur in Andhra Pradesh, Belāri in Kuppugālu hill range, Gotgiriletta hill (Bongalore) of Karnataka, and Edkālmāl hills in Kerala. In these rock paintings, food gathering, hunting, and food producing motifs are predominant.

The Kāimur pictures are primarily hunting scenes, for example, a bison hunt by a number of men armed with clubs and spears. The paintings also depict the gathering of flowers, fruit, and honey; hunters with spear and nets, and other men and women climbing a tree.

In Bhimbeṭkā hills, pictures of a furious boar attacking a man, a woman mourning for a deceased child, cow-boys gathering the cowherd, hunters running after the game, and half-clad hunters with masks on their faces are prominent. Also depicted are royal processions; warriors on elephants or horses; warriors with bows and arrows, spears, or swords; and a group of men interlocking their hands while dancing to the tune of music.

In Mahādeo mountain range, the paintings represent cowboys, men working in the field, a man playing with a bear and monkey, women playing and dancing with a harp, and women carrying water. These images reflect the activities of the neolithic culture of the prehistoric age.

The Gudhandi hills are situated in the district of Kalahandi in Orissa. Here pictographic paintings in red and black appear at the entrance of the cave. The paintings are decorated with drawings mostly of esoteric geometrical designs—squares, rectangles, and circles. The most fascinating painting is a hunting scene that depicts a hunter throwing a stone missile at a running deer. The missile strikes at the deer. The wounded deer casts a pathetic glance at the hunter turning its head toward him. The face of the man is beaming with joy and his curly hair dances, revealing his thrill at his success.

The paintings in the Jogimath Dongar near Khariar town in the Nawapara district in Orissa consist of domestic animals, a plow, a bullock, and the musical instrument *dambaru,* with some obscure lines representing pastoral scenes of the late Neolithic age.

The colors used in all these rock paintings are black, red, white, green, and gray. All the paintings date from the Paleolithic to the late Neolithic age.

References

Dash, Rabinarayan. 1987. *Pre-historic Art of Orissa.* In *RANGAREKHA* (Silver jubilee Publication) Orissa Lalit Kala Akademy Bhubaneswar, 51–66.

———. 1988. *Prageitihasika Bharatiya Chitrakala* (Prehistoric art of India). In *RANGAREKHA* (Oriya) Ed. Kanungo J. C. (Silver Jubilee Publication) Lalitkala Akademy, Bhubaneswar.

Ghosh, Rai Sahib Manoranjan. 1982. *Rock paintings and other antiquities of pre-historic and later times.* Patna Museum IB Corporation, Patna.

Pathy, D. N. 1984. Orissan paintings. In *Glimpses of Orissan art and culture,* Golden Jubilee volume of Orissa Historical Research journal (*OHRJ*) Vol. XXX Nos. 2, 3 & 4 Orissa State Museum, 149.

Sahu, N. K. 1974. Odia Jatra Itihasa (Oriya). *History of Orissa* Bhubaneswar, 28–29.

Singh Deo, J. P. 1976. Pre-historic cave paintings of Joginath Dongar *OHRJ* vol. XXII, no. 2, 21–22, Orissa.

MAHENDRA KUMAR MISHRA

SEE ALSO
Painting

ROMA (GYPSY)

Perhaps the South Asian population with the most direct effect upon Western folklore is the Romani people, commonly though inaccurately referred to in English as "Gypsies." Roma first appeared in Europe toward the end of the thirteenth century, their entry into the West being the result of Islamic expansion under the Ottoman Turks, in whose migration the Roma took part, either as a labor force or possibly as captives.

During the medieval period Christian Europe was being encroached upon on three sides by Muslim and non–Muslim Asians and North Africans; trade routes to the East were blocked, as was access to the Holy Land. The dark-skinned Roma were assumed to be a part of this threat, and from the beginning were given such exonyms (names applied to a group by outsiders) as "Saracen," "Turk," "heathen," "Egyptian," and so on. It is from the last name that the English misnomer "Gypsy" derives (as do the Spanish *gitano,* the French *gitan,* the Slavic *gjupci,* etc.).

Balkan populations came to realize early on that the Roma in fact were not Muslims or Turks or Egyptians; nor did they turn out to be Christians or Jews or Tatars. Their tendency to keep at a distance from non–Romani populations earned them the nickname *Atsingani,* Greek for "[the] don't touch [people]," from which a whole new set of exonyms was derived, the Slavic *cigan,* the German *Zigeuner,* and the Turkish *çingene* among them. The only name not used for them was the name they called themselves: *Roma,* a Sanskrit-derived word meaning "men." And though there was a proliferation of guesses as to the true identity of this population, it was not until the end of the eighteenth century that their Indian origin was recognized, through an examination of their ethnic language, Romani.

Once their Indian identity had been ascertained, scholars throughout the following century attempted to learn when and why an Indian people would have left their home to come to Europe, though their hypotheses were for the most part highly imaginative and Eurocentric. It was only in the twentieth century that historical and linguistic evidence provided more credible insight into Romani history.

On such evidence, one can posit that the exodus from India took place during the first half of the eleventh century, and that the ancestors of the Roma were a composite, non–Aryan population called Rājpūts who had been assembled in previous centuries and trained as a martial force to defend the northern borders of India. They were also assembled to resist a series of raids led by Mahmud of Ghazni (997–1027). The Rājpūts had been given warrior caste *Kśatriya* status, and were drawn principally from the Dravidian populations of northern India, such as the Lohars and the Gujjars. Other populations that contributed recruits were the Pratihara, originally from an area north of India, and possibly the Siddis or Habshis, Africans who served as mercenaries for both the Muslim and the Hindu armies. Today, the Rājpūts of Rajasthan recognize themselves as the descendants in India of those early warriors; the Roma are descended from those who left and moved West.

Though nearly a millennium has passed since the exodus from India, and the Roma have absorbed many other peoples during their dispersal, so that local Romani culture and physical type can differ considerably from place to place, there is much in *Romanipen* (the Romani way of life) that is clearly Indian. Most obvious is the language, which, although it has many dialects, has been preserved with remarkable tenacity to the present day, having over six million speakers (about half of the global Romani population). The basic structure and vocabulary of Romani are clearly of Indian origin, Hindi being the language most closely related to it. In addition to the language, the Romani worldview rests firmly on the perception of a universe that is divided into Roma and *gadjé* (everyone else). Furthermore, the Romani world is safe and clean, while the non–Romani world and everything in it are dangerous and defiling. Care must be taken in the preparation of food, in washing oneself and one's clothing, in male-female relationships, and above all in contact with non–Roma, which can ritually pollute. Indigenous Romani music retains the Indian or *bhairava* scale; internal disputes are settled at a tribunal similar to the Indian *panchayat*; possessions may be burned after death as in India, and the female deity *Kāliz* is still revered and remembered by name.

It would be a mistake to assume that all Romani populations exhibit the same degree of "Indianness," or that they are even aware of their Indian heritage. Mainly because of a lack of any resistance to it from Roma, since the mid-nineteenth century in the West a romanticized and exotic image of the "Gypsy" has grown that is quite different from the actual population. Most Roma are not nomadic, for example. Most do not live in wagons. Most do not tell fortunes. Most neither play a violin nor own a tambourine. Rather, Roma are members of their national governments, and are lawyers and professors and writers; Roma have their own representatives in the United Nations and the Council of Europe; a multivolume Romani-language encyclopedia is being compiled; and a Romani university is being considered for central Europe.

After about seven centuries in the West, Roma remain a people of Asian origin, speaking an Asian language through which they express an Asian point of view in interpreting the world around them. This, together with their status as a nonterritorial people, means that they are outsiders culturally and ideologically, as well as physically, wherever they live. Attempts to destroy the Roma in Europe have occurred since the sixteenth century, reaching a high point with Hitler's final solution of the Gypsy question and continuing to the present day in the new, ethnically divided Europe where Roma form a huge and growing refugee population.

Others were transported involuntarily to North, Central, and South America by various western European governments during the colonial period. The largest single Romani population in the Americas today is the Vlax (or Vlach) Roma, descended from the slaves liberated from the Romanian estates in the 1850s and 1860s. Including all groups, those of Romani descent number some one million in North America, and a similar number in South America. Vlax Roma, in particular, rigorously maintain their social separateness from the non–Romani population, engaging in traditional occupations such as stove repair, fortune-telling, and the trading of vehicles. Yet there are Vlax Roma who attend college and are represented in the mainstream professions, but who do not compromise their ethnic language and culture. Such individuals are beginning to interact with the non–Romani establishment, and to speak out against the anti–Gypsy sentiment that is increasing in the United States.

As politicians and scholars alike begin to recognize Roma as a "real" people, concern will grow for this several-million-strong population without a country or a government. But at present the long-term prospects for their survival and equal treatment, particularly in Europe, do not look encouraging.

References

Crowe, David, and John Kolsti, eds. 1989. *The Gypsies of eastern Europe*. Armonk, N.Y.: M. E. Sharpe.
Fraser, Angus. 1993. *The Gypsies*. Oxford: Blackwell.
Hancock, Ian. 1987. *The pariah syndrome: An account of Gypsy slavery and persecution*. Ann Arbor, Mich.: Karoma.
———. 1995. *A handbook of Vlax Romani*. Columbus, Ohio: Slavica.

IAN HANCOCK

SEE ALSO
Character Stereotypes; *Dom*

S

SACRED GEOGRAPHY

Sacred geography is an aspect of a people's cosmology, part of the way they see the world as ordered and significant. In South Asia this topic encompasses religious valuations of nature; ideas about the earthly locations of gods and goddesses; memories of the locations of events in the lives of saints, founders, and divine incarnations; notions of center and periphery, and ideas about directional orientation; notions of replication and microcosm; and ideas about the holiness of certain regions and territories.

The religious valuation of nature in South Asia focuses on mountains, rivers, and the wilderness. Mountains and rivers are not only the abodes of deities but also, in some cases, themselves divine. Mountains are most often associated with the god Śiva, by virtue of his ascetic nature and their appropriateness for asceticism and because their shape identifies them with the *liṅga,* the aniconic or phallic representation of Śiva. Rivers are most often goddesses, or the homes of goddesses. The sexual imagery is at its most explicit in the portrayal of Śiva as a male human with the Ganges (India's holiest river, worshipped as a goddess) as a small female figure entwined in his hair.

Other religious values are associated with forests and the wilderness. From within the settled agricultural village, these areas appear dangerous and frightening, the abode of tigers, serpents, hunters, and robbers. But forests and wilderness are also another preferred abode of ascetics and hermits and an important source of renewal of life in the village and kingdom. Trees in temple courtyards and elsewhere bring an element of wild nature into the settlement and are sometimes worshipped as deities or abodes of deities.

Gods are located at other places as well. In brahmanical temple religion, priests invoke the life (*prāṇa*) of the deity into an image that artisans have prepared to house it; the temple can therefore be located wherever its patron desires. In folk religion, by contrast, gods manifest themselves at particular spots in "self-formed" (*svayambhū*), unhewn rocks. People recognize the manifestation because the place is marked by a spontaneous flow of blood, by a cow lactating onto the ground, or by some other natural wonder.

In many cases, a particular place of worship of a deity is understood to be the locus of some event in the deity's life—the killing of a demon, for instance, or the deity's wedding. When a god (or, less often, a goddess) is understood to have descended to earth in human form (as an *avatāra*), a number of different spots are identified as loci of specific episodes in the avatāra's life story. The same is true of places associated with the lives and deaths of religious founders (whether divine or not), saints, and holy persons. Such places are particularly important in Buddhist, Jain, and Muslim religious geography, as well as in the religious geography of Hindu devotional (*bhakti*) and ascetic groups.

A more abstract kind of sacrality inheres in places that are viewed as the center of the world or of some part of it. In Southeast as well as South Asia, such places are sometimes seen as analogous to Mount Meru, the cosmic mountain at the center of the world in some versions of Sanskrit cosmology. Often a holy place will be surrounded by a sacred precinct, its *pañcakrośī,* the area within a radius of approximately ten miles of it; sometimes the periphery of such a sacred area will be marked by shrines of guardian deities in the four cardinal and four intermediate directions. The direction in which a temple or shrine faces is also often significant: east, for instance, toward the rising sun, for most temples of Śiva and many other gods; south, toward the realm of death, for less auspicious deities and some guardian figures. In paying honor to a deity, shrine, or city, one circumambulates it, keeping one's right side toward it.

Major holy places are often replicated elsewhere, and they frequently contain replicas of other holy places. The best example of this is Vārāṇasī (Banaras, Kāśī). This most holy city contains shrines of important gods from all over India and is itself replicated in many other cities and towns. Most frequently, it is holy places and rivers of North India with which other places and rivers are identified or connected. In addition to Kāśī, places that are particularly prominent in this respect include Prayāg (Allahabad), Gayā, and the Ganges river. The replication can take the form of a simple assertion of identity (a local place *is* Gayā, or it is the "Southern Gayā"); of an expression of the power of the local place in terms of the power of the distant, more famous place (the local place destroys as many sins as, or provides ten times as much merit as, Prayāg); of evidence of the physical connection of the local place to the more distant, more famous one (a lemon dropped into the Ganges comes out in the tank of a local temple far to the south); of a story indicating a god's preference for the local place (Śiva left Vārāṇasī and came to stay at the local place because he liked it better); and so on.

In some cases, it is not only individual places but whole areas that are viewed as holy. Such, for example, is the Braj area for devotees of Kṛṣṇa, who lived there, or the Godāvarī river valley for Mahānubhāvs, whose founder, Cakradhar, wandered there. In other cases, holy places are thought of and visited in sets: the twelve *jyotirliṅga*s ("liṅgas of Light"), for instance, spread throughout India, or the five or six holy places of the god Murukan in Tamil Nadu. By encouraging pilgrims to travel throughout the area in which they are scattered, by enabling the pilgrims to meet others from that area, and even by allowing people who do not travel to the places to *think* of the area as a whole, such sets of places can foster the development of regional or national consciousness.

References

Clothey, Fred W. 1972. Pilgrimage centers in the Tamil cultus of Murukan. *Journal of the American Academv of Religion* 40: 79–95.

Eck, Diana. 1982. *Banaras: city of light*. New York: Alfred A. Knopf.

Feldhaus, Anne. 1995. *Water and womanhood: religious meaninqs of rivers in Maharashtra*. New York: Oxford University Press.

Parry, Jonathan. 1994. *Death in Banaras*. Cambridge: Cambridge University Press.

ANNE FELDHAUS

SEE ALSO

Buddhist Sacred Geography, Sri Lanka; *Dargāh;* Fairs and Festivals; Goddesses, Place, and Identity in Nepal; *Melā;* Pilgrimage; Sacred Geography, Afghanistan; Sacred Places; Shrines; Water Lore; Worship; Ziyārat

SACRED GEOGRAPHY, AFGHANISTAN

The tradition of associating hallowed locations with the esteemed is widely manifest in Islamic Afghanistan, despite the fact that Islam does not encourage saint cults and numbers of Islamic societies actively suppress the veneration of shrines.

Sites all over Afghanistan are honored because of their linkage with events or personalities mentioned in the Qur'ān, with relics of the Prophet Muḥammad, or with eminent early Islamic heroes. A few may be exploited simply for commercial or political advantage, but typically, in addition to offering hope for sought-after boons, cures, or solace, sites connected with the renowned serve to bond individuals to their heritage and strengthen personal identities by adding significance to their immediate surroundings. Pilgrims to Chishmah-i Ḥayāt (Spring of Life) in Samangan Province, north of the Hindu Kush, hope to meet there the green-robed Khwaja Khiẕr, the only being who can show the way to the spring of eternal life. While Khwaja Khiẕr may roam the world to succor the lost and needy, many believe his abode is actually at this spring of northern Afghanistan. Those afflicted with boils visit Chismah-i Ayyūb, a shrine built over a hot spring in Balkh Province where Ayyūb (Job) is believed to have rested while journeying through Afghanistan.

Similarly, according to Surah 18 in the Qur'ān, certain Seekers of Truth were put to sleep in a cave by Allah to await the day of Revelation. Jordan and Iraq also claim the site of this cave, but the brotherhood at the Aṣḥāb al-Kahf (People of the Cave) near Maymanah in northern Faryab Province, reverently lead pilgrims to a cave where the Seekers and their faithful hound still slumber under shrouded mounds.

Paramount among the locations associated with such venerated figures or events are those honoring the life and miraculous exploits of 'Alī ibn Abi Ṭālib, cousin and son-in-law of the Prophet Muḥammad, fourth caliph of Sunni Islam (656–661 C.E.) and first legitimate imām in the Shī'a tradition. Ḥaẕrat 'Alī is revered for his role as an intermediary against tyranny.

Mazār-i Sharif (Noble Shrine), from which the capital city of Balkh Province in Northern Afghanistan takes its name, is a shrine held sacred as the tomb of Ḥaẕrat 'Alī, although many Sunni and Shī'a Muslims believe that after he was assassinated in 661 C.E., 'Alī was buried in Najaf, Iraq. According to Afghan legend, 'Alī was interred in Balkh because his followers, fearing desecration by his enemies, placed the body on the back of a white she-camel and allowed her to wander until she

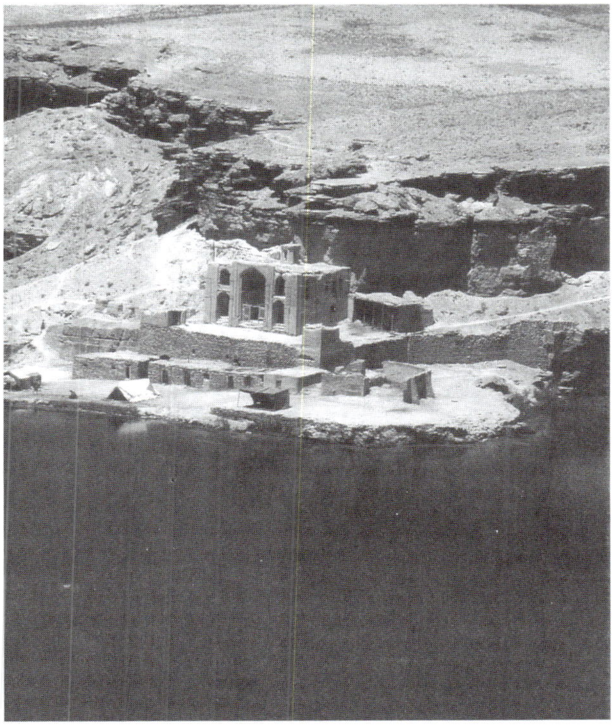

Band-l-Amir, Bamiyan Province, Afghanistan, 2000, © Karla Schefter

fell exhausted. On this spot the remains were buried, but all knowledge of it was lost until the twelfth century C.E.

The tradition recounting the rediscovery of the burial is recorded by Abu Hamīd al-Gharnati, an Andalusian visiting Balkh in 1153. In 530 H. / 1135–1136 C.E. the Prophet Muhammad revealed the site to several Balkh citizens in their dreams. Religious leaders at first discounted the revelations until ʻAlī himself appeared in the dreams of a noted jurist. The governor then opened the tomb and found the body in its shroud intact, next to an identifying inscription. The first magnificent shrine was built at this time.

Local lore credits Chingiz Khan with the destruction of this structure in 1220, but written sources are silent. Ibn Battuta in about 1333 described Balkh as "completely dilapidated and uninhabited." Oral and literary sources revive the story late in the fifteenth century C.E. In oral accounts the location of the tomb is again revealed through a dream, but the standard written account, Khwandmir's *Ḥabīb al-Siyār,* states that in 885 H. / 1480–1481 C.E. Shams al-Din Muhammad Bastami arrived in Balkh from Kabul carrying the work of al-Gharnati. Bastami and Balkh's governor opened a domed tomb described in the early work and there found an inscribed tablet corroborating the identification.

So great was the rejoicing when the Timurid ruler Sultan Husayn Bayqara (1468–1506) came from Herat to offer his respects and comission the construction of another splendid building. The form of this building survives today, albeit extensively reconstructed and redecorated. Afghanistan's most elaborate religious gathering is held here during the annual celebrations of the Gul-i Surkh (Red Blossom, a wild desert tulip) festival on Naw Ruz (New Year, 21 March).

Band-i Amīr (Dam of the Amir) is a chain of six lakes in the Hazarajat mountains of the Western Hindu Kush range in Bamiyan Province. The magical combination of sparkling sapphire-blue lakes nestled at the foot of sheer magenta-hued cliffs in a vast barren landscape calls for miraculous explanations. For the Hazāra people living in the region, the answer lies in the intercession of Ḥaẕrat ʻAlī.

The oral traditions describing the creation of the dams that separate the lakes center around Barbar, an irascible infidel king whose conduct became increasingly overbearing when the thousand slaves sent to dam a raging river consistently failed to contain the flood. Everywhere, the people suffered great hardship because of the king's frustration. One victim in desperate need of money to release his unjustly imprisoned wife and children sought the aid of Ḥaẕrat ʻAlī, who instructed the young man to offer him as a slave to the king without revealing his identity. Barbar agreed to the purchase on condition that the slave build the dam he so desired. Ḥaẕrat ʻAlī strode over the mountain and with a colossal kick brought down masses of rock to form Band-i Haībat (Dam of Awe). With a mighty stroke of his sword, he sliced off another huge hunk for Band-i Ẕulfiqār (Dam of the Sword of ʻAlī) and uprooted bushes in great number to shape Band-i Pudinah (Dam of Mint).

Meanwhile, ʻAlī's groom assisted his master by constructing Band-i Qambar (Dam of the Groom) and the thousand slaves who had labored so long in vain were amazed to find Band-i Ghulamān (Dam of the Slaves) completed. As a token of esteem, a passing nomad woman offered the miracle worker a round of fresh cheese, which Ḥaẕrat ʻAlī placed in the river to form Band-i Panīr (Dam of Cheese). Finally, in order that villagers down river might not suffer, ʻAlī drew his fingers across Band-i Ḥaībat to create channels for the river to flow through to irrigate the fields. His work done, Ḥaẕrat ʻAlī revealed his true identity to the king, who was so overcome he immediately embraced Islam.

Darra-yi Azhdahār (The Valley of the Dragon) is a small valley five miles west of Bamiyan, the capital of Bamiyan Province. The valley is sacred because of its association with another miraculous victory that continues Ḥaẕrat ʻAlī's feats undertaken at Band-i Amīr, some forty miles to the northwest.

According to legend, this narrow, barren valley was once the residence of a dragon who roamed the countryside, breathing fire and devouring all that passed his way. Noting the distress of his subjects, the king of the region promised to provide the dragon one beautiful damsel, two live camels, and six hundred pounds of other foodstuffs every single day. In return, the dragon agreed to remain within his valley. Once this bargain was struck, peace reigned throughout the kingdom.

Many years later, the duty of giving up a daughter fell to the lot of an old woman whose ravishingly beautiful daughter was all she had in life. Hand in hand, they proceeded to the mouth of the dragon's lair where their bitter sobs awoke a young man who sprang to the maiden's defense as the dragon emerged. Tulips fell to the ground from his sword as he delivered the fatal blow, splitting the dragon down its entire length. To this day, the body blocks of western exit of the valley. Recognizing that their deliverer could be none other than Ḥaẓrat ʻAlī, the king and his subjects came bearing gifts, only to find that their hero had been spirited away on the back of his faithful horse Duldul. Some eighty miles due south of here an even more realistic rock formation represents the dragon's baby, similarly dispatched by the Ḥaẓrat. Scores of pilgrims picnic at both these shrines in the spring.

Aside from the New Year festivities held at Mazār-i Sharīf, the only other formally organized fair takes place, also on Naw Roz, in the capital city of Kabul at the Ziyārat-i Sakhī (Shrine of the Generous One, another title bestowed upon Ḥaẓrat ʻAlī). It commemorates the time in 1768 when Ḥaẓrat ʻAlī came to pay his respects to the Cloak of the Prophet, which had been placed for a few days in a natural basin on the hillside. The cloak had been obtained by Ahmad Shah Durrani (1747–1772) from the Amīr of Bukhara as part of a treaty settling the northern boundaries. It is now enshrined at Kandahar in the lavishly adorned Da Khirqah-i Sharīf Ziyārat, one of the holiest shrines in Afghanistan.

Most shrines in Afghanistan are, however, simple, even humble, constructions cared for by single custodians. Afghans characteristically dislike ostentation in any form. The most elaborate ritual conducted at Mazār-i Sharīf and at Ziyārat-i Sakhī in Kabul is the raising of the heavy pole carrying the Jandah (Banner) symbolizing the renaissance of spring, the blossoming of renewed hopes with the coming of a new year. Elsewhere, religious occasions eschew set ceremonial performances and are most popularly celebrated with family outings, picnics, new clothes, culinary specialties, and games, plus much spirited socializing among family and friends.

References

Dunn, Ross E. 1986. *The adventures of Ibn Battuta: a Muslim traveler of the 14th century*. London: Croom Helm.

Dupree, Louis. 1976. Saint cults in Afghanistan. *American Universities Field Staff Reports,* South Asia Series (Afghanistan) 20: 1. Hanover, N.H.: American Universities Field Staff.

———. 1978. The role of folklore in modern Afghanistan: Silas Marner revisited. *American Universities Field Staff Reports,* Asia 46. Hanover, N.H.: American Universities Field Staff.

Dupree, Nancy Hatch. 1967. *The valley of Bamiyan*. Kabul: Afghan Tourist Organization.

———. 1977. *A historical guide to Afghanistan*. Kabul: Afghan Tourist Organization.

Hakin, R. and A. A. Kohzad. 1953. *Legendes et Coutumes Afghanes*. Paris: Imprimerie Nationale, Presses Universitaires de France.

McChesney, Robert D. 1991. *Waqf in central Asia: four hundred years in the history of Muslim shrine,* 1480–1889, Princeton: Princeton University Press.

Safa, A. Ghafoor. 1999. *The tomb of Hazrat-e Ali: historical background and recent events*. Peshawar: Society for the Preservation of Afghanistan's Cultural Heritage.

Shank, Christopher C. and John Y. Larsen. 1977. *A strategy for the establishment and development of Bande Amir National Park*. Kabul: FO: DP/AFG/74/016 Field Document 38, UNDP/FAO/Ministry of Agriculture.

NANCY HATCH DUPREE

SEE ALSO
Afghanistan; ʻAlī; Dreams; Islam; Muslim Folklore

SACRED PLACES

The idea and institution of sacred places is one of the most complex and powerful expressions of religion in South Asia. The traditional Sanskrit term for sacred place is *tīrtha,* a word etymologically derived from the verbal root *tṝ* (to cross over). There are a number of words connected to tīrtha via the root *tṝ* that mean "raft," "boat," "wave," "escape," "cross a river," "be saved," etc. All these meanings point collectively to the idea of a sacred place being a ford or crossing, at which an individual undergoes a spiritual transformation. The tīrtha also is conceptualized as a doorway connecting the world of the gods and the world of humans. Given the strong metaphoric use of images of rivers and crossings, tīrthas are, in fact, in many cases located near flowing water. Beyond that, they are associated with other natural objects such as mountains (Arunacala in South India), lakes (Manasarovar in Tibet), or stretches of land (Kuruksetra in North India).

The power to transform and heal is thus primarily connected to specific places. The specificity of place has led to tīrthas being described as the "locative strand" of Hinduism (Eck 1980). In fact, in historical terms, the association of a sacred place with a particular deity, his or her mythology, rituals, and worship can be considered to be a secondary development. Tīrthas today, however, are inextricably linked to narratives and worship centering around gods and goddesses. Depending upon which deity dominates, tīrthas are usually classified as being either Śaivite or Vaiṣṇavite. Those associated with manifestations of Devi are called *Śākta pīṭha*s and are connected to various bodily parts of Śiva's consort, Sati. The most important of the śākta pīṭhas are Kamakhya (Assam), Kalighat (Calcutta), and Jvalamukhi (Himachal Pradesh). Examples of important Śaiva tīrthas are Kasi (Benares) and Cidambaram (Tamilnadu). Mathura (Madhya Pradesh) and Vrindavan (Gujarat) are examples of Vaiṣṇava tīrthas, where Kṛṣṇa, an incarnation of Viṣṇu, is worshipped.

A further indigenous classification of tīrthas is found in the *Brahmapurāṇa* in which tīrthas are ranked according to their origins. Thus, those that were created through the deeds of gods (*daiva tīrtha*s) are considered to be the highest of all. After them follow the *āsura tīrtha*s (created in connection with anti-gods), the *ārṣa tīrtha*s (created through the deeds of seers and holy men), and *mānuṣa tīrtha*s (created by mortals such as kings).

Another distinction can be drawn between pan-Indian, regional, and local tīrthas. Although these types tend to differ, for example, in their construction of ritual space and time, in the class of ritual specialists, in ritual offerings, mythology, and devotees, they do, as a whole, form a crucial network for the dissemination of cultural and religious ideas within South Asia. In fact, certain pan-Indian sacred places, such as Kasi, Puskara (where Brahmā is worshipped), and Cidambaram, are major centers of the merger of religious symbols such as temples, forms of worship, religious narratives, and renunciatory groups. Alongside their religious significance, sacred places have also continuously formed the focus of political interest of kings and dynasties.

The sacred place or a pilgrimage to a sacred place is considered to be a viable alternative to the performance of Vedic rituals (*yajña*). Already in texts such as the *Mahābhārata* (composed between 400 B.C.E–400 C.E.) we are told that a "visitation to the sacred fords" is the path ordinary folk can take in order to gain religious merit. This line of praise is taken up in many subsequent purāṇic texts. Notwithstanding the replacement of the yajña through the tīrtha, both remain connected in conceptually important ways. Thus, for example, the *tīrtha-phala* (fruit of action at a sacred place) is measured in terms of the merit generated by different kinds or even multiple yajñas. Sometimes, the origins of a sacred place are explained in terms of a yajña performed at that place by a deity, most often Prajāpati or Brahmā. Thus, the five pilgrimage centers of Kuruksetra, Prayaga, Gaya, Puskara, and Viraja are considered to be Brahmā's five *vedī*s (sacrificial pits).

The main rituals associated with pan-Indian tīrthas are *snāna* (ritual bathing), *dāna* (ritual offering), *pradakṣiṇa* (ritual circumambulation of the sacred space), *darśana* (seeing the divine), *prasāda* (receiving offerings from the deity), *tapas* (ascetic practice), *vrata* (religious vow or observance), *pitṛ-tarpaṇa* (satisfying the ancestors), and *śrāddha* (rites for the deceased). At many sacred places, a festival (*melā*) is held on astrologically determined dates. These periods are considered particularly auspicious, attracting hundreds of thousands of pilgrims.

References

Bhardwaj, S. M. 1973. *Hindu places of pilgrimage in India.* Berkeley: University of California Press.

Eck, D. L. 1980. India's *Tīrthas*: "crossings" in sacred geography. *History of Religions* 20: 323–343.

Ensink, J. 1974. Problems of the study of pilgrimage in India. *Indologica Taurenensia* 2: 57–79.

Kulke, Hermann. 1970. *Cidambaramāhātmya.* Wiesbaden: Otto Harrassowitz.

Turner, Victor. 1973. The center out there: pilgrims' goal. *History of Religions* 12: 191–230.

Aditya Malik

SEE ALSO

Darśan; Fairs and Festivals; Gods and Goddesses; *Mēla;* Pilgrimage; Sacred Geography

SACRIFICE

In South Asian contexts, sacrifice is discussed primarily in relation to the Sanskrit term *yajña* and its vernacular derivatives, from the root *yaj* (to offer). However, the pre-Vedic Indus Valley religion probably also practiced sacrifices connected with goddess worship, and sacrificial practices are found in South Asian tribal religions and Islam and Christianity as well.

Vedic Sacrifice

The Ṛg Vedic Puruṣa hymn tells how the universe with all its hierarchies and correspondences was created by dismembering Puruṣa (primordial "Man"), whose form thereby enters all parts and whose essence yet transcends the whole. Man, created in four classes, becomes the exemplary animal victim, since he alone can both sacrifice and be sacrificed. The four other suitable victims (horse, bull, ram, he-goat), substitutes for man, are classified among domesticated village animals, but man is "of the forest." Other substances (*dravya*) suitable for sacrifice include the divine soma plant, grain and milk products, and speech (recited Vedic *mantras*). Man is the measure of sacrifice; the sacrificial stake (*yūpa*) is measured by the sacrificer's (*yajamāna*'s) height.

Vedic sacrifice has two aspects: *śrauta,* "connected with *śruti*" (Vedic revelation), and *gṛhya,* "domestic" and based on *smṛti* (tradition). Gṛhya sacrifice requires one fire, śrauta three. Animal sacrifices are included in both types. The śrauta prototype was the goat sacrifice and the royal horse sacrifice. Typical domestic animal sacrifices were hospitality rites, and a controversial one, performed yearly in autumn or spring, was a "spit ox" (*śūlagāva*) offered to Rudra, northeast of the village. The gṛhya fire, brought from the bride's home to the couple's new household, should be tended for family ceremonies (*saṃskāras*) through to the "final sacrifice" of the husband's cremation. Householders must also perform five daily "great sacrifices" (*mahāyajñas*): to brahman (offering sacred words or mantra), ancestors, gods, other "beings," and humans (hospitality rites).

Entitlement to perform either type of sacrifice is open only to married "twice-born" men: Brahmans, Kṣatriyas, Vaiśyas. Householders can perform gṛhya rites themselves or hire a domestic priest. Śrauta rites require specialized Vedic priests, who conduct sacrifice to fulfill a desire of the *yajamāna* who engages them. The yajamāna and his wife alone reap the benefit: food, cows, sons, victory, and, ultimately, heaven. Contests may be arranged so the yajamāna wins, with rivals often represented by his priests or a relative. Sacrificial implements are regularly compared with weapons. Magical rites (*abhicāra*) are designed to harm or kill a rival.

Sacrifice in Classical Hinduism and Folk Religion

Aside from a school of ritual exegesis (*Mīmāṃsa*), post-Vedic traditions designate yajña as the religious virtue of the bygone previous age to our "age of discord" (*kali yuga*), which is characterized by "giving." Purāṇic texts say the twice-born no longer perform sacrifice, leaving it to Śūdras and others of low birth. But sacrificial concerns and imagery pervade the lawbooks, epics (including the *Bhagavad Gītā*), *purāṇas*, *āgamas*, and many hagiographies. The folklore of saints continues to be full of sacrificial tales, not only in Hindu but Muslim and Christian circles. South Asian folk religion retains elements of Vedic sacrifice, most obviously audial (mantra) and visual ones. Although Vedic sacrifice was mobile, without permanent structures, and aniconic, its geometric shapes and principles are reconfigured in popular ritual forms (such as altars and posts) and temple design. Vedic gṛhya ceremonies—especially marriage and funerary ones—not only continue, but have been transformed in non-twice-born circles, with great regional, community, and even tribal variations.

More controversially, features of śrauta ritual may continue in festivals. Vows taken for folk deities—self-impalement with needles, hook swinging, fire walking, and other forms of self-mortification—are self- offerings, and raise the question of continuities with Vedic weapons, posts, and fires. Goddess worship, with blood sacrifice and victim beheading, characteristic of medieval royal Dasarā sacrifices and village buffalo and goat sacrifices, may redefine aspects of Vedic royal sacrifices around new understandings of the relation between king, territory, community, and goddess. Similar sacrificial themes are found in South Asian Muslim and Christian folklores of martyrdom, and especially in Muslim Muḥarram ceremonies.

Reconstructions of a presystematized Vedic sacrifice compete with explanations by diffusion from non-Vedic sources (both from beyond and within South Asia) to account for features of buffalo sacrifices, the victim's beheading at the sacrificial stake, revivals of the victim, agonistic opposition between double sacrificers, the sacrificial practices of warrior bands (initially, post-Ṛg Vedic *Vrātyas*), and the relation between sacrificial violence and social instability. One thus hears arguments, for instance, that buffalo sacrifices at Dasarā are transformations of the Vedic horse sacrifice and explanations that they derive from a Dravidian substratum. Similarly, Vedic, Dravidian, and tribal prototypes are sought for highly specialized medieval forms of sacrifice (including self-sacrifice) to Śiva and the goddess by such violent means as dismemberment, beheading, and impalement.

References

Bayly, Susan. 1989. *Saints, goddesses and kings: Muslims and Christians in South Indian society 1700–1900*. Cambridge: Cambridge University Press.

Biardeau, Madeleine. 1989. *Histoires de poteaux: variations védiaues autour de la déesse Hindoue*. Paris: École Française d'Extrême Orient.

Heesterman, J. C. 1993. *The broken world of sacrifice: an essay in ancient Indian ritual*. Chicago: University of Chicago Press.

Hiltebeitel, Alf. 1991. *The cult of Draupadi,* Vol. 2. *On Hindu Ritual and the Goddess*. Chicago: University of Chicago Press.

Shulman, David Dean. 1980. *Tamil temple myths: sacrifice and divine marriage in South Indian Śaiva tradition*. Princeton: Princeton University Press.

Alf Hiltebeitel

SEE ALSO
Buffalo; Circumcision; *Dāsara;* Goddesses, Hindu; Gods and Goddesses; Hook-swinging; *Muḥarram; Śamī;* Self-sacrifice

SADHU

Commonly translated as "holy man" or "ascetic," the term *sadhu* lumps together men initiated into any one of the myriad Hindu sects dedicated to spiritual pursuits. (The less common female sadhus are called *sadhvis*). A sadhu's identity is defined by opposition to the householder (*grahastha*). A sadhu is ideally celibate, possessionless, has no blood ties or settled abode, and does not work for wages. Living off alms, by renouncing worldly pleasures and attachments he pursues release from the cycle of death and rebirth. However, departures from these ideals are common, and the degree of accepted variation may differ between sects.

As persons of spiritual power, in folklore sadhus often figure as donors granting boons. They may also be portrayed as fakes capitalizing on the role. Sadhus help spread folklore by drawing on oral traditions to instruct disciples, and by wandering between regions.

Sadhu; Karnataka, India, © Mimi Nichter

References

Bloomfield, Maurice. 1924. On false ascetics and nuns in Hindu fiction. *Journal of the American Oriental Society* 44: 202–42

Gold, Ann. 1993. *A carnival of parting. The tales of King Bharthari and King Gopi Chand as sung and told by Madhu Natisar Nath of Ghatiyali, Rajasthan*. Berkeley: University of California Press.

Narayan, Kirin. 1989. *Storytellers, saints, and scoundrels: folk narrative in Hindu religious teaching*. Philadelphia: University of Pennsylvania Press.

KIRIN NARAYAN

SEE ALSO
Malang; Qalandar

SAINTS

Saints (termed *Ṣūfī, pīr,* or *walī* by Muslims; guru, *sānt,* swami, and *yogī* by Hindus; Buddha and bodhisattva by Buddhists; guru or *sānt* by Sikhs) play a key role in South Asian folk religious practices. Although the terminology, attributes, and contexts of saintship differ among major religious groups, there is much in common.

Saints are popularly thought to possess more spiritual power than ordinary human beings. Among Muslims, for example, this power, or *barkat,* has its source in the human spirit, or *rūḥ,* created by Allah. Among Hindus power, or *Śaktī* (shakti), arises from the particular biomoral nature (*dhātu-dharma*) of the person. In either case this power is thought to be an ethereal force concentrated in the person of the saint; it may be deliberately focused for specific purposes, and it gives the saint the ability to accomplish extraordinary deeds or miracles.

In South Asia saints have generally been male, but there are occasional female saints. People are recognized as saints while alive, but their power often continues beyond their death in their successors, or adheres to objects, relics, and places closely associated with them. Saintship is recognized by followers, who may be formally initiated though rituals that suggest birth and make the saint their spiritual father. Some saints claim only a handful of followers. Others, like Pīr Pagaro in Pakistan, claim millions. Followers generally describe themselves as being touched by the saint's gaze (*naẓar* among Muslims) or bathed in the saint's sight (*darśan* among Hindus), and they are often given a new name, and sometimes a meditative phrase or formula.

The spiritual power of the saint generally distinguishes him from other good teachers, religious functionaries, or exemplary leaders. The power effects transformations—curing illness, calming natural disaster, relieving human misery, prompting new insight and understanding. Saints are renowned for countering the effects of mischievous spirits such as *jinn,* malevolent deities, ghosts, and ghouls. Both hagiographic and contemporary legends abound of saints competing against each other, performing superhuman feats. The Baloch, for example, tell of one pīr who stopped a bullet; another pīr, to prove himself more powerful, supposedly then stopped a train.

Some saints are highly regarded for the social development of groups and communities. For example, Kabir (1440–1518), a medieval Indian saint, elevated the dignity of his own caste of weavers by drawing out the metaphorical mystical significance of their artistry. Other saints may be highly regarded for their civilizing influence in opening up barren or inhospitable lands for cultivation and settlement. For example, the Muslim saints of the Sundarbans, a swampy mangrove region of Bengal, are reputed to have had uncanny knowledge of the dangerous tigers, and how settlers could avoid them.

Saints in South Asia are renowned for converting populations to new forms of religious practice. They spread Buddhism across the subcontinent during the reign of Aśoka (d. 232 B.C.E.). Muslim saints converted Buddhists, artisans, and lower caste Hindus to Islam largely after 1000 C.E. Saintly teachers and mystics advocating devotional reformations of Hinduism (bhakti) led popular movements that changed mass religious practice in India from the eleventh through the sixteenth centuries.

In South Asia, except for the Roman Catholic Church, saints are not canonized. There are no formal, bureaucratic, hierarchical, or centralized corporate religious institutions to recognize sainthood. Saints are recognized and accepted by followers; their sainthood may be, and often is, disputed by others.

South Asian traditions of sainthood are manifested in Mahayana Buddhism, Tamil Saivism, Hindu bhakti, Ṣūfism, Sikhism, and Indian Catholicism. Generally the personal veneration of the saint is thought to be a vehicle for the spiritual satisfaction of the follower. Saints are typically more concerned with the spiritual life of their followers than with explicating and enforcing the formal rules, dogma, and congregational practices of a religion. Indeed, in some cases, saints are regarded by priestly and scholarly authorities as hindering the teaching of the more formal written, legal, and normative practices of religion. The tension between saints and such religious authorities as Hindu Brahman priests and Muslim *'ulamā'* (teacher-scholars) is a common theme in South Asian religious life. So is the conflict and competition between between saints, as powerful holy men, and kings, emperors, and local rulers.

The distinctive appeal of saints to the populace is founded upon the concept of spiritual power as immanent and accessible, rather than as transcendent and unobtainable. Saints have the ability to tap and direct spiritual power so that it can be personally experienced in physical, mental, and emotional ways. This ability comes through personal, mystical, devotional experience—meditation, physical trials and discipline, devotional singing, ecstatic dancing, ingestion of empowered substances, chanting of *mantra* and *ẕikr* (devotional formulas in Hindu and Muslim traditions, respectively)—under the guidance of or through the mediation of a saint. If these practices are successful, the person becomes a vehicle for the power, a channel through which it may suffuse others.

Beyond that the person may become united with the power—attaining *nirvāṇa* (nirvana) in Buddhist terms, *mokśa* or release in Hindu terms, or *fanā* (dissolution) in Ṣūfī terms—after death. Saints may achieve the merging of individuated existence with a larger universal whole. This merging, variously characterized in different religious traditions as blissful joy, sexual-type ecstasy, or pure serenity, may itself be celebrated. *Murīd*s (followers of Muslim pīrs), for example, annually celebrate the *'urs* (union; literally, wedding) of the saint with Allah.

Saints aid others in the achievement of this merging and of intermediate goals. In ancient Buddhist tradition, bodhisattva and their wives postpone their own achievement of nirvāṇa in order to perform acts of mercy and kindness so that others may attain enlightenment. Guru and pīr dutifully help their followers, as spiritual offspring, to connect with this power.

While sociologists might regard the power of the saint as "charismatic," an abstract suasive power over behavior, South Asians, and indeed others, tend to act as though saintly power is materially instantiated. Power is transmitted from the eye of the saint to the countenance of the follower through active gazes, sightings, and visual blessings (*darśan* among Hindus, *naẓar* among Muslims). Devotees acquire doses of saintly power through physical contact—touching the body, a relic, or (for Muslims) the grave of a saint—listening to the saint's words, drinking his leftover water, eating his leftover food, and breathing his exhaled air. Devotees have to be in a clear state to receive these doses of power. Some devotees go to extraordinary lengths to receive the power of their saint, including drinking the bathwater of a guru, eating the dirt from the grave of a Ṣūfī pīr, and listening to the toilet noises of a sānt.

Much of this behavior occurs at Hindu pilgrimage and holy sites, Ṣūfī shrines, and ancient (relic-holding)

Buddhist stūpas. Hindus may take *prasād,* or spiritually infused food, from holy men in order to perfect their own state. At the *mazār* (shrines) of physically deceased (but spiritually living) Ṣūfī saints, tabarak—sweets that have acquired the blessedness of the saint through physical contact with his grave—are distributed to visitors. Once tabarak are ingested, visitors acquire some of the blessedness, which can affect a variety of life circumstances. Large numbers of South Asians visit saints and saintly sites daily, weekly, and annually.

Yearly festivals and fairs (*melā*) are held at sites of saintly achievement and interment, to commemorate the feats of saints. These attract large numbers of people to access and share in the power of the saint. Some hope that the saint's power will cure their child's illness. Others hope the power will enable them to win a lottery, give birth to a son, do well in school, win an election, find a wife or husband. Still others come to fulfill a vow resulting from a previous efficacious exercise of saintly power.

In South Asia, where earthly power is often restricted on the basis of birth, gender, and wealth, access to spiritual power through saints is exceedingly broad. The immanence of power and its dissemination make saints a broad, populist, egalitarian force in South Asia. Sainthood has promoted the decentralization of religion, its local ownership and development, a diversity of belief, and the formation of groups that cut across caste, status, and rural/urban categories of identity.

Saint–follower relationships are largely dyadic. There are some institutions based on these relationships—the *āśram* (retreat) of guru, the *waqf* and *dargāh* (shrines, property, and headquarters) of pīr, for example. Saints may form chains of succession. Among Ṣūfī, for example, *tarīqa* or orders, such as the Chishtiyah, Suhrawardi, Firdausi, and Naqsbandi, have a long history. Hindu families, and occupational and caste groups, may have long associations with particular successions of holy men. Yet, for the most part, saintly institutions are numerous, particularized, nonhierarchical, and decentralized. Such institutions have mitigated confederation, elaborate organization, and broad authoritative control, leaving the emphasis upon the power and accomplishments of the individual saint.

While most saints are identified with a particular major religion, there are many exceptions at the level of local religious practice, particularly before the partition of the subcontinent. Notable saints sometimes blurred the lines between Hinduism, Buddhism, and Islam among the general populace. In sixteenth-century Punjab, for example, Guru Nanak (c. 1469–c. 1538) articulated a synthesis of Hindu and Muslim religious elements that developed into Sikhism. A popular saying refers to Nanak as "A guru to Hindus, a pīr to Muslims." Modern-day saints also have been ecumenical, seeking adherents from beyond South Asia. Maharishi Mahesh Yogī, A. C. Swami Bhaktivedanta, and Sānt Kirpal Singh are widely known in the United States and Europe through transcendental meditation, Krishna Consciousness, and other forms of spiritual practice.

References

Ahmed, Imtiaz. 1985. *Ritual and religion among Muslims of the sub-continent.* Lahore: Vanguard.

Bharati, Agehananda. 1962. *The ochre robe.* Seattle: University of Washington Press.

Contributions to Indian sociology (new series). 1989. Special issue, *Toward an ethnosociology of India* 23 (1).

Metcalf, Barbara D., ed. 1984. *Moral conduct and authority: the place of adab in South Asian Islam.* Berkeley: University of California Press.

Schimmel, Annemarie. 1975. *Mystical dimensions of Islam.* Chapel Hill: University of North Carolina Press.

RICHARD KURIN

SEE ALSO

'Alī; Bhakti Saints; Buddhism and Buddhist Folklore; *Darśan;* Fāṭima; Festival of St. Francis; Gūrū Nanak, Life Stories of; Imām Ḥusayn; Jain Folklore; Jewish Folklore; *Jinn; Mādēśvara* Epic; *Melā; Pīr;* Sikhism; Ṣūfī Folk Poetry; *'Urs*

SAINTS, CHRISTIAN, KERALA

Reflecting past and present West Asian ecclesial ties, Portuguese and British colonial influence, and contemporary Vatican relations, Kerala Christian saint devotion offers valuable insight into the domestic management of a many-layered foreign presence in southwest India.

The earliest "saint cults"—in actuality the veneration of hero-bishops—emerged from posthumous devotion to Chaldean and, later, Antiochene bishops who visited Kerala from these foreign ecclesiastical centers. Definitive evidence of Syrian Christianity in Kerala can be traced back to the fourth century C.E., although the tradition marks its beginnings with the apostle Thomas and his first-century C.E. mission to south India. Claiming hereditary ties to clergy appointed by St. Thomas, Malayali Syrian Christian archdeacons controlled hero-bishops' grave-shrines as a means of maintaining priestly authority from at least the twelfth century (although probably earlier) through the nineteenth century. A 1947 Orthodox synod, comprised jointly of Jacobite and Orthodox Syrian branches, officially canonized two of these foreign prelates, Elias III (d. 1585) and Baselius Yeldo (d. 1932), along with a Malayali bishop, Gregorios of Parumala (1848–1902). Reflecting a contemporary split in Kerala's Syrian

Festival image of Sr. Alphonsa before annual feast day procession. Bharananganam, Kerala, India, © Corinne Dempsey

Church, devotion to the two foreign bishop-saints is greater among the Antioch-based Jacobite denomination; the preferred saint for Kerala-based Orthodox Syrians is St. Gregorios.

Within Roman Catholicism, Eastern rite Malabar Catholics (a faction within Syrian Christianity resulting from sixteenth-century Portuguese missionary activity) are promoting seven Malayali candidates for canonization. The Vatican has beatified three of them, so that they are one step removed from sainthood. Among the contenders the cult of Blessed Alphonsa of Bharananganam (1910–1946), a Clarist nun, has the widest appeal. While Sister Alphonsa's reputation as a posthumous miracle worker is key to her popularity, she is also known for her lifelong endurance of excruciating pain, both physical and emotional. Her heroic suffering fits squarely within the parameters of (European) Christian sainthood, particularly for women, yet details of her story also echo themes found in the lives of Indian holy women. Most strikingly, Alphonsa's tale enacts the South Asian folk-heroine theme of self-immolation: She deliberately burned herself in her family's ash pit. Her resulting disfigurement rendered Alphonsa unmarriageble, thus clearing the way for life in the convent.

The non-Syrian, or Latin, contingent of Kerala's Catholic community, largely made up of low-caste Hindu converts, has little of the political and economic clout necessary to support campaigns for its own Malayali saints. Nonetheless, practices at shrines honoring European saints belonging to both Latin and Syrian rite Catholics reflect devotees' domestication and reinterpretation of these imported cults. For instance, saints' festivals usually integrate a number of South Indian practices, such as the use of decorated umbrellas (*muttukuṭa*) and Hindu drumming (*ceṇdamēḷam*) during procession ceremonies. Devotees also assign the more popularly invoked "European" saints particular efficacies and vow practices, largely agreed upon throughout the state. For instance, St. Sebastian has been known to cure smallpox and, more recently, other infectious diseases. His designated vow is the circumambulation of a church or shrine while carrying a small arrow on a plate.

Of considerable significance to Kerala Catholics, as well as to other non–Protestant denominations (including Hindus), is the cult of St. George, patron of Portugal and Britain, likely brought to Kerala by Syrian merchants as early as the fourth century C.E. In spite of this complex foreign legacy, devotees invoke St. George—iconographically depicted as riding a white horse and thrusting his spear into a dragon's mouth—for protection against an indigenous threat: poisonous snakes. At major centers of St. George devotion scattered throughout Kerala, roosters are the commonly designated vow offering. Rooster sacrifice was once an integral part of festival ceremonies, but church officials currently sell the fowl through festival auctions. In spite of the Vatican's demotion of St. George's cult status during the 1960s (George's local veneration was condoned while he was deprived of a place on any official calendar), the cult continues to be one of the most vibrant throughout Kerala.

References

Bayly, Susan. 1989. *Saints, goddesses and kings: Muslims and Christians in south Indian society 1700–1900*. Cambridge: Cambridge University Press.

Chacko, K. C. 1990. *Sister Alphonsa*. Bharananganam, Kerala: The Vice Postulator, Cause of the Blessed Alphonsa.

Dempsey, Corinne. 2001. *Kerala Christian sainthood: collisions of culture and worldview in south India*. New York: Oxford University Press.

———. 2002. Lessons in miracles: three 'Christian' saints in Kerala, South India. *Popular Christianity in India: riting between the lines,* eds. Selva Raj and Corinne Dempsey. Albany, N.Y.: Suny Press.

Neill, Stephen. 1984. *A history of Christianity in India*. Vol. 1, *The beginnings to AD 1707*. London: Cambridge University Press.

———. 1985. *A history of Christianity in India*. Vol. 2, 1707–1858. London: Cambridge University Press.

CORINNE G. DEMPSEY

SEE ALSO

Festival of St. Francis

ŚĀKTA SONG

In Bengali devotional *Śākta* songs known as *Śāktapadābalī,* the Goddess or *Śakti* (female power) is conceived of as the supreme divinity. Rāmprasād Sen (ca. 1718–1775), considered the best of the Śākta poets, is credited with introducing the genre. Śākta songs are composed, for the most part, in simple, colloquial Bengali. They have end rhymes, and generally conclude in a signature line (*bhaṇitā*).

The first of two types concerns the myth of the Goddess Umā, the young daughter of the poverty-stricken king of the Himalayas, Giribar, and his wife, Menakā. Umā is married to the God Śiva, who is an old, grisly drug addict. Once a year, during *Durgā Pūjā* (the ten-day autumn festival), she is said to visit her parents for three days. The songs known as *āgamanī* (welcome) celebrate the Goddess's homecoming, and those known as *bijayā* (literally, "victory," the last day of Durgā pūjā, when the images of the Goddess are immersed in the water) lament her departure for her husband's house on Mount Kailasa. The songs are frequently presented in the persona of Menakā, who describes her anxieties about her daughter's welfare and her longing for her.

The second type of Śākta song is often termed *Śyāmāsaṅgīt* (songs about Śyāmā). Śyāmā (the Dark One) is an epithet of Kālī, the terrifying black Goddess. The songs use imagery drawn from the activities of everyday life to express religious beliefs, to symbolize the body, or to describe the tantric yogic *sādhanā* (method of realization) centering on the body that many Śākta poets practiced. For example, in one famous song, "Mā āmāy ghurābe kato?" (Mother, How Many Times Will You Make Me Go Round?), Rāmprasād compares the endless cycle of death and rebirth to an oil press, himself to the ox who crushes the seeds, and the vices of lust, anger, greed, infatuation, vanity, and envy to six oilmen:

> Mother, how many times
> will you make me go round
> like the oilman's blindfolded ox?
>
> You tethered me to the tree of the world
> and keep walking me in circles.
> What did I do wrong
> that you've made me obey
> the six oilmen? (Rāy 1971: 114; song no. 165)

Rāmprasād and the Śākta poets who followed him humanized the image of Kālī, softening her fearsome aspect and turning her into an adored, although somewhat neglectful, mother. These songs are unique in that the poets take the role of a child and express filial love for the Goddess.

References

Dāsgupta, Śaśibhūṣan. 1960. *Bhārater Śakti-sādhanā o Śākta Śāhitya* (The Śakti in Indian religious practice and Śākta literature). Calcutta: Sāhitya Samsad.

McDermott, Rachel Fell. 1995. Bengali songs to Kālī. In *Religions of India in practice,* ed. Donald S. Lopez, Jr., 55–76. Princeton, N.J.: Princeton University Press.

———. 2001. *Mother of my heart, daughter of my dreams: Kālī and Umā in the devotional poetry of Bengal*. New York: Oxford University Press.

———. 2001. *Singing to the goddesses: poems to Kalī and Umā from Bengal*. New York: Oxford University Press.

Rāy, Amarendranāth, ed. 1971. *Śāktapadāvalī* (Śākta poetry). 9th ed. Calcutta: Calcutta University.

Śen, Rāmprasād. 1982. *Grace and mercy in her wild hair: selected poems to the Mother Goddess*. Translated by Leonard Nathan and Clinton Seely. Boulder, CO: Great Eastern.

Sinha, Jaduath. 1966. *Ramprosad's devotional songs: the cult of Shakti*. Calcutta: Sinha Publishing House.

Thompson, Edward J., and Arthur Marshman Spencer, trans. 1923. *Bengali religious lyrics, Śākta*. The Heritage of India Series. London: Oxford University Press.

CAROL SALOMON

SEE ALSO
Goddesses, Hindu; Song

ŚAMĪ

The *śamī* is a tree (and its wood), variously identified as *Prosopis spicigera* or *Mimosa suma,* used in Vedic ritual, classical mythology, folklore, and regional ritual. The Vedic śamī and *pipal* (Sanskrit, *aśvattha*) sticks are used to produce sacrificial fire, *Agni*. Either the fire sticks are both made of pipal, said to be *śamīgarbhāt,* "from the womb of the śamī," or the vertical male stick is pipal and the horizontal, female one, śamī. In either case, Śamī is understood as a feminine source of Agni as sacrificial fire.

Since its use in sacrificial contexts during Vedic times, the śamī has come to be associated with fiery weapons, war, death, and the goddess. These themes have been linked in the *Mahābhārata*. There, the Pāṇḍavas hide their weapons in a "big śamī close to the cremation ground" to begin their year of hiding. To keep away the curious, they say that the male corpse that they tie up along with the weapons is, following a family custom, their 180-year-old mother's odorous cadaver. In the Sanskrit epic "vulgate," they conceal their weapons with a prayer to Durgā for victory in the forthcoming war.

In medieval kingdoms, worship of the śamī (*śamīpūjā*) forms part of royal rituals of Dasarā or Vijayādaśamī. Seventeenth- and eighteenth-century Sanskrit manuals, and eyewitness accounts from Rajasthan, Mysore, Ramnad, and elsewhere from the early seventeenth century on, connect śamīpūjā with three related rites: *sīmollanghana* ("crossing the boundary" of the capital), *Aparājitāpūjā* (worshiping the Unvanquished goddess), and *āyudhapūjā*) (worship of weapons). Dasarā, the "tenth day," preceded by Navarātrī (nine nights), marks the end of the rainy season and opening of military campaigns. The king may make an effigy of his enemy, or bring him before his mind. The śamī, feminine itself, invoked as Aparājitā, embodies the "unvanquished" goddess worshiped in conjunction with the crossing of the boundary to obtain victory and is a regarded as a form of the goddess Durgā-Vijayā ("Victory") herself, whose defeat of the Buffalo Demon Mahiṣāsura is celebrated during Navarātri. Thus we may say there is an equivalence between the śamī and Durgā, and that the śamī is one of the goddess's ritually embodied multiforms.

In later folkloric developments, both the *Rāmāyaṇa* and *Mahābhārata* oral epic traditions recount the śamīpūjā's origins. In the Rām Līlā at Banaras, three days before Vijayadāśamī, the Banaras Mahārāja, doubling for Rāma, worships a śamī on procession toward effigies of Rāma's enemies. Rāma worships Durgā to defeat Rāvaṇa and purify his rusted weapons, then honors her with a śamīpūjā before returning to Ayodhya. The Pāṇḍavas do the rite to defeat the Kauravas when they retrieve their weapons from the śamī after their year incognito. In the Pāṇḍav Līlā, śamīpūjā is enacted in connection with the Pāṇḍavas' post-war *Aśvamedha* (horse sacrifice). The Sanskrit epics have no corresponding episodes.

In certain oral martial epics, under vernacular names—Telugu *jammi* in the *Epic of Palnāḍu;* Tamil *vaṉṉi* (probably from Sanskrit *vahni,* "fire") in the *Aṇṇaṉmār Kathai* (*Elder Brothers Story*); Rajasthani *khejaṛī* in *Pābūjī*—the śamī figures in sacrificial death scenes.

In the Deccan, a "popular śamīpūjā" simulates combat. Men of all castes including untouchables assemble at a śamī tree, or, where it is rare, a bush is made of branches from the *āpaṭā* (*bauhinia tomentosa*). There is mock scuffling, and people cast śamī (or āpaṭā) leaves beneath the tree or bush. Then, at home, women perform an *ārati* (waving of a lit lamp) for the men of the family, and friends visit each other, exchanging śamī and *āpaṭā* leaves, saying, "It's gold." An explanatory story links indirectly with the *Rāmāyaṇa* through Rāma's ancestor Raghu. A young Brahman had to pay a guru's fee of fourteen crores (1 crore = 100,000,000) of gold coins, and asked King Raghu to supply it. Raghu was out of gold after a great sacrifice, but the sacrifice guaranteed victory over anyone. Remembering that Indra owed him "gifts," he prepared to fight him. Alarmed, Indra asked aid from Kubera, god of riches, who showered gold pieces onto a śamī. Raghu collected what he needed for the young Brahman and let his people loot the rest. The latter believed it came from the śamī.

In Tamilnadu, where Vijayādaśamī is usually detached from any prior Navarātri that would explicitly link it with the mythical and ritual killing of a buffalo, the śamī (or vaṉṉi), still often associated with boundaries, comes to represent the "king's" adversary himself, or a demon. The "kings" are usually royal deities, male or female, who ride a horse (vehicle or *vāhana*) to a boundary location where a priest shoots arrows in various directions before aiming at a śamī, a plantain tree, or some combination of the two. The target tree represents the demon enemy: sometimes Mahiṣāsura; usually Vaṉṉiyācuraṉ, whose name derives from the śamī-vaṉṉi.

The Pōta Rāju post in front of goddess temples in Andhra, representing the god Pōta Rāju (probably, "buffalo king") as guardian of village goddesses, is made of śamī-*jammi* wood. Śamī-related ritual and folklore remain linked with him there; with Pōttu Rāja (Tamil) as guardian of the goddess Draupadī; and with untouchable priests called Pōtrāj in parts of Andhra, Karnataka, and Maharashtra.

References

Biardeau, Madeleine. 1984. The *śamī* tree and the sacrificial buffalo. *Contributions to Indian Sociology,* (n.s.) 18(1): 1–23.

———. 1989. *Histoires de poteaux: variations védiaues autour de la déesse Hindoue*. Paris: École Française d'Extrême Orient.

Hiltebeitel, Alf. 1991. *The cult of Draupadī*. Vol. 2. *On Hindu ritual and the goddess*. Chicago: University of Chicago Press.

———. 1999. *Rethinking India's oral and classical epics: Draupadi among Rajputs, Muslims, and Dalits*. Chicago: University of Chicago Press.

ALF HILTEBEITEL

SEE ALSO

Aṇṇaṇmār Kathai; Dasarā; Goddesses, Hindu; *Mahābhārata;* Navarātrī; *Pābūjī; Palnāḍu; Pāndav Līla;* Processions; *Rām Līlā; Rāmāyaṇa;* Sacrifice; Worship

SATĪ

Satī, literally, a "good woman," refers to a wife who immolates herself on her husband's funeral pyre. Her death is deemed by devotees a manifestation and proof of goodness/purity (*sat*), which she developed by being loyal to her husband and by scrupulously fulfilling her duties as a wife. The satī's immolation reaffirms the union of husband and wife that was symbolically established at the sacrificial wedding fire. There are, however, many stories of women becoming satīs by throwing themselves down wells or jumping from roof tops.

Although the satī dies after the husband, she if often referred to as a *sahagāminī,* one who "goes together with" her husband. She is considered the very embodiment of auspiciousness. Whereas the widow breaks her bangles and discards other ornamentation when she hears of her husband's death, the satī dons her finest attire, usually her wedding clothes, and her best jewelry. The satī is frequently described as processing to the pyre with a happy countenance; her meditation on her husband as she perishes is said to prevent her from feeling pain.

In Western India the wives of warriors repelling invaders sometimes became satīs before their husbands died. Certain that their husbands faced imminent death, the wives died in group immolations known as *jauhar*s. Such sacrifices were intended to inspire the warriors to fight bravely, as they had little left to lose.

Opinions about the after-death destiny of the satī vary. It is widely believed that satīs achieve *mokṣa,* liberation from rebirth. While such a fate is often assumed to follow a single instance of self-immolation, in some stories a woman concludes numerous lives as a satī before winning liberation. Often the satī's death is represented as securing places in heaven for herself and her husband, even if he would otherwise have been reborn in a wretched condition because of past sins.

In many stories, a woman takes a vow to become a satī when she learns of her husband's death or she suspects he will die soon. This vow is usually interpreted as an indication of the sincerity of her devotion to her husband and of her willingness to share his fate. When she has taken such a vow, her sat begins to manifest itself as power, which enables her to grant boons to reverent petitioners and to curse people who annoy her. Typical boons are the birth of babies and recovery from illness. The curses are seemingly endless in variety: many involve infertility and sickness, but there are also property losses, family quarrels, and other misfortunes. Both blessings and curses are taken to verify the satī's possession of sat and to validate the tradition of veneration that ensues after her death. Despite the capacity to curse, satīs are described by people in many communities across India as utterly benevolent.

After the satī dies, she is worshiped as a supernatural guardian. In some cases satīs are associated with, or homologized to, well-known deities. Satī monuments in the Mewar region of Rajasthan are often placed near images of *lingam*s and *yoni*s, emblems of Śiva and Śakti. There have also been Vaiṣnavite satīs, including Godāvarī Satī in the Marwar region of Rajasthan and many satīs in Bengal.

Satīs are usually worshiped by members of their lineages. Their cult is centered around memorial stelae with representations of themselves and sometimes of their husbands as well. Many stelae contain crude relief images and are located at the borders of villages or near wells and tanks. The satī stelae of aristocratic families are often expertly carved in marble and enshrined in imposing pavilions. In central and southern India satīs are not only worshiped by lineage members, but also transformed by lineage members into *kuldevi*s, goddesses who either found a lineage or adopt an already existing lineage.

Frequently, however, the veneration of a satī extends beyond her lineage. People from various caste backgrounds may worship a satī who is considered the guardian of a village or even a larger area. Rānī Satī, whose temple in Jhumjhunu attracts pilgrims from many parts of India, has subsidiary shrines in places as far away as Calcutta.

Satī immolation was banned by the Bengal Presidency in 1829. The Republic of India kept the statute, and in 1988 passed an anti-glorification statute after the Rajput Roop Kanwar burned on her husband's pyre in 1987. Although satī immolation is all but extinct, rare incidents have attracted widespread media attention and have led to debates among scholars and activists about the rights of women and freedom of expression.

Recent years have seen the development of a tradition of worshiping *jivit* or "living" satīs. Having desired to die as satīs, these women nevertheless concluded that they were duty-bound to live. Their followers explain that because satī immolation is illegal and family members can be tried as accomplices, the living satī unselfishly sacrifices her desire to die. The living satī's power is such that she no longer requires nourishment or sleep: she lives by sat alone.

References

Courtright, Paul, 1995. Satī, sacrifice, and marriage: the modernity of tradition. In *From the margins of Hindu marriage: essays on gender, religion and culture,* 184–203. New York: Oxford University Press.

Harlan, Lindsey. 1992. *Religion and Rajput women: the ethic of protection in contemporary narratives.* Berkeley: University of California Press.

Hawley, John Stratton, ed. 1994. *Sati: the blessing and the curse.* New York: Oxford University Press.

Sangari, Kumkum and Sudesh Vaid. 1981. Satī in modern India: a report. *Economic and Political Weekly* 16(31): 1284–1288.

van den Bosch, Lourens P. 1992. Pilgrimage, prestige and protest: on the origin of recent satī temples in India. In *The sacred centre as the focus of political interest,* ed. Hans Bakker. Groningen: Egbert Forsten.

LINDSEY HARLAN

SEE ALSO

Gods and Goddesses; Heroes and Heroines; *Pēranṭālu;* Self-Sacrifice

SATYA NĀRĀYAṆA VRAT KATHĀ

The vow (*vrat*) and story (*kathā*) of *Nārāyaṇa* (*Viṣṇu*) worshipped as truth (*Satya*) is a Hindu religious ritual popular throughout India found from the Punjab to Tamilnadu and from Bengal to Gujarat. The copious display of three-rupee pamphlets located at bookstalls in the environs of many temples in India supplies the textual source used in the performance of the ritual. The pamphlets have Sanskrit text at the top of each page and vernacular translation at the bottom. In Banares alone at least seven different publishers, all within the nearby environs of Uttar Pradesh, present their versions of the SNVK. Its popularity among the Hindu diaspora is also a phenomenon of increasing interest as numerous temples across the U.S.—the Devi Mandir in Napa, California, and the Venkateshwar Mandir in Bridgewater, New Jersey, for example—perform the ritual for patrons both in temple precincts and in sponsors' homes. One Indian store in Fremont, California, Pooja International, even advertises mail-order pre-packaged Satya Nārāyaṇa Vrat Kathā *pūjā* supply kits.

The ritual, a part of the tradition of votive offering, involves primarily five elements: (1) the vow to do the worship, (2) the fasting, (3) the ceremonial worship (pūjā), (4) the storytelling, and (5) the feasting. The ritual is generally, though not necessarily, performed on the full moon with the requisite fasting on the day of the rite. Nārāyaṇa's image is then worshipped more or less elaborately depending upon the financial means and desires of the patron, but a particular sweet dish made of wheat flour and ghee is always included in the feast. A priest often conducts the pūjā by reciting one of several variants of standard Āgamic verses in Sanskrit while various substances such as flowers are offered. Following this the officiant tells the kathā, first reciting from the Sanskrit text and then following this by reading the vernacular rendering for the participants. The ritual concludes with a communal feast, providing the context for a social gathering.

As part of the tradition of vrat kathā, however, the SNVK stands out as an anomaly. In contrast to the traditional folk emphasis of the vrat kathā tradition, the SNVK fuses within itself elements and appeals of both brahminical culture and folk tradition. For instance, its popularity is not confined to women as a significant number of the traditional performers of vrat kathās are men. The text is in Sanskrit, the traditional literary language of the brahminical elite, while most vrat kathās are in the vernacular. Most vrat kathās focus on a female protagonist, emphasizing the empathy with a mostly female practitioner audience that we would expect, but the SNVK displays a predominantly male cast. Further, the structure of the story, the frame, and the use of the ubiquitous Purāṇic character Narada all maintain a brahminical hegemony for the ritual, as does its claim to the prestige concomitant with its status as part of the *Skanda Purāṇa.* On the other hand, within the story, elements of folk culture undermine the authority of brahminical tradition. For instance, a Brahmin violates caste injunctions by teaching the rite to a Bhīl, a low caste tribal.

Within the frame story, Narada relates four other stories of men who see someone performing the SNVK. The men then perform it themselves and attain wealth or children, or both, thus illustrating the efficacy of Satya Nārāyaṇa's worship. The central story involves a merchant and deviates from the brevity and protocol of the other three stories by giving a prominent role to a female character and suggesting the traditional performance of the ritual by women which we find in other vrat kathās. The merchant obtains a daughter, but neglects to perform the rite and displeases Satya Nārāyaṇa. Imprisoned overseas, he is only released when his daughter and wife fulfill the vow. The daughter also displeases Satya Nārāyaṇa by neglecting his *prasad;* after she loses her husband, she decides to drown herself, but Satya Nārāyaṇa saves her. Here, as in other vrat kathās, devotion is a resonant virtue enjoined upon the female characters and the links of the folk tradition to a grass roots *bhakti* movement is emphasized. Conversely, the male characters' attitude toward the deity departs from the emphasis on devotion to the deity typically found in vrat kathā literature.

The performance of the ritual displays the juxtaposition of folk and brahminical. The fasting and the pūjā in Sanskrit, a language which the participants do not understand, align as symbols of the power of tradition and of brahminical authority. During the pūjā, the priest excludes the audience by facing away from them. This is in contrast to the kathā portion where he physically shifts to expand the sacred space of the ritual to include the audience. Perhaps the appeal of the SNVK to the diaspora community lies in its fusion of brahminical and folk. The participants empathize with the merchant's adventures abroad, while the brahminical element provides the aura of respectability necessary to assert a diaspora identity.

LORILAI BIERNACKI

SEE ALSO

Gender and Folklore; Gods and Goddesses; *Satya Pīr; Vrat Katha;* Worship

SATYA PĪR

The mythic figure of Satya Pīr has engaged the frontier populations of Bengal and the northeastern section of the South Asian subcontinent for at least four centuries. He appeals to all segments of the population as an aide to survival, his intercession being sought primarily for the material basics of human existence. His primary mode of assistance comes through the creation or outright granting of wealth, but extends to include a more general weal that embraces the health and success of the entire family. Not to worship him, especially once that honor is promised, is to incur his wrath and punishment, usually through the loss of wealth and status, banishment, and even death. But Satya Pīr, when appeased either directly or by a loving spouse, can just as quickly reverse those fortunes; and that, it would seem, constitutes much of his broad appeal. It is more generally his universal accessibility that makes him stand out from the hosts of powerful deities and holy figures.

As his name suggests, Satya Pīr (*satya* the Sanskrit term for truth and *pīr* the Perso-Arabic designation for a Sufi guide) is a figure that has a significant standing in all religious communities. Beginning in the early 1600s, the Bengali and later the Oriya literature represents Satya Pīr as a combined form of a Muslim holy man, generally a Sufi mendicant or *fakīr,* and a sometime Hindu Brahman sometime ascetic *sannyāsī.* His dress, which often eclectically combines elements of each of these powerful institutional personas, serves as a visual metaphor of his basic message: pay respect to the all-encompassing power of the ultimate reality, regardless of its articulation as Allah, God of the Muslims, or as Nirañjana, the Stainless One of the Hindus, especially of the Vaiṣṇavas and Nāths. The impulse to honor the supreme in this interchangeable form through the figure of Satya Pīr is often styled as "syncretism" but a close analysis of the literature suggests other processes at work. All communities recognize the power resident in the morally righteous institution of the holy man. Each community seeks to appropriate that moral purity, with its concomitant worldly power, to lay claim to the territories under Satya Pīr's sway, for much of the land where he is popular is along the frontiers of the northeast that only began to come under full settlement in the seventeenth through the nineteenth centuries. Satya Pīr's adherents do not abandon their other religious proclivities or commitments by following him.

Hindus promote the worship of Satya Pīr by identifying him with Satya Nārāyaṇa, a celestial form of Kṛṣṇa / Viṣṇu who is popular throughout the subcontinent. By this identification, Vaiṣṇavas insert Satya Pīr into the purāṇic incarnational theory of the *avatāra,* with Satya Pīr descending to earth to guide the struggling survivors of the degraded Kali age. The stories depicting this descent are part of a troika of frontier narratives: the saga of the poor brahman, the conversion of the woodcutters, and the mad adventures of the ocean-faring merchant. In each the message is unambiguous: worship Satya Pīr by offering his preferred śirnī/śinnī (traditionally a simple mixture of rice, sugar, milk, and spices) and you will get rich. Because of his appearance as a Muslim mendicant, he does encounter resistance from his would-be Hindu converts, and so is forced to reveal his celestial form as Nārāyaṇa to convince them. While some segments of the population have in recent times denigrated the cult and its goals, the literature is extensive, suggesting its broad-based appeal. These three tales, composed in the form of Bengali *pālā-gān* or *pāñcālī* style, very much akin to the semi-epic *maṅgal-kāvya,* comprise approximately 90 percent of the extant manuscript and printed literature devoted to the figure of Satya Pīr. More than 180 authors tell these stories in just as many different ways, with those of Rāmeśvar Bhaṭṭācārya and Śaṅkarācārya most often employed by Hindu women to perform the monthly *brata* or household ritual vow to ensure the family's prosperity.

In what appears to be an overt attempt to legitimize this identification of Satya Pīr with Viṣṇu, these episodes have been incorporated into the Sanskrit *Skanda Purāṇa* (5.233–36) and *Bhaviṣya Purāṇa* (3.2.24–29) as late additions. This apparent act of Sanskritization clearly serves to incorporate Satya Pīr into brahmanical culture, and the initially simple ritual of an ordinary devotee offering śirnī becomes in at least one twentieth-century example, so elaborate as to require more than sixty ritual articles and the action of three brahmans to execute. At the same time, however, this act of appropriation becomes a not-so-subtle act of communal accommodation. Vaiṣṇavas, while justifying Satya Pīr in sophisticated theological terms, pragmatically acknowledge the power of the Muslim pīr to tame the frontier and make it habitable for settlement, that is, to create an environment where *dharma* can flourish.

This mutual recognition is precisely what lies at the heart of the Muslim stories, although their plots tend to be much more in the genre of the fabulous folk- or fairy-tale. Many of the Muslim narratives comprise singular episodes which conjure a Mecca-dwelling Satya Pīr to precipitate crises that serve to frame the plot, a narrative thread that is more commonly about humans struggling to make sense of a world that does not always adhere to ideals of order. *The Saga of Lālmon* (*Lālmoner kāhinī*) by Kabi Āriph, is typical in that it explores the desperate antics of a heroine who because of her father's egregious conduct, must endure numerous trials of gender confusion and humiliations of personal and marital status to maintain her honor.

A major exception to this trend of disconnected or independent narratives is the neatly interwoven set by Haridās, whose *Great Tale of the Youthful Sandhyābatī and Satya Pīr (Baṛa satyapīr o sandyābatī kanyār puṅthi)* strings together stories that trace the life of Satya Pīr from his conception to his later peregrinations around Bengal. These tales depict a mischievous and often cantankerous tiger-taming magician-pīr who makes it his duty to humble and educate arrogant brahmans and the kings who support them. With the various traditional Hindus depicted in the role of the intolerant, the result is their recognition, albeit often grudging, of the power of Satya Pīr's offices and the legitimacy of the Muslim presence in Bengal.

While the forms and audiences vary widely, it is clear that every tale, whether Hindu or Muslim, speaks to the accommodation and interdependence of the different frontier communities in their struggle to survive in an often hostile world. After a brief downturn in popularity in the middle of the twentieth century, interest in Satya Pīr is again resurging throughout Bengal.

References

Bühnemann, Gudrun. 1998. Examples of occasional pūjās: Satyanārāyaṇ avrata. In *Pūjā: A study in Smarta ritual.* The De Nobili Research Library Publications, vol. 15. 200–213. Vienna: Institute for Indology, University of Vienna.

Chandola, Anoop. 1991. *The way to true worship: a popular story of Hinduism.* Lanham, Md.: University Press of America.

Mitra, S. C. 1927. On a Satya Pīr legend in Śāntatī guise. *Journal of the Bihar and Orissa Research Society* 13:145–67.

———. 1919. On the worship of the deity Satyanārāyaṇa in northern India. *The Journal of the Anthropological Society of Bombay* 9, no. 7: 768–811.

Panda, Bishnupada, ed. and trans. 1991. *Pālās of Śrī Kavi Karṇa.* 4 vols. Kalāmūlaśāstra Series, vols. 4–7, ed. Kapila Vatsyayan. Delhi: Indira Gandhi National Centre for the Arts and Motilal Banarsidass Publishers, Pvt., Ltd.

Sen, Dinesh Chandra. 1920. Satya Pīr. 99–113. In *The folk literature of Bengal.* Calcutta: University of Calcutta.

Stewart, Tony K. 1995. Satya Pīr: Muslim holy man and Hindu god. 578–97. In *The religions of south Asia in practice,* ed. Donald S. Lopez, Jr. Princeton, N.J.: Princeton University Press.

TONY K. STEWART

SEE ALSO

Gods and Goddesses; *Maṅgalkāvya; Nāth;* Saints; *Satya Nārāyaṇa Vrat Kathā;* Syncretism; *Vrat Kathā*

SELF-SACRIFICE

Mythic, folkloric, and iconographic expressions of self-sacrifice are widespread in South Asia. They are evident in every religious tradition and are of varied origins, including historic examples of religious practice. On one hand, moral or religious suicide, or self-immolation, is a voluntary offering of life for a declared moral or spiritual goal. It may be an active self-destruction, an act of violence involving all the ambiguities of killing and its consequences, as in the case of someone jumping from a cliff in dedication to Śiva during *Mahāśivarātri,* or performing self-decapitation in the fervor of devotion to a goddess. Alternatively, self-immolation may be a passive relinquishment of life, in renunciation of life-sustaining food and water, for example, or altruistically feeding the body to needy beings, or entering martyrdom by nonresistance to hostile force. The law codes of almost all religions proscribe "secular" suicide while finding a way to extol self-offering in special circumstances.

The phenomenon of suicide bombing has introduced a new and horrific dimension to the folklore of self-sacrifice. Since 1983 the violent war in Sri Lanka between Tamil Hindus and the Sinhala government has updated martyrdom with the Tamil Tigers (LTTE) celebrating men and women suicide bombers. Similarly, certain extremist factions of Muslims, particularly in the disputed territory of Kashmir, have extolled martyrdom for "freedom fighters" in continuing confrontations with the Indian government. In both instances, Tamil independence or Islamic *jihād,* older strata of heroic legend have been cited for authority.

On the other hand, symbolic self-sacrifice plays a central role in all the religious traditions of South Asia and is a prominent motif in folklore. A part of the body may suffice for the whole. Unlike the Sanskrit epic heroine Sītā, who rejoins the Earth from which she came in the sequel to the Vālmīki *Rāmāyaṇa,* or the Purāṇic goddess Satī, who enters her self-created sacrificial fire, or Kanaka, a Brahman woman who threw herself into a well when falsely accused of adultery and now is worshiped as a regional form of Durgā, the Tamil epic *Śilappatikāram* produces a more aggressive self-sacrificer. Kannaki becomes a reluctant warrior heroine to punish an unjust kingdom, tears off her left breast, and hurls it at the city of Madurai in divine all-consuming wrath. Another form of partial sacrifice is declared in popular *vrata*s (vows), particularly among Hindus and Jains, in which normal bodily functions are given up for a higher purpose. Fasting, celibacy, breath-control, meditation, wakefulness, and other austerities demonstrate on the folk level a creative asceticism (*tapas*) long prized by tradition. Symbolic self-sacrifice is also declared spiritually in unqualified devotion to a deity or, in the case of Buddhists, to a recognition of existence itself as fundamentally selfless.

The earliest and best-known account of self-sacrifice in South Asia is the *Puruṣa-sūkta, Ṛgveda* 10.90, a hymn addressed to the divine being Puruṣa who sacrifices himself to himself in cosmogonic projection. His paradigmatic sacrifice (*yajña*) establishes the first cosmic laws. Parts of his self-dismembered body become not only cosmic elements but also the hierarchic social classes of humans, the four *varṇa*s derived respectively from his mouth, arms, thighs, and feet. The sixteen verses of this 3,000-year-old Vedic hymn have been perpetuated in myths, rituals and symbols in a variety of forms (in the structure of sixteen steps of *pūjā* [worship of a deity], for example) or in meditations and personal recitations. In addition to the creative self-sacrifice of Puruṣa (or Agni-Prajāpati in the Brāhmaṇas and later texts) and other mythic paradigms of self-sacrifice in the Vedas, basic elements of the Vedic sacrificial worldview stress initiatory death and rebirth, as in the *dīkṣā* consecration; abandonment of this world for the next, as in a moment when the sacrificer (*yajamāna*) ascends the cosmic pole to attain heaven and declares himself immortal; and renunciation, as in *tyāga,* the formal relinquishment of the fruits of sacrifice by the sacrificer himself. The fundamental Vedic system of correspondences repeatedly accents the identity of sacrificer and victim: Death is overcome by self-offering.

The Upaniṣadic doctrine of transmigration (*saṃsāra*) brought a new perspective to notions of self-sacrifice: Life is a moment in a series of existences concluded by liberation (*mokṣa, nirvāṇa*). The late *Maitri Upaniṣad* reveals the power of *ātmayajña,* the sacrifice of the self to the eternal Self (*ātman*). The *ātmayājī* (self-sacrificer) has descendants on one hand in the emergence of *bhakti* as a favored path to salvation (in *Bhagavadgītā* 9.28, Kṛṣṇa declares the ātman to be the proper offering of the worshipper to him) and on the other hand in multiple renunciant traditions. The renunciate, or *saṃnyāsin,* when entering the fourth and final *āśrama* (stage) of life, interiorizes his sacrificial fires and abandons society. Buddhism and Jainism also understand renunciation as a sacrifice of worldly existence. Like the Upaniṣadic poet-philosophers, they go beyond the ritual killing of victim-as-self, an action that brings only further bondage to *saṃsāra,* by renouncing the killing. The Jainas take such renunciation to ultimate lengths. Even for laity, short of the monastic vows, a lifetime of progress through cultivated austerities in twelve vows may be deliberately ended in the vow of *sallekhanā,* whereby food, water, and mobility are altogether abandoned and the body completes its life-span, often subsisting for weeks in ideal stasis without injury to any other being before release of the *jīva*, the eternal self.

Popular lore also celebrates the offering of the body as gift, as in the *Mahābhārata* tale of King Śibi who cut away his own flesh piece by piece to rescue a hunted dove, or the *Jātaka* account of a previous existence of the Buddha in which he sacrificed himself to a starving tigress. Restoration is usually the reward for ultimate altruism. Shamanic themes of dismemberment and rememberment became a staple of folklore in several religions, from Aśvaghoṣa's *Buddhacarita* account of the Buddha slicing himself to pieces, then assembling himself whole, to contemporary *mantravādins* and fakirs who work such magic for a fee. Here might also be mentioned thousands of female and male spirit mediums who offer their bodies as vehicles of possession by deities and spirits of the deceased. They consider themselves self-sacrificers in the sense that their bodies are used up in service to constant demands of clients, deities, and spirits.

Many Hindu, Jaina, and Mahāyāna Buddhist devotional traditions elevate symbolic self-sacrifice to prominence as the ultimate goal of a path of disciplined spiritual transformation. Quite as often, however, Hindu folklore highlights accounts of sudden, dramatic, physical self-immolation, often in the intoxication and madness of love for a deity. The fervor of devotion might be illustrated by one who wishes to bind a god to his own place, as in the case of a Mātaṇga who offered himself to Śiva as foundation sacrifice for the temple in Jejuri, where he is found today as guardian deity of the main gate. Self-decapitation before a goddess, Śiva, or local deity is a favored theme in iconography and folklore. Ecstatic devotees of goddesses may be seen today in this extreme form of worship, serving up her ideal food, human blood, by swinging a sword to strike their heads.

The warrior-hero (*vīra*) self-offered in battle is a conspicuous motif. In Sanskrit epics and their subsequent regional counterparts, warfare itself is at times a metaphor for human existence, with the slain simultaneously victims of, and victors over, the enigma of *saṃsāra*. Identification with the warrior ethos by many non-Brahman communities, only a few of them actual *Kṣatriya-varṇa* (warrior) lineages, allows widespread voice to heroic themes of ultimate devotion. Mannappan (Kativānur Vīraṉ) is an example from Kerala of a low-caste deified martial hero, self-sacrificed in combat. In the Tamil *Śilappatikāram* the warriors' self-decapitations are dedicated in the festival of Indra to provide victory for the king's army. In the medieval period, introduction of various ethnic forms of Islam to South Asia provided further opportunities for cross-fertilization in tales of heroes and heroines whose careers were elevated to spiritual models. The tenth-century hero Shāh Dola, nephew of Maḥmūd of Ghazni, decapitated himself into martyrdom in Maharashtra in a battle against a Hindu king. The most influential example of passive self-offering in the history of the Shī'a sect of Islam is that of Ḥusayn, son of 'Alī and grandson of the Prophet Muḥammad. According to tradition, he allowed himself to be murdered at Karbala in 680 C.E., a martyrdom and blood sacrifice reenacted annually in the pageantry of the Muharram festival.

Satī, in regional Hinduism, the self-immolation of a widow on the cremation pyre of her husband, is a special, now infamous, case of ritualized devotion. The husband, according to traditionalists, is a deity deserving of a wife's worship throughout marriage, and her self-abandonment upon his demise. From this perspective, a wife's existence is synchronous with that of her spouse, and the funeral or *antyeṣṭi,* literally "last offering," should be both bodies together and not his alone.

References

Coomaraswamy, Ananda K. 1941. Ātmayajña: self-sacrifice. *Harvard Journal of Asiatic Studies* 6: 358–398.

Freeman, John R. 1991. Purity and violence: sacred power in the teyyam worship of Malabar. Ph.D. diss., University of Pennsylvania.

Hiltebeitel, Alf, ed. 1989. *Criminal gods and demon devotees. essays on the guardians of popular Hinduism.* Albany: State University of New York Press.

Murty, M. L. K. 1982. Memorial stones in Andhra Pradesh. In *Memorial stones—a study of their origin, significance and variety,* ed. S. Settar and Günther D. Sontheimer Heidelberg: South Asia Institute.

Sircar, D. C. 1967. *The śakti cult and tārā.* Calcutta: University of Calcutta.

Williams, R. 1963. *Jaina yoga. A survey of the mediaeval Sravakacaras.* London: Oxford University Press.

DAVID M. KNIPE

SEE ALSO

Gorava/Goramma; Heroes and Heroines; Jainism; Mailāra; *Majlis; Mātam; Muḥarram; Pattini; Satī;* Sacrifice

SEN, DINESH CHANDRA

Sen (1866–1939) held the Ramtanu Lahiri professorship at Calcutta University for much of his academic career, and is best known for his scholarship on Bengali literature and folklore. His most important contributions to the study of Bengali folklore studies are *Folk-Literature of Bengal* (1920) and *Eastern Bengal Ballads* (1923–1932). The former was based on his 1917 Ramtanu Lahiri lectures at Calcutta University, while the latter was based on fieldwork conducted in East Bengal (what is now Bangladesh) by Chandra Kumar De, whom Sen commissioned to collect ballads that were widely sung in the early decades of the twentieth century.

Sen's Major Works

Folk-Literature of Bengal was Sen's most theoretical work. In it, he not only contextualized Bengali folklore by situating it in the social, religious, and political history of Bengal, but also compared Bengali folklore with similar work in Europe and elsewhere. In drawing parallels between Bengali folk tales and European ones, Sen posited three possible routes of diffusion from India to Europe. The first was via Buddhist missionaries who carried the stories out of eastern India on their proselytizing missions. The second channel of dissemination was through gypsy musicians who were sent to the Persian court of Behram Gor in the fifth century C.E. Sen argued that many of the minstrels later settled in Europe to continue performing their craft there. Lastly, he suggests that tales may have spread via seafaring merchants who sailed from eastern seaports to Europe for economic trade. Although all three routes are presented in a speculative manner, they parallel those of Theodor Benfey (1809–1881) and other European scholars who postulated an Indian origin for certain genres of folklore. The real value of these lectures rests not as much in Sen's theorizing and comparisons as in his extensive presentation of lore grounded in local forms of popular Islam. Prior to Sen's groundbreaking work, very little had been published on the distinct genres comprising the expressive culture of Bengali Muslims.

Eastern Bengal Ballads, consisting of four volumes, was Sen's magnum opus. In addition to the fifty-five valuable translations he provided, Sen included a lengthy introduction in which he provided linguistic, aesthetic, social, historical, and political analyses of the songs and their performances. Within the course of a few decades, however, Nandagopal Sengupta (1940: 35–38) raised the question of the antiquity and authenticity of the ballads, which led Dušan Zbavitel to author a book in 1963 defending Sen's scholastic integrity and the value of the collection.

Whether one accepts the authenticity of Sen's collection is a matter of scholarly debate, but one cannot deny his important contribution to the overall study of Bengali literature. The sincerity of his work must also be analyzed against the backdrop of nationalism that was developing in Bengal during Sen's career. Sen's love of vernacular literature was grounded in his patriotic love of Bengal. Like other scholars, this may have led him to romanticize the folk. Nonetheless, his romanticism yielded a quintessential corpus of work upon which contemporary scholars may draw for more refined analysis.

References

Sen, Dinesh Chandra. 1920. *Folk-literature of Bengal*. Calcutta: University of Calcutta Press.

———. 1923–1932. *Eastern Bengal ballads*. 4 vols. Calcutta: University of Calcutta Press [reprinted as *The ballads of Bengal*. 4 vols. 1988. Delhi: Mittal Publications].

Sengupta, Nandagopal. 1940. Bāṅglā Sāhityer Bhūmikā (Introduction to Bengali literature). Calcutta: Chakravarty, Chatterji and Company.

Siddique, Ashraf H. 1966. Bengali folklore collections and studies during the British period (1800–1947): A critical survey. 2 vols. Ph.D. dissertation, Folklore Institute, Indiana University.

Zbavitel, Dušan. 1963. *Bengali folk-ballads from Mymensingh and the problem of their authenticity*. Calcutta: University of Calcutta Press.

PABITRA CHAKRABORTY

SEE ALSO

Bangladesh; Benfey, Theodor; Folklorists; Nationalism and Folklore

SHADOW PUPPETRY

Shadow puppetry was once thought to have vanished from its Indian birthplace as it migrated and flourished elsewhere in Asia. Old Sanskrit texts mentioned shadow puppetry, or so it appeared, but no one had documented it in modern India. This led half a century of Indologists to debate whether shadow puppetry, despite those textual references, had ever existed in the subcontinent. Research beginning in the 1930s has shown that the vanishing act had been an illusion and that shadow puppetry is vigorously practiced in central Kerala, throughout Karnataka, northern Andhra Pradesh, on a limited scale in southern Tamil Nadu, and, until the 1970s, in southern Maharashtra and Orissa. All the South Indian traditions, with the exception of Kerala, derive from forms of visual storytelling (including shadow puppetry) in the northern Deccan and southern Maharashtra. As evidence of this, puppeteers in Andhra Pradesh, Karnataka, and Tamil Nadu speak Maṛathi as their mother tongue.

Most puppeteers are low-caste, itinerant performers who erect temporary stages and hang kerosene lamps (or light bulbs) to throw shadows on white cloth screen during temple festivals; only in Kerala is the performance held in a permanent building. Puppeteer troupes are often families, and women play an important part in every tradition except in Kerala and Maharashtra. Stories from the *Rāmāyaṇa* and *Mahābhārata* and pan-Indian myths dominate the repertoire of performances, although local material is introduced, particularly in Andhra Pradesh and Tamil Nadu. With the exception of Orissa, puppets are made of tanned leather, preferably deer skin, but whereas those in Karnataka, Andhra Pradesh, and Tamil Nadu are translucent, in Kerala and Orissa they are opaque. Again with the exception of Orissa, puppets are painted and articulated. Approximately one hundred different figures and objects form a complete set of puppets in most traditions. These central and southern Indian shadow puppet traditions are the source of better-known traditions in Southeast Asia, and possibly in the Mediterranean world.

References

Blackburn, Stuart. 1996. *Inside the drama house: Rāma stories and puppet plays in south India*. Berkeley: University of California Press.

Mair, Victor. 1988. *Painting and performance: Chinese picture recitation and its Indian genesis*. Honolulu: University of Hawaii Press.

GoldbergeBelle, Jonathan. 1984. Tōlubommalāṭa: the Andhra shadow puppet theater. Ph.D. diss. University of Wisconsin-Madison.

Seltmann, Friedrich. 1985. *Schatten- und marionettenspiel in Savantvadi (Sud-Maharashtra)*. Franz Steiner: Wiesbaden & Stuttgart.

STUART BLACKBURN

SEE ALSO

Marionettes; Theater and Drama

SHAMANISM, ISLAM

The term "shaman" is derived from the word *saman* (or *vaman*), used by the Tungus-speaking people of Siberia to refer to a particular type of magico-religious specialist, a part-time practitioner whose services are sought during times of personal or social crisis. The shaman, more popularly known as "medicine man," is adept at personally communicating with the spiritual world. Such practitioners often serve as healers, diviners, and guardians of the psychic equilibrium of their communities. Shamanism is more often a male occupation, although in some parts of South Asia, such as in the western Karakoram Mountains, both men and women are practitioners.

Shamanism has a long history and is considered by many anthropologists to be the most ancient of all religious practices. Although the term "shaman" has sometimes been used in an imprecise and indiscriminate way in the ethnographic literature (Kehoe 2000: 37–71), the concept of shamanism is widely used by anthropologists to refer to a basic configuration of beliefs and practices that appears cross-culturally among geographically distant societies. The shaman has been described as a magician, healer, diviner, mystic, poet, and performer of miracles. Not every magician, diviner, miracle worker, or healer, however, is a shaman. Similarly, not every shaman is a healer. In other words, in any given culture one seldom finds a shaman engaged in all activities associated with shamanism. Thus it is difficult to define shamanism according to the precise professional functions of its practitioners.

The shaman has also been described as a religious practitioner who employs specific techniques of ecstasy. But shamanism does not encompass all varieties of ecstatic experience. For example, the Sufi orders, or *tarīqat,* found in many parts of Central and South Asia, use a number of techniques for inducing *hāl* (ecstasy) and *fanā-fil-haq* (mystical union with the divine). These techniques include music, rhythmic dancing, seclusion, and, more frequently, *ẓikir,* the recitation or repetition of mystical formulas and sentences. Sufi mystical states, however, cannot be equated with shamanic ecstasy, which necessarily involves contact with particular spiritual entities rather than with an all-enveloping Godhead. As Hultkrantz correctly points out, in shamanism "we never find mystical union with the Divinity so typical for the ecstatic experiences in the 'higher' forms of religious mysticism" (42). Where Sufi *hāl*-evoking techniques appear in connection with shamanic rituals—as they do, for example, in Afghanistan—their purpose is to gain control of particular spirits rather than to obtain mystical union with the divine.

Despite the conceptual difficulties noted, it is possible to distinguish a shaman from other religious specialists according to a specific, cross-culturally recurring and interrelated configuration of elements. These include a belief in the presence of helpful and harmful supernatural entities, supernatural causes and cures for illness, spirit or soul loss, and the belief that some people—by virtue of inherent qualities, the use of hallucinogenic substances, or through other ecstatic techniques—are able to interact with, and establish personal control over, supernatural entities. A shaman's diagnostic, healing, or magical abilities stem directly from his or her control over particular supernatural beings. The role of spirit helpers is a crucial element of the shamanic configuration. Indeed, the ecstatic who communes with the supernatural world without the intercession of spirits should not be considered a shaman. On the other hand, a person's ability to contact spirits outside the total shamanic configuration does not in itself justify the use of the term "shaman." There must also be unique ritual paraphernalia, a specialized mystical language, and operational procedures such as working for a fee.

Shamanism is usually associated with hunting and foraging societies that lack complex technical and social organization. Nevertheless, its presence within stratified societies that are economically based on agriculture and animal husbandry, and religiously monotheistic, is not unusual. Shamanism excludes neither other magico-religious elements nor (necessarily) belief in a Supreme Being. As Eliade (1972: 8) has observed in his classic study, "We frequently find the shamanic (that is, ecstatic) experience attempting to express itself through an ideology that is not always favorable to it." Indeed, shamanic beliefs have shown a remarkable ability to persist alongside major religious traditions, not only Islam but also Buddhism and Hinduism. From Islam's point of view, its traditional tolerance for *ādat* (from the Arabic for "customary practices") has allowed it to accommodate shamanism as well as other indigenous cultural practices and beliefs.

Shamanism was once prevalent among the Turkic peoples who originally occupied the area of the Altai Mountains. By the sixth century C.E., the Turks had invaded the Central Asian steppes, bringing with them their shamanistic beliefs along with cults of ancestors, stones, mountains, and the earth goddess Otukan. Such beliefs seem to have been shared by the Uzbeks of the Oxus delta, the Mongols, and the Turkmen. The concept of Tanggri, the heaven or sky deity, along with associated shamanistic beliefs, was brought to Central Asia by the Hsiun-Nu. These people originally inhabited the Mongolian steppes to the northwest of China, but by the middle of the sixth century C.E. they had conquered the Central Asian steppes and defeated the Hephthalites of Afghanistan. An indigenous shamanistic religion, the cult of Zhun, which survived until the ninth century C.E., was already present in Zamindawar and Zabulistan, in southeastern Afghanistan, at this time.

Despite the Muslim hegemony that was established over a large part of Central Asia after the seventh century C.E., many of the preexisting shamanic practices survived. In some places these beliefs and practices persisted intact; elsewhere they were incorporated into the framework of Muslim cosmology. The ecstatic techniques associated with Islam's mystical Sufi tradition must have lent themselves particularly well to the assimilation of indigenous shamanistic practices.

Nineteenth-century Russian ethnographers reported the presence of shaman-sorcerers and exorcists in Tajikistan (former Soviet Central Asia) who employed human skullcaps (the top part of the human skull, used as a bowl), drums, smoke, and animal blood in their rituals. Similarly, the Uzbeks and Kazakhs, up until the nineteenth century, had religious specialists who beat sacred drums and were adept at divination and healing. Among the Kazakhs these specialists were referred to as *bakshi* (*baxsi*). They were said to have been able to communicate with *jinn* who acted as their familiars, helping them to cure illness, foretell the future, and counteract the influence of evil spirits. Following the Kazakhs' acceptance of Islam in the nineteenth century, such shamanic practices were taken up by the *mullā,* Muslim religious guides. The Turkmen also retained many shamanistic beliefs, some of which still persist in Afghan Turkestan. Among the Kirghiz and Uighur, shamans were known as bakshi. While curing illness and foretelling the future, they beat drums, entered into trances, and invoked Allah as well as Adam, Noah, and other representatives of the Biblical-Qur'ānic prophetology.

The shamanistic configuration also survived in parts of what is now modern Afghanistan. Muslim mystics and mendicants known as *malang* practiced a variety of ecstatic techniques clearly affiliated with shamanism. The beliefs and practices of these rural ascetics, some researchers have argued, represent "carryovers" of a shamanistic tradition once present in the Hindu Kush, the western Himalayan region, and throughout the mountains of central Afghanistan. The *malang,* some of whom claim to be Muslim Sufis, are still found in some regions of Afghanistan.

Ecstatic shamanism was also present in Kafiristan (the area of present-day Nuristan in the Hindu Kush of northeastern Afghanistan) until the end of the nineteenth century. Such beliefs and practices still exist among the Kalasha Kafir people in Chitral. Farther east, in the Karakoram Mountains of northern Pakistan, shamans continued to operate into the present era. These practitioners, known locally as *bitan* or *daniyal,* danced to the rhythm of beating drums, inhaled the smoke of sacred juniper leaves, entered into violent trances, and communed with supernatural beings believed to inhabit upland pastures and mountain peaks. A few bitan can still be found in villages in Gilgit, Hunza, and neighboring valleys.

Vestiges of what was once a widespread shamanistic complex can still be found in parts of Central and South Asia. In some places, such as the former Soviet Central Asia, and parts of the Hindu Kush and the Karakoram Mountains, local shamanistic practices survived as a distinct tradition well into the modern era. Elsewhere, such beliefs and practices were incorporated into, and are now expressed within, the framework of Islam and in the persons of mendicants and mystics. These religious specialists operate under various Muslim titles, and conduct their rituals in the idiom of Muslim mysticism. Nevertheless, they are easily distinguished from other religious practitioners by the criteria established above.

References

Baldick, Julian. 2000. *Animal and shaman: ancient religions of central Asia*. New York: New York University Press.

Balzer, Marjorie M. 1990. *Shamanism: Soviet studies of traditional religion in Siberia and central Asia*. Armonk, N.Y.: M.E. Sharpe.

Eliade, Mircea. 1972. *Shamanism: archaic techniques of ecstasy*. Princeton, NJ: Princeton University Press.

Gilberg, R. 1984. How to recognize a shaman among other religious specialists. In *Shamanism in Eurasia,* ed. Mihaly Hoppel. Partone, Germany: Herodot.

Hultkrantz, Åke. 1978. Ecological and phenomonological aspects of shamanism. In *Shamanism in Siberia,* ed. Mihaly Hoppel. Budapest: Akademiai Kiado.

Kehoe, Alice Beck. 2000. *Shamans and religion: an anthropological exploration in critical thinking*. Prospect Heights, Ill.: Waveland.

Lewis, David C. 2000. *After atheism: religion and ethnicity in Russia and central Asia*. Surrey, England: Curzon Press.
Sidky, H. 1990. Malang, Sufis, and mystics: An ethnographic and historical study of shamanism in Afghanistan. *Asian Folklore Studies* 49: 275–301.
———. 1994. Shamans and mountain spirits in Hunza. *Asian Folklore Studies* 53: 67–96.
——— and Janardan Subedi. 2000. *Bitan, oracles and healers in the Karakorams*. Jaipur, India: Illustrated Publishers.

H. SIDKY

SEE ALSO
Divination; Islam; Jinn; Malang; Supernatural Beings

SHAMANISM, NEPAL

There is no "shamanism" in Nepal, not in the sense of a coherent religious system, neither one paralleling those religious complexes found among the Ural-Altaic peoples (as the term was originally applied), nor as some systematic institution whose specialists perform priestly life-cycle functions for their clientele. However, even with a rigorous definition of this frequently misapplied term, there are "shamans" in many communities of Nepal, ritual intercessors whose divination, exorcism, and healing practices incorporate a mastery over spirits.

To distinguish clearly these intercessors from other ritual specialists, such as the *dhāmī* oracles of western Nepal or Newari Tantric priests (*vajrācārya*) of the Kathmandu Valley, this discussion follows Shirokogoroff's 1935 definition of shamans: persons of either sex who are masters of spirits, who can at will introduce these spirits into themselves, and who use this power over the spirits in their own interests, particularly to help other people. Shirokogoroff lists the essential characteristics of a shaman as the following: (1) the shaman is a master of spirits; (2) he has mastered a group of spirits; (3) there is a complex of methods and paraphernalia recognized and transmitted; (4) there is a theoretical justification of the practice; (5) the shaman has a special social position. Additional characteristics include a predilection to undertake soul journeys to the underworlds and the heavens, trance states (sometimes described as "ecstasy"), dramatically staged performances including specific initiation and death ceremonies, and an extensive repertoire of memorized oral texts, both long, publicly chanted recitals and short, whispered, secretive incantations (*mantra*s).

In Nepal, practitioners who most closely match this full set of conditions are *kāmī* (blacksmith), *jhāṅgrī*, and Magar *rammā* of the western hills. In the first publication on western Nepalese shamans, John T. Hitchcock noted the striking similarities between their symbols and practices and those of Central Asian shamans, clear parallels also demonstrated in a spectacular ethnographic film by Michael Oppitz. Elsewhere in Nepal ritual specialists who meet most of the basic features of this definition (although each type of specialist has distinct characteristics) include Tamang *lambu* and *bonpo,* Gurung *poju* and *hlewri,* Yolmo *bonpo,* Tharu *gurau,* Rai *bijuwā,* Limbu *yeba,* Sunuwar *puimbo,* and Chepang *pande.*

Throughout Nepal most shamans are male, although in some communities, women also become shamans. Though many future shamans undergo disturbing possession crises as adolescents, training of new shamans concentrates on their memorizing oral texts, particularly the secret mantras that control the many spirits which shamans manipulate in their rituals. Unlike other circumstances that involve spirit possession, shamans thoroughly control these spirits in their ceremonies, forcing, flattering, bribing, cajoling, and threatening them until they obey the shaman's will. One line of a mantra used to summon dead souls clearly demonstrates the hierarchical relation between a shaman and his spirits: "Come when I say come, go when I say go" (Maskarinec 1995: 101).

Spirits summoned by shamans belong to many different classes, including local gods and goddesses (*deutā, debī*); spirits of animals and inanimate forces (*bir*); souls of human suicides, particularly spirits seeking vengeance (*barmā, bājyū*); souls of other dead humans (*massān, syāuryā*); familiars of living entities (*barāṅg*); familiars of dead entities (*māphī*); crossroads ghosts (*dhām, dhuwā*); and the souls of other shamans (*gel*). Some of these groups are protective, solicitous, benign, and undemanding; others are malicious, oppressive, and threatening. Nearly all demand blood sacrifices, a key element of all major shamanic rituals. Communicating with these spirits allows shamans to diagnose problems, treat afflictions, and restore order and balance to the lives of their clients and their communities.

Shamans' diagnoses of their patients' afflictions commonly involve some combination of seven categories of origin: (1) curses and spells, particularly the actions of witches and other shamans; (2) misfortune-causing astrological configurations, foremost of which are dangerous planetary configurations called star obstructions; (3) the intrusion of alien substances into the body; (4) weakened life forces, including soul loss, distracted wits, and madness; (5) social disorder, especially disputes within families and communities; (6) fevers of autonomous origin (self-originating, not necessarily within the person); (7) the activities of spirits. While witches are the traditional enemies of shamans, Nepal's legal codes of the past hundred years (1834–1960) set such strict criteria to determine bewitchment, along with severe punishments for unproved accusations, that cases specifically involving bewitchment are a small percentage of most shaman consultations; treatments involving astrological crises, soul loss, or the afflictions caused by spirits appear to be the most frequent.

Shaman repertoires clarify major traditional concerns of Nepalese society. They demonstrate the interrelatedness of illness, death, witchcraft, sorcery, land disputes, astrological impasses, political opportunism, childlessness, problems with in-laws, and accidents. Publicly recited narratives explain the origin of the world, its inhabitants, and their afflictions. In archaic but understandable language they clarify symptoms and provide explanations of the causes of problems, and they carefully describe the methods of intervention, detailing the proper ways to conduct rituals. The public narratives preserve the knowledge necessary to act as a shaman. Providing audiences with a perspective on their misfortunes that provides hope of possible relief, the results of public recitals parallel the ways that the whispered mantras seek to manipulate and change the world.

Shamans perform at their patients' homes, after being personally invited by a member of the patient's family. The latter must arrange for an assistant, called a *curmi,* to carry the basket of the shaman's paraphernalia; the shaman never carries this basket himself, insisting on the formal social recognition of the Shaman's social status. Crucial paraphernalia, besides the drum, includes an elaborate costume whose elements deliberately suspend the shaman's identity between male and female, human and animal, living and dead, natural and cultural. These ambiguous states are emphasized in both initiations, which take place with the shaman suspended on a pole between heaven and earth, and in burial practices, with the shaman's corpse seated in a mound half in the earth, half out of it, comparable to the tombs of Kānphaṭa yogin.

References

Hitchcock, John T. 1967. A Nepalese shamanism and the classic inner Asian tradition. *History of Religions* 7, no 2: 149–158.

Maskarinec, Gregory G. 1995. *The rulings of the night: an ethnography of Nepalese shaman oral texts*. Madison: University of Wisconsin Press.

Shamanen in blinden land (Shamans of the blind country). 1980. A film by Michael Oppitz. WSK Productions, New York. 16 mm.

Shirokogoroff, Sergei M. 1935. *Psychomental complex of the Tungus*. London: K. Paul Trench & Trubner.

GREGORY G. MASKARINEC

SEE ALSO

Divination; *Gurav;* Sacrifice; Spirit Possession and Mediumship; Witches and Sorcerers; Witches, Nepal

SHRINES, HINDU

A Hindu shrine is a place for showing reverence to a god or goddess, an ancestor, a spiritual leader, or a spirit greater than ordinary man. The term incorporates an infinite variety of types of spaces, from the intimate to the magnificent, the elemental to the ornate, the almost imperceptible to the grandiose. Each is equally valid as a means for conducting *pūja,* or worship. Hindus commonly perform pūjas in shrines in three different environments: in the home, outside on the street or in conjunction with an element of nature, and within larger temple structures.

The heart of every Hindu home is its shrine room: the sacred space delineated for honoring and worshiping the gods. The pūjas that take place in the household shrine are the foundation of all family actions and decisions. Everything begins and ends here. The size and description of this shrine is immaterial. It may be large and impressive, an entire room or a beautifully designed edifice, or it may be simply a tiny niche, or even just a row of religious prints pasted on a wall. As the area in which food is prepared is considered sacred, the family shrine is often inside or next to the kitchen.

Although children grow up following family beliefs, they are encouraged as young adults to make their own choices of which gods or goddesses they find personally inspiring. They will continue to practice many family rituals, but they also conduct their own personal worship in whatever manner seems most beneficial to them, often based upon the advice of respected religious teachers and priests. Consequently, household shrines contain those images that pertain to the belief systems of the home's inhabitants, and it is not uncommon to find several small individual shrines in one household.

Every day members of the family perform personal rituals at this shrine. During the year, it also becomes the focus of seasonal and special pūjas involving the entire family. As in a temple, the energy of the deity is invoked to enter the image. During the pūja, the god or goddess is fully present, incarnate, within the home. That presence is believed to protect the family and to engender a positive future.

At all other times, except during worship, most household shrines are closed from view by a drawn curtain or door. These doors are frequently carved or painted with sacred designs, so that those from Rajasthan, for example, may be painted with images of the flute-playing Kṛṣṇa and his *gōpis;* or those from Orissa carved with images of Lord Jagannāth and his brother and sister. Many shrines contain a *maṇḍapa,* or platform, that holds the principal images for worship. Often these maṇḍapa are of unadorned wood; however, some in Gujarat, for example, are architecturally ornate with tiered roofs decorated with parrots, and shrines in

Community tree shrine to Durga near Cumbum, Tamil Nadu, India, © Stephen Huyler

Karnataka are sometimes versions of Hoysala temples, intricately carved in sandalwood.

As the shape, size, and contents vary from house to house, each family chooses to place in its shrine those objects which are specific to the family's devotion. Chosen at random, a niche shrine to Viṣṇu in Andhra Pradesh contains a simple wooden platform upon which are placed a small bronze image of Vēnugōpāla, two *sālagrāma* (sacred fossilized ammonites), a sandalwood carving of Lakṣmī, and a stone sculpture of Ganeśa. Beneath it, on the floor of the shrine is a brass bell, a brass and copper *lōṭa* (water pot) with a small sculpted spoon for ladling holy water onto the images, a box of *āgarbati* (incense), and a brass *āraṭi* tray containing offerings of flowers, a container of *sindhur* (powdered vermillion), and a small bottle of *ghī* (clarified butter). The wall behind holds framed posters of Venkateswara, Lakṣmī, and Jagannāth, and a calendar print of Bālakṛṣṇa (the baby Kṛṣṇa stealing butter).

The second category of shrines includes a wide variety of those that are unstructured, most often in the open air. They are usually devoted to honoring *grāmadevatā,* the spirits of a community or a place, deities that govern the myriad facets of mundane life and death. A small hamlet will have one grāmadevatā, while a town may have several, with an individual shrine for each of its subsections. A large city usually has hundreds of such shrines: a sacred stone grappled by the roots of a banyan tree, a tiny niche tucked into the side of a building, and an ancient carving resting upon a cement platform at a crossroads. Frequently, the deity honored is a goddess. The shrine may not have a full time priest or caretaker. Instead, members of the community alternately take turns cleaning and caring for the image, replacing fresh flowers and offerings as part of vows to the goddess in return for her beneficence.

India is filled with millions of these outdoor shrines. Some shrines are worshipped daily, others weekly, seasonally, or even annually. Most do not contain a man-made image. The deity is worshipped in a natural, aniconic form: a tree, a stone, or a spring. Yet even these unchanged elements of nature will be adorned with the accoutrements of traditional pūja: with flowers, sacred substances such as ghī, sandalpaste, or vermillion (*kumkum*), and clothes when possible. Shrines to Tākurāṇī (the generic term in Oriya for the goddess who is the local grāmadevī) are found in every community in Orissa. Usually, she is represented by a sacred tree under which are one to seven ancient stones daubed with vermillion. The tree may or may not be encompassed by a short walled enclosure and a stone or cement platform upon which pūjas are performed. Similarly, shrines to *Di Baba,* a grāmadevatā in eastern Uttar Pradesh, may be a small grove of venerable trees or an unornamented brick wall around a natural spring. Shrines to goddess Mātajī abound in Gujarat and Rajasthan, honored as the protective goddess of each community.

Many outdoor shrines also contain images carved of stone. Sculptures of Hanumān, painted brilliant red in worship, are particularly popular in the Deccan. Throughout the south, steles sculpted with images of single or entwined *nāga*s (snakes) and usually grouped at the base of *pīpal* trees herald shrines dedicated to the health and fertility of women. Communities throughout western India have shrines containing "hero stones": granite slabs carved with the figures of men and women sometimes on horse or camelback that represent the deified spirits of long dead local heroes (*vīra*). They too are accorded specific pūja rituals.

A further subsection is that of impermanent images, those sculpted of clay or some other ephemeral substance that is intended to last for only a short while. Sometimes the primary icon may be created in this fashion; for example, the large clay sculptures of Ganeśa made for the festival of *Gaṇeś Caturthi* in Maharashtra or those of Durgā made for her pūja in Bengal. In each case temporary shrines are constructed by the community using available materials (wood, cloth, paper, scrap metal) to house the temporary image for several days of worship and celebration, after which the images are thrown into a nearby water source and the shrine dismantled. In the outdoor shrines dedicated to Ayyanār, the Protector of Boundaries, the deity is sometimes sculpted in fragile terra-cotta, although more frequently his image is made of brick-based stucco. However, small terra-cotta horses are placed before his image as symbolic offerings to his *Vīraṉ* (soldiers) for their nightly rides to protect the community from evil. Some shrines contain as many as several hundred of these colorful sculptures. They are important for the moment of their donation only, after which time they gradually break and disintegrate. Similarly terra-cotta sculptures of horses or elephants are placed in outdoor rural shrines in every Indian state as votive offerings to local grāmadevatā.

The final category of shrine is the structure built to house an image. There are many reasons for building such a structure. One is the community's proud response to the strength and power of its grāmadevatā. Money will be raised from local devotees and landowners to erect a building on the site. Often when an image or sacred spot begins to gain a reputation for its efficacy in answering many devotees' prayers, its fame spreads further than just the immediate community, and it may begin to accrue its own revenue. An outdoor shrine will then be roofed over and various outbuildings erected to meet the pilgrims' needs. A third reason is the patronage of a wealthy individual or an influential family that wishes to acknowledge the local deity for aid in gaining prestige and, through building a temple, thereby accrue further merit, both sacred and mundane. Most, if not all, of the major temples in South Asia began as minor shrines to local deities, the size and grandeur of the edifice growing in just such a manner.

Simple, flat-roofed buildings house sacred images throughout the subcontinent, their architecture elemental and non-descript. An architect or craftsman with imagination will add ornamentation to that prototype that unconsciously gives the shrine an indigenous style. Consequently, rural brick shrines in Orissa have the rounded stepped roofs reminiscent of the magnificent temples of Bhubaneshwar and Orissa; laterite block shrines in northern Karnataka are often built with a tower, hall, and porch reflecting Chalukyan influence; stone shrines in villages in northern Madhya Pradesh reveal towered structures similar to the sacred mountain shapes of nearby Khajuraho's great temples.

Larger structures require the maintenance of one or more priests to care for the image and administer the pūjas. Depending upon the size, popularity, and wealth of the temple, other shrines secondary to that of the principal deity may be built. In some cases these smaller buildings will house sacred stones or images that have already been in worship at the shrine. Otherwise, new images will be commissioned and consecrated, each with its own carefully prescribed rituals of care and devotion. South Asia has always been a land of cycles of change and renewal. Many older shrines become less popular or even abandoned, due to the breaking or damage of the central image, the perception that the deity is no longer considered effective, or the fact that the population may have shifted elsewhere.

Similarly, new shrines are constantly being built everywhere. Burgeoning population growth demands new communities, each of which needs its own local shrines. New cults, such as that of Ayyappa in south India or the recent resurgence of Rāma devotion in north India, require new buildings to house new images. Many of these structures repeat the traditional architectural norms of the vicinity. Others utilize the classical styles of other regions: for example, the current popularity in Kerala for Tamil-style shrines, or the Chandela-style architecture that one now finds in the western Gangetic Plain. Many contemporary shrines draw upon what might be called "Bombay-cinema style," where elements of architectural design are distinctly influenced by the latest fads for film sets. An Ayyanar shrine in South Arcot District, Tamil Nadu, is decorated with sculptural images clearly reminiscent of the Statue of Liberty, and a shrine to Rāma outside Delhi is painted with scenes of the Rāmāyaṇa with the Pāṇḍava brothers and Sītā in form and dress remarkably like that of a film dance line.

References

Anand, Uma, ed. 1982. *Gods of the byways: wayside shrines of Rajasthan, Madhya Pradesh and Gujarat*. Oxford: Museum of Modern Art.

Blurton, Richard T. 1992. *Hindu art*. London: British Museum Publications.

Fischer, Eberhard, Sitakant Mahapatra, and Dinanath Pathy, eds. 1980. *Orissa: kunst und kultur in Nordost-Indien*. Zurich: Museum Rietberg.

Gold, Ann Grodzins. 1989. *Frutiful journeys: the ways of Rajasthani pilgrims*. Berkeley: University of California Press.

Huyler, Stephen P. 1996. *Gifts Of earth: terracottas and clay sculptures of India*. Seattle: University of Washington Press.

———. 1994. *Painted Prayers: Women's Art In Village India*. New York: Rizzoli.
Lewis, Norman. 1991. *A Goddess In The Stones*. Calcutta: Rupas & Co.
Maury, Curt. 1969. *Folk Origins of Indian Art*. New York: Columbia University Press.
Meister, Michael, W., ed. 1995. *Cooking For The Gods: the Art of Home Ritual in Bengal*. Newark: The Newark Museum.
Torbert, Natalie, and Teague, Ken. 1994. *Sacred Lands, Devoted Lives: Hinduism and Daily Life in a South Indian Village*. London: Horniman Museum.

STEPHEN P. HUYLER

SEE ALSO

Goddesses, Place, and Identity in Nepal; Gods and Goddesses; Heroes and Heroines; Kataragama; *Nāga; Pūjā;* Sacred Places; Stūpa; Worship

SHRINES, MUSLIM

In the Islamic tradition shrines may be identified by various terms: *qabar* (grave), *maqbarā* (place of burial), *mazār* (place of visitation), *dargāh* (royal court). Muslim shrines most often house the purported remains of a *pīr* (saint) or, on occasion, those of a *shahīd* (martyr). Shrines also have been erected on sites dedicated to a saint. Thus Ghāzī Miyān (Sayyid Sālār Mas'ūd, d. 1034), believed to be the first martyr of Islam in South Asia, has shrines at Bahraich, Gorakhpur, and Bhadohi in northern India. Pīr Zākī (d. ca. 1250) has two adjacent shrines in Lahore, Pakistan. Popular legend has it that he was killed defending the city from the Mongols and, though he was beheaded during the battle, his body continued fighting on. One shrine is believed to contain his head and the other, some fifteen yards away, was built on the grave containing his body.

Shrines of pīr and shahīd are frequented by South Asian Muslims to seek their intercession before God in some temporal matter. The most popular days for visits are Thursdays and the death anniversary (*'urs*) of the deceased. Shrines may also be visited because of the popular belief that the *barakat* (blessing) accumulated by the saint during his or her lifetime infuses the area surrounding the grave and is transferable, in a general way, to those who visit. This *barakat* may promote health: for instance, in Pakistan, the shrine of Shāh Sufaid in the Jhelum District of Pakistan is visited for the cure of leprosy. For venereal disease dust from the shrine of Pīr Bukhārī in the city of Quetta, Pakistan, is efficacious. Women who are childless may visit the shrine of Shaikh Salīm Chistī (d. 1571) in the town of Fatehpur Sikri, India, in the belief that they may receive the same boon granted the Mughal Emperor Akbar (r. 1556–1605): the birth of a boy whom Akbar named Salīm after the saint. The boy later became Emperor Jahāngīr. Likewise the shrine of Shāh Jamāl (d. 1612) in Lahore is visited by childless women familiar with the story that this saint granted a son to a childless couple.

Some Muslim shrines forbid the entry of women, while others are very popular among them. For example, the shrine of Bībī Pāk Dāman (Ladies of the Pure Hem) in Lahore purportedly contains the graves of the six "Ladies" (*Bībī*)—Hāj, Tāj, Nūr, Hūr, Gohar, and Shāhbāz—who were sent away from the battlefield of Karbalā (in Iran) by the Shī'ite Third Imām, Ḥusayn, prior to his martyrdom in 680 C.E. They found their way to Lahore, where they were brought before the Hindu ruler. Threatened with great indignities, they prayed to God to save them; as a result the ground opened up and swallowed them. Only the hem of one saint's garment remained aboveground, and their shrine was erected upon the site. Women revere these martyrs for the high morals they represent.

The funds for the maintenance and upkeep of many larger Muslim shrines in South Asia come from donations made by visitors and the revenue of attached *awqāf* (pious endowments; singular, *waqf*). For the latter revenue-producing properties are donated to the shrine. For instance the Mazār-i Shahīd-i Sālis (Shrine of the Third Martyr) in Agra is fronted by property leased to stores. The supervision of the shrine and any attached properties may be in the hands of a disciple of the saint who is buried there, or of one of the saint's descendants (*pīrzāda*).

References

Qādarī, Muhammad Kalīm. n.d. *Madīnat al-awlīya* (*City of saints*). Lahore: Islamic Book Foundation.
Shārb, Zuhūrulḥasan. n.d. *Tazkīra-yi awlīya pāk-i hind* (*Lives of the pure saints of India*). Lahore: Al-Faizal Publishing Co.
Subhan, John A. 1970. *Sufism, its saints and shrines*. New York: S. Weiser.

WAYNE R. HUSTED

SEE ALSO

Dargāh; Martyrdom; *Pīr;* Saints; *Ziyārat*

SIKH FOLKLORE

The Sikh religion originated within the varied ethnic, religious, and cultural districts of northern India, especially within Punjab. Hinduism and Islam, with their diverse schools of thought and practices, provided many of the elements that were brought together to form this vibrant religion, from the time of the First Gūrū (Nānak, 1469–1539) to the Tenth Gūrū (Gobind Singh, 1666–1708). Many of the prevalent manners, customs, and oral traditions of the Punjab became a part of Sikh life, and in turn received a new impulse from Sikhism. Since Punjab has been predominantly an agrarian society, Sikh folk art, song and dance, and fairs and festivals are marked by the agricultural cycle and seasonal moods.

Art

Ikk oan kār ("One Being is"), the most pervasive religious symbol in Sikh arts, crafts, and architecture, signifies the one transcendent Reality. The Tenth Gūrū's emblem of the *khālsā* is another very visible symbol in Sikh life. These two images, along with Gurmukhī script (based on the Devanāgrī), are used extensively as a form of ornamentation in Sikh art and architecture. They are embroidered on ox covers and garments; appear on jewelry; and are painted on walls, doors, and windows of homes, shrines, and shops. Especially favored in rural areas are bright posters depicting the Sikh holy book, *Ādi Granth,* and the lives of the ten gūrūs (spiritual teachers). Blue and saffron are the most commonly used colors.

The basic design in Sikh folk art is *phulkārī,* literally, "a spread of flowers." With its simple arabesque patterns, phulkārī is a visual rendering of the Sikh concept of the transcendent reality (*Ikk oan kār*). Bright colors in thread or paint or wool or jute come together in simple, abstract forms. Without a visible beginning and end, these designs have a dynamic momentum that leads the eye toward infinity. Items in a dowry—including mats (*darī*), quilts (*razāī*), shawls, hand fans (*pakhī*), sheets, cushions, and bread baskets (boīā)—all have embroidered, woven, or painted phulkārī patterns on them. The Punjab emporiums in Chandigarh and Delhi have abundant displays of Sikh folk art; both shops are named Phulkārī.

Song and Dance

Sikhs are known for their heartiness and zest. *Kheṛā* (cheerfulness), their prized virtue, manifests itself in their song and dance. *Bhangṛā* and *giddā* are the folk dances of the Sikhs, and central to all their celebrations.

Bhangṛā, performed by a group of men, dates back to the fourteenth century, and originated in the Gujrānwālā and Sialkot regions of West Punjab (now part of Pakistan). Dressed in bright colors, the group dances to the beat of a large drum and songs. The vigorous steps and sounds create a primal connection with the soil. The audience encircles the dancers, clapping and joining in the dancing and singing. The songs extol heroism, love, and hard work. They exalt the beauty of the cotton fields, the resplendent yellow mustard, and the fields of sugarcane. Bhangṛā acquires extra verve during *Baisākhī,* the Sikh New Year. Seeing the ripened wheat ready for harvest, the farmer's joy is uncontrollable. Bhangṛā is also popular at the Indian Republic Day and Independence Day celebrations.

Interestingly, this folk dance has migrated into the West with Sikh communities, and has become the latest rage with young music lovers in the United Kingdom, Europe, and Canada. The modern form of bhangṛā combines northern Indian folk music with contemporary styles including reggae and Western pop.

The women perform *giddhā,* choreographed in gentle and lithe movements. Their dresses reflect the brilliance of the flora and fauna around them. Like bhangṛā, giddhā celebrates nature and her bountiful gifts through the seasons. It captures simple agrarian activities: milking cows, cooking mustard greens, doing needlework, fanning in the summer, buying glass bangles, churning milk in the morning, carrying water in earthenware pitchers steadily balanced on heads, helping with plowing and harvesting.

Giddhā affords women a means of self-expression through dancing. The patriarchal structure of Punjabi society, combined with the rigidity of the joint family system, closely restricts the life of the newlywed wife. Giddhā opens the way to articulate her oppression, her hopes and dreams. The individual anguish is rendered a collective idiom. Women sing freely and vent their frustration with their in-laws. In a popular folk song a woman asks her father for "a cow, a buffalo, two bulls with bells, and a female camel with anklets" so that she can break away from her in-laws and start life independently with her husband.

During weddings Sikh homes resound with music. In the evenings female friends and relatives on both sides gather and sing songs to the accompaniment of a drum. While the lead singer sits cross-legged on the floor and plays the drum placed in the crook of her knee, a companion beats upon the wooden side with a spoon and the friends sing Punjabi folk songs. The songs on the groom's side are called *ghoriān* (literally, "mares"), and those on the bride's are called *suhāg* (crimson).

Also popular are Sufi poets like Bullhe Shāh (1680–1752) and Wāris Shāh (1730–1790). They wrote in Punjabi, expressing their yearning for the Divine in language and metaphors grounded in earthly relationships. Punjabis love reciting, and even shedding tears at, the tragic romances "*Hīr-Rānjhā,*" "*Sassī-Punnu,*" and "*Sohnī-Māhiwal.*"

Fairs and Festivals

Baisākhī is New Year's Day on the Indian calendar. For Sikh farmers it is the last day to relax before the beginning of the harvest, so they make the most of it. They hold a large fair at which goats, buffaloes, camels, and other livestock are bought and sold.

Basant Panchamī is another spring festival. The color yellow dominates in all spheres of life: yellow mustard blooms in the Punjabi fields; people wear yellow; and they eat yellow rice. The village rooftops are full of youngsters flying kites. There are competitions to see whose kite will fly highest, and part of the fun is to sabotage rivals' kites.

Holā Mohallā is a variation of the Hindu festival of *Holī*. During Holī people throw brightly colored powder, paint, and dye on one another. Friends and strangers alike are sprayed, splashed, and smeared with yellows, greens, reds, and blues. Gūrū Gobind Singh gave this traditional spring festival a Sikh character. In Anandpur, he initiated the Holā Mohallā, a three-day festival during which Sikhs trained as soldiers. There were contests in horsemanship, wrestling, and archery as well as mock battles and military exercises. The gūrū also encouraged competitions in music and poetry. Sikhs still celebrate the festival annually at Anandpur. They hold a large fair with singing, discussions, and athletic competitions.

There are several important festivals celebrated by women. The festival of *Rakṛī* comes in mid-August. A rakṛī is a bright band that a sister ties around her brother's right wrist as she puts something sweet in his mouth. In turn the brother gives his sister a gift of money, clothing, or jewelry. This brief ritual symbolizes the bond between the siblings.

Tīāṉ is another important celebration for women. When the cool monsoon showers arrive in the month of *Sāvan* (July–August), after the sizzling summer, women dress in their finest garments and leave their homes to enjoy picnics, joy rides, swings, sweet bread (*pūrī*), rice pudding (*khīr*), music, and dancing. Through songs that have been passed down orally through the generations, they remember and celebrate their history. For example, they show affection for the martyred sons of Gūrū Gobind Singh—"*cum cum rakhān kalgī jujhār dī*." This is a major occasion when women buy the brightly colored glass bangles so popular in the Punjab.

Karvā Chauth is a ritual during which women fast the entire day to bring their husbands long life and prosperity. They are not even supposed to sip water. The fast is a way for women to build positive energy that they can transfer to their husbands and families. Starting with Gūrū Nānak, Sikh gūrūs rejected the observance of fasts. However, some ritual fasts, like the Karvā Chauth, have become a part of Sikh life.

Dīvālī is the festival of lights. It is an ancient Hindu festival, commemorating the return of Lord Rāma and his wife Sītā to their kingdom of Ayodhyā after fourteen years of exile. In Sikhism, Dīvālī is a reminder of the time when the Sixth Gūrū returned to Amritsar after the Mogul rulers released him from the fort of Gwalior. During Dīvālī, people whitewash and paint their homes, and decorate them with earthenware lamps and candles. Fireworks light the night sky. Candles and lanterns float in the pools of *gurdwaras*. People exchange gifts and distribute sweets.

Lorī is celebrated in the winter, when the nights are long and cold. Bonfires are lit. Men, women, and children throw sesame seeds and peanuts into the fires. Children go around the neighborhood, collecting money and sweets. The wife's family sends gifts and money for the husband and his family.

There are many multipurpose fairs like *shapar dā melā* and *dhanaule dā melā*. Such gatherings last for several days and draw huge village crowds. There are camel races, bull races, *kabaddī* games (wrestling matches), films, and bazaars. Along with sales of cows and bulls, tractor sales are becoming an important part of these rural fairs.

References

Axel, Brian Keith. 2001. *The nation's tortured body: violence, representation, and the formation of a Sikh diaspora.* Durham: Duke University Press.

Bhachu, Parminder. 1985. *Twice migrants: East African Sikh settlers in Britain.* New York: Tavistock.

Cole, W. O., and Sambhi, Piara Singh. 1978. *The Sikhs, their religious beliefs and practices.* London: Routledge.

Gill, Harjit Singh. 1977. *A phulkari from Bhatinda.* New Delhi: Department of Anthropological Linguistics, Punjabi University Patiala.

Mahmood, Cynthia, and Brady, Stacy. 2000. *The guru's gift: exploring gender equality with North American Sikh women.* Mountain View: Mayfield.

McLeod, W. H. 1991. *Popular Sikh art.* Delhi: Oxford University Press.

Singh, Harbans. 1985. *The heritage of the Sikhs.* New Delhi: Manohar Publishers.

Singh, Nikky-Guninder. 1993. *Sikhism.* N.Y.: Facts on File.

Strong, Susan (ed). 1999. *The arts of the Sikh kingdoms.* London: Victoria and Albert Museum.

Tandon, Prakash. 1968. *Punjabi century.* Berkeley: University of California Press.

NIKKY-GUNINDER KAUR SINGH

SEE ALSO

Character Stereotypes; *Dīvālī/Dīpāvalī;* Gūrū Nānak, Life Stories of; Holī; Punjab; Sikhism

SIKHISM

There are more than twenty-two million Sikhs in the world today, and about twelve million of them live in the Punjab, in northwestern India. There is an intimate link between the soil and soul of the Sikhs: Mother

"Guru Nanak at Mecca." A Muslim Mulla chides Guru Nanak for sleeping with his feet toward Mecca, © Painting by Alam Chand Ram, 1773 A.D. By permission of the British Library

Earth (*mata dharati*), is also the spiritual realm where moral action is performed (*dharam khand*). The Sikh religion rejects spiritual asceticism and affirms the value of daily occupations, marriage, and friendships. In fact, according to the teachings of the ten Sikh *gūrūs*, the deeper the awareness of the Infinite One, the more vibrant is participation in daily life. Spiritual awareness and everyday schedules are integrated, and the division between "official" and "folk" dissolves. Sikhs living in Amritsar, the center of Sikh culture, or in a metropolis like New York, have a work ethic, a worldview, a pattern of worship, and even a code of dress similar to those in rural areas of Punjab.

Gūrū Granth

Gūrū Granth, the holy book, is the sole visual and aural icon for the Sikhs. Its language is simple. The Sikh Gūrūs chose vernacular Punjabi, rather than scholarly and elitist Sanskrit and Persian, as the medium to convey their longing for the Divine. Since reading, reciting, hearing, and seeing the sacred text are equally efficacious, an illiterate peasant is on equal footing with a scholar.

The *Gūrū Granth* is treated with the highest respect and veneration. It is draped in cloth, called *rumālā,* placed on quilted mats, and supported by cushions. A canopy hangs over it for protection, and a whisk is waved over it as a sign of respect. The fabric of the rumālā and canopies may vary: tinsel in small village shrines; silks and brocades in rich urban areas. Sikhs bow before the *Gūrū Granth* and seat themselves on the floor. Shoes are removed and heads are covered in the presence of the holy book. Every day in shrines (and homes), Sikhs open the *Gūrū Granth* at dawn. This act of opening the holy book is called *prakāsh,* "making the light manifest." *Vāk* (the order of the day) is obtained by opening the book at random and reading the passage on the top of the left-hand page. After dusk the *Gūrū Granth* is closed. The closing ritual is called *sukhāsan* (to sit comfortably).

The *Gūrū Granth* is read for rites of passage, for family events, and at times of both difficulty and celebration. The reading may be *saptāh* (a seven-day reading), or it may be *akhand* (a forty-eight-hour, nonstop reading of its 1,430 pages), during which several readers, called *granthī,* take turns. Any Sikh, male or female, who can read Gurmukhī script may read the *Gūrū Granth.*

Kīrtan is the singing of the scriptural verses. The harmonium and tabla (a type of drum) are the most common musical accompaniments. Occasionally sitar and veena (stringed instruments) are used in "highbrow" circles.

Special functions culminate with the bhog ceremony. The word bhog literally means "pleasure." It is similiar to the Greek word "eucharist," which means thanksgiving and, in the spiritual sense, refers to the Christian sacrament of Holy Communion. Bhog involves reading the concluding pages of the *Gūrū Granth,* reciting *ardā* (liturgical prayer said while standing), and sharing the Sikh sacrament of *karāhprashād,* which concludes every religious ceremony.

Karāhprashād is a sweet sacrament made of butter, flour, sugar, and water. During its preparation Sikh men and women have their heads covered and their feet bare, and they recite hymns from the *Gūrū Granth.* When the karāhprashād is ready, it is put in a large, flat dish and placed on the right side of the *Gūrū Granth.* The aromatic sacrament is shared among the entire congregation.

The Five Ks

On *Baisakhī* day in 1699, Gurū Gobind Singh (1675–1708) inaugurated the *Khālsā,* the Order of the Pure.

Since then Sikh men and women around the globe have maintained their identity through five external signs, all beginning with the letter K:

1. *Kesha,* uncut hair—denoting the way of nature.
2. *Kanghā,* a comb tucked into the *kesha* to keep it tidy (in contrast with recluses, who keep it matted as a token of their having renounced the world).
3. *Karqā,* a steel bracelet worn on the right arm. The steel of the bracelet represents spiritual courage and strength, and its circular form, the unity of the Ultimate One, with no beginning or end.
4. *Kaccha,* short breeches worn by the soldiers at the time of the Tenth Gūrū, stand for chastity and moral restraint.
5. *Kirpān,* a sword symbolizing self-defense and the fight against injustice. Often it is represented on a comb or a necklace.

Sikh men have the last name Singh, meaning lion-hearted; the women have Kaur, meaning princess. All Sikhs greet one another by joing their hands together and saying, *Sat Srī Akāl,* which means "Truth is the Timeless One." The men are easily recognized by their untrimmed beards and colorful turbans. Women and girls refrain from cutting their hair as well. Young girls wear long braids, and women tie up their hair in a variety of styles. Sikh women dress in loose trousers (*salvār*), a shirt that reaches to the knees (*kamīz*), and a long, sheer scarf wound around the neck or over the head (*dupattā*).

Sacred Stories

The biographical accounts of the founder, Gūrū Nānak (1469–1539), and of the nine subsequent *Gūrūs*, are important to the Sikh popular imagination. *Janamsākhī* are the contemporary stories (*sākhī*) of Gurū Nānak's life (*janam*) and teachings. They are collected from various oral traditions, *Purātan, Bālā,* and *Meharbān* being among the most popular. They convey altruism and social interaction. Through *Janamsākhī* children are introduced to Sikh morality from a very early age, often through brightly illustrated books.

Sikh Institutions: Sevā, Langar, and Sangat

The highest ideal in Sikh ethics is *sevā,* voluntary manual labor in the service of the community. Beginning with Gūrū Nānak, it has been seen as an essential condition of spiritual discipline. Through sevā Sikh believers cultivate humility, overcome ego, and purify their body and mind. Sevā may take the form of attending to the holy book, sweeping and dusting shrines, preparing and serving food, or looking after (even cleaning the shoes of) worshipers. Young and old, rich and poor, engineers and peasants take on and perform the different tasks.

Langar is both the community meal and the kitchen in which it is prepared. It is a central practice of Sikhism. It testifies to the social equality and familyhood of all people. This fundamental institution involves preparing meals together and eating them together. The food prepared and served at langar is vegetarian. Both men and women participate in preparation and cleanup—chopping vegetables, kneading and rolling out dough, cleaning utensils. Then they sit in *pangat,* a long row, without regard to caste, race, or religion, and eat the meal that they have prepared together.

Sikhs consider langar to be a way of earning merit toward rebirth and their next life. Whether in Amritsar, London, Paris, or Toronto, Sikhs stress the community meal. So long as they observe the basic guidelines, non–Sikhs and foreigners are welcome. Often langar extends beyond the shrines. During certain celebrations, such as the birthday of a gūrū, the celebration of an important historical event, or the martyrdom of a Sikh hero, langar is everywhere, even on the highways and byways. Sikhs of all ages arrange themselves in rows to block the road, or they lay tree trunks across it to stop the flow of traffic. They stop the speeding buses, cars, and trucks, the slow bullock carts, rickshaws, and pedestrians, and they enthusiastically serve langar that includes tea, *chapātī* (flat bread), dāl (cooked pulses), and vegetables to the drivers and passengers.

Sangat is the Sikh gathering, or local community. It is a democratic community without priests or ordained ministers. Like langar, sangat is open to all. Members of the Sikh congregation sit on the floor as they sing hymns, listen to readings from the holy text, recite verses, and pray—with no restrictions as to gender, race, creed, or caste. The inclusive nature of sangat dates to the time of Gūrū Nānak, who welcomed everyone who wished to follow his teachings.

Sacred Space and Time

Sikh sacred space is called *gurdwārā,* literally a door to enlightenment. A gurdwārā may be a simple rustic structure in a small village, or an elegant, multistory building surrounded by a reflecting pool in a city. One identifying mark of a gurdwārā is the flag that flies over it. The flag is yellow in color and triangular in shape, and it is emblazoned with the *Khālsā* emblem: a double-edged sword set in a circle, surrounded by two semicircular swords. A gurdwārā has four doors, indicating welcome to people of all four castes. The focus of attention is the *Gūrū Granth.*

Harimandir, the Golden Temple, at Amritsar, India, is the most sacred of all Sikh holy places. In addition to the Golden Temple, the five *takht,* or seats of temporal authority, are of major importance. In those places, Sikh leaders traditionally make decisions about the secular and religious aspects of Sikhism. The five seats are the Akāl Takht, Patnā Sāhib, Keshgarh Sāhib, Hazīr Sāhib, and Damadamā Sāhib. Several of these places are associated with Sikh history, especially with the life of the Tenth Gūrū, Gobind Singh. Sikhs from across the globe regard it as a special privilege to visit these spots.

Sangrānd is the first day of the month on the Indian solar calendar. Many Sikhs who do not regularly go to the gurdwārā do so on this occasion. They pray for prosperity, health, and peace throughout the month. In the village gurdwārā, warm karāhprashād replaces the sugar puffs more commonly used for the sacrament. *Masiā,* the darkest night of the month, is thought by many Sikhs to be an especially good time for bathing in the holy pool of the gurdwārā. Bathing (*isnān*) is regarded as a means of physical and spiritual refreshment. Sangrānd and masiā celebrations help Sikhs to stay in harmony with the natural rhythms of the month.

Gūrpurabs are Sikh anniversaries. The birth dates of gūrūs, important historical events, and the martyrdom of Sikh heroes are remembered annually. Sikhs all over the world celebrate Baisakhī as a social, political, and religious occasion. The Khālsā community initiates new members on this birthday of the Khālsā itself. At the gurdwārā a new yellow Sikh flag replaces the old one. In the month of Jaith (May–June), Sikhs commemorate the martyrdom of Gūrū Arjan. In August they celebrate the installation of the *Gūrū Granth* in the Golden Temple. As winter comes, Sikhs celebrate the birthdays of the First and Tenth Gūrū, only a month apart. The martyrdom of the Tenth Gūrū's young sons falls during December, preceded by the day of the martyrdom of his father, Gūrū Teg Bahādur.

During the various gūrpurabs, a float decorated with flowers carries the *Gūrū Granth* in a procession through the city or village. Wherever the procession goes, people come out of their homes to see it. They cover their heads and remove their shoes to show respect to the holy book. Along the way Sikhs recite scriptural hymns and serve langar. On the anniversary of Gūrū Arjan's martyrdom, Sikhs serve a blend of cold milk and water, a welcome refreshment in a hot month. Millions gather in the Sirhind area of the Punjab to honor the memory of Gūrū Gobind Singh's young sons who died as martyrs. Farmers bring out wheat, grain, milk, butter, and vegetables. Also during gūrpurabs, Sikh scholars deliver lectures, and uninterrupted readings of the scripture take place, followed by bhog ceremonies. People often attend exhibits of Sikh treasures at shrines like the Golden Temple.

These festivities enable Sikhs to share in their heritage and keep the foundations of the community strong and lively. They can celebrate by participating in the festival atmosphere or simply by praying in a gurdwārā. For the Sikhs, sacred space and sacred time are not two different or separate things. Rather, they merge into the singular experience of the sacred that is beyond all space and time.

References

Cole, W. O., and Sambhi, P. S. 1978. *The Sikhs, their beliefs, and practices*. London: Routledge, and Kegan Paul.

McLeod, W. H. 1989. *Who is a Sikh?* Oxford: Clarendon Press.

Singh, Harbans. 1994. *Heritage of the Sikhs*. New Delhi: Manohar Publishers.

Singh, Nikky-Guninder Kaur. 1995. *The name of my beloved: Verses of the Sikh gurus*. San Francisco: HarperCollins.

NIKKY-GUNINDER KAUR SINGH

SEE ALSO
Gūrū Nānak, Life Stories of; *Kirtana;* Sikh Folklore

SILOK

Silok, a derivative of the Sanskrit *śloka* (verse), is a term commonly applied to folk poetry in Nepali. Though Nepali folk poets are supposed to follow the guidelines of the Sanskrit classical meters, they seldom do so. Nevertheless, it is highly desirable to maintain the same number of syllables in each line, and to have rhymes in the final syllable. In performance, however, the formal structure of a *silok* is usually a minor consideration for poets and their audiences.

Silok are composed, read, and recited by common people to express their emotions and ethos, as in the following silok in which a woman laments her unhappy marriage. Like some of the Nepali folk songs, the first line of the silok may be nonsensical. Nevertheless, it sets an appropriate melodic background to reinforce the statement of the second line. In the following silok, the first line establishes the scene.

> *Madhu ra banamā pāt tipna gaithemṭīkī khasyo pātamā.*
> *Ek dinko lahanā duī dinko sahanā, sindur paryo rātamā.*
>
> Once I went to fetch some green leaves from the Madhuvana, and [unfortunately] my *tīkā* [a decorative mark put on the forehead] was lost on the fallen leaves.
>
> The deal of one day has caused me trouble forever, since I was made wife without my consent by just having *sindur* [a ritual in which the groom puts vermilion powder on the bride's head where her hair is parted, as a symbol of making her his wife] put on my head at night.

Since the meter and rhymes make a text memorable, silok functions as a depository of folk knowledge and wisdom, especially for those who are illiterate. By reciting silok people can retrieve knowledge useful in their daily lives, as in this silok that describes the characteristics of a good buffalo.

Pailā bhaisīṃ nirog, jīu khadamiī asal aṇga ṭhāṅgai mileko.
Kwaile thun patalā hun, siṅghumī kalase, bharī thaile kalchauḍo.
Duī thunko tīna manā dudha-ghīu saṅgako, beta duī kākha paḍī.
Baigun khun kyai nabhāko, duhuna pani sajilo bhaiṇ sī kinnu nachādī.

First the buffalo should be healthy and well built, and her limbs should be in proportion.

Her teats should be black and slender, the horns should be cylindrical and curved, and the udder should be big and heavy.

If she gives almost a liter of milk per teat, if her milk is full of fat, if she is on her second delivery with a she-calf, if she has no bad habits, and if she is easy to milk, then buy her, do not miss.

In villages one of the criteria for measuring a person's intellectual ability is his or her ability to compose, remember, or recite silok. A person can demonstrate his or her talent at the silok *hālne* program held during marriage ceremonies, in which the parties of the bride and groom compete with each other. One party challenges the other by reciting a silok. The other has to respond by starting a silok with the last syllable of the recited silok. Occasionally the silok are made complicated by quizzes and riddles. Finally one party has to yield when it is unable to provide an appropriate and timely response. If both parties are equally talented, the program goes on and is terminated by mutual consent only when the bride departs.

References

Bhattarai, Harihar P. 1985. Folklore studies in Nepal. *Himalayan Culture* 3, no. 1: 10–14.

Pradhan, Kumar. 1984. *A history of Nepali literature*. New Delhi: Sahitya Akademi.

HARIHAR P. BHATTARAI

SEE ALSO
Lament; Nepal; Verbal Dueling; Wedding Songs

SILSILA

Literally "chain" in Persian and Urdu, the term *silsila* designates, in a technical sense, the lineage of individuals through which authority and knowledge are transmitted or transferred, usually orally, by direct personal contact, instruction and initiation. The term is used by Sufi orders to refer to the spiritual genealogy by which a master (*shaykh* or *pīr*) is linked to all his predecessors. Since every Sufi silsila culminates with the Prophet Muḥammad himself, and through him connects to God, it is the most important means by which the *pīr* legitimizes his authority to guide disciples. Through the silsila, the Sufi master inherits the spiritual charisma, knowledge, and *baraka* (blessings, spiritual power) of his predecessors and the Prophet Muḥammad. The disciple (*murīd*), through an oath of allegiance to the pīr during initiation, is also bound to the silsila and gains access to its cumulative store of esoteric wisdom. The concept of an institutionalized tradition of transmission, in the form of a lineage chain legitimizing authority, occurs in other Islamic contexts as well—the authenticity of *ḥadīth* literature, literature that records the sayings and actions of the prophet Muḥammad, is validated by chains of transmitters (*isnād*) whereas the Shī'ī imām bases his authority on lines of direct physical descent from 'Alī, the first Sh'ī'ī imām. In the cultural sphere, the transmission of the various arts of the Muslim world is also based on the concept of the silsila.

References

Graham, William A. 1993. Traditionalism in Islam: an essay in interpretation. *Journal of Interdisciplinary History*. 23:3, 495–522.

Gramlich, Richard. 1981. *Die Schiitischen Derwischorden Persiens*. vols. I, II. Wiesbaden: Kommissionverlag Steiner.

Trimingham, John S. 1971. *Sufi orders in Islam*. Oxford: Clarendon Press.

ALI S. ASANI

SEE ALSO
Ḥadith; Pīr

SINDH

One of the four provinces of Pakistan, Sindh includes the lower 350 miles of the Indus River valley, plus Kohistan, a mountainous region to the west of the river, and the Thar desert, also called Registan, to the east of the Indus delta. Prior to Partition in 1947, which created the states of India and Pakistan from the former British India, Muslim and Hindu groups intermingled in Sindh. With Partition and its accompanying violence, many Hindus emigrated to India, and Indian Muslim refugees (*Muhājir*) came to be a substantial, self-identifying ethnic group in Sindh and elsewhere in Pakistan. Meanwhile, regional Sindhi culture areas and some local populations were divided by the new state borders.

Archaeologically renowned as the primary locale of the Indus Valley civilization (second millennium B.C.E.), which flourished prior to the arrival of Indo-European language speakers in the subcontinent, Sindh is seen by its scholars as the inheritor of this great civilization which left no written history but had trade contacts as far afield as the Mesopotamian cities (for example, Tell Asmar) by 2000 B.C.E. Significant research includes efforts to trace connections of current customs and beliefs, folk art motifs, architectural features, and other traditional institutions with archaeologically revealed ancient roots. These claims to authenticity and cultural continuity are pursued with full acknowledgement of a complex succession of cultural and political influences in the region: "pre-Indus Valley" (exemplified by Bronze-Age Nal pottery styles, 3500–2500 B.C.E.), Indus Valley or Harappan, "Aryan" (including Hellenistic Greek, Persian, and Indo-European language–speaking Central Asians), "Arab" (after the Muslim conquest of Sindh in 721 C.E.), "Mongol" (Mughal as they became in India, with Delhi as their capital), plus Baloch in the fifteenth or sixteenth century C.E., and Pashtun thereafter.

In a region hitherto startling for the range and abundance of its verbal art and material culture productions, another common thread in writings on the region in the mid- to late twentieth century is concern for the survival of verbal art traditions and certain highly demanding crafts in competition with mass manufactured items and mass media entertainment (film, then video and satellite TV).

Verbal Arts

Sindh is one of many locales where it is most productive to regard written literature as a subcategory of verbal arts in general, where much of written literature depends on oral performance for its life and lives alongside related oral forms, with connections to oral tradition in form, composition, and transmission. Any discussion of Sindhi oral tradition must begin with the exhaustive and foundational documentary work of Dr. N. A. Baloch, who along with a series of publications on Sindhi history, traditional music, and material culture, has also edited, under the sponsorhip of the Sindhi Adabi Board, a monumental series of documentary studies of Sindhi verbal genres, numbering more than three dozen volumes. The project began in 1956 and continued for two decades, assembling materials from both oral and written sources. No such systematic archive exists in print for any other region of the country. The volumes listed below have English summary introductions by Dr. Baloch, which comprise an introduction to the extensive system of Sindhi verbal genres. Among the genres documented are:

- Riddles, particularly richly represented, with several named genres differentiated on the basis of their poetic form (stanza form, rhymes, alliteration, etc.), content (religious, secular), and performance contexts.
- Proverbs, with and without narrative substrates.
- Romances devoted to named heroes and heroines: Dodo and Chanesar, Suhni and Mehar, Noori and Jam Tamachi, Lilan and Chanesar, and Sasui and Punhu, among whom Sasui is the most universally known. Sasui's story claims the greatest age, traditionally dated to the eleventh century C.E. and later maintained in performance by professional minstrels, in three main verse versions composed by known poets. It received various written treatments by other Sindhi poets as well. Sasui is a Brahmin girl baby abandoned to the Indus by her parents and rescued and raised by a Muslim washerman. She is the beloved of Punhu, a Baloch prince who becomes a washerman to win her father's consent to marry her. Punhu is later drugged and abducted by his brothers. Sasui, abandoned, follows him into the Kohistan wilderness. Lost, she meets a shepherd who approaches her sexually and she prays to be protected, whereupon she is swallowed up by the earth, except for a bit of her headscarf. Punhu, escaping, comes back to find her, hears the grieving shepherd's story, and prays to be joined with her, whereupon the earth opens and swallows him as well. The geography of the story is recognizable, including a pilgrimage site at the spot where Sasui disappeared. The theme of Sasui's total commitment in love is at the core of the story and has received Sufi mystical interpretations.

  Other named romances regarded by their audience as historical include *Mokhi the Barmaid and the Matara* (Drinkers) and *Muree and Mongthar.* In "Mokhi the Barmaid" a group of connoisseur drinkers is served very old wine into which a cobra has fallen and been dissolved. They love the wine and clamor for more until they learn that cobra venom has flavored it, at which point they all fall dead. In *Muree and Mongthar* a great hunter feeds his beloved wife a piece of his thigh when he fails at hunting, yet she falls in love with a black-haired shepherd and kills her husband to get rid of him; the shepherd is horrified and cuts off his hair and gives it to her, telling her to leave him alone.
- Folk tales: Seven volumes are devoted to summarized prose folk tales, categorized as (1) Kings, Queens, Princes and Princesses; (2) Kings, Ministers and Merchants; (3) Fairies, Demons, Magicians, Witches, and Sooth-Sayers; (4) Kings, Rich Men, Wise Men, Cheats, etc.; (5) Tales for the Young; (6) Tales of Birds and Animals; (7) *Cante Fable* or prosimetric narratives, prose stories with individual titles pertaining to personal names of the characters and containing

composed verse, which in the Sindhi genre system are a bridge between the prose folktale and the romances described above, including like the romances allusions to historical details and some claims to historicity.

- Religious poetic genres, including separate volumes on *mu'jaza* (compositions pertaining to miracle tales of prophets and saints), *madāhoon* and *munājāroon,* and *manāqibī* (two volumes on three distinct poetic forms in praise of the Prophets and revered saints, with biographical content), and *maulood* songs for the Prophet, sung with musical accompaniment on the occasion of his birth but also celebrating other aspects of his life. All of these genres comprise poems by named poets, some previously in print, others not.
- *Baita* and *wāqiātī baita,* couplet compositions, the latter defined as compositions commemorating events.
- Other genres are represented by a volume devoted to *Hafta, Deenhan, Ratiyoon,* and *Maheena,* clusters of lyric poems devoted to praise of the beloved and named after days of the week, numbered days or nights of the month, months, etc., attributed to named poets, many identified historically, including the foremost of Sindhi literary poets, Shah Abdul Latif of Bhit.
- Obviously related to literacy is the poetic genre of *teeha akhanyoon,* "thirty-lettered compositions," with each stanza or couplet beginning with a letter of the alphabet in order, and full of alliteration, following a Persian model (*sī harfī*) but often using indigenous Sindhi meters and stanza forms. Of fifty-three poems presented, all by known poets, thirty-two had not been printed previously, indicating the importance of oral performance to this very large corpus of material.
- *Munāzirā,* or disputations in verse, also called *jherra.* The disputants may be abstracts (for example, love and reason), two figures from well-known romances (heroines Sasui and Marui), generic characters (husband and wife), or animals or objects. Eventually a third character is introduced as referee. The speech style of the parties is shaped according to modal personality (for example, farmer and landlord) to demonstrate the poet's acuteness of observation. This collection of 157 poems by 117 poets was predominantly orally transmitted at the time it was documented, only nine having been printed before. About half of the named poets were traced historically by the editor.
- *Geecha* or women's songs, also called *giya* or *gawan.* Within the genre, *saatth-giya* or marriage songs are judged to be of great antiquity, while others are estimated to date prior to 1350 C.E. on the basis of internal evidence. The collection includes songs in three languages. Sindhi, Siraiki, and the Tharī of the Tharparkar desert district. *Sihra* is a related genre composed in a more literary style by known male poets; all female-composed songs are anonymous.

The women's songs begin with a verse which becomes a refrain, separating individual verses strung together. They can be categorized in two subgenres: songs of celebration, invoking blessings with praise for God, the Prophet, and saints, sung on any happy occasion, and marriage songs sung by the bridegroom's women relatives, who sing praises for the expensive preparations for the wedding, the virtues of the bride and groom, etc., at each stage of the wedding ceremonies. Geecha are always sung in chorus, in groups of up to ten or twelve women, sometimes accompanied by dance by the groom's nearest relatives. About three traditional melodies predominate in this nonprofessional singing, accompanied by *dholak,* a small drum, or *thall,* a large brass platter used for percussion accompaniment.

Geecha of the bride's party are said to have almost died out by the 1960s, but to have formerly been given a distinct genre term, *kamin,* which literally means "magic." Baloch speculates that the magic was once incantation sung on behalf of the bride, to give her control over the groom, but was later replaced by more acceptable forms of praise and injunctions to the groom to treat the bride well and be loyal. They are sung in the voice of the mother-in-law (paraphrased by Baloch, 1964 p. v):

> *Kamins* shall have their effect.
> They shall be effective in fact.
> Like fragrant oil they still apply.
> Like sandal-wood powder they shall apply.
> Like red henna they shall apply.
>
> Dear son! Our *kamins* had their effect on you
> Do not depart from us, be true!
> The previous ones will give up your hand,
> the "new ones" will stick to the end,
> Dear son! our *kamins* have an effective wand.

Of about 5000 geecha collected, many of them variants of each other over a broad regional distribution, 1467 complete texts in three languages, Sindhi, Siraiki, and Tharī, were printed in the volume.

Material Culture

"Folk arts" is a problematical distinguishing term where production is *all* artisanal, just as "folklore" is a problematical concept in an exclusively or predominantly oral culture. Yet some distinctions have been made, perhaps only to be unmade in favor of a continuum model on further reflection. From earliest times, elite patronage, now largely disappeared in the wake of the colonial period, played a formative role in crafts production, creating a "high end" market for skills and types of products that also had basic general-market and domestic-production forms. G. A. Allana notes that the fifth century B.C.E. Sanskrit grammarian Pāninī distinguished between *raj shilpin* (royal crafts/artisans) and *grama shilpin* (village crafts/artisans) and listed five artisans to be found in every village: potter, blacksmith, carpenter, barber, and washerman, all to one degree or another marginalized or "lower caste" professions in historical times.

In 1966, the recently formed Mehran Arts Council organized a seminar to inventory traditional arts and crafts in the central, Hyderabad region of Sindh, which to an extent reflects the range of production in the province. At that time, the scholars noted the effects of colonial as well as post-colonial social, economic, and political change on the lives of artisans and on production and markets. National and provincial government schemes for craftspeople's income generation and for maintaining the viability of traditional crafts were underway but were of concern because, as the Mehran workshop concluded, "It is not the mass production but production by the masses which brings prosperity to the nation" (Baloch 1966, p. 15). While government handicrafts–income generation schemes have remained in place for the rest of the century, supplemented with efforts by certain non-governmental organizations (NGOs), they have not achieved the national viability of similar regional/provincial schemes in India, where a larger and growing middle class seems to form a healthier domestic market for handwork, a more elaborated national marketing network has been created, and private export trade has also been more systematically developed.

Among the handicrafts profiled in 1966 were:

- Pottery, wheel-thrown and molded, including more than forty named domestic utility articles still marketed, as well as musical instruments, toys, and architectural elements such as roof and drain tiles, and glazed tile for architectural decoration of mosques and fine houses, the latter developed under Persian influence in design and technique.
- Needle arts, including many styles of embroidery: mirror work; *gajj* embroidery in silk on small cloth squares with geometric patterns of running and satin stitches, incorporated into a fitted blouse called *gajj; zardozī* gold and silver metallic thread work on velvet (formerly a major industry for elite women's dress and men's caps; down to one aged master craftsman in 1966); sequin and beadwork, including beadweaving; woolen embroidery on winter shawls; the elaborate appliqued and embroidered quilts called *rallī,* a salvage art originally sewn by women for domestic use, the varied color schemes bespeaking their locales of origin; cotton, silk, and metallic thread embroidery on leather (primarily a male activity), often for shoes, prayer mats, and small personal items, but also on large squares of camel or deer hide (*nutt*) for table covers and wall decorations.
- Textiles; several kinds of hand-loomed materials, plus tie-dye and block printing, especially the regionally-unique *ajrak,* a block-print technique involving multiple steps of both resist and mordant printing using hand-carved wooden blocks and successive rounds of vat-dyeing with madder and indigo.
- Carpet weaving, including indigenous striped flatweave forms made of goat hair or camel hair on a cotton warp, later augmented by geometric and floral-design, knotted pile carpet production introduced from Central Asia perhaps during the period of Moghul invasion of India (fifteenth-century C.E.).
- Decorative painting on walls, ceilings, and architectural trim, as well as on cloth, leather, and pottery. Most is floral or geometric and may integrate calligraphy. Predominant colors were green, red, sky blue, and white. This art form lost its elite patronage during the British colonial era.

Other Sindhi indigenous crafts to be added to this list include stone- and wood-carving for architectural and decorative use, lacquer work on wood, jewelry making (gold- and silversmithing, lapidary work, bead-making, glass bangle making), calligraphy, and the local production of materials in support of the above crafts, such as tools supplied by blacksmiths, wood blocks for block printing, dyes, paints, glazes, and other chemicals for textiles and pottery, locally produced fiber for textiles as well as basketry and mat-weaving, and tanning of leather.

Neither sufficiently current and comprehensive inventories nor properly detailed ethnographies of individual crafts and communities have been produced for this region. Lok Virsa, the National Folk Heritage institution, and its museum in Islamabad continue to sponsor and spotlight master craftspeople from Sindh as well as other locales as exhibitors at the annual folk festival, Lok Mela, and in other venues as opportunity permits, but concern for the survival and economic viability of highly skilled indigenous crafts is well-founded.

References

Allana, Ghulam Ali, n.d. *Art of Sind.* Islamabad: Lok Virsa.

Allana, Ghulam Ali, ed. 1982. *Folk music of Sind.* Jamshoro, Pakistan: University of Sindh Institute of Sindhology.

Baloch, N. A. 1975. *Musical instruments of the lower Indus Valley of Sind.* Hyderabad, Sindh, Pakistan: Zeb Adabi Markaz.

———. 1982. Prehistoric to early historic period; Developments under Islamic civilization; developments in the sub-continent: Evolution of the music tradition in Sind. In *Folk music of Sind*, ed. G. A. Allana, 1–26. Jamshoro, Pakistan: University of Sindh Institute of Sindhology.

Baloch, N. A., ed. 1961. *Baita compositions.* Sindhi folklore and literature, Book XVIII. Hyderabad, Pakistan: Sindhi Adabi Board.

———. 1960. *Folk tales–I. (Kings, queens, princes and princesses.)* Sindhi Folklore and Literature, Book XXI. Hyderabad, Pakistan: Sindhi Adabi Board.

———. 1963. *Folk tales–II. (Kings, ministers and merchants.)* Sindhi Folklore and Literature, Book XXII. Hyderabad, Pakistan: Sindhi Adabi Board.

———. 1963. *Folk tales–III. (Fairies, demons, magicians, witches and sooth-sayers.)* Sindhi Folklore and Literature, Book XXIII. Hyderabad, Pakistan: Sindhi Adabi Board.

———. 1961. *Folk tales–IV. (Kings, rich men, wise men, cheats, etc.)* Sindhi Folklore and Literature, Book XXIV. Hyderabad, Pakistan: Sindhi Adabi Board.

———. 1962. *Folk tales–V. (Tales for the young.)* Sindhi Folklore and Literature, Book XXV. Hyderabad, Pakistan: Sindhi Adabi Board.

———. 1962. *Folk tales–VI. (Tales of birds and animals.)* Sindhi Folklore and Literature, Book XXI. Hyderabad, Pakistan: Sindhi Adabi Board.

———. 1964. *Folk tales–VII. Gāhana Sān Galhyūn. (Stories in narrative form).* Sindhi Folklore and Literature, Book XXI. Hyderabad, Pakistan: Sindhi Adabi Board.

———. 1964. *Geecha. The homely songs of the women-folk.* Sindhi Folklore and Literature, Book XVI. Hyderabad, Pakistan: Sindhi Adabi Board.

———. 1961. *Hafta, deenhan, ratiyoon, maheena. (Poems entitled weeks, days, nights and months.)* Sindhi Folklore and Literature, Book VII. Hyderabad, Pakistan: Sindhi Adabi Board.

———. 1961. *Manāqibā. Compositions in praise of the prophets, and the revered saints.* Sindhi Folklore and Literature, Book II. Hyderabad, Pakistan: Sindhi Adabi Board.

———. 1961. *Maulood.* Sindhi Folklore and Literature, Book IV. Hyderabad, Pakistan: Sindhi Adabi Board.

———. 1961. *Mu'jazā. Compositions pertaining to miracles of the prophets and the saints.* Sindhi Folklore and Literature, Book III. Hyderabad, Pakistan: Sindhi Adabi Board.

———. 1961. *Munāzirā (Disputations).* Sindhi Folklore and Literature, Book X. Hyderabad, Pakistan: Sindhi Adabi Board.

———. 1964. *Popular folk stories. The romantic stories of Sind-I.* Sindhi Folklore and Literature, Book XXIX. Hyderabad, Pakistan: Sindhi Adabi Board.

———. 1971. *Popular folk stories. The romantic stories of Sind-II. The romance of Lilan-Chanesar.* Sindhi Folklore and Literature, Book XXXI. Hyderabad, Pakistan: Sindhi Adabi Board.

———. 1972. *Popular folk stories. The romantic stories of Sind-III. Suhni-Mehar and Noori-Jam Tamachi.* Sindhi Folklore and Literature, Book XXX. Hyderabad, Pakistan: Sindhi Adabi Board.

———. 1976. *Popular folk stories. The romantic stories of Sind-IV. Sasui-Punhu.* Sindhi Folklore and Literature, Book XXXII. Hyderabad, Pakistan: Sindhi Adabi Board.

———. 1971. *Riddles and proverbs.* Sindhi Folklore and Literature, Book XXXI. Hyderabad, Pakistan: Sindhi Adabi Board.

———. 1960, 1961. *Teeha Akhanyoon, The thirty-lettered compositions*, 2 vols. Sindhi Folklore and Literature, Books V and VI. Hyderabad, Pakistan: Sindhi Adabi Board.

———. 1966. *The traditional arts and crafts of Hyderabad region. Proceedings of the seminar, Mehran Arts council, Hyderabad, May 22, 1966.* Hyderabad, Sindh, Pakistan: Mehran Arts council.

———. 1961. *Wāqiātī Baita. (Compositions commemorating events).* Sindhi Folklore and Literature, Book IX. Hyderabad, Pakistan: Sindhi Adabi Board.

Bunting, Ethel-Jane. 1980. *Sindhi tombs and textiles: The persistence of pattern.* Albuquerque, N.M.: University of New Mexico Press.

Cousin, Francoise. 1981. Some data on block-printing in Sind. In *Sind through the centuries*, ed. Hamida Khuhro, 228–236. Karachi: Oxford University Press.

Doktor, Roma, 1985. Sindhi folklore: An introductory survey. *Folklore* 96:2: 223–233.

Duarte, Adrian. 1982. *The crafts and textiles of Sind and Baluchistan.* Jamshoro, Pakistan: University of Sindh Institute of Sindhology.

Khuhro, Hamida, ed. 1981. *Sind through the centuries.* Karachi: Oxford University Press.

Kincaid, C. A. 1925 (1976). *Folk tales of Sind and Guzerat.* London: Oxford University Press (reprint Ahmedabad: New Order Book Company).

Schimmel, Annemarie. 1974. Sindhi literature. In *A history of Indian literature*, ed. Jan Gonda. Vol. VIII, Wiesbaden: Otto Harrassowitz.

Westphal-Hellbusch, Sigrid, and Westphal, Heinz. n.d. *The Jat of Pakistan.* Islamabad: Lok Virsa.

Wheeler, Mortimer. 1972. *The Indus civilization.* Cambridge: Cambridge University Press.

MARGARET A. MILLS

SEE ALSO

Bait/Bayt; Folk Art; Glass; *Kāfī;* Maternal Culture, Pakistan; *Munazira*

SIRI

Siri is the name of a goddess worshiped in the Tulu-speaking of region Karnataka, where the same term (siri) can also refer to a class of deities. In both senses, there are sacred oral traditions (*pāḍḍana*) that tell the deities' stories. Siri and the siri deities are worshiped in connection with regionally organized annual rituals (*jātras*), which entail the mass possession of participants by the siri spirits. The women who participate in the cult are also sometimes referred to as siris.

An oral narrative, mythic in quality, epic in length, called the *Siri Pāḍḍana,* tells the lives of the siri spirits, beginning with the miraculous birth of Siri, and continues through her disastrous marriage to an unfaithful husband and her subsequent remarriage. By her first husband, Siri has a son, Kumar, and by her second, a daughter, Sonne. The myth continues into subsequent generations of this matrilineal family. Sonne gives birth to twin daughters, Abbaga and Daraga, who, in the end, die tragically, playing a game of *cenne (mancala),* one killing the other in a fit of jealousy and then taking her own life. The life of Ginde, step-sister of Sonne, is described in a related myth.

The annual ceremonies take place at fifteen or twenty locations, called *āluḍe* (most likely from *āl-,* "to rule" plus "*-aḍe,*" "place"), or *mūlasthāna* (*mūla,* "root, origin" plus *sthāna,* "place"). At some locations the rituals are preceded with a dramatization of the myth. During the rituals, up to a thousand or more women and men, gathering into groups of twenty to thirty individuals, are possessed by spirits. Except for men possessed by the spirit of Siri's son, Kumar, the participants are not regarded as professionals and come from different villages, different castes, different backgrounds, and usually have little or no contact with one another at other times of the year.

The bulk of the ritual at the annual ceremonies consists of cases of spirit investigation. Novices (first-time participants), mostly young women, are brought to the Siri festival because they have been experiencing spirit possession in their homes, which can be embarrassing and disruptive and is regarded as undesirable. During the rituals, such cases are dealt with, one at a time, through an investigation of the young woman and her family. The investigations are led by Kumar with the assistance of one or more of the Siris. The process normally involves getting the young woman into a state of possession and then inquiring into the identity of the Siri spirit and why it is giving her trouble. At the end of each "case" the spirit in the young woman is expected to identify itself and make clear why it has been intruding on the lives of the family. The family promises to meet whatever demands the spirit might be making. Although her home life usually stabilizes and she subsequently behaves according to social norms, the young woman is required to return to the Siri festival annually. She becomes a medium for the spirit and joins the ranks of the other women as an adept.

All of this takes place in a sing-song speech style characteristic of the Siri rituals. Some of Kumar's discourse uses fragments of the *Siri Pāḍdana,* but most of it is impromptu (sung) speech. Meanwhile, women (adepts), possessed by one of the Siri spirits, may be reciting various episodes from the *Siri Pāḍdana,* either alone or with another woman.

The Siri ritual can be documented at least as far back as the sixteenth century. An earlier form of the Siri cult may have consisted of the worship of twins, variously identified as Abbaga and Daraga, Sonne and Ginde, or Mayage and Maipage, and may have revolved around fertility and the perpetuity of matrilineal lines. Portions of variants of the Siri myth are found in other Tulu genres and some of these suggest links with Malayali myths and rituals revolving around *nāga* (cobra) worship.

References

Bhatt, Gururaja, 1969. *Antiquities of South Kanara.* Udupi: Milagres College, Kallianpur.

Claus, Peter J. 1975. Siri myth and ritual: description of a mass possession cult of south India. *Ethnology,* 14(1): 47–58.

———. 1987. Mancala (cenne) in Tulu myth and cult. In *Indian folklore II,* eds. Peter J. Claus, D. P. Pattanayak, and J. Handoo. Mysore: Central Institute of Indian Languages Press.

———. 1993. Text variability and authenticity in the Siri cult. In *Flags of fame: studies in south Asian folk culture,* ed. Heidrun Brückner, et al. Delhi: The Inter-regional Seminar, South Asia Institute, University of Heidelberg.

———. 1997. Ritual transforms a myth. *South Indian Folklorist.* 1(1): 37–57.

Honko, Lauri, Chinnappa Gowda, Anneli Honko, and Viveka Rai. 1998. *The Siri epic as performed by Gopala Naika. Parts I and II.* Folklore Fellows' Communications No. 265–266. Helsinki: Suomalainen Tiedeakatemia (Academia Scientiarum Fennica).

PETER J. CLAUS

SEE ALSO

Epic; Gods and Goddesses; Mancala; *Nāga; Pāḍdana; Pāmpin Tuḷḷal;* Rituals; Spirit Possession and Mediumship

SĪTALĀ

Sītalā, "The Cool One," is best known as the goddess of smallpox and other diseases involving skin eruptions, such as measles and chicken pox. Every part of India has a goddess concerned with smallpox, and in northern India (from Gujarat to Bengal) she is commonly known by the name Sītalā. (In most of southern India, the goddess of smallpox is known as Māriamman, "Giver of Death or Rain.") While best known as the giver of the pox to those who have angered her, Sītalā is also known as the protector of children and the giver of good fortune. The Sītalā cult is perhaps most highly developed in Bengal, where there are major all-village *pūjā*s (devotional rituals) in her honor, lengthy poems (*maṅgal*) written to praise her, and numerous temples constructed for her worship. Her connections to the dreaded pox are clearest in Bengal. In contrast, in Gujarat, Sītalā is primarily the giver of good fortune, husbands, and sons. There is no literary tradition about Sītalā, and her temples are not numerous.

In all areas where she is worshiped, Sītalā is "the Cool One," a goddess who abhors heat and seeks coolness. Born from cooled ashes, she is by nature cool.

Sītalā rewards those who make her cool, and "burns" with fever those who cause her to burn. She is portrayed riding an ass, carrying a broom and water vessel, with a winnowing fan on her head. She is usually dressed as a married woman or an elderly Brahman woman, a favorite disguise, although sometimes she is portrayed naked.

In Bengal there is no fixed date for Sītalā's worship, but in the Hindi-speaking regions she is generally worshiped during the month of Caitra or Baisakh (April or May), the hot, dry season, when smallpox epidemics were most common and other diseases with skin eruptions, like chicken pox, are prevalent. In the Hindi-speaking regions her worship, sometimes called *basorā* (literally, "leftover food worship"), involves offerings of cool or stale food. Cooking on the day of Sītalā's worship is forbidden. In Bengal cooking for Sītalā is allowed. In Gujarat, cooking is banned, and Sītalā is worshiped mostly during the rainy season.

The *vrat kathā*s (stories) for Sītalā are many and varied, and her worship is clearly established by the medieval period, when both the proper ritual actions and the supporting stories are given in the Hindu lawbooks known as the *nibandha*s. What unites these many tales is the theme of heating and cooling, and maintaining the proper bodily balance between these. The theme of the proper balance between heat and coolness pervades Hindu thought, whether regarding food habits or Āyurvedic medicine. Whatever else Sītalā may be now or in the future—the goddess of smallpox, the protector of children, the giver of good fortune—it is clear that she will always be a reminder to her human worshipers of the necessity to maintain the proper balances of heat and coolness.

References

Kolenda, Pauline. 1982. Pox and the terror of childlessness: images and ideas of the smallpox goddess in a north Indian village. In *Mother worship: themes and variations* ed., James J. Preston. Chapel Hill: University of North Carolina Press.

Wadley, Susan S. 1980. Sītalā: The cool one. *Asian Folklore Studies* 39(1): 33–62.

SUSAN S. WADLEY

SEE ALSO

Goddesses, Hindu; Hot/Cold; *Māriyamma;* Medicine, Āyurveda; *Vrat Kathā*

ŚIVA

Along with Viṣṇu and the Goddess, Śiva is one of three great forms of deity in Hinduism. All three have multiple names, forms, and expressions in regional as well as pan-Indian folklore and folk ritual. Śiva strongly contrasts with the more urbane, gracious Viṣṇu and is sometimes identified as supreme god of rural India. An "outsider" god, he inhabits the wilderness, mountains, dry plains, cemeteries, and remote crossroads. Some of his roots are in the *ugra* (powerful, ferocious) Ṛgvedic wilderness god Rudra of the late second millennium B.C.E, a god at first excluded from the great sacrificial system but gradually accepted. In the late Vedic *Śvetaśvatara Upaniṣad,* a poet carefully addresses the terrifying, death-dealing Rudra as *Śiva* ("auspicious"), the name by which the god is best known today. The litany of Rudra's names in the *Śatarudrīya-stotra,* chapter 16 of the *Vājasaneyī-samhitā* (also known as the White or *Śukla Yajurveda*) became formative and is still a basic liturgy in Śiva temples today. It echoes in cults of major folk deities, for example, in western India's Khāṇḍobā. And the ferocious ritual *gaṇa* (horde) of Vīrabhadra-Śiva's minions in southeast India recalls the destructive Rudras or Rudriyas of ancient myths.

Other roots of Vedic-Hindu Rudra-Śiva may go deeper than the Vedas and into the third millennium B.C.E. Speculation on archeological and linguistic evidence has led some scholars to suggest links to the religions of the Indus Valley, for example, in steatite seals depicting a powerful male figure seated in "yogic" *padmāsana,* lotus posture, apparently animal-masked and ithyphallic, or in representations of fig tree deities. In another direction there is speculation that the myths and cult of an Indo-Iranian archer deity may have played a role in the early history of both Śarva (an epithet of Rudra) and Saurva of ancient Iran.

Well before the Common Era, Śiva secured a permanent place in the developing Hindu pantheon. His roles are displayed in the *Mahābhārata, Purāṇas, Tantra*s, *Āgama*s, vernacular *bhakti* traditions such as the sixty-three Tamil Nāyānmārs, regional sects, theological and philosophical schools, such as the Pāśupatas, Kāpālikas, Vīraśaivas (Liṅgāyats), Śaiva Siddhānta, and various systems in Kashmir, and folklore of every region of South Asia and much of Southeast Asia. His stature grew until, for many, he became simply *Mahāśvara* (Great Lord), *Mahādeva* (Great God), and *Parameśvara* (Highest Lord). Śiva's Sanskrit names include, among many others, Ardhanārīśvara, Bhava, Bhīma, Hara, Īśāna, Kapardin, Naṭarāja, Śambhu, Śaṅkara, and Sthāṇu. Powerful, virtually independent deities born from his uncontrollable rage include Bhairava and Vīrabhadra. Regional deities more or less clearly connected to his traditions and cults, even when they are scarcely addressed as Śiva, are plentiful. To cite an example that is widespread and interregional (Andhra, Karnataka, and Maharashtra), the gods Mallaṇṇa (or Mallikārjuna), Mailāra, Khaṇḍobā (or Mallāri, Malhāri, Mairāḷ) all adhere to a particular folk deity rather than sectarian or purāṇic Śiva.

Pārvātī, also known as Umā or Gaurī, is Śiva's most frequent consort, but Satī, Gaṅgā, and others play similar roles. Gaṇeśa, son of Śiva and Pārvātī, provides a popular family trio, but another son of Śiva, Skanda or Kārttikeya, identified with Murukan in Tamil tradition, is almost as favored. Colorful "god-posters" commonly include Śiva's *vahana* (mount), the bull Nandi, lying contentedly near Śiva, Pārvātī, and Gaṇeśa.

Few deities in the history of religions are as complex and ambiguous. The central paradox in the mythology of Śaivas (worshipers of Śiva), according to Wendy Doniger O'Flaherty, is that Śiva, prototype of renunciant, celibate ascetics such as *yogi*s and *sādhu*s, is god of the *liṅga* (phallus). Many other paradoxes endure in popular tales either descended from Sanskrit epic and purāṇic myths or emergent from regional vernacular lore. Śiva obliterates the world with his dance of destruction, yet saves it from catastrophe by catching the flooding torrent of the Ganges in his hair, or by drinking poison that turns his throat blue. He makes passionate love to Pārvātī for 36,000 years, yet destroys the god of love for disturbing his meditation. As Mahāyogin he renounces the householder's world of sacrifice, yet he destroys Dakṣa's sacrifice because he has not been invited. He is Ardanārīśvara, the Lord who is Half Female. He is Mahāliṅga god of the great liṅga, yet he is a god who is castrated. Śiva's rival as supreme male divine power is Viṣṇu and tales of their competition are legion, yet the two become one as Harihara.

Śiva in Space and Time

The space of Śiva is "outside" in both geographic and social senses. He is found in remote, uninhabited spaces, untamed lands where he associates with wild animals, including those he has killed. Seated on an elephant or tiger hide, with venomous *nāga*s (cobras) encircling his body, a meditating Śiva wears a necklace of human skulls. White ants (termites) in stone-hard mounds (all nāga residences in popular belief), play in his domain, reinforcing his links to death and regeneration in the netherworld. The fierce composite beast Śarabha is the form he takes to defeat Viṣṇu as Nārasiṁha (Man-Lion). But conversely, Śiva is also known as Paśupati, Lord of (domestic) animals, and his inseparable companion is a benign bull.

In the wild space of Śiva, several trees are noteworthy. The *bilva* or *bel* (wood apple) is sacred to Śiva, its trifoliate leaves (recalling his three eyes) a favored item in *pūjā* to his liṅga form. The *pipal* (*aśvattha*) fig is another abode for Śiva as well as nāgas and ghosts. One should shade every burning and burial ground as, one hopes, a temporary haven for migratory *preta*s (spirits of the dead). Another fig tree associated with Śiva is the *vaṭa* (*nyagrodha*), or banyan, with its phallic aerial roots. Flowers of the *aśoka* were offered by Pārvātī to Śiva, and the god then granted immortality to this enduring tree. Devotees of Śiva often wear *rudrākṣa* beads, berries of *Elaeocarpus ganitrus,* fingered during *japa* (recitations), for example, when counting his hundred names.

Figuring prominently in Saiva folklore and ritual are both fire and ashes, the remnants of fire, sacrifice, destruction, cremation. As Naṭarāja, King of the Dance, a dancing Śiva holds a flame in his upper right hand. Ecstatically possessed devotees with flying *jaṭās* (matted locks of Śiva) may handle fire in this manner, walk on fires of wood or camphor, swallow burning coals or skewer cheeks and tongue with lances tipped with burning wicks, (these skewers represent Śiva's most prominent weapon, the *triśūla* [trident]). Śiva's semen is fiery, as is his third eye with its capacity to burn someone to ashes. Kāma, god of erotic love, suffered this fate, and the triple city of the demons was incinerated by Śiva's fire. In his *śmaśāna* home Śiva is ghostly white, covered with ashes of the dead. In widespread ritual use, *vibhūti* is a sacred ash, often of burnt cow dung, but understood to be the cremation ashes from Śiva's body and therefore endowed with his grace, his healing and regenerative powers, his cooled fire.

Śiva's perpetually erect liṅga is most often stone, the element of his cosmic mountain residence, and in folk belief frequently perceived as *svayambhū* (self-manifest, i.e. natural and unworked). There are countless tales of an endless liṅga or a liṅga that bleeds and harms when damaged or slighted, but speaks and rewards when honored. Every home of his devotees displays a liṅga, as do nearly every village and many crossroads. On wilderness roads travelers on foot may honor a great boulder or fig tree as locus of Śiva, and long-distance truck drivers do not neglect his shrines. Liṅgāyats carry or wear a small liṅga.

Śiva is sometimes known as Kāla—time itself—that ambiguous abstraction that appears endless, yet cyclical. In his Naṭarāja form, during his dance that destroys the world, the white crescent moon shines in his hair, signifying cycles of time in which Śiva not only destroys but regenerates. The crescent is a waxing moon, symbol of growth and increase. In the Hindu calendar of lunar months, nights of Śiva (*Śivarātri*), special for his worship, occur on the eve of each new moon day *(amāvāsyā)*, the fourteenth of each dark fortnight. Once each solar year, in Māgha (January-February) or Phālguna (February-March), there is his great night, Mahāśivarātri. Śaivas, and indeed most Hindus, remain awake in *jāgara* (vigil) all night in worship, meditation, and fasting. Of the weekdays it is Monday, the day of the moon and of the sacred plant of immortality, *soma,* that is most auspicious for the worship of Śiva.

Śiva himself, powerful Mahādeva, is subject to the influence of planets. In particular, the gaze of the malevolent planet Śani (Saturn) causes anxiety. Common are tales of Śiva, immediately after his boast that he fears no one, found hiding in a hollow tree by a mocking Śani. Every being is subject to a baleful glance from this awesome planet. It was Sani's stare that decapitated Śiva's son Gaṇeśa. Another of the *navagrahas* (nine major planets) feared by Śiva is Sūrya, the Sun, whose blaze daily obliterates the Moon in Śiva's hair.

Worship and Meditation

Devotion to and worship of Śiva takes place in a wide range of castes and communities. Śiva is identified in folklore as a hunter, woodsman, herder, farmer, warrior, trader, artisan, healer, vagabond, bandit, leper, and so on, and numerous castes claim a special relationship. For many devotees the distinctive appeal of folk Śaivism is access to the god without mediation of Brahmans or brahmanic regulations.

Śiva's liṅga generally serves as center for pūjā directed to the great god. Often the popular paradigm is Pārvātī's or Lakṣmī's simple offering of *bilva* leaves, water, and flowers to Śiva as liṅga or in a bilva tree. Milk, honey, and other usual pūjā items may augment worship. Liquid offerings onto the liṅga run off in a north-directed channel in the *yoni* (female genitals) or *pīṭha* (seat) in which the liṅga is positioned. Recitations of the names of Śiva and a favored Vedic five-syllable mantra, *namaḥ śivāya,* praise him. More elaborate worship might consist of a *homa* fire offering, *naivedya* (cooked food), meditation upon Śiva as fire, light, and regenerative seed, and *nyāsa,* touching different bodily parts to transfer powers from the five faces of Śiva.

In former times, but less frequently today, *bali* offerings of meat to Śiva were prominent, as they were in cults of the dead and in magic and sorcery. Again, continuities with ancient Rudra surface here, as well as in Śiva's close links to fierce *(raudra)* goddesses and the blood sacrifices they demand. Bhairava and Vīrabhadra are alloforms of the god at the extreme, violent end of his *ghora* (awful) spectrum. Meat offerings still today figure in the esoteric rituals of the tantric tradition's left-hand *(vāmācāra)* path, where Śiva's *saumya* (mild) aspects surface while feminine power is highlighted. Śiva, the Goddess, and their union are the focus of this form of tantrism in which a male adept identifies with Śiva, while his female partner is ritually transformed into the Goddess, her *śakti* serving as redemptive power. The *kuṇḍalinī* female serpent force is awakened to rise up through the levels of the male's cosmicized body. In these tantric rituals four substances proscribed by orthoprax brahmanic worship, each beginning with the letter "m" in Sanskrit, are offered with the left hand: meat, fish, an intoxicating beverage, parched grain. The fifth "m" of this *pañcamakāra* ritual is *maithuna,* sexual intercourse, performed either physically or meditatively. This ultimate union at the top of the yogic body accomplishes a divine transcendence of all dualities. While the number of *vāmācāra* adepts remains small today, tantric ideology and symbolism in general have exerted a pervasive and continuing influence upon regional folklore and ritual.

Music and dance also play a part in Śaiva worship. Śiva is known for his *tāṇḍava* dance of destruction, a ritual erasure of the world to the beat of a drum. A drum beat accompanies a corpse to the cemetery. Cymbals, the blowing of flutes and conch shells, ecstatic dancing as writhing cobras or as fiercely stomping heroes imitating Śiva all play a role. Women possessed and animated by Vīrabhadra-Śiva may involuntarily dance strenuous *vīrāṅga* steps as powerful heroines.

Śiva is often portrayed seated cross-legged, eyes closed in deep meditation *(dhyāna).* A devotee may employ this as a form of worship, even identification, or persist in extended periods of dhyāna to impress Mahādeva and force a boon. In the Tamil martial folk epic *Aṇṇaṇmār* the barren heroine Tāmarai doggedly meditates for twenty-one years on Mt. Kailāsa before Śiva grants her pregnancy with triplets. Such devotional *tapas* (austerity, creative heat) may go to extremes. When narrating their personal histories, possession ritualists frequently speak of falling into comas for five, seven, or nine days. Unknown to their families, who considered them all but dead, they received instructions from Śiva and Pārvātī on Mt. Kailāsa. Dedicated tapas can reach the point of more or less violent self-sacrifice to Śiva, parallel to self-immolations to goddesses. Often these willing victims become foundation sacrifices or hero-stone guardians of temples.

Not surprisingly, Śiva is also invoked for the purposes of magic, sorcery, countersorcery, alchemy. The *Atharvaveda* and other texts *abhicāra* make clear that spells and charms were employed three thousand years ago. Today every region has counterpart names and variants for these nearly universal beliefs and practices, most relying upon the efficacy of the spoken word as mantra, incantation, curse, defensive shield, as well as formulaic rituals that may sometimes include states of possession.

In sum, although dreaded for his terrifying demeanor, destructive behavior, and wrathful punishment of those who withhold offerings or impede others intending to worship, Śiva is also loved and praised, particularly by recipients of his grace. Those who, for example, keep awake in vigil on Śivarātri expect divine favor. The Tamil tale of *Ciruttoṇṭar* illustrates Śiva's power: The terrible god, disguised as an ascetic, demands for food the only son of Ciruttoṇṭar and his wife. Religious duty obliges them to comply. After eating the child cooked and served by the dutiful mother, a pleased Śiva reveals himself, restores the boy, and, as reward for supreme devotion, takes the reunited family to heaven.

References

Abbott, John. 1932. *The keys of power. a study of Indian ritual and belief*. London: Methuen.

Blackburn, Stuart *et al.*, ed. 1989. *Oral epics in India*. Berkeley: University of California.

Clothey, Fred W., and J. Bruce Long, ed. 1983. *Experiencing Śiva: encounters with a Hindu deity*. New Delhi: Manohar.

Eliade, Mircea. 1969. *Yoga: immortality and freedom*. 2d ed. Trans. Willard R. Trask. Princeton: Princeton University.

Freeman, John R. 1991. Purity and violence: sacred power in the Teyyam worship of Malabar. Ph.D. Diss., University of Pennsylvania.

Gonda, Jan. 1970. *Viṣṇuism and Śivaism. A comparison*. London: Athlone.

Hiltebeitel, Alf, ed. 1989. *Criminal gods and demon devotees. Essays on the guardians of popular Hinduism*. Albany: State University of New York.

Kramrisch, Stella. 1981. *The presence of Śiva*. Princeton: Princeton University.

O'Flaherty, Wendy Doniger. 1973. *Asceticism and eroticism in the mythology of Śiva*. New York: Oxford.

Parpola, Asko. 1992. The "fig deity seal" from Mohenjo-daro: its iconography and inscription. In *South Asian Archaeology 1989*. Papers from the Tenth International Conference of South Asian Archaeologists in Western Europe, Paris, 1989, ed. by Catherine Jarrige. Madison Wisc.: Prehistory Press.

Ramanujan, A. K., tr. 1973. *Speaking of Śiva*. Baltimore: Penguin.

Sen Gupta, Sankar, ed. 1965. *Tree symbol worship in India. A new survey of a pattern of folk-religion*. Calcutta: Indian Publications.

Shulman, David, ed. 1995. *Syllables of sky. Studies in South Indian Civilization*. Delhi: Oxford.

Sontheimer, Günther-Dietz. 1989. *Pastoral deities in western India*, trans. Ann Feldhaus. New York: Oxford.

David M. Knipe

SEE ALSO

Aṇṇanmār Katai; Fire-walking; Goddesses, Hindu; Gods and Goddesses; *Nāga; Navarātri; Pūjā; Sādhu;* Self-sacrifice

SKANDA (KATARAGAMA)

Skanda is a Hindu deity who is the son of Śiva and Umā, and the brother of Gaṇeśa. One of the most powerful deities in Sri Lanka, Skanda is popularly known as Kataragama, after the site of his principal shrine on the southeast coast. In the Kandy region Skanda is one of the four guardian deities of the island, along with Nātha, Viṣṇu, and Pattini.

Skanda is a warlike, fiery deity whose power and anger are to be feared. Unlike the other guardian deities, who are seen as well on their way to attaining Buddhahood, Kataragama is viewed as immoral, a "heretic," far from achieving *Nibbāna* (Nirvāṇa; in Sanskrit meaning "release from the cycle of life and death"). While the other major deities follow Buddhist ethical principles, Skanda is known to do anything to help his devotees, thus making him a favorite of businessmen, politicians, and criminals, and contributing to his widespread popularity among Sri Lankans of virtually all classes and professions.

Skanda has a long history in Sri Lanka. He is first mentioned in the Buddhist chronicle the *Mahāvaṃsa,* in relation to a seventh-century prince. However, it appears that he did not become one of the more powerful deities until the immigration of South Indian priests in the fifteenth and sixteenth centuries. Robert Knox (1984 [1681]), in his account of seventeenth-century Kandy, mentions Skanda as the "great god" who was widely feared by the Sinhalas. Subsequently his popularity declined to such an extent that by the early 1800s, his main shrine was in decay. Since the 1930s, however, Skanda has again risen to power, and Kataragama is the most popular pilgrimage site in Sri Lanka.

The annual festival of Kataragama is held in the month of *Ăsala* (July/August). It commemorates the union of Skanda with his mistress, the wild Vădda princess Valli Ammā. Each night of the fifteen-day festival, the god is taken to unite with Vallī Ammā at her shrine, bypassing that of his legitimate spouse, Tēvānī Ammā. Thousands of pilgrims attend the festival. Possession trances, firewalking, flesh-piercing, and dancing with *kāvaḍi* (wooden peacock arches symbolic of Skanda) are part of the unrestrained atmosphere at Kataragama. Tamils, Sinhalas, and Muslims participate, though recently Sinhala Buddhists have taken over many of the ritual practices, such as fire walking, that previously were under the control of Tamil Hindus.

References

Gombrich, Richard, and Gananath Obeyesekere. 1988. *Buddhism transformed: Religious change in Sri Lanka*. Princeton, NJ: Princeton University Press.

Knox, Robert. 1984 [1681]. *An historical relation of the island of Ceylon in the East Indies*. New Delhi: Navrang Publishers. First published in London, 1681.

Obeyesekere, Gananath. 1977. Social change and the deities: Rise of the Kataragama cult in modern Sri Lanka. *Man*, n.s., 12 nos. 3/4: 377–396.

———. 1981. *Medusa's hair*. Chicago: University of Chicago Press.

Pfaffenberger, Bryan. 1979. The Kataragama pilgrimage: Hindu–Buddhist interaction and its significance in Sri Lanka's polyethnic social system. *Journal of Asian Studies* 38, no. 2: 253–270.
Wirz, Paul. 1972. *Kataragama: The holiest place in Ceylon*. Translated from the German by Davis Berta Pralle. Colombo: Lake House.

SUSAN A. REED

SOKARI

Sokari is one of the most popular Sinhalese folk plays, serves as both entertainment and ritual. It incorporates many cultural, religious, and theatrical features. This play is most frequently performed in the northwestern and up-country villages in Sri Lanka. Unlike most other Sinhalese folk plays, this one does not tell a Buddhist story.

Although manuscripts exist, the play has prevailed in the oral tradition: Villagers know it by heart because almost every year it is played after the harvest for several nights. At the culmination of the *Sokari* play season, a procession called *Sokari perahăhra* winds its way through the village, carrying the insignia of the goddess Pattini. Important gods such as Kataragama and Alutnuwara are invoked to be present and protect both dancers and audience.

The play is set in Sri Lanka a few centuries ago. The title *Sokari* may be an adaptation of an Indian name meaning "girl"—it is not a common Sinhalese name. In the play the title character, Sokari, is a flirtatious young woman married to an eccentric old Brahman who loses his fortune, then migrates to Sri Lanka to earn a living with the help of the god Kataragama. Although Sokari is first presented as promiscuous, she is later made to represent the chaste goddess Pattini.

Sokari includes miming, dancing, singing, and chanting. The actors wear simple costume and makeup; only a few wear masks made of leaves or cardboard. At certain points in the play the chief actors enter a trance and begin to dance in ecstasy. In the dialogue everyday language is mixed with obscene words and ribald jokes, arousing laughter from the audience.

One of the important themes in *Sokari* is harmony and reconciliation among rival ethnic groups. The immigrant Indians and the suspicious Sinhalese villagers sit together on a mat woven by Sokari, caress her baby, partake of the rice she has cooked, and pass around a ganja cigar to show friendship and solidarity.

Another important theme of the play is that of poking fun at the wealthy and powerful. The play ends with a vigorous dance by the master, who turns a coconut flower around his head, scattering hundreds of seeds around the stage, symbolizing fertility. Another character in *Sokari* is the Vedarāḷa, the village physician, whose prosperity is signaled by his belly, made huge by being full of farm animals.

Sokari is considered to have strong links with the caste system because mat-weaving people in a certain village believe that they are the custodians of *Sokari*. While laughing at themselves as well as at their superiors, the village folk perform this play as a ritual petitioning the gods for protection, fertility, and peace, as well as a form of entertainment.

Reference

Saracchanira, Ediriweera. 1966. *The folk drama of Ceylon*. 2nd ed. Colombo, Sri Lanka: Department of Cultural Affairs.

UDAYA MEDDEGAMA

SONG

See Angaẏ; *Bait/Bayt;* Balandaẏ; Balochistan: Oral Tradition; Bāul Song; *Bhajan;* Bhakti; Bhakti Saints; Bhāoyāiyā Song; Bhāṭiẏālī Song; Bīcār Gān; Bihar; Birth Songs; Bow Songs (*Vil Pāṭṭu*); Brahui Folk Literature; Brass Bands; British Folklore (in South Asia); *Candaini (Lorik-Candā)*; Cassettes; Chahārbayti; Christianity, Kerala; Film Music; Gāzir Gān; *Ghazal;* Ginan; *Gondhaḷa;* Govindevji, Temple of; Jainism; Jihād Poetry; *Kāfī, Kamsāle; Kīrtana;* Lalan Fakir; Lament; *Landaẏ; Lāvaṇt; Mārphatī* and *Murśīdī* Songs; *Munazira;* Song, Sinhala; *Ovī; Pāḍdana;* Parsi Folklore; *Qawwālī;* Sindh; Song, Bengal; Song, Nepal; Song, Sinhala; *Tij* Songs; *Tōṟṟam;* Wedding Songs; Women's Songs; *Yakṣagāna*

SONG, BENGAL

The folksongs of Bangladesh and West Bengal, India, are extremely rich and varied in their tunes, themes, and forms, expressing many folk religious traditions, including both Hindu and Muslim. The general terms used in Bengali to refer to folksongs are *lokgīti* (songs of the people) or *pallīgīti* (village songs). Since it is not possible to give a complete survey of Bengali folksongs in the present article, only some of the more widespread and well-known song traditions will be introduced.

There are three major types of regional Bengali folksongs: *bhāoẏāiẏā, bhāṭiẏāli,* and *jhumur*. Their tunes are among the most popular in Bengali folk music and are used in other Bengali song genres as well, including those of the Bāul religious tradition. (The *bhāoẏāiẏā* and *bhāṭiẏāli* genres are discussed in separate articles in this encyclopedia.) The *jhumur* songs of West Bengal are performed in the districts of Puruliya, Bankura, and Medinipur. Sung by both men and women, they originated from songs of the Santali tribal people and today preserve the original Santali *jhumur* tune. The main theme of these songs is typically the love story of Rādhā and Kṛṣṇa. A *jhumur* performance may take the form of a bawdy exchange between two groups of singers, with one group taking Rādhā's role and the other group, Kṛṣṇa's. Dancing is often a part of the performance, and musical accompaniment may include *khol* (a double-headed barrel drum) and *kartāl* (small metal cymbals) as well as flute and *mādal* (another type of double-headed barrel drum). Bhabānī was a famous female singer and composer of *jhumur* in the mid-nineteenth century who also led her own troupe. Bhabaprītā Ojhā is one of the best known twentieth century *jhumur* composers.

Calendrical songs, or those sung on the occasion of a cyclical religious festival, are another type of Bengali folksong. For example, *jāri gān* (lamentation songs) are dirges sung in Bangladesh in connection with the Shī'a Muslim holiday of Muḥarram. These songs, for the most part, tell the story of the battle at Karbalā, Iraq (680 C.E.) and the martyrdom of Muhammad's grandson Ḥusayn. They are emotionally charged and highly dramatic, evoking the sufferings, bravery, and self-sacrifice of the Karbalā martyrs. *Jāri gān* are sung by a group of men, including a lead singer (*bayātī*) and a chorus (*dohār*). They are particularly popular in the district of Mymensingh where the singers dance to the songs and beat their chests with the palms of their hands even to the point of drawing blood. Besides songs connected with Muḥarram, *jāri* may also refer to songs composed on secular and even humorous subjects that have no relation to any particular celebration.

Songs are also sung during the festivals for the Hindu folk goddesses Ṭusu (also Tuṣu and Tuṣ-tuṣalī) and Bhādu, who are worshipped by women in West Bengal in Puruliya, Birbhum, Bankura, and Medinipur districts. The Ṭusu and Bhādu festivals each last for one month. The former is a harvest festival that is held throughout the month of Pauṣ (December-January), and the latter takes place during the rainy season in the month of Bhādra (August-September), whence the name Bhādu. The songs, which are composed extemporaneously and sung on each night of the festival, depict the goddesses as young girls. They describe Bhādu and Ṭusu and tell in loving detail how they will be entertained, even mentioning the brand of oil that will be used to anoint Tuṣu's hair. They also mention local events that happened during the year. The main differences between Bhādu and Ṭusu and their festivals are that Bhādu is unmarried, her songs are sung mostly by unmarried girls, and her wedding is an important theme in the songs about her, whereas Ṭusu is a child-wife and her songs are sung by married, unmarried, or widowed women. Bhādu is always worshipped iconically (with an image) but Ṭusu may be worshipped either iconically or aniconically (without an image). Moreover, dancing and the playing of drums may accompany Bhādu, but not Ṭusu songs. In addition, Bhādu songs are also sung by unmarried men in courtship rituals.

Other songs are sung during the festivals of Gājan, Nīlpūjā, Gambhīrā, and Gamīrā, which are festivals connected with Śiva, or in the case of Gājan, also with the folk deity Dharma. These festivals are held at the end of the month of Caitra (March-April) and are characterized by physical austerities such as body piercing or swinging from the top of a tall pole (*caṛak*). Similar songs are sung during Gājan in West Bengal and during Nīlpūjā, its counterpart in Bangladesh. The songs begin with praise of the deities and then describe the rituals of the festival. The main theme of Gājan and Nīlpūjā songs is the wedding of Śiva and Parvatī and their married life, particularly their quarrels. They are sung in the style of *pāñcāli* (devotional narrative poetry) to the accompaniment of the *ḍhol* (a double-headed cylindrical drum). Gambhīrā and Gamīrā festivals are held in West Bengal, in Malda and Jalpaiguri districts respectively. Distinctive to both these festivals is a type of song that gives an account of the events of the year. One of the main differences between the songs in these two festivals is that, in Gambhīrā, the songs are addressed to Śiva, whereas, in Gamīrā, they are not. They also typically include social and political commentary.

Songs about the snake goddess Manasā are sung all over Bengal during the rainy season month of Śrāvaṇī (July-August). They recount the famous story of Behulā and Lakhindar told in the medieval narrative poems *Manasāmaṅgal*. The songs have many local variants including *jhāṁpān, raẏāṇī,* and *bhāsān*. *Jhāṁpān* is sung by snake catchers (*bede*) in West Bengal (particularly in Murshidabad District), who go from house to house, charming snakes and singing these songs. *Raẏāṇī* is sung by professional groups of men and women in Barisal District, Bangladesh, and *bhāsān* is sung in *pāñcāli* style by groups of men to the accompaniment of musical instruments in the districts of Nadiya, 24 Parganas, and Birbhum, West Bengal

Occasional songs are sung by women in connection with life-cycle rituals. Of these rituals, the marriage ceremony is the most elaborate and has the greatest variety of songs. Wedding songs are sung all over West Bengal and Bangladesh by Hindu and Muslim women as each *strī-ācār* (woman's ritual) is performed, beginning on the day the marriage is arranged and ending the day the bride is ritually welcomed into the groom's house. They describe such rituals as the smearing of turmeric paste on the bride and groom and the bathing of the couple. Joking songs full of sexual innuendo that make fun of the groom are sung in the bridal chamber (*bāsar ghar*) after the marriage ceremony.

Devotional songs belong to many different religious traditions and include: *Śākta* songs; Sufi and Vaiṣṇava songs; Bāul songs; and songs of other syncretic Hindu-Muslim traditions in Nadiya District, West Bengal and Kushtia District, Bangladesh, such as *Kartābhajā* and *Balarāmī*. Bāul, Sufi (Islamic mysticism), and Vaiṣṇava (worship of the Hindu gods Viṣṇu/Kṛṣṇa) songs are not mutually exclusive categories: Bāuls compose songs that reflect the influence of both Sufism and Vaiṣṇavism. Moreover, songs composed by Sufis may be on Vaiṣṇava themes. Most of these traditions share a type of song called *dehattattva* (truth in the body) that depicts the body symbolically. The body is a central theme because it is conceived of as a microcosm of the universe in which the Divine resides and is the means to conquer death and gain liberation.

The following Bengali terms are used to designate Sufi songs (including Bāul songs influenced by Sufism): *maramī* (mystic in general), *mārphatī, phakīrī, darbeśī* (about the Sufi mystic path), and *murśidī* (about the *murśid,* or spiritual guide). Sufi songs are composed all over Bengal by poets belonging to a variety of traditions. For example, Māij Bhāṇḍārī songs are composed by Sufis whose religious center is in the village Māij Bhāṇḍār in Chittagong, Bangladesh. The songs of the various Sufi traditions are often sung to Bāul tunes, and generally, the same instruments are used to accompany them, including: *dotārā* (a four-stringed instrument played with a plectum), *sārindā* (a three-stringed instrument played with a bow), *khañjani* (a small frame drum), and flute, in addition to the more usual Bāul instruments, the *ektārā* (a one-stringed instrument) and *ḍugi* (a small clay kettle drum).

The influence of Vaiṣṇavism on Bengali folksongs is reflected in the Bengali proverb "*Kānu chāṛā gīt nāi*" ("There are no songs without Kṛṣṇa"). Among the several genres that include songs on Vaiṣṇava themes, in addition to those already mentioned, are *nāmkīrtan* (singing the names of the deities Rādha and Kṛṣṇa, and Caitanya, the sixteenth-century Vaiṣṇava reformer) and other devotional songs sung by Vaiṣṇava devotees, including *bairāgī* (songs of Vaiṣṇava mendicants). *Padābalī kīrtan,* songs based on the texts of medieval Vaiṣṇava poets and on Indian classical *rāga,* are sung in a variety of styles by amateur village groups, as well as by highly trained specialists. These songs have had great influence on the music and poetry of many folk song traditions. Instruments associated with Vaiṣṇava songs are *khol*, flute, *ektārā, dotārā, khañjani,* and *kartāl*.

Specialist songs are those sung by paid performers. The *paṭuyā* are scroll painters who live in the West Bengal districts of Medinipur, Bankura, and Birbhum, and who combine Hindu and Muslim customs and practices. They earn their living by selling their scrolls and singing the stories depicted in them. Typical themes include episodes from the epic *Rāmāyaṇa,* the narrative poems *Manasāmaṅgal,* and the Kṛṣṇa tales, as well as stories about modern society that are often critical of the changing roles of women. The songs are sung in *pāñcālī* style, without musical accompaniment. In Bangladesh, singers specializing in songs about the folk saint Gājī (Arabic: *ghāzi*, "warrior") go from house to house showing paintings of Gājī and singing stories to both Muslims and Hindus about his supernatural powers, particularly his miraculous ability to subdue tigers.

Kabi songs are composed extemporanously in competitions lasting as long as two to three days, held throughout Bengal. The competitions are in the form of a debate or "duel" (*laṛāi*) in song between two groups. Although the heydey of the *kabi* tradition was in the late eighteenth to early nineteenth centuries, it continues to be a popular form of village entertainment to this day. The songs, which are on secular as well as religious topics, are noted for their bawdy humor, witty puns, and satirical portrayals of deities, heroes, and men. They are sung at *pūjā* (worship events) and *melā* (fairs) by amateur and professional groups of men (and sometimes also women). Each *kabi* group consists of a *kabiẏāl* (the lead singer and principal composer), a chorus, and musicians. The main instruments used in a *kabi* performance are *ḍhol* and *kām̐sī* (a metal plate-like instrument struck with a stick). *Tarjā* songs are similar to *kabi* in method of composition and performance contexts. *Tarjā,* however, is a West Bengal song tradition that concerns primarily Hindu mythological themes.

Narrative songs are another type of Bengali folksong. *Jāg gān* (vigil songs) are so named because a performance lasts the entire night. They are sung in the north of Bangladesh in Rangpur, Pabna, and Rajshahi districts by groups of peasant boys, particularly in the month of Pauṣ (December-January). They recount stories about *pīr* (Muslim saints) such as Māṇikpīr and Sonāpīr, Lord Kṛṣṇa, and Caitanya.

Narrative songs of the *Nāth* tradition are sung in Rangpur and Dinajpur, Bangladesh, to the accompaniment of *gopiẏantra* (a one-stringed instrument similar to an ektārā) by *Nāth* yogī, as well as by Muslim farmers. The songs "*Māṇikcandra Rājār Gān*" ("The Song of King Māṇikcandra"), "*Maẏnāmatīr Gān*" ("The Song of Maynāmatī"), and "*Gopicām̐der Gān*" ("The Song of Gopicandra") relate the legend of Gopīcandra, son of Queen Maynāmatī and King Māṇikcandra, who renounced the world to become a yogī at the insistence of his mother.

Fifty-five ballads of varying length from Mymensingh and other districts in present-day Bangladesh were published from 1923 to 1932 by Dinesh Chandra Sen under the titles *Maimansiṁha-gītikā* ("Folk Songs of Mymensingh") and *Pūrbabaṅga-gītikā* ("Folk Songs of East Bengal"). They are unusual in Bengali folk literature in that they concern secular themes, particularly romantic love, and are of remarkably high literary quality. These ballads, which reflect the folk culture of Bengal common to Hindus and Muslims, were sung by Muslim and low-caste Hindu men and women, some of whom were professional singers. A typical performance consisted of a lead singer and a chorus of eight to ten members, playing the cymbals, drum, violin, and occasionally, harmonium. The ballads, having lost patronage, were already in danger of disappearing at the time of publication. However, according to Shamsuzzaman Khan, this ballad tradition continued in Mymensingh at least until 1960 when the specimens in the Bangla Academy Folklore Archives in Dhaka were collected.

Work songs are another type of Bengali folksong. The best-known and most-collected work songs are *sāri gān,* rowing songs sung by East Bengal boatmen. For the most part, they concern the story of Rādhā and Kṛṣṇa. *Chād peṭār gān* (roof-beating songs) are sung in Dhaka by a lead singer playing the violin and by male and female workers who repeat his lines, keeping time with their hammers. The main theme is lost love. Work songs are also sung by men without musical accompaniment in connection with agricultural labor, such as cutting jute or paddy, plowing fields, and planting seeds. One such song praises the land as the farmer's mother and father, and another describes the gifts that the farmer will give his wife if the harvest is good.

Topical songs are composed on subjects ranging from corrupt officials, plagues, and murder to heroes and patriotic causes. Some have already been mentioned in connection with *jāri,* Gambhīrā, Ṭusu, and Bhādu. Topical songs are often composed and sung by beggars on trains in West Bengal to the accompaniment of an *ektārā,* or a clay rice pot played as a drum. In Bangladesh, narrative songs describing local scandals and calamities, known as *bayātīr gān* (songs of poets), are sung by Hindus and Muslims at fairs and markets. Although topical songs usually have short lifespans, a few have had lasting popularity, such as the famous song about Khudiram Bose, who in 1908 became the first Bengali revolutionary to be hanged by the British.

The *bāromāsī* (literally, "song of the twelve months"; Hindi *bārahmāsā*) is a poetic structural technique found in art poetry, as well as in folk poetry. Nowadays, folk bāromāsī are predominantly found in Bangladesh. Although not associated with any particular occupation, they are often sung by farmers to the accompaniment of a *dotārā*. The songs can be sung by women as well as by men. In the most common type of bāromāsī, a woman abandoned by her husband or lover describes the characteristics of each month of the year and tells how she suffers with each change.

References

Bhaṭṭācārya, Āśutoṣ. 1962. *Bāṃlār lok-sāhitya* (The folk literature of Bengal). 3rd ed. Vol. 3. Calcutta: Calcutta Book House.

———. 1967. *Baṅgīẏa lok-saṅgīt ratnākar* (A treasury of Bengali folk songs). Calcutta: Paścimbaṅga lok-saṃskṛti ratnākar.

Biswas, Hemango, et al., eds. 1967. *Folkmusic and folklore: An anthology*, Vol. 1. Calcutta: Folkmusic and Folklore Research Institute.

Capwell, Charles. 1974. *The music of the Bāuls of Bengal*. Kent, Ohio: Kent State University Press.

Datta, Gurusaday, and Nirmalendu Bhoumik, eds. 1966. *Śrīhaṭṭer loksaṅgīt* (The folk songs of Sylhet). Calcutta: Calcutta University.

Deb, Cittarañjan. 1966. *Bāṅglār Pallīgīti* (The folk songs of Bengal). Calcutta: National Book Agency.

Dunham, Mary Frances. 1997. *Jārigan: Muslim epic songs of Bangladesh.* Dhaka: The University Press Limited.

Khan, Shamsuzzaman. 1995. Folklore fieldwork, problems and prospects: Perspective on Bangladesh. *Daily Star.* 1 December: 10–11.

Ray, Sukumar. 1988. *Folk-music of eastern India with special reference to Bengal*. Calcutta: Naya Prokash.

Shahidullah, Muhammad, and Muhammad Abdul Hai. 1963. *Traditional Culture of East Pakistan*. Dhaka: Department of Bengali, University of Dacca.

Zbavitel, Dusan. 1961. The Development of the Bāromāsī in the Bengali Literature. *Archiv Orientalni* 29(4): 582–619.

———. 1963. *Bengali Folk-Ballads from Mymensingh and the problem of their authenticity*. Calcutta: University of Calcutta.

CAROL SALOMON

SEE ALSO

Bārahmāsā; Bāul Song; *Bhāoẏāiẏā* Song; *Bhātiẏalī* Song; Fairs and Festivals; *Gāmbhīra; Gāzīr/Gājīr Gān;* Goddesses, Hindu; *Gopī Cand; Jārī Gān;* Kṛṣṇa; Life Cycle Rituals; Marriage; *Muḥarram;* Music; Narative Scroll Painting; *Nāth; Pīr;* Śiva; Sufi Folk Poetry; Syncretism; Wedding Songs

SONG, NEPAL

Folk song—a lyric poem set to melody, regarded as common property, and performed and transmitted orally by the people—is called *lokagīt* in Nepali. Folksongs can express a variety of moods and feelings and, hence, mark the celebration of birth as well as the mourning of death. They also enhance a wide range of everyday activities: porters sing to ease their exhausting long journeys, peasants sing while working in the fields to make their work less tiring, and young people sing to express symbolically and aesthetically their innermost desires of love and courtship. Because of the wide range of expression afforded by folk songs, this genre is more popular than classical or mass-mediated popular songs, and Nepali folk songs have been circulated orally for centuries.

Nepali folk songs share common ground with other folklore genres. Folk songs are generally accompanied by instrumental music and/or dance and often share the same name with these genres. Furthermore, folk song also overlaps with ballad and epic. Indeed, the narrative versions of many Nepali ballads and epics are lost. However, elements of them (a few lyrical segments, names of characters, other references to the narrative, but without the full story) survive in some folk songs. For instance, the refrain of the *Sītārānī* epic or ballad, *Sītā rānī banaimā laharī chalyo manaimā,* can be found in many folk songs having no relation to the character of Sītā.

Nepali folk songs can be classified into three categories: wordless, recited, and lyrical. Vocal music without words is commonly heard in the trails and forests, in which the people whistle a tune, whistle with a rolled tender leaf (*pipirī*) as an instrument, yodel, or sing nonsense syllables such *as lā li lā le lā li, lā li lā le lā li*. These wordless folk songs may have been the basis for various ethnic melodies, such as *Tamaṅ Selo* (Tamang Melody), *Durā Bhākā* (Dura Melody), and *Guruṅ Bhākā* (Gurung Melody).

In recited folk song, melody is weak and words predominate. Numerous Nepali folk songs—especially those in children's play and rhymes—fall into this twilight zone of verse and song. An example is the chants of Tihār (an autumn festival of lights and prosperity), when at night people go from house to house and chant the *Deusire* song. (The following examples were collected and translated by the author.) The chorus chants "*Deusire*" (a name of Lakṣmī, goddess of prosperity) after each of the leader's lines, including:

Bhana bhana bhāi ho!
Deusire.
Barsai dinko,
Deusire.
Cāḍai ṭhulo,
Deusire.

Raise your voice, O brothers!
Deusire.
In this year,
Deusire.
The festival is great,
Deusire.

Lyrical folk songs have both music and verse. Each stanza has two or four lines. The first and third lines may or may not have real meaning, but they always set an appropriate melodic background and mood to reinforce the sentiment of the second and fourth lines. The final syllables in a pair of lines always rhyme, as in this song, for example:

Mero māyā cha bhane tyatā,
Pānī khāne niu pārī āu yatā.

Khara chaina ghar ke le chāune ho.
Tirkhā chaina ke niule āune ho.

Boy: If you love me, my dear,
Come here as if you are just heading to drink water.
Girl: There is not enough thatch for the roofing of my house.
I am not thirsty, and hence I cannot justify my going thither.

Many lyrical folk songs express feelings of love and courtship. In the popular duets, *deuḍā, dohorī, juhārī, rasiyā,* and *roilā,* boys and girls express their love and commitment and also test each other's wit and intelligence. Not uncommonly, these duets have led couples to marriage.

According to the context of their performance, lyrical folk songs may be categorized as follows: religious songs, work songs, lullabies, ritual songs, and festival songs. *Bholāulo, pravātī, stuti, bhajan, maṅgal, sanje,* and *āratī* are religious songs and emphasize the supremacy of the God, the impermanence of human life, the grace of the saints, and the importance of love, compassion, and charity in social life. *Bholāulo* and *pravātī* are sung early in the morning, even in bed. *Bhajan, maṅgal, stuti, sanje,* and *āratī* can be sung in any sacred place or occasion. However, they are sung regularly in temples and *pūjākoṭhā* (room for worship, prayer, and meditation) where *āratī* are sung as the concluding part of the worship. *Sanje* are sung at evening when people are ready to light their lamps.

Nidarī gīt (lullabies) are smooth and rhythmic and make children sleep. *Cāncarī, jeṭhe, asāre, rasiyā, ohālī, jiriyā,* and *dāīṃ* are work songs performed during the agricultural chores of sowing, transplanting, weeding, and harvesting. In general, these songs are sung in groups. The subject of these songs are social and often tragic. For example, an *ohālī* song portrays the plea of children to their cruel mother who puts them in termite hills so that she could be free to marry another man.

Śirai lāmne śirphūlaā hāmī dimlā āmai
Najāu āmai arikāko des
Aiyā āmai aiyā, dhamirīle khāyo.
Kānai lāmne kunnala hāmī dimlā āmai
Najāu āmai arikāko des
Aiyā āmai aiyā, dhamirīle khāyo.

When we grow up, we will buy you a golden flower for your head.
Mother! Don't go to another's house.

Oh, mother! it is extremely painful, the termites
 are eating us.
When we grow up, we will buy you a pair of earrings for
 your ears.
Mother! Don't go to another's house.
Oh, mother! it is extremely painful, the termites are
 eating us.

Maṅgal, sagun, phāg, and *ratyaulī* songs enhance rites and rituals such as birth and marriage. *Tij, malsirī, bhailī,* and *horī* songs are performed during important festivals such as *Tij, Daśaiṃ, Tihār,* and *Phāgu* respectively. The themes of these songs are typically joy, happiness, and prosperity; nevertheless, some of them also express the voices of the oppressed and helpless people. For example, in a maṅgal song a daughter complains to her father about his unwise decision which led her to an unhappy marriage.

Suna hũ ta merā bābā jokhī taulī dindā hau.
Malāī diyau timle bābā ekai bacana.
Rupa huṃ ta merā bābā jokhī taulī dindā hau.
Malāī diyau timle bābā ekai bacana.

If I were gold, father! you would have given me only after
 meticulously weighing me.
Alas! I was given by you just as a response of a single
 word to a stranger.
If I were silver, father! you would have given me only after
 meticulously weighing me.
Alas! I was given by you just as a response of a single
 word to a stranger.

Some Nepali castes earn their living by performing folk songs. *Ḍholī,* the tailor caste musicians, are hired to perform folk songs in festivals and celebrations. *Gāine,* minstrels who accompany song with the music of the *saraṅgī* (stringed instrument similar to the fiddle), entertain their patrons singing all manner of folk songs from hymns to romantic *jhyāure* songs (named for the very popular lyric meter jhyāure). Other musical castes, Bādī and Bhāñnda, are not confined to folk song and also perform other popular genres.

Modern technologies enable Nepali folk songs to reach audiences by means other than live oral performance. Print, audio, and video recording, and broadcasting have all disseminated folk songs to wider audiences. Since folk songs are so popular, audiovisual production of Nepali folk songs has become a lucrative business. However, broadsides and chapbooks of folk songs—while previously very popular—are now on the decline.

Various Nepali institutions such as the Royal Nepal Academy, Tribhuvan University, Himalaya Institute, Radio Nepal, and National Sports Council have been actively organizing folk song research and folk song competitions. Nevertheless, academic training in fieldwork, collection, documentation, archiving, and analysis of folk songs is still conspicuously absent. Not a single manual exists to facilitate the work. The Nepali folk song, therefore, promises to be a particularly fruitful area of research.

References

Bhattarai, Harihar P. 1985. Folklore studies in Nepal. *Himalayan culture* 3(1): 10–14.

Lienhard, Siegfried. 1992 [1974]. *Songs of Nepal: An anthology of Nevar folksongs and hymns*. Delhi: Motilal Banarsidass.

Lohani, Laxman. 1968. Spotlight on folk songs. In *Nepal monograph on Nepalese culture,* 6–64. Kathmandu: HMG of Nepal, Department of Information.

Pradhan, Kumar. 1984. *A history of Nepali literature*. New Delhi: Sahitya Akademi.

Sharma, M. M. 1978. *Folklore of Nepal*. New Delhi: Vision Books.

HARIHAR P. BHATTARAI

SEE ALSO
Chapbooks; Folk Music; Folk Music, Nepal; *Silok*

SONG, SINHALA

Folk poems and songs are known in Sinhala as *jana kavi* and *jana gī*. These terms cover a wide range of poems, songs, ballads, and recitative compositions. What we mean here by folk poetry and songs are those anonymous compositions for which the date and place of origin are untraceable. Sinhala folk poetry is quite vast and varied, existing in oral as well as written forms. Most folk songs and poems in Sinhala are of recent origin although there have been such compositions in existence for millennia.

Sinhala folk poetry employs a variety of meters. Almost all the compositions can be sung in many different tunes. On certain occasions involving group singing and dancing, these folk songs are accompanied by musical instruments such as a hand-held drum called *uḍakki,* and cymbals. There are different kinds of work songs, including, for example, *păl kavi* (watch-hut poems), quatrains sung by the watchers of paddy and other fields. Watch-hut songs and carters' songs are generally sung solo while *nelum kavi* and miners' songs are sung by groups.

The whole community in a given area knows by heart the poems and songs typical to that area. However, some songs and poems are regional or confined to certain professions, castes, or communities, such as those sung by the Veddas (a forest dwelling tribe), the Rodiyas (a low caste community now fast disappearing), and the Kinnarayas (mat weavers). Songs that are not confined to any particular group are known all over the island. Along with trends of modernization, urbanization, and with vanishing taboos and discrimination against caste and creed, folk poems and songs of different traditions are now sung by anyone who appreciates them solely for their musical and literary qualities.

Sinhala folk songs and poems vividly reflect local scenes and environment. These creations are born out of genuine feelings and experiences of the people who paint realistic vignettes of their life, coloring them with the natural hues of the countryside. The poems employ actual speech of ordinary people and imagery full of symbolic significance drawn from their physical surroundings. The Sinhala villager, whether farmer or ferryman, sings in order to keep himself awake and to ward off fear and loneliness.

These songs and poems clearly reflect the problems faced by ordinary men and women. Some express criticism of the feudal lords of centuries past, as in this poem wherein a farmer aims a subtle attack on his landlord Atappattu, who was at one time an officer of the king:

Behold! the injustice done to me by the saintly Atapattu
by not allowing me to cultivate my field.
How I suffered by toiling to weed it.
O sun! Why do you shine on a land like this?

Some other poems strike us as genuine expressions of the plight of poor village women, as in this poem in which a village woman expresses her sufferings under the merciless sun, the village urchins, and her husband:

Even if I go to the chena, the sun beats upon me.
Even if I go to the village water tank the children
harass me.
Even if I stay home, that devil [of a husband] tortures me.
So, I'll make him eat unsalted *roti* [bread] tonight too.

A picture of a passive, but tolerant and understanding farmer emerges from these poems. For his suffering and misfortune he does not blame anyone but his own *karma,* as in these two poems:

I sow seeds like stars in the sky.
Grains appear like sand upon earth.
Why is it only my field that the boar attacks?
Gods Viṣṇu and Saman please hear my case.

I drive my pair of bullocks yoked together.
They suffer as I do not let them rest at Katukele.
My belly burns upon seeing the hill at Haputale.
O bull the sinner, pull on, we are going to Haputale.

Poetry is one of the finest Sinhala arts. As Godakumbura notes: "Of all their arts, the Sinhalese people have excelled in poetry, and as we study the development of arts in which the nation tried to express itself we see poetry standing supreme." He further observes that, by temperament, the Sinhalese is a poet: "He speaks in poetry." This is true especially with regard to the ordinary Sinhalese villagers who created thousands of poems and songs attuned to the pulsations of the heart. In any village in the island it is possible to find a man or a woman who can recite verses impromptu. This may be immediately added to the vast body of already documented folk songs and poems.

UDAYA MEDDEGAMA

SPIRIT POSSESSION AND MEDIUMSHIP

Possession by deities, the deified dead, ghosts, or demons is an important feature of South Asian folk culture and religion. Supernatural entities are not only present in inanimate objects, such as the image of a deity, but also manifest themselves in human form. The phenomenology of possession shows a vast number of different forms, ranging from possession by spirits and demons to different forms of oracular possession by deities and to possession in ritual drama.

Two forms of possession are often mentioned in the research on South Asian folk culture. Depending on the possessing entities, a distinction is made between spirit possession and possession mediumship. The term "spirit possession" is used when a person is possessed involuntarily by an undesired, harmful, and malevolent entity. Possession mediumship is defined as the "legitimate, expected possession of a specialist by a spirit or a deity, usually for the purpose of soliciting the aid of the supernatural for human problems" (Claus 1979: 29).

Although established in academic discourse, the term "possession" is nevertheless questionable. In those South Asian languages in which terms for the various forms of possession are documented, there is no literal equivalent for "possession" or "being possessed." What is translated with the participle construction "to be possessed" is originally described with verbs of movement such as "to enter, come, join, mount, ride, descend." Often the entities do not enter the body as a whole, but only parts of it (head, shoulders, back). Possession mediumship is called *angāt yeṇe* (to come into the body) in Marathi, *bhāv ānā* ([the deity's] feeling is coming) in Rajasthani, "*darṣana* had happened to so and so" in Tulu, and *jāgar* (waking [the deity]) in Hindi. In Malayalam, the onset of possession during Teyyam dance is described as a "coming to" (*varuka*), "joining" (*kūṭuka*), or "mounting" (*kēruka*) of the body. A person on or in whose body a deity comes, is called *bhaktuḍu* (male) or *bhakturālu* (female) (devotee) in Telugu and *camiyāti* (god dancer) in Tamil. Spirit possession is referred to as *bhūt bādhā* (harmful effect of the spirit) in Marathi or *upadra* (trouble) in Tulu. There seem to be no native terms for persons who are afflicted by a spirit. In English they are described as victims or patients.

Cutalaimatan Temple Festival, © Richard Rapfogel

In the scholarly interpretation of spirit possession, most attention is paid to the possessed person, and the different forms of possession are analyzed and interpreted through various approaches. The psychic or social condition of the individual is often taken into consideration in order to determine the probable causes of the person's behaviour. It has been noted, for example, that persons afflicted by evil spirits are usually of younger or middle age, and the majority are women. Young women are particularly exposed to stress on marrying a stranger and living as a stranger in the household of their affines. Several case studies in the literature depict women in hopeless situations. Spirit possession is sometimes explained as the symptom of a psychic illness or is described as an expression of psychic stress which occurs and recurs in the life cycle of an individual.

Folk cultural interpretation pays more attention to the possessing entities. Spirit possession is seen as a chance for malevolent cosmic forces to interfere with human beings. Possessing spirits and demons constitute the lower part of the cosmic hierarchy and have a constant desire for worship. In accordance with the cosmology, they only trouble people who are in some kind of liminal state such as ritual impurity or social vulnerability. If their demands are fulfilled in the form of a sacrifice or intensified worship, their status as a tutelary being is verified. Even if they are merely exorcised, their minor cosmological status as a malevolent entity is equally confirmed.

Possession mediumship takes place in a ritual context. Preparations include ritual purification of the body of the medium and the space where the possession is to take place. The devotion of the medium to his or her personal deity is another precondition for the deity to come. Similar to a shaman, it takes several years until a medium is able to cope with the divine power and to control the words of the gods.

Entities who are able to possess a medium include deities of local and regional origin as well as deified dead. After a premature or violent death, children or young adults may be incorporated as "heroes" (Sanskrit, *vīra;* Telugu, *vīruḍu*), as *vīrabhadra,* or as *pēranṭālu* into the divine realm. They are worshipped by their relatives and can be invoked to enter the medium's body in order to explain causes and to suggest solutions for individual problems, such as ill health, misfortune, or distress. Generally, it can be observed that local and regional gods and goddesses are much more powerful than the deified dead. But the amount of power turns out to be of limited value for the clients. Deities may be more powerful, but they are also very demanding and strict with their devotees. Deified children, on the other hand, are much more lenient. Although their power usually is only sufficient to help their family members, they are sympathetic with the needs of their relatives and try to help them without demanding too much remuneration. The worship of the deified dead and their ability to communicate with human beings is not only a matter of getting help in times of distress but also a matter of consolation in the tragic situation of losing one's child. It may even be seen as a (partial) victory over death, since the child remains within reach and can be contacted in times of need. As long as it is not neglected but worshipped properly, the bereaved family members can secure the benevolent divine status of their deceased child.

The main characteristic of possession mediumship is its problem-solving mechanism. Individuals hope to get an explanation and support for various problems such as illness, childlessness, or misfortune. Scholars have only recently considered the utterances of the divinity in detail. This has led to a more integral understanding of possession mediumship since, as Nuckolls argues, "Possession is, after all, a phenomenon which usually expresses itself in language and which people interpret *through* explanation" (Nuckolls 1991:58 [emphasis in original]). The shift in attention from the "*outcome*" to the "*process*" of possession mediumship leads to new insights, Nuckolls says. For the audience, the divine speech not only offers ways to interpret and solve various problems, but it also confirms the cosmological order and ensures that divine beings are worshipped properly.

As a social practice, the phenomenon of possession cannot be easily reified. Each form is an ecstatic experience, an encounter with transcendent entities. Anybody can serve as a temporary vessel for a divine or demonic being, although the embodiment is never accidental. Each entity needs certain preconditions to be able to interact with human beings. The meaning of each form of possession depends on its social and ritual context.

References

Claus, Peter J. 1979. Spirit possession and spirit mediumship from the perspective of Tulu oral traditions. *Culture, Medicine and Psychiatry* 3(1): 29–52.

———. 1984. Medical anthropology and the ethnography of spirit possession. *Contributions to Asian Studies* 18: 60–72.

Freeman, Richardson J. 1993. Performing possession: ritual and consciousness in the Teyyam complex of northern Kerala. In *Flags of fame. Studies in south Asian folk culture,* ed. Heidrun Brückner, Lothar Lutze, and Aditya Malik, 109–138. Delhi: Manohar.

Gold, Ann Grodzins. 1988. Spirit possession perceived and performed in rural Rajasthan. *Contributions to Indian Sociology* 22(1): 35–63.

Knipe, David M. 1990. Night of the growing dead: a cult of Virabhadra in coastal Andhra. In *Criminal gods and demon devotees. Essays on the guardians of popular Hinduism,* ed. Alf Hiltebeitel, 123–156. Delhi. Manohar.

Nuckolls, Charles. 1991. Deciding how to decide: possession mediumship in Jalari divination. *Medical Anthropology* 13: 57–82.

Obeyesekere, Gananath. 1977. Psychocultural exegesis of a case of spirit possession in Sri Lanka. In *Case studies in spirit possession,* ed. V. Crapanzano and V. Garrison, 235–295. New York: Wiley.

Schoembucher, Elisabeth. 1993. Gods, ghosts and demons: possession in south Asia. In *Flags of fame: studies in south Asian folk culture,* ed. Heidrun Brückner, Lothar Lutze, and Aditya Malik, 239–267 Delhi: Manohar.

———. 1999. Death as the beginning of a new life. Hero worship among a south Indian fishing caste. In *Ways of dying. Death and its meanings in south Asia,* ed. Elisabeth Schoembucher and Claus Peter Zoller, 162–178. Delhi: Manohar.

Stanley, J. M., 1988. Gods, ghosts and possession. In *The experience of Hinduism. Essays on religion in Maharashtra,* ed. Eleanor Zelliot and M. Berntsen, 26–59. Albany: State University of New York Press.

ELISABETH SCHOEMBUCHER

SEE ALSO

Bakshi; Bhagavati Ritual Traditions of Kerala; *Bhūta;* Buddhism, Sri Lanka; *Darśan;* Exorcism; Gods and Goddesses; *Malang;* Maldives; *Muṭiyēṭṭu; Parī; Pēraṇṭālu;* Shamanism, Islam; Shamanism, Nepal; Siri; *Teyyam; Tōṟṟam*

SRI LANKA, SINHALA

Sri Lanka is a part of the South Asian culture area. However, just as there are many internal variations within the Indian subcontinent, resulting from factors such as geography, history, language, religion, and ethnicity, so too in Sri Lanka there is marked differentiation. The island is situated at the southernmost tip of the Indian subcontinent, separated from it by the Gulf of Mannar. The proximity to India has significantly influenced the development of Sri Lanka's history, culture, and ethnic mix.

Sri Lanka's population reflects a long history of contact. To the earliest inhabitants of the island, remnants of which are believed to be the present-day Veddas, were added immigrant groups from different parts of India who settled on the island at different times. The groups that settled in the southern regions quickly integrated into the Buddhist culture and adopted the Sinhala (earlier known as Sinhalese) language. Areas in the north, in closer contact with southern India, developed a Tamil identity, while in the northeast small groups of Arab (and later Muslim) settlers retained an Islamic identity.

Buddhism came originally from India and became a major unifying force for the island's peoples. The Sinhala language, derived from Sanskrit and Prakrit roots, quickly developed distinctive characteristics and became the language of the island's majority community. Long-term interaction with Tamil also left its mark on Sinhala, so that the language, like the culture, shows traces of multiple influences.

The spread of Buddhism and the Sinhala language helped to unify many immigrant groups, thus creating a distinctive identity among the majority population that one might label "Sinhala Buddhist." The Sinhala Buddhist culture that developed over the centuries was the product of a dynamic tension created, on the one hand, by a sense of a distinctive identity (self-consciously fostered by kings and by the Buddhist clergy) and, on the other, by the island's proximity to the mainland, which resulted in invasions, alliances, peaceful migrations, ongoing cultural contacts, and influences and cross-influences, all of them inevitable in such a context of contiguity. Buddhism, once established, rapidly became the single most important sociopolitical dynamic in the country's 2300-year history. Influences from the mainland were continually absorbed, modified, and integrated into the overall Buddhist culture of the island.

Nowhere is this dynamic tension better exemplified than in folk rituals and performances that symbolically "incorporate" Hindu or pre–Buddhist gods and demons into popular Buddhism. The structure of many ritual performances is based on the theme of a deity or demon from a "foreign" country who tries to enter the island at a coastal city. He or she is stopped by a (makeshift) barricade. The deity or demon acts and talks like a stranger unfamiliar with the local language and customs, undergoes questioning by the exorcist keeper of the barricade, and after much punning and horseplay over linguistic misunderstandings, he or she finally accepts the supremacy of the Buddha, obtains the keeper's permission or *varan* (a warrant), and enters the country. He or she is then incorporated into the local Buddhist pantheon, worshiped, and propitiated.

Theravada Buddhism in its doctrinal form downplayed religious ritual, and its orthodoxy did not produce or support the rich and varied communal rituals and performance culture that characterized Hindu India. Yet such rituals quickly developed as part of popular Buddhism, the religion as it was practiced by laymen seeking this-worldly help with the problems of everyday life.

One performance ritual that was incorporated very early into orthodox Theravada Buddhism was the ceremony of *pirit* (from the Pali *paritta*). Monks, seated in a sacred arena, chant in unison (often with considerable vocal musical variations) certain set doctrinal texts in order to protect and bless the individual and/or the community. At the end of the chanting, water and thread, empowered by the words uttered during the ritual, and thought thus to have magical potency, are distributed to the participants. This is followed by ceremonial offerings of food and gifts from the laity to the monks. This early incorporation of magical practice into Theravada Buddhism suggests how fluid the lines were between the anti-ritualistic doctrine of Theravada orthodoxy and the pressures for magical and protective rituals.

The *upasampadā* ceremony performed when a lay person is initiated into the monastic order is another such ritual. The initiate, accompanied by his relatives, is richly dressed like a prince (a replay of the renunciation by Prince Siddartha [the Buddha]) and then, with much ceremony, is inducted into the monastic order.

Singing and dancing were not initially considered an integral part of Buddhist temple worship. But over time rituals such as the offering of flowers, food, incense, and lights to Buddha images were introduced. At first the ritual practices were simple, minimalist, meditative ceremonies of worship intended to be performed by the individual rather than the group; later they became more elaborate with the input of pre–Buddhist folk practices and periods of strong Hindu influence on the Sinhala courts. Offerings of music, known as *śabdha pujā* or sound offerings (which involved drumming and the blowing of conch shells and horns) and dancing (especially by men) as a form of offering were introduced into Buddhist temples. The rituals at the Temple of the Tooth in Kandy, still performed today, illustrate such influences. Throughout the history of Buddhism in Sri Lanka there has been tension between the highly individualized form of the religion as it was expected to be practiced by monks or individuals seeking salvation, and the ongoing pressure to transform it into a religion of this-worldly support for lay folk in their daily activities.

Performance in the Folk Ritual Tradition

There is no record of plays or of a performance tradition in the classical literature of the early period, but a rich folk repertoire of dance and dramatic performance rituals associated with the worship of gods and demons has come down to modern times. They were preserved first in the oral tradition, and later also in a folk textual tradition: committed to writing and handed down by ritual specialists. These rituals were for propitiating mainly the "lesser" deities, who were seen as more directly involved in the day-to-day well-being of mortals.

Unlike the Buddha, who had achieved nirvana, and so could no longer play the role of a personal savior, these lesser gods and demons could be invoked, placated, and asked to intervene in human affairs. This was done not only with food offerings but also with dance, music, and performance rituals.

The practice of such propitiatory rituals probably predated the coming of Buddhism to Sri Lanka. Even after Buddhism was firmly established, such practices remained embedded in the folk imagination, and they continue to influence the manner in which the religion is perceived and practiced by laymen. Curing rituals and demon exorcisms that involve dancing, music, and dramatic interludes are performed by ritual specialists or "lay priests" who have never been fully accepted by the Buddhist clergy, but have not been actively discouraged either. These ritual specialists (*kapurālas* and *kaṭṭāḍiyā*s) are viewed as distinct from Buddhist monks. They engage in normal lay occupations, for the most part, but claim to have special powers. In the ritual context the gods or demons possess them, and they become their vehicle or representative. They remain part of the popular belief system and are incorporated into Buddhism as practiced at the folk level. All folk rituals commence with an invocation to the Buddha, who is head of a pantheon composed of a hierachy of lesser deities and demons. Local and "Hindu" deities have been incorporated into this "Buddhist" pantheon.

Paul Wirz, Nur Yalman, E. R. Sarachchandra, Gananath Obeyesekere, and Bruce Kapferer are noted scholars who have made exhaustive studies of these folk ritual performances. Most folk rituals are in the form of song and mimetic dances, accompanied by drums, that narrate the birth of one or more deities and the origin of the ritual. This body of serious ritual enactments is punctuated at intervals by comic and satiric prose interludes. These are most often extemporaneous, their content sometimes a parody of the main ritual and often only tangentially related to it. In these comic interludes the satire is directed at kings, or figures of authority or of high social status in the village, exposing them to the community's laughter. The ritual arena has thus become a "permitted space," in which political and social criticism is given public expression through satire, comedy, lampooning, and banter. Over time such comic interludes led to the development of secular folk dramas such as *Sokari* and *Maname.*

Just as folk beliefs and practices were absorbed into popular Buddhism, so Buddhist values filtered into popular culture. Buddhist texts, especially the dialogues and *suttas,* were permeated by the reflexive, ironic, skeptical voice of the speaking Buddha. This was repeated by generations of Buddhist monks in their sermons, and reached the village level through sermons, stories such as the *Jātaka*s, and popular Buddhist writings such as the *Saddharmaratnāvaliya.* This critical tradition entered ritual performances and folk dramas, where divine and secular authority was both implicitly and explicitly satirized and parodied. Thus pre–Buddhist folk ritual practices were incorporated into popular Buddhism and simultaneously the skeptical critical attitudes encouraged by the Buddhist doctrinal tradition influenced the content and the manner of ritual performances.

Folk Poetry

The four-line, end-rhymed stanza or *sivpada* (four rhymes), also referred to as *kavi* (poem), was the most common and popular form of poetry. *Sivpada,* called *sīpada* in colloquial speech, are generally chanted or sung, and though the musical score is relatively simple, it can be varied and made more complex according to the skill of the singer. The Sinhala language lends itself readily to rhyme, so such verses can be readily composed by people from all walks of life for all manner of occasions and experiences. The ease with which Sinhala peasants composed poetry was remarked on by the Englishman John Davy in his account of the interior of the island (176).

Sinhala has a rich tradition of folk poetry—love poems, erotic poems, narrative poems from the *Jātaka* stories, eulogies, battle poems, poems associated with agrarian events—and of tales of gods and demons. The poetry is traditionally sung, whether by an individual in the isolation of his fields or in public places for the benefit of listeners. In the nineteenth century a British administrator, Hugh Nevill, gathered a large collection of Sinhala folk poetry. The manuscripts are in the British Museum, and selections from them have been edited, translated, and published (Nevill; Jayasuriya). There are only a few scattered English translations of Sinhala folk poetry (Disanayaka 1984; Keyt; R. Obeyesekere 1972).

Folk Tales

There is an equally rich tradition of folk tales in the Sinhala language, both oral and written. Many of them are folk versions of the *Jātaka* tales that have become part of the culture; others are humorous tales that make fun of human foibles and the vanities, desires, loves, and hates experienced in daily living. Many deal with archetypal figures: the *gamarāḷa* (farmer), the stepmother (*para ammā*), the court jester (named Andare), devils, demons, and gods. Yet others are about common birds and beasts, such as the crow, the fox, the tortoise, and the lion. The most comprehensive collection of Sinhala folk tales translated into English is the three volumes collected and edited by H. Parker. A few other translations exist (Disanayaka 1984; Liyanaratne).

As in many traditional cultures, riddles, proverbs, omens and auguries, and word games form an important part of popular culture. This is particularly so with the Sinhala people, whose fascination with the play of language probably stems from the fact that they have a long tradition of exposure to a complex written literature. The monastic institutions of Buddhism carried this literature to the villages along with a tradition of education and literacy. Access to this literature in turn replenished and enriched the folk imagination.

References

Davy, John. 1983 [1821]. *An account of the interior of Ceylon and of its inhabitants.* London. First published 1821.

Disanayaka, J. B. 1984. *Aspects of Sinhala folklore.* Colombo: Lake House Investments.

———. 1993. *The monk and the peasant: A study of the traditional Sinhalese village.* Colombo: Lake House Investments.

Jayasuriya, Shirhan de Silva. 1995. Portuguese and English translations of some Indo-Portuguese songs in the Hugh Nevill collection. *Journal of the Royal Asiatic Society, Sri Lanka Branch* 40: 1–102.

Kapferer, B. 1977. First class to Maradana: Secular drama in Sinhala healing rites. In *Secular Ritual*, eds. Sally Moore and Barbara Myerhoff. Assen: Van Gorcum.

———. 1979a. Emotion and feeling in Sinhalese Healing rites. *Social Analysis* 1 (February).

———. 1979b. Entertaining demons: Comedy, interaction and meaning in Sinhala healing rites. *Social Analysis* 2.

———. 1983. *A celebration of demons:* exorcism and the aesthetics of healing in Sri Lanka. Bloomington: Indiana University Press.

Keyt, George. 1954. *Sinhala folk poetry.* Colombo: Lake House Investments.

Liyanaratne, J. 1995. Five Sinhala folk tales. *Journal of the Royal Asiatic Society, Sri Lanka Branch,* 329–366.

Nevill, Hugh. 1954–1955. *Manuscript collections of Sinhala verse.* Edited by P. E. P. Deraniyagala. *Ethnology,* vols. 2 and 3. Ceylon National Museum manuscript Series, vol. 6.

Obeyesekere, Gananath. 1969. Ritual drama and the Sanni demons: Collective representation of disease in Ceylon. *Comparative Studies in Society and History* 11: 175–216.

———. 1980. The goddess Pattini: A Jaina-Buddhist deity. In *Buddhist studies in honour of Walpola Rahula,* ed. S. Balasooriya. London.

———. 1984. *The cult of the goddess Pattini.* Chicago: University of Chicago Press.

Obeyesekere, Ranjini. 1973. [1972]. Sinhalese folk poetry. In *New Ceylon Writing,* ed. Y. Gooneratne. Vol. 2. First printed in *ARIEL* 3, no. 2 (1972):

———. 1974. *Sri Lankan Writing and the New Critics.* Colombo.

———. 1990. The significance of performance for its audience: An analysis of three Sri Lankan Rituals. In *By means of performance,* ed. Schechner and Apfel. Cambridge.

Parker, H. 1997 [1910]. *Village folk tales of Ceylon.* London.

Pertold, O. 1930. The ceremonial dance of the Sinhalese: An inquiry into Sinhala folk religion. *Archive Orientalia* 2: 108–137, 201–254, 385–424.

Sarachchandra, E. R., 1966. *Folk drama of Ceylon.* Columbo: Dept. of Cultural Affairs.

Wirz, Paul. 1954. *Exorcism and the art of healing in Ceylon.* Leiden: E. J. Brill.

Yalman, Nur. 1964. The Structure of Sinhalese Healing Rituals. In *Religion in South Asia,* ed. E. B. Harper. Seattle, WA: University of Washington Press.

RANJINI OBEYESEKERE

SEE ALSO

Buddhism and Buddhist Folklore; Buddhism, Sri Lanka; Character Stereotypes; Folk Literature, Sinhala; Jākata Tales; *Pirit; Sokari*

SRI LANKA, TAMIL

Jaffna refers to the northernmost peninsula of Sri Lanka and to the ancient Tamil city (pop. 200,000) which is located there. The Tamil word for Jaffna is *Yālppāṇam,* derived from the legend of a blind minstrel from the Chola country who played the *yāḻ,* an ancient stringed instrument. In terms of educational achievement, public virtues, and cultural politics, the Jaffna peninsula has always been regarded as the center of Tamil civilization in Sri Lanka. Many of the earliest leaders of the Tamil literary and religious revival of the nineteenth century came from Jaffna, including Arumuga Navalar (1822–1879), whose teaching and scholarship on Śaiva Siddhanta philosophy and whose early efforts to found Hindu schools and to publish Tamil literature were highly influential in South India. Even the poorest Jaffna vegetable farmer is extolled as a paragon of thrift and hard work, the Scotsman of Sri Lanka. Both the Tamil dialect of Jaffna as well as the Tamil dialect spoken in the eastern Batticaloa region are distinct from that of Tamilnadu, preserving a more archaic vocabulary and a colloquial pronunciation which is closer to the literary standard. Yet it is also in Jaffna that the most bitterly fought battles for low caste and Untouchable temple entry rights raged in the twentieth century against the vested powers of conservative *Vēḷāḷar* caste landowners and temple managers. In the eyes of many Sri Lankans, the image of Jaffna society suffers from an impression of rigidity, hierarchy, and an attitude of superiority, but there is also well-earned respect for the sons and daughters of Jaffna who have achieved so much on the basis of their initiative, cleverness, and hard work.

To many non-Sri Lankans, the term "Jaffna" is loosely applied to the entire Tamil-speaking portion of the island, extending from north of Chilaw on the west coast, across the northern quarter of the island, and down the eastern coastline as far as Trincomalee, Batticaloa, and Pottuvil. This northeastern arc is conceived by Tamil nationalists in Sri Lanka as "Tamil Eelam" (*Īḻam* is a Tamil name for the island), a historic zone of Tamil ethnic settlement dating back before the formation of the Kingdom of Jaffna in 1200–1400, C.E., and before the period of imperial Chola conquest and colonization around 1000 C.E., to even earlier periods of Sri Lankan civilization. Unfortunately, modern archaeology, which could shed a great deal of light on these ancient multi-ethnic settlements, has been severely hampered by twentieth-century ethnic politics. The "Estate Tamils" whom the British recruited in the late nineteenth and early twentieth century from Tamilnadu to pick tea in the central Kandyan highlands are culturally and socially distinct from the much older Tamil communities in the northeast.

Śaivite Hinduism is the predominant religion of Tamils everywhere in Sri Lanka, and non-Brahmin priesthoods are common. In both the Jaffna and the Batticaloa regions the cult of the goddess *Kaṇṇaki* (Sinhala *Pattini*), heroine of the Tamil epic *Cilappatikāram,* is a popular tradition, and several famous temples reenact the story of Draupadī (*Turōpatai*) from the Mahābhārata epic. Christianity has also been an important factor for the Tamils. As early as 1813 the American Missionary Society launched western-style Christian schools in the heart of Hindu Jaffna. This gave the educated children of high caste Jaffna Tamil families favored access to professional careers during the colonial era, a pattern of conspicuous achievement which provoked an anti-Tamil backlash from the majority Sinhalese community in the decades following Independence in 1949.

Tamil-speaking Sunni Muslims of the Shāfi'ī legal school (termed *Moros* or "Moors" by Portuguese, Dutch, and British rulers; *Cōṉakar* or *Muslīm* in Tamil) are found throughout the island, but their largest settlements in the northeast are in Puttalam, Mannar, Trincomalee, and especially the Batticaloa and Amparai districts. The Muslims owe their religion and part of their ancestry to medieval Arab spice traders plying the Indian Ocean, but both Tamils and Muslims also have historical connections to South India. Scholars have noted a mixture of Tamilnadu and Kerala-derived customs and social practices in Jaffna, but the distinctive matrilineal and matrilocal family patterns as well as popular oral traditions of sorcery (*mantras*) associated with the Malabar Coast are strongest among Tamils and Muslims in the eastern Batticaloa region.

References

Manogaran, Chelvadurai, and Bryan Pfaffenberger, eds. 1994. *The Sri Lankan Tamils: ethnicity and identity*. Boulder: Westview Press.

McGilvray, Dennis B., 1989. Households in Akkaraipattu: dowry and domestic organisation among the matrilineal Tamils and Moors of Sri Lanka. In *Society from the inside out: anthropological perspectives on the South Asian household*, ed. John N. Gray and David J. Mearns, 192–235. New Delhi: Sage Publications.

DENNIS B. MCGILVRAY

SEE ALSO

Muslim Folklore, Sri Lanka; Pattini

SRI PADA

Sri Pada (*śrī pāda,* Sinhala, *Siri pāda*), mountain of "the sacred footprint," is located in southwestern Sri Lanka. Sri Pada is a pilgrimage site for Buddhists, Hindus, and Muslims, who regard the imprint in the rock at the summit as that of the Buddha, Śiva, and Adam, respectively. Legends of the origin of the footprint and accounts of pilgrimage to the cone-shaped mountain have been passed down over the centuries. Hindus and Buddhists alike regard the mountain, also known as Adam's Peak and Samanala Kanda, as the domain of the deity Saman, a vanquisher of demons. According to early legends it was at the behest of the deity that the first of the four Buddhas of the present era visited the peak, leaving his footprint.

The annual pilgrimage season lasts from December to the full moon of Vesak in April / May. The climb is usually made at night in order for pilgrims to arrive at the summit shortly before dawn. The two major routes, the shorter Maskeliya path and the more arduous climb through the Carney estate, are marked by the presence of sites related to the Buddha and earlier pilgrims. For example, a rock known to Buddhists as *iňḍi-kaṭu-pāna* (place of the needle) is said to have been the site where the Buddha was mending his robe when Māra, the tempter, caused a flood to rush down the mountain. When the waters reached the rock, however, they parted, thus sparing the Buddha's life. To commemorate this incident, pilgrims make offerings of needles and thread that are draped on nearby trees.

The pilgrimage culminates in a series of steep steps, enclosed by a parapet about five feet high, that lead to the summit. In the early morning pilgrims huddle together in the cold air to watch the sun rise and to view the extraordinary triangular shadow that is cast on the clouds below. The sound of a large bell rings through the mists as pilgrims mark the number of times they have successfully climbed the peak.

References

Brohier, R. L. 1965. *Seeing Ceylon*. Pt. 3. Colombo: Lake House.

Paranavitana, S. 1958. The god of Adam's peak. Ascona, Switzerland: Artibus Asiae Publishers.

Skeen, William. 1870. *Adam's peak: Legendary, traditional and historic notices of the Samanala and Sri Pada.* Colombo: W. L. H. Skeen.

SUSAN A. REED

SEE ALSO

Buddhism and Buddhist Folklore; Sacred Geography; Sri Lanka, Sinhala

STORY LITERATURE, PERSIAN

Moral instruction through telling stories constitutes a long tradition in Persian literature, and has resulted in a large body of narrative literature. During the period of Islamic rule in South Asia, when the Persian language was used for official correspondence, a great deal of this type of literature spread into South Asia.

In the pre–Islamic period Persian narrative literature was already closely related to Indian sources. Burzōe, the court physician of the Persian emperor Anūshīvān (c. 531–579), who traveled to India to obtain copies of Indian medical works, brought back to Iran the *Pañcatantra.* In an adapted form (incorporating tales from the *Mahābhārata*) this book later earned international fame as *Kalīla wa-Dimna.* It constitutes an early example of the literary category "mirrors for princes," a genre of didactic literature for the ruling class. Also in this category is the book of the wiles of women known as *Sindbād-nāma,* which, though it originated in Persian literature, incorporates many tales of Indian origin.

Other literary works were meant to provide a more general moral education. These include the Sanskrit *Shukasaptatī* (The Seventy Tales of the Parrot), adapted into Persian in the Islamic period under the titles *Javāhir al-asmār* (Jewels of Night Entertainment, 1314 C.E.) and *Ṭūtī-nāma* (Book of the Parrot, 1330 C.E.), by Ẓīā'ud-dīn Nakhshabī and Muḥammad Qādirī (seventeenth century), respectively. Works of Buddhist teaching also have been passed on to (or via) Persian literature, such as the collection of jocular tales contained in Somadeva's *Kathāsaritsāgara* (eleventh century), part of the earlier *Tripiṭaka,* a collection of Buddhist tales translated into Chinese in the fifth century.

Narrative works of Persian origin also exerted a considerable influence on South Asian literature. Compilations like the Sanskrit *Kathāsaritsāgara* by the Gujarat Jainist Hemavijaya, made in 1600, contain a considerable number of tales from Persian sources. Even during British dominion in South Asia, Persian narrative literature left distinctive traces: In his grammar of the Persian language (1795), under the heading of Ḥikāyāt-i laṭīf, ("Pleasant Stories in an Easy Style"), Francis Gladwin, an English diplomat serving at Fort William College in Bengal, appended a selection of jocular tales for language practice. This appendix eventually was separated from the grammar and became a chapbook; it was translated into various Indian languages and is documented to have influenced the Indian (oral) tradition.

At a more general level narrative literature in the Persian language can be divided into the categories of prose and poetry. Poetic works like Jalāluddīn Rūmī's *Masnavī* employ stories in order to further moral education and the attainment of mystical enlightenment, whereas prose works elaborate stories that are predominantly entertaining. In the context of relations between South Asian and Persian story literature, it is interesting to note that after the establishment of lithographic printing of Persian texts, some of the most efficient and productive printing houses were located in India, notably in Bombay, Cawnpore (Kampur), and Newal Kishor. While these printing houses primarily produced books for the Iranian market, they also served the Persian-speaking community in South Asia and thus constitute another important means for transmitting Persian story literature. Narrative works printed in India since about the middle of the nineteenth century include Firdawsī's *Shāh-nāma,* Niẓāmī's *Khamsah,* and especially Sa'dī's *Golestān.* Through the mid-twentieth century Persian booklets such as *Chihil-Tūtī,* a popular adaptation of *Ṭūtī-nāma,* were printed in India and exported to Iran.

Yet another facet of the close relation between Persian and South Asian story literature is the genre of popular romance (*dāstān*) in the Urdu language. Its dominant example, both written and orally recited, is *Dāstān-i Amīr Ḥamza,* also known as *Ḥamza-Nāma,* the story of Ḥamza ibn 'Abdulmuṭṭālib, the prophet Muḥammad's paternal uncle, who in Persian literature since at least the eleventh century has developed into the protagonist of a narrative tradition modeled in part on the classical romance of Alexander. The *Ḥamza-Nāma* is reported to have been Emperor Akbar's (1556–1605) favorite narrative; a number of lavishly illustrated leaves from Akbar's personal copy survive in libraries worldwide. In the twentieth century the *Ḣamza-Nāma* has been more popular in South Asia than in Iran. There are also a number of Urdu adaptations of similar works of Persian origin, mostly compiled in the eighteenth and nineteenth centuries, such as *Bustān-i Khiyāl* by Mīr Taqī Khān, *Chahār Darvīsh,* and popular romances originating from the Arabian Nights or the narrative cycle Ḥātim at-Tā'ī.

In South Asia story literature of Persian origin is by no means an exclusively, and perhaps not even a predominantly, written genre. Numerous relations exist between written or printed versions and performances in the oral tradition. Professional or semiprofessional storytellers use notebooks (Persian; *daftar*) and exploit the huge stock of narrative motifs available from published sources. On the other hand many written items of story literature rely to a certain extent on orally transmitted material. Even Persian narratives written down as late as the nineteenth century have some of the structural qualities of oral performance, such as text markers and a traditional stock of narrative formulas.

References

Marzolph, Ulrich. 1992. *Arabia ridens: Die humoristische Kurzprosa der früuhen Adab-Literatur im internationalen Traditionsgeflecht*. Vol. 1, 89–152. Frankfurt am Main: Klostermann.

———. 1995. "Pleasant stories in an easy style." Gladwin's Persian grammar as an intermediary between classical and popular literature. *Proceedings of the Second European Conference of Iranian Studies;* held in Bamberg, 30 September to 4 October 1991. Ed. Bert G. Fragner et al. Rome: Istituto Italiano per il Medio ed Estremo Oriente.

Pritchett, Frances W. 1985. *Marvelous encounters: Folk romance in Urdu and Hindi*. New Delhi: Manohar.

Schimmel, Annemarie. 1975. *Classical Urdu literature from the beginning to Iqbal*. Wiesbaden: Harrassowitz.

ULRICH MARZOLPH

SEE ALSO
Amīr Ḥamza; *Dāstān;* Folk Literatūre; *Qiṣṣa*

STORY LITERATURE, SANSKRIT

In India, stories are attested to have existed since the beginning of literary memory. However in Vedic literature (1550 B.C.–500 B.C.), stories are part of ritual and therefore appear only in fragments or in allusions. Scholars such as Oldenburg have argued that the Vedic hymns are only the metric skeleton of stories which we have now lost. Nevertheless a sizable number of collections of Vedic stories, myths and legends have been translated into Western languages.

The same use of stories for ritual purpose is also found in post-Vedic story literature. For example, the birth stories of the Buddha, called *Jātaka,* contain a wealth of stories narrated for didactic or missionary purposes. The same can be said of the rich story material found in the Jain religious tradition. A clear didactic purpose is also connected with most of the stories in the great Indian epics, the *Mahābhārata* and *Rāmāyaṇa,* which extol the excellence and propitiousness of Hindu ethics. For example, the story of Sāvitrī and Satyavant illustrates the virtues of chaste marriage and the narrative of Nala and Damayanti teaches the dangers of gambling.

Collections of stories for enjoyment only started to appear during the second century B.C.E. The lost *Bṛhatkathā* is believed to be the source for numerous later collections, the most famous of which is the *Kathāsaritsāgara* (Ocean Stream of Stories). Some of these collections were purportedly used for the education of princes, such as the *Pañcatantra* and *Hitopadeśa.* Nineteenth century scholars such as Theodor Benfey traced many of the stories from these collections to those found later in the Near East and in Europe, proposing the theory that *Märchen,* fictional folk tales of magic, originated in India. This led to a debate among folklorists about the single or multiplex origins of stories.

In the Indian middle ages (circa 670 C.E.–1800 C.E.), the modern Indian languages of today first manifested themselves in literary form. The stories from this period retained some of the ritual and didactic purposes of former times, and drew much from the earlier Sanskrit stories. These traditions are vast and span all regions of India. Devotional (*bhaktī*) cults used the classical legends of the great gods of Hinduism, Viṣṇu and Śiva, to spread their doctrines among illiterate believers, furthering the development of oral story telling traditions. Especially rich are the accounts of the various incarnations of Viṣṇu as Kṛṣṇa and Rāma. We also find many stories of the lives of bhaktī saints in languages such as Tamil.

A tradition of sanguinary battles against the Muslims, most often with a clear bias in praising Rajput courage and their upholding of *dharma* ("rules of correct behavior") are found in the Rajput story literature of Western India. A caste of bards is famous for its rendering of the *Ālhā Khand,* telling about the battles between Hindus and Muslims and about local heros such as Pābūjī, who is most popular among the lower castes.

Caste heros often figure as chief protaganists in local story-telling traditions. Many of these stories are adapted from the epic traditions, made to serve as local expressions of identity and pride. This type of hero features in the famous Punjabi epic of *Hīr Rānjhā.* A separate tradition is the Bengali *Maṅgala* poems, most of which tell about the hardships befalling a man who neglected to worship his local goddess (Candi), god (Dharma), or the snake goddess (Manaśa) or who has enraged the goblins (Citra and Gupta).

Another important story-telling tradition is narratives told among women while observing fasts and taking part in other ritual activities, known as *vrat kathā.* The richness and variety of vernacular story-telling traditions in India is quite staggering.

Another very interesting set of stories are those which appear in Muslim Sufi texts, some of which follow the Persian tradition of the *Khamsah* (set of five stories) of Niẓāmi. Especially well-known are the stories of Yusūf and Zulaykhā, Laila and Majnūn, and the Alexander story. There is also an attempt made to convey the Sufi message in a more Indian context using Indian as opposed to Persian names for characters and places. Since no Indian sources for these stories have been found, it is assumed that they are of Sufi origin.

While the rich Near Eastern and Persian material that embellishes medieval Muslim *mathnavī* (narrative poems in rhymed couplets) has been widely forgotten, in modern times, stories of the Prophet in historic form are known by most Muslims. In the Isma'īlī tradition there still lives rich devotional story material of Indian and non-Indian origin, collected in the *ginan* which only recently became accessible to non-Ismā'īlī scholars.

PETER GAEFFKE

SEE ALSO
Ālhā (Ālhā-Ūdal); Benfrey, Theodor; *Ginān; Kathāsaritsāgara;* Pābūjī; *Pañcatantra;* Vrat Katha

STŪPA

Stūpas are dome-, bell-, or egg-shaped reliquaries, usually constructed out of brick and mortar (miniature stūpas are usually made out of bronze), and range in size from a few inches to hundreds of feet in height. They are among the most visible symbols of Buddhism in South and Southeast Asia, simultaneously symbolizing the presence of the Buddha and the Buddhist worldview.

The Sanskrit term stūpa first appears in the ancient Brahmanic Vedas, where it means "top" or "summit," perhaps deriving from a reference to a topknot or tuft of hair. By the time the interchangeable Pali terms *thūpa* and *dhātugarbha* were used in Buddhist literature in the early centuries B.C.E., the meaning clearly refers to molded mounds constructed over the bodily relics of the Buddha. The etymology of dhātugarbha provides a more precise meaning: *dhātu* means "element" or "material reality," and *garbha* means "womb" or "treasury." Thus, stūpa or dhātugarbha (later glossed in Sinhala as *dāgäba*) means "the womb of what is real." The "mound" of the stūpa is a symbol of the origins of material, conditioned reality; and the spire emanating from its top and pointing skyward is symbolic of the spiritual path realized by the Buddha to transcend the limits of this phenomenal world. The stūpa is, therefore, both a cosmogonic and a soteriological symbol.

In the canonical *Mahāparinibbāna Sutta,* an early Pali text (first century B.C.E) purportedly recounting the final months of his life, the Buddha instructs his monastic disciples to preserve his *dhammakāya* (body of teaching or truth) and to regard it as their guiding spiritual focus. At the same time he declares that when he dies, he will be cremated in the manner accorded to cosmic or universal kings (*rājā cakkavattī*), and that the remains of his *rūpakāya* (form body or phenomenal body) will be cared for by the laity. According to this text, following the Buddha's "royal" cremation, his relics were divided and enshrined in stūpas by leaders of the eight republican clans of central and eastern India. Further, the Buddha introduced the cult of *cetiya* (Sanskrit, *caitya*), or sacred places, where stūpas without relics should be constructed. He designated these as places to which laity might journey, so that feelings of reverence and awe might be cultivated.

Four places are especially identified by the Buddha in the *Mahāparinibbāna Sutta* for this purpose: his birthplace at Lumbini (just within the modern Nepalese border); the site of his enlightenment under the *bodhi* tree at Buddha Gaya (near modern Gaya in Bihar); the place of his first sermon, where he turned the "wheel of dharma" at the Deer Park in Sarnath (near Varanasi or Benares), and the place where he died or entered his final *nirvāṇa* (nirvana) at Kusinagara. In the *Mahāparinibbāna Sutta* account, then, there is an early textual reference to the origins of the cult of the Buddha in the form of stūpa veneration and the first Buddhist practices of pilgrimage. Pilgrimages to sacred places associated with the "presence" of the Buddha, places marked either by the enshrinement of his relics in stūpas or by *cetiya,* remain a staple of popular lay Buddhist practice today.

Stūpas are the most ubiquitous symbol of the spread of the Buddhist religion and culture throughout Asia. They are the architectural precursors of the pagoda in China, and are found within the temple compound of virtually every Buddhist monastic establishment in South and Southeast Asia. In modern Sri Lanka it is said that every temple or monastic complex must contain a stūpa, a bodhi tree, and a meditation/preaching hall in order to completely symbolize the *triratna* ("triple gem"—Buddha, dharma, and *sangha* [monastic community]), the three objects in which Buddhists take refuge from suffering in this world. The stūpa stands for the Buddha, the bodhi tree stands dharma, and the meditation/preaching hall stands for sangha.

The widespread incorporation of the stūpa within Buddhist tradition and its consequent importance to lay Buddhist practice may owe much to Aśoka, the great Indian emperor of the third century B.C.E., who is said (in the *Aśokāvadāna* and other popular sources written in the next centuries B.C.E.) not only to have made a pilgrimage to the four great sites associated with the life of the Buddha but also, purportedly, to have ordered that the eight stūpas originally erected by the republican clans of India be opened and that the relics contained within be enshrined in 84,000 newly built stūpas throughout his vast empire.

With the emergence of Mahayana Buddhism in the early centuries C.E., scriptures such as the *Saddharmapuṇḍarīka Sūtra* (Lotus Sūtra) declared that worshiping at, making offerings at, and constructing stūpas were to be regarded as means to the attainment of Buddhahood. The architectural and spatial elements of the stūpas provided a model, or became a cosmologically projected sacred space, on which the cosmic Buddha Amitābha's idealized afterlife land of bliss, *Sukhāvatī* (Pure Land), was imagined by early Māhayāna adherents. This popular conception of the "Pure Land," a place of rebirth in which nirvāṇa is believed to be easily attained, was aspired to over many centuries by thousands of East Asian Buddhists in China, and continues in contemporary Buddhist practice in Japan as the most popular form of the religion.

In eschatological traditions concerning the future Buddha Maitreya, it is believed that at the moment of his enlightenment, all of the bodily relics of the Buddha (*rūpakāya*) enshrined in stūpas throughout the world will miraculously came together under the bodhi tree in India to form the new body of this next Buddha. Stūpas are, therefore, not only a symbol of the past Buddha or of his continuing "presence," but also a symbol of the future of the tradition.

References

Akira Hirakawa. 1963. The rise of Mahayana Buddhism and its relationship to the worship of stupas. *Memoirs of the Research Department of the Toyo Bunko* 22: 57–106.

Bareau, André. 1962. La construction et le culte des stupas d'après les Vinayapitaka. *Bulletin de l'Ecole française d'Extrême-Orient* 50: 229–274.

JOHN CLIFFORD HOLT

SEE ALSO

Buddhism and Buddhist Folklore; Buddhism, Sri Lanka; Pilgrimage; Sacred Places; Shrines; Worship

SUFI FOLK POETRY

Sufi folklore in South Asia developed predominantly as folk poetry in a variety of vernacular languages such as Hindi, Punjabi, Sindhi, Bengali, Kashmiri, and Tamil. As early as the thirteenth century, Sufis initially began composing short poems in local languages for the *samā'*. This was a ritual involving singing and dancing that attracted large audiences to Sufi shrines. Subsequently, they adopted a broad range of popular indigenous verse forms to communicate mystical ideas to local populations. These were derived from folk poetic traditions that were oral in nature.

Since women were closely associated with folk traditions in many regions of South Asia, Sufi poetry frequently borrowed the structure of songs sung by women as they performed daily tasks such as grinding, spinning, weaving or putting children to bed. Drawing parallels and metaphors from the activity in which the women were engaged, Sufi poets would explain their basic precepts in a simple language. The high frequency with which vocabulary, similes and technical terms associated with women's activities occur in this poetry indicate the importance of women as transmitters of Islamic/Sufi ideas in rural households (Eaton 1974–5: 125–6). The feminine element is manifest in another significant manner. In consonance with local literary conventions, Sufi folk poetry always represents the soul as a *virahinī*, a loving woman who yearns for her absent beloved. The woman-soul becomes for the folk poet a standard symbol to express the core message of Sufi thought, the yearning of the human soul for God.

Sufis also used popular Indian folk romances and legends to express different aspects of the human-divine relationship by giving them mystical and allegorical interpretations. Thus, in Bengal, the Rādha-Kṛṣṇa romance from Hindu devotional poetry was furnished with a Sufi meaning while in Punjab and Sind, poets provided mystical overtones to folk romances such as Hīr-Rānjhā or Sassui-Puṅhuṅ, always portraying the heroine as the parable of the soul who seeks divine union. In Hindi-speaking areas, Sufi poets composed long mystical epics based on traditional romances, some of which, like Jaisī's *Padmāvat*, are counted among the classics of medieval Hindi.

Beyond these epic romances, Sufi folk-poetry drew on a repertoire of symbols derived from a range of everyday activities including fishing and seafaring as well as the world of nature to express its love mysticism so that even the *papiha* bird that constantly cries out (in Hindi!) *piu kahāṅ*, "where is the beloved?" evokes images of the searching soul.

Sufi folk poetry strongly condemns bookish learning and ritualism as a means of approaching God. The main targets of criticism are religious scholars and jurists who are portrayed as being narrow-minded and intolerant. Far more instrumental in nurturing an individual's relationship to God was the instruction of the mystical preceptor, the *pīr*, in whose guidance total trust was necessary. He was God's "friend" and representative of the prophet Muḥammad. Naturally the *ʿulamā*, the guardians of religious orthodoxy, objected to the exaggerated importance accorded to the Sufi master in this poetry. Even more unacceptable to them were the pantheistic-sounding verses declaring the fundamental unity of all forms of creation. Though very likely composed under the influence of the *waḥdat al-wujūd* "unity of existence," theory associated with the Iberian Sufi Ibn 'Arabī (d. 1240), this philosophy is reminiscent of the Hindu philosophical doctrine of *advaita* "non-dualism," leading some scholars to detect Vedantic Hindu influences in Sufi folk poetry.

Whatever the case may be, the strong reverence that this poetry accords Muḥammad, the Prophet of Islam, gives it a distinctively Islamic hue. He is variously portrayed as the loyal and trustworthy friend, the bridegroom of Medina, the merciful intercessor on the day of judgement, and the protector and guide through whose example human beings can attain the ultimate goal of complete submission to God.

References

Asani, Ali. 1988. Sufi poetry in the folk tradition of Indo-Pakistan. *Religion and Literature*. 20:1, 81–94.

———. 1993. Folk romance in Sufi poetry from Sind. *Islam and the Indian Regions,* ed. A. Dallapiccola and S. Lallemant, Beitrage zur Sudasienforschung, vol. 145:1, 229–237. Stuttgart: Franz Steiner Verlag.

Eaton, Richard. 1974–5. Sufi folk poetry and the expansion of Islam. *History of Religions*. 14:2, 115–27.

Schimmel, Annemarie. 1982. Reflections of popular Muslim poetry. In *Islam in Local Contexts,* ed. Richard C. Martin. Contributions to Asian Studies (genl. eds. I. Ishwaran and Bardwell L. Smith). vol. 117, 17–26. Leiden: E. J. Brill.

———. 1982. *As through a veil: mystical poetry in Islam*. New York: Columbia University Press.

ALI S. ASANI

SEE ALSO

Hīr/Rānjhā; Islam; *Pīr*

SUPERNATURAL BEINGS

***See** Āl;* Ancestor Worship; *Baiṭhak; Bandara* Cults; *Bakshi; Bhūtā; Bhūta Kōla; Daha-Ata-Sanniya; Dev;* Exorcism; Ghosts; Ghūl; Gods and Goddesses; Heroes and Heroines; *Jinn;* Malignant Spirits, Nepal; *Mammā;* Myth; *Parī; Pīr; Pirit; Purāṇa; Satī; Satya Pir;* Spirit Possession and Mediumship; Supernatural Beings, Nepal; Witches and Sorcerers; Witches, Nepal

SUPERNATURAL BEINGS, NEPAL

Events and beings that defy the laws of "nature" or normalcy as it is conceived of, and are thus difficult to comprehend rationally, may be classified as "supernatural." Belief in the supernatural is characteristic of all religions and societies, yet there is no single agreed-upon definition among scholars. In folklore studies the term "supernaturals" generally refers to nonsacred beings such as nature spirits, fairies, witches, ghosts, ancestral spirits, and vampires, as distinct from sacred deities. However, in practice these distinctions are not always clear.

Both Hinduism and Mahāyān Buddhism—the state religion and the second most practiced religion in Nepal, respectively—are polytheistic and integrate the deities of other indigenous religions of Nepal. Both revere countless gods, goddesses, and other celestial entities, all of which are considered sacred. In addition Nepali also believe in "supernaturals," which can generally be classified into two types. The first type is by nature benevolent but can be troublesome if offended, while the other is evil by nature but can be appeased, and hence manipulated to fulfill human desires. Nepali folktales, legends, and memorates are filled with accounts of these supernaturals.

The benevolent spirits most widely believed in are *sime* (water spirits), *bhūme* (earth spirits), and *nāg* (supernatural serpents). The nāg, in particular, are thought to attract rain and impart fecundity. Bhūme and sime are generally believed to dwell in mountains, rivers, fields, or forests, and are thought to protect the pious, orphans, lost travelers, battered women, and others in times of need. People who frequently encounter and have benefited from such supernaturals may build shrines in their honor. In times of crisis some people promise to make offerings and sacrifices to these spirits; if they fail to fulfill their promises, the spirits will usually remind them in dreams, or punish them by inflicting illness or other misfortunes. All of these spirits are very sensitive to pollution. Those who pollute land or water sources may be punished with a fatal illness.

The spirits of ancestors, called *pitr,* are venerated as equal to gods. If pleased, they bless the family by bringing them good fortune. People believe that their own life stems from that of their anscestors, so they have a responsibility to care for them even after death. If a family can afford it, it will devote one day each year to *śraddha* rituals in which they offer food to the departed ancestors. If people neglect to make offerings, or if they criticize the character of their ancestors, the ancestors may inflict illness or other misfortunes.

Among the malevolent supernaturals, bhūt (ghosts) are widely believed in. However, not all bhūt are considered bad. For example, the Newars of Kathmandu Valley desire to have a *tuyu khyā* (white ghost) in their home because it brings prosperity. There are many kinds of bhūt. Lustful women who die in their youth turn into *kicakannī* ghosts and roam about, seducing men. *Murkaṭṭā* (headless ghosts) are ghosts of people who were murdered or of soldiers killed in battle. They threaten people with knives. *Rāṇke bhūt* resemble fire, and threaten people with burning. *Bhakuṇḍe bhūt* look like soccer balls, and harass people by constantly blocking their way. All these murkaṭṭā, rāṇke, and bhakuṇḍe bhūt do not kill people. *Tarsāune*, a rather passive ghost, amuses itself by frightening children, cowherds, and animals, and by throwing stones and making weird sounds even in daylight. However, the fright caused by seeing these tarsāune may occasion a fatal nervous breakdown.

Other catagories of bhūt include *piśaca* and *pret,* which are ghosts that live in solitude, especially in ruins, forests, and caves, and *masāne bhūt,* which dwell in cremation grounds. These three kinds of bhūt feed upon animal and human remains. When they feel hungry or disturbed by humans and animals, they possess their bodies, causing illness; chronic possession can lead to death. *Pacabhaiyā* is a group of five very rich and powerful ghosts who ride horses and conduct a tour every fortnight. If one sees them coming, one must yield immediately; otherwise the confrontation may cause illness or instant death. The pacabhaiyā are very sensitive about their prestige. Those who worship them as deities may be blessed with money and power.

Bīr, the most powerful ghosts, are hard to appease because they have a direct link with the real world through human masters (*bīr khelāune mānche*). The bīr and their human masters benefit from each other's services and patronage. For example, the bīr have power to kill but cannot kill by their own will, so they need orders from living people. The human masters have the capacity to order the killing but not the power to kill directly. Both are cruel, and will not hesitate to kill a person.

To satisfy their selfish desires malicious people learn to manipulate ghosts and spirits. *Bokso* (sorcerers) and *boksī* (witches) learn to create their own *putalā* (a psychic counterpart that may resemble a doll) and train black cats, both of which help them to summon bhūt, especially the powerful bīr. The putalā, black cats, and bhūt help them harass or take revenge; in turn they demand to be fed. Sometimes the bīr asks to be fed with human blood, and on such occasions the bokso or boksī may give them permission to possess their husband, wife, or children because they are bound to maintain their relationships with their supernatural helpers at any cost.

In contrast those collectively called *jānne* (one who is familiar with the supernatural), including *pandit* (priests), *jyotishī* (astrologers), *jhā̃krī* (shamans), protect people from boksa, boksī, and bhūt. To determine whether the afflicted person's misfortune has a natural or a supernatural cause, they analyze dreams, interpret horoscopes, read pulses, read the *ākhat* (a kind of divination involving counting unbroken kernels of rice), or invoke their gurus and deities. If they find the cause to be supernatural, a power struggle ensues between the jānne and the malevolent agent. A weak bhūt may depart immediately or suffer censure from the jānne, whereas strong bīr can demand a buffalo sacrifice (which, in some cases, may be bargained down to a rooster sacrifice by the jānne).

Sacred books, mantras, incense, and amulets are used to control supernatural beings. For example, amulets such as a tiger's claw, knife, porcupine quill, clove, and mustard seed may repel evil supernaturals. Interestingly, Nepali folklore attests that not only can bhūt possess people, but human beings may also possess bhūt, although unknowingly. If a pious person encounters a bhūt, the bhūt will be possessed. The person will become aware that he or she has possessed a bhūt only when the bhūt appears and offers wealth and service to appease the person. Hence, as the Nepali proverb says, *Baliyākā āge bhūt bhāge* (Ghosts flee when they see a strong person coming). Indeed, no supernatural being can match the potential strength of a human; it is said that everything in the universe, whether good or bad, is controlled by deities and supernaturals, who are controlled by *mantra*s, which in turn are known only by certain learned people. Nepalis believe that humans have ultimate control over deities as well as less powerful beings. They also believe that both deities and humans have control over the supernaturals.

References

Bharati, Agehananda. 1975. *The tantric tradition*. Rev. ed. New York: Samuel Weiser.

Hitchcock, John T., and Rex L. Jones, eds. 1976. *Spirit possession in the Nepal Himalayas*. New Delhi: Vikas Publishing House.

Levy, Robert I. 1990. *Mesocosm: Hinduism and the organization of a traditional Newar city in Nepal*. Berkeley: University of California Press.

Sharma, Prayag R., ed. 1976. *Contributions to Nepalese studies: anthropology, health, and development*. Kathmandu: Research Centre for Nepal and Asian Studies.

HARIHAR P. BHATTARAI

SEE ALSO

Bhūta; Divination; Ghosts; Spirit Possession and Mediumship; Witches and Sorcerers; Witches, Nepal

SWADESHI

Swadeshi (self-reliance) refers to a movement in India based on a preference for Indian-made goods rather than imported ones and the constructive encouragement of India-based production. Together with *swaraj* (self-rule) and nonviolent resistance, swadeshi was a core principle of the Indian independence movement.

By the end of the nineteenth century declining Indian handicraft production and limited industrial growth were blamed on British colonial rule by the economic historians R. C. Dutt and Dadabhai Naoraji, among others. Discriminatory tariff and excise policies had allowed imported goods to flood markets, and as a result the Indian economy had been impoverished. Indian machine loom and hand loom cloth, in particular, faced overwhelming competition from imported Lancashire cloth made from cheaply obtained Indian raw cotton. At the same time British and Indian art critics lamented the near extinction of indigenous industries as Indian tastes shifted toward the consumption of foreign commodities. Early nationalist intellectuals of the late nineteenth century proposed swadeshi ideals to counter these economic and cultural trends.

The partition of Bengal by the British imperial regime sparked the 1905–1908 swadeshi movement, organized and dominated by an educated elite frustrated at the failure of the politics of persuasion to alter colonial policy. Protests of partition initially took the form of boycotting British imports, complemented by intensified efforts to produce commodities inside India and calls (sometimes backed by coercion) to consume home-produced goods. A forerunner of later and more successful mass mobilizations, the swadeshi movement was an important watershed in the nationalist movement, contributing to awareness of the cultural and political issues at stake in opposing British rule. It included, for example, some of the earliest explorations of handicrafts and a life of rustic simplicity as alternatives to industrialization and consumption-oriented urbanization. There was a revival of interest in the folk arts and folklore of Bengal and other regions of India, and a prodigious output of patriotic literature, music, and song.

However, producing and consuming Indian goods rather rapidly proved to be of limited impact. The complete replacement of imported products proved to be an unattainable ideal; there were the practical difficulties of offering alternatives to foreign goods, and it was impossible to match them in price or, in the case of English cotton textiles, to replicate their texture. It became apparent that swadeshi by itself was insufficient to solve more fundamental problems stemming from colonial rule, although its potential as part of a larger political movement was glimpsed. The swadeshi movement as a whole foundered on its inability to sustain a mass movement, and it succumbed to fragmentation in its ranks and suppression by British authorities. In addition the Hindu religious associations of the swadeshi movement's populist efforts alienated many Muslims. Nevertheless, seeds of subsequent nationalist movements had been sown.

Many elements of the swadeshi movement were recycled in the 1920s and 1930s by the Congress Party as it crafted its anticolonial politics. Swadeshi ideals epitomized economic independence, self-reliance, and national pride. Ultimately swadeshi and swaraj were linked as a fully independent India became imaginable and nationalist leaders were measured by their devotion to swadeshi ideals. A leading figure in the development of these ideals was Mohandas K. Gandhi (1869–1948), whose profound understanding of the symbolic and moral appeal of swadeshi was critical to the popular success of the independence movement. His commitment to swadeshi forms—for example, khadi (homespun cloth) and traditional Indian garments—led directly to the Congress Party's adoption of the spinning wheel as its symbol and a characteristic style of dress using khadi. Gandhi also saw in swadeshi a model for a future India that would turn toward handicraft production in a revival of village life, and turn away from industrial manufacture and urbanization. His objection was not just to British manufactured goods but to all manufactured goods, whatever their source. This particular interpretation of swadeshi has had lasting influence until the present day.

The emotional and economic appeal of swadeshi in post–Independence India is arguably as strong as it was prior to 1947, and in the rest of South Asia the exploration of traditional arts is similarly strong. In India the influence of Gandhian philosophy persists in state patronage of indigenous handicrafts, which, it is argued, are culturally and economically indispensable in a country that is still largely agricultural. The showcasing of Indian handicrafts and folk performing arts occupies a sizable portion of Indian public culture. India has undergone marked industrial development; it is scarcely believable that the country will pursue the return to village life envisaged by Gandhi. Nevertheless swadeshi ideals continue to be voiced in debates about what degree of dependence and enjoyment of imported goods is acceptable, and what patterns of consumption and production most epitomize India's past and its future.

References

Bayly, C. A. 1986. The origins of *swadeshi* (home industry): cloth and Indian society, 1700–1930. In *The social life of things: commodities in cultural perspective,* ed. Arjun Appadurai. Cambridge: Cambridge University Press.

Dutt, Romesh Chunder. 1902. *The economic history of India.* London: K. Paul Trench and Trubner.

Gandhi, M. K. 1922 [1908]. *Indian home rule.* 5th ed. Madras: Ganesh.

Sarkar, Sumit. 1973. *The swadeshi movement in Bengal, 1903–1908.* New Delhi: People's Publishing House.

Tagore, Rabindranath. 1919. *The home and the world.* Trans. Surendranath Tagore. New York: Macmillan.

CLARE M. WILKINSON-WEBER

SEE ALSO

Bangladesh; Crafts; Nationalism and Folklore

SYNCRETISM

In its most common form in the study of South Asian cultures, syncretism denotes the combination or alliance of religious or philosophical doctrines, often with political undertones, that results in public and private rituals and commonly accepted local practices which appear to the observer to link orientations that are normally disparate, if not disjunctive. The term favors the description of a state or condition of uneasy union, but can be extended to describe the process by which such conciliations occur. Syncretism as both process and description hinges on the assumption that those observed have inappropriately mixed cultural and religious categories that are intrinsically alien to each other, but the expression of this combination is almost never made directly, but metaphorically. With several notable exceptions—the Mughal emperor Akbar, Dārā Shikūh, Kabīr, the Sikhs—scholars have tended to locate examples of syncretistic religion and ritual at the non-textual, village, or local level, and especially in areas that are deemed remote from the centers of high culture. While the term is occasionally used to delineate the mixing of sectarian positions, for example the fusion of Śaiva and Vaiṣṇava theologies within the Hindu traditions, it is more often than not associated with the products of inter-sectarian or inter-religious encounters, such as that of Hindu and Muslim, producing a mixed product that mysteriously exhibits features of both.

Although scholars sometimes use the term positively, in the sense of "synthesis," more often than not the term is derogatory. The first modern use of the term (1615 C.E.) described "misguided" attempts at reunion of the Protestant and Catholic churches as syncretism. In the history of religions, syncretism was applied particularly to the "mixed" religions of the Hellenistic and Roman eras, in implicit or explicit contrast with "pure" Christianity. Historically it has not been the syncretistic outcome of this process of combination that has concerned scholars, as much as the basic "elements" leading to this strange combination. Because of its ahistoricism and underlying essentialist bias, syncretism is only just beginning to lose favor as an explanatory model in critical scholarship. On examination every "pure" tradition turns out to contain mixed elements; if everything is syncretistic, nothing is syncretistic, and the term loses its power to describe. The basic problem stems from the fact that the initial categories that are established in opposition can never be natural, nor can they be sufficiently comprehensive to accommodate the incredible variety of human religious and cultural experience. Consequently, nearly every cultural product suffers from this lack of categorical purity, and will to a greater or lesser degree participate in syncretism. When a religious ritual, theology, symbol, or text fails to measure to this standard of purity, it is designated as tainted, diluted, corrupt, or otherwise divergent (a favorite of way of describing the interaction of mainstream and high culture with so-called "folk" traditions); when the taint or dilution can be positively identified with another main stream tradition, it becomes syncretic. Either way, the designation is nearly always negative.

Part of the power and appeal of syncretism as a descriptor, however, lies in the fact that it never describes directly, but indirectly through metaphors with generally negative valuation. This valuation emerges only by examining the entailments of the metaphoric constructs, which will invariably seek to explain the abstract through concrete analogies, forcing the interpreter to rely on a model that reifies and objectifies its subject. The metaphors of syncretism presuppose original, essential, and axiomatic categories of cultural and religious experience. Yet the pristine and exclusive identities given to various religious and social groups in South Asia today through primordial narratives are frequently themselves the products of modern political processes. The first Indian census of 1871 attempted to define exclusive religious identities; the gazetteers and related official and semi-official documents created by colonial officials such as W. Crooke, H. Rose, and L. S. S. O'Malley served much the same purpose for the recording of ritual processes and the charting of social organization. A similar logic has justified the attempts of reformers (whether Muslim, Hindu, or Sikh) to "purify" their religions of foreign accretions. Invocations of syncretism inevitably use the broad strokes of monolithic cultural and religious categories, as opposed to the historically specific forms that would require more subtle and nuanced distinctions. The argument reduces complex forms to simplistic terms that have but a dubious analytic value and which serve to instantiate existing stereotypes.

Precisely because of its effective use of clichéd metaphors and in- or mis-direction, however, syncretism continues to shape much of the scholarship that examines the popular and folk cultures which fail to adhere to the dominant religious and social constructs of South Asian society at large. The metaphors can be reduced to four broad models of interaction and encounter: (1) influence and borrowing; (2) the overlay or "cultural veneer"; (3) alchemy; and (4) organic or biological reproduction. The first two are rudimentary and focus on the description of a static condition, while the latter attempt to define both the condition and process.

Borrowing and Influence

These terms describe transactions in which two groups or individuals are affected by each other through direct and indirect contact, respectively. Borrowing suggests that one group has taken and incorporated an idea, custom, or specific item from another. The implication of this model of physical exchange is that the borrowing group is dependent, lacking in creativity, and fundamentally incapable of defining itself. This model does not, however, adequately encompass the complex process that can perhaps better be described as "appropriation," wherein the borrowed item is transformed through the process of incorporation, thus fundamentally altering both the appropriated and the appropriator (true synthesis). The same holds for the model of "influence," which originally derived from the astrological concept of emanations from the stars and the parallel inflow or affluence of waters. Influence as the exertion of action through unseen forces by one thing on another is a decidedly more sophisticated model than borrowing because of its astral or hydraulic base metaphor (celestial radiations or mixing of flowing waters vs. the exchange of concrete objects). But the advantage gained concomitantly dissolves into mechanistic vagueness, precisely because the factors are understood to be unstated or unconscious, without any acknowledgement of selectivity or volition on the part of the "influenced" person or culture. Examples of influence (which pervade much of the secondary literature in the history of art, ideas, and literature) nearly always define the "source" as dominant over the passive recipient, which is also therefore "derivative" and less authentic.

The "Cultural Veneer" or Overlay

Syncretism is often used to describe the product of the large-scale imposition of one alien culture, religion, or body of practices over another that is already present. This spatial model (also known as "envelope") creates a politicized topography that describes a state or condition, but does not explain any of the processes by which this condition has been achieved. The entailments of the metaphor of veneer, however, reveal a decided ambiguity. Veneer is, of course, a thin and delicate layer of ornamental wood laid over and bonded to a thicker, sturdier foundation of courser wood or other material. When juxtaposed, the two parts are only artificially joined; they can be delaminated at any moment, and they will always retain their intrinsic characteristics. One need only think of the many theories describing the advent of Islam in South Asia to see the pervasiveness of this model. Although Muslims have shared the geographical space of South Asia with Hindus and others for more than a thousand years, many still deny to their religion any kind of indigenous status, which is reserved exclusively for Hindus who, the argument runs, were there first. Analyses of other large-scale contacts (e.g., Christian "rice-conversions") follow similar patterns.

Alchemy

Perhaps the most popular model of syncretism is that of alchemy, which secondarily shares in the hydraulic metaphor of influence, while maintaining a chemical basis of interaction (reaction). There are two types of combinations that can be forged in the alchemical crucible, one irreversible, the other not. The irreversible combination of fluids or the dissolution of a compound results in the creation of a solution, which is a new entity; chemically the resulting reaction would produce a new substance with by-products, such as heat and light. This syncretic end-product is a new creation, which may or may not have any use; it may, in fact, be lethal to those who come into contact with it. The more common alchemical model of syncretism, however, is that of the mixture, a colloidal suspension of two ultimately irreconcilable substances. The result is a temporary mixture that will invariably separate over time, because the component parts are unalterable and must remain forever distinct and apart. The implication is that the parts remain recognizable, the concoction requires constant agitation to remain viable; it cannot endure without outside intervention. What remains, as in all of the models of syncretism, are the original component parts that have been mixed against what was intended by nature; in this model, religious or cultural essence triumphs over history.

Biological Model

The biological model of syncretism generally articulates two or more contributing "parents" that produce offspring through a mysterious miscegenation. The offspring is either an obvious blend of the parents containing clearly identifiable characteristics or features, or it is deemed to be a hybrid (plant) or halfbreed (animal). The implication is that like all hybrids, the result is sterile or does not "breed true," but disaggregates in the next generation rather than reproducing itself, thereby ending the lineage or species. This form of syncretism, while acknowledging the viability of the immediate result, holds little hope for continuation, and is, therefore, usually discounted as unviable. But the appeal of this model is its reliance on the organic metaphor which has served to organize so much of our (pseudo-) science of culture since its application to languages and societies following evolutionary morphologies of the natural sciences.

When applied to South Asian cultures, it is easy to see how the explanations that hinge on syncretism often tend only to concretize the initial religious or cultural categories presumed to be self-evident by the interpreter. Folk culture, precisely because it frequently does not adhere to the strictures of dominant religious and ideological modes of organization, is frequently described in such demeaning terms. While syncretism has often been invoked to explain what does not "fit" into the dominant intellectual and cultural categories, it has almost without fail served to relegate its subjects to a secondary status.

It should be added that in the mid-1990s in the state of India, the term syncretism has been successfully used in the popular media by intellectuals and other outspoken proponents of cultural and political pluralism as a positive alternative conceptual structure to the insular and exclusive ideological positions of religious nationalist groups, especially the Bharatiya Janata Party (BJP). While the ramifications of such usage have yet to be fully gauged, this appears to be one of the first positive valuations of the term in religious or political discourse and should be noted as a potential shift in its semantic field.

Reference

Lakoff, G. and M. Johnson. 1980. *Metaphors we live by*. Chicago: University of Chicago Press.

TONY K. STEWART AND CARL W. ERNST

SEE ALSO

Colonialism and Folklore; Crooke, William C.; Nationalism and Folklore; Religion

T

TA'AWĪZ

See Islam

TABĀRRAK

Tabārrak, or *tabarrūk* ("Sanctified food"), is a traditional Islamic ritual meal. During various religious festivities (e.g., the day of *'Urs*) a dish called *khicuṛi* (rice mixed with pulses) or *biranī* (rice with meat and spices) is cooked. After it is cooked, some of the food is taken out of the pot. The devotees sit together and the *fātiḥa* (opening verse of the Qur'ān) is repeated. After the prayer is completed, this portion of the food is mixed back into the pot. Only then does the *tabārrak* become sacred. The *tabārrak* is distributed among the devotees and poor people. It is believed that those who eat this food become purified in body and mind, and may be cured of a disease.

SHAFIQUR RAHMAN CHOWDHURY AND LAURI HARVILAHTI

SEE ALSO

Foodways; Islam

TAGORE, RABINDRANATH

Best known as the 1913 Nobel Prize winning writer of fiction and poetry, Tagore (1861–1941) drew heavily on his native Bengali folklore for inspiration. Much of his knowledge of Bengali genres came at an early age, while he was growing up in the family mansion at Jorashanko, near Calcutta. The young Tagore was exposed to a great deal of verbal art performed for him by the family's household servants. In fact, many scholars have speculated that this early exposure resulted in Tagore's later activities as a collector and a proponent of folklore an unifying agent of romantic nationalism.

After going abroad to England between 1878 and 1880, Tagore returned to Bengal to begin a career as an activist in the Indian Freedom Movement. The years between 1880 and 1910 were his most active time in the political arena. It was during this period that Tagore realized the important role that folklore could play in creating both a national and regional identity, and in bridging the widening gap between urban and rural dwellers. Influenced by the British oppression of the Irish during his first visit to England in 1878, Tagore returned there in 1890 to gather more material for his sociopolitical writings. His work from that period suggests a strong orientation towards the propagation of folk traditions and vernacular language as unifying agents of change. This second trip inspired him to take up the linguistic cause to have Bengali reinstated as the official language in Bengal. Related to this was his conviction that a "national literature" based on Bengali folk traditions needed to be consciously cultivated in order to create a common political and aesthetic ideology for all Bengalis, a theme he developed in a lecture on Bengali National Literature delivered in Calcutta in 1894.

Tagore's increasing activity as a spokesman for the Freedom Movement led to the formation of a number organizations and journals concerned with the rediscovery and preservation of Bengal's oral heritage. In the same year as his monumental lecture, Tagore, along with other wealthy and powerful literary figures in Calcutta, founded the Baṅgīya Sāhitya Pariṣad (Bengali Literature Society), which published the *Sāhitya Pariṣad Patrikā (Journal of the Literature Society)*. The society and its publication created a strong impetus for later collectors of folkore, not to mention the great effect they had on the formation of a united Bengali ethnic identity.

After 1894 Tagore himself was engaged in the collection and analysis of local folkloric traditions. He feared that the forms he heard as a child might be disappearing due to the use of English by the elite classes. Beginning with urban rhymes collected in and around Calcutta, he went on to collect folk ballads (*pallīgīti*), dramas (*jātrā*), local myths (*paurāṇik kāhinī*), legends (*upakathā*) and fairy tales (*rūpkathā*). Like many European collectors before him, Tagore "rewrote" many of the items he collected in order to create a standard form of the language. He also drew heavily on English printed sources of folklore from other regions of India to create what we might term a "localized universalism," as Arabinda Poddar (1977, 182) has pointed out. But this universalism eventually led Tagore away from politics and into a spiritual realm of "world humanism." By 1910 Tagore's nationalistic period of folklore collection and production was over.

Tagore's contribution to the development of folklore studies in Bengal was very important for the development of an indigenous and applied folklore studies movement. Because he was a product of a specific urban, class-oriented milieu, however, his conception of *lok sāhitya* (folk literature) was limited in scope. The context of his affluent social life in Calcutta played a critical role in his folkloristic formulations, which were further shaped by his readings of books published by British ethnographers and civil servants. His recasting of local folklore infused with pan-Indian elements was thus a literary creation for the purpose of constructing a unique Bengali identity. Nonetheless, his career was a necessary step, not only in the development of folklore studies in Bengal but also in the history of Indian nationalistic movements.

References

Haque, A. S. Zaharul. 1981. *Folklore and nationalism in Rabindranath Tagore*. Dacca: Bangla Academy.

Korom, Frank J. 1989. Inventing traditions: folklore and nationalism as historical process in Bengal. In *Folklore and historical process,* eds. D. Rihtman-Auguštin and M. Povrzanović, 57–84. Zagreb: Institute of Folklore Research.

Poddar, Arabinda. 1977. *Renaissance in Bengal: search for identity*. Simla, India: Indian Institute for Advanced Studies.

Sengupta, Sankar. 1963. Rabindranath Tagore's role in Bengal's folklore movement. *Folklore* (Calcutta) 4: 137–152.

Tagore, Rabindranath. 1917. *Nationalism*. New York: The Macmillan Company.

———. 1945. *My boyhood days*. Trans. Marjorie Sykes. Calcutta: Visva-Bharati Publishing Department.

Zbavitel, Dušan. 1961. Rabindranath and the folk-literature of Bengal. *Folklore* (Calcutta) 2: 9–14.

FRANK J. KOROM

SEE ALSO

Bangladesh; Colonialism and Folklore; Folklorists; Jātrā/Yātrā; Myth; Nationalism and Folklore; West Bengal

TAMĀŚA

Tamāśa is a Persian word meaning a show, play, farce, or other diverting entertainment, but in Maharashtra, it means a specific form of folk theater. Although tamāśa as theatre dates from the period of Mughal influence, probably the end of the sixteenth century, it incorporates elements of Maharashtrian folk culture from much earlier times. A tamāśa performance begins with a *gāṇ,* a devotional song to the God Gaṇeśa. It is followed by a *gauḷaṇ,* a farce centered around the stories of Kṛṣṇa and the *gopīs*, with added characters such as Kṛṣṇa's friend, Peṇḍya and an "auntie" character, always played by a male dressed as a woman. The *vag*, a play with a definite story line, often depicting situations from daily life, with laughter as its chief aim follows. The two sided *ḍhōlki* drum is chief among tamāśa instruments, and a singer of *lāvāṇī* is essential to the performance. Stock characters include the *songādyā,* a witty clown. The *tuṇtuṇa* (one-stringed instrument) and the cymbals of the traditional Gondhal singers are used to accompany a *powāḍā,* the narrative ballad form that predates tamāśa. The riddle found in Marathi folklore is also an important part of tamāśa.

The eighteenth century was the classical era of tamāśa, and some of the *śāhīrs* (creators and singers of lāvāṇī and powāḍā, a ballad form) of the Peshwa period are themselves the subject of song and theater. Famous śāhīrs of that time include Anant Phandi, who seems to be the first Brahman involved in the very non-Brahman, non-elite tamāśa. Another Brahman, Ram Joshi, sang of the great famine of 1802 and the raid of Holkar and in this century became the subject of a Marathi movie. Honaji, a barber at the Peshwas' court, composed lāvāṇī still sung today and is the hero of a popular play written in 1954. The important elements of Peshwai period tamāśa were the major actor-singer characters of the *sardār,* the songādyā and the *nācyā,* young boys dancing female roles. At the end of the Peshwa period (1796–1818), women began to replace the boys as dancers.

After the Peshwas, there was a decline in tamāśa, although it continued to be the most important form of entertainment in the rural areas, and it seems to have resumed its totally folk form. However, during the British period, probably due to the inspiration of English theater, the vag became more highly developed, and a revival of tamāśa under yet another

Brahman, Patthe Bapurao (1866–1942), took place in the early twentieth century. Bapurao's marriage to an untouchable Mahār dancer, Pavala, became the stuff of drama in itself, and the presence of women in predominant acting roles dates to his time. The Mahār and Māng untouchable castes were the backbone of tamāśa, and Mahār women dominated the erotic female dance roles. Kolhātis (an acrobat caste) were also important players.

The caste composition of tamāśa continues to contemporary times. A traditional Mahār *tamasgīr,* Dadu Indirikar, was among the last of the great tamasgīrs (leaders of troupes). The best-known post-independence troupe was that of the late Bhau Māng. In the revival of tamāśa for social messages in the 1930s, the Marxists Śāhīrs Amar Shaikh and Annabhau Sathe, a Māng, were leaders. Sathe's *Akkalecī goṣṭa* (Tale of Wisdom) is probably the most popular Marathi folk drama of all time. In the 1950s tamāśa was adapted to government messages on such subjects as birth control and to issues such as the campaign for a Marathi language state. Although B. R. Ambedkar, a leader of untouchables, had urged women not to take part in tamāśa since doing so, he believed, contributed to their image as low women, some troupes spread his message of equality and protest against injustice. In an effort to make tamāśa less "vulgar," a board, created in 1960 censored tamāśa scripts, which resulted as well in the writing down and subsequent publication of many Marathi scripts.

Around 1971, according to Teva Abrams, there were ten thousand tamāśa artists performing in five hundred or so itinerant troops. Balwant Gargi's somewhat earlier study (1962) estimates eight hundred troupes with forty thousand people making their living by tamāśa; three thousand women actresses, most of them Mahārs, performed in tamāśa. Until recently, there were very popular daily performances of tamāśa at theatres in Bombay and Pune, and tamāśa centers in the Jalgaon, Kolhapur, and Sholapur areas were devoted to that form. Until the advent of television, tamāśa troupes constituted the chief form of entertainment in rural Maharashtra. Although tamāśa as a folk form has declined, its influence on Marathi film and theatre continues strong. Dozens of films made about tamāśa have been enormously popular, and such well known playwrights as Venkatesh Madgulkar, P. L. Deshpande, and Vijay Tendulkar have used tamāśa forms with great effect in their dramas.

References

Abrams, Teva. 1974. Tamāśa: people's theatre of Maharashtra, India. Ph.D. dissertation. Michigan State University.

Gargi, Balwant. 1991 [1962]. Tamāśa. In *Folk theatre of India,* 73–88. Calcutta: Rupa and Company.

Varadpande, M. L. 1992. *History of Indian theatre.* Vol. 2: Loka Ranga. Panorama of Indian Folk Theatre. 163–172. New Delhi: Abhinav.

Vatsyayan, Kapila. 1980. *Traditional Indian theatre: multiple streams,* 169–177. New Delhi: National Book Trust.

ELEANOR ZELLIOT

SEE ALSO

Comedians, Jesters, and Clowns; Ganeśa; Kṛṣṇa; Lāvaṇī; Maharashtra; *Nācā; Nauṭanki*

TAMIL NADU

Tamil Nadu, one of the southern most states of India, located in the extreme southeast, has an area of 130,058 square kilometers. It stretches from the Bay of Bengal in the east to Kerala in the west, to the Indian Ocean in the south, to Andhra Pradesh in the north and Karnataka in the northwest.

Divided between the flat country along the eastern coast and the hilly regions in the north and west, Tamil Nadu's major mountain range is the western Ghats. The eastern Ghats, located in central Tamil Nadu, are referred to as Javadu Hills, Kalrayan Hills, and Shervarayan Hills. Rivers such as the Palaru, Cauvery or Ponni, Vaigai, and Tambraparani irrigate majors parts of the state; legends about the rivers abound.

According to the 1991 census, Tamil Nadu's population is approximately 60 million. Followers of the major religions—Hinduism, Christianity, and Islam—are found in all districts, but the Jains live primarily in North and South Arcot Districts and Madras City. Hindus make up the majority of the population and belong to two significant traditions: the folk and the classical. Christians are divided between Catholics and Protestants, each tradition having its own folklore.

Even though some parts of Tamil Nadu are industrialized, agriculture is the predominant economic occupation. Rice-based foodways, one of the important traits of South Asia, are also predominant.

Eighty-three percent of the population of Tamil Nadu speaks Tamil; Telugu is spoken by approximately 10 percent, and Kannada by 3 percent. The land is divided into several cultural *maṇḍalams* (regions): Thondai, Chola, Chera, Kongu, and Pandia, each one having its own significant folk art forms, folk cults, rituals and festivals which highlight the heterogeneity of Tamil folklore.

Puppetry

In Tamil, the native term for puppetry is *pavaikkūtu.* This folk art form is performed throughout the state by a community called the Marathi Raos, who migrated to Tamil Nadu from Maharashtra centuries ago. It is a family tradition in which each and every family member is a full-time performer playing *surappeṭṭi, mattalam,* and *jalra*. Puppets, made of leather, occasionally paper, and more recently, plastic, are used. Well-known and popular stories such as the abduction of Sīta, *Vāli Vatai, Sūrpānagai Chaṇḍai, Rāmar Paṭṭabishekam, Nallataṅgaḷ Kathai* are performed in the puppetry tradition.

Pommalāṭṭam (wooden puppets) is another type of puppetry performed throughout Tamil Nadu. Only a few groups are engaged in this art form. Up to seventy-five puppets are used in this tradition in the enactment of mythical tales.

Terukkūttu

Terukkūttu is a ritual folk theater performed during the festivals of the Goddess of Draupadī in Thondaimandalam. The term *Terukkūttu* literally means "street" (*teru*) "drama" (*kūttu*), but it is different from *Vīti Nātakam,* which uses Sanskrit words conveying same literal meaning, or the more recently introduced forms that go under the English term "street theatre." *Terukkūttu* employs poetry and prose, as well as music and dance. Since the performance begins with the singing of *Naṭṭai Rāga* it is sometimes called *Naṭṭaikkūttu,* "dance drama." The musical instruments accompanying this dance drama are: harmonium, *mirutankam, ḍōlak* (both are kinds of drums), and *mukavīnai,* a small wind instrument. The stylistic performance of this art form varies as *karṇāṭakam* (Karnataka style), *vekujāveli, vadakkūtti* (northern style), and *tekkūtti* (southern style). Altogether, this widespread tradition has three hundred texts based on the *Mahābhārata*.

Vilpāṭṭu

Vilpāṭṭu, named after the bow used in the musical and narrative tradition, is primarily confined to Tirunelveli-Kattabomman, V. O. C., and Kanyakumari Districts, a region collectively known as Thenpandi mandalam. There are two distinct regional stylistic traditions, namely Nanchil Nadu and Tirunelvely. The *Vilpāṭṭu* is performed by five persons. Each of them sings and plays instruments: a bow, a hand drum, a large earthen pot, a pair of slim wooden blocks, and a pair of brass cymbals. The performers are semi-professionals and semi-literate. This tradition is performed and supported by low- and middle-caste people such as Nāḍars, Maravars, Konars, Pillaimars, and Mūpanars. The Bow Song is performed in the Kodai Festivals organized for the local deities, namely Sudalai Madaswamy, Essakkiamman, Muthu Pattan. These deities are indigenously called *Vettupatta Vathi* (cut up spirits), *Peipadaikal,* and *Padukalangal*. Of these, one sect is called *matans* (male) and the other, *ammans* (female).

Kaṇiyankūttu

Kaṇiyankūttu, also known as *Magutāṭṭam,* is another ritualistic dance performed by a group of five to six people of the Kaṇiyan caste in the Kodai rituals of Thenpandi Maṇḍalam. *Magutāṭṭam* is named after the one-sided drum played in this art form. The stories narrated in the *Vilpāṭṭu* tradition are also used in this ritualistic tradition. While the lead singer narrates, two drummers (one believed to be a male and the other a female) will play the two *Magudam;* two other males will dance dressed as transvestites.

Udukkai Pāṭṭu

Udukkai Pāṭṭu is a tradition of narrating a legend or local epic to the accompaniment of a hand drum, performed mainly in Kongumandalam and northern Tamil Nadu. *Aṇṇanmar Kathai* or *Kunnudayan Kathai, Katavarayan Kathai, Maduraivīraswāmi Kathai,* and *Desingu Rājan Kathai* are some of the folk epics narrated in verse-narratives.

Oyil Āttam

The word *oyil* means beauty. This narrative dance is performed in Paṇḍi maṇḍalam, at the festivals for Āyyanār and at Life Cycle ceremonies; it is only performed by a minimum sized group of twelve males. *Rāmāyaṇa* and *Mahābhārata* episodes and Biblical stories are narrated. The lead singer sings while the others will follow and dance.

Folk Dances

Karakāṭṭam is a dance performed through Tamil Nadu. A *karakam* is a small vessel made of copper or brass. Balancing the decorated vessels on their heads, the performers (male or female) dance to the rhythm of *nayyandi mēlam*.

Poykkāl Kutirai āṭṭam literally means "hobby horse dance." With two wooden sticks tied to their legs, performers dance to the tune of a *mēlam*.

Chilambāṭṭam

Chilambāṭṭam, a martial art, uses long sticks for self-defense and is practiced in every village, whereas *Kaliyalāṭṭam,* which uses two small sticks, is only found in the southernmost part of Tamil Nadu. *Kōtāṭṭam* is a similar dance/sport form performed by girls and boys in Tamil Nadu.

Dēvarāṭṭam

Dēvarāṭṭam is performed by the Chillavār sect of the Telugu-speaking community of Rajakambalam caste in the contexts of festivals like Kodai (gift), folk cults, and life cycle ceremonies. It is performed in the districts of Chidambaranar, Nellai-Kattabomman, Kamarajar, Madurai, Anna, Trichi, Coimbatore, Periyar, Salme, and Dharmapuri, or wherever the Kambalathu Nayakkars live in large numbers. This dance is performed with the help of a drum called *Deva Dundubi* or *Urumi.* There are two or three aetiological myths about this performance.

Bull-baiting

Pongal (Ponkal), a national festival of the Tamils, is celebrated on January 14th. The next day is "Mattu Pongal" (celebration for cows and bulls). On that day, Manji Virattu, a kind of bull-baiting is conducted in the central part of Tamil Nadu: mostly in Madurai, Pasumpon Devar, Pudukottai and Ramnad Districts. Another type of bull-baiting known as *Jallikkaṭṭu* is aranged in this region. After tying a *calli* (copper coin) on the foreheads of the bulls-trained specially for this, the bulls are set loose. The competitors then try to recapture the fierce bulls. In the ancient extant texts of Sangam Tamil literature and the famous grammar *Tolkappiyam,* this is mentioned as "erukotal" or "eru taluvutal." Another form of bull-baiting, *eruthukattu* is conducted at an Ayyanar festival called *Puravi Eduppu* (taking horse).

Moḍiyāṭṭam

Moḍiyāṭṭam is a kind of performance ridiculing black magic, and is performed on the day of Dīpāwali, and the day after as well, and only in Nallān Pillai Petral Village in the South Arcot District. One person dressed as a buffoon acts like a black magician. He will tie a doll made out of clothes, called *Kutty Chattan,* to a pedestal (*moḍi*) and place it in front of the temple street and challenge the people to remove it. Persons pretending to be from the royal family will come and try to remove the moḍi. But the magician will make them pretend to die by vomiting blood. Finally, their sister, Mantira Cikkamani, will remove the moḍi and pretend to kill the magician.

References

Beck, Brenda E. F. 1982. *The three twins*. Bloomington: Indiana University Press.

———. 1979. *Perspectives on a regional culture: essays about the Coimbatore area of south India*. New Delhi: Vikas.

Blackburn, Stuart H. 1980. *Performance as paradigm: the Tamil folk song tradition*. USA: University Microfilm International.

Frasca, Richard A. 1990. *The theater of Mahabharata*. Honolulu: University of Hawaii Press.

Hiltebeital, Alf. 1988. *The cult of Draupati,* vol. 1. Chicago: Chicago University Press.

S. D. Lourdu

SEE ALSO

Aṇṇanmār Katai; Bow Songs (*Vil Pāṭṭu*); *Dīvālī/Dīpāvalī;* Draupadī; *Jallikaṭṭu;* Marionettes; *Ponkal;* Shadow Puppetry; Terukkūttu

TARANNUM

Tarannum (Urdu: chanting of poetry) is integral to the performance and dissemination of Urdu poetry. It is a melodic, rhythmic style of recitation created and performed by poets, because poetry traditionally is presented and experienced orally.

Primarily associated with the widely favored *ghazal* genre, tarannum musically articulates formal aspects of the poem while enhancing its emotional or experiential content. Musical elements are strictly subordinated to the text; indeed tarannum is not considered to be music, and is therefore respectably dissociated from the negative Islamic valuation of music. Melodically, however, tarannum belongs in the context of north Indian light music, though voice production and performance style render its tunes distinct.

Tarannum is strictly strophic. Following the couplet structure of the ghazal, the first nonrhyming line and the concluding rhyming line are marked with a higher-pitched and a lower-pitched tune, respectively, corresponding to the *antarā* and *asthāyī* principles of classical and light classical songs. Tarannum rhythm is directly linked to the complex metric system of Urdu poetry, which in turn is rooted in Arabic-Persian prosody. Its diverse patterns of long and short syllables are realized musically by corresponding long and short durational units. The result is "metric tunes," or "pattern *dhun,*" articulating specific meters that also serve as templates for poets when composing their verses. Tarannum tunes can be adapted to different meters as required. Poets are the principal innovators, if not composers, of tarannum.

The principal occasion for performing tarannum is the *mushā'ira,* a private or public assembly at which poets present their work to connoisseurs as well as general audiences. For listeners these simple text-based musical settings not only heighten the sense of poetic structure, but also leave room for highly personal recitation styles, including the freedom to respond to listeners' reactions with appropriate interruptions and repetitions. The result is an intensely shared experience of poetry through music.

References

Qureshi, Regula Burckhardt. 1969. Tarannum, the chanting of Urdu poetry. *Ethnomusicology* 13, no. 3: 425–469.

———. 1990. Musical gesture and extra-musical meaning: Words and music in the Urdu ghazal. *Journal of the American Musicological Society* 43, no. 3: 472–496.

REGULA BURCKHARDT QURESHI

SEE ALSO

Ghazal; *Mushā'ira;* Song

TATTOOING

The art of tattooing is an important folk art form found all over the world. ("Tattoo" is derived from the Polynesian term "ta," meaning to strike). According to Anantha Krishna Iyer and H. V. Nanjundayya (1935, 436) "The art is of Polynesian origin, and the word *tatoo* is derived from *ta* (to strike). It suggests the primitive method of operation which is caused by beating into flesh with a fine pointed bone dipped in a mixture which leaves an indelible mark behind."

The origin of the art of tattooing is a matter of speculation. Primitive man, living with beasts, may have developed a desire to put on colours similar to those on the bodies of the beasts. To start with, our earliest ancestors might have applied some pigments to their bodies, but the short duration of these applications must have disappointed them. Looking about for lasting pigments to decorate the body, they must have gradually discovered methods of tattooing.

An expressly ritualistic context is also attached to tattooing. It was customary for primitive man to make offerings of his own blood to ghosts and *bhūta*s (souls of dead men that help the living) or to the soul of the dead leaders of the group. The marks left behind by such bloodletting might have given rise to the art of tattooing. Many cultures have traditions of making oblations of their life blood or mutilating parts of their bodies as sacrificial or penitential offerings. Thus, tattooing developed against the background of religion, ritual, and belief.

Tattooing is done by pricking the skin and inscribing indelible designs on it. One method is to remove bits of skin, and rub black pigment on the inner layer of skin, with repeated prickings, the desired pictorial shapes are drawn. This method is called cicatrization and is practised in many countries. The other method is to use nails or other sharp tools to prick the skin at various places and then apply pigment to the spots. This is the method of tattooing common in India and most parts of the world. In countries like Sumatra, some people still practise the art of applying red hot iron rods to the face and other parts of the body to cause the scars needed for pictorial designs.

Those who follow tattooing as a profession in India do it as a part-time occupation and belong such tribes as Korma, Karegār, Besta, Kiḷḷekyāta, Mēdar, Oḍḍa, Gondaliga, Jātigār, Domba, and to other tribes. It is their custom to go around the countryside between March and July practising their art, since the period between the beginning of new year and the advent of the monsoon is a time of leisure for village women when they prefer to be tattooed.

Tattoo artists bring with them sheets of paper containing designs and pictures to guide them in their work, although some can draw the designs from memory. For tattooing, three to nine needles are arranged side by side and clamped together between two flat metal pieces with thread wrapped round them. This assembly of needles is called *chakra*. In some countries sharp and strong thorns form this assembly of tools; in Burma and Japan a brass stylus is used. Electric gadgets are now also used for tattooing. The linear arrangement of needles placed side by side makes linear sketching very convenient. The more intricate the design, the less the number of needles required in the assembly.

In the process of tattooing, the blood oozes and causes intense pain. The tattoo artists, however, know how to alleviate pain through their stories and songs. In the pricked holes they rub the colouring pigment. This pigment penetrates to the bottom of the holes and settles there as a permanent design.

Tattoo artists in India generally prepare two types of colouring pigments. One is green mixed with yellow and the other, black mixed with blue. In New Zealand, Burma, and Japan, all sorts of colours are used. The process of preparing the pigments for tattooing comes from ancient times. The artists themselves rub *mani-avare* leaves against the surface of country tiles and hold them against the flame of a castor lamp. The soot produced by this process is mixed with water. This produces a black coloured dye. Alternatively, betel leaves are rubbed against the tiles and held against a lamp flame, yielding a black soot; this is mixed with cow's milk for obtaining the tattooing dye. A third method of dye preparation is to add breast milk to the carbon on the burnt wick of gingelly oil lamp. In some cases, dye is prepared by pounding charcoal into a fine powder and mixing it with juice of *hacce soppu* (tattooing leaves). In addition to these methods and processes, there are several other ways of obtaining dye since nature offers a rich supply of plants and roots suitable for this purpose.

People choose to have various designs tattooed on different parts of their bodies. On the forehead, designs like the sun, moon, cross, conch, or flower, are favoured. Between their eyebrows, some people like to have a dot of beauty, a mark expected to offset the evil eye. On either side of the eyes, mango leaves may be inscribed. The cheeks may be tattooed with fine dots. Drawings of the saree-border, shoulder-band, pearly creeper, and *toṇḍe* creeper are made on the upper arm. On the right elbow are inscribed such designs as the plantain tree, the pearl lamp (*muttinārati*), the serpent, Hanumān, Hanumān's chariot, Sīta's saree-border, or Rāma's cradle; on the left, Gouri's throne, Jogi's knotted hair, the lotus, a chariot, Śiva's head, an ornament *bāsinga* (crown worn by a bride or groom), etc. Some tribal members have a horse rider or some dotted design tattooed on their forearms. On the back of their palms they may have figures of Hanumān's chariot, Śiva's hair, or a pearl lamp. The back of the left palm could displays drawings of *nandi kōlu* (a large bamboo pole with a metal bull idol) or cockroach. The back of the right palm has the husband's name for the wife and the wife's name for the husband or the names of friends and relatives. A woman's breasts may have designs of the peacock, and on her buttocks, various designs of flowers. Some women have a dragon, ship, butterfly, bird, or mating serpents sketched on their genitals. In the modern age, objects like a train, rail track, etc., have come to be included among tattooed objects, adding to the versality of the art.

More than two hundred tattoo designs have been identified in Karnataka (South India), and the majority of them are distinct to this region. The art of tattooing still flourishes because of the support it has from strong religious and psychological beliefs. When a pregnant woman gets a *kirīṭa* (crown) design tatooed, for example, she believes she will have a beautiful daughter. There is also a belief that tattooing on the waist of a woman will prevent the death of her children and that widowhood can be avoided by getting tattooed early.

References

Claus, Peter J. and Frank J. Korom 1991. *Folkloristics and Indian folklore*. Udupi: Regional Resource Center.

Gupte, B. A. 1902. Notes on female tattoo designs in India. *The Indian Antiquary*.

Iyer, Anantha Krishna and H. V. Nanjundayya 1935. *The Mysore tribes and castes* (Vol. I). Mysore: Mysore University Press.

Maheshwaraiah, H. M. 1988. *Hacce: ondu jānapada kale*. Bangalore: IBH Publication.

Rose, H. A. 1902. Notes on female tattooing in the Punjab. *Indian Antiquary*. Delhi: Swati Publication.

H. M. MAHESWARAIAH

SEE ALSO

Bhūta; Jewelry and Adornment; Self-sacrifice

TA'ZIYA

Ta'ziya is a Persian term based on an Arabic root used to denote "condolence" or "expression of grief." It is used in many contexts by Shī'a Muslims for the rituals associated with the annual remembrance of Ḥusayn ibn 'Alī's martyrdom at Karbalā (in modern Iraq) during the Islamic month of Muḥarram in 680 C.E. Ḥusayn and a small party of followers were killed by the forces of the Umayyad caliphate in a dispute concerning the rightful spiritual and political successor to the Prophet Muhammad. Although the historical event is central to Shī'a religious expression, participation in the annual commemoration is by no means restricted to Shī'a Muslims. Sunnī Muslims and people of other faiths have played an ancillary role in the development of the rituals and have contributed to the term's usage worldwide.

In Iran, where the term first gained a concrete theological sense during the rule of the Safavid dynasty (1200–1786), ta'ziya was used to refer primarily to the dramatic enactments of the historical events surrounding the death of Ḥusayn. These "passion plays" remain a focus of Muḥarram observance in Iran, whereas dramatic commemorations are less significant in South Asian observances. Eventually, in South Asia and among overseas South Asians, ta'ziya came to refer specifically to the miniature mausoleums used in processions held during Muḥarram.

Numerous local traditions of ta'ziya construction have emerged over the centuries. Ta'ziyas vary in shape and size according to region. Although some were originally made of precious materials for royal and wealthy patrons, to be housed permanently in specially designed buildings, the majority of ta'ziyas were what might be termed "disposable sacred art." Such disposable structures predominate on the popular level today. Materials used to build ta'ziyas include wood and bamboo for the frame and paper, tin foil, mica, and glass for the ornamental exterior.

How the meaning of ta'ziya became transformed in the South Asian context is not completely clear, but oral legends from the fifteenth century—still repeated today—concerning the Timurid invaders suggest that carrying model tombs in procession came to replace actual pilgrimages to Karbalā, a practice well established by the time the Timurids entered the subcontinent. This may partially explain the use of ta'ziyas in processions, but it also hints at the symbolism of constructing these ornate objects of veneration. Building miniature replicas of Ḥusayn's actual tomb in Karbalā became not only an act of sacrificial devotion but also a re-creation of sacred space on local soil, replete with a variety of associated rituals and beliefs.

Participants say, for example, that the ta'ziyas are conduits between earth and heaven imbued with *baraka,* a healing power bestowed by Allah upon human beings through physical objects. The belief is an innovative interpretation of the Shī'a doctrine asserting Ḥusayn's position as intermediary between humans and Allah on *qiyāmat,* the Day of Judgment: The faithful who have remembered Ḥusayn's suffering on earth may enter Paradise through his intercession. This understanding suggests that Ḥusayn is embodied in the ta'ziya and that its veneration could have salvational effects. Further evidence for the corporeal nature of the ta'ziya appears in the funerary ritual symbolism, most vivid on the tenth day of Muḥarram, when the objects are either buried or immersed in a body of water.

Ta'ziya construction has spread from India to many other countries, including parts of Indonesia and the Caribbean. For example, Trinidadian ta'ziyas (locally known as *tadjahs*) reflect South Asian origins; their shapes, designs, and ritual usages all bear strong resemblances to Indian prototypes while displaying local influences, such as the incorporation of Afro-Caribbean elements into the rituals performed for Husayn. The labor migrations that occurred within colonial empires transplanted this sacred tradition to places far removed from the major centers of Shi'ite observance. Today Trinidadian ta'ziya builders live in New York and Ontario, continuing a tradition thrice removed from the homeland. All of this suggests a global vitality rooted in common theological orientations but mediated through localized ritual practices and artistic traditions.

References

Chelkowski, Peter J., ed. 1979. *Ta'ziyeh: Ritual and drama in Iran.* New York: New York University Press.

Korom, Frank J. 2002. *Hosay Trinidad: Muḥarram performances in an Indo-Caribbean diaspora.* Philadelphia: University of Pennsylvania Press.

Monchi-Zadeh, Devoud. 1967. *Ta'ziya. Das persische Passionsspiel.* Stockhom: Almqvist and Wiksell.

Pelly, Lewis. 1879. *The miracle play of Hasan and Husain.* Collected and translated by Lewis Pelly. 2 vols. London: William H. Allen.

FRANK J. KOROM

SEE ALSO

Death Rituals; Diaspora, Caribbean; Imām Ḥusayn; Islam; Muḥarram; Processions

TĒJAJI

Tējaji is a folk hero deity worshiped in Rajasthan and other parts of Western India. His cult has much in common with others in the area in its relation to snake worship and propitiation, as well as to the veneration of heroes, as is common in many parts of Western India. Tējaji is renowned as a snake god who is called upon to protect devotees from and cure snake bites. Other folk hero-deities of Rajasthan, such as Gūgā, are known for similar efficacies.

Tējaji was a Jāt of Karnala near Nagaur, in Marwar. Various traditions relate different historical times for his life, from the eleventh to the fifteenth centuries. Although many versions of Tējaji's life exist, all of them focus on the intervention of snakes. Tējaji is forced to make a pact with a snake who has threatened to bite him. In a Gazetteer version of the story, this happens because Tējaji has agreed to feed the snake some milk, and he has forgotten to do so one day. So, the snake demands that he be allowed to bite Tēja. Other versions give other reasons for the snake's demand. Tēja convinces the snake to allow him to pay his respects to his father-in-law. Tējaji is allowed to go. During his journey, he rescues the cows of his in-law's village from a band of robbers and is terribly injured. He struggles on to return to the snake. The snake is unable to find a place to bite him until Tējaji offers his tongue. Tējaji thus dies of a snakebite to his tongue, and this motif is common to many versions of his life.

The worship of Tējaji takes place within the rich cultural fabric of hero worship present in Rajasthan and other parts of India. Although Tēja is unlike many of the other heroes of Rajasthan in that he is not a Rājpūt, his cult is similar in its focus on fairs, songs, and charms that make the power of the hero-deity effective in the world. Fairs, called *Tējaji ka mela,* are associated with his worship and are held in different parts of Rajasthan around the time of his festival, *Tēja Daśami,* the tenth day of the bright half of the month of Bhādon (August-September). It is no coincidence that his worship takes place at this time; during the wet months of August and September, snakes are a serious problem in Rajasthan. Ballads are sung, describing the life of the hero and his ability to protect and save. Charms and protective talismans are worn in his name. In these ways, the worship and celebration of his cult have an effect in the world of his adherents.

References

Dhoundiyal, B. N. 1966. *Rajasthan district gazetteers: Ajmer.* Jaipur: Government Central Press.

Kothari, Komal. 1982. The shrine: an expression of social needs. In *Gods of the byways*, ed. Anand et al. Oxford: Museum of Modern Art.

ANNE MURPHY

SEE ALSO

Devnārāyaṇ; Fairs and Festivals; Gūgā; Heroes and Heroines; *Melā; Nāga; Pābūjī;* Rāmdev

TERUKKŪTTU

Terukkūttu is an important form of mythic reenactment performed in several regions of Tamil-speaking South India. It utilizes poetry and prose as well as music, rhythm, and dance to present highly sacralized dramatizations of important mythic episodes drawn from the Hindu epics and puranas. The vast majority of these performances are put on in connection with ritual celebrations relating to Tamil village deities or to important rites of passage, such as marriage, that mark the lives of Tamil Hindus.

The operative word in the genre title terukkūttu is the term *kūttu, teru* (street) simply indicating that this form is performed outdoors. Looking through Tamil religious literature as far back as the Sangam anthologies (first century C.E.), it is clear that kūttu means more than just "dance" or "drama," the meanings accorded this concept in modern dictionaries. Kūttu in the most ancient period had a direct reference to rituals of enactment (or reenactment) that involved the sacred possession or entrancement of individuals by deities or sacred entities immanent in the religious milieu. These possessions were brought about through the use of poetry, music, and rhythm. Parallel conceptualizations characterize terukkūttu performances of the present day in which important mythic episodes are dramatically ecstaticized in the context of ritual celebrations relating to numerous Hindu village cults of Tamil-speaking South India.

The most important performative context for the *terukkūttu* is the *Mahābhārata* cult of the northeastern portion of the Tamil region. Two major foci of this cult are the epic female figure Draupadī, conceptualized as the Tamil village goddess Tiraupataiyamman, and the epic hero Dharmarāja, the eldest of five heroic Pāṇḍava brothers who marry her as a spouse in common. Dharmarāja is referred to as Yudhiṣṭhira in Sanskrit versions of the epic. Both Draupadī and Dharmarāja are worshiped in the form of icons housed in Draupadī temples (also called Dharmarāja temples) found in villages throughout this region. The *Mahābhārata* cult represents a complex fusion of elements from epic mythology—Tamil village goddess worship and the devotional worship of the god Kṛṣṇa, her protector. It effectively transforms Draupadī of the epic into Draupadī the village *amman,* a powerful goddess who presides over and protects a village.

Annually, or as finances dictate, a village with a Draupadī temple will conduct an eighteen to twenty day festival called the *Pāratam* (Tamil for *Mahābhārata*) that ritually reenacts the sacred mythology of the epic in a cycle of selected episodes spread over the entire span of the celebration. This reenactment takes place in three modes: musical recitation (*Piracankam*) of epic verses, formal temple ritual, and most importantly, the sacred, ecstatic dramatizations of the terukkūttu. A typical cycle of terukkūtu *Mahābhārata* performances would be nine nights long and include the vital episodes of *The Wedding of Draupadī, The Dicegame and the Disrobing, Ārjuna's Penance* and *The Battle of the Eighteenth Day*.

The Dicegame and the Disrobing exemplifies the sacred and ecstatic elements in the terukkūttu. In the sequence reenacting the dicegame in which Draupadī is wagered and lost, Dharmarāja prays to Kṛṣṇa while his opponent, Śakuni, in a frenzied dance, conjures a local demon. Both actions transform the dice table into a confrontation between the divine and demonic. In its final scene, at the moment when Duḥśāsana's attempts to dishonor Draupadī by disrobing her in public are defeated by the god Kṛṣṇa's intercession, both Draupadī and Duḥśāsana will often lapse into states of deep possession.

The terukkūttu, through its ritually charged performances, recreates the sacred time and space of the mythology of the *Mahābhārata,* sheltering and blessing the entire village. Its ritual reenactment of the *Pāratam* restores Dharmarāja to the position of just kingship in the world of the epic and the goddess Draupadī to the pure, re-empowered state in which she can protect and nurture the village.

References

Frasca, Richard A. 1990. *The theater of the Mahābhārata: Terukkūttu performances in South India*. Honolulu, Hawaii: University of Hawaii Press.

Hiltebeital, Alf. 1988. *The cult of Draupadī: mythologies; from Gingee to Kuruksetra*. Chicago, Ill.: The University of Chicago Press.

RICHARD A. FRASCA

SEE ALSO

Draupadī; Epic; Goddesses, Hindu; Myth; Ritual; Theater and Drama

TEYYAM

Teyyam is a term designating a variety of Hindu deities propitiated during festivals (*kaḷiyāṭṭam*) held throughout the northern part of Kerala State and the border areas of Dakshina Kannada (South Kanara) and Kodagu (Coorg) Districts, Karnataka. During the months of November through June, sponsors organize the festivals in both lineage and community shrines to invoke ancestors, local heroes, and *purāṇic* deities, who are worshiped through the orchestration of many performative modes—drumming, singing, possession, dancing, feasting, and entertainment. Teyyam ritual performances both please a deity and maintain its *śakti,* or power. This power is potentially unstable and capable of creating disorder if humans do not contain, visualize, and placate it.

Performances are of several types. Large regular community festivals have fixed auspicious dates and repeat themselves periodically, depending upon the costs of the performance and economic status of the community. Members of a particular caste usually host a festival, and draw the participants and resources from the entire village. Other regular festivals are sponsored by an extended family or lineage (*taravād*) of means and status on behalf of the kin group for ensuring its continued prosperity. A *nērcca kōlam* or "vow to god" is an unscheduled performance commissioned after a deity has gratified the wishes of a devotee. For example, devotees may offer a nērcca after the safe delivery of a child, on receiving a good job, or when constructing a new house. *Ōṭṭa kōlam* is a performance commissioned by an entire village to ward off an epidemic.

The central performance passes through a series of stages during which a low-caste male dancer (*kōlakārran*) transforms into a deity who ultimately bestows blessings on the assembled devotees. Although performance structures may vary from shrine to shrine and according to the particular deity, teyyam ritual is organized around a basic six-part sequence: (1) beginning (*totannal*), (2) recitation of the deity's story (*tōṟṟam*), (3) possession of the performer by the deity who then dances (teyyam), (4) first person recitation of additional history (*mumbasthānam*), (5) giving out blessings to participants in order of their social status (*vavivākku*), and (6) removing the crown (*muṭiyēṭṭukkal*). As teyyam is understood to be a visitation of the divine in the present, the ritual sequence facilitates this transformation as it shifts from third-person narrative, in which the performer recites the story about the deity, to a state in which he embodies the deity and participates in an actual and dynamic world. Costuming and makeup play an important part in marking this gradual transformation. The performer wears only a partial costume for the invocation and recitation of the deity's story. He wears no makeup. He dons a full costume when he appears as the deity incarnate.

Teyyam festivals not only provide an occasion for devotees to make physical contact with the divine; they can also bring into focus the moral and economic responsibilities of the members of the lineage or community toward one another.

References

Ashley, Wayne. 1993. Recordings: ritual, theatre, and political display in Kerala State, South India. Ph.D. dissertation, Department of Performance Studies, New York University.

Freeman, J. R. 1993. Performing possession: ritual and consciousness in the Teyyam Complex of Northern Kerala. In *Flags of fame: studies in south Asian folk culture,* eds. Heidrun Bruckner, Lothar Lutze, and Aditya Malik, 109–138. New Delhi: Manohar.

Gough, Kathleen. 1958. Cults of the dead Among the Nayars. *Journal of American Folklore*. 71(281): 446–478.

Holloman, Regina and Wayne Ashley. 1983. Caste and cult in Kerala. *South Asian Anthropologist* 4(2): 93–104.

WAYNE ASHLEY

SEE ALSO

Bhagavati Ritual Traditions of Kerala; *Bhūta Kōla;* Gods and Goddesses; Karnataka; Kerala; *Pāḍdana;* Ritual; Spirit Possession and Mediumship; *Tōṟṟam*

THEATER AND DRAMA

Theater and drama date from antiquity on the Indian subcontinent. The myth of the origins of theater and drama is attributed to Bharata, a great sage, and begins the most comprehensive treatment of all aspects of theater and drama ever written, the *Nāṭyaśāstra* (200 B.C.E.–200 C.E.). The story relates how Indra organized a group of the gods to approach the creator, Lord Brahma, to request that he create a pastime that would provide all manner of people with visual as well as auditory pleasures. Since the Vedas were accessible only to those males of the highest birth, Brahma accepted their argument, and, using his yogic powers, he took in mind the four Vedas and resolved to

> make a fifth Veda on the Nāṭya [drama] with the Semi-historical Tales (*itihāsa*), which will conduce to duty (*dharma*), wealth (*artha*) as well as fame, will contain good counsel and collection [of traditional maxims], will give guidance to people of the future as well, in all their actions, will be enriched by the teaching of all authoritative works (*śāstra*) and will give a review of all arts and crafts (Bharata 1967, I:15).

The drama discussed in the *Nāṭyaśāstra* is known as Sanskrit drama since Sanskrit was spoken by the major male characters. The themes, social organization, and behavior of characters reflect the implicit values, social perspective, and aesthetic associated with the privileged hierarchies of court and temple life in which the Sanskrit theater flourished. All characters other than the male heroes spoke various forms of Prakrits, the local languages and dialects of the period in which the dramas were written. From the *Nāṭyaśāstra* and the extant Sanskrit dramas, we learn that performances were complex integrations of music, dance, interpretive movement, literal and symbolic hand-gestures, and dramatic narrative which attempted to create for the audience a unique aesthetic experience in which they savored or tasted (*rasa*) the essences or flavors imbedded in the composition of the dramas and their realization in performance. Although the ideal audience member was one whose tastes had been cultivated to a state of ideal appreciation, it is clear that the dramas and their performances have always existed in a dialectical relationship with other extant modes of noncourtly performance and that they were not intended to appeal exclusively to connoisseurs. By the ninth century C.E., the Sanskrit theater was in decline, and, by the tenth century, it had died out except for a few pockets, most notably in the *kūṭiyāṭṭam* tradition of performing Sanskrit dramas in Kerala temples and the much later *ankīya nāṭ* tradition of Assam. Its place was gradually subsumed by performances in regional languages, the vast majority of which did not appear until after the sixteenth century.

Drama and theater on the South Asian subcontinent have never been limited to the formal and well-patronized Sanskrit theater, but range across a broad spectrum of public arts from the bardic traditions of rendering oral epics, to puppetry, to magicians and street performers, to troupes of itinerant regional-language performers. Each traditional genre of performance is known by its genre-specific local name—*kathakaḷi, cavittu nāṭakam, bhavāi, nauṭanki, yakṣagāna*. For the vast majority of South Asians, their experience and understanding of performance is constructed out of their local experience of the specific set of oral performances available in their own region, or those genres that might be experienced while on religious pilgrimage to sacred sites. Often from childhood, audiences are enculturated to appreciate, and understand, the codes and meanings of performance from complex makeup types (as in kathakaḷi, yakṣagāna and *terukuttu*) to the use of a complete language of hand-gestures (*mudrās*) that at first seem so complex to outsiders. As Kathryn Hansen suggests, each genre of performance is part of a "'community of forms'... a historically specific set of practices located in an evolving social environment" (1992: 56).

Although many genres have written texts and require literate performers, the performances of the texts are intended to appeal to the senses and stress aural and visual modes of communication. Many of the theatrical conventions of the early Sanskrit theater are still in evidence in these traditions, including the sanctification of the stage and preliminary pre-performance rituals; the use of a "stage manager" (*sūtradhāra*); the appearance of a buffoon or clown character (*vidūṣaka*) who provides commentary or comic commentary; the interweaving of music, dance or movement, and gesture in the interpretation of narrative; the use of a relatively neutral and open playing space, where time is marked by conventionalized use of that space, and through the use of a hand-held curtain; and the dramatization of stories based on epics, myths, or ballads. But unlike the Sanskrit theater (or the kūṭiyāṭṭam of Kerala), where performances took place in formal theater buildings constructed according to specific codes, most traditional modes of performance were traditionally performed on temporary stages—either a simple clearing on the ground in the middle of a paddy field (yakṣagāna) or on a temporarily constructed raised stage (cavittu nāṭakam). With the introduction of the modern proscenium theater, most of these genres are performed both out-of-doors on temporary stages, as well as inside modern theater buildings.

As reflected in the *Nāṭyaśāstra,* training in traditional forms of South Asian performance can be a long, arduous, and full-time occupation, especially when performers are born into a tradition of performance and begin their training as children. Such is still the case with kūṭiyāṭṭam and kathakaḷi of Kerala. For other genres, training is intense, but seasonal.

So diverse is the array of dramatic and theatrical forms in South Asia that any form of classification ultimately proves unsatisfactory. However, the Sanskrit terms, *lokadharmī* and *nāṭyadharmī* have been usefully applied to Indian arts and drama. Vidya Niwas Misra and Prem Lata Sharma translate lokadharmī as the "ordinary" or "concrete," or that from which the "extraordinary" or "ideational" (nāṭyadharmī) is elaborated, abstracted, transformed, and distilled. In more specific theatrical terms, the lokadharmī are those elements of a performance which tend toward "realistic... or suggestive" conventions and modes of representation, while nāṭyadharmī suggests a greater degree of stylization. Any specific performance genre can be examined to see which aspects are more "concrete" or "ordinary" and which aspects are more "extraordinary." Even in a genre like kathakaḷi, which is generally more "stylized," or nāṭyadharmī, there are nevertheless some specific plays-in-performance, or specific characters, scenes, or gestures which are very "concrete" *and* "ordinary."

The traditional genres of performance have been caught up in India's contemporary struggles with its own identity as a modern nation-state, as well as in the internal sociopolitical and economic struggles for survival in a newly emergent market economy, where traditional forms of patronage (of courts, temples, and the landed aristocracy) have shifted to state or private sources. During the course of the twentieth century, the politics of representation of traditional perfomances has had a profound impact on those arts that received some form of state-sponsored patronage and those that do not. Performances that were interpreted as exhibiting a more lokadharmī quality were often denigrated during the early-to mid-twentieth century as India's cultural revival movement celebrated what became identified as the "classical" (or nāṭyadharmī) to the disparagement of the "folk" (lokadharmī). As Frederique Marglin has pointed out, the category "Indian Classical Dance" was invented as a result of the turn-of-the-century social reform movements which helped create modern performing arts institutions: "the adjective classical reflects the Western model of the reformers: Indian Classical Dance connotes a status on a par with Western Classical Ballet" (1985: 2–3).

As folklorist Richard Bauman noted long ago, traditions of performance, like yakṣagāna, cavittu nāṭakam, *rām līlā,* kathakaḷi, have always stood available to participants and spectators "as a set of conventional expectations and associations" which can be "manipulated in innovative ways, by fashioning novel performances and adaptations which turn performance into something else" (1977: 34–35). Although each individual genre or tradition of performance often shows a great deal of continuity through the generations, as cultural performances these are not fixed sets of conventions or attributes, but rather, dynamic systems open to negotiation. Therefore, many of these traditional genres of theater, dance, and dance-drama continue to evolve in unique and interesting ways.

References

Bauman, Richard. 1977. *Verbal art as performance.* Rowley, Mass.: Newbury Books.

Bharata. 1967, 1961. *Natyasastra.* Trans. and ed. Manmohan Ghosh. 2nd rev. ed. Vol. 1. Calcutta; Manisha Granthalaya; Vol. 2. Calcutta: Asiatic Society.

Emigh, John, and Ulrike Emigh. 1986. Hajari Bhand of Rajasthan: a joker in the deck. *The Drama Review* 30(1): 101–130.

Frasca, Richard Armando. 1990. *The theater of the Mahabharata: terukkuttu performances in South India.* Honolulu: University of Hawaii Press.

Hansen, Kathryn. 1992. *Grounds for play: the Nautanki Theatre of North India.* Berkeley: University of California Press.

Hawley, John Stratton. 1981. *At play with Krishna: pilgrimage dramas from Brindavan.* Princeton: Princeton University Press.

Kapur, Anuradha. 1990. *Actors, pilgrims, kings and gods: the Ramlila at Ramnagar.* Calcutta: Seagull Press.

Marglin, Frederique. 1985. *Wives of the god-king.* New Delhi: Oxford University Press.

Misra, Vidya Niwas and Prem Lata Sharma. 1992. *Kalatattvakosa (concepts of space and time).* New Delhi: Indira Gandhi National Centre for the Arts.

Richmond, Farley P., Darius L. Swann, and Phillip B. Zarrilli, eds. 1990. *Indian theatre: traditions of performance.* Honolulu: University of Hawaii Press.

Shulman, David. 1985. *The king and the clown in south Indian myth and poetry.* Princeton: Princeton University Press.

Siegel, Lee. 1991. *Net of magic: wonders and deceptions in India.* Chicago: University of Chicago Press.

Vatsyayan, Kapila. 1980. *Traditional Indian theatre: multiple streams.* New Delhi: National Book Trust.

PHILLIP B. ZARRILLI

SEE ALSO

Bhagavati Ritual Traditions of Kerala; *Bhānd Paṭhar; Bharat Līlā; Bhavāi; Cavittu Nāṭakam;* Conjuring; Dance; Folk Drama, Afghanistan; *Jātrā/Yātrā; Jhumur Jātrā;* Karnataka; *Kathakaḷi; Laḷita; Mukhos Nāc; Muṭiyēttu; Nācā;* Nationalism and Folklore; *Nauṭaṅki; Pañdar Līla; Prahlāda Nāṭak; Rām Līlā; Sokari; Terrukkūttu;* Theater and Drama, Sri Lanka; *Vīthī Nāṭakam; Yakṣagāna*

THEATER AND DRAMA, SRI LANKA

Sri Lanka has a rich tradition of ritual performances whose roots probably go back to pre-Buddhist practices. Over time, the deities and demons these rituals propitiated were integrated through the performance tradition into the Buddhist pantheon. Ritual performances thus became an important part of popular Buddhism. Performances consisted mainly of chanting, masked dancing to drum music, acts of propitiation and dramatic enactments. Comic, satiric, prose interludes were included for entertainment.

These comic interludes in rituals generated more secular forms of entertainment. Folk dramas known as *Kōlam, Nāḍagam,* and *Sokari* became popular entertainment in villages. They were still tied to the harvest festivities and rituals, but there was a clearly discernible shift of emphasis from the religious to the secular.

The kōlam (Comic Impersonation), a genre of folk drama found mainly in the coastal areas of South Sri Lanka, is patterned on exorcist rituals. A narrator introduces each character (in verse) who then enters the arena, costumed and masked, and dances and mimes his/her role. Kōlam plays were no more than a masquerade of motley characters (wearing distinctive masks), dancing and miming in a circular arena. From time to time a story or dramatic event was spliced in, and sometimes snatches from verse dramas of Buddhist legends such as the *Maname* story or the *Sañdakiñduru* story were included. Village personages and authority figures were often stereotyped and caricatured and the masks provided an added level of satire. Performances were fluid and could be lengthened or shortened as the occasion demanded, and contemporary characters included for further comic effect. The humor was often obscene, and an enormous degree of license was permitted.

Sokari, a folk drama found mainly in the central hill country, has the story element more clearly defined. The satire is aimed at dominant personae of the rural community such as the crafty physician (Vedarāḷa); the exploitative trader and money lender (Heṭṭirāḷa); the king's representative and law enforcer (Gamarāḷa); a learned Brahmin from Kalinga (Bamuṇā); the village virago (Mahalla); the ritual specialist (Guruhāmi).

There are many versions and extant texts of this folk drama. The core story is as follows: Sokari is the beautiful but barren wife of a ritual specialist named Guruhami. She and her husband, accompanied by a servant, Parayā, decide to come to Lanka to the shrine of god Kataragama to ask for a boon of a child. They are shipwrecked, but land in Lanka. The landing place varies with the different versions. They cannot speak the language and have difficulty trying to obtain food and lodging. In all the versions Sokari is unfaithful, whether she elopes with a merchant, and/or (as in most versions) with a village doctor, or has an affair with the servant, Parayā. However the play ends with Sokari and her husband reconciled.

Sokari is performed as part of the harvest festivities and is linked to the fertility rituals associated with the goddess Pattini. But it is an ironic parody or reversal of the Pattini story. Pattini is the chaste, faithful, long-suffering wife of Guru Palanga. Sokari is the young, attractive, unfaithful wife of Guruhāmi. She abandons her husband and elopes with the merchant, Heṭṭirāḷa, and later again with a local doctor, Vederāḷa. In some versions there is an earlier seduction episode with Guruhami's servant, Parayā.

In the story of the goddess, faithful and devoted Pattini goes in search of Palangā, finds him dead, laments over the body and by the power of her virtue, finally resurrects him. In contrast, Guruhāmi curses as he searches for Sokari, complaining of her infidelity. He finds her and brings her back. She cleverly convinces Guruhāmi that she was the innocent victim of a spell cast by the physician. They weave a mat (to sleep on) symbolizing their union.

Another item of satiric reversal in the Sokari performances is that Guruhāmi's servant, Parayā (low-caste fellow) is often also named Rāma (avatar of Viṣṇu) and Sokari's maid, Mahalla ("Old One"), is named Kāli (Hindu mother goddess). In the Buddhist village dramas of Sri Lanka both Rāma and Kāli are "demoted" to servant status and made the butt of satire.

The nāḍagam, a form of folk opera with a large element of dance, was popular in the eighteenth and nineteenth centuries in the southwestern coastal areas of Sri Lanka. Because of its Christian themes scholars believed it was derived from the *naṭṭukūttī* folk plays of the Tamils of the north and spread by Christian and Catholic missionaries active in the South-Western regions. Others argue that nāḍagam was an earlier pre-fifteenth century poetic drama tradition, linked to the South Indian street dramas which spread to Sri Lanka with successive waves of South Indian migrants between the twelfth through fifteenth centuries. As these migrant communities became "Sinhalized" their performance tradition too was absorbed into the folk culture. Extant texts that date from the eighteenth century were probably only the first written versions of an older, well-established tradition. The Christian themes of nāḍagam plays were a likely transformation of the older form resulting from colonial missionary contact (Daalabandara: 1993). Phillipu Sinno was one of the earliest and best known nāḍagam writers.

Puppet plays were another form of folk entertainment performed at carnivals and amusement stalls during religious or other festivities. Puppeteers performed nāḍagam texts and nāḍagam players and musicians were part of the troupe. As nāḍagam performances lost popularity, puppet plays took their place.

The Passion Play, or *pasu,* originated in the Catholic areas of the north and spread to the west coast. Today the most famous performance is held at Duwa (an island off the west coast) during Holy Week. Statues as well as actors are used as cast and while a stage is constructed for the performance much of the action takes place outside amidst the crowds who actively participate. On Palm Sunday the statue of Christ is taken in procession around the village. The trial scene before Pilate is in prose and enacted on the stage. On Good Friday the statue of Christ carrying a cross is taken around in procession. Encounters with the Virgin Mary and Mary Magdalen take place amidst weeping women singing hymns. The statue is then placed on stage and after three hours of "The Agony," the statue is again taken in procession accompanied by hymn singing. On Saturday, village boys representing devils blacken their faces and playfully loot and vandalize shops and stores in the vicinity. The celebrations conclude with the Easter service.

These forms of folk drama are fast dying out even in the villages. The modern secular theatre, evolved from a blend of folk and contemporary dramatic traditions, seems to have taken its place.

References

Daalabandara, Gamini. 1993. *Siṅhala Nāḍagam Sampradāya* [The Sinhala Nadagam tradition]. Colombo.

Kapferer, B. 1977. First class to maradana: Secular drama in Sinhalese healing rites. In *Secular ritual*, ed. Sally Moore and Barbara Myerhoff. Amsterdam: Van Gorcum: Assen.

Obeyesekere, Gananath. 1984. *The cult of the goddess Pattini*. Chicago: University of Chicago Press.

Pieris, Edmund. 1949. A Sinhalese nativity play. *The Ceylon Fortnightly Review*.

Pertold, O. 1930. The ceremonial dances of the Sinhalese. *Archiv Orientalni,* 11: 1, 2, 3, pp. 224ff.

Raghavan, M. D. 1967. *Siṅhala nǎṭum* [Sinhala dance]. Colombo: Gunasena Press.

Sarachchandra, E. R. 1952. *The Sinhalese folk play*. (Reprinted as *The Folk Drama of Ceylon* [1966].)

Wickremesinghe, Martin. 1970. *Siṅhala Nātakaya hā Saňda-kiňdurava* [The Sinhala drama and the Saňdakiňdura Story]. Colombo.

RANJINI OBEYESEKERE

SEE ALSO
Kataragama; Pattini; Sokari

THURSTON, EDGAR

Edgar Thurston (1855–1935) was appointed head of the Government Museum in Madras in 1885. Experienced in ethnology and museum work, and particularly interested in anthropometry, he sought to reorient the museum toward ethnographic materials and research. Soon after his arrival he set up an anthropometrical laboratory at the museum. With the addition of his extended field research beginning in 1893, and more serious institutional attention to publishing anthropological findings through museum bulletins and the like, Thurston was able to transform the museum into a research center in its own right by the 1890s. He also expanded the museum collections to include both ancient materials from the area and contemporary ethnographic materials collected by himself, his Indian assistants, and other European scholars. This expansion was given a boost by Thurston's research as a participant in the Ethnographic Survey of India, begun in 1901 and completed in 1909.

As head of the survey for the Madras presidency, Thurston traveled widely across southern India with his assistants, collecting materials, conducting interviews, taking photographs, and measuring skulls for his anthropometric charts and diagrams. The result of his and others' efforts were three publications, the best-known of which is the eight-volume report of the Ethnographic Survey, *Castes and Tribes of Southern India*. Modeled on Risley's *Tribes and Castes of Bengal,* Thurston's work offers an alphabetical listing of all of the castes and tribes of the south and provides details of occupations, marriage customs, death rites, religious affiliations, and relative social ranking. Particular attention is paid to hill tribes and martial groups.

In 1906, prior to the release of the eight-volume work, Thurston published the much shorter *Ethnographic Notes in Southern India*. This focuses on some of the more obscure and "exotic" customs of the south, including torture, slavery, fire walking, hook swinging, infanticide, and human sacrifice, as well as more mundane topics like dress, names, weighing instruments, and native clocks. Finally, as an expansion of one of the chapters in *Ethnographic Notes,* Thurston published *Omens and Superstitions of Southern India* in 1912. He retired from the Government Museum in 1920 and died in 1935.

References

Harinarayana, N., and N. Devasahayam. 1991. Anthropological collections in Government Museum, Madras: Notable efforts of Thurston, Gravely & Aiyappan. In *Anthropological research and tribal situation*, ed. L. K. Bala Ratnam. Palghat: Centram.

Thurston, Edgar. 1912. *Omens and superstitions of southern India*. New York: McBride, Nast and Co.

———. 1975a. [1906]. *Castes and tribes of southern India*. 8 vols. Delhi: Cosmo. Written with the assistance of K. Rangachari.

———. 1975b. [1906]. *Ethnographic notes in southern India*. Delhi: Cosmo.

ABIGAIL MCGOWAN

SEE ALSO
Colonialism and Folklore; Folklorists

TIBET

Many of the folktales, riddles, proverbs, song contests, epics, secular rituals, games, and dramas of Tibet emerge from a culture steeped in a two-thousand-year heritage and displaying a remarkable continuity from the far western province of Ngari to the eastern provinces of Khams and Amdo.

Folktales

Tibetan folktales incorporate a wide range of genres including parables, animal fables, trickster cycles, tales of abominable snowmen, zombies, gamblers, and pilgrims, and fairy tales replete with witches, ogres, clever shepherds, princes, princesses, or sorcerers' apprentices.

Parables often illustrate pragmatic applications of Buddhism or episodes from the lives of great Buddhist teachers. One important parable genre, which spans literary and folk traditions, is that of the *'das-log,* a person who returns from the dead to instruct the living about *bar-do,* the limbo-like state through which all souls must pass on their path to future rebirth and hell. Another parable genre lampoons devotees' insistence upon correct ritual form as opposed to the sincerity of spiritual piety. The *phra-men-ma,* seemingly pious women whose evil thoughts harm others, are one example.

Animal fables may offer straightforward moral lessons or venture into the more subtle messages arising from trickster stories. Major cycles of trickster stories recount the adventures of Agu Tompa (*A-khu sTon-pa*) or Uncle Tompa, who defies all social conventions, and the unusual didactic strategies of saintly madmen such as *'Brug-pa Kun-legs.*

Monsters of several orders abound in Tibetan folklore. Among them are various "abominable snowmen," such as the *mi-rgod,* or wild man, *dred-mo,* and *mentri.* These creatures, living at the fringe of the habitable world and blending the features of humans and bears or humans and monkeys, consider humans to be prey or potential mates. Another major monster is the *ro-langs,* or "walking corpse," a corpse animated by an evil spirit. Wylie classifies ro-langs stories into legendary ro-langs, epidemic ro-langs, and comatose ro-langs. Other popular horrific subjects include ghosts, witches, and sundry evil spirits. Of the latter, one impish spirit, *thebs-rang,* is renowned among gamblers for his ability to confer luck on anyone defeating him in a wrestling match.

Many Tibetan folktale genres are linked by the common theme of the traveler's tale, whether emerging from the rivalries of the central Tibetan provinces of *Dbus* and *Gtsang,* the bawdy escapades of Agu Tompa, the rustic pilgrim's initiation into urban life, the missions of animal protagonists, or the well-prepared soul's indifference to horrific beings lining the path of the journey through bar-do. Much of the humor in these travelers' tales results from cross-cultural encounters and misperceptions.

The Gesar Epic

Gesar, often referred to as Ling (*gLing*) Gesar, after a former state in the eastern region of Khams, is a culture hero whose praises are sung and exploits recounted in many parts of the country. Some evidence suggests that the Gesar epic may have its origins in Tibet's far west (Nagari), where the ancient Tibetan kingdom of Zhangzhung flourished in pre-Buddhist times.

The epic begins with the hero dispatched by the gods to subdue evil in the world. Gesar wins the fiercely contested hand of *'Brug-mo* in marriage and begins his conquest of kingdoms neighboring Ling in all directions. His initial victory over a giant in the north is sabotaged when the giant's wife administers a potion to Gesar causing him to lose his memory. The resulting delay in Gesar's return to Ling enables the King of Hor (Turkish tribes to the northeast) to subdue Ling and kidnap 'Brug-mo. Discovering his bride missing and his home destroyed, Gesar mounts an elaborate attack against the King of Hor and is eventually victorious. Gesar's valiant exploits continue in his conquest of Jang to the east, Mon to the south, and *sTag-gZig* (Persia), suggesting his equivalence with the universal emperor (*chakravartī*) in the Indian tradition.

The Gesar epic is encoded in oral tradition, manuscript, and abridged printed versions. All versions retain the core plot, but there are many variations in the subplots of both oral and written renditions. Although some Gesar bards rely upon a manuscript for reference, others may compose additional passages as they recite the epic over a three- to ten-day period. Many Tibetans believe that the spirit of Gesar takes possession of certain individuals, causing them to gain sudden knowledge of the epic along with the vocal ability to communicate it.

Song Duels

Song duels occurred traditionally at weddings, district village competitions, certain monastic dance performances, the celebration of the Great Prayer Festival (*sMon-lam*), picnics, parties, or wherever two people decided to challenge each other. Song competitions in Tibet gave vent to social criticism and political exchange, or provided an organized opportunity for sexual banter. Although singers often drew upon a wealth of Tibetan proverbs and riddles for inspiration, they also composed verses on the spot. In Ngari (far western Tibet), for example, the creativity of song duel rivals could prolong the contest for a week or more, compelling participants to request the local judge to determine the victor.

In Central Tibet, song duels are known as *tshig-kyag,* "teasing words," and are a specific form of *glu-gzhas.* Glu-gzhas songs, typically comprised of "twenty-four syllable verses divided into four phrases of six contextually related syllables," form a major category of Tibetan oral and enscribed folk tradition (Snyder 1968, 1). Tshig-kyag poetry heavily influenced the famous songs of the Tibetan saint *Milaraspa* and the unconventional performances of the "mad saint" 'Brugpa Kun-legs. Moreover, tshig-kyag circulating at the time of the Sixth Dalai Lama (1683–1706) most likely inspired the structure and content of his famous love songs.

The Opera Season

Snyder (1979) defines *lha-mo* as Tibetan classical secular theater closely paralleling Western opera. Lha-mo has ancient Tibetan antecedents that were probably associated with ensuring crop fertility, but its specific origin is traditionally attributed to the inventiveness of a "mad" saint, Thangstong rGyalpo (1385–1464), who devised it as a spectacular diversion for demons who were destroying the iron bridges he was building throughout Tibet. One legend holds that the saint tutored seven beautiful sisters, who were bridge workers, in dancing and singing until their proficiency encouraged their comparison to goddesses; hence, the alternative name for Tibetan opera, *a-lce lha-mo* (sister goddess). Indeed, the role taken in Tibetan opera by the sisters' successors is that of *mkha'-'gro-ma* (sky-going goddesses), who sing Thangstong rGyalpo's praises in opera performances. In early lha-mo troupes, these goddesses were joined by auspicious hunters (*rngon-pa*), who purify and tame the earth, and by venerable, well-wishing headmen (*gya-lu*). Later lha-mo troupes retained the actors' ritual obeisance to Thangstong rGyal-po and the auspicious introduction by the goddesses, hunters, and headmen, but developed lha-mo performances into day-long spectacles presenting classical plays based on historical events or the lives of Buddhist saints.

Although lha-mo troupes were extant throughout Tibet, the Lhasa region celebrated the theater season, spanning nearly two months in the late summer and early fall, in great style. This celebration became known as the *Sho-ton* (Great Yogurt) festival because it coincided with the nomads' grand offering of the year's finest yogurt to Drepung monks returning from their annual retreat. The monks invited theater groups to entertain at this annual feast, and the festival's subsequent popularity resulted in its expansion into a major event organized and sponsored by the Tibetan government and drawing the population of Lhasa. By the twentieth century, five days of operas, staged in the garden of the Norbulinkga, the summer palace of the Dalai Lama, followed the Sho-ton festival.

New Year Portents

The official Tibetan New Year (*lo-sar*), also known as King's New Year, usually falls sometime in February, but villagers in towns like Shigatse observe the Farmer's New Year associated with the winter solstice and marked by rituals of status reversal. Apart from the religious and state rituals traditionally conducted at New Year are folk rituals centering on predictions for the family and the individual. These include a ritual house cleansing conducted two days prior to the onset of the New Year, the consumption of a special soup, which contains a dumpling encasing a symbol of one's fortune for the coming year (for example, the sun signifies that one will be compassionate and free of demerits), and the casting out of a female dough effigy, representing the matron of the house.

Householders offer one fortune dumpling in a bit of soup to the family altar and often draw fortune dumplings for absent relatives. Following the disclosure of the fortunes, each person rubs a ball of dough all over his or her body to draw out any illnesses or pains. He or she then spits into the dough ball and utters "*thu-'trel-lo*" ("rolling the spit") to rid the body of any ills. Female householders squeeze the dough balls in their left hands while males squeeze them in their right hands to imprint the patterns of their individual fingers on the balls before contributing them, along with bits of lint from old clothing, coins, and leftover soup from each person's bowl, to the matron dough effigy. Male householders then carry the effigy out of the house and leave it at the crossing of three roads. Taking care not to look back at the effigy, the men fire guns or make some other noise to frighten off evil spirits intent upon returning to the household.

As an exorcism, this house cleansing ritual appears to parallel the casting out of the great effigy (*gtor-gyag*) conducted on the same day at temples by monks for the benefit of the community and the entire world. However, the two rituals represent different strategies of exorcism. The matron effigy, usually less than a foot in height, symbolizes the nurturing mother, who is perceived as the primary household attraction for both family members and evil spirits. To convince evil spirits that the effigy is actually the mother is to rid the house of its annual accumulation of undesirable entities. The great effigy, although also made of dough, is constructed by monks preparing to conduct a pre-New Year exorcism at a major temple. It is a conical structure reaching six or more feet in height, topped with a molded skull, and embellished with wooden carvings of flames and entrails, images of nude humans, and other symbols of wrongful desires and actions. The exorcism is designed to trap the evil that has afflicted the community during the past year in the great effigy, which is ultimately conveyed from the temple and destroyed by fire. Thus, rather than simply luring evil spirits away as in the house cleansing ritual, the casting out of the great effigy is intended to destroy (or transform) evil.

Another secular ritual primarily associated with the celebration of the New Year is the visit of a masked, well-wishing bard known as *'bras-dkar* (*'bras:* older person; *dkar:* white). Though many Tibetans assume that 'bras-dkar is simply a costumed beggar wearing a white mask framed with goat hair who appears at the New Year to sing verses promising good luck to those who reward him, the 'bras-dkar drew his name from traveling bards, old men who wore no masks, recounted myths, legends, and folktales, and brought good luck to those who listened.

Other Portents and Invocations

Tibetan folk divination incorporates dream interpretations, numerous omens, a translation of the language of ravens, and beliefs about the properties of precious stones. Tibetans, for example, prize turquoise and etched agate (*dzi*) for their magical properties as well as for their beauty. Turquoise secures the secondary soul (*bla*) in the wearer's body, purifies the blood, and counteracts jaundice. Dzi beads, featuring striped, wave, or "eye" patterns, are believed to have mystical origins. While some Tibetans describe dzi as the cast-off ornaments of the demigods, others believe dzi are petrified worms. Dzi beads ward off epilepsy, sudden illness, and death, but anyone who sells a valuable dzi risks sudden sickness or death. The most powerful dzi features a nine-eyed pattern, a pattern also woven into a legendary invincible slingshot. Small prehistoric bronze figurines, known as *rnam-chags* (sky iron) believed to have been formed by lightning, bring luck to their finders.

Tibetans also assign magical efficacy to certain poetic invocations used to plead for the desired outcome of a dice roll in the game of *sho,* which parallels the logic of backgammon, and is played with cowrie shells, coins, two dice, a leather dice shaker, and pad.

References

Ardussi, John, and Lawrence Epstein. 1978. The saintly madman in Tibet. In *Himalayan anthropology: The Indo-Tibetan interface,* ed. James F. Fisher, 327–338. The Hague and Paris: Mouton Publishers.

Chophel, Norbu. 1984. *Folktales of Tibet*. New Delhi: Library of Tibetan Works and Archives.

———. 1989. [1983.] *Folk culture of Tibet*. New Delhi: Library of Tibetan Works and Archives.

Devahuti. 1987. The Gesar Epic. *The Tibet Journal* 12(2): 16–24.

Dorje, Rinjing. 1975. *Tales of Uncle Tompa: the legendary rascal of Tibet*. San Rafael, Calif.: Dorje Ling Press.

Eppinghouse, David, and Michael Winsten. 1988. Tibetan dZi (gZi) Beads. *Tibet Journal* 13(1): 38–56.

Epstein, Lawrence. 1982. On the history and psychology of the *'Das-log. The Tibet Journal* 7(4): 20–85.

Gergan, J. 1991. [Reprint, n.d.] *A thousand Tibetan proverbs and wise sayings*. Kathmandu, Nepal: Tiwari's Pilgrims Book House.

O'Connor, W. F. 1977. [1906.] *Folk tales from Tibet*. Kathmandu, Nepal: Ratna Pustak Bhandar.

Samuel, Geoffrey. 1993. *Civilized shamans: Buddhism in Tibetan societies*. Washington, D.C.: Smithsonian Institution Press.

Snyder, Jeanette Marie. 1968. *Tshig Kyag,* A Tibetan alternate song competition. M.A. thesis. University of Washington.

———. 1979. Preliminary study of the *lha mo. Asian Music* 10(2): 23–62.

Stein, R. A. 1972. *Tibetan civilization*. Trans. J. E. Stapleton Driver. Stanford, Calif.: Stanford University Press.

Tucci, Giuseppe. 1966. *Tibetan folk songs from Gyantse and Western Tibet*. 2nd ed. Ascona, Switzerland: Artibus Asiae.

Wylie, Turrell. 1964. Ro-langs: the Tibetan zombie. *History of Religions* 4(1): 69–80.

Marcia S. Calkowski

SEE ALSO

Beads; Buddhism and Buddhist Folklore; Divination; Exorcism; Folktale; Kevar; Life Cycle Rituals; Masks; Theater and Drama

TIJ SONGS

Tij songs are a genre of folk song composed for the annual Tij festival celebrated throughout Nepal and parts of India by Hindu women. The rites of Tij are associated with Pārvati's devotion to Śiva. Women, in remembrance of the austerities Pārvati undertook to obtain Śiva as a husband, ritually bathe and fast during Tij. While fasting they sing and dance. Tij refers both to the festival and to the songs created by women (and sometimes men) specifically for this day.

Tij songs in Nepal share a similar rhythm, rhyming pattern, and melody, but their composers distinguish four subtypes according to the song's content: *deutā* (god), *dukha* (hardship), ghaṭanā (incident), and *rājnīti* (political). In deutā songs women pledge their devotion to a Hindu god or goddess and sing of the deity's feats. This type of Tij song is rarely sung today; younger women say deutā songs are uninteresting. Incident songs chronicle major events of the past year, such as suicides, bus accidents, or landslides.

The dukha song depicts the hardships women face as daughters, daughters-in-law, and wives. An example of a dukha song follows.

(Daughter): I rose in the morning to pick flowers,
But did not pick them because they were covered by dew.
Parents just keep the daughters to do work at home,
But not even a small piece of courtyard [i.e., land] is given [to daughters].
(Parents): The small piece of courtyard is needed to dry the paddy,
Go, daughter, to your husband's house to get your property.
(Daughter): We have to go empty-handed [to our husband's home],
The brothers fence in their property.
Brothers' clothes are so many that they rot away in a box,
But when they have to give us a single cloth, tears come to their eyes. (Skinner et al. 1994: 268)

This dukha song, like those recorded in India, contains an explicit critique of male privilege. In their dukha songs women challenge ideologies and practices that place them in disadvantaged and vulnerable positions vis-à-vis men. They attribute their problems to abusive husbands, unkind in-laws, jealous co-wives and sisters-in-law, and parents' favoring sons over daughters. In both India and Nepal images of the ideal and docile wife are questioned in the texts of Tij songs. Women characters in the songs recount and redress injustices against them, and provide a moral evaluation of the malefactors.

After the 1991 revolution in Nepal, political songs became more predominant in the Tij festival. Women (and some men) composed songs that were critical of governmental politics and in favor of women's rights. Although dukha songs share accounts of injustices and inequalities with rājnīti songs, the latter are more revolutionary in content. Talk of exploitation and calls to action are more explicit. An excerpt from a rājnīti song composed by a Nepali girl of thirteen follows.

Listen sisters, listen society,
Today I am going to speak about tyranny over women.
The male and female born from the same womb,
Do not have equal rights.
The son gets the ancestral property at the age of fourteen,
Whereas the daughter has to get married when she is only twelve . . . .
Parents send the son to school,
Whereas they are afraid to provide education to the daughter.
Father bought books and pens for my younger brother,
Whereas he wove a basket [for carrying loads] for me, the daughter . . . .
We women are also energetic and want justice,
We also have the right to hold a job. . . .
We women are always deprived in Nepal.
Women have even climbed Mt. Everest and reached the moon,
Women have done so many things in this world.
Women of other countries are pilots.
We Nepalese women will be happy if we get the chance to be great women.
Therefore, women of Nepal, this is not the time to be silent,
Let's fight to obtain our rights. (Skinner and Holland 1996: 286–287)

In Nepal political Tij songs chronicle abuses by those in power, their exploitation of women and the poor, the treacheries of political parties, and the violence perpetrated in other countries by political regimes.

Although performed in a ritual space where an ideal Hindu femininity is represented, Tij songs—whether about hardships or politics—contest this ideal, challenging male privileges and governmental policies and practices. They provide a critical voice on the social and political world, and are a basis for women's critical self-consciousness and social action. For as long as women can remember, both dukha and rājnīti songs have been in the Tij repertoire, providing a critical commentary on women's lives, and visions of alternative femininities and subjectivities.

References

Bennett, Lynn. 1983. *Dangerous wives and sacred sisters: Social and symbolic roles of high-caste women in Nepal.* New York: Columbia University Press.

Bhatnagar, Manju. 1988. The monsoon festival Teej in Rajasthan. *Asian Folklore Studies* 47: 63–72.

Bista, Khem Bahadur. 1969. Tij ou la fête des femmes. *Objets et mondes* 9: 7–18.

Holland, Dorothy, and Debra Skinner. 1995a. Contested ritual, contested femininities: (Re)forming self and society in a Nepali women's festival. *American Ethnologist* 22, no. 2: 279–305.

———. 1995b. Not written by the Fate-Writer: The agency in women's critical commentary in Nepal. *Folk: The Journal of the Danish Ethnographic Society* 37: 103–133.

Holland, D., and D. Skinner. 2001. From women's suffering to women's politics: Re-imagining women's problems after Nepal's 1990 Pro-Democracy Movement. In *History in person: Enduring struggles, contentious practice, intimate identities,* ed. Dorothy Holland and Jean Laue. Sante Fe, N.M.: School of American Research Press.

Holland, Dorothy, William Lachiotte, Debra Skinner, and Carole Cain. 1998. *Identity and agency in cultural worlds.* Cambridge: Harvard University Press.

Raheja, Gloria Goodwin, and Ann Grodzins Gold. 1994. *Listen to the heron's words: Reimagining gender and kinship in north India.* Berkeley: University of California Press.

Skinner, Debra, and Dorothy Holland. 1996. Schools and the cultural production of the educated person in a Nepalese hill community. In *The cultural production of the educated person: Critical ethnographies of schooling and local practice,* ed. Bradley A. Levinson, Douglas E. Foley, and Dorothy C. Holland. Albany: State University of New York Press.

Skinner, Debra, Dorothy Holland, and G. B. Adhikari. 1994. The songs of *Tij*: A genre of critical commentary for women in Nepal. *Asian Folklore Journal* 53, no. 2: 259–305.

DEBRA SKINNER

SEE ALSO
Gender and Folklore; Song

TILES AND TILE MAKING, TERRA-COTTA

The oldest terra-cotta tiles on the Indian subcontinent date to the Indus Valley civilization (2600–1900 B.C.E.), where they were used as flooring. At the site of Balakot, located west of Karachi, Pakistan, a small room had a floor of tiles with an impressed design of intersecting circles. During the Vedic period (roughly 1800–800 B.C.E.) flat tiles in square or triangular shapes were used by Brahmanic priests to construct ritual platforms for the *agnichayana* ritual sacrifice. Miniature tiles incised with sacred lines were used to make smaller household sacrificial altars.

Terra-cotta tiles with molded scenes from the life of the Buddha were used to decorate stūpas during the early historic period (300 B.C.E.–300 C.E.). Plaster or stucco tiles were used to decorate religious buildings of both Buddhist and Hindu sects. One of the regions most famous for sculptural terra-cotta tiles was Bengal during the eleventh century. The temples of Bishnupur are particularly well known for the narrative scenes depicted on terra-cotta tiles. Similar tile-making traditions continue to be practiced in many parts of the subcontinent, particularly Rajasthan and Gujarat.

Famous glazed terra-cotta tiles come from Pakistan and northern India. Designs painted in blue, blue-green, black, and yellow are quite common. Tiles with geometric and calligraphic designs are used almost exclusively for Muslim tombs and mosques, while figurative designs are found on Hindu temples and palaces. Many scholars attribute the specific technology of making glazed terra-cotta tiles to workmen brought to the subcontinent from Iran or elsewhere in western Asia between roughly 700 and 1400 C.E. However, glazing technology was used during the early historic period (300 B.C.E.–300 C.E.) to produce glass bangles as well as glass utensils and glazed tiles. At present the most famous tile-making centers in Pakistan are at Multan and Hala, while in northern India they are scattered between Delhi and Agra.

References

Fischer, Eberhard, and Haku Shah. 1970. *Rural craftsmen and their work*. Ahmadabad: National Institute of Design.

Haider, Sajjad. 1982. *Tilework in Pakistan*. Islamabad: Lok Virsa, National Institute of Folk Heritage.

Rye, Owen S., and Clifford Evans. 1976. *Traditional pottery techniques of Pakistan*. Smithsonian Contributions to Anthropology no. 21. Washington, D.C.: Smithsonian Institution Press.

JONATHAN MARK KENOYER

SEE ALSO
Material Culture; Pottery; Stūpa

TIRUVĀTIRA

Tiruvātira is a traditional festival of Kerala in which high-caste women commemorate the death of Kāmadēvan, the god of sexual love. Characterized by bathing, singing, playing, and feasting, Tiruvātira is performed by virgin girls in order to get husbands and by married women to achieve a happy marital life. The mythological event commemorated in the festival is the burning of the god of lust, Kāma, by the fire of Śiva's third eye. Śiva's wife Pārvati enlisted Kāma's help to distract Śiva from his ascetic meditations so that he might fulfil his marital duties toward her as a lover. In his anger on being disturbed, Śiva opened his third eye and burned Kāma. On Tiruvātira day Śiva gives rebirth to Kāma on hearing the mournful cries of lust of the bathing women. Thus the main theme of the festival is fertility and auspicious marital sexuality.

On the day of Tiruvātira, said to be Śiva's birth star, in the winter month of Dhanu (December–January), young women of the matrilineal Nāyar caste awake well before dawn and go to the nearest bathing tank or river together to bathe. While in the water, the women sing *Tiruvātira pāṭṭu,* songs about the marital relations of Śiva and Pārvati and the god of love, while beating the water in a unique style with the hands. The left hand is cupped under the water and struck obliquely with the right, causing a large splash and a deep noise. This rhythmic singing and beating of the water symbolizes the women's mournful beating of their breasts upon hearing of Kāma's death. With great enjoyment the women play in the water and then return home to decorate themselves with eye-black, flowers, sandalpaste, and other cosmetics. The women sing, dance, and play games all day, taking rest from household chores. The chief entertainment is swinging from a bamboo swing. Until evening, the women refrain from eating rice, the ordinary staple food of their diet, taking only fruits and water. At night they enjoy a feast prepared from plantains, tubers, and cereals.

The singing, bathing, swinging, dancing, playing, and eating of phallic shaped foods all celebrate the women's auspicious connection to married sexual life and fertility. On Tiruvātira, men must do all household work, including cooking, and must serve the ladies in the evening. Husbands are also required to be present in their wives' bedchambers without fail in the evening for sexual enjoyment.

References

Fawcett, F. 1901. Nayars of Malabar. *Madras Government Museum Bulletin* 3(3): 299–301.

Iyer, L. K. Anantha Krishna. 1981 [1912]. *The Tribes and Castes of Cochin*. Vol. II, 70. New Delhi: Cosmo Publications.

Raghavan, M. D. 1947. *Folk Plays and Dances of Kerala,* 11–14. Trichur, Kerala: Magalodayam Press.

SARAH CALDWELL

SEE ALSO
Fairs and Festivals; Gender and Folklore; Kerala; Śiva

TŌṞṞAM

Tōṟṟam is a word principally used with reference to a variety of songs of praise, invocation, and spirit possession addressed to various Hindu deities in a variety of contexts of worship in different parts of Kerala. It is in the northern Kerala tradition of worshipping local deities known as *teyyam*s, however, that *tōṟṟam-pāṭṭu*s (-songs) are most elaborated as a separate genre. In this generic usage, tōṟṟam comprises the many hundreds of descriptive and narrative songs, each dedicated to the particular teyyam deity whose worship through possession-dance these songs help effect. Lastly, tōṟṟam is also often used for the preliminary phase of worshipping the teyyam itself, a ritual which entails the dancer singing tōṟṟam songs while wearing a light and standardized costume, as opposed to the highly elaborated and individuated costume and makeup for the full form of teyyam worship. By extension, tōṟṟam may refer to this form of the costume itself.

The word's etymology is important to an understanding of its semantic range, for it derives from a Dravidian root meaning "to make something appear" (*tōrr-*), in the peculiar sense of effecting as a physical presence what takes shape as a mental conception. The uses of this verb and its noun, tōṟṟam, thus pertain both to creative acts of deities themselves, in mythological accounts, and to the invocation of a divine presence through acts of worship or routines of spirit possession. Further, by a false etymological convergence with the Sanskrit word, *stotra,* meaning a hymn of praise, the word tōṟṟam has come to refer as well to the songs of worship by which a deity's presence is invoked in worship and manifested through possession.

In this latter sense, tōṟṟam is used for a variety of songs of worship and possession for other individual deities throughout the state. Prominently, for instance, it is used in the ritual mode called *pāṉa,* where the tōṟṟam recounts the origins of the goddess Bhagavati worshipped in those rites. But as noted, tōṟṟam finds its greatest conceptual elaboration and extended range of application in the northern Kerala worship of teyyams, where the tōṟṟam-pāṭṭās are correlated descriptively and performatively with each phase of the worship and possession-dance for these deities. There are thus tōṟṟams of invocation (*varaviḷi*), of praise (*stuti*), and of description of the deity's appearance and its life history (variously titled), all culminating in the onset of the performer's possession (*uṟaccil*), effected through a tōṟṟam of that same name (uṟaccil-tōṟṟam).

A substantial part of the richly narrative and descriptive corpus of tōṟṟam songs has been collected and published by various Kerala folklorists in their native Malayalam, both for the southern traditions of worshipping Bhagavati (Achyuta Menon 1959) and for the northern tradition of teyyam worship. For sources on the teyyam tradition in English, Kurup (1973) provides a schematic narrative summary of tōṟṟams in their ritual context for a number of the most prominent deities, while the present author's dissertation (Freeman 1991) provides the most in-depth treatment of tōṟṟams in their ritual and cultural-historical context. More readily accessible studies which help situate tōṟṟams in the context of teyyam ritual generally, can be found in Kurup (1977), Ashley, and Ashley and Holloman.

References

Achyuta Menon, C. 1943. *Kali worship in Kerala.* Madras University Malayalam Series, No. 8. Madras: University of Madras.

Ashley, Wayne. 1979. The teyyam kettu of northern Kerala. *Drama Review* 23(2): 99–112.

Ashley, Wayne, and Regina Holloman. 1990. Teyyam. In *Indian theatre: traditions of performance,* eds. Farley Richmond, Darius Swann, and Phillip Zarrilli, 131–150. Honolulu: University of Hawaii Press.

Freeman, J. R. 1991. Purity and violence: sacred power in the teyyam worship of Malabar. Ph.D. dissertation, Department of Anthropology, University of Pennsylvania.

———. Performing possession: ritual and consciousness in the teyyam complex of northern Kerala. In *Flags of Fame: Studies in South Asian Folk Culture,* eds. Heidrun Bruckner, Lothar Lutze, and Aditya Malik, 109–138. New Delhi: Manohar.

Kurup, K. K. N. 1973. *The cult of teyyam and hero worship in India.* Calcutta: Indian Publishing House.

———. 1977. *Aryan and Dravidian elements in Malabar folklore.* Trivandrum, Kerala: Kerala Historical Society.

RICH FREEMAN

SEE ALSO

Bhagavati Ritual Traditions of Kerala; Kerala; *Pāḍdana;* Spirit Possession and Mediumship; *Teyyam*

TOYS

Essentially children's playthings, some of which also serve as teaching aids, toys range from any natural object or ordinary artifact that may catch the child's imagination to the most sophisticated product turned out by a machine. Those which are manually fashioned in the traditional manner and reflect the life and culture of a community are classed as folk or traditional toys. The function of such toys extends beyond the child's amusement and instruction: Forming a segment of physical folklife, they shed light on other aspects of culture in general and of folk culture in particular.

The place of traditional toys in the cultural history of South Asia—particularly of the Indian subcontinent—is significant on several counts. First, such toys bear an excellent testimony to the unbroken continuity of the cultural tradition of the region. Second, today the impressive array of traditional or folk toys available in the region ranges from the crude and plain to the highly finished and artistic. Third, the fact that traditional toys have been holding their own, however tenuously, against the onslaught of modern, mass-produced, and aggressively marketed toys demonstrates both the resilience of folklore forms and their continued relevance.

The toys of South Asia can be traced back to the terra-cotta figurines of human females and animals, and bird-shaped whistles recovered from ancient sites like Kulli and Zhob (in Pakistan) that have been placed in the fourth and third millennia B.C.E. The largest group of ancient terra-cotta toys was found in Mohenjo-daro, Harappa, and Chanhu-Daro (also in Pakistan), which are important sites of the Indus Valley civilization (c. 3000–1800 B.C.E.). The finds include figures representing human beings (mostly female) and various animals and birds, as well as objects like carts, rattles, balls, and whistles. Some had mechanical devices that facilitated movement, and others had wheels attached to them. Scholars believe that many of these figures were cult objects, but a considerable proportion must have certainly been children's playthings. While the bulk of the toys display excellent workmanship and artistic sensibility, the visible crudeness of some indicates that they could be the handiwork of children themselves.

That the tradition of terra-cotta toys has been carried down through the centuries is borne out by the fact that more or less similar toys have been unearthed from various sites of later periods in northern India (Kosam, Varanasi, Sarnath, Mathura, Basahr, Pataliputra), Bangladesh (Rangamati and Rajshahi), and southern India (Chandra-valli, Brahmapuri, and Arikamedu, where some foreign influences have been discerned).

Information about the use of toys in ancient India is available from literary and sculptural evidence. Ancient literary works like the *Mahābhārata,* some Buddhist and Jain texts, and two of Kalidasa's (fourth or fifth century C.E.) plays contain references not only to games and amusements but also to toys or playthings (dolls, balls, and drums). Significantly the title of one of the earliest Sanskrit plays is *Mṛcchakaṭika* (literally, The Clay Toy Cart). Some ancient sculptures depict children playing with toys.

In the making of traditional toys today, various materials—clay, wood, ivory, pith, bamboo, grass, cloth, stone, metal, and papier-mâché—are used; there is also much diversity in form, technique, style, and finish. A high degree of stylization characterizes the forms and decorative motifs of the great body of toys, although certain types are remarkable for their lifelike representation of objects.

On the basis of workmanship and artistic excellence, as well as links with the traditional culture, scholars and experts have paid special attention to certain categories of toys. These include terra-cotta toys from West Bengal, Assam, Uttar Pradesh, Saurashtra, and Rajasthan; wooden toys from Andhra Pradesh, Tamil Nadu, Karnataka, West Bengal, Orissa, and Maharashtra; papier-mâche toys from Orissa and Rajasthan; cloth toys from Rajasthan and Manipur; soapstone toys from Madhya Pradesh; and pith toys from Assam. Most of these toys have steady local markets, sales being particularly heavy during fairs and festivals. However, some classes with special reputations have much wider markets.

Today the making of folkish toys with commercial techniques and in commercial quantities is being encouraged by various government, semiofficial, and private agencies that are promoting the products as examples of "local handicraft" or "ethnic art." They are doing well as "tourist folklore."

Such commercialization has not, however, snapped the intimate links of the genuine folk toys with traditional life. For example, certain classes of toys are still integral to belief and ritual systems at the folk level. Some may serve as idols, some others are meant as votive offerings to local deities and shrines, and still others are part of the paraphernalia of festivals and ceremonies. Many toys also help in integrating the child into the sociocultural ethos of the community. For instance there are pieces that facilitate acquaintance with characters and episodes from popular mythological, legendary, and fictional literature. Among dolls those representing brides are the most numerous. Mock weddings with toy brides and grooms are a popular pastime of children. These toys, along with those representing various utensils and other household articles, are particularly popular with girls and indirectly impart early lessons in household management. As a medium of artistic expression folk toys also reflect the traditional aesthetic ideals at the folk level.

Puppets and marionettes, which may be considered animated toys, are made in different forms and styles in India (Rajasthan, the southern states, Orissa, West Bengal, and Assam), Bangladesh, and Sri Lanka.

References

Chattopadhyay, K. 1975. *Handicrafts of India.* New Delhi: Indian Council for Cultural Relations.

Dhavlikar, M. K. 1977. *Masterpieces of Indian terra-cotta.* Bombay: D. B. Taraporevala Sons.

Dongerkery, K. S. 1954. *A journey through toyland.* Bombay: Popular Book Depot.

Majumdar, R. C., ed. 1951. *Vedic age.* Bombay: Bharatiya Vidya Bhavan.

Mehta, R. J. 1960. *The handicrafts and industrial arts of India.* Bombay: D. B. Taraporevala Sons.

Mookerji, A. 1956. *Folk toys of India*. Calcutta and New Delhi: Oxford Book & Stationery Co.
Swarup, S. 1968. *5000 years of arts and crafts of India and Pakistan*. Bombay: D. B. Taraporevala Sons.

BIRENDRANATH DATTA

SEE ALSO
Fairs and Festivals; Games and Contests; Marionettes; Material Culture

TRIBAL COMMUNITIES, NORTHEAST INDIA

The geographic area of northeast India is 255,083 square kilometers, and mountains, hills, and plateaus cover 70 percent of this region. There are more than eighty main tribes with numerous subdivisions who often claim separate identity. They are mongoloid in racial feature and, with the exception of the Austric-speaking Khasi-Jaintia tribes, speak Sino-Tibetan languages of Tibeto-Burman and Siamese-Chinese branches. Tibeto-Burman speakers belong to Boṛo-Garo, Naga, Kuki-Chin, and North Assam groups, whereas a small Tai-speaking group belongs to Siamese-Chinese branch. Tribal populations vary from a few hundred to one hundred thousand, except six tribes, each with more than a quarter million population. Percentages of tribals are in Arunachal Pradesh, Meghalaya, Mizoram, and Nagaland around 80 percent; in Manipur and Tripura around 30 percent; and in Assam below five percent of the total populations of these states. On the basis of linguistic, ethnographic, and administrative considerations, these tribes are divided into generic groups such as Boṛo, Naga, Kuki, Mizo, Khasi-Jaintia, Arunachal, and some intermediate tribes. Boṛo tribes mainly live in Assam and Tripura; Naga tribes in Nagaland, Manipur, and Assam; Kuki tribes in Manipur, Mizoram, and Assam; Mizo tribes in Mizoram, Manipur, and Tripura; and matrilineal Khasi-Jaintia and Garo tribes in Meghalaya.

Tribal populations entered this area from Bhutan, south China, and Burma, and some tribes spread to Bangladesh. Khasi-Jaintias settled first and were followed by the Boṛos and Garos before the commencement of the common era. Naga and some Kuki tribes also settled long ago, but the rest of the migration occured in the last thousand years, ending with some Kukis and Mizos in the eighteenth century. In recent years, a large number of Indian tribes from other regions have settled as workers in tea plantations.

In Assam, there are twenty-two tribes, of which the Boṛo-Kachari, Dimasa-Kachari, and Rabha are the members of the Boṛo group. There are also Karbis, Misings, and some tribes of the adjoining states. In Meghalaya, apart from the Khasi-Jaintias and Garos, Hajongs are also an important tribe. In Manipur, there are twenty-nine Naga, Kuki, and Mizo tribes who shift their alignments with the broader groups; some prefer to identify themselves separately. Bigger tribes are Thadou, Tangkhul, Kabui, Mao, and Paite. There are twenty-one Naga tribes—Angami, Ao, Chakhesang, Chang, Jeme, Kabui, Kacha, Khiamngan, Konyak, Lotha, Mao, Maram, Maring, Phom, Pochury, Rengma, Sangtam, Sema, Tangkhul, Yimchunghir, and Zeliang. In Mizoram, Lushai, Ralte, Hmar, Piate, Pawi, and eleven minor tribes denoted by the term *Awzia* forged a common identity as Mizos after the 1950s. Among the non-Mizos there are Buddhist Chakmas, Kukis, and allied groups. Among the nineteen tribes of Tripura, Tripuri, a Boṛo tribe, and Riang are dominant. The tribes of Arunachal Pradesh along the northern frontier, such as Monpa, Momba, and Sherdukpen, are Buddhist, and Aka and Miji are also influenced by Buddhism. Tribes of the central area, such as Adi, Apatani, Hill Miri, Mishmi, Sulung, Tangin, and Tangsa, are at a low level of socio-political integration. The rest of the tribes, those along the southeastern and southern border, such as Khampti, Singpho, and Wancho have been influenced by Burmese Buddhism. Noctes have adopted Assamese Vaiṣnavism. There are altogether 110 groups, including the above major tribes and their subdivisions.

The tribes broadly occupy two ecological zones: hills and plains. In the hills, many practice slash and burn (*jum*) cultivation, with a few exceptions such as Angami Nagas and Apatanis, who cultivate wet rice in the terraces. In the plains plough cultivation is typical.

In the plains, Hinduisation produced a tribe-caste continuum in Assam, Tripura, Manipur, and some parts of Meghalaya. Hinduisation also occurred through evolution of some tribes, between the thirteenth and sixteenth centuries C.E., into a rudimentary state society. Three levels of growth have been identified:

- consolidation of chiefdom without religious conversion
- expansion of chiefdom and adoption of Hinduism by the rulers (Jaintia and Dimasa Kings) who through their conversion maintained a liaison and balance between the hills and plains, and
- further evolution of Hinduism in the Koch kingdom of the Boṛo-Kacharis, Tripura state, and the state of the Meiteis (Hinduised Naga-Kukis of Manipur).

The spread of Hinduism and Buddhism brought their respective great traditions. Various media of oral communications and performance flourished to transmit great traditions. Attempts were also made to connect tribal kings with the famous lineages of Hindu myths and legends.

In this ecology of varying cultural developments, certain tribes took up the role of bridge by promoting exchange between various cultural levels, and some tribes acted as buffers for reducing conflicts. Where the tribes living at the low techno-economic level could not evolve such symbiotic relationships, head-hunting and war flourished, as happened among the Nagas and some Mizo tribes.

Rice is the staple food of these tribes. Most of them live in raised platform houses made of bamboo, wood, and thatch; prepare rice-beer in their homes; and chew areca nuts. Bride-price, an age-grade system, and youth dormitories are widespread social institutions. Except in three matrilineal tribes, organization is patrilineal. Social structures are based on clan and lineage, and the segmentary system extends up to phratry and dual organisations among some Naga, Mizo, and Arunachal tribes. A few tribes are organised into separate divisions. In the marriage system, mother's-brother's-daughter marriage, levirate, and sororate are common. Among some tribes of Arunachal and Mizoram, stratification based on internal class divisions is present. Slavery was prevalent in many areas. Broadly, there are two types of polities, based on chiefdom and democratic council of the village elders. Tribal households possess looms and weave colorful cloth, and specialisation is nearly absent. Like clothes, bamboo crafts, masks, and wood carvings are popular artistic traditions.

Belief in traditional religion persists in spite of large-scale conversion to Hindu, Christian, and Buddhist faiths. Monpas and Sherdukpens have been influenced by Māhayāna Buddhism from Tibet, and Khamptis and Singphos by Hinayāna Buddhism from Burma. Belief in a supreme being (creator or principal), ancestral and natural spirits, and minor deities characterizes traditional religion. Priests and medicine men control and appease them. Divinition, spirit-possession, and oracle-telling through ritualistic dances are widespread. The most elaborate system of taboo, called *genna,* is observed by the Nagas for prosperity. Change in religions on the model of bigger religions is also observed, such as in the Heraka faith of Zeliang Nagas and Donyi-Polo (the sun and moon) worship of the tribes of central Arunachal.

Modernisation of the tribals began first in the colonial period and then increased after Independence. Extension of networks of market, politics, and education has transformed many tribals into peasants. Historical patterns of continuum have been disrupted and mobilisation of the tribes on ethnic lines has taken place. In this process folklore is playing an important role.

References

Benedict, Paul and Dipankar, Moral. *Boro-Garo handbook.*

Bhagabati, Annada C. 1988. Tribal transformation in Assam and north-east India: An appriasal of emerging ideological dimensions. *Presidential address, section of anthropology and archeology,* Calcutta, Indian Science Congress Association.

Chatterjee, Suniti K. 1951. *Kirāta Jana Kriti.* Calcutta: Asiatic Society of Bengal.

Elwin, Verrier. 1958. *Myths of the north-east frontier of India.* Shillong: Director of Information North-East Frontier Agency.

Roy Burman, B. K. 1970. *Demographic and socio-economic profiles of the hill areas of north-east India* (Census of India 1961 Monograph). New Delhi: Office of the Registrar General of Census of India.

Singh, K. S., ed. 1994. *The scheduled tribes.* People of India National Series, Vol. 3. Delhi: Oxford University Press.

Sinha, Surajit, ed. 1987. *Tribal polities and state systems in precolonial eastern and north eastern India.* Calcutta: K. P. Bagchi and Company.

KISHORE BHATTACHARJEE

SEE ALSO
Bangladesh

TRIBAL COMMUNITIES, SOUTHERN INDIA

The communities of South India designated scheduled tribes share many of the same socioeconomic and cultural characteristics and face many of the same problems as those found throughout India. Unlike the tribes of central and northern India, who speak languages of Austro-Asiatic, Indo-Aryan, and Dravidian origin, almost all of the tribes of South India speak Dravidian languages. Most of them speak dialects of major languages such as Tamil, Telugu, Malayalam, Kanada, and Tulu. Others, often small populations such as the Kotas (roughly 1,500) and Todas (roughly 1,200) of the Nilgiris, speak distinct languages that appear to have split away from ancient Tamil as early as two thousand or more years ago.

South Indian tribals employ a variety of terms for self-description, including the English word tribe, the Hindi word *ādivāsi* (original inhabitant), and regional language terms that variously translate as hill people, ancient people, and so forth. Tribal terms for their own communities usually differ from those imposed by outsiders. Some of these terms indicate a base-level "us-them" distinction common also among north Indian tribals. Todas, for example, call themselves *O·ḷ,* or "men"; Nāyakas call themselves "our own." Others have names for themselves that may have once had lexical meaning but now exist simply as proper names. For example, Kotas call themselves "*ko·v.*"

Women in a tribal community, © Mimi Nichter

Some tribal societies have incorporated into their own self-representation what now appear to be widely held stereotypes of so-called primitive peoples, introduced in part during the colonial period. Stereotypically, tribals are cast as, for example, hunter-gatherers or practitioners of ecstatic rituals who are comparatively egalitarian and sexually uninhibited. There are other stereotypes as well; some, for example, attribute to tribals laziness and childlike innocence. Only certain attributes are singled out for tribal self-representation. Symbols of hunting such as the spear or bow and arrow, and of traditional music like frame drum and oboe types, are popular emblems for modern intertribal organizations and often appear as sacralized artifacts associated with tribal deities.

In fact, the cultural characteristics of tribals are highly diverse in South India. Since some tribes self-identify as Hindus, they are in many cases virtually indistinguishable from nontribals. There are some seventy-five distinct tribal populations in South India that appear in recent cultural surveys, such as Hockings's (1992), varying in number from only five (the Araṇḍan in 1971) to nearly 160,000. Census lists do not always correspond with ethnographically determined cultural entities, and some tribal communities argue that they have been historically undercounted. For example, whereas ethnographic literature suggests Kerala hosts at least forty-eight distinct tribal populations (25 percent of them represented in Kozhikode district), the Scheduled Castes and Scheduled Tribes Orders (Amendment) Act of 1976 listed thirty-five. The same census schedules list forty-nine tribes in Karnataka, thirty-six in Tamilnadu, and thirty-three in Andhra Pradesh. Out of about 165 million people in the four southern states, about six million (3.5 percent) were listed as belonging to scheduled tribes.

Of the roughly seventy-five tribal populations described in the recent cultural survey, about twenty-five of these communities subsist almost entirely as cultivators or farm laborers; an additional twenty-five or so are cultivators or laborers who either are reported to have once been hunter-gatherers, or who continue to supplement their income/subsistence by hunting or collecting forest produce. It is common for tribals most closely connected to forest life to be employed as mahouts, or elephant drivers, especially, if not exclusively, in wildlife sanctuaries. Some tribals, castelike, specialize in particular occupations or engage in a lifestyle that features stone masonry, smithing, weaving, carpentry, animal husbandry, pastoralism, toddy-tapping, and even wrestling. Some tribals are nomadic; of these, a few still sleep in, or ritually employ, rock shelters. Other nomadic tribes, like certain Hindu castes and Muslim communities, wander the countryside, begging, telling fortunes, and acting as astrologers.

The ways in which tribals interact with each other and with surrounding Indian populations are diverse. Although tribes stereotypically are egalitarian, with weakly articulated pollution ideologies and strongly articulated forms of social solidarity, there are tribes such as the Todas in which gender divisions as well as grades of purity and pollution are strongly marked. Communities such as the Kotas perform rituals signifying unity of clan, village, and tribe, based frequently on demonstrating unity of the male population—men and women also dance separately from one another. This strongly contrasts with the practices of larger tribal populations in North India, such as the Mundas, among whom men and women participate in communal dance. Several tribes in South India, such as the Nāyakas (or Jēnu Kurumbas) and Malapaṇṭāram, are characterized by individual autonomy and focus on the conjugal family as the relevant corporate unit; in some cases, brothers tend to avoid one another and do not cooperate in subsistence activities.

Tribal/nontribal relations also vary. In the Nilgiri hills, for instance, one may observe a great deal of social and cultural interaction between Irula plantation workers and Tamilians of low caste who have been imported as laborers from the plains. This has led to an "ever-increasing diffusion of Tamil non-Brahmin, low caste, or Harijan cultural traits among the Irulas . . ." (Zvelebil 1988: 83). Among more affluent tribes such as the Todas and Kotas, who have been able to secure land rights, diffusion of cultural traits has certainly occurred, but social relations are decidedly different. Kotas, for example, may hire untouchable laborers to till their fields; in some cases, they may also work side by side with them. Kotas do not ordinarily interdine with or invite these laborers into their houses. They also tend to limit the degree to which and times during which non-Kotas may enter their villages. But like the Goṇḍs of Andhra Pradesh, restrictions on accepting food from outsiders and allowing them to enter their villages and homes have decreased in recent decades.

It has been suggested that, unlike scheduled castes, scheduled tribes are not considered to be polluting to other Hindus. Part of this stems from the custodial role some tribals have long played in remote temples; another reason may be the popular association of tribals with the oldest inhabitants of India—thus, as it were, bestowing a sort of sacredness on a presumed primevality. Śiva worship and Goddess worship are believed by some to be tribal in origin; thus, tribal priests at temples devoted to what are now explained to be manifestations of Śiva or Śakti appear to be "natural." However, tribals such as the Irulas of the Nilgiris also serve as priests for Vaiṣnava temples. Inscriptions suggest that Irula temples for Rangasami and a variety of goddesses came under Irula control and were not, as it might be assumed, primordially Irula.

One of the more fascinating features of tribal social organization is the local system of interaction in a predominantly tribal area. Perhaps the most well known of these traditional systems is found in the Nilgiris, where well into the twentieth century there was an integrated, hierarchically arranged, sociocultural system in which Toda pastoralists provided milk products, hereditarily linked Badagas (an immigrant *jāti* cluster from what is now Karnataka) provided grain, and Kotas, their services as artisans (providing tools, jewelry, music, etc.). These communities occupy the Nilgiri plateau; less directly involved in the system were the Kurumbas, hunter-gatherers who live on the Nilgiri slopes. They provided services as magicians, watchmen, and providers of forest products. All of these ties were articulated and meaningful, ritually as well as socially. Thus, for example, until recent times, Todas felt a funeral was not proper unless accompanied by Kota music. Changes in demography, industrialization, and the homogenizing forces of a monetary economy, along with other factors, eventually led to the demise of this system, but traces of it still exist.

References

Demmer, Ulrich. Voices in the forest: The field of gathering among the Jēnu Kuṟumba. In *Blue Mountains revisited: cultural studies of the Nilgiris,* ed. Paul Hockings. Delhi: Oxford University Press.

Emeneau, Murray Barnson. 1944–46. *Kota texts*. 4 Parts. University of California Publications in Linguistics 2 & 3. Berkeley: University of California Press.

Fürer-Haimendorf, Christoph von, and Elizabeth von Fürer-Haimendorf. 1979. *The Gonds of Andhra Pradesh: tradition and change in an Indian tribe*. School of Oriental and African Studies Studies on Modern Asia and Africa, no. 12. London: George Allen & Unwin.

Hockings, Paul, ed. 1992. *Encyclopedia of world cultures*. Vol. III, *South Asia*. Boston: G. K. Hall.

———. 1989. *Blue Mountains: the ethnography and biogeography of a south Indian region*. Delhi: Oxford University Press.

Misra, Rajalakshmi. 1971. *Mullukurumbas of Kappala*. Calcutta: Anthropological Survey of India.

Morab. S. G. 1977. *The Soliga of Bilgiri Rangana Hills*. Calcutta: Anthropological Survey of India.

Padmanabha, P. 1984. *Census of India 1981*. Series-1, paper 2, General population and population of scheduled castes and scheduled tribes. Delhi: Controller of Publications Civil Lines.

Singh, K. S. 1985. *Tribal society in India: an anthropo-historical perspective*. New Delhi: Manohar.

Vitebsky, Piers. 1993. *Dialogues with the dead: the discussion of mortality among the Sora of eastern India*. Cambridge: Cambridge University Press.

Walker, Anthony. 1986. *The Toda of south India: a new look*. Delhi: Hindustan Publishing Corporation.

Yorke, Michael. 1989 [1982]. The situation of the Gonds of Asifabad and Lakshetipet Taluks, Adilabad District. In *Tribes of India: the struggle for survival,* by Christoph von Fürer-Haimendorf, 203–249. Delhi: Oxford University Press; Berkeley: University of California Press.

Zvelebil, Kamil V. 1988. *The Irulas of the Blue Mountains*. Foreign and Comparative Studies. South Asian Series 13. Syracuse N.Y.: Maxwell School of Citizenship and Public Affairs, Syracuse University.

RICHARD KENT WOLF

SEE ALSO
Character Stereotypes

TRIBAL FOLKLORE, CENTRAL INDIA

The term "tribe" applied to certain ethnic groups in South Asia is a controversial one, originating as a product of British administrative jargon and nineteenth century orientalism. Tribal peoples are also referred to as "aboriginals" (*ādivāsīs* in Hindi-Urdu), implying that they are descendants of the original inhabitants of the land, those who occupied the Indian subcontinent before Aryan immigration from central Asia beginning about 1500 B.C.E. In India the term tribe has also received a certain bureaucratic legitimacy in the form of "Scheduled Tribe," as identified in Article 342 of the constitution. "Scheduled Tribes and Castes" are conceptualized as peoples outside of, or occupying low positions within, the traditional caste hierarchies of many regions, and are characterized as "backward" or underprivileged in terms of socioeconomic status and education, and marginal in relation to dominant cultural features of Indian civilization.

In some areas of central India, as well as elsewhere, tribals occupy relatively isolated hilly, forested tracts and have developed and maintained rather distinct cultural characteristics and institutional forms, such as elaborate dance and adolescent dormitories. But in many instances groups conventionally identified as "tribal" are well-integrated into rural life, occupying specific caste (*jāti*) strata in village hierarchies, and are fully assimilated into the regional culture. For example, the "tribal" group known as Goṇḍ Ṭhākur in southern Chattīsgaṛh occupies a specific (low or middle range) position in the caste hierarchy of village communities in the region, and its members participate fully in the economic, social, and ceremonial life of these communities. At the annual fall festival of Dīvālī, the Goṇḍ Ṭhākurs are responsible for performing elaborate Gaura-Gaurī rituals, which celebrate the marriage of Śiva and Pārvatī, important "great tradition" Hindu deities. Of course they do follow specific traditions which set them apart somewhat from other castes, such as the performance of weddings in the groom's rather than the bride's house, but many similar examples of distinctive caste culture are evident among all castes of this and other regions, whether "tribal" or not.

According to the 1981 Census of India figures, scheduled tribes constitute 51,628,638 persons, or 7.76 percent of the total population of the country. There are over two hundred tribes, distributed throughout many geographical regions, with particularly large concentrations along the northeast frontier and in central India, especially within the area sometimes referred to as the "central tribal belt." Most of the central Indian tribal languages belong to the Mundari (or Austric) language family or to the Dravidian family. Mundari languages are distinct and have no known affiliation with those of any other region. Dravidian tribal languages, however, are closely related to the major Dravidian languages of south India, such as Telugu and Tamil, suggesting that their speakers originally migrated into central India from areas farther south. Many tribal people are bilingual in their mother tongue and a regional language such as Hindi-Urdu, Bihari, Bengali, or Oriya. In many instances the mother tongue is no longer spoken at all.

A major concentration of tribals is found in the Chhota Nagpur plateau, an area of 86,239 square kilometers, running across the southern part of Bihar and extending eastward into part of West Bengal. About twenty-five tribes occupy this region, including such populous groups as the Santhals, Mundas and Oraons. Together Bihar and West Bengal have a tribal population exceeding twelve million, or about 14 percent of the total population of the two states combined. South of this plateau is the state of Orissa, the population of which is nearly one fourth tribal, including fairly large tribes such as the Konds, Saoras, and Binjhwars, and at least a dozen smaller ones, some of them former hunter-gatherers. Bordering both Bihar and Orissa to the west is India's largest state, Madhya Pradesh (literally, "central state" in Hindi-Urdu), which has a tribal population numbering over twelve million, or nearly one-fourth of the total, concentrated particularly within the districts of Bastar and Maṇḍlā. In the year 2000 the new state of Chattīsgaṛh was created out of certain districts of Madhya Pradesh, resulting in a redistribution of the tribal population figures. The various Goṇḍ groups, such as the Muṛīā and Māṛīā, are the most important tribals in this region.

Because of the great diversity of central Indian tribal cultures, there is no single folklore tradition characteristic of all of them. Nevertheless, as elsewhere in India and perhaps in all folk cultures, there are myths, legends, songs, jokes, and riddles which serve to entertain and instruct. There are also common themes, such as origins of the world, of humankind and different creatures, of foods and food taboos, of tribal customs and various institutions such as clans, marriage, and adolescent dormitories; the conflicts between brothers, parents and children, or in-laws; the problems of love and marriage; proper conduct and moral dilemmas. In many instances very similar elements and episodes are discernible across tribal cultures, but these often are shared by non-tribal peoples, so it is difficult to identify any broad characteristics which are distinctly "tribal."

A case in point is the widespread legend of Lingo Pen. There are many versions of this myth among the Goṇḍs and other related tribal people of central India. It explains variously the origins of the world, the gods, ethnic groups and clans, and illustrates a basic conflict between elder and younger brothers. In one Muṛīā Goṇḍ version, the youngest of seven brothers was exiled due to the jealousy of the others. After performing various heroic feats, he was allowed back into the house. In gratitude he decided to help his brothers with their farm chores. He tied two buffaloes to a harrow with his own loin-cloth and, naked, climbed on the harrow and drove the buffaloes across the field to break the clods of earth. As he was driving the buffaloes back, he came face to face with his sisters-in-law who were bringing him his food. His *ling* (penis) stood up stout and strong before him, and when the girls saw it, they said, "Look how stout and strong is his ling; from today his name must be Lingo" (Elwin 1947, 241). The connection of this tribal god (*pen*) with the Hindu deity Śiva (usually represented by a *liṅga,* or phallic symbol), is evident, and has been noted by many folklorists.

References

Census of India. 1981. *Primary census abstract: scheduled tribes*. Series 1, Part 2B, Volume 3.

Culshaw, W. J. 1949. *Tribal heritage*. London: Lutterworth Press.

Elwin, Verrier. 1947. *The Muria and their Ghotul*. London: Oxford University Press.

———. 1950. *Myths of middle India*. London: Oxford University Press.

———. 1954. *Tribal myths of Orissa*. London: Oxford University Press.

Herrenschmidt, Oliver. 1966. *Le cycle de Lingal*. Paris: École des Hautes Études.

EDWARD J. JAY

SEE ALSO

Bangladesh; *Cait Parab; Dīvālī/Dīpāvalī;* Epic, Tribal, Central India; Elwin, Verrier, Tribal Communities, Northeast India; Tribal Music Nilgiris; Tribalism and Tribal Identity

TRIBAL MUSIC, NILGIRIS

The Nilgiris, a hill range running along the borders of the states of Tamilnadu, Kerala, and Karnataka host some fifteen tribal populations whose musical traditions are intricately linked with traditions of dance, verbal art, and ritual. Some small populations, like the Kotas and Todas, are unique to the Nilgiris; most of the others, Irulas, Kurumbas (of which there are many sub-groupings whose historical relation to one another is questionable), and Paniyas extend elsewhere into the states of Kerala, Karnataka, and Tamilnadu; nevertheless, an argument can be made for the Nilgiris as a tribal musical area.

Two systems of ritual interaction among tribes and castes were evident in the Nilgiris. Although these systems, particularly on the plateau, are nearly dissolved, their historical role has been significant in shaping musical life. The best-known economic, social, and ritual system involved the Badagas (an immigrant *jāti* cluster from Karnataka), Todas, Kotas, Irulas, and Kurumbas Ālu and Pālu).

Just as on the plains, where ritual musicians (especially drummers) tended to be lower in caste than their patrons, so too in the hills did lower-ranking tribal communities (Kotas, Irulas, Kurumbas) provide music for funerals and occasional functions of the ritually elite Todas and economically powerful Badagas. This system of interaction covered the Nilgiri plateau and involved trade with plainspeople through such Hindu communities as the Chettis (a trading caste). The Chettis would import a variety of items, the most prominent of which was cloth; after the advent of this trade, presumably, the Kota practice of weaving cloth from plant fiber became no more than a ritual remembrance. Some groups of Irulas and Kurumbas, living on the steep slopes of the Nilgiris, appeared to have participated in both plains and hill economic systems.

The Wynad, a region of Kerala lying along the foothills of the Nilgiris, hosts another hierarchically organized intertribal system. At the top of the system are the Wynad Chettis (a farming caste) and the Mullu Kurumbas (a cultivating and field-laboring tribe with a cultural history that includes hunting). These landowning communities employ Kāṭṭu Nāyakas (Jēnu Kurumbas) for field labor and Ūrāḷis for crafts (much as the Kotas on the plateau). The Paṇiyas were formerly bonded laborers and are still, unfortunately, treated as ritually and socially inferior.

Both in the plateau and foothill systems, the two communities vying for the top of the hierarchy ("top" as viewed, in part, from the perspective of the economically powerful, a view reinforced, to an extent, by colonial policy), the Todas and Badagas, and Mullu Kurumbas and Wynad Chettis, claim as their own traditions of oral performance (sung or chanted poetry, ritual formulai, prayers, songs) and movement (dancing, rhythmic stepping, and clapping). Communities such as the Badagas now play a variety of popular Indian instruments such as the harmonium, but they have expressed reservations about drums. Although these communities exhibit various responses to technological modernity and popular Hinduism, nothing really prohibits anyone from picking up an instrument. However, Nilgiri people consider the artisan and laborer communities of Kotas, Iruḷas, Kurumbas (other than Mullu), and Paṇiyas to be the indigenous instrumental musicians.

The unity of the Nilgiris as a musical area is demonstrated most strongly in its instrumental music—its ritual association, material, and structure—rather than in its songs and other forms of oral performance. All of the instrument-playing tribes share a basic music ensemble consisting of one or more frame drums, cylindrical drums, and shawm-types. The percussion ensembles exhibit some variety; the Paniyas, for example, employ a series of small hourglass-shaped pressure drums, and the Irulas of different regions include additional drums in their ensembles and omit others. Most of the shawm types feature six holes. The structure of the instrument limits pitch intonation to some extent, but the tonal systems also have a significant cognitive element because the reeds (made by the musicians themselves) allow for significant pitch fluctuation.

Diatonic melodies of more than four tones, or melodies employing common Indian forms of embellishment (folk, classical, or cinema music styles), are very difficult to play on these instruments. Portions of Kota instrumental melodies may appear to a Western ear as major or minor because the central pitches produced on the instrument outline intervals that are close to semitones and whole tones (the positions of these intervals vary depending on the piece). The upper range is squeezed, however, and thus the arrangement of tones in a given piece does not seem to "add up" in Western terms. It is not the difference between Kota and European systems that is interesting here, however, but the difference between Kota instrumental music and 1) mainstream forms of Indian subcontinental music, which in theory or practice are largely based on a twelve-fold division of the octave, and 2) Kota song, whose tonal system is nearly diatonic and is thus closer in some ways to other forms of Indian folk music.

Not surprisingly, melodic influence from cinema songs and popular folk genres has significantly penetrated Kota vocal music, but instrumental music almost not at all. However, there are instrumental pieces based on some of the simpler (four notes) vocal melodies in certain Kota genres of instrumental music—thus retaining the contour of the original composition if not the precise tonal relations. Some songs are also based on instrumental pieces. Yet there are a significant number of instrumental pieces that are not associated with songs per se, and this too is rather unique in the Indian context, where vocal, and thus textual, models are the norm. When these instrumental pieces are rendered vocally, for purposes of teaching or practice, vocables (gag, gaggil, lil lil, e, etc.) are employed. Vocables differ from tribe to tribe.

One of the peculiarities of the instrumental pitch arrangement is the lowest pitch, which usually lies somewhere between a major and minor third below the next pitch. This pitch, particularly in Kota music, serves a rhythmic function and punctuates sections between and within musical phrases. All of the pitches are subject to possible bending or ambiguity in intonation. The lowest pitch is sometimes given a great deal of weight, through pulsing air pressure on the reed, thus bending the pitch a few semitones. Instrumental music of all the tribes consists of discrete pieces (the word for instrumental piece in each language is the same as that for shawm), usually short (roughly one to twelve phrases), repeated continuously, with or without subtle variation, against one of several rhythmic ostinati.

The rhythmic ostinati are relatively homogeneous among all the tribes. The most important consist of ten beats (divided //.//././.) eight beats (/../../..), six beats (/.//..), and seven beats (/.//./.). The Kotas (and probably other tribes as well) have also incorporated a rhythm they believe to be Cakkiliyar (a Telugu-speaking scheduled caste) in origin of twelve beats (main beats articulated by the right hand on a frame drum are, for example, /././../.../); the interesting feature of these rhythms is that the former are used for indigenous Kota deities and the latter exclusively for the worship of Hindu deities—either those whose temples lie outside of Kota villages or those who have been adopted into Kota village pantheons.

Most ten-beat cycles and some eight-beat cycles accompany relatively slow melodies, some of them relatively long, and usually associated with an important ritual activity, not a dance. Other eight-beat cycles, and all those in six or seven beats are fast and tend to be associated with dance. The tessitura of Irula and Kurumba music is higher and the tempo more rapid than in Kota music. The performance of pieces associated with Kota men's dances is faster than those of the women.

All the tribes perform circle dances, usually gender-segregated in some way. Among the Kotas, a set of men's dances always precedes a set of women's dances. Women's song, dance, and play usually takes place at the end of long ritual cycles, or at the end of structural units within a complex ceremony. Some Paniya dances feature men in one circle and women in another; some Irula dances feature concentric circles of men and women. Most of the pieces in all these tribal repertoires are associated with the dance. The remaining pieces are attached to specific rituals, such as those associated with worship or death. The Kota system of melody/ritual relationships constitutes a hierarchized, highly differentiated moral and religious classification system. Other tribal music/ritual systems in the Nilgiris appear to be less complex (only four or five ritually associated melodies rather than twenty or thirty), possibly owing to economic degradation and hence severe time constraints on expressive culture. Yet the ritual/melodic systems should be viewed as part of a large regional musical culture because they articulate the same sorts of things—usually beginnings and endings, ritual perambulation between significant places, and spiritually transformational moments.

The Todas, Mullu Kurumbas, and Wynad Chettis perform forms of vocal performance that are quite unique. Toda singing style is characterized by raspy and guttural delivery of melodies that consist entirely of wide, undulatingly contoured pairs of balanced melodic phrases. There are three types of melodic song: men's songs (*po·ṭ* and *nöw*) and women's work songs (*ti·m*). A relatively homogeneous melodic style is now shared by men and women, and much has changed in recent years in the practice of music and dance, in the memory of old songs, and in the ability to compose new songs based on traditional formulai.

The primary distinction in oral performance style (disregarding textual content and ritual context) is between what Emeneau terms dance songs (*koṇ*) and melodic types; but the description of the koṇ as a dance song is slightly confusing in the present-day context because dances also accompany the performance of melodic songs. The koṇ is rendered less in a melody than in a formulaic shout with a distinct rhythmic character, of which there are two or three varieties. All the tribes in the Nilgiris, and even the Badagas, perform a similar kind of ritual chanting (syllable "ho ko" or "ho ho"), sometimes accompanied by a circle dance similar to that of the Todas. All these Nilgiri varieties of chanting (called *edykd* or "jumping" in Kota) appear similar in style, but, with few exceptions, only the Toda koṇ actually possesses textual content; thus, one might argue that the style originated in Toda performance and was adopted only in external form by others. The koṇ texts often recount the ritual procedure with which the performance is associated. Emeneau noted that in some cases a single text could be rendered as a *po·ṭ* using one particular melody, a nöw using another, and a koṇ by rendering it in the characteristic shouting style. Nowadays, the po·ṭ is considered the older, heavier, and rarer form of composition.

Mullu Kurumbas and Wynad Chettis also perform a distinct circle-dance and chanting form the Mullu Kurumbas call *vaṭṭakaḷi* (circle-art). This dance-chant is performed exclusively by men who step in a circle around a sacred lamp, at first slowly, and gradually increasing in speed until finally unable to hold together in a circle. These two communities also perform several types of stick dance around the lamp.

Paṇiyas appear to be unique to the area in that they once practiced an indigenous form of drama in their own language. (Recent efforts have been made to revive this dramatic form). The songs associated with drama are called *nāḍagapāṭu* and *kuratipāṭu*. Kotas of the now nearly defunct village of Kurgo·j in the modern town of Gudalur used to perform Tamil drama.

References

Aiyappan, A. 1992. *The Paniyas: an ex-slave tribe of south India*. Calcutta: Institute of Social Research and Applied Anthropology.

Deva, B. C. and J. Kuckertz. 1978. Songs of the Todas of the Nilgiris. *Sangeet Natak* 50: 5–25.

Emeneau, Murray B. 1971. *Toda Songs*. Oxford: Oxford University, Clarendon Press.

Gramophone records of the languages and dialects of the Madras presidency. 1927. Records and Text of Passages, pp. 22–50; plate nos. 122–131. Madras: Government Museum.

Kuckertz, J. 1973. Music and dance in the Nilgiris. *Bulletin of the Ramakrishna Mission Institute of Culture,* Feb 24(2): 54–59.

Wolf, Richard K. I. P. Rain, God and unity among the Kotas. In *Blue Mountains revisited: cultural studies of the Nilgiris,* ed. Paul Hockings. Delhi: Oxford University Press.

———. Forthcoming. Three perspectives on music and the idea of tribe in India. [*Asian Music*]

———. Forthcoming. Of God and death: music in ritual and everyday life, a musical ethnography of the Kotas of south India. Ph.D. Diss. School of Music, University of Illinois at Urbana-Champaign.

———. 1990–1992. The Richard Wolf Collection [video and audio recordings of Nilgiri music and dance]. Archives and Research Center for Ethnomusicology, Defence Colony, Delhi.

Zvelebil, Kamil. 1982. *The Irula language, part III: Irula lore, texts and translations*. Wiesbaden: Otto Harrassowitz.

RICHARD KENT WOLF

SEE ALSO
Tribal Communities, Southern India

TRIBALISM AND TRIBAL IDENTITY: THE BHĪLS OF WESTERN CENTRAL INDIA

Contemporary Bhīls are a diverse ethnic group of several million people in Gujarat, Madhya Pradesh, Maharashtra, and Rajasthan. They engage in many different occupations in both urban and rural settings, although they are primarily agricultural workers and laborers. Many social and economic activities in Bhīl communities are based on kinship and lineage connections; marriages are generally arranged between Bhīl *jāti* members, as determined through male lineages, in other villages. Life cycle rituals and religious festivals are enacted within these local clusters of related villages and lineages. Contemporary Bhīls generally self-identify as Hindus, and incorporate Hindu rituals, myths, and deities into localized religious practices. Gavarī, a forty-day religious performance cycle of Bhīls and Bhīl Minas in Rajasthan's Udaipur district, illustrates this blending of local Bhīl beliefs and rituals with Hindu deities and epic stories.

The designation "Bhīl" is controversial and laden with myths and stereotypes of tribal identity in India. The widely held assumption that contemporary people designated as Bhīls are the descendants of ancient indigenous South Asians is based largely on references in the *Mahābhārata* and *Rāmāyaṇa* to short, dark skinned, forest dwellers. The English language translations of these Sanskrit texts influenced colonial discourse that subsequently linked these mythic forest dwellers to contemporary Bhīls. In the nineteenth and early twentieth centuries, Tribals were generally categorized as a "race" consistent with prevailing assumptions about phenotypic (physical) and linguistic characteristics. Although all the observers of Bhīl communities throughout Central Western India during this period noted physical, economic, and linguistic diversity, as well as the physical resemblance of Bhīls to other local caste group members, the idea of the Bhīls as a separate race of people with distinct physical, linguistic, and social characteristics persists.

Scholars now suggest much more recent, localized processes of class-based differentiation to account for the separation and subsequent marginalization of Bhīls from caste-based Hindu society. Contemporary research challenges the assumption of the historical existence of "tribal" society in relation to its presumed opposite, "caste" society, and the presumed isolation of Bhīls from agricultural and entrepreneurial castes and classes. Evidence of economic interaction between Bhīls and merchants of other caste and religious groups pre-dates the colonial period, and often shows the Bhīls at a disadvantage in these commercial transactions. Bhīl agriculturalists historically practiced slash and burn, or swidden agriculture, and frequently relocated in small family groups. This may account for their subsequent social marginalization as well as their settlement patterns on less desirable hilltop farmland.

Historical research suggests that some Bhīl communities in pre-colonial India have a long history of political autonomy and secured alliances with dominant Rajputs in western central India. The historians of Rajasthan for example cite examples in which Bhīls fought in the armies of the Maharanas (Rajput ruling princes). In return for this military support they were given rewards of land over which they exerted total control, including the right to charge tolls to non-Bhīls traveling through their areas.

Flexibility in group self-designation terminology was reported by colonial census administrators and continues among contemporary Bhīls. In Rajasthan, tribal people may refer to themselves as Mīnās, a higher status tribal group, while outsiders believe them to be Bhīls; Gameti and Gameti-Bhīl are also terms of local self-designation which, due to their frequency of use, have been incorporated into census designations and the Government of India's Schedule of Tribes.

In some geographical areas of central India, Bhīls have politically mobilized around the identity of Ādivāsī, a pan-Indian term for tribals coined during the Independence movement, as well as around the identity category of Dalit which expresses alliance with other Scheduled Tribe and Scheduled Caste groups throughout India. In many parts of western India the right of access to forestland controlled by the state and national governments is linked to demonstration of tribal identity. These issues all demonstrate the ongoing economic and political significance of the categories of tribal and Bhīl, and their continuous renegotiation in light of contemporary national events.

References

Census of India. 1981. Special tables for scheduled tribes on mother tongue and bilingualism. Series 1, Part 9 vol. 2. New Delhi: Registrar General, Government of India.

Deliege, Robert. 1985. *The Bhils of western India: Some empirical and theoretical issues in anthropology in India.* New Delhi: National Publishing House.

Dowson, John. 1989 (1891). *A classical dictionary of Hindu mythology and religion, geography, history, and literature.* Calcutta: Rupa & Co.

Hardiman, David. 1987. *The coming of the Devi: Ādivāsī assertion in western India.* Delhi: Oxford University Press.

The Imperial gazetteer of India. 1908. New Edition. Oxford: Clarendon Press.

Webb, A. W. T. 1941. *These ten years: A short account of the 1941 census operations in Rajputana and Ajmer-Merwara.* Rajputana Census Volume XXIV–Part 1. Bombay: Census Department of India.

MAXINE WEISGRAU

SEE ALSO

Colonialism and Folklore; Epic, Tribal, Central India; Tribal Communities, Northeast India; Tribal Communities, Southern India; Tribal Folklore, Central India

TUKKĀ

Tukkā is a Nepali term referring to idiomatic expressions. It also can refer more broadly to proverbial phrases, comparisons, and conventional similes and metaphor. Hence a tukkā, which may be a compound word or a group of words, is a building block of aesthetic folk expression. Tukkā are frequently used as aesthetic devices in Nepali folk song and narrative.

An example of tukkā is *lāhure dāi,* formed from the words *lāhure* (a person from Lahore) and *dāi* (elder brother). When they are combined, they suggest a romantic and adventurous person: The phrase is (sometimes derogatorily) used by a girl to address a boy or lover who has just returned from a foreign land. Likewise bāramāse, formed from bāra (twelve) and *mās* (month), means "twelve months" or "all seasons." Hence the bāramāse songs describe the twelve months, or can be sung at any time of year. In another context *bāramāse phūl* may denote habiscus (*Hibiscus rosa-sinensis*), a common flower that blooms all year, or an everlastingly beautiful thing, such as beautiful young girl.

The real meanings of these figures of speech emerge from the context of the utterance, as in the following folk song:

Lāhuredāi kahā jāna ḍhalkeko?
Bāramāse phūl tipna palkeko.

Where is the romantic adventurer [*lāhure dāi*] going?
He loves to entice the beautiful girls [*bāramāse phūl*].

Some tukkā are popular and lasting; others appear, then go out of fashion. For example, the patriotic *Jaya deśa, jaya nareśa* (Hail to the Country, Hail to the Crown) went out of fashion in 1990 when the sovereignty of Nepal was transferred from the king to the people.

References

Bhattarai, Harihar P. 1985. Folklore studies in Nepal. *Himalayan Culture* 3, no. 1: 10–14.
Pradhan, Kumar. 1984. *A history of Nepali literature*. New Delhi: Sahitya Akademi.

HARIHAR P. BHATTARAI

TULSI (BASIL)

Virtually every account of popular Hinduism mentions the cultivation of the *tulsi* or sacred basil plant (*Ocymum sanctum,* linn.). Tulsi, "the incomparable one," is worshiped as a goddess in various regions across the length and breadth of India and is also known by more localized names as Hāriprīya (Hāri: a name of Viṣṇu; *prīya:* beloved), Viṣṇuprīya, Vṛṇda, Bruṇḍabati, Briṇḍa Devī, and Saili. (Here *tulsi* indicates the plant; Tulsi indicates the Goddess.) In addition to having ritual, purificatory uses, tulsi leaves are also thought to have medicinal properties, which include remedies for cough, asthma, malarial fever, and stress. Juice of the tulsi plant is also believed to keep away mosquitoes.

Tulsi is a consort of Viṣṇu and thus is a form of Mahalakṣmī—the Goddess of Good Fortune. Devotees of Viṣṇu may wear necklaces made of tulsi seeds. There are many mutually contradictory myths in Saṇskrit Purāṇas and in local folklore about how Viṣṇu and Tulsi came to be paired. While some of the Purāṇic myths describe Tulsi as originally having been the wife of a demon who was tricked by Viṣṇu, in women's oral variants she may be depicted as a virgin girl who chooses Viṣṇu (or Kṛṣṇa) as her spouse.

In many parts of India, the cultivation of the plant is associated with upper castes; the presence of a tulsi plant in the courtyard may thus be an index of caste status or aspirations. Often, women tend the household plant with regular watering, the muttering of incantations, and the lighting of lamps at specified times of year. Rich women's oral traditions cluster around the plant. In Kārttik (October-November) pious women may celebrate Tulsi's marriage. Though Tulsi is associated with the deity Viṣṇu in his form of a *sālagrāma* or sacred ammonite stone, married women are not supposed to touch this stone because, for them, their husband is their lord. In women's rituals the sālagrāma is substituted with other iconic forms of Viṣṇu. For the wedding, the plant may be dressed up as a bride, with a small image of Kṛṣṇa (a form of Viṣṇu) as her groom. This divine marriage opens the winter marriage season for humans.

References

Acworth, H. A. 1890–91. On the tulsi plant. *Journal of the Anthropological Society of Bombay* 2: 109–112.
Chandool, Sudha. 1976. Tulsi plant in Indian folklore. *Folklore* (Calcutta) 17: 107–114.
Gupta, S. L. 1964. Sacred plants in Hindu religion: tulsi. *India Cultures Quarterly* 21: 2–11.
Gupta, Shakti M. 1991. *Plant myths and traditions in India*. 2nd rev. ed. New Delhi: Munshiram Manoharlal Publishers.
Narayan, Kirin. 1995. How a girl became a sacred plant. In *Readings in Indian religion*, ed. Donald Lopez. Princeton University Press.
Sankar Sen Gupta, ed. 1965. *Tree symbol worship in India*. Calcutta: Indian Publications.

KIRIN NARAYAN

SEE ALSO

Gender and Folklore; Goddesses, Hindu; Marriage Ceremonies; *Purāṇa*

TURMERIC

Turmeric is the root of a plant (*Curcuma longa*) from the ginger family that is widely cultivated in India for its use as a dye, spice, and stimulant. Its name may be derived from the Sanskrit *kunkuma* (saffron), a belief supported by its application as an alternative to saffron for yellow dyes.

Because of its yellow color, turmeric is a sacred plant in Hindu beliefs and rituals. It plays a very important role in women's life cycle ceremonies in south India. The puberty ritual is a turmeric bathing ceremony. Because of its erotic significance, turmeric is used in wedding rites. Among the Tamils, married women wear *tāli,* a string smeared with turmeric and tied with a piece of turmeric, but widows are prohibited from using turmeric. On all occasions when *pūjā*—worship of the gods—is made, turmeric is a necessity. During an adoption ceremony, the new parents drink turmeric water as an important part of the ritual. Many south Indians customarily apply a bit of turmeric paste at the corner of a garment upon wearing it for the first time because they believe any dress marked with turmeric becomes auspicious. In addition, women apply turmeric paste to their faces.

Centuries ago, turmeric was offered to the gods when assigning a young sacred prostitute to a temple. The *Rāmāyaṇa* states that turmeric is one of the constituents of the *Arghya,* a respectful offering given to gods and elders. Among the Khonds in Bengal, human sacrifices were previously made in the cultivation of turmeric because of the belief that it could not have its deep color unless blood were poured.

Different kinds of turmeric are used for different kinds of purposes, and in different ways. Supernatural beings, particularly evil spirits, hate the smell of burning turmeric. In Bengal, this aversion is still sometimes used to test whether a person is an ordinary human or a ghost. In many parts of India married women dip their hands in turmeric water, then dab it lightly over their cheeks to avoid the infliction of evil spirits. Turmeric is also used in South India for various curative purposes: treating injuries, preventing diarrhea in children, curing coughs and sore eyes, and so forth.

A. CHELLAPERUMAL

SEE ALSO
Life Cycle Rituals

U

UKHĀN

Ukhān and *ahan,* derived from the Sanskrit words *upākhyāna* and *ākhyāna* (short story or episode), are the Nepali terms for "proverb." They are thought of as encapsulating knowledge culled from past human experiences. In fact, *ukhān hālnu* or *āhān hālnu* (to cite a proverb) means using the past as a guide to grasp the meaning of the current situation and to decide upon the appropriate course of action. Since human experiences are diverse, ukhān do not express a unified and single-minded collective consciousness or code of conduct for all of Nepali society; rather, they reflect different, and sometimes contradictory, views on the same subject. For instance, two proverbs regarding polygamy represent contradictory viewpoints: *Tīn goruko ko hal pakkā, duī joiko ghar pakkā* (Three oxen make plowing guaranteed [an extra ox, in case of emergency]. Similarly the presence of two wives ensures that a home will run smoothly, because one falls sick, the other will take care of the domestic chores). Similarly *Duī joīko poi, kunā pasī roi* (The husband of two wives has to cry in private. [He can get no sympathy; both his wives and others taunt him]).

In general ukhān are one sentence long, though they also can be shorter phrases or a couple of sentences or rhymes. Some ukhān are literal, while others are metaphorical. For instance, *Ki paḍhera jānincha, ki parera jānincha* (One learns either by studying or by experience) is a literal ukhān. A metaphorical one is *Ek hātle tālo bajdaina* (One hand cannot clap), which can be interpreted as "Cooperation is needed in any worthwhile effort." *Phūlko subās wariparo, māncheko subās ḍāḍā pārī* contains both literal and metaphorical elements. Literally it means "The fragrance of a flower is sensed only near it, but the fragrance of a person wafts across the mountain," but it is taken to mean that the fame of a person is recognized across his or her sociocultural and national boundaries.

Many ukhān have existed for centuries. New proverbs continue to arise, however, as people reflect upon the meanings of their experiences. *Cansmāḍāns* is a modern ukhān incorporating the English words "chance" and "dance." Literally it means "Dance whenever there is a chance," and figuratively that one should seize every opportunity.

References

Bhattarai, Harihar P. 1985. Folklore studies in Nepal. *Himalayan Culture* 3, no. 1: 10–14.

Lall, Kesar. 1985. *Nepalese book of proverbs*. Kathmandu: Sashi M. Shrestha.

Pradhan, Kumar. 1984. A *history of Nepali literature*. New Delhi: Sahitya Akademi.

HARIHAR P. BHATTARAI

SEE ALSO
Proverbs

'URS

For South Asian Muslims, an *'urs* (Arabic,"wedding") is the celebration of the anniversary, fixed according to the Muslim lunar calendar, of the union of the soul of a deceased saint with God at death. This event stands in contrast to *mīlād* (Arabic,"birthday"), the celebration of the birth of a Muslim saint, commonly observed in Western Asia and North Africa. The 'urs of a saint is typically celebrated over one to three days and begins with the laying on of a new cloth shroud over the cenotaph (tomb) by some high official, the singing of devotional songs such as *qawwālī* in the evening, and the distribution of food. Shops are set up in the shrine environs, selling various sweets, tape cassettes of devotional songs, perfume, toys, trinkets, and crockery. Many celebrations have an accompanying fair *(melā)* with carnival rides.

The 'urs of a major saint such as Data Ganj Bakhsh (Sayyid 'Alī Hujwīrī, d. 1072 C.E.) in Lahore, Pakistan, or Nizāmuddīn Awliyā (d. 1318 C.E.) in Delhi, India, is attended by Muslims from throughout South Asia. In the case of the former, many of the thousands attending the three-day event sleep in the streets surrounding the shrine, which are closed off for this purpose. The 'urs of Madho Lal Husayn is one of the largest in Lahore, and is celebrated concurrently with *Melā Cirāghān* (Festival of the Lights) at that location. It takes place on the first weekend of March, that is around the time of the Spring equinox, and is the only 'urs fixed by the solar calendar.

In Bangladesh, on the day of the *oras* (Bangla for Arabic 'urs), the inner sides of the *mājār* or shrine are washed with perfumes. The resident *pīr* or other enlightened persons drape the tomb with new cloth shrouds (Bangla *cādar* or *gilāp*), often beautifully embroidered on high quality local silk, and decorate the grave with flowers. The large gathering of devotees is expected to create an atmosphere of harmony and amity. The animals for sacrifice and other food offerings (called *mānat*), brought by both rich and poor, are prepared and consumed together as sanctified food (Bangla *tabārrak,* Arabic *tabārruk*). Offerings may take the form of cash money, goats, cows, buffaloes, chickens, fruit, or rice, depending on the means of the donor, and are often given as part of a vow connected with a request for help from the saint. Prepared dishes may include *khicuṛi* (rice mixed with pulses) or *biranī* (rice with meat and spices), both typical ritual foods. After the food is cooked, some of it is removed from the pot, and assembled devotees sit together to recite over it the *fātiḥa*, the opening verse of the Qur'ān, which also constitutes the Muslim profession of faith ("There is no God but God and Muhammad is His Prophet"), as a prayer of consecration. After the prayer is completed, this portion of the food is mixed into all the pots, thus making all the food tabārrak. The sanctified food is distributed among devotees and poor people.

People from all walks of life, irrespective of caste or religion, including politicians, bureaucrats, army officers, students, teachers, farmers, and rickshaw pullers, both give offerings and receive sanctified food. Eating this food is believed to purify mind and body, and to cure illness. Believers pray to the saint, not only on oras days but on shrine visits at all times of the year, for, among other things, success in business or in finding work, recovery from diseases, happiness in matrimony, and children. The mass gathering of the oras allows for the conversational exchange of information and ideas, spiritual and mundane. Touring musicians and those serving and working in the mājār also derive income from these events.

WAYNE R. HUSTED, SHAF IQUR RAHMAN CHOWDHURY, AND LAURI HARVILAHTI

SEE ALSO

Maulid; Melā; Pīr; Qawwālī; Shrines, Muslim; *Tabarrak*

UTTAR PRADESH

With well over 160 million residents, the state of Uttar Pradesh (UP) in northern India has a population that is larger than all but five countries in the world. Increasingly urban, almost thirty percent of its residents now live in cities, six of which contain more than one million people (Kanpur, Lucknow, Agra, Varanasi, Meerut, and Allahabad). Yet seventy percent of UP's residents remain in rural areas, mostly employed in farming. Education has slowly penetrated the rural countryside, but literacy remains low, with only forty-three percent of women and seventy percent of men considered to be literate. This vast population and rural/urban differences complicate any attempt to sketch the folklore of the region.

What is common across Uttar Pradesh are complex multicaste farming communities, many of which have distinctive caste-based folk traditions that vary from region to region, even within the state itself. In these rural (and their urban counterpart) communities, two social factors mark lines of cleavage in folk traditions: caste and gender (with its attendant rules of purdah, the seclusion of women).

Divisions along lines of caste (*jāti*) are common to both rural and urban areas. Rural communities often have twenty or more resident caste groups, with each locale having its own understanding of the hierarchical ranking of these groups. These rankings are based both on conceptions of purity/pollution and on economic and political power. Urban areas lose the sense of a community understanding of rank, though the broad outlines of rural ranking systems remain in these communities of migrants. Broadly conceived, there are a cluster of castes, mostly Brahman, at the top of local hierarchies (and also at the top of all visions of caste hierarchies in India). Some communities have groups, often landowners, that are classified as warriors (Kṣatriya). Whereas tradesmen are most common in the urban areas, many village communities also have a few Banya or Mahajan families, members of trading castes associated with the Vaiṣya *varna*. Below them are a large number of service castes (Śūdra), such as water carriers or grain parchers or shepherds, often ranked according to their economic clout. Lowest are numerous untouchable castes, such as leatherworkers and sweepers. Some communities have groups of Muslims that are locally thought of as castes. In both urban and rural UP, patterns of sociality are constrained by these caste differences, despite the highly nucleated villages and packed urban areas. Family connections, which are by definition caste-based, dominate the social lives of both men and women, but especially women.

Gender segregation is another facet of UP lifestyles that contributes to the distribution of folklore. Women and men lead highly segregated lives, with houses and courtyards being the domains of women, and lanes, verandahs, and fields being the domains of men. Upper caste rural communities follow strict rules of purdah, which mandate that women speak in whispers in front of male affines older than their husbands, that their faces be covered before these same men, and that they remain within the walls of house and courtyard, except for the daily trip to the village fields (which serve as a latrine). These strictures are lessened as a woman ages. Yet upper caste women's functions, such as song fests in honor of marriages or births, are filled with elderly women and teenage girls, as younger daughters-in-law are not allowed to move through the village lanes and attend these events. Hence, UP folklore is gender-based, with the traditions of males and females seldom common or crossing gender lines.

Nevertheless, vibrant traditions of male and female folk performances are found throughout both rural and urban UP. Both men and women, in separate groups, meet over fires in the winter, on verandahs in the summer, around events such as weddings and births, or just a rainy day or cold evening, to tell stories and sing songs. In addition, a number of more professional singers and performers (almost always men) entertain in folk theater, oral epic, curing ceremonies, or other religious events.

Folk performances follow the seasons and the ritual cycle, both of the annual calendar and the human life cycle. A few illustrative examples will demonstrate the wide range of folk performances in UP, and also the distinctions made by caste and gender.

Ritual Cycles

Ritual cycles are daily, weekly, monthly, and yearly. Daily folk rituals include offering the first bread of the day to the family's cow by the women of the house, or the high caste man's worship of the sun. Women are quite likely to celebrate weekly rituals, choosing the day of the week associated with the god or goddess they wish to honor. Typical is the worship of Santoshi Mā, the goddess of benevolence and prosperity. On Fridays women fast, tell her story (her *vrat kathā*) either from memory or by reading it from a cheap pamphlet bought in the bazaar, and worship her, often before a *tulsi* (basil) plant in their courtyards. Monthly rituals revolve around the named days of the month, and are often performed by elderly men or women or by women in urban households with greater leisure time. Annual cycle rituals include major events such as Holī or Dīvālī, with their separate gendered and caste traditions. For example, in western UP, men of the *kaci* caste (farmers or vegetable growers, often petty landowners) go to every house in their community where a death occurred during the previous year to sing a song called *anarya*. Singing anarya at Holī is believed to "cut the sorrow" of that family and allow them to reenter normal village life. Further, Holī is celebrated with a village bonfire in which Holikā, the demon aunt of Prahlād, is burned. Women, at least in much of UP, must light separate Holī fires in their courtyards because purdah rules forbid their participation in the communal event. Some cycles of folk ritual focus on women's concerns for and power over family prosperity, especially that of male kin.

Human life cycles also provide a myriad of occasions for folk events, especially for women who are excluded from the male-dominated Sanskrit-based core ritual events. (Note that many Muslim women participate in traditions that mirror those of Hindu women.) These include numerous song fests that celebrate bride (*varnī*) or groom (*varnā*) and articulate women's concerns about the changes occurring in their families. These song fests are also sites where women contest the conditions of their lives. Numerous genres of wedding songs exist, some named for specific ritual events of the wedding process.

Another set of folk performances is more tied to the annual cycle. Both the heat of summer and the cold of winter provide time for storytelling and song. Groups of men, from a number of different families or even castes, often gather around fires in the lanes on cold evenings and share songs or stories. Women of a single household will warm themselves around fires in their courtyard, or perhaps with women from a nearby house that can be reached without going in the lanes. In the summer heat or monsoon rains, men and women gather indoors to stay cool or dry. If a community has a renowned resident singer, he might be called upon to sing an epic such as *Ḍholā* or *Ālhā*. Women have several named genres of song associated with the rainy season, such as *malhar* or *sāvan*. Men are more likely to sing genres like *kajri* or *bārahmasī* (songs of the twelve months).

Curing Rituals

Several forms of folklore revolve around curing rituals. One common form involves cures for snake bite, sometimes just evoking a ritual saying (*mantra*) or sometimes by a ritual such as *ḍank,* involving drums, singing, and a lower caste male ritual specialist who acts as the exorcist, for the snake is believed to possess his victim. Various folk medicines exist, ranging from cooling a fever victim's body with leaves of the neem tree to elaborate possession rituals for mental illness.

Finally, a number of wandering mendicants traverse both city and countryside, singing songs in praise of god and surviving off of donations from local households. Other times a community or family may hire a folk opera troupe to perform, such as a *nauṭanki* group or a "ḍhola company." Other times a expert in religious traditions is hired to expound on a particular text or epic. Finally, many communities, both urban and rural, organize and perform their own versions of the story of the god Rāma, the Rām Līlā, every October in the ten to thirty days leading up to the festival of Dásahrā. The most famous of these is the thirty-day Rām Līlā organized by the Maharaja of Banaras.

Globalization

Nowadays, many of these events are transformed through processes of globalization (or universalization as this process was known earlier). Some have moved through print into audio cassettes, while others were directly transferred to audio cassettes. Some folk practices, such as the ritual cleansing of a floor by smearing it with cow-dung prior to a ritual, have given way in urban areas to cement and tile floors, and modern cleaning products. Some new practices have crept into middle-class practices, such as the Western birthday party, but with decidedly local overtones such as anointing the birthday child with a *tika* (a ritual mark made on the forehead with rice and turmeric) and an egg-less birthday cake made of an Indian halva-like sweet, though decorated with candles to be blown out and "Happy Birthday" written in pink frosting. Yet despite these changes, the folk traditions of UP remain heavily influenced by caste and gender divisions.

References

Crooke, William. 1896. *The popular religion and folk-lore of northern India.* A new edition, revised and illustrated. London: A. Constable & Co.

Gold, Ann Grodzins. 2000. From Demon aunt to gorgeous bride: Women portray female power in a north Indian festival cycle. In *Invented identities: The interplay of gender, religion and politics in India,* ed. Julia Leslie and Mary McGee, 203–230. South Asia: Understandings and Perspectives Series. Delhi: Oxford University Press.

Henry, Edward O. 1988. *Chant the names of God: Music and culture in Bhojpuri-speaking India.* San Diego: San Diego State University Press.

Manuel, Peter. 1993. *Cassette culture: Popular music and technology in north India.* Chicago: University of Chicago Press.

Marriott, McKim. 1955. Little communities in an indigenous civilization. In *Village India: Studies in the little community, Papers by Alan R. Beals (and others),* ed. McKim Marriott. Chicago: University of Chicago Press.

Raheja, Gloria Goodwin, and Ann Grodzins Gold. 1994. *Listen to the heron's words: Reimagining gender and kinship in north India.* Berkeley: University of California Press.

Wadley, Susan S. 2000. From sacred cow dung to cow "shit": Globalization and local religious practices in rural north India. *Journal of the Japanese Association for South Asian Studies* 12: 1–28.

———. 2001. Popular Culture and the North Indian Oral Epic *Dhola. Indian Folklore Research Journal* 1(1): 13–24.

SUSAN WADLEY

SEE ALSO

Ālhā (Ālhā-Ūdal); Bārahmasā; *Candaini (Lorik-Candā); Ḍhola; Dīvālī/Dīpāvalī;* Gender and Folklore; *Holī; Tulsi* (Basil); *Vrat Kathā;* Wedding Songs

V

VĀGHYĀ/MURAḶĪ

Vāghyā and *Muraḷī* are Maharashtrian devotees of Khaṇḍobā, the pastoral deity known by the name of Mailāra in Karnataka and Mallāṇṇā in Andhra Pradesh, who has come to be identified with Śiva. Vāghyā is a male child and Muraḷī is a female child offered to Khaṇḍobā for life. Parents with several children often offer one of them to Khaṇḍobā as an act of piety but also to reduce need. Such children are called *khāndānī Vāghye* (high born). Men keen to serve the god who also devote themselves this way from childhood are called *hause Vaghye* (volunteer Vāghye). Those given to Khaṇḍobā in fulfillment of *navasa* (vow) are called *navase Vaghye*. The same applies to Muraḷis. The Vāghyā/Muraḷī tradition is also found in Karnataka and parts of Andhra Pradesh.

The ritual of offering a male child is performed in the month of Caitra (April). The child is taken to Khaṇḍobā temple, where a Gurav priest applies turmeric to his forehead, ties a bag full of turmeric around his neck, and asks the god to accept the child as a Vāghyā. In the making of a Muraḷī, the girl undergoes the marriage ceremony with the icon of Khaṇḍobā in the presence of all her relations. After the wedding, her head is shaved and she spends the rest of her life with Vāghyās as her brothers. While some Muraḷīs prefer to stay at the temple, others roam the country singing praises of Khaṇḍobā and begging for survival. During the months of April and May, when most Hindu weddings take place, the Vāghyās and Muraḷīs get many assignments to perform the *jāgaraṇa* (staying awake all night). This observance is not unlike a *gondhaḷa,* in that the performers dance the whole night, sing praises of Malhāri Mārtaṇḍa (another name of Khaṇḍobā) and tell purāṇic stories about the god. They may also perform acts of mortification such as standing on boards studded with sharp nails or beating themselves with leather thongs. The highlight of the evening is the breaking of an iron chain (*langara*) tied to a crowbar. The host then gives them money and other presents. Vāghyā-Muraḷī performances are also done during the Khaṇḍobā *jātrā*s (annual festivals).

Vāghyā and Muraḷī have a wide repertoire of songs. The humorous ones often describe the constant bickering between Khaṇḍobā's co-wives. Others such as the one below are descriptive of the Muraḷī's ecstatic existence.

My pot is full of turmeric and kumkum
I have become the Muraḷī of Khaṇḍobā
Having taken the turmeric of devotion
I have followed the god
I shout "Jaya Malhāra"
I become the Muraḷī of Khaṇḍobā

My parents made this vow
They offered their daughter to Malhāri
The sweetness of his name is exceptional
I become the Muraḷī of Khaṇḍobā

I look only at him
My five lives are with him
I throw turmeric on the yellow flag
I become the Muraḷī of Khaṇḍobā

All my relationships are with god only
He ordered me to come here
He is always near me
I become the Muraḷī of Khaṇḍobā

JAYANT BHALCHANDRA BAPAT

SEE ALSO
Gondhaḷa; Goravā/Goramma; Mailāra/Mallanna/ Khandoba; Turmeric

VEDDAS [VĂDDO]

The Veddas of Sri Lanka, whose origins may be traced to the Old Stone Age, have retained their physical and cultural distinctiveness from the other communities, including Sinhalese, Tamil, and Muslim. Comparison of the genetic and cultural traits of the Veddas with those of similar "relict" communities in South Asia has shown that they are part of the group of Australoid peoples found from Southeast Asia down to Australia.

Sinhalese historical chronicles trace the origin of the Veddas to the miscegenous union of the progeny of Vijaya, the leader of the first Indo-Aryan immigrants, and Kuveni, a princess of the superhuman *yakkha* who previously inhabited the island. This imputed high birth of the Veddas has drawn respect from the other communities and has helped them maintain a racial and cultural distinctiveness for over two millennia.

According to the Sri Lankan census of 1881, there were 2,228 Veddas out of a total population of 2.7 million. Two-thirds of them lived in the forest regions of Uva, Bintenna, and Polonnaruwa, with the remainder along the east coast. Later census figures indicate a gradual decline in numbers until they reached four hundred in 1963. Thereafter they were grouped with other small communities in the category "other races." Today only a few Vedda families remain at Dambana, near Mahiyangana; at Ratugala, near Monerangala, in the majority Sinhalese area; and in a few villages on the east coast, such as Vakarai.

Văddā (plural *văddo*) is a Sinhala word meaning "user of bow and arrow." The Veddas call themselves *Vanniyalātto,* meaning "forest dwellers." Traditionally the Veddas were hunter-gatherers, and there is evidence that this way of life was retained by some until the early twentieth century. Veddas hunted with bow and arrow and a small pickax. They occasionally fished by using poisonous herbs in water holes. They prepared meat by roasting or baking it, rather than boiling. Honey was a favorite food. The staple starch food was the wild yam, harvested with a digging stick. Of late the Veddas have adopted slash-and-burn agriculture to grow rice and *kurakkan* (Indian millet).

Until the early twentieth century many Veddas lived in rock caves. Socially they were grouped into nonhierarchical clans (*variga*), such as Morana (a fruit), Ambela (ant), and Uuru (wild boar). Although the *variga* were not hierarchical like the castes found among the Sinhalese and the Tamils, a preference for cross-cousin marriage led to clan endogamy.

Traditionally Vedda women gave birth in the caves, with the help of midwives. There were no puberty ceremonies or beliefs in pollution (*kili*) at birth and menstruation, as is the case with the Sinhalese and the Tamils. Marriage was contracted by gift exchange. Funeral ceremonies were minimal; the body was covered with leaves at the site of death; if the person had died in a cave, it was abandoned for a period of time.

Traditional Vedda religion consists largely of ancestor worship. The deceased join the ranks of "relative deities" (*nâl yaku*), whose presiding deity is Kande Yaka (mountain god). There are several other leading deities, including the chief female deity, Indigolle Kiriamma (grandmother of Indigolle [a place]). The most prominent ritual in the Vedda religion is *kiri koraha* (vessel of milk), performed annually to appease the ancestors. Other rituals, related to specific occasions, include *añguru mas yahana* (bed of embers and meat), a thanksgiving ritual following a successful hunt; *pattayak* (deity of the bark), a ceremony for safety during pregnancy; and *doleyak* (deity of streams), a ceremony before a honey-gathering excursion.

Today the Veddas speak a creole language whose base is Sinhalese, with an admixture of phonological, grammatical, and lexical features of the original Vedda language. The coastal Veddas have adopted the Tamil language.

References

Deraniyagala, S. U. 1992. *The prehistory of Sri Lanka*. Colombo: Department of Archaeology Survey.

Dharmadasa, K. N. O. 1974. The creolization of an aboriginal language: The case of Vedda in Sri Lanka. *Anthropological Linguistics* 16, no.1: 79–106.

Ellepola, S. B. 1990. A genetic analysis of the Veddas. In *The vanishing aborigines: Sri Lanka's Veddas in transition*, ed. K. N. O. Dharmadasa and S. W. R. de A. Samarasinghe. New Delhi: Vikas.

Goonetilleke, H. A. I. 1960. A bibliography of the Veddah: The Ceylon aboriginal. *Ceylon Journal of Historical and Social Studies* 3, no. 1: 96–106.

Seligman, Charles Gabriel, and Brenda Seligman. 1911. *The Veddas*. Cambridge: Cambridge University Press.

K. N. O. DHARMADASA

VEHICLE PAINTING

The painted vehicle is a prominent venue for the expression of both individuality and popular sentiment throughout the subcontinent. Although the particular standards of content and expression vary widely by region and culture, the importance of vehicle painting as a popular art form has grown everywhere.

The modern practice of vehicle painting has its aesthetic roots in the simple embellishment of cart handles and wagon wheels, as well as in the tradition of elaborately decorating wagons, carriages, animal harnesses, and draft animals themselves, for such auspicious occasions as weddings and religious pilgrimages. Today, however, vehicle painting is no longer limited to

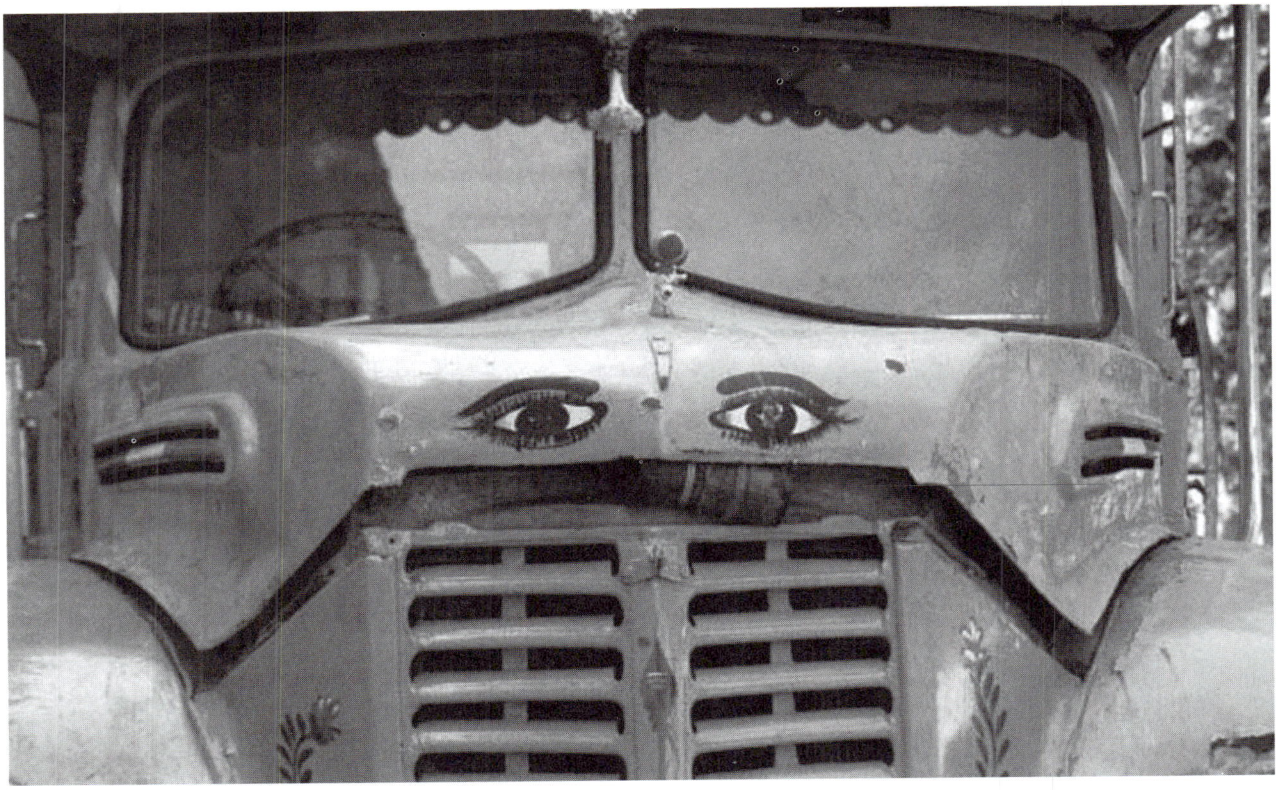

Painted truck. Kochi, Kerala, India, © Richard Rapfogel

special or ceremonial occasions. Commercially owned vehicles in daily use—tongas, rickshaws, buses, and cargo trucks—commonly bear designs intended to reflect the aesthetic tastes, personalities, attitudes, and political opinions of their owners and drivers.

Some of the most elaborate forms of vehicular art are the large trucks particularly prevalent in Pakistan and Afghanistan. There, the history of the flourishing popular art genre parallels that of the trucking industry itself. The earliest pictorial representations began to appear on trucks with the expansion of the trucking industry on an interprovincial scale during the early 1950s. Calligraphers, originally hired only to paint license numbers and legal payload limits on trucks, introduced such motifs as the ribbon and globe, bearing the name and telephone number of the owner, to symbolize interprovincial transport and its more worldly character. This rapidly grew to more elaborate painting and decoration as a means of conspicuously displaying the success and wealth of truck owners. Much impetus also came from the eventual elevation of the truck driver himself to the status of popular folk hero, a romantic, foot-loose figure traveling far and wide, across sun-backed deserts and through mountain passes to link the towns and villages of Pakistan.

Today, a fully adorned truck results from the work of up to nine specialists, beginning with the carriage-maker, who adds to the truck chassis a towering walled bed constructed of sheet metal, pine and rosewood, and carved rosewood cab doors. Other specialists add etched and painted mirror to the doors, upholster the cab interior with leather and colored vinyl appliques, install colored lights and translucent panels, apply hammered brass and chrome exterior trim, add wrought-iron designs and good luck charms, and apply a paint undercoat.

The truck carriage is generally divided into four decorative planes. Each of two towering sides, averaging between fourteen and sixteen feet long and up to seven feet high, is divided into narrower panels by vertical and horizontal iron supports required for excessively heavy payloads. Though of suitable mural size, each side typically houses up to twenty miniature representations from the secular world of wild animals, jet aircraft, ocean liners, and idyllic country scenes. Each scene includes its own painted frame, and is thus not a direct representation of nature, but a painting of a painting. The most common sources of inspiration for the miniature scenes are the stock of postcards, bazaar posters, photographs, and English-language children's story and alphabet books shared between artists. It is by way of the particular selection, layout, and execution of scenes that the artist's persuasive influence and reputation are expressed.

Another design area is the upper portion of the tailgate, composed of lumber slats arranged horizontally, with runners on each end to facilitate removal. This area is usually dedicated to a mural size representation of an idyllic landscape, a painting of a truck on a country road, or less often the Muslim hero 'Alī's horse, Duldul, or the winged being *Al Buraq*. Beneath the rear mural may be a traditional proverb or two, a few fancy calligraphed verses from Iqbal or another poet-hero, some humorous jibes such as "Move you Rattletrap," and a blessing from Allah. Beneath these often hang tin representations of fish or other amulets for good luck.

The most sacred area of the truck is the wooden overhang above the driver's cab. There one typically finds representations of the mosque of the holy city of Medina and the Kaaba stone of Mecca, as well as the Kalīma (Islamic profession of faith) and one or more verses from the Holy Qur'ān. If space does not suffice, Qur'ānic verses may be reduced to mere reference numbers. Amulets to ward off the Evil Eye frequently adorn the sacred space, sometimes illuminated for night time driving.

Though denigrated by some indigenous scholars as a "true *ars vulgaris*" (H. Khan 1975: 187) and ignored by others as neither traditional nor pristine, the ever-present painted truck constitutes a highly visible folk art edifice. It articulates a mixture of religious and popular icons, of traditional sayings, romantic verses, and images of modernity, creating a juxtaposition of the sacred and the secular otherwise not commonly seen in South Asia.

References

Centlivres-Demont, M. 1976. *Popular art in Afghanistan: Paintings on trucks, mosques, and tea houses*. Graz, Austria: Druck.

Khan, Hasan-Uddin. 1975. Mobile shelter in Pakistan. In *Shelter, sign and symbol,* ed. Paul Oliver, 183–196. London: Barrie & Jenkins.

Kirkpatrick, Joanna and Kevin Bubriski. 1994. Transports of delight: Ricksha art of Bangladesh. *Aramco World* 45(1): 33–35.

Rich, George W. and Shahid Khan. 1980. Bedford painting in Pakistan: the aesthetics and organization of an artisan trade. *Journal of American Folklore* 93(369): 257–275.

GEORGE W. RICH

SEE ALSO
Muslim Folklore

VERBAL DUELING

Verbal dueling, or competitive oral exchanges of witticisms—usually delivered in rhyme—covers a wide gamut in South Asia, drawing upon a variety of folk styles and a diversity of topics, ranging from the romantic to the political. The duelists can be professional poets and folk singers, as well as the common villagers, including women, who have a high degree of verbal dexterity and skill in coming up with appropriate retorts to provocative insults. Since cheers from supporters of the respective contending groups are an essential part of such duels, the performances are held in public on occasions such as festivals, wedding ceremonies, and cultural soirees especially organized for competition among poets. The duelists take on pairing roles of lovers, rivals, or political or religious contestants.

In Bengali folk culture (which is shared by both Bangladesh and the neighboring Indian state of West Bengal), the most widespread form of such extempore versification of retorts is *tarja.* This was institutionalized by an elaborate set of rules in the eighteenth and nineteenth centuries in the form of *kobir ladai* (contests between poets), which became a highly popular form of folk entertainment, giving rise to well-known songwriters and versifiers called *kobial*s such as Horu Thakur (1738–1808), Nityananda Boiragi (1751–1818), Ram Bosu (1787–1829), and their contemporaries Bhola Moira, Antuny Firingi, and the poetess Jogyeshwari. Antuny Firingi was a Portuguese man named Hensman Antony, who adopted local social and religious manners and acquired enough command over the Bengali language to be a force to reckon with in the kobir ladais. In one such contest, Ram Bosu made fun of Antuny's self-righteous devotion to the Hindu deity Kṛṣṇa in the following couplet.

Saheb, mithye tui Kṛṣṇa-padey matha mudali,
O tōre padri saheb shuntey peley galey debey chunkali!

It is in vain, white man, that you shaved your head to show respect to the god Krishna.
If your Christian priest hears of it, he will blacken your face!

Antuny retorted with a syncretistic interpretation of religious unity by playing on the Bengali pronunciation of both Christ and the Hindu deity as *Krishta:*

Khrishtey aar Krishtey kichhu probhed nairey, bhai
Shudhu namer pherey manush pherey, eo kotha shuni nai!

Dear brother, there's no difference between Christ and Krishna.
I haven't ever heard of people running after mere differences of names.

Antuny then added, using another name of Kṛṣṇa's—Hari:

Amar Khoda jey̆, Hindu Hari shey—

The One who is my God is the same Hari of the Hindus
(verse quotations from Mitra 1962: 1054–55)

While kobir ladai today primarily remains a Bengali rural entertainment, the popularity of the poetic contest known as *mushā'ira* is mainly urban, cutting across class and religious barriers among the Urdu-speaking population of both north India and Pakistan. Here, two poets or groups exchange couplets back and forth, each being required to respond with a couplet, usually composed around a single word or syllable found in the opponent's couplet. A typical example is the following exchange between two famous rival poets of nineteenth century Lucknow, the first couplet being on a woman's face by Khvaja Haidar Ali Atish (1774–1846) and the second by Shaikh Imam Baksh Nasikh (1771–1838).

Zakhm-i dil bharta hai jalva chahra-i pur nūr kā
Chāndnī men yāñ asar hai marham-i kāfūr kā

The sight of that lustrous face heals my wounded heart.
Glowing moonbeams soothe like dressings soaked in camphor.

Nasikh responded by taking off from the word *nūr* (light):

Kyā asar merī siyah-bakhtī ke āge nūr kā
Māh hai ik khāl-i rukhsāra shab-i daijūr kā

What use is radiance in the face of my black fate?
The moon is but a mole on the cheek of winter's longest, darkest night.
(Petievich 1992: 153)

Women play an important role in verbal dueling during wedding ceremonies in the form of songs that make fun of the bride's and groom's parties, such as the *sanjina gīt* and *fatana* among the Gujarati-speaking population of western India, and in songs of courtship which involve exchanges between the lovers, such as those between the *Lahuray* and *Maruni* in Nepal.

Whether as an exclusive form of poetic contests, such as kobir ladai and *mushā'ira,* or as a part of a ritual, such as wedding songs, verbal dueling in South Asia is marked by certain common characteristics—competition in boasting, exchange of abuses, vivid imagery, instant improvisation, and appropriate selection of retorts from a vast reservoir of inherited knowledge of myths and allegories.

References

Edwards, Viv and Thomas Sienkewicz. 1990. *Oral cultures. Past and present.* Malden, Mass.: Basil Blackwell.
Mitra, Sudhir Chandra. 1962. *Hugli jelar itihash* (History of the Hugli district). Calcutta: Mitrali Prakashan.
Petievich, Carla. 1992. *Assembly of rivals. Delhi, Lucknow and the Urdu ghazal.* Delhi: Manohar.
Sharma, Man Mohan. 1982. *Folklore of Nepal.* New Delhi: Vision Books.

Sumanta Banerjee

SEE ALSO
Cait Parab; Munazira; Mushā'ira; Qawwālī; Riddle, Balochi; Riddle, Nepal; *Silok;* Song, Bengal; Syncretism; Tibet

VESSANTARA

The story of the Buddha's penultimate birth as the Bodhisttava Vessantara, whose unstinted generosity led him to give away his children and wife, has captured the folk imagination throughout the Buddhist world. Depicted in temple murals, popular art, folk poetry, and drama, it permeates Buddhist culture in the way Homer's work permeates European culture.

Vessantara succeeds his father as king of Sivi and immediately orders that the kingdom's treasury be opened to the needy. The populace rejoices, but when he gives away the country's greatest treasure, an elephant with magic powers, they are angry and demand his exile. He is banished, and leaves for the Vaṅka forest with his wife, Queen Maddī (who insists on accompanying him with their children, Jāli and Kaṇhājinā). There they live as ascetics. One day, while Maddī is in the forest gathering food, Jūjaka, a cruel and ugly Brahman arrives and asks for the children as slaves for his wife. Hard though it is, and steeling himself against the pleading of the children, Vessantara grants the Brahman's request.

When Queen Maddī returns, she finds the children missing and her husband silent. Wracked by grief, she searches the forest for them. Finally, exhausted and distraught, she collapses at Vessantara's feet. He revives her and tells her what he has done, and why. She accepts the act as necessary for Buddhahood and for the salvation of suffering humanity. Meanwhile the god Sakra, concerned that another supplicant may ask for Queen Maddī, intervenes. Disguised as an old man, he asks for the queen. When she is given to him, he reveals himself and restores her to Vessantara. He also intervenes by magically directing Jūjaka to the kingdom of the children's grandparents, where they are bought back at great cost. Jūjaka, enjoying his sudden wealth, dies of overeating. Vessantara's father regrets his order of banishment, and sets out with a great retinue to recall his son. Vessantara and Maddī return, and rule over the land.

In Sri Lanka a moving folk poem on the mother's lament over the loss of her children is sung at funerals, especially over the coffin of a dead child.

References

Keith, A. B. 1928. *History of Sanskrit literature.* Oxford: The Clarendon Press.

Sarach chandra, E. R. 1966. *The folk drama of Ceylon.* Colombo: Dept. of Cultural Affairs.

Spiro, Melford E. 1970. *Buddhism and society.* New York: Harper & Row.

Vessantara Jātaka. 1907. Translated by E. B. Cowell and W. H. D. Rouse. Cambridge: Vol. 6.

Vessantara Jātaka. 1964 [1896]. Edited by V. Fausboll. Pali Text Society, vol. 6.

RANJINI OBEYESEKERE

SEE ALSO

Buddhism and Buddhist Folklore; *Jātaka* Tales

VĪTHI NĀṬAKAM

In classical texts the term *vīthi* (or *vīdhi*) *nāṭakam* (street play, or street drama) appears to have referred to a specific form of Sanskrit drama, but today, in the rural areas of Andhra Pradesh, it is used as a general term to refer to a broad range of open-air dance/drama forms. The use of the term in the sense of folk drama was probably introduced by Viraśaivas sometime in the fifteenth century, and the broad classificatory use of the term probably has a scholarly origin. The formal characteristics—staging, props, costume, acting method, and some of the characters (for example, a stage manager and a clown), musical instruments (the two-headed wooden *maddela* drum, cymbals, and harmonium) and the presence of a chorus—are common to all of the forms. It is primarily in the core repertoire of their stories and in the caste of the performers that they differ.

Most of the forms are associated with a particular caste. The specific traditions are inherited within families and belong to a hereditary subsection of the larger caste or to a separate, dependent caste, which is closely associated with that of the patron caste. In either case, each drama tradition specializes in the mythological stories (*purāṇa*) of a particular caste. The dependent castes are itinerant troupes who spend a portion of the year traveling to villages where there are members of patron castes. Although the series of performances they present in a given village may include a variety of stories drawn from regional and pan-Indian epic traditions, the presentation of the caste purāṇa is both mandatory and a right (*hakku*) and will include worship of the patron caste's ancestral deities (*kula dēvata*). During their stay in the locality, they may demand by right that the patron community gives them room and board and a gift in kind and cash at the end of the series. Other communities in the village may also give them gifts, but as a token of their appreciation rather than by right.

Cindu Bhāgavatam, for example, is a form of *vīthi nāṭakam* (street drama) exclusively performed by the Cindu Māḍiga, a subset of the Māḍiga caste, which many other castes regard as untouchable. A story performed only for Māḍiga caste patrons is called the *Jāmba Purāṇam,* but other stories from the *Mahābhārata* and *Rāmāyaṇa* are performed for the general public and is called *cindu yakṣagānam.* Although most of the characters are played by male actors, one, Ellamma, is always played by a woman in Jāmbapurāṇam.

The form known as *Cencu Nāṭakam* is performed only by the Cencu, a tribe found in the region surrounding the Nallamallai Hills in central Andhra Pradesh. They specialize in performing the story of Cencu Lakṣmi, a regional extension of the story of Narasiṃha, one of the ten incarnations (*avatārās*) of Viṣṇu, one of the central gods of Hinduism. In the pan-Indian version, Viṣṇu took the ferocious form of a being half man, half lion, to kill the seemingly invincible demon Hiraṇyakasyapa. After this was accomplished, the other gods feared that Narasimha, himself, might destroy the world with his ferocity. They appealed to Lakṣmi, Viṣṇu's wife, to "cool" him. She incarnated herself as the daughter of a Cencu king. Lured into her forest kingdom, Narasimha fell in love with her, and, under the power of her domesticity, he was finally controlled. Lakṣmi and Viṣṇu resumed their original form, and the world returned to normal.

Similarly, *Yānādi Bhāgavatam* is a drama form of the Yānādi community, a tribe from the region of Guntur and Chittur Districts. The speciality of this form is that it allows Yānādi women to become actors.

One of the most distinctive forms in the category of *vīthi nāṭakam* is the *Kuppam Sampradāyam Vīthi Nāṭakam* of Chittoor District. Performed over a ten-day period annually, its only story is that of the great war between the Pāṇḍavās and the Kaurava from the *Mahābhārata.* Although the costuming and acting are similar to other forms of *Vīthi Nāṭakam,* it falls more clearly in the category of ritual drama. During the performance, the "actor" representing Arjuna sits on a tree performing *tapassu* (meditation) during the night and at the end of the performance throws bananas to devotees as prasādam.

In addition to the above, *bayalāṭa* (*bayalu* means open place, āṭa means play or drama) is the regional name in Anamtapur district; *Vīthi* Bhagavatham is the regional name in coastal districts, and *Yakṣaganam* (played by Miltiri *dasarulu,* a caste of Harijan) is the regional name in Telangana districts for Vīthi Nāṭakam.

Reference

Rama, Raju B. 1991. *Glimpses into Telugu folklore*. Hyderabad: Janapada Vijnana Prachuranalu.

BITTU VENKATESWARLU

SEE ALSO

Dependent Performing Castes; Ellamma; Gods and Goddesses; Mahābhārata; *Purāṇa;* Theater and Drama; Yakśagāna

VRAT KATHĀ

Vrat kathā (from the Sanskrit *vrata,* "vow," derived from the root *vr,* "to choose or will," and *kathā,* "story" or "telling") are stories associated with Hindu rituals aimed at obtaining a boon or marking a spiritual goal. *Vrat* as practiced by present-day Hindus is part of the *bhakti* (devotional) tradition. The basic aim of a vrat is to influence a deity to come to one's aid as one stuggles across the ocean of existence. A vrat usually involves fasting, a *pūjā* (worship) ceremony, and the telling of a kathā (story). The corpus of vrat kathā is enormous, with stories in many variants in both Sanskrit and regional languages.

Vrat and their associated stories became very popular, especially with the rise of bhakti after the ninth century. They are commonly found in the *Purāṇa*s and the works of Hindu law digest writers (*nibandhakara*). The *Śrīvratarājā,* composed in Sanskrit in Banaras (Varanasi) in the eighteenth century and now available in translation into modern Hindi, contains both the rules for performing various vrats and their associated vrat kathā. It is a primary scriptural source for vrat kathā. However, vrat kathā have always been orally transmitted in vernacular languages alongside the Sanskrit renditions, most probably influencing the textual variants.

Vrat and their associated kathā exist for numerous deities and occasions: There are vrat kathā for specific annual festivals (such as Dīvālī), for each day of the week (such as the vrat kathā of *Sanicār,* Saturday), for each day of the month (the *ekadashi* vrat kathā for the eleventh day of the month), and for particular deities (*Santoṣī Mā kā vrat kathā*). Many regional variants of vrat kathā for the days of the week or other popular rituals are available as inexpensive chapbooks. Collections of vrat kathā for the monthly and yearly festivals are available in slightly more expensive chapbooks.

One of the most popular vrat kathā is that of Satya Narayan, a kathā read by a Brahman priest to alleviate a difficulty or accrue merit in a petitioner's household. This ceremony is often held when building a new house, when a child is born, or on some other important occasion. It is one of the more popular rituals among Hindus everywhere, including those residing in Europe and the Americas.

While the vrat kathā of Satyā Nārāyaṇ is almost always read by a Brahman male while officiating at a ritual ceremony, most vrat kathā are told by women as part of their vrat observances. After fasting and doing pūjā, a knowledgeable woman will tell the kathā associated with the deity being worshiped that day. These orally transmitted versions have the widest currency in South Asia today.

The kathā emphasizes the qualities of the deity being worshiped and the boons that the worshiper will receive from the ritual observance. The stories often end with a phrase such as "From performing such a good ceremony, the worshiper will gain happiness and salvation [*mokśa*]." The vrat kathā counter the claims that Hindus believe in a fixed fate, determined at or prior to birth. The content of the vrat kathā continuously reinforces the value of action in this life in order to receive instant, or almost instant, rewards.

Recent scholarship by folklorists has found that Muslim women in central India and in the region extending to Iran also have vrat kathā, but little is known about the topic.

References

Jamzadeh, Laal, and Margaret Mills. 1986. Iranian *sofreh* from collective to female ritual. In *Gender and religion: on the complexity of symbols* ed. C. W. Bynum, S. Harvell, and P. Richman, Boston: Beacon, pp. 23–65.

Kane, P. V. 1974. *History of Dharmasastra*. 2nd ed. Poona: Bhandarkar Oriental Institute.

Pearson, Anne. 1996. *Because it gives me peace of mind: Ritual fasts in the religious lives of Hindu women*. Albany: State University of New York Press.

Visvanatha. 1963. *Srivrataraja*. Bombay: Srivenkateshvar Press. In Sanskrit with Hindi translation.

Wadley, Susan S. *Shakti: Power in the conceptual structure of Karimpur religion*. Chicago: The University of Chicago series in social, cultural and linguistic anthropology, no. 2.

———. 1981b. Vrats: Transformers of destiny. In *Karma: An anthropological inquiry,* ed. V. Daniels and Charles Keyes. Berkeley: University of California Press.

SUSAN S. WADLEY

SEE ALSO

Bhakti; Dīvalī/Dīpāvalī; Folktale; *Mu'jizāt Kahānī; Pūjā; Puraṇa; Satya Narāyana Vrat Kathā*

VYĀS

Vyās, from Sanskrit *vyāsa* (one who separates or divides) is a respectful title used in many parts of India to denote a storyteller or expounder specializing in Hindu religious lore, particularly that associated with the preserver-god, Viṣṇu, and his earthly incarnations.

Such a performer may also be known as a *kathāvācak* or *kathākār,* a narrator of *kathā* or sacred story; those who specialize in the popular Rāma-narrative sometimes style themselves *rāmāyaṇī* or "Rāmāyaṇa-specialist." The mythical archetype for such narrators is the sage Kṛṣṇa Dvaipāyana, also known as Veda Vyāsa, the reputed author of the Sanskrit epic *Mahābhārata* and one of its prominent characters. A liminal figure born at the juncture of two cosmic epochs, on an island in the Yamuna River, of the union between a Brahman sage and a fisher-girl, Vyāsa seems to embody mediation and cultural synthesis. Apart from his role in creating the martial epic, his legendary credits include the "division" of the unitary sacred wisdom, or Veda, into four parts to render it more comprehensible, and the composition of the *Brahma sūtra* and of the Sanskrit *purāṇa*s, voluminous compendia of ritual and lore that became influential scriptures for medieval Hinduism.

Historical antecedents of the contemporary vyās may include the *sūta,* or bard, mentioned in Sanskrit literature, who combined the roles of royal charioteer, genealogist, and panegyrist. In later times, these activities became the specialty of regional Cāraṇ and Bhāṭ castes, while the role of sacred expounder was taken up by the *paurāṇika,* who recited and explained the purāṇas, and who was often an itinerant mendicant and/or Brahman scholar. Modern performers include both male ascetics and householders, as well as a small number of women. A vyās may be engaged by an individual patron or a community for a variable period to expound a scripture such as the Sanskrit *Bhagavad Gītā* or *Bhāgavata purāṇa,* or the Hindi version of the Rāma-story, the *Rāmcaritmānas* of Tulsidas, now the most popular text for kathā performances in Hindi-speaking regions. However, once the performer assumes a seat on the sanctified dais (*vyās-pīṭh*), and with it the archetypal persona of Veda Vyāsa, the chosen text typically provides no more than an outline for an extemporaneous and often tour-de-force performance comprising scriptural quotations, dramatized anecdotes, and homely sermonizing, sometimes accompanied by music. Audiences respond with such enthusiasm that the most renowned contemporary expounders have become celebrities who command large fees and whose discourses circulate on audio and videocassette. Regional variations on this performance genre include the *harikathā* associated with the Maharashtran Vaiṣṇavite Vārkarī tradition and the *kathākālakṣepam* of Tamil Nadu. A comparatively recent trend is the vyās festival (*sammelan*), at which a variety of invited speakers address large, usually urban, audiences in nighttime performances that resemble classical music recitals.

References

Bonazzoli, Giorgio. 1983. Composition, transmission, and recitation of the *Purāṇas. Purāṇa* 25 (July): 254–280.

Damle, Y. B. 1960. Harikatha—a study in communication. *Bulletin of the Deccan College Research Institute* 20: 63–107.

Lutgendorf, Philip. 1991. *The life of a text: performing the Rāmcaritmānas of Tulsidas.* Berkeley and Los Angeles: University of California Press, esp. 113–247.

PHILIP LUTGENDORF

SEE ALSO

Bhakti; Epic; *Mānas Kathā; Purāṇa;* Rāma; Rāmāyaṇas

W

WATAṆḌĀRI SYSTEM

The *wataṇḍāri* system is a social system that has existed in the villages of the Telingana region of Andhra Pradesh since at least the regime of Nizams (rulers). Watan is an Urdu word that means "land," but in this context refers to certain rent-free, or tax-free land that is given to a person for performance of a service to government officials, or to the village community as a whole. *Watan* also referred to a hereditary right to perform a service that is distributed among heirs of the holder.

The wataṇḍāri social system is an officially recognized mechanism of the village administration introduced in 1853 by Sir Salarjung-1 as one of his administrative reformations when he was the prime minister to the Nizam (head of state). The wataṇḍāri organisation consists of at least fifteen persons. Generally, there are two categories of wataṇḍārs: village officers, called *paṭwāris* and *paṭēls,* and *balutedars* (*Baluta* means gift), composed of various kinds of village servants. The latter category, in particular, draws upon traditional village castes and caste specializations.

The paṭwāri is the village revenue officer who keeps the village records, while the paṭēl looks after matters concerning law and order. The Paṭwāri post is higher in rank than the paṭēl. These village officers get remuneration in the form of monthly salaries, a percentage of the taxes collected, income from the rent free lands given by the government, and remunerations (*mamul*) from the villagers for specific services.

Village servants are called balutēdārs. Balutā is a right to take remunerations and to give services. There are twelve kinds of balutēdār, so they are called *bārāh* (Urdu for twelve) balutēdārs. Among these twelve *Mōtādu* or *Sethsindhi* or *Maikūri* are village watchman. This servant helps the village officials in village administration. He watches the village and reports all happenings. The *Nīruḍi* is a watchman of government irrigation sources in the village. A *Talāri* is the watchman of the government lands of the village. All these servants are drawn from any traditional non-peasant castes.

Apart from these three kinds of watchman there are nine other service personnel without which the wataṇḍari is not complete. They are 1) *purōhit,* or *Brahman* priest, 2) carpenter (*Viśwakarma* or *Waḍla*), 3) blacksmith (*Viśwakarma* or *Kammari*), 4) potter (*Kummari*), 5) barber (*Maṅgali*), 6) washerman (*cākali*), 7) *bēgari,* or grave digger, of the untouchable Māḍiga or Māla castes, 8) *dappu* or drum beater (a Māḍiga), and 9) *veṭṭimāḍiga,* who serves as a laborer to the village officials. All these service personnel offer their traditional occupational services and some additional services to the government officials whenever they visit the village, and also give their occupational services for the village-wide rituals (*jātara*s and *tirunāḷḷa*s). They enjoy rent-free and hereditary right-holding land given by the government for their services and, in addition, some get monthly remuneration from the village revenue. The hereditary right can be abolished or changed by the government in case of dereliction of duties or a right holder does not have heirs.

Although the wataṇḍāri system has experienced several changes in successive governments, the bārāh balutēdārs still hold their rights to perform duties and receive payment from the government. In many respects, however, the government has introduced changes in the mode of services and remunerations for these service personnel in order to reduce its originally feudal way of functioning.

References

Dube, S. C. 1957. *Indian village.* London: Routledge Kegan Paul, Ltd.

Raju, M. V. T. 1980. Persistence and change, A study of Watanḍāri system in rural Telingana with Special reference of Medak district. Ph.D. diss., Department of Anthropology, Andhra University, Visakhapatnam, India.

PULIKONDA SUBBACHARY

SEE ALSO
Jamānī

WATER LORE

Rivers, wells, and lakes are the focus of rich traditions in South Asia. Bathing is emphasized in Brahmanical Hindu traditions, and appears to have been important in the ancient Harappan civilization as well. The most common term for a holy place, *tīrtha,* has as its root meaning "ford" or "crossing place on a river." Most major Hindu pilgrimage places have either a series of broad steps (a *ghāṭ*) leading down to a nearby river, or a temple "tank" (a water reservoir) for bathing. Sanskrit texts praising rivers and pilgrimage places along them assert the power of the water to demolish sin or to bring peace to ancestors whose ashes are immersed in the water.

Equally importantly, water is viewed as a source of fecundity. In accord with this view, the vast majority of rivers in India are seen as feminine, and both rivers and wells are the homes of a variety of female divinities. In Maharashtra, for instance, there are a number of locally or regionally important goddesses whose temples are found on the banks of a river and whose original home is an underwater palace in a deep, still, perennial river pool. Such pools, whether the abode of a particular goddess or not, are frequently understood to hold food, gold, or other forms of wealth and plenty. In particular, they are said to be the home of special fish such as extremely large fish with nose-rings the size of cart wheels or fish of certain species that fishermen are not supposed to catch. Such a pool is frequently said to be unfathomably deep; even if the rope from twelve rope-cots is tied end to end, people say, it will not be long enough to plumb the water hole.

Dangerous beings also inhabit some water holes. Besides crocodiles, these beings include water spirits who can cause drownings or interfere with human fertility. In Maharashtra, such spirits, classified as *paryā* (a word that may be etymologically related to the English word "fairy"), are most frequently called *āsarā,* or *māvalayā.* Invisible, but located quite precisely at some particular spot in a river, on a riverbank, or at a well, the āsarās can easily be offended by an unwitting young woman who goes too close to their place when she is menstruating. She may learn of her infraction only later in life, when she has difficulty conceiving children, or when her children are born sickly or die young. The Sanskrit cognate of āsarā is *apsaras,* the term for a kind of water nymph who lives in the heaven of Indra, the king of the gods, and whom Indra sends to tempt male ascetics.

The most religiously important river of South Asia is the Ganges. In the best-known story about this river's descent to earth, the river falls first onto Mount Meru, at the center of the earth, and from there onto the head of the god Śiva. Because it flows through his matted hair, the Ganges is also seen as a second wife to Śiva, and, in oral traditions in regional languages, as a rival of his first wife, Pārvatī. Other rivers are often identified, more or less explicitly, with the Ganges, and, in many cases, the places identified as their origin spots are located on mountaintops near temples of Śiva. Rivers that flow into the ocean are also understood to have the ocean as their husband.

References

Eck, Diana L. 1996 [1982]. Ganga: The Goddess Ganges in Hindu sacred geography. In *Devī: Goddesses of India,* ed. John Stratton Hawley and Donna M. Wulff, 137–153. Berkeley: University of California Press.
Feldhaus, Anne. 1995. *Water and womanhood: religious meanings of rivers in Maharashtra.* New York: Oxford University Press.
Gold, Ann Grodzins. 1988. *Fruitful journeys: the ways of Rajasthani pilgrims.* Berkeley: University of California Press.

ANNE FELDHAUS

SEE ALSO
Bhāṭiyālī Song; *Mēla;* Sacred Geography; Sacred Geography, Afghanistan

WEDDING SONGS

The marriage ceremony is the most ritually elaborate of all the life-cycle transitions in South Asia. Since the act of singing is considered auspicious (*maṅgal*), wedding songs are indispensable to Hindu marriage ceremonies, particularly in rural regions. Wedding songs are performed by groups of women—relatives and neighbors who cluster together around ritual action. Songs are part of the action rather than a demarcated performance event.

There are many different indigenous genres which can be lumped together under the rubric "wedding songs." The names and delineations of these genres vary between regions. Most broadly, songs for the bride differ from songs for the groom. There are also songs that describe the experience of marriage in general terms which can be sung at any time, and songs keyed to specific phases of ritual action. Bawdy insults are addressed to the groom from the bride's female relatives and neighbors and at the bride from her new in-laws.

The singing of wedding songs may start several weeks in advance, especially in a bride's home. When the actual marriage rituals are taking place, women typically sing amid a din of activity—the Brahman priest's sonorous chant, the piping clamor of a brass wedding band, the blaring recorded music of a loudspeaker, the cries and shrieks of children, and the conversations of adults.

Most wedding songs are textually and musically repetitive. Lines of text are usually repeated twice, enabling other women who may not know the song to join in. The text may also be repeated again and again, each time inserting a different keyword into the same slot. For example, in a slot for relatives, a wedding song may be repeated to include father and mother, father's elder brother and his wife, the father's younger brother and his wife, the mother's brother and his wife, paternal grandfather and grandmother, brother and sister-in-law, sister and brother-in-law, and so on. Alternately, in a slot for objects, one may hear about the groom's tinsel crown, his shoes, watch, handkerchief, socks, and so on. Thus, songs can be expanded or contracted, adapting to the performers' interest or the length of a particular ritual procedure.

Sung by women, even when describing events on the groom's side, wedding songs enshrine women's points of view. Apart from ritual insults, whose humor draws on systematic inversions of the expected, wedding songs portray conventional emotions associated with the kinship roles that are brought into focus by the rite of passage. In North India where village exogamy and patrilocality are practiced, songs depict a bride lamenting her departure from all that has been familiar. Her father, mother, and brother may weep, but her brother's wife is usually triumphant. A mother-in-law and husband's sister are presented as tyrannical creatures to whom the new bride must submit. These songs thus underscore kinship arrangements as given and natural. They envelope individual experience in culturally approved symbolism. When performed by unmarried girls, wedding songs serve as a powerful agent of socialization.

Many Hindu wedding songs naturalize their content by recourse to mythology. The groom is frequently compared to Rām, Kṛṣṇa, or occasionally Śiva; the bride to Sīta, Rukmānī or Pārvatī. These gods of Sanskritic mythology become domesticated around regional practises, giving contemporary weddings an aura of mythic timelessness.

Other wedding songs directly invoke present social conditions. They may speak of changing practices (for example a bride being taken off in a bus rather than a red palanquin), objects, or events (such as the election of the current Prime Minister). It is sometimes possible to date a song through such references.

Although wedding songs have been extensively studied among Hindus of North India, studies from South India, from tribal groups, and from religious minorities are scant.

References

Archer, William. 1985. *Songs for the bride: wedding rites of rural India*. New York: Columbia University Press.

Henry, Edward O. 1988. *Chant the names of God: musical culture in Bhojpuri-Speaking India.* San Diego: San Diego State University Press.

Narayan, Kirin. 1986. Birds on a branch: girlfriends and wedding songs in Kangra. *Ethos* 14: 47–75.

Raheja, Gloria, and Ann Gold. 1994. *Listen to the heron's words: reimagining gender and kinship in North India.* Berkeley: University of California Press.

Kirin Narayan

SEE ALSO

Angay; Balanday; Gender and Folklore; Marriage Ceremonies; Song; Women's Songs

WEDDING VIDEOS

Wedding videos are fast becoming the most common locally produced representation of social life in South Asia. These two-to-three-hour cassettes are produced by professional videographers hired by families to record wedding ceremonies and receptions. Video technology has been available in South Asia since the early 1970s, but wedding videos became popular only in the 1980s, and production exploded in the 1990s. Although at first only the richest families could afford them, increasingly competitive videographers have caused prices to drop sharply, putting wedding videos within the reach of even middle- and lower-middle-class families in many parts of South Asia. Indeed, wedding videos and videographers have become expected at middle-class Hindu, Muslim, and Christian weddings, both urban and rural.

Wedding videos compete with photography, which has been common in South Asia for over a century. Early images of weddings were confined to one or two black-and-white studio photographs, but with the increasing popularity of location photography and color film, representations of weddings expanded to include full-color albums of twenty-five to two hundred photographs. In the early 1980s both clients and photographers began to see video as the next step, and many photographers became videographers.

However, wedding videos differ significantly from photographic representations of weddings. First, videos incorporate movement and allow for continuous coverage of events. The wedding video industry in South Asia is known as "video coverage," and videographers and their clients often cite "full coverage" as the measure of the professional video. Some consumers apparently see videos as very long series of still photographs, so they find wedding photographs redundant. For them, videos provide more "pictures" more cheaply than any photographer could.

Second, videos allow the producer much more freedom to manipulate images than photography does. Although hand photo retouching has a long history in South Asia, it cannot compare with the videographers' fluid use of camera effects, video editing, mixing, and special effects to reshape images. Using these tools, videographers craft images that fit aesthetic ideals drawn from cinema and photography, emphasize culturally significant moments in the wedding, and focus on particular symbols for dramatic effect. This creates a distinctive video narrative form. Since weddings are increasingly experienced through this video narrative, the audience's expectations of and reactions to weddings are to some extent the product of the videographer's craft.

Third, videos add sound to images. Often videographers replace the original wedding sound track with cinema songs, which link the wedding video to cinema through lyrics and through implicit references to film plots. Such links are sometimes emphasized by repeated switching between wedding images and film excerpts, using song to connect the two. This makes the bride and groom film stars, and gives the video a distinctly cinematic, "romantic" tone. Such videos may either reflect or create a new emotional and cultural conception of marriage, particularly arranged marriage, the contours of which can be glimpsed in cinema lyrics and scripts, and in the form and content of wedding videos.

References

Gutman, Judith Mara. 1982. *Through Indian eyes.* New York: Oxford University Press/International Center of Photography.

Zeff, Adam. 1999. Marriage, film, and video in Tamil Nadu. Ph.D. diss., Department of Anthropology, University of Pennsylvania.

ADAM ZEFF

SEE ALSO

Cassettes; Film Music; Song

WEST BENGAL

A part of Eastern India, West Bengal (87,853 sq. kms) extends from the Himalayan ranges in the North to the Bay of Bengal in the South and from Bihar and Orissa in the West to Bangladesh in the east. The land includes the Northern hill tracts, Western plateau region, Southern Coastal region and Middle alluvial Gaṅgā (Ganges) basin. The Bengali people have evolved out of Proto-Australoid, Dravidian, Mongoloid and Indo-Aryan ethno-racial stocks. Both autochthonous and immigrant races and cultures have woven the life-pattern and cultural profile of Bengal. The vast and varied folklore of Bengal is the result of the fusion of the different ethnic traits and cross-cultural relations which conditioned its emergence. The range of vernacular expressive culture in the region is very hard to describe in summary fashion. The major folklore genres of West Bengal may be grouped as folk literature, folk song, drama, dance, religion and festival, belief and superstition, art and craft, foodways, games and sports, transport, medicine and ethno-therapeutics etc.

Folk literature of West Bengal is manifested in different genres such as narrative (myth, ritual tale or *bratakathā,* legend, "frolic tale" or *raṅgakathā,* hearsay, fables etc), ballad, nursery rhyme, doggerel verse, song, riddle, proverb, dramatic narrative, folk epic, etc. All these exist in two modes, oral and written, and operate in three-fold directions: classical-folk-popular as well as tribal-folk-elite exchange. Folk literature expresses fantasy as well as practical experiences of life and presents religious, secular and didactic elements in different genres.

The traditions of Bengali folk song are numerous and diverse in content and musical patterns. Major identified genres include *Bhāoẏaiẏā, Caṭkā Hudumā, Gamīrā; Jhumur, Bhādu, Ṭusu; Kheur, Kȧbi, Pālā gīt;* Marriage songs; *Murśidā, Mārphatī, Bāul, Bhābergīt, Mātuẏagīt, Pāgalgīt; Pāñcāli, Kathakathā, Kīrtan;* Work songs; etc. All forms exhibit different regional variations and ethno-ecological peculiarities. The devotional songs of para-folkloric religious sects express their own philosophies mainly in *Saoẏāl-Jabāb* (question and answer) forms. *Pālāgīt* constitutes an oral epic tradition. *Jhumur* originated from agricultural work songs. *Kheuṛ gīt* is rooted in weaving work songs. Changes are taking place in folksongs in terms of Lok-calan, their folk or ethno-musicological features. Supporting instruments of folksongs are made of string, skin, pipe, metal and clay or wood of which *dhāṅsā-kāṛā-nākaṛā, ḍhol, mādal, khol, kartāl, gopiẏantra, gābgubī, ektārā, dotārā,* etc. are important.

Several living folk dramas are popular in West Bengal: *Jātrā, Song, Gambhīrā, Bolān, Aṣṭak, Ālkāp, Khan, Palatia, Kushan, Cor-curni, Mecheni, Halẏā-Haluẏāni, Banbibipālā, Ḍomni, Bahurupī,* puppetry, etc. are noteworthy. Folk plays are performed, in open fields, courtyards, small platforms, or proscenium stages with the aid of music and dance. Usually males play the female roles. Mythological, historical, and socio-political themes are played out following written or unwritten texts. Traditional folk play scripts make necessary changes in consistency with the performance contexts and the issues of the day.

Bengal is rich in folk dance, among which *chau, gambhīrā, bhaktyā, bau, baraṇ, mukha-khel, hudumādeo, bhādu, ṭusu, hijra, khemṭī, nācni, naṭuẏā, lāṭhi-kāṭhi, rāibeṁśe, pāik, ḍhālī, carak-gājan* dances, and mask dances, are important. Chau is *mār-rukh* (attack and resist) dance, and its nomenclature is derived from Mundari language *Chutao* (to stop, kill, etc). *Baunāc* and *Nācnīnāc* are not originally entertainment dances, but magico-ritual in origin. Folk dances of Bengal are generally performed in the context of cultural and magico-religious ceremonies, but presently the functional value of them is entertainment.

Innumerable religious ceremonies and folk festivals take place all over Bengal throughout the year; among them *Carak-Gājan* (Hook swinging), *Dakṣinrāy-Baraṭhākur, Banbibi, Manasā-Jhaṁpān-Biṣarā, Bhādu-Ṭusu, Beṛābhāsān, Daksaṁkrānti, Lakṣmī-Alakṣmī, Kārtiklaṛāi, Āuni-Bāuni, Hur, Hālakātā, Nabānna, Bhīm, Gheṅṭu, Śītalā, Olābibi, Sātbon, Jarāsur, Caṇḍī, Dharma, Tistāburi, Hudumdeo, Pāñcānanda, Biśālākṣī Mākāl, brata*-rites, etc. are popular. Folk festivals are generally celebrated in relation to fertility beliefs, healing-cults to ward off evil spirits, and to solicit good fortune. *Manasā* is the snake-cult and *Jhāṁpān* is a convention of snake charmers. Bhādu is a festival for the *Bhādui* crop and Ṭusu is a post-harvest festival of the *Pouṣālī* crop. *Carak-Gājan* is a Sun and Mother Earth-cult related to agriculture. Dakṣinrāy-Bara cult is noted in human sacrifice for good rain and crops. Banbibi is a sylvan deity. Bhīm refers not to the epic hero, Bhīma of the Mahābhārata, but is an ancestor worship for the well-being of the community. *Pīr, Gājī, Fakir,* and *Darbeś* (types of Muslim saints) are revered by both Hindus and Muslims. Para-folkloric religious sects represent unorthodox human impulses. In spite of their shastric (orthodox) connections, *Durgāpūjā, Raṭhayātrā,* and *Rās* festivals all contain folkloric residues. People participate irrespective of caste and creed in all festivals and fairs. Folk festivals are dedicated to earthly happiness and the welfare of the community and activities include ceremonial bathing, fasting, sacrifices, music, dance, drama, symbolic art, and activity independent of any priest-cult. Many *melā* (fairs with sales of goods, etc.) are held on the occasion of these festivals.

There exist countless folk beliefs in Bengal to ward off evil and bring good fortune. Beliefs about inauspicious and auspicious numbers, days, months, directions, animals, travel, barrenness, pregnancy, childbirth, death, dreams, itching, sneezing, calling, etc. are many and varied. *Ojhā, Guṇin,* and *Deẏāsī* are types of skilled sorcerers who make charms in connection with these matters. Folk beliefs prevail till now.

West Bengal is renowned for its beautiful folk arts and crafts among which alpana, clay modeling, wood carving, cutlery, terra-cotta, paṭcitra, *kāṅthā, ḍhokṛa,* weaving and needle craft, mats, *sikā, pākhā,* wall paintings, basketry, toys, masks, idols, votive offerings, *gaynābaṛi* (ornamental sundried paste), flower and pandel decorations, *jarī* goldwork, fireworks, etc. are popular. Folk arts and crafts of Bengal are both artistic and utilitarian, working in clay, stone, ivory, wood, cane, bamboo, conch shell, varieties of reeds and grasses, old cloth, cotton, silk, etc. The folk arts of Bengal traditionally represent magico-religious beliefs, cosmic and fertility symbols, ritual and decorative motifs. But of late changes are occurring in the arts due to social and economic change.

Foodways are a special branch of Bengali folklore, a conceptual system classifying major or minor foods and sick or healing diets. Various preparations of rice, vegetarian and non-vegetarian items are cooked using grains, edible herbs, vegetables, fruits and roots, pigeon-peas, fish, crab, meat, etc. Among named folk dishes, are *sukto, cacari, lābṛā, kormā, ghaṇṭo, caṅcra, dāl, ambal, cāṭni,* etc. and among sweet items *piṭhā* (sweet pie) and *pāẏas* (sweet rice porridge) are popular. Among the many sweets made of posset or flour are *rasagollā, lāṅgcā, sandeś, gajā, manoharā, nikhunti, sītābhog-mihidānā, babarsaw, sarpuryā, kalojām, moticur,* etc. *Morabbā (sweetened fruit conserve), moyā, nāru, āmsatta, kāsundi, baṛi, ācār* (pickles), etc. are also prominent. Besides good taste, food items become visual art objects through their ornamentation and design.

Several kinds of folk games and sports prevail in Bengal, on land, water, or air; indoor or outdoor; boys' or girls'; or male-female mixed group. The most popular folk games are boat races, wheel races, fire play, kite flying, swimming, stick and spear games, plays of colour, cowrie, leaf, ring, mud marble, games, and named games including *dāṅguli, laṭṭu, buṛi-basanta, dools, lukocuri, ekkā-dokkā, kānā-māchi, khelamkuchi, rumāl-cor, kumir-kumir, gadi, cor-puliś, kit-kit, kābādi,* cards, *luḍu, bāgbandi, golakdhām,* etc. Folk games incorporate psycho-physical practices, magico-ritualistic symbolic actions, and allusions to ways of life or life struggle. Rhymes, songs, and dances are inseparable parts of many folk games. In spite of the popularity of some Western sports, the folk games are still popular and living phenomena.

There are several kinds of traditional vehicles and folk transport systems in West Bengal. They are categorized as sthalāyānā (land-vehicles) and *jalāyānā* (water vehicles) in this land of rivers and streams and freguent inundations. Among land vehicles *raṇ-pā* (stilts), *dolā-duli* (litter), *pālki* (palanquin), *thelāgāṛi* (hand-barrow), bullock cart, buffalo cart, horse carriage, *rath* (chariot), and rickshaw are well-known. Among water-vehicles *velā* (raft), *ḍoṅgā* (canoe), *ḍiṅgi* and *naukā* (two types of boats), etc. are noteworthy. Folk transports are still widely used in remote areas, and on ceremonial occasions folk vehicles are customarily used. In recent years mechanical aids are being added to folk vehicles, such as outboard motors on traditional boats formerly powered by pole or sail.

Folk medicines and ethno-theraputics are important components of folklore. Evil spirits and black magic are considered as the roots of diseases. The major treatment processes are witch-therapy, fire and water therapy, metal therapy, and herbal therapy. These techniques stand in between Āyurvedic-Ḥakīmī (traditional herbal) and western scientific systems. *Mantra* (mystic words), *jhār-phuk* (thrashing and blowing on evil spirits, to dispel them), *tābij-kabac* (amulets and charms), *jaṛi-buṭi* (medicinal herbs and drugs) etc. are all used in curing crafts. Generally *ojhā* or *guṇin* healers and quacks are accepted as folk medical practioners. Folk drugs are prepared with herbs, honey, oil or sap, metal or mineral objects, human or non-human waste, etc. *Pacan* (a decoction of indigenous ingredients) is an omnipotent nostrum. *Pathya,* the "sick" or "cure" diet is a part of folk therapies. Folk pathology contains age-old knowledge which merits western scientific exploration. In spite of the challenges of western sciences, folk medicine and ethno-theraputics are acquiring extensive recognition.

The folklore of West Bengal has undergone changes due to socio-environmental causes. In certain cases original ritualistic features and significance have been lost and decorative, entertaining and commercial orientations have emerged. In the changing situation, though different genres have suffered, yet folklore in general and urban folklore, folklorism (public performances for nontraditional audiences, often government-sponsored), and immigrant folklore in particular have expanded in West Bengal. In respect of developing identity consciousness, group awareness, immigrant solidarity, and emancipatory efforts, folklore is playing a major role in West Bengal especially in regional, marginal, and ethnic communities. Governmental and non-governmental enterprises have helped to increase the popularity of folklore on the one hand and have caused deviation and intensified sectarianism in many ways on the other. The establishment of a full-fledged Folklore Department in the University of Kalyani (1990) opened a new chapter in the history of folklore study in Bengal as well as in India. In spite of politico-commercial hindrances, folklore is gaining wider ground in the trichotomous emerging patterns of tribal-folk-elite interaction and adaptive mechanisms. Of late folklore is being used for socio-political ends in applied contexts as a popular modality of mass communication. The study of folklore in West Bengal, to a great extent, has by now crossed beyond the past-oriented diachronic approach and colonial nationalistic paradigms in pursuit of the theoretical and methodological concerns of modern academic folkloristics.

TUSHAR CHATTOPADHYAY

SEE ALSO

Chau; Crafts; Gāmbhīrā; Handloom Weaving; Jātrā/ Yātrā; Jhumur Jātrā Drama; *Kāñthā;* Marionettes; Masks; Medicine, Āyurveda; *Melā;* Pottery; *Ratha Jātrā;* Saints; Satya Pīr; Song, Bengal; *Vrat Kathā*

WITCHES AND SORCERERS

In anthropological terminology witches and sorcerers are defined as human beings with the ability to harm or kill another person through magical means. When this ability stems from an inherently evil disposition, it is generally ascribed to a witch. Sorcerers, by contrast, are understood to work evil indirectly, through memorized knowledge and manipulation of symbolic and ritual procedures for causing misfortune. This witch-sorcerer distinction can be useful in interpreting the categories of specialists whom South Asians believe capable of evil doing.

The Hindi word *tonhi,* for example, describes a woman who meets the anthropological criteria of witch. Indistinguishable from other women in appearance, the tonhi in Madhya Pradesh is said to possess powers of metamorphosis (for example, she can change gender at will). She can also magically turn stones into wax and ride on the backs of ghosts from place to place. In addition, tonhis appear genetically programmed to behave in ways that are fundamentally aberrant and antisocial. At night, they congregate in graveyards, dig up newly buried corpses, sit on them, suck their blood, and eat their flesh. A dance that they perform nude is said to please Bhairava (a fierce manifestation of the God Śiva), who then grants them stronger powers to accomplish their wicked ends.

Witches are also believed to threaten the fertility of human beings, domesticated animals, cultivated plants, and the flow of water. Above all, they prey on newly married couples, women who have just given birth, and young children. Given their mysterious powers, it is not surprising that precisely how these witches actually injure their victims is not amenable to empirical observation. In Madhya Pradesh most tonhis are said to work malevolence through evil glances. But in Karnataka, village women are rumored to be driven by possessing evil spirits to poison other people. Since it is generally impossible to present convincing evidence of presumed witchcraft, accusations are rare. However, widows, barren women, female members of ethnic minorities (like Muslims in a Hindu community), and women who take on male-oriented professions (like money lending) often fall under suspicion.

In contrast to the witch who acts out of an uncontrollable, female impulse, the Indian sorcerer draws upon an esoteric corpus of incantations and ritual techniques that have been transmitted under a shroud of secrecy since Vedic times, as described in the *Atharva Veda*. Whereas the witch is often unaware of her evil power, the sorcerer is consciously focused upon controlling his craft. The "rationality" of his crimes is evidenced by the fact that, typically, he is paid by clients to injure an enemy. Since conflicts over sorcery accusations in South Asia often have to do with competition and tension over money, land, and property, it is men, and particularly urban middle-class men, who are likely to be its victims.

In order to control his clients' enemies, the Indian sorcerer uses spells. In fact, the native term that is closest to the anthropological notion of sorcerer derives from the Sanskrit *mantiravāti,* which means "one who utters *mantras*" or spells, which may include syllables, words, formulas, names, curses, prayers, invocations, or songs. When uttered by a trained specialist who is ritually pure, they can thereby take "command," as suggested by the Tamil word for sorcery spell (*ēval*), or "to bind" (*jing-*) their designated victims, as the Soras of eastern India put it.

The Indian sorcerer also manipulates homeopathic and contagious magic. In the first instance, he may work upon small effigies, operating on the principle that "like produces like," that whatever is said or done to these dolls will affect their human targets. In the second case, he may inject certain organic substances (for instance, an egg or a lime) with sickness, and then bury them near the victim's house, working under the assumption that affliction may then be transmitted to him or her via physical contact. But the sorcerer may also work without such mechanical devices, soliciting the aid of spiritual beings, such as the Hindu Goddess Kālī or the Sinhalese demon Sūniyama, by means of sacrificial offerings, in order to secure their powers on behalf of his clients.

However most South Asian theories of sorcery also emphasize the dire risks of misusing this knowledge. A sorcerer can go mad or die in some violent way. Despite these consequences, in Sri Lanka, the Indian state of Kerala, and among the Sora of Eastern India, sorcery seems actually to be practiced by priests of the dominant religious tradition (as by Buddhist monks in Sri Lanka). As with witchcraft, when sorcery stems from a system of beliefs rather than an underground practice, it is often outsiders (such as Muslim priests within Hindu communities) who are the ones to be accused of it.

References

Babb, Lawrence A. 1975. *The divine hierarchy: popular Hinduism in central India.* New York: Columbia University Press.

Epstein, Scarlett. 1967. A sociological analysis of witch beliefs in a Mysore village. In *Magic, Witchcraft, and Curing,* ed. John Middleton 135–154. American Museum Sourcebooks in Anthropology. Garden City, N.Y.: The Natural History Press.

Kapferer, Bruce. 1991 [1983]. *A celebration of demons: exorcism and the aesthetics of healing in Sri Lanka.* Oxford/Washington D.C.: Berg Publishers Limited and Smithsonian Institution Press.

Obeyesekere, Gananath. 1975. Sorcery, premeditated murder, and the canalization of aggression in Sri Lanka. *Ethnology,* 14(1): 1–23.

Vitebsky, Piers. 1993. *Dialogues with the dead: the discussion of mortality among the Sora of eastern India.* Cambridge: Cambridge University Press.

Isabelle Nabokov

SEE ALSO

Divination; *Dṛṣti;* Gender and Folklore; Spirit Possession and Mediumship; Supernatural Beings

WITCHES, NEPAL

Nepalis commonly distinguish three grades of witches: *ḍaṁkī, boksī,* and *kapṭī,* categories that are frequently further subdivided using diminutives: *ḍaṁkinī, boksinī,* and *kapṭinī.* Ḍaṁkī—sometimes identified as spirits of dead witches, and sometimes confused with *ḍankinī*—are the most dangerous: They may cause sudden death, even of a bird flying overhead, with just a glance. Kapṭinī are the weakest; they cause only minor harms, such as tense stomachs, skin blemishes, or swelling, usually in children. Most common are boksī, the term most often used for witches throughout Nepal. Boksī may cause the death of their victims, but more often are responsible for less dramatic difficulties. At night they prey sexually on victims, who sometimes wake up unable to move or breathe because the witch is sitting on their chest, a condition called *aiṭhan lāgnis.* Bluish tooth bites on the skin, progressive weakness, fevers, headaches, muscle and joint aches, dry coughs, and deafness are some of the conditions frequently attributed to boksī. Unable to destroy their victims by reciting *mantras* and oaths, they pour oil into ears, contaminate food, blow on open wounds, deposit filth (*putlā*) into victims, and resort to other forms of physical attack.

Mantras give witches control over spirit familiars, such as *masān* (spirits of dead humans), *bir* (spirits of animals), and *maphī* (bloodthirsty spirits of both animate and inanimate objects). The most powerful witch mantra is called the *Indra Jāl* (Indra's Net) because Indra taught it to the original witches when the gods required their assistance to churn the nectar of immortality from the primordial ocean.

Ever since the battles between the first shaman and the first witches, who are known as the "The Nine Skillful Little Sisters," the two groups have been celebrated antagonists, with cases of witchcraft the special therapeutic domain of shamans. Witches, who are almost always women, learn their craft from other witches; daughters most frequently are taught the spells and rituals by their mothers or grandmothers, who sometimes sing the secret knowledge to them before the child realizes that the training has begun. To complete their training, witches must harm someone dear to them, such as a son or husband, before their guru will teach them the most powerful mantras. Failure to complete the course, once begun, results in madness. Every witch must train at least one *celā* (disciple) before she can die. Though one witch can train several disciples completely before her death, many, in their death agonies, must part with their secrets.

Nepal's first legal code, the *Muluki ain* of 1853/1854, enforced for over a century and still quoted in local discussions, contained severe punishments not only for acts of witchcraft but also for accusations that could not be conclusively proven, along with strict criteria for determining acceptable proofs of bewitchment. These include vicariously branding the witch by directly branding the patient, vicariously causing the witch's head to be shaved by shaving the patient's head, and using a reversal mantra to make the witch dance in public.

References

Gellner, David N. 1994. Priests, healers, mediums and witches: The context of possession in the Kathmandu Valley, Nepal. *Man* 29, no. 1: 27–48.

Glover, Jessie R. 1972. The role of the witch in Gurung society. *Eastern Anthropologist* 25, no. 3: 221–226.

Levine, Nancy E. 1982. Belief and explanation in Nyimba women's witchcraft. *Man* 17, 259–274.

Maskarinec, Gregory G. 1995. *The rulings of the night: An ethnography of Nepalese shaman oral texts*. Madison: University of Wisconsin Press.

GREGORY G. MASKARINEC

SEE ALSO

Shamanism, Nepal; Supernatural Beings, Nepal

WOMEN'S SONGS

Women's songs are important statements of women's identity and must be understood in terms of a society's gender norms. Most oral performances in South Asia are segregated by gender (as well as by social class and/or caste). In part due to this social separation, women's social and cultural issues often differ from those of men. These two factors have resulted in female song traditions that are markedly different from those of men in terms of context, content, and texture (especially melody and meter).

Due to rules of female seclusion, social events in which women sing together, or women's song fests, almost always occur in an enclosed space, whether the courtyard of a house or a temple, or a room. Men are generally excluded from these events, although small boys usually attend with their mothers and grandmothers. One exception is weddings, when women relatives of the bride and groom sing from the sidelines while the male priest conducts the formal ceremony. Also, in many South Asian wedding traditions, when the groom's kin arrive at the bride's house, women from the bride's side typically sing loud, bawdy insults at them. Women's song fests are often associated with life cycle events—childbirth, puberty rituals (sacred thread ceremonies for Hindu males and celebrations of a girl's first menses in southern India), and weddings. Women also sing funeral laments that are less formal than other songs and are more individual than group songs.

In Nepal, Tamang women sing a life narrative called *bomsang* that is individual in composition but communal in its telling and its themes. Other women's song fests are associated with calendrical rituals and events, such as the celebration of the start of the monsoon season or festivals such as *Dīvālī* or *Mahāvīr Jayanti*. Women's vernacular songs provide an important counterpoint to the male-dominated Sanskrit rituals that often take place during important life cycle ceremonies or religious festivals, thus articulating the concerns of women.

The songs that women sing present a distinctly female view of the world, whether a birth, a wedding, or a ritual. Women's birth songs, sung by the new mother's female relatives, often focus on the mother's pain and the inability of those around to aid her. These songs also acknowledge the important role played by kin in childbirth and its associated rituals. In Hindu families the birth songs may compare the newborn boy to the boy-god Kṛṣṇa, whereas birth songs for girls, in much of the region, are all but nonexistent. Muslim women sing similar songs, associating the newborn with the Prophet Muhammad instead of the Hindu gods.

One woman's song that recounts the pain of childbirth and the help of female companions and male kin goes like this:

(Wife): Oh, my dearest husband, my knee trembles from the pain,
On account of the pain, I am dying,
Oh my dearest husband, a clever midwife is needed.
(Husband): I don't know the name of the midwife: I don't know her village!
(Wife): Ask her name of your mother or sister,
Or, my dearest husband, ask her name of the water carrier at the well . . . .

Since most of South Asia is patrilineal and patrilocal, wedding songs often speak of the girl's unhappiness at being sent away while her brothers remain in their natal home. They also may describe the bride and groom (in Hindu households usually identifying them as the god Rām and the goddess Sītā), and express women's concerns at losing a daughter or integrating a daughter-in-law into the household. Women's rainy season songs often focus on the married woman's desire to visit her natal kin and her anxious longing for her brother to come and take her there. Thus women's songs play with kinship relations and family. Women's songs also express an active sexuality, despite the dominant ideology that downplays any positive female sexuality.

Women use many song genres, though these are often female-only genres, such as birth or wedding songs. In much of India song genres are melody-specific, that is, there is a given melody that is used for a variety of texts which deal with similar themes and belong to a named genre. Hence melody alone often defines a genre, and women's melodies are often distinct from those of men. Further, the form of women's songs differs from those of many male songs. Women, who are often segregated in households except on special occasions, use textual and melodic devices that allow for a community of singers, unlike many male genres, which highlight a solo singer using complicated melodic and textual structures. Women's songs are also highly repetitious, with frequently repeated chorus lines that permit easy participation by all attending the event. (Male songs that aim to create community, like some *bhajan*s or work songs, follow the less complicated forms that prevail in women's song fests.)

Women's songs respond easily to changing socioeconomic circumstances; for instance, songs in the 1960s contained lines about wearing lipstick and riding a bicycle. This one, from the 1980s, concerns the English-educated daughter-in-law:

I am English-educated, but my luck is bad, oh, Mommy dearest.
My mother-in-law said, "*Bahu* [son's wife], cook the breads."
My sari worth thousands of rupees,
It was burned up, oh, Mommy dearest.
I am English-educated, but my luck is bad, oh, Mommy dearest . . . .

Most important, women's songs resist and counter the viewpoints of men, whether women are singing about the *Rāmāyaṇa* or a marriage or their own lives. Song provides an opportunity for a communal articulation of female self-perceptions and self-fashionings. In this song a woman laments the loss of her lover-husband:

I did not meet him for whom I slave.
In my palace I stood alone.
Tears came to my eyes, crying loudly: Oh, I did not meet him.
I did not meet him for whom I slave.
On the branch of the mango tree the cuckoo [a symbol of love] spoke,
Hearing its voice, my heart broke: Oh, I did not meet him . . . .

In a society where most marriages are arranged, and love and sexual passion are often thought of as being outside of marriage, the thoughts of women focus on the absence of a loving husband and the drudgery of daily lives where women indeed feel enslaved. But though they are not hidden or covert, the messages in women's songs are either not "heard" by men or are used as further proof of the fickle and slothful nature of women. But for women themselves these communally produced statements of the workings of their world are an important affirmation of femaleness as they understand it.

References

Archer, William G. 1985. *Songs for the bride: Wedding rites of rural India*. New York: Columbia University Press.
Harlan, Lindsay. 1995. Women's songs for auspicious occasions. In *Religions of India in practice*, ed. Donald S. Lopez. Princeton, NJ: Princeton University Press.
Raheja, Gloria Goodwin, and Ann Grodzins Gold. 1994. *Listen to the heron's words: Reimaging gender and kinship in north India*. Berkeley: University of California Press.
Trawick, Margaret. 1988. Spirits and voices in Tamil songs. *American Ethnologist* 15(2): 193–215.
Wadley, Susan S. 1993. Beyond texts: Tunes and contexts in Indian folk music. In *Texts, tunes and tones*, ed. Bonnie Wade. New Delhi: Oxford and IBH *Publishing Company*.

SUSAN S. WADLEY

SEE ALSO
Angay; Dīvālī/Dīpāvalī; Folk Literature; Gender and Folklore; Lament; Song; Wedding Songs

WORSHIP

The enormous diversity of patterns of worship in South Asia is rivaled only by the wealth of South Asian mythologies. The earliest oral textual sources are the four Vedic *saṁhitā*s composed in the last half of the second millennium B.C.E. One of the four, the *Atharvaveda,* reveals in its hymns in that early period considerable documentation for folk worship, that is, patterns of worship of major and minor deities and abstract entities, and the use of spells, curses, incantations, and healing remedies, all meant for domestic religious goals. Folk worship was quite aware of and yet mainly separate from the concerns of the other three Vedic saṁhitās: the official, priestly schedules of the sacrificial network and worship of dominant gods such as Agni, Soma, and Indra. Most of the concerns of the *Atharvaveda* are those of people today. Over the next three millennia, where worship is concerned, the oral and eventually written textual traditions of Vedic and classical Hinduism, Buddhism, Jainism, and the later traditions of Christianity, Islam, Parsis (Zoroastrians), and Sikhs displayed similar complex interweavings of regional popular expressions with the "classical" formulations of the official faith.

The earliest substantial archeological evidence for worship is far older. Third and second-millennium B.C.E. artifacts from cities of the Indus Valley civilization suggest continuities with certain religious traditions that survive today, particularly in popular Hinduism: worship of the bull and other animals, of the *pipal* (sacred fig), *vaṭa* (banyan) and other trees, of *liṅga* and *yoni* stones; the use of bathing tanks and ghats for individual worship; and the ritual use of fire. Without literary or inscriptional evidence, however, continuities remain speculative. The Vedic sacrificial paradigm evolved after the collapse of the Indus civilization. Its portable fires, temporary altars, and invited or dismissed deities—convenient for pastoral nomads—eventually gave way to *devapūjā,* the worship of a vast array of gods and spirits in household and public shrines and temples understood to be permanent residences for divine powers.

A sacrificial worldview became the foundation for a complex system of domestic and official rituals and philosophical speculations in an increasingly stratified society dominated by Brahmans and royalty. At times this worldview has been seen as definitive "high" religion for ancient and classical South Asia. From such a perspective, "folk" religion is a non-Brahmanic, non-Sanskritic, agrarian-based perpetuation of elements of indigenous religions traditions that may have preceded the arrival of Indo-Aryan pastoral nomads and continued to develop with little or no interaction with classical Hinduism. However, a viewpoint that defines folk worship in Hinduism as non-Brahmanical (unsupervised by Brahmans) or non-Sanskritic (without oral or written Sanskrit guidance) would be wide of the mark. Brahmans participate in many regional forms of worship and ritual practice that have neither Brahman supervision nor Sanskrit textual bases. Conversely, the vast non-Brahman majority of Hindus elects forms of worship from a broad range of Sanskritic and non-Sanskritic sources. The same multiformity applies to South Asian Muslims regarding patterns of worship derived from the Arabic Qur'ān and Ḥadīth on one hand and those derived from local, vernacular traditions on the other.

An illustration of this interactive diversity might be a crucial period of drought. Whereas authorities in great temples employing Sanskrit liturgies might request Vaidika Brahmans to come from their remote enclaves to recite Vedic *mantras* in praise of the god Varuṇa, folk religion reaches for its own considerable resources. One remedy calls for tying a frog to a stone pestle that is carried by two people house to house throughout the village, with someone from each household sprinkling water and turmeric and red powders on the frog and its ritual bearers. In general, folk will look to both procedures—and many others, both private and public—as potential solutions.

Among the striking features of worship in Hinduism that more or less have carried over into other South Asian religions are not only diversity but freedom of choice. Apparent is a broad division between personal and family worship on one hand, and public or semipublic worship on the other. Such a distinction, however, is easily blurred. For example, the concept of *iṣṭadevatā,* or chosen deity, is nested within the concept of *kuladevatā,* family or clan deity, and that too is harbored within a nation of *grāmadevatā,* village or neighborhood deity. An individual may have a special, personal relationship with a goddess or god but still worship one or more deities recognized by other family members and participate with the entire clan, subcaste, caste, and neighborhood in routine or festival occasions for deities of wider spheres of devotion. The kuladevatās of folk worship may take many forms, often as animals, perhaps the cow most of all, but also a bull buffalo, house cobra, forest tiger, boar, crocodile, duck, swan, or other animal. No one in the community should ever kill such a divinized creature.

In certain languages of the subcontinent, folk deities and spirits, such as these devatās, are sometimes characterized as *kṣudra śakti,* of less power than such great classical deities as Śiva, Viṣṇu, and the major goddesses. For many, however, it is precisely their local and immediate authority that has promoted them to constant ritual attention. Understandably, the home is the locus for the worship of a great variety of deities, ancestors, and other spirits. Some household gods and goddesses may have small images in the

Community tree shrine to Thakurani in Puri District, Orissa, India, © Stephen Huyler

kitchen or elsewhere; others may be aniconic. The terrifying goddess *Gaṅgāmma,* for example, may be thick jute ropes coiled in a covered wicker basket that swings from a granary rafter in coastal Andhra. In Maharashtra, Kansari, the principal goddess for the Kokna, is represented by a bronze figure with millet in her right hand, rice in her left, appropriate for one also called Annadevata, goddess of food. Many Hindu, Jain, Muslim, and Christian families have a *tulsī* "square" or "fort" in their compounds, a substantial container for a basil plant that is circumambulated and worshipped daily by the women of the household. Tens of thousands of homes in coastal Andhra attribute their prosperity and harmony to the presence of deceased children who continue to live in the form of "ashfruits," worshipped as *vīrabhadras* or *vīrakanyakas* in the cult of the powerful god Vīrabhadra.

Although such multifaceted opportunity has led to unlimited personalized choices for worship, most traditions have defined borders to such an extent that basic methods of worship are easily recognizable throughout the subcontinent. For example, folk worship in Hinduism seems to pay more attention to neighborhood goddesses than to male deities, the latter frequently serving as guardians or kin of a goddess. Many *raudra* (fierce) goddesses demand blood sacrifices, chickens and goats most often, but also sheep, buffalo, pigs, or cooked rice with blood. In return they protect the entire village from disease and other misfortunes, as well as individuals from their enemies, women from infertility or failed pregnancy, children from untimely death.

Possession ritualism is one popular means of access to a wide range of such goddesses. Female and male mediums may be possessed by a single or a dozen or more goddesses special to them, as well as by spirits of deceased individuals. Clients may walk all day to reach a favored medium who then becomes a temporary container for the worshipped supernatural being, one who provides a rhythmic supernatural voice to be heard by the assembled group. Possession ritualism creates an alternate reality for the audience as well as for the one possessed, and important messages from the spirit world are received and taken home by departing clients to share with family and friends.

One of the most common forms of religious exercise is the individual vow (*vrata*). Often crisis-oriented, a vow may be made in time of peril (destitution, drought, flood, cyclone, epidemic disease). In coastal Andhra, for example, if cholera is rampant, a few coins may be tied in a new yellow cloth with a vow to Paiditalli, one of the powerful disease goddesses. This dedication is put aside with the intention later to go on pilgrimage to a certain great temple, not expressly to perform *pūjā* to the god or goddess in that temple but to worship Paiditalli in a small adjoining shrine. On the other hand, a vow may serve as thanks for an invaluable experience in connection with a first visit to a particular temple, mosque, or church. It may also be fasting or sexual abstinence on certain days or complete shaving of the head in forms of *tapas* (austerity), or remaining awake through festivals of Śiva or a local goddess or on Good Friday eve, offering one's weight in sugar to a deity, prostration in *daṇḍam* by repeatedly measuring out one's body on pilgrimage. A vow might also be a more-or-less severe form of self-mortification with branding, skewering the flesh, fire-walking, or even a long-term contract demanding lengthy pilgrimages away from home over a period of years. Jain lay folk are perhaps the foremost adepts at maintaining increasingly rigorous scales of fasts and other vratas en route toward monastic vows.

Special art forms constitute a sizeable arena for folk worship. In every language of India and Nepal are words for threshold and floor designs (*alpona, kolam, maṇḍana, muggu, raṅgoli,* etc.) drawn with rice or other powder in predawn darkness by girls and women to protect and purify the house for the day. They reach colorful, dramatic proportions at junctures in time such as Sankrānti, close to the winter solstice. Many regions of India display multicolored wall paintings and other arts as components of worship.

Folk worship enters into segments of sacred time as well as space. Life-cycle rituals (*saṃskāra*s), a classical set of ten to sixteen from conception to cremation, all have Sanskrit manuals with ample provision for the insertion of "local customs." This open invitation to regional interpolations puts on hold, albeit temporarity, the remarkable pan-Indian homogeneity that saṃskāras enjoy. Aside from constant modifications to the brahmanic schedules descended from the late Vedic period, there are folk traditions supporting a number of rituals marking the passages of individuals, females in particular, that never were included as saṃskāras. One example is first menstruation, observed ceremonially by some in virtually every religion and every level of society. Women's oral traditions serve as authority for the passage of a girl into sexual and maternal competence and readiness (*samartha*). Another example from Hinduism, performed by all Brahmans and non-Brahmans in areas of coastal Andhra, is a special ritual observed on the tenth or eleventh day after the cremation of an auspicious wife who dies before her husband. Contrary to the brahmanic program for her afterlife among the ancestors and then rebirth, she is transformed by a female Brahman ritualist into Gauri and dispatched to that goddess's heaven.

The lunar calendars within the solar year also have their segments of sacred time writ large, and folk customs enter into countless local and regional festivals as well as those observed more or less at the same time throughout the subcontinent. The Census of India regularly publishes long, detailed reports on the fairs (*melā*s) and festivals (*utsava*s) of selected districts. Closings of public institutions for observance of statewide and nationwide holidays and the publication of particularized multifaith calendars have both brought increased awareness of the various religious festivals of major faiths and expanded an already considerable interfaith level of folk worship.

Cosmic time also has an important place. People of all religions and communities are concerned with astrology, planetary horoscopes in particular. The *navagraha*s (nine planets) include several troublesome beings who require constant or occasional pūjās and *dāna*s (ritual offerings) in order to avert misfortune. Śani (Saturn), Maṅgala (Mars), and the two lunar eclipse nodes, Rāhu and Ketu, are among the malevolent planets most worrisome in folk traditions.

Finally, it is evident that much of South Asian folk worship is interfaith in character. Hindus worship in Jain temples and at the *dargāh*s (tombs/cult centers) of Muslim saints; Sikhs and Muslims join in *bhajan*s and *kīrtaṇa*s (devotional music and singing); Christians frequently participate in possession ritualism at the seats of Hindu deities and sometimes dance, possessed by their own deceased children, in nocturnal processions. Folk worship draws fewer lines between faiths than mainstream institutional literature cares to admit.

References

Ahmad, Imtiaz, ed. 1984. *Ritual and religion among Muslims in India*. New Delhi: Manohar.

Babb, Lawrence A. 1975. *The divine hierarchy: popular Hinduism in central India*. New York: Columbia University.

Brückner, Heidrun, Lothar Lutze, and Aditya Malik, eds. 1993. *Flags of fame: studies in south Asian folk culture*. Delhi: Manohar.

Claus, Peter J. 1984. Medical anthropology and the ethnography of spirit possession, In Judy Pugh and Valentine Daniel, ed., *Contributions to Asian Studies* 18: 60–72.

Diehl, Carl Gustav. 1956. *Instrument and purpose, studies on rites and rituals in South India*. Lund: Gleerup.

Elmore, W. T. 1915. *Dravidian gods in modern Hinduism*. Lincoln: University of Nebraska.

Freeman, John R. 1991. Purity and violence: sacred power in the teyyam worship of Malabar. Ph. D. diss., University of Pennsylvania.

Fuller, Christopher J. 1992. *The camphor flame. Popular Hinduism and society in India.* Princeton: Princeton University Press.

Glushkova, Irina and Anne Feldhaus, eds. 1998. *House and home in Maharashtra.* Delhi: Oxford.

Gonda, Jan. 1970. *Viṣṇuism and Śivaism. A Comparison.* London: Athlone.

Hiltebeitel, Alf, ed. 1989. *Criminal gods and demon devotees. Essays on the guardians of popular Hinduism.* Albany: State University of New York.

Huyler, Stephen P. 1994. *Painted prayers. Women's art in village India.* New York: Rizzoli.

Jayakar, Pupul. 1980. *The earthen drum: an introduction to the ritual arts of rural India.* New Delhi: National Museum.

Knipe, David M. 2002. When a wife dies first: the mūsivāyanam and a female Brahman ritualist in coastal Andhra. In *The living and the dead: the social dimensions of death in south Asian Religions,* ed. Liz Wilson. Albany: State University of New York.

Kramrisch, Stella. 1968. *Unknown India: ritual art in tribe and village.* Philadelphia.

Michaels, Axel, Carnelia Vogelsanger and Annette Wilke, eds. 1996. *Wild goddesses of India and Nepal.* Bern/New York: Peter Lang.

Östör, Ákos. 1980. *The play of the gods. Locality, ideology, structure and time in the festivals of a Bengali town.* Chicago: University of Chicago.

Reiniche, Marie-Louise. 1993 [1981]. Popular Hinduism. In *Asian Mythologies,* trans. under the direction of Wendy Doniger from the French edition compiled by Yves Bonnefoys, 68–75. Chicago: University of Chicago.

Shulman, David, ed. 1995. *Syllables of sky. Studies in south Indian civilization. In honour of Velcheru Narayana Rao.* Delhi: Oxford.

Sontheimer, Günther-Dietz. 1989. *Pastoral deities in western India.* Trans. Anne Feldhaus. New York: Oxford.

Tiwari, Laxmi G. 1991. *The splendor of worship. Women's fasts. rituals, stories and art.* Delhi: Manoharlal.

Waghorne, Joanne Punzo and Norman Cutler, ed. 1985. *Gods of flesh/gods of stone. The embodiment of divinity in India.* Chambersburg Penn.: Anima.

Werbner, Phina and Helenc Basu, eds. 1998. *Embodying charisma. Modernity, locality, and performance of emotion in Sufi cults.* New York: Routledge.

Whitehead, Henry. 1921. *The village gods of south India.* Calcutta: Association.

David M. Knipe

SEE ALSO

Ancestor Worship; *Darśan; Dāsara;* Floor Designs; Gāvarī; God-Boxes, Painted; Gods and Goddesses; *Gondhaḷa; Gorava/Goramma;* Govindji, Temple of; *Gurav;* Life Cycle Rituals; *Mandeccula; Pūjā;* Religion; Ritual; Sacred Places; *Samī;* Self-sacrifice; Spirit Possession and Mediumship; Syncretism; Tulsi (Basil); *Vrat Kathā*

Y

YAKṢAGĀNA

In Sanskrit, *yakṣa* refers to a chubby dwarf servant of Kubera, the Hindu god of wealth, and *gāna* designates a particular kind of vocal music. The term *yakṣagāna* came to refer to both an old style of South Indian music and a musical dance-drama in which this style of music is performed. Yakṣagāna troupes exist in the Indian states of Andhra Pradesh and Karnataka. The styles of the yakṣagānas of Karnataka's Kanara Districts, however, are the most well known and documented. The following description applies primarily to contemporary Kanara styles of yakṣagāna: *teṇku* (southern style), the *baḍaga* (northern style) of South Kanara, and the North Kanara style which is a distinctive variation of the baḍaga style. Teṇku is noted for spectacular demonic make-up, striped skirts, intense *caṇḍe* drumming, whirling dance, and intellectual and philosophical dialogue. Baḍaga is famous for elaborate, painstakingly wrapped, tear-drop shaped headdresses, checkered clothing, *maddaḷe* drumming, and vigorous dance, including twirling on the knees. The North Kanara styles are noted for their bravado stance, vigorous dance, and exaggerated eye and facial movements. All troupes' costumes include intricately carved and decorated crowns, and neck, shoulder, chest, wrist, and waist ornaments. Dancers wear bells tied either at the ankles or knees.

During the yakṣagāna season, from end of November to first week in June (or first monsoon rain), advertisements for some yakṣagāna performances appear in the local Kannada-language newspapers. Others advertise in the traditional way. In the late afternoon, near the place of performance, drummers perform a specific pattern known to local people as an invitation to the performance that night. The drums' sounds can be heard for several miles.

The traditional place of a yakṣagāna performance is in a harvested rice field. An area about 20 ft. × 20 ft. is marked off at each corner with bamboo poles and joined at the top with strings of mango leaves, flowers, and sometimes fruits and areca nuts. Nearby is the dressing room made of palm frond-matted floors and walls. Here the actors dot their faces with rice-paste on thorns and don their gilded wooden crowns and ornaments. Originally, both these areas were lighted only by fire torch and oil lamps. Sponsored by a wealthy landlord, yakṣagāna was free for all to see. It was, and still is, a casual affair where people eat, drink, enjoy their favorite scenes, and talk or sleep through the rest.

Over time, additional types of staging and lighting have emerged. First, kerosene lanterns were added to supplement traditional firelight. Then came a decorated, raised, mud platform stage. Next, a large tent covered the stage and audience area, and admission was charged. Then an indoor theatre with proscenium stage was introduced, complete with electric lighting, sound system, and admission fees. Today, yakṣagāna is performed in combinations of all of these formats. The latest addition has been the staging required for television presentations.

At sunset, rituals are perfomed and songs are sung in the dressing room, prayers are said for a successful performance, young artists are costumed, and the audience is on its way. Drummers play again to inform people that the songs in praise of the gods and comic interludes are beginning.

About 10 p.m. drums send the message that the story is about to begin. Yakṣagāna texts are based on old stories and legends that expound Hindu beliefs, rituals, and proper way of life. The majority of the audience has some knowledge of the stories. Baḍaga troupes mostly perform stories from India's epics—the

Yakṣagāna, badaga style traveling dance, Karnataka, India, © Martha Ashton-Sikora

Mahābhārata and *Rāmāyaṇa,* from the *Jaimini Bhārata* and the *purāṇas* (myths), particularly *Bhagavata Purāṇa*. Teṇku troupes perform stories from the epics and purāṇas, as well as stories from *dēvi mahātme* (mother goddess legends), stories about the origins of the deities whose temples sponsor these troupes, and stories of local heroes and spirits. The North Kanara troupes perform stories mostly from the epics and purāṇas, inserting their local traditions, such as the lion dance of the Hasyagar troupe.

The performance consists of vocal and instrumental music, dance, costumes and make-up, and extemporaneous dialogue. There are two singers: the *saṅgītagāra,* who sings the ritual songs prior to the presentation of the story, and the *bhāgavata,* who sings the story. The vocal music includes the text and folk songs not in the text; instrumental music is performed on two drums—the *maddaḷe* and the *caṇḍe*—and either a small pair of metal cymbals or a gong. Hand gestures are mainly those commonly used in everyday conversation, and facial expressions are more realistic than stylized.

Before the story begins, the story's major characters, elaborately costumed, perform a choreographed dance, first behind a handheld curtain, and then in front of the curtain. At the conclusion of this dance, the singer (*bhāgavata*) asks who they are and why they have come. The spokesperson (usually the actor playing the king) responds for the group. The singer then sings the story's first song, to which the characters dance. When the song is finished, the dancer-actors speak extemporaneously about the content of the song. The singer sings the next song, and the story proceeds with the dancer-actors conversing after each song. This pattern is broken when new characters enter the performance area behind the curtain and perform their special introductory dances, when there are traveling and battling sequences, and when there are scenes with women playing water games.

After these interspersions, the story resumes the song/dance/dialogue pattern. When an actor is performing alone, he speaks his thoughts to the singer.

It is the responsibility of the singer to direct the performance so that the story comes to an end at dawn. Performers, through the concluding rituals, then thank the deities for a successful performance and offer their respect to the members of the audience, who believe they have received the deities' blessing for having attended. The patron pays for the performance, and a night of theatre is over.

The troupe and staff pack and move on to the place of the next performance. There, the patron provides food and a place for the troupe to rest and prepares the performance area and dressing room for the coming night's performance.

References

Ashton, Martha B., and Bruce, Christie. 1977. *Yakshagana*. New Delhi: Abhinav Publications.

Awasthi, Suresh. 1983. Traditional dance-drama in India: an overview in *dance and music in south Asian drama*. Tokyo: The Japan Foundation.

Karanth, K. Shivarama. 1975. *Yakṣagāna*. Mysore: Institute of Kannada Studies.

Ranganath, H. K. 1960. *The Karnataka Theatre*. Dharwar: Karnatak University.

MARTHA ASHTON-SIKORA

SEE ALSO

Dance; Folk Music; India; Karnataka; *Pāḍdana; Purāṇa;* Theater and Drama

YAKṢI

*Yakṣi*s (female tree spirits) and their male counterparts, *yakṣa*s, are ancient mythological figures in South Asia.

These nature spirits populate both Jain and Buddhist sculpture and mythology from the fourth century B.C.E., as harbingers of fertility. In iconography *yakṣis* are often portrayed as either feminine tree spirits or snake goddesses, and in contemporary folklore they are often regarded as sexually voracious tricksters.

References

Chandra, M. 1952–53. Some aspects of Yaksha cult in ancient India. Bulletin of the *Prince of Wales Museum* 3: 53–62.

Coomaraswamy, A. K. [1928–1931] 1993. *Yakṣas: Essays in the water cosmology*. Revised and enlarged edition. Delhi: Oxford University Press.

Sutherland, G. H. 1991. *The disguises of the demon: the development of the Yakṣa in Hinduism and Buddhism.* Albany: State University of New York Press.

SARAH CALDWELL

SEE ALSO

Buddhism and Buddhist Folklore; Jain Folklore; *Nāga;* Water Lore; *Yakṣagāna*

YĀTRĀ

See Jātrā/Yātrā

Z

ZIYĀRAT

For the Sunni Muslims of South Asia, *ziyārat* is the act of visiting the shrine of a saint. (The term comes from the Arabic meaning "visitation.") Ostensibly this is done to offer prayers to the deceased saint for his or her intercession before God in some temporal matter. Often a vow is made to increase the possibility of one's request being granted. As a reminder to the saint, a piece of colored string or cloth may be tied to the grating surrounding the cenotaph. It is believed that the string or cloth will be loosed when the saint accepts or grants the request. At frequently visited shrines padlocks may be affixed to the grating surrounding the saint's grave, possibly indicating a substantial request. On the popular level the *barakat* (blessing) of the deceased saint is thought to permeate the environs of his or her grave and to be transferred to those who visit the site.

For Shī'a Muslims *ziyārat* specifically refers to visiting the shrine of one of the Twelve Imāms (spiritual leaders) and to the ancillary liturgical prayers to the imams. The Shī'ī also attribute substantial religious merit to the action, which may earn the intercession of the imāms before God on Judgment Day (made possible by the redemptive self-sacrifice of the Third Imām, Ḥusayn ibn 'Alī on the battlefield of Karbalā in 680 C.E.). This religious merit is considered equal to a thousand pilgrimages to Mecca (*hajj*).

Many of the Shī'a Muslims of South Asia find it difficult to perform *ziyārat* to Ḥusayn's shrine at Karbalā in distant Iraq. However, the religious merit remains available (e.g., through the recitation of liturgical prayers connected with the rite; these prayers also are termed *ziyārat*). Another option open to South Asian Shī'a Muslims is the performance of *ziyārat* to the shrine of a local martyr that popular traditions hold to be equivalent to Imām Ḥusayn's shrine, such as the shrine of Qāzī Nūrullāh Shūstarī (d. 1610) in Agra, annually visited by thousands of Shī'a Muslims.

References

Ayoub, Mahmoud. 1978. *Redemptive suffering in Islam*. The Hague: Mouton.

Crooke, W. 1894. *An introduction to the popular religion and folklore of northern India*. Allahabad: Government Press.

Subhan, John A. 1970. *Sufism, its saints and shrines*. New York: S. Weiser.

WAYNE R. HUSTED

SEE ALSO

Muḥarram; Mu'jizāt Kahāni; Pilgrimage; Saints; Shrines, Muslim

Index

Note: Page numbers in **boldface** indicate primary discussion of the topic.